MediaGuardian

Media Directory

2005

Edited by **Chris Alden**

Researched by
Toni Hanks

Additional Research
Mo Smith, Pauline Hughes, Janice Wood

Guardian Books is an imprint of Guardian Newspapers Ltd.

A CIP record for this book is available from the British Library

ISBN: 1-84354-049-5

Distributed by Atlantic Books
An imprint of Grove Atlantic Ltd
Ormond House
26–27 Boswell Street
London WC1N 3JZ

Cover design: Two Associates
Text design: Bryony Newhouse

Sub-edited by: Mike McNay
Proofread by: Peter Gibbs and Amelia Hodsdon
Indexed by: Diana Le Core

Data researched and updated on behalf of Guardian Newspapers Ltd by Toni Hanks

Disclaimer
We have taken all steps possible to ensure the accuracy of the data in this directory. If any information is incorrect, please send an email with updated details to mediadirectory@guardian.co.uk

Printed by Cambridge University Press

Contents

Introduction

Welcome to the second edition of the MediaGuardian Media Directory, the indispensable guide to the industry for journalists, students and media professionals.

This book is really three books in one. First, it is a comprehensive guide to the major trends in every media sector – with a wealth of useful statistics, a new "State of the media" section, plus comment from Guardian journalists and other industry figures. This year we pick through the Hutton report, the process of BBC charter renewal, the ITV merger, the Independent's decision to go tabloid, the sale of the Telegraph, the advertising revival, the rise of digital – and a thousand other issues that will shape the future of the industry. Whether you are student looking for a job or just want to keep up to date, you will find our straightforward analysis invaluable.

Second, it is a directory of more than 7,000 contacts in every media sector – essential for freelancers, producers, PRs and other media professionals. New this year, we publish names of the senior editorial staff at newspapers and magazines; commissioning contacts at broadcasters; listings of post-production companies; a hierarchical guide to book publishers and their imprints; more global media outlets; and most usefully for students, a revised, expanded guide to courses in media, journalism, TV, publishing and PR.

Last but by no means least, at the back of the directory you will find a Contacts Book aimed particularly at journalists – with more than 6,000 contacts for the most high-profile public and private organisations in the UK. Whether you want a government department, a local police press office, a football team, charity, campaign group or FTSE-listed company, you will find a number and a website here. Our primary criterion for selection is this: if journalists might want to write about it, it goes in.

With more than 13,000 contact phone numbers, this year's Media Directory is the most comprehensive yet. We hope you find it useful.

Chris Alden

State of the media

Top five media events 2003–04	
1. The Hutton report	**page 116**
2. Piers Morgan is sacked	**pages 5, 14**
3. Independent ditches its broadsheet	**pages 15, 19**
4. Barclay brothers buy Telegraph	**page 15**
5. ITV merger goes ahead	**page 123**

It has been a year of inquiry for the media industry. After the rows and trauma of last year – the Iraq dossier, the war, the row between the BBC and the government, the death of Dr David Kelly – this year we had the verdict, and the fallout. We had the Hutton report into that affair, the Butler report into WMD (page 119), the Phillis review of government PR (page 284), and countless other reviews at the BBC including the Graf report, the Neil report, and the Ofcom review of public service broadcasting (all listed on page 120).

January 2004, of course, was the month of the **Hutton report**, the controversial verdict of a retiring law lord into the circumstances surrounding the death of Dr David Kelly. Dr Kelly, an expert on Iraqi weapons, had apparently committed suicide at the height of a row between the government and the BBC, about a key dossier which had helped justify war in Iraq. At issue was a Today programme report by Andrew Gilligan, in which the journalist reported a conversation he had held with the then anonymous Dr Kelly; in it, Gilligan said the government "probably knew" that a key claim about WMD – that Iraq could use them in 45 minutes – was wrong before it put it in the dossier, and that Downing Street had ordered the dossier to be "sexed up". Although most of those who looked over the evidence expected both the government and the BBC to be criticised, Hutton in fact cleared Downing Street of any wrongdoing, finding Gilligan's key claims to be unfounded. The verdict led to the resignations of the BBC director general, Greg Dyke, the chairman of governors, Gavyn Davies, and Gilligan himself – and led to a period of sustained blood-letting and introspection within the corporation. For more on the Hutton report, how the BBC reacted to it – and the possible implications for the licence fee as the BBC seeks to have its charter renewed – see page 120.

As the BBC searched its soul, there was renewed strength at ITV – or rather **ITV plc**, the result of the merger between Carlton and Granada that was completed in January 2004. The newly formed company controls 11 of the 15 regional television franchises, and is expected to provide serious competition to both BBC and BSkyB. For more on that, turn to page 123.

Whole-year trends	2003	2002
Total national newspaper circulation (per week)	89.3 million	90.7 million
Total regional newspaper circulation/distribution	68.4 million	68.6 million
Total consumer magazine circulation (per week)	25.4 million	25.3 million
Total households with multichannel TV*	13.4 million	11.4 million
Total radio reach	44.0 million	44.2 million
... total number of digital radios sold*	435,000	135,000
Total households with internet access*	12.5 million	11 million
... total broadband connections*	3.4 million	1.4 million
Total volume of books sold	286 million	273 million
Total measured ad spend	£17.2bn	£16.4bn

*Figures at the end of year. For statistics up to spring and summer 2004, see individual chapters of the book.

Media stocks: capitalisations and prices, 2 July 2004

Company	Capitalisation	Sector	Share price
Aegis	£976.1m	advertising & PR	87p
Bloomsbury	£172.7m	publishing	£2.45
BSkyB	£11.9bn	broadcasting	£6.15
Capital Radio	£373.4m	broadcasting	£4.30
Chrysalis	£329.3m	broadcasting	£1.97
Daily Mail & General Trust	£2.7bn	publishing and broadcasting	£7.10
Datamonitor	£93.8m	market information	£1.33
Emap	£1.9bn	publishing and broadcasting	£7.28
EMI	£1.9bn	music	£2.43
Euromoney	£327.1m	publishing	£3.70
Future Network	£207.2m	publishing	61p
GWR Group	£336.4m	broadcasting	£2.65
Highbury House	£53.5m	publishing	17p
Hit Entertainment	£352.6m	broadcasting	£2.18
Incepta	£170.4m	PR & marketing	88p
Incisive Media	£125.2m	publishing	£1.36
ITE	£176.1m	exhibitions & publishing	65p
iTouch	£119.9m	new media	29p
ITV	£4.7bn	broadcasting	£1.12
Johnston Press	£1.6bn	publishing	£5.58
Maiden	£101.6m	advertising	£2.20
Metal Bulletin	£121.0m	market information	£2.24
Pearson	£5.2bn	publishing	£6.55
Photo-Me International	£395.8m	photo booths	£1.07
Reed Elsevier	£6.6bn	publishing	£5.23
Reuters	£5.1bn	news and market information	£3.50
Sanctuary Group	£130.9m	music	48p
Scottish Radio	£332.4m	broadcasting	£9.25
SMG	£354.6m	publishing and broadcasting	£1.14
St Ives	£392.1m	printing	£3.82
T&F Informa	£1.2bn	publishing	£3.87
TNS	£951.2m	market information	£2.11
Trinity Mirror	£1.9bn	publishing	£6.52
Ulster TV	£211.0m	broadcasting	£3.95
United Business Media	£1.7bn	publishing	£4.90
Wilmington	£88.2m	market information	£1.06
Wireless Group	£75.0m	broadcasting	92p
WPP	£6.3bn	advertising & PR	£5.55
Yell Group	£2.4bn	publishing	£3.42

It was also an extraordinary year in newspapers. It was the end of the line for **Piers Morgan**, the bullish Daily Mirror editor who presided over an increasing number of scoops and controversies alike as his editorship drew to a close. It was Iraq, again, that cost him his job: or rather, his decision to run photographs purporting to show British soldiers torturing Iraqi prisoners; photographs which turned out to be fake. For more on how Morgan was forced out, see page 5. It was the end too for **Conrad Black**, the newspaper mogul who was ousted from the board of Hollinger International, owners of the Daily and Sunday Telegraph, for making "unauthorised payments" to himself and other executives. The Telegraphs were ultimately sold to the Barclay brothers; for more on that saga, see page 15. And it was a happy end for the broadsheet Independent – the newspaper **switched to tabloid** format over the course of the year, breathing new life into its circulation figures as it did so. To read Peter Preston on why that is a real piece of newspaper history, turn to page 19.

2004 was also the year that the advertising industry started to haul itself **out of recession**, breathing confidence back into every media sector after a lean few years. Sir Martin Sorrell, the often pessimistic chief executive of advertising supergroup WPP, confirmed the good news when he said in January that his company has climbed out of its "bath-shaped" slump. For more on the advertising revival, see page 271.

2003–04: key trends

The key trends of 2003 and 2004 have been the increase in **advertiser confidence**, and the increase in uptake of **new media technologies**. Advertisers spent £17.2bn on UK media in 2003, up from £16.7bn in 2002; this was all the more remarkable given that advertiser confidence had been shattered at the start of the year by the Iraq war. See page 271 for more on how advertiser confidence grew at the start of 2004.

Multichannel TV, digital radio and broadband internet access continued to become more important parts of the media landscape. The number of households receiving multichannel TV rose to 13.4 million by the end of 2003, up from almost 12 million in June; Freeview, the free-to-view digital terrestrial television service, was largely responsible for the rise (see page 129). Digital radio became ever more popular, with almost 500,000 sets sold by the end of 2003, a figure expected to double by the end of 2004 (page 178). And as internet access grew to more than 12.5 million households at the end of 2003, the number of broadband connections more than doubled (page 211).

Newspaper circulations continued to decline; 1.4 million fewer national newspapers a week – or some 200,000 a day – were sold in 2003 than in the previous year. Books, however, were more popular: Britons bought 13 million more books in the year, or almost 36,000 extra a day.

Finally, the FTSE media and photography index mirrors increased advertiser confidence. By summer 2004, share prices had broadly risen to those of spring 2002 – below the level they had been before the dot.com crash, below even the levels they reached after the September 11 attacks; but comfortably up on the prices to which they had fallen in early 2003. Companies that fitted the broad trends included **WPP**, whose share price recovered from a £4 low in spring 2003 to a stable £6 in 2004; and the **Daily Mail & General Trust**, which recovered to about £7, after slipping to £5.50 in the spring of 2003. **Pearson**, the publisher of the Financial Times and Penguin Books – whose share price is often a barometer of the wider markets – recovered only slightly to almost £7 by summer of 2004, from below £6 in spring 2003.

There was strong recovery at **Reuters**, as shares quadrupled from below £1 in spring 2003 to about £4 in the spring of 2004; but then, its price had been about £10 in 2001. The company had been through a major reorganisation after losing almost £500m in 2002, and identified some 3,000 job losses; in February 2004 it revealed it had made a profit for the year of almost £50m.

Johnston Press was once again the stock market star; its shares climbed steadily to above £5, rising from £3 in 2000: an extraordinary performance given the state of the rest of the market. The company, which has grown by buying other regional publishers, made a £128m profit in 2003, up 38 per cent on the previous year.

Forced out

Some of the most high-profile names in the UK media business were forced out of their jobs in 2003 and 2004. We examine who they were, why they had to go – and whether they will be back.

L–R: David Levene; Eamonn McCabe; Lisa Carpenter; Clive Postlethwaite

GREG DYKE

Old job: Director general of the BBC
Forced out: January 2004

- **Why did he have to go?** Publicly backed the Radio 4 journalist Andrew Gilligan in his row with the government over the September 2002 Iraq dossier, which culminated in the death of the weapons scientist David Kelly. Left exposed when the Hutton inquiry said Gilligan's claims were "unfounded" and criticised "defective" editorial system at the BBC.
- **Manner of his leaving?** Forced out by governors after key ally, Gavyn Davies, had resigned as chairman. Heralded by 900-strong crowd of BBC staff outside White City.
- **Soft landing?** Yes: received a pay-off of more than £400,000, and signed a book deal with HarperCollins worth at least as much.
- **Fond memories?** BBC staff took him to their hearts after he promised to "cut the crap" – and succeeded.
- **Will he be back?** He already is. He's presented Have I Got News For You?; his book is out soon; and he's been linked with almost every high-profile TV job.

PIERS MORGAN

Old job: Editor of the Daily Mirror
Forced out: May 2004

- **Why did he have to go?** Published fake pictures of British soldiers supposedly abusing an Iraqi prisoner. Refused to apologise.
- **Manner of his leaving?** Sacked and escorted from the building. Not even allowed to go back for his jacket.
- **Fond memories?** His sharp tongue will never be forgotten. "This is a very good day for lying drug-abusing prima donnas who want to have their cake with the media, and the right to then shamelessly guzzle it with their Cristal champagne," he said after losing a privacy case to Naomi Campbell at the House of Lords.
- **Soft landing?** Maybe – hired Campbell's lawyers in an attempt get his hands on a £2m pay-off.
- **Will he be back?** Yes. Had already started his TV presenting career before he left the Mirror.

CONRAD BLACK

Old job: Chairman and chief executive of Hollinger International, publisher of the Telegraph titles and others around the world.
Forced out: January 2004

- **Why did he have to go?** An internal investigation found £17m in payments to executives, including Lord Black himself, that weren't authorised by the board.
- **Manner of his leaving?** Not quiet. Denied any wrongdoing, and tried to sell his 73 per cent stake in the Telegraph titles to the Barclay brothers without the approval of the rest of the Hollinger International board.
- **Fond memories?** Not many. He's the man Canadians love to hate, according to the Globe and Mail – rival to his paper, the National Post.
- **Soft landing? Will he be back?** Both hard to say. Depends on the outcome of his legal battles to protect his name and assets.

MICHAEL GREEN

Old job: Chairman of Carlton Television, briefly chairman-elect of ITV plc.
Forced out: October 2003

- **Why did he have to go?** Presided over the ITV Digital disaster in 2002 – thus losing the confidence of investors.
- **Manner of his leaving?** Ousted by institutional shareholders – particularly Anthony Bolton, UK boss at Fidelity – who was keen to bring in an external chairman.
- **Soft landing?** Positively bouncy. Received a £15m pay-off.
- **Fond memories?** Yes and no. Carlton was a powerful force in British television but failed to build a reputation for innovative programming. Never really forgiven for beating Thames to the London weekday franchise in 1993.
- **Will he be back?** Wants to be. There was talk in 2003 of his launching a bid for ITV, alongside the US entrepreneur Haim Saban.

MediaGuardian 100

The MediaGuardian 100 list is the definitive guide to the most powerful movers and shakers in one of Britain's most vibrant industries. In this, the fourth year of its publication, there has been more upheaval than ever before, with the cataclysmic events at the BBC emasculating last year's most powerful person in the media – Greg Dyke. He is not the only one to go into freefall – Piers Morgan, the Unilever boss Niall Fitzgerald, and Charles Allen are all heavy fallers this year.

Rupert Murdoch is back on top, but his political editor at the Sun, Trevor Kavanagh, is the big winner with the position of newspapers considered particularly strong in this upcoming election year. Channel 4 is also well represented – with three new executives, Kevin Lygo, Luke Johnson and the newly minted chief executive Andy Duncan, all coming into their own. Women are less prominent, while the arrival in Britain of James Murdoch, aged 31, gives a lift to the number of under-40s with power in the media. This year the panel retained the BBC at the top – in number two position – but decided that in charter renewal year more power was vested in the chairman Michael Grade than new director general Mark Thompson.

1. Rupert Murdoch

Job: chairman and chief executive, News Corporation *Age:* 73 *Industry:* broadcasting, publishing, new media *Annual revenue:* US$17.5bn *Staff:* 35,000 *Salary:* US$12m *2003 ranking:* 2

It was one of Rupert Murdoch's greatest triumphs. Twelve years after it was the Sun wot won the 1992 general election, it was the Sun again wot won a referendum on the European constitution.

It was a sign that Mr Murdoch's power, at the grand old age of 73, shows no sign of diminishing just yet. Indeed, his son James's installation as chief executive of BSkyB, which provoked a furious rebellion among some shareholders, suggests his grip on the UK media may be firmer than ever. In global terms, Mr Murdoch remains the most powerful man in television. NewsCorp controls 35.4 per cent of BSkyB in Britain and owns News International, home of the Sun, News of the World, the Times and the Sunday Times. Three of them are market leaders, the other one wants to be, and between them they have an audience of more than 20 million readers a week.

2. Michael Grade

Job: chairman, BBC *Age:* 61 *Industry:* broadcasting, publishing, new media *Salary:* £81,320 *2003 ranking:* new entry

After completing the unlikeliest of TV comebacks, Michael Grade's task is nothing less than restoring the reputation of the BBC and securing its future in the run-up to charter renewal in 2006. He'll be hoping the odds of success are rather better than winning the lottery jackpot. It was a sign of Mr Grade's prestige and charisma that his appointment was so warmly welcomed by corporation staff, whose morale sank to an all-time low in the wake of the Hutton report and the departure of the director general Greg Dyke and chairman Gavyn Davies. Personable, confident and "one of the people" – despite his wealth – Mr Grade was described by an executive as having the "Greg factor". "Do give me a shout if you see me walking around," he told staff. "I'm the one with the red socks (but no cigar these days)."

Michael Grade: man of the people

3. David Currie

Job: chairman, Ofcom *Age:* 57 *Industry:* media regulation *Annual budget:* £144m *Staff:* 880 *Salary:* £133,000 *2003 ranking:* 3

As chairman of Ofcom, David Currie is one of the most powerful people in the media. Ofcom oversees everything from the future of public service broadcasting to digital television, broadband internet, newspaper mergers and the consolidation of the TV and radio industries.

4. Sir Peter Burt

Job: chairman, ITV *Age:* 60 *Industry:* broadcasting *Annual revenue:* £3bn *Salary:* £200,000 *2003 ranking:* new entry

Sir Peter Burt, formerly Bank of Scotland chief executive, filled the gap left by Michael Green, ousted in a dramatic shareholder coup. The spectre of investor unrest has hung over his appointment, which was welcomed by the City institutions that have never stopped grumbling about the network's management since the ITV Digital fiasco of 2002.

5. Tessa Jowell

Job: culture secretary *Age:* 56 *Industry:* politics *Staff:* 480 *Salary:* £130,347 *2003 ranking:* 31

The last 12 months have made Tessa Jowell one of the most prominent politicians in the media. And her job as secretary of state for culture, media and sport has been even busier with a succession of media events, from the Communications Act and the creation of a single ITV, to the setting up of Ofcom, the destructive fallout from the Hutton report and the BBC's ongoing charter review process.

6. Mark Thompson

Job: director general, BBC *Age:* 46 *Industry:* broadcasting, publishing, new media *Income:* £3.53bn (£2.65bn licence fee, £627m BBC Worldwide and other commercial activities, £223m BBC World Service) *Staff:* 29,200 *Salary:* as yet undisclosed (predecessor Greg Dyke earned £464,000) *2003 ranking:* 23

When Mark Thompson was appointed chief executive of Channel 4 two years ago, he took charge of a broadcaster that had slightly lost its way and needed reassurance about its future and confirmation of its role in the public service landscape. In many ways it echoes the challenges he now faces as director general of the BBC, except the scale of his task has increased exponentially.

7. Paul Dacre

Job: editor-in-chief, Associated Newspapers *Age:* 55 *Industry:* publishing *Circulation:* Daily Mail 2.3 million, Mail on Sunday 2.25 million (Dec 2003–Apr 2004), London Evening Standard 387,609 (May 3–May 30 2004) *Salary:* £899,000 *2003 ranking:* 7

"Why are you so obsessed with the Daily Mail?" Paul Dacre asked MPs at a Commons select committee. "We're just one paper." But what a paper. Love it or hate it, Dacre's Daily Mail is the newspaper success story of the decade. While its rivals have been shedding sales by the vanload, the Mail has piled on nearly a million copies over the last 10 years.

8. Trevor Kavanagh

Job: political editor, the Sun *Age:* 61 *Industry:* publishing *2003 ranking:* 56

The Sun's political editor Trevor Kavanagh is the most influential journalist in Britain. As one panellist put it: "Editors of the Sun come and go but Kavanagh will always be there as long as Rupert Murdoch is." As Lord Hutton was preparing to deliver his report into the death of David Kelly, most of us had already read its conclusions – courtesy of Kavanagh in the Sun.

9. Martin Sorrell

Job: group chief executive, WPP *Age:* 59 *Industry:* advertising, marketing *Company turnover:* £4.1bn *Staff:* 54,324 (72,000 including associates) *Salary:* £2.13m *Worth:* £130m *2003 ranking:* 45

Sir Martin Sorrell is the country's most influential advertising man. As the head of WPP, Sir Martin is in charge of the third largest advertising and marketing services group in the world. It encompasses such familiar names as J Walter Thompson, Ogilvy & Mather and Young & Rubicam, and among its global clients are IBM, Ford, Kellogg's, Unilever and Shell.

10. Stephen Carter

Job: chief executive, Ofcom *Age:* 40 *Industry:* regulation *Annual budget:* £144m *Staff:* 880 *Salary:* £250,000 *2003 ranking:* 8

It's not called a super-regulator for nothing. As chief executive of Ofcom, Stephen Carter is charged with overseeing a media, telecom and communications industry worth £40bn.

11–100: job INDUSTRY *(2003 ranking)*

11. Sir David and Sir Frederick Barclay owners of the Telegraph Group, Press Holdings PUBLISHING *(new entry)*

12. James Murdoch chief executive, BSkyB BROADCASTING *(new entry)*

13. Viscount Rothermere chairman, Daily Mail & General Trust PUBLISHING *(new entry)*

14. Richard Desmond chief executive, Northern and Shell, Express Newspapers PUBLISHING *(9)*

15. Andy Duncan chief executive, Channel 4 BROADCASTING *(new entry)*

PA

Barclay brothers (11): new Telegraph owners

16. **Nigel Pickard** director of programmes, ITV BROADCASTING *(44)*

17. **Simon Cowell** TV presenter, producer BROADCASTING *(new entry)*

18. **Les Hinton** executive chairman, News International PUBLISHING *(19)*

19. **Sly Bailey** chief executive, Trinity Mirror PUBLISHING *(18)*

20. **Larry Page and Sergey Brin** founders, Google NEW MEDIA *(new entry)*

21. **Tom Moloney** chief executive, Emap BROADCASTING, PUBLISHING *(37)*

22. **Alan Rusbridger** editor of the Guardian, executive editor of the Observer PUBLISHING, NEW MEDIA *(38)*

23. **Kevin Lygo** director of television, Channel 4 BROADCASTING *(47)*

24. **Ed Richards** senior partner, strategy and market development, Ofcom MEDIA REGULATION *(new entry)*

25. **Jana Bennett** director of television, BBC BROADCASTING *(22)*

26. **Luke Johnson** chairman, Channel 4 BROADCASTING *(new entry)*

27. **Jeremy Deedes** interim chief executive, the Telegraph Group PUBLISHING *(new entry)*

28. **David Frank** chief executive, RDF Media BROADCASTING *(new entry)*

29. **Steve Jobs** co-founder and chief executive, Apple Computer; co-founder and chief executive, Pixar Animation NEW MEDIA, FILM *(13)*

30. **Charles Allen** chief executive, ITV BROADCASTING *(14)*

31. **Dame Marjorie Scardino** chief executive, Pearson PUBLISHING, NEW MEDIA *(27)*

32. **Dawn Airey** managing director, Sky Networks BROADCASTING *(16)*

33. **Ashley Highfield** director of new media, BBC BROADCASTING, NEW MEDIA *(25)*

34. **Ralph Bernard** executive chairman, GWR BROADCASTING *(34)*

35. **Jenny Abramsky** director of BBC radio and music BROADCASTING *(32)*

36. **David Mansfield** chief executive, Capital Radio BROADCASTING *(33)*

37. **Ivan Fallon** UK chief executive, Independent News & Media PUBLISHING *(new entry)*

38. **Dennis Stevenson** chairman, Pearson PUBLISHING, NEW MEDIA *(new entry)*

39. **Rebekah Wade** editor, the Sun PUBLISHING *(6)*

40. **Gerhard Zeiler** chief executive, RTL Group BROADCASTING *(new entry)*

41. **Sir Christopher Meyer** chairman, Press Complaints Commission MEDIA REGULATION *(21)*

42. **Dan Chambers** director of programmes, Channel Five BROADCASTING *(new entry)*

43. **Richard Huntingford** chief executive, Chrysalis BROADCASTING, MUSIC *(new entry)*

44. **Richard Wallace** editor, Daily Mirror PUBLISHING *(new entry)*

45. **David Hill** director of communications, Downing Street PUBLIC RELATIONS *(new entry)*

46. **Gail Rebuck** chairman and chief executive, Random House PUBLISHING *(new entry)*

47. **John Humphrys** presenter, Today, On the Ropes, BBC Radio 4 BROADCASTING *(new entry)*

48. **John Witherow** editor, the Sunday Times PUBLISHING *(53)*

49. **Roger Parry** chief executive, Clear Channel International BROADCASTING, ADVERTISING *(42)*

50. **Roly Keating** controller, BBC2 BROADCASTING *(new entry)*

51. **Andy Coulson** editor, News of the World PUBLISHING *(new entry)*

52. **Mark Frith** editor, Heat PUBLISHING *(88)*

53. **Maurice Saatchi** partner, M&C Saatchi; co-chairman, Conservative party ADVERTISING, POLITICS *(new entry)*

54. **Lorraine Heggessey** controller, BBC1 BROADCASTING *(46)*

55. **Crispin Davis** chief executive, Reed Elsevier PUBLISHING, NEW MEDIA *(55)*

56. **Jonathan Ross** TV and radio presenter, independent producer BROADCASTING *(64)*

57. **Richard Freudenstein** chief operating officer, BSkyB BROADCASTING *(new entry)*

58. **Simon Kelner** editor, Independent PUBLISHING *(84)*

59. **Richard Curtis** TV and film director FILM, TV, FUNDRAISING *(new entry)*

60. **Jane Lighting** chief executive, Five BROADCASTING *(58)*

61. **Robert Thomson** editor, the Times PUBLISHING *(49)*

62. **David Bergg** director of strategy, ITV BROADCASTING *(new entry)*

63. **Tony O'Reilly** executive chairman, Independent News & Media PUBLISHING *(61)*

64. **Niall Fitzgerald** chairman, Unilever (incoming chairman, Reuters) CONSUMER GOODS *(30)*

65. **Max Clifford** founder, Max Clifford Associates PUBLIC RELATIONS *(57)*

66. **Alan Parker** owner/founder/senior partner, Brunswick PUBLIC RELATIONS *(new entry)*

67. **Guy Black** press secretary to Michael Howard MEDIA RELATIONS *(new entry)*

68. **Martin Newland** editor, Daily Telegraph PUBLISHING *(new entry)*

69. **Andrew Gowers** editor, Financial Times PUBLISHING *(71)*

70. **Terry Wogan** presenter, BBC Radio 2 BROADCASTING *(new entry)*

71. **Jeremy Paxman** presenter, Newsnight and University Challenge on BBC2; author BROADCASTING *(72)*

72. **Tim Bowdler** chief executive, Johnston Press PUBLISHING *(74)*

73. **Doug McCorkindale** chairman, president and chief executive, Gannett PUBLISHING *(75)*

74. Roger Alton editor, Observer PUBLISHING *(80)*

75. Lesley Douglas controller, BBC Radio 2 and 6 Music BROADCASTING *(new entry)*

76. Nicholas Coleridge managing director, Condé Nast PUBLISHING *(79)*

77. Peter Fincham chief executive, Talkback Thames BROADCASTING *(new entry)*

78. Dominic Lawson editor, Sunday Telegraph PUBLISHING *(77)*

79. Stef Calcraft partner, Mother ADVERTISING *(83)*

80. John Birt special adviser to No 10 GOVERNMENT *(new entry)*

81. Johnny Hornby managing partner, Clemmow Hornby Inge ADVERTISING *(new entry)*

82. Bob Phillis chief executive, Guardian Media Group PUBLISHING, BROADCASTING, NEW MEDIA *(92)*

83. Peter Hill editor, Daily Express PUBLISHING *(new entry)*

84. Helen Boaden director, BBC news BROADCASTING *(87)*

85. Andrew Neil TV presenter, columnist PUBLISHING, BROADCASTING *(new entry)*

86. Kelvin MacKenzie chairman and chief executive of the Wireless Group BROADCASTING *(93)*

87. Nick Pollard head of Sky News BROADCASTING *(new entry)*

88. Duncan Edwards managing director, the National Magazine Company PUBLISHING *(new entry)*

89. Greg Dyke former director general, BBC BROADCASTING *(1)*

90. Paul Abbott writer BROADCASTING *(new entry)*

91. Sylvia Auton chief executive, IPC Media PUBLISHING *(98)*

92. Piers Morgan TV presenter, unemployed tabloid editor BROADCASTING, PUBLISHING *(29)*

93. Richard Woolfe director of programmes, LivingTV, Bravo and FTN BROADCASTING *(new entry)*

94. Daisy Goodwin editorial director, Talkback BROADCASTING *(new entry)*

95. Stephen Glover columnist, publisher-in-waiting PUBLISHING *(new entry)*

96. Richard Littlejohn columnist, the Sun PUBLISHING *(73)*

97. Steve Coogan and Henry Normal founders, Baby Cow Productions BROADCASTING *(new entry)*

98. Bob Shennan controller, BBC Radio 5 Live BROADCASTING *(new entry)*

99. Haim Saban chairman/CEO, Saban Capital Group BROADCASTING *(new entry)*

100. The institutional investor causing trouble for company chairmen and chief executives CITY *(new entry)*

■ Panellists

Lord Alli Founded Big Breakfast, produced Planet 24 with his partner, Charlie Parsons, and made some of Channel 4's best-known hits, including TFI Friday and Don't Forget Your Toothbrush. Chairman of Noddy owner Chorion.

Emily Bell Editor-in-chief of Guardian Unlimited, named editor of the year by the Association of Online Publishers last year. Previously worked for Observer as advertising correspondent, media business editor and finally business editor.

Lorraine Candy Editor of Elle magazine. At Cosmopolitan earlier this year, won best non-weekly women's magazine at British Society of Magazine Editors awards. Former editor of B magazine, features editor of the Times and woman's editor of the Sun.

Janine Gibson Editor-in-chief of MediaGuardian; has previously written for the Independent, Broadcast, and Televisual. Oversees the Guardian's weekday G3 sections – Society, Media, Life, and Education.

Janet Goldsmith Former managing director of Universal Studios Networks UK, Janet Goldsmith is a partner at Mediatique, the media consultancy run by former City analyst Mathew Horsman.

Jim Hytner Has had some of media's most high-profile marketing jobs. As marketing chief of ITV he oversaw a £100m facelift for the channel, while at Five he developed a reputation for high-profile stunts. Worked at BSkyB under Sam Chisholm; now moves to Barclays.

Carolyn McCall Chief executive of Guardian Newspapers. Previously deputy managing director and communications director.

Richard Park As a judge on the BBC1 talent show Fame Academy, Richard Park became a household name. Spent 14 years at Capital Radio where he was instrumental in its growth, hiring DJs including Chris Tarrant. Now works as a consultant at Emap and has a chatshow on Magic.

Jeff Randall BBC business editor. Joined three years ago from Sunday Business, which he edited from launch in 1998. Former City editor, assistant editor and sports editor on Sunday Times. Presents Weekend Business, Sunday night programme on Radio Five Live.

Press

The nationals

Britain is famous for the quality, energy and diversity of its national press. According to the Newspaper Marketing Agency, some 86 per cent of British adults say they read a national paper on a daily basis, and 80 per cent read one every week; and according to ABCs, some 87 million national papers are sold each week. But the market is crowded: there are now ten daily papers and eleven Sundays, as listed in the table on page 15; and over the past 50 years, national dailies have lost some 2 million readers a day, largely under the challenge of competing media. Many of the changes in national papers over the past decades – increased pagination, more supplements, price wars and now the "compact" broadsheet – have been efforts to reverse this long-term circulation decline.

About half the daily papers sold in Britain are accounted for by the red-top tabloids: that is, the Sun, the Daily Mirror and the Daily Star. Of these, the Sun is the most popular, selling 3.4 million. The mid-market tabloids, the Daily Mail and the Daily Express, account for more than a quarter of daily sales: of these, the Mail sells more than twice as many papers as its rival, and outsells the Daily Mirror too. The quality press – the Daily Telegraph, the Times, the Guardian, the Independent and the Financial Times – all started 2003 as broadsheets, but the Independent and the Times launched tabloid or "compact" versions during the year, with the Independent abandoning the broadsheet altogether in 2004. The Telegraph, however, leads the market.

The Sunday market is similar. The News of the World leads the popular sales march, far outselling Trinity Mirror's Sunday Mirror and

■ Explainer: ABCs

- **What are ABCs?**
  ABCs are circulation figures published by the Audit Bureau of Circulation, an independent company that monitors and verifies sales of newspapers and magazines.
- **How often do ABCs come out?**
  National newspaper ABCs are published each month. Regional newspaper and magazine ABCs are published every six months, covering January–June and July–December each year.
- **What do the ABCs include?**
  The ABC publishes the number of copies of a publication sold at full price and sent to subscribers. They used also to include "bulks" – copies distributed free to targeted places such as hotels and airlines – but now bulks must be reported by target audience, and the number of "actively purchased" copies is more often considered the headline figure.

Sunday People, and the new Daily Star Sunday. In the middle market, the Mail on Sunday outstrips the Sunday Express; but the Sunday Times leads broadsheet sales ahead of the Sunday Telegraph, the Observer and the Independent on Sunday.

Red tops

The Sun may be the market leader among the red-top tabloids, but there hardly seemed a moment in 2003 and 2004 when the media headlines were not dominated by the **Daily Mirror**. After the failed attempt by the editor, Piers Morgan, to cover serious news in the run-up to the Iraq war, the paper turned instead into an extension of Morgan's personality: bold, forthright and controversial in the extreme. The strategy seemed to work in late 2003, when, as the paper celebrated its centenary, it paid for the story of a convicted killer, Tony Martin, and then ran an extraordinary scoop by a reporter who had been working for two months as a Buckingham Palace footman. But in 2004, things started to unravel. First, in April, the model Naomi Campbell won a 3-2 privacy judgment against the paper at the House of Lords (see page 305); and then on May 1, the newspaper published pictures purporting to show British soldiers torturing a prisoner in Iraq. The pictures looked a bit too pristine, and although Morgan stood by them to the end, he lost his job two weeks later as Trinity Mirror bosses accepted that they were fakes. His replacement, Richard Wallace, is a popular choice in the Morgan mould, although the appointment did prompt the acting editor and deputy editor, Des Kelly, to quit. Wallace takes over a paper that has suffered a decline in circulation of more than 5 per cent year-on-year.

Richard Wallace: Mirror editor

Elsewhere in the Mirror stable, the **Sunday Mirror** and the **People** were the losers of the tabloid market, shedding more than 140,000 readers between them.

The Sun maintained its irreverence under Rebekah Wade, who kept a lower personal profile as she entered her second year as editor. There were gaffes: the headline "Bonkers Bruno locked up" led to a public outcry in September 2003, and the paper made a £10,000 donation to the mental health charity Sane, in an attempt to defuse the crisis. There was bad taste: "Ship Ship Hooray", the paper gloated, when mass murderer Harold Shipman committed suicide in his cell. There were disappointments: circulation fell below 3.3 million in December 2003, a 30-year low. But there was humour: on hearing of Morgan's sacking from the Daily Mirror, the Sun put up one of its own staff for the job – from its postroom. And there was one almighty scoop: thanks to the political editor, Trevor Kavanagh, the Sun was able to get a leaked copy of the Hutton report.

The **News of the World** stuck closely to its time-honoured recipe of good sport and better sex – and brought both together in 2004, as one woman and then another claimed to have bedded England's football captain David Beckham. Most entertaining were a series of sexually explicit text messages supposedly sent by the footballer, peppered with asterisks for added reader interaction; Beckham himself called the media's depiction of him an "absolute disgrace".

The **Daily Star** appointed Dawn Neesom as editor in December 2003, promoting her from deputy after Peter Hill had become editor of the Express. The paper's circulation even rose to more than that of the Express, reaching 898,000 in the first six months of 2004. The Daily Star Sunday also increased its sales, to more than 500,000 copies.

Quality press

In the quality market, all eyes were on the **Independent**, which launched its tabloid version in September 2003, in an attempt to improve profitability and reverse a sales decline. The new size contained the same copy as the broadsheet, and was originally sold alongside its big brother within the M25 only. As sales grew, the newspaper expanded the tabloid to the north-west, the south and eventually nationwide. More than 40,000 readers a day (22 per cent) were added to circulation, at a cost of more than £4m – described by the chief executive of Independent Newspapers, Ivan Fallon, as "the best money we've ever spent". In May, the newspaper announced that it was killing off the broadsheet.

Life at the **Telegraph** and **Sunday Telegraph** was clouded by change and uncertainty at the top. First, the daily editor Charles Moore resigned in October, to be replaced by Martin Newland – a former deputy editor of the National Post in Canada, a stablemate of the Telegraph at Hollinger International. Then in November the chief executive of Hollinger, Lord Black, was forced to resign from the company he controlled, after it said it had found improper payments worth about £20m. Lord Black effectively had to put the Telegraph titles up for sale

National daily circulations

	Editor	Jan–Jun 04	Jan–Jun 03	% change
Popular & midmarket				
Sun	Rebekah Wade	3,365,844	3,525,993	–4.54
Daily Mail	Paul Dacre	2,322,970	2,350,541	–1.17
Daily Mirror	Richard Wallace	1,883,274	1,989,174	–5.32
Daily Star	Dawn Neesom	898,692	851,781	5.51
Daily Express	Peter Hill	892,388	904,325	–1.1
Quality press				
Daily Telegraph	Martin Newland	878,030	911,584	–3.68
Times	Robert Thomson	616,706	616,308	0.06
Financial Times	Andrew Gowers	414,377	434,907	–4.72
Guardian	Alan Rusbridger	358,625	386,585	–7.23
Independent	Simon Kelner	224,499	184,016	22

Source: ABC

National Sunday circulations

	Editor	Jan–Jun 04	Jan–Jun 03	% change
Popular & midmarket				
News of the World	Andy Coulson	3,840,584	3,875,857	–0.91
Mail on Sunday	Peter Wright	2,269,271	2,278,959	–0.43
Sunday Mirror	Tina Weaver	1,594,143	1,643,936	–3.03
People	Mark Thomas	1,029,364	1,120,222	–8.11
Sunday Express	Martin Townsend	889,973	881,556	0.95
Daily Star Sunday	Gareth Morgan	515,200	472,228	9.1
Quality press				
Sunday Times	John Witherow	1,347,665	1,369,130	–1.57
Sunday Telegraph	Dominic Lawson	672,554	710,581	–5.35
Observer	Roger Alton	425,317	430,546	–1.21
Independent on Sunday	Tristan Davies	174,573	182,646	–4.42
The Business	Andrew Neil	61,144	75,524	–19.04

Source: ABC

– and although he thought he had sold the papers in January, when he tried to tie up a quick deal with the Barclay brothers, it was scotched when a US court blocked the deal and demanded due process, branding Black "cunning and calculated". Hollinger International finally did conclude a deal with the Barclay brothers, although in July 2004, Black was planning to challenge it in court.

The **Times** was the only paper to follow the Independent's switch in size. It launched its own tabloid version in the London area from November 2003, and went nationwide in June 2004 as staff came in earlier to hit the earlier production deadlines necessary. Circulation, however, remained virtually constant year-on-year in the first six months of 2004. Taken together with the **Sunday Times**, it lost more than £28m in 2003.

The **Guardian**'s circulation dipped to below 360,000, leading to speculation that it might too turn tabloid; but editor Alan Rusbridger ruled out such a move in February 2004. "The Independent's a better tabloid than it was a broadsheet," he said. "I don't think the same would be true of the Guardian." The paper was thought to be investigating a quality mid-size version, similar to Le Monde. The **Observer**, meanwhile, lost ground slightly, even though it launched the Observer Music Monthly magazine, complementing Food Monthly and Sport Monthly.

The **Financial Times** continued its global expansion, announcing plans to print its FT Asia edition in Sydney, targeting Australian readers in the process. But UK circulation dipped by more than 20,000, despite a redesign in 2003.

Midmarkets

The **Daily Mail** continued to dominate the middle market. The Daily Mail and General Trust's bid for the Telegraph titles attracted most attention: it bid £690m, although it admitted it was prepared to take a minority stake in order to avoid opposition from the Office of Fair Trading. It also achieved a coup in December 2003 by poaching Express editor Chris Williams, making him editor of the Scottish Daily Mail. The Mail's editor, Paul Dacre, continued to be well rewarded: he took home £899,000 in 2003, making him the best-paid editor on Fleet Street for another year.

The **Daily Express** vacancy was filled quickly enough – Peter Hill, the Daily Star editor, being rewarded for his success at the Daily Star – but there is no doubt where the power really lies at either paper. Richard Desmond, the Express proprietor who also owns OK!, continued to bag the headlines with his bizarre management style. April was the weirdest month: first staff threatened to strike over proposed £2m cuts at the paper – on top of the 150 jobs already lost – and then Desmond shocked a meeting with Telegraph executives, with whom his titles share a printing press, by goose-stepping around the room implying that all Germans were Nazis. His antics took the edge off the Express's decision to switch allegiance from Labour to the Conservative party.

Even though the Daily Express was overtaken in circulation by the Daily Star, the market share figures (see table) show that Desmond's tactics may be effective. His papers increased share, and closed to within 2.1 percentage points of the Trinity Mirror titles, down from 3.3 percentage points the year before.

The bottom line

The past year has seen a rise in revenue from national newspaper advertising, after the dip during the Iraq war. The first quarter of 2004 saw spend rise to £511m, a 1.9 per cent increase in real terms; though this represented only 14 per cent of the total advertising market. The Newspaper Marketing Agency, formed in 2002 to market newspapers to advertisers, launched its website in July 2003 – with the result that all the nationals' ratecards are now available for the first time in one place.

The PCC

The self-regulatory body for the newspaper industry is the press complaints commission, or PCC: it operates a code of practice by which newspapers agree to abide, and according to which members of the public may complain. Some 3,649 people complained to the commission in 2003 – an increase of 39 per cent on the previous year, and a reflection of the steps the PCC has taken to raise its own profile under chairman Sir Christopher Meyer. Remarkably, 400 of the complaints were made about a single case: the front-page tabloid photographs of the Manchester City footballer, Marc Vivien Foe, as he lay dying on a football pitch in July of that year.

The commission has continued to face calls to act as a tougher regulator. There has been some reform: a "charter compliance" panel, led by Sir Brian Cubbon, was appointed to scrutinise the PCC's handling of complaints; and its code was also updated to improve the way newspapers label reports of negative adjudications against them, and to ban newspapers from intercepting mobile phone calls, text messages, and emails. But sanctions against newspapers remain slight: they merely agree to publish the results of adjudications against them, and there is no financial compensation for those who successfully complain.

In March 2004, the commission appointed a 29-year-old as its director. Tim Toulmin, who has worked at the PCC for his entire career, was appointed after Guy Black stepped down in 2003 to become press secretary for the Conservative leader, Michael Howard.

Major PCC rulings

- **July 2003:** The commission finds the Sun guilty of "one of the most serious forms of physical intrusion into privacy", after it published taped phone calls between the Australian conman Peter Foster – the boyfriend of Cherie Blair's lifestyle guru, Carole Caplin – and his mother.
- **July 2003:** PCC rejects a complaint by the star of Pearl Harbor, Kate Beckinsale, against the Daily Mail for publishing pictures of her daughter without consent.
- **September 2003:** PCC clears the News of the World for paying a convicted conman £10,000 for details of an alleged plot to kidnap Victoria Beckham.
- **October 2003:** Commission clears Daily Mirror over its decision to pay Tony Martin, the farmer convicted of manslaughter, for his story.
- **November 2003:** The footballer Jermaine Pennant complains to the PCC about a People headline saying his "mum" was a prostitute. Pennant points out that the woman is not his biological mother; but the complaint is rejected on the grounds that the article makes this clear.
- **May 2004:** Sunday Express apologises to the prime minister, Tony Blair, after he complained that an article about his son Nicky was intrusive.
- Total number of complaints to commission in 2003: 3,649

Awards

British Press Awards, March 2004

- National newspaper of the year: The Independent
- Front page of the year: News of the World, "Huntley in his cell"
- Scoop of the year: Ryan Parry, Daily Mirror, "Intruder at Palace"

Regional Press Awards, July 2004

- Regional newspaper of the year: Kent on Sunday
- Front page of the year: Lincolnshire Echo, "When will our suffering end?"
- Scoop of the year: Yorkshire Evening Post, the Sergeant Roberts tapes

What the Papers Say Awards, December 2003

- Editor of the year: Simon Kelner, The Independent

PPA Awards, May 2004

- Consumer magazine of the year: InStyle (IPC)
- Editor of the year, consumer magazines: Jane Johnson, Closer (Emap)
- Consumer specialist magazine of the year: Uncut (IPC)
- Consumer lifestyle magazine of the year: Country Living (Natmags)
- Business and professional magazines of the year: Building (CMP); Financial Director (VNU)
- Customer magazine of the year: Home (Redwood)

National newspaper ownership

Group name	Market share		Titles	Executive control
	Jan–Jun 03	Jan–Jun 02		
News International	34.6%	35.2%	Sun Times Sunday Times News of the World	Rupert Murdoch
Daily Mail and General Trust	19.3%	19.0%	Daily Mail Mail on Sunday	Lord Rothermere
Trinity Mirror	16.6%	17.1%	Daily Mirror Sunday Mirror People	Victor Blank
Northern and Shell	14.5%	13.8%	Daily Express Daily Star Sunday Express Daily Star Sunday	Richard Desmond
Telegraph Group (& The Business)	7.2%	7.2%*	Daily Telegraph Sunday Telegraph The Business	Barclay brothers
Guardian Media Group	3.1%	3.2%	Guardian Observer	Scott Trust
Pearson	3.0%	3.0%	Financial Times	Pearson board
Independent Newspapers	1.8%	1.5%	Independent Independent on Sunday	Tony O'Reilly

*Then owned by Hollinger International; Telegraph titles only

Turning tabloid **Peter Preston**

Some media upheavals, of course, are personal. So this was the year when, kicking and struggling, Piers Morgan and Conrad Black went down the memory hole (though not together). But some upheavals are structural, profound and hugely influential. The birth of the quality tabloid is just such an event. Size really does matter.

Ivan Fallon, the CEO at the Independent, set the gossip going in July 2003. Simon Kelner, his editor, had had an extremely bright idea, Fallon told anyone interested in the paper's travails. It might even add 10,000 copies a day. From 220,000 to to 230,000? That sounded a useful lift after years of stagnation, but it wasn't exactly a thunderclap.

The wheeze, when it came in September, was better than that, though. The Independent began publishing in two sizes, broadsheet or what was coyly called "compact". You choose, Kelner told his readers: and within three months they'd effectively done exactly that. Not only was Independent circulation nudging 30,000 or more ahead, but the Times had followed the same route in a wild dash of action, the Guardian was investigating a Berliner (or mid-size) format, and the Telegraph was pondering its options with growing anxiety.

By spring there was no doubt about it. The Independent was entirely tabloid everywhere and on every day (including Saturday). The Guardian was investing heavily in new (Berliner) presses, the Times was pushing its tabloid with almost hectic fervour – and though the Telegraph still stood to one side, no-one was betting against eventual catch-up.

What did it – and does it – all mean? The temptation is to see the whole trend as little more than a fad, just one of those fashionable things in a daily market which is, literally, here today and gone tomorrow. Didn't the Daily Mail do something similar over thirty years ago, turning tabloid with great eventual success – and provoking a wave of copycats, from the Daily Express down, who found no instant salvation in size change? Surely it's the words and pictures and editorial flair that count in the end?

Of course this is true. But there are factors that help and omissions that don't. One – seldom included in the argument as carefully as it should be – is the mushroom growth of the free morning Metro titles in London and most of Britain's big cities, not to mention Europe and the US. Around a million of them go out in the UK every morning. They're there for a quick commuter ride by bus or train, and their audience is overwhelmingly young and busy and in work. An ABC1 advertisers' dream. The readers here, on careful research, are mostly under-30s who don't read a paid-for daily on any regular basis. They're the young who are passing newspapers by, because print is too thick, too much, too cumbersome in a digital world. A quick, tersely constructed tabloid suits them well.

What happens when they want something more than that, to graduate to a better spread of information, debate and feature coverage? Tabloid is still the natural, expected shape. So is a paper with proper tabloid pacing: not too stodgy, not too oblivious to the need to keep pages turning. Does that paper, though, have to be a conventional British tabloid, full of large headlines, bosoms and football? There is no remote reason why that should be so. Look at Newsday in America, La Repubblica in Rome, Gazeta Wyborska in Poland: look even at Le Monde. Some of those papers, to be sure, are Berliner rather than squashed tabloid, but they all use tabloid editing techniques, full of pace and variety. Not big headlines, but a big concentration on content. They demonstrate, absolutely, how you can cut down page sizes without dumbing down. They're just as much quality papers as any competing broadsheet. And in some countries, moreover, there are no broadsheets left. Go to Spain – one of the most vibrant competitive press arenas in Europe – and El Pais, El Mundo and the rest are all tabloids. That is the universally chosen way.

Tabloid, then, is an assumption of mind, a habit that changes at national borders. It doesn't have to equal downmarket. In many places, it signals completely the reverse. The question for Britain has been whether the ingrown British equation of tabloid and trash could be successfully questioned. The Guardian began to do that over a decade ago with its tabloid features sections. The Metro series broadened the point. The Independent – by giving readers a choice over months – let the punter decide. Any residual prejudice is gone.

But that's by no means the end of the affair. Does a paper's print run have to be entirely tabloid or entirely broadsheet? There's no reason why it should be any longer. Continuing choice, large or compact according to commuting circumstances, may be an alternative option. El Periodico in Barcelona appears each morning in two different languages after all: a reader service like any other. Can a range of tabloids on the news-stand look sufficiently different to generate casual sale? So far the British compacts seem a bit quiet and dull. Will front pages, as in Europe, become more contents posters than news? Watch this space – and never forget that what you're seeing, in a small, profound way, is a bit of newspaper history.

The regionals

The past few years have been difficult for the regional press. Circulation has been on a slow but persistent slide: nearly 68.2 million newspapers were sold or distributed in the six months to December 2003, compared to more than 70 million three years before. The problems are most noticeable at the top end of the market: none of the top 20 regional papers posted an increase in circulation in the same period, and most posted significant falls. The figures can only partly be explained by the decision by many papers to stop giving away copies for free or at discounted prices; although as the Newspaper Society points out, three-quarters of regional newspapers now post 100 per cent actively purchased ABCs (see explainer, page 13).

The Newspaper Society, which lobbies for the publishers of regional and local newspapers, is nevertheless passionate about the health of the industry. Some 84 per cent of British adults read a regional newspaper, it boasts; since 2000, it says, readership has grown by 2.3 per cent, while that of national press has fallen by 4.3 per cent. There were signs, too, of a recovery in advertising: ad spend on regional newspapers was £796m in the first quarter of 2004, according to the Advertising Association, a growth of almost 6 per cent in real terms. Regional newspapers accounted for 21.8 per cent of total advertising spend in that quarter.

Of the 1,300 titles in Britain at the beginning of 2004, only 100 were dailies: but together, dailies commanded more than half of the circulation (35.6 million copies a week). By contrast there were 21 Sunday papers, circulating 2.2 million copies; 529 weekly paids, selling almost 6.3 million; and 650 weekly frees, distributing just over 24 million. The industry employs about 34,000 people, nearly a quarter of whom are editorial staff.

The regional press remains a highly consolidated market. At the beginning of 2004, 64 per cent of regional newspaper circulation was controlled by just four newspaper groups – Trinity Mirror, Newsquest, the Daily Mail & General Trust, and Johnston Press – and in the second half of 2003, these same publishers sold or distributed more than 43 million of the 68 million papers circulated each week, owning 801 of the 1,300 titles.

Partly as a result of this consolidation, further mergers and acquisitions tend to attract the attention of regulators. Independent News & Media had particular trouble selling its 27 papers in greater London: it first tried to offload them to Newsquest in 2003 for £60m, but the Competition Commission said parts of the deal were against the public interest, so the sale collapsed. Next the Daily Mail and General Trust tried to buy the papers; but just as regulators gave it the go-ahead to do so, the rival publisher Archant made a £62m bid of its own. Finally in April 2004, the Office of Fair Trading stepped in again, referring

In the regions

- **July 2003:** Britain's largest regional newspaper publisher, Trinity Mirror, says it will cut 550 jobs in an attempt to save £25m a year by 2005.
- **December 2003:** Regulators block the owners of the Shropshire Star, the Midlands News Association, from taking over a radio station in Telford, citing public interest grounds.
- **February 2004:** Yorkshire Post journalists pass a vote of no-confidence in their editor, Rachael Campey, in a row over compulsory redundancy for the woman's editor, Jill Armstrong. Campey responded by appointing Armstrong as editor of the monthly magazine Absolute Leeds, which appeared to defuse the row.
- **May 2004:** Newsquest journalists protest against what they call "poverty pay", at AGM of the US parent group, Gannett.

the Archant deal to the Competition Commission. A decision was not expected until October 2004.

In 2004, Johnston Press nevertheless indicated that it would like to buy more papers, after announcing a 38 per cent increase in profits for 2003 – some £128m before tax.

The biggest-selling regional daily was once again the Daily Record in Scotland; but it continued to lose circulation in the six months to December 2003, selling 503,489 copies on average: the psychologically important half-million mark beckons. The biggest selling Sunday title was again the Sunday Mail.

London's Evening Standard was again the biggest selling regional evening title; but like other regional papers, its circulation was in decline, at just below 400,000 for the six months to December 2003. It lost more than £10m in 2003, its finance director admitted, so the editor, Veronica Wadley, was forced to make cuts: 13 staff were axed in April 2004, including two long-serving reporters, Colin Adamson and Richard Holliday, while the paper also scrapped its New York correspondent. The Standard still faced the prospect of competition from Richard Desmond's Northern & Shell: Desmond promised his new London evening title as long ago as 2002, but in 2004 he was awaiting an Office of Fair Trading ruling into Associated's exclusive distribution contracts with London's rail and underground stations. Scepticism remained about whether the paper, provisionally titled PM, would ever be launched.

The Standard's free morning sister title, Metro, distributed almost 450,000 papers in London in the second half of 2003, an increase of some 13 per cent.

Top 10 regional publishers

	Number of papers	Weekly circulation (m)	Share
Trinity Mirror	235	15.6	22.9%
Newsquest	215	10.6	15.6%
Northcliffe Newspapers Group*	110	9.1	13.4%
Johnston Press	241	8.3	12.2%
Associated Newspapers*	7	6.4	9.4%
Archant**	85	3.0	4.4%
Guardian Media Group	44	2.6	3.8%
The Midland News Association	19	2.1	3.1%
DC Thomson	3	1.2	1.8%
Scotsman Publications	6	1.1	1.6%
Top 10	**965**	**60.0**	**88.1%**
All regional publishers	**1,300**	**68.1**	

*owned by Daily Mail and General Trust

** includes purchase of Independent News & Media's greater London titles; subject to Competition Commission ruling

Data for 1 January 2004, based on ABCs for second half of 2003

Source: Newspaper Society

Top 20 paid regionals

	Circulation	% change	Frequency	Editor
Sunday Mail, Scotland	618,312	−5.2%	Sunday	Allan Rennie
Sunday Post, Dundee	530,168	−5.8%	Sunday	David Pollington
Daily Record, Scotland	503,489	−6.5%	morning	Bruce Waddell
Evening Standard, London	398,966	−2.9%	evening	Veronica Wadley
West Midlands Express & Star*	163,543	−2.5%	evening	Adrian Faber
Manchester Evening News*	153,125	−4.1%	evening	Paul Horrocks
Liverpool Echo*	135,845	−5.3%	evening	Mark Dickinson
Birmingham Evening Mail*	107,410	−6.1%	evening	Roger Borrell
Belfast Telegraph*	103,103	n/a	evening	Edmund Curran
Leicester Mercury	93,156	−3.7%	evening	Nick Carter
Evening Times, Glasgow*	92,716	−3.0%	evening	Charles McGhee
Newcastle Evening Chronicle*	90,813	−4.1%	evening	Paul Robertson
Aberdeen Press & Journal	90,379	n/a	morning	Derek Tucker
Sunday Life, Belfast	87,132	−5.7%	Sunday	Martin Lindsay
Sunday Sun, Newcastle	86,400	−6.0%	Sunday	Peter Montellier
Sunday Mercury, Birmingham	85,934	−6.2%	Sunday	David Brookes
Scotland on Sunday	83,229	−1.0%	Sunday	John McLellan
Dundee Courier & Advertiser	83,084	−3.4%	morning	Arthur Adrian
The Herald, Glasgow*	83,083	−7.9%	morning	Mark Douglas-Home
Shropshire Star	82,862	−3.3%	evening	Sarah Jane Smith

Average net circulation July–Dec 2003 *Monday to Friday Source: Newspaper Society, ABC

Top 10 frees

	Average net circulation, July–Dec 2003	Frequency
Metro London	449,616	morning
Manchester Metro News	301,914	weekly
Nottingham & Long Eaton Topper	208,690	weekly
The Glaswegian	154,890	weekly
Nottingham Recorder	154,060	weekly
Southampton Advertiser	151,021	weekly
Wirral Globe	134,669	weekly
Bexley Dartford & Gravesend News Shopper	130,455	weekly
Herald & Post Edinburgh	128,847	weekly
Derby Express	122,173	weekly

Sources: Newspaper Society, VFD

The weekly revival **Toby Granville**

Duran Duran have done it. So has John Travolta. Even "cabriolet" cars are back in vogue. But one thing stands out above the rest when you consider the comebacks of late – the weekly regional press.

That's not to say that they've ever been out of fashion; it's just that this year the trusted weekly has enjoyed something of a renaissance. And while managing directors of newspaper publishers across the land count the profits as their titles hit unprecedented ABC sales increases, the question is: why are the weeklies doing so well – and at what cost?

The Newspaper Society says that readership of paid-for-weeklies has grown by 15 per cent over the past decade – and shows "no sign of a slowdown". They also say that more than half of all paid-for-weeklies increased their circulation between January and June this year, despite reducing bulk sales.

There is no single reason for the rise of the weekly. One factor is that more weekly editors than ever are launching slip editions, and pushing back the boundaries of their circulation areas. They have broken into new market areas, and been rewarded with hikes in circulation.

There's also the notion – sadly to the detriment of national and regional dailies – that lifestyles in Britain are changing. No matter how many competitions and offers that are puffed on the front pages, there's no getting away from the fact that there are simply not enough hours in the day for people who have constant access to news via the internet and TV. The "work hard" lifestyle means they want to spend their free time in other ways than reading the local paper.

There's also the cost. We're inundated with doom and gloom about interest rates, rip-off Britain and petrol prices going through the roof. Readers are holding on to their change rather than splashing out 35p a day, when they can buy a weekly packed with motoring, property and jobs supplements for 50p to read over the weekend. And, as I'm often told, for many communities there's buying a daily newspaper – or buying a loaf of bread.

It's about added value. There's no doubt that readers turn to their weekly for the full story – the in-depth piece that they've only heard a snippet of on the TV or radio.

Dailies, by comparison, can sometimes lack that human touch. And it's the campaigns and crusading for the little person that has helped the weekly become an increasingly credible force in homes across the land. They want to know what's going on in their street, and to see pictures of their children in the school panto. They want to know that when they call the news desk with a problem, something will be done. They rely on the paper, and expect weekly papers to stand up for them – and deliver. Communities have grown up with their ever-faithful weeklies; they feel they own them, and they trust them.

When radio launched, people said it was the death knell for newspapers. When TV launched they said it was the death knell for newspapers. When the internet launched they said it was the death knell for newspapers. Can you see a pattern forming? The newspaper is the great survivor, and the weekly is the greatest survivor of them all. And while the likes of Duran Duran and John Travolta will dip in and out of stardom, the weekly will always be in fashion.

Toby Granville is the editor of the Wiltshire Times Series

Magazines

Launches and folds

Launches

- Sorted, monthly for teenage boys – Oct 2003
- Nuts, men's weekly from IPC – January 2004
- Zoo Weekly, its Emap rival – January 2004

Folds:

- J17, Emap's long-running teen weekly – March 2004
- 19, its IPC counterpart – April 2004
- The Face, Emap style magazine – April 2004
- Sorted, after barely seven months – May 2004
- Jack, handbag-sized men's magazine – July 2004

The magazine market is once again growing. There are more than 8,000 separate periodical titles in Britain, of which about two-thirds are business titles and one-third consumer – and according to the Periodical Publishers' Association, the industry is worth some £6.4bn.

Consumer magazines again performed well: circulation rose 1.6 per cent year on year in the six months to December 2003, while ad spend rose to £191m in the first quarter of 2004, a 5 per cent increase in real terms. TV magazines continued to top the newsstand ABCs: What's On TV remained the number one seller, with more than 1.6 million readers, ahead of Take A Break, Radio Times and TV Choice. Celebrity magazines also maintained their popularity, with Now maintaining its market leadership over Heat and OK!: Hello! slipped to fifth, overtaken by Emap's Closer – edited by the former Sunday Mirror hack Jane Johnson.

The most hyped magazine launches were the two men's weeklies, IPC's Nuts and Emap's Zoo Weekly, which hit the newsstands together in January 2004. According to early reports, Nuts, with its lower nipple count and slightly less racy features, was thought to be in the lead, with a circulation of about 225,000 to Zoo's 150,000. "Nuts is outselling Zoo, but we are only 10 minutes into the first half," Tom Moloney, chief executive of Emap, told the Observer at the end of May.

The most high-profile folds were Jack, the men's mini magazine which died in July 2004, after Dennis Publishing bought it last year from James Brown's I Feel Good Publishing; and the style magazine the Face, which went under in April. Two once popular teen magazines, 19 and J17, were also axed.

The men's weekly launches were expected to hurt the monthly market: even before 2004, monthlies had seen a sharp fall in circulation, with the top three men's titles – FHM, Loaded and Maxim – losing a combined total of 50,000 readers a month in the second half of the previous year. In an attempt to reverse the slide, Maxim appointed Greg Gutfeld, the former editor of Stuff magazine in the US. Bucking the trend, Arena put on 28 per cent to bring its circulation back over 40,000.

In the women's monthly market, news was dominated by a series of editorial changes. First Sarah Bailey left the helm at Elle to join Harper's Bazaar in New York; she was replaced by Cosmopolitan's editor Lorraine Candy; Cosmo then poached Company's editor, Sam Baker; and as the wheel stopped spinning, the Company job went to Victoria White. But it was Glamour, under the editorship of Jo Elvin, that once again posted the most impressive ABCs: it sold more than 582,000 copies on average in the second half of 2003, extending its lead over Cosmo.

Music titles continued to suffer, leading Emap to make several senior staff redundant at its music magazine division, Emap Performance.

Top 50 consumer magazines

	Title	Average circulation/issue Jan–Jun 04	Jan–Jun 03	Year-on-year
1	Sky the magazine	6,600,677	6,124,572	7.8%
2	Asda Magazine	2,453,133	2,012,733	21.9%
3	O Magazine – Group	2,093,641	2,500,025	-16.3%
4	Boots Health & Beauty	1,834,270	1,870,390	-1.9%
5	**What's on TV**	**1,635,023**	**1,689,621**	**-3.2%**
6	The National Trust Magazine	1,573,615	–	
7	Saga Magazine	1,244,002	1,239,221	0.4%
8	**Take a Break**	**1,208,473**	**1,225,116**	**-1.4%**
9	The Somerfield Magazine	1,130,743	1,345,789	-16.0%
10	**Radio Times**	**1,104,767**	**1,161,019**	**-4.8%**
11	**TV Choice**	**1,082,654**	**967,807**	**11.9%**
12	**Reader's Digest**	**822,780**	**860,562**	**-4.4%**
13	Birds	616,477	–	
14	**Chat**	**606,599**	**575,585**	**5.4%**
15	**Glamour**	**605,747**	**576,832**	**5.0%**
16	**Now**	**580,007**	**590,544**	**-1.8%**
17	**That's Life**	**573,966**	**592,036**	**-3.1%**
18	**FHM**	**573,713**	**600,568**	**-4.5%**
19	**OK! Magazine**	**553,777**	**489,882**	**13.0%**
20	Club News	543,175	582,346	-6.7%
21	**Heat**	**540,556**	**565,484**	**-4.4%**
22	**Woman**	**536,364**	**571,482**	**-6.1%**
23	**Closer**	**480,187**	**334,542**	**43.5%**
24	**TV Times**	**473,379**	**529,632**	**-10.6%**
25	Legion	456,744	–	
26	**Cosmopolitan**	**456,447**	**462,157**	**-1.2%**
27	**Woman's Weekly**	**451,690**	**465,500**	**-3.0%**
28	Homebase Ideas	447,500	497,090	-10.0%
29	**Woman's Own**	**446,194**	**484,705**	**-7.9%**
30	VM The Vauxhall Magazine	422,907	478,018	-11.5%
31	**Auto Exchange**	**420,167**	**441,790**	**-4.9%**
32	**Good Housekeeping**	**417,893**	**400,253**	**4.4%**
33	**Bella**	**414,984**	**398,009**	**4.3%**
34	**Yours**	**413,855**	**386,591**	**7.1%**
35	**New!**	**403,864**	**339,035**	**19.1%**
36	**Best**	**401,678**	**414,739**	**-3.1%**
37	Motability Lifestyle Magazine	384,227	–	
38	**Marie Claire**	**380,760**	**376,476**	**1.1%**
39	**People's Friend**	**369,430**	**375,443**	**-1.6%**
40	Motoring & Leisure	365,010	–	
41	**BBC Gardeners' World**	**360,342**	**360,236**	**0.0%**
42	**TV Quick**	**354,620**	**394,251**	**-10.1%**
43	**Auto Trader***	**351,654**	**365,549**	**-3.8%**
44	**National Geographic Magazine**	**341,565**	**334,478**	**2.1%**
45	**The Garden**	**332,033**	**312,183**	**6.4%**
46	Unlimited	330,520	349,500	-5.4%
47	**Prima**	**330,179**	**330,045**	**0.0%**
48	**Company**	**325,185**	**330,617**	**-1.6%**
49	The Caravan Club Magazine	322,820	–	
50	**Candis**	**315,803**	**279,517**	**13.0%**

* Guardian Media Group   Newsstand titles in bold   Source: ABC

Business press

Perhaps two-thirds of magazines in the country are business titles: Brad lists more than 5,300 business magazines that accept advertising, but some estimates say there are as many as 10,000, if every journal and newsletter is taken into account, with more than 175,000 people employed.

The business press depends on advertising for more than three-quarters of its revenue – so it was disappointing that, even a year after the Iraq war, ad spend in business magazines actually dipped in real terms year-on-year in the first quarter of 2004, despite a 3.5 per cent increase in the advertising market as a whole. Ignoring inflation, spend in the sector rose 1 per cent to £227m (a 6.2 per cent share).

Customer magazines

Customer magazines – publications produced on contract for companies, and often distributed free of charge for marketing purposes – are a fast-growing industry. The sector was worth £366m in 2003, up from £313m in 2002; and the top five circulating consumer titles from July to December 2004 were all customer magazines. None of these titles, however, was actively purchased.

Top 10s

Title	Average circulation/issue Jan–Jun 04	Jan–Jun 03	Year-on-year	Title	Average circulation/issue Jan–Jun 04	Jan–Jun 03	Year-on-year
TOP 10 WOMEN'S WEEKLIES							
1 Take a Break	1,208,473	1,225,116	–1.4%	6 Heat	540,556	565,484	–4.4%
2 Chat	606,599	575,585	5.4%	7 Woman	536,364	571,482	–6.1%
3 Now	580,007	590,544	–1.8%	8 Closer	480,187	334,542	43.5%
4 That's Life	573,966	592,036	–3.1%	9 Woman's Weekly	451,690	465,500	–3.0%
5 OK! Magazine	553,777	489,882	13.0%	10 Woman's Own	446,194	484,705	–7.9%
TOP 10 WOMEN'S LIFESTYLE							
1 Glamour	605,747	576,832	5.0%	6 Prima	330,179	330,045	0.0%
2 Cosmopolitan	456,447	462,157	–1.2%	7 Company	325,185	330,617	–1.6%
3 Good Housekeeping	417,893	400,253	4.4%	8 Woman & Home	303,701	283,025	7.3%
4 Yours	413,855	386,591	7.1%	9 New Woman	290,913	275,648	5.5%
5 Marie Claire	380,760	376,476	1.1%	10 Real	204,455	180,680	13.2%
TOP 10 MEN'S LIFESTYLE – including weeklies							
1 FHM	573,713	600,568	–4.5%	6 Zoo	200,125	–	
2 Nuts	290,337	–		7 GQ	124,685	120,741	3.3%
3 Loaded	235,140	261,937	–10.2%	8 Wallpaper	107,800	110,920	–2.8%
4 Maxim	227,017	251,117	–9.6%	9 Front	100,259	110,323	–9.1%
5 Men's Health	221,049	218,756	1.0%	10 Bizarre	87,331	101,209	–13.7%

Source: ABC

Spoilt for choice **Marie O'Riordan**

The women's magazine market has always been a touchstone for change in society, since the launch of Cosmo in the 60s signalled the birth of feminism. As Britain has been a more stable, economically sound and classless society, our magazines have become ever more indulgent of female desire. Gone are the days of "how to" articles with subjects ranging from haberdashery tips to "satisfying your man between the sheets"; instead we have articles various on "me time", stress relief and the joys, after all, of not having it all. It's official: women's magazine readers are a cash-rich, time-poor demographic.

These days our only difficulty lies in multiple choice. Where on the high street shall I shop? Which anti-ageing cream is right for my skin? Why is my nanny so irritating? Which man should I marry – or shall I just date him and have more time with my girlfriends in All Bar One? These and all decisions are helpfully managed with the help of your personal life coach: your magazine.

But with so many to choose from, which one? The magazine market has never been so crowded, with each title vying for an audience that has never been less disparate. Gone are the days when a reader was identified by her class (traditional weeklies have seen serious decline), the state of her uterus (a kiddie-friendly environment used to be a major signifier of your reader) and her career trajectory (housewife or not is no longer appropriate). Now the new weeklies are trendy, like Heat, and some glossies seem just a tad old-fashioned – being the large, heavy objets that used to litter our coffee table.

Age has traditionally been the mechanism for editors to carve out their share of the marketplace. You were 13 and you started with J17 (closed in '04), through to your first glossy, 19 (also closed in '04), quickly moving onto More! for some prepubescent but frank sex advice before you arrived into glossies where you went from Cosmopolitan (orgasm central) to She (when you juggled your life) and finally Good Housekeeping, where you went out to pasture. Then along came handbag-sized Glamour in '01 – and its success signified another gear shift in women's lives.

"The teenager is dead," declared experts following the closure of J17 – and to an extent they were right. Teens are some of Heat and Glamour's keenest consumers. Current readers are not feminists so much as post-feminist ("feminism – is that, like, Carrie Bradshaw?"). Marie Claire defines a reader only by her intelligence, and prides itself on celebrating an eclectic 21st-century woman who has a curiosity beyond her postcode – but will be as passionate about Big Brother or Pop Idol as she will be about whether Blair fooled the electorate in the run-up to the war.

A woman will punish the editor who dares define her in too narrow a way. Her media landscape is busy and she likes dipping in and out of all that's on offer. Now mothers and daughters each want to dress like Beyoncé (she graced teen titles as well as Elle and InStyle covers this past year) and listen to the same music (Red readers pride themselves on playing Radiohead on the school run), while boss and PA swap Heat gossip over lunch.

All the growth in the market has been driven by new titles: Glamour, InStyle, Eve, Closer et al. Linguistically, the currency in our magazines is "me me me" – see InStyle, where every inch of your fashion and beauty routine is expertly dissected and advised upon. There are Eve and Red who subtly speak to the wife/mother who spends all her life pandering to her nanny/cleaner/children/boss/colleagues/husband. Poor you, enthuse these magazines.

And then there is celebrity. It used to be that Kylie belonged to Smash Hits, and Julia Roberts was for the grown-up glossy brigade – but now Robbie Williams bares his backside in Vogue, and Victoria Beckham's marriage crisis is Marie Claire's biggest scoop. Reality TV means everyone's a celebrity, and Closer (the brilliant success of '04) bridges the gap between celebrity and "civilians" by persuading celebrities to share their real-life dramas and diet secrets.

In many ways, women's magazines have not changed at all. They will always be a treat, a bit of escapism from day-to-day mundanity. Yet the editors' rulebook has been cast aside like a dog-eared copy of Jackie. Why oh why does Jade Goody deserve to grace – and sell – so many magazine covers?

The titles that don't adapt quickly enough to this confident, sussed reader have gone and will continue to go to the wall. And marketing budgets, both for above-the-line and increasingly bizarre shrink-wrapped gifts, constantly threaten editorial investment.

Yet a good editorial mix will win out. Glamour and Heat would not be leading their marketplace if they weren't good products. And that's something that will never change. This reader is too powerful a consumer to be disregarded. The women's magazine market is here to stay. Amen to that.

Marie O'Riordan is the editor of Marie Claire

Further reading

■ Press

MediaGuardian
media.guardian.co.uk/presspublishing

Press Gazette: weekly trade magazine
www.pressgazette.co.uk

■ Books

The Shipping News E ANNIE PROULX, FOURTH ESTATE 1993 The tale of Quoyle, who finds his peace through car wrecks on the front page

Scoop EVELYN WAUGH, PENGUIN MODERN CLASSICS 1938 Classic Fleet Street satire

In Print: A Career in Journalism CHRIS ALDEN, GUARDIAN BOOKS 2004 The essential careers guide to newspapers and magazines

Stick it Up Your Punter, The Uncut Story of the Sun Newspaper PETER CHIPPINDALE AND CHRIS HORRIE, POCKET BOOKS (1999)

The Guardian Stylebook DAVID MARSH AND NIKKI MARSHALL, GUARDIAN BOOKS £9.99 (2004)

Orwell: The Observer Years GUARDIAN BOOKS £8.99 (2004)

The Elements of Journalism: What the people should know and what the public should expect BILL KOVACH AND TOM ROSENTIEL, GUARDIAN BOOKS, £8.99 (2003)

■ Web only

World News: newspaper search engine
www.worldnews.com

DotJournalism
www.journalism.co.uk

■ Other resources

Audit Bureau of Circulations
www.abc.org.uk

Newspaper Society
www.newspapersoc.org.uk

Periodical Publishers' Association
www.ppa.org.uk

Association of Publishing Agencies
www.apa.co.uk

National press Contacts

National daily newspapers

Daily Express
Express Newspapers
Ludgate House, 245 Blackfriars Rd
London SE1 9UX
020 7928 8000
www.express.co.uk
firstname.surname@express.co.uk
Editor: Peter Hill

- *Deputy editor: Hugh Whittow; news editor: Howard Smith; home affairs correspondent: James Slack; political editor: Patrick O'Flynn; chief political correspondent: Alison Little*
- Section editors – *city: Stephen Kahn (deputy: Peter Cunliffe; associate city ed: Robert Lindsay; markets: David Shand); comment: Jennifer Selway; Express Woman: Tina Moran; defence: John Ingham; features: Fergus Kelly; foreign: Gabriel Milland; health: Julia Wheldon/Rachael Baird; personal finance: David Prosser; showbusiness: Mark Jagasia; sport: Bill Bradshaw; transport: John Ingham; TV & radio: Charlotte Civil*
- *Production editor: Bob Smith; chief sub: Keith Ging*
- *Publicity: Brian MacLaurin Associates, 020 8834 1034*

Daily Mail
Associated Newspapers
Northcliffe House, 2 Derry St
Kensington, London W8 5TT
020 7938 6000
www.dailymail.co.uk
firstname.surname@dailymail.co.uk
Editor: Paul Dacre

- *Deputy editor: Alistair Sinclair; news editor: Tony Gallagher (assistant: Chris Evans); political editor: David Hughes (deputy: Paul Eastham); chief reporter: David Williams*
- Section editors – *city: Alex Brummer; diplomatic: Richard Kay; features: Leif Kalsayan; Money Mail: Tony Hazell; royal: Richard Kay; sport: Peter Ferguson; transport: Ray Massey; TV: Tara Conlan*
- Correspondents – *consumer affairs: Sean Poulter; education: Sarah Harris; health: Beezy Marsh; industry: Darren Behar; political: James Chapman, Graeme Wilson; social affairs: Steve Doughty*
- *Production editor: Hugh Dawson; chief subs: Gerry Williams (news); Robin Popham (features)*
- *Publicity: Laurence Sear, 020 7938 6000*

Daily Mirror
Trinity Mirror
1 Canada Square, Canary Wharf
London E14 5AP
020 7293 3000
www.mirror.co.uk
firstname.surname@mirror.co.uk
Editor: Richard Wallace

- *Deputy editor: Conor Hanna; news editor: Chris Boffey (deputy: James Mellor); political editor: Oonagh Blackman (group political editor: David Seymour)*
- Section editors – *3am columnists: Jessica Callan, Eva Simpson, Caroline Hedley; business: Clinton Manning; consumer: Ruki Sayid; fashion: Ollie Picton Jones (deputy: Amber Graafland); features: Alison Phillips (assistant editor - features, Matt Kelly); foreign: Mark Ellis; health: Caroline Jones; letters: Fiona Parker; money: John Husband; sport: Dean Morse; TV: Nicola Methven*
- *Executive editor (production): Jon Moorhead; chief news sub: Pratima Sarwate; chief features sub: James Rettie; assistant editor (pictures): Ian Down; picture editor: Greg Bennett*
- *Publicity: Sarah Vaughan-Brown, 020 7293 3222*

Daily Sport
Sport Newspapers
19 Great Ancoats St
Manchester M60 4BT
0161 236 4466
www.dailysport.net
firstname.surname@
sportsnewspapers.co.uk
Publicity: Jane Field, 0161 238 8135

Daily Star
Express Newspapers
Ludgate House, 245 Blackfriars Rd
London SE1 9UX
020 7928 8000
www.dailystar.co.uk
firstname.surname@dailystar.co.uk
Editor: Dawn Neesom

- *Deputy editor: Jim Mansell; news: Kieron Saunders; political: Macer Hall; features: Samantha Taylor; sport: Howard Wheatcroft; Cashpoint: Michelle Carter*
- *Production editor: Bob Hadfield (deputy: Brian Kelly)*
- *Publicity: Brian MacLaurin Associates, 020 8834 1034*

Daily Telegraph
Telegraph Group
1 Canada Square, Canary Wharf
London E14 5DT
020 7538 5000
www.telegraph.co.uk
firstname.surname@telegraph.co.uk
Editor: Martin Newland

- *Deputy & Saturday editor: Sarah Sands; news: Fiona Barton; political: George Jones (chief political correspondent: Toby Helm); home affairs: Philip Johnston; managing editor: Sue Ryan; executive editor: Neil Darbyshire; night editor: David Lucas*
- Section editors – *arts & books: Tom Horan; city: Kate Rankine (deputy); Alistair Osborne & Andrew Cave (associate eds); diplomatic: Anton La Guardia; environment: Charles Clover; fashion: Hilary Alexander; features: Richard Preston; foreign: Alan Philps; health/medical: Celia Hall; health & style: Rachel Forder; legal: Joshua Rozenberg; personal finance: Ian Cowie; science: Roger Highfield; sport: David Welch; Weekend: Rachel Simhom*
- *Production editor: Steve Greaves*
- *Publicity: Victoria Higham, 020 7538 6259*

Financial Times
The Financial Times Group
1 Southwark Bridge
London SE1 9HL
020 7873 3000
www.ft.com
firstname.surname@ft.com
Editor: Andrew Gowers

- *Deputy editor: Chrystia Freeland; news: Edward Carr; political: James Blitz*
- Section editors – *Asia: John Ridding; FT magazine: John Lloyd; FT Weekend: Emma Tucker; Europe: Brian Groom; features: Andrew Hill; media: Tim Burt; public policy: Nicholas Timmins*
- *Production editors: Jo Russ, Ken Tough (day); Andy Anderson, Matthew Pettipher (night). Chief subs: Jeremy Hart (news); Andrew Hill (features)*
- *Communications director: Jo Manning-Cooper, 020 7873 3829*

The Guardian
Guardian Media Group
119 Farringdon Rd
London EC1R 3ER
020 7278 2332
www.guardian.co.uk
firstname.surname@guardian.co.uk
Editor: Alan Rusbridger

- *Deputy editor (news): Paul Johnson; home affairs: Alan Travis; home news: Ed Pilkington, Andrew Culf; political: Michael White (chief political corr: Patrick Wintour)*
- Section editors – *arts: Charlie English (Friday Review: Merope Mills); books: Claire Armistead; city: Julia Finch (deputy: Jill Treanor); economics: Larry Elliott; education: Will Woodward; environment: John Vidal; features: Ian Katz; foreign: Harriet Sherwood; health: Sarah Boseley; media: Charlie Burgess; northern: Martin Wainright; obituaries: Phil Osborne; Online: Vic Keegan; regional affairs: Peter Hetherington; social affairs: John Carvel; sport: Ben Clissit; travel: Andy Pietrasik; Weekend magazine: Katherine Viner; women's page: Clare Margetson*
- *Assistant editor (production): David Marsh; production editor, G2: Paul Howlett; production editor, Weekend: Bill Mann; chief sub, city: Rob Firth*
- *Publicity: Anna Sinfield, 020 7239 9818*

The Independent
Independent News and Media (UK)
Independent House, 191 Marsh Wall
London E14 9RS
020 7005 2000
www.independent.co.uk
firstletter.surname@independent.co.uk
firstname.surname@independent.co.uk
Editor: Simon Kelner

- *Deputy editor: Ian Burrell; news editor: Danny Groom; political editor: Andrew Grice (deputy: Colin Brown; chief political corr: Marie Woolf)*
- Section editors – *business: Michael Harrison; city: Damian Reece; diplomatic: Mary Dejevsky; education: Richard Garner; environment: Michael McCarthy; features: Lisa Markwell; foreign: Leonard Doyle (international news: Anne Penketh); health: Jeremy Laurance; labour: Barrie Clement; media: Ian Burrell; science: Steve Connor; sport: Paul Newman; technology: Charles Arthur; transport: Barrie Clement*
- *Production editor: Louis Jebb; chief news sub: Andrew Webster*
- *Marketing manager: Johnathan Grogan, 020 7005 2000*

The Sun
News Group Newspapers
1 Virginia St, London E98 1SN
020 7782 4000
www.thesun.co.uk
firstname.surname@the-sun.co.uk
Editor: Rebekah Wade

- *Deputy editor: Fergus Shanahan; assistant editor (news): Graham Dudman; political editor: Trevor Kavanagh (deputy: George Pascoe-Watson, Whitehall editor: David Wooding); chief reporter: John Kay*
- Section editors – *Bizarre: Victoria Newton; business: Ian King; crime: Mike Sullivan; defence: Tom Newton Dunn; deputy features editor: Ben Jackson; motoring: Ken Gibson; sport: Steve Waring; Sun Woman: Sharon Hendry; TV: Emily Smith*
- *Chief production editor (night): John Perry; chief sub, news: Jim Holgate*
- *Publicity: Lorna Carmichael, 020 7782 5000*

The Times
Times Newspapers
1 Pennington St, London E98 1TT
020 7782 5000
www.timesonline.co.uk
firstname.surname@thetimes.co.uk
Editor: Robert Thomson

- *Deputy editor: Ben Preston; news: John Wellman; home: Ian Cobain; political: Philip Webster (deputy: Rosie Bennett; assistants: Peter Riddell, Tom Baldwin; Whitehall: Jill Sherman; chief political corr: David Charter)*
- Section editors – *business: Patience Wheatcroft (international business: Carl Mortished); comment: David Finkelstein; countryside: Valerie Elliott; defence: Michael Evans; diplomatic: Richard Beeston; education: Tony Halpin; fashion: Lisa Armstrong; features: Michael Harvey; financial: Graham Searjeant; foreign: Bronwen Maddox; health: Nigel Hawkes; personal finance: Anne Ashworth; sport: David Chappell*
- *Executive editors/chief subs: Chris McKane, Simon Pearson*
- *Communications director: Anoushka Healy, 020 7782 5000*

National Sunday newspapers

The Business
Sunday Business Publishing
PA News Centre
292 Vauxhall Bridge Rd
London SW1V 1AE
020 7961 0000
www.thebusinessonline.com
firstinitialsurname@thebusinesspress.net
Also published on Monday
Publisher: Andrew Neil

- *Deputy editor: Ian Watson*
- *Economics: Allister Heath; technology: Tony Glover; transport: Tracey Boles*
- *Production: Graham Penn: chief sub: Phil Swift*
- *Publicity: Grant Clelland, 020 7961 0029*

Daily Star Sunday
Express Newspapers
Ludgate House, 245 Blackfriars Rd
London SE1 9UX
020 7928 8000
www.megastar.co.uk
firstname.surname@dailystar.co.uk
Editor: Gareth Morgan

- *Deputy editor: David Harbord; news editor: Michael Booker; political editor: Macer Hall*
- *Features: Julia Etherington; sport: Ray Ansbro*
- *Chief sub: Mike Woods; picture editor: Tomassina Brittain*
- *Publicity: Brian MacLaurin Associates, 020 8834 1034*

The Independent on Sunday
Independent News and Media (UK)
Independent House, 191 Marsh Wall
London E14 9RS
020 7005 2000
www.independent.co.uk
initial.surname@independent.co.uk
Editor: Tristan Davies

- *Deputy editor: Michael Williams; news editor: Robert Mendick; political editor: Andy McSmith (deputy: Francis Elliott)*
- Sections – *education: Richard Garner; environment: Geoffrey Lean; features: Nick Coleman; sport: Neil Morton; Time Off: Simon O'Hagan; women's: Elizabeth Heathcote*
- *Production editor: Keith Howitt*
- *Marketing manager: Johnathan Grogan, 020 7005 2000*

The Mail on Sunday
Associated Newspapers
Northcliffe House, 2 Derry St
Kensington, London W8 5TT
020 7938 6000
www.mailonsunday.co.uk
firstname.surname@mailonsunday.co.uk
Editor: Peter Wright
- *Deputy editor: Rod Gilchrist; news: Sebastian Hamilton; home affairs: Christopher Leake; political: Simon Walters*
- Sections – *education: Glen Owen; defence: Christopher Leake; environment: Jo Knowsley; features: Sian James; showbusiness: Katie Nicholl; sport: Malcolm Vallerius*
- *Production editor: Tim Smith; chief sub: Nick Petkovic*
- *Managing editor: John Wellington, 020 7938 7015*

News of the World
News Group Newspapers
1 Virginia St, London E98 1NW
020 7782 4000
www.thenewsoftheworld.co.uk
firstname.surname@notw.co.uk
Editor: Andy Coulson
- *Deputy editor: Neil Wallis; news editor: James Weatherup; assistant editor (news): Greg Miskiw; associate news editors: Ian Edmondson, Gary Thompson; political editor: Ian Kirby; investigations: Mazher Mahmood; senior associate editor: Harry Scott*
- *Production editor: Richard Rushworth*
- *Publicity: Hayley Barlow, 020 7782 4000*

The Observer
Guardian Media Group
119 Farringdon Rd
London EC1R 3ER
020 7278 2332
www.observer.guardian.co.uk
firstname.surname@observer.co.uk
Editor: Roger Alton
- *Deputy editors: John Mulholland, Paul Webster; executive editor, news: Andy Malone; political editor; Kamal Ahmed; chief political corr: Gaby Hinsliff*
- Sections – *business: Frank Kane; comment: Mike Holland; foreign news: Andy Malone; health: Jo Revill; media: Vanessa Thorpe; Observer Food Monthly: Nicola Jeal; Observer Music Monthly: Caspar Llewellyn Smith; Observer Review: Louise France; personal finance: Maria Scott; public affairs: Anthony Barnett; Scottish editor: Stephen Khan; social affairs: Jamie Doward; sport: Brian Oliver; travel: Jeannette Hyde*
- *Production editor: Bob Poulton; chief news sub: David Pearson*
- *Publicity: Anna Sinfield, 020 7239 9818*

The People
MGN, 1 Canada Square
Canary Wharf, London E14 5AP
020 7293 3000
www.people.co.uk
firstname.surname@people.co.uk
Editor: Mark Thomas
- *Deputy editor: Alan Edwards; news editor: Ian Edmondson; deputy news editor: Ben Proctor; associate news editor: David Jeffs; political editor: Nigel Nelson*
- *Features: Katie Weitz; investigations: Roger Insall; showbiz: Sean O'Brien; sport: Lee Horton*
- *Chief sub: Trisha Harbord; night editor: Matt Clarke; picture editor: Paula Derry*
- *Publicity: Sarah Vaughan-Brown, 020 7293 3222*

The Sunday Express
Express Newspapers
Ludgate House, 245 Blackfriars Rd
London SE1 9UX
020 7928 8000
www.express.co.uk
firstname.surname@express.co.uk
Editor: Martin Townsend
- *Deputy editor: Richard Dismore; news: James Murray; political: Julia Hartley-Brewer*
- Sections – *arts: Rachel Jane; business: David Parsley; crime: Andrea Perry; defence & diplomatic: Tim Shipman; environment: Stuart Winter; features: Janie Lawrence; health: Hilary Douglas; royal: Keith Perry; sport: Scott Wilson; travel: Jane Memmler*
- *Night editor: Andy Hoban; assistant night editor (features): Stuart Kershaw; chief news sub: Keith Ging*
- *Publicity: Brian MacLaurin Associates, 020 8834 1034*

Sunday Mirror
MGN, 1 Canada Square
Canary Wharf, London E14 5AP
020 7293 3000
www.sundaymirror.co.uk
firstname.surname@sundaymirror.co.uk
Editor: Tina Weaver
- *Associate editor: Mike Small; assistant editor (news): Nick Buckley; news editor: James Scott; political editor: Paul Gilfeather; chief reporter: Euan Stretch*
- Sections – *features: Nicky Dawson (deputy: Deborah Sherwood); investigations: Graham Johnson; show business: Ben Todd; sport: Craig Tregurtha*
- *Chief subs: Brian Hancill (news/features); Phil Davies (sport). Picture editor: Mike Sharp*
- *Publicity: Sarah Vaughan-Brown, 020 7293 3222*

Sunday Sport
Sport Newspapers
19 Great Ancoats St
Manchester M60 4BT
0161 236 4466
www.sundaysport.com
firstname.surname@sportsnewspapers.co.uk
Publicity: Jane Field, 0161 238 8135

The Sunday Telegraph
Telegraph Group, 1 Canada Square
Canary Wharf, London E14 5DT
020 7538 5000
www.telegraph.co.uk
firstname.surname@independent.co.uk
Editor: Dominic Lawson
- *Deputy editor: Matthew d'Ancona; news editor: Richard Ellis (chief reporter: Andrew Alderson); home affairs: David Bamber; political: Patrick Hennessy (deputy: Melissa Kite)*
- Sections – *city: Robert Peston; features: Emma Gosnell; foreign: Topaz Amoore; sport: Jon Ryan*
- *Chief subs: Justin Williams (news), John Morgan (features)*
- *Publicity: Victoria Higham, 020 7538 6259*

The Sunday Times
Times Newspapers
1 Pennington St, London E98 1ST
020 7782 5000
www.sunday-times.co.uk redirected to timesonline.co.uk
firstname.surname@sunday-times.co.uk
Editor: John Witherow
- *Deputy editor: Martin Ivens; managing editor: Richard Caseby; news: Charles Hymas; associate editor: Bob Tyrer; managing editor, news: Mark Skipworth; political editor: David Cracknell (deputy: Andrew Porter)*
- Sections – *business: William Lewis; city: Paul Durman; culture: Helen Hawkins; economics: David Smith; environment: Jonathan Leake; foreign: Sean Ryan; medical: Lois Rogers; money: Naomi Caine; News Review: Eleanor Mills; science: Jonathan Leake; sport: Alex Butler; Sunday Times magazine: Robin Morgan; travel: Christine Walker*
- *Managing editor (production): Ian Coxon; chief subs: David Paton; Denise Boutall (features)*
- *Publicity: Mary Fulton (Townhouse Publicity), 020 7226 7450*

Regional press Contacts

Main publishers

Archant

Prospect House, Rouen Rd
Norwich NR1 1RE
01603 628311
www.archant.co.uk

Daily Mail & General Trust

www.dmgt.co.uk

Associated Newspapers
Northcliffe House, 2 Derry St
London W8 5TT
020 7938 6000
www.associatednewspapers.co.uk

Northcliffe Newspapers Group
31–32 John St,
London WC1N 2QB
020 7400 1100
www.thisisnorthcliffe.co.uk

DC Thomson

185 Fleet St
London EC4A 2HS
020 7400 1030
www.dcthomson.co.uk

Guardian Media Group

164 Deansgate
Manchester M3 3RN
0161 832 7200
www.gmgplc.co.uk

Independent News and Media

2023 Bianconi Avenue
Citywest Business Campus
Naas Road
Dublin 24, Ireland
00 353 1 466 3200
www.independentnewsmedia.com

Johnston Press

53 Manor Place
Edinburgh EH3 7EG
0131 225 3361
www.jptalk.co.uk

Midland News Association

51–53 Queen St
Wolverhampton WV1 1ES
01902 313131
www.expressandstar.com

Newsquest Media

58 Church Street, Weybridge
Surrey KT13 8DP
01932 821212
www.newsquest.co.uk

Scotsman Publications

Barclay House, 108 Holyrood Road
Edinburgh EH8 8AS
0131 620 8620
www.scotsman.com

Trinity Mirror

4th Floor, Rear Wing
191–197 North Circular Rd
Dublin 7
00 353 1 868 8600
www.trinitymirror.com

UK head office
Chronicle House, Commonhall Street
Chester CH1 2AA
01244 687000

Regional newspapers – England

Main regionals

Birmingham Evening Mail
Weaman St, Birmingham
West Midlands B4 6AT
0121 236 3366
www.icbirmingham.co.uk
Daily. Editor: Roger Borrell
News editor: Andy Richards
Features editor: Alison Handley

Bristol Evening Post
Temple Way
Bristol BS99 7HD
0117 934 3000
www.thisisbristol.co.uk
Daily. Editor: Mike Lowe
News editor: Kevin Blackadder
Features editor: Bill Davis
Chief sub-editor: Helen Lawrence

Coventry Evening Telegraph
Corporation St
Coventry CV1 1FP
024 7663 3633
www.iccoventry.co.uk
Daily. Editor: Alan Kirby
News editor: John West
Features editor: Steven Chilton

Derby Evening Telegraph
Northcliffe House, Meadow Rd
Derby, Derbyshire DE1 2DW
01332 291111
www.thisisderbyshire.co.uk
Daily. Editor: Mike Norton
News editor: Nicola Hodgson
Features editor: Cheryl Hague
Chief sub-editor: Peter Pheasant

Eastern Daily Press
Archant Norfolk, Prospect House
Rouen Rd
01603 628311
www.edp24.co.uk
Daily. Editor: Peter Franzen

Evening Chronicle
Groat Market
Newcastle Upon Tyne NE1 1ED
0191 232 7500
www.icnewcastle.co.uk
Daily (Mon–Fri)
Editor: Paul Robertson
News editor: Mick Smith
Features editor: Richard Ord
Chief sub-editor: Adrian Hogg

Evening Standard
Associated Newspapers
Northcliffe House, 2 Derry St
020 7938 6000
www.thisislondon.co.uk
Daily. Editor: Veronica Wadley
News editor: Ian Walker
Features editor: Guy Eaton

Express & Star
51–53 Queen St, Wolverhampton
West Midlands WV1 1ES
01902 313131
www.expressandstar.com
Daily. Editor: Adrian Faber
News editor: Mark Drew
Features editor: Dillion Evans
Chief sub-editor: Tony Reynolds

Leicester Mercury
St George St
Leicester LE1 9FQ
0116 251 2512
www.leicestermercury.co.uk
Daily. Editor: Nick Carter
News editor: Richard Bettsworth

Liverpool Post & Echo
Old Hall St, Liverpool L3 9JQ
0151 227 2000
www.icliverpool.co.uk
Daily. Editor: Mark Dickinson
News editor: Alison Gow

Manchester Evening News
164 Deansgate
Manchester M3 3RN
0161 832 7200
www.manchesteronline.co.uk
Daily. Editor: Paul Horrocks
News editor: Ian Woods
Chief sub-editor: John Whittaker

The News (Portsmouth)
Portsmouth Publishing & Printing
The News Centre, Military Rd
Hilsea, Portsmouth
Hampshire PO2 9SX
023 9266 4488
www.thenews.co.uk
Daily. Editor: Mike Gilson
News editor: Colin McNeill
Features editor: John Millard
Chief sub-editor: Steve Matthews

Northern Echo (Darlington & South West Durham)
Priestgate, Darlington
County Durham DL1 1NF
01325 381313
www.thisisthenortheast.co.uk
Daily. Editor: Peter Barron
News editor: Nigel Burton
Features editor: Nick Morrison
Chief sub-editor: Ken Farrier

The Sentinel (Stoke-On-Trent)
Staffordshire Sentinel Newspapers
Sentinel House, Etruria
01782 602525
www.thesentinel.co.uk
Daily. Editor: Sean Dooley
News editor: Robert Cotterill
Features editor: Charlotte Little-Jones

Shropshire Star
Shropshire Newspapers, Ketley
Telford, Shropshire TF1 5HU
01952 242424
www.shropshirestar.com
Daily. Editor: Sarah Jane Smith
News editor: John Simcock
Features editor: Carl Jones
Chief sub-editor: Lisa Bailey

Southern Daily Echo
Newsquest (Southern)
Newspaper House, Test Lane
Redbridge, Southampton SO16 9JX
023 8042 4777
www.dailyecho.co.uk
Daily. Editor: Ian Murray
News editor: Gordon Sutter
Chief sub-editor: Colin Jenkins

The Star (Sheffield)
York St, Sheffield
South Yorkshire S1 1PU
0114 276 7676
www.sheffieldtoday.net
Daily. Editor: Peter Charlton
News editor: Bob Westerdale
Features editor: John Highfield
Head of content: Paul License

Sunday Mercury
Weaman St, Birmingham
West Midlands B4 6AT
0121 236 3366
www.icbirmingham.co.uk
Sunday. Editor: David Brookes
News editor: Tony Larner
Features editor: Paul Cole

Sunday Sun (Newcastle)
Groat Market
Newcastle Upon Tyne NE1 1ED
0191 232 7500
www.icnewcastle.co.uk
Sunday. Editor: Peter Montellier
News editor: Mike Kelly
Chief sub-editor: Lesley Oldfield
Production editor: Colin Patterson

Yorkshire Evening Post
PO Box 168, Wellington St
Leeds LS1 1RF
0113 243 2701
www.leedstoday.net
Daily. Editor: Neil Hodgkinson
News editor: Gillian Howorth
Features editor: Anne Pickles
Production editor: Howard Corry

Yorkshire Post
PO Box 168, Wellington St
Leeds LS1 1RF
0113 243 2701
www.yorkshireposttoday.co.uk
Daily. Editor: Rachael Campey
News editor: Hannah Start
Features editor: Catherine Scott
Head of production: Dick Porter

Other local and regional papers

London

Barnes, Mortlake & Sheen Times
020 8940 6030
www.richmondandtwickenhamtimes.co.uk
Weekly (Fri). Editor: Paul Mortimer
News editor: Andrew Raine

Barnet & Potters Bar Times
020 8203 0411
Weekly (Thu). Editor: John Killeen
News editor: Ian Lloyd

Barnet & Whetstone Press
020 8367 2345
Weekly free (Thu). Editor: Simon Jones
News editor: Jonathan Lawn

Brent & Wembley Leader
020 8427 4404
www.trinitymirrorsouthern.co.uk
Weekly free (Fri). Editor: Jo Makosinski
News editor: Caroline Lord
Features editor: Victoria Prewer
Production editor: Andre Erasmus

Brentford, Chiswick & Isleworth Times
020 8940 6030
www.richmondandtwickenhamtimes.co.uk
Weekly (Fri). Editor: Paul Mortimer
News editor: Andrew Raine

Bromley & Beckenham Times
020 8269 7000
Weekly (Thu). Editor: Melody Ryall
Production editor: Mick Taylor

Bromley & Orpington Express
020 8269 7000
Weekly free (Wed). Editor: Melody Ryall
Production editor: Mick Taylor

Bromley News
01959 564766
www.bromley-today.co.uk
Weekly (Thu). Editor: Bridger Hogan

Bromley News Shopper
020 8646 6336
www.newsshopper.co.uk
Weekly (Thu). Editor: Andrew Parkes
News editor: Matthew Ramsden
Chief sub-editor: Tim Miles

Camden Chronicle
020 8340 6868
Weekly (Thu). Editor: Tony Allcock

Camden New Journal
020 7419 9000
www.camdennewjournal.co.uk
Weekly (Thu). Editor: Eric Gordon
News editor: Dan Carrier
Features editor: Claire Davies
Chief sub-editor: Obi Jilani
Production editor: Sarah Roberts

Camden Times
020 8962 6800
Weekly (Wed). Editor: Tim Cole

Caterham & District Advertiser
020 8763 6666
www.icsurrey.co.uk
Weekly (Fri). Editor: Ian Carter
News editor: Mike Hawkins

Chingford Guardian
020 8498 3400
Weekly (Thu). Editor: Pat Stannard

The Chiswick
020 8940 6030
Weekly (Wed). Editor: Paul Mortimer
News editor: Andrew Raine

City of London & Dockland Times
07957 961520
Fortnightly (Mon)
Editor: Richard Alvin

Croydon Advertiser
020 8763 6666
www.iccroydon.co.uk
Weekly (Fri). Editor: Ian Carter
News editor: Mike Hawkins

Croydon Borough Post
020 8763 4433
Weekly (Wed). Editor: Ian Carter
News editor: Mike Hawley

Croydon Guardian
020 8774 6565
www.croydonguardian.co.uk
Weekly (Wed). Editor: Alison Hepworth
News editor: Helen Barnes

Docklands & City Recorder
020 8472 1421
Weekly (Wed). Editor: Colin Grainger
News editor: Pat Cougherey
Chief sub-editor: John Finn

Docklands News
020 7473 2488
www.docklandsnews.co.uk
Weekly (Thu). Editor: Richard Alvin

Ealing & Acton Gazette
020 8579 3131
Weekly (Fri). Editor: Linda Coulson
News editor: Sarah Graham
Features editor: Victoria Prewer
Chief sub-editor: Joyce McKim

Ealing & Uxbridge Times
01494 755000
www.hillingdontimes.co.uk
Weekly free (Thu). Editor: Steve Cohen
News editor: Kelly Clayton

Ealing Informer
020 8579 3131
Weekly (Wed). Editor: Linda Coulson
News editor: Sarah Graham
Features editor: Victoria Prewer
Chief sub-editor: Joyce McKim

Ealing Leader
01895 451000
Weekly (Fri). Editor: Linda Coulson
News editor: Sarah Graham
Features editor: Victoria Prewer
Chief sub-editor: Joyce McKim

Ealing Times
01494 755000
www.ealingtimes.co.uk
Weekly (Thu). Editor: Steve Cohen
News editor: Kelly Clayton

East End Life
020 7364 3059
Sunday free. Editor: Lorraine Clay
News editor: Helen Watson

East London Advertiser
020 7790 8822
Weekly (Thu). Editor: Richard Tidiman

East London Enquirer
01277 627300
Weekly (Thu). Editor: Carol Driver

Edgware & Mill Hill Press
020 8367 2345
Weekly free (Thu). Editor: Simon Jones
News editor: Jonathan Lawn

Edgware & Mill Hill Times
020 8203 0411
Weekly (Thu). Editor: John Killeen
News editor: Ian Lloyd

Eltham and Greenwich Times
020 8269 7000
Weekly (Wed). Editor: Melody Ryall
Production editor: Mick Taylor

Enfield Advertiser
020 8367 2345
Weekly (Wed). Editor: Simon Jones
News editor: Jonathan Lawn

Enfield Gazette
020 8367 2345
Weekly (Thu). Editor: Simon Jones
News editor: Jonathan Lawn

Enfield Independent
020 8362 1431
www.enfieldindependent.co.uk
Weekly (Wed). Editor: Kate Russell

Erith & Crayford Times
020 8269 7000
Weekly (Wed). Editor: Melody Ryall
Production editor: Mick Taylor

Evening Standard
020 7938 6000
www.thisislondon.co.uk
Daily. Editor: Veronica Wadley
News editor: Ian Walker
Features editor: Guy Eaton

Fulham Chronicle
020 8572 1816
Weekly (Thu). Editor: Kim Chapman
News editor: Janice Raycroft
Features editor: Gerri Besgrove

Fulham Gazette
020 8579 3131
Weekly (Fri). Editor: Sarah Graham
News editor: Lindsay Coulson

Greater London Advertiser
024 7625 1627
Weekly (Wed). Editor: Sam Lee

Greenford & Northolt Gazette
020 8579 3131
Weekly (Fri). Editor: Sarah Graham
News editor: Lindsay Coulson

Greenwich Borough Mercury
020 8769 4444
Weekly (Wed)
Editor-in-chief: Hannah Walker
Editor: Douglas Nel

Hackney Gazette
020 7790 8822
Weekly (Thu). Editor: Mick Ferris
News editor: Ross Lawrence

Hammersmith & Fulham Chronicles
020 8572 1816
Weekly (Thu). Editor: Kim Chapman
News editor: Janice Raycroft
Features editor: Gerri Besgrove

Hammersmith & Shepherd's Bush Gazette
020 8579 3131
Weekly (Fri). Editor: Sarah Graham
News editor: Lindsay Coulson

Hammersmith Times
020 8962 6800
Weekly (Wed). Editor: Tim Cole

Hampstead and Highgate Express
020 7433 0000
www.hamhigh.co.uk
Weekly (Fri). Editor: Geoff Martin
News editor: Bridget Galton
Features editor: Melanie Smith

Harefield Gazette
01895 451000
Weekly (Wed). Editor: Adrian Seal
News editor: Liz Bellchambers
Features editor: Neil Dhot

Haringey Advertiser
020 8367 2345
Weekly (Wed). Editor: Simon Jones
News editor: Jonathan Lawn

Haringey Independent
020 8359 5959
www.haringeyindependent.co.uk
Weekly (Fri). Editor: Kate Russell

Harrow & Sudbury Chronicle
020 8962 6800
Weekly (Wed). Editor: Tim Cole

Harrow Leader
020 8427 4404
www.trinitymirrorsouthern.co.uk
Weekly free (Fri). Editor: Jo Makosinski
News editor: Caroline Lord
Features editor: Victoria Prewer
Production editor: Andre Erasmus

Harrow Observer
020 8427 4404
Weekly (Thu). Editor: Jo Makosinski
News editor: Caroline Lord
Features editor: Victoria Prewer
Production editor: Andre Erasmus

Harrow Times
01923 216216
www.harrowtimes.co.uk
Weekly (Thu). Editor: Charlie Harris

Havering Herald
01708 771500
Weekly (Wed)
Editor: Mark Sweetingham

Hayes and Harlington Gazette
01895 451000
Weekly (Wed). Editor: Adrian Seal
News editor: Liz Bellchambers
Features editor: Neil Dhot

Hendon & Finchley Press
020 8367 2345
Weekly free (Thu). Editor: Simon Jones
News editor: Jonathan Lawn

Hendon Times
020 8359 5959
www.hendontimes.co.uk
Weekly (Thu). Editor: John Kileen
News editor: Colin O'Toole

Highbury & Islington Express
020 7433 0000
www.islingtonexpress.co.uk
Weekly (Fri). Editor: Geoff Martin
News editor: Bridget Galton
Features editor: Melanie Smith

Hillingdon Times
01494 755000
www.hillingdontimes.co.uk
Weekly (Thu). Editor: Steve Cohen

Hornsey & Crouch End Journal
020 8340 6868
Weekly (Thu). Editor: Tony Allcock

Hounslow, Brentford & Chiswick Informer
020 8572 1816
Weekly free (Fri). Editor: Kim Chapman
News editor: Ben Harvey

Hounslow Chronicle
020 8572 1816
Weekly (Thu). Editor: Kim Chapman
News editor: Ben Harvey
Features editor: Gerri Besgrove

Hounslow Guardian
020 8940 6030
www.hounslowguardian.co.uk
Weekly (Thu). Editor: Paul Mortimer
News editor: Andrew Raine

Hounslow Informer
020 8572 1816
Weekly free (Fri). Editor: Kim Chapman
News editor: Janice Raycroft
Features editor: Gerri Besgrove

Hounslow, Feltham & Hanworth Times
020 8940 6030
Weekly (Fri). Editor: Paul Mortimer
News editor: Andrew Raine

Hoxton & Stamford Hill Express
020 7790 8822
Weekly (Thu). Editor: Clara Wiseman

Ilford Recorder
020 8478 4444
www.recorderonline.co.uk
Weekly (Thu). Editor: Chris Carter
News editor: Antigone Forder
Production editor: Mike Cubitt

Islington Gazette
020 8340 6868
Weekly (Thu). Editor: Tony Allcock

Islington Tribune
020 7419 9000
Weekly (Thu). Editor: Eric Gordon
News editor: Dan Carrier
Features editor: Claire Davies
Chief sub-editor: Obi Jilani
Production editor: Sarah Roberts

Kensington & Chelsea Informer
020 8572 1816
Weekly (Fri). Editor: Kim Chapman
News editor: Janice Raycroft
Features editor: Gerri Besgrove

Kensington Times
020 8962 6800
Weekly (Wed). Editor: Tim Cole

Kilburn Times
020 8962 6800
Weekly (Wed). Editor: Tim Cole

Kingston & Surbiton Times
020 8940 6030
Weekly (Fri). Editor: Paul Mortimer
News editor: Chris Briddon

Kingston Guardian
020 8940 6030
www.kingstonguardian.co.uk
Weekly (Thu). Editor: Sean Duggan

Kingston Informer
020 8572 1816
www.trinitymirrorsouthern.co.uk
Weekly (Fri). Editor: Kim Chapman
News editor: Janice Raycroft
Features editor: Gerri Besgrove

Lewisham and Greenwich Mercury
020 8769 4444
www.icsouthlondon.co.uk
Weekly free. Editor: Hannah Walker
News editor: Shujal Azam

Lewisham Borough Mercury
020 8692 1122
Weekly (Wed). Editor: Douglas Nel

Lewisham News Shopper
020 8646 6336
www.newsshopper.co.uk
Weekly (Thu). Editor: Andrew Parkes
News editor: Matthew Ramsden
Chief sub-editor: Tim Miles

Leyton & Leytonstone Guardian
020 8498 3400
www.leytonguardian.co.uk
Weekly (Thu). Editor: Pat Stannard

Marylebone & Paddington Informer
020 8572 1816
Weekly (Fri). Editor: Kim Chapman
News editor: Janice Raycroft
Features editor: Gerri Besgrove

Marylebone & Paddington Mercury
020 8572 1816
Weekly (Fri). Editor: Kim Chapman
News editor: Janice Raycroft
Features editor: Gerri Besgrove

Mayfair Times
020 7839 2455
Monthly free (1st Mon)
Editor: Eric Brown

Metro London
020 7651 5200
www.metro.co.uk
Daily. Editor: Kenny Campbell
News editor: Mark Dorman
Features editor: Kieran Meeke
Production editor: Jason Kent

Mitcham, Morden & Wimbledon Post
020 8769 4444
www.icsouthlondon.co.uk
Weekly free (Fri)
Editor: Hannah Walker
News editor: Shujal Azam

Muswell Hill Journal
020 8340 6868
Weekly (Thu). Editor: Tony Allcock

New Addington Advertiser
020 8763 6666
www.icsurrey.co.uk
Weekly (Fri). Editor: Ian Carter
News editor: Mike Hawkins

Newham Recorder
020 8472 1421
www.recorderonline.co.uk
Weekly (Thu). Editor: Colin Grainger
News editor: Pat Cougherey
Chief sub-editor: John Finn

North London Herald
020 8340 6868
Weekly (Thu). Editor: Tony Allcock

Paddington Times
020 8962 6800
Weekly (Wed). Editor: Tim Cole

Pinner Observer
020 8427 4404
Weekly (Thu). Editor: Jo Makosinski
News editor: Caroline Lord
Features editor: Victoria Prewer
Production editor: Andre Erasmus

Potters Bar Press
020 8364 4040
Weekly free (Thu)
Editor: Jonathan Lawn
News editor: Joseph Lee

Richmond & Twickenham Informer
020 8572 1816
Weekly (Fri). Editor: Kim Chapman
News editor: Janice Raycroft
Features editor: Gerri Besgrove

Richmond & Twickenham Times
020 8940 6030
www.richmondandtwickenhamtimes.co.uk
Weekly (Fri). Editor: Paul Mortimer
News editor: James Adlam

Richmond Borough Guardian
020 8940 6030
www.kingstonguardian.co.uk
Weekly (Thu). Editor: Paul Mortimer
News editor: James Adlam

Ruislip & Northwood Gazette
01895 451000
Weekly (Wed). Editor: Adrian Seal
News editor: Liz Bellchambers
Features editor: Neil Dhot

Ruislip & Northwood Informer
01895 451000
Weekly free (Fri). Editor: Adrian Seal
News editor: Liz Bellchambers
Features editor: Neil Dhot

South London Press
020 8769 4444
www.icsouthlondon.co.uk
Twice-weekly (Tue, Fri)
Editor: Hannah Walker
News editor: Shujal Azam

Southall Gazette
020 8579 3131
Weekly (Fri). Editor: Sarah Graham
News editor: Lindsay Coulson

Southwark News
020 7231 5258
Weekly (Thu). Editor: Chris Mullany
News editor: Kevin Quinn

St John's Wood & Maida Vale Express (Wood & Vale)
020 7433 0000
Weekly (Fri). Editor: Geoff Martin
News editor: Bridget Galton
Features editor: Melanie Smith

Stanmore Observer
020 8427 4404
Weekly (Thu). Editor: Jo Makosinski
News editor: Caroline Lord
Features editor: Victoria Prewer
Production editor: Andre Erasmus

The Star
01494 755000
Weekly free (Thu). Editor: Steve Cohen
News editor: Julie Voyce
Features editor: Clare Bourke

Stratford & Newham Express
020 7790 8822
Weekly (Wed). Editor: Richard Tidiman

Streatham Guardian
020 8646 6336
www.streathamguardian.co.uk
Weekly (Thu). News editor: Dave Tilley
Features editor: June Simpson

Streatham, Clapham & West Norwood Post
020 8769 4444
www.icsouthlondon.co.uk
Weekly free (Thu)
Editor: Hannah Walker
News editor: Shujal Azam

Teddington & Hampton Times
020 8940 6030
Weekly (Fri). Editor: Paul Mortimer
News editor: James Adlam

Tottenham & Wood Green Journal
020 8340 6868
Weekly (Thu). Editor: Tony Allcock

Tower Hamlets Recorder
020 8472 1421
www.recorderonline.co.uk
Weekly (Thu). Editor: Colin Grainger
News editor: Pat Cougherey
Chief sub-editor: John Finn

Uxbridge & Hillingdon Leader
01895 451000
Weekly free (Thu). Editor: Adrian Seal
News editor: Liz Bellchambers
Features editor: Neil Dhot

Uxbridge & W Drayton Gazette
01895 451000
Weekly (Tue). Editor: Adrian Seal
News editor: Liz Bellchambers
Features editor: Neil Dhot

Uxbridge Informer
01895 451000
Weekly (Wed). Editor: Adrian Seal
News editor: Liz Bellchambers
Features editor: Neil Dhot

Uxbridge Leader
01895 451000
Weekly free (Wed). Editor: Adrian Seal
News editor: Liz Bellchambers
Features editor: Neil Dhot

Walthamstow Guardian
020 8498 3400
www.walthamstowguardian.co.uk
Weekly (Thu). Editor: Pat Stannard

Wandsworth Guardian
020 8646 6336
www.wandsworthguardian.co.uk
Weekly (Thu). News editor: Dave Tilley
Features editor: June Simpson

Wembley & Kingsbury Chronicle
020 8962 6800
Weekly (Wed). Editor: Tim Cole

Wembley Leader
020 8427 4404
Weekly (Thu). Editor: Jo Makosinski
News editor: Caroline Lord
Features editor: Victoria Prewer
Production editor: Andre Erasmus

Wembley Observer
020 8427 4404
Weekly (Thu). Editor: Jo Makosinski
News editor: Caroline Lord
Features editor: Victoria Prewer
Production editor: Andre Erasmus

West End Extra
020 7419 9000
Weekly (Fri). Editor: Eric Gordon
News editor: Dan Carrier
Features editor: Claire Davies
Chief sub-editor: Obi Jilani
Production editor: Sarah Roberts

Westender
020 7607 6060
Monthly free (last week in month)
Editor: Eileen Martin
News editor: Bina Gowrea
Features editor: Eileen Duff
Production editor: Jason Kent

Westminster & Pimlico News
020 8572 1816
Weekly (Fri). Editor: Kim Chapman
News editor: Janice Raycroft
Features editor: Gerri Besgrove

Westminster Independent
020 8961 3345
www.londonlocals.co.uk
Weekly (Fri). Editor: Jan Mappin

Westminster Times
020 8962 6800
Weekly (Wed). Editor: Tim Cole

The Wharf
020 7510 6306
www.icthewharf.co.uk
Weekly free (Thu)
Editor: Ann Stenhouse

Willesden & Brent Chronicle
020 8962 6800
Weekly (Wed). Editor: Tim Cole

Willesden Observer
020 8427 4404
Weekly (Thu). Editor: Jo Makosinski
News editor: Caroline Lord
Features editor: Victoria Prewer
Production editor: Andre Erasmus

Wimbledon Guardian
020 8646 6336
www.wimbledonguardian.co.uk
Weekly (Thu). News editor: Dave Tilley
Features editor: June Simpson

Wimbledon News
020 8646 6336
Weekly (Wed). News editor: Dave Tilley
Features editor: June Simpson

South-east England

Bedfordshire, East Sussex, Hertfordshire, Kent, Surrey, West Sussex

Addlestone and Byfleet Review
01483 508700
www.surreyad.co.uk
Weekly (Wed). Editor: Marnie Wilson

Adscene – Ashford & Tenterden
01227 767321
Weekly (Thu). Editor: Lesley Finlay
News editor: Julia Rogers
Chief sub-editor: Mark Silva

Adscene (Canterbury)
01227 767321
Weekly (Thu). Editor: John Nurden
News editor: Ian Reed
Features editor: Julia Rogers
Chief sub-editor: Paul Taylor
Production editor: Mark Silva

Adscene (Folkestone & Dover)
01227 767321
Weekly (Thu). Editor: Simon Finlay

Adscene (Maidstone)
01622 690339
www.kent-online.co.uk
Weekly free (Thu). Editor: Diane Nicholls

Adscene (Medway)
01227 767321
Weekly (Thu). Editor: Diane Nicholls
News editor: Nicola Jordan

Adscene (Sittingbourne & Sheppey)
01227 767321
Weekly (Thu). Editor: Christine Rayner
News editor: Steve Waite

Adscene (Thanet)
01227 767321
Weekly (Thu). Editor: Mike Pearce

Aldershot News
01483 508700
www.aldershot.co.uk
Weekly (Tue). Editor: Marnie Wilson

Ashford KM Extra
01233 623232
Weekly (Tue). Editor: Brian Lewis
News editor: Leo Whitlock
Features editor: Leo Whitlock
Chief sub-editor: Claire Stevens
Production editor: Gary Barker

Baldock Crow
01763 245241
Weekly (Thu). Editor: Les Baker

Barnet & Potters Bar Times
020 8359 5959
www.barnettimes.co.uk
Weekly (Thu). Editor: John Kileen
News editor: Colin O'Toole

Bedford Times & Citizen
01234 405060
www.bedfordtoday.co.uk
Weekly (Fri). Editor: Chris Hall
News editor: Mark Lewis
Features editor: Olga Norford

Bedfordshire on Sunday
01234 300888
www.seriousaboutnews.com
Sunday. Editor: Steve Lowe
News editor: Liz Ashton
Production editor: Phil Umney

Bexhill AdNews
01424 730555
www.bexhilltoday.co.uk
Weekly free (Wed). Editor: Michael Beard
Deputy editor: John Dowling
News editor: Rob Hustwaype

Bexhill-On-Sea Observer
01424 730555
www.bexhilltoday.co.uk
Weekly (Fri). Editor: Michael Beard
Deputy editor: John Dowling
News editor: Rob Hustwaype

Bexley & Eltham Express
020 8269 7000
Weekly free (Wed). Editor: Melody Ryall
Production editor: Mick Taylor

Bexley Dartford & Gravesham News Shopper
01689 885701
Weekly (Wed). Editor: Andrew Parkes

Bexley Mercury
020 8769 4444
www.icsouthlondon.co.uk
Weekly free. Editor: Hannah Walker
News editor: Douglas Mill

Bexleyheath & Welling Times
020 8269 7000
Weekly (Wed). Editor: Melody Ryall
Production editor: Mick Taylor

Biggin Hill News
01959 564766
www.biggin-hill-today.co.uk
Weekly (Thu). Editor: Bridger Hogan

Biggleswade & Sandy Comet
01462 420120
www.thecomet.net
Weekly (Thu). Editor: Darren Isted
News editor: John Adams

Biggleswade Advertiser
01462 441020
www.hitchinadvertiser.co.uk
Weekly (Wed)
No editorial

Biggleswade Chronicle
01767 222333
www.biggleswadetoday.co.uk
Weekly (Fri). Editor: Jim Stewart

Bishops Stortford Citizen
01992 572285
Weekly (Thu). Editor: David Jackman

Bishops Stortford Herald
01279 624331
Weekly (Thu). Editor: Peter Jeffery
News editor: Tracey Hubbard
Features editor: James Wilmore

Bognor Regis Guardian
01243 534133
Weekly free (Wed). Editor: Alicia Denny

Bognor Regis Observer
01243 828777
www.chichester.co.uk
Weekly (Thu). Editor: Keith Newberry
Features editor: Kevin Smith

Borehamwood & Elstree Times
020 8359 5959
www.borehamwoodtimes.co.uk
Weekly (Fri). Editor: John Kileen
News editor: Colin O'Toole

Brighton & Hove Leader
01273 544544
www.thisisbrightonandhove.co.uk
Weekly (Fri). Editor: Chris Chandler
News editor: Mike Dunford

Brighton Evening Argus
01273 544544
www.thisisbrightonandhove.co.uk
Daily. Editor: Simon Bradshaw
News editor: Simon Freeman
Features editor: Jacqui Phillips
Chief sub-editor: Pat Lewis
Production editor: Chris Heath

Camberley Courier
01252 339760
www.camberley.co.uk
Weekly free (Wed). Editor: James Taylor
News editor: Adam Clark

Camberley News & Mail
01252 339760
www.camberley.co.uk
Weekly (Fri). Editor: James Taylor
News editor: Adam Clark

Canterbury KM Extra
01227 768181
Weekly (Tue). Editor: Bob Bounds
News editor: Trisha Jaimeson
Production editor: Gary Barker

Cheshunt & Waltham Mercury
01992 414141
Weekly (Fri). Editor: Ian Rogerson
News editor: Pat Roberts

Chichester & Selsey Journal
01243 534133
www.chichester.co.uk
Weekly free (Wed). Editor: Alicia Denny

Chichester Observer
01243 539389
www.chiobserver.co.uk
Weekly (Thu). Editor: Keith Newberry
Features editor: Peter Homer

Chislehurst Times
020 8269 7000
Weekly (Thu). Editor: Melody Ryall
Production editor: Mick Taylor

Cranleigh Times
01483 508700
Weekly free (Wed). Editor: Marnie Wilson

Crawley News
01737 732000
www.icsurrey.co.uk
Weekly (Wed). Editor: Ian Carter
News editor: John Keeble

Crawley Observer
01293 562929
www.crawleyobserver.co.uk
Weekly (Wed). Editor: Graham Campbell
News editor: Allan Norbury
Chief sub-editor: Mark Dunford

Crowborough Courier
01892 681000
www.thisiskentandeastsussex.co.uk
Weekly (Fri). Editor: Giles Broadbent
News editor: Melanie Whittaker
Features editor: Lucia Blash
Chief sub-editor: Lindsey Jones
Production editor: Richard Page

Croydon Advertiser
01737 732000
www.iccroydon.co.uk
Weekly (Fri). Editor: Mike Hawkins

Croydon Guardian
020 8774 6590
www.croydonguardian.co.uk
Weekly (Wed). Editor: Alison Hepworth
News editor: Helen Barnes
Chief sub-editor: Ali Mased

Croydon Post
01737 732000
Weekly (Thu). Editor: Mike Hawkins

Dartford & Swanley Extra Informer
01322 220791
Weekly (Thu). Editor: Sandra Hembury
News editor: Teresa Gaines

Dartford Express
020 8269 7000
Weekly free (Wed). Editor: Melody Ryall
Production editor: Mick Taylor

Dartford Messenger
01322 220791
www.kent-online.co.uk
Weekly (Thu). Editor: Sandra Hembury
News editor: Denise Eaton

Dartford Times
020 8269 7000
Weekly (Thu). Editor: Melody Ryall
Production editor: Mick Taylor

Dover & Deal Extra
01233 623323
Weekly (Wed). Editor: Brian Lewis
News editor: Leo Whitlock
Features editor: Leo Whitlock
Chief sub-editor: Claire Stevens
Production editor: Gary Barker

Dover Express
01227 767321
Weekly (Thu). Editor: Simon Finlay

Dover Mercury
01304 240380
Weekly (Thu). Editor: Graham Smith

Downs Mail
01622 630330
www.downsmail.co.uk
Monthly (variable)
Editor: Geoff Manners

Dunstable Gazette
01582 526000
www.lutontoday.co.uk
Weekly (Wed). Editor: John Buckledee

Dunstable On Sunday
01582 707707
www.seriousaboutnews.com
Sunday. Editor: Aylia Fox
News editor: Gaynor Selby
Production editor: Phil Umney

Eastbourne & District Advertiser
01323 722091
www.eastbournetoday.co.uk
Weekly free (Thu). Editor: Peter Lindsay
News editor: Robin Emanuel
Features editor: Andrew Bennett

Eastbourne Gazette
01323 722091
www.eastbournetoday.co.uk
Weekly (Wed). Editor: Peter Lindsay
News editor: Robin Emanuel
Features editor: Andrew Bennett

Eastbourne Herald
01323 722091
www.eastbournetoday.co.uk
Weekly (Fri). Editor: Peter Lindsay
News editor: Robin Emanuel
Features editor: Andrew Bennett

East Grinstead Courier
01892 681000
Weekly (Thu). Editor: Giles Broadbent
News editor: Melanie Whittaker
Features editor: Lucia Blash
Chief sub-editor: Lindsey Jones
Production editor: Richard Page

East Grinstead Observer
01737 732000
www.icsurrey.co.uk
Weekly (Wed). Editor: Ian Carter
News editor: Catherine Simmons

East Kent Gazette
01227 767321
Weekly (Thu). Editor: Christine Rayner
News editor: Steve Waite

East Kent Mercury
01304 365526
Weekly free. Editor: Graham Smith
Production editor: Gary Barker

Edenbridge Chronicle
01959 564766
Weekly (Thu). Editor: Signid Sherrell

Edenbridge County Border News
01959 564766
www.edenbridge-today.co.uk
Weekly (Thu). Editor: Kevin Black

Edenbridge Courier
01892 681000
www.thisiskentandeastsussex.co.uk
Weekly (Fri). Editor: Giles Broadbent
News editor: Melanie Whittaker
Features editor: Lucia Blash
Chief sub-editor: Lindsey Jones
Production editor: Richard Page

Edgware & Mill Hill Times
020 8359 5959
www.edgwaretimes.co.uk
Weekly (Thu). Editor: John Kileen
News editor: Colin O'Toole

Elmbridge Guardian
020 8646 6336
Weekly (Thu). Editor: Sean Duggan

Epsom Guardian
020 8646 6336
www.epsomguardian.co.uk
Weekly (Thu). Editor: Sean Duggan

Epsom, Ewell & Banstead Post
020 8763 6666
www.icsurrey.co.uk
Weekly (Fri). Editor: Ian Carter
News editor: Mike Hawkins

Esher News & Mail
01483 508700
www.esher.co.uk
Weekly (Fri). Editor: Marnie Wilson

Farnham Herald
01252 725224
www.farnham-herald-today.co.uk
Weekly (Fri). Editor: Vic Robbie
News editor: James Bowman
Chief sub-editor: Sandy Baker

Farnham Post
01420 88949
Fortnightly free (Mon)
Editor: Alan Wooler

Faversham KM Extra
01227 768181
Weekly (Tue). Editor: Bob Bounds
News editor: Trisha Jaimeson
Production editor: Gary Barker

Faversham News
01227 475901
www.faversham.org/GENERAL/favnews.htm
Weekly (Thu). Editor: Bob Bounds
News editor: Trisha Jaimeson
Production editor: Gary Barker

Faversham Times
01227 767321
Weekly (Thu). Editor: Christine Rayner
News editor: Steve Waite
Features editor: Julia Rogers

Folkestone & Hythe Extra
01303 850676
Weekly (Wed). Editor: Brian Lewis
Production editor: Gary Barker

Folkestone Express
01233 623232
Weekly (Wed). Editor: Brian Lewis
News editor: Leo Whitlock
Features editor: Leo Whitlock
Chief sub-editor: Claire Stevens

Folkestone Herald
01227 767321
Weekly (Thu). Editor: Simon Finlay

Friday-Ad
0870 162 9999
www.friday-ad.co.uk
Weekly (Fri). Editor: David Sommerville

Gatwick Skyport
01932 561111
Weekly free (Fri). Editor: Liz Billings

Godalming Times
01483 508700
Weekly free (Wed)
Editor: Marnie Wilson

Gravesend Express
020 8269 7000
Weekly free (Wed). Editor: Melody Ryall
Production editor: Mick Taylor

Gravesend KM Extra
01474 333381
www.kent-online.co.uk
Weekly (Fri). Editor: Sandra Hembury
News editor: Denise Eaton

Gravesend Messenger
01474 333381
www.kent-online.co.uk
Weekly (Thu). Editor: Sandra Hembury
News editor: Denise Eaton

Gravesend Reporter
020 8269 7000
Weekly (Thu). Editor: Melody Ryall
Production editor: Mick Taylor

Guildford Times
01483 508700
www.surreyad.co.uk/news/guildford-times.html
Weekly free (Wed)
Editor: Marnie Wilson

Hailsham Gazette
01323 722091
Weekly (Wed). Editor: Peter Lindsay
News editor: Robin Emanuel
Features editor: Andrew Bennett

Harpenden Observer
01727 834411
Weekly (Wed). Editor: Deborah Williams

Haslemere Times & Mail
01252 716444
Weekly free (Tue). Editor: Jean Parrat

Hastings & St Leonards Observer
01424 854242
www.hastingstoday.co.uk
Weekly (Fri). Editor: Michael Beard
News editor: Ann Terry
Associate editor: Russell Claughton

Hastings AdNews
01424 854242
www.hastingstoday.co.uk
Weekly (Fri). Editor: Michael Beard
News editor: Ann Terry
Associate editor: Russell Claughton

Hemel Hempstead Gazette
01442 262311
www.hemelonline.co.uk
Weekly (Wed). Editor: David Feldstein
News editor: Ann Traynor

Hendon & Finchley Times
020 8359 5959
www.hendontimes.co.uk
Weekly (Thu). Editor: John Kileen
News editor: Colin O'Toole

Herne Bay Gazette
01227 475901
Weekly. Editor: Bob Bounds
News editor: Trisha Jaimeson
Production editor: Gary Barker

Herne Bay KM Extra
01227 768181
Weekly (Tue). Editor: Bob Bounds
News editor: Trisha Jaimeson
Production editor: Gary Barker

Herne Bay Times
01227 771515
Weekly (Thu). Editor: John Nurden
News editor: Ian Reed
Features editor: Julia Rogers
Chief sub-editor: Paul Taylor
Production editor: Mark Silva

Hertford Times
01727 327551
www.hertsad.co.uk
Weekly (Wed). Editor: Terry Mitchinson

Hertfordshire Mercury
01992 526625
www.herts-essex-news.co.uk
Weekly (Fri). Editor: Paul Winspear

Hertfordshire News
01926 431601
Weekly (Mon). Editor: Funsho Ajibade

Hertfordshire on Sunday
01582 700800
Sunday. Editor: Liz Reilly

Hertfordshire Star
01992 526625
www.herts-essex-news.co.uk
Weekly (Wed). Editor: Chris Bristow

Herts & Essex Observer
01279 866355
www.herts-essex-news.co.uk
Weekly (Thu). Editor: Val Brown
News editor: Sandra Perry

Herts Advertiser
01727 865165
www.hertsad.co.uk
Weekly (Thu). Editor: Noel Cantillon

Hitchin Advertiser
01462 441020
www.hitchinadvertiser.co.uk
Weekly (Wed)
General manager: Ricky Allan

Hitchin Comet
01462 420120
www.thecomet.net
Weekly (Thu). Editor: Darren Isted
News editor: John Adams

Hoddesdon & Braxbourne Mercury
01992 414141
Weekly (Fri). Editor: Ian Rogerson
News editor: Pat Roberts

Horley Life
01273 544544
Weekly (Thu). Editor: Chris Chandler
News editor: Mike Dunford

Horsham Advertiser
01403 751200
www.horshamtoday.co.uk
Weekly (Fri). Editor: Gary Shipton
Chief sub-editor: Steve Payne
Production editor: Jonathan Taylor

Hythe Herald
01227 767321
Weekly (Thu). Editor: Simon Finlay

Isle of Thanet Gazette
01227 767321
Weekly (Thu). Editor: Mike Pearce

Kent & Sussex Courier
01892 681000
www.thisiskentandeastsussex.co.uk
Weekly (Fri). Editor: Giles Broadbent
News editor: Melanie Whittaker
Features editor: Lucia Blash
Chief sub-editor: Lindsey Jones
Production editor: Richard Page

Kent Messenger
01622 695666
www.kent-online.co.uk
Weekly (Fri). Editor: Ron Green
News editor: Cathy Tyce

Kent on Sunday
01227 732223
www.kentonsunday.co.uk
Sunday. Editor: Ian Patel
News editor: Gary Wright
Chief sub-editor: Dave Hobday
Production editor: Jason Pyne

Kentish Express
01233 623232
Weekly (Thu). Editor: Brian Lewis
News editor: Leo Whitlock
Features editor: Leo Whitlock
Chief sub-editor: Claire Stevens
Production editor: Gary Barker

Kentish Gazette
01227 768181
Weekly (Thu). Editor: Bob Bounds
News editor: Trisha Jaimeson
Production editor: Gary Barker

Kentish Times Newspapers
020 8269 7000
Weekly (Thu). Editor: Melody Ryall
Production editor: Mick Taylor

Kingston Guardian
020 8646 6336
www.kingstonguardian.co.uk
Weekly (Thu). Editor: Sean Duggan

Lea Valley Star
01992 526625
Weekly (Wed). Editor: Chris Bristow

Leatherhead Advertiser
01737 732000
www.icsurrey.co.uk
Weekly (Thu). Editor: Ian Carter
News editor: Monica Hawley

Leatherhead Guardian
020 8646 6336
Weekly (Thu). Editor: Sean Duggan

Leighton Buzzard & Linslade Citizen
01908 651200
www.miltonkeynestoday.co.uk
Weekly free (Thu). Editor: Alan Legg

Leighton Buzzard Observer
01525 858400
www.miltonkeynestoday.co.uk
Weekly (Tue). Editor: Nick Wormley
News editor: Mike King

Leighton Buzzard On Sunday
01908 809000
www.seriousaboutnews.com
Sunday. Editor: Liz Aston

Letchworth & Baldock Comet
01462 420120
www.thecomet.net
Weekly (Thu). Editor: Darren Isted
News editor: John Adams

Limited Edition – Hertfordshire
01923 216220
Monthly (1st Tue)
Editor: Deborah Aspinall

Littlehampton Gazette
01903 230051
www.littlehamptontoday.co.uk
Weekly (Thu). Editor: Roger Green

Luton Herald & Post
01582 700600
www.lutontoday.co.uk
Weekly (Thu). Editor: John Francis

Luton News
01582 526000
www.lutontoday.co.uk
Weekly (Wed). Editor: John Buckledee
Assistant editor: Geoff Cox

Luton on Sunday
01582 707707
www.seriousaboutnews.com
Sunday. Editor: Aylia Fox
News editor: Gaynor Selby

Maidstone KM Extra
01622 695666
www.kent-online.co.uk
Weekly free (Fri). Editor: Ron Green
News editor: Cathy Tyce

Medway Messenger (Rochester, Chatham, Maidstone, Gravesend)
01634 830600
www.kent-online.co.uk
Weekly. Editor: Bob Diamond
News editor: Nikke White
Features editor: Lynn Cox
Chief sub-editor: Digby Kennard

Medway News
01227 767321
Weekly (Thu). Editor: Diane Nicholls
News editor: Nicola Jordan

Medway Standard
01227 767321
Weekly (Fri). Editor: Diane Nicholls
News editor: Nicola Jordan

The Messenger (Haslemere)
01428 653999
www.messenger-online.co.uk
Weekly free (Wed). Editor: Guy Butchers
News editor: Sheila Checkley

Mid Sussex Citizen
01444 452201
www.midsussextoday.co.uk
Weekly free (Wed). Editor: Paul Watson

Mid Sussex Leader
01273 544544
www.thisismidsussex.co.uk
Weekly (Thu). Editor: Chris Chandler
News editor: Mike Dunford

Mid Sussex Times
01444 452201
www.midsussextoday.co.uk
Weekly (Thu). Editor: Paul Watson

Midhurst & Petworth Observer
01730 813557
www.midhurstandpetworth.co.uk
Weekly (Thu). Editor: Keith Newberry
News editor: Jane Hurt

News in Focus
01732 228000
www.thisiskentandeastsussex.co.uk
Weekly (Tue). Editor: Frank Baldwin

News & Mail
01483 508900
www.surreyad.co.uk/aboutus.htm
Weekly (Wed). Editor: Marnie Wilson

News Shopper Guide
020 8646 6336
Weekly (Thu). Editor: Andrew Parkes
News editor: Matthew Ramsden
Chief sub-editor: Tim Miles

Orpington & Petts Wood Times
020 8269 7000
Weekly (Thu). Editor: Melody Ryall
Production editor: Mick Taylor

Paddock Wood Courier
01892 681000
www.thisiskentandeastsussex.co.uk
Weekly (Fri). Editor: Giles Broadbent
News editor: Melanie Whittaker
Features editor: Lucia Blash
Chief sub-editor: Lindsey Jones
Production editor: Richard Page

Redhill & Reigate Life
020 8646 6336
Weekly (Wed). Editor: Alison Hepworth
News editor: Helen Barnes
Chief sub-editor: Ali Mased

Reigate Post
020 8770 7171
Weekly (Thu). Editor: Ian Carter
News editor: Helen Backway

Reigate, Redhill & Horley Post
01737 732000
www.icsurrey.co.uk
Weekly (Wed). Editor: Ian Carter
News editor: Glen Mitchell

Romney Marsh Herald
01227 767321
Weekly (Wed). Editor: Diane Nicholls
News editor: Nicola Jordan

Royston & Buntingford Mercury
01992 526600
Weekly (Fri). Editor: Paul Winspear
News editor: Paul Brackley
Features editor: Bridget McAlpine

Royston Crow
01763 245241
Weekly (Thu). Editor: Les Baker

Rye & Battle Observer
01424 854242
www.ryeandbattletoday.co.uk
Weekly (Fri). Editor: Michael Beard
News editor: Ann Terry
Associate editor: Russell Claughton

St Albans & Harpenden Review
01727 834411
www.stalbansobserver.co.uk
Weekly free (Wed)
Editor: Deborah Williams

St Albans Observer
01727 834411
www.stalbansobserver.co.uk
Weekly (Thu). Editor: Deborah Williams

Seaford Gazette
01323 722091
Weekly (Wed). Editor: Peter Lindsay
News editor: Robin Emanuel
Features editor: Andrew Bennett

Sevenoaks Chronicle
01732 228000
www.thisiskentandeastsussex.co.uk
Weekly (Thu). Editor: Frank Baldwin

Sheerness Times Guardian
01795 580300
Weekly (Thu). Editor: Duncan Marsh
News editor: Linda Mitchell

Sheppey Gazette
01227 767321
Weekly (Thu). Editor: Christine Rayner
News editor: Steve Waite

Shoreham Herald
01903 230051
www.shorehamtoday.co.uk
Weekly (Thu). Editor: Michelle Neville

Sidcup & Blackfen Times
020 8269 7000
Weekly (Wed). Editor: Melody Ryall
Production editor: Mick Taylor

Sittingbourne KM Extra
01795 580300
Weekly (Wed). Editor: Duncan Marsh
News editor: Linda Mitchell

South Coast Leader
01273 544544
www.thisisbrightonandhove.co.uk
Weekly (Fri). Editor: Chris Chandler
News editor: Mike Dunford

Staines & Ashford News
01932 561111
www.trinitymirrorsouthern.co.uk
Weekly free (Wed). Editor: Kim Chatman
News editor: Judy Parsons

Staines & Egham News
01932 561111
www.trinitymirrorsouthern.co.uk
Weekly free (Wed). Editor: Kim Chatman
News editor: Judy Parsons

Staines Guardian
020 8940 6030
www.stainesguardian.co.uk
Weekly (Thu). Editor: Paul Mortimer
News editor: James Adlam

Staines Informer
01932 561111
www.trinitymirrorsouthern.co.uk
Weekly free (Thu). Editor: Kim Chatman
News editor: Judy Parsons

Staines Leader
01932 561111
www.trinitymirrorsouthern.co.uk
Weekly free (Thu). Editor: Kim Chatman

Star Classified (Bishops Stortford)
01279 866355
www.herts-essex-news.co.uk
Weekly (Thu). Editor: Val Brown
News editor: Sandra Perry

Stevenage Advertiser
01462 441020
www.hitchinadvertiser.co.uk
Weekly (Wed)
General manager: Ricky Allan

Stevenage Comet
01462 420120
www.thecomet.net
Weekly (Thu). Editor: Darren Isted
News editor: John Adams

Stevenage Herald
01462 420120
www.thecomet.net
Weekly free (Wed). Editor: Darren Isted
News editor: John Adams

Stevenage Mercury
01992 526600
Weekly (Fri). Editor: Paul Winspear
News editor: Paul Brackley
Features editor: Bridget McAlpine

Surrey & Hants News
01252 716444
Weekly free (Tue). Editor: Jean Parrat

Surrey Advertiser
01483 508700
www.surreyad.co.uk
Weekly (Fri). Editor: Marnie Wilson

Surrey Comet
020 8646 6336
Weekly (Wed). Editor: Sean Duggan

Surrey Hants Star
01252 316311
www.shstar.co.uk
Weekly free (Thu). Editor: Alan Franklin

Surrey Herald
01932 561111
Weekly (Wed). Editor: Kim Chatman

Surrey Mirror
020 8770 7171
www.icsurrey.co.uk
Weekly (Wed). Editor: Ian Carter
News editor: Glen Mitchell
Features editor: Caroline Harrap
Chief sub-editor: Sherif El Alfay

Sussex Express
01273 480601
www.sussexexpress.co.uk
Weekly (Fri). Editor: Peter Austin
Deputy editor: Kevin Penfold

Sutton Advertiser
020 8763 6666
www.icsurrey.co.uk
Weekly (Fri). Editor: Ian Carter
News editor: Mike Hawkins

Sutton Borough Post
020 8763 6666
www.icsurrey.co.uk
Weekly (Wed). Editor: Ian Carter
News editor: Mike Hawkins

Sutton Guardian
020 8646 6336
www.suttonguardian.co.uk
Weekly (Thu). Editor: Marie Jackson

Swanley Messenger
01322 220791
www.kent-online.co.uk
Weekly (Thu). Editor: Sandra Hembury
News editor: Teresa Gains

Swanley Times
020 8269 7000
Weekly (Thu). Editor: Melody Ryall
Production editor: Mick Taylor

Tandridge Chronicle
01959 564766
www.tandridge-today.co.uk
Weekly (Thu). Editor: Signid Sherrell

Tandridge County Border News
01959 564766
www.tandridge-today.co.uk
Weekly (Thu). Editor: Kevin Black

Tenterden Express
01233 623232
Weekly (Tue). Editor: Brian Lewis
News editor: Leo Whitlock
Features editor: Leo Whitlock
Chief sub-editor: Claire Stevens

Tenterden KM Extra
01233 623232
Weekly (Tue). Editor: Brian Lewis
News editor: Leo Whitlock
Features editor: Leo Whitlock
Chief sub-editor: Claire Stevens

Thanet KM Extra
01843 221313
Weekly (Fri). Editor: Rebecca Smith
News editor: Sarah Munday
Production editor: Gary Barker

Thanet Times
01227 767321
Weekly (Thu). Editor: Mike Pearce
News editor: Sarah Murdey

Tonbridge Courier
01892 681000
www.thisiskentandeastsussex.co.uk
Weekly (Fri). Editor: Giles Broadbent
News editor: Melanie Whittaker
Features editor: Lucia Blash
Chief sub-editor: Lindsey Jones
Production editor: Richard Page

Tunbridge Wells Courier
01892 681000
www.thisiskentandeastsussex.co.uk
Weekly (Fri). Editor: Giles Broadbent
News editor: Melanie Whittaker
Features editor: Lucia Blash
Chief sub-editor: Lindsey Jones
Production editor: Richard Page

Tunbridge Wells Extra
01892 525111
Weekly (Fri). Editor: Ron Green
News editor: Nigel Jarrett

Virginia Water Villager
01753 523355
Fortnightly (Thu). Editor: Martin Biddle
News editor: Mike Sim

Walton & Weybridge Informer
01932 561111
www.trinitymirrorsouthern.co.uk
Weekly free (Thu). Editor: Kim Chatman
News editor: Abbi Dornan

Watford Free Observer
01923 216216
www.watfordobserver.co.uk
Weekly (Thu)
Editor: Peter Wilson-Leary
News editor: Frazer Ansell

Watford Review
01727 834411
www.stalbansobserver.co.uk
Weekly free (Wed)
Editor: Deborah Williams

Watford Times
01788 543077
Weekly free (Wed)
Editor: Stephen Williams
News editor: Stuart Platt

Weald Courier
01892 681000
www.thisiskentandeastsussex.co.uk
Weekly (Fri). Editor: Giles Broadbent
News editor: Melanie Whittaker
Features editor: Lucia Blash
Chief sub-editor: Lindsey Jones
Production editor: Richard Page

Wealden Advertiser
01580 753322
www.wealdenad.co.uk
Weekly free (Fri). Editor: Graham Thorn

Weekend Herald (Crawley, Horsham, Horley)
01293 562929
www.crawleyobserver.co.uk
Weekly free (Fri)
Editor: Graham Campbell
News editor: Allan Norbury
Chief sub-editor: Mark Dunford

Welwyn & Hatfield Review
01727 834411
www.stalbansobserver.co.uk
Weekly (Thu). Editor: Deborah Williams
Features editor: Paul Collins

Welwyn & Hatfield Times
01727 327551
www.whtimes.co.uk
Weekly (Wed). Editor: Terry Mitchinson

Westerham County Border News
01959 564766
www.westerham-today.co.uk
Weekly (Thu). Editor: Kevin Black

West Sussex County Times
01403 751200
www.horshamonline.co.uk
Weekly (Fri). Editor: Gary Shipton
Chief sub-editor: Steve Payne
Production editor: Jonathan Taylor

West Sussex Gazette
01243 534155
www.chichester.co.uk
Weekly (Wed). Editor: Dorothy Blundell
News editor: Jeannie Knight
Chief sub-editor: Tony Jackman

Weybridge Villager
01753 523355
Fortnightly (Thu). Editor: Martin Biddle
News editor: Mike Sim

Whitstable Gazette
01227 768181
Weekly (Thu). Editor: Bob Bounds
News editor: Trisha Jaimeson
Production editor: Gary Barker

Whitstable KM Extra
01227 768181
Weekly (Tue). Editor: Bob Bounds
News editor: Trisha Jaimeson
Production editor: Gary Barker

Whitstable Times
01227 771515
Weekly (Thu). Editor: John Nurden
News editor: Ian Reed
Features editor: Julia Rogers
Chief sub-editor: Paul Taylor
Production editor: Mark Silver

Woking Informer
01932 561111
www.trinitymirrorsouthern.co.uk
Weekly free (Thu). Editor: Kim Chatman
News editor: Irlene Watchmore

Woking News & Mail
01483 755755
www.woking.co.uk
Weekly (Thu). Editor: Penny Bray
News editor: Lisa Porter

Woking Review
01483 508700
www.surreyad.co.uk
Weekly (Wed). Editor: Penny Bray
News editor: Lisa Porter

Worthing Advertiser
01903 230051
www.worthingtoday.co.uk
Weekly (Wed). Editor: Tony Mayes

Worthing Guardian
01903 282398
www.worthingtoday.co.uk
Weekly (Fri). Editor: Nikki Jeffrey

Worthing Herald
01903 230051
www.worthingtoday.co.uk
Weekly (Thu). Editor: John Buss
News editor: Harriet Shelley

South England

Berkshire, Buckinghamshire, Hampshire, Oxfordshire, Wiltshire

Abingdon Herald
01865 425262
www.thisisoxfordshire.co.uk
Weekly (Thu). Editor: Derek Holmes

The Advertiser (Newbury)
01635 524111
www.newburynews.co.uk
Weekly (Tue). Editor: Brian Beharrell
News editor: Martin Robertshaw

Aldershot Courier
01252 339760
www.aldershot.co.uk
Weekly free (Wed). Editor: James Taylor
News editor: Adam Clark

Aldershot Mail
01252 339760
www.surreyad.co.uk
Weekly (Tue). Editor: James Taylor
News editor: Adam Clark

Aldershot News
01252 339760
www.aldershot.co.uk
Weekly (Fri). Editor: James Taylor
News editor: Adam Clark

Alresford Advertiser
01252 716444
Weekly (Tue)
Editor: Christine McDermott
News editor: Paul Ferguson

Alton Gazette
01420 84446
Weekly (Wed)
Editor: Christine McDerment
News editor: Paul Ferguson

Alton Times & Mail
01252 716444
Weekly free (Tue). Editor: Jean Parrat

Amersham & Chesham Free Press
01494 755081
Weekly (Fri). Editor: Steve Cohen
News editor: Julie Voyce
Features editor: Clare Bourke

Amersham Examiner
01753 888333
Weekly (Thu). Editor: Peter Krinks
News editor: Estelle Sinkins
Features editor: Rachael Double

Andover Advertiser
01264 323456
www.andoveradvertiser.co.uk
Weekly (Fri). Editor: Joe Scicluna
News editor: Judy Belbin
Features editor: Simon Reeve
Chief sub-editor: Judith Hughes

Andover Advertiser Midweek
01264 323456
www.andoveradvertiser.co.uk
Weekly (Wed). Editor: Joe Scicluna
News editor: Judy Belbin
Features editor: Simon Reeve
Chief sub-editor: Judith Hughes

Ascot News
01344 456611
Weekly (Wed). Editor: Paul Ryan
Features editor: James Osborne

Ash & Farnham Mail
01252 339760
Weekly (Tue). Editor: James Taylor
News editor: Adam Clark

Banbury Cake
01295 256111
www.thisisoxfordshire.co.uk
Weekly (Thu). Editor: Derek Holmes
News editor: Stephanie Preece

Banbury Citizen
01295 227777
www.banburyguardian.co.uk
Weekly free (Fri). Editor: Bridget Dakin
News editor: Ben Kendall

Banbury Guardian
01295 227777
www.banburyguardian.co.uk
Weekly (Thu). Editor: Bridget Dakin
News editor: Ben Kendall

Basingstoke Extra
01256 461131
www.thisishampshire.net
Weekly free (Wed). Editor: Mark Jones
News editor: Simon Pluckrose
Chief sub-editor: Jonathan Lee
Production editor: Alan Cranham

Basingstoke Observer
01256 694121
www.basingstoke.co.uk
Weekly (Thu). Editor: Steve Davies

Beaconsfield Advertiser
01753 888333
www.buckinghamtoday.co.uk
Weekly (Thu). Editor: Peter Krinks
News editor: Estelle Sinkins
Features editor: Rachael Double

Bicester Advertiser
01865 425262
www.thisisoxfordshire.co.uk
Weekly (Fri). Editor: Derek Holmes

Bicester Review
01280 813434
Weekly (Fri). Editor: Rob Giddard
Assistant editor: Mark Pendred
Deputy editor: Clare Wale

Bordon Post
01730 264811
Weekly (Wed). Editor: David Garlant
Features editor: Will Parsons

Bordon Times & Mail
01252 716444
Weekly free (Tue). Editor: Jean Parrat

Bracknell & Ascot Times
0118 936 6180
www.getbracknell.co.uk
Weekly (Thu). Editor: Keith Redbourn
News editor: Matt Blackman

Brackley & Towcester Advertiser
01280 813434
Weekly (Fri). Editor: Rob Giddard
Assistant editor: Mark Pendred
Deputy editor: Clare Wale

Bracknell & Wokingham Standard
0118 936 6180
www.getbracknell.co.uk
Weekly (Thu). Editor: Adam D Smith

Bracknell Midweek News
01344 456611
Weekly (Wed). Editor: Paul Ryan
News editor: James Osborne

Bracknell News
01344 456611
Weekly (Wed). Editor: Paul Ryan
News editor: James Osborne

Buckingham & Winslow Advertiser
01280 813434
Weekly (Fri). Editor: Rob Giddard
Assistant editor: Mark Pendred
Deputy editor: Clare Wale

Buckinghamshire Advertiser
01753 888333
www.buckinghamtoday.co.uk
Weekly (Thu). Editor: Peter Krinks
News editor: Estelle Sinkins
Features editor: Rachael Double

Buckinghamshire Echo
0116 233 3635
Weekly (Tue). Editor: Paul Clark

Buckinghamshire Examiner
01753 888333
www.buckinghamtoday.co.uk
Weekly (Thu). Editor: Peter Krinks
News editor: Estelle Sinkins
Features editor: Rachael Double

Bucks Free Press
01494 755000
www.bucksfreepress.co.uk
Weekly (Fri). Editor: Steve Cohen
News editor: Julie Voyce

Bucks Herald
01296 318300
www.bucksherald.co.uk
Weekly (Wed). Editor: David Summers

Chippenham, Corsham Advertiser
01225 760945
www.wiltshirepublications.com
Weekly (Thu). Editor: David Gledhill
News editor: Paul Wiltshire
Features editor: George McCready
Production editor: Marion Wild

The Citizen
01908 371133
Twice-weekly free (Tue/Thu)
Editor: Jan Henderson

Crowthorne & Sandhurst Times
0118 936 6180
Weekly (Wed). Editor: Keith Redbourn
News editor: Matt Blackman

Crowthorne, Sandhurst, Owlsmoor Newsweek
01344 456611
Weekly (Wed). Editor: Paul Ryan
News editor: James Osborne

Devizes, Melksham and Vale of Pewsey News
01793 528144
www.thisisswindon.co.uk
Weekly free (Wed). Editor: Mark Waldron

Didcot Herald
01865 425262
www.thisisoxfordshire.co.uk
Weekly (Thu). Editor: Derek Holmes

Eastleigh News Extra
01962 841772
www.thisishampshire.net
Weekly free (Thu). Editor: Mary Payne

Eton Observer
01753 523355
Weekly (Fri). Editor: Martin Biddle
News editor: Mike Sim

Evening Advertiser
01793 528144
www.thisisswindon.co.uk
Daily. Editor: Mark Waldron
News editor: Cath Turnbull

Fareham & Gosport Journal
023 9266 4488
www.thisisportsmouth.co.uk
Weekly free (Thu). Editor: Mike Gilson
News editor: Colin McNeill
Features editor: John Millard

Fareham & Gosport News
023 9266 4488
www.thisisportsmouth.co.uk
Daily. Editor: Mike Gilson
News editor: Colin McNeill
Features editor: John Millard

Farnborough News & Mail
01252 339760
www.farnborough.co.uk
Weekly (Tue). Editor: James Taylor
News editor: Adam Clark

Fleet News & Mail
01252 339760
www.fleet-online.co.uk
Weekly (Tue). Editor: James Taylor
News editor: Adam Clark

Gazette Extra
01256 461131
www.thisishampshire.net
Weekly (Wed). Editor: Mark Jones
News editor: Simon Pluckrose
Chief sub-editor: Jonathan Lee
Production editor: Alan Cranham

Hamble Valley Journal
023 9266 4488
www.thisisportsmouth.co.uk
Weekly free (Thu). Editor: Mike Gilson
News editor: Colin McNeill
Features editor: John Millard

Hampshire Chronicle
01962 841772
www.thisishampshire.net/hampshire/winchester
Weekly (Fri). Editor: Alan Cleaver
News editor: Kit Neilson

Hants & Dorset Avon Advertiser
01722 426500
Weekly (Wed). Editor: Bill Browne
News editor: David Vallis
Features editor: Lesley Bates
Chief sub-editor: Sarah Elderkin

Hants and Surrey Post Dispatch
01420 88949
Fortnightly free (Mon)
Editor: Alan Wooler

Hart Courier
01252 339760
www.surreyad.co.uk
Weekly (Fri). Editor: James Taylor
News editor: Adam Clark

Havant & Waterlooville Journal
023 9266 4488
www.thisisportsmouth.co.uk
Weekly free (Thu). Editor: Mike Gilson
News editor: Colin McNeill
Features editor: John Millard

Havant & Waterlooville News
023 9266 4488
www.thisisportsmouth.co.uk
Daily. Editor: Mike Gilson
News editor: Colin McNeill
Features editor: John Millard

Hemel Hempstead Herald & Express
01442 262311
www.hemelonline.co.uk
Weekly (Thu). Editor: David Feldstein
News editor: Ann Traynor
Sports editor: Graham Caygill

Henley Standard
01491 419444
www.henleystandard.co.uk
Weekly (Fri). Editor: George Tuckfield
News editor: David Dawson

Isle of Wight County Press
01983 521333
www.iwcp.co.uk
Weekly (Fri). Editor: Brian Dennis
News editor: Phil Wolsey

Liphook Times & Mail
01252 716444
Weekly free (Tue). Editor: Jean Parrat

Lymington Times
01425 613384
Weekly (Fri). Editor: Charles Curry

Maidenhead Advertiser
01628 680680
www.maidenhead-advertiser.co.uk
Weekly (Fri). Editor: Martin Trepte

Marlow Free Press
01494 755081
Weekly (Fri). Editor: Steve Cohen
News editor: Julie Voyce
Features editor: Clare Bourke

The Midweek (Reading)
01494 755081
Weekly (Tue). Editor: Steve Cohen
News editor: Julie Voyce
Features editor: Clare Bourke

Meon Valley News
023 9263 2767
Monthly (Mon). Editor: Christine Miller

Melksham Independent News
01225 704761
www.melkshamnews.com
Fortnightly free (Thu). Editor: Ian Drew
News editor: Loraine Ward

Mid Hampshire Observer
01962 859559
www.hantsmedia.co.uk
Weekly (Wed). Editor: Pete Harvey

Milton Keynes Citizen
01908 651200
www.miltonkeynes.co.uk
Weekly free (Thu)
Editor: Jan Henderson

Milton Keynes Journal
0116 233 3635
Weekly (Tue). Editor: Paul Clark

MK News
01908 809000
www.seriousaboutnews.co.uk
Weekly (Wed). Editor: David Gale

Monday Gazette
01256 461131
www.thisishampshire.net
Weekly (Mon). Editor: Mark Jones
News editor: Simon Pluckrose
Chief sub-editor: Jonathan Lee
Production editor: Alan Cranham

New Forest Post
01590 613888
www.thisishampshire.net/
Weekly (Thu). Editor: Sue Edwins

New Milton Advertiser
01425 613384
Weekly (Fri). Editor: Charles Curry

Newbury & Thatcham Chronicle
01635 32812
www.icberkshire.co.uk
Weekly free (Wed). Editor: Brian Mustoe

Newbury Weekly News
01635 524111
www.newburynews.co.uk
Weekly (Thu). Editor: Brian Beharrell
News editor: Martin Robertshaw

The News (Portsmouth)
023 9266 4488
www.thenews.co.uk
Daily. Editor: Mike Gilson
News editor: Colin McNeill
Features editor: John Millard
Chief sub-editor: Steve Matthews

Oxford Courier
01235 553444
www.courier-newspapers
-oxford.co.uk
Weekly (Thu). Editor: Lawrence Web
Production editor: Howard Taylor

Oxford Journal
01235 553444
www.courier-newspapers
-oxford.co.uk/journal.htm
Weekly (Fri). Editor: Lawrence Web
Production editor: Howard Taylor

Oxford Mail
01865 425262
www.thisisoxfordshire.co.uk
Daily. Editor: Simon O'Neil

Oxford Star
01865 425262
www.thisisoxfordshire.co.uk
Weekly (Thu). Editor: Simon O'Neil

Oxford Times
01865 425262
www.thisisoxfordshire.co.uk
Weekly (Fri). Editor: Derek Holmes
News editor: Stephanie Preece
Chief sub-editor: Marc Evans

Oxfordshire Guardian
01926 431601
Weekly (Thu). Editor: Paul Gleeson

Oxfordshire Weekly
01865 425262
www.thisisoxfordshire.co.uk
Weekly (Wed). Editor: Derek Holmes

Petersfield Mail
01252 716444
Weekly free (Tue). Editor: Jean Parrat

Petersfield Post
01730 264811
www.petersfield.co.uk
Weekly (Wed). Editor: David Garlant
Features editor: Will Parsons

Portsmouth & Southsea Journal
023 9266 4488
www.thisisportsmouth.co.uk
Weekly free (Thu). Editor: Mike Gilson
News editor: Colin McNeill
Features editor: John Millard

Property Chronicle (Berkshire)
0118 950 3030
www.icberkshire.co.uk
Weekly (Wed, Thu)
Editor: Anthony Longden
News editor: Maurice O'Brien
Features editor: Paul Kirkley
Production editor: Jeremy Drakes

Reading Central
0118 918 3000
www.readingcentral.co.uk
Weekly (Thu). Editor: Hiliary Scott
Chief sub-editor: Keir Rithie

Reading Chronicle
0118 950 3030
www.icberkshire.co.uk
Weekly (Thu). Editor: Anthony Longden
News editor: Maurice O'Brien
Features editor: Paul Kirkley
Production editor: Jeremy Drakes

Reading Evening Post
0118 918 3000
www.getreading.co.uk
Daily (Mon–Fri). Editor: Andy Murrill
News editor: Lucy Rimmer
Features editor: Kate Magee
Chief sub-editor: Alan Blayney

Romsey Advertiser
023 8042 4777
www.thisishampshire.net
/hampshire/romsey
Weekly (Fri). Editor: Ian Murray
News editor: Gordon Sutter
Chief sub-editor: Colin Jenkins

Salisbury Avon Advertiser
01722 426500
www.thisiswiltshire.co.uk
Weekly (Wed). Editor: Bill Browne
News editor: David Vallis
Features editor: Lesley Bates

Salisbury Journal
01722 426500
www.thisissalisbury.co.uk
Weekly (Thu). Editor: Bill Browne
News editor: David Vallis
Features editor: Lesley Bates

Sandhurst & Crowthorne Mail
01252 339760
Weekly (Tue). Editor: James Taylor
News editor: Adam Clark

Sandhurst & Crowthorne News
01252 339760
Weekly (Fri). Editor: James Taylor
News editor: Adam Clark

Slough Express
01753 825111
www.icberkshire.co.uk
Weekly (Thu). Editor: Paul Thomas
News editor: Francis Batt
Features editor: Sarah Larch

Slough Observer
01753 523355
www.thisisslough.com
Weekly (Wed). Editor: Martin Biddle
News editor: Mike Sim

South Bucks, Wycombe & Chiltern Star
01494 755000
www.hillingdontimes.co.uk
Weekly (Thu). Editor: Steve Cohen
News editor: Clare Bourke

South Oxfordshire Courier
01235 553444
www.courier-newspapers
-oxford.co.uk
Weekly (Thu). Editor: Lawrence Web
Production editor: Howard Taylor

Southampton Advertiser
023 8042 4777
Weekly (Thu). Editor: Ian Murray
News editor: Gordon Sutter
Chief sub-editor: Colin Jenkins

Southern Daily Echo
023 8042 4777
www.dailyecho.co.uk
Daily. Editor: Ian Murray
News editor: Gordon Sutter
Chief sub-editor: Colin Jenkins

Surrey & Hampshire Guardian
02476 631911
Daily. Editor: Jag Basra
News editor: Keith Brailford
Features editor: Andrew Woods

Swindon Star
01793 528144
www.thisisswindon.co.uk
Weekly free (Thu). Editor: Mark Waldron
News editor: Cath Turnbull

Tadley Gazette
01256 461131
www.thisishampshire.net
Weekly free (Wed). Editor: Mark Jones
News editor: Simon Pluckrose
Chief sub-editor: Jonathan Lee
Production editor: Alan Cranham

Thame Gazette
01296 318300
www.aylesburytoday.co.uk
Weekly (Fri). Editor: David Summers

Thames Valley Weekly
01235 553444
www.courier-newspapers
-oxford.co.uk/tvw.htm
Weekly (Fri). Editor: Lawrence Web
Production editor: Howard Taylor

Thatcham News
01635 524111
www.newburynews.co.uk
Weekly (Thu). Editor: Brian Beharrell
News editor: Martin Robertshaw

Trowbridge, Melksham, Bradford-On-Avon Advertiser
01225 760945
www.wiltshirepublications.com
Weekly (Thu). Editor: David Gledhill
News editor: Paul Wiltshire
Features editor: George McCready
Production editor: Marion Wild

Twyford Times
0118 936 6180
Weekly (Wed). Editor: Keith Redbourn
News editor: Matt Blackman

Wallingford Herald
01865 425262
www.thisisoxfordshire.co.uk
Weekly (Thu). Editor: Derek Holmes

Wantage Herald
01865 425262
www.thisisoxfordshire.co.uk
Weekly (Thu). Editor: Derek Holmes

Warminster Journal
01985 213030
Weekly (Fri). Editors: RC Shorto and DJ Watkins

Weekend Express
01753 825111
www.icberkshire.co.uk
Weekly (Fri). Editor: Paul Thomas
News editor: Francis Batt
Features editor: Sarah Larch

West & North Wilts Star
01225 777292
www.thisiswiltshire.co.uk
Weekly free (Thu)
Editor: Toby Granville
News editor: Holly Robinson
Features editor: Claire Waring

Westbury, Warminster Advertiser
01225 760945
www.wiltshirepublications.com
Weekly (Thu). Editor: David Gledhill
News editor: Paul Wiltshire
Features editor: George McCready
Production editor: Marion Wild

White Horse News
01225 704761
www.wiltshirepublications.com
Fortnightly free (Thu)
Editor: Ian Drew
News editor: Loraine Ward

Wilts & Gloucestershire Standard
01285 642642
www.thisiscirencester.com
Weekly (Thu). Editor: Jeff Eames
News editor: Lindi Roberts
Production editor: Mark Jones

Wiltshire Gazette and Herald
01793 528144
www.thisisswindon.co.uk
Weekly (Thu). Editor: Mark Waldron
News editor: Gary Lawrence

Wiltshire Guardian
024 7663 1911
Weekly free (Thu). Editor: Jag Basra
News editor: Keith Brailford
Features editor: Andrew Woods

Wiltshire Times
01225 777292
www.thisiswiltshire.co.uk
Weekly (Fri). Editor: Toby Granville
News editor: Holly Robinson
Features editor: Claire Waring

Winchester News Extra
01962 841772
www.thisishampshire.net
Weekly free (Thu). Editor: Mary Page

Winchester Shopper
023 8042 4777
Sunday. Editor: Ian Murray
News editor: Gordon Sutter
Chief sub-editor: Colin Jenkins

Windsor Express
01753 825111
www.icberkshire.co.uk
Weekly free (Thu)
Editor: Paul Thomas
News editor: Francis Batt
Features editor: Sarah Larch

Windsor, Ascot & Maidenhead Observer
01753 523355
www.thisiswindsor.com
Weekly (Fri). Editor: Martin Biddle
News editor: Mike Sim

Witney & West Oxfordshire Gazette
01865 425262
www.thisisoxfordshire.co.uk
Weekly (Wed). Editor: Derek Holmes

Wodley Times
0118 936 6180
Weekly (Wed). Editor: Keith Redbourn
News editor: Matt Blackman

Wokingham News
01344 456611
Weekly (Wed). Editor: Paul Ryan
News editor: James Osborne

Wokingham Times
0118 366180
www.getwokingham.co.uk
Weekly (Wed). Editor: Keith Redbourn
News editor: Matt Blackman

Woodley & Earley Chronicle
0118 963 3151
www.icberkshire.co.uk
Weekly (Thu). Editor: Anthony Longden
News editor: Maurice O'Brien
Features editor: Paul Kirkley
Production editor: Jeremy Drakes

Yateley Mail
01252 339760
Weekly (Tue). Editor: James Taylor
News editor: Adam Clark

Yateley News
01252 339760
Weekly (Fri). Editor: James Taylor
News editor: Adam Clark

South-west England

Cornwall, Devon, Dorset, Somerset & Avon

Bath Chronicle
01225 322322
www.thisisbath.co.uk
Daily. Editor: David Gledhill
News editor: Paul Wiltshire
Features editor: George McCready
Chief sub-editor: Graham Holburn
Production editor: Marion Wild

Bath Times
01225 322322
www.thisisbath.co.uk
Weekly (Wed). Editor: David Gledhill
News editor: Paul Wiltshire

Bournemouth Advertiser
01202 554601
www.thisisdorset.net
Weekly free (Thu)
Editor: Neal Butterworth
News editor: Andy Martin
Features editor: Kevin Nash

Bridgwater Mercury
01823 365151
www.thisisthewestcountry.co.uk
Weekly (Tue). Editor-in-chief: Ken Bird
News editor: Bob Drayton

Bridgwater Star
01823 365151
www.thisisthewestcountry.co.uk
Weekly (Thu). Editor-in-chief: Ken Bird
News editor: Bob Drayton

Bridgwater Times
01749 672430
www.thisissomerset.co.uk
Weekly (Thu). Editor: Carol Deacon
News editor: Juliette Auty

Bridport & Lyme Regis News
01308 425884
www.thisisdorset.net/dorset/bridportandlyme
Weekly (Fri). Editor: Margery Hookings

Bristol Evening Post
0117 934 3000
www.thisisbristol.co.uk
Daily. Editor: Mike Lowe
News editor: Kevin Blackadder
Features editor: Bill Davis
Chief sub-editor: Helen Lawrence

Bristol Observer
0117 934 3401
www.thisisbristol.co.uk
Weekly free (Fri). Editor: Peter O'Reilly
News editor: Sharon Kelly
Chief sub-editor: Mike Chart

Brixham News
01584 856353
www.thisisthewestcountry.co.uk
Weekly (Thu). Editor: Gina Coles

Bude & Stratton Post
01566 772424
Weekly (Thu). Editor: Geoff Secombe
News editor: Keith Whitford

Burnham & Highbridge Mercury
01823 365151
www.thisisthewestcountry.co.uk
Weekly (Tue). Editor-in-chief: Ken Bird
News editor: Bob Drayton

Burnham & Highbridge Times
01749 672430
www.thisissomerset.co.uk
Weekly (Thu). Editor: Carol Deacon
News editor: Juliette Auty

Burnham & Highbridge Weekly News
01823 365151
www.thisisthewestcountry.co.uk
Weekly (Thu). Editor-in-chief: Ken Bird
News editor: Bob Drayton

Camborne and Redruth Packet
01326 213333
www.thisisthewestcountry.co.uk
Weekly free (Wed). Editor: Terry Lambert
News editor: Stephen Ivall
Chief sub-editor: David Robinson

Camelford & Delabole Post
01566 772424
Weekly (Thu). Editor: Geoff Secombe
News editor: Keith Whitford

Camelford & Delabole Journal Gazette
01566 772424
Weekly (Fri). Editor: Geoff Secombe
News editor: Keith Whitford

Central Somerset Gazette
01749 832300
www.thisissomerset.co.uk
Weekly (Fri). Editor: Philip Welch

Chard & Ilminster News
01823 365151
www.thisisthewestcountry.co.uk
Weekly (Wed). Editor-in-chief: Ken Bird
News editor: Bob Drayton

Chard & Ilminster News (Somerset)
01460 67474
www.thisisthewestcountry.co.uk
Weekly (Wed). Editor: Bryan Armstrong
News editor: Alan Hall

Chard Advertiser
01935 471764
www.chard-today.co.uk
Weekly free (Fri). Editor: Philip Edwards

Cheddar Valley Gazette
01749 832300
www.thisissomerset.co.uk
Weekly (Thu). Editor: Philip Welch

Chew Valley Gazette
01275 332266
www.chewvalleygazette.co.uk
Last monthly (Fri)
Editor: Rowland Janes
Features editor: Anne Collier

Clevedon Mercury
01275 335142
www.thisissomerset.co.uk
Weekly (Thu). Editor: Carol Deacon
News editor: Juliette Autey
Chief sub-editor: Kevin Lee

Cornish & Devon Post
01566 772424
Weekly (Thu). Editor: Geoff Secombe
News editor: Keith Whitford

Cornish Guardian
01208 78133
www.cornishguardian.co.uk
Weekly (Thu). Editor: Alan Cooper
News editor: Ian Sheppard
Chief sub-editor: Anne Witney

Cornish Times
01579 342174
www.liskeard-today.co.uk
Weekly (Fri). Editor: John Noble

The Cornishman
01736 362247
www.thisiscornwall.co.uk
Weekly (Thu). Editor: Jeremy Ridge
Features editor: Joyce Channon

Crewkerne Advertiser
01935 471764
www.crewkerne-today.co.uk
Weekly free (Fri). Editor: Philip Edwards

Culm, Crediton & Tiverton Gazette
01884 252725
Weekly (Tue)
Editor: Mary-Ann Bloomfield

Daily Echo
01202 554601
www.thisisbournemouth.co.uk
Daily. Editor: Neal Butterworth
News editor: Andy Martin
Features editor: Kevin Nash

Dartmouth Chronicle
01548 853101
www.dartmouth-today.co.uk
Weekly (Fri). Editor: Gina Coles
Chief sub-editor: Lucy Baker-Kind

Dawlish Gazette
01626 353555
www.dawlish-today.co.uk
Weekly (Fri). Editor: Ruth Davey
News editor: John Belment
Chief sub-editor: Steven Taylor

Dawlish Post
01626 353555
www.dawlish-today.co.uk
Weekly (Fri). Editor: Ruth Davey
News editor: John Belment
Chief sub-editor: Steven Taylor

Dorchester Advertiser
01305 830930
www.thisisdorset.net
Weekly (Thu). Editor: David Murdock
News editor: Paul Thomas
Features editor: Dirmaid Macdonagh
Chief sub-editor: Nick Horton

Dorset Echo
01305 830930
www.thisisdorset.net
Weekly (Thu). Editor: David Murdock
News editor: Paul Thomas
Features editor: Dirmaid Macdonagh

Exeter Express and Echo
01392 442211
www.thisisexeter.co.uk
Daily. Editor: Steve Hall
News editor: Sue Kemp
Features editor: Lynne Turner
Production editor: Jerry Charge

Exeter Leader
01392 442211
www.thisisexeter.co.uk
Weekly free (Wed). Editor: Steve Hall
News editor: Sue Kemp
Features editor: Lynne Turner

Exmouth Herald
01392 888444
www.archantdevon.co.uk
/exmouthherald.asp
Weekly free (Fri)
Chief sub editor: Mary Evans

Falmouth Packet
01326 213333
www.thisisthewestcountry.co.uk
Weekly (Thu). Editor: Terry Lambert
News editor: Stephen Ivall
Chief sub-editor: David Robinson

Frome Times
01225 704761
www.frometimes.com
Fortnightly free (Thu). Editor: Ian Drew
News editor: Loraine Ward

Hayle Times
01736 795813
www.thisiscornwall.co.uk
Weekly (Fri). Editor: Toni Carver
News editor: Paul Popcock
Features editor: Tricia Carver

Helston Gazette
01326 213333
www.thisisthewestcountry.co.uk
Weekly free (Wed)
Editor: Terry Lambert
News editor: Stephen Ivall
Chief sub-editor: David Robinson

Holsworthy Post
01566 778220
Weekly (Fri). Editor: Keith Whitford

Honiton Advertiser
01297 33034
www.pulmansweekly.co.uk
Weekly (Wed). Editor: Philip Evans
News editor: Tony Woodman
Production editor: Jacqui Evans

Ivybridge, South Brent and South Hams Gazette
01548 853101
www.ivybridge-today.co.uk
Weekly (Fri). Editor: Gina Coles
Chief sub-editor: Lucy Baker-Kind

Journal (Exmouth)
01392 888444
www.archantdevon.co.uk/journal.asp
Weekly (Thu). Editor: Mary Evans

Kingsbridge and Salcombe Gazette
01548 853101
Weekly (Fri). Editor: Gina Coles
Chief sub-editor: Lucy Baker-Kind

Launceston Journal Gazette
01566 772424
Weekly (Fri). Editor: Geoff Secombe
News editor: Keith Whitford

Liskeard Gazette & Journal
01579 342174
Weekly (Wed). Editor: Mary Richards

Mid Cornwall Advertiser
01726 66755
www.midcornwall-today.co.uk
Monthly (middle of month)
Editor: Fiona Jolley

Mid Devon Advertiser
01626 353555
www.dawlish-today.co.uk
Weekly (Fri). Editor: Ruth Davey
News editor: John Belment
Chief sub-editor: Steven Taylor

Mid Devon Star
01823 365151
www.thisisthewestcountry.co.uk
Weekly (Fri). Editor-in-chief: Ken Bird
News editor: Bob Drayton

Mid Somerset Times
01749 672430
www.thisissomerset.co.uk
Weekly (Thu). Editor: Philip Welch

Midweek Herald
01392 888444
www.archantdevon.co.uk
Weekly (Wed). Editor: Andre Gibbons

North Cornwall Advertiser
01208 815096
www.northcornwall-today.co.uk
First week of month
Editor: Tony Gregan

North Devon Gazette & Advertiser
01392 888444
www.northdevongazette.co.uk
Weekly (Wed). Editor: David Tanner

North Devon Journal
01271 347420
www.thisisnorthdevon.co.uk
Weekly (Thu). Editor: Andy Cooper
News editor: Richard Best
Features editor: Sue Robinson
Chief sub-editor: Chris Machin

North Somerset Times
01934 422622
www.thewestonmercury.co.uk
Weekly (Wed). Editor: Heather Pickstock
News editor: Andy Ridgeway

Newquay Voice
01637 878298
www.newquayvoice.co.uk
Weekly (Wed). Editor: Andrew Laming
News editor: Matt Bond

North Cornwall Advertiser
01208 815096
www.northcornwall-today.co.uk
Monthly (first wed) free
Editor: Tony Gregan

Okehampton Times
01822 613666
www.okehampton-today.co.uk
Weekly (Thu). Editor: Colin Brent

Ottery Advertiser
01297 33034
Weekly (Wed). Editor: Philip Evans
News editor: Tony Woodman
Production editor: Jacqui Evans

Penwith Pirate
01326 213333
www.thisisthewestcountry.co.uk
Weekly free (Wed)
Editor: Terry Lambert
News editor: Stephen Ivall
Chief sub-editor: David Robinson

Plymouth Evening Herald
01752 765529
www.thisisplymouth.co.uk
Daily. Editor: Alan Qualtrough
News editor: John Casey
Features editor: Mike Bramhall

Plymouth Extra
01752 765525
www.thisisthewestcountry.co.uk
Weekly free (Thu). Editor: Paul Atkins
News editor: Pam Guyatt

Plympton Plymstock & Ivybridge News
01548 853101
Weekly (Fri). Editor: Gina Coles
Chief sub-editor: Lucy Baker-Kind

Poole Advertiser
01202 675413
Weekly free (Thu)
Editor: Neal Butterworth
News editor: Andy Martin
Features editor: Kevin Nash

Post Advertiser
01305 830900
Monthly free (Mon). Editor: Bob Conway

Princetown Times
01822 613666
www.thisisthewestcountry.co.uk
Weekly (Thu). Editor: Colin Brent

St Ives Times & Echo
01736 795813
www.thisiscornwall.co.uk
Weekly (Fri). Editor: Toni Carver
News editor: Paul Pocock
Features editor: Tricia Carver

Shepton Mallet Journal
01749 832300
www.thisissomerset.co.uk
Weekly (Thu). Editor: Philip Welch

Sidmouth Herald
01392 888444
www.archantdevon.co.uk
Weekly (Fri). Editor: Emma Silverthorne

Somerset County Gazette
01823 365151
www.thisisthewestcountry.co.uk
Weekly (Fri). Editor-in-chief: Ken Bird
News editor: Bob Drayton

Somerset Guardian
01225 322322
www.thisissomerset.co.uk
Weekly (Thu). Editor: Joanne Roughton
Features editor: Pip Larkham

Somerset Standard
01225 322322
www.thisissomerset.co.uk
Weekly (Thu). Editor: Joanne Roughton
Features editor: Pip Larkham

South Devon & Plymouth Times
01584 856353
www.thisisthewestcountry.co.uk
Weekly (Thu). Editor: Gina Coles

Sunday Independent
01752 206600
www.thisisthewestcountry.co.uk
Sunday. Editor: John Noble
News editor: Nikki Rowland

Swanage and Wareham District Advertiser
01929 427428
www.thisisdorset.net
Weekly free (Thu)
Editor: Neil Butterworth
News editor: Paula Tegerdine

Taunton Star
01823 365151
www.tauntonstar.co.uk
Weekly (Wed). Editor-in-chief: Ken Bird
News editor: Bob Drayton

Taunton Times
01823 250500
www.thisissomerset.co.uk
Weekly free (Thu). Editor: Debbie Rundle
News editor: Matt Chorley

Tavistock Times Gazette
01822 613666
www.tavistock-today.co.uk
Weekly (Thu). Editor: Colin Brent

Teignmouth News
01626 353555
www.dawlish-today.co.uk
Weekly (Fri). Editor: Ruth Davey
News editor: John Belment
Chief sub-editor: Steven Taylor

Teignmouth Post & Gazette
01626 353555
www.dawlish-today.co.uk
Weekly (Fri). Editor: Ruth Davey
News editor: John Belment
Chief sub-editor: Steven Taylor

Torbay Weekender
01803 676000
www.thisissouthdevon.co.uk
Weekly (Thu)
Editor: Bendan Hanrahan
News editor: Jim Parker
Features editor: Nick Pannell
Chief sub-editor: Nigel Lines

Torquay Herald Express
01803 676000
www.thisissouthdevon.co.uk
Daily. Editor: Bendan Hanrahan
News editor: Jim Parker
Features editor: Nick Pannell
Chief sub-editor: Nigel Lines

Totnes News
01548 853101
Weekly (Fri). Editor: Gina Coles
Chief sub-editor: Lucy Baker-Kind

Totnes Times Gazette
01584 856353
www.thisisthewestcountry.co.uk
Weekly (Thu). Editor: Gina Coles

Trader News (West Somerset)
01984 632731
Weekly free (Wed). Editor: Gareth Purcell

Truro Packet
01326 213333
www.thisisthewestcountry.co.uk
Weekly (Wed). Editor: Terry Lambert
News editor: Stephen Ivall
Chief sub-editor: David Robinson

Wellington Weekly News
01823 250500
www.thisissomerset.co.uk
Weekly (Wed). Editor: Debbie Rundle
News editor: Matt Chorley

Wells Journal
01749 832300
www.thisissomerset.co.uk
Weekly (Thu). Editor: Philip Welch

The West Briton
01872 271451
www.thisiscornwall.co.uk
Weekly (Thu)
Editor: Richard Vankinsbergh
News editor: Mark Binnersley

West Somerset Free Press
01984 632731
www.west-somerset-today.co.uk
Weekly (Fri). Editor: Gareth Purcell

Western Daily Press (Bristol)
0117 934 3223
www.westpress.co.uk
Daily. Editor: Terry Manners
News editor: Cathy Ellis
Features editor: Steve White
Chief sub-editor: Dave Web
Production editor: Tony Wills

Western Gazette
01935 700500
www.westgaz.co.uk
Weekly (Thu). Editor: Martin Heal
News editor: Zena O'Rourke
Features editor: Carla Gale

Western Morning News
01752 765500
www.thisisplymouth.co.uk
Daily. Editor: Barrie Williams
News editor: Philip Reynolds
Features editor: Sue Carroll

Weston and Worle News
01275 335140
www.thisissomerset.co.uk
Weekly (Thu). Editor: Carol Deacon
News editor: Juliette Autey
Chief sub-editor: Kevin Lee

Weston Mercury
01934 422622
www.thewestonmercury.co.uk
Weekly (Fri). Editor: Judy Kisiel
News editor: Andy Ridgeway

Weston Super Mare Admag
01934 422622
www.thewestonmercury.co.uk
Weekly (Wed). Editor: Judy Kisiel
News editor: Andy Ridgeway

Weymouth & Dorchester Advertiser
01305 830930
www.thisisdorset.net
Weekly (Thu). Editor: David Murdock
News editor: Paul Thomas
Features editor: Dirmaid Macdonagh

Yeovil Express
01823 365151
www.thisisthewestcountry.co.uk
Weekly (Thu). Editor-in-chief: Ken Bird
News editor: Bob Drayton

Yeovil Independent Clarion
01935 471764
www.yeovil-clarion-today.co.uk
Weekly free (Fri). Editor: Philip Edwards

Yeovil Times
01935 700500
Weekly free (Wed). Editor: Martin Heal
News editor: Zena O'Rourke
Features editor: Carla Gale

East of England

Cambridgeshire, Essex, Lincolnshire, Norfolk, Suffolk

Alford Standard
01754 897120
Weekly (Wed). Editor: John Coupe

Axholme Herald
01427 874417
Weekly (Fri). Editor: Ron Shipley

Barking & Dagenham Post
020 8491 2000
Weekly (Thu). Editor: Dave Russell
News editor: Scott Morrow
Chief sub-editor: Graham Whitmore

Barking & Dagenham Recorder
020 8478 4444
www.recorderonline.co.uk
Weekly (Thu). Editor: Chris Carter
News editor: Antigone Forder
Production editor: Mike Cubitt

Barking & Dagenham Weekender
020 8491 2000
Weekly (Fri). Editor: Dave Russell
News editor: Scott Morrow
Chief sub-editor: Graham Whitmore

Barking & Dagenham Yellow Advertiser
01268 503400
www.trinitymirrorsouthern.co.uk
Weekly (Thu). Editor: Graham Allen
News editor: Paula Dady
Features editor: Pat Jones

Basildon and Wickford Recorder
01268 522792
www.thisisessex.co.uk
Daily. Editor: Martin McNeil
News editor: Chris Hatton
Features editor: Sally King
Chief sub-editor: Neal Reeve

Basildon Yellow Advertiser
01268 503400
www.trinitymirrorsouthern.co.uk
Weekly (Thu). Editor: Graham Allen
News editor: Paula Dady
Features editor: Pat Jones

Beccles & Bungay Journal
01603 628311
www.edp24.co.uk
Weekly (Fri). Editor: Terry Redhead

Billericay & Wickford Gazette
01277 219222
www.thisisessex.co.uk
Weekly (Wed). Editor: Roger Watkins
News editor: Sheelagh Bree
Features editor: Josie Stephenson

Boston Citizen
01205 311433
www.bostontoday.co.uk
Weekly (Fri). Editor: Julia Ogden
News editor: Pam Browne
Chief sub-editor: Warren Moody

Boston Focus
01205 354547
www.bostonuk.com/focus
Monthly free. Editor: Irene Kettle
News editor: Sally Tetheridge
Features editor: Iris Clapp
Chief sub-editor: Will Bramhill

Boston Standard
01205 311433
www.bostontoday.co.uk
Weekly (Wed). Editor: Julia Ogden
News editor: Pam Browne
Chief sub-editor: Warren Moody

Boston Target
01522 820000
www.thisislincolnshire.co.uk
Weekly (Wed). Editor: Glynn Belsher

Braintree & Witham Times
01376 343344
www.thisisessex.co.uk
Weekly (Thu). Editor: Neil Thomas
News editor: Veronica Balls

Braintree Chronicle
01245 600700
www.thisisessex.co.uk
Weekly (Wed/Thu)
Editor: Stuart Rawlins
News editor: Matt Adams
Features editor: Darryl Webber

Brentwood Gazette
01277 219222
www.thisisessex.co.uk
Weekly (Wed). Editor: Roger Watkins
News editor: Sheelagh Bree
Features editor: Josie Stephenson

Brentwood Weekly News
01268 522792
www.thisisessex.co.uk
Weekly (Thu). Editor: Martin McNeil
News editor: Chris Hatton
Features editor: Sally King
Chief sub-editor: Neal Reeve

Brentwood Yellow Advertiser
01268 503400
www.trinitymirrorsouthern.co.uk
Weekly free (Fri). Editor: Graham Allen
News editor: Paula Dady
Features editor: Pat Jones

Brentwood, Billericay & Havering Recorder
01708 771500
www.recorderonline.co.uk
Weekly (Fri). Editor: Mark Sweetingham
News editor: Ross Hindley

Bury Free Press
01284 768911
www.buryfreepress.co.uk
Weekly. Editor: Barry Peters
News editor: Lesley Anslow
Features editor: Claire Brown

Bury St Edmunds Citizen
01284 768911
www.edp24.co.uk
Weekly. Editor: Barry Peters
News editor: Lesley Anslow
Features editor: Claire Brown

Bury St Edmunds Mercury
01284 702588
www.edp24.co.uk
Weekly (Fri). Editor: James Mortlock
News editor: David Desilva

Cambridge Crier
01223 434434
www.cambridge-news.co.uk
Weekly (Fri). Editor: Nigel Brookes
Features editor: James Fuller

Cambridge Evening News
01223 434434
www.cambridge-news.co.uk
Daily. Editor: Colin Grant
News editor: John Deex
Features editor: Debbie Tweedie

Cambridge Weekly News
01223 434434
www.cambridge-news.co.uk
Weekly (Wed). Editor: Nigel Brookes

Cambridgeshire Times
01354 652621
Weekly (Thu). Editor: Brian Asplin
News editor: John Elworthy
Features editor: Maggie Gibson

Castle Point Yellow Advertiser
01268 503400
www.trinitymirrorsouthern.co.uk
Weekly free (Thu). Editor: Graham Allen
News editor: Paula Dady
Features editor: Pat Jones

Castlepoint & Rayleigh Standard
01268 522792
www.thisisessex.co.uk
Weekly (Wed). Editor: Martin McNeil
News editor: Chris Hatton
Features editor: Sally King
Chief sub-editor: Neal Reeve

Chatteris Times
01354 652621
www.cambs-times.co.uk
Weekly (Thu). Editor: Brian Asplin
News editor: John Elworthy
Features editor: Maggie Gibson

Chelmsford Chronicle
01245 600700
www.thisisessex.co.uk
Weekly (Wed/Thu)
Editor: Stuart Rawlins
News editor: Matt Adams
Features editor: Darryl Webber

Chelmsford Weekly News
01245 493444
www.thisisessex.co.uk
Weekly (Thu). Editor: James Wills
News editor: Denise Rigby

Chelmsford Yellow Advertiser
01268 503400
www.trinitymirrorsouthern.co.uk
Weekly free (Thu). Editor: Graham Allen
News editor: Paula Dady
Features editor: Pat Jones

Clacton & Frinton Gazette
01255 221221
www.thisisessex.co.uk
Weekly (Fri). Editor: Neal Harrington
Chief sub-editor: Nigel Brown

Colchester Evening Gazette
01206 506000
www.nqe.info
Daily. Editor: Irene Kettle
News editor: Sally Tetheridge
Features editor: Iris Clapp
Chief sub-editor: Will Bramhill

Dereham & Fakenham Times
01603 628311
www.edp24.co.uk
Weekly (Thu). Editor: Terry Redhead

Diss Express
01379 642264
Weekly (Fri). Editor: Nicola Brown
Deputy editor: Fraser McKay

Diss Mercury
01603 628311
www.edp24.co.uk
Weekly (Fri). Editor: Terry Redhead

Dunmow & Stansted Chronicle
01245 600700
www.thisisessex.co.uk
Weekly (Wed/Thu)
Editor: Stuart Rawlins
News editor: Matt Adams
Features editor: Darryl Webber

Dunmow Broadcast and Recorder
01371 874537
www.dunmow-broadcast.co.uk
Weekly free (Thu)
Editor: Jenny Oliveira

Dunmow Observer
01279 866355
www.herts-essex-news.co.uk
Weekly (Thu). Editor: Val Brown
News editor: Sandra Perry

East Anglian Daily Star
01284 702588
www.eveningstar.co.uk
Daily. Editor: Nigel Pickover
News editor: Martin Davey

East Anglian Daily Times
01284 702588
www.eadt.co.uk
Daily. Editor: Terry Hunt
News editor: Aynsley Davidson
Features editor: Julian Ford
Chief sub-editor: Mike Crookwell

Eastern Daily Press
01603 628311
www.edp24.co.uk
Daily. Editor: Peter Franzen

Ely Standard
01353 667831
www.ely-standard.co.uk
Weekly (Thu). Editor: John Ison
News editor: Debbie Davies

Epping & Waltham Yellow Advertiser
01268 503400
www.trinitymirrorsouthern.co.uk
Weekly free (Fri). Editor: Graham Allen
News editor: Paula Dady
Features editor: Pat Jones

Epping Guardian
01992 572285
Weekly (Thu). Editor: David Jackman

Epping Independent
020 8498 3400
Weekly (Fri). Editor: David Jackman

Epping Star
01279 838111
www.thisisessex.co.uk
Weekly (Thu). Editor: Ken Morley
News editor: Beverley Rouse

Epworth Bells & Crowle Advertiser
01427 872202
Weekly (Thu). Editor: Mandy McSorley

Essex Chronicle
01245 600700
www.thisisessex.co.uk
Weekly (Wed/Thu)
Editor: Stuart Rawlins
News editor: Matt Adams
Features editor: Darryl Webber

Essex County Standard
01206 506000
www.nqe.info
Weekly (Fri). Editor: Jo Robinson
News editor: David Grocott
Features editor: Iris Clapp
Chief sub-editor: Will Bramhill

Essex Enquirer
01277 627300
www.thisisessex.co.uk
Weekly (Thu). Editor: Carol Driver

Evening Echo
01268 522792
www.thisisessex.co.uk
Daily. Editor: Martin McNeil
News editor: Chris Hatton
Features editor: Sally King
Chief sub-editor: Neal Reeve

Evening News
01603 628311
www.eveningnews24.co.uk
Daily. Editor: David Bourn

Evening Star
01284 702588
www.eveningstar.co.uk
Daily. Editor: Nigel Pickover
News editor: Martin Davey
Features editor: Tracy Sparling

Fenland Citizen
01945 586100
Weekly (Wed). Editor: Keith Drayton

Gainsborough Standard
01427 615323
Weekly (Thu). Editor: Mandy McSorley

Gainsborough Target
01427 810148
Weekly (Fri). Editor: Mike Sass

Goole Courier
01405 782400
www.gooletoday.co.uk/
Weekly (Thu). Editor: Janet Harrison
News editor: Stephanie Bateman

Goole Times/Selby Post
01405 720110
www.horshamonline.co.uk
Weekly (Thu). Editor: Peter Butler

Grantham Citizen
01476 562291
Weekly (Tue). Editor: Nick Woodhead
News editor: John Pinchbeck

Grantham Journal
01476 562291
Weekly (Fri). Editor: Nick Woodhead
News editor: John Pinchbeck

Great Yarmouth & Gorleston Advertiser
01493 601206
www.advertiser-online.co.uk
Weekly (Thu)
Senior reporter: Leanne Boast

Great Yarmouth Mercury
01603 628311
www.edp24.co.uk
Weekly (Tue). Editor: Terry Redhead

Grimsby Evening Telegraph
01472 360360
www.thisisgrimsby.co.uk
Daily. Editor: Michelle Lalor
News editor: Dave Atkin
Features editor: Lorraine Johnson

Grimsby Target
01472 360360
www.thisisgrimsby.co.uk
Weekly free (Wed)
Editor: Michelle Lalor
News editor: Dave Atkin
Features editor: Lorraine Johnson

Halstead Gazette
01376 343344
www.thisisessex.co.uk
Weekly (Fri). Editor: Neal Thomas
News editor: Veronica Balls

Harlow Herald
01279 624331
www.thisisessex.co.uk
Weekly (Thu). Editor: Peter Jeffery
News editor: Tracey Hubbard
Features editor: James Wilmore

Harlow Star
01279 866355
www.herts-essex-news.co.uk
Weekly (Thu). Editor: Val Brown
News editor: Sandra Perry

Harold Gazette
01277 219222
www.thisisessex.co.uk
Weekly (Wed). Editor: Roger Watkins
News editor: Sheelagh Bree
Features editor: Josie Stephenson

Harold Recorder
01708 771500
www.recorderonline.co.uk
Weekly (Fri). Editor: Mark Sweetingham
News editor: Ross Hindley

Haverhill Echo
01440 703456
www.buryfreepress.co.uk
Weekly (Thu). Editor: Heather Turner
News editor: David Hart

Haverhill Weekly News
01223 434434
www.cambridge-news.co.uk
Weekly (Thu). Editor: Nigel Brookes

Havering Herald
01603 628311
Weekly free (Fri)
Editor: Richard Thompson

Havering Yellow Advertiser
01268 503400
www.trinitymirrorsouthern.co.uk
Editor: Graham Allen
News editor: Paula Dady
Features editor: Pat Jones

Horncastle News
01507 353200
www.horncastletoday.co.uk
Weekly (Wed). Editor: Janet Richardson

Hornsea Gazette
01964 612777
Weekly (Thu)
News editor: Andrew Swales
Features editor: David McAughtrie

Huntingdon Town Crier
01480 402100
www.cambridge-news.co.uk
Weekly (Thu)
Editor: Anthony Hawkswell

Huntingdon Weekly News
01480 467670
www.cambridge-news.co.uk
Weekly (Wed). Editor: Colin Grant
News editor: John Deex

Hunts Post
01480 411481
www.huntspost.co.uk
Weekly (Wed). Editor: Paul Richardson
Deputy editor: Angela Singer

Ilford & Redbridge Post
020 8491 2000
Weekly free (Wed). Editor: Dave Russell
News editor: Scott Morrow
Chief sub-editor: Graham Whitmore

Ipswich Advertiser
01473 324700
www.advertiser-online.co.uk
Weekly (Thu). Editor: Paul Couch
News editor: Nicola Durrant

Island Times
01702 477666
www.thisisessex.co.uk
Monthly (Tue). Editor: Michael Guy

Leigh Times
01702 477666
www.thisisessex.co.uk
Fortnightly (Tue). Editor: Michael Guy

Lincoln Target
01522 820000
www.thisislincolnshire.co.uk
Weekly (Wed). Editor: Mike Sassi

Lincolnshire Echo
01522 820000
www.thisislincolnshire.co.uk
Daily. Editor: Mike Sassi

Lincolnshire Free Press
01775 725021
www.spaldingtoday.co.uk
Weekly (Tue). Editor: Alan Salt
News editor: David Crossley
Features editor: Julie Williams
Chief sub-editor: Tracey Vale

The Local
01778 425876
Weekly (Fri). Editor: Lisa Bruen

Loughton & Epping Herald
01279 624331
www.thisisessex.co.uk
Weekly (Thu). Editor: Peter Jeffery
News editor: Tracey Hubbard
Features editor: James Wilmore

Loughton, Chigwell & Buckhurst Hill Guardian
01992 572285
Weekly (Thu). Editor: David Jackman

Louth Citizen
01507 353200
www.louthtoday.co.uk
Weekly (Fri). Editor: Charles Ladbrooke

Louth Leader
01507 353200
www.louthtoday.co.uk
Weekly (Wed)
Editor: Charles Ladbrooke

Lowestoft Journal
01603 628311
www.edp24.co.uk
Weekly (Fri). Editor: Terry Redheard

Lynn News
01553 761188
www.lynnnews.co.uk
Weekly (Tue, Fri)
Editor: Malcolm Powell
News editor: Donna Semmens

Maldon & Burnham Chronicle
01245 600700
www.thisisessex.co.uk
Weekly (Wed/Thu)
Editor: Stuart Rawlins
News editor: Matt Adams
Features editor: Darryl Webber

Maldon & Burnham Standard
01621 852233
Weekly (Thu). Editor: James Wills

Market Rasen Mail
01507 353200
www.marketrasentoday.co.uk
Weekly (Wed). Editor: Jason Hipsley

Newmarket Journal
01638 564104
Weekly (Thu). Editor: Colin Lucas

Newmarket Weekly News
01223 434434
www.cambridge-news.co.uk
Weekly (Thu). Editor: Nigel Brookes

Norfolk Citizen
01553 761188
Weekly (Fri). Editor: Chris Hornby

Norfolk North Advertiser
01603 740222
www.advertiser-online.co.uk
Weekly (Fri). Editor: Sharon Richardson

Norfolk South Advertiser
01603 740222
www.advertiser-online.co.uk
Weekly (Fri). Editor: Sara Hardman

North Essex Advertiser
01473 324700
www.advertiser-online.co.uk
Weekly (Fri). Editor: Paul Couch
News editor: Nicola Durrant

North Norfolk & Broadland Town & Country News
01692 582287
Monthly (Fri nearest 1st)
Editor: Lawrence Watts

North Norfolk News
01603 628311
www.edp24.co.uk
Weekly (Thu). Editor: Terry Redhead

Norwich Advertiser
01603 740222
www.advertiser-online.co.uk
Weekly (Fri). Editor: Lisa Horton

Ongar and North Weald Gazette
01277 219222
www.thisisessex.co.uk
Weekly (Wed). Editor: Roger Watkins
News editor: Sheelagh Bree
Features editor: Josie Stephenson

Ongar Guardian
01992 572285
Weekly (Thu). Editor: David Jackman

Peterborough Citizen
01733 555111
www.peterboroughnow.co.uk
Weekly (Wed). Editor: Rebecca Stephens
News editor: James Kelly
Features editor: Rachael Gordon
Chief sub-editor: Tracey Crampton
Production editor: Brad Barnes

Peterborough Evening Telegraph
01733 555111
www.peterboroughnow.co.uk
Daily. Editor: Rebecca Stephens
News editor: James Kelly
Features editor: Rachael Gordon
Chief sub-editor: Tracey Crampton

Peterborough Herald & Post
01733 318600
www.peterborough.net/heraldandpost
Weekly (Thu). Editor: Steve Rose
Features editor: Amanda Franklin

Ramsey Post
01480 411481
Weekly (Thu). Editor: Paul Richardson
Deputy editor: Angela Singer

Rayleigh Times
01702 477666
www.thisisessex.co.uk
Monthly (Tue). Editor: Michael Guy

Redbridge Yellow Advertiser
01268 503400
www.trinitymirrorsouthern.co.uk
Editor: Graham Allen
News editor: Paula Dady
Features editor: Pat Jones

Redbridge, Waltham Forest & West Essex Guardian
020 8498 3400
Weekly (Thu). Editor: Pat Stannard

Romford & Havering Post
020 8491 2000
Weekly free (Wed). Editor: Dave Russell
News editor: Scott Morrow
Chief sub-editor: Graham Whitmore

Romford Recorder
01708 771500
www.recorderonline.co.uk
Weekly (Fri). Editor: Mark Sweetingham

Royston Weekly News
01223 434434
www.cambridge-news.co.uk
Weekly (Thu). Editor: Nigel Brookes

Rutland & Stamford Mercury & Citizen
01780 762255
www.stamfordmercury.co.uk
Weekly (Fri). Editor: Tor Clark
News editor: Suzanne Moon

St Ives Town Crier
01480 402100
www.cambridge-news.co.uk
Weekly (Thu)
Editor: Anthony Hawkswell

St Ives Weekly News
01223 434434
www.cambridge-news.co.uk
Weekly (Thu). Editor: Nigel Brookes

St Neots Town Crier
01480 402100
www.cambridge-news.co.uk
Weekly (Thu)
Editor: Anthony Hawkswell

St Neots Weekly News
01480 467670
www.cambridge-news.co.uk
Weekly (Wed). Editor: Nigel Brookes

Saffron Walden Observer
01279 866355
www.herts-essex-news.co.uk
Weekly (Thu). Editor: Val Brown
News editor: Sandra Perry

Saffron Walden, Stansted & Sawston Reporter
01763 245241
www.thisisessex.co.uk
Weekly (Thu). Editor: Les Baker

Saffron Walden Weekly News
01223 434434
www.cambridge-news.co.uk
Weekly (Thu). Editor: Nigel Brookes

Sawbridgeworth Star
01279 838111
www.thisisessex.co.uk
Weekly (Thu). Editor: Ken Morley
News editor: Beverley Rouse

Scunthorpe Target
01724 273273
www.thisisscunthorpe.co.uk
Weekly (Thu). Editor: John Grubb
News editor: Matthew Finch
Chief sub-editor: John Curtis

Scunthorpe Telegraph
01724 273273
www.thisisscunthorpe.co.uk
Daily. Editor: John Grubb
News editor: Matthew Finch
Chief sub-editor: John Curtis

Skegness Citizen
01507 353200
Weekly (Fri). Editor: John Calpe

Skegness Standard
01507 353200
www.skegnesstoday.co.uk
Weekly (Wed)
Editor: Charles Ladbrooke

Skegness Target
01205 315000
Weekly (Wed). Editor: Glyn Belsher
News editor: Katy Roberts

Sleaford Citizen
01529 413646
Weekly (Fri). Editor: John Lavery
News editor: Andy Hubbert

Sleaford Standard
01529 413646
Weekly (Wed). Editor: John Lavery
News editor: Andy Hubbert

Sleaford Target
01522 820000
www.thisislincolnshire.co.uk
Weekly (Wed). Editor: Glynn Belsher

Soham Standard
01353 667831
www.ely-standard.co.uk
Weekly (Thu). Editor: John Ison
News editor: Debbie Davies

South Woodham & Maldon Weekly News
01621 852233
www.thisisessex.co.uk
Weekly (Thu). Editor: James Wills

Southend Standard
01268 522792
www.thisisessex.co.uk
Weekly (Thu). Editor: Martin McNeil
News editor: Chris Hatton
Features editor: Sally King
Chief sub-editor: Neal Reeve

Southend Times
01702 477666
www.thisisessex.co.uk
Weekly (Tue). Editor: Michael Guy

Southend Yellow Advertiser
01268 503400
www.trinitymirrorsouthern.co.uk
Weekly free (Thu)
Editor: Graham Allen
News editor: Paula Dady
Features editor: Pat Jones

Spalding Guardian
01775 725021
www.spaldingtoday.co.uk
Weekly (Thu). Editor: Alan Salt
News editor: David Crossley
Features editor: Julie Williams
Chief sub-editor: Tracey Vale

Spalding Herald
01775 713723
www.spaldingtoday.co.uk
Monthly free (1st of month)
Editor: Natalie Ward

Spilsby Standard
01754 897120
Weekly (Wed). Editor: John Coupe

Spilsby Target
01205 315000
Weekly (Wed). Editor: Glyn Belsher
News editor: Katy Roberts

Stamford Citizen
01780 762255
www.stamfordmercury.co.uk
Weekly free (Tue). Editor: Tor Clark
News editor: Suzanne Moon

Stamford Herald & Post
01733 318600
Weekly (Thu). Editor: Steve Rose
Features editor: Amanda Franklin

Stansted Observer
01279 866355
www.herts-essex-news.co.uk
Weekly (Thu). Editor: Val Brown
News editor: Sandra Perry

Sudbury Mercury
01284 702588
www.edp24.co.uk
Weekly (Fri). Editor: Terry Hunt
News editor: Ainsley Davidson
Features editor: Julian Ford
Chief sub-editor: Mike Crookwell

Suffolk Advertiser
01473 324700
www.advertiser-online.co.uk
Weekly (Fri). Editor: Paul Couch
News editor: Nicola Durrant

Suffolk Free Press
01787 375271
www.sudburytoday.co.uk
Editor: Phil Minett
News editor: Nick Wells

Swaffham Mercury
01603 628311
www.edp24.co.uk
Monthly. Editor: Terry Redhead

Swaffham News
01553 761188
Weekly (Fri). Editor: Malcolm Powell
News editor: Donna Semmens

Tendring Weekly News
01206 506000
www.thisisessex.co.uk
Weekly free (Wed). Editor: Irene Kettle
News editor: Sally Teatheredge

Thetford & Brandon Times
01603 628311
www.edp24.co.uk
Weekly (Wed). Editor: Terry Redhead

Thetford Citizen
01284 768911
www.johnstonpress.co.uk/anglia
Weekly. Editor: Barry Peters
News editor: Lesley Anslow
Features editor: Claire Brown

Thurrock Gazette
01375 411502
www.thisisessex.co.uk
Weekly free (Fri). Editor: Neil Speight

Thurrock Recorder
01708 771500
www.recorderonline.co.uk
Weekly (Fri). Editor: Mark Sweetingham
News editor: Ross Hindley

Thurrock Yellow Advertiser
01268 503400
www.trinitymirrorsouthern.co.uk
Weekly free (Thu). Editor: Graham Allen
News editor: Paula Dady
Features editor: Pat Jones

Thurrock, Lakeside & Grays Post
020 8491 2000
Weekly (Thu). Editor: Dave Russell
News editor: Scott Morrow
Chief sub-editor: Graham Whitmore

Walden Local
01799 516161
www.thisisessex.co.uk
Weekly (Wed). Editor: John Brooker

Waltham Forest Guardian
020 8498 3400
Weekly (Thu). Editor: Pat Stannard

Waltham Forest Independent
020 8498 3400
Weekly (Fri). Editor: Pat Stannard

Watton & Swaffham Times
01603 628311
www.edp24.co.uk
Weekly (Fri). Editor: Terry Redhead

Waveney Advertiser
01493 601206
www.advertiser-online.co.uk
Weekly (Fri)
Managing editor: Mike Almond

Whittlesey Times
01354 652621
www.cambs-times.co.uk
Weekly (Thu). Editor: Brian Asplin
News editor: John Elworthy
Features editor: Maggie Gibson

Wisbech Standard
01354 652621
www.wisbech-standard.co.uk
Weekly (Thu). Editor: Brian Asplin
News editor: John Elworthy
Features editor: Maggie Gibson

Witham Chronicle
01245 600700
www.thisisessex.co.uk
Weekly (Wed/Thu)
Editor: Stuart Rawlins
News editor: Matt Adams
Features editor: Darryl Webber

Woodham Chronicle
01245 600700
www.thisisessex.co.uk
Weekly (Wed/Thu)
Editor: Stuart Rawlins
News editor: Matt Adams
Features editor: Darryl Webber

Wymondham & Attleborough Mercury
01603 628311
www.edp24.co.uk
Weekly (Fri). Editor: Terry Redhead

Midlands

Derbyshire, Leicestershire, Northamptonshire, Nottinghamshire, Staffordshire

The Advertiser
01782 602525
Weekly free (Thu). Editor: Sean Dooley
News editor: Robert Cotterill
Features editor: Charlotte Little-Jones

Alfreton Chad
01623 456789
www.johnstonpress.co.uk/yorkshire.asp
Weekly (Fri). Editor: Jeremy Plews
News editor: Joy Thompson
Chief sub-editor: Karen Robinson

Alfreton & Ripley Echo
01773 834731
Weekly (Fri). Editor: David Hopkinson

Ashbourne News Telegraph
01283 512345
www.ashbournenewstelegraph.co.uk
Weekly (Wed). Editor: Paul Hazeldine
News editor: Steve Doohan
Features editor: Bill Pritchard
Chief sub-editor: Steve Davies
Production editor: Diane Finn

Ashfield Chad
01623 456789
www.ashfieldtoday.co.uk
Weekly (Wed). Editor: Jeremy Plews
News editor: Joy Thompson
Chief sub-editor: Karen Robinson

Ashby & Coalville Mail
0116 251 2512
www.thisisleicestershire.co.uk
Weekly (Tue). Editor: Nick Carter
News editor: Richard Bettsworth

Ashby Times
01530 813101
Weekly (Fri). News editor: Mark Good
Features editor: Kay Moon
Chief sub-editor: Mark Good

Atherstone Herald
01827 848535
Weekly (Thu). Editor: Sam Holliday

Belper Express
01332 291111
Weekly free (Tue). Editor: Andy Machin

Belper News
01629 582432
Weekly (Wed). Editor: Amanda Hatfield
News editor: Helen Taylor

Biddulph Advertiser
01260 281012
Weekly (Thu). Editor: Harri Ashton

Biddulph Chronicle
01260 273737
Weekly (Fri). Editor: Jeremy Condliffe

Birstall Post
0116 267 4213
www.birstallpost.co.uk
Monthly free (1st of month)
Editor: Jerry Jackson
News editor: Mrs E M Jackson

Brackley Post
01604 614600
Weekly (Fri). Editor: Richard Howarth
Production editor: Julie Fisher

Burntwood Mercury
01827 848535
Weekly (Thu). Editor: Sam Holliday

Bolsover & District Advertiser
01246 202291
Fortnightly free (Wed)
Editor: Mike Wilson
Assistant editor: Phil Bramley
News editor: Tracy Mitchell
Entertainment editor: Gay Bolton
Assistant news editor: Sean Boyle

Burton Mail
01283 512345
www.burtonmail.co.uk
Daily. Editor: Paul Hazeldine
News editor: Steve Doohan
Features editor: Bill Pritchard
Chief sub-editor: Steve Davies
Production editor: Diane Finn

Burton & South Derbyshire Advertiser
01283 512345
www.uttoxeteradvertiser.co.uk
Weekly (Wed). Editor: Paul Hazeldine
News editor: Steve Doohan
Features editor: Bill Pritchard
Chief sub-editor: Steve Davies
Production editor: Diane Finn

Burton Trader
01283 512200
Weekly (Wed). Editor: Paul Thomas
News editor: Paul Henshall
Chief sub-editor: Alan Payne

Buxton Advertiser
01298 22118
www.buxtontoday.co.uk
Weekly (Thu). Editor: John Phillips
News editor: Emma Downes

Buxton Times
01298 22118
www.buxtontoday.co.uk
Weekly free (Fri). Editor: John Phillips
News editor: Emma Downes

Cannock & Rugeley Mercury
01827 848535
Weekly (Thu). Editor: Linda Young

Cannock & Rugeley Chronicle
01543 506311
Weekly (Fri). Editor: Susan Attwater

Cannock Chase & Burntwood Post
01543 501700
Weekly (Thu). Editor: Mike Lockley

Cheadle & Tean Times
01538 753162
Weekly (Wed). Editor: Nigel Titterton

Cheadle Post & Times
01538 750011
Weekly (Wed). Editor: Doug Pickford

Chesterfield Advertiser
01246 202291
Weekly free (Fri). Editor: Mike Wilson
Assistant editor: Phil Bramley
News editor: Tracy Mitchell
Entertainment editor: Gay Bolton
Assistant news editor: Sean Boyle

Chesterfield Express
01246 504500
Weekly free (Wed). Editor: Mike Wilson
Assistant editor: Phil Bramley
News editor: Tracy Mitchell
Entertainment editor: Gay Bolton
Assistant news editor: Sean Boyle

Chronicle and Echo (Northampton)
01604 467000
www.northantsnews.com
Daily. Editor: Mark Edwards
News editor: Richard Edmondson
Features editor: Sarah Freeman
Chief sub-editor: Joanne Cartwright
Production editor: Graham Tebbutt

Coalville & Ashby Echo
01509 635807
Weekly (Tue). Editor: Pete Warrington

Coalville Times
01530 813101
Weekly (Fri). News editor: Mark Good
Features editor: Kay Moon
Chief sub-editor: Mark Good

Coleshill Herald
01827 848535
Weekly (Thu). Editor: Sam Holliday

Corby Citizen
01536 506100
www.northantsnews.com
Weekly (Thu). Editor: David Penman
News editor: Nick Shaw
Features editor: Alistair Whitfield
Chief sub-editor: Andy Wynham
Production editor: Richard Yetman

Corby Herald & Post
01604 614600
Weekly (Thu). Editor: Richard Howarth
Production editor: Julie Fisher

Daventry Express
01327 703383
www.daventryonline.co.uk
Weekly (Thu). Editor: Jason Gibbons
News editor: Adam Hollier

Derby Evening Telegraph
01332 291111
www.thisisderbyshire.co.uk
Daily. Editor: Mike Norton
News editor: Nicola Hodgson
Features editor: Cheryl Hague
Chief sub-editor: Peter Pheasant

Derby Express
01332 291111
Weekly free (Tue). Editor: Andy Machin

Derby Trader
01332 253999
Weekly (Thu). Editor: Patrick O'Connor
Features editor: Steve Eyley
Chief sub-editor: Richard Taylor

Derbyshire Guardian
01909 500500
Weekly (Fri). Editor: George Robinson
News editor: Jackie Laver

Derbyshire Times
01246 504500
www.derbyshiretimes.co.uk
Weekly (Thu). Editor: Mike Wilson
Assistant editor: Phil Bramley
News editor: Tracy Mitchell
Entertainment editor: Gay Bolton
Assistant news editor: Sean Boyle

Dronfield Advertiser
01246 202291
Weekly free (Wed). Editor: Mike Wilson
Assistant editor: Phil Bramley
News editor: Tracy Mitchell
Entertainment editor: Gay Bolton
Assistant news editor: Sean Boyle

Dukeries Advertiser
01636 681234
Weekly (Fri)
Editor: Harry Whitehouse
News editor: Lucy Millard
Chief sub-editor: Chris Prine

Eastwood & Kimberley Advertiser
01773 713563
www.eastwoodadvertiser.co.uk
Weekly (Fri). Editor: John Shawcroft

Eckington Leader
01246 434343
Weekly (Fri). Editor: Mike Wilson
Assistant editor: Phil Bramley
News editor: Tracy Mitchell
Entertainment editor: Gay Bolton
Assistant news editor: Sean Boyle

The Evening Telegraph
01536 506100
www.northantsnews.com
Daily. Editor: David Penman
News editor: Nick Shaw
Features editor: Alistair Whitfield
Chief sub-editor: Andy Wynham
Production editor: Richard Yetman

Glossop Chronicle
0161 304 7691
Weekly (Thu). Editor: Nigel Skinner

Harborough Mail
01858 462626
www.harboroughmail.co.uk
Weekly (Thu). Editor: Brian Dodds
News editor: Maria Thompson

High Peak Courier
01298 22118
www.buxtontoday.co.uk
Weekly free (Fri). Editor: John Phillips
News editor: Emma Downes

Hinckley Herald & Journal
01455 891981
www.hinckley-times.co.uk
Weekly (Wed). Editor: Paul Webb

Hinckley Times
01455 891981
www.hinckley-times.co.uk
Weekly (Thu). Editor: Paul Webb

Hucknall & Bulwell Dispatch
01623 456789
www.hucknalltoday.co.uk
Weekly (Fri)
Editor: Richard Silverwood

Ilkeston & Ripley Trader
01332 253999
Weekly (Fri). Editor: Patrick O'Connor
Features editor: Steve Eyley
Chief sub-editor: Richard Taylor

Ilkeston Advertiser
0115 944 4411
www.derbyshiretimes.co.uk
Weekly (Thu). Editor: David Horne

Ilkeston Express
01332 291111
Weekly free (Tue). Editor: Andy Machin

Ilkeston Shopper
0115 944 4411
www.derbyshiretimes.co.uk
Weekly free (Tue). Editor: David Horne

Kettering Citizen
01536 506100
www.northantsnews.com
Weekly (Thu). Editor: David Penman
News editor: Nick Shaw
Features editor: Alistair Whitfield
Chief sub-editor: Andy Wynham
Production editor: Richard Yetman

Kettering Evening Telegraph
01536 506100
www.northantsnews.com
Daily. Editor: David Penman
News editor: Nick Shaw
Features editor: Alistair Whitfield
Chief sub-editor: Andy Wynham
Production editor: Richard Yetman

Kettering Herald & Post
01604 614600
Weekly (Thu). Editor: Richard Howarth
Production editor: Julie Fisher

Leek Post & Times
01538 399599
Weekly (Wed). Editor: Doug Pickford
News editor: Jane Griffiths

Leicester Mail
0116 251 2512
www.thisisleicestershire.co.uk
Weekly free (Tue). Editor: Nick Carter
News editor: Richard Bettsworth

Leicester Mercury
0116 251 2512
www.leicestermercury.co.uk
Daily. Editor: Nick Carter
News editor: Richard Bettsworth

Leicestershire Times Today
0115 982 7338
Weekly (Fri). Editor: Matthew Palmer

Lichfield and Burntwood Edition Express and Star
01902 313131
www.expressandstar.com
Daily. Editor: Adrian Faber

Lichfield Mercury
01827 848535
Weekly (Thu). Editor: Sam Holliday

Lichfield Post
01543 258523
Weekly (Thu). Editor: Pam Thomas

Long Eaton Advertiser
0115 946 2837
Weekly (Wed). Editor: David Godsall

Long Eaton Recorder
0115 948 2000
www.thisisnottingham.co.uk
Weekly free (Thu). Editor: Graham Glen
News editor: Claire Catlow
Features editor: Jeremy Lewis

Long Eaton Trader
0115 946 9909
Weekly (Thu). Editor: Patrick O'Connor
Features editor: Steve Eyley
Chief sub-editor: Richard Taylor

Loughborough Echo
01509 232632
Weekly (Thu). Editor: John Ripon
News editor: John Brindley

Loughborough Mail
0116 251 2512
www.thisisleicestershire.co.uk
Weekly (Tue). Editor: Nick Carter
News editor: Richard Bettsworth

Lutterworth Mail
01858 462626
www.harboroughtoday.co.uk
Weekly (Thu). Editor: Brian Dodds
News editor: Maria Thompson

Mansfield & Ashfield Observer
01623 456789
Weekly free (Thu). Editor: Tony Spittles

Mansfield & Ashfield Recorder
01623 420000
Weekly free (Wed)
Editor: Graham Glenn

Mansfield Chad
01623 456789
www.mansfieldtoday.co.uk
Weekly (Wed). Editor: Jeremy Plews
News editor: Joy Thompson
Chief sub-editor: Karen Robinson

Market Harborough Herald & Post
01604 614600
Weekly (Fri). Editor: Richard Howarth
Production editor: Julie Fisher

Matlock Mercury
01629 582432
www.matlockmercury.co.uk
Weekly (Thu). Editor: Amanda Hatfield
News editor: Helen Taylor

Melton Citizen
01664 410041
www.meltontoday.co.uk/
Weekly free (Tue). Editor: Andrew Plaice
Melton Times
01664 410041
www.meltontoday.co.uk/
Weekly (Thu). Editor: Andrew Plaice
Mid Staffs Edition Express and Star
01543 506311
www.expressandstar.com
Daily. Editor: Adrian Faber
News editor: Mark Drew
Mountsorrel Post
0116 267 4213
4pa. Editor: Jerry Jackson
News editor: Mrs E M Jackson
Newark Advertiser
01636 681234
www.newarkadvertiser.co.uk
Weekly (Fri). Editor: Harry Whitehouse
News editor: Lucy Millard
Newcastle Advertiser
01782 619830
Daily. Editor: Sean Dooley
News editor: Robert Cotterill
Features editor: Charlotte Little-Jones
North West Leics & South Derbyshire Leader
01530 813101
Weekly (Wed). News editor: Mark Good
Features editor: Kay Moon
Chief sub-editor: Mark Good
Northampton Herald & Post
01604 614600
Weekly (Thu). Editor: Richard Howarth
Production editor: Julie Fisher
Northampton Mercury
01604 467000
www.northantsnews.com
Weekly (Thu). Editor: Mark Edwards
News editor: Richard Edmondson
Features editor: Sarah Freeman
Chief sub-editor: Joanne Cartwright
Production editor: Graham Tebbutt
Northamptonshire Journal
0116 233 3635
Weekly (Tue). Editor: Paul Clark
Northants on Sunday
01536 467000
www.northantsnews.com
Sunday. Editor: Steve Scoles
Nottingham & Trent Valley Journal
0115 982 7337
Weekly (Fri). Editor: Matthew Palmer
Nottingham and Long Eaton Topper
0115 969 6000
www.toppernewspapers.co.uk
Weekly free (Wed). Editor: John Howarth
Nottingham Evening Post
0115 948 2000
www.thisisnottingham.co.uk
Daily. Editor: Graham Glen
News editor: Claire Catlow
Features editor: Jeremy Lewis
Nottingham Recorder
0115 948 2000
www.thisisnottingham.co.uk
Weekly free (Wed). Editor: Graham Glen
News editor: Claire Catlow
Features editor: Jeremy Lewis

Oadby & Wigston Mail
0116 251 2512
www.thisisleicestershire.co.uk
Weekly (Tue). Editor: Nick Carter
News editor: Richard Bettsworth
Peak Advertiser
01629 812159
Fortnightly free (Thu)
Editor: Steve Wild
Peak Times
01629 582432
Weekly free (Fri)
Editor: Amanda Hatfield
News editor: Helen Taylor
Potteries Advertiser
01782 602525
Weekly free (Thu). Editor: Sean Dooley
News editor: Robert Cotterill
Features editor: Charlotte Little-Jones
Retford and Bawtry Guardian
01909 500500
www.retfordtoday.co.uk
Weekly (Thu)
Editor: George Robinson
News editor: Jackie Laver
Retford Trader
01909 500500
Weekly free (Thu)
Editor: George Robinson
News editor: Jackie Laver
Retford, Gainsborough & Worksop Times
01777 702275
Weekly (Thu). Editor: Nick Purkiss
Ripley & Heanor News
01629 582432
Weekly (Thu). Editor: Amanda Hatfield
News editor: Helen Taylor
Rothley Post
0117 267 4213
6pa. Editor: Jerry Jackson
News editor: Mrs E M Jackson
Rugeley Mercury
01543 414414
Weekly (Thu). Editor: Tim Hewitt
News editor: Andy Kerr
Rugeley Post
01543 258523
Weekly (Thu). Editor: Pam Thomas
Rutland Times
01572 757722
www.rutlandtimes.co.uk
Weekly (Thu). Editor: Brian Martin
The Sentinel (Stoke-On-Trent)
01782 602525
www.thesentinel.co.uk
Daily. Editor: Sean Dooley
News editor: Robert Cotterill
Features editor: Charlotte Little-Jones
Sentinel Sunday
01782 602525
www.thesentinel.co.uk
Sunday. Editor: Sean Dooley
News editor: Robert Cotterill
Features editor: Charlotte Little-Jones
Shepshed Echo
01509 232632
Weekly (Thu). Editor: John Ripon
News editor: John Brindley

Sherwood/Rainworth Chad
01623 456789
Weekly (Wed). Editor: Jeremy Plews
News editor: Joy Thompson
Chief sub-editor: Karen Robinson
Shirebrook & Bolsover Chad
01623 456789
Weekly (Wed). Editor: Jeremy Plews
News editor: Joy Thompson
Chief sub-editor: Karen Robinson
South Notts Advertiser
01636 681234
Weekly (Fri)
Editor: Harry Whitehouse
News editor: Lucy Millard
Stafford & Stone Chronicle
01785 247290
Daily. Editor: Klooran Wills
Stafford Post
01543 501700
Weekly (Thu). Editor: Mike Lockley
Staffordshire Newsletter
01785 257700
www.staffordshirenewsletter.co.uk
Weekly (Thu). Editor: Klooran Wills
Stapleford & Sandiacre News
0115 946 2837
Weekly (Wed). Editor: David Godsall
Stratford & Banbury Why
01527 588000
Weekly free (Fri). Editor: Claire Smith
Swadlincote Times
01530 813101
Weekly (Fri). News editor: Mark Good
Features editor: Kay Moon
Chief sub-editor: Mark Good
Tamworth Herald
01827 848535
www.tamworthherald.co.uk
Weekly (Thu). Editor: Sam Holiday
Tamworth Times
01827 308000
Weekly (Thu). Editor: Pam Thomas
Trader Pictorial
01636 681234
Weekly (Wed)
Editor: Harry Whitehouse
News editor: Lucy Millard
Towcester Post
01604 614600
Weekly (Fri). Editor: Richard Howarth
Production editor: Julie Fisher
Uttoxeter Advertiser
01889 562050
www.uttoxeteradvertiser.co.uk
Weekly (Tue). Editor: Alan Harris
Uttoxeter Post & Times
01889 568999
Weekly (Thu). Editor: Alan Harris
Warsop Chad
01623 456789
Weekly (Wed). Editor: Jeremy Plews
News editor: Joy Thompson
Chief sub-editor: Karen Robinson

Wellingborough & East Northants Evening Telegraph
01536 506100
www.northantsnews.com
Daily. Editor: David Penman
News editor: Nick Shaw
Features editor: Alistair Whitfield
Chief sub-editor: Andy Wynham
Production editor: Richard Yetman

Wellingborough & Rushden Citizen
01536 506100
www.northantsnews.com
Weekly (Thu). Editor: David Penman
News editor: Nick Shaw
Features editor: Alistair Whitfield
Chief sub-editor: Andy Wynham
Production editor: Richard Yetman

Wellingborough & Rushden Herald & Post
01604 614600
Weekly (Thu). Editor: Richard Howarth
Production editor: Julie Fisher

Worksop Guardian
01909 500500
www.worksoptoday.co.uk
Weekly (Fri). Editor: George Robinson
News editor: Jackie Laver

Worksop Trader
01909 500500
Weekly free (Wed)
Editor: George Robinson
News editor: Jackie Laver

West Midlands

West Midlands, Warwickshire

Ad News – Willenhall, Wednesbury & Darlaston
01543 501700
Weekly (Wed). Editor: Mike Lockley

Bedworth Echo
024 7663 3633
www.iccoventry.co.uk
Weekly (Fri). Editor: Alan Kirby
News editor: John West
Features editor: Steven Chilton

Birmingham Evening Mail
0121 236 3366
www.icbirmingham.co.uk
Daily. Editor: Roger Borrell
News editor: Andy Richards
Features editor: Alison Handley

Birmingham News
0121 234 5073
www.icbirmingham.co.uk
Weekly (Thu). Editor: David Brook
News editor: Damien O'Laughlin

Birmingham Post
0121 236 3366
www.icbirmingham.co.uk
Daily. Editor: Fiona Alexander
News editor: Carole Cole
Features editor: Sid Langley

Black Country Bugle
01384 567678
www.blackcountrybugle.co.uk
Weekly (Thu). Editor: Robert Taylor

Coventry Citizen
024 7663 3633
www.iccoventry.co.uk
Weekly (Thu). Editor: Alan Kirby
News editor: John West
Features editor: Steven Chilton

Coventry Evening Telegraph
024 7663 3633
www.iccoventry.co.uk
Daily. Editor: Alan Kirby
News editor: John West
Features editor: Steven Chilton

Coventry Observer
024 7649 5900
www.coventryobserver.co.uk
Weekly free (Fri). Editor: Mike Green

Daventry Express
01788 535363
www.daventryonline.co.uk
Weekly (Thu). Editor: Jason Gibbons

Dudley Chronicle
01384 353211
www.expressandstar.com
Weekly (Fri). Editor: Leon Burakowski
Features editor: Dave Pearce
Chief sub-editor: Jane Reynolds

Dudley Edition Express & Star
01384 355355
www.expressandstar.com
Daily. Editor: Adrian Faber
News editor: Mark Drew
Features editor: Dylan Evans
Chief sub-editor: Tony Reynolds

Dudley News
01384 358050
www.dudleynews.co.uk
Weekly (Fri). Editor: Jeff Gepheott
Features editor: Lynn Taylor

Express & Star
01902 313131
www.expressandstar.com
Daily. Editor: Adrian Faber
News editor: Mark Drew
Features editor: Dylan Evans
Chief sub-editor: Tony Reynolds

Express & Star (Stourbridge)
01384 399914

Express & Star (Walsall)
01922 444444

Great Barr and Erdington Chronicle
0121 553 7171
Weekly free (Wed). Editor: Caroline Jones

Great Barr Observer
01827 848535
Weekly (Fri). Editor: Mark Eustace

Halesowen Chronicle
01384 353211
Weekly (Fri). Editor: Leon Burakowski
Features editor: Dave Pearce
Chief sub-editor: Jane Reynolds

Halesowen News
01384 358050
www.halesowennews.co.uk
Weekly (Fri). Editor: Jeff Gepheott
Features editor: Lynn Taylor

Heartland Evening News
024 7635 3534
www.hen-news.com
Daily. Editor: Tony Parrott
News editor: Jack Linsted
Features editor: John Jevons
Production editor: Bob Clemens

Kenilworth Weekly News
01926 457777
www.kenilworthonline.co.uk
Weekly (Fri). Editor: Martin Lawson
News editor: Calista Lewis

Leamington Spa Courier
01926 457777
www.leamingtononline.co.uk
Weekly (Fri). Editor: Martin Lawson
News editor: Calista Lewis

Leamington Spa Observer
01926 451900
www.leamington-now.com
Weekly free (Thu). Editor: Ian Hughes

Leamington Spa Review
01926 457777
www.leamingtonspatoday.co.uk
Weekly (Thu). Editor: Martin Lawson
News editor: Calista Lewis

Metro Birmingham
020 7651 5200
www.metrobirmingham.co.uk
Daily. Editor: Kenny Campbell
News editor: Mark Dorman
Features editor: Kieran Meeke

Nuneaton Weekly Tribune
024 7663 3633
www.iccoverntry.co.uk
Weekly (Thu). Editor: Alan Kirby
News editor: John West
Features editor: Steven Chilton

Rugby Advertiser
01788 535363
www.rugbyadvertiser.co.uk
Weekly (Thu)
Editor: Peter Hengenheister

Rugby Observer
01788 535147
www.therugbyobserver.co.uk
Weekly free (Fri). Editor: Chris Smith

Rugby Review
01788 535363
www.rugbyreviewtoday.co.uk
Weekly (Thu)
Editor: Peter Hengenheister

Sandwell Chronicle
0121 553 7171
Weekly free (Wed). Editor: Caroline Jones

Solihull News
0121 711 3993
www.midlandweeklymedia.co.uk
Weekly (Fri). Editor: Ross Crawford

Solihull Times
0121 711 3993
www.midlandweeklymedia.co.uk
Weekly (Fri). Editor: Roland Wilson

Stourbridge Chronicle
01384 399914
www.expressandstar.com
Weekly (Fri). Editor: Leon Burakowski
Features editor: Dave Pearce
Chief sub-editor: Jane Reynolds

Stourbridge News
01384 358050
www.thisisstourbridge.co.uk
Weekly (Thu). Editor: Jeff Gepheott
Features editor: Lynn Taylor

Stratford-upon-Avon Herald
01789 266261
www.stratford-herald.co.uk
Weekly (Thu). Editor: Chris Turner
News editor: Dale Levack

Stratford-upon-Avon Journal
01442 386555
www.thisisstratford-upon-avon.co.uk
Weekly (Thu). Editor: John Murphy
News editor: Pat Smith

Stratford-upon-Avon Midweek
01789 266261
www.stratford-herald.co.uk
Weekly (Tue). Editor: Chris Turner
News editor: Dale Levack

Stratford-upon-Avon Observer
01789 415717
www.stratfordstandard.co.uk
Weekly free (Thu). Editor: Sarah Halford

Sunday Mercury
0121 236 3366
www.icbirmingham.co.uk
Sunday. Editor: David Brookes
News editor: Tony Larner
Features editor: Paul Cole

Sutton Coldfield News
0121 355 7070
Weekly (Fri). Editor: Pam Thomas

Sutton Coldfield Observer
01827 848535
Weekly (Fri). Editor: Gary Phelps

Walsall Advertiser
01827 848535
Weekly (Thu). Editor: Natalie Missenden

Walsall Chronicle
01922 444444
Weekly (Thu). Editor: Mike Caldicott

Walsall Observer
01922 636666
www.thisiswalsall.co.uk
Weekly (Fri). Editor: Mike Lockley

Why Coventry, Nuneaton & Hinckley
01527 588000
Weekly free (Fri). Editor: Claire Smith

Why Solihull & District
01527 588000
Weekly free (Fri). Editor: Claire Smith

Why Warwick & Leamington
01527 588000
Weekly free (Fri). Editor: Claire Smith

Wolverhampton Ad News
01543 501700
Weekly (Wed). Editor: Mike Lockley

Wolverhampton Chronicle
01902 313131
www.yourchronicle.com
Weekly free (Thu). Editor: Adrian Faber
News editor: Mark Drew
Features editor: Dillion Evans
Chief sub-editor: Tony Reynolds

West of England

Gloucestershire, Herefordshire, Shropshire, Worcestershire

Alcester Chronicle
01527 453500
www.thisisworcestershire.co.uk
Weekly (Wed). Editor: Paul Walker
News editor: Sarah Cross

Alcester Standard
01789 415717
Weekly (Fri). Editor: Sarah Halford

Berrow's Worcester Journal
01905 748200
www.berrowsjournal.co.uk
Weekly. Editor: Stewart Gilbert
News editor: Sala Lloyd
Chief sub-editor: Jim Collins

Bridgnorth Journal
01746 761411
www.bridgnorthjournal.co.uk
Weekly (Fri). Editor: Colin Northway

Bromsgrove Advertiser
01527 837000
www.thisisworcestershire.co.uk
Weekly (Wed). Editor: Alan Wallcroft
News editor: Peter Lammas

Bromsgrove Messenger
01527 837000
www.thisisworcestershire.co.uk
Weekly (Wed). Editor: Alan Wallcroft
News editor: Peter Lammas

Bromsgrove Standard
01527 574111
www.bromsgrovestandard.co.uk
Weekly free (Fri)
Editor: Charlotte Beavers

Cheltenham Independent
01453 762412
www.thisisstroud.com
Weekly (Wed). Editor: Skip Walker
News editor: Sue Smith

Cheltenham News
01452 424442
Weekly free (Thu). Editor: Anita Syvrat

Cheltenham/Tewkesbury News
01452 420632
Weekly free (Thu). Editor: Chris Hill

Chipping Sodbury/Yate Gazette
01453 544000
Weekly (Fri). Editor: David Cullimore
News editor: Carole Taylor

Cotswold Journal
01886 442555
www.thisistewkesbury.com
Weekly (Thu). Editor: John Murphy
News editor: Pat Smith

County Independent
01453 762412
www.thisisstroud.com
Weekly (Wed). Editor: Skip Walker
News editor: Sue Smith

Droitwich Spa Advertiser
01905 795097
www.thisisdroitwichspa.co.uk
Weekly (Wed). Editor: Alan Wallcroft
News editor: Peter Lammas

Droitwich Standard
01527 574111
Weekly (Fri). Editor: Charlotte Beavers

Evesham Journal
01886 442555
www.thisisworcestershire.co.uk
Weekly (Thu). Editor: John Murphy
News editor: Pat Smith

Express and Star (Kidderminster)
01902 313131
www.expressandstar.com
Daily. Editor: Adrian Faber
News editor: Mark Drew
Features editor: Dylan Evans
Chief sub-editor: Tony Reynolds

Forest of Dean and Wye Valley Review
01594 841113
www.forest-and-wye-today.co.uk
Weekly free (Wed). Editor: John Powell

The Forester
01594 820600
www.thisisgloucestershire.co.uk
Weekly (Thu). Editor: Viv Hargreaves

Gloucester Citizen
01452 424442
www.thisisgloucestershire.co.uk
Daily. Editor: Ian Mean

Gloucester Independent
01453 762412
www.thisisstroud.com
Weekly (Wed). Editor: Skip Walker
News editor: Sue Smith

Gloucester News
01452 424442
Weekly free (Thu). Editor: Anita Syvrat

Gloucestershire County Gazette
01453 544000
www.thisisthesouthcotswolds.co.uk
Weekly (Fri). Editor: David Cullimore
News editor: Carole Taylor

Gloucestershire Echo
01242 271821
www.thisisgloucestershire.co.uk
Daily. Editor: Anita Syvret
News editor: Tanya Gledhill
Features editor: Ian Akerman
Chief sub-editor: Jason Clare

Hereford Admag
01432 376120
Weekly (Wed). Features editor: Clare Fry

Hereford Journal
01432 355353
www.herefordjournal.co.uk
Weekly free (Wed)
Editor: Mike Robinson
Assistant editor: Colin Osborne

Hereford Times
01432 274413
www.thisisherefordshire.co.uk
Weekly (Thu). Editor: Liz Griffin
News editor: Nigel Heins

Jobs Today – Cheltenham and Gloucester
01453 544000
Daily. Editor: David Cullimore
News editor: Carole Taylor

Kidderminster Chronicle
01562 829500
www.thisisworcestershire.co.uk/worcestershire/kidderminster
Weekly (Wed). Editor: Brian Gough

Kidderminster Shuttle and Times and Stourport News
01562 633333
www.thisisworcestershire.co.uk/worcestershire/kidderminster
Weekly (Thu). Editor: Clive Joyce

Ledbury Reporter
01684 892200
Weekly (Fri). Editor: Nick Howells
News editor: Ally Hardy

Leominster Journal
01432 355353
www.shropshirestar.co.uk
Weekly free (Wed)
Editor: Mike Robinson
Assistant editor: Colin Osborne

Ludlow Advertiser
01584 873796
www.thisisludlow.co.uk
Weekly (Wed). Editor: Jean Kingdon
News editor: Michael Baws
Features editor: Arun Marsh

Ludlow Journal
01743 248248
www.ludlowjournal.co.uk
Weekly free (Fri)
Editor: Mike Robinson
News editor: Vince Buston

Malvern Gazette
01684 892200
Weekly (Fri). Editor: Nick Howells

Market Drayton Advertiser
01630 698113
www.marketdraytonadvertiser.co.uk
Weekly (Fri). Editor: Sam Taylor

Newport Advertiser
01952 811500
www.newportadvertiser.co.uk
Weekly (Fri). Editor: Samantha Taylor
News editor: Terry Morris

North Shropshire Chronicle
01743 248248
www.northshropshirechronicle.com
Weekly (Thu). Editor: John Butterworth

Oswestry & Border Counties Advertiser
01691 655321
www.bordercountiesadvertiser.co.uk
Weekly (Wed). Editor: Sue Perry

Redditch Advertiser
01527 453500
www.thisisworcestershire.co.uk/worcestershire/redditch
Weekly (Wed). Editor: Paul Walker
News editor: Sarah Cross

Redditch Standard
01527 588688
www.redditchstandard.co.uk
Weekly free (Fri)
Editor: Andrew Powell

Ross Gazette
01989 562007
www.ross-today.co.uk
Weekly (Thu). Editor: Chris Robertson
News editor: Pat Roberts

Ross-on-Wye Journal
01432 355353
www.shropshirestar.co.uk
Weekly free (Wed)
Editor: Mike Robinson
Assistant editor: Colin Osborne

Shrewsbury Admag
01743 241414
www.northshropshirechronicle.com
Weekly (Thu). Editor: Jan Edwards

Shrewsbury Chronicle
01743 248248
www.shrewsburychronicle.co.uk
Weekly (Thu). Editor: John Butterworth

Shropshire Star
01952 242424
www.shropshirestar.com
Daily. Editor: Sarah Jane Smith
News editor: John Simcock
Features editor: Carl Jones
Chief sub-editor: Lisa Bailey

South Shropshire Journal
01584 876311
www.southshropshirejournal.co.uk
Weekly (Fri). Editor: Mike Robinson
News editor: Vince Buston

Stourport News
01562 633330
Weekly free (Thu). Editor: Clive Joyce
News editor: Peter McMillan
Chief sub-editor: Alison Grange

Stroud News & Journal
01453 762142
www.thisisstroud.com
Weekly (Wed). Editor: Skip Walker
News editor: Sue Smith

Telford Journal
01743 248248
www.telfordjournal.co.uk
Weekly free (Thu). Editor: David Sharpe

Tenbury Wells Advertiser
01584 873796
www.thisistenbury-wells.co.uk
Weekly (Wed). Editor: Jen Green

Thornbury Gazette
01453 544000
www.thisissouthgloucestershire.co.uk
Weekly (Fri). Editor: David Cullimore
News editor: Carole Taylor

Why Evesham
01527 588000
Weekly free (Fri). Editor: Claire Smith

Why Redditch & District
01527 588000
Weekly free (Fri). Editor: Claire Smith

Why Worcester, Malvern & Kidderminster
01527 588000
Weekly free (Fri). Editor: Claire Smith

Wilts & Gloucestershire Standard
01285 642642
www.thisiscirencester.com
Weekly (Thu). Editor: Peter Davidson
News editor: Charlotte White

Worcester Evening News
01905 748200
www.thisisworcestershire.co.uk
Daily. Editor: Stewart Gilbert
News editor: Sala Lloyd
Chief sub-editor: Jim Collins

Worcester Standard
01905 726200
www.worcesterstandard.co.uk
Weekly free (Thu). Editor: James Illes
News editor: David Dunham

North England

East, North, South & West Yorkshire

Aire Valley Target
01274 729511
Weekly (Thu)
Editor: Perry Austin-Clarke
News editor: Martin Heminway
Features editor: David Barnett
Chief sub-editor: Neal Jones

Axholme Herald
01427 874417
Weekly (Fri). Editor: Ron Shipley

Barnsley Chronicle
01226 734734
www.barnsley-chronicle.co.uk
Weekly (Fri). Editor: Robert Cockcroft
News editor: Andrew Harrod
Features editor: Maureen Middleton
Chief sub-editor: John Threlkeld

Barnsley Independent
01226 734734
www.barnsley-chronicle.co.uk
Weekly (Tue). Editor: Robert Cockcroft
News editor: Andrew Harrod
Features editor: Maureen Middleton
Chief sub-editor: John Threlkeld

Batley News
01924 468282
www.dewsburytoday.co.uk
Weekly (Thu). Editor: John Wilson
News editor: Christine Littlewood

Beverley Advertiser
01482 327111
Weekly (Thu). Editor: Alex Leys
Production editor: Rosie Goodman

Beverley Guardian
01377 241122
www.beverleytoday.co.uk
Weekly free (Fri). Editor: David Sissons
News editor: Steve Petch
Chief sub-editor: Gill Pick

Birstall News
01924 468282
www.dewsburytoday.co.uk
Weekly (Thu)
Editor: John Wilson

Bradford Target
01274 729511
Weekly (Tue)
Editor: Perry Austin-Clarke
News editor: Martin Heminway
Features editor: David Barnett
Chief sub-editor: Neal Jones

Bridlington Free Press
01262 606606
www.bridlingtontoday.co.uk
Weekly (Thu). Editor: Nick Procter
News editor: Simon Haldenbee
Features editor: Jenny Norton

Bridlington Gazette & Herald
01262 606606
www.bridlingtontoday.co.uk
Weekly free (Tue). Editor: Nick Procter
News editor: Simon Haldenbee
Features editor: Jenny Norton

Brighouse Echo
01422 260200
www.brighousetoday.co.uk
Weekly (Fri). Editor: Stephen Firth

Calderdale News
01422 260200
www.halifaxtoday.co.uk
Weekly free (Wed)
Editor: John Furbisher
Production editor: Gordon Samson

Colne Valley Chronicle
01484 437747
www.ichuddersfield.co.uk
Weekly (Fri). Editor: Chris Burgess

Craven Herald & Pioneer
01756 794117
www.cravenherald.co.uk
Weekly (Fri). Editor: Ian Lockwood
News editor: Lindsey Moore

Dearne Valley Weekender
01709 571111
www.rotherhamadvertiser.com
Weekly (Fri). Editor: Doug Melloy

Dewsbury Reporter
01924 468282
www.dewsburytoday.co.uk
Weekly (Fri). Editor: John Wilson
News editor: Christine Littlewood

Dinnington & Maltby Guardian
01909 550500
www.dinningtontoday.co.uk
Weekly (Fri). Editor: George Robinson
News editor: Jackie Laver

Dinnington & Maltby Trader News
01909 550500
Weekly (Thu). Editor: George Robinson
News editor: Jackie Laver

Doncaster Advertiser
01302 564500
Weekly (Thu). Editor: Martin Edmunds
News editor: John Hepperstall

Doncaster Free Press
01302 819111
www.doncastertoday.co.uk
Weekly (Thu). Editor: Merrill Diplock
News editor: Keith Finlay
Features editor: Eddie Mardell
Production editor: David Crossland

Doncaster Star
01302 819111
www.doncastertoday.co.uk
Daily. Editor: Rob Hollingworth
News editor: David Kessen

Driffield Post
01377 241122
www.driffieldtoday.co.uk
Weekly (Fri). Editor: David Sissons
News editor: Steve Petch
Chief sub-editor: Gill Pick

Driffield Times
01377 241122
www.driffieldtoday.co.uk
Weekly (Wed). Editor: David Sissons
News editor: Steve Petch
Chief sub-editor: Gill Pick

Easingwold Advertiser & Weekly News
01347 821329
www.ghsmith.com/advertiser
Weekly (Thu). Editor: Margery Smith

East Hull Advertiser
01482 327111
Weekly (Wed). Editor: Alex Leys
Production editor: Rosie Goodman

East Riding Advertiser
01482 327111
Weekly (Thu). Editor: Alex Leys
Production editor: Rosie Goodman

East Riding News
01482 887700
Monthly (1st week)
Editor: Andrew Milner

Elmsall & South Elmsall Express
01977 640107
www.wakefieldexpress.co.uk
Weekly free (Fri). Editor: Delia Kitson

Epworth Bells & Crowle Advertiser
01427 615323
Weekly (Thu)
Editor: Amanda McForley
News editor: Stephanie Bateman

Filey & Hunmanby Mercury
01723 363636
www.scarboroughtoday.co.uk
Weekly (Sat). Editor: Ed Asquith
News editor: Neil Pickford
Chief sub-editor: Steve Banbridge
Production editor: Pete Hodgson

Gainsborough News
01427 872202
Weekly free (Fri)
Editor: Amanda McForley
News editor: Stephanie Bateman

Gainsborough Standard
01427 615323
Weekly (Thu)
Editor: Amanda McForley
News editor: Stephanie Bateman

Halifax Evening Courier
01422 260200
www.halifaxtoday.co.uk
Daily. Editor: John Furbisher

Harrogate Advertiser
01423 564321
www.harrogatetoday.co.uk
Weekly (Fri). Editor: Jean Macquarrie
Assistant editor: Rita Sobot
Chief sub-editor: Michael Molsher

Harrogate Herald
01423 564321
www.harrogatetoday.co.uk
Weekly (Tue). Editor: Jean Macquarrie
Assistant editor: Rita Sobot
Chief sub-editor: Michael Molsher

Hebden Bridge Times
01422 260200
www.halifaxtoday.co.uk
Weekly (Fri). Editor: Sheila Tordoff

Heckmondwike Herald
01924 468282
www.dewsburytoday.co.uk
Weekly (Fri). Editor: John Wilson

Holderness Advertiser
01482 327111
Weekly (Wed). Editor: Alex Leys
Production editor: Rosie Goodman

Holderness Gazette
01964 612777
holderness-online.com/
Weekly (Thu)
News editor: Andrew Swales
Features editor: David McAughtrie

Huddersfield Daily Examiner
01484 437747
www.ichuddersfield.co.uk
Daily. Editor: Roy Wright
News editor: Neil Atkinson
Features editor: Andrew Flynn

Huddersfield District Chronicle
01484 437747
www.ichuddersfield.co.uk
Weekly (Fri). Editor: Chris Burgess

Huddersfield District News
01484 437747
www.ichuddersfield.co.uk
Weekly free (Tue). Editor: Chris Burgess

Hull Daily Mail
01482 327111
www.hulldailymail.co.uk
Daily. Editor: John Meehan
News editor: Jeremy Deacon
Features editor: Paul Johnson
Chief sub-editor: Sarah Main-Prize

Ilkley Gazette
01943 607022
www.ilkleygazette.co.uk
Weekly (Thu). Editor: Mel Vasey
News editor: Paul Langan

The Journal
01482 327111
Monthly (24th). Editor: Roy Woodcock

Keighley & Craven Target
01274 729511
Weekly (Tue)
Editor: Perry Austin-Clarke
News editor: Martin Heminway
Features editor: David Barnett
Chief sub-editor: Mel Jones

Keighley News
01274 729511
www.keighleynews.co.uk
Weekly (Thu). Editor: Malcolm Hoddy
News editor: Alistair Shand
Chief sub-editor: Ralph Badham

Knaresborough Post
01423 564321
www.knaresboroughtoday.co.uk
Weekly (Fri). Editor: Jean Macquarrie
Assistant editor: Rita Sobot
Chief sub-editor: Michael Molsher

Leeds and Yorkshire Times
01926 431601
Weekly (Fri). Editor: Dennis Draper

Leeds Weekly News
0113 243 2701
Weekly (Thu). Editor: Sheila Holmes

Look Local
0114 283 1100
Weekly (Wed). Editor: Phil Dolby
Head of production: Adrian von Werzbach

Malton and Pickering Mercury
01723 363636
www.maltontoday.co.uk
Weekly (Wed). Editor: Ed Asquith
News editor: Neil Pickford
Chief sub-editor: Steve Banbridge
Production editor: Pete Hodgson

Metro Yorkshire
020 7651 5200
www.metro.co.uk
Daily. Editor: Kenny Campbell
News editor: Mark Dorman
Features editor: Kieran Meeke

Mexborough & District Leader
01709 303030
www.doncastertoday.co.uk
Weekly (Fri). Editor: Linda Wasildge
News editor: Keilly Ball
Features editor: Kevin Rogers

Mirfield Reporter
01924 468282
www.dewsburytoday.co.uk
Weekly (Fri). Editor: John Wilson

Morley Advertiser
0113 252 4020
www.wakefieldexpress.co.uk
Weekly (Wed). Editor: Robert Evans
News editor: Sarah Hall

Morley Observer
01924 468282
www.dewsburytoday.co.uk
Weekly (Fri). Editor: John Wilson

North Yorkshire Advertiser
01325 381313
www.thisisdarlington.co.uk/the_north_east/advertiser/ny
Weekly free (Tue). Editor: Peter Barron
News editor: Nigel Burton
Features editor: Nick Morrison
Chief sub-editor: Ken Farrier

North Yorkshire Herald & Post
01642 245401
www.ncjmediainfo.co.uk
Weekly (Fri). Editor: Sue Giles

North Yorkshire News
01765 601248
Weekly free (Wed). Editor: Steve Barton
News editor: Stephen Pass

Northallerton, Thirsk & Bedale Times
01765 601248
Weekly (Fri). Editor: Steve Barton
News editor: Stephen Pass

Ossett Observer
01924 375111
www.wakefieldexpress.co.uk
Weekly free (Fri). Editor: Mark Bradley
News editor: Mark Lingard

Pateley Bridge & Nidderdale Herald
01423 564321
www.nidderdaletoday.co.uk
Weekly (Fri). Editor: Jean Macquarrie
Assistant editor: Rita Sobot
Chief sub-editor: Michael Molsher

Pocklington Post
01723 363636
www.pocklingtontoday.co.uk
Weekly (Fri). Editor: Ed Asquith
News editor: Neil Pickford
Chief sub-editor: Steve Banbridge
Production editor: Pete Hodgson

Pontefract & Castleford Express
01977 737200
www.wakefieldexpress.co.uk
Weekly (Thu). Editor: David Ward
News editor: Julie Hawksworth

Pontefract & Castleford Extra
01977 737200
www.wakefieldexpress.co.uk
Weekly free (Fri). Editor: David Ward
News editor: Julie Hawksworth

Pudsey Times
01943 466750
Weekly (Thu). Editor: Kate Evans

Ripon Gazette & Boroughbridge Herald
01423 564321
www.ripontoday.co.uk
Weekly (Fri). Editor: Jean Macquarrie
Assistant editor: Rita Sobot
Chief sub-editor: Michael Molsher

Rotherham & South Yorkshire Advertiser
01709 364721
www.rotherhamadvertiser.com
Weekly (Fri). Editor: Doug Melloy
News editor: Ann Charlton

Rotherham Record
01709 364721
www.rotherhamadvertiser.com
Weekly (Wed). Editor: Doug Melloy
News editor: Ann Charlton

Scarborough Evening News
01723 363636
www.scarborougheveningnews.co.uk
Daily. Editor: Ed Asquith
News editor: Neil Pickford
Chief sub-editor: Steve Banbridge
Production editor: Pete Hodgson

Scarborough Trader
01723 352269
www.scarboroughtoday.co.uk
Weekly free (Thu). Editor: Ed Asquith

Selby Chronicle
01757 702198
www.selbytoday.co.uk
Weekly free (Fri). Editor: Chris Page
News editor: Richard Parker

Selby Post
01405 720110
www.selbypost.co.uk
Weekly (Thu). Editor: Peter Butler

Selby Star
01904 653051
www.yorkandcountypress.co.uk/york/ycp/star
Weekly free (Wed). Editor: Lynne Martin

Selby Times
01757 702802
www.selbytoday.co.uk
Weekly (Thu). Editor: Chris Page
News editor: Richard Parker

Sheffield & South Yorkshire Times Today
0115 956 8858
Weekly free (Wed)
Editor: Matthew Palmer

Sheffield Journal
0114 276 7676
www.sheffieldtoday.nct
Weekly free (Thu). Editor: Peter Charlton
News editor: Bob Westerdale
Features editor: John Highfield
Head of content: Paul License

Sheffield Mercury
0114 274 6555
Weekly (Fri). Editor: David Hayes

Sheffield Telegraph
0114 276 7676
www.sheffieldtoday.net
Weekly (Fri). Editor: Alan Powell
News editor: Peter Kay
Head of content: Paul License

Sheffield Weekly Gazette
0114 276 7676
www.sheffieldtoday.net
Weekly (Thu). Editor: Peter Charlton
News editor: Peter Kay
Features editor: John Highfield
Head of content: Paul License

South Yorkshire Times
01709 303050
Weekly (Fri). Editor: Linda Waslidge

Spenborough Guardian
01924 468282
www.dewsburytoday.co.uk
Weekly (Fri). Editor: John Wilson

The Star (Sheffield)
0114 276 7676
www.sheffieldtoday.net
Daily. Editor: Peter Charlton
News editor: Bob Westerdale
Features editor: John Highfield
Head of content: Paul License

Telegraph and Argus (Bradford)
01274 729511
www.thisisbradford.co.uk
Daily. Editor: Perry Austin-Clarke
News editor: Martin Heminway
Features editor: David Barnett
Chief sub-editor: Neal Jones

The Town Crier
01274 729511
Weekly (Thu)
Editor: Perry Austin-Clarke
News editor: Martin Heminway
Features editor: David Barnett
Chief sub-editor: Mel Jones

Todmorden News & Advertiser
01422 260200
www.halifaxtoday.co.uk
Weekly (Fri). Editor: Sheila Tordoff

Wakefield Express
01924 375111
www.wakefieldexpress.co.uk
Weekly free (Fri). Editor: Mark Bradley
News editor: Mark Lingard

Wakefield, Rothwell & Alton Extra
01924 375111
www.wakefieldexpress.co.uk
Weekly free (Thu). Editor: Mark Bradley
News editor: Mark Lingard

Weekly Advertiser
01924 468282
www.dewsburytoday.co.uk
Weekly free (Fri). Editor: John Wilson

West Hull Advertiser
01482 327111
Weekly (Wed). Editor: Alex Leys
Production editor: Rosie Goodman

Wetherby, Boston Spa & Tadcaster News
01423 564321
www.harrogatetoday.co.uk
Weekly (Fri). Editor: Jean Macquarrie
Assistant editor: Rita Sobot
Chief sub-editor: Michael Molsher

Wharfe Valley Times
01943 466750
Weekly (Thu). Editor: Kate Evans

Wharfedale & Airedale Observer
01943 465555
www.wharfedaleobserver.co.uk
Weekly (Thu). Editor: Mel Vasey
News editor: Jim Jack

Whitby Gazette
01947 602836
www.whitbytoday.co.uk
Twice weekly (Tue, Fri)
Editor: Damien Holmes

Yorkshire Evening Post
0113 243 2701
www.leedstoday.net
Daily. Editor: Neil Hodgkinson
News editor: Gillian Howorth
Features editor: Anne Pickles
Production editor: Howard Corry

York Evening Press
01904 653051
www.yorkandcountypress.co.uk/york/ycp/ad
Daily. Editor: Kevin Booth
News editor: Francine Slee
Features editor: Chris Titley
Chief sub-editor: Steve Nelson

York Star
01904 653051
www.yorkandcountypress.co.uk/york/ycp/star
Weekly free (Wed). Editor: Lynne Martin

Yorkshire Express
0115 956 8858
Weekly free (Wed)
Editor: Matthew Palmer

Yorkshire Gazette & Herald
01904 653051
www.thisisryedale.co.uk
Weekly (Wed). Editor: Bob McMillan

Yorkshire Post
0113 243 2701
www.yorkshireposttoday.co.uk
Daily. Editor: Rachael Campey
News editor: Hannah Start
Features editor: Catherine Scott
Head of production: Dick Porter

North-east England

Cleveland, Durham, Northumberland, Tyne & Wear

Berwick Advertiser
01289 306677
www.berwicktoday.co.uk
Weekly (Thu). Editor: Janet Workershaw
News editor: Ian Smith
Features editor: Thomas Baldwin
Chief sub-editor: Keith Hamblin

Berwick Gazette
01289 306677
www.tweedalepress.co.uk
Weeekly free. Editor: Willie Mack

Chester-le-Street Advertiser
01325 381313
www.thisisthenortheast.co.uk
Weekly free (Thu). Editor: Peter Barron
News editor: Nigel Burton
Features editor: Nick Morrison
Chief sub-editor: Ken Farrier

Citylife
0191 211 5093
www.newcastle.gov.uk/citylife
Monthly (last week of month)
Editor: Jane Byrne

Consett & Stanley Advertiser
01325 381313
www.thisisthenortheast.co.uk
Weekly free (Thu). Editor: Peter Barron
News editor: Nigel Burton
Features editor: Nick Morrison
Chief sub-editor: Ken Farrier

Darlington & Stockton Times
01325 381313
www.thisisthenortheast.co.uk
Weekly (Fri). Editor: Peter Barron
News editor: Nigel Burton
Features editor: Nick Morrison
Chief sub-editor: Ken Farrier

Darlington Herald & Post
01325 262000
www.icteesside.co.uk
Weekly (Fri). Editor: Sue Giles

Darlington, Aycliffe & Sedgefield Advertiser
01325 381313
www.thisisthenortheast.co.uk
Weekly free (Wed). Editor: Peter Barron
News editor: Nigel Burton
Features editor: Nick Morrison
Chief sub-editor: Ken Farrier

Durham Advertiser
01325 381313
www.thisisthenortheast.co.uk
Weekly free (Thu). Editor: Peter Barron
News editor: Nigel Burton
Features editor: Nick Morrison
Chief sub-editor: Ken Farrier

East Cleveland Advertiser
01325 381313
www.theclarion.co.uk
Weekly free (Fri). Editor: Peter Barron
News editor: Nigel Burton
Features editor: Nick Morrison
Chief sub-editor: Ken Farrier

East Cleveland Herald & Post
01642 245401
www.icteesside.co.uk
Weekly (Wed). Editor: Sue Giles

Evening Chronicle
0191 232 7500
www.icnewcastle.co.uk
Daily (Mon–Fri)
Editor: Paul Robertson
News editor: Mick Smith
Features editor: Richard Ord
Chief sub-editor: Adrian Hogg

Evening Gazette
01642 245401
www.icteesside.co.uk
Daily. Editor: Steve Dyson
News editor: Jim Horsley
Features editor: Kathryn Armstrong

Gateshead Herald and Post
0191 201 6405
Weekly (Wed). Editor: Catherine Welford
News editor: Roger Woodcock

Hartlepool Mail
01429 239333
www.hartlepoolmail.co.uk
Daily. Editor: Paul Napier
News editor: Brian Nuttley

Hartlepool Star
01429 239333
www.hartlepoolmail.co.uk
Weekly free (Thu). Editor: Paul Napier
News editor: Brian Nuttley

Hexham Courant
01434 602351
www.hexham-courant.co.uk
Weekly (Fri). Editor: Eve Fuller
News editor: Brian Tilley

Houghton Star
0191 501 5800
Weekly free (Thu). Editor: Betty Long

The Journal (Newcastle Upon Tyne)
0191 201 6230
www.icnewcastle.co.uk
Daily. Editor: Brian Aitken
News editor: Stephen Rouse
Features editor: Jane Hall
Chief sub-editor: Roger Brown

Metro North East
0191 477 8200
www.metronortheast.co.uk
Daily. Editor: Deane Hodgson

Middlesbrough Herald & Post
01642 245401
www.icteesside.co.uk
Weekly (Wed). Editor: Sue Giles

Morpeth Herald
01670 510522
www.morpethtoday.co.uk
Weekly (Thu). Editor: Terry Hackett

Newcastle Herald & Post
0191 201 6405
www.icnewcastle.co.uk
Weekly (Wed). Editor: Catherine Welford
News editor: Roger Woodcock

Newcastle Times
01332 205900
Weekly (Thu). Editor: Ruth Dhanda
News editor: Simon Howorth
Features editor: Emily Clarke
Chief sub-editor: Fatt Basra
Production editor: Sonia Watters

News Post Leader
0191 251 8484
www.blyth-wansbecktoday.co.uk
Weekly. Editor: Ross Weeks

North Tyneside Herald & Post
0191 201 6405
www.icnewcastle.co.uk
Weekly (Wed). Editor: Catherine Welford
News editor: Roger Woodcock

Northern Echo
01325 381313
www.thisisthenortheast.co.uk
Daily. Editor: Peter Barron
News editor: Nigel Burton
Features editor: Nick Morrison
Chief sub-editor: Ken Farrier

Northumberland Gazette
01665 602234
www.northumberlandtoday.co.uk
Weekly (Thu). Editor: Andrew Smith

Northumberland Herald and Post
0191 201 6405
Weekly (Wed). Editor: Catherine Welford
News editor: Roger Woodcock

Peterlee Star
0191 501 5800
Weekly free (Thu). Editor: Betty Long

Seaham Star
0191 501 5800
Weekly free (Thu). Editor: Betty Long

South Durham Herald & Post
01642 245401
www.icteesside.co.uk
Weekly (Fri). Editor: Sue Giles

South Shields Gazette
0191 455 4661
www.southtynesidetoday.co.uk
Daily. Editor: John Syzmanski

South Tyne Star
0191 455 4661
Weekly free (Thu)
Editor: John Syzmanski

South Tyneside Herald & Post
0191 201 6405
www.icnewcastle.co.uk
Weekly (Wed). Editor: Catherine Welford
News editor: Roger Woodcock

Stockton & Billingham Herald & Post
01642 245401
www.icteesside.co.uk
Weekly (Wed). Editor: Sue Giles

Sunday Sun (Newcastle)
0191 232 7500
www.icnewcastle.co.uk
Sunday. Editor: Peter Montellier
News editor: Mike Kelly
Chief sub-editor: Lesley Oldfield
Production editor: Colin Patterson

Sunderland Echo
0191 501 7208
www.sunderland-today.co.uk
Daily. Editor: Rob Lawson
News editor: Patrick Lavelle
Features editor: Paul Taylor
Chief sub-editor: Paul Woods
Production editor: Paul Larkin

Sunderland Star
0191 501 5800
Weekly free (Thu). Editor: Betty Long

Teesside Focus
01332 365811
Weekly free (Mon). Editor: Sean Peaty
News editor: Fiona Smith

Teesside Herald & Post
01642 245401
www.icteesside.co.uk
Weekly (Wed). Editor: Sue Giles

Wallsend News Guardian
01670 517171
www.northtynesidetoday.co.uk
Weekly free (Thu). Editor: Terry Hackett

Washington Star
0191 501 5800
Weekly free (Thu). Editor: Betty Long

Whitley Bay News Guardian
0191 251 8566
www.northtynesidetoday.co.uk
Weekly free (Thu). Editor: Ross Weeks

North-west England

Cheshire, Cumbria, Lancashire, Manchester, Merseyside

Accrington Observer
01254 871444
www.accringtonobserver.co.uk
Weekly (Fri). Editor: Mervyn Kay
News editor: Michells McKenna

Anfield and Walton Star
0151 236 2000
Weekly (Thu)
News editor: Kevin Mathews

Ashton-under-Lyne Reporter
0161 303 1910
Weekly (Thu). Editor: Nigel Skinner

Asian News
01706 354321
www.theasiannews.co.uk
Monthly (4th Fri)
Editor: Steve Hammond

Barnoldswick & Earby Times
01282 426161
www.eastlancashireonline.co.uk
Weekly (Fri). Editor: Roy Penton
News editor: Peter Dewhurst
Features editor: Barry Bradshaw
Chief sub-editor: Rebecca Smith
Production editor: Paul Watson

Barrow Advertiser
01229 840150
www.cumbria-online.co.uk
Weekly free (Thu). Editor: Steve Brauner
News editor: Steve Hartley
Features editor: Peter Leach
Chief sub-editor: Sarah Farrell
Production editor: Bill Myers

Bentham Guardian
01524 32525
Weekly (Fri). Editor: Sue Riley
News editor: Louise Bryning
Features editor: Paul Collins
Chief sub-editor: Bryan Carter

Birkenhead News
0151 647 7111
Weekly (Wed). Editor: Sue McCann
News editor: Louise Powney

Blackburn Citizen
01254 678678
www.thisislancashire.co.uk
Weekly (Thu)
Editor-in-chief: Kevin Young
News editor: Andrew Turner
Features editor: John Anson

Blackpool & Fylde Citizen
01253 292005
www.thisislancashire.co.uk
Weekly (Thu). Editor: Greg Morgan
News editor: Steve Dunthorne
Features editor: Nikki Smith

Blackpool Gazette & Herald
01253 400888
www.blackpoolonline.co.uk
Daily. Editor: David Halliwell
News editor: Adrian Derbyshire
Features editor: Paul McKenzie
Chief sub editor: Linda Chatburn

Blackpool Reporter
01253 400800
www.blackpoolonline.co.uk
Daily. Editor: David Halliwell
News editor: Adrian Derbyshire
Chief sub-editor: Linda Chatburn

Bolton Evening News
01204 522345
www.thisisbolton.co.uk
Daily. Editor: Steve Hughes
News editor: John Horn
Features editor: Andrew Mosley
Production editor: John Bird

Bolton Journal
01204 522345
www.thisisbolton.co.uk
Weekly (Thu). Editor: Steve Hughes
News editor: John Horn
Features editor: Andrew Mosley
Production editor: John Bird

Bootle Times
0151 932 1000
Weekly (Thu). Editor: Peter Harvey
News editor: Peter Elliott

Bromborough & Bebington News
0151 647 7111
Weekly (Wed). Editor: Sue McCann
News editor: Louise Powney

Burnley Citizen
01254 678678
www.thisislancashire.co.uk
Weekly (Thu)
Editor-in-chief: Kevin Young
News editor: Andrew Turner
Features editor: John Anson

Burnley Express
01282 426161
www.burnleytoday.co.uk
Weekly (Tue & Fri)
Editor: Chris Daggett
News editor: Margaret Parsons
Features editor: Barry Bradshaw
Chief sub-editor: Rebecca Smith
Production editor: Paul Watson

Bury Journal
0161 764 9421
www.thisisbury.co.uk
Weekly (Wed). Editor: Bill Allen
News editor: Steve Orrell
Chief sub-editor: John Ellavy

Bury Times
0161 764 9421
www.thisisbury.co.uk
Weekly (Tue, Fri). Editor: Bill Allen
News editor: Steve Orrell
Chief sub-editor: John Ellavy

Buy Sell Cheshire
01928 736200
www.cheshirenews.co.uk
Weekly (Thu). No editorial

Carlisle News & Star
01228 612600
www.news-and-star.co.uk
Daily (Mon–Thu). Editor: Keith Sutton
News editor: Sue Crawford
Features editor: Kath Smart
Chief sub-editor: Phil Taylor
Production editor: Richard Eccles

Carnforth Guardian
01524 32525
Weekly (Fri). Editor: Sue Riley
News editor: Louise Bryning
Features editor: Paul Collins
Chief sub-editor: Bryan Carter

Chester & District Standard
01244 304500
Weekly (Thu). Editor: Jonathan White

Chester Chronicle
01244 340151
www.cheshirenews.co.uk
Weekly (Fri). Editor: Barry Elans

Chester Mail
01244 340151
www.cheshirenews.co.uk
Weekly (Fri). Editor: Barry Elans

Chorley Citizen
01257 269313
www.thisislancashire.co.uk/lancashire/chorley
Weekly (Wed)
Editor-in-chief: Kevin Young

Chorley Guardian
01257 264911
www.chorleytoday.co.uk
Weekly (Wed). Editor: Tracy Bruce
News editor: Vanessa Taylor
Chief sub-editor: Mal Morris

Chronicle Weekend (Oldham)
0161 633 2121
www.oldham-chronicle.co.uk
Daily. Editor: Jim Williams
News editor: Mike Attelborough
Chief sub-editor: Jim Austin

Clitheroe Advertiser & Times
01282 426161
www.clitheroe.co.uk
Weekly (Thu). Editor: Vivien Meath
News editor: Duncan Smith

Clitheroe Express
01200 422324
Weekly (Fri). Editor: Vivien Heath
News editor: Margaret Parsons
Features editor: Barry Bradshaw
Chief sub-editor: Rebecca Smith
Production editor: Paul Watson

Colne Times
01282 612561
www.eastlancashireonline.co.uk
Weekly (Fri). Editor: Roy Preston
News editor: Peter Dewhurst
Features editor: Barry Bradshaw
Chief sub-editor: Rebecca Smith
Production editor: Paul Watson

Community News
01625 503322
Weekly (Thu). Editor: Jean Ellis

Congleton Advertiser
01782 602525
Weekly free (Thu). Editor: Sean Dooley
News editor: Robert Cotterill
Features editor: Charlotte Little-Jones

Congleton Chronicle
01260 273737
www.beartown.co.uk
Weekly (Fri). Editor: Jeremy Condliffe

Congleton Guardian
01260 280686
www.thisischeshire.co.uk
Weekly (Fri). Editor: Paul Smith
News editor: Ian Ross

Crewe & Nantwich Guardian
01925 434000
www.thisischeshire.co.uk
Weekly (Thu). Editor: Jan Lever

Crewe Chronicle
01270 256631
www.cheshirenews.co.uk
Weekly (Wed). Editor: Dave Fox
News editor: Jan Roberts
Chief sub-editor: Neil Avery

Crewe Mail
01270 211767
www.cheshirenews.co.uk
Weekly (Fri). Editor: Dave Fox
News editor: Jan Roberts
Chief sub-editor: Neil Avery

Crosby Herald
0151 932 1000
Weekly (Thu). Editor: Peter Harvey
News editor: Peter Elliott

Cumberland and Westmorland Herald
01768 862313
www.cwherald.com
Weekly (Sat). Editor: Colin Maughan
News editor: Liz Stannard
Features editor: Helen Phillips

Cumberland News
01228 612600
www.cumberland-news.co.uk
Weekly (Fri). Editor: Keith Sutton
News editor: Sue Crawford
Features editor: Kath Smart
Chief sub-editor: Phil Taylor
Production editor: Richard Eccles

Deeside Chronicle
01244 340151
www.cheshirenews.co.uk
Weekly (Fri). Editor: Paul Cook

East Cumbrian Gazette
01228 612600
www.cumbria-online.co.uk
Weekly free (Thu). Editor: Keith Sutton
News editor: Sue Crawford
Features editor: Kath Smart
Chief sub-editor: Phil Taylor
Production editor: Richard Eccles

Ellesmere Port Pioneer
0151 355 5181
www.cheshirenews.co.uk
Weekly (Wed). Editor: Phil Robinson

Ellesmere Port Standard
01244 304500
www.ellesmereportstandard.co.uk
Weekly (Thu). Editor: Jonathan White

Evening Leader – Chester
01352 707707
Daily. Editor: Richard Williams
Features editor: Joanne Shone
Chief sub-editor: Joanne Shone
Production editor: Karen Perry

Fleetwood Weekly News and Chronicle
01253 772950
Weekly (Wed). Editor: Gary Miller
News editor: Karen Evans
Chief sub-editor: Linda Chatburn

Flint and Holywell Chronicle
01244 821911
www.cheshirenews.co.uk
Weekly (Fri). Editor: Paul Cook
News editor: Kevin Hughes

Formby Champion
01704 392392
www.championline.net
Weekly (Wed). Editor: Martin Horden

Formby Times
01704 872237
Weekly (Thu). Editor: Hazel Shaw

Freestyle
01704 392392
Monthly (Fri). Editor: Erica Dillon

Frodsham & Helsby Chronicle
01244 340151
www.cheshirenews.co.uk
Weekly (Fri). Editor: Paul Cook

Garstang Courier
01995 602494
Weekly (Fri). Editor: Richard Machin
News editor: Tony Coppin

Garstang Guardian
01524 32525
www.prestontoday.net/
Weekly (Fri). Editor: Sue Riley
News editor: Louise Bryning
Features editor: Paul Collins
Chief sub-editor: Bryan Carter

Heswall News
0151 647 7111
Weekly (Wed). Editor: Sue McCann
News editor: Louise Powney

Heywood Advertiser
01706 360626
www.heywoodadvertiser.co.uk
Weekly (Wed)
Editor: Margaret Cheesebrough

Hoylake & West Kirby News
0151 647 7111
Weekly (Wed). Editor: Sue McCann
News editor: Louise Powney

Huyton & Roby Star
0151 236 2000
Weekly (Thu)
News editor: Kevin Mathews

Keswick Reminder
01768 772140
www.keswickreminder.co.uk
Weekly (Fri). Editor: Jane Grave

Kirkby Extra
07831 090566
Monthly (1st Wed). Editor: Chris O'Shea

Kirkham Express
01253 724236
Weekly (Thu). Editor: Gary Miller
News editor: Chris Dixon

Knowsley Challenge
0151 236 2426
www.knowsleychallenge.co.uk
Monthly (15th). Editor: Alan Birkett

Knutsford Guardian
01925 434000
www.thisischeshire.co.uk
Weekly (Wed). Editor: Jan Lever

Lakeland Echo
01524 833111
www.lakelandtoday.co.uk
Weekly (Fri). Editor: David Waddington

Lancashire Evening Post
01772 838103
www.lep.co.uk
Daily. Editor: Simon Reynolds
News editor: Suzanne Ellsworth

Lancashire Evening Telegraph
01254 298220
www.thisislancashire.co.uk
Daily. Editor-in-chief: Kevin Young
News editor: Andrew Turner
Features editor: John Anson

Lancaster & Morecambe Citizen
01524 382121
www.thisislancashire.co.uk
Weekly (Thu). Editor: Phil Fleming

Lancaster Guardian
01524 32525
www.lancastertoday.co.uk
Weekly (Fri). Editor: Sue Riley
News editor: Louise Bryning
Features editor: Paul Collins
Chief sub-editor: Bryan Carter

Leigh Journal
01942 672241
www.thisislancashire.co.uk
Weekly (Thu). Editor: Mike Hulme

Leigh Reporter
01942 603334
www.leightoday.co.uk
Weekly free (Thu). Editor: Wendy Moss

Leyland Guardian
01257 264911
www.leylandtoday.co.uk
Weekly (Wed). Editor: Tracy Bruce
News editor: Vanessa Taylor
Chief sub-editor: Mal Morris

Liverpool Post & Echo
0151 227 2000
www.icliverpool.co.uk
Daily. Editor: Mark Dickinson
News editor: Alison Gow

Longridge News
01772 783265
www.thisislancashire.co.uk
Weekly (Thu). Editor: Richard Machin

Lytham St Annes & Fylde Express
01253 724236
Weekly (Thu). Editor: Gary Miller
News editor: Chris Dixon

Macclesfield Express
01625 424445
www.macclesfield-express.co.uk
Weekly (Wed). Editor: Mike Quilley
News editor: Pat Hills

Macclesfield Times
01625 424445
www.manchesteronline.co.uk/news papers/macctimes.html
Weekly (Thu). Editor: Mike Quilley
News editor: Pat Hills

Maghull & Aintree Star
0151 236 2000
Weekly (Thu)
News editor: Kevin Mathews

Maghull Champion
01704 392392
www.championline.net
Weekly (Wed). Editor: Martin Horden

Manchester Evening News
0161 832 7200
www.manchesteronline.co.uk
Daily. Editor: Paul Horrocks
News editor: Ian Woods
Chief sub-editor: John Whittaker

Marketplace
0151 906 3000
Weekly (Thu). Editor: Leigh Marles

Metro North West
0161 832 7200
www.metronorthwest.co.uk
Weekly free (Fri). Editor: Richard Butt

Middleton & North Manchester Guardian
0161 643 3615
www.middletonguardian.co.uk
Weekly (Thu). Editor: Gerry Sammon

Middlewich Chronicle
01244 340151
www.cheshirenews.co.uk
Weekly (Fri). Editor: Paul Brown

Middlewich Guardian
01925 434000
www.thisischeshire.co.uk
Weekly (Wed). Editor: Jan Lever

Midweek Advertiser
01695 572501
Weekly (Thu). Editor: Rob Hopkins
News editor: Clifford Birchall

Mold & Buckley Chronicle
01244 340151
www.cheshirenews.co.uk
Weekly (Fri). Editor: Paul Cook

Morecambe Guardian
01524 32525
Weekly (Fri). Editor: Sue Riley
News editor: Louise Bryning
Features editor: Paul Collins
Chief sub-editor: Bryan Carter

Morecambe Visitor
01524 833111
www.morecambetoday.co.uk
Weekly (Wed). Editor: Glen Cooper
News editor: Ingrid Kent

Nantwich Chronicle
01244 340151
www.cheshirenews.co.uk
Weekly (Fri). Editor: Alan Jarvis

Nelson Leader
01282 612561
www.burnleytoday.co.uk
Weekly (Fri). Editor: Roy Preston
News editor: Peter Dewhurst
Features editor: Barry Bradshaw
Chief sub-editor: Rebecca Smith
Production editor: Paul Watson

Neston News
0151 647 7111
Weekly (Wed). Editor: Sue McCann
News editor: Louise Powney

Newton & Golborne Guardian
01925 434000
www.thisischeshire.co.uk
Weekly (Thu). Editor: Jan Lever

Northwest Evening Mail (Barrow)
01229 821835
www.nwemail.co.uk
Daily. Editor: Steve Brauner
News editor: Steve Hartley
Features editor: Peter Leach
Chief sub-editor: Sarah Farrell
Production editor: Bill Myers

Northwich & District Guardian
01925 434000
www.thisischeshire.co.uk
Weekly (Wed). Editor: Jan Lever

Northwich Chronicle
01244 340151
www.cheshirenews.co.uk
Weekly (Fri). Editor: Paul Brown

Northwich Herald & Post
01244 340151
www.cheshirenews.co.uk
Weekly (Fri). Editor: Paul Brown

Northwich Mail
01606 42272
Weekly (Thu). Editor: Paul Brown

Oldham Evening Chronicle
0161 633 2121
www.oldham-chronicle.co.uk
Daily. Editor: Jim Williams
News editor: Mike Attelborough
Chief sub-editor: Jim Austin

Ormskirk Advertiser
01695 572501
Weekly (Thu). Editor: Rob Hopkins
News editor: Clifford Birchall

Ormskirk Champion
01704 392392
www.championline.net
Weekly (Wed). Editor: Malcolm Hindle

Padiham Express
01282 426161
Weekly (Tue & Fri)
Editor: Chris Daggett
News editor: Margaret Parsons

Pendle Express
01282 426161
Weekly (Tue & Fri). Editor: Roy Preston
News editor: Peter Dewhurst
Features editor: Barry Bradshaw
Chief sub-editor: Rebecca Smith
Production editor: Paul Watson

Pendle View
01282 612561
Weekly free (Fri). Editor: Roy Preston
News editor: Peter Dewhurst
Features editor: Barry Bradshaw
Chief sub-editor: Rebecca Smith
Production editor: Paul Watson

Poynton Times
01625 424445
Weekly (Wed). Editor: Mike Quilley
News editor: Pat Hills

Preston & Leyland Reporter
01772 838103
Weekly free (Thu)
Editor: Simon Reynolds
News editor: Suzanne Ellsworth

Preston and Leyland Citizen
01772 824631
www.thisislancashire.co.uk
Weekly (Thu). Editor: Jill Ellis
News editor: Jill Willis

Prestwich Advertiser
0161 789 5015
www.manchesteronline.co.uk/newspapers/prestwich.html
Weekly (Fri). Editor: Vince Hale

Prestwich & Whitefield Guide
0161 764 9421
www.thisisbury.co.uk
Weekly (Fri). Editor: Bill Allen
News editor: Steve Orrell
Chief sub-editor: John Ellavy

Radcliffe Times
0161 764 9421
www.thisisbury.co.uk
Weekly (Thu). Editor: Bill Allen
News editor: Steve Orrell
Chief sub-editor: John Ellavy

Rochdale Express
01706 354321
www.manchesteronline.co.uk/news papers/rochdaleexpress.html
Weekly free (Fri). Editor: Claire Mooney

Rochdale Observer
01706 354321
www.rochdaleobserver.co.uk
Weekly (Wed, Sat)
Editor: Claire Mooney

Rossendale Free Press
01706 213311
www.therossendalefreepress.co.uk
Weekly (Thu). Editor: Adrian Purslow

Runcorn and Widnes Herald & Post
0151 424 5921
Weekly (Fri). Editor: Ian Douglas
News editor: Simon Drury

Runcorn Weekly News
0151 424 5921
www.cheshireonline.icnetwork.co.uk
Weekly (Thu). Editor: Ian Douglas
News editor: Simon Drury

Runcorn World
0151 907 8525
Weekly (Wed). Editor: Carla Flynn
News editor: Barbara Jordan
Chief sub-editor: Graham Bailey

St Helens Star
01925 434000
www.thisisst-helens.co.uk
Weekly (Thu). Editor: Jan Lever

St Helens, Prescot & Knowsley Reporter
01744 22285
Weekly (Wed). Editor: Julie McCormick

Sale & Altrincham Messenger
0161 908 3360
www.thisistrafford.co.uk/trafford/sale__altrincham
Weekly (Thu). Editor: Lyn Hughes

Salford Advertiser
0161 789 5015
www.manchesteronline.co.uk/newspapers/salford.html
Weekly (Fri). Editor: Vince Hale

Skelmersdale Advertiser
01695 572501
Weekly (Thu). Editor: Rob Hopkins
News editor: Clifford Birchall

Skelmersdale Champion
01704 392392
www.championline.net
Weekly (Wed)
Editor: Malcolm Hindle

South Cheshire Advertiser
01782 602525
Weekly free (Thu). Editor: Sean Dooley
News editor: Robert Cotterill
Features editor: Charlotte Little-Jones

South Cheshire Guardian
01925 434000
www.thisischeshire.co.uk
Weekly (Wed). Editor: Jan Lever
News editor: Richard Babbington

South Cheshire Mail
01270 256631
www.cheshirenews.co.uk
Weekly (Wed). Editor: Dave Fox
News editor: Jan Roberts
Chief sub-editor: Neil Avery

South Lakes Citizen
01539 720555
www.thisisthelakedistrict.co.uk
Weekly free (Wed). Editor: Mike Glover
News editor: Mike Addison
Chief sub-editor: Richard Belk

South Liverpool Merseymart
0151 734 4000
Weekly (Thu)
News editor: Kevin Mathews

South Manchester Reporter
0161 446 2213
www.southmanchesterreporter.co.uk
Weekly (Thu)
Editor: Laurence Matheson
News editor: Andy Cranshaw

South Wirral News
0151 355 5181
Weekly free. Editor: Phil Robinson

Southport Champion
01704 392392
www.championline.net
Weekly (Wed). Editor: Martin Horden

Stockport Citizen
0161 491 5700
www.thisislancashire.co.uk
Fortnightly (Thu). Editor: Mike Shields

Stockport Express
0161 480 4491
Weekly (Wed). Editor: Mike Quilley
News editor: Craig Archer
Features editor: Clare Sheridan

Stockport Times
0161 480 4491
www.manchesteronline.co.uk/newspapers/stockporttimeseast.html
Weekly free (Thu). Editor: Mandy Leigh
News editor: Craig Archer
Features editor: Clare Sheridan

Stockport Times East
0161 475 4834
Weekly (Thu). Editor: Mandy Leigh
News editor: Duncan Porter
Features editor: Clare Sheridan

Stockport Times West
0161 475 4834
Weekly (Thu). Editor: Mandy Leigh
News editor: Duncan Porter
Features editor: Clare Sheridan

Stretford & Urmston Messenger
0161 908 3360
www.thisistrafford.co.uk/trafford/stretford__urmston
Weekly (Thu). Editor: Ian Probert

Tameside Advertiser
0161 339 7611
www.tamesideadvertiser.co.uk
Weekly free (Thu). Editor: David Porter

Tameside Reporter
0161 304 7691
Weekly (Thu). Editor: Nigel Skinner

Thornton, Cleveleys & Poulton Citizen
01253 292005
www.thisislancashire.co.uk
Weekly (Thu). Editor: Greg Morgan
News editor: Steve Dunthorne
Features editor: Nikki Smith

Village Visiter
01695 572501
Weekly (Thu). Editor: Rob Hopkins
News editor: Clifford Birchall

Wallasey News
0151 647 7111
Weekly (Wed). Editor: Sue McCann
News editor: Louise Powney

Warrington Guardian
01925 434000
www.thisischeshire.co.uk
Weekly (Thu). Editor: Jan Lever
News editor: Gareth Dunning

Warrington Guardian Midweek
01925 434000
www.thisischeshire.co.uk
Weekly free (Tue). Editor: Jan Lever

Warrington Mercury
01925 434000
www.thisischeshire.co.uk
Weekly free (Fri). Editor: Jan Lever

West Cumberland Times and Star
01900 607600
www.times-and-star.co.uk
Weekly (Fri). Editor: Stephen Johnson
Deputy editor: Ian Brogden

West Cumbrian Gazette
01228 612600
www.cumbria-online.co.uk
Weekly free (Thu). Editor: Keith Sutton
News editor: Sue Crawford
Features editor: Kath Smart
Chief sub-editor: Phil Taylor
Production editor: Richard Eccles

West Derby and Tuebrook Star
0151 236 2000
Weekly (Thu)
News editor: Kevin Mathews

Westmorland Gazette
01539 720555
www.thisisthelakedistrict.co.uk
Weekly (Fri). Editor: Mike Glover
News editor: Mike Addison
Chief sub-editor: Richard Belk

Westmorland Messenger
01539 720555
www.thisisthelakedistrict.co.uk
Weekly (Wed). Editor: Mike Glover
News editor: Mike Addison
Chief sub-editor: Richard Belk

Whitchurch Herald
01948 662332
Weekly (Thu). Editor: Andrew Bowan

Whitehaven News
01946 595100
www.whitehaven-news.co.uk
Weekly (Thu). Editor: Colin Edgar
News editor: Christine Peacock

Widnes Weekly News
0151 424 5921
Weekly (Thu). Editor: Ian Douglas
News editor: Adrian Short

Widnes World
0151 907 8525
Weekly (Wed). Editor: Carla Flynn
News editor: Barbara Jordan
Chief sub-editor: Graham Bailey

Wigan Courier
01257 400026
Monthly (last Fri). Editor: Mark Ashley

Wigan Evening Post
01772 838103
www.wigantoday.net
Daily. Editor: Simon Reynolds
News editor: Gillian Gray

Wigan Observer
01772 838103
www.wigantoday.net
Weekly (Tue). Editor: Gillian Gray

Wigan Reporter
01772 838103
www.wigantoday.net
Weekly (Thu). Editor: Gillian Gray

Wilmslow Citizen
0161 491 5700
Fortnightly (Thu). Editor: Mike Shields

Wilmslow Express
01625 529333
www.thewilmslowexpress.co.uk
Weekly (Wed). Editor: Mike Quilley
News editor: Betty Anderson

Winsford Chronicle
01244 340151
www.cheshirenews.co.uk
Weekly (Fri). Editor: Richard Ault

Winsford Guardian
01925 434000
www.thisischeshire.co.uk
Weekly (Wed). Editor: Jan Lever

Wirral Chronicle
01244 340151
www.cheshirenews.co.uk
Weekly (Fri). Editor: Richard Ault

Wirral Globe
0151 906 3000
www.thisiswirral.co.uk
Weekly (Wed). Editor: Leigh Marles

Wirral Target
0151 906 3000
www.thisiswirral.co.uk
Fortnightly free (Wed)
Editor: Leigh Marles

Wythenshawe World
0161 998 4786
Fortnightly free (Fri)
Editor: John Oatway

Isle of Man

Isle of Man Courier
01624 695695
www.iomonline.co.im
Weekly (Thu). Editor: Lionel Cowin
News editor: Jo Overty
Chief sub-editor: Dave Corbett

Isle of Man Examiner
01624 695695
www.iomonline.co.im
Weekly (Tue). Editor: Lionel Cowin
News editor: Jo Overty
Chief sub-editor: Dave Corbett

The Manx Independent
01624 695695
www.iomonline.co.im
Weekly (Fri). Editor: Lionel Cowin
News editor: Jo Overty
Chief sub-editor: Dave Corbett

Regional newspapers – Wales

Wales on Sunday
Thomson House, Havelock St
Cardiff CF10 1XR
029 2058 3583
www.icwales.co.uk
Sunday. Editor: Tim Gordon
News editor: Laura Kemp

Western Mail
Thomson House, Havelock St
Cardiff CF10 1XR
029 2058 3583
www.icwales.co.uk
Daily. Editor: Allan Edmunds
News editor: Duncan Higgitt

North Wales

Abergele Visitor
01492 584321
www.icnorthwales.co.uk
Weekly (Thu). Editor: Alan Davies

Bangor Chronicle
01248 387400
www.northwaleschronicle.co.uk
Weekly (Thu). Editor: Emlyn Roberts
News editor: Helen Speddy
Features editor: Tony Coates

Bangor Spectator
028 9127 0270
Weekly (Thu). Editor: Paul Flowers

Bangor/Anglesey Mail
01286 671111
www.icnorthwales.co.uk
Weekly (Wed). Editor: Jeff Eames
News editor: Lindi Roberts
Production editor: Mark Jones

Buy Sell (Flintshire Edition)
01978 290400
Weekly (Wed). No editorial

Caernarfon & Denbigh Herald
01286 671111
www.icnorthwales.co.uk
Weekly (Thu). Editor: Jeff Eames
News editor: Lindi Roberts
Production editor: Mark Jones

Daily Post
01492 574455
www.icnorthwales.co.uk
Daily. Editor: Alastair Macrae

Denbighshire Free Press
01745 813535
www.denbighshirefreepress.co.uk
Weekly (Thu). Editor: Alistair Syme

Flintshire Chronicle
01244 821911
www.icnorthwales.co.uk
Weekly (Fri). Editor: Paul Cook
News editor: Kevin Hughes

Flintshire Leader
01244 304500
www.chesterstandard.co.uk
Weekly (Thu). Editor: Jonathan White

Flintshire Leader & Standard
01352 707707
www.flintshirestandard.co.uk
Weekly (Thu). Editor: Richard Williams
Features editor: Joanne Shone
Chief sub-editor: Joanne Shone
Production editor: Karen Perry

Gwynedd Chronicle
01248 387400
www.chroniclenow.co.uk
Weekly (Thu). Editor: Emlyn Roberts
News editor: Helen Speddy
Features editor: Tony Coates

Holyhead and Anglesey Mail
01286 671111
www.icnorthwales.co.uk
Weekly (Wed). Editor: Jeff Eames
News editor: Lindi Roberts
Production editor: Mark Jones

North Wales Chronicle
01248 387400
www.chroniclenow.co.uk
Weekly (Thu). Editor: Emlyn Roberts
News editor: Helen Speddy
Features editor: Tony Coates

North Wales Pioneer
01492 531188
www.northwalespioneer.co.uk
Weekly (Thu). Editor: Steve Rogers

North Wales Weekly News
01492 584321
www.icnorthwales.co.uk
Weekly (Thu). Editor: Alan Davies

Rhyl & Prestatyn Visitor
01745 334144
www.icnorthwales.co.uk
Weekly free (Wed). Editor: Alan Davies
News editor: Dave Jones

Rhyl Prestatyn & Abergele Journal
01745 357500
Weekly (Thu). Editor: Steve Rogers
Deputy editor: Diane Ashton

Vale Advertiser
01492 584321
icnorthwales.icnetwork.co.uk
/news/valeadvertiser
Weekly (Fri). Editor: Alan Davies

Wrexham Evening Leader
01978 355151
www.eveningleader.co.uk
Daily. Editor: Richard Williams

Wrexham Leader
01978 355151
www.bigleader.co.uk
Weekly free (Fri)
Editor: Richard Williams

Wrexham Mail
01978 351515
www.icnorthwales.co.uk
Weekly (Thu). Editor: Paul Cook
News editor: Kevin Hughes

Y Cymro
01970 615000
www.y-cymro.co.uk
Weekly (Mon). Editor: Rob Jones

Ynys Mon Chronicle
01248 387400
www.chroniclenow.co.uk
Weekly (Thu). Editor: Emlyn Roberts
News editor: Helen Speddy
Features editor: Tony Coates

Yr Herald
01286 671111
www.icnorthwales.co.uk
Weekly (Sat). Editor: Jeff Eames
News editor: Lindi Roberts
Production editor: Mark Jones

South Wales

South Wales Echo
Thomson House, Havelock St
Cardiff CF10 1XR
029 2058 3583
www.icwales.co.uk
Daily. Editor: Alistair Milburn
News editor: Nick Machin

South Wales Evening Post
PO Box 14, Adelaide St
Swansea SA1 1QT
01792 510000
www.swep.co.uk
Daily. Editor: Spencer Feeney
News editor: Peter Lee
Features editor: Catherine Ings
Chief sub-editor: Lynne Fernquest

Abergavenny Chronicle
01873 852187
www.abergavenny.co.uk
Weekly (Thu). Editor: Liz Davies

Abergavenny Free Press
01873 857497
www.thisismonmouthshire.co.uk
Weekly (Wed). Editor: Carl Difford
News editor: Lesley Flynn

Barry & District News
01446 704981
www.thisisbarry.co.uk
Weekly (Thu). Editor: Carl Difford
News editor: Sue Vincent-Jones

Barry Gem
01446 774484
www.barry-today.co.uk
Weekly (Thu). Editor: Don John

Brecon & Radnor Express
01874 610111
www.brecon-radnor.co.uk
Weekly (Wed). Editor: Dave Meechan

Bridgend & District Recorder
01446 774484
Weekly (Tue). Editor: Don John

Cambrian News
01970 611611
www.aberystwyth-today.co.uk
Weekly (Wed). Editor: Beverley Davis
News editor: Simon Middlehurst

Campaign Blackwood
01633 777212
www.thisisgwent.co.uk
Weekly (Fri). Editor: Carl Difford
News editor: Andy Sambridge

Campaign Caerphilly
01633 777212
www.thisisgwent.co.uk
Weekly (Fri). Editor: Carl Difford
News editor: Andy Sambridge

Campaign North Gwent
01633 777212
www.thisisgwent.co.uk
Weekly (Fri). Editor: Carl Difford
News editor: Andy Sambridge

Campaign Pontypridd
01633 777212
www.thisisgwent.co.uk
Weekly (Fri). Editor: Carl Difford
News editor: Andy Sambridge

Cardiff Advertiser & Property Times
029 2030 3900
www.icwales.co.uk
Weekly (Fri). Editor: David Hynes

Cardigan & Tivyside Advertiser
01239 614343
www.thisistivyside.net
Weekly (Wed). Editor: Areurin Evans
News editor: Sue Lewis

Carmarthen Herald
01267 227222
www.carmarthenjournal.co.uk
Weekly free (Fri). Editor: David Hardy
News editor: Diane Williams

Carmarthen Journal
01267 227222
www.carmarthenjournal.co.uk
Weekly (Wed). Editor: David Hardy
News editor: Diane Williams

Chepstow Free Press
01291 621882
www.thisismonmouthshire.co.uk
Weekly (Wed). Editor: Carl Difford
News editor: Jacqui Carole

County Echo
01348 874445
www.newport-today.co.uk
Weekly (Fri). Editor: Chris Taylor

County Times & Gazette
01938 553354
www.countytimes.co.uk
Weekly (Thu). Editor: Martin Wright

Courier
01792 510000
Weekly (Tue). Editor: Paul Turner

Cowbridge Gem
01446 774484
www.cowbridge-today.co.uk
Weekly (Thu). Editor: Don John

Cynon Valley Leader
01685 873136
Weekly (Wed). Editor: Gary Marsh

Glamorgan Gazette
01656 304924
Weekly (Thu). Editor: Paul Jones

Gwent Gazette
01495 304589
www.buckinghamtoday.co.uk
Weekly (Tue). Editor: Sarah Harris

Heart of Wales Chronicle
01874 610111
Weekly (Mon). Editor: Dave Meechan

Llanelli Star
01554 745300
www.thisissouthwales.co.uk
Weekly (Wed, Thu)
Editor: Andy Pearson
News editor: Laura Grime

Llantwit Major Gem
01446 774484
www.llantwit-major-today.co.uk
Weekly (Thu). Editor: Don John

Merthyr Express
01685 856500
Weekly (Fri). Editor: Gordon Caldicott

Mid Wales Journal
01597 828060
www.midwalesjournal.co.uk
Weekly (Fri). Editor: Mike Robinson
News editor: Karen Evans

Milford & West Wales Mercury
01646 698971
Weekly (Thu)
News editor: Richard Harris

Monmouth Free Press
01600 713631
www.thisismonmouthshire.co.uk
Weekly (Wed). Editor: Carl Difford
News editor: Sarah Wood

Monmouthshire Beacon
01600 712142
www.monmouth-today.co.uk
Weekly (Thu). Editor: Robert Williams

Narbeth & Whitland Observer
01834 843262
Weekly (Fri). Editor: Neil Dickinson

Neath & Port Talbot Guardian
01639 778885
Weekly (Thu). Editor: Fay Harris

Neath & Port Talbot Tribune
01792 510000
Monthly (2nd Fri). Editor: Paul Turner

Penarth Times
029 2070 7234
www.thisispenarth.co.uk
Weekly (Thu)
News editor: Susan Vincent Jones
Chief reporter: Jessica Hinton

Pontypool Free Press
01495 751133
www.thisismonmouthshire.co.uk
Weekly (Wed). Editor: Carl Difford
News editor: Adrian Osmond

Pontypridd Observer
01443 665161
www.icwales.com
Weekly (Wed). Editor: Dean Powell

Rhondda Leader
01443 665151
Weekly (Thu). Editor: Kiyrin Davis
News editor: Dave Edwards

South Wales Argus
01633 810000
www.thisisgwent.co.uk
Daily. Editor: Gerry Keightley
News editor: Mark Templeton
Chief sub-editor: Caroline Woolard

South Wales Echo
029 2058 3583
www.icwales.co.uk
Daily. Editor: Alistair Milburn
News editor: Nick Machin

South Wales Evening Post
01792 510000
www.swep.co.uk
Daily. Editor: Spencer Feeney
News editor: Peter Lee
Features editor: Catherine Ings
Chief sub-editor: Lynne Fernquest

South Wales Guardian
01269 592781
www.thisisammanford.co.uk
Weekly (Wed). Editor: Steve Robbins
News editor: Emma Evans
Features editor: Richard Sharpe

Swansea Herald
01792 514630
Weekly (Thu). Editor: David Robbins

Tenby Observer
01834 843262
Weekly (Fri). Editor: Neil Dickinson

Tenby Times
01834 843262
Monthly free (first Wed)
Editor: Neil Dickinson

Weekly Argus
01633 810000
www.thisisgwent.co.uk
Weekly (Thu). Editor: Gerry Keightley
News editor: Mark Templeton
Chief sub-editor: Caroline Woolard

Western Telegraph
01437 763133
www.thisispembrokeshire.net
Weekly (Wed). Editor: Fiona Phipps

Regional newspapers – Scotland

Main papers

Aberdeen Press and Journal
Aberdeen Journals
Lang Stracht, Mastrick
Aberdeen AB15 6DF
01224 690222
www.pressandjournal.co.uk
Daily. Editor: Derek Tucker
News editor: Fiona McWair
Features editor: Richard Neville
Chief sub-editor: Jim Urquart

Courier and Advertiser
DC Thomson & Co, 2 Albert Square
Dundee DD1 9QJ
01382 223131
www.thecourier.co.uk
Daily. Editor: Bill Hutcheon
News editor: Arliss Rhind
Features editor: Catriona Macinnes
Production editor: Brian Clarkson

Daily Record
One Central Quay, Glasgow G3 8DA
0141 309 3000
www.dailyrecord.co.uk
Daily. Editor: Bruce Waddell
News editor: Tom Hamilton
Features editor: Melanie Harvey

Edinburgh Evening News
Barclay House, 108 Holyrood Rd
Edinburgh EH8 8AS
0131 620 8620
www.edinburghnews.com
Daily. Editor: Ian Stewart
News editor: Ewan McGrory
Features editor: Jeanne Davidson
Chief sub-editor: Howard Dorman
Production editor: Mark Endie

Glasgow Evening Times
200 Renfield St, Glasgow G2 3QB
0141 302 7000
www.eveningtimes.co.uk
Daily. Editor: Charles McGhee
News editor: Hugh Boag

Glasgow Herald
200 Renfield St, Glasgow G2 3QB
0141 302 7000
www.theherald.co.uk
Daily. Editor: Mark Douglas-Home

Scotland On Sunday
Barclay House, 108 Holyrood Rd
Edinburgh EH8 8AS
0131 620 8620
www.scotlandonsunday.com
Sunday. Editor: John McLellan
News editor: Peter Laing
Chief sub-editor: Martin Allen
Production editor: Chris Dry

The Scotsman
Barclay House, 108 Holyrood Rd
Edinburgh EH8 8AS
0131 620 8620
www.scotsman.com
Daily. Editor: Ian Martin
News editor: Nick Drainey

Sunday Herald
200 Renfield St, Glasgow G2 3QB
0141 302 7800
www.sundayherald.com
Sunday. Editor: Andrew Jaspan
News editor: David Milne
Features editor: Charlene Sweeney

Sunday Mail
One Central Quay, Glasgow G3 8DA
0141 309 3230
www.sundaymail.co.uk
Sunday. Editor: Allan Rennie
News editor: Brendan McGinty
Features editor: Susie Cormack
Chief sub-editor: George Welsh

Sunday Post
DC Thomson & Co, 2 Albert Square
Dundee DD1 9QJ
01382 223131
www.thesundaypost.co.uk
Sunday. Editor: David Pollington
News editor: Tom McKay
Features editor: Brian Wilson
Chief sub-editor: Alastair Bennett

Other Scottish newspapers

Aberdeen & District Independent
01224 618300
www.aberdeen-indy.co.uk
Weekly (Thu). Editor: Derek Piper
News editor: Donna Morrison

Aberdeen Citizen
01224 690222
Weekly (Wed). Editor: Donald Martin

Aberdeen Evening Express
01224 690222
Daily. Editor: Donald Martin
News editor: Richard Prest
Chief sub-editor: James Donaldson

The Advertiser
0131 561 6600
Weekly (Wed). Editor: Roy Scott
News editor: Alex Hogg

Airdrie & Coatbridge Advertiser
01236 748648
www.icScotland.co.uk
Weekly (Wed). Editor: John Murdoch

Alloa & Hillfoots Advertiser
01259 214416
Weekly (Thu). Editor: Kevin McRoberts
News editor: Karen Payton

Annandale Herald
01461 202078
www.thisisthewestcountry.co.uk
Weekly (Thu). Editor: Bryan Armstrong
News editor: Alan Hall

Annandale Observer
01461 202078
www.thisisthewestcountry.co.uk
Weekly (Fri). Editor: Bryan Armstrong
News editor: Alan Hall

Arbroath Herald
01241 872274
Weekly (Fri). Editor: Craig Nisbet
News editor: Brian Forsythe

Ardrossan & Saltcoats Herald
01294 464321
www.threetowners.com/Herald/herald_files.htm
Weekly (Fri). Editor: Alex Clarke
News editor: Craig Nisbet

Argyllshire Advertiser
01631 563058
www.argyllshireadvertiser.co.uk
Weekly (Fri). Editor: Stewart Mackenzie
News editor: Joanne Simms

Arran Banner
01631 568000
www.obantimes.co.uk
Weekly (Sat). Editor: Stewart Mackenzie

Ayr Advertiser
01292 267631
Weekly (Wed). Editor: Alex Clarke
News editor: Caroline Paterson

Ayrshire Extra
01292 611666
Weekly (Thu). Editor: Scott Back

Ayrshire Post
01292 261111
www.icScotland.co.uk
Weekly (Wed). Editor: Cheryl McEvoy
Features editor: Yonnie McInnes

Ayrshire Weekly Press
01294 464321
Weekly (Fri). Editor: Alex Clarke
News editor: Craig Nisbet

Ayrshire World
01294 272233
www.icScotland.co.uk
Weekly free (Wed)
Editor: Alan Woodison
News editor: Lex Brown
Chief sub-editor: Murray Stevenson

Banff Gazette
01224 618300
www.aberdeen-indy.co.uk
Weekly (Fri). Editor: Derek Piper
News editor: Donna Morrison

Banffshire Herald
01542 886262
www.bannfshireherald.com
Weekly (Fri). Editor: Morven Macneil

Barrhead News
0141 887 7055
Weekly (Wed). Editor: Tom McConigley

Bearsden, Milngavie and Glasgow Extra
0141 427 7878
www.icscotland.co.uk
Weekly (Thu). Editor: Allan Hodge
News editor: Colin Macdonald
Chief sub-editor: John Mathews

Bellshill Speaker
01698 264611
Weekly (Thu). Editor: Archie Fleming

Berwick Gazette
01289 306677
www.berwicktoday.co.uk
Weekly (Thu). Editor: David Johnstone
News editor: Sandy Brydon
Features editor: Janice Gillie
Chief sub-editor: Diane Welsh

Berwickshire News
01289 306677
www.berwickshiretoday.co.uk
Weekly (Fri). Editor: David Johnstone
News editor: Sandy Brydon
Features editor: Janice Gillie
Chief sub-editor: Diane Welsh

Blairgowrie Advertiser
01250 872854
www.icScotland.co.uk
Weekly (Tue, Fri). Editor: Alison Lowson

Border Telegraph
01896 758395
www.bordertelegraph.com
Weekly (Tue). Editor: Atholl Innes

Brechin Advertiser
01356 622767
www.brechinadvertiser.com
Weekly (Thu). Editor: Alan Ducat
News editor: Gregor Wilson
Features editor: Jenny Hill

Buchan Observer
01779 472017
www.buchanie.co.uk
Weekly (Tue). Editor: Ken Duncan

The Buteman
01700 502503
www.icScotland.co.uk
Weekly (Fri). Editor: Craig Borland

Caithness Courier
01955 602424
www.caithness-courier.co.uk
Weekly (Wed). Editor: Alan Henry
News editor: Karen Macdonald

Campbell Times Courier
01631 563058
Weekly (Sat). Editor: Stewart Mackenzie
News editor: Joanne Simms

Campbeltown Courier & Argyllshire Advertiser
01586 554646
www.campbeltowncourier.co.uk
Weekly (Fri). Editor: Ronald Watson

Carrick Gazette
01671 402503
Weekly (Thu). Editor: Peter Jeal

Central Fife Times & Advertiser
01383 728201
Weekly (Wed). Editor: Jim Stark
Chief sub-editor: Susan Dryburgh

Clyde Post
01475 720511
Weekly free (Wed)
Editor: David Carndess
News editor: Wilma Riley

Clyde Weekly News
01294 273421
www.icScotland.co.uk
Weekly (Wed). Editor: Alex Clarke

Clydebank Post
0141 952 0565
Weekly (Thu). Editor: James Walsh

Craigmillar Chronicle
0131 661 0791
www.craignet.org.uk/chronicle
Monthly free (1st of month)

Cumbernauld News & Advertiser
01236 725578
www.falkirktoday.co.uk
Weekly free (Fri)
Editor: Archie Fleming
Chief sub-editor: Neil Smith

Cumbernauld News & Kilsyth Chronicle
01236 725578
www.falkirktoday.co.uk
Weekly (Wed). Editor: Archie Fleming
Chief sub-editor: Neil Smith

Cumnock Chronicle
01290 421633
Weekly (Wed). Editor: Douglas Skelton
News editor: Amanda Smith

Deeside Piper
01330 824955
www.deesidepiper.com
Weekly (Fri). Editor: Phil Allan

Donside Piper & Herald
01330 824955
www.donsidepiper.com
Weekly (Fri). Editor: Phil Allan

Dumbarton & Vale Of Leven Reporter
01436 673434
Weekly (Tue). Editor: Julian Calvert
News editor: Steve MacIlroy

Dumfries & Galloway Standard
01387 240342
www.icScotland.co.uk
Weekly (Wed)
Editor: Adrian Barnfather
News editor: Ian Pollock

Dumfries and Galloway Today
01387 240342
www.icScotland.co.uk
Weekly (Wed)
Editor: Adrian Barnfather
News editor: Ian Pollock

Dumfries Courier
01461 202078
www.thisisthewestcountry.co.uk
Weekly free (Fri)
Editor: Bryan Armstrong
News editor: Alan Hall

Dunfermline Press & West of Fife Advertiser
01383 728201
www.snpa.org.uk
Weekly (Thu). Editor: Tom Davidson
News editor: Simon Harris

Dunoon Observer & Argyllshire Standard
01369 703218
www.dunoon observer.co.uk
Weekly (Fri). Editor: Bill Jardin
Features editor: Michelle Robertson
Chief sub-editor: Gerald Deveney
Production editor: Michelle Robertson

East End Independent
0141 647 6156
www.iclanarkshire.icnetwork.co.uk
Weekly free (Wed). Editor: Gordon Bury
Features editor: Gary Thomas

East Fife Mail
01592 261451
www.fifenow.co.uk
Weekly free (Wed)
Editor: Ian Muirhead

East Kilbride News
01355 265000
www.berwickshire-news.co.uk
Weekly (Wed). Editor: Gordon Bury
News editor: Lynda Nichol

East Kilbride World
01698 283200
Weekly free (Fri). Editor: Joseph Kelly
East Lothian Courier
01620 822451
www.eastlothiancourier.com
Weekly (Fri). Editor: Elaine Reid
East Lothian Herald
01289 306677
www.berwickshire-news.co.uk
Weekly (Thu). Editor: David Johnstone
News editor: Sandy Brydon
Features editor: Janice Gillie
Chief sub-editor: Diane Welsh
East Lothian News
0131 561 6600
Weekly (Thu). Editor: Roy Scott
News editor: Alex Hogg
East Lothian Times
0131 561 6600
Weekly free (Fri). Editor: Roy Scott
News editor: Alex Hogg
Ellon Advertiser
01888 563589
Weekly (Fri). Editor: Joyce Summers
Ellon Times & East Gordon Advertiser
01779 472017
Weekly (Thu). Editor: Anne Robertson
Eskdale and Liddesdale Advertiser
01387 380012
Weekly (Thu). Editor: Rachael Norris
Evening Telegraph
01382 223131
Daily. Editor: Alan Proctor
News editor: Elaine Harrison
Features editor: Phillip Smith
The Extra
01292 611666
Weekly (Thu). Editor: Scott Back
Falkirk Herald
01324 624959
www.falkirktoday.co.uk
Weekly (Thu). Editor: Colin Hume
News editor: Duncan McCullum
Features editor: Alan Muir
Falkirk, Grangemouth & Linlithgow Advertiser
01324 638314
Weekly (Wed). Editor: Colin Hume
News editor: Duncan McCullum
Features editor: Alan Muir
Fife & Kinross Extra
01383 728201
Weekly free (Fri). Editor: Andrew Cowie
Fife Free Press
01592 261451
www.fifenow.co.uk
Weekly free (Thu). Editor: Allen Crow
Fife Herald
01592 261451
www.fifenow.co.uk
Weekly free (Fri). Editor: Graham Scott
Fife Leader
01592 261451
www.fifenow.co.uk
Weekly free (Tue). Editor: Jack Snedden
Forfar Dispatch
01307 464899
www.forfardispatch.com
Weekly (Tue). Editor: Alan Ducat
Forres Gazette
01309 672615
www.forres-gazette.co.uk
Weekly (Wed). Editor: Ken Smith
Fraserburgh Herald
01779 472017
Weekly (Fri). Editor: Alex Shand
Galloway Gazette
01671 402503
www.gallowaygazette.com
Weekly (Thu). Editor: Peter Jeal
Galloway News
01556 504141
www.icScotland.co.uk
Weekly (Thu). Editor: Elizabeth Martin
Chief sub-editor: Chris McIntyre
The Gazette
0141 887 7055
Weekly (Wed). Editor: Tom McConigley
Glasgow East News
0141 573 5060
Weekly free (Fri)
Editor: Christine McPherson
News editor: Jim Holland
Glasgow South & Eastwood Extra
0141 427 7878
www.icscotland.co.uk
Weekly (Thu). Editor: Allan Hodge
News editor: Colin Macdonald
Chief sub-editor: John Mathews
Glasgow West Extra
0141 427 7878
www.icscotland.co.uk
Weekly (Thu). Editor: Allan Hodge
News editor: Colin Macdonald
Chief sub-editor: John Mathews
The Glaswegian
0141 309 3132
Weekly free. Editor: Trevor Walls
Glenrothes Gazette
01592 261451
www.fifenow.co.uk
Weekly free (Wed)
Editor: Brian Stormont
Gorgie Dalry Gazette
0131 337 2457
Monthly (Fri)
Editor: Brian Montgomery
Greenock Telegraph
01475 726511
www.greenocktelegraph.co.uk
Weekly (Wed). Editor: David Carndess
News editor: Wilma Riley
Hamilton Advertiser
01698 283200
www.icScotland.co.uk
Weekly (Thu). Editor: Joseph Kelly
Hamilton Extra People
01698 261321
Weekly (Fri). Editor: Martin Clark
Hawick News
01750 21581
www.hawicktoday.co.uk
Weekly (Fri). Editor: Willie Mack
Helensburgh Advertiser
01436 673434
Weekly (Thu). Editor: Julian Calvert
News editor: Steve Macllroy
Herald & Post Edinburgh
0131 620 8620
Weekly free (Thu)
Editor: Stuart Farquhar
News editor: Adrian Mather
Highland News
01463 732222
www.highland-news.co.uk
Weekly (Thu). Editor: Helen Macrae
Huntly Express
01466 793622
Weekly (Fri). Editor: Helen Macrae
Ileach (Islay)
01496 810355
www.ileach.co.uk
Weekly (Sat). Editor: Stuart Todd
Inverness & Nairnshire Herald
01463 732222
Weekly (Thu). Editor: Helen Macrae
Inverness Courier
01463 233059
www.inverness-courier.co.uk
Weekly (Tue, Fri). Editor: Jim Love
Inverurie Advertiser
01888 563589
Weekly (Fri). Editor: Joyce Summers
Inverurie Herald
01467 625150
www.inverurieherald.com
Weekly (Thu). Editor: David Duncan
Irvine and North Ayrshire Extra
01292 611666
Weekly (Thu). Editor: Scott Back
Irvine Herald
01294 222288
www.icScotland.co.uk
Weekly (Wed). Editor: Alan Woodison
News editor: Lex Brown
Chief sub-editor: Murray Stevenson
Irvine Times
01294 273421
Weekly (Wed). Editor: Alex Clarke
John O'Groat Journal
01955 602424
www.johnogroat-journal.co.uk
Weekly (Fri). Editor: Alan Henry
News editor: Karen Macdonald
Kilmarnock & District Extra
01292 611666
Weekly (Thu). Editor: Scott Back
Kilmarnock Standard
01563 525115
www.icScotland.co.uk
Weekly (Wed). Editor: Alan Woodison
News editor: Lex Brown
Kincardineshire Observer
01561 377283
Weekly (Fri). Editor: Charles Wallace
Kirkintilloch Herald
0141 775 0040
www.kirkintillochtoday.co.uk
Weekly (Wed)
Editor: Christie McPherson
Chief sub-editor: Jim Holland
Kirriemuir Herald
01307 464899
www.kirriemuirherald.com
Weekly (Wed). Editor: Alan Ducat
Lanark Gazette
01555 663937
Weekly (Thu). Editor: Aileen McCulloch

Lanarkshire Extra
01698 261321
www.icscotland.co.uk
Weekly (Thu). Editor: Martin Clark

Lanarkshire World
01698 283200
www.icScotland.co.uk
Weekly (Wed). Editor: Joseph Kelly

Largs & Millport Weekly News
01475 689009
Weekly (Wed)
Editor: Andrew Cochrane

Lennox Herald
01389 742299
www.icScotland.co.uk
Weekly (Wed)
Editor: Graham Crawford

Linlithgowshire Journal & Gazette
01506 844592
www.icScotland.co.uk
Weekly (Fri). Editor: Jack Shennan
Features editor: Julie Currie

Lochaber News
01463 732222
www.lochaber-news.co.uk
Weekly (Thu). Editor: Helen Macrae

Lothian Times East
0131 561 6600
Weekly free (Fri). Editor: Roy Scott
News editor: Alex Hogg

Mearns Leader
01569 762139
www.mearnsleader.com
Weekly (Fri). Editor: John McIntosh

Metro Scotland
020 7651 5200
www.metroscot.co.uk
Daily. Editor: Kenny Campbell
News editor: Mark Dorman
Features editor: Kieran Meeke

Mid Lothian Times
0131 561 6600
Weekly free (Fri). Editor: Roy Scott
News editor: Alex Hogg

Midlothian Advertiser
0131 561 6600
Weekly (Wed). Editor: Roy Scott
News editor: Alex Hogg

Milngavie and Bearsden Herald
0141 956 3533
Weekly (Fri). Editor: Alistair Blyth
News editor: Rena O'Neill

Moffat News
01461 202078
www.thisisthewestcountry.co.uk
Weekly (Thu). Editor: Bryan Armstrong
News editor: Alan Hall

Montrose Review
01674 672605
www.montrosereview.net
Weekly (Thu). Editor: Douglas Hill

Motherwell Extra
01698 261321
Weekly (Fri). Editor: Martin Clark

Motherwell Times
01698 264611
Weekly (Thu). Editor: Archie Fleming

Musselburgh News
0131 561 6600
Weekly (Thu). Editor: Roy Scott
News editor: Alex Hogg

North Ayrshire World
01294 272233
www.icScotland.co.uk
Weekly (Wed). Editor: Alan Woodison
News editor: Lex Brown
Chief sub-editor: Murray Stevenson

North Edinburgh News
0131 467 3972
www.northedinburghnews.co.uk
Monthly free (2nd Wed)
Editor: Mary Burnside

North Star
01463 732222
www.highland-news.co.uk
Weekly (Thu). Editor: Helen Macrae

North West Highlands Bratach
01641 521227
www.bratach.co.uk
Monthly (1st Thu)
Editor: Donald McCloud

Northern Scot
01343 548777
www.northern-scot.co.uk
Weekly (Fri). Editor: Pauline Taylor

Northern Times
01408 633993
www.northern-times.co.uk
Weekly (Thu). Editor: Duncan Ross

Oban Times
01631 563058
www.obantimes.co.uk
Weekly (Thu). Editor: Stewart Mackenzie
News editor: Joanne Simms

The Orcadian
01856 879000
www.orcadian.co.uk
Weekly (Thu). Editor: Stuart Laurdy

Paisley & District People
0141 887 7055
Weekly free (Fri)
Editor: Tom McConigley

Paisley & Renfrewshire Extra
0141 427 7878
www.icscotland.co.uk
Weekly (Thu). Editor: Allan Hodge
News editor: Colin Macdonald
Chief sub-editor: John Mathews

Paisley Daily Express
0141 887 7911
www.icScotland.co.uk
Daily. Editor: Jonathan Russell
News editor: Anne Dalrymple
Chief sub-editor: Wendy Slavin

Peebles Times
0131 561 6600
Weekly free (Fri). Editor: Roy Scott
News editor: Alex Hogg

Peeblesshire News
01896 758395
www.peeblesshirenews.com
Weekly (Fri). Editor: Atholl Innes

Perth Shopper
01738 626211
www.northshropshirechronicle.com
Weekly (Fri). Editor: Alison Lowson

Perthshire Advertiser
01738 626211
www.northshropshirechronicle.com
Weekly (Tue/Fri). Editor: Alison Lowson

Ross-shire Herald
01463 732222
Weekly (Thu). Editor: Helen Macrae

Ross-shire Journal
01349 863436
www.rsjournal.co.uk
Weekly (Fri). Editor: Caroline Bham
Features editor: Jacqui McKenzie

Rutherglen Reformer
0141 647 2271
www.icscotland.co.uk
Weekly (Thu). Editor: Louise Reilly

Selkirk Advertiser
01750 21581
www.selkirktoday.co.uk
Weekly (Fri). Editor: Willie Mack

Shetland Life
01595 693622
www.shetlandtoday.co.uk
Monthly (1st Fri)
Editor: Andrew Morrison

Shetland News
01806 577332
www.shetland-news.co.uk
Daily, online. Editor: John Daly

Shetland Times
01595 693622
www.shetlandtoday.co.uk
Weekly. Editor: Viala Wishart

South West News & Star
01228 612300
www.news-and-star.co.uk
Daily. Editor: Keith Sutton
News editor: Sue Crawford
Features editor: Kath Smart
Chief sub-editor: Phil Taylor
Production editor: Richard Eccles

Southern Reporter
01750 21581
www.borderstoday.co.uk
Weekly (Fri). Editor: Willie Mack

St Andrews Citizen
01592 261451
www.fifenow.co.uk
Weekly free (Fri)
Editor: Mike Rankin

Stirling News
01259 214416
Weekly free (Wed)
Editor: Andrew Cowie

Stirling Observer
01786 451110
Twice-weekly free (Wed, Fri)
Editor: Alan Rennie
News editor: Donald Morton

Stirling/Alloa & Hillfoots Shopper
01786 451110
Weekly free (Fri). Editor: Alan Rennie
News editor: Donald Morton

Stornoway Gazette & West Coast Advertiser
01851 702687
www.stornowaygazette.co.uk
Weekly (Thu). Editor: Juliette Conway

Stranraer & Wigtownshire Free Press
01776 702551
www.stranraer.org/freepress
Weekly (Wed). Editor: John Neil

Strathearn Herald
01738 626211
www.northshropshirechronicle.com
Weekly (Fri). Editor: Alison Lowson

Strathkelvin Advertiser
0141 775 0040
Weekly (Sat)
Editor: Christie McPherson
Chief sub-editor: Jim Holland

Strathspey Herald
01479 872102
Weekly (Wed). Editor: Gavin Musgrove

Turriff Advertiser
01888 563589
Weekly (Fri). Editor: Joyce Summers

Wee County News
01259 724724
www.wee-county-news.co.uk
Weekly (Thu). Editor: Joan McCann
Chief sub-editor: Susan Carden
Production editor: Bryan Watson

West Highland Free Press
01471 822464
www.whfp.co.uk
Weekly (Thu). Editor: Ian McCormack

West Lothian Courier
01506 633544
www.icScotland.co.uk
Weekly (Thu). Editor: Mike Barr

West Lothian Herald & Post
0131 620 8620
Weekly free (Thu)
Editor: Stuart Farquhar

Wishaw Press
01698 373111
www.icScotland.co.uk
Weekly (Wed). Editor: John Murdoch

Wishaw World
01698 283200
www.icScotland.co.uk
Weekly (Fri). Editor: Joseph Kelly

Regional newspapers – Northern Ireland

Main papers

Belfast Telegraph
124–144 Royal Avenue
Belfast BT1 1EB
028 9026 4000
www.belfasttelegraph.co.uk
Daily. Editor: Edmund Curran
News editor: Paul Connolly
Features editor: John Caruth

Sunday Life
124–144 Royal Avenue
Belfast BT1 1EB
028 9026 4000
www.sundaylife.co.uk
Sunday. Editor: Martin Lyndsey
News editor: Martin Hill
Features editor: Audrey Watson

Belfast

Belfast News
028 9068 0000
www.icnorthernireland.co.uk
Weekly (Thu). Editor: Julie McClay
News editor: Rick Clarke
Features editor: Jeff Hill

The Daily Mirror (NI)
028 9056 8000
Daily. Editor: Jerry Miller
News editor: Morris Fitzmaurice
Features editor: Jilly Beattie

Derry Journal
028 7127 2200
www.icnorthernireland.co.uk
Weekly (Tue & Fri). Editor: Pat Meart
News editor: Sioban McEleney

Farming Life
028 9068 0000
www.farminglife.com
Weekly (Wed, Sat)
Editor: David McCoy
News editor: Rick Clarke
Features editor: Jeff Hill

Irish News
028 9032 2226
www.irishnews.com
Daily. Editor: Noel Doran
News editor: Steven O'Reilly
Features editor: Joanna Braniff

News Letter
028 9068 0000
www.icnorthernireland.co.uk
Daily. Editor: Austin Hunter
News editor: Rick Clarke
Features editor: Jeff Hill

North Belfast News
028 9058 4444
www.irelandclick.com
Weekly (Fri). Editor: John Ferris
News editor: Andrea McKernon
Features editor: Aine Mcentee

The People (Northern Ireland editions)
028 9056 8000
Sunday. Editor: Greg Harkin
News editor: Jason Johnson

South Belfast News
028 9024 2411
www.irelandclick.com
Weekly (Fri). Editor: Maria McCourt

Sunday Mirror
028 9056 8000
www.sundaymirror.co.uk
Sunday. Editor: Christian McCashin
Assistant editor: Donna Carton

Sunday World (Northern Ireland edition)
00 353 1 406 3500
www.sundayworld.com
Sunday. Editor: Colm McGinty
News editor: John Donlon
Features editor: John Sheils

Other newspapers

Andersonstown News
028 9061 9000
www.irelandclick.com
Weekly (Mon/Thu)
Editor: Robin Livingstone

Antrim Guardian
028 9446 2624
www.ulster-ni.co.uk
Weekly (Wed). Editor: Liam Hesfron

Antrim Times
028 3839 3939
www.mortonnewspapers.com
Weekly (Wed). Editor: David Armstrong
Assistant editor: Dessie Blackadder

Armagh-Down Observer
028 8772 2557
Weekly (Thu). Editor: Desmond Mallon
News editor: Desmond Mallon Junior

Armagh Observer
028 8772 2557
Weekly (Wed). Editor: Desmond Mallon
News editor: Desmond Mallon Junior

Ballycastle Chronicle
028 7034 3344
www.ulsternet-ni.co.uk/chronicle
/pages/ballycastle.htm
Weekly (Wed). Editor: John Fillis

Ballyclare Advertiser
028 9336 3651
www.ulster-ni.co.uk
Weekly (Wed). Editor: Raymond Hughes

Ballymena Chronicle
028 8772 2557
Weekly (Wed). Editor: Desmond Mallon
News editor: Desmond Mallon Junior

Ballymena Guardian
028 2564 1221
www.macunlimited.net
Weekly (Wed). Editor: Maurice O'Neil
Assistant editor: Shaun O'Neil

Ballymena Times
028 2565 3300
www.mortonnewspapers.com
Weekly (Wed). Editor: David Armstrong
Assistant editor: Dessie Blackadder

Ballymoney & Coleraine Chronicle
028 7034 3344
www.ulsternet-ni.co.uk/chronicle
/pages/ballymoney.htm
Weekly (Wed). Editor: John Fillis

Ballymoney Times
028 2766 6216
www.mortonnewspapers.com
Weekly (Wed). Editor: David Armstrong
Assistant editor: Lyle McMullen

Banbridge Chronicle
028 4066 2322
Weekly (Wed). Editor: Bryan Hooks

Banbridge Leader
028 4066 2745
www.bambridgeleader.com
Weekly (Wed). Editor: Damien Wilson
Features editor: Cathy Wilson

Carrick Gazette
028 9336 3651
www.ulster-ni.co.uk
Weekly (Wed). Editor: Raymond Hughes

Carrick Times
028 3839 3939
www.mortonnewspapers.com
Weekly (Thu). Editor: David Armstrong
Assistant editor: Lyle McMullen

Carrickfergus Advertiser
028 8772 2274
www.ulsternet-ni.co.uk/carrick/CPAGES/CMAIN.htm
Weekly (Wed). Editor: Raymond Hughes

City News
028 7127 2200
Weekly (Wed). Editor: Pat McArt
Deputy editor: Siobhan McEleney

Coleraine Times
028 7035 5260
www.mortonnewspapers.com
Weekly (Wed). Editor: David Armstrong
Assistant editor: David Rankin

County Down Spectator
028 9127 0270
Weekly (Thu). Editor: Paul Flowers

Craigavon Echo
028 3839 3939
www.mortonnewspapers.com
Weekly free (Wed)
Editor: David Armstrong
Assistant editor: Hugh Vance

Derry Journal
028 7127 2200
Twice-weekly (Tues/Fri)
Editor: Pat McArt
Deputy editor: Siobhan McEleney

Derry Journal (Sunday)
028 7127 2200
Weekly (Sunday). Editor: Pat McArt
Deputy editor: Siobhan McEleney

Derry News
028 7129 6600
Twice-weekly (Thu/Sat)
Editor: Joanne McCool

Down Democrat
028 4461 4400
www.downdemocrat.com
Weekly (Tue). Editor: Terry McLaughlin

Down Recorder
028 4461 3711
www.thedownrecorder.com
Weekly (Wed). Editor: Paul Symington

Dromore Leader
028 3839 3939
www.mortonnewspapers.com
Weekly (Wed). Editor: David Armstrong

Dungannon News & Tyrone Courier
028 8772 2271
www.ulsternet-ni.co.uk/courier/cpages/CMAIN.htm
Weekly (Wed). Editor: Ian Grear

Dungannon Observer
028 8772 2557
Weekly (Fri). Editor: Desmond Mallon
News editor: Desmond Mallon Jr

East Antrim Advertiser
028 2827 2303
www.mortonnewspapers.com
Monthly. Editor: David Armstrong
Assistant editor: High Vance

East Antrim Guardian
028 2564 1221
www.macunlimited.net
Weekly (Wed). Editor: Maurice O'Neil
Assistant editor: Shaun O'Neil

Fermanagh Herald
028 8224 3444
www.fermanaghherald.com
Weekly (Wed). Editor: Pauline Leary

Fermanagh News
028 8772 2557
Weekly (Fri). Editor: Desmond Mallon
News editor: Desmond Mallon Junior

Foyle News
028 7127 2200
www.icderry.icnetwork.co.uk/ournewspapers/foylenews/
Weekly (Wed). Editor: Pat McArt
Deputy editor: Siobhan McEleney

The Guardian
028 7034 3344
Weekly (Wed). Editor: John Fillis

Impartial Reporter
028 6632 4422
www.impartialreporter.com
Weekly (Thu). Editor: Denzil McDaniel

Lakeland Extra
028 6632 4422
www.impartialreporter.com
Monthly free (3rd Mon)
Editor: Denzil McDaniel

Larne Gazette
028 9336 3651
www.ulster-ni.co.uk
Weekly (Wed). Editor: Raymond Hughes

Larne Times
028 3839 3939
www.mortonnewspapers.com
Weekly (Thu). Editor: David Armstrong
Assistant editor: Hugh Vance

The Leader
028 2827 2303
www.mortonnewspapers.com
Weekly (Wed). Editor: David Armstrong
Assistant editor: Damien Wilson

The Leader (Coleraine)
028 7034 3344
www.ulsternet-ni.co.uk/leader/pages/leader.htm
Weekly (Mon). Editor: John Fillis

Limavady Chronicle
028 7034 3344
www.ulsternet-ni.co.uk/chronicle/pages/limavady.htm
Weekly (Wed). Editor: John Fillis

Lisburn Echo
028 3839 3939
www.mortonnewspapers.com
Weekly free (Wed)
Editor: David Armstrong
Assistant editor: Hugh Vance

Londonderry Sentinel
028 7134 8889
www.mortonnewspapers.com
Weekly (Wed). Editor: David Armstrong
Assistant editor: Chris McNabb

Lurgan & Portadown Examiner
028 8772 2557
Weekly (Wed). Editor: Desmond Mallon
News editor: Desmond Mallon Junior

Lurgan Mail
028 3832 7777
www.mortonnewspapers.com
Weekly (Thu). Editor: David Armstrong
Assistant editor: Richard Elliott

Magherafelt & Limavady Constitution
028 7034 3344
www.ulsternet-ni.co.uk/ncon/pages/limavady.htm
Weekly (Wed). Editor: John Fillis

Mid-Ulster Echo
028 8676 2288
www.mortonnewspapers.com
Weekly free (Wed)
Editor: David Armstrong
Assistant editor: John Fillis

Mid-Ulster Mail
028 8676 2288
www.mortonnewspapers.com
Weekly (Thu). Editor: David Armstrong
Assistant editor: John Fillis

Mid-Ulster Observer
028 8772 2557
Weekly (Wed). Editor: Desmond Mallon
News editor: Desmond Mallon Junior

Mourne Observer & County Down News
028 4372 2666
www.mourneobserver.com
Weekly (Wed). Editor: Terrance Bowman

Newry Advertiser
028 8772 2557
Monthly free. Editor: Desmond Mallon
News editor: Desmond Mallon Junior

Newry Democrat
028 3025 1250
www.newrydemocrat.com
Weekly (Tue). Editor: Caroline McEvoy
News editor: John Grant
Features editor: Patrick Ryan

Newtownabbey Times
028 3839 3939
www.mortonnewspapers.com
Weekly (Thu). Editor: David Armstrong
Assistant editor: Hugh Vance

Newtownards Chronicle
028 9127 0270
Weekly (Thu). Editor: Paul Flowers

Newtownards Spectator
028 9127 0270
Weekly (Thu). Editor: Paul Flowers

Adult

Asian Babes
020 7308 5092
Monthly. Editor: Phil Brock
Escort
020 7292 8000
Monthly. Editor: James Hundleby
Fiesta
01376 534500
13pa. Editor: Ross Gilfillan
For Women
020 7308 5363
Editor: Liz Beresford
Forum
020 7308 5363
13pa. Editor: Elizabeth Coldwell
Knave
01376 534500
13pa. Editor: Ross Gilfillan
Mayfair
020 7292 8000
Monthly. Editor: David Rider
Men Only
020 7292 8000
Monthly. Editor: David Rider
Skin Two
020 7498 5533
4pa. Editor: Tony Mitchell
Viz
020 7907 6000
www.viz.co.uk
Monthly

Children and teenage

2000 AD
01865 200603
www.2000adonline.com
Weekly. Editor: Matt Smith
Action Man
01892 500100
www.paninicomics.co.uk
17pa. Editor: Rob Jones
Angel Magazine
020 7250 0750
Monthly. Editor: Mark Kebble
Animal Action
0870 754 0145
www.rspca.org.uk
Bi-monthly. Editor: Simon Corrall
Animals and You
01382 223131
www.dcthomson.co.uk
Monthly. Editor: Margaret Monaghan
Aquila Children's Magazine
01323 431313
www.aquila.co.uk
Monthly. Editor: Jackie Berry
Art Attack
01892 500100
www.paninicomics.co.uk
17pa. Editor: Karen Brown
Barbie
020 7380 6430
www.egmontmagazines.co.uk
Every 3 weeks. Editor: Beckie Brookes
BBC Toybox
020 8433 3442
www.bbcmagazines.com/toybox/
Monthly. Editor: Coralie Noakes
Beano
01382 223131
www.beanotown.com
Weekly. Editor: Euan Kerr
Bliss
020 7208 3791
www.blissmag.co.uk
Monthly. Editor: Helen Johnston
Breakout
01235 553444
www.couriergroup.com
6pa. Editor: Lawrence Webb
Chill Out
01908 651270
2pa. Editor: Liz Slee
CosmoGirl!
020 7439 5000
www.cosmogirl.co.uk
Monthly. Editor: Celia Duncan
Dandy
01382 223131
www.dandy.com
Weekly. Editor: Morris Heggie
Digimon
01892 500100
www.paninicomics.co.uk
13pa. Editor: Ed Hammond
Disney & Me
020 7380 6430
www.egmontmagazines.co.uk
Fortnightly. Editor: Jeanette Ryall
Elle Girl
020 7150 7000
www.hf-uk.com
Monthly. Editor: Claire Irvin
Fresh Magazine
01392 677321
Monthly. Editor: Joanne Trump
Girl
01392 664141
Monthly. Editor: Joanne Trump
Girl Talk
020 8433 2758
www.bbcmagazines.com/girltalk
Fortnightly. Editor: Samantha McEvoy
Go Girl
020 7380 6430
www.egmontmagazines.co.uk
13pa. Editor: Sarah Delmege
Guiding
020 7592 1821
www.girlguiding.org.uk
Monthly. Editor: Wendy Kewley
Mizz
020 7261 7358
Weekly. Editor: Sharon Christal
Plus/Eagles' Wings
01903 824174
10pa. Editor: Donald Banks
Pokemon World
01202 299900
www.paragon.co.uk
10pa. Editor: Charlotte Martyn
Pony
01428 601020
www.horseandridermagazine.co.uk
Monthly. Editor: Janet Rising
Rugrats
0161 624 0414
13pa. Editor: Patris Gordan
Scouting Magazine
020 8433 7100
www.scoutingmagazine.org
Bi-monthly. Editor: Anna Sorensen
Shout Magazine
01382 223131
www.dcthomson.co.uk
Fortnightly. Editor: Ria Welch
Simpsons Comic
020 7620 0200
www.titanmagazines.com
Monthly. Editor: Paul Terry
Sindy
01892 500100
www.paninicomics.co.uk
13pa. Editor: Jan Comley
Sneak
020 7312 8932
www.sneakmagazine.com
Weekly. Editor: Michelle Garnett
Spectacular Spiderman
01892 500100
www.paninicomics.co.uk
17pa. Editor: Tom O'Malley
Sugar
020 7150 7000
www.sugarmagazine.co.uk
Monthly. Editor: Nick Chalmers
Young Scot
0131 313 2488
www.youngscot.org
Monthly. Editor: Fiona McIntyre

Computing

.net
01225 442244
www.netmag.co.uk
13pa. Editor: Paul Douglas
Computer & Video Games
020 7907 6000
www.dennis.co.uk
Monthly. Editor: Alex Simmons
Computer Arts
01225 442244
www.computerarts.co.uk
13pa. Editor: Gillian Carson
Computer Buyer
020 7907 6000
www.computerbuyer.co.uk/
Monthly. Editor: James Nixon
Computer Music
01225 442244
www.computermusic.co.uk
13pa. Editor: Ronan MacDonald
Computer Shopper
020 7907 6000
www.computershopper.co.uk
Monthly. Editor: Paul Sanders
Computeractive
01858 438881
www.computeractive.co.uk
Fortnightly. Editor: Dylan Armbrust
Computing Which?
0845 301 8000
www.computingwhich.co.uk
Bi-monthly. Editor: Jessica Ross
Cube
01202 299900
www.totalgames.net
13pa. Editor: Miles Guttery

Digital Creative Arts
01202 299900
www.paragon.co.uk
9pa. Editor: Paul Newman

Edge
01225 442244
www.edge-online.co.uk
13pa. Editor: Tony Mott

Games Domain
0121 326 0900
www.gamesdomain.com
Website, updated daily

Games TM
01202 299900
www.totalgames.net
13pa. Editor: Simon Philips

GamesMaster
01225 442244
www.futurenet.com/gamesmaster
13pa. Editor: Robin Alway

iCreate
01202 299900
www.paragon.co.uk
9pa. Editor: Paul Newman

Internet and Broadband Advisor
01225 442244
www.netadvisor.co.uk
13pa. Editor: Graham Barlow

Internet User
01202 299900
www.paragon.co.uk
13pa. Editor: Dominic Brookman

Internet World
020 8232 1600
www.internetworld.co.uk
Monthly. Editor: Janine Milne

It's On The Net
01689 887200
www.iotn.co.uk
4pa. Editor: Annette Connor

Login Magazine
01702 582895
Monthly. Editor: Rick Haynes

MacFormat
01225 442244
www.macformat.co.uk
13pa. Editor: Rachel Spooner

MacUser
020 7907 6000
www.macuser.co.uk
Fortnightly. Editor: Nick Rawlinson

Macworld
020 7831 9252
www.macworld.co.uk
13pa. Editor: David Fanning

Max
01225 442244
www.futurenet.com/macmagazine
13pa. Editor: Adam Waring

Micro Mart
0121 233 8712
www.micromart.co.uk
Weekly. Editor: Simon Brew

Official Playstation 2 Magazine
01225 442244
www.playstation.co.uk
13pa. Editor: Richard Keith

Official Xbox Magazine
020 7317 2471
www.officialxboxmagazine.co.uk
Monthly

P2
01202 299900
www.totalgames.net
13pa. Editor: Roy Kimber

PC Advisor
020 7291 5939
www.pcadvisor.co.uk
Monthly. Editor: Guy Dixon

PC Answers
01225 442244
www.pcanswers.co.uk
13pa. Editor: Simon Pickstock

PC Basics
01202 299900
www.paragon.co.uk
13pa. Editor: Geoff Spick

PC Essentials
01202 299900
www.paragon.co.uk
9pa. Editor: Geoff Spick

PC Format
01225 442244
www.pcformat.co.uk
13pa. Editor: Adam Oxford

PC Gamer
01225 442244
www.pcgamer.co.uk
13pa. Editor: Mark Donald

PC Home
01202 299900
www.paragon.co.uk
13pa. Editor: Paul Lester

PC Plus
01225 442244
www.pcplus.co.uk
13pa. Editor: Ian Robson

PC Pro
020 7907 6000
www.pcpro.co.uk
Monthly. Editor: Tim Danton

PC Utilities
01625 855086
www.pc-utilities.co.uk
13pa. Editor: Gavin Burrell

PC Zone
020 7907 6000
www.pczone.co.uk
Monthly. Editor: David Woods

PDA Essentials
01202 299900
www.paragon.co.uk
9pa. Editor: David Harfield

Personal Computer World
01858 438881
www.pcw.co.uk
Monthly. Editor: Rob Jones

Play
01202 299900
www.totalgames.net
13pa. Editor: Nick Jones

Pokemon World
01202 299900
www.paragon.co.uk
10pa. Editor: Charlotte Martyn

Powerstation
01202 299900
www.totalgames.net
13pa. Editor: Mike O'Sullivan

Practical Web Projects
01202 299900
www.paragon.co.uk
10pa. Editor: James Thornton

PSM2
01225 442244
www.futurenet.com/psm2
13pa. Editor: Daniel Griffith

Solutions
01202 299900
www.totalgames.net
13pa. Editor: Phil King

Web Designer
01202 299900
www.paragon.co.uk
13pa. Editor: Thomas Watson

Web Pages Made Easy
01202 299900
www.paragon.co.uk
9pa. Editor: Rob Clymo

WebUser
020 7261 7376
www.web-user.co.uk/
Fortnightly. Editor: Richard Clark

What Laptop & Handheld PC
020 8334 1600
www.whatlaptop.co.uk
Monthly. Editor: Michael Browne

Windows XP Made Easy
01202 299900
www.paragon.co.uk
13pa. Editor: Stuart Tarrant

Windows XP: The Official Magazine
01225 442244
www.windowsxpmagazine.co.uk
13pa. Editor: David Bradley

XBM
01202 299900
www.totalgames.net
13pa. Editor: Ian Dean

XP First Aid
01202 299900
www.paragon.co.uk
4pa. Editor: Geoff Spick

Current affairs

AFF Families Journal
01980 615517
www.aff.org.uk
4pa. Editor: Sue Bonney

The American
01297 561147
www.the-american.co.uk
Monthly. Editor: Catherine Russell

Big Issue
020 7526 3200
www.bigissue.com
Weekly. Editor: Matt Ford

Big Issue in Scotland
0141 418 7000
www.bigissuescotland.com
Weekly. Editor: Claire Black

Big Issue in the North
0161 834 6300
www.bigissueinthenorth.com
Weekly. Editor: Ato Erzan

Challenge Newsline
0800 195 7969
Monthly. Editor: Debbie Bunn

Connect Magazine (Greenpeace)
020 7865 8100
www.greenpeace.org.uk
4pa. Editor: Stokeley Webster

EarthMatters (Friends of the Earth)
020 7490 1555
www.foe.co.uk
3pa. Editor: Adam Bradbury/ Nicola Baird

Ecologist
020 7351 3578
www.theecologist.org
10pa. Editor: Zac Goldsmith

Economist
020 7830 7000
www.economist.com
Weekly. Editor: Bill Emmott

Glasgow Magazine
0141 287 0901
Bi-monthly. Editor: Jim Clark

Granta
020 7704 9776
www.granta.com
4pa. Editor: Ian Jack

Green Futures
020 7324 3660
www.greenfutures.org.uk
Bi-monthly. Editor: Martin Wright

The House Magazine
020 7878 1520
www.epolitix.com
Weekly. Editor: Sir Patrick Cormack

Impact International
020 7263 1417
Monthly. Editor: Ahmad Irfan

Index on Censorship
020 7278 2313
www.indexoncensorship.org
4pa. Editor: Judith Bidal-Hall

Liberty
020 7403 3888
www.liberty-human-rights.org.uk
4pa. Editor: Lincoln E Steed

Middle East Expatriate
020 8943 3630
www.middleeastexpatonline.com
10pa. Editor: Babu Kalyanpur

New African
020 7713 7711
www.africasia.com
Monthly. Editor: Baffour Ankomah

New Internationalist
01865 728181
www.newint.org
Monthly. Editor: Adam Ma'anit

New Statesman
020 7730 3444
www.newstatesman.com
Weekly. Editor: Peter Wilby

News Africa
020 7713 8135
www.newsafrica.net
Monthly. Editor: Moffat Ekoriko

Newsweek
020 7851 9799
www.newsweek.com
Weekly. Editor: Fareed Zakaria

Nexus
01342 322854
www.nexus.com
Bi-monthly. Editor: Duncan Roads

Outrage – magazine of Animal Aid
01732 364546
www.animalaid.co.uk
4pa. Editor: Mark Gold

Party Politics
020 7324 8500
www.sagepub.co.uk
6pa. Editor: Lucy Robinson

Private Eye
020 7437 4017
www.private-eye.co.uk
Fortnightly. Editor: Ian Hislop

Prospect
020 7255 1281
www.prospect-magazine.co.uk
Monthly. Editor: David Goodhart

Red Pepper
020 7281 7024
www.redpepper.org.uk
Monthly. Editor: Hilary Wainwright

Report
020 7930 6441
www.askatl.org.uk
10pa. Editor: Heather Pinnell

SchNews
01273 685913
www.schnewsatbrighton.co.uk
Weekly. Editor: Jo Makepeace

Socialism Today
020 8988 8782
www.socialistparty.org.uk
Monthly. Editor: Lynn Walsh

The Socialist
020 8988 8782
www.socialistparty.org.uk
Weekly. Editor: Ken Smith

Socialist Review
020 7538 3308
www.socialistreview.org.uk
11pa. Editor: Peter Morgan

Socialist Worker
020 7538 0828
www.socialistworker.co.uk
Weekly. Editor: Chris Harman

Spectator
020 7405 1706
www.spectator.co.uk
Weekly. Editor: Boris Johnson

The Sticks Magazine
01462 486810
www.the-sticks.com
Monthly. Editor: John Boston

Time
020 7499 4080
www.time.com
Weekly. Editor: Eric Pooley

Tribune
020 7433 6410
www.tribuneweb.co.uk
Weekly. Editor: Mark Seddon

The Week
020 7907 6000
www.theweek.co.uk
Weekly. Editor: Jeremy O'Grady

The World Today
020 7957 5712
www.theworldtoday.org
Monthly. Editor: Graham Walker

WWF News
01483 426444
www.wwf.org.uk
Quarterly. Editor: Guy Jowett

Arts & entertainment

All About Soap
020 7150 7000
www.allaboutsoap.co.uk
Fortnightly. Editor: Lorna Cowan

Amateur Photographer
020 7261 5100
www.amateurphotographer.com
Weekly. Editor: Garry Coward-Williams

AN Magazine
0191 241 8000
www.a-n.co.uk
Monthly. Editor: Gillian Nicol

The Art Book
01323 811759
4pa. Editor: Sue Ward

The Art Newspaper
020 7735 3331
www.theartnewspaper.com
Monthly. Editor: Cristina Ruiz

Art Quarterly
020 7225 4818
www.artfund.org
4pa. Editor: Caroline Bugler

Art Review
020 7246 3350
www.art-review.com
Monthly. Editor: Rebecca Wilson

The Artist
01580 763315
www.theartistmagazine.co.uk
Monthly. Editor: Sally Bulgin

Artists & Illustrators
020 7700 8500
www.aimag.co.uk
Monthly. Editor: James Hobbs

Arts East
01284 701190
www.acornmagazines.co.uk
Monthly. Editor: Unity Norwak

BBC Music Magazine
020 8433 3283
www.bbcmagazines.com/music
Monthly. Editor: Harriet Smith

The Big Cheese
020 7607 0303
www.bigcheesemagazine.com
Monthly. Editor: Eugene Butcher

Billboard
020 7420 6000
www.billboard.com
Weekly. Editor: Emmanuel Legrand

Blues & Soul
020 7402 6869
www.bluesandsoul.com
Fortnightly. Editor: Bob Killbourn

The Brighton Source
01273 561617
Monthly. Editor: Marcus O'Dair

Buzz Magazine
029 2025 6883
Monthly. Editor: Emma Clark

Camcorder User
020 7331 1000
www.camuser.co.uk
13pa. Editor: Robert Hull

Cineworld
01225 737300
Bi-monthly. Editor: Sally Thomson

Classic FM – The Magazine
020 8267 5000
www.haymarketpublishing.co.uk
Monthly. Editor: Emma Baker

Classic Rock
020 7317 2654
www.classicrockmagazine.com
13pa. Editor: Mick Wall

Classical Music
020 7333 1742
www.rhinegold.co.uk
Fortnightly. Editor: Keith Clarke

Country Music People
020 8854 7217
www.countrymusicpeople.com
Monthly. Editor: Craig Baguley

Country Music Round-up
01472 821707
www.cmru.co.uk
Monthly. Editor: John Emptage

The Crack
0191 2303038
www.thecrackmagazine.com
Monthly. Editor: Robert Meddes

Cult Times
020 8875 1520
www.visimag.com
Monthly. Editor: Paul Spragg

Dance Europe
020 8985 7767
www.danceeurope.net
Monthly. Editor: Emma Manning

Dance Gazette
020 7326 8000
www.rad.org.uk
3pa. Editor: Olivia Swift

Desi
020 8571 7700
www.snooplife.com
Monthly. Editor: Raj Kaushal

Digital Camera Buyer
01202 299900
www.paragon.co.uk
13pa. Editor: James Broomfield

Digital Camera Magazine
01225 442244
www.dcmag.co.uk
13pa. Editor: Adam Evans

Digital Music Maker
01202 299900
www.paragon.co.uk
Monthly. Editor: Karl Foster

Digital Photo
01733 282748
www.greatmagazines.co.uk
Monthly. Editor: Jon Adams

Digital Photographer
01202 299900
www.paragon.co.uk
13pa. Editor: Michael Roscoe

Digital Photography Made Easy
01202 299900
Monthly. Editor: Jo Cole

Digital Video Made Easy
01202 299900
www.paragon.co.uk
13pa. Editor: Mark Hattersley

DJ
020 7331 1000
www.djmag.com
Fortnightly. Editor: David Eserin

DMC Update
020 7262 6777
www.dmcworld.com/update
Weekly. Editor: Nick Darby

DVD Monthly
01392 434477
www.predatorpublishing.co.uk
Monthly. Editor: Tim Isaac

DVD Review
01202 299900
www.dvdreview.net
13pa. Editor: Paul Morgan

DVD World
020 7331 1000
www.highburywv.com
13pa. Editor: Richard Marshall

Early Music Today
020 7333 1744
www.rhinegold.co.uk
Bi-monthly. Editor: Lucien Jenkins

Edge
01225 442244
www.edge-online.co.uk
13pa. Editor: Tony Mott

Empire
020 7182 8000
www.empireonline.co.uk
Monthly. Editor: Colin Kennedy

Entertainer
01302 819555
www.doncastertoday.co.uk
Weekly. Editor: Martin Edmonds

EP Magazine
0118 958 1878
10pa. Editor: Jon Ewing

Essential Hi-fi and Home Cinema
020 7331 1000
www.highburywv.com
13pa. Editor: Adrian Justins

Film Review
020 8875 1520
www.visimag.com
Monthly. Editor: David Richardson

First on Video
020 7608 6789
www.firstonvideo.co.uk
Monthly. Editor: Sharon Lacey

The Fly
020 7691 4555
Monthly. Editor: Will Kinsman

Freetime
01252 621513
www.freetimemag.co.uk
4pa. Editor: Vic Robbie

fRoots
020 8340 9651
www.frootsmag.com
Monthly. Editor: Ian Anderson

Future Music
01225 442244
www.futuremusic.co.uk
13pa. Editor: Andy Jones

Gramophone
020 8267 5000
www.gramophone.co.uk
Monthly. Editor: James Jolly

Granta
020 7704 9776
www.granta.com
4pa. Editor: Ian Jack

Guitar Buyer
01954 252983
Monthly. Editor: Mick Taylor

Guitar Techniques
01225 442244
www.futurenet.com/guitartechniques
13pa. Editor: Cliff Douse

Guitarist
01225 442244
www.guitarist.co.uk
13pa. Editor: Michael Leonard

Hi-Fi Choice
020 7317 2495
www.hifichoice.co.uk
13pa. Editor: Tim Bowern

Hi-Fi News
020 8774 0850
www.hifinews.com
Monthly. Editor: Steve Harris

Hi-Fi World
01275 371386
www.hi-fiworld.co.uk
Monthly. Editor: David Price

Hip Hop Connection
01223 210536
www.hiphop.co.uk
Monthly. Editor: Andy Cowan

Hollywood Reporter
020 7420 6000
www.hollywoodreporter.com
Weekly. Editor: Stuart Kemp

Home Cinema Choice
020 7331 1000
www.homecinemachoice.com
Monthly. Editor: Steve May

Hotdog
01202 299900
www.paragon.co.uk
13pa. Editor: Andy McDermott

Impact
01484 435011
www.martialartsltd.co.uk
Monthly. Editor: John Mosby

Inside Soap
020 7150 7000
www.insidesoap.co.uk
Weekly. Editor: Steven Murphy

It's Hot
020 8433 1432
www.bbcmagazines.com/hot
Monthly. Editor: Peter Hart

Jazz at Ronnie Scott's
020 7485 9803
www.ronniescotts.co.uk
Bi-monthly. Editor: God Bolt

Jazz Guide
01908 312392
Monthly. Editor: Bernie Tyrrell

Jazz UK
029 2066 5161
www.jazzservices.org.uk
Bi-monthly. Editor: John Fordham

Kerrang!
020 7436 1515
www.kerrang.com
Weekly. Editor: Ashley Bird

Knowledge
020 8533 9300
www.knowledgemag.co.uk
10pa. Editor: Colin Steven

Leisure Gazette
01782 860800
Monthly. Editor: Terry Winter
Leisure Painter
01580 763315
www.leisurepainter.co.uk
Monthly. Editor: Ingrid Lyon
The List
0131 550 3050
www.list.co.uk
Fortnightly; extra festival issues in August. Editor: Nick Barley
London Review of Books
020 7209 1101
www.lrb.co.uk
Fortnightly. Editor: Mary-Kay Wilmers
London Theatre Guide
020 7557 6700
www.officiallondontheatre.co.uk
Fortnightly. Editor: Richard Embray
M8
0141 840 5980
www.m8magazine.com
Monthly. Editor: Kevin McFarlane
Magpie
0870 071 1611
www.magpiedirect.com
Bi-monthly. Editor: Mark Rye
Metal Hammer
020 7317 2691
www.metalhammer.co.uk
13pa. Editor: Alex Burrows
Mixmag
020 7182 8000
www.mixmag.net
Monthly. Editor: Viv Craske
Mojo
020 7312 8716
www.mojo4music.com
Monthly. Editor: Phil Alexander
Movie Mag International
020 8574 2222
www.movie-mag.net
Monthly. Editor: Bharathi Pradhan
Musician
020 7840 5531
www.musiciansunion.org.uk
Quarterly. Editor: Keith Ames
National Gallery Season Guide
020 7747 2836
www.nationalgallery.org.uk
3pa. Editor: Andrea Easey
Night & Day – The Essential Visitor Guide
0121 212 4141
www.icbirmingham.co.uk
Yearly. Editor: Stacey Barnfield
NME
020 7261 5564
www.nme.com/
Weekly. Editor: Conor McNicholas
NW
020 7792 2626
www.hhc.co.uk
Monthly. Editor: Cathy Levy
Official Elvis Presley Fan Club Magazine
0116 253 7271
www.elvisweb.co.uk
Bi-monthly. Editor: Todd Slaughter
Opera
020 8563 8893
www.opera.co.uk
Monthly. Editor: John Allison
Opera Now
020 7333 1740
www.rhinegold.co.uk
6pa. Editor: Ashutosh Khandekar
Piano
020 7333 1724
www.rhinegold.co.uk
Bi-monthly. Editor: Jeremy Siepmann
Practical Photography
01733 282736
www.greatmagazines.co.uk
Monthly. Editor: Andrew James
Q
020 7312 8182
www.q4music.com
Monthly. Editor: Paul Rees
RA Magazine
020 7300 5820
www.ramagazine.org.uk
4pa. Editor: Sarah Greenberg
Radio Times
020 8433 2235
www.radiotimes.com
Weekly. Editor: Gill Hudson
Record Buyer
01522 511265
Monthly. Editor: Paul Rigby
Rock Sound
020 7278 5559
www.rock-sound.net
Monthly. Editor: Darren Taylor
Rolling Stone
001 212 484 1616
www.rollingstone.com
26pa. Editor: Jann S Wenner
Satellite and Digital Choice
020 7331 1000
www.bettersat.com
8pa. Editor: Grant Rennell
Satellite TV Monthly
020 7226 2222
www.satellitetvtoday.com
Monthly. Editor: Paul Hirons
Screen International
020 7505 8080
www.screendaily.com
Weekly. Editor: Tim McLoughlin
SFX
01225 442244
www.sfx.co.uk
13pa. Editor: Dave Golder
Shivers
020 8875 1520
www.visimag.com
Monthly. Editor: David Miller
Sight & Sound
020 7255 1444
www.bfi.org.uk/sightandsound
Monthly. Editor: Nick James
Sky Customer Magazine
020 7565 3000
www.jbcp.co.uk
Monthly. Editor: Liz Murphy
Smash Hits
020 7436 1515
www.smashhits.com
Fortnightly. Editor: Lisa Smosarski
Soaplife
020 7261 7568
www.soaplife.co.uk/
Fortnightly. Editor: Hellen Gardner
Songlines
01753 865342
www.songlines.co.uk
Bi-monthly. Editor: Simon Broughton
Sound on Sound
01954 789888
www.soundonsound.com
Monthly. Editor: Ian Gilby
The Stage
020 7403 1818
www.thestage.co.uk
Weekly. Editor: Brian Attwood
Starburst
020 8875 1520
www.visimag.com
Monthly. Editor: Stephen Payne
Stardust International
020 8795 5318
www.stardustindia.com
Monthly. Editor: Ashwin Warde
The Strad
020 7203 6731
www.thestrad.com
Monthly. Editor: Naomi Sadler
Straight No Chaser
020 8533 9999
www.straightnochaser.co.uk
Bi-monthly. Editor: Paul Bradshaw
Theatregoer
020 7684 7111
www.theatregoer.net
Monthly. Editor: Deirdre Vine
This is London Magazine
020 7434 1281
www.thisislondon.com
Weekly. Editor: Julie Jones
Time Out
020 7813 3000
www.timeout.com
Weekly. Editor: Laura Lee Davies
Time Out Student Guide
020 7813 3000
www.timeout.com
Annually. Editor: Sharon Lougher
Times Literary Supplement
020 7782 3000
www.the-tls.co.uk
Weekly. Editor: Peter Stothard
Top of the Pops Magazine
020 8433 3701
www.bbcmagazines.com/totp
Monthly. Editor: Corinna Shaffer
Total DVD
020 7331 1000
www.totaldvd.net
13pa. Editor: Chris Jenkins
Total Film
020 7317 2449
www.totalfilm.co.uk
13pa. Editor: Matt Mueller
Total Guitar
01225 442244
www.totalguitar.co.uk
13pa. Editor: Scott Rowley
TV & Satellite Week
020 7261 7534
www.tvandsatelliteweek.com/
Weekly. Editor: Jonathan Bowman

TV Choice
020 7241 8000
www.bauer.co.uk
Weekly. Editor: Lori Miles
TV Hits!
020 7150 7000
www.tvhits.co.uk
Monthly. Editor: Helen Lamont
TV Quick
020 7241 8000
www.bauer.co.uk
Weekly. Editor: Lori Miles
TV Times
020 7261 7740
Weekly. Editor: Mike Hollingsworth
TV Zone
020 8875 1520
www.visimag.com
Monthly. Editor: Jan Vincent-Rudzki
Twenty 4-seven
01752 294130
www.twenty4-seven.co.uk
Monthly. Editor: Lucy Griffiths
Ultimate DVD
020 8875 1520
www.visimag.com
Monthly. Editor: David Richardson
Uncut
020 7261 6992
www.uncut.net
Monthly. Editor: Allan Jones
Unlimited
0117 927 9009
www.originpublishing.co.uk
Monthly. Editor: Pat Reed
Unreel
01225 737300
www.unreelmovies.co.uk
Bi-monthly. Editor: Sally Thomson
V&A Magazine
020 7942 2505
4pa. Editor: Charlotte Mullins
Variety
020 7611 4580
www.variety.com
Daily and weekly. Editor: Steven Gaydos
What Camcorder
020 7331 1000
www.whatcamcorder.net
Monthly. Editor: Jake Williams
What Camera?
020 7261 5266
4pa. Editor: Joel Lacey
What Digital Camcorder
020 7331 1000
www.whatcamcorder.net
13pa. Editor: Ali Upham
What Digital Camera
020 7261 7284
www.whatdigitalcamera.com/
Monthly. Editor: Nigel Atherton
What Guitar?
01225 442244
www.whatguitar.co.uk
13pa. Editor: Stephen Lawson
What Hi-Fi? Sound and Vision
020 8267 5000
www.whathifi.com
Monthly, plus awards issue
Editor: Clare Newsome
What Home Cinema
020 7331 1000
www.whathomecinemamag.com
Monthly. Editor: Rob Lane
What Satellite and Digital TV
020 7331 1000
www.wotsat.com
Monthly. Editor: Alex Lane
What Satellite TV
020 7331 1000
www.wotsat.com
Monthly. Editor: Grant Rennell
What Video and Widescreen TV
020 7331 1000
www.whatvideomag.com
Monthly. Editor: Danny Phillips
What's on in London
020 7278 4393
www.whatsoninlondon.co.uk
Weekly. Editor: Michael Darvell
What's on TV
020 7261 7535
Weekly. Editor: Colin Tough
Where London
020 7242 5222
Monthly. Editor: Mary-Anne Evans
The Wire
020 7422 5010
www.thewire.co.uk
Monthly. Editor: Chris Bohn
Word
020 7520 8625
www.wordmagazine.co.uk
Monthly. Editor: Mark Ellen
Writers' News
0113 200 2929
www.writersnews.co.uk
Monthly. Editor: Derek Hudson
The X Files
020 7620 0200
Monthly. Editor: Martin Eden
X-pose
020 8875 1520
www.visimag.com
Bi-monthly. Editor: Anthony Brown
The Zone
mail@zone-sf.com
www.zone-sf.com
Website. Editor: Tony Lee

Food & drink

BBC Good Food
020 8433 3781
www.bbcmagazines.com/goodfood
Monthly. Editor: Gillian Carter
Decanter
020 7261 3929
www.decanter.com/
Monthly. Editor: Amy Wislocki
Food & Travel
020 8332 9090
www.fox-publishing.com
Monthly. Editor: Nicky Symington
Food Chain
01603 274130
www.foodchain-magazine.com
Bi-monthly. Editor: Libbie Hammond
Foodie Magazine
01202 535666
www.foodiemag.com
Monthly. Editor: Karleh Light
Italian Wines & Spirits
020 8458 4860
www.iwines.it
Website updated monthly
Editor: Bruno Roncarati
M&S Magazine
020 7747 0871
www.redwoodgroup.net
4pa. Editor: Diane Kenwood
Sainsbury's Magazine
020 7633 0266
www.sainsburysmagazine.co.uk
Monthly. Editor: Sue Robinson
Somerfield Magazine
0117 989 7800
www.somerfield.co.uk
13pa. Editor: Hannah Smith
The Vegetarian
0161 925 2000
www.vegsoc.org
4pa. Editor: Jane Bowler
Waitrose Food Illustrated
020 7565 3000
www.jbcp.co.uk
Monthly. Editor: William Sitwell
What's Brewing
01727 867201
www.camra.org.uk
Monthly. Editor: Ted Bruning
Whisky Magazine
01603 633808
www.whiskymag.com
8pa. Editor: Dominic Roskrow
Wine
020 7549 2567
www.wineint.com
Monthly. Editor: Catharine Lowe

Gay and lesbian

►► see **Diversity**, page 327

General interest

American in Britain
020 8661 0186
www.americaninbritain.com
4pa. Editor: Helen Elliott
Another Magazine
020 7336 0766
www.anothermag.com
2pa. Editor: Jefferson Hack
Asian Image
01254 298263
www.asianimage.co.uk
Monthly. Editor: Shuiab Khan
Astronomy Now
01903 266165
www.astronomynow.com
Monthly. Editor: Steven Young
BBC History Magazine
020 8433 3289
www.bbchistorymagazine.com
Monthly. Editor: Greg Neale

Choice
01733 555123
Monthly. Editor: Norman Wright
Contemporary
020 7740 1704
www.contemporary-magazine.com
Monthly. Editor: Roger Tatley
Der Spiegel
020 8605 3893
www.spiegel.de
Weekly. Editor: Matthias Matussek
DV8
01202 388388
www.dv8online.co.uk
Monthly. Editor: Nina Tsang
Epicurean Life
020 7376 5959
www.epicureanlife.co.uk
4pa. Editor: Azzy Asghar
Expression
01392 263052
www.exeter.ac.uk/alumni
2pa. Editor: Karen Lippoldt
Focus Magazine
0117 927 9009
www.originpublishing.co.uk
Monthly. Editor: Paul Parsons
Folio
0117 942 8491
Monthly. Editor: Rebecca Dean
Forward
0118 983 8243
www.guidedogs.org.uk
4pa. Editor: Tracey Gurr
Freemasonry Today
01284 754155
www.freemasonrytoday.co.uk
4pa. Editor: Michael Baigent
Fresh Direction
020 7424 0400
www.freshdirection.co.uk
3pa. Editor: Paul Russell
The Green
020 7792 2626
www.hhc.co.uk/thegreen
Monthly. Editor: Hugh Fasken
Guide Magazine
020 7792 2626
www.hhc.co.uk
Monthly. Editor: Ed Ewing
H&E Naturist
01405 769712
www.henaturist.co.uk
Monthly. Editor: Mark Nisbet
Harrods
020 7152 3842
2pa. Editor: Darius Sanai
Harvey Nichols Magazine
020 7747 0700
www.redwoodgroup.net
4pa. Editor: Deborah Bee
The Hill
020 7792 2626
www.hhc.co.uk/thehill
Monthly. Editor: Jane Turney
History Today
020 7534 8000
www.historytoday.com
Monthly. Editor: Peter Furtado
Hot Press
00 353 1 241 1500
www.hotpress.com
Fortnightly. Editor: Niall Stokes
Hotline (Virgin Trains)
020 7306 0304
www.riverltd.co.uk
Quarterly. Editor: Rod Stanley
i-D
020 7490 9710
www.i-dmagazine.com
Monthly. Editor: Avril Mair
Illustrated London News
020 7805 5555
www.ilng.co.uk
Bi-annual. Editor: Alison Booth
The Insight
01273 245956
www.theinsight.co.uk
Monthly. Editor: Nic Compton
Kindred Spirit
01803 866686
www.kindredspirit.co.uk
6pa. Editor: Richard Beaumont
The Lifeboat
01202 663188
www.rnli.org.uk
4pa. Editor: Liz Cook
Limited Edition
01689 885661
www.thisislimitededition.co.uk
Monthly. Editor: Andrew Parkes
Living South
020 7223 0022
www.hhc.co.uk/livingsouth
Monthly. Editor: Pendle Harte
Magnet – The Village Communicator
01825 732796
www.magnetpublications.com
Monthly. Editor: Mary Hillyar
Majesty
020 7436 4006
www.majestymagazine.com
Monthly. Editor: Joe Little
Mayfair and St James's Life
020 7344 9121
www.mayfairlife.co.uk
Monthly. Editor: Stephen Goringe
New Humanist
020 7436 1151
www.newhumanist.org.uk
Bi-monthly. Editor: Frank Jordans
North Magazine
020 7250 0750
Monthly. Editor: Mark Kebble
O Magazine
020 7565 3000
www.jbcp.co.uk
Monthly. Editor: Dan Linstead
Occasions
020 7650 2000
www.occasions-mag.com
4pa. Editor: Raza Sharma
The Oldie
020 7436 8801
www.theoldie.co.uk
Monthly. Editor: Richard Ingrams
Password
020 7261 9878
Bi-monthly. Editor: Alistair Gordon
Perth Life
01738 567700
Monthly. Editor: Steven Lavery
Platform
0115 848 1510
www.su.ntu.ac.uk/platform
Fortnightly. Editor: Loay El Hady
Quicksilver Magazine
020 7747 9390
www.quicksilvermagazine.co.uk
Bi-monthly. Editor: Alex Johnson
Reader's Digest
020 7715 8000
www.readersdigest.co.uk
Monthly. Editor: Katherine Walker
Reform
020 7916 8630
www.urc.org.uk
11pa. Editor: David Lawrence
The Resident
020 7384 9124
www.theresident.co.uk
Monthly. Editor: Amanda Constance
Ritz Magazine
020 7269 7416
www.electricink.net
2pa. Editor: Giles Morgan
Royalty
020 8201 9978
www.royalty-magazine.com
Monthly. Editor: M Houston
Saga Magazine
01303 771523
www.saga.co.uk
Monthly. Editor: Emma Soames
Salvationist
020 7367 4897
www.salvationarmy.org.uk/salvationist
Weekly. Editor: Dean Pallant
Scots Magazine
01382 223131
www.scotsmagazine.com
Monthly. Editor: John Methven
Select
01484 437737
www.ichuddersfield.co.uk
Bi-monthly. Editor: Julian Pratt
Sixer
0114 267 9686
www.northernlifestyle.com
Monthly. Editor: Chris Wilson
Snoop Magazine
020 8571 7700
www.snooplife.com
Monthly. Editor: Raj Kaushal
The Spark
0117 914 3434
www.thespark.co.uk
4pa. Editor: John Dawson
Tank
020 7434 0110
www.tankmagazine.com
Quarterly. Editor: Masoud Golsorkhi
Toni & Guy
020 7462 7777
www.publicis-blueprint.co.uk
4pa. Editor: Scarlett Brady
Town & Country News
01692 582287
Monthly. Editor: Laurence Watts

Trafford Magazine
020 7387 9888
www.babersmith.co.uk
2pa. Editor: Debbie Hyams
The Visitor
01963 351256
Monthly. Editor: Helen Dunion
Vivid
020 7307 8620
www.vivid-magazine.com
Quarterly. Editor: Anna Westermann
Vivid Magazine
020 7307 8620
Quarterly. Editor: Anna Westermann
Wavelength
01637 878629
Monthly. Editor: Steve Bough
Weekly News
01382 223131
www.dcthomson.co.uk
Weekly. Editor: Dave Burness
Which?
0845 307 4000
www.which.co.uk
Monthly. Editor: Malcolm Coles
The World of Yachts & Boats (pan-Arab)
020 7625 8030
www.worldofyachts.com
Bi-monthly. Editor: Nabil Farhat
You Can! Magazine
01242 544873
3pa. Editor: Anthony McClaran
Your Family Tree
01225 442244
www.yourfamilytreemag.co.uk
13pa. Editor: Garrick Webster
Yours
01733 264666
www.emap.com
Monthly. Editor: Valerie McConnell

Home and garden

25 Beautiful Homes
020 7261 5718
www.25beautifulhomes.co.uk
Monthly. Editor: Rhoda Parry
Amateur Gardening
01202 440840
Weekly. Editor: Tim Rumball
BBC Gardeners' World
020 8433 3593
www.gardenersworld.com
Monthly. Editor: Adam Pasco
BBC Good Homes
020 8433 2337
www.bbcmagazines.com/goodhomes
Monthly. Editor: Lisa Allen
BBC Homes & Antiques
020 8433 3483
www.bbcmagazines.com/homesandantiques
Monthly. Editor: Mary Carroll
Country Homes & Interiors
020 7261 6451
www.countryhomesandinteriors.co.uk
Monthly. Editor: Deborah Barker
Country House & Home
01689 887200
Monthly. Editor: Jennifer Morgan
Country Living
020 7439 5000
www.countryliving.co.uk/
Monthly. Editor: Susy Smith
Country Market
01273 837703
www.country-mkt.co.uk
Monthly. Editor: David Somerville
Elle Decoration
020 7150 7000
www.hf-uk.com
Monthly. Editor: Michelle Ogunadehin
The English Garden
020 7751 4800
www.theenglishgarden.co.uk
Monthly. Editor: Janine Wookey
The English Home
020 7751 4800
www.theenglishhome.co.uk
Monthly. Editor: Charlotte Coward-Williams
The Essential Kitchen, Bathroom & Bedroom Magazine
01206 851117
www.essentialpublishing.co.uk
Monthly. Editor: Gail Major
Essential Water Garden
01206 505900
www.essentialwatergarden.co.uk
10pa. Editor: Georgina Wroe
Fabric
020 7747 0700
www.redwoodgroup.net
Monthly. Editor: Steven Short
The Garden
01733 775775
www.rhs.org.uk
Monthly. Editor: Ian Hodgson
Garden Answers
01733 282683
www.greatmagazines.co.uk
Monthly. Editor: Nicola Dela-Croix
Garden News
01733 282680
www.greatmagazines.co.uk
Weekly. Editor: Sarah Page
The Gardeners' Atlas
01603 633808
www.gardenersatlas.co.uk
Website. Editor: Matthew Page
Gardening Which?
0845 903 7000
www.which.co.uk/gardeningwhich
10pa. Editor: Julia Bolton
Gardens Illustrated
020 8433 1354
www.bbcmagazines.com/gardensillustrated
10pa. Editor: Clare Foster
Gardens Monthly
01689 887200
Monthly. Editor: Helen Griffin
Good Housekeeping
020 7439 5000
www.goodhousekeeping.co.uk
Monthly. Editor: Lindsay Nicholson
Home
01689 887200
Monthly. Editor: Jocelyn Garside
Home & Country
020 7731 5777
www.womens-institute.co.uk
Monthly. Editor: Susan Seager
Home Building & Renovating
01527 834400
www.homebuilding.co.uk
Monthly. Editor: Michael Holmes
Home DIY
01689 886677
www.highburyleisure.co.uk
Monthly. Editor: John McGowen
Home Efficiency
01753 884216
www.4ecotips.com
Bi-monthly. Editor: Andrew Leech
Home Furnishing News (HFN)
020 7240 0420
www.hfnmag.com
Weekly. Editor: Warren Shoulberg
Home Life Magazine
028 3832 4006
Monthly. Editor: M Kinsella
Home View
01277 366134
www.homeviewpropertymagazine.com
Bi-monthly. Editor: Garry Clarke
Homebase Magazine
020 7462 7777
www.publicis-blueprint.co.uk
Quarterly. Editor: Ward Hellewell
Homebuilding & Renovating
020 7970 4000
www.centaur.co.uk
Monthly. Editor: Michael Holmes
Homes & Gardens
020 7261 5678
www.homesandgardens.com/
Monthly. Editor: Isobel McKenzie-Price
Homes & Interiors Scotland
0141 331 2221
www.homesandinteriorsscotland.com
Bi-monthly. Editor: Sandra Colamartino
Homes Overseas
020 7939 9888
www.homesoverseas.co.uk
Monthly. Editor: Mike Hayes
Homes Review
01206 506250
Monthly
HomeStyle
01206 851117
www.essentialpublishing.co.uk
Monthly. Editor: Sally Narraway
House & Garden
020 7499 9080
www.houseandgarden.co.uk
Monthly. Editor: Susan Crewe
House Beautiful
020 7439 5000
www.housebeautiful.co.uk
Monthly. Editor: Kerryn Harper
Housing Association Magazine
0121 682 8881
Bi-monthly. Editor: Bruce Meecham
Ideal Home
020 7261 6474
www.idealhomemagazine.co.uk
Monthly. Editor: Susan Rose

Inside Readers Homes
01689 887200
Monthly. Editor: Karen Bray
Inspirations for your Home
01689 887200
Monthly. Editor: André Frieze
International Homes
01245 358877
www.international-homes.com
9pa. Editor: Jill Keene
International Relocation
01295 255177
www.intrel.co.uk
Yearly. Editor: Martin Coomber
Ireland's Homes Interiors & Living
028 9147 3979
Monthly. Editor: Mike Keenan
KBB – Kitchens, Bedrooms & Bathrooms Magazine
020 8515 2000
www.dmgworldmedia.com
Monthly. Editor: Rosalind Anderson
Key
020 7494 3155
2pa. Editor: Clare Weatherall
Livingetc
020 7261 6603
www.livingetc.com
Monthly. Editor: Suzanne Imre
Perfect Home
01342 828700
www.brooklandsgroup.com
Monthly. Editor: Sarah Giles
Period House
01206 851117
www.essentialpublishing.co.uk
Monthly. Editor: Sarah Wiltshire
Period Ideas
01206 505900
www.periodideas.com
Monthly. Editor: Jeannine McAndrew
Period Living & Traditional Homes
020 7182 8775
Monthly. Editor: Sharon Parsons
Real Homes Magazine
020 7226 2222
www.hhc.co.uk
Monthly. Editor: Karen Williams
Renovations
020 7384 1985
4pa. Editor: Liz Cowley
Rooms, Rooms, Rooms
01206 851117
www.essentialpublishing.co.uk
Monthly. Editor: Sarah Gallaher
Traditional Homes & Interiors
01795 599191
www.cplmedia.co.uk
10pa. Editor: Lisa Perry
What House?
020 7939 9888
www.whathouse.co.uk
Monthly. Editor: Lisa Isaacs
World of Interiors
020 7499 9080
www.worldofinteriors.co.uk
Monthly. Editor: Rupert Thomas
Your New Home
020 8349 1380
www.yournewhome.co.uk
Bi-monthly. Editor: Karen Keeman

Leisure

Absolute Horse
01473 461515
www.ahmagazine.com
Monthly. Editor: Sandy Lee
Adrenalin (International Edition)
020 7345 5066
www.adrenalin.com
4pa. Editor: Mike Fordham
Aeroplane
020 7261 5849
www.aeroplanemonthly.com/
Monthly. Editor: Michael Oakey
Air Enthusiast
01780 755131
www.airenthusiast.com
Bi-monthly. Editor: Ken Ellis
Air Transport World
01628 477775
www.atwonline.com
Monthly. Editor: Perry Flint
Aircraft Illustrated
01932 266600
www.aircraftillustrated.com
Monthly. Editor: Alan Burney
Airliner World
01780 755131
www.airlinerworld.com
Monthly. Editor: Tony Dixon
Allotment & Leisure Gardener
01425 616459
4pa. Editor: David Gibbs
Animal Life
0870 010 1181
www.rspca.org.uk
Quarterly. Editor: Amanda Bailey
Antique Collecting
01394 389950
www.antique-acc.com
Monthly. Editor: Susan Wilson
Antique Dealer & Collectors Guide
020 8691 4820
www.antiquecollectorsguide.co.uk
Bi-monthly. Editor: Philip Bartlam
Argos
01732 848499
www.prodogs.org
2pa. Editor: Mike Findlay
Asda Magazine
020 7462 7777
www.publicis-blueprint.co.uk
Monthly. Editor: Amanda Morgan
At Home in Cardiff Bay
029 2045 0532
4pa. Editor: Andy Meredith
Aviation News
01424 720477
www.aviation-news.co.uk
Monthly. Editor: Barry Wheeler
Aviation Week & Space Technology
020 7409 1482
www.aviationnow.com/
Weekly. Editor: Anthony L Velocci Jr
Award Journal
01753 727470
www.theaward.org
3pa. Editor: Dave Wood

BBC Wildlife Magazine
0117 973 8402
www.bbc.co.uk/nature/animals/
Monthly. Editor: Sophie Stafford
Bird Life
01767 680551
www.rspb.org.uk
Bi-monthly. Editor: Derek Niemann
Bird Watching
01733 465972
www.greatmagazines.co.uk
Monthly. Editor: David Cromack
Birds
01767 680551
www.rspb.org.uk
4pa. Editor: Rob Hume
Birdwatch
020 8881 0550
www.birdwatch.co.uk
Monthly. Editor: Dominic Mitchell
Black Beauty & Hair
020 7720 2108
www.blackbeautyandhair.com
Bi-monthly. Editor: Irene Shelley
BMFA News
0116 244 0028
www.bmfa.org/news
Bi-monthly. Editor: Eric Clark
Boat International
020 8547 2662
www.boatinternational.co.uk/
Monthly. Editor: Amanda McCracken
Boats & Yachts for Sale
01243 533394
www.boats-for-sale.com
Monthly. Editor: Sue Milne
Book & Magazine Collector
0870 732 8080
13pa. Editor: Jonathan Scott
Bridge Magazine
020 7388 2404
www.bridgemagazine.co.uk
Bi-monthly. Editor: Mark Horton
British Birds
01580 882039
www.britishbirds.co.uk
Monthly. Editor: Roger Riddington
British Horse
0870 120 8880
www.bhs.org.uk
Bi-monthly. Editor: David Prince
British Naturism
01604 620361
www.british-naturism.org.uk
4pa. Editor: Tracey Major
Budgerigar World
01678 520262
Monthly. Editor: G Evans
Buy a Boat (for under £20,000)
01243 533394
www.boats-for-sale.com
Monthly. Editor: Sue Milne
Cage & Aviary Birds
020 7261 6201
www.cageandaviarybirds.com
Weekly. Editor: Donald Taylor
Cakes & Sugarcraft
0845 225 5671/2
www.squires-shop.com
4pa. Editor: Beverley Dutton

Camping & Caravanning
024 7669 4995
www.campingandcaravanningclub.co.uk
Monthly. Editor: Nick Harding
Camping Magazine
01778 391000
www.campingmagazine.co.uk
Monthly. Editor: Darren Webb
Canal & Riverboat
01603 708930
www.canalandriverboat.com
Monthly. Editor: Chris Cattrall
Canal Boat & Inland Waterways
0118 977 1677
www.canalboatmagazine.com
Monthly. Editor: Emrhys Barrell
Caravan Club Magazine
01342 336804
www.caravanclub.co.uk
Monthly. Editor: Barry Williams
Caravan Life
01778 391000
www.caravanlife.co.uk
Monthly. Editor: Michael Le Caplain
Caravan Magazine
020 8774 0737
Monthly. Editor: Steve Rowe
The Cat
01403 221936
www.cats.org.uk
Bi-monthly. Editor: Clare Jeater
Cat World
01403 711511
www.catworld.co.uk
Monthly. Editor: Jo Rothery
Chess
020 7388 2404
www.chess.co.uk
Bi-monthly. Editor: Jimmy Adams
Christmas Cakes – A Design Source
0845 225 5671/2
www.squires-shop.com
Yearly. Editor: Beverley Dutton
Church Music Quarterly
01306 872800
www.rscm.com
4pa. Editor: Esther Jones
Club News
020 8469 9700
www.swanpublishing.co.uk
6pa. Editor: David Tickner
Coast
020 7287 0035
www.coastmagazine.co.uk
Monthly. Editor: Jo Denbury
Coin News
01404 46972
www.tokenpublishing.com/
Monthly. Editor: John Mussell
Coin Yearbook
01404 46972
www.tokenpublishing.com/
Yearly. Editor: John Mussell
Collect it!
01206 851117
www.collectit.info
Monthly. Editor: Charlotte Barber
Collections
020 7870 9000
www.bostonhannah.co.uk
3pa. Editor: Charles Ford

Collector
020 8740 7020
www.artefact.co.uk
Bi-monthly. Editor: Paul Hooper
Collectors Gazette
01778 391124
Monthly. Editor: Denise Burrows
Companions Magazine
01952 290999
www.pdsa.org.uk
4pa. Editor: Clare Evans
Continental Modeller
01297 20580
www.peco-uk.com
Monthly. Editor: Andrew Burnham
Country Illustrated
020 7255 3330
www.countryclubuk.com
Monthly. Editor: Julie Spencer
Country Life
020 7261 6969
www.countrylife.co.uk/
Weekly. Editor: Clive Aslet
Country Market
01273 837703
www.country-mkt.co.uk
Monthly. Editor: David Somerville
Country Smallholding
01392 888475
www.countrysmallholding.com
Monthly. Editor: Diane Cowgill
Country Walking
01733 282614
www.greatmagazines.co.uk
Monthly. Editor: Jonathan Manning
The Countryman
01756 701033
www.countrymanmagazine.co.uk
Monthly. Editor: Bill Taylor
The Countryman's Weekly
01822 855281
www.countrymansweekly.co.uk
Weekly. Editor: David Venner
Countryside La Vie
0116 212 2555
www.countryside-lavie.com
Bi-monthly. Editor: Marlene Bowley
Crafts
020 7806 2500
www.craftscouncil.org.uk
Bi-monthly. Editor: Geraldine Rudge
Crafts Beautiful
01206 505900
www.crafts-beautiful.com
Monthly. Editor: Lynn Martin
Crafty Carper
0114 258 0812
www.anglingpublications.com
Monthly. Editor: Simon Crow
Cross Stitch Collection
01225 442244
www.crossstitchcollection.co.uk
13pa. Editor: Debora Bradley
Cross Stitch Gallery
01227 750215
Bi-monthly. Editor: Mary Hickmott
Cross Stitcher
01225 442244
www.cross-stitchermagazine.co.uk
13pa. Editor: Cathy Lewis

Cumbria
01756 701033
www.dalesman.co.uk
Monthly. Editor: Terry Fletcher
Dalesman
01756 701033
www.dalesman.co.uk
Monthly. Editor: Terry Fletcher
Dartmoor Magazine
01822 614899
www.dartmoormagazine.co.uk
4pa. Editor: Elisabeth Stanbrook
Dog World
01233 621877
www.dogworld.co.uk
Weekly. Editor: Stuart Baillie
Dogs Today
01276 858880
Monthly. Editor: Beverley Cuddy
Doll Magazine
01403 711511
www.dollmagazine.com
Monthly. Editor: Emma Brown
Dollond & Aitchison Magazine
020 7747 0700
www.redwoodgroup.net
2pa. Editor: Laurence Weinberger
Dolls House World
01403 711511
www.dollshouseworld.com
Monthly. Editor: Laura Quiggan
Engineering in Miniature
01926 614101
www.engineeringinminiature.co.uk
Monthly. Editor: CL Deith
EOS Magazine
01869 331741
www.eos-magazine.com
4pa. Editor: Angela August
EQ
01986 782368
www.feedmark.com
4pa. Editor: Clare Macleod
Erotic Review
020 7907 6404
www.theeroticreview.co.uk
Monthly. Editor: Rowan Pelling
ESP Magazine
01733 253477
www.espmag.co.uk
Monthly. Editor: Sharon McAllister
Evergreen
01242 537900
www.thisengland.co.uk
4pa. Editor: Roy Faiers
Everyday Practical Electronics
01202 873872
www.epemag.co.uk
Monthly. Editor: Mike Kenward
Families East
020 8694 8694
www.familiesonline.co.uk
Bi-monthly. Editor: Mewe Mechese
Families Edinburgh
0131 552 6005
www.familiesonline.co.uk
Bi-monthly. Editor: Louise Armour
Families Liverpool
0151 522 9361
www.familiesonline.co.uk
Bi-monthly. Editor: Jennifer-Paige Deenihan

Families North
020 7794 5690
www.familiesonline.co.uk
Bi-monthly. Editor: Cathy Youd
Families Together
01903 821082
www.cfnetwork.co.uk
3pa. Editor: Clive Price
Families Upon Thames
01932 254584
www.familiesonline.co.uk
Bi-monthly. Editor: Francis Loates
The Flower Arranger
020 7247 5567
www.theflowerarrangermagazine .co.uk
4pa. Editor: Judith Blacklock
Flyer
01225 481440
www.flyer.co.uk
Monthly. Editor: Nick Wall
FlyPast
01780 755131
www.flypast.com
Monthly. Editor: Ken Ellis
Fortean Times
020 7907 6000
www.forteantimes.com
Monthly. Editor: David Sutton
Galleries
020 8740 7020
www.artefact.co.uk
Monthly. Editor: Andrew Aitken
Gardens of England & Wales Open for Charity
01483 211795
www.ngs.org.uk
Yearly. Editor: Julia Grant
Gibbons Stamp Monthly
01425 472363
www.gibbonsstampmonthly.com
Monthly. Editor: Hugh Jefferies
Goodtimes
020 7431 2259
www.arp050.org.uk
6pa. Editor: Susi Rogol
Goodwood Magazine
01243 755000
www.goodwood.co.uk
Yearly. Editor: Kathryn Bellamy
The Great Outdoors
0141 302 7700
Monthly. Editor: Cameron McNaish
Gulliver's World
01228 404350
www.lilliputlane.co.uk
4pa. Editor: Jean Mounsey
Gun Mart
01206 505900
www.gunmart.net
Monthly. Editor: Pat Farey
Heritage Magazine
020 7751 4800
www.heritagemagazine.co.uk
Bi-monthly. Editor: Penelope Rance
Home DIY
01689 887200
Monthly. Editor: John McGowan
Hoofprint
01565 872107
www.hoofprint.co.uk
Monthly. Editor: Barry Hook
Horoscope
01202 873872
www.horoscope.co.uk
Monthly. Editor: Mike Kenward
Horse
020 7261 7969
www.horsemagazine.co.uk
Monthly. Editor: Jaki Bell
Horse & Hound
020 7261 6453
www.horseandhound.co.uk
Weekly. Editor: Lucy Higginson
Horse & Rider
01428 601020
www.horseandridermagazine.co.uk
Monthly. Editor: Alison Bridge
Jane Greenoff's Cross Stitch
01225 442244
www.futurenet .com/janegreenoffscrossstitch
Bi-monthly. Editor: Faye Dixon
K9 Magazine
0870 011 4115
www.k9magazine.com
Quarterly. Editor: Ryan O'Meara
Kew
020 8332 5906
www.rbgkew.org.uk
4pa. Editor: Sue Seddon
Koi Carp
01202 735090
www.koi-carp.com
Monthly. Editor: Louise Harper
Lakeland Walker
01778 391000
www.lakelandwalker.co.uk
Bi-monthly. Editor: Michael Cowton
Legion – Royal British Legion
020 7296 4200
Bi-monthly. Editor: Claire Townley-Jones
Leisure Painter
01580 763315
www.leisurepainter.co.uk
Monthly. Editor: Ingrid Lyon
Leisure Scene
01494 888433
www.cssc.co.uk
3pa. Editor: Gemma Thomson
Lifewatch Magazine
020 7449 6241
www.zsl.org
3pa. Editor: Debbie Curtis
Machine Knitting News
01273 400425
www.machineknittingnews.co.uk
Monthly. Editor: Christine Richardson
Marine Modelling International
01684 588604
www.traplet.com
Monthly. Editor: Chris Jackson
Microlight Flying
01524 841010
www.bmaa.org
6pa. Editor: David Bremner
Military Illustrated Past & Present
0870 870 2345
www.publishingnews.co.uk
Monthly. Editor: Tim Newark
Military Model Craft International
01494 799982
www.modelactivitypress.com
Monthly. Editor: Tony Little
Military Modelling
01689 887200
www.militarymodelling.com
15pa. Editor: Ken Jones
Miniature Wargames
01202 297344
www.miniwargames.com
Monthly. Editor: Iain Dickie
Model & Collectors Mart
0121 233 8712
www.modelmart.co.uk
Monthly. Editor: Dean Shepherd
Model Boats
01689 887200
www.modelboats.co.uk
Monthly. Editor: John Cundell
Model Collector
020 8774 0600
Monthly. Editor: Lindsey Amrani
Model Engineer
01689 887200
26pa. Editor: Mike Chrisp
Model Engineers' Works
01689 887200
8pa. Editor: David Fenner
Model Helicopter World
01684 588612
www.traplet.com
Monthly. Editor: Jon Tanner
Motor Boat & Yachting
020 7261 5308
www.ybw.com/
Monthly. Editor: Tom Isitt
Motor Boats Monthly
020 7261 7257
www.motorboatsmonthly.com/
Monthly. Editor: Hugo Andreae
Motor Caravanner
01480 496130
www.motorcaravanners.org.uk
Monthly. Editor: Susan Lomax
Motorcaravan & Camping Mart
01778 391000
www.caravanmart.co.uk
11pa. Editor: Peter Sharpe
Motorhome Monthly
020 8302 6150
www.stoneleisure.com
Monthly. Editor: R Griffiths
National Trust Magazine
020 7222 9251
www.nationaltrust.org.uk
3pa. Editor: Gaynor Aaltonen
New Stitches
01227 750215
www.newstitches.com
Monthly. Editor: Mary Hickmott
Our Dogs
0870 731 6500
www.ourdogs.co.uk
Weekly. Editor: William Moores
Paddles
01202 735090
www.freestyle-group.com
Monthly. Editor: Richard Parkin

Patchwork & Quilting
01684 588601
www.traplet.com
Monthly. Editor: Dianne Huck
Paws
020 7627 9293
www.dogshome.org
4pa. Editor: Helen Tennant
The Peak
01756 701033
www.dalesman.co.uk
Monthly. Editor: Terry Fletcher
The People's Friend
01382 223131
www.dcthomson.co.uk
Weekly. Editor: Margaret McCoi
Pet Patter
020 7212 9000
www.mediamark.co.uk
Quarterly. Editor: Emily Bamber
Pilot
01799 544200
www.pilotweb.co.uk
Monthly. Editor: Dave Calderwood
Popular Crafts
01689 887200
www.popularcrafts.com
13pa. Editor: Dawn Frosdick-Hopley
Popular Patchwork
01689 887200
13pa. Editor: Stacey Kerr
Practical Boat Owner
01202 680593
www.pbo.co.uk
Monthly. Editor: Sarah Norbury
Practical Caravan
020 8267 5000
www.practicalcaravan.com
Monthly. Editor: Alex Newby
Practical Fishkeeping
01733 282764
www.greatmagazines.co.uk
Monthly. Editor: Karen Youngs
Practical Wireless
01202 659910
www.pwpublishing.ltd.uk/pw
Monthly. Editor: Rob Mannion
Practical Woodworking
01689 887200
www.getwoodworking.com
Monthly. Editor: Mark Chisholm
Prediction
020 8774 0600
www.predictionmagazine.co.uk
Monthly. Editor: Tania Ahsan
Quick & Easy Cross Stitch
01225 442244
www.futurenet.com/quickandeasycrossstitch
13pa. Editor: Jenny Dixon
RA Magazine
020 7300 5820
www.ramagazine.org.uk
4pa. Editor: Sarah Greenberg
RadCom
01707 659015
www.rsgb.org
Monthly. Editor: Steve Telenius-Lowe
Radio Control Jet International
01684 594505
www.traplet.com
Bi-monthly. Editor: Simon Delaney
Radio Control Model Flyer
01525 222573
Monthly. Editor: Ken Shepherd
Radio Control Model World
01684 588500
www.traplet.com
Monthly. Editor: Peter Dawson
Radio Race Car International
01684 588605
www.traplet.com
Monthly. Editor: Chris Deakin
Rail Express
01780 470086
www.railexpress.co.uk
Monthly. Editor: Philip Sutton
Railway Modeller
01297 20580
www.peco-uk.com
Monthly. Editor: John Brewer
Raw Vision
01923 856644
www.rawvision.com
4pa. Editor: John Maizels
RC Scale International
01684 588606
www.traplet.com
Bi-monthly. Editor: Simon Delaney
RCM & E
01689 887200
www.modelflying.co.uk
Monthly. Editor: Graham Ashby
RIB International
01884 266100
www.ribmagazine.com
Bi-monthly. Editor: Hugo Montgomery-Swan
Routing
01689 887200
www.getwoodworking.com
6pa. Editor: Neil Mead
RYA Magazine
023 8060 4100
www.rya.org.uk
Quarterly. Editor: Deborah Cornick
Sailing Today
01489 585225
www.sailingtoday.co.uk
Monthly. Editor: John Goode
Scale Aviation Modeller
0870 733 3373
www.sampublications.com
Monthly. Editor: Richard Franks
Scamp's Diary
01628 771232
www.scampsdiary.co.uk
2pa. Editor: Phillip Sheahan
Sew Bridal
0870 777 9955 x105
www.sewbridal.co.uk
Annually. Editor: Rosemary Sellers
Sewing With Butterick
0870 777 9955 x105
www.sewdirect.com
4pa. Editor: Rosemary Sellers
Sewing World
01684 588608
www.traplet.com
Monthly. Editor: Wendy Gardiner
Ships Monthly
01283 542721
www.shipsmonthly.co.uk
Monthly. Editor: Iain Wakefield
Short Wave Magazine
01202 659910
www.pwpublishing.ltd.uk/swm
Monthly. Editor: Kevin Nice
Stamp Magazine
020 8774 0600
www.stampmagazine.co.uk/
Monthly. Editor: Steve Fairclough
Steam Days
01202 304849
www.steamdaysmag.co.uk
Monthly. Editor: Douglas Kennedy
Steam Railway
01733 282719
www.greatmagazines.co.uk
Monthly. Editor: Tony Streeter
Surrey Nature Line
01483 488055
www.surreywildlifetrust.co.uk
3pa. Editor: Christine Reeves
The Teddy Bear Club International
01206 505979
www.planet-teddybear.com
12pa. Editor: Lorna Floyde
Time Out Shopping Guide
020 7813 3000
www.timeout.com
Annually. Editor: Janice Fuscoe
Today's Fishkeeper
01234 714644
Monthly. Editor: Christina Guthrie
Toy Soldier & Model Figure
01403 711511
www.toy-soldier.com
Monthly. Editor: Stuart Hessney
Treasure Hunting
01376 521900
www.greenlightpublishing.co.uk
Monthly. Editor: Gregg Payne
Trends
020 8340 6868
www.independentregionals.com
4pa. Editor: Ollie Lane
Used Bike Guide
01507 525771
www.usedbikeguide.com
Monthly. Editor: Brian Tarbox
Vogue Patterns
0870 777 9955 x105
www.sewdirect.com
Bi-monthly. Editor: Rosemary Sellers
Wag
020 7837 0000
www.dogstrust.org.uk
3pa. Editor: Joanna Bould
Walk
020 7339 8500
Quarterly. Editor: Christopher Sparrow
Waterways
01283 790447
www.waterways.org.uk
Quarterly. Editor: Harry Arnold
Waterways World
01283 742970
Monthly. Editor: Hugh Potter
Wild Times
01767 680551
www.rspb.org.uk
6pa. Editor: Derek Niemann

Wildfowl & Wetlands
01453 891900
www.wwt.org.uk
4pa. Editor: Mike Daw

Wolverine & Gambit
01892 500100
www.paninicomics.co.uk
13pa. Editor: Scott Gray

Woodcarving
01273 477374
Bi-monthly. Editor: Stuart Lawson

The Woodturner
01689 887200
www.getwoodworking.com
6pa. Editor: Nick Hunton

Woodturning
01273 477374
13pa. Editor: Mark Baker

The Woodworker
01689 887200
www.getwoodworking.com
Monthly. Editor: Mark Ramuz

Workbox
01579 340100
www.ebony.co.uk/workbox
Bi-monthly. Editor: Victor Briggs

The Yorkshire Journal
01756 701033
www.dalesman.co.uk
Quarterly. Editor: Mark Whiteley

You & Your Vet
020 7636 6541
www.bva-awf.org.uk
4pa. Editor: Martin Alder

Your Cat
01780 766199
www.yourcat.co.uk
Monthly. Editor: Sue Parslow

Your Dog
01780 766199
www.yourdog.co.uk
Monthly. Editor: Sarah Wright

Your Horse
01733 282750
www.greatmagazines.co.uk
Monthly. Editor: Natasha Simmonds

Men's interest

Arena
020 7520 6518
www.emap.com
Monthly. Editor: Anthony Noguera

Arena Homme Plus
020 7520 6571
www.emap.com
2pa. Editor: Ashley Heath

Bizarre
020 7907 6000
www.bizarremag.com
Monthly. Editor: Alex Godfrey

Boys Toys
01202 735090
www.boystoys.co.uk
Monthly. Editor: Mark Nuttall

Dazed & Confused
020 7336 0766
www.confused.co.uk
Monthly. Editor: Callum McGeoch

Details
020 7240 0420
www.details.com
10pa. Editor: Daniel Peres

DNR
020 7240 0420
www.dnrnews.com
Weekly. Editor: Jon Birmingham

Esquire
020 7439 5000
www.esquire.co.uk
Monthly. Editor: Simon Tiffin

FHM
020 7436 1515
www.fhm.com
Monthly. Editor: David Davies

FHM Collections
020 7436 1515
www.fhm.com
Monthly. Editor: Gary Kingsnorth

Front
020 7288 7500
www.hhc.co.uk
Monthly. Editor: Ioin McSorley

GQ
020 7499 9080
www.gq.com
Monthly. Editor: Dylan Jones

Jack
020 7907 6000
www.jackmagazine.co.uk
Monthly. Editor: Michael Hodges

Loaded
020 7261 5562
www.uploaded.com
Monthly. Editor: Martin Daubney

Maxim
020 7907 6000
www.maxim-magazine.co.uk
Monthly. Editor: Greg Gutfeld

Men's Fitness
020 7907 6000
www.mensfitnessmagazine.co.uk
Monthly. Editor: Peter Muir

Men's Health
020 7439 5000
www.menshealth.co.uk
11pa. Editor: Morgan Rees

Menz
020 2039 6600
www.hilspublications.com
4pa. Editor: Hilary Ferda

Muscle & Fitness
01423 504516
www.muscle-fitness-europe.com
Monthly. Editor: Geoff Evans

Musclemag International
0121 327 7525
www.tropicanahealthandfitness.com
Monthly. Editor: Gary Hill

Nuts
020 7261 5661
www.nutsmag.co.uk
Weekly. Editor: Phil Hilton

Stuff
020 8267 5000
www.stuffmagazine.co.uk
Monthly. Editor: Tom Dunmore

T3
020 7317 2433
www.t3.co.uk
13pa. Editor: James Beechinor-Collins

The Veteran
01582 663880
www.pensioneronline.com
8pa. Editor: Lee Wilson

Wallpaper
020 7322 1592
www.wallpaper.com
Monthly. Editor: Jeremy Langmead

Zoo Weekly
020 7208 3797
www.zooweekly.co.uk
Weekly. Editor: Paul Merrill

Money and property

Bloomberg Money
020 7484 9771
www.bloomberg.com
Monthly. Editor: Julian Marr

Business Week
020 7176 6060
www.businessweek.com
Weekly. Editor: Stanley Reed

Complete Guide to Homebuying
020 7827 5454
www.homebuying.co.uk
Monthly. Editor: Nia Williams

Country Land & Business Magazine
020 7235 0511
www.cla.org.uk
Monthly. Editor: Tom Quinn

Euroslot
01622 687031
www.datateam.co.uk
Monthly. Editor: Alan Campbell

Forbes
020 7534 3900
www.forbes.com
Fortnightly. Editor: Tim Ferguson

Fortune
020 7322 1074
www.fortune.com
Fortnightly. Editor: Nelson Schwartz (European editor of Fortune Europe)

Investment International
020 7827 5454
www.investmentinternational.com
Monthly. Editor: James Featherstone

Investors Chronicle
020 7382 8000
www.investorschronicle.co.uk
Weekly. Editor: Matthew Vincent

ISA Direct
020 7409 1111
www.alanbridge.co.uk
2pa. Editor: Anthony Yadgaroff

London Property News
01933 271611
www.londonpropertynews.co.uk
Monthly. Editor: Julia Read

The MBA Career Guide
020 7554 3350
www.mba.com
2pa. Editor: Nunzio Quacquarelli

Money Observer
020 7713 4188
www.moneyobserver.com
Monthly. Editor: Andrew Pitts

Moneywise
020 7715 8303
www.moneywise.co.uk
Monthly. Editor: Ben Livesey
Mortgage Advisor & Home Buyer
020 8334 1600
www.mortgageadvisormag.co.uk
Monthly. Editor: Ruth Bell
The Mortgage Edge
020 7404 3123
www.mortgageedge.co.uk
Monthly. Editor: Andy Stuart
Mortgage Finance Gazette
020 7827 5454
www.mfgonline.co.uk
Monthly. Editor: John Murray
Mortgage Introducer
020 7827 5454
www.mortgageintroducer.com
Fortnightly. Editor: Rob Griffiths
Negotiator
020 7772 8300
www.negotiator-magazine.co.uk
Fortnightly. Editor: Rosalind Renshaw
Optima
020 8420 4488
www.optimamagazine.co.uk
Fortnightly. Editor: Kathryn Michaels
Personal Finance Confidential
020 7447 4000
www.fleetstreetpublications.co.uk
Monthly. Editor: tbc
Personal Finance Magazine
020 7827 5454
www.pfmagazine.co.uk
Monthly. Editor: Martin Fagan
Post Magazine
020 7484 9700
www.postmagazine.co.uk
Weekly. Editor: Jonathan Swift
The Property Magazine
01480 494944
www.property-platform.com
Monthly. Editor: Malcolm Lindley
What House?
020 7939 9888
www.whathouse.co.uk
Monthly. Editor: Lisa Isaacs
What Investment
020 7827 5454
www.what-investment-mag.co.uk
Monthly. Editor: Sally Wright
What Investment Trust
020 7827 5454
www.charterhouse-communications.co.uk
3pa. Editor: Kieran Root
What ISA
020 7827 5454
www.charterhouse-communications.co.uk
3pa. Editor: Amanda Jarvis
What Mortgage
020 7827 5454
www.what-mortgage-mag.co.uk
Monthly. Editor: Hilary Osborne
Your Money: Savings & Investments
020 7404 3123
www.yourmoney.com
Quarterly. Editor: Mike Collins
Your Mortgage
020 7404 3123
www.yourmortgage.co.uk
Monthly. Editor: Paula John
Your New Home
020 8301 9311
www.yournewhome.co.uk
Bi-monthly. Editor: Jon Wadeson

Motoring

100% Biker
01244 663400
www.100-biker.co.uk
Monthly. Editor: Pat Ringwood
4x4
020 8774 0600
www.offroad4wd.co.uk/
Monthly. Editor: John Carroll
911 & Porsche World Magazine
01844 260959
www.chpltd.com
Monthly. Editor: Chris Horton
Advanced Driving
01483 230323
3pa. Editor: Ian Webb
American Motorcycle Dealer
01892 511516
www.dealer-world.com
Monthly. Editor: Fraser Addecott
Audi Driver
01525 750500
www.autometrix.co.uk
Monthly. Editor: Paul Harris
The Audi Magazine
01590 683222
2pa. Editor: Clive Richardson
Auto Express
020 7907 6000
www.autoexpress.co.uk
Weekly. Editor: David Johns
Auto Italia
01707 273999
www.auto-italia.co.uk
Monthly. Editor: Philip Ward
Auto Weekly
01392 442211
www.autoweekly.co.uk
Weekly. Editor: Steve Hall
Autocar
020 8267 5000
www.autocarmagazine.co.uk
Weekly. Editor: Steve Sutcliffe
The Automobile
01483 268818
www.oldcar-discoveries.com
Monthly. Editor: Michael Bowler
AutoTrader
020 8544 7000
www.autotrader.co.uk
Weekly. Editor: Graham Luff
Back Street Heroes
020 7772 8300
Monthly. Editor: Stu Garland
Banzai
01732 748000
www.banzaimagazine.com
Monthly. Editor: Joe Clifford
BBC Top Gear
020 8433 3710
www.topgear.com
Monthly. Editor: Michael Harvey
Bike
01733 468000
www.emap.com
12pa. Editor: Tim Thompson
BMW Car
01732 748000
www.bmwcarmagazine.com
Monthly. Editor: Bob Harper
BMW Magazine
020 7534 2400
www.cedarcom.co.uk
Quarterly. Editor: Jason Barlow
Car
01733 468000
www.car-magazine.co.uk
12pa. Editor: tbc
Car Mechanics
01959 541444
www.carmechanicsmag.co.uk
Monthly. Editor: Peter Simpson
Carbuyer
01689 887200
www.highburyleisure.co.uk
Monthly. Editor: Carlin Gerbick
CarSport Magazine
028 9078 3200
www.carsportmag.net
Monthly. Editor: Pat Burns
Classic & Sports Car
020 8267 5000
www.classicandsportscar.com/
Monthly. Editor: James Elliott
Classic American
0161 836 4457
www.classic-american.com
Monthly. Editor: Ben Klemenzson
Classic Bike
01733 468000
www.emap.com
12pa. Editor: Hugo Wilson
The Classic Bike Guide
01507 524004
www.classicbikeguide.com
Monthly. Editor: Tim Britton
Classic Car
01733 468000
www.classiccarsmagazine.com
12pa. Editor: Martyn Moore
Classic Car Mart
0121 233 8712
www.classic-car-mart.co.uk
Monthly. Editor: Frank Westworth
Classic Car Weekly
01733 347559
www.classic-car-weekly.co.uk
Weekly. Editor: Russ Smith
Classic Ford
01452 317765
www.classicfordmag.co.uk
Monthly. Editor: Marc Stretton
Classic Military Vehicle
01959 541444
www.kelsey.co.uk
Monthly. Editor: Pat Ware
Classic Motor Monthly
01204 657212
www.classicmotor.co.uk
Monthly. Editor: John Hodson

Classic Motorcycle
01507 525771
www.classicmotorcycle.co.uk
Monthly. Editor: James Robinson

Classic Racer
01507 525771
www.classicracer.com
Bi-monthly. Editor: Nigel Clark

Classics
01689 887200
13pa. Editor: Dan Harris

Custom Car
01959 541444
www.kelsey.co.uk
Monthly. Editor: Kev Elliott

Dirt Bike Rider
01524 834077
www.dirtbikerider.co.uk
Monthly. Editor: Sean Lawless

Enjoying MG
01954 231125
www.mgcars.org.uk
Monthly. Editor: Richard Ladds

Evo
020 7907 6000
www.evo.co.uk
Monthly. Editor: Peter Tomalin

Fast Bikes
01689 887200
www.fastbikesmag.com
13pa. Editor: Dan Harris

Fast Car
01689 887200
www.fastcar.co.uk
13pa. Editor: Gez Jones

Fast Ford
01452 307181
www.fastfordmag.co.uk
Monthly. Editor: Paul Wager

Good Motoring
01342 825676
www.motoringassist.com
Quarterly. Editor: Derek Hainge

Ignition
020 8420 1210
www.ignitionmotoringforwomen.co.uk
Quarterly. Editor: Claire Bowen

Intersection
020 7608 1166
www.intersectionmagazine.com
Bi-monthly. Editor: Emma E Forrest

Jaguar Driver
01582 419332
www.jaguardriver.co.uk
Monthly. Editor: Steve Fermore

Jaguar World Monthly
01959 541444
www.jaguar-world.com
Monthly. Editor: Phil Weeden

Kit Car
01924 469410
www.kit-cars.com
Monthly. Editor: Ian Hyne

Land Rover Enthusiast
01379 890056
www.landroverenthusiast.com
Monthly. Editor: James Taylor

Land Rover Owner International
01733 468000
www.lro.com
13pa. Editor: John Pearson

Land Rover World
020 8774 0976
www.landroverworld.co.uk
Monthly. Editor: Luke Evans

Lexus Magazine
020 7837 8337
www.justcomm.net
4pa. Editor: Lucy Reid

LRM – Land Rover Monthly
01359 240066
www.lrm.co.uk
Monthly. Editor: Richard Howell-Thomas

Max Power
01733 468000
www.maxpower.co.uk
13pa. Editor: Roger Payne

Mercedes
01789 490530
3pa. Editor: Eric Lafone

Mercedes Enthusiast
020 8639 4400
www.mercedesenthusiast.co.uk
Monthly. Editor: Dan Trent

MG Enthusiast Magazine
01924 499261
www.mgcars.org.uk/mgmag
10pa. Editor: Martyn Wise

MiniWorld
020 8774 0600
www.miniworld.co.uk
Monthly. Editor: Monty Watkins

Motor Cycle News (MCN)
01733 468000
www.motorcyclenews.com
53pa. Editor: Marc Potter

Motor Sport
020 8267 5000
www.haymarketpublishing.co.uk
Monthly. Editor: Paul Fearnley

Motorcycle Mechanics
01507 523456
www.classicmechanics.com
Monthly. Editor: Rod Gibson

Motorcycle Racer
01353 616000
www.motorcycleracer.net
Monthly. Editor: Tony Carter

Motorcycle Rider
01652 680060
www.rbp-ltd.co.uk
4pa. Editor: Andy Dukes

Motorcycle Sport & Leisure
01353 616000
www.motorcyclemag.co.uk
Monthly. Editor: Rod Chapman

Motoring & Leisure
01273 744759
www.csma.uk.com
10pa. Editor: David Arnold

The Motorist
020 8994 3239
Weekly. Editor: BJ Charig

Performance Bikes
01733 468000
www.emap.com
12pa. Editor: Simon Hargreaves

Performance VW
01732 748000
www.performancevwmag.com
Monthly. Editor: Elliot Roberts

Peugeot Rapport
0117 925 1696
www.specialist.co.uk
3pa. Editor: Karen Ellison

Porsche Post
01608 652911
www.porscheclubgb.com
Monthly. Editor: Stephen Mummery

Post Office Motoring
0191 418 3970
4pa. Editor: Alan Fairbairn

Practical Classics
01733 468000
www.emap.com
13pa. Editor: Martyn Moore

Rally XS
020 8267 5000
www.haymarketpublishing.co.uk
Bi-monthly. Editor: Oliver Peagam

Redline
01225 442244
www.redlinemag.co.uk
13pa. Editor: Dan Lewis

The Renault Magazine
01342 828700
4pa. Editor: Ann Wallace

Revs
01733 468000
www.revs.co.uk
13pa. Editor: Nigel Grimshaw

Ride
01733 468000
www.emap.com
13pa. Editor: Stefan Bartlett

Saab Magazine
01603 664242
www.archantdialogue.co.uk
2pa. Editor: Charlie Watson

Safety Fast!
01235 555552
www.mgcc.co.uk
Monthly. Editor: Peter Browning

Scootering
01507 525771
www.scootering.com
Monthly. Editor: Andy Gillard

Street Fighters
020 7772 8300
Monthly. Editor: Stu Garland

SuperBike
020 8774 0670
www.superbikemagazine.co.uk
Monthly. Editor: Kenny Pryde

Torque
01455 891515
www.triumph.co.uk
Quarterly. Editor: Neil Webster

Total Car Audio
01452 317773
www.totalcaraudio.co.uk
Bi-monthly. Editor: Chris Anderson

Toyota's In Front
020 7837 8337
www.justcomm.net
4pa. Editor: Oliver Parsons

Twist & Go Scooter Magazine
01507 524004
www.twistngo.com
Monthly. Editor: Mau Spencer

TWO – Two Wheels Only
020 8267 5000
www.haymarketpublishing.co.uk
Monthly. Editor: Bertie Simmonds

The Used Bike Guide
01507 524004
www.usedbikeguide.com
Monthly. Editor: Brian Tarbox

VM – Vauxhall
020 7212 9000
www.mediamark.co.uk
Quarterly. Editor: Zeta Eldridge

Volks World
020 8774 0600
www.volksworld.com
Monthly. Editor: Ivan McCutcheon

Volkswagen Driver
01525 750500
www.autometrix.co.uk
Monthly. Editor: Neil Birkitt

The Volvo Magazine
020 7747 0700
www.redwoodgroup.net
4pa. Editor: Zac Assemakis

VW Magazine
01778 391000
www.warners.co.uk
Monthly. Editor: Peter Rosenthal

What Car?
020 8267 5000
www.whatcar.co.uk
Monthly. Editor: Rob Aherne

Which Kit?
01737 222030
www.which-kit.com
Monthly. Editor: Peter Filby

Puzzles

100 Crosswords
01737 378700
www.puzzler.co.uk
13pa. Editor: Debbie Hardy

Cross Reference
01737 378700
www.puzzler.co.uk
13pa. Editor: Charles Sloan

Kriss Kross
01737 378700
www.puzzler.co.uk
13pa. Editor: Jo MacLeod

Logic Problems
01737 378700
www.puzzler.co.uk
13pa. Editor: Steve Bull/Catherine Bygrave

Pocket Puzzler Crosswords
01737 378700
www.puzzler.co.uk
13pa. Editor: Maggie Ayres

Puzzle Compendium
01737 378700
www.puzzler.co.uk
10pa. Editor: Birgitta Bingham

Puzzle Corner Special
01737 378700
www.puzzler.co.uk
10pa. Editor: Debbie Hardy

Puzzler
01737 378700
www.puzzler.co.uk
13pa. Editor: Catherine Filby

Puzzler Quiz Kids
01737 378700
www.puzzler.co.uk
11pa. Editor: Jenny Anstruther

Take a Break
020 7241 8000
www.bauer.co.uk
Weekly. Editor: John Dale

Sport

Ace
020 7381 7000
Monthly. Editor: Nigel Billen

Air Gunner
0118 977 1677
www.romseypublishing.net
Monthly. Editor: Nigel Allen

Airgun World
0118 977 1677
www.romseypublishing.net
Monthly. Editor: Adam Smith

Angler's Mail
020 7261 5829
Weekly. Editor: Tim Knight

Angling Times
01733 465520
www.greatmagazines.co.uk
Weekly. Editor: Richard Lee

Angling Times Advanced
01733 465705
Monthly. Editor: Steve Cole

The Arsenal Magazine
020 7704 4010
www.arsenal.com
Monthly. Editor: Andy Exley

Athletics Weekly
01733 898440
www.athletics-weekly.com
Weekly. Editor: Jason Henderson

Autosport
020 8267 5000
www.autosport.com
Weekly. Editor: Lawrence Foster

Badminton Magazine
020 8866 6517
Monthly. Editor: William Kings

Bogey
020 7987 6166
www.bogeymag.com
Quarterly. Editor: Richard Redmond

Boxing Monthly
020 8986 4141
www.boxing-monthly.co.uk
Monthly. Editor: Glyn Leach

Boxing News
020 7618 3456
www.boxingnewsonline.net
Weekly. Editor: Claude Abrams

British Homing World
01938 552360
www.pigeonracing.com
Weekly. Editor: Cameron Stansfield

British Waterski & Wakeboard
01932 570885
www.britishwaterski.org.uk
5pa. Editor: Gill Hill

Bunkered
0141 950 2216
www.bunkered.co.uk
8pa. Editor: Martin Dempster

Calcio Italia
020 7005 2000
www.independent.co.uk
Monthly. Editor: Bill Williamson

Canoe Focus
01480 465081
www.canoefocus.demon.co.uk
Bi-monthly. Editor: Peter Tranter

Carpworld
0114 258 0812
www.anglingpublications.com
Monthly. Editor: Simon Crow

Carve Surfing Magazine
01637 878074
www.orcasurf.co.uk
8pa. Editor: Chris Power

Celtic View
0141 551 4218
www.celticfc.com
Weekly. Editor: Paul Cuddihy

Clay Shooting
01264 889533
www.clay-shooting.com
Monthly. Editor: Keith Fisher

Climber
01778 391000
www.climber.co.uk
Monthly. Editor: Jo Cooke

Coarse Fisherman
07971 241484
www.coarse-fisherman.co.uk
Website, updated daily
Editor: Phil Runciman

Combat
0121 344 3737
www.martialartsinprint.com
Monthly. Editor: Paul Clifton

Combat & Survival
01484 435011
www.combatandsurvival.com
Monthly. Editor: Bob Morrison

Corporate Golf Magazine
01273 777994
www.golfnews.co.uk
4pa. Editor: Nick Bayly

Country Walking
01733 282614
www.greatmagazines.co.uk
Monthly. Editor: Jonathan Manning

Cricket World Magazine
01476 561944
www.cricketworld.com
Quarterly. Editor: Alistair Symondson

Cycle
0870 873 0060
www.ctc.org.uk
Bi-monthly. Editor: Dan Joyce

Cycle Sport
020 8774 0703
Monthly. Editor: Robert Garbult

Cycling Plus
01225 442244
www.cyclingplus.co.uk
13pa. Editor: Tony Farrelly

Cycling Weekly
020 8774 0703
www.cyclingweekly.co.uk/
Weekly. Editor: Robert Garbult

Daily Mail Ski & Snowboard Magazine
020 8515 2000
www.skiingmail.com
6pa Sep–Mar. Editor: Henry Druce

Darts World
020 8650 6580
www.dartsworld.com
Monthly. Editor: Tony Wood

Direct Hit
020 7953 7473
www.surreycricket.com
5pa. Editor: Matt Thacker

Dirt MTB Magazine
01305 251263
www.dirtmag.co.uk
Bi-monthly. Editor: Mike Rose

Distance Running
0141 810 9000
www.inpositionmedia.co.uk/publishing/drun.html
3pa. Editor: Hugh Jones

DIVE Magazine
020 8940 3333
www.divemagazine.co.uk
Monthly. Editor: Simon Rogerson

Diver
020 8943 4288
www.divernet.com
Monthly. Editor: Nigel Eaton

Document Skateboard
01305 251263
www.documentskateboard.com
9pa. Editor: Percy Dean

Document Snowboard
dickie@fall-line.co.uk
www.thesnowboardmag.co.uk
Bi-annual. Editor: Ian Samson

Dog Training Weekly
01348 875011
www.dogtrainingweekly.co.uk
Weekly. Editor: Angela Barrah

England Rugby
01707 273999
www.trmg.co.uk
Quarterly. Editor: Howard Johnson

Equi-Ads
01738 567700
www.equiads.net
Monthly. Editor: Mary Moore

Evening Times Wee Red Book
0141 302 6606
Yearly. Editor: Philip Joyce

Eventing
020 7261 5388
www.eventing.com
Monthly. Editor: Amanda Gee

The Evertonian
0151 227 2000
Monthly. Editor: Steve Hanrahan

F1 Racing
020 8267 5000
www.haymarketpublishing.co.uk
Monthly. Editor: Anthony Rowlinson

The Fairway Golfing News
01633 666700
www.fairway.org.uk
Monthly. Editor: John Doherty

Fall Line (skiing)
dickie@fall-line.co.uk
www.fall-line.co.uk
Bi-annual. Editor: Ian Samson

The Field
020 7261 5198
www.thefield.co.uk/
Monthly. Editor: Jonathan Young

First Down
020 7005 2000
www.first-down.co.uk
Weekly. Editor: Keith Webster

Fitness First
01932 841450
www.fitnessfirst.com
Quarterly. Editor: Iain Mackie

FitPro
0870 513 3434
www.fitpro.com
Bi-monthly. Editor: Gemma Carr

Flex
01423 504516
www.flex-europe.com
Monthly. Editor: Geoff Evans

Football First
020 7878 1007
www.sportfirst.com
Sunday. Editorial director: Chris Mann

Football Insider
020 7937 3759
www.sportservicesgroup.com
Quarterly mag, daily email
Editor: Jay Stuart

Football Italia
01494 564564
www.channel4.co.uk/sport/football_italia
Monthly. Editor: John D Taylor

FourFourTwo
020 8267 5000
www.haymarketpublishing.co.uk
Monthly. Editor: Mat Snow

Glory Glory Man United
020 7317 2614
www.futurenet.com
13pa. Editor: Sarah Shaddick

Go Tenpin
01502 560445
Monthly. Editor: Eric Hayton

Going for Golf
01268 554100
www.goingforgolf.com
Quarterly. Editor: Neil Webber

The Golf Guide: Where to Play/Where to Stay
0141 887 0428
www.holidayguides.com
Yearly. Editor: Anne Cuthbertson

Golf International
020 7828 3003
www.golfinternationalmag.co.uk
10pa. Editor: Robert Green

Golf Monthly
020 7261 7237
www.golf-monthly.co.uk
Monthly. Editor: Jane Carter

Golf News
01273 777994
www.golfnews.co.uk
Monthly. Editor: Nick Bayly

Golf Weekly
01733 288035
www.greatmagazines.co.uk
Weekly. Editor: Peter Masters

Golf World
01733 288011
www.greatmagazines.co.uk
Monthly. Editor: Andy Carlton

Good Ski Guide
020 7332 2000
www.goodskiguide.com
4 issues in the winter. Editor: Kate Langmuir

Greenside
0870 900 6415
www.foremostonline.com
Quarterly. Editor: Jenni O'Connor

The Gymnast
0116 247 8766
www.british-gymnastics.org
Bi-monthly. Editor: Trevor Low

High Mountain Sports
0114 236 9296
www.planetfear.com/climbing/highmountainmag
Monthly. Editor: Geoff Birtles

Improve Your Coarse Fishing
01733 465822
www.greatmagazines.co.uk
Monthly. Editor: Kevin Wilmot

In The Know
0870 513 3345
www.itkonline.com
Monthly. Editor: Darren Croft

The Informer
01923 821909
www.middlesexrugby.com
4pa. Editor: John King

International Rugby News
020 7005 2000
www.independent.co.uk
Monthly. Editor: Graeme Gillespie

Ireland's Equestrian Magazine
028 3833 4272
www.equestrian.co.ni
Bi-monthly. Editor: Diane Wray

Irish Golf Review
00 353 1 662 2266
www.worldsfair.co.uk
Quarterly. Editor: Robert Heuston

Karting
01689 897123
www.kartingmagazine.com
Monthly. Editor: Mark Burgess

The Kop
0151 285 8412
Monthly. Editor: Chris McLoughlin

Lady Golfer
01274 851323
Monthly. Editor: Mickey Walker

LFC
0845 143 0001
Weekly. Editor: Steve Hanrahan

Liverpool Monthly
01392 664141
Monthly. Editor: Joanne Trump

London Cyclist
020 7928 7220
www.lcc.org.uk
Bi-monthly. Editors: Jonathan Hewett, Rebecca Lack

Manchester United Magazine
020 7317 2614
www.manunited.com/magazine
13pa. Editor: Sarah Shaddick

Martial Arts Illustrated
01484 435011
www.martialartsltd.co.uk
Monthly. Editor: Bob Sykes
Match
01733 288138
www.greatmagazines.co.uk
Weekly. Editor: Simon Caney
Match Fishing Magazine
01327 311999
www.total-fishing.com
Monthly. Editor: Dave Harrell
Moto
01305 251263
www.motomagazine.co.uk
Bi-monthly. Editor: Rob Walters
Motor Sport
020 8267 5000
www.haymarketpublishing.co.uk
Monthly. Editor: Paul Fearnley
Motorsport News
020 8267 5385
Weekly. Editor: Tim Bowdler
Motorsports Now!
01753 765000
www.msauk.org
Quarterly. Editor: Dave Hancock
Mountain Bike Rider
020 8774 0600
Monthly. Editor: John Kitchiner
Mountain Biking UK
01225 442244
www.mbuk.com
13pa. Editor: Mat Brett
Muscle & Fitness
01423 504516
www.muscle-fitness-europe.com
Monthly. Editor: Geoff Evans
Muscle & Fitness Hers
01423 504516
www.muscle-fitness-europe.com
Bi-monthly. Editor: Geoff Evans
Musclemag International
0121 327 7525
www.tropicanahealthandfitness.com
Monthly. Editor: Gary Hill
National Club Golfer
01274 851323
www.nationalclubgolfer.com
Monthly. Editor: Chris Bertram
The Non-League Paper
020 8971 4333
www.thenon-leaguepaper.com
Twice weekly (Aug–May), weekly (May–Aug). Editor: David Emery
The Official Tour de France Guide
020 7331 1000
www.procycling.com
Yearly. Editor: Jeremy Whittle
On The Edge
01298 72801
www.ontheedgemag.co.uk
10pa. Editor: Neil Pearsons
Pool Industry
01420 563602
www.spata.co.uk
Quarterly. Editor: Stephen Delany
PQ International
020 7924 2550
www.poloworld.co.uk
4pa. Editor: Roger Chatterton-Newman
Procycling
020 7331 1000
www.procycling.com
Monthly. Editor: Jeremy Whittle
Pull!
01780 754900
www.countrypursuits.co.uk
10pa. Editor: Mike Barnes
Raceform Update
020 7293 3000
www.racingpost.co.uk
Weekly. Editor: Bernie Ford
Racing Calendar
0870 871 2000
www.britishcycling.org.uk
Quarterly. Editor: Phil Ingham
Racing Pigeon Weekly
01689 600006
www.racingpigeon.co.uk
Weekly. Editor: Steve Dunn
Racing Post
020 7293 3000
www.racingpost.co.uk
Daily. Editor: Chris Smith
Rally XS
020 8267 5000
www.haymarketpublishing.co.uk
Bi-monthly. Editor: Oliver Peagam
Ride BMX
01305 251263
www.ridebmxmag.co.uk
9pa. Editor: Mark Noble
Rugby League World
01484 401895
www.totalrl.com
Monthly. Editor: Tim Butcher
Rugby Leaguer & League Express
01484 401895
www.totalrl.com
Weekly. Editor: Martyn Sadler
Rugby Times
01484 401895
www.rugbytimes.com
Weekly. Editor: Jon Newcombe
Rugby World
020 7261 6810
www.rugbyworld.com/
Monthly. Editor: Paul Morgan
Runner's World
020 7439 5000
www.runnersworld.co.uk
Monthly. Editor: Steven Seaton
Running Fitness
01733 347559
www.running-fitness.co.uk
Monthly. Editor: Paul Larkins
Salmon & Trout Association Newsletter
020 7283 5838
www.salmon-trout.org
2pa. Editor: Carmel Jorgensen
Scottish Rugby
0141 309 1400
Bi-monthly. Editor: Scott Monroe
Scuba World
01202 735090
www.freestyle-group.com
Monthly. Editor: Frank Raines
Sea Angler
01733 465702
www.greatmagazines.co.uk
Monthly. Editor: Mel Russ
Seahorse
01590 671899
www.seahorsemagazine.com
Monthly. Editor: Andrew Hurst
Shoot Monthly
020 7261 7452
www.shootmonthly.co.uk
Monthly. Editor: Colin Mitchell
Shooting Gazette
01780 754900
www.countrypursuits.co.uk
Monthly. Editor: Will Hetherington
Shooting Sports
01206 505900
www.shooting-sports.net
Monthly. Editor: Peter Moore
Shooting Times and Country Magazine
020 7261 7659
www.shootingtimes.co.uk
Weekly. Editor: Robert Gray
Sidewalk Skateboarding Magazine
01235 536229
www.sidewalkmag.com
Monthly. Editor: Ben Powell
The Skier and Snowboarder Magazine
0845 310 8303
5pa. Editor: Frank Baldwin
Snooker Scene
0870 220 2125
Monthly. Editor: Clive Everton
Speedway Star
020 8335 1100
www.speedwaystar.net
Weekly. Editor: Richard Clark
Sport Cities and Venues
020 7937 3759
www.sportservicesgroup.com
Quarterly. Also a weekly email Editor: Jay Stuart
Sport Diver
01799 544200
www.sportdiver.co.uk
Monthly. Editors: Mark Evans, Rebecca Corbally
Sporting Gun
020 7261 7199
www.sportinggun.co.uk
Monthly. Editor: Robin Scott
Sportsbetting Update
020 7937 3759
www.sportservicesgroup.com
Quarterly. Also a weekly email Editor: Jay Stuart
Sportsmedia
020 7937 3759
www.sportservicesgroup.com
Quarterly. Also a daily email Editor: Jay Stuart
Sportsmedia Report
020 7937 3759
www.sportservicesgroup.com
Monthly. Editor: Jay Stuart
Spurs Monthly
01708 379877
Monthly. Editor: Tony McDonald
The Squash Player
01753 775511
www.squashplayer.co.uk
10pa. Editor: Ian McKenzie

Summit
0161 438 3308
www.thebmc.co.uk
Quarterly. Editor: Alex Messenger

Super Reds
01392 664141
Monthly. Editor: Joanne Trump

Surf News
01637 876474
www.britsurf.co.uk
4pa. Editor: Chris Power

The Surfer's Path
01235 536229
www.surferspath.com
Bi-monthly. Editor: Alex Dick-Read

Swimming
01509 632230
www.britishswimming.org
Monthly. Editor: Peter Hassall

Swimming Pool News
01353 777656
www.swimmingpoolnews.co.uk
Bi-monthly. Editor: Christina Connor

Taekwondo & Korean Martial Arts Magazine
0121 344 3737
www.martialartsinprint.com
Monthly. Editor: Paul Clifton

Target Sports
01905 795564
www.targetsportsmag.com
Monthly. Editor: Richard Atkins

Thoroughbred Owner and Breeder
020 7408 0903
www.racehorseowners.net
Monthly. Editor: Michael Harris

Today's Golfer
01733 288016
www.greatmagazines.co.uk
Monthly. Editor: Paul Hamblin

Today's Pilot
01780 755131
www.todayspilot.co.uk
Monthly. Editor: Dave Unwin

Total Carp
01327 311999
www.total-fishing.com
Monthly. Editor: Mark Coulson

Traditional Karate
0121 344 3737
www.martialartsinprint.com
Monthly. Editor: Paul Clifton

Trail
01733 282620
www.greatmagazines.co.uk
Monthly. Editor: Guy Procter

Trials & Motorcross News
01524 834029
www.tmxnews.co.uk
Weekly. Editor: John Dickinson

Trout & Salmon
01733 465821
www.greatmagazines.co.uk
Monthly. Editor: Sandy Leventon

Ultra-Fit
01736 350204
www.ultra-fitmagazine.com
8pa. Editor: Charles Mays

Unity
01993 811181
www.unitymag.co.uk
8pa. Editor: Steve Glidewell

Warren Miller's Impact
020 7240 4071
www.blackdiamond.co.uk/tour
Yearly. Editor: Guy Chambers

What Mountain Bike
01225 442244
www.whatmtb.co.uk
13pa. Editor: Jane Bentley

When Saturday Comes
020 7729 1110
www.wsc.co.uk
Monthly. Editor: Andy Lyons

White Lines Snowboarding Magazine
01235 536229
www.whitelines.com
6pa (Oct–Mar). Editor: Matt Barr

Windsurf Magazine
01993 811181
www.windsurf.co.uk
10pa. Editor: Mark Kasprowicz

Women & Golf
020 7261 7237
Monthly. Editor: Jane Carter

World Soccer
020 7261 5714
www.worldsoccer.com/
Monthly. Editor: Gavin Hamilton

Yachting World
020 7261 6800
www.ybw.com/
Monthly. Editor: Andrew Bray

Yachts & Yachting
01702 582245
www.yachtsandyachting.com
Fortnightly. Editor: Gael Pawson

Travel

Activity Wales
01437 766888
www.activitywales.com
Yearly. Editor: Matthew Evans

Adventure Travel
01789 450000
www.atmagazine.co.uk
Bi-monthly. Editor: Alun Davies

Arab Traveller
01621 842745
Bi-monthly. Editor: Jeremy Wright

Australian News
01323 726040
www.australian-news.co.uk
Monthly. Editor: Paul Beasley

BA Impressions
020 7269 7480
www.impressions-ba.com
Quarterly. Editor: Charlotte Methven

Best of Britain
020 8740 2040
www.morriseurope.com
Yearly. Editor: Leonora Peralta

Big City
020 7212 9000
www.mediamark.co.uk
Bi-monthly. Editor: Zeta Eldridge

Bradmans Business Travel Guides
020 7269 7416
www.bradmans.com
Yearly. Editor: Giles Morgan

Canada News
01323 726040
www.canadanews.co.uk
Monthly. Editor: Paul Beasley

City to Cities
020 8469 9700
www.swanpublishing.co.uk
Bi-monthly. Editor: David Tickner

CN Traveller (Condé Nast Traveller)
020 7499 9080
www.cntraveller.com
Monthly. Editor: Sarah Miller

Destination New Zealand
01323 726040
www.destination-newzealand.com
Monthly. Editor: Paul Beasley

Easyjet Magazine
020 7269 7480
www.easyjetinflight.com
Monthly. Editor: Michael Keating

Edinburgh Shopping & Tourist Guide
01506 508001
2pa. Editor: Roger Sadler

Education Travel Magazine
020 7440 4025
www.hothousemedia.com
Bi-monthly. Editor: Amy Baker

Enjoy Dorset & Hampshire Magazine
01202 737678
www.enjoydorset.co.uk
Yearly. Editor: Zoe Wilson

Ensign
01202 414200
Yearly. Editor: Karen Portnall

Essentially America
020 7243 6954
www.phoenixip.com
Quarterly. Editor: Mary Moore Mason

Essex Life & Countryside
01206 571348
www.archant.co.uk
Monthly. Editor: Robin Bechelet

Everything France Magazine
01342 828700
www.efmag.co.uk
Monthly. Editor: Ann Wallace

Flybe. Uncovered
020 8649 7233
www.bmipublications.com
Bi-monthly. Editor: Alan Orbell

Food & Travel
020 8332 9090
Monthly

France
01242 216050
www.francemag.com
Monthly. Editor: Kate McNally

French Property News
020 8543 3113
www.french-property-news.com
Monthly. Editor: Karen Tate

Gap Year
0870 241 6704
www.gapyear.com
Website. Editor: Tom Griffiths

Geographical
020 8960 6400
www.geographical.co.uk
Monthly. Editor: Nick Smith

Going USA
01323 726040
www.goingusa.com
Bi-monthly. Editor: Paul Beasley

Greece
01225 786800
www.merricksmedia.co.uk
Bi-monthly. Editor: Diana Cambridge

High Life
020 7534 2400
www.cedarcom.co.uk
Monthly. Editor: Alex Finer

Holiday & Events Guide
0870 444 2702
www.nealsyardagency.com
4pa. Editor: Ulriche Speyer

Holiday Which?
0845 309 4000
4pa. Editor: Patricia Yates

Holiday, The RCI Magazine
01536 310101
3pa. Editor: Simon McGrath

Homes Overseas
020 7939 9888
www.homesoverseas.co.uk
Monthly. Editor: Mike Hayes

In Britain
020 7751 4800
www.romseypublishing.net
Bi-monthly. Editor: Andrea Spain

In London
020 8740 2040
www.morriseurope.com
Bi-monthly. Editor: Chris Johnson

Italy
01305 266360
www.italymag.co.uk
Monthly. Editor: Fiona Tankard

Kuoni World Magazine
01306 744247
www.kuoni.co.uk
4pa. Editor: Mary Donovan

LAM – Living Abroad Magazine
020 7005 5000
www.lam-online.co.uk
Monthly. Editor: Bill Williamson

The London Guide
020 8740 2040
www.morriseurope.com
Monthly. Editor: Leonora Peralta

London Hotel Magazine
020 7373 7282
Bi-monthly. Editor: E R Spence

London Planner
020 7751 4800
www.londonplanner.co.uk
Monthly. Editor: Nick Buglione

Mediterranean Life
020 7415 7020
Quarterly. Editor: Glyn Wilmshurst

Msafiri-Kenya Airways
01442 875431
www.dfadesign.com
4pa. Editor: Dennis Fairey

My Travel Recline & Life Magazines
020 7269 7480
www.electricink.net
Quarterly. Editor: Chloe Wilson

National Geographic
01483 522068
www.nationalgeographic.com
Monthly. Editor: Bill Allen

Orient-Express Magazine
020 7805 5555
www.ilng.co.uk
4pa. Editor: Alison Booth

Overseas
020 7016 6905
4pa. Editor: Pat Treasure

Pride of Britain
020 7739 1434
www.prideofbritainhotels.com
2pa. Editor: Sophie MacKenzie

The Railway Magazine
020 7261 5821
www.railwaymagazine.co.uk
Monthly. Editor: Nick Pigott

Redhot Magazine
020 7269 7480
www.ontoeurope.com
Quarterly. Editor: Charlotte Methven

South Africa News
01323 726040
www.southafricanews.co.uk
Bi-monthly. Editor: Paul Beasley

Spain
0131 226 7766
www.spainmagazine.info
Monthly. Editor: Nicola McCormack

Sunday Times Travel
020 7306 0304
www.sundaytimestravel.co.uk
Bi-monthly. Editor: Jane Knight

TNT Magazine
020 7373 3377
www.tntmagazine.com
Twice weekly. Editor: Lyn Eyb

Travel & Leisure
020 8554 4456
4pa. Editor: Terry Stafford

Travel Australia
01424 223111
www.consylpublishing.co.uk
2pa. Editor: Bill Deacon

Travel GBI
020 7729 4337
Monthly. Editor: Richard Cawthorne

Traveller
020 7589 3315
www.travelleronline.com
Quarterly. Editor: Jonathan Lorie

Travelmag
01672 810202
www.travelmag.co.uk
Online magazine. Editor: Jack Barker

Wanderlust
01753 620426
www.wanderlust.co.uk
Bi-monthly. Editor: Lyn Hughes

Welcome to London
020 8297 4444
www.welcometolondon.com
Bi-monthly. Editor: Melanie Armstrong

Women and health

Accent Magazine
0191 284 9994
Monthly. Editor: Kevin Wright

Al Jamila
020 7831 8181
www.alkhaleejiahadv.com.sa/srpc/jamila
Weekly. Editor: Sanaa Elhadethee

Allergy Magazine
020 7269 7416
www.allergymagazine.com
Bi-monthly. Editor: Charmaine Yabsley

Asian Woman
0870 755 5501
Quarterly. Editor: Beena Nadeem

Asthma News
020 7226 2260
www.asthma.org.uk
4pa. Editor: Jenny Cockin

A–Z of Calories
01984 623014
Bi-monthly. Editor: Gertude Pertl

B
020 7150 7000
www.bmagazine.co.uk
Monthly. Editor: Frances Sheen

Baby & You
020 7226 2222
www.hhc.co.uk
Monthly. Editor: Amanda Burney

Balance
020 7424 1000
www.diabetes.org.uk
Bi-monthly. Editor: Martin Cullen

Be Slim
01984 623014
4pa. Editor: Gertude Pertl

Beautiful Brides
0117 934 3742
www.thisisbristol.co.uk/beautifulbrides
4pa. Editor: Harry Mottram

Bella
020 7241 8000
www.bauer.co.uk
Weekly. Editor: Jayne Marsden

Best
020 7439 5000
www.natmags.co.uk
Weekly. Editor: Louise Court

Blackhair
01376 534500
Bi-monthly. Editor: Jane MacArthur

Bliss for Brides
01376 534500
Bi-monthly. Editor: Abbey Marjoram

Boots Health and Beauty
020 7747 0960
www.redwoodgroup.net
6pa. Editor: Jan Boxshall

Bride & Groom
020 8477 3771
www.recorderonline.co.uk
2pa. Editor: Emma Rice

Brides
020 7499 9080
www.bridesuk.net
Bi-monthly. Editor: Liz Savage

Caduceus Journal
01926 451897
www.caduceus.info
4pa. Editor: Sarida Brown

Candis
0151 632 3232
www.candis.co.uk
Monthly. Editor: Jenny Campbell

Chat
020 7261 6559
Weekly. Editor: June Smith-Sheppard

Closer
020 7859 8463
www.emap.com
Weekly. Editor: Jane Johnson

Company
020 7439 5000
www.company.co.uk/
Monthly. Editor: Victoria White

Cosmopolitan
020 7439 5000
www.cosmopolitan.co.uk/
Monthly
Acting editor: Nina Ahmad

Cosmopolitan Hair & Beauty
020 7439 5000
www.cosmohairandbeauty.co.uk/
Monthly. Editor: Melanie Goose

Elle
020 7150 7000
www.hf-uk.com
Monthly. Editor: Lorraine Candy

Essentials
020 7261 6970
www.essentialsmagazine.com
Monthly. Editor: Karen Livermore

Eve
020 8433 2041
www.bbcmagazines.com/eve
Monthly. Editor: Jane Bruton

Executive Woman
020 8420 1210
www.execwoman.com
Bi-monthly. Editor: Angela Giveon

Family Circle
020 7261 6195
www.familycircle.co.uk
Monthly. Editor: Julie Barton-Breck

Family Magazine
01200 453000
Bi-monthly. Editor: Jeremy Nicholls

For the Bride
01376 534500
Bi-monthly. Editor: Abbey Marjoram

For Women
020 7308 5363
9pa. Editor: Liz Beresford

Glamour
020 7499 9080
www.glamour.com
Monthly. Editor: Jo Elvin

Good Health Magazine
01376 534500
www.gh-online.co.uk
Monthly. Editor: Jane MacArthur

Hair
020 7261 6974
www.hairmagazine.co.uk
Bi-monthly. Editor: Zoe Richards

Hair & Beauty
020 7436 9766
Bi-monthly. Editor: Laura Curtis

Hair Now
020 7436 9766
Bi-monthly. Editor: Tim Frisby

Hairflair
01376 534500
Bi-monthly. Editor: Ruth Page

Hairstyles Only
01376 534500
Bi-monthly. Editor: Ruth Page

Harpers & Queen
020 7439 5000
www.harpersandqueen.co.uk
Monthly. Editor: Lucy Yeomans

Health & Fitness
020 7226 2222
www.hfonline.co.uk
Monthly. Editor: Mary Comber

The Health Store Magazine
0115 955 5259
www.thehealthstore.co.uk
Bi-monthly. Editor: Jane Garton

Healthy
020 7306 0304
www.riverltd.co.uk
Bi-monthly. Editor: Annabel Meggeson

Healthy Times
020 7819 1111
www.squareonegroup.co.uk
Quarterly. Editor: Sharon Gray

Heat
020 7437 9011
www.emap.com
Weekly. Editor: Mark Frith

Hello!
020 7667 8901
www.hellomagazine.com
Weekly; website updated daily
Editor: Ronnie Whelan;
website editor: Tree Elven

Hia
020 7539 2270
Monthly. Editor: Mai Badr

Holistic London Guide
020 8672 7111
www.healthyinfo.co.uk
3pa. Editor: Samantha Stent

In Style
020 7261 4747
Monthly. Editor: Louise Chunn

Jane
020 7240 0420
www.janemag.com
Monthly. Editor: Jane Pratt

Junior
020 7761 8900
www.juniormagazine.co.uk
Monthly. Editor: Catherine O'Dolan

Junior Pregnancy & Baby
020 7761 8900
www.juniormagazine.co.uk
Bi-monthly. Editor: Debora Stottor

Ladies First
029 2039 6600
www.hilspublications.com
4pa. Editor: Hilary Ferda

The Lady
020 7379 4717
www.thelady.co.uk
Weekly. Editor: Arline Usden

Marie Claire
020 7261 5177
Monthly. Editor: Marie O'Riordan

Memsahib
020 8571 7700
www.snooplife.com
Quarterly. Editor: Jay Kumar

More!
020 7208 3165
www.moremagazine.co.uk
Fortnightly. Editor: Ali Hall

Mother & Baby
020 7347 1869
www.emapmagazines.co.uk
Monthly. Editor: Eleanor Dalrymple

Ms London
020 7005 2000
www.independent.co.uk
Daily. Editor: Bill Williamson

MS Matters
020 8438 0700
www.mssociety.org.uk
Bi-monthly. Editor: Debbie Reeves

My Weekly
01382 223131
www.dcthomson.co.uk
Weekly. Editor: Harrison Watson

New Woman
020 7437 9011
www.newwoman.co.uk
Monthly. Editor: Claire Baylis

Now
020 7261 6274
www.nowmagazine.co.uk/
Weekly. Editor: Jane Ennis

Now Star Diet & Fitness
020 7261 7366
www.ipcmedia.com
3pa. Editor: Jane Ennis

Now Star Style
020 7261 7366
www.ipcmedia.com
3pa. Editor: Jane Ennis

Number Ten
020 7439 9100
www.numberten.co.uk
Bi-annual. Editor: Laura Sheed

OK!
020 7928 8000
Weekly. Editor: Nic McCarthy

Parent News UK
020 8337 6337
www.parents-news.co.uk
Monthly. Editor: Penny McCarthy

Parent Talk
020 7450 9073
www.parentalk.co.uk
Website updated weekly
Editor: Maggie Doherty

People
020 7322 1134
www.people.com
Weekly. Editor: Bryan Alexander

Practical Parenting
020 7261 5058
www.practicalparenting.co.uk
Monthly. Editor: Sara Pates

Pregnancy and Birth
020 7347 1885
www.emapmagazines.co.uk
Monthly. Editor: Charlotte Coleman

Pregnancy Magazine
020 7226 2222
www.hhc.co.uk
Monthly. Editor: Amanda Hemmings

Pride Magazine
020 7228 3110
www.pridemagazine.com
Monthly. Editor: Amina J Taylor

Prima
020 7439 5000
www.primamagazine.co.uk/
Monthly. Editor: Maire Fahey

Prima Baby
020 7439 5000
www.primababy.co.uk/
Monthly. Editor: Julia Goodwin

Real
020 7241 8000
www.bauer.co.uk
Fortnightly. Editor: Sian Rees

Real Health & Fitness
020 7306 0304
www.riverltd.co.uk
Bi-monthly. Editor: Andrea Hammett

Red
020 7150 7000
www.redmagazine.co.uk
Monthly. Editor: Trish Halpin

Rosemary Conley Diet & Fitness Magazine
01509 620444
www.conley.co.uk/magazine
Bi-monthly. Editor: Gerri Hosier

Sayidaty
020 7539 2242
www.sayidaty.net
Weekly. Editor: Hani Nakshabandi

Sayidaty Fashion
020 7539 2242
www.sayidaty.net
4pa. Editor: Lucy Habib

Scottish Home & Country
0131 225 1724
www.swri.org.uk
Monthly. Editor: Liz Ferguson

Select Magazine
0121 212 4141
www.icbirmingham.co.uk
Monthly. Editor: Ann Roberts

Shape
020 7907 6531
Monthly. Editor: Liz Jarvis

She
020 7439 5000
www.she.co.uk
Monthly. Editor: Terry Tavner

Slimmer, Healthier, Fitter
01206 505900
www.slimmerrecipes.co.uk
10pa. Editor: Helen Mulley

Slimming Magazine
020 7347 1854
www.emapmagazines.co.uk
Monthly. Editor: Marie Farqharson

Slimming World
01773 546360
www.slimming-world.com
7pa. Editor: Christine Michael

Spirit of Superdrug
020 7306 0304
www.riverltd.co.uk
Bi-monthly. Editor: Brigid Moss

Take a Break
020 7241 8000
www.bauer.co.uk
Weekly. Editor: John Dale

Tatler
020 7499 9080
www.tatler.co.uk
Monthly. Editor: Geordie Greig

That's Life!
020 7241 8000
www.bauer.co.uk
Weekly. Editor: Jo Checkley

Tiara
029 2039 6600
www.hilspublications.com
3pa. Editor: Hilary Ferda

Top Santé Health & Beauty
020 7208 3772
www.emap.com
Monthly. Editor: Marina Gask

Twins, Triplets & More Magazine
01909 500874
3pa. Editor: Sheila Payne

Ulster Bride
028 9068 1371
www.ulstertatler.com
Bi-monthly. Editor: Christopher Sherry

Ulster Tatler
028 9068 1371
www.ulstertatler.com
Monthly. Editor: Richard Sherry

Ultra-Fit
01736 350204
www.ultra-fitmagazine.com
8pa. Editor: Charles Mays

Vanity Fair
020 7499 9080
www.vanityfair.co.uk
Monthly. Editor: Henry Porter

Vogue
020 7499 9080
www.vogue.com
Monthly. Editor: Alexandra Shulman

W
020 7240 0420
www.wmagazine.com
Monthly. Editor: John B Fairchild

Wave
01273 818160
www.wavemagazine.co.uk
Monthly. Editor: Emma Amyatt-Leir

Wedding & Home
020 7261 7470
www.weddingandhome.co.uk
Monthly. Editor: Kate Burlow

Wedding Cakes– A Design Source
0845 225 5671/2
www.squires-shop.com
4pa. Editor: Beverley Dutton

Wedding Day
020 7761 8980
www.beachpublishing.co.uk
Bi-monthly. Editor: Alice Kodell

Wedding Journal
028 9045 7457
www.weddingjournalonline.com
Quarterly. Editor: Tara Craig

Weight Watchers
020 8882 2555
www.weight-watchers.co.uk
8pa. Editor: Barbara Raine-Allen

WM
029 2058 3592
www.icwales.co.uk
Quarterly. Editor: Nina Rabaiotti

Woman & Home
020 7261 5176
www.womanandhome.co.uk/
Monthly. Editor: Sue James

Woman Alive
01903 821082
www.womanalive.co.uk
Monthly. Editor: Jackie Stead

Woman's Own
020 7261 5500
Weekly. Editor: Elsa McAlonan

Woman's Weekly
020 7261 6131
Weekly. Editor: Gilly Sinclair

Women's Health
020 7226 2222
www.hhc.co.uk
Monthly. Editor: Tracey Smith

Women's Wear Daily (WWD)
020 7240 0420
www.wwd.com
Daily. Editor: James Fallon

Yoga and Health
020 7480 5456
www.yogaandhealthmag.co.uk/
Monthly. Editor: Jane Sill

You & Your Wedding
020 7439 5000
www.youandyourwedding.co.uk
6pa. Editor: Carole Hamilton

Zest
020 7439 5000
www.zest.co.uk
Monthly. Editor: Alison Pylkkanen

Business and trade press

Business

Accountancy
020 8247 1387
www.accountancymagazine.com
Monthly. Editor: Chris Quick

Accountancy Age
020 8606 7505
www.accountancyage.com
Weekly. Editor: Damian Wild

Accounting & Business
020 7396 5966
www.accaglobal.com
10pa. Editor: John Prosser

Accounting Technician
020 7880 6200
www.accountingtechnician.co.uk
Monthly. Editor: Martin Allen-Smith

Assessment
020 7801 2884
www.pcs.org.uk/revenue
Monthly. Editor: Dennis Calnan

Bradmans Business Travel Guides
020 7269 7416
www.bradmans.com
Yearly. Editor: Giles Morgan

Brand Strategy
020 7970 4000
www.mad.co.uk
Monthly. Editor: Elen Lewis

Business Informer
0191 518 4281
Bi-monthly. Editor: Alan Roxborough

Business Traveller
020 7778 0000
www.businesstraveller.com
10pa. Editor: Tom Otley

CFO Europe
020 7830 7000
www.cfoeurope.com
11pa. Editor: Janet Kersnar

CIMA Insider
020 8849 2313
www.cimaglobal.com
Monthly. Editor: Ruth Prickett

Creative Review
020 7970 4000
www.mad.co.uk
Monthly. Editor: Patrick Burgoyne

Design Week
020 7970 4000
www.mad.co.uk
Weekly. Editor: Lynda Relph-Knight

Director
020 7766 8950
www.iod.com
Monthly. Editor: Joanna Higgins

Euromoney
020 7779 8888
www.euromoneyplc.com
Monthly. Editor: Peter Lee

European Business
020 7269 7416
www.electricink.net
Monthly. Editor: John Lawless

Financial Advisor
020 7382 8000
www.ftadvisor.com
Weekly. Editor: Hal Austin

Financial Management
020 8849 2313
www.cimaglobal.com
Monthly. Editor: Ruth Prickett

Financial News
020 7426 3333
www.efinancialnews.com
Weekly. Editor: William Wright

Financial World
01227 818609
www.financialworld.co.uk
Monthly. Editor: Denise Smith

First Voice of Business
01223 477411
www.campublishers.com
Bi-monthly. Editor: Warren Clark

Growing Business
020 8334 1600
www.gbmag.co.uk
Monthly. Editor: Marcus Austin

Human Resources
020 8267 5000
www.humanresourcesmagazine.com
11pa. Editor: Trevor Merriden

Industrial Focus
020 7014 0300
www.industrialfocus.co.uk
Bi-monthly. Editor: Mike Wearing

Institutional Investor – International Edition
020 7779 8888
www.iilondon.com
Monthly. Editor: Andrew Capon

In-Store
020 7970 4000
www.mad.co.uk
Monthly. Editor: Matthew Valentine

Insurance Age
020 7484 9700
www.insuranceage.com
Monthly. Editor: Michelle Worvell

Investor Relations
020 7637 3579
www.ironthenet.com
Monthly. Editor: Claire Hunte

The Journal
020 7534 2400
www.cedarcom.co.uk
Bi-monthly. Editor: Martin Baker

Landscape and Amenity Product Update
01952 200809
www.landscapespecification.com
6pa. Editor: David Stiles

Management Today
020 8267 5000
www.mtmagazine.co.uk
Monthly. Editor: Matthew Gwyther

Marketing Week
020 7970 4000
www.marketing-week.co.uk/
Weekly. Editor: Stuart Smith

MiD
020 7612 9300
www.infoconomy.com
Bi-monthly. Editor: Graeme Burton

Money Marketing
020 7970 4000
www.moneymarketing.co.uk
Weekly. Editor: John Lappin

New Business
020 7407 9800
www.newbusiness.co.uk
Quarterly. Editor: Chris Head

New Media Age
020 7970 4000
www.nma.co.uk/
Weekly. Editor: Michael Nutley

OS Magazine
0141 567 6000
www.peeblesmedia.com
Bi-monthly. Editor: Clare Bodel

Overseas Trade
020 7368 9600
www.overseas-trade.co.uk
Monthly. Editor: Janet Tibble

Pensions & Investments
020 7457 1430
www.pionline.com
Fortnightly. Editor: Nancy Webman

Pensions Age
020 7426 0101
www.pensions-age.com
Monthly. Editor: Francesca Fabrizi

People Management
020 7880 6200
www.peoplemanagement.co.uk
Fortnightly. Editor: Steve Crabb

Personnel Today
020 8652 3705
www.personneltoday.com
Weekly. Editor: Jane King

Professional Manager
020 7421 2705
www.managers.org.uk
Bi-monthly. Editor: Sue Mann

Real Business
020 7828 0733
www.realbusiness.co.uk
Monthly. Editor: Adam Leyland

Recruiter Magazine
020 7296 4200
www.recruiter.co.uk
Fortnightly. Editor: Karen Dempsey

StartUps.co.uk
20 8334 1600
www.startups.co.uk
Website, updated hourly
Editor: Matthew Thomas

Supply Management
020 7880 6200
www.supplymanagement.co.uk
Fortnightly. Editor: Geraint John

What's New In Industry
020 7970 4000
www.centaur.co.uk
Monthly. Editor: David Keighly

Construction and engineering

ABC&D
01527 834451
www.abc-d.co.uk
Monthly. Editor: Barry Cook

Architecture Today
020 7837 0143
www.architecturetoday.co.uk
10pa. Editors: Ian Latham, Mark Swenarton

Builder & Engineer
0161 236 2782
www.excelpublishing.co.uk
Monthly. Editor: Alex Kearns

Building
020 7560 4000
www.building.co.uk
Weekly. Editor: Denise Chevin

Building Design
01732 364422
www.cmpinformation.com
Weekly. Editor: Robert Booth

Building Products
020 8565 4387
www.buildingproducts.co.uk
Monthly. Editor: Phil Stronach

Civil Engineering
020 7665 2448
www.ice.org.uk
6pa. Editor: Simon Fuller-Love

Construction Manager
020 7560 4000
www.construction-manager.co.uk
10pa. Editor: Rod Sweet

Construction News
020 7505 6600
www.cnplus.co.uk
Weekly. Editor: Aaron Morby

Construction Products
020 7505 6868
www.cnplus.co.uk
Bi-monthly. Editor: Julian Birch

Contract Journal
020 8652 4756
www.contractjournal.com
Weekly. Editor: Rob Willock
Electronics
01474 565625
www.connectingindustry.com
11pa. Editor: Jo Bennett
Electronics Weekly
020 8652 3650
www.electronicsweekly.com
Weekly. Editor: Richard Wilson
Gas Installer
020 7401 4101
Monthly. Editor: Ian McManus
IEE Review
01438 313311
www.iee.org/review
Monthly. Editor: Svetlana Josifovska
New Civil Engineer
020 7505 6600
www.nceplus.co.uk
Weekly. Editor: Antony Oliver
Offshore
020 8946 7783
www.offshore-mag.com
Monthly. Editor: Eldon Ball
Offshore Engineer
020 8956 2835
www.offshore-engineer.com
Monthly. Editor: David Morgan
Pipeline World
01245 496321
www.pipemag.com
Bi-monthly. Editor: John Tiratsoo
PIR Construction
01234 348878
www.pirnet.co.uk
6pa. Editor: Derek Cooper
Professional Electrician & Installer
01923 237799
www.hamerville.co.uk
11pa. Editor: Richard Pagett
Professional Engineering
020 7973 1299
www.profeng.com
Fortnightly. Editor: John Pullin
Professional Heating & Plumbing Installer
01923 237799
www.hamerville.co.uk
11pa. Editor: Stuart Hamilton
Public Sector Building
020 7970 4000
www.centaur.co.uk
6pa. Editor: Derek Rogers
RIBA Journal
020 7921 8000
www.ribajournal.com
Monthly. Editor: Amanda Baillieu
The Engineer
020 7970 4000
www.e4engineering.com
Fortnightly. Editor: George Coupe
What's New In Building
01732 364422
www.cmpinformation.com
Monthly. Editor: Mark Pennington

Defence

Airforces Monthly
01780 755131
www.airforcesmonthly.com
Monthly. Editor: Alan Warnes
Jane's Defence Weekly
020 8700 3700
www.janes.com
Weekly. Editor: Peter Felstead
Navy News
023 9272 4194
www.navynews.co.uk
Monthly. Editor: Jim Allaway
Soldier
01252 347356
www.soldiermagazine.co.uk
Monthly. Editor: John Elliott

Education

Child Education
01926 887799
www.scholastic.co.uk
Monthly. Editor: Michael Ward
Education Today
020 7947 9536
www.collegeofteachers.ac.uk
Quarterly. Editor: Brychan Thomas
Education Travel Magazine
020 7440 4025
www.hothousemedia.com
Bi-monthly. Editor: Amy Baker
FE Now
01458 830033
www.feonline.net
4pa. Editor: Sara Clay
Gair Rhydd
029 2078 1400
www.cardiffstudents.com
Weekly. Editor: Sally Strachan
Governors' News
0121 643 5787
www.nagm.org.uk
5pa. Editor: Gillian Stunell
Higher Education Review
020 8341 1366
www.highereducationreview.com
3pa. Editor: John Pratt
ICT for Education
020 8334 1600
www.ictforeducation.co.uk
Monthly. Editor: Ian Delaney
The Lecturer
020 7837 3636
www.natfhe.org.uk
5pa. Editor: Midge Purcell
London Student
020 7664 2054
Fortnightly during term
Editor: Alexi Duggins
LSE Magazine
020 7955 7582
www.lse.ac.uk
2pa. Editor: Judith Higgin
The Magic Key
020 8433 2883
Monthly. Editor: Stephanie Cooper
Nursery Education
01926 887799
www.scholastic.co.uk
Monthly. Editor: Sarah Sodhi
Nursery World
020 7782 3120
www.nurseryworld.co.uk
Weekly. Editor: Liz Roberts
Open Learner
01223 400359
www.nec.ac.uk
Website. Editor: Jo McGowan
Oxford Today
01865 280545
www.oxfordtoday.ox.ac.uk
3pa. Editor: Georgina Ferry
Report
020 7930 6441
www.askatl.org.uk
10pa. Editor: Heather Pinnell
Right Start
020 7878 2338
www.rightstartmagazine.co.uk
Bi-monthly. Editor: Lynette Lowthian
Scottish Educational Journal
0131 225 6244
www.eis.org.uk
5pa. Editor: Simon MacAulay
Sesame
01908 652451
www.open.ac.uk/sesame
6pa. Editor: Debbie Dixon
Special Schools Guide
020 7970 4000
www.centaur.co.uk
Annual. Editor: Derek Rogers
Student Direct
0161 275 2943
www.student-direct.co.uk
Weekly during term
Editor: Alexa Gainsbury
The Teacher
020 7380 4708
www.teachers.org.uk
8pa. Editor: Mitch Howard
Teaching Today
0121 453 6150
www.teachersunion.org.uk
5pa. Editor: Joe Devo
Times Educational Supplement
020 7782 3000
www.tes.co.uk
Weekly. Editor: Bob Doe
Times Higher Education Supplement
020 7782 3000
www.thes.co.uk
Weekly. Editor: John O'Leary

Farming

Arable Farming
01728 687970
18pa. Editor: Dominic Kilburn
British Dairying
01438 716220
Monthly. Editor: Judie Allen

Crop Production Magazine
01743 235594
www.cpm.gb.net
Monthly Feb–Oct
Editor: Angus McKirdy

Crops
020 8652 3500
www.reedbusiness.co.uk
Fortnightly. Editor: Charles Able

Dairy Farmer
01732 377273
16pa. Editor: Peter Hollinshead

Farmers Guardian
01772 799411
Weekly. Editor: Liz Falkingham

Farmers Weekly
020 8652 4911
www.fwi.co.uk
Weekly. Editor: Stephen Howe

Feed International
01730 261951
www.wattnet.com
Monthly. Editor: Clay Gill

Living Earth
0117 914 2434
www.soilassociation.org
3pa. Editor: Elisabeth Winkler

NFU Horticulture
020 7331 7359
www.nfuonline.com
3pa. Editor: Martin Stanhope

Poultry International
01730 261951
www.wattnet.com
Monthly. Editor: Jackie Linden

Scottish Farmer
0141 302 7700
Weekly. Editor: Alistair Fletcher

Tractor & Machinery
01959 541444
www.kelsey.co.uk
Monthly. Editor: Peter Love

Health and social care

Ambulance Today
0151 708 8864
www.eclipsepublishing.co.uk
Quarterly. Editor: Declan Heneghan

Arthritis News
020 7380 6500
www.arthritiscare.org.uk
Bi-monthly. Editor: Kate Llewelyn

BMJ
020 7387 4499
www.bmj.com
Weekly. Editor: Richard Smith

CareandHealth
0870 907 7773
www.careandhealth.com
Weekly
Managing editor: Marcia White

Community Care
020 8652 3500
www.communitycare.co.uk
Weekly. Editor: Polly Neate

Doctor
020 8652 3500
www.doctorupdate.net
Weekly. Editor: Charles Creswell

GP
020 8267 5000
www.gponline.com
Weekly. Editor: Colin Cooper

Health Service Journal
020 7874 0253
www.hsj.co.uk
Weekly. Editor: Alastair McLellan

Hospital Doctor
020 8652 3500
www.hospital-doctor.net
Weekly. Editor: Mike Broad

The Lancet
020 7611 4100
www.lancet.com
Weekly. Editor: Richard Horton

Medeconomics
020 8267 5000
www.gponline.com
Monthly. Editor: Julian Tyndale-Biscoe

MIMS
020 8267 5000
www.gponline.com
Monthly. Editor: Colin Duncan

NHS Magazine
0113 306 0000
www.nhs.uk/nhsmagazine
10pa. Editor: Richard Spencer

Nursing Standard
020 8423 1066
www.nursing-standard.co.uk
Weekly. Editor: Jean Gray

Nursing Times
020 7874 0500
www.nursingtimes.net
Weekly. Editor: Rachel Downey

The Pharmaceutical Journal
020 7572 2420
www.pjonline.com
Weekly. Editor: Olivia Timbs

The Practitioner
020 7921 8113
www.practitioner-i.co.uk
Monthly. Editor: Gavin Atkin

The Psychologist
0116 252 9573
www.bps.org.uk/publications/thepsychologist.cfm
Monthly. Editor: John Sutton

Pulse
020 7921 8102
www.pulse-i.co.uk
Weekly. Editor: Phil Johnson

RCN Bulletin
020 8423 1066
www.nursing-standard.co.uk
Weekly. Editor: Ken Edwards

Update
020 8652 8878
www.doctorupdate.net
Fortnightly. Editor: Andrew Baxter

▶▶ see also **disability**, page 325

Law

Law Society Gazette
020 7320 5820
www.lawgazette.co.uk
Weekly. Editor: Jonathan Ames

The Lawyer
020 7970 4000
www.centaur.co.uk
Weekly. Editor: Catrin Griffiths

Legal Week
020 7566 5600
www.legalweek.com
Weekly. Editor: John Malpas

Media Lawyer
01229 716622
www.medialawyer.press.net
Bi-monthly. Editor: Tom Welsh

Police

Constabulary Magazine
01932 820123
Monthly. Editor: Chris Lock

Police Magazine
020 8335 1000
www.polfed.org
Monthly. Editor: Metin Enver

Police Review
020 8276 4701
www.policereview.com
Weekly. Editor: Katriona Marchant

Property

The Estate Agent
01926 496800
www.naea.co.uk
10pa. Editor: June Warner

Estates Gazette
020 7411 2540
www.reedbusiness.co.uk
Weekly. Editor: Peter Bill

Facilities Management Journal
020 8771 3614
www.fmarena.com
Monthly. Editor: Mark Povey

Facilities Management UK
0161 683 8032
www.worldsfair.co.uk
Bi-monthly. Editor: Mike Appleton

Scotland's New Home Buyer
0131 556 9702
4pa. Editor: Anna Baird

Retail and catering

Asian Trader
020 7928 1234
www.gg2.net
Fortnightly. Editor: R Solanki

Caterer and Hotelkeeper
020 8652 3500
www.caterer-online.com
Weekly. Editor: Mark Lewis

Caterer and Licensee News
01202 552333
Monthly. Editor: Peter Adams

Catering Update
020 8652 3500
www.reedbusiness.co.uk
Monthly. Editor: Kathy Bowry
Class
01293 610442
www.william-reed.co.uk
Monthly. Editor: Paul Wootton
Convenience Store
01293 610277
www.william-reed.co.uk
Fortnightly. Editor: Sonia Young
DNR
020 7240 0420
www.dnrnews.com
Weekly. Editor: Jon Birmingham
Drapers
020 7391 3300
Weekly. Editor: Eric Musgrave
Food Manufacture
01293 610231
www.foodmanufacture.co.uk
Monthly. Editor: Rick Pendrous
Footwear News (FN)
020 7240 0420
www.footwearnews.com
Weekly. Editor: Michel Atmore
Forecourt Trader
01293 610219
www.william-reed.co.uk
Monthly. Editor: Merrill Boulton
The Franchise Magazine
01603 620301
www.franchise-group.com
8pa. Editor: Stuart Anderson
The Grocer
01293 610259
www.grocertoday.co.uk
Weekly. Editor: Julian Hunt
Hospitality
0161 236 2782
www.excelpublishing.co.uk
Monthly. Editor: Lucy Bryson
Independent Retail News
01322 660070
www.irn-talkingshop.co.uk
Fortnightly. Editor: Richard Siddle
Leisure Report
01293 846569
www.martin-info.com
Monthly. Editor: Mel Flaherty
MA Scotland
0131 247 7542
www.william-reed.co.uk
Fortnightly. Editor: Mairi Clarke
MBR
01293 610268
www.william-reed.co.uk
Monthly. Editor: Mary Carmichael
Morning Advertiser
01293 610344
www.william-reed.co.uk
Weekly. Editor: Andrew Pring
Off Licence News
01293 610344
www.william-reed.co.uk
Weekly. Editor: Graham Holter
Party Times
020 7819 1200
www.partytimes.biz
Bi-monthly. Editor: Andrew Maiden
The Pub Business
01474 574435
www.dewberry-boyes.co.uk
Monthly. Editor: Tim Palmer
PubChef
01293 610487
www.william-reed.co.uk
Monthly. Editor: Jo Bruce
Publican
020 8565 4200
www.thepublican.com
42pa. Editor: Lorna Harrison
The Restaurant Business
01474 574436
www.dewberry-boyes.co.uk
Monthly. Editor: David Foad
Shopping Centre
01293 610294
www.william-reed.co.uk
Monthly. Editor: Pat Morgan
Supermarket News
020 7240 0420
www.supermarketnews.com
Weekly. Editor: David Orgel
The Trader
01202 445320
www.thetrader.co.uk
Monthly. Editor: Angela Boyer
Women's Wear Daily (WWD)
020 7240 0420
www.wwd.com
Daily. Editor: James Fallon
WWDBeautyBiz
020 7240 0420
www.wwd.com
9pa. Editor: Peter Born

Science

Clinical Laboratory International
01442 877777
www.cli-online.com
8pa. Editor: Alan Barclay
Nature
020 7833 4000
www.nature.com
Weekly. Editor: Phil Campbell
New Scientist
020 7331 2735
www.newscientist.com
Weekly. Editor: Jeremy Webb
Science
01223 326500
www.sciencemag.org
Weekly. Editor: Andrew Sugden

Technology

Computer Bulletin
01793 417474
www.bcs.org
Bi-monthly. Editor: John Cavanagh
Computer Business Review
020 7919 5000
www.cbronline.com
Monthly. Editor: Jason Stamper
Computer Weekly
020 8652 8979
www.reedbusinessinformation.co.uk
Weekly. Editor: Karl Schneider
Computing
020 8606 7505
www.computing.co.uk
Weekly. Editor: Mike Gubbins
Developer Network Journal
0117 930 0255
www.dnjonline.com
Website. Editor: Matt Nicholson
Information Age
020 7612 9300
www.infoconomy.com
Monthly. Editor: Kenny MacIver
IT Week
020 8606 7505
www.itweek.co.uk
Weekly. Editor: Toby Wolpe
Scientific Computing World
01223 477411
www.europascience.com
Bi-monthly. Editor: Tom Wilkie

Travel trade

Travel Trade Gazette
020 7921 8029
www.ttglive.com
Weekly. Editor: John Welsh
Travel Weekly
020 8652 8230
www.travelweekly.co.uk
Weekly. Editor: Martin Lane

Transport

Aerospace International
020 7670 4300
www.aerosociety.com
Monthly. Editor: Richard Gardner
Air International
01780 755131
www.airinternational.com
Monthly. Editor: Malcolm English
Automotive Engineer
020 7304 6809
www.pepublishing.com
Monthly. Editor: William Kimberley
Autowired
01565 872107
www.autowired.co.uk
Daily. Editor: Barry Hook
Commercial Motor
020 8652 3252
Weekly. Editor: Andy Salter
Flight International
020 8652 3842
www.flightinternational.com
Weekly. Editor: Kate Sarsfield
Helicopter International
01934 822524
www.helidata.rotor.com
Bi-monthly. Editor: Elfan ap Rees
Motor Trader
01322 660070
www.motortrader.co.uk
Weekly. Editor: Curtis Hutchinson
Motor Transport
020 8652 3284
www.reedbusinessinformation.co.uk
Weekly. Editor: Andrew Brown

Professional Motor Mechanic
01923 237799
www.hamerville.co.uk
11pa. Editor: Nick Holt

Rail
01733 282718
www.greatmagazines.co.uk
Fortnightly. Editor: Nigel Harris

Railnews
020 7278 6100
www.railnews.co.uk
Monthly. Editor: David Harding

Truck
020 8652 3251
Monthly. Editor: Peter Shakespeare

Truck & Driver
020 8652 3251
Monthly. Editor: Dave Young

Trucking
01452 317753
www.truckingmag.co.uk
Monthly. Editor: Richard Simpson

Trade press

Best Sellers
Newtrade Publishing
11 Angel Gate, City Road
London EC1V 2SD
020 7689 3357
robin.parker@newtrade.co.uk
www.newtrade.co.uk
2pa. Consumer magazine data and ABC results. Editor: Robin Parker

CPU News
Commonwealth Press Union
17 Fleet Street, London EC4Y 1AA
020 7583 7733
cpu@cpu.org.uk
www.cpu.org.uk
6pa. In-house newspaper of the Association of Commonwealth Newspapers.
Editorial contact: Rosie Vlasto

The Journal
The Chartered Institute of Journalists
2 Dock Offices, Surrey Quays Road
London SE16 2XU
020 7252 1187
memberservices@ioj.co.uk
www.ioj.co.uk
Quarterly. reports the activities of the Institute and industry developments
Editor: Andy Smith

The Journalist
National Union of Journalists
Acorn House, 308–312 Gray's Inn Rd
London WC1X 8DP
020 7278 7916
timg@nuj.org.uk
www.nuj.org.uk
10pa. free to union members
Editor: Tim Gopsill

Magazine Retailer
Newtrade Publishing
11 Angel Gate, City Road
London EC1V 2SD
020 7689 3357
robin.parker@newtrade.co.uk
www.newtrade.co.uk
2pa. Information on magazine sales in all sectors. Editor: Robin Parker

Magazine World
FIPP
Queens House
55–56 Lincoln's Inn Field
London WC2A 3LJ
020 7404 4169
info@fipp.com
www.fipp.com
Quarterly. International consumer and b2b publishing trends.
Editor: Arif Durrani

Media Moves
Quantum Business Media
Quantum House, 19 Scarbrook Road
Croydon CR9 1LX
020 8565 4333
www.mediamoves.co.uk
Website. Online selection of jobs in the media industry.
Editorial contact: Kevin May

News from NewstrAid
Newstraid Benevolent Society
PO Box 306, Great Dunmow
Essex CM6 1HY
01371 874198
oldben@newstraid.demon.co.uk
www.newstraid.org.uk
Annual. Charity for the newspaper industry.
Editorial contact: Tansey Davis

Press Gazette
Quantum Business Media
Quantum House, 19 Scarbrook Road
Croydon CR9 1LX
020 8565 4448
pged@pressgazette.co.uk
www.pressgazette.co.uk
Weekly. Editor: Ian Reeves

Ulrich's Periodical Directory
Bowker
3rd Floor, Farringdon House
Wood Street, East Grinstead
West Sussex RH19 1UZ
01342 310450
sales@bowker.co.uk
www.ulrichsweb.com
Updated annually in print, quarterly on cd, monthly on website
International directory

►► **SEE OTHER CHAPTERS FOR MORE MEDIA TRADE PRESS**

Useful associations

Association of American Correspondents in London
c/o Time Life International
Brettenham House, Lancaster Place
London WC2E 7TL
020 7499 4080
elizabeth_lea@timemagazine.com

Association of British Science Writers (ABSW)
Wellcome Wolfson Building
165 Queen's Gate
London SW7 5HE
0870 770 3361
absw@absw.org.uk
www.absw.org.uk

Association of Freelance Writers
Sevendale House, 7 Dale Street
Manchester M1 1JB
0161 228 2362
fmn@writersbureau.com
www.writersbureau.com/resources.htm

Audit Bureau of Circulations (ABC)
Saxon House, 211 High Street
Berkhamsted
Hertfordshire HP4 1AD
01442 870800
marketing@abc.org.uk
www.abc.org.uk

Authors' Club
40 Dover Street, London W1S 4NP
020 7499 8581
circles@author.co.uk
www.author.co.uk

British Copyright Council
29–33 Berners Street
London W1T 3AB
01986 788122
secretary@britishcopyright.org
www.britishcopyright.org

British Guild of Beer Writers
68B Elmwood Rd
London SE24 9NR
020 8853 8585
peterhaydon@onetel.net.uk
www.beerguild.com

British Guild of Travel Writers
51B Askew Crescent
London W12 9DN
020 8749 1128
charlotte.c@virtualnecessities.com
www.bgtw.org

British Newspaper Library
The British Library
Newspaper Library, Colindale Avenue
London NW9 5HE
020 7412 7353
newspaper@bl.uk
www.bl.uk/catalogues/newspapers.html

British Society of Magazine Editors (BSME)
137 Hale Lane, Edgware
Middlesex HA8 9QP
020 8906 4664
admin@bsme.com
www.bsme.com

Broadcasting Press Guild
Tiverton, The Ridge, Woking
Surrey GU22 7EQ
01483 764895
torin.douglas@bbc.co.uk

Bureau of Freelance Photographers
Focus House, 497 Green Lanes
London N13 4BP
020 8882 3315
info@thebfp.com
www.thebfp.com

Campaign for Freedom of Information
Suite 102, 16 Baldwins Gardens
London EC1N 7RJ
020 7831 7477
admin@cfoi.demon.co.uk
www.cfoi.org.uk

Campaign for Press and Broadcasting Freedom
2nd Floor, Vi and Garner Smith House, 23 Orford Road
Walthamstow, London E17 9NL
020 8521 5932
freepress@cpbf.org.uk
www.cpbf.org.uk

Chartered Institute of Journalists
2 Dock Offices, Surrey Quays Road
London SE16 2XU
020 7252 1187
memberservices@ioj.co.uk
www.ioj.co.uk

The Critics' Circle
51 Vartry Road, London N15 6PS
info@criticscircle.org.uk
www.criticscircle.org.uk

Foreign Press Association in London
11 Carlton House Terrace
London SW1Y 5AJ
020 7930 0445
secretariat@foreign-press.org.uk
www.foreign-press.org.uk

Garden Writers' Guild
c/o Institute of Horticulture
14/15 Belgrave Square
London SW1X 8PS
020 7245 6943
gwg@horticulture.org.uk
www.gardenwriters.co.uk

Guild of Agricultural Journalists
Charmwood, 47 Court Meadow
Rotherfield, East Sussex TN6 3LQ
01892 853187
don.gomery@farmingline.com
www.gaj.org.uk

Guild of Food Writers
020 7610 1180
guild@gfw.co.uk
www.gfw.co.uk

Guild of Motoring Writers
39 Beswick Avenue
Bournemouth BH10 4EY
01202 518808
gensec@gomw.co.uk
www.guildofmotoringwriters.co.uk

International Newspaper Marketing Association
10300 North Central Expressway
Suite 467, Texas 75231 USA
00 1 214 373 9111
inma@inma.org
www.inma.org

Medical Writers' Group
The Society of Authors
84 Drayton Gardens
London SW10 9SB
020 7373 6642
info@societyofauthors.org
www.societyofauthors.org

National Union of Journalists
Acorn House, 308–312 Gray's Inn Rd
London WC1X 8DP
020 7278 7916
info@nuj.org.uk
www.nuj.org.uk

Newspaper Marketing Agency
Berkeley Square House
Berkeley Square, London W1J 6BD
020 7887 6112
enquiries@nmauk.co.uk
www.nmauk.co.uk

Newspaper Society
Bloomsbury House
74–77 Great Russell St
London WC1B 3DA
020 7636 7014
ns@newspapersoc.org.uk
www.newspapersoc.org.uk

Outdoor Writers' Guild
PO Box 118, Twickenham TW1 2LR
info@owg.org.uk
www.owg.org.uk

Periodical Publishers Association (PPA)
Queens House, 28 Kingsway
London WC2B 6JR
020 7404 4166
info1@ppa.co.uk
www.ppa.co.uk

The Picture Research Association
c/o 1 Willow Court, off Willow Street
London EC2A 4QB
chair@picture-research.org.uk
www.picture-research.org.uk

Press Complaints Commission
1 Salisbury Square
London EC4Y 8JB
020 7353 1248
complaints@pcc.org.uk
www.pcc.org.uk

Scottish Newspaper Publishers Association
48 Palmerston Place
Edinburgh EH12 5DE
0131 220 4353
info@snpa.org.uk
www.snpa.org.uk

Scottish Print Employers Federation and Scottish Daily Newspaper Society
48 Palmerston Place
Edinburgh EH12 5DE
0131 220 4353
info@spef.org.uk
www.spef.org.uk

Society of Editors
University Centre, Granta Place
Mill Lane, Cambridge CB2 1RU
01223 304080
info@societyofeditors.org
www.societyofeditors.org

Society of Women Writers & Journalists
swwriters@aol.com
www.swwj.co.uk

The Sports Journalists' Association of Great Britain
c/o Victoria House
Bloomsbury Square
London WC1B 4SE
020 7273 1589
petta.naylor@sportengland.org
www.sportsjournalists.co.uk

News and picture agencies Contacts

Key contacts

National Association of Press Agencies
41 Lansdowne Crescent
Leamington Spa
Warwickshire CV32 4PR
01926 424181
secretariat@napa.org.uk
www.napa.org.uk

24/7 Media (Photography)
200 St Andrews Road
Bordesley Village, Birmingham
West Midlands B9 4JG
0121 753 1329
Photographer covering news, sports, features, PR and commercial

7 Day Press
132 West Nile Street
Glasgow G1 2RQ
0141 572 0060
daypress@aol.com
www.7daypress.co.uk
Scottish sport

AFX News
Finsbury Tower
103–105 Bunnhill Row
London EC1Y 8TN
020 7422 4870
john.manley@afxnews.com
www.afxpress.com
Financial news, pan-European

Agence France-Presse, UK
78 Fleet Street, London EC4Y 1NB
020 7353 7461
london.bureau@afp.com
www.afp.com
Major agency

Airtime Television News
PO Box 258, Maidenhead SL6 9YR
01628 482763
info@airtimetv.co.uk
www.airtimetv.co.uk
Heathrow airport

Allscot News Agency
PO Box 6, Haddington EH41 3NQ
01620 822578
allscotnewsuk@compuserve.com
Scottish news

Anglia Press Agency
17A Whiting Street
Bury St Edmunds, Suffolk IP33 1NR
01284 702421
East Anglia, words and pictures

ANSA News Agency
Essex House, 12–13 Essex Street
London WC2R 3AA
020 7240 5514
ansalondra@yahoo.com
www.ansa.it
News worldwide

Apex News and Picture Agency
Priests Court, Main Road
Exminster, Exeter EX6 8AP
01392 824024
apex@apexnewspix.com
www.apexnewspix.com
South-west. All news

APTN
The Interchange, Oval Road
Camden Lock, London NW1 7DZ
020 7482 7400
aptninfo@ap.org
www.aptn.com
International newsgathering

Associated Press News Agency
12 Norwich Street
London EC4A 1BP
020 7353 1515
www.ap.org
Worldwide all news

Associated Sports Photography
21 Green Walk, Leicester LE3 6SE
0116 232 0310
asp@sports-photos.co.uk
www.sporting-heroes.net
Worldwide sports, politics, travel

Australian Associated Press
Associated Press Building
12 Norwich Street
London EC4A 1QJ
020 7353 0153
news.london@aap.com.au
www.aap.com.au
Overseas news to London & New York

Bellis News Agency
14B Kenelm Road
Rhos on Sea, Colwyn Bay
North Wales LL28 4ED
01492 549503
bellisd@aol.com
North Wales (excluding Deeside)

Big Picture Press Agency
50–54 Clerkenwell Road
London EC1M 5PS
020 7250 3555
picturedesk@bigpictures.com
www.bigpicturesphoto.com
Celebrities

Bloomberg LP
City Gate House
39–45 Finsbury Square
London EC2A 1PQ
020 7330 7500
newsdesk@bloomberg.net
www.bloomberg.com
Worldwide financial

Bournemouth News & Picture Service
1st Floor Offices
5–7 Southcote Road
Bournemouth BH1 3LR
01202 558833
news@bnps.co.uk
www.bnps.co.uk
News and features

Calyx Multimedia
41 Churchward Avenue
Swindon SN2 1NJ
01793 520131
richard@calyxpix.com
www.calyxpix.com
Stills, news and freelance cameraman

Canadian Press
Associated Press House
12 Norwich Street
London EC4 1QE
020 7353 6355
www.cp.org

Capital Press Agency
14 Canongate Venture
New Street, Edinburgh EH8 8BH
0131 652 3999
capitalnews@hemedia.co.uk;
capitalpix@hemedia.co.uk
www.hemedia.co.uk
Edinburgh, Lothians and Borders

Capital Pictures
85 Randolph Avenue
London W9 1DL
020 7286 2212
sales@capitalpictures.com
www.capitalpictures.com
International celebrities

Cassidy & Leigh Southern News Service
Exchange House, Hindhead Road
Hindhead GU26 6AA
01428 607330
denis@cassidyandleigh.com
News and pictures

Caters News Agency
Queens Gate, Suite 40
121 Suffolk Street Queensway
Birmingham B1 1LX
0121 616 1100
news@catersnews.com;
features@catersnews.com;
pix@catersnews.com
West Midlands news, featuring pictures and sport

Cavendish Press and CPMedia
3rd Floor, Albert House
17 Bloom Street
Manchester M1 3HZ
0161 237 1066
newsdesk@cavendish-press.co.uk
www.cavendish-press.co.uk;
www.cpmedia.co.uk
News & pictures

Celtic News
PO Box 26, Llangadog
Carmarthenshire SA19 9YR
01550 740 209
features@celticnews.co.uk
www.celticnews.co.uk
UK-wide features for nationals and magazines

Central News Network
Suite 7, 350 Main Street
Canelon, Falkirk FK1 4EG
01324 630505
jimdavisofcnn@aol.com
Central Scotland news features

Central Press Features
5th Floor, BEP Building
Temple Way, Bristol BS99 7HD
0117 934 3600
mail@central-press.co.uk
www.central-press.co.uk
Worldwide editorial syndication

Centre Press Agency
2 Clairmont Gardens
Glasgow G3 7LW
0141 332 8888
centrenews@hemedia.co.uk;
centrepix@hemedia.co.uk
www.hemedia.co.uk
Central and southern Scotland

Chapman & Page
Dengate House, Amber Hill
Boston PE20 3RL
01205 290477
chapmanpage@internett.demon.co.uk

Chester News Service
Linen Hall House, Stanley Street
Chester CH1 2LR
01244 345562
news@chesterstandard.co.uk
www.chesterstandardnow.co.uk
North Wales area

Chester Press Bureaux
Riverside House
Brymau 3 Trading Estate
River Lane Saltney
Chester CH4 8RQ
01244 678575
ron@chesterpb.freeserve.co.uk
Chester area

Computer Wire
Charles House
108–110 Finchley Road
London NW3 5JJ
020 7675 7000
kevin.white@computerwire.co.uk
www.computerwire.com
Worldwide IT index links

Copyline Scotland
Second Floor, 17 Queensgate
Inverness IV1 1DF
copylinescotland@aol.com
Scottish Highlands

Cotswold & Swindon News Service
Oxford House, 101 Bath Road
Swindon SN1 4AX
01793 485461
cotswin@stares.co.uk
www.stares.co.uk
Swindon area

Coventry News Service
7 Queen Victoria Road
Coventry CV1 3JS
024 7663 3777
adent@advent-communications.co.uk
www.advent-communications.co.uk
Coventry area

David Hoffman Photo Library
c/o BAPLA, 18 Vine Hill
London EC1R 5DZ
020 8981 5041
lib@hoffmanphotos.com
www.hoffmanphotos.com
Social issues in UK & Europe

DBSP
112 Cornwall Street South
Glasgow G41 1AA
0141 427 5344
stewart.mcdougall@btclick.com
Worldwide sport

DobsonAgency.co.uk
20 Seafield Avenue, Osgodby
Scarborough YO11 3QG
01723 585141
pix@dobsonagency.co.uk
www.dobsonagency.co.uk
Press and PR, around UK

Double Red Photographic
The Old School, Thorn Lane
Goxhill
Barrow upon Humber DN19 7JE
01469 531416
doublered@atlas.co.uk
www.doublered.co.uk
Motorsport photography

Dow Jones Newswires
10 Fleet Place, Limeburner Lane
London EC4M 7QN
020 7842 9900
djequitiesnews.london@dowjones.com
www.djnewswires.com
International financial news

DPA (German Press Agency)
30 Old Queen Street
St James's Park
London SW1H 9HP
020 7233 2888
london@dpa.com
www.dpa.com
Global media services

Dragon News & Picture Agency
21 Walter Road
Swansea SA1 5NQ
01792 464800
mail@dragon-pictures.com
www.dragon-pictures.com
All news & PR

Edittech International (IT News Agency)
5 Exeter Close
Chippenham SN14 0YG
01249 444416
elspethwales@aol.com
www.edittech.com
Articles and publications from US to Australia

Emirates News Agency
The Studio, 143 Lavender Hill
London SW11 5QJ
020 7228 1060
mia@mia.gb.com
www.mia.gb.com
News from Arab emirates

Empics Sports Photo Agency
Pavilion House, 16 Castle Boulevard
Nottingham NG7 1FL
0115 844 7447
info@empics.com
www.empics.com
Sports worldwide

Entertainment News
Dragon Court, 27–29 Mackin Street
London WC2B 5LX
020 7190 7795
info@entnews.co.uk
www.entnews.co.uk

Essex News Service
121 High Street
Witham CM8 1BE
01206 211413
perfect@essexnews.freeserve.co.uk
Essex area news

Evertons News Agency
Cavalier House
202 Hagley Road, Edgbaston
Birmingham B16 9PQ
0121 454 2931
clive.everton@talk21.com
News and pictures

Feature Story News
The Interchange, Oval Road
London NW1 7DZ
020 7485 0303
drewc@featurestory.com
www.featurestory.com
Domestic & international radio & TV stories

Ferrari Press Agency
7 Summerhill Road, Dartford
Kent DA1 2LP
01322 628444
news@ferraripress.com
www.ferraripress.com
Kent, south London, south Essex, East Sussex, Calais and Boulogne etc

Fleetline News Service
Southern House
1a Bedford Road, East Finchley
London N2 9DB
020 8444 9183
fleetlinenews@hotmail.com
Law courts, magistrates courts, appeals. Employment tribunals throughout London

Foresightnews
Dragon Court, 27–29 Mackin Street
London WC2B 5LX
020 7190 7799
info@foresightnews.co.uk
www.foresightnews.co.uk

Frank Ryan News Service
Cargenriggs, Islesteps
Dumfries DG2 8ES
01387 253700
smeddum@btinternet.com
South-west Scotland, general news and features

Freemans Press Agency
Raleigh House, 1 Mill Road
Barnstable EX31 1JQ
01271 324000
tonyfreemanpressagency@bp.com
www.bipp.com
All news, north Devon

Front Page News Agency
The Whitehouse
24 the Ridgeway, Astwood Bank
Worcestershire B96 6HT
01527 892123
saralain@btopenworld.com
www.frontpagenewsagency.co.uk
True life, human interest stories UK

Future Events News Service
FENS House, 8–10 Wiseton Road
London SW17 7EE
020 8672 3191
uk@fens.demon.co.uk
www.fens.com
Diary news service, UK/international. Entertainment and business

Getty Images
116 Bayham Street
London NW1 1OG
0800 376 7981
allsportlondon@gettyimages.com
www.gettyimages.com

Gloucestershire News Service
Maverdine Chambers
26 Westgate Street
Gloucester GL1 2NG
01452 522270
john.hawkins@glosnews.com
www.glosnews.com
Gloucester general news

Gosnay's Sports Agency
Park House, 356 Broadway
Horsforth, Leeds LS18 4RE
0113 258 5864
gosnays@aol.com

Government News Network
London
River Wall House, 157–161 Millbank
London SW1P 4RR
020 7217 3091
london@gnn.gsi.gov.uk
www.gnn.gov.uk
Government press office
West Midlands
Five Ways House
Islington Row Middleway
Birmingham B15 1SL
0121 626 2033
birmingham@gsi.gov.uk
www.gnn.gov.uk
East Midlands
Belgrave Centre, Stanley Place
Talbot Street, Nottingham NG1 5GG
0115 971 2780
nottingham@gnn.gov.uk
www.gnn.gov.uk
North-west
27th Floor, Sunley Tower
Picadilly Plaza, Manchester M1 4BD
0161 952 4500
manchester@gnn.gov.uk
www.gnn.gov.uk
All North-west, Carlisle to Stoke
North-east
Wellbar House, Gallowgate
Newcastle upon Tyne NE1 4TB
0191 202 3600
newcastle@gsi.gov.uk
www.gnn.gov.uk
Yorkshire & Humber
1st Floor, City House
New Station Street
Leeds LS1 4JG
0113 283 6599
leeds@gnn.gsi.gov.uk
www.gnn.gov.uk

Harrison Photography
37/39 Great Northern Street
Belfast BT9 7FJ
028 9066 3100
mail@harrisonphotography.co.uk
www.harrisonphotography.co.uk
All Northern Ireland. Business, PR, photography

Hayters Teamwork
Image House, Station Road
London N17 9LR
020 8808 3300
sport@haytersteamwork.com
www.haytersteamwork.co.uk
Home and international sports

IPS Photo Agency
21 Delisle Road
London SE28 0JD
020 8855 1008
info@ips-net.co.uk
Agents in Japan, Italy, Germany, Spain, France, Scandinavia

Independent Radio News (IRN)
ITN Radio, 200 Gray's Inn Road
London WC1X 8XZ
020 7430 4814
irn@itn.co.uk
www.irn.co.uk
National and international news

Independent Sports Network
London Television Centre
Upper Ground, London SE1 9LT
020 7827 7700
jane.tatnall@isntv.co.uk
www.Isntv.co.uk
UK sport transmissions

Islamic Republic News Agency (IRNA)
3rd Floor, Imperial Life House
390–400 High Road
Wembley, Middlesex HA9 6AS
020 8903 5531
irna@irna.com
www.irna.com
Islamic Republic news agency

Information Telegraph Agency of Russia (ITAR-TASS)
Suite 12–20, 2nd Floor, Morley House
314–320 Regent Street
London W1B 3BD
020 7580 5543
iborisenko@yahoo.co.uk
www.itar-tass.com
Russian business news agency

Jarrold's Press Agency
68 High Street, Ipswich IP1 3QJ
01473 219193
jarroldspress@cix.compulink.co.uk
Suffolk, north Essex, south Norfolk, East Anglia and football coverage

Jenkins Group
Berkeley House, 186 High Street
Rochester ME1 1EY
01634 830888
nickand marion@hotmail.com
PR worldwide

Jewish Chronicle News Agency
25 Furnival Street
London EC4A 1JT
020 7415 1500
marketing@thejc.com
www.thejc.com
Worldwide all news

JIJI Press
4th Floor, International Press Centre
76 Shoe Lane, London EC4A 3JB
020 7936 2847
edit@jiji.co.uk
www.jiji.co.jp
London economic news

John Connor Press Associates
57a High Street, Lewes BN7 1XE
01273 486851
news@jcpa.co.uk
News and features in Sussex

John Fairfax (UK)
1 Bath Street, London EC1V 9LB
020 7688 2777
linda@fairfaxbn.com
www.f2.com
Worldwide news

John Wardle Agency
Trafalgar House, 5 High Lane
Manchester M21 9DJ
0161 861 8015
iwhittell@aol.com
Sports agency nationwide

Kuwait News Agency (KUNA)
6th Floor, New Premier House
150 Southampton Row
London WC1B 5AL
020 7278 5445
kuwait@btclick.com
www.kuwait-info.com
News around the world

Kyodo News
5th Floor, 20 Orange Street
London WC2H 7EF
020 7766 4400
london@kyodonews.jp
www.kyodo.co.jp
Japan news, worldwide news

Lakeland Press Agency
16 Stonecroft, Ambleside
Lancashire LA22 0AU
01539 431749
craigwilson23@yahoo.co.uk
Cumbria/Lake District. All news and features

Lappas of Exeter
IVA House, 13 South Grange
Clyst Heath, Exeter
Devon EX2 7EY
01392 446670
lappas@freeuk.com
Devon, Cornwall, Somerset, Dorset

M&Y News Agency
65 Osborne Road, Southsea
Portsmouth PO5 3LS
023 9282 0311
mynews@dircon.co.uk
www.mynewsagency.co.uk
News, sports & pictures. Hants, Sussex, Dorset

M2 Communications
PO Box 475, Coventry CV1 1ZB
024 7623 8200
m2pw@m2.com
www.m2.com
Global all news

Maghreb Arabe Press
35 Westminster Bridge Road
London SE1 7JB
020 7401 8146
mapldn@aol.com
www.map.co.ma
North Africa, Middle East & Mediterranean. All news

Market News International
Ocean House
10–12 Little Trinity Lane
London EC4V 2AR
020 7634 1655
ukeditorial@marketnews.com
www.marketnews.com
International economics, politics and financial markets

Marshall's Sports Service
2 Newfield Drive
Kingswinford DY6 8HY
01384 274877
marshall@bham-sport.demon.co.uk
West Midlands sports

Masons News Service
Unit 2, Clare Hall, Parsons Green
St Ives, Cambs PE27 4WY
01480 302302
newsdesk@masons-news.co.uk
www.campix.co.uk
General news from East Anglia

Media Features
36 Holcroft Court, Carburton Street
London W1W 5DJ
020 7436 3678
leozanelli@aol.com
Worldwide press syndication

Mercury Press Agency
7th Floor, Cotton Exchange
Old Hall Street, Liverpool L3 9LQ
0151 236 6707
reporters@mercurypress.co.uk
Merseyside, Lancashire, Cheshire, parts of North Wales

National News Agency
4–5 Academy Buildings
Fanshaw Street, London N1 6LQ
020 7684 3000
news@nationalnews.co.uk
www.nationalpictures.co.uk
General news. London and South-east

News of Australia
1 Virginia Street, London E98 1NL
020 7702 1355
anne.wall@newsint.co.uk
www.news.com.au

News Team International
41–43 Commercial Street
Birmingham B1 1RS
0121 246 5511
commercial@newsteam.co.uk
www.newsteam.co.uk
Midlands, London news

Newsflash Scotland
1st Floor, Viewfield Chambers
Viewfield Place, Stirling FK8 1NQ
01786 477310
news@nflash.co.uk
www.newsflashscotland.com
Scotland

North News and Pictures
The Newgate Centre
69 Grainger Street
Newcastle upon Tyne NE1 5JE
0191 233 0223
pictures@northnews.co.uk;
news@northnews.co.uk
North-east England, Cumbria and borders

Northscot Press Agency
18 Adelphi, Aberdeen AB11 5BL
01224 212141
northnews@hemedia.co.uk;
northpix@hemedia.co.uk
www.hemedia.co.uk
Grampian and Highlands

Nunn Syndication
13a Shade Thames, Butlers Wharf
London SE1 2PU
020 7407 4666
production@nunn-syndication.com
www.nunn-syndication.com
London Press agency

Press Association (PA)
292 Vauxhall Bridge Road
London SW1V 1AE
020 7963 7000
information@pa.press.net
www.pa.press.net
National news agency of UK and Ireland; provider of real-time news and sports information and images

PA News Birmingham
312–313 The Custard Factory
Gibb Street, Digbeth
Birmingham B9 4AA
0121 224 7686
pa_birmingham@hotmail.com
www.pa.press.net

PA News Liverpool
PO Box 48, Old Hall Street
Liverpool L69 3EB
0151 472 2548
paliverpool@pa.press.net
www.pa.press.net

PA News Scotland
1 Central Quay, Glasgow G3 8DA
0870 830 6725
pascotland@pa.press.net
www.pa.press.net

Pacemaker Press International
787 Lisburn Road, Belfast BT9 7GX
028 9066 3191
david@pacemakerpressintl.com
www.pacemakerpressintl.com
Northern Ireland, Republic of Ireland

Parliamentary & EU News Service
19 Douglas Street, Westminster
London SW1P 4PA
020 7233 8283
info@parliamentary-monitoring.co.uk
www.parliamentary-monitoring.co.uk
Parliamentary news service

PPP News Service
109 Conway Road, London N14 7BH
020 8886 2721
wkastor@compuserve.com
Germany and its politics

Press Agency (Gatwick)
1a Sunview Avenue
Peacehaven BN10 8PJ
01273 583103
Gatwick & south coast, national press

Press Team Scotland
22 St John's Street, Coatbridge
Lanarkshire ML5 3EJ
01236 440077
news@pressteam.co.uk
Lanarkshire, Glasgow and West of Scotland

Press Trust of India
Suite 303, Radnor House
93–97 Regent Street
London W1B 4ET
020 7494 0602
ptilondon@aol.com
www.ptinews.com
Worldwide news and photos

Profile Group (UK)
Dragon Court
27–29 Macklin Street
London WC2B 5LX
020 7190 7777
info@profilegroup.co.uk
www.profilegroup.co.uk
Future events info and business leads

Racenews
85 Blackstock Road
London N4 2JW
020 7704 0326
racenews@compuserve.com
www.racenews.co.uk
Worldwide horse racing

Raymonds Press Agency
3rd Floor Abbots Hill Chambers
Gower Street, Derby DE1 1SD
01332 340404
news@raymondspress.com
Sports, news and photography

Reuters
85 Fleet Street, London EC4P 4AJ
020 7250 1122
robert.woodward@reuters.com
www.reuters.com
Worldwide news and features

Rex Features
18 Vine Hill, London EC1R 5DZ
020 7278 7294
rex@rexfeatures.com
www.rexfeatures.com
International & USA picture agency

Richard Harris News
Woody Glen, How Mill
Branton CA8 9JY
01228 670381
richardwjharris@aol.com
News in north Cumbria

Ross Parry Agency
40 Back Town Street
Farsley, Leeds LS28 5LD
0113 236 1842
newsdesk@rossparry.co.uk
www.rossparry.co.uk
Yorkshire, news features and photos

Russian Information Agency – Novosti (RIA-Novosti)
3 Rosary Gardens
London SW7 4NW
020 7370 3002
ria@novosti.co.uk
www.rian.ru
Russia

Scottish News Agency
Avian House, 4 Lindsay Court
Dundee Technology Park
Dundee DD2 1SW
01382 427035
g.ogilvy@scottishnews.com
East and central Scotland, Perthshire, Fife, Edinburgh, Lothians and Borders

Scottish News & Sport
15 Fitzroy Place, Glasgow G3 7RW
0141 221 3602
info@snspix.com
www.snspix.com
Scotland sport

Smith Davis Press
Queens Chambers
8 Westport Road, Burslem
Stoke on Trent ST6 4AW
01782 829850
smith-davis@smith-davis.co.uk
www.smith-davis.co.uk
Photography, graphic design and freelance journalists

Snowmedia Consultancy
Unit G4, Broadway Studio
28 Tooting High Street
London SW17 0RG
020 8672 9800
info@snowmedia.net
www.snowmedia.net
Nationwide lifestyle profiles on health and sport

Solent News and Photo Agency
23 Mitchell Point
Ensign Way, Hamble
Southampton SO31 4RF
023 8045 8800
news@solentnews.biz
www.solentnews.biz
Hants, Wilts, Isle of Wight news features for all media

Somerset News Service
3 Lewis Road, Taunton
Somerset TA2 6DU
01823 331856
somersetnews@boltblue.com
Contact: Richard Briers

Somerset Photo News
12 Jellalabad Court
The Mount, Taunton
Somerset TA1 3RZ
01823 282053, 07860 207333
somersetnews@boltblue.com
somersetphotonews@boltblue.com
Somerset

South Beds News Agency
Bramingham Park Business Centre
Enterprise Way, Bramingham Park
Luton, Beds LU3 4BU
01582 572222
south.b@virgin.net;
southbedsnews@btconnect.com
Herts, Beds, Bucks, Northants

South West News & Picture Service
Media Centre
Emma-Chris Way, Abbeywood Park
Bristol BS34 7JU
0117 906 6500
news@swns.com
www.swns.com
South-west general news, features and photos

Space Press News and Pictures
Bridge House, Blackden Lane
Goostrey, Cheshire CW4 8PZ
01477 533403
scoop2001@aol.com
Knutsford, Macclesfield, Crewe, Nantwich, Wilmslow, Alderley Edge, Northwich, Cheshire, Shropshire and North-west

Specialist News Services
27 Newton Street
London WC2B 5EL
020 7831 3267
desk@snsnews.co.uk
National. Consumer, media, city, travel and motor industry, advertising and marketing, new products, science and nature

Speed Media One
3 Kings Court, Horsham RH13 5UR
01403 259661
info@speedmediaone.co.uk
www.speedmediaone.co.uk
General news and features. Sport, sport development, education, local government

Sport & General Press Agency
63 Gee Street, London EC1V 3RS
020 7253 7705
info@alphapress.com
www.alphapress.com

Sportsphoto
20 Clifton Street
Scarborough YO12 7SR
01723 367264
library@sportsphoto.co.uk
www.sportsphoto.co.uk
All sport and entertainment, national and international

Tim Wood Agency
Press Room, Central Criminal Courts
London EC4M 7EH
020 7248 6858
Court cover at Old Bailey and Southwark and Knightsbridge crown courts

Tony Scase News Service
Little Congham House
Congham, Kings Lynn PE32 1DR
01485 600650
news@scase.co.uk
www.scase.co.uk
East Anglia news

TV News
Feature Story News
The Interchange
Oval Road, London NW1 7DZ
020 7485 0303
london.bureau@featurestory.com
www.fsntv.com
TV news for north America, south-east Asia, southern Africa

UK Press
Unit 27, The Limehouse Cut
46 Morris Road, London E14 6NQ
020 7515 3878
info@ukpress.com
www.ukpress.com
Europe/UK photography

Unique Entertainment News
50 Lisson Street, London NW1 5DF
020 7453 1650
amie.oconnor@unique.com
www.unique.com
Nationwide general news and features

Universal Pictorial Press & Agency
29–31 Saffron Hill
London EC1N 8SW
020 7421 6000
contacts@uppa.co.uk
www.uppa.co.uk
Press and worldwide commercial photography

Wales News & Picture Service
Market Chambers, St Mary's Street
Cardiff CF10 1AT
029 2066 6366
news@walesnews.com
www.walesnews.com
Wales. General news and features

Warwickshire News & Picture Agency
41 Lansdowne Crescent
Leamington Spa CV32 4PR
01926 424181
barrie@tracynews.co.uk
Midlands. General news, features and pictures

Wessex Features and Photos Agency
Neates Yard, 108 High Street
Hungerford RG17 0NB
01488 686810
news@britishnews.co.uk
www.britishnews.co.uk
Women's news, nationwide

West Coast News
Renaissance House, Parracombe
Barnstaple, Devon EX31 4QH
01598 763296
westcoast.news@dial.pipex.com
Devon, Cornwall, west Somerset

White's Press Agency
446 London Road
Heeley, Sheffield S2 4HP
0114 255 3975
newsdesk@press-agency.com
Men's sport, south Yorkshire

World Entertainment News Network
35 Kings Exchange
Tileyard Road, London N7 9AH
020 7607 2757
sales@wenn.com
www.wenn.com
Worldwide entertainment & photos

Xinhua News Agency of China
8 Swiss Terrace, Belsize Road
Swiss Cottage, London NW6 4RR
020 7586 8437
xinhua@easynet.co.uk
www.xinhuanet.com

Picture libraries

Key contacts

British Association of Picture Libraries and Agencies
18 Vine Hill, London EC1R 5DZ
020 7713 1780
enquiries@bapla.org.uk
www.bapla.org

Picture Research Association
Head Office, 2 Culver Drive
Oxted, Surrey RH8 9HP
020 7739 8544
pra@lippmann.co.uk
www.picture-research.org.uk

A1PIX Digital Picture Library
Finsbury Business Centre
40 Bowling Green Lane
London EC1R 0NE
020 7415 7045
london@a1pix.com
www.a1pix.com
Travel, business, lifestyle, children, nature, animals & illustrations. Hi-res download facility, personal search service

Advertising Archives
45 Lyndale Avenue
London NW2 2QB
020 7435 6540
suzanne@advertisingarchives.co.uk
www.advertisingarchives.co.uk
British and American press ads, magazine illustration

Allstar Picture Library
20 Clifton Street
Scarborough YO12 7SR
01723 367264
library@allstarpl.com
www.allstarpl.com
Worldwide sports, politics, travel

Alvey & Towers
Springboard centre
Mantle Lane, Coalville
Leicestershire LE67 3DW
01530 450011
alveytower@aol.com
www.alveyandtowers.com
Transport

Andes Press Agency
26 Padbury Court
London E2 7EH
020 7613 5417
apa@andespressagency.com
www.andespressagency.com
Travel and social documentary worldwide, Latin America, UK, Middle East

AP Photo Archive
12 Norwich Street
London EC4A 1BP
020 7427 4263
london_photolibrary@ap.org
www.apwideworld.com
Archive of global news agency

Art Directors & Trip Photo Library
57 Burden Lane, Cheam
Surrey SM2 7BY
020 8642 3593
images@artdirectors.co.uk
www.artdirectors.co.uk
Worldwide countries and religion

Artbank Illustration Library
114 Clerkenwell Road
London EC1M 5SA
020 8906 2288
info@artbank.com
www.artbank.com
Online library

Aviation Images – Mark Wagner
42B Queens Road
Wimbledon, London SW19 8LR
020 8944 5225
pictures@aviation-images.com
www.aviation-images.com
Aviation and aerial photography

Aviation Picture Library
116 The Avenue
West Ealing, London W13 8JX
020 8566 7712
avpix@aol.com
www.aviationpictures.com
Aviation pictures

Axel Poignant Archive
115 Bedford Court Mansions
Bedford Avenue
London WC1B 3AG
020 7636 2555
Rpoignant@aol.com
Anthropology, ethnography

BBC Picture Archives
Room B116, Television Centre
Wood Lane, London W12 7RJ
020 8225 7193
research-central@bbc.co.uk
www.bbcresearchcentral.com
Worldwide

BFI Stills, Posters and Designs
21 Stephen Street
London W1T 1LN
020 7957 4797
stills.films@bfi.org.uk
www.bfi.org.uk/collections/stills/index.html
Images, film and TV

British Library Picture Library
96 Euston Road
London NW1 2DB
020 7412 7614
imagesonline@bl.uk
www.bl.uk/imagesonline
Images/maps/historical and engravings

Bryan & Cherry Alexander Photography
Higher Cottage
Manston Sturminster, Newton
Dorset DT10 1EZ
01258 473006
alexander@arcticphoto.co.uk
www.arcticphoto.co.uk
Arctic and Antarctic specialists

Camera Press
21 Queen Elizabeth Street
London SE1 2PD
020 7378 1300
a.golding@camerapress.com
www.camerapress.com
Worldwide photographic library

Cephas Picture Library
Hurst House, 157 Walton Road
East Moseley, Surrey KT8 0DZ
020 8979 8647
pictures@cephas.co.uk
www.cephas.com
Wine and vineyards, whisky and brandy, food and drink

Chris Howes/Wild Places Photography
51 Timber Square
Cardiff CF24 3SH
029 2048 6557
photos@wildplaces.co.uk
Travel, topography and natural history, plus action sports and caving

Christie's Images
1 Langley Lane, Vauxhall
London SW8 1TJ
020 7582 1282
imageslondon@christies.com
www.christiesimages.com
Fine and decorative art

Chrysalis Images
The Chrysalis Building
Bramley Road, London W10 6SP
020 7314 1469
Tforshaw@chrysalisbooks.co.uk
www.chrysalisbooks.co.uk
History, transport, cookery, crafts, space

Collections
13 Woodberry Crescent
London N10 1PJ
020 8883 0083
collections@btinternet.com
www.collectionspicturelibrary.com
Britain and Ireland: people and traditional culture

Country Life Pictures/Library
Kings Reach Tower
Stamford Street, London SE1 9LS
020 7261 6337
camilla_costello@ipcmedia.com
www.countrylifelibrary.co.uk
Architecture, country pursuits, gardens, crafts, 1897 black and white pictures

David Hoffman Photo Library
c/o 18 Vine Hill
London EC1R 5DZ
020 8981 5041
info@hoffmanphotos.com
www.hoffmanphotos.com
Social issues, built from journalistic work since 1970s

Double Red Photographic
The Old School, Thorn Lane, Goxhill
Barrow upon Humber DN19 7JE
01469 531416
doublered@atlas.co.uk
www.doublered.co.uk
Motorsport photography

E&E Picture Library (Religion)
Beggars Roost, Wooltackle Hill
Smeeth, Kent TN25 6RR
01303 812608
isobel@picture-library.freeserve.co.uk
www.picture-library.freeserve.co.uk
World religion

Edifice
14 Doughty Street
London WC1N 2PL
020 7242 0740
info@edificephoto.com
www.edificephoto.com
Buildings and architecture

Education Photos
April Cottage, Warners Lane
Albury Heath, Guildford
Surrey GU5 9DE
01483 203846
johnwalmsley@educationphotos.co.uk
www.educationphotos.co.uk
Education, work, homes, signs

English Heritage Photo Library
23 Saville Row, London W15 2ET
020 7973 3338
celia.sterne@english-heritage.org.uk
www.english-heritage.org.uk
English Heritage properties, locations

Exile Images
1 Mill Row, Weston Hill Road
Brighton, East Sussex BN1 3SU
01273 208741
pics@exileimages.co.uk
www.exileimages.co.uk
Refugees, protest, asylum seekers, conflict. Middle East, Balkans, south-east Asia

ffotograff
10 Kyveilog Street, Cardiff CF11 9JA
029 2023 6879
ffotograff@easynet.co.uk
www.ffotograff.com
Travel, exploration, arts, architecture, culture, Wales, Middle East, Far East

Financial Times Pictures
1 Southwark Bridge
London SE1 9HL
020 7873 3000
photosynd@ft.com
www.ft.com
Business

Fogden Wildlife Photographs
16 Lochetort, North Uist
Western Isles HS6 5EU
01876 580245
susan.fogden@virgin.net
www.fogdenphotos.com
Natural history

Food Features
5 Upper Church Lane
Farnham, Surrey GU9 7PW
01252 735240
frontdesk@foodpix.co.uk
www.foodpix.co.uk
Food and drink

Forest Commission Life Picture Library
231 Corstorphie Road
Edinburgh EH12 7AT
0131 314 6411
neil.campbell@forestry.gsi.gov.uk
www.forestry.gov.uk
Image bank of the Forestry Commission

Frank Lane Picture Agency
Pages Green House, Pages Green
Wetheringsett, Suffolk IP14 5QA
01728 860789
pictures@flpa-images.co.uk
www.flpa-images.co.uk
Natural history, environment, pets, weather

Galaxy Picture Library
34 Fennels Way, Flackwall Heath
High Wycombe, Bucks HP10 9BY
01628 521338
robin@galaxypix.com
www.galaxypix.com
Astronomy & the sky

Garden Picture Library
Unit 12 Ransome Dock
35 Parkgate Road
London SW11 4MT
020 7228 4332
info@gardenpicture.com
www.gardenpicture.com
Gardening

Geo Aerial Photography
4 Christian Fields
London SW16 3JZ
020 8764 6292
geo.aerial@geo-group.co.uk
www.geo-group.co.uk
Aerial photographs

Geo Science Features Picture Library
6 Orchard Drive, Wye
Kent TN25 5AU
01233 812707
gsf@geoscience.demon.co.uk
www.geoscience.demon.co.uk
Natural science and natural history

Geoslides Photography
4 Christian Fields, London SW16 3JZ
020 8764 6292
geoslides@geo-group.co.uk
www.geo-group.co.uk
Landscape and human interest

Getty Images
116 Bayham Street
London NW1 1OG
0800 376 7981
allsportlondon@gettyimages.com
www.gettyimages.com

Heather Angel/Natural Visions
6 Vicarage Hill
Farnham, Surrey GU9 8HJ
01252 716700
info@naturalvisions.co.uk
www.naturalvisions.co.uk
Online images of worldwide wildlife

Holt Studios International
The Courtyard, 2499 High Street
Berkshire RG17 0NF
01488 683523
library@holt-studios.co.uk
www.holt-studios.co.uk
World agriculture and horticulture. Wildlife, pests and diseases

Hutchison Picture Library
65 Brighton Road, Shoreham on sea
West Sussex BN43 6RE
01273 440113
library@hutchisonpictures.co.uk
www.hutchisonpictures.co.uk
Worldwide contemporary images

Images of Africa Photobank
11 The Windings, Lichfield
Staffordshire WS13 7EX
01543 262898
info@imagesofafrica.co.uk
www.imagesofafrica.co.uk
130,000 images of 20 African countries

Imperial War Museum Photograph Archive
Lambeth Road, London SE1 6HZ
020 7416 5333
photos@iwm.org.uk
www.iwm.org.uk/collections/photos.htm
20th- and 21st-century conflicts

International Photobank
Unit D, Roman Hill Business Park
Broadmayne, Dorset BT2 8LY
01305 854145
peter@internationalphotobank.co.uk
www.internationalphotobank.co.uk
400,000 travel images

Jacqui Hurst
66 Richford Street, London W6 7HP
020 8743 2315
jacquih@dircon.co.uk
www.jacquihurstphotography.co.uk
Designers and applied artists, regional food producers and markets

James Davis Worldwide
65 Brighton Road, Shoreham on sea
West Sussex BN43 6RE
01273 452252
library@eyeubiquitous.com
www.eyeubiquitous.com
Travel collection

Jessica Strang Photo Library
504 Brody House, London E1 7LQ
020 7247 8982
jessica.strang@virgin.net
Architecture, interiors and gardens

Jim Henderson Photographer & Publisher
Crooktree Lincardine O'Neil
Aboyne, Aberdeenshire AB34 4JD
01339 882149
JHende7868@aol.com
www.jimhendersonphotography.com
Aberdeenshire, aurora borealis, ancient Egypt

Forthill Gifford
Nr Salisbury, Wiltshire SP3 6QW
01747 820320
cleare@btinternet.com
www.mountaincamera.com
Landscapes for UK and worldwide – mountains and trekking

John Heseltine Archive
Mill Studio, Frogmarsh Mills
South Woodchester
Gloucester GL5 5ET
01453 873792
john@heseltine.co.uk
www.heseltine.co.uk
Landscapes, architecture, food and travel: Italy and UK

David King Collection
90 St Pauls Road, London N1 2QP
020 7226 0149
davidkingcollection@btopenworld.com
www.bapla.org
Soviet Union and other Communist movements

Kos Picture Source
7 Spice Court, Plantation Wharf
London SW11 3UE
020 7801 0044
images@kospictures.com
www.kospictures.com
Water-based images

Lebrecht Music and Art
58b Carlton Hill, London NW8 0ES
020 7625 5341
pictures@lebrecht.co.uk
www.lebrecht.co.uk
Musical and art images

Lesley & Roy Adkins
10 Acre Wood, Whitestone
Exeter EX14 2HW
01392 811357
mail@adkinsarchaeology.com
www.adkinarchaeology.com
Archaeology and heritage

London Aerial Photo Library
Studio D, West Entrance
Fairoaks Airport, Chobham
Surrey GU24 8HU
01276 855997
info@londonaerial.co.uk
www.londonaerial.co.uk
Aerial imagery (oblique and vertical) covering most UK

Mary Evans Picture Library
59 Tranquil Vale, Blackheath
London SE3 0BS
020 8318 0034
pictures@maryevans.com
www.maryevans.com
Historical images

Monitor Picture Library
The Forge, Roydon
Essex CM19 5HH
01279 792700
info@monitorpicturelibrary.com
www.monitorpicturelibrary.com
UK and international personalities

Morocco Scapes
Seend Park, High Street
Seend, Wiltshire SN12 6NZ
01380 828533
chris@realmorocco.com
www.realmorocco.com
Collection of Moroccan material

National History Museum of London Picture Library
National History Museum
Cromwell Road, London SW7 5BD
020 7942 5041
nhmpl@nhm.ac.uk
www.nhm.ac.uk/piclib
History of London, museum's collection

National Galleries of Scotland Picture Library
The Dean Gallery, Belford Road
Edinburgh EH4 3DS
0131 624 6260
picture.library@nationalgalleries.org
www.nationalgalleries.org
Art

National Portrait Gallery Picture Library
39–45 Orange Street
London WC2H 0HE
020 7312 2474
picturelibrary@npg.org.uk
www.npg.org.uk
Portraits

Nature Photographers
West Wit, New Road, Little London
Tadley, Hampshire RG26 5EU
01256 850661
info@naturephotographers.co.uk
www.naturephotographers.co.uk
Worldwide natural history

Nature Picture Library
Broadcasting House
White Lady's Road
Bristol BS8 2LR
0117 974 6720
info@naturepl.com
www.naturepl.com
Wildlife

Neil Williams Classical Collection
22 Avon Hockley, Tamworth
Staffordshire B77 5QA
01827 286086
neil@classicalcollection.co.uk
Classical music

NHPA
57 Hish Street, Ardingley
West Sussex RH17 6TB
01444 892514
nhpa@nhpa.co.uk
www.nhpa.co.uk
Natural history

Novosti Photo Library
3 Rosary Gardens
London SW7 4NW
020 7370 1873
photos@novosti.co.uk
www.rian.ru
Russia

PA Photos
292 Vauxhall Bridge Road
London SW1V 1AE
020 7963 7990
paphotos@pa.press.net
www.paphotos.com
News, entertainment, celebrity and sports

Panos Pictures
Studio 3B, 34 Southwark Street
London SE1 1UN
020 7234 0010
pics@panos.co.uk
www.panos.co.uk
Documentary library specialising in developing world

Papilio
155 Station Road, Herne Bay
Kent CT6 5QA
01227 360996
library@papiliophotos.com
www.papiliophotos.com
Natural history subjects worldwide

Phil Sheldon Golf Picture Library
40 Manor Road, Barnet
Herts EN5 2JQ
020 8440 1986
phil@philsheldongolfpics.co.uk
www.philsheldongolfpics.co.uk
More than 500,000 images of golf

Photofusion
17a Electric Lane, London SW9 8LA
020 7733 3500
library@photofusion.org
www.photofusion.org
Contemporary social and environmental issues

Photogold
40 Dunvegan Place, Polmont
Falkirk FK2 0NX
01324 720038
sales@photogold.co.uk
www.castlepictures.com
Scotland

Photolibrary Wales
2 Bro-Nant, Church Road
Pentrych, Cardiff CF15 9QC
029 2089 0311
info@photolibrarywales.com
www.photolibrarywales.com
Wales

PPL Photo Agency
Bookers Yard, The Street, Walberton
Arundel, West Sussex BN18 0PF
01243 555561
ppl@mistral.co.uk
www.pplmedia.com
Watersports, sub-aqua, business, travel, Sussex scenes and historical images

Premaphotos Wildlife
1 Kirland Road, Bodmin
Cornwall PL30 5JQ
01208 78258
library@premaphotos.co.uk
www.premaphotos.com
Natural history worldwide

Raymond Mander & Joe Mitchenson Theatre Collection
Jerwood Library of Performing Arts
Trinity College of Music
King Charles Court
Old Royal Naval College
London SE10 9JF
020 8305 4426
rmangan@tcm.ac.uk
www.mander-and-mitchenson.co.uk
Theatre

Redferns Music Picture Library
7 Bramley Road, London W10 6SZ
020 7792 9914
info@redferns.com
www.musicpictures.com
Music photography

Retna Pictures
West Complex, Pinewood Studios
Pinewood Road, Iver Heath
Bucks SL0 0NH
01753 785450
ukinfo@retna.com
www.retna.com
Celebrity music and lifestyle

Retrograph Archive Collection
10 Hanover Street, Brighton
East Sussex BN2 9SB
01273 687554
retropix1@aol.com
www.retrograph.com
Vintage consumer advertising, art, decorative art

Robbie Jack Photography
45 Church Road, London W7 3BD
020 8567 9616
robbie@robbiejack.com
www.robbiejack.com
Performing arts

Robert Forsythe Picture Library
16 Lime Grove, Prudhoe
Northumberland NE42 6PR
01661 834511
robert@forsythe.demon.co.uk
www.forsythe.demon.co.uk
Original ephemera and transparencies of industrial and transport heritage

Royal Air Force Museum Hendon
Grahame Park Way, Hendon
London NW9 5LL
020 8205 2266
hendon@rafmuseum.org
www.rafmuseum.org.uk/
History of aviation

Royal Collection Photographic Services
Windsor Castle, Berkshire SL4 1NJ
01753 868286
photoservices@royalcollection.org.uk
www.the-royal-collection.org.uk
Royal family

RSPB Images
POBox 7515, Billericay
Beds CM11 1WR
01268 711471
rspb@thatsgood.biz
www.rspb-images.com
Wildlife

RSPCA Photolibrary
Wilberforce Way, South Water
Horsham, West Sussex RH13 9RS
0870 754 0150
pictures@rspcaphotolibrary.com
www.rspcaphotolibrary.com
Natural history

S&O Mathews Photography
Little Pit Place, Brighstone
Isle of Wight PO30 4DZ
01983 741098
oliver@mathews-photography.com
www.mathews-photography.com
Gardens, plants and landscapes

Science & Society Picture Library
Science Museum, Exhibition Road
London SW7 2DD
020 7942 4400
piclib@nmsi.ac.uk
www.nmsi.ac.uk/piclib/
Science museum, national railway museum; photography, film and television

Skishoot-Offshoot
Hall Place, Upper Woolcott
Hampshire RG28 7TY
01635 255527
skishootsnow@aol.com
www.skishoot.net
Winter sports

Skyscan Photolibrary
Oak House, Coddington
Cheltenham
Gloucestershire GL54 5BY
01242 621357
info@skyscan.co.uk
www.skyscan.co.uk
Aviation & aerial sports

Snookerimages (Eric Whitehead Photography)
25 Oak Street, Windermere
Cumbria LA23 1EN
015394 48894
eric@snookerimages.co.uk
www.snookerimages.co.uk
Snooker

SOA Photo Library
Lovelly Farm, Dark Lane
St Gregory, Taunton TA3 6EU
0870 333 6062
info@soaphotoagency.com
www.soaphotoagency.com
Humour, sports, travel, modern European

Still Moving Picture Company
1c Castlehill, Doune
Edinburgh FK16 6BU
01786 842790
info@stillmovingpictures.com
www.stillmovingpictures.com
Scotland and sport

Still Pictures Photolibrary
199 Shooters Hill Road
London SE3 8UL
020 8858 8307
info@stillpictures.com
www.stillpictures.com
Environment, nature, social and third-world issues

Stockfile
5 High Street, Sunningdale
Berkshire SL5 0LX
01344 872249
info@stockfile.co.uk
www.stockfile.co.uk
Mountain biking and cycling

Sylvia Cordaiy
45 Rotherstone, Devizes
Wiltshire SN10 2DD
01380 728327
info@sylvia-cordaiy.com
www.sylvia-cordaiy.com
160 countries, from obscure to stock images

The National Archives
Kew, Richmond, Surrey TW9 4DU
020 8876 34444
image-library@nationalarchives.gov.uk
www.nationalarchives.gov.uk
British and colonial history

True North Photo Library
26 New Road, Hebden Bridge
West Yorkshire HX7 8ER
07941 630420
john@trunorth.demon.co.uk
Landscape and life of the North

Ulster Museum Picture Library
Botanic Gardens, Belfast BT9 5AB
028 9038 3000
patricia.mclean.um@nics.gov.uk
www.ulstermuseum.org.uk
Art, archaeology, ethnography, natural history, Irish history

V&A Images
Victoria & Albert Museum
South Kensington, London SW7 2RL
020 7942 2966
vaimages@vam.ac.uk
www.vandaimages.com
Design imagery

Valley Green
Barn Ley, Valley Lane, Buxhall
Stowmarket IP14 3EB
01449 736090
pics@valleygreen.co.uk
Perennials

Vaughan Williams Memorial Library
Cecil Sharpe House
Regents Park Road
London NW1 7AY
020 7485 2206
library@efdss.org
www.efdss.org
Traditional music and culture

VinMag Archive
Vin May House, 84–90 Digby Road
London E9 6HX
020 8533 7588
piclib@vinmag.com
www.vinmagarchive.com
20th-century history. Books, newspapers, posters, adverts, photos, film, ephemera

Waterways Photo Library
39 Manor Court Road
Hanwell, London W7 3EJ
020 88401659
watphot39@aol.com
www.waterwaysphotolibrary.com/
Inland waterways

World Pictures
25 Gosfield Street
London W1W 6HA
020 7437 2121
worldpictures@btinternet.com
www.worldpictures.co.uk
Travel

York Archaeological Trust Picture Library
Cromwell House, 13 Ogleforth
York YO1 7FG
01904 663000
enquiries@yorkarchaeology.co.uk
www.yorkarchaeology.co.uk
Archaeology in York area

Media monitoring

BBC Monitoring
Marketing Dept, Caversham Park
Reading RG4 8TZ
0118 948 6289
marketing@mon.bbc.co.uk
www.monitor.bbc.co.uk
News, information and comment gathered from mass media around the world

BMC Extreme Information
89 Worship Street, London E2A 2BF
020 7377 1742
info@extremeinformation.com
www.extremeinformation.com
European press monitoring

CIS Information Services
16 Hatton Wall, London EC1N 8JH
020 7242 5886
info@cisclip.co.uk
www.cisclip.com
Press monitoring service

Daryl Willcox Publishing
Melrose House, 42 Dingwall Road
Croydon CR9 2DX
0870 774 0777
info@dwpub.com
www.dwpub.com
Information services for journalists and PR

DigiReels Media Monitoring
45 Fouberts Place
London W1F 7QH
020 7437 7743
info@digireels.co.uk
www.digireels.co.uk
Online database of TV, radio, poster and press ads

Durrants Press Cuttings
Discovery House
28–42 Benner Street
London EC1Y 8QE
020 7674 0200
contact@durrants.co.uk
www.durrants.co.uk
All print media plus internet, newswire and broadcast monitoring

International Press-Cutting Bureau
224–236 Walworth Road
London SE17 1JE
020 7708 2113
ipcb2000@aol.com
National, provincial, trade, technical and magazine press

John Frost Newspapers
22b Rosemary Avenue, Enfield
Middlesex EN2 0SS
020 8366 1392
andrew@johnfrostnewspapers.com
www.johnfrostnewspapers.co.uk
Original newspapers and press cuttings

Ludvigsen Library
Scoles Gate, Hawkedon
Bury St Edmonds IP29 4AY
01284 789246
library@ludvigsen.com
www.ludvigsen.com
Photographic archive and research facilities for writers and publishers

Media Tenor
Kurt-Schumacher-Strasse 2
D-53113 Bonn, Germany
00 49 228 93 444 31
f.blase@innovatio.de
www.mediatenor.com
Analysis of new and traditional media content

Melanie Wilson
72 High Street, Syston
Leicester LE7 1GQ
0116 260 4442
melaniewilson@bigfoot.com
Research service across all media; free worldwide booksearch service

PA News Library
The Press Association
292 Vauxhall Bridge Road
London SW1V 1AE
020 7963 7000
palibrary@pa.press.net
www.pa.press.net
Digital library

Parliamentary Monitoring Services
19 Douglas Street
London SW1P 4PA
020 7233 8283
info@parliamentary-monitoring.co.uk
www.parliamentary-monitoring.co.uk/
Confidential monitoring and research services

Romeike Media Intelligence
Romeike House, 290 Green Lanes
London N13 5TP
0800 289543
info@romeike.com
www.romeike.com
Monitors all media; back research; analysis and editorial summary service

Television Research Partnership (TRP)
Nightingale Lodge, East Reach
Taunton TA1 3EN
01823 424260
partners@trponline.co.uk
www.trponline.co.uk
Media measurement information

TV

Good news for the television industry: more TV is being watched than at any stage in the past decade. According to a Trends in Television report from the Institute of Practitioners in Advertising, viewers watched an average of four hours' television a day in the first quarter of 2004 – matching levels last seen in the first quarter of 1993. The rise is attributed to the growing audience for digital channels: in March and April 2004 total multichannel audience share exceeded that of any terrestrial channel for two consecutive months, for the first time ever.

The television landscape is still dominated by three major players. There is the BBC, the main public service broadcaster, still fresh from its mauling in the Hutton report (see next page); BSkyB, the main satellite broadcaster; and now ITV plc, the biggest commercial terrestrial broadcaster, which was formed in 2004 by the mergers of the two biggest ITV franchise holders, Carlton and Granada. The two smaller terrestrial channels are the semi-public Channel 4 and the downmarket Five; these flirted with each other about a possible merger.

Hundreds of other channels are available on the digital television platforms: that is, satellite, cable and digital terrestrial. There are also hundreds of independent production companies, which compete with broadcasters' own programme-making divisions; and post-production houses, which compete with companies' in-house facilities.

With the exception of the BBC, television is regulated by Ofcom – the watchdog organisation formed by the merger of the two former television regulators, the ITC and the Broadcasting Standards Commission, and three other bodies in December 2003. The BBC, for its part, does submit statements of its programme policy to Ofcom, but is regulated by its governors.

Television audiences are measured by Barb, the Broadcasters Audience Research Board.

Analogue terrestrial ownership

BBC	BBC1, BBC2	publicly owned; board of governors answerable to government
ITV	ITV Anglia, ITV Border, ITV Central, ITV Granada, ITV London, ITV Meridian, ITV Wales, ITV West, ITV Westcountry, ITV Yorkshire, Tyne Tees TV GMTV (75%)	ITV plc
	Grampian, Scottish	Scottish Media Group
	Ulster	Ulster TV
	Channel	Channel TV
Channel 4	Channel 4, S4C	semi-public
Channel 5	Five	RTL, owned by Bertelsmann

The BBC

The BBC is the nation's public broadcaster. In television, it runs the two national terrestrial channels, BBC1 and BBC2; two free-to-air digital channels, BBC3 and BBC4; a rolling news service, BBC News 24; and other channels including children's services and BBC Parliament. It has its own programme-making departments, and a division called BBC Resources which provides production and post-production support both internally and on a commercial basis. It also has extensive interests in radio, new media and, commercially, magazines.

It has, however, been a traumatic year for the corporation. Already facing criticism over its **commercial and new media activities**, and fighting to save the **licence fee** as its main source of funding, it was hit for six in January by the **Hutton report**, which found it to be almost entirely at fault over the Kelly affair; that is, the high-level, long-running row with Downing Street that culminated in the death of a BBC source, the government weapons scientist Dr David Kelly. The crisis led to the resignations of both the director general, Greg Dyke, and the chairman of governors, Gavyn Davies, mass protests among BBC staff, a divisive internal review, and ultimately a new start as two popular ex-Channel 4 men, Michael Grade and Mark Thompson, were appointed to the two top jobs.

Hutton: verdict and fallout

The Hutton report, in January 2004, was a body blow to BBC journalism. For the best part of 2003, the corporation – led from the front by its then director general, Greg Dyke, and his board of governors – had stood by claims made by BBC Radio 4 correspondent Andrew Gilligan that, according to its source, the government had "sexed up" a dossier into Iraqi weapons capabilities (see box for the full background) and inserted a claim that Iraq could use weapons of mass destruction within 45 minutes when it probably knew that the claim was false. When that source, Dr David Kelly, was outed by the government and was found dead, there was a public inquiry. The resulting report by Lord Hutton – that Gilligan's claims were "unfounded", the editorial system "defective" – led to the biggest crisis the corporation had faced in decades.

First came the **resignations**. The chairman of the governors, Gavyn Davies, quit on the day of the report, hoping that would draw a line under events. Not so. Despite widespread criticism from the press – see box – the crisis deepened. On the night of January 28, Greg Dyke, the director general, handed in his resignation to the governors; he said later that he expected it to be rejected. But with Davies gone, the resignation was accepted by the remaining governors, effectively forcing Dyke out, a move as unpopular as it was startling. Dyke announced his departure in an email to staff next day; and up to 900 staff at Television Centre immediately took to the streets to demand his reinstatement, shouting "We Want Greg" and "Bring Back Greg".

Perhaps buoyed by that support, Dyke did not go quietly. "We were shocked that it was so black and white," he said of the report on an interview on GMTV next morning. "We knew mistakes had been made by us but we didn't believe they were only by us." He even went so far as to attack it in the clearest terms: "There are points of law in there where he is quite clearly wrong." Dyke later signed a book deal with HarperCollins, rumoured to be worth between £500,000 and £1m; readers

■ Hutton: the background

From the BBC's perspective, the David Kelly affair started on May 22, 2003, when Andrew Gilligan, then defence correspondent for BBC Radio 4's Today programme, met Mr Kelly in the lobby of a London hotel. There the two men discussed the justification for war in Iraq; and, particularly, a September 2002 government dossier which claimed incorrectly that Iraq was able to deploy weapons of mass destruction "within 45 minutes". At 6:07am on May 29, as a result of his conversation with Dr Kelly, Gilligan made two damaging allegations live on Today. In a conversation with the presenter John Humphrys, he reported that according to his source – then unnamed – the government "probably, erm, knew that that 45-minute figure was wrong"; and that Downing Street ordered it to be "sexed up".

When Gilligan expanded on his allegations in the Mail on Sunday – naming Alastair Campbell, Tony Blair's then PR boss, as the man responsible for inserting "unreliable" information into the dossier – Downing Street went on the counter-attack. Blair's spokesman listed what he called a series of inaccuracies in Gilligan's report; but the BBC, citing "unprecedented" pressure from Number 10, stood by its story. For almost a month, neither side budged. Then on July 4, the government said an unnamed official had come forward to say he was the BBC's source; and within a few days, the MoD was confirming to any journalist who guessed correctly that it was Dr Kelly. On July 15, Dr Kelly told a foreign affairs committee that Gilligan's claims were "not a factual record" of his views.

Two days later, Dr Kelly was found dead in woods near his home, and Lord Hutton subsequently found that he had committed suicide. He was buried on August 6.

The public inquiry led by Lord Hutton had a brief but inexact remit: to investigate the "circumstances surrounding" Dr Kelly's death. It did so by calling nearly 90 witnesses – including the prime minister, the director general of the BBC, Greg Dyke, the chairman of governors, Gavyn Davies, and senior figures in the intelligence services – and by looking at thousands of pages of emails, letters and memos. Unprecedentedly, all the evidence was posted on the internet: which meant, in theory, that anyone with a few spare hours or days on their hands could come to a view themselves. Many did.

The press, for its part, came to wildly differing conclusions. While the anti-Blair papers (the Mail, the Mail on Sunday) reported every scrap of evidence that was damaging in any way to the government, the pro-Blair camp (the Sun, the Times) reported every scrap that was damaging to the BBC. And there was plenty to fuel both schools of thought. The inquiry heard how the dossier had been drafted and redrafted in the weeks leading up to publication, and from those in public service who told of concern about the role of "spin merchants" and the "tendency ... to over-egg" intelligence claims. On the other hand, Gilligan came under fire for making notes on a palmtop computer, while BBC editors had privately criticised his "loose use of language and lack of judgment". The final report, most commentators thought, would come down heavily on both sides.

But that was not what happened. "Hutton report LEAKED," boasted the Sun newspaper on January 28 2004, the day Hutton was to reveal his verdict. "Tony Blair is today sensationally cleared of any 'dishonourable or underhand' conduct leading to the suicide of tragic scientist David Kelly... Lord Hutton's long-awaited report ... also exonerates ex-Downing Street media boss Alastair Campbell ... But the document is a devastating indictment of the BBC and its defence correspondent Andrew Gilligan..."

Hutton's report ran to 740 pages, but its effect was exactly as the Sun reported. Citing a narrow remit, the law lord had refused to be drawn on intelligence issues; but Gilligan's key allegations about the dossier, he said, were "unfounded". Saying the BBC should have vetted Gilligan's story more thoroughly, he described the editorial system as "defective". For the government he reserved one minor criticism: that they should have told David Kelly that they were going to release his name if a journalist suggested it.

Almost as soon as the report was released, Mr Campbell put the knife in. Mr Campbell, who had himself quit in September, said that if similar official criticisms had been aimed at it as had been made of the BBC, there would have been "several resignations at several levels". He was soon to get his wish: Mr Davies resigned on the day of the report, Mr Dyke was forced out the day after; and the third to leave, on January 30, was Andrew Gilligan.

were warned to "expect fireworks". He was later backed by the BBC's senior legal adviser, Glenn del Medico, who went so far as to call Lord Hutton's report "biased"; and Davies later criticised the government for leading a "witch hunt" against the corporation.

Without its leaders, though, the BBC itself back-pedalled. On January 30 Andrew Gilligan resigned, becoming the third scalp in three days. The same day Lord Ryder, acting chairman of the governors, issued an **apology**: "On behalf of the BBC I have no hesitation in apologising unreservedly for our errors and to the individuals whose reputations were affected by them." It was a humiliating climbdown, and galling for those staff whose sympathies lay with Dyke.

With deputy director general Mark Byford at the helm, the BBC began its own **internal review** into what went wrong. That review brought its own divisions: staff told MediaGuardian that hearings resembled a kangaroo court; and in April, it was reported that three of the most senior managers – director of television Jana Bennett, director of radio Jenny Abramsky, and director of drama Alan Yentob – asked Byford to stop the process on the basis that it was tearing staff apart. When the review finally reported back in May, it denied that editorial systems had been defective; instead it put the blame on Gilligan, saying he had veered from his agreed script.

Nevertheless a further review, conducted by the former BBC executive Ron Neil in June, focused on lessons to learn from the whole affair. It attempted to define the corporation's core journalistic values; it recommended a **journalism training college** – measures to which the corporation agreed. Neil also said BBC news programme editors should be able to demand that journalists name their sources before broadcasting stories – a move that raised concerns at the National Union of Journalists.

Also in June, Mark Thompson – the new director general who, as chief executive of Channel 4, turned the station back into profit at the

BBC protest: staff in Manchester demonstrating a week after the Hutton verdict

PA

cost of more than 200 jobs – warned that the corporation would have to change "more rapidly and radically over the next three to five years than at any previous point in its history". He began by **downsizing the executive committee** from 17 members to nine; instead setting up three boards to oversee creative output, commercial activities and journalism. In the most notable appointment, Mark Byford was brought in over the head of the then director of news, Richard Sambrook, to chair the journalism board – thus bringing national news, regional news and the World Service under the same leadership. Finally, in July, Sambrook became head of the World Service, while Helen Boaden was promoted to director of news.

In July, the BBC announced a long-awaited change in its complaints procedures – saying it would set up a corrections website, and a weekly feedback programme on which editors would defend their decisions to the public.

Finally, also in July, came the **Butler report** into the intelligence surrounding the Iraq war, which appeared to confirm Gilligan's central claim that the September dossier was indeed "sexed up" – but not his stuttering remark that Downing Street "probably knew" the 45-minute claim was false. Gilligan said he felt "substantially vindicated" by the Butler report; while Dyke was even firmer, saying he would defend his decision to back Gilligan for ever.

"Dr Kelly told Andrew Gilligan that the document had been 'sexed up' and one of the examples of it having been 'sexed up'; the most significant example was the 45-minute claim," Dyke told Channel 4 News. "Here, we are told today, with the Butler report saying that the 45-minute claim should not have been in the document without a set of caveats — caveats that were there in early drafts and disappeared. The question is who took out the caveats, and it appears that Butler doesn't tell us and nobody is owning up."

■ Hutton: the press reaction

The Hutton inquiry was designed to get to the bottom of the row between the BBC and the government that culminated in the death of David Kelly. But judging by the reaction of the press in the days and weeks after the report – in particular with regard to the law lord's narrow interpretation of his remit — the inquiry could not be said to have ended the debate.

"Whitewash?" asked the Independent, on an otherwise blank front page; the verdict bordered "on what looks like naivete", said Donald Macintyre in the same paper; it "stinks to high heaven", said Paul Routledge in the Daily Mirror; "Blair without flaw – official!", laughed Simon Hoggart in the Guardian; while in the same paper on February 1, four out of five lawyers questioned said the judgment would give grounds for appeal were his inquiry a court of law. Only the pro-Blair (or anti-BBC) Sun and Times thought Hutton had got it wholly right.

But there was support for Hutton too. The Telegraph, while acknowledging that there Hutton could have widened his remit, backed the inquiry's criticisms about the BBC. In the FT, Philip Stephens defended the law lord against his critics: "Had the inquiry pronounced the prime minister a liar, Lord Hutton's words would have been held up as if inscribed on a tablet of stone."

But it was Lord Hutton himself who had the last word – at a Commons select committee inquiry into, yes, public inquiries. "The duty of a judge is to decide on the issues before him without fear or favour and without having regard to the political consequences – and without having regard to the comments that may be made by editorial writers," he told the committee.

Charter review panel

- Sly Bailey, Trinity Mirror chief executive
- Tim Gardam, former Channel 4 programming chief
- Howard Davies, the director of the London School of Economics
- Alan Budd, provost of Queen's College, Oxford
- Janet Finch, the vice-chancellor of Keele University
- Alice Rawsthorn, director of the Design Museum, former FT journalist

Charter renewal and the licence fee

The first job for the BBC's new bosses was to defend the licence fee, the corporation's main system of funding. Every person who watches television must buy a TV licence, which cost £121 in 2004; this licence made up £2.8bn of the BBC's income in 2003 – with the rest coming from commercial enterprises (£645m) and the Foreign Office for the World Service (£243m). But the system is under threat, first because many of the BBC's competitors oppose it, and second because the BBC's charter – the government rulebook, effectively, which establishes how the corporation is funded and run – is up for renewal in 2006. The government's review of the charter renewal process is conducted by the Labour peer Lord Burns and a six-strong panel (left).

In its submission to the charter review panel, the BBC announced a nine-point plan for its future, in an effort to protect the licence fee. It promised to build a public digital archive of TV programmes; to "eliminate derivative and cynical programmes"; set up a new "governance unit"; establish tests of public value; ensure the corporation has the right scale and scope; invest in the regions; become more open and audience-focused; reduce overheads to 10 per cent of expenditure; and ensure partnerships it enters into are part of this overall strategy.

Commercial broadcasters, for their part, have used the charter renewal process to argue that the licence fee in its present form should

■ The paper trail

It was a BBC journalist, Gavin Esler, who said on Newsnight in July 2004 that the BBC has inquiries "the way some people have mice". As charter renewal approaches, the past year has certainly seen a confusing array of reports into the way the corporation conducts its affairs – here are most of them.

- **January 2004: Hutton report into David Kelly affair** Law lord deals blow to BBC journalism, saying editorial system is "defective"
- **April 2004: Ofcom review of public service broadcasting** Super-regulator Ofcom says licence fee should be shared with other broadcasters, says every BBC programme should set out public service value, and says corporation should work harder to be standard-bearer for excellence. It also wants to "take a lead" in regulating BBC content
- **May 2004: BBC review into Kelly affair** Editorial system defended; journalist Andrew Gilligan is blamed
- **June 2004: Neil report into lessons from Kelly affair** Internal team led by former BBC executive Ron Neil, redefines journalistic values and recommends journalism training college
- **July 2004: Graf report into BBC's online services** Former Trinity Mirror boss Philip Graf calls bbc.co.uk "impressive", but says online remit was too widely drawn, too broadly interpreted, and some sites should close. See new media chapter, page 209
- **July 2004: Internal overhaul of complaints system** BBC announces review of complaints process, led by Mark Byford and begun before Hutton verdict. Complaints website to be set up; feedback programme to be launched
- **July 2004: BBC manifesto** Corporation announces charter review submission. Nine-point plan promises to eliminate derivative programming, and to set out public service test for programmes
- **July 2004: annual report** Annual report promises independent review into BBC1, amid falling approval ratings from viewers; but it praises the "challenging" BBC2.
- **By August 2004: Gardam report into BBC's digital services** Former Channel 4 director of programmes, Tim Gardam, and academic Patrick Barwise, to report on BBC's digital TV and radio services

BBC directors' remuneration, 2003–04

		Salary	Bonus	Benefits	2004	2003
Current directors		**£k**	**£k**	**£k**	**£k**	**£k**
Mark Thompson	director general	salary not yet known				
Jenny Abramsky	radio and music		40	18	276	274
Jana Bennett	television		43	27	305	444*
Helen Boaden	news	salary not yet known				
Mark Byford	deputy director general	270	100	14	384	306
Stephen Dando	human resources	231	61	2	294	272
Carolyn Fairbairn	strategy and distribution	202	53	16	271	169
Rupert Gavin	BBC Worldwide	287	59	27	373	362
Ashley Highfield	new media	238	53	17	308	294
Pat Loughrey	nations and regions	205	46	36	287	280
Peter Salmon	sport	212	49	28	289	279
Richard Sambrook	World Service (formerly news)	235	43	14	292	287
John Smith	chief operating officer	238	63	26	327	300
Caroline Thomson	policy and legal; charter review	187	48	15	250	236
John Willis	factual and learning	183	47	91**	321	–
Alan Yentob (appointed Jun 2003)	creative director; drama, entertainment, children	235	45	21	301	321
Former directors						
Glenwyn Benson (resigned Jun 2003)	factual and learning	36	–	3	39	238
Andy Duncan (appointed Channel 4 boss, July 2003)	marketing	239	55	15	309	301
Greg Dyke † (resigned Jan 2004)	director general	316	–	5	321	464
Roger Flynn § (resigned 31 March 2004)	BBC Ventures	239	61	15	315	314
Michael Stevenson (resigned Jan 2003)	factual and learning	–	–	–	–	175
Incentive plans					**39**	**45**
Total		**4,006**	**866**	**390**	**5,301**	**5,361**

* includes £167,000 relocation package ** includes £72,440 relocation package † Received £488,416 payoff § Receives £301,625 payoff in Sep 2004
NB Directors are no longer automatic members of the executive committee

be scrapped. ITV, in particular, has advocated "top-slicing" the fee – allowing other broadcasters to bid for public money to produce public service programming. A more radical plan was commissioned by the Conservative party from the former chief executive of Five, David Elstein: he proposed scrapping the fee and replacing it with a subscription system. Tessa Jowell, the Culture secretary, dismissed the idea, saying it would lead to a "weak and insignificant" BBC. "We regard the BBC as a British success story," she said, "admired round the world and highly regarded at home."

Also at issue is the BBC's system of regulation. The media super-regulator, Ofcom, currently has no powers over the BBC governors; although the BBC does submit annual statements of its programme policy. The BBC's rivals, though, would like to see the BBC under Ofcom control. Ofcom, for its part, seems keen to take such control: in its ongoing review of public service broadcasting, it said it would assess whether the BBC should continue with "non-core" activities such as its commercial arm, BBC Worldwide – and even, surprisingly enough, its in-house production and post-production departments.

Digital broadcasting is another controversial area: the BBC spent more than £15 of every licence fee on digital projects, a spokesman said in 2003, as it prepares for the switch-off of the terrestrial analogue signal by 2010. As part of its submission for charter renewal, though, the BBC said the switch-off should be put back to 2012.

The BBC has spent 2004 trying to demonstrate its public service commitments in time for 2006. In February it launched an £8m series of prime time arts programming, to fight accusations that it is dumbing down. And there are also plans to move major services to Manchester; proposals which give a much-needed boost to broadcasting in the north-west, but which will not please many London-based workers.

"We regard the BBC as a British success story, admired round the world and highly regarded at home."

Tessa Jowell

Annual report

The BBC annual report, published in July 2004, was a chance for the new management team to set the agenda for the future. The report was more self-critical than usual. It also said BBC1 – which only had five of the top 20 programmes in 2003 – was to undergo an independent review to establish whether its balance of peak-time programmes was right. But there was praise for BBC2, which was judged to have offered a "more challenging mix of output than on BBC1", according to its remit.

The report also revealed that Greg Dyke had received more than £800,000 from the BBC over the year; his £488,416 came on top of £321,000 salary and benefits.

BBC programming and channels

If you include digital services, BBC channels attracted just over 37 per cent of the total television audience in the last four months of 2003. Terrestrial channels still accounted for the vast majority of this; but their share of the overall market has been slipping. BBC1's share was 24.9 per cent in the first quarter of 2004, down from 25.4 per cent in the previous quarter and from 26.5 per cent in the same period of the previous year; while BBC2's was 10.9 per cent, down from 11.2 per cent year on year.

BBC1's top programme of 2003 was again EastEnders, which reached a peak of 16.7 million. In 2004, football was a big ratings success – a peak of 20.7 million saw England's 2-1 defeat by France. It also shifted Saturday morning cartoons to BBC2 for summer 2004, replacing them with sport instead. The BBC also celebrated the return of Match of the Day on Saturday nights in 2004; but in April it lost the rights to the Boat Race to ITV, following a row with the organisers over plans to commercialise it. It later hung on to the Grand National and Six Nations rugby until the end of the decade.

In daytime, bosses axed Kilroy, the show presented by Robert Kilroy-Silk, because of anti-Arab remarks he made in the Sunday Express; and then axed its replacement, Now You're Talking, which was presented by Nicky Campbell and made by Mr Kilroy-Silk's production company.

In news, Kevin Bakhurst was confirmed as the editor of the 10 O'Clock News; while Mark Popescu was made permanent head of BBC News 24. Meanwhile, in April, Peter Barron – who launched BBC2's acclaimed If series of documentaries, was announced as the new editor of Newsnight.

In the same month in which it celebrated its 40th birthday, BBC2 lost its controller. Jane Root left to head the Discovery channel in the US in April 2004. The channel replaced her with the BBC4 controller Roly Keating, who promised to "build the next generation of unforgettable programmes" – with a particular focus on drama.

Award-winning programmes

Baftas

- *Drama series:* Buried (World Productions, Channel 4)
- *Drama serial:* Charles II, the Power and the Passion (BBC and A&E, BBC1)
- *Feature:* Wife Swap (RDF, Channel 4)
- *Current affairs:* The Secret Policeman (BBC1)
- *Sitcom:* The Office Christmas Special (BBC1)
- *Soap:* Coronation Street (Granada, ITV1)

Broadcast awards

- *Best popular factual, best new programme:* Wife Swap (RDF, Channel 4)
- *Best drama series or serial:* State of Play (BBC & Endor, BBC1)
- *Best documentary series:* Operatunity (Diverse, Channel 4)
- *Best comedy:* Bo Selecta (Talkback, Channel 4)
- *Best news programme:* Newsnight Blair special (BBC2)
- *Best independent production company:* RDF Media

National TV awards

- *Most popular comedy:* My Family (BBC1)
- *Most popular drama:* A Touch of Frost (ITV1)
- *Most popular soap:* EastEnders (BBC)
- *Most popular reality programme:* I'm A Celebrity … Get Me Out of Here! (ITV1)
- *Most popular entertainment programme:* Ant and Dec's Saturday Night Takeaway (Granada, ITV1)

Royal Television Society awards

- *Drama serial:* State of Play (BBC & Endor, BBC1)
- *Drama series:* Spooks (Kudos, BBC1)
- *Entertainment:* Little Britain (BBC3)
- *Single documentary:* The Secret Policeman (BBC1)
- *Soap:* Coronation Street (Granada, ITV1)
- *Sitcom and comedy drama:* The Office Christmas Special (BBC1)
- *Judges' award:* Greg Dyke, ex-director-general of the BBC

BBC4 replaced Keating by making a raid for Janice Hadlow, Channel 4's head of specialist factual. It was the second boss the BBC had poached from the channel in quick succession, after appointing Mark Thompson as director general. Ms Hadlow promised to bring more "big, ambitious, authoritative" factual shows to the channel, whose audience share remained low at about 0.2 per cent.

BBC3 achieved a vastly improved audience of about 0.6 per cent in 2004 – but it was criticised in the corporation's own annual report for tending "to be dominated by celebrity, relationship and lifestyle content".

BBC Technology row

The threat of strikes and blackouts loomed over the BBC in 2004, over its plans to sell off its IT division, BBC Technology, to Siemens in a 10-year, £2bn deal. The broadcasting union, Bectu, opposed the deal, in the belief that it contained a blueprint for cutting up to 350 jobs. It argued in a letter that BBC Technology constituted the nerve centre of the BBC and because it was "central to the convergence of broadcasting and information technology, it is a proposal which makes no sense".

BBC Technology provides services not only to its own channels, but to other clients including BSkyB, DirecTV and ESPN.

ITV

The ITV network is made up of 15 regional franchises; but in 2004, with the merger of the media giants Carlton and Granada, 11 of those franchises came under the control of a single company, ITV plc. The new company now controls 92 per cent of the ITV network – that is, all of the franchises in England and Wales, plus Border in Scotland – and accounts for more than 50 per cent of the television advertising market.

The £4bn merger had first been mooted in 2002, but was opposed by advertisers on the grounds that it was anti-competitive. The trade and industry secretary, Patricia Hewitt, agreed that there would indeed be adverse effects for advertisers; but she also said a merged ITV would give healthy competition to the BBC and BSkyB. So she let the deal go ahead, but said ITV had to guarantee to advertisers that they could pay proportionally for the same airtime if ITV's ratings declined. She also told Ofcom to appoint an adjudicator to referee disputes between ITV and advertisers; and she also required the company to treat the other ITV licensees – Scottish Media Group (which controls Scottish TV and Grampian), Ulster TV and Channel – fairly.

There is also a national breakfast-time service, GMTV – now controlled by ITV plc, after Scottish Media Group sold its 25 per cent stake in the company for £31m. ITV now owns 75 per cent, and the other 25 per cent is owned by Disney.

All change at the top

No sooner had the ITV merger been announced than the founder of one of the companies involved was out of a job. Michael Green, founder of Carlton, had been due to be chairman of the newly merged ITV; but he was ousted from the company by shareholders in November. Ostensibly, the move was payback for the ITV Digital disaster; but another major Carlton shareholder, Gary Channon, alleged that the move was actually part of a "de facto takeover" by Granada investors who may have bought

Charles Allen: chief executive of ITV plc

into their merger partner. But there was financial solace for Mr Green: he was given a golden handshake of £15m, it was announced in March, a pay-off that shareholders called "unreasonable and obscene".

With Green out, ITV appointed Sir Peter Burt, the former Bank of Scotland chief executive, as its chairman; and then began the process of restructuring. All Carlton and Granada bosses were made to reapply for their jobs; you stood a healthier chance of success, it seemed, if you worked at Granada. The company made Simon Shaps head of its main programme-making arm, now called Granada; created a single ITV News boss, Clive Jones, whose job is to oversee all 11 regional news services; and rebranded most of its regional franchises, merging LWT and Carlton into ITV London, headed by Christy Swords.

The bottom line

Even after the merger was complete, speculation surrounded the future of Charles Allen, the Granada chairman turned ITV chief executive. Mr Allen had, after all, collaborated on ITV Digital; so he was under particular pressure from investors to secure the company's long-term financial health – and in particular, to make £100m of cost savings in the first year.

The first result of that pressure was a brutal series of job cuts. First, 300 jobs went, mostly to create a merged sales house; then 175 jobs at Meridian, as network factual and sports production departments were closed in Southampton; and most controversially of all, up to 400 jobs at Central, including the closure of studios in Nottingham and the transfer of production and news departments to Birmingham. This last move led MPs as senior as Geoff Hoon and Kenneth Clarke to protest to the media watchdog, Ofcom; and when Ofcom did nothing about it, the culture select committee criticised it for accepting ITV's "glib" justifications. Gerald Kaufman, leader of the committee, also warned Ofcom not to misinterpret its remit: "Light touch is not the same as no touch," he said.

Mr Allen also hopes to persuade the government to reduce what it pays in licensing costs – what he calls its "super tax" burden.

The ex-BBC chairman, Gavyn Davies, said it was the rise of multichannel TV that meant ITV was losing money; and film-maker Roger Graef seemed to agree, criticising the company for agreeing to charge lower rates if its ratings went down. "ITV has made a rod for its own back," he told the Media Society in June, "or certainly a rod for the backs of people who want to make more challenging work. They've really trapped themselves on this unnecessary and impossible promise."

Overall, ITV plc said, advertising revenues were down 2 per cent year-on-year in 2003; but in the first quarter of 2004, television advertising as a whole was worth £880m, according to the Advertising Association,

Terrestrial audience share, year to June 2004

	2003–04	2002–03	2002*	2000–01	1999–2000	1998–99
BBC1	25.0	26.3	26.4	26.6	27.8	28.7
BBC2	10.7	11.3	11.3	10.9	10.6	11.2
ITV	23.4	24.0	24.6	28.2	30.2	31.4
Channel Four	9.8	9.6	9.9	9.9	10.1	9.9
Five	6.6	6.4	6.4	5.6	5.7	4.9

* figures cover six months to June 2002

Sources: ITC archive, Barb

a rise of 2.4 per cent in real terms year-on-year. Post-merger, ITV shares rose to between £1 and £1.50 – about half the value of Granada's shares in spring 2000, just before the advertising slump.

ITV programming

ITV1's audience share was stable in the first quarter of 2004; it held on to 23.9 per cent, the same share as in the first quarter of 2003, against a background of decline. It did, however, record 15 of the top 20 programmes in 2003. Its most notable performer was I'm A Celebrity ... Get Me Out Of Here!, whch topped 10 million night after night in February, peaking at 15.7 million at the end of the last show; by way of comparison, England's Euro 2004 football match against France peaked at 20.7 million in June. There was more reality success for Hell's Kitchen, starring Angus Deayton, Gordon Ramsay and a host of celebrities, which peaked at 8.1 million in June; but Trouble in Paradise flopped, dipping below 3 million and being moved out of peak time.

ITV also dominated in drama, with 14 of the top 20 shows in the genre in the first half of 2004. A notable newcomer was Life Begins, by Mike Bullen, the writer of Cold Feet, and starring Caroline Quentin.

ITV1's most consistent ratings success is Coronation Street, which secured a new £10m sponsorship deal with Cadbury in January 2004.

In a surprise coup in April, ITV poached Michael Parkinson from the BBC. Parky will go head-to-head with Match of the Day on Saturday nights from autumn 2004.

In news, ITV1's main evening news bulletin settled in at 10.30pm, ending its "News at When" tag; but the culture select committee said it deplored Ofcom's decision to allow it to broadcast so late.

Finally, the ITV3 digital channel was due to launch in September 2004, focusing on classic repeats. The channel is due to replace Granada Plus, a joint venture with BSkyB.

Channel 4

Channel 4 was created in 1982 as a publicly owned corporation, with a remit to foster diversity and innovation. After restructuring and job cuts in 2002, it tripled its profits in 2003, taking them to £45m, their highest level for five years; and ratings were also up, to 9.4 per cent year-on-year in the first quarter of 2004. It was a successful series of results for chief executive Steve Thompson, before he stepped down to become director general of the BBC.

Thompson's replacement was a surprise choice: Andy Duncan, the BBC's marketing boss, who had helped to make Freeview such a success. Before the BBC, Duncan had worked at Unilever, and is the first chief executive in Channel 4's history not to come from a broadcasting background.

Much of the talk this year, however, was of a possible merger between Channel 4 and its terrestrial rival, Five. How any deal might look is difficult to predict, as Channel 4 is barred by statute from being bought or sold; it would take a change in the law for a deal to go ahead. Another possibility is that the two companies' sales houses could merge: in December 2003, Ofcom removed the ban on Channel 4, Five and BSkyB selling advertising airtime jointly.

In February 2004, Ofcom appointed Luke Johnson as Channel 4

chairman. The head of news and current affairs, David Lloyd, stepped down after illness in October; but Andrew Newman and Sue Murphy, two executives who followed the director of television, Kevin Lygo, to Five in 2001, followed him back in 2003.

Channel 4 put its faith in Big Brother 5, devoting almost twice as much terrestrial airtime to the reality show as it did last year; as a result, it continued to attract the 16- to 34-year-olds who allow it to attract premium rates from advertisers. "Black Friday", on which the channel scheduled both the Big Brother 5 launch and the last ever episode of Friends, hit 8.9 million viewers at its peak. But Channel 4 also faced criticism over its sleep deprivation experiment show, Shattered, in which contestants competed for £100,000 by going without sleep for up to a week. The programme, produced by Endemol, was criticised by the British Association for Counselling and Psychotherapy as "misconceived and dangerous".

Channel 4 also signed a three-year deal for Richard & Judy, after competition from their former employers, ITV.

In news, Channel 4 News has won an international Emmy award for its coverage of the war in Iraq; while in sport, Channel 4 agreed to continue to show racing from Cheltenham, Newmarket, Kempton Park, Sandown, Haydock Park and six smaller courses.

The company's 4Ventures commercial arm, meanwhile, said in April 2004 that it was close to announcing a new interactive betting service, after the collapse of the Attheraces racing consortium.

Five

Five, a more downmarket national channel launched in 1997, is ultimately owned by German media giant Bertelsmann. It grew its ratings share again in the first quarter of 2004 – to 6.7 per cent, up from 6.4 per cent – but there is much speculation about its immediate future. Its main problem is its share of the advertising market, which at 8 per cent is now dwarfed by that of ITV. It could merge, or merge its sales house, with Channel 4 – Lord Hollick, chief executive of Five shareholder United Business Media, said discussions were being held about a deal – or it could even do a deal with BSkyB, a prospect which seemed more likely after Five handed its £35m, five-year news contract to Sky News (who appointed Mark Calvert as editor); and when Nick Milligan, Five's deputy chief executive, joined BSkyB as head of sales.

Good news for independents: controller Jane Lighting did also manage to secure an increased programming budget for 2004, some £170m.

Multichannel TV

The multichannel market has come of age. In April 2004, non-analogue channels beat BBC1 and ITV1 in the ratings for the second month in a row; they scored 26.1 per cent of the share, compared with 24.3 per cent for BBC1 and ITV1's 22.8 per cent. And by the end of March 2004, according to Ofcom, just over 13 million people (53 per cent) had access to digital TV, through satellite, cable or digital terrestrial; this compared to 50 per cent in the previous quarter and 43 per cent a year before. Each platform offers different pricing structures and different packages of channels, so see the table for a round-up of the providers and options.

The government has committed to switching off the terrestrial analogue signal by 2010, and is already working to set a precise date – a move which will only increase multichannel share. It has promised that all viewers who can receive analogue television now (more than 99 per cent) must be able to receive the main free-to-air channels digitally, and 95 per cent of people must be able to afford it. The BBC, for its part, wants the date put back to 2012.

Top 20 programmes, 2003

		Channel	Audience
1	Coronation Street	ITV1	19.4m
2	EastEnders	BBC1	16.7m
3	Only Fools and Horses	BBC1	16.2m
4	Millionaire Tonight Special	ITV1	16.1m
5	Michael Jackson Tonight Special	ITV1	15.3m
6	Heartbeat	ITV1	12.8m
7	I'm a Celebrity ... Get Me Out of Here!	ITV1	12.7m
8	Rugby World Cup Final	ITV1	12.7m
9	Billy Elliott	BBC1	12.7m
10	A Touch of Frost	ITV1	12.2m
11	The Royal	ITV1	12.0m
12	Emmerdale	ITV1	11.9m
13	Comic Relief	BBC1	11.7m
14	Rosemary & Thyme	ITV1	11.1m
15	Pop Idol: Final	ITV1	11.1m
16	Cold Feet	ITV1	10.7m
17	Prime Suspect 6	ITV1	10.5m
18	Man Utd v Real Madrid	ITV1	10.5m
19	Children In Need	BBC1	10.5m
20	The Bill	ITV1	10.4m

% of viewing (individuals): terrestrial channels/other	BBC1	BBC2	ITV	CH4	CH5	OTHERS (Cable/Sat/RTE)
1983	37.0	11.0	48.0	4.0	–	–
1988	38.0	11.0	42.0	9.0	–	–
1993	33.0	10.0	40.0	11.0	–	6
1998	29.5	11.3	31.7	10.3	4.3	12.9
2003	25.6	11.0	23.7	9.6	6.5	23.6

Source: Barb

BSkyB and satellite

Satellite services provided by BSkyB lead the way in digital TV. The company is a "vertically integrated" business: that is, it both charges viewers to access its subscription services – about 7.3 million of them in March 2004, paying a maximum of £40 a month – and also controls the platform, setting the price at which rival channels can access it. It is therefore in a position to offer more than 375 channels – of which 23, at the latest count, are Sky own-brand or spin-off channels – and still make £283m of pre-tax profits in the second half of 2003, up 84 per cent on the previous year.

But BSkyB is in the process of dynamic change. First, chief executive Tony Ball stepped down in September 2003, after four years in charge, and for a £10.7m pay-off; that cleared the way for James Murdoch, son of owner Rupert Murdoch, to step in at the age of 31. The succession was not short – after a protracted row, one in three shareholders voted against the appointment – but it was certainly sweet: James stands to make more than £10m in pay and bonuses before his 34th birthday.

There has also been a rethink of the company's digital strategy. The number of subscribers added to Sky Digital was just 66,000 in the first quarter of 2004, the second lowest growth rate since its launch, which leaves the company in danger of missing its target of 8 million subscribers by December 2005. There is also the threat from Freeview which, although co-owned by BSkyB, attracted more than 3.5 million subscribers for its free-to-view service by December 2003 (see below). So in June, James Murdoch unveiled plans for a free-to-air satellite package, with 116 TV and 81 radio channels. The service will be available for the cost of the installation of a satellite dish and receiver — around £150. The idea, it is thought, is to corral potential subscribers – especially the 27 per cent of viewers who cannot yet receive Freeview.

James Murdoch: Sky CEO at 31

There were also changes at the Sky-brand channels. Sara Ramsden, head of Sky One, left the channel in October 2003 – barely six months after the head of Sky Networks, Dawn Airey (responsible for all the Sky channels bar sport), had brought her in. Sky One's ratings were about 20 per cent down in the first three quarters of 2003 compared to 2002; and in September they were dismal, as the channel recorded its three lowest weekly audience share figures for the past nine years. Mark Sharman, Ms Airey's deputy, also left in November, to be replaced by Sophie Turner Laing. But there was good news in April 2004, when the channel bought an interview with Rebecca Loos, the woman alleged to have had an affair with David Beckham; more than 2 million people tuned in, the channel's fourth highest audience so far.

Exclusive rights to Premiership football have been one of the cornerstones of Sky Digital's success, so it was noteworthy when the European commission forced BSkyB to auction eight games a season to rival broadcasters; none of the bids it received, however, reached the minimum level Sky had agreed with the regulators. The commission, a goal down but not beaten, promised to force the broadcaster to break its monopoly in three years' time.

BSkyB shares, which had hit a £4 low in October 2002, recovered to a high of £7.50 at the beginning of 2004; only to slip back to £6 at the beginning of June.

Digital terrestrial

The success of Freeview in the past year has been extraordinary. The digital terrestrial service – launched in October 2002, as a joint venture between the BBC, BSkyB, and transmitter operator Crown Castle – offers 26 TV channels and 21 digital radio stations for the cost of a £50–£60 set-top box. In the first quarter of 2004, it increased the number of subscribers to 3.5 million; up from 2.9 million at the end of 2003, and 1.3 million in March 2003. Challenges remain, though; Freeview still only covered 73 per cent of Britain in June 2004.

Meanwhile a new company, Top-Up TV, hopes to cash in on the success of Freeview, by offering 10 new subscription channels to Freeview customers, including E4, at £7.99 a month plus a £20 installation charge. The company, set up by former Sky executives David Chance and Ian West, has targeted 250,000 subscribers within two years.

Cable

Cable television is a subscription-based service, usually offered in conjunction with telephone or internet, all broadcast through an analogue or digital cable into the home. Some 3.3 million people in the country subscribed in March 2004, mostly in urban or suburban areas. NTL, which broadcasts to homes in Oxford, Cambridge, Surrey, Hampshire and Teesside, had 2 million subscribers; losses fell by 63 per cent in the first quarter of 2004. President and chief executive Barclay Knapp quit in August 2003, taking home a £1.3m payoff after leading the firm out of bankruptcy. Meanwhile Telewest – which broadcasts to London and the south-east, the Midlands and parts of northern England and Scotland – had 1.3 million subscribers.

At the end of March 2004, 900,000 cable subscribers still received television through an analogue line.

Digital & multichannel TV: the options

	Main operators	Connected homes 31 Mar 04	Comments
Satellite	Sky Digital	6.96m*	subscription
	Free-to-view	231,000	Solus card viewers; ex-Sky
Digital terrestrial	Freeview	3.47m	free-to-view; requires digital-compatible TV or set-top box
Cable	NTL, Telewest	3.33m	subscription, usually including phone or internet
	of which digital:	*2.41m*	
ADSL		9,000	
Total digital		**13.07m**	
Total multichannel		**13.99m**	

*plus 318,000 homes in Republic of Ireland

Source: Ofcom

Multichannel audience share, year to June 2004

Channel	2003–04	2002–03	2002*	2000–01	1999–2000	1998–99
Animal Planet	0.2	0.1	0.1	0.1	0.1	–
Animal Planet +1	0.1	–	–	–	–	–
At the Races	0.2	0.1	–	–	–	–
BBC3	0.6	0.1	–	–	–	–
BBC4	0.2	0.1	–	–	–	–
BBC News 24	0.5	0.4	0.3	0.2	0.1	0.1
Bid-Up TV	0.1	0.1	–	–	–	–
Biography Channel	0.1	0.1	0.1	–	–	–
Boomerang	0.7	0.4	0.3	0.2	–	–
The Box	0.2	0.2	0.2	0.3	0.2	0.1
Bravo	0.3	0.2	0.3	0.2	0.2	0.2
Bravo +1	0.2	–	–	–	–	–
Cartoon Network	0.5	0.3	0.4	0.7	0.7	0.8
Cartoon Network Plus	0.2	0.1	0.1	–	–	–
CBBC	0.4	0.1	–	–	–	–
CBeebies	1.3	0.7	0.4	–	–	–
Challenge TV	0.5	0.3	0.2	0.3	0.2	0.2
Channel U	0.1	–	–	–	–	–
Chart Show TV	0.1	–	–	–	–	–
Discovery	0.5	0.3	0.4	0.3	0.3	0.3
Discovery +1	0.2	–	–	–	–	–
Discovery Civilisation	0.1	–	–	–	–	–
Discovery Health	0.3	0.1	0.1	–	–	–
Discovery Kids	0.1	–	–	–	–	–
Discovery Science	0.1	–	–	–	–	–
Discovery Travel & Adventure	0.1	–	–	–	–	–
Discovery Wings	0.1	–	–	–	–	–
Disney Channel	0.3	0.3	0.3	0.4	0.4	0.4
Disney Channel +1	0.2	–	–	–	–	–
Disney Playhouse	0.1	0.1	0.1	0.1	–	–
Disney Toon	0.2	0.1	0.1	–	–	–
E!	0.1	–	–	–	–	–
E4	1.0	0.7	0.9	0.2	–	–
E4 +1	0.3	–	–	–	–	–
Eurosport	0.4	0.2	0.3	0.3	0.3	0.3
Fox Kids	0.3	0.2	0.2	0.2	0.2	0.1
Fox Kids +1	0.2	–	–	–	–	–
FTN	0.1	–	–	–	–	–
FX	0.1	–	–	–	–	–
Men & Motors	0.2	0.1	0.1	0.1	0.1	–
Plus	0.7	0.4	0.4	0.3	0.3	0.3
Hallmark	0.9	0.4	0.3	0.1	–	–
History Channel	0.2	0.1	0.1	0.2	0.1	0.1
History Channel +1	0.1	–	–	–	–	–
The Hits	0.3	0.1	–	–	–	–
Home and Leisure	0.5	0.3	0.3	0.2	0.2	0.2
Home and Leisure +1	0.2	–	–	–	–	–
ITN News	0.1	0.1	0.1	–	–	–
ITV2	1.7	0.7	0.5	0.1	0.1	–
Kerrang	0.1	0.1	0.1	–	–	–
Kiss TV	0.1	0.1	0.1	0.1	–	–
Living	0.8	0.6	0.6	0.5	0.6	0.6
Living TV +1	0.3	–	–	–	–	–
Magic TV	0.2	0.1	0.1	–	–	–
Motors TV	0.1	–	–	–	–	–
MTV	0.4	0.2	0.2	0.3	0.4	0.4
MTV Base	0.1	0.1	0.1	0.1	–	–
MTV Dance	0.1	–	–	–	–	–
MTV Hits	0.2	0.1	0.1	0.1	–	–

Channel	2003–04	2002–03	2002*	2000–01	1999–2000	1998–99
MTV2	0.1	0.1	0.1	–	–	–
National Geographic	0.1	0.1	0.1	0.1	0.1	0.1
National Geographic +1	0.1	–	–	–	–	–
National Geographic Adventure One	0.1	–	–	–	–	–
Nickelodeon	0.4	0.5	0.4	0.7	0.7	0.7
Nickelodeon Replay	0.2	–	–	–	–	–
Nick Jr	0.5	0.2	0.2	0.2	0.1	–
Nick Toons	0.2	0.1	–	–	–	–
Paramount	0.4	0.3	0.3	0.2	0.1	0.1
Paramount 2	0.1	–	–	–	–	–
Q Channel	0.1	–	–	–	–	–
QVC	0.2	0.1	0.1	0.2	0.2	0.2
Reality TV	0.1	–	–	–	–	–
The Sci-Fi Channel	0.5	0.3	0.3	0.3	0.2	0.2
Sky Cinema	0.2	0.1	0.1	0.2	0.2	0.2
Sky Cinema 2	0.1	0.1	0.1	0.1	–	–
Sky Movies	0.7	0.4	0.4	0.6	0.7	0.8
Sky Movies 2	0.5	0.2	0.3	0.4	0.5	0.5
Sky Movies 3	0.3	0.2	0.3	0.2	0.1	–
Sky Movies 4	0.3	0.1	0.1	0.1	–	–
Sky Movies 5	0.3	0.2	0.2	0.2	0.1	–
Sky Movies 6	0.3	0.1	0.1	0.1	–	–
Sky Movies 7	0.3	0.2	0.2	0.2	0.1	–
Sky Movies 8	0.2	0.1	0.1	0.1	–	–
Sky Movies 9	0.2	0.1	0.1	0.1	–	–
Sky News	0.7	0.7	0.3	0.3	0.3	0.4
Sky One	2.6	1.7	2.1	1.8	1.7	1.5
Sky One Mix	0.5	0.1	–	–	–	–
Sky Premiership Plus	0.1	–	–	–	–	–
Sky Sports 1	1.8	1	0.8	0.9	0.8	0.8
Sky Sports 2	0.9	0.3	0.4	0.5	0.6	0.6
Sky Sports 3	0.2	0.2	0.1	0.2	0.2	0.3
Sky Sports Extra	0.2	0.1	0.1	0.1	–	–
Sky Sports News	0.7	0.2	0.2	0.1	0.1	–
Sky Travel	0.2	–	–	–	–	–
Sky Travel 2	0.1	–	–	–	–	–
Smash Hits	0.2	0.1	0.1	–	–	–
TCM (Turner Classic Movies)	0.4	0.2	0.2	0.1	–	–
TMF (The Music Factory)	0.3	0.1	–	–	–	–
Toonami	0.2	–	–	–	–	–
Trouble	0.3	0.2	0.2	0.2	0.2	0.2
Trouble Reload	0.1	–	–	–	–	–
UKTV Bright Ideas	0.1	–	–	–	–	–
UKTV Drama	0.1	–	–	–	–	–
UKTV Food	0.2	0.1	0.1	–	–	–
UKTV Food +1	0.1	–	–	–	–	–
UKTV Gold	1.5	0.9	0.9	1.2	1.0	0.8
UKTV Gold +1	0.5	–	–	–	–	–
UKTV G2	0.2	0.1	0.1	–	–	–
UKTV History	0.3	0.1	–	–	–	–
UKTV History +1	0.1	–	–	–	–	–
UKTV Documentary	0.2	0.2	0.3	0.1	0.1	0.1
UKTV People	0.1	–	–	–	–	–
UKTV Style	0.7	0.6	0.6	0.3	0.1	0.1
UKTV Style +1	0.3	–	–	–	–	–
VH-1	0.2	0.1	0.1	0.2	0.2	0.3
VH-1 Classic	0.2	0.1	0.1	0.1	–	–
VH-2	0.1	–	–	–	–	–
Wrestling Channel	0.1	–	–	–	–	–

– figures unavailable   * figures cover six months to June 2002   Sources: ITC archive, Barb

Independent TV production

There are 1,000 independent TV producers in Britain, most of whom are members of Pact, the producers' alliance for cinema and television. Of these, only 20 or 30 companies have the resources to compete regularly for the major budgets. Televisual magazine conducts an annual peer poll of the most successful production companies; see the panel for its top 20 and the work they do. According to that magazine, the top 10 per cent of production companies – the "superindies" – are responsible for almost 60 per cent of the turnover of the sector, win more than 40 per cent of the commissions, and employ more than half the staff.

The Communications Act 2003 has had a hugely beneficial effect on the way independent production companies do business. Under new codes of practice agreed by Ofcom, indies can now exploit the rights in the ideas they sell, a development which will no doubt be reflected in the balance sheet of the most successful companies. This makes the "returnable format" – the programme that, like Faking It or Who Wants to be a Millionaire?, can be sold internationally as well in Britain – ever more valuable to the independent producer.

Perhaps because of this, there has also been a rash of consolidation in the past year. The former ITV director of channels, David Liddiment, together with two former Granada executives, Steve Morrison and Jules Burns, bought Chrysalis TV, makers of Richard & Judy and Midsomer Murders, for £51m in August 2003. Under the new name of All3Media, it then acquired another highly respected indie, Lion TV, in June 2004. In Scotland, meanwhile, Ideal World and Wark Clements merged, creating the biggest indie outside London; the new company is to be called IWC Media. Hat Trick, however, ditched plans to buy Shed in a £20m deal.

Top 20 independent production companies

	Company	Last year	Credits
1	Endemol	(1=)	Big Brother, Fame Academy, Changing Rooms
2	TWI	(1=)	Wimbledon, The Olympics
3	TV Corporation	(4)	Robot Wars, Britain's Worst Driver
4	Talkback Thames	(5)	Family Affairs, Bo Selecta
5	RDF	(6)	Faking It, Wife Swap
6	Lion**	(8)	Bad Behaviour, Days that Shook the World
7	Tiger Aspect	(7)	Teachers, Murphy's Law
8	Chrysalis*	(3)	Richard and Judy, Midsomer Murders
9	Wall to Wall	(10)	1940s House
10	Princess	(9)	Back to Reality, Rise, Wright Stuff
11	Ideal World	(11)	Location, Location, Location
12	Celador	(15=)	Who Wants to be a Millionaire?
12	September	(15=)	Holiday Homes Nightmares, The Bottom Line
14=	Diverse	(20)	Operatunity
14=	Zig Zag		Fashion is Football Challenge, Inside the Mind of Frank Bruno
16	Zenith	(14)	Byker Grove, 2000 Acres of Sky
17	Prospect	(12)	Saturday Kitchen, Straight Dates by Gay Mates
18=	At It		T4, LA Pool Party, Sun Sea and Silicone
18=	Hat Trick	(19)	Have I Got News For You?, Room 101, Kumars
20	Two Four	(18)	G Girls, Gardens Through Time, City Gardener

*Now All3Media **now part of All3Media

Source: Production 100 survey, September 2003, Televisual monthly magazine (www.televisual.com). Survey takes into account industry peer poll.

Top 10 independent facilities

	Facility	Last year	Credits
1	Framestore CFC	(2)	Thunderbirds; Walking with Sea Monsters
2	MPC	(3)	Troy; Dunkirk; Guinness moth commercial
3	The Mill	(1)	Commercials: Mercedes; Honda; O2
4	The Farm Group	(4)	Dunkirk; Friday Night with Jonathan Ross
5	Blue Post	(9)	BBC Imagine; Pompeii: The Last Day
6	Barcud Derwen	(6)	Celebrity Poker; Mountains and Man
7	VTR	(4)	Christine Aguillera; McDonalds; Persil
8	Oasis	(7)	State of Play
9	Resolution	(19)	Big Brother; Top Gear; Fame Academy
10=	Evolutions	(16)	Top of the Pops titles; Jump London
10=	Rushes	(7)	Commercials: HP; Offspring; Ford Mondeo

Source: Facilities 50 survey, October 2003, Televisual monthly magazine (www.televisual.com). Survey takes into account industry peer poll.

Terrestrial broadcasters are in theory supposed to commission at least a quarter of their programming hours from independents; although in October 2003, the BBC missed this quota for a third successive year, according to the Office of Fair Trading, commissioning only 21 per cent. Indies accused the corporation of having a "callous disregard" for their industry – and the media secretary, Tessa Jowell, stepped in to express her concern. Meanwhile, Pact is calling for the BBC to outsource 50 per cent of its programming to external companies, although 25 per cent would still be provided by indies.

Channel 4 remains the broadcaster with the closest relationship with independent production companies; but Five's extra 8 per cent of funding for programme-making will increase the budget available to independents.

The new chairman of Pact is Andrew Zein, the chief executive of Tiger Aspect.

Further reading

■ Press

MediaGuardian
media.guardian.co.uk/broadcast

Broadcast: weekly trade magazine
www.broadcastnow.co.uk

Screen International: film trade magazine
www.screendaily.com

Televisual: monthly trade magazine
www.mad.co.uk/publication/tv

■ Web only

Digital Spy
www.digitalspy.co.uk

■ Books

Strange Places, Questionable People JOHN SIMPSON; PAN 1999
Autobiography of the ubiquitous BBC television journalist

Life On Air DAVID ATTENBOROUGH; BBC 2002
Autobiography of the ubiquitous BBC television naturalist

Broadcast Journalism ANDREW BOYD; FOCAL PRESS 2000
Widely recommended guide.

John Birt: the Harder Path TIME WARNER PAPERBACKS 2003
Autobiography of a director general.

On Air: A Career in TV & Radio CHRIS ALDEN, GUARDIAN BOOKS 2004
The essential careers guide to television and radio

■ Other resources

Barb
www.barb.co.uk

British Film Institute
www.bfi.org.uk

Digital television (government site)
www.digitaltelevision.gov.uk

Pact
www.pact.co.uk

Why Auntie needs to detox **Janine Gibson**

When you're in the middle of it, it's like a swamp fog (I saw a programme on Discovery) – something so all-consuming that you can't see any way out. No path back, the only way forward is to press on blindly, confident that eventually it will end. Alternatively you can stand still and sob. The end result seems to be the same.

Every 10 years we go through this process of renewing the BBC's royal charter. Sometimes, in between, we have a broadcasting or communications bill just to keep us limber and in shape. Otherwise, a good debate about what constitutes public service broadcasting or licence-fee-funded services could throw a regulator off his game, and mistakes could happen. There is a theory that this is how BBC Choice was first conceived.

This charter renewal (and let me tell you that if you can remember the last, it's time to be doing something else) has been characterised by more arguments about money, and fewer debates about quality television. To give Michael Grade and Mark Thompson their due, they have tried to focus the money-grabbing opposition on questions such as "public value" and "distinctiveness".

Grade has pledged no more copycat programmes on the BBC, which must immediately put the kibosh on half the schedule. And "public value" means socially conscious event programming, so instead of derivative Fame Academy, we get good-for-you Fat Nation, where half of Birmingham will be fed lettuce for three months until they've lost 55 stone. If this sounds of dubious interest, try and remember the full name of the government ministry which is in charge of the media, and consequently the BBC. Yes, that's right: it's culture, media and sport. The media minister is also in charge of getting us more active. Immediately after doing that, the minister will decide on the BBC's future funding. Sports Relief night, anyone?

None of this is bad, though. It is simply the correction at the end of a swing towards the commercial end of the market. In between communications bills and charter review, the BBC, shall we say, drifts a bit. Programmes that should never be commissioned, such as Britain's Best Sitcom, are allotted 10 weeks of primetime Saturday nights. An ascetic period of purging – or lettuce-eating – is necessary now and then to get us back on track.

The danger is that during the binge, when the Fame Academy, Holby City, Oh-go-on-let's-have-another-episode-of-EastEnders period gets out of hand, one really stupid idea gains currency. This time round, it's called top-slicing the licence fee, or "contestable funding". Pick a name, it's still stupid. It involves arresting the BBC's income, putting the rest of the cash in a pot and allowing other broadcasters or producers to apply for it in order to make quality television. Independent producers love these funds: there are several thousand of them in Europe, available for everything from animation produced in Scandinavia to filming in widescreen or promoting the image of Lithuania. In fact Fifteen to One was heavily subsidised, entirely because it was one of the first programmes in Europe to be filmed in widescreen. (Let's never discuss the absolute futility of filming a quiz show in letterbox format when no one had a widescreen television.) Of course the problem is that in the real world, the fund's ability to create interesting and good programmes that would not otherwise be made is dwarfed by its ability to eat money in administration and invest in terrible ideas that no one else wants to fund because they're terrible. First witness for the prosecution: the national lottery film fund.

So in order to swerve these truly terrible "funding solutions", the BBC has to detox, purge and prove to us all that it's perfectly capable of making good programmes on its own, without money being hived off and given to someone else.

It's because of this natural phenomenon – the binge and purge – that some media brains are proposing that the charter should be reviewed every five years. This is a bit like the idea floated every August in the tabloids, that marriage should consist of a number of renewable licences of five years in duration in answer to the problem of rising divorce rates. It doesn't really solve the problem. And, God knows, the rest of us really can't take charter review every five years. It's a three-year process as it is. We'd be in a permanent state of review. The BBC would be discussing its purposes constantly. Please, no.

Janine Gibson is editor of the Guardian's G3 sections – Media, Society, Life and Education

TV Contacts

Key contact

Office of Communications (Ofcom)
Riverside House
2A Southwark Bridge Road
London SE1 9HA
020 7981 3000
www.ofcom.gov.uk

Ofcom Media Office
020 7981 3033
mediaoffice@ofcom.org.uk

BBC

MAIN BBC ADDRESSES

Television Centre
Wood Lane, London W12 7RJ

BBC White City
201 Wood Lane, London W12 7TS

Broadcasting House
Portland Place, London W1A 1AA

www.bbc.co.uk
020 8743 8000

BBC Television

Television Centre
020 8743 8000
General enquiries: info@bbc.co.uk
www.bbc.co.uk/television
Director of television: Jana Bennett

General press enquiries
press.office@bbc.co.uk
www.bbc.co.uk/pressoffice

Media TV enquiries
020 8576 9900
publicity.frontdesk@bbc.co.uk
www.bbc.co.uk/pressoffice

BBC channels

BBC One
Television Centre
020 8743 8000
www.bbc.co.uk/bbcone
Controller: Lorraine Heggessey; controller of daytime: Alison Sharman (daytime.proposals@bbc.co.uk)

BBC Two
Television Centre
020 8743 8000
www.bbc.co.uk/bbctwo
Controller: Roly Keating; controller of daytime: Alison Sharman

BBC Three
Television Centre
020 8743 8000
www.bbc.co.uk/bbcthree
Controller: Stuart Murphy

BBC Four
Television Centre
020 8576 3193
www.bbc.co.uk/bbcfour
Controller: Janice Hadlow

CBBC
Television Centre
020 8743 8000
www.bbc.co.uk/cbbc
Controller: Dorothy Prior

CBeebies
Television Centre
020 8743 8000
www.bbc.co.uk/cbeebies
Controller: Dorothy Prior

BBC America
7475 Wisconsin Avenue, 11th Floor
Bethesda, USA MD 20814
00 1 301 347 2222
bbcamerica@bbc.co.uk
www.bbcamerica.com
Programme executive: Alison Fredericks

BBC Canada
121 Bloor Street East, Suite 200
Toronto, Ontario, Canada M4W 3M5
00 416 934 7800
feedback@bbccanada.com
www.bbccanada.com

BBC Food
PO Box 5054, London W12 0ZY
020 8433 2221
bbcfood@bbc.co.uk
www.bbcfood.com
Editor: David Weiland

BBC News 24
Television Centre
020 8743 8000
bbcnews24@bbc.co.uk
www.bbc.co.uk/bbcnews24
Editoral director: Mark Popescu

BBC Parliament
4 Millbank, London SW1P 3JA
020 7973 6216
parliament@bbc.co.uk
www.bbc.co.uk/bbcparliament

BBC Prime
PO Box 5054, London W12 0ZY
020 8433 2221
bbcprime@bbc.co.uk
www.bbcprime.com
Editor: David Weiland

BBC World
Television Centre
020 8576 2308
bbcworld@bbc.co.uk
www.bbcworld.com
Editorial director: Sian Kevill

BBC nations and regions

Director of nations and regions
Pat Loughrey
Controller of English regions
Andy Griffee
Network development, nations and regions
Colin Cameron, room 3187
BBC Scotland, 0141 338 2424

BBC Scotland
Broadcasting House
Queen Margaret Drive
Glasgow G12 8DG
0141 339 8844
www.bbc.co.uk/scotland
Controller: Ken MacQuarrie

BBC Wales
Broadcasting House
Llandaff, Cardiff CF5 2YQ
029 2032 2000
www.bbc.co.uk/wales
Controller: Menna Richards

BBC Northern Ireland
Broadcasting House
Ormeau Avenue, Belfast BT2 8HQ
028 9033 8000
www.bbc.co.uk/northernireland
Controller: Anna Carragher

BBC East
The Forum, Millennium Plain
Norwich NR2 1BH
01603 619 331
look.east@bbc.co.uk
www.bbc.co.uk/england/lookeast/
Head of regional and local programmes: Tim Bishop

BBC East Midlands
London Road, Nottingham NG2 4UU
0115 955 0500
emt@bbc.co.uk
www.bbc.co.uk/england/eastmidlandstoday/
Head of regional and local programmes: Alison Ford

BBC London
35c Marylebone High Street
London W1U 4QA
020 7224 2424
yourlondon@bbc.co.uk
www.bbc.co.uk/london/
Head of regional and local programmes: Michael MacFarlane

BBC North
Broadcasting Centre
Woodhouse Lane, Leeds LS2 9PX
0113 244 1188
look.north@bbc.co.uk
www.bbc.co.uk/england/looknorthyorkslincs/
Head of regional and local programmes: Colin Philpott

BBC North East and Cumbria
Broadcasting Centre, Barrack Road
Newcastle upon Tyne NE99 2NE
0191 232 1313
look.north.northeast.cumbria@bbc.co.uk
www.bbc.co.uk/england/looknorthnecumbria/
Head of regional and local programmes: Wendy Pilmer

BBC North West
New Broadcasting House
Oxford Road, Manchester M60 1SJ
0161 200 2020
nwt@bbc.co.uk
www.bbc.co.uk/manchester/
Head of regional and local programmes: Martin Brooks

BBC South
Broadcasting House, Havelock Road
Southampton SO14 7PU
02380 226201
south.today@bbc.co.uk
www.bbc.co.uk/england/southtoday/
Head of regional and local programmes: Eve Turner

BBC South East
The Great Hall, Mount Pleasant Road
Tunbridge Wells TN1 1QQ
01892 670000
southeasttoday@bbc.co.uk
www.bbc.co.uk/england/southeasttoday/
Head of regional and local programmes: Laura Ellis

BBC South West
Broadcasting House, Seymour Road
Mannamead, Plymouth PL3 5BD
01752 229201
spotlight@bbc.co.uk
www.bbc.co.uk/england/spotlight/
Head of regional and local programmes: John Lilley

BBC West
Broadcasting House
Whiteladies Road, Bristol BS8 2LR
0117 973 2211
pointswest@bbc.co.uk
www.bbc.co.uk/england/pointswest/
Head of regional and local programmes: Andrew Wilson

BBC West Midlands
The Mailbox, Birmingham B1 1XL
0121 567 6767
midlands.today@bbc.co.uk
www.bbc.co.uk/birmingham
Head of regional and local programmes: David Holdsworth

BBC News

Television Centre
020 8743 8000
http://news.bbc.co.uk

Director of BBC News
Helen Boaden
Deputy director of BBC News
Mark Damazer
Head of communications
Janie Ironside Wood

BBC Television News
Room 1502, Television Centre
020 8624 9043
Head of television news: Roger Mosey; deputy: Rachael Attwell

BBC Newsgathering
020 8743 8000
Head of newsgathering: Adrian Van Klaveren

Current affairs
Head of current affairs: Peter Horrocks

Political programmes unit
BBC Westminster, 4 Millbank
London SW1P 3JA
020 7973 6000
Head of political programmes: Fran Unsworth; political editor: Andrew Marr

BBC News Online
Television Centre
http://news.bbc.co.uk
Head of new media: Richard Deverell

BBC EDITORS & CORRESPONDENTS

Home editor: Mark Easton
Political editor: Andrew Marr
Business editor: Jeff Randall
World affairs editor: John Simpson
Diplomatic editor: Brian Hanrahan

HOME AND ABROAD

Home affairs: Margaret Gilmore; education: Mike Baker; health: Karen Allen; social affairs: Daniel Sandford; royal: Nicholas Witchell, Peter Hunt; political: Laura Trevelyan; defence: Paul Adams; security: Frank Gardner; rural affairs: Tom Heap; diplomatic: Bridget Kendall, James Robbins; environment and science: David Shukman; media: Torin Douglas; technology (BBC News Online): Alfred Hermida, Mark Ward

Special correspondents
Jeremy Bowen, Fergal Keane, Gavin Hewitt; TV news: Ben Brown; BBC News 24: Philippa Thomas

WORLD

World affairs
Peter Biles

Europe
Europe: Tim Franks, Chris Morris, Stephen Sackur; Paris: Allan Little, Caroline Wyatt; Berlin: Ray Furlong;

Rome: David Willey; Greece: Richard Galpin; Moscow: Damian Grammaticas; south Europe: Brian Barron; central Europe: Nick Thorpe

Middle East
Orla Guerin, James Reynolds, Paul Wood; Turkey: Jonny Dymond

Americas
Washington: Nick Bryant, Matt Frei, Jon Leyne, Clive Myrie, Ian Pannell, Justin Webb; California: David Willis; Mexico and central America: Claire Marshall; South America: Elliott Gotkine

Other
Africa: Hilary Andersson; east Africa: Andrew Harding; south Asia: Adam Mynott; south-east Asia: Kylie Morris; central Asia: Monica Whitlock; world media: Sebastian Usher; also Dominic Hughes, Jill McGivering, Rageh Omaar, Matthew Price

FLAGSHIP NEWS AND POLITICS PROGRAMMES

Breakfast
Room 1605, News Centre
Television Centre
020 8624 9700
breakfasttv@bbc.co.uk
Editor: Richard Porter; presenters: Dermot Murnaghan, Natasha Kaplinsky

Newsnight
Television Centre
020 8624 9800
Editor: George Entwhistle; presenters: Jeremy Paxman, Kirsty Wark, Gavin Esler

Panorama
Room 1118, BBC White City
020 8752 7152
panorama@bbc.co.uk
Editor: Mike Robinson; deputy editors: Andrew Bell and Sam Collyns

Politics Show
4 Millbank, London SW1P 3JQ
020 7973 6199
politicsshow@bbc.co.uk
Presenter: Jeremy Vine

Question Time
Mentorn, 43 Whitfield Street
London W1T 4HA
020 7258 6800
Presenter: David Dimbleby

Six O'Clock News
Television Centre
020 8624 9996
Presenters: George Alagiah, Sophie Raworth

Ten O'Clock News
Television Centre
020 8624 9999
Editor: Kevin Bakhurst; presenters: Huw Edwards, Fiona Bruce

Factual and learning

Director of factual and learning
John Willis 020 8752 6501

Controller, factual TV
Glenwyn Benson 020 8743 8000

PROGRAMMES

Arena
Room 2168, BBC White City
020 8752 5172
Series editor: Anthony Wall

Everyman
Room 5048, BBC Manchester
Broadcasting House, Oxford Road
Manchester M60 1SJ
0161 244 3321
ruth.pitt@bbc.co.uk
Creative director: Ruth Pitt

Horizon
Room 4523, BBC White City
020 8752 6134
horizon@bbc.co.uk
Editor: Matthew Barrett

Imagine
Arts Department, 2nd Floor
BBC White City
020 8752 4092
ian.macmillan@bbc.co.uk
Series Producer: Ian Macmillan

Money programme
Room 4116, BBC White City
020 8752 7400
Executive editor: Clive Edwards

One Life
Room 5503, BBC White City
020 8752 6608
todd.austin@bbc.co.uk
Commissioning editor: Todd Austin

Panorama
Room 1118, BBC White City
020 8752 7152
Editor: Mike Robinson

Storyville
Room 201, 1 Mortimer Street
London W1T 3JA
020 7765 5211
storyville@bbc.co.uk
Commissioning editor: Nick Fraser

This World
Room 1362, BBC White City
020 8752 7500
thisworld@bbc.co.uk
Editor: Karen O'Connor

Timewatch
Room 3150, BBC White City
020 8752 7079
Editor: John Farren

FACTUAL & LEARNING CONTACTS

Arts
2nd Floor, BBC White City
020 8752 4092
claire.lewis.02@bbc.co.uk
Executive producer: Claire Lewis; commissioner, arts and culture: Franny Moyle

Arts (Wales)
Room 4001, BBC Wales
029 2032 2943
paul.islwyn.thomas@bbc.co.uk
Head of arts, Wales: Paul Islwyn Thomas

Classical music
Room EG09, Television Centre
020 8895 6541
Head of TV, classical music and performance: Peter Maniura

Music (Wales)
Room E4113, BBC Wales
029 2032 2111
davidm.jackson@bbc.co.uk
Head of music, Wales: David Jackson

Current affairs
Room 1172, BBC White City
020 8752 7005
Head of current affairs: Peter Horrocks

Documentaries and contemporary factual
Room 3559, BBC White City
020 8752 5766
genfact.proposals@bbc.co.uk
Head of documentaries: Alan Hayling; acting commissioner: Tom Archer; development executives: Nicky Colton & Sara Brailsford

Factual (Northern Ireland)
2nd Floor, BBC Northern Ireland
028 9033 8207
Head of factual and learning, NI: Bruce Batten; editor, network factual, NI: Eamon Hardy, 020 8576 7045
Head of factual network production, NI: Fiona Campbell, 020 8752 6074

Factual (Scotland)
Room 3178, BBC Scotland
0141 338 3646
andrea.miller.01@bbc.co.uk
Head of factual programmes, Scotland: Andrea Miller

Factual (Wales)
Room 4020, BBC Wales
029 2032 2976
Head of factual programmes, Wales: Adrian Davies

Education
Room 3416, BBC White City
020 8752 5241
Executive editor: Karen Johnson

Education (Northern Ireland)
Education Unit, First Floor
BBC Northern Ireland
028 9033 8445
Head of factual and learning, NI: Bruce Batten; editor, learning, NI: Kieran Hegarty

Education (Scotland)
Room 230, BBC Scotland
0141 338 1507
Editor, education, Scotland: Moira Scott

Education (Wales)
Room E3106, BBC Wales
029 2032 2834
Head of education and learning, Wales: Dr Eleri Wyn Lewis

Lifeskills TV
Room 2308, BBC White City
020 8752 4574
Head of Lifeskills TV: Seetha Kumar

Specialist factual, current affairs and arts
Room 2156, BBC White City
020 8752 6810
specfact.proposals@bbc.co.uk
Head of independent commissioning: Adam Kemp; commissioner, specialist factual: Emma Swain; senior commissioning executives: Krishan Arora, Lucy Hetherington; executive editor: Jacquie Hughes

Drama and entertainment

Director of drama, entertainment and CBBC
Alan Yentob 020 8743 8000

DRAMA & ENTERTAINMENT CONTACTS

Comedy
Room 4045, Television Centre
020 8743 8000
Head of comedy commissioning: *Mark Freeland; head of comedy entertainment: Jon Plowman*

Comedy and entertainment (Scotland)
Room 3167, BBC Scotland
0141 338 2370
Head of comedy and entertainment, Scotland: Mike Bolland

Daytime
Room 3560
BBC White City
020 8752 6225
Senior commissioning executive, daytime: Dominic Vallely

Daytime entertainment
Room 6070, Television Centre
020 8576 9960
Commissioning executive, daytime entertainment: Gilly Hall

Drama
Room D333, Centre House
56 Wood Lane, London W12 7SB
020 8576 4935
Controller, commissioning, drama: Jane Tranter; head of drama serials: Laura Mackie; controller of continuing drama series: Mal Young; head of drama commissioning: Gareth Neame

Drama (Northern Ireland)
BBC Northern Ireland
020 8576 1664
Head of drama, NI: Patrick Spence

Drama (Scotland)
Room 2170, BBC Scotland
0141 338 2517
Head of television drama, Scotland: Barbara McKissack

Drama (Wales)
Room E2106, BBC Wales
029 2032 2935
Head of drama, Wales: Julie Gardner

Entertainment
Room 6070, Television Centre
020 8225 6992
Controller, entertainment, commissioning: Jane Lush

Entertainment (Northern Ireland)
Room 229, BBC Northern Ireland
028 9033 8375
mike.edgar@bbc.co.uk
Head of entertainment, events and sport, NI: Mike Edgar

CBBC

Room E1012, Television Centre
020 8576 1280
Controller of CBBC: Dorothy Prior

Acquisitions
Room 360 DB, Television Centre
020 8576 1105
Head of acquisitions and co-productions: Theresa Plummer Andrews

CBBC Creates
Room E1200, Television Centre
020 8576 1040
Development executive, CBBC Creates: Amanda Gabbitas

CBBC Scotland
Room 2104, BBC Scotland
0141 338 2012
Head of Scotland: Donalda MacKinnon

Drama
Room E817, Television Centre
020 8576 8245
Head of drama: Elaine Sperber

Entertainment
Room E701, Television Centre
020 8225 9269
Head of entertainment: Anne Gilchrist

News and factual
Room E111, Television Centre
020 8576 3118
Head of news and factual: Roy Milani

Pre-school
Room N105, Neptune House
BBC Elstree, Clarendon Road,
Borehamwood, Herts WD6 1JF
020 8228 7072
Head of pre-school: Clare Elstow

Sport

Director of sport
Peter Salmon

Finance controller
Richard Jones 020 8225 6173

Live sport and highlights
Room 5060, Television Centre
020 8225 8400
andrew.thompson.01@bbc.co.uk

Head of new media, sports news and development
Andrew Thompson

Ceefax

Television Centre 020 8225 7022

Programme acquisition

Controller, programme acquisition
George McGhee 020 8743 8000

New media and technology

BBC Bush House
Strand, London WC2B 4PH
020 8743 8000
Director of new media and technology: Ashley Highfield

bbc.co.uk
Controller, internet: Tony Ageh

Emerging platforms
Controller: Angel Gambino

BBCi (interactive TV)
Controller, 24/7 interactive television: Rahul Chakkara; head, interactive TV programming: Emma Somerville

BBC Kingwood Warren (R&D)
Acting head: Ian Childs

BBC Films

1 Mortimer Street, London W1T 3JA
020 7765 0251
Head of BBC Films: David Thompson; executive producer & head of development: Tracy Scoffield 020 7765 0475

Business services

BBC International Unit
020 8576 1963
international.unit@bbc.co.uk
www.bbc.co.uk/international/
Manager: Peter James
Supplies TV facilities to overseas broadcasters transmitting from UK

BBC Monitoring
Marketing Unit, Caversham Park
Reading RG4 8TZ
0118 948 6289
csu@mon.bbc.co.uk
www.bbcmonitoringonline.com
and www.monitor.bbc.co.uk
Monitors world media

BBC Research Central
Broadcasting House
020 7557 2452
research-central@bbc.co.uk
www.bbcresearchcentral.com
Senior researchers: Helen Turner, Huw Martin, Guy Watkins, Angie Francis, Kyla Thorogood, Richard Jeffery, Jacqueline Faulkner, Michael Paige
Information, footage, pronunciation, radio and photo research services

BBC Training and Development
35 Marylebone High Street
London W1U 4PX
0870 122 0216
training@bbc.co.uk
www.bbctraining.co.uk
Press contact:
Louise Findlay-Wilson
01993 823011
louise@energypr.co.uk
Training solutions in programme-making, broadcasting and new media
Elstree
Clarendon Road, Borehamwood
Herts WD6 1JF
Wood Norton Training Centre
Evesham, Worcestershire WR11 4YB

BBC Ventures Group
020 7765 2938
bbcventuresgroup@bbc.co.uk
Commercial director: David Moody; head of press and PR: Alison Jeremy
Wholly owned commercial subsidiary, comprising BBC Vecta, BBC Broadcast, BBC Resources and BBC Technology
BBC Broadcast
Television Centre
020 8225 6666
bbcbroadcast@bbc.co.uk
www.bbcbroadcast.com
Managing director: Pam Masters
Offers range of play-out and channel management services across multiple media platforms; planning to move in 2004 to: Media Village, BBC White City, 201 Wood Lane, London
BBC Resources
0870 010 0883
bbcresources@bbc.co.uk
www.bbcresources.com
Managing director: Mike Southgate
Production facilities

BBC Costumes and Wigs
Victoria Road, London W3 6UL
020 8576 1761
costume@bbc.co.uk;
wigs@bbc.co.uk
www.bbcresources.com

BBC Outside Broadcasts
Kendal Avenue, London W3 0RP
020 8993 9333
ob@bbc.co.uk
www.bbcresources.com

BBC Post-Production
Television Centre
020 8225 7702
postproduction@bbc.co.uk
www.bbcresources.com
Bristol
Broadcasting House
White Ladies Road
Bristol BS8 2LR
0117 974 6666
postproduction@bbc.co.uk
www.bbcresources.com
Birmingham
BBC Pebble Mill
Birmingham B5 7QQ
0121 432 8621
postproduction@bbc.co.uk
www.bbcresources.com

BBC Studios
Television Centre
020 8576 7666
tvstudio.sales@bbc.co.uk
www.bbcresources.com

BBC Technology
3rd Floor, Brock House
19 Langham Street, London W1 1AA
020 7765 4748
bbctechnology-sales@bbc.co.uk
www.bbctechnology.com
Managing director: Ann Wilson
Offers solutions in media, broadcast and interactive applications to the BBC and other companies

BBC Vecta
The Studio, 1 Mortimer Street
London W1T 3JA
020 7765 0850
amanda.harris@bbc.co.uk
www.bbcvecta.com
Managing director: Mark Popkiewicz; communications manager: Amanda Harris
Represents BBC in commercial exploitation of rights; works with BBC Research and Development to bring developments to market

BBC Worldwide
Woodlands, 80 Wood Lane
London W12 0TT
020 8433 2000
www.bbcworldwide.com
Managing director: Peter Phippen
Commercial arm: businesses include distribution, TV channels, magazines, books, videos, spoken word, music, DVDs, licensed products, CD-ROMs, English language teaching, videos for education and training, interactive telephony, co-production, library footage sales, magazine subscription exhibitions, live events, film and media monitoring

Advisory bodies

Broadcasting Council for Scotland
The Secretary, Broadcasting House
Queen Margaret Drive
Glasgow G12 8DG
0141 339 8844

Broadcasting Council for Wales
The Secretary, Broadcasting House
Llandaff, Cardiff CF5 2YQ
029 2032 2000

Broadcasting Council for Northern Ireland
Head of Public Affairs and Secretary,
Broadcasting House, Ormeau Avenue
Belfast BT2 8HQ
028 9033 8000

Central Religious Advisory Committee
The Secretary, Broadcasting House
London W1A 1AA
020 7580 4468

English National Forum
Head of Press and Public Affairs,
English Regions
BBC Broadcasting Centre
Pebble Mill Road
Birmingham B5 7QQ
0121 432 8888

Governors' World Service Consultative Group
BBC World Service, Bush House
Strand, London WC2B 4PH
020 7240 3456

BBC governors

Chairman of governors:
Michael Grade
Vice-chairman:
Anthony Salz
Governors:
Deborah Bull
Dame Ruth Deech
Dermot Gleeson
Professor Merfyn Jones
Professor Fabian Monds
Dame Pauline Neville-Jones
Angela Sarkis
Sir Robert Smith (until end of 2004)
Ranjit Sondhi
Richard Tait

ITV Network

200 Grays Inn Road
London WC1X 8HF
020 7843 8000
Controls commissioning and scheduling across entire ITV network, including non-ITV plc regions

NETWORK CONTROLLERS

Acquisitions
Jeremy Boulton 020 7843 8120

Arts, current affairs and religion
Steve Anderson 020 7843 8110

Children's and youth
Steven Andrew 020 7843 8132

Comedy
Sioned Wiliam 020 7843 8093

Drama
Nick Elliot 020 7843 8202
Head of network drama:
Jenny Reeks 020 7843 8211

Entertainment
Claudia Rosencrantz 020 7843 8105

Factual
Bridget Boseley 020 7843 8297
Head of continuing series
Corrine Hollingworth 020 7843 8211

Sport
Brian Barwick 020 7843 8113

ITV 50th Anniversary
Liam Hamilton 020 7843 8107

ITV channels

ITV1
020 7843 8000
www.itv.com/itv1

ITV2
020 7843 8000
www.itv.com/itv2
Channel editor: Zai Bennett, 020 7843 8129; controller of commissioned programmes: Daniella Neumann, 020 7843 8101

ITV News
200 Grays Inn Road
London WC1X 8XZ
020 7833 3000
Press: itvplanning@itn.co.uk
www.itv.com/news
Editor-in-chief: David Mannion

ITV plc

London Television Centre
Upper Ground, London SE1 9LT
Chief executive: Charles Allen; chairman: Sir Peter Burt
Controls 11 of the 15 ITV franchises

ITV plc board
Chief executive: **Charles Allen**
Chairman: **Sir Peter Burt**
Deputy chairman: **Sir George Russell**
Directors:
Henry Staunton
David Chance
James Crosby
John McGrath
Sir Brian Pitman
Etienne de Villiers

ITV PLC DIVISIONS

ITV News Group
020 7306 6000
Chief executive: Clive Jones
Includes ITV1's national and international news output, and regional news for ITV plc franchises; plus ITV plc's 40% stake in ITN

ITV Broadcasting
020 7843 8000
Chief executive: Mick Desmond; head of programmes: Nigel Pickard
Runs ITV plc's 11 regional ITV1 franchises; runs ITV2; runs sales house
ITV sales
200 Grays Inn Road WC1X 8XZ
020 7396 6000
Managing director: Graham Duff; director of ITV sales: Gary Digby; director of sales operations: Jill Kerslake; director of knowledge management: Andy Bagnall

Granada
020 7620 1620
Chief executive: Simon Shaps
Production arm
Press office 020 7843 8218/8219

ITV News
ITN, 200 Grays Inn Road
London WC1X 8XZ
020 7833 3000
Editor-in-chief: David Mannion; editor: Deborah Turness; deputy editor: Jonathan Munro; managing editor: Robin Elias; head of ITV News channel: Dominic Crossley-Holland

Key presenters: Sir Trevor McDonald; Mary Nightingale; Katie Derham; Mark Austin; Nicholas Owen; Alastair Stewart

Editors and correspondents
UK editor: Tom Bradby
Political editor: Nick Robinson
Consumer affairs editor: Chris Choi
International news editor: Bill Neely
Business and economics editor: Caroline Kerr
Science editor: Lawrence McGinty
Sports editor: Tim Ewart
Senior correspondent: James Mates

Home and abroad
News correspondents: Shiulie Ghosh, Joyce Ohajah, Mark Webster, Helen Wright; news reporters: Catherine Jacob, Philip Reay-Smith, Romilly Weeks; political: Angus Walker, Libby Wiener; north of England: Tim Rogers; south of England: Adrian Britton; Wales and west of England: Geraint Vincent; Scotland: Martin Geissler; medical: Sue Saville; crime: Dan Rivers; media and arts: Nina Nannar; sport: Felicity Barr

World
International news: Andrea Catherwood; Europe: Juliet Bremner; Washington: Robert Moore; Middle East: Julian Manyon; Africa: Neil Connery; Asia: John Irvine
Press officer: Saskia Wirth
020 7430 4825
saskia.wirth@itn.co.uk
Press releases to:
itvplanning@itn.co.uk

ITV regions

OWNED BY ITV PLC

ITV Anglia
Anglia House, Norwich NR1 3JG
01603 615151
firstname.lastname@itv.com
www.angliatv.com
Managing director: Graham Creelman; controller of programmes: Neil Thompson; head of regional affairs: Jim Woodrow; press officer: Lisa Munghan-Gray
News at Anglia
0870 240 6003
news@angliatv.com
Controller of news: Guy Adams
Cambridge regional office
ITV Anglia
26 Newmarket Road
Cambridge CB5 8DT
01223 467076
Chelmsford regional office
64–68 New London Road
Chelmsford CM2 0YU
01245 357676
Ipswich regional office
Hubbard House
Ipswich IP1 2QA
01473 226157
Luton regional office
16 Park Street
Luton LU1 2DP
01582 729666
Northampton regional office
77b Abington Street
Northampton NN1 2BH
01604 624343

Peterborough regional office
6 Bretton Green
Peterborough PE3 8DY
01733 269440

ITV Border
The Television Centre
Durranhill, Carlisle CA1 3NT
01228 525101
www.border-tv.com
Managing director: Paddy Merrall; production controller: Neil Robinson; head of news: Ian Proniewicz; press officer: Louise Maving

ITV Central
Gas Street, Birmingham B1 2JT
0121 643 9898
firstname.lastname@itv.com
www2.itv.com/central/
Managing director: Ian Squires; controller of news and operations: Laurie Upshon; head of regional programming: Duncan Rycroft; press officer: Christopher Strange; editor Central News West: Dan Barton

Central News East
Carlton Studios, Lenton Lane
Nottingham NG7 2NA
0115 986 3322
News editor: Mike Blair
Studios marked for closure; operation to move to Birmingham office

Central News South
9 Windrush Court
Abingdon Business Park, Abingdon
Oxford OX14 1SA
01235 554123
News editor: Ian Rumsey

ITV Granada
Quay Street, Manchester M60 9EA
0161 832 7211
firstname.lastname@itv.com
www.granadatv.com
Managing director: Susan Woodward; controller of programmes: Kieron Collins; executive producer regional programmes: Eamonn O'Neal; controller of regional affairs: Jane Luca; news editor: Cerys Griffiths

Blackburn regional news centre
Daisyfield Business Centre
Appleby Street
Blackburn BB1 3BL
01254 690099

Chester regional news centre
Bridgegate House, 5 Bridge Place
Lower Bridge Street
Chester CH1 1SA
01244 313966

Lancaster regional news centre
White Cross, Lancaster LA1 4XQ
01524 60688

ITV London
London Television Centre
Upper Grounds, London SE1 9LT
020 7620 1620
firstname.lastname@itv.com
www2.itv.com/london/
Managing director: Christy Swords; controller of regional programming: Emma Barker; head of regional affairs: Helen Andrews

London News Network
200 Gray's Inn Road
London WC1X 8HF
020 7430 4000
firstname.lastname@itvlondon.com
www.itvlondon.co.uk
Planning editor: Arti Lukha; head of news: Stuart Thomas; news editors: Brendan McGowan and Robin Campbell

ITV Meridian
Television Centre, Southampton
Hampshire SO14 0PZ
023 8022 2555
news@meridiantv.com
firstname.lastname@
granadamedia.com
www.meridiantv.co.uk
Managing director; Lindsay Charlton; controller of programmes: Mark Southgate; head of regional affairs: Alison Pope; head of news: Guy Phillips

Maidstone news office
ITV Meridian, Westpoint
New Hythe, Kent ME20 6XX
01622 882244

Newbury news office
ITV Meridian, Strawberry Hill House
Strawberry Hill, Newbury
Berkshire RG14 1NG
01635 552266

Tyne Tees Television
City Road
Newcastle Upon Tyne NE1 2AL
0191 261 0181
news@tynetees.tv;
firstname.lastname@itv.com
www.tynetees.tv
Managing director and controller of programmes: Graeme Thompson; head of regional affairs and press contact: Norma Hope; head of news: Graham Marples

Tees Valley & North Yorkshire news office
Tyne Tees Television
Belasis Hall Technology Park
Billingham, Teesside TS23 4EG
Newsroom: 01642 566999
newstoday@tynetees.tv
Senior editor: Bill Campbell

ITV Wales
The Television Centre
Culverhouse Cross
Cardiff CF5 6XJ
029 2059 0590
info@itvwales.com;
news@itvwales.com;
firstname.lastname@itvwales.com
www.itvwales.com
Acting managing director and controller of programmes: Elis Owen; head of regional affairs and press contact: Mansel Jones; head of news: John G Williams

Carmarthen news office
ITV Wales
Top Floor, 19–20 Lammas Street
Carmarthen SA31 3AL
01267 236809
West Wales correspondent: Giles Smith

Colwyn Bay news office
ITV Wales
Celtic Business Centre, Plas Eirias,
Heritage Gate, Abergele Road
Colwyn Bay LL29 8BW
01492 513888
colwyn@itvwales.com
North Wales correspondents: Carole Green and Ian Lang

Newtown news office
ITV Wales, St David's House
Newtown SY16 1RB
01686 623381
Mid-Wales correspondent: Rob Shelley

Wrexham news office
ITV Wales, Crown Buildings
31 Chester Street
Wrexham 01978 261462
North Wales correspondent: Paul Mewies

ITV West
Television Centre, Bath Road
Bristol BS4 3HG
0117 972 2722
reception@itv.com;
firstname.lastname@itv.com
www.itv1west.com
Managing director: Mark Haskell; controller of programmes: Jane McCloskey; head of regional affairs: James Garrett

Newsdesk
0117 972 2151/2152
itvwestnews@itv.com
Head of news: Steve Egginton

Press office
0117 972 2214
Head of press and community relations: Richard Lister

ITV Westcountry
Langage Science Park
Western Wood Way
Plymouth PL7 5BQ
01752 333333
firstname.lastname@itv.com
www.westcountry.co.uk
Managing director: Mark Haskell; director of programmes: Jane McCloskey; controller – business affairs: Peter Gregory; controller – technical operations: Mark Chaplin; press contact: Rebecca Turner

Main newsdesk
01752 333329
news@westcountry.co.uk
Controller of news: Phil Carrodus

Barnstaple news office
ITV Westcountry, 1 Summerland
Terrace, Barnstaple EX32 8JL
01271 324244

Exeter news office
ITV Westcountry, St Luke's Campus
Magdalene Road, Exeter EX4 4WT
01392 499400

Penzance News Office
ITV Westcountry, Parade Chambers
10 Parade Street
Penzance TR18 4BU
01736 331483

Taunton news office
ITV Westcountry, Foundry Cottage
Riverside Place, St James Street
Taunton TA1 1JH
01823 322335

Truro news office
ITV Westcountry, Courtleigh House
Lemon Street, Truro TR1 2PN
01872 262244

Weymouth news office
ITV Westcountry, 8 King Street
Weymouth DT4 7BP
01305 760860

ITV Yorkshire
The Television Centre, Kirkstall Road
Leeds, West Yorkshire LS3 1JS
0113 243 8283
firstname.lastname@itv.com
www.yorkshiretv.com
Managing director: David Croft, 0113 222 7184; controller of regional programmes: Clare Morrow, 0113 222 8724; head of regional affairs: Sallie Ryle, 0113 222 7118

Calendar (ITV Yorkshire News programme)
0845 121 1000
calendar@yorkshiretv.com
Head of news: Will Venters 0113 222 8822

Grimsby office
Immage Studios, Margaret Street
Immingham, Grimsby DN40 1LE
01469 510661

Hull office
23 Brook Street, Hull HU2 8PM
01482 324488

Lincoln office
88 Bailgate, Lincoln LN1 3AR
01522 530738

Sheffield office
23 Charter Square
Sheffield S1 3EJ
0114 272 7772

York office
York St John's College
Lord Mayors Walk
York YO31 7EX
01904 610066

Press office
0113 222 7129
Press officer: Jo Gough

OWNED BY SCOTTISH MEDIA GROUP

Grampian TV
Television Centre
Craigshaw Business Park
West Tullos, Aberdeen AB12 3QH
01224 848848
firstname.lastname@smg.plc.uk
www.grampiantv.co.uk
Managing director and controller of regional programmes: Derrick Thomson; head of news: Henry Eagles

Scottish TV
200 Renfield Street, Glasgow G2 3PR
0141 300 3000
firstname.lastname@smg.plc.uk
www.scottishtv.co.uk
Managing director and controller of regional programmes: Bobby Hain

Press office
0141 300 3670
Press officer: Kirsten Elsby

Newsdesk
0141 300 3360
Head of news: Paul McKinney

INDEPENDENTLY OWNED

Channel Television
Television Centre, La Pouquelaye
St Helier, Jersey JE1 3ZD
01534 816816
news room: 01534 816688
broadcast@channeltv.co.uk
www.channeltv.co.uk
Managing director: Michael Lucas; director of programmes: Karen Rankine (karen.rankine@channeltv.co.uk); director of special projects: Gordon de Ste Croix (gordon@channeltv.co.uk); director of resources and transmission: Kevin Banner

Guernsey office
Television House, Bulwer Avenue
St Sampson, Guernsey GY2 4LA
01481 241888
broadcast.gsy@channeltv.co.uk

London office
Unit 16A, 3rd Floor, Enterprise House
59–65 Upper Ground
London SE1 9PQ
020 7633 9902

UTV
Ormeau Road, Belfast BT7 1EB
028 9032 8122
firstinitiallastname@utvplc.com
www.u.tv
Group chief executive: John McCann; director of television: Alan Bremner; head of press and PR: Orla McKibbin; head of news: Rob Morrison

Channel 4

124 Horseferry Road
London SW1P 2TX
020 7396 4444

Chief executive
Andy Duncan

Managing director
David Scott 020 7306 6590; assistant: Lee Bassett 020 7306 8637

Commercial director
Andy Barnes 020 7306 8200; assistant: Dee Caldwell 020 7306 8201

Director of television
Kevin Lygo 020 7306 6907; assistant: Helen Pickett 020 7306 3771

Managing director, 4 Ventures
Rob Woodward 020 7306 3777; assistant: Olga Boff 020 7306 3740

PRESS

Head of press & publicity: Matt Baker 020 7306 8666; assistant: Pip Lowe 020 7306 8523

COMMISSIONING

Director of television
Kevin Lygo 020 7306 3775

Comedy
Head of comedy & comedy films: Caroline Leddy 020 7306 8718; assistant: Cathy Mason 020 7306 8066

Daytime and features
Commissioning editor, daytime: Adam MacDonald 020 7306 8033
Editor, daytime and features: Mark Downie 020 7306 5150

Documentaries
Head: Peter Dale 020 7306 8314; assistant: Emily Renshaw-Smith 020 7306 8676
Commissioning editors: Hilary Bell 020 7306 5173; Danny Cohen (Cutting Edge) 020 7306 6912; deputy: Sam Bickley 020 7306 1044; assistant editor: Katie Speight 020 7306 8727
Editor, independent film and video: Jess Search 020 7306 8312

Drama
Head: John Yorke 020 7306 6970; assitant: Beverley Booker 020 7306 3647; deputy: Lucy Richer 020 7306 6970
Editors: Camilla Campbell (series) 020 7306 3783; Hannah Weaver (events) 020 7306 5536; assistant editor: Liz Pilling 020 7306 8621

E4
Head, programming, E4 & digital: Murray Boland 020 7306 8671 (assistant Sasha Phillips 020 7306 8672)
Commissioning editor: Deborah O'Connor 020 7306 3649; head of scheduling: David Booth 020 7306 6582; planner: Shireen Tayabali 020 7306 5591

Entertainment
Head: Andrew Newman 020 7306 6342
Commissioning editor: Katie Taylor 020 7306 8679; deputy: Ruby Kuraishe 020 7306 6950

Factual entertainment
Head: Julian Bellamy 020 7306 6436 (assistant Claudia Emery 020 7306 5537)
Editors: Sharon Powers 020 7306 5379; Nav Raman 020 7306 8746; Andrew Mackenzie 020 7306 3680; Debbie Searle (cross-platform development) 020 7306 2656

Features
Head: Sue Murphy 020 7306 8616 (assistant Daniella Eversby 020 7306 5192)
Commissioning editor: Emma Westcott 020 7306 8476; executive producer: Philippa Ransford 020 7306 8424

Music, youth & T4
Head: Jules Oldroyd 020 7306 8229
Editor: Neil McCallum 020 7306 8588; assistant editor: Cath Lovesey 020 7306 5622

Nations and regions
Director: Stuart Cosgrove 0141 568 7105; assistant: Debbie Walker

News and current affairs
Head: Dorothy Byrne 020 7306 8588 (assistant: Louise Platel 020 7306 8132)
Editors: Kevin Sutcliffe (investigations) 020 7306 1068; Mark Rubens 020 7306 8771

Science and education
Head: Simon Andreae 020 7306 8289; assistant: Katie Vogel 020 7306 8431
Editor, education: Simon Dickson 020 7306 3799; commissioning editor, 4Learning, schools and youth: Deborah Ward 020 7306 8499; deputy CE: Bridget Bakokodie 020 7306 6043; reader: Clare Boyd 020 7306 3781

Specialist factual
Head TBA (assistant: Ebona Eastmond-Henry 020 7306 8745)
History: head Hamish Mykura 020 7306 1036; assistant: Edwina Waddy 020 7306 8303; editor Ralph Lee 020 7306 3863. Religion: Aaqil Ahmed 020 7306 8065. Arts & performance: Jan Younghusband 020 7306 5153.

Sport
Head: David Kerr: 020 7306 6581
Deputy commissioning editor: Deborah Poulton 020 7306 8501
Commissioning support
Managing editor: Janey Walker 020 7306 8623 (assistant: Melissa Hameed 020 7306 8282); manager, commissioning & suppliers: Helen Robertson 020 7306 6433; manager, talent development: Charlotte Black 020 7306 5505; editorial manager, cultural diversity: Mary Fitzpatrick 020 7306 6454; disability advisor: Alison Walsh 020 7306 8125

Programme acquisition
June Drumgoole 020 7306 8050; assistant: Sarah Lloyd 020 7306 8733

BROADCASTING

Controller: Rosemary Newell 020 7306 8620; head of schedules: Jules Oldroyd 020 7306 8229; deputy scheduler: John Williams 020 7306 8257; planner: Lynne Jarrett 020 7306 8231; senior planner: Lucy Rogers 020 7306 8536; finance planning: Steve Harding 020 7306 8511, Ray Banks 020 7306 6965, Gayle Higginbotham 020 7306 5362; Paul Matias 020 7306 8042
Agency sales: Matt Shreeve 020 7306 8240; airtime management: Merlin Inkley 020 7306 8254; channel operations: Steve White 020 7306 8403; commercial affairs: Sara Geater 020 7306 8619; client & strategic sales: Mike Parker 020 7306 8242; corporate development: Michael Hodgson 020 7306 5356; finance: Sue Ford 020 7306 8234; marketing: Bill Griffin 020 7306 6583; sales, marketing & research: Hugh Johnson 020 7306 8633; research & insight: Claire Grimmond 020 7306 8779; sponsorship: David Charlesworth 020 7306 8043; strategy: Jonathan Thompson 020 7306 8799

4Ventures

124 Facilities
Tony Chamberlain 020 7306 8110

4Channels
Dan Brooke 020 7306 6497; assistant: Wendy Foster 020 7306 6448

4Creative
Richard Burdett 020 7306 8110; assistant: Clare Wells 020 7306 1005

4Learning
Heather Rabbatts 020 7306 5125; assistant: Louise Ann Cotter 020 7306 5541

4Rights (C4I)
Paul Sowerbutts 020 7306 6459; assistant: Karol Roker 020 7306 6905

4Rights (consumer products)
Mike Morris 020 7306 5364; assistant: Kristell Farr 020 7306 5510

4Ventures
Anmar Kawash 020 7306 5350; assistant: Clare Brown 020 7306 6461

E4
Murray Boland 020 7306 8671; assistant: Sasha Phillips 020 7306 8672

Film Four channel
Tom Sykes 020 7306 6442; assistant: Jolene Yeo 020 7306 3691

Interactive
Andy Taylor 020 7306 3651

Media projects
Graeme Mason 020 7306 3796; assistant: Rebecca Turner 020 7306 6588

Channel 4 News

ITN, 200 Grays Inn Road
London WC1X 8XZ
020 7833 3000
www.channel4.com/news
Editor: Jim Gray; deputy editor: Martin Fewell; managing editor: Gay Flashman

Newsdesk 020 7430 4601

Press 020 7430 4220
Fiona.Railton@itn.co.uk
Press & publicity manager: Fiona Railton

Presenters
Anchor: Jon Snow; noon anchor: Krishnan Guru-Murthy; Sue Turton, Samira Ahmed

Senior home news editor
Evette Edwards

Political editor
Elinor Goodman

Senior foreign news editor
Deborah Rayner

International editor
Lindsey Hilsum

Commissioning editor, independent productions
Fiona Campbell

Correspondents Chief correspondent: Alex Thomson; home affairs: Simon Israel; political: Gary Gibbon; social affairs: Victoria Macdonald; science: Tom Clarke; science/defence: Julian Rush; economics: Liam Halligan; arts: Nicholas Glass; Midlands: Carl Dinnen; Scotland: Sarah Smith; foreign affairs: Jonathan Miller; Washington: Jonathan Rugman; Asia: Ian Williams; reporters: Katie Razzall, Stephen Smith, Darshna Soni; sport: Sue Turton

Five

22 Long Acre, London WC2E 9LY
020 7550 5555
firstname.lastname@five.tv
www.five.tv
Director of programmes: Dan Chambers, 020 7550 5673 (PA Sarah Jackson, 020 7550 5522); controller of broadcast services: David Burge, 020 7691 6260; head of marketing: Simon Downing, 020 7550 5531; brand manager: Jo Fuller, 020 7550 5528 Five, address as above; Tel: 020 7550 5551; head of sales: Nick Milligan; email: nick.milligan@five.tv

Press office 020 7550 5558
Head of press & corporate affairs: Paul Leather, 020 7550 5541; deputy head of press: Tracey O'Connor, 020 7550 5553; marketing & publicity executive: Louise Bowers, 020 7550 5662; entertainment publicist: Nick Dear, 020 7550 5634; drama serials: Marie Louise Pumfrey, 020 7550 5538; factual and features: Louise Plank, 020 7550 5659; acquisitions & youth: Tamara Bishopp, 020 7550 5539

GENRES

Arts Controller: Kim Peat, 020 7421 7107
Children Controller of children's programmes: Nick Wilson
Drama Temporary controller of drama: Jane Harris;
Daytime Controller: Kim Peat, 020 7421 7107
Factual entertainment Controller: Steve Gowans; deputy controller: Liam Humphreys, 020 7550 5628; deputy commissioning editor: Ian Dunkley, 020 7550 5659
Features & entertainment Controller: Ben Frow, 020 7421 7118
History Controller: Alex Sutherland
News & current affairs Senior programme controller: Chris Shaw, 020 7421 7122; deputy controller of news, current affairs and documentaries: Ian Russell, 020 7550 5529
Religion Controller: Kim Peat, 020 7421 7107
Science Controller: Justine Kershaw, 020 7421 7112
Sport Controller: Robert Charles, 020 7421 7185
Youth & music Controller: Sham Sandhu, 020 7421 7184

Other departments
Acquisitions Director: Jeff Ford, 020 7421 7166
Interactive Controller: Sham Sandhu, 020 7421 7184; producer: Steven Bonner, 020 7550 5663
Scheduling and planning Director: Susanna Dinnage, 020 7550 5588

five news

Until 2005: ITN
200 Grays Inn Road
London WC1X 8XZ
020 7833 3000
www.itn.co.uk/fivenews
Editor: Gary Rogers; political editor: Andy Bell; presenters: Kirsty Young, Charlie Stayt, Rob Butler, Katie Ledger Defence and foreign affairs correspondent: James Bays; consumer: Charlotte Hume; north of England: Ben Scotchbrook; senior reporters: Ben Ando, Mark Jordan; reporters: Colin Campbell, Keith Doyle, Catherine Jones
From January 2005: Sky News (see page 145)

ITN

200 Grays Inn Road
London WC1X 8XZ
020 7833 3000
www.itn.co.uk
Chief executive: Mark Wood; director of corporate affairs: Sophie Cohen; managing director, multimedia content: Nicholas Wheeler; head of production, ITN Factual: Marilyn Bennett; head of ITN factual: Philip Dampier; managing director, ITN Archive: Alwyn Lindsay

RTÉ

Radio Telefís Éireann
New Library Building, Donnybrook
Dublin 4, Ireland
00 353 1 208 3111
info@rte.ie
www.rte.ie
Irish national broadcaster. Communications manager, TV: Kathriona Edwards

Press and information:
00 353 1 208 3434
firstname.lastname@rte.ie
Press contacts: acquisitions and drama: Sharon Brady; entertainment: Dympna Clerkin; factual: Dervla Keating; Fair City (soap): Tara O'Brian; music, sport and young people: Richie Ryan; news and current affairs: Carolyn Fisher

Multichannel

KEY GOVERNMENT CONTACTS FOR DIGITAL TV

Department for Culture, Media and Sport
2–4 Cockspur Street
London SW1Y 5DH
020 7211 6000
enquiries@culture.gov.uk;
broadcasting@culture.gov.uk
www.culture.gov.uk/broadcasting
Culture secretary: Tessa Jowell
Press: *Mark Devane 020 7211 6267; Mark.devane@culture.gsi.gov.uk digitaltelevision@culture.gov.uk www.digitaltelevision.gov.uk*

Department for Trade and Industry
1 Victoria Street, London SW1H 0ET
020 7215 5000
dti.enquiries@dti.gsi.gov.uk
www.dti.gov.uk/industries/broadcasting
Head of broadcasting policy and director of digital television project: Jane Humphreys; deputy project manager, digital television: David Fuhr; broadcasting policy advisor: John Franck; head of broadcasting technology: Ian Dixon
Press: *Nic Fearon 020 7215 5952; nic.fearon@dti.gsi.gov.uk digitaltelevision@culture.gov.uk www.digitaltelevision.gov.uk*

BSkyB

British Sky Broadcasting
Grant Way, Isleworth TW7 5QD
0870 240 3000
www.sky.com
Chief executive: James Murdoch; chief operating officer: Richard Freudenstein: managing director, sales, marketing & interactive: Jon Florsheim; managing director, Sky Sports: Vic Wakeling; director of corporate communications: Julian Eccles
Press office 0870 240 3000
Director of publicity: Adrian Lee; head of programme publicity: Richard Turner; Sky One: Stephen Browning; Sky Movies: Phil Evans; Sky News: Stella Tooth; Sky Sports: Chris Haynes; consumer PR: Gabby Bennett

SKY CHANNELS

Sky Networks
Managing director, Sky Networks: Dawn Airey; deputy managing director, Sky Networks/director of film channels & acquisitions: Sophie Turner-Laing; director of commercial affairs: Delia Bushell
All Sky channels bar sport

Sky One, Sky One Mix
www.skyone.co.uk
Controller: James Baker

Sky Box Office
www.skymovies.com
Director of film channels & acquisitions: Sophie Turner-Laing

Sky Cinema 1 & 2
www.skymovies.com
Director of film channels & acquisitions: Sophie Turner-Laing

Sky Movies 1 & 2
www.skymovies.com
Director of film channels & acquisitions: Sophie Turner-Laing

Sky Sports 1, 2 & 3; Extra; News
www.skysports.com
Managing director, Sky Sports: Vic Wakeling

Sky Travel, Travel Extra, Shop
www.skytravel.co.uk
General manager, Sky Travel: Barbara Gibbon

Sky Vegas Live, Sky Bet
www.skyvegaslive.com
Managing director, Sky Bet: Nick Rust

The Amp
www.theamp.tv
Head of music: Jo Wallace

Scuzz
www.scuzz.tv
Head of music: Jo Wallace

Flaunt
www.flaunt.tv
Head of music: Jo Wallace

Sky Active
www.sky.com/skyactive
Managing director, Sky Interactive: Ian Shepherd
Interactive

Sky Business
www.sky.com/business
Commercial marketing director: Iain Holden
Sales to non-domestic clients

Sky Ventures
www.sky.com/ventures
Head of Sky Ventures & commercial management: Matthew Imi
Joint venture channels and services

Sky News
www.skynews.co.uk
Head of Sky News: Nick Pollard
Key presenters
Afternoon: Kay Burley, Mark Longhurst; Live at Five: Anna Botting, Jeremy Thompson
Correspondents
Political: Adam Boulton, Jon Craig, Jenny Percival, Peter Spencer, Glen O'Glaza; business: Michael Wilson, Heather Scott, Juliet Errington, Alex Crawford; crime: Martin Brunt; health: Nicola Hill, Thomas Moore; foreign: Richard Bestic, Colin Brazier, Keith Graves, Emma Hurd, Laurence Lee, Tim Marshall, Stuart Ramsay, Dominic Waghorn, Andrew Wilson; entertainment: Georgie Arnold, Neil Sean, Matt Smith; royal: Geoff Meade; other: David Bowden, David Chater, Michelle Clifford, Lisa Holland, Peter Sharp; also regional bureaux and 25 other reporters

Cable

NTL UK
NTL House
Bartley Wood Business Park
Bartley Way, Hook
Hampshire RG27 9UP
01256 752000
www.ntl.com
Managing director, NTL Home: Aizad Hussain; managing director, NTL Business: Tom Bennie
Press: 01256 752000
Contact: Justine Parrish

NTL Broadcast
Crawley Court, Winchester
Hampshire SO21 2QA
01962 823434
www.ntlbroadcast.com/
Managing director: Peter Douglas
Press: 01962 822582
Contact: Bruce Randall

Telewest Communications
Export House, Cawsey Way
Woking, Surrey GU21 6QX
01483 750900
www.telewest.co.uk
Acting chief executive: Barry Elson
Press: 020 7299 5888
Contact: Jane Hardman

Cablecom Investments
The Coach House, Bill Hill Park
Wokingham
Berks RG40 5QT
0118 979 2076
customer@cablecom.co.uk
www.cablecom.co.uk
Managing director: Charles Tompkins

WightCable
56 Love Lane, Cowes
Isle of Wight PO31 7EU
01983 242424
enquiries@wightcable.com
www.wightcable.com
Managing director: Duncan Kerr
WightCable North
3 Chalmers Place
Riverside Business Park
Irvine, North Ayrshire KA11 5DH
01294 230000
enquiries@wightcablenorth.com
www.wightcablenorth.com
Press: 01294 231145
pr@wightcablenorth.com
Contact: Emma Dawson

Video Networks
205 Holland Park Avenue
London W11 4XB
020 7348 4000
info@videonetworks.com
www.videonetworks.com/
Chairman and CEO: Roger Lynch
Press: 020 7348 4110
Contact: Nick Southall

Digital terrestrial

Freeview
Broadcast Centre, (BC3 D5)
201 Wood Lane, London W12 7TP
0870 880 9980
www.freeview.co.uk
General manager: Lib Charlesworth
Free-to-view digital terrestrial service, owned by Crown Castle, BBC and BSkyB
Press: 020 7229 4400
nick.clark@nelsonbostock.com
Contact: Nick Clark

Crown Castle UK
Warwick Technology Park
Gallows Hill, Heathcote Lane
Warwick CV34 6TN
01926 416000
MarketingUK@crowncastle.com
www.crowncastle.com
Managing director: Peter Abery
Digital terrestrial transmitter operator; part-owner of Freeview
Press: 01926 416870
Contact: Stephen Arnold

Top-Up TV
PO Box 208, Twickenham TW1 2YF
0870 054 5354
enquiries@topuptv.com
www.topuptv.com
Chairman: David Chance
Offers top-up pay channels for Freeview viewers

TV channels

Adventure One
Grant Way, Isleworth TW7 5QD
020 7705 3000
natgeoweb@bskyb.com
www.nationalgeographic.co.uk
General manager: Simon Bohrsmann

African and Caribbean TV
28F Lawrence Road
London N15 4EG
020 8809 7700
info@actv.org.uk
www.actv.org.uk
Programme controller: Rose McDonald

The Amp
Grant Way, Isleworth TW7 5QD
0870 240 3000
www.theamp.tv
Head of music: Jo Wallace

Artsworld
Great West House (15th floor)
Great West Road, Brentford
Middlesex TW8 9DF
020 7805 2404
Press: judith.holmes@artsworld.com
www.artsworld.com
Programme controller: Alison Martin

AsiaNet
Studio complex, Puliyarakonam PO
Trivandrum 695 573
India
00 91 471 237 8407
webmaster@asianetglobal.com
www.asianetglobal.com

attheraces
11–13 Charlotte Street
London W17 1RH
020 7705 3000
team@attheraces.co.uk
www.attheraces.co.uk
Managing director: Sir Iain Hogg; head of betting: David Stewart

B4U
Transputec House
19 Heather Park Drive
Wembley HA0 1SS
020 8795 7171
Press: sajnit@b4unetwork.com
www.b4utv.com
Programme controller: Anita Roy

B4U Music
Transputec House
19 Heather Park Drive
Wembley HA0 1SS
020 8795 7171
Press: sajnit@b4unetwork.com
www.b4utv.com
Programme controller: Anita Roy

BBC America
7475 Wisconsin Avenue, 11th Floor
Bethesda, USA MD 20814
00 1 301 347 2222
bbcamerica@bbc.co.uk
Press: press.office@bbc.co.uk
www.bbcamerica.com
Programme executive: Alison Fredericks

BBC Canada
121 Bloor Street East, Suite 200
Toronto, Ontario, Canada M4W 3M5
00 416 934 7800
feedback@bbccanada.com
Press: press.office@bbc.co.uk
www.bbccanada.com

BBC Food
PO Box 5054, London W12 0ZY
020 8433 2221
bbcfood@bbc.co.uk
Press: press.office@bbc.co.uk
www.bbcfood.com
Editor: David Weiland

BBC Four
Television Centre, Wood Lane
London W12 7RJ
020 8576 3193
Press: press.office@bbc.co.uk
www.bbc.co.uk/bbcfour
Controller: Janice Hadlow

BBC News 24
Television Centre, Wood Lane
London W12 7RJ
020 8743 8000
bbcnews24@bbc.co.uk
Press: press.office@bbc.co.uk
www.bbc.co.uk/bbcnews24
Editoral director: Mark Popescu

BBC One
Television Centre, Wood Lane
London W12 7RJ
020 8743 8000
Press: press.office@bbc.co.uk
www.bbc.co.uk/bbcone
Controller: Lorraine Heggessey; controller of daytime: Alison Sharman daytime.proposals@bbc.co.uk

BBC Parliament
4 Millbank, London SW1P 3JA
020 7973 6216
parliament@bbc.co.uk
Press: press.office@bbc.co.uk
www.bbc.co.uk/bbcparliament

BBC Prime
PO Box 5054, London W12 0ZY
020 8433 2221
bbcprime@bbc.co.uk
Press: press.office@bbc.co.uk
www.bbcprime.com
Editor: David Weiland

BBC Three
Television Centre, Wood Lane
London W12 7RJ
020 8743 8000
bbcthreefeedback@bbc.co.uk
press: press.office@bbc.co.uk
www.bbc.co.uk/bbcthree
Controller: Stuart Murphy

BBC Two
Television Centre, Wood Lane
London W12 7RJ
020 8743 8000
Press: press.office@bbc.co.uk
www.bbc.co.uk/bbctwo
Controller: Roly Keating

BBC World
Television Centre, Wood Lane
London W12 7RJ
020 8576 2308
bbcworld@bbc.co.uk
Press: press.office@bbc.co.uk
www.bbcworld.com
Editorial director: Sian Kevill

Biography Channel
Grant Way, Isleworth TW7 5QD
0870 240 3000
Press: biographychannelpress@bskyb.com
www.thebiographychannel.co.uk
Channel director: Richard Melman

Bloomberg Television
City Gate House
39–45 Finsbury Square
London EC2A 1PQ
020 7330 7797
Press: dwachtel@bloomberg.net
www.bloomberg.com/tv
Executive editor, broadcast: Ken Cohn

Boomerang
Turner House
16 Great Marlborough Street
London W1F 7HS
020 7693 1000
Press: lucy.amos@turner.com
www.cartoonnetwork.co.uk
press website:
www.europe.turnerinfo.com
Channel manager: Dan Balaam

The Box
Mappin House, 4 Winsley Street
London W1W 8HF
020 7182 8000
Press: maureen.corish@emap.com
www.emap.com
Programme director: Dave Young; director of music: Simon Sadler

Bravo
160 Great Portland Street
London W1W 5QA
020 7299 5000
Press: jakki_lewis@flextech.co.uk
www.bravo.co.uk
Programme controller: Richard Woolfe

British Eurosport
55 Drury Lane, London WC2B 5SQ
020 7468 7777
Press: swalker@eurosport.com
www.eurosport.co.uk
Programming director: Pierre Jean Sebert

Cartoon Network
Turner House
16 Great Marlborough Street
London W1F 7HS
020 7693 1000
Press: lucy.amos@turner.com
www.cartoonnetwork.co.uk; press website: www.europe.turnerinfo.com
Channel manager: Don Gardiner

CBBC
Television Centre, Wood Lane
London W12 7RJ
020 8743 8000
Press: press.office@bbc.co.uk
www.bbc.co.uk/cbbc
Controller: Dorothy Prior

CBeebies
Television Centre, Wood Lane
London W12 7RJ
020 8743 8000
Press: press.office@bbc.co.uk
www.bbc.co.uk/cbeebies
Controller: Dorothy Prior

Challenge
160 Great Portland Street
London W1W 5QA
020 7299 5000
Press: jakki_lewis@flextech.co.uk
www.challenge.co.uk
Programme controller: Jonathan Webb

Chelsea TV
Stamford Bridge, Fulham Road
London SW6 1HS
020 7915 1980
chelseatv@chelseafc.com
www.chelseafc.com
Managing director: Chris Tate

Chinese Channel
Teddington Studios, Broom Road
Teddington TW11 9NT
020 8614 8364
newseditor@chinese-channel.co.uk
www.chinese-channel.co.uk
Head of programming: Desmond Ng

CNBC Europe
10 Fleet Place, London EC4M 7QS
020 7653 9300
Press: cblenkinsop@cnbceurope.com
www.cnbceurope.com
Programme controller: Harry Fuller

CNN
Turner House
16 Great Marlborough Street
London W1F 7HS
020 7693 1000;
Press: 020 7693 0942
Press: chris.dwyer@turner.com
http://edition.cnn.com
International managing editor for EMEA: Nick Wrenn

The Community Channel
3–7 Euston Centre, Regent's Place
London NW1 3JG
020 7874 7626
Press: helenad@communitychannel.org
www.communitychannel.org
Channel controller: Jane Mote

Discovery Animal Planet
160 Great Portland Street
London W1W 5QA
020 7462 3600
Press: becky_weathers@discovery-europe.com
www.discoverychannel.co.uk
Channel director: Eliza Burrows

Discovery Channel
160 Great Portland Street
London W1W 5QA
020 7462 3600
Press: lee_hobbs@discovery-europe.com
www.discoverychannel.co.uk
Channel director: Katy Thorogood

Discovery Civilisation
160 Great Portland Street
London W1W 5QA
020 7462 3600
Press: jo_march@discovery-europe.com
www.discoverychannel.co.uk
Channel director: Katy Thorogood

Discovery Health
160 Great Portland Street
London W1W 5QA
020 7462 3600
Press: libby_rowley@discovery-europe.com
www.discoverychannel.co.uk
Channel director: Clare Laycock

Discovery Home and Leisure
160 Great Portland Street
London W1W 5QA
020 7462 3600
Press: claire_phillips@discovery-europe.com
www.discoverychannel.co.uk
Channel director: Paul Welling

Discovery Kids
160 Great Portland Street
London W1W 5QA
020 7462 3600
Press: libby_rowley@discovery-europe.com
www.discoverychannel.co.uk
Channel director: Clare Laycock

Discovery Science
160 Great Portland Street
London W1W 5QA
020 7462 3600
Press: jo_march@discovery-europe.com
www.discoverychannel.co.uk
Channel director: Katy Thorogood

Discovery Travel and Adventure
160 Great Portland Street
London W1W 5QA
020 7462 3600
Press: claire_phillips@discovery-europe.com
www.discoverychannel.co.uk
Channel director: Paul Welling

Discovery Wings
160 Great Portland Street
London W1W 5QA
020 7462 3600
Press: jo_march@discovery-europe.com
www.discoverychannel.co.uk
Channel director: Katy Thorogood

Disney Channel
Chiswick Park, Building 12
566 Chiswick High Road
London W4 5AN
020 8636 2000
Press: rachel.babington@disney.com
www.disneychannel.co.uk
Director of programming and acquisitions: James Neal

E4
124 Horseferry Road
London SW1P 2TX
020 7396 4444
Press: mbeake@channel4.co.uk
www.channel4.com/e4
Head of programming: Murray Boland

Eurosport International
55 Drury Lane, London WC2B 5SQ
020 7468 7777
Press: swalker@eurosport.com
www.eurosport.com
Programming director: Pierre Jean Sebert

Eurosportnews
55 Drury Lane, London WC2B 5SQ
020 7468 7777
Press: swalker@eurosport.com
www.eurosport.co.uk
Programming director: Pierre Jean Sebert

Extreme Sports Channel
The Media Centre
19 Bolsover Street
London W1W 5NA
020 7886 0770
Press: zoe@extremesportschannel.com
www.extreme.com
Head of acquisitions: Andy Warkman

Fantasy Channel
Suite 14, Burlington House
St Saviours Road, St Helier
Jersey JE2 4LA
01534 703700
admin@nasnet.je
Programme controller: Peter Farell

Filmfour
124 Horseferry Road
London SW1P 2TX
020 7396 4444
Press: spinder@channel4.co.uk
www.filmfour.com
Head of film: Tessa Ross

Flaunt
Grant Way, Isleworth TW7 5QD
0870 240 3000
www.flaunt.tv
Head of music: Jo Wallace

FTN
160 Great Portland Street
London W1W 5QA
020 7299 5000
Press: judy_wells@flextech.co.uk; jessica_alder@flextech.co.uk
www.ftn.tv
Programme controller: Richard Woolfe

God TV
Crown House, Borough Road
Sunderland SR1 1HW
0191 568 0800
info@god.tv
www.GOD.tv
Network controller: Wendy Alec

Granada Men and Motors
Franciscan Court, 16 Hatfields
London SE1 8DJ
020 7578 4040
Press: malcolm.packer@gsb.co.uk
www.menandmotors.co.uk
Director of programming: Gary Shoefield

Hallmark
234a Kings Road
London SW3 5UA
020 7368 9100
info@hallmarkchannel.co.uk
Press: janemuirhead@hallmarkchannel.com
www.hallmarkchannel.co.uk
Director of acquisitions: Rosy Hill-Davies

History Channel
Grant Way, Isleworth TW7 5QD
0870 240 3000
Press: historychannelpress@bskyb.com
www.thehistorychannel.co.uk
Channel director: Richard Melman

Hits Channel
Mappin House, 4 Winsley Street
London W1W 8HF
020 7182 8000
Press: maureen.corish@emap.com
www.emapadvertising.com
Programme director: Dave Young; director of music: Simon Sadler

ITV1
200 Grays Inn Road
London WC1X 8XZ
020 7843 8000
www.itv.com/itv1
Director of programmes: Nigel Pickard; director of programme strategy: David Bergg

ITV2
200 Grays Inn Road
London WC1X 8XZ
020 7843 8000
www.itv.com/itv2
Channel editor: Zai Bennett, 020 7843 8129; controller of commissioned programmes: Daniella Neumann, 020 7843 8101

ITV News
200 Grays Inn Road
London WC1X 8XZ
020 7833 3000
Press: itvplanning@itn.co.uk
www.itv.com/news
Editor-in-chief: David Mannion

Kerrang TV
Mappin House, 4 Winsley Street
London W1W 8HF
020 7182 8000
Press: maureen.corish@emap.com
www.emapadvertising.com
Programme director: Dave Young; director of music: Simon Sadler

Kiss TV
Mappin House, 4 Winsley Street
London W1W 8HF
020 7182 8000
Press: maureen.corish@emap.com
www.emapadvertising.com
Programme director: Dave Young; director of music: Simon Sadler

Living
160 Great Portland Street
London W1W 5QA
020 7299 5000
Press: judy_wells@flextech.co.uk; jessica_alder@flextech.co.uk
www.livingtv.co.uk
Programme controller: Richard Woolfe

Magic TV
Mappin House, 4 Winsley Street
London W1W 8HF
020 7182 8000
Press: maureen.corish@emap.com
www.emapadvertising.com
Programme director: Dave Young; director of music: Simon Sadler

MTV Base
MTV, Hawley Crescent
London NW1 8TT
020 7284 7777
Press: parker.eleanor@mtvne.com
www.mtv.co.uk
Head of development (for programme commissions): Chris Sice

MTV Dance
MTV, Hawley Crescent
London NW1 8TT
020 7284 7777
Press: parker.eleanor@mtvne.com
www.mtv.co.uk
Head of development (for programme commissions): Chris Sice

MTV UK & Ireland
MTV, Hawley Crescent
London NW1 8TT
020 7284 7777
Press: parker.eleanor@mtvne.com
www.mtv.co.uk
Head of development (for programme commissions): Chris Sice

MTV2
MTV, Hawley Crescent
London NW1 8TT
020 7284 7777
Press: parker.eleanor@mtvne.com
www.mtv.co.uk
Head of development (for programme commissions): Chris Sice

Music Choice Europe
Fleet House
57–61 Clerkenwell Road
London EC1M 5AR
020 7014 8700
Press: djones@musicchoice.co.uk
www.musicchoice.co.uk/
Head of music and PR: Dylan Jones

MUTV
4th Floor, 274 Deansgate
Manchester M3 4JB
0161 834 1111
mutv@mutv.com
www.manutd.com/mutv
Editor-in-chief: Bob Farrer

Nation 217
6&7 Princes Court
Wapping Lane, London E1W 2DA
020 7942 7942
william.van.rest@nation217.tv
www.nation217.tv
Head: William van Rest

National Geographic Channel
Grant Way, Isleworth TW7 5QD
020 7705 3000
natgeoweb@bskyb.com
www.nationalgeographic.co.uk
General manager: Simon Bohrsmann

Nick Jr
Nickelodeon House
15-18 Rathbone Place
London W1T 1HU
020 7462 1000
www.nickjr.co.uk
Director of programming: Howard Litton

Nickelodeon
Nickelodeon House
15–18 Rathbone Place
London W1T 1HU
020 7462 1000
www.nick.co.uk
Director of programming: Howard Litton

Nicktoons TV
Nickelodeon House
15–18 Rathbone Place
London W1T 1HU
020 7462 1000
www.nick.co.uk/toons/
Director of programming: Howard Litton

Paramount Comedy
UK House, 4th Floor
180 Oxford Street
London W1D 1DS
020 7478 5300
Press: zoe.diver@paramountcomedy.com
www.paramountcomedy.co.uk
Director of programming: Heather Jones

Plus
Franciscan Court, 16 Hatfields
London SE1 8DJ
020 7578 4040
Press: malcolm.packer@gsb.co.uk
www.plustv.co.uk
Director of programming: Gary Shoefield

Q TV
Mappin House, 4 Winsley Street
London W1W 8HF
020 7182 8000
Press: maureen.corish@emap.com
www.emapadvertising.com
Programme director: Dave Young; director of music: Simon Sadler

QVC
Marco Polo Hous
346 Queenstown Road
Chelsea Bridge, London SW8 4NQ
020 7705 5600
Press: 020 7886 8440
www.qvcuk.com
Planning manager: Susan Hellyar

Revelation TV
117a Cleveland Street
London W1T 6PX
020 7631 4446
howard@revelationtv.com
leslie@revelationtv.com
www.revelationtv.com
Head of programming: Howard Conder

Sci-Fi
5–7 Mandeville Place
London W1U 3AR
020 7535 3500
Press: 020 7535 3591
www.uk.scifi.com
Head of programming & acquisitions: Monica Iglesias

Scuzz
Grant Way, Isleworth TW7 5QD
0870 240 3000
www.scuzz.tv
Head of music: Jo Wallace

Setanta Sport Europe
52 The Haymarket, St James's
London SW1Y 4RP
020 7930 8926
setantauk@setanta.com
www.setanta.com
Joint managing director: Leonard Ryan

Sky Bet
Grant Way, Isleworth TW7 5QD
0870 240 3000
www.skybet.com;
www.skybetvegas.com
Head of programme publicity: Richard Turner – richard.turner@bskyb.com

Sky Box Office
Grant Way, Isleworth TW7 5QD
0870 240 3000
www.skymovies.com
Director: Sophie Turner-Laing

Sky Cinema 1 & 2
Grant Way, Isleworth TW7 5QD
0870 240 3000
www.skymovies.com
Director: Sophie Turner-Laing

Sky Movies 1
Grant Way, Isleworth TW7 5QD
0870 240 3000
www.skymovies.com
Director: Sophie Turner-Laing

Sky Movies 2
Grant Way, Isleworth TW7 5QD
0870 240 3000
www.skymovies.com
Director: Sophie Turner-Laing

Sky News
Grant Way, Isleworth TW7 5QD
0870 240 3000
www.skynews.co.uk
Head of Sky News: Nick Pollard

Sky One
Grant Way, Isleworth TW7 5QD
0870 240 3000
www.skyone.co.uk
Controller: James Baker

Sky One Mix
Grant Way, Isleworth TW7 5QD
0870 240 3000
www.skyone.co.uk
Controller: James Baker

Sky Sports 1, 2 & 3
Grant Way, Isleworth TW7 5QD
0870 240 3000
www.skysports.com
Managing director: Vic Wakeling

Sky Sports Extra
Grant Way, Isleworth TW7 5QD
0870 240 3000
www.skysports.com
Managing director: Vic Wakeling

Sky Sports News
Grant Way, Isleworth TW7 5QD
0870 240 3000
www.skysports.com
Managing director: Vic Wakeling

Sky Travel
Grant Way, Isleworth TW7 5QD
0870 240 3000
www.skytravel.co.uk
General manager: Barbara Gibbon

Sky Travel Extra
Grant Way, Isleworth TW7 5QD
0870 240 3000
www.skytravel.co.uk
General manager: Barbara Gibbon

Sky Travel Shop
Grant Way, Isleworth TW7 5QD
0870 240 3000
www.skytravel.co.uk
General manager: Barbara Gibbon

Sky Vegas Live
Grant Waym Isleworth TW7 5QD
0870 240 3000
www.skyvegaslive.com

Smash Hits Channel
Mappin House, 4 Winsley Street
London W1W 8HF
020 7182 8000
Press: maureen.corish@emap.com
www.emapadvertising.com
Programme director: Dave Young; director of music: Simon Sadler

Sony Entertainment TV Asia
34 Foubert's Place
London W1V 2BH
020 7534 7575
Press: ash_jaswal@spe.sony.com
www.setasia.tv
Head of UK and Europe: Nilam Panchal

Star TV
Great West House
Great West Road, Brentford
Middlesex TW8 9DF
020 7805 2326
Press: rinku.devgun@bskyb.com
www.uk.startv.com
UK marketing executive: Rinku Devgun

SUBtv
4th Floor
140 Buckingham Palace Road
London SW1W 9SA
020 7881 2540
info@jvtv.net
www.jvtv.net
Commercial manager: Joy Golden; creative director: Jon Kingdon

TMF (available on Freeview)
MTV, Hawley Crescent
London NW1 8TT
020 7284 7777
Press: hershon.mandy@mtvne.com
www.vh1.co.uk
Acting general manager (for programme commissions): Steve Shannon

Toonami
Turner House
16 Great Marlborough Street
London W1F 7HS
020 7693 1000
Press: lucy.amos@turner.com
www.cartoonnetwork.co.uk; press website: www.europe.turnerinfo.com
Channel manager: Paul Cackett

Travel Channel
66 Newman Street
London W1T 3EQ
020 7636 5401
Press: petra@travelchannel.co.uk
www.travelchannel.co.uk
Head of programming: Angela Taylor

Trouble
160 Great Portland Street
London W1W 5QA
020 7299 5000
Press: jakki_lewis@flextech.co.uk
www.trouble.co.uk
Programme controller: Jonathan Webb

Turner Classic Movies
Turner House
16 Great Marlborough Street
London W1F 7HS
020 7693 1000
Press: ann.rosen@turner.com
www.tcmonline.co.uk; press website: www.europe.turnerinfo.com
Channel manager: Alan Musa

UKTV Bright Ideas
UKTV, 2nd Floor, Flextech Building
160 Great Portland Street
London W1W 5QA
020 7299 6200
Press: dorita.hollins@uktv.co.uk
www.uktv.co.uk
Head of lifestyle: Nick Thorogood

UKTV Documentary
UKTV, 2nd Floor, Flextech Building
160 Great Portland Street
London W1W 5QA
020 7299 6200
Press: rebecca.hook@uktv.co.uk
www.uktv.co.uk
Head of factual: Charlotte Ashton

UKTV Drama
UKTV, 2nd Floor, Flextech Building
160 Great Portland Street
London W1W 5QA
020 7299 6200
Press: carolyn.ball@uktv.co.uk
www.uktv.co.uk
Head of entertainment: Matt Tombs

UKTV Food
UKTV, 2nd Floor, Flextech Building
160 Great Portland Street
London W1W 5QA
020 7299 6200
Press: dorita.hollins@uktv.co.uk
www.uktvfood.co.uk
Head of lifestyle: Nick Thorogood

UKTV G2
UKTV, 2nd Floor, Flextech Building
160 Great Portland Street
London W1W 5QA
020 7299 6200
Press: carolyn.ball@uktv.co.uk
www.uktv.co.uk
Head of entertainment: Matt Tombs

UKTV Gold
UKTV, 2nd Floor, Flextech Building
160 Great Portland Street
London W1W 5QA
020 7299 6200
Press: carolyn.ball@uktv.co.uk
www.uktv.co.uk
Head of entertainment: Matt Tombs

UKTV History
UKTV, 2nd Floor, Flextech Building
160 Great Portland Street
London W1W 5QA
020 7299 6200
Press: rebecca.hook@uktv.co.uk
www.uktv.co.uk
Head of factual: Charlotte Ashton

UKTV People
UKTV, 2nd Floor, Flextech Building
160 Great Portland Street
London W1W 5QA
020 7299 6200
Press: rebecca.hook@uktv.co.uk
www.uktv.co.uk
Head of factual: Charlotte Ashton

UKTV Style
UKTV, 2nd Floor, Flextech Building
160 Great Portland Street
London W1W 5QA
020 7299 6200
Press: dorita.hollins@uktv.co.uk
www.uktvstyle.co.uk
Head of lifestyle: Nick Thorogood

VH1
MTV, Hawley Crescent
London NW1 8TT
020 7284 7777
Press: hershon.mandy@mtvne.com
www.vh1.co.uk
Acting general manager (for programme commissions): Steve Shannon

VH1 Classic
MTV, Hawley Crescent
London NW1 8TT
020 7284 7777
Press: hershon.mandy@mtvne.com
www.vh1.co.uk
Acting general manager (for programme commissions): Steve Shannon

VH2
MTV, Hawley Crescent
London NW1 8TT
020 7284 7777
Press: hershon.mandy@mtvne.com
www.vh1.co.uk
Acting general manager (for programme commissions): Steve Shannon

Zee TV
64 Newman Street
London W1T 3ES
020 7637 4502
media@zeenetwork.com
www.zeetelevision.com
Programmes manager: Pranab Kapadia

Data services

Teletext
Building 10, Chiswick Park
566 Chiswick High Road
London W4 5TS
0870 731 3000
editor@teletext.co.uk
www.teletext.co.uk
Has a licence to use spare capacity within the Channel 3 (ITV) signal

Data Broadcasting International
Allen House, Station Road
Egham, Surrey TW20 9NT
01784 471515
sales@databroadcast.co.uk
www.databroadcast.co.uk

Other broadcasters

6TV Southampton
023 8023 2400
feedback@southamptontv.co.uk
www.southamptontv.co.uk

Abacus TV
01508 570970
sales@abacustv.co.uk
www.abacustv.co.uk

BFBS Forces Radio and TV
01494 878290
sarah.dornford-may@ssvc.com
www.ssvc.com

Bloomsbury Television (BTV)
020 7387 3827
btv@ucl.ac.uk
www.homepages.ucl.ac.uk/~uczxbts/

BVTV
01582 581753
info@bvtv.co.uk
www.bvtv.co.uk

C4TV
c4tv@cant.ac.uk
www.c4online.co.uk

Caledonia Television
01463 790310
george.cocker@tvaye.co.uk
www.tvaye.co.uk

Capital TV (Wales)
02920 488500
capitaltv@newsnet.co.uk
www.newsnet.co.uk

Channel M
0161 475 4855
info@channelM.co.uk
www.channelm.co.uk

EBS New Media
01462 895999
ben@newmedia.co.uk
www.ebs.newmedia.com

Glasgow University Student Television (GUST)
0141 341 6216
gust@src.gla.ac.uk
www.src.gla.ac.uk/gust

Glasgow's Own Television Channel Limited
0141 331 0077
rockettvf@aol.com

Leeds University Union TV (LUUTV)
0113 3801423
nick.smith@luutv.co.uk
www.luutv.co.uk/

Loughborough Students Union TV (LSUTV)
01509 635045
manager@lsutv.co.uk
www.lsutv.co.uk/

Middlesex Broadcasting Corporation (MATV Channel 6)
0116 253 2288
info@matv.co.uk
www.matv.co.uk/

Nerve TV
01202 595765
sucptomms@bournemouth.ac.uk
www.subu.org.uk/nerve

Nexus UTV
01603 456161
sunexus@uea.ac.uk
www.uea.ac.uk/~sunexus/

North West Television Services (Channel 9 – Coleraine, Limavady, Londonderry/Derry)
028 7131 4400
info@c9tv.tv
www.c9tv.tv

Northern Visions
028 9024 5495
info@northernvisions.org
www.northernvisions.org

Oxford Broadcasting Limited (Six TV)
01865 557000
admin@oxfordchnnel.com
www.oxfordchannel.com

Red TV
01223 722722
tim@dawemedia.co.uk
www.redtv.co.uk

Solent TV (Isle of Wight)
01983 522344
info@solent.tv
www.solent.tv

STOIC Student Television of Imperial College
020 7594 8104
james@stoictv.com
www.stoictv.com/

Thistle Television
01698 833773
andrew.everitt@thistletv.com
www.thistletv.com

TV Portsmouth
023 8023 2400
enquiries@portsmouthtv.co.uk
www.portsmouthtv.co.uk

XTV
01392 263598
gareth@xtv.org.uk
www.xtv.org.uk/

YCTV - Youth Culture Television
020 8964 4646
stuartr@yctv.org
www.yctv.org

York University St John Student Television (YSTV)
01904 624624
station.director@ystv.york.ac.uk
www.ystv.york.ac.uk

Independent production companies

Key companies

ALL3MEDIA
87–91 Newman Street
London W1T 3EY
020 7907 0177
www.allthreemedia.com
Chief executive: Steve Morrison; chief operating officer: Jules Burns; creative director: David Liddiment
Formerly Chrysalis TV

Assembly TV
Riverside Studios
Crisp Road, London W6 9RL
020 8237 1075
judithmurrell@riversidestudios.co.uk
www.allthreemedia.com
Chief executive: William Burdett-Coutts
- *Black Books; Jo Brand's Hot Potatoes; In Exile*

Bentley Productions
Pinewood Studios, Pinewood Road
Iver, Bucks SL0 0NH
01753 656594
www.allthreemedia.com
Managing director: Brian True-May
- *Midsomer Murders; Ultimate Force*

Cactus TV
373 Kennington Road
London SE11 4PS
020 7091 4900
touch.us@cactustv.co.uk
www.cactustv.co.uk
Managing directors: Simon Ross, Amanda Ross
- *Richard & Judy*

Lion Television
Lion House, 26 Paddenswick Road
London W6 0UB
020 8846 2000
mail@liontv.co.uk
www.liontv.co.uk
Scotland: 0141 331 0450
New York: +1 212 206 8633
LA: +1 310 566 7940
Managing directors: Richard Bradley, Nick Catliff, Shahana Meer, Jeremy Mills; director of production: Patsy Blades; executive producers: Bill Locke, Hilary Rosen
- *Bad Behaviour; Days That Shook the World; Britain's Finest; Castles; Royal Deaths and Diseases; Passport to the Sun*

North One TV
Maywood House
46–52 Pentonville Road
London N1 9HF
020 7502 6000
annelise.unitt@northonetv.com
www.allthreemedia.com
Managing director: Neil Duncanson; chief executive: John Wohlgemuth; head of production, entertainment: Pip Haddow; production logistics manager: Robert Gough
- *Formula One; World Rally; The Top Ten series; Speed Sunday; Fifth Gear*

Celador Productions
39 Long Acre, London WC2 9LG
020 7845 6999
tvhits@celador.co.uk
www.celador.co.uk
Managing directors: Paul Smith, Danielle Lux; head of entertainment: Colman Hutchinson; head of production: Heather Hampson; development executives, comedy: Vanessa Haynes, Humphrey Barclay; marketing manager: Michael Seres
- *You Are What You Eat; It's Been A Bad Week; Who Wants To Be a Millionaire?; Winning Lines; Britain's Brainiest*

Diverse
Gorleston Street, London W14 8XS
020 7603 4567
reception@diverse.tv
www.diverse.tv
Head of post-production: Paul Bates; director of programmes: Narinder Minhas; creative director: Roy Ackerman; head of production: Janet Smyth; bookings: Fay Searl
- *Operatunity; The Plot to Kill Hitler; The House of War; The Real George V; The Truth About Gay Animals*

Endemol UK
Shepherds Building Centre,
Clarecroft Way, Shepherds Bush
London W14 0EE
0870 333 1700
info@endemoluk.com
www.endemoluk.com
Chief executive: Tom Barnicoat; managing director: Nikki Cheetham; director of production: Clare Pickering; heads of production: Petrina Good, Richard Thomson
- *Big Brother; Fame Academy; Orange British Academy Film Awards; Ground Force; Changing Rooms; Restoration; The Salon 2; The Games*

Hat Trick Productions
10 Livonia Street, London W1F 8AF
020 7434 2451
info@hattrick.com
www.hattrick.com
Managing directors: Denise O'Donoghue, Jimmy Mulville; head of production: Laura Djanogle
• *Have I Got News For You; Bodies; Bromwell High; Room 101; The Kumars at No. 42; Father Ted; Jeffrey Archer - The Truth; Underworld; Drop The Dead Donkey*

IWC Media
St George's Studio
93-97 St George's Road
Glasgow G3 6JA
0141 353 3222
info@iwcmedia.co.uk
www.iwcmedia.co.uk
London: 020 7684 1661
Chairman: Alan Clements; managing director: Sue Oriel; creative directors: Zad Rogers, Hamish Barbour; head of documentaries: Charlotte Moore; news editor: Kirsty Walk; head of factual: Adam Barker
• *Ultimate Cars; 18th Street; Other Side; Location, Location, Location; The Planman; Changemakers; Hunt for Jill Dando's Killer*

Princess Productions
Whiteley's Centre, 151 Queensway
London W2 4SB
020 7985 1985
reception@princess.tv.com
www.princess.tv.com
Managing director: Sebastian Scott; head of production: Sarah Buckenham
• *Ruby Does the Business; Back to Reality; Bump 'n' Grind; Ri:se; The Wright Stuff*

Prospect Pictures
Wandsworth Plain
London SW18 1ET
020 7636 1234
rhys@prospect-uk.com
www.prospect-uk.com
Wales 029 2055 1177
Capital studios, London:
020 8877 1234
Directors: Rhys John, Tony McAvoy; managing director: Barry Lynth; head of production: Louise Doffman
• *Saturday Kitchen; Good Food Live; Under One Roof; Straight Dates by Gay Mates; A-list Diet with Food Doctor*

Ragdoll (UK)
Timothy's Bridge Road
Stratford Upon Avon CV37 9NQ
01789 404100
pinewood@ragdoll.co.uk
www.ragdoll.co.uk
USA: +1 212 966 4477
Director of production: Sue James
• *Open a Door; Rosie and Jim; Tots TV; Brum; Teletubbies; Teletubbies Everywhere; Boohbah*

RDF Media
The Gloucester Building
Kensington Village, Avonmore Road
London W14 8RF
020 7013 4000
contactus@rdfmedia.com
www.rdfmedia.com
LA: +1 818 817 5200
Head of production: Jane Wilson; production executive: Jo Crawley; press and marketing executive: Alice Robertson; senior producer: David Wise; executive producers: Jenny Crowther, Martin Davidson, Jill Robinson
• *Faking It 4; Wife Swap & Celebrity Wife Swap; Scrapheap Challenge 5; Century of the Self; Holiday Showdown*

September Films
Glen House, 22 Glenthorne Road
London W6 0NG
020 8563 9393
september@septemberfilms.com
www.septemberfilms.com
USA: +1 323 960 8085
Chief executive: Marcus Plantin; director of production: Elaine Day; director of factual and digital channels: Sam Brick; head of drama and film development: Nadine Mellor
• *Holiday Homes Nightmares; Clubbing on the Frontline; The Bottom Line; New Tycoons; Secrets and Lies; Instant Wedding; Making It*

Talkback Thames Productions
20–21 Newman Street
London W1T 1PG
020 7861 8000
reception@talkbackthames.tv
www.talkbackthames.tv
Chief executive: Peter Fincham; executive editor: Daisy Goodwin
• *Family Affairs; Bo' Selecta!; I'm Alan Partridge; Smack the Pony; Jamie's Kitchen; Property Ladder; Perfect Strangers*

The Television Corporation
30 Sackville Street, London W1S 3DY
020 7478 7300
tvcorp@tvcorp.co.uk
www.tvcorp.co.uk
Mentorn London: 020 7258 6800;
Oxford Mentorn: 01865 318 450;
Glasgow Mentorn: 0141 204 6600
Director of programmes: George Carey; managing director, Mentorn: Charles Thompson; head of programmes, Mentorn Scotland: Jane Rogerson; head of Mentorn Midlands: Eamonn Matthews; head of communications: Mark Ogle
• *Robot Wars; Britain's Worst Driver; Botham's Ashes; Gillette World Sport; Hitler's Legacy; Club Culture; Question Time; The Real Monty*

Tiger Aspect Productions
7 Soho Street, London W1D 3DQ
020 7434 6700
general@tigeraspect.co.uk
www.tigeraspect.co.uk
Managing director: Andrew Zein; executive producer, entertainment: Anastasia Mouzas; head of factual: Paul Sommers; head of comedy: Clive Tulloh; head of history and features: Charles Brand
Comedy, drama, entertainment, factual and animation.
• *Teachers; Murphy's Law; Fat Friends; Streetmate; Gimme Gimme Gimme*

TWI (Trans World International)
Pier House, Strand on the Green,
London W4 3NN
020 8233 5000
kmullins@imgworld.com
www.imgworld.com
Managing director: Andrew Hampel; head of production: Graham Fry
• *Japan's War (in colour series); Wimbledon; The Olympics; Premier League; PGA European Tour; Colour of War*

Twofour Productions
Quay West Studios, Old Newnham
Plymouth PL7 5BH
01752 333900
enq@twofour.co.uk
www.twofour.co.uk
Managing director: Charles Wace; director of business communications: Charles Mills; director of broadcast programming: Jill Lourie; director of production: Shireen Ward; director of broadcast development: Melanie Leach
• *G Girls; Gardens Through Time; Dead Famous; The City Gardener; Ideal Home Show*

Wall To Wall
8–9 Spring Place, Kentish Town
London NW5 3ER
020 7485 7424
mail@walltowall.co.uk
www.walltowall.co.uk
Head of production: Helena Ely
• *Life Beyond the Box: Norman Stanley Fletcher; New Tricks; The Regency House Party*

Zenith Entertainment
43–45 Dorset Street
London W1U 7NA
020 7224 2440
general@zenith-entertainment.co.uk
www.zenith-entertainment.co.uk
Managing director of production; Ivan Rendall
• *Byker Grove, 2000 Acres of Sky, CD:UK; RE-Covered; Headliners; Garden Rivals, Room Rivals; Brian's Boyfriends; Murder Most Foul*

Other production companies

12 Yard Productions
020 7432 2929
contact@12yard.com
www.12yard.com
Managing director: David Young
• *Dog Eat Dog; Weakest Link; In It To Win It; Without Prejudice?; Double Cross; EggHeads; Here Comes The Sun; Three's A Crowd*

1A Productions
01360 620855
langshot@nildram.co.uk
Managing director; Norman Stone
• *Tales From the Madhouse; Man Dancin'*

3BM Television
020 7251 2512
3bmtv@3bmtv.co.uk
www.3bmtv.co.uk
Managing director: Daniel Korn
• *War Lords; Children of Abraham; Zero Hour: Ten Days to D-Day*

The 400 Company
020 8746 1400
info@the400.co.uk
www.the400.co.uk
Managing director: Mark Sloper
• *The Real TT Heroes; Full Throttle Famous*

A Works TV
0118 934 2380
adrian@aworks.tv
www.aworks.tv
• *Sergeant Stripes (BBC)*

Absolutely Productions
020 7930 3113
info@absolutely-uk.com
www.absolutely-uk.com
Managing director: Miles Bullough
• *Barry Welsh; Pub Quiz; Stressed Eric; Trigger Happy TV*

Acacia Productions
020 8341 9392
projects@acaciaproductions.co.uk
www.acaciaproductions.co.uk
Managing director: J Edward Milner
• *Documentary and news, environment, current affairs and human rights*

Accomplice Television
00 353 1 660 3235
office@accomplice-tv.com
www.iftn.ie
Managing director: David Collins
• *Bachelors Walk Series 1, 2, 3*

Addictive Television
020 7700 0333
mail@addictive.com
www.addictive.com
Head of production: Nik Clarke; Graham Daniels
• *Spaced Out; Transambient; Night Shift; The Web Review, Mixmasters (ITV1), Visual Stings (Magnetic Channel)*

Aimimage Production Company
020 7482 4340
atif@aimimage.com
www.aimimage.com
Managing director: Ahmad Zadeh
• *Terra Circa; Balls to Basra; The Family Portrait*

Alibi Productions
020 7845 0400
rogerholmes@alibifilms.co.uk
www.alibifilms.co.uk
Chief executive officer: Roger Holmes
• *Sir Gadabout; The Safe House; Goodbye Mr Steadman*

Angel Eye Film and Television
020 7437 0082
office@angeleye.co.uk
www.angeleye.co.uk
Managing director: Richard Osborne
• *Beginners Luck; Estate Agents; Lady Macbeth; The Last Chances*

Antelope
01243 370806
mick.csaky@antelope.co.uk
www.antelope.co.uk
31 Willow Road, London NW3 1TL
Chief executive and creative director: Mike Csaky
• *Docs: Mozart in Turkey; Rebel Music: The Bob Marley Story; Geiko Girl, Africa Live; Epic Journey; 13-part series about Kyoto*

APT Films
020 7284 1695
admin@aptfilms.com
www.aptfilms.com
Managing director: Jonny Persey
• *Wondrous Oblivion (feature); Solomon and Gaenor (Oscar nomination, best foreign film); The Chosen Ones, Solo One, When I Lived in Modern Times*

At It Productions
020 8964 2122
enquiries@atitproductions.com
www.atitproductions.com
Managing directors: Martin Cunning, Chris Fouracre
• *T4; LA Pool Party; Sun Sea and Silicone; Perfect Getaway; Chancers; Popworld, 25 Years of Smash Hits*

Atlantic Productions
020 7371 3200
info@atlanticproductions.tv
www.atlanticproductions.tv
Managing director: Anthony Geffen
• *Spartans; The Queen of Sheba; Nefertiti Resurrected; Mystery of the Tibetan Mummy; The Real Jules Verne; Tutankhamen: a murder mystery*

Big Bear Films
020 7229 5982
office@bigbearfilms.co.uk
www.bigbearfilms.co.uk
Managing directors: John Stroud, Marcus Mortimer
• *My Hero (BBC1), Strange (with BBC1); Agatha Raisin; Hairy Bikers Cookbook*

Big Heart Media
020 7608 0352
info@bigheartmedia.com
www.bigheartmedia.com
Managing director: Colin Izod
• *Grid Club/music Studio; Spin 'n Groove; Street Corner Symphony; Rewind; Cape Farewell*

Big Umbrella Media
01225 817500
production@bigumbrellamedia.co.uk
www.bigumbrellamedia.co.uk
Third Floor, 37 Foley Street
London W1W 7TN
020 7631 2050
Managing director: Martin Head
• *Living with the New Cross Fire; Sir Frank Whittle: The Man who Shrank the World*

Big Wave Productions
01243 532531
info@bigwavetv.com
www.bigwavetv.com
Managing director: Sarah Cunliffe
• *Bug Attack; Death on the Amazon; Secret Weapons*

Black Coral Productions
020 8520 2881
bcp@coralmedia.co.uk
www.m4media.net
Managing director: Lazell Daley
• *Killing Time; Phil's Job; Which Witch is Which*

Blackwatch Productions
0141 222 2640
info@blackwatchtv.com
www.blackwatchtv.com
Managing director: Nicola Black
• *Boys with Breasts; Snorting Coke with the BBC; Designer Vagina*

Blakeway Productions
020 8743 2040
admin@blakeway.co.uk
www.blakeway.co.uk
Managing director: Denys Blakeway
• *Empire: how Britain made the modern world; Strike: When Britain Went to War; American Colossus; Prince William; Winston's War; The Major Years*

Blast! Films
020 7267 4260
blast@blastfilms.co.uk
www.blastfilms.co.uk
Managing director: Edmund Coulthard
• *Principles of Lust; The Death of Klinghoffer; Tales from Pleasure Beach*

Blue Egg Television/Blue Egg Studios
0870 765 0007
info@blueegg.tv
www.blueegg.tv
Managing director: Jill Scott
• *James Bond: Die Another Day; San Antonio, Orange Commercial*

Brechin Productions
020 8876 4333
clive@brechin.com
www.brechin.com
Managing director: Clive Doij
• *See it, Saw it; Turnabout; Eureka*

Brian Waddell Productions
028 9042 7646
strand@bwpltv.co.uk
www.bwpltv.co.uk
Managing director: Brian Waddell
• *The Craig Doyle Show; Carhunt; Chasing Time In... (13-part travel series, National Geographic); Ulster Fly; Boffins (6×30'); Life After*

Brighter Pictures
020 8222 4100
info@brighter.co.uk
www.brighter.co.uk
Managing director: Gavin Hay
• *Take the Mike; Bombay Blush; Diet Another Day*

Brighter Pictures Scotland
0141 572 0861
scotland@brighter.co.uk
www.brighter.co.uk
Managing director: Gavin Hay
• *Get a New Life (BBC2), Tabloid Tales (BBC1), Nick Nairn and the Dinner Ladies (BBC Scotland)*

Brighton TV
01273 224260
info@brighton.tv
www.brighton.tv
Managing director: David Pounds
• *Tales of the Living Dead; Big Boutique*

Brook Lapping Productions
020 7428 3100
info@brooklapping.com
www.brooklapping.com
Managing director: Brian Lapping
• *I met Osama Bin Laden; The fall of Milosevic; Avenging Terror; Before the Booker; I Met Adolf Eichmann*

Cactus TV
202 7091 4900
touch.us@cactustv.co.uk
www.cactustv.co.uk
Managing directors: Amanda Ross, Simon Ross
• *The Spirit of Diana, The Debate; Songs of Bond; Cliff Richard, The Hits I Missed; Richard & Judy; British Soap Awards*

Caledonia, Sterne And Wyld
0141 564 9100
info@caledonia-tv.com
www.caledonia-tv.com
Managing director: Seona Robertson
• *Sun Worshippers; King Jamie and the Angel; The Real Tartan Army II*

Carnival (Films and Theatre)
020 8968 0968
info@carnival-films.co.uk
www.carnival-films.co.uk
Managing director: Brian Eastman
• *Shadowlands; Firelight; Bugs; As If; Poirot; Rosemary and Thyme*

Channel X
020 7428 3999
info@channelx.co.uk
www.channelx.co.uk
Managing director: Alan Marke
• *Reeves & Mortimer; Date That; Popetown*

Cicada Films
020 7266 4646
cicada@cicadafilms.com
www.cicadafilms.com
Managing director: Frances Berrigan
• *Ancient inventions; NYPD Animal Squad; Fat Fiancees; The Abyss; Beyond Pompeii; Bikini*

Circle Multimedia
01243 601482/01628 509501
circlemultimedia@hotmail.com
www.circlemultimedia.com
Director: Jenny Burgess
• *Wire in the Blood; Alchemist's Cat (feature film), Afterlife (feature film), Conqueror (feature film), The Cloak (TV-DVD)*

Clearcut Communications
0161 427 3052
info@clearcut.freeserve.co.uk
Managing director: Robin Anderson
• *Sex and the Village; On the Edge (Granada); Sense of Place (BBC1); Shanghai'd (BBC2); Proof Positive (pilot for Discovery America)*

Clerkenwell Films
020 7608 2726
andy@clerkenwellfilms.com
Managing director: Murray Ferguson
• *Quite Ugly One Morning; Dr Jekyll and Mr Hyde (Universal TV); Inspector Rebus, Parlabane (ITV1)*

Collinwood O'Hare Entertainment
020 8993 3666
info@crownstreet.co.uk
www.collingwoodohare.com
Managing director: Christopher O'Hare
• *Animal Stories, Eddy and the Bear, The King's Beard, Yoko! Jakamoko! Toto!*

COLOUR Television
0141 222 2442
mail@colour-tv.com
www.colour-tv.com
• *EX-S; Edinburgh Nights; Love Bites; Fully Booked; Dali and the Doctor; Silicone Soul*

The Comedy Unit
0141 305 6666
comedyunit@comedyunit.co.uk
www.comedyunit.co.uk
Managing directors: Colin Gilbert, April Chamberlain
• *Still Game; The Karen Dunbar Show; Offside; Yo! Diary!; Taxi for Cowan Spanish Special; New Year specials: Chewin' The Fat; Only An Excuse?*

Company Pictures
020 7380 3900
enquiries@companypictures.co.uk
www.companypictures.co.uk
Managing directors: Charlie Pattinson, George Faber
• *Life and Death of Peter Sellers; Shameless; Forty; White Teeth; Anna Karenina*

Cosgrove Hall Films
0161 882 2500
animation@chf.co.uk
www.chf.co.uk
Managing director; Lee Marriott
• *Andy Pandy; Bill & Ben; Postman Pat; Enjie Benji; Dangermouse*

CTVC
020 8950 4426
ctvc@ctvc.co.uk
www.ctvc.co.uk
Head of programmes: Ray Bruce
• *Imber, Britain's Lost Village; Tonight; Shariah TV; Victim 001; Bethlehem Year Zero; John Meets Paul; A Mediterranean Journey; Understanding Islam*

Dai4Films
07976 819611
info@dai4films.com
www.dai4films.com
Managing director: Neil Davies
• *The Montserrat Volcano; Islands in the Sun; Working Machines; Double or Nothing; Raw Spice; Dirty Streets*

Dan Films
020 7916 4771
enquiries@danfilms.com
www.danfilms.com
Director: Julie Baines
• *Creep; Sons of the Wind; The Republic of Love*

Darlow Smithson Productions
020 7482 7027
mail@darlowsmithson.com
www.darlowsmithson.com
Managing director: John Smithson
• *Touching the Void; We Built the City; Dragons World.*

Darrall Macqueen
020 7407 2322
info@darrallmacqueen.com
www.darrallmacqueen.com
Managing directors: Maddy Darrall, Billy Macqueen
• *The Crust; Play the Game; Smile series 1,2,3 (BBC2); U Get Me series 1,2,3 (CBBC)*

Dazed Film and TV
020 7549 6840
info.film&tv@dazegroup.com
www.dazedfilmtv.com
Managing director: Laura Hastings-Smith
• *Perfect; Stop for a Minute; Untold Beauty, BBC3*

DLT Entertainment UK
020 7631 1184
jbartlett@dltentertainment.co.uk
www.dltentertainment.com
Managing director: John Bartlett
• *As Time Goes By; Love on a Branch Line; My Family, BBC1; Meet My Folks, BBC1*

DNA Films
020 7292 8700
info@dnafilms.com
www.dnafilms.com
Managing director: Andrew MacDonald
• *28 Days Later*

Double Exposure
020 7490 2499
reception@doublex.com
www.doublex.com
Managing director: Andrew Bethell
• *The House; Culloden; Pleasure Beach*

Eagle and Eagle
020 8995 1884
producer@eagletv.co.uk
www.eagletv.co.uk
Producer: Robert Eagle
• *The Nuclear Boy Scout (C4); Robo Sapiens (Discovery/TLC); Big Questions (C4 Learning)*

Eagle Films
01372 844484
enquiries@eaglefilms.co.uk
www.eaglefilms.co.uk
Producer: Katrina Moss
• *Bitter Honey; The Sins of the Father; It Started with a Kiss; The Road to Somewhere*

Ecosse Films
020 7371 0290
webmail@ecossefilms.com
www.ecossefilms.com
Managing director: Douglas Rae
• *Amnesia; Like Father Like Son; Monarch of the Glen; The Ambassador; Mrs Brown; Charlotte Gray*

Educational Broadcasting Services Trust
020 7613 5082
enquiries@ebst.co.uk
www.ebst.co.uk
Chief executive: Dr Jim Stevenson
• *Looking at Learning; Maths for Engineers; Maths tutor – Algebra*

Electric Sky
01273 224240
info@electricsky.com
www.electricsky.com
Managing director: David Pounds
• *Myths of Mankind; Iraq – in the Shadow of the Palms; First Human Clone*

The Elstree Production Company
01932 572680
enquiries@elsprod.com
www.elsprod.com
Producer: Greg Smith
• *Agnes Brown; George Orwell's Animal Farm; David Copperfield*

Extreme Production
028 9080 9050
dmalone@extremeproduction.com
www.extremeproduction.com
Managing director: David Malone
• *Macintyre's Millions; Clash of the Celtic Giants; Ballykissanything; Country Practice*

FACE Television
01256 350022
paula@facetv.co.uk
www.facetv.co.uk
Managing director: Paul Friend
• *Wildlife SOS series 1,2; Lifeboat Rescue; Wildlife Photographer*

Faction Films
020 7690 4446
faction@factionfilms.co.uk
www.factionfilms.co.uk
Managing directors: David Fox, Sylvia Stevens, Peter Day
• *Aphrodite's Drop; Murder in the Family; Love for Sale (BBC); Resistencia; Cinematic Orchestra (C4); Sonic Revolution (C4/Levi's); Point Annihilation (surf drama)*

The Farnham Film Company
01252 710313
info@farnfilm.com
www.farnfilm.com
Managing director: Ian Lewis
• *Dance with the Devil; Intergalactic Kevin; Mona the Vampire; The Druid's Tune*

Festival Film and TV
020 8297 9999
info@festivalfilm.com
Managing director: Ray Marshall
• *Feature films: Man Dancin'; The Colour*

Film and Music Entertainment
020 7636 9292
info@fame.uk.com
www.fame.uk.com
Managing director: Mike Downey
• *Guy X; Deathwatch; The Enemy*

Fireside Favourites
020 7439 6110
info@firesidefavourites.co.uk
www.firesidefavourites.co.uk
Managing director: Gavin Claxton
• *House of Rock; Infamous Five series 1 and 2*

Flame Television
020 7713 6868
contact@flametv.co.uk
www.theflamegroup.co.uk
Managing director: Roger Bolton
• *Discovery Health 2 bulletins; Cage Combat (Carlton); Crime Team (C4); Square Planet (Discovery Europe); Roadies 2 (UK Horizons); Ann Summers Uncovered (Carlton); Dim Crims (Five); Jane Goldman Investigates (Living TV); Wild Prince (C4)*

Flashback Television
020 7490 8996
mailbox@flashbacktv.co.uk or
bristol@flashbacktv.co.uk
www.flashbacktv.co.uk
1–2 Fitzroy Terrace
Lower Redland Road, Bristol BS6 6TF
0117 973 8755
Managing director: Taylor Downing
• *D-Day: The lost evidence; Regency Feast; The badness of King George IV; Nigella Bites; Speed Machines; Battlestations*

Flick features
020 7855 3697
info@flickfeatures.com
www.flickfeatures.co.uk
Director: John Deery
• *Hell4Leather; Feature film : Conspiracy of Silence; Pictures of Anna (in development)*

Flying Elephant Films
020 8230 6920
info@flyingelephant.co.uk
www.flyingelephant.co.uk
Managing director: Preeyf Nair
• *A Story That Begins at the End; A Different Life; You Know What I'm Saying*

Focus Productions
0117 904 6292
martinweitz@focusproductions.co.uk
or maddern@focusproductions.co.uk
www.focusproductions.co.uk
PO Box 173
Stratford-upon-Avon CV37 7ZA
01789 298948
Managing director: Martin Weitz
• *Pharaoh's Holy Treasure (BBC2), This Sceptred Isle, The Jewish Journey (BBC R4). Winner Sony Gold Award. Projects 2003: Witness on Saint-making (C4), The Godfather of the Blues (BBC4)*

Footstep Productions
020 7836 9990
info@footstep-productions.com
www.footstepproductions.com
Managing director: Collette Thomson
• *Worktalk; Voces Espanolas*

Free@Last TV
020 7242 4333
barry@freeatlasttv.co.uk
www.freeatlasttv.co.uk
Executive producer: Barry Ryan
• *The Spiderman Story; Making Of Jackass The Movie; Rock 'n' Roll Myths; Blackadder@20; Adored:The Stone Roses Story; Mobo Unsung; Dr Who@40*

Fresh One Productions
020 7359 1000
andrew@freshone.tv
Managing director: Andrew Conran
• *Jamie's School Dinners; Oliver's Twist; Jamie's Kitchen*

Fulcrum TV
020 7939 3160
info@fulcrumtv.com
www.fulcrumtv.com
Managing directors: Christopher Hird, Richard Belfield
• *The State of Texas; The Christmas Truce; The Utimate Psychic Challenge; Belonging; The Man from the Met*

Genesis Media Group
029 2066 6007
alan@genesis-media.co.uk
www.genesis-media.co.uk
Producer and programme director: Alan Torjussen
• *Peter Warlock; Ceiri and his Music; Love Talk; Leila Megane; corporate & govt projects plus travel, arts, music and docs for TV*

Ginger Television
020 7663 2300
production@ginger.tv
www.ginger.tv
Managing director: Elisabeth Partyka
• *Czech Mates; High School Projects USA; Extreme lives – My Right Foot; Don't Drop the Coffin (ITV), Timewatch – The Secrets of Enzo Ferrari (BBC2)*

Glasshead
020 8740 0024
media@glasshead.co.uk
www.glasshead.co.uk
Managing director: Lambros Atteshlis
• *Blue Dragon; Watch Magic Grandad; Real Science*

Green Bay Media
029 2064 2370
john-geriant@green-bay.tv
www.green-bay.tv
Managing director: Phil George, John Geraint
• *An Archbishop Like This; A Bloody Good Friday; Do Not Go Gentle*

Green Umbrella Ltd
0117 973 1729
postmaster@umbrella.co.uk
www.umbrella.co.uk
Managing director: Nigel Ashcroft
• *Journey to Centre of the Earth; Escape from Berlin; Galileo's Daughter*

Greenlit Productions
020 7287 3545
info@greenlit.co.uk
www.greenlit.co.uk
Managing director: Jill Green
• *Foyle's War; The Swap; Menace; Trust*

Greenpoint Films
020 7240 7066
info@greenpointfilms.com
www.greenpointfilms.co.uk
Managing directors: Patrick Cassavetti, Ann Scott, Simon Relph
• *Only Human; Hideous Kinky; The Land Girls*

Grosvenor Park Productions
020 7529 2500
chris.chrisafis@grosvenorpark.com
www.grosvenorpark.com
Managing director: Daniel Taylor
• *Reign of Fire; Being Julia; Colour Me Kubrick; Count of Monte Cristo; Spider*

Gruber Films
0870 366 9313
office@gruberfilms.com
www.gruberfilms.com
Managing director: Richard Holmes
• *Shooting Fish; Waking Ned; The Abduction Club*

Hand Pict Productions
0131 346 1111
ask@handpict.com
www.handpict.com
Director: George Cathro
• *Adoption Stories; East Coast Boy, West Coast Man; Numero Una*

Hanrahan Media
01789 450182
info@hanrahanmedia.com
www.hanrahanmedia.tv
Managing director: Will Hanrahan
• *Your Stars; Renovation Creation; Star Lives (ITV); World's Biggest Ghost Hunt; Most Haunted Live (LivingTV); Men's Health (Bravo)*

Hasan Shah Films
020 7722 2419
hsfilms@blueyonder.co.uk
Managing director: Hasan Shah
• *Short: Art Of The Critic. Feature in development 2003: A Little Scary*

Hopscotch Films
0141 334 5576
info@hopscotchfilms.co.uk
www.hopscotchfilms.co.uk
Managing directors: Charlotte
• *Wontner, Clara Glynn, John Archer Writing Scotland; Detox or Die; Last Train to Beechwood*

Hot Shot Films
028 9031 3332
info@hotshotfilms.com
www.hotshotfilms.com
Managing directors: Brendan J. Byrne, Jimmy McAleavey
• *Living History; Blind Vision; Street Detectives; So You Thought You Knew the Plantation; Heroes*

Hotbed Media
0121 248 3900
mail@hotbedmedia.co.uk
Managing director: Johannah Dyer
• *Under the Hammer; Songs of Praise; Real Brassed Off; 100 Worst Britons; Everything Must Go; 100 Worst Pop Records; Star Portraits with Rolf Harris*

Hourglass Productions
020 8540 8786
productions@hourglass.co.uk
www.hourglass.co.uk
Managing director: Martin Chilcott
• *Energy for Nature; DNA and Rocket Science, Living Donation*

HRTV
020 7494 3011
mail@hrtv-online.com
www.hrtv-online.com
Managing director: Jerry Hibbert
• *Tractor Tom; Stressed Eric series II*

Hyphen Films
020 7734 0632
nmk@hyphenfilms.com
Managing director: N.M. Kabir
• *Spotlights and Saris; Bollywood Dancing; Bollywood Women – Intros; Bismillah of Benarus; Bollywood Celebrities; Bollywood 2004*

Icon Films
0117 924 8535
info@iconfilms.co.uk
www.iconfilms.co.uk
Managing director: Laura Marshall
• *Belgrano; King Cobra; Einstein's Brain*

Illumina Digital
020 8600 9300
info@illumina.co.uk
www.illumina.co.uk
Managing director: Andrew Chitty
• *DFES; National Theatre; Culture; Net Cymru*

Illuminations Films
020 7288 8400
griff@illumin.co.uk
www.illumin.co.uk
Managing director: Keith Griffiths
• *The Piano Tuner of Earthquakes; London Orbital; Little Otik*

Images Of War
020 7267 9198
derek@dircon.co.uk
www.warfootage.com
Managing director: Derek Blades
• *Mass for Peace; Invasion; D-Day; Footage for Hitler's Britain; 300 hours of war-related material*

Imago Productions
01603 727600
mail@imagoproductions.tv
www.imagoproductions.tv
Managing director: Vivica Parsons
• *Grudge Match; Perfect Man; The Coach; Sporty Facts; Bryan's Olde and Bitter*

Independent Image
01883 654867
info@indimage.com
www.indimage.com
Managing director: David Wickham
• *Chefs in the City; Cannabis from the Chemist; Interpol's Most Wanted*

Infinite Pictures
01752 830000
info@infinitepictures.com
www.infinitepictures.com
Managing director: David Nottage
• *Boy's Toys; Civvie to Sailor; Centre Stage*

Infonation
020 7370 1082
mail@infonation.org.uk
www.infonation.org.uk
Managing director: Ron Blythe
• *Under One Umbrella; Protected Meal Times; Challenge UK*

Intelfax
020 7928 2727
billskirrow@intelfax.co.uk
www.intelfax.co.uk
Managing director: Bill Skirrow
• *Subtitles for: 21st Century War; A Band Called Treacle*

Intermedia Film and Video (Nottingham)
0115 955 6909
info@intermedianotts.co.uk
www.intermedianotts.co.uk
Managing director: Ceris Morris
• *One For The Road; Slot Art; Shifting Units; The Entertainer; DV Shorts; First Cut*

International Media Productions (IMP)
020 8690 9674
improductions@tiscali.co.uk
www.improductions.co.uk
Producer/director: Paul Moody
• *Arriva; Tiny Lives; A Beacon for Culture*

ITN factual
020 7430 4511
itn.factual@itn.co.uk
www.itn.co.uk
Head of ITN Factual: Philip Armstrong
• *Hunt for The Hood/Bismarck; Leonardo's Dream Machines; Sars – Global Killer; Are Your Kids on Drugs?*

IWC Media
0141 429 1750
info@iwcmedia.co.uk
www.warkclements.com
Managing director: Sue Oriel
• *Relocation, Relocation, Relocation; Location, Location, Location; Jeopardy; The First World War (C4)*

Jay Media
01270 884453
media@jaymedia.co.uk
www.jaymedia.co.uk
Managing director: Nigel Jay
• *Skill City; Manchester Evening News; Preston City Council*

The Jim Henson Company
020 7428 4000
fanmail@henson.com
www.henson.com
Managing director: Pete Coogan
• *Muppet series; Aliens in the Family; Bear in the Big Blue House*

Keo Films
020 7490 3580
keo@keofilms.com
www.keofilms.com
Managing director: Andrew Palmer
• *River Cottage Diner; Surviving Extremes; 10 Years Younger*

The Kilroy Television Company
020 7893 7900
info@kilroy.co.uk
Head of production: Graham Walters
• *Panorama; Now You're Talking!; The Kilroy Programme*

Landmark Films
01865 297220
info@landmarkfilms.com
www.landmarkfilms.com
Managing director: Nick O'Dwyer
• *Extraordinary Illness; Beauty School; Real Life Swap*

Landseer Productions
020 7485 7333
mail@landseerfilms.com
www.landseerfilms.com
Managing director and producer: Derek Bailey
• *Resurrecting St Luke's; South Bank Show – Johnnie Ray; The Magic Mountain*

Leopard Films
0870 420 4232
mail@leopardfilms.com
www.leopardfilms.com
Managing director: James Burstall
• *Car Booty; Cash in the Attic; Money Spinners; Elvis Mob*

Liberty Bell Productions
0191 222 1200
info@libertybell.tv
www.libertybell.tv
Managing directors: Stuart Prebble, Andrea Wonfor; head of features: Judith Holder
• *Grumpy Old Men; Victoria Wood's Big Fat Documentary; Stella's Story; For the Benefit of Mr Parris*

Libra Television
0161 236 5599
hq@libratelevision.com
www.libratelevision.com
Managing directors: Madeline Wiltshire, Louise Lynch
• *Gross; Citizen Power; How to be a Bully; Copycat Kids; History Busters*

Little Bird
00 353 1 613 1710
info@littlebird.ie
www.littlebird.ie
Co Chairmen: James Mitchell, Jonathan Cavendish
• *Bridget Jones 2 – The Edge of Reason; Trauma; Churchill the Hollywood Years; In my Father's Den*

Loose Moose
020 7287 3821
info@loosemoose.net
www.loosemoose.net
Managing director: Glenn Holberton
• *Pepperoni; Chips Ahoy!; Brisk Iced Tea*

Lupus Films
020 7419 0997
info@lupusfilms.net
www.lupusfilms.net
Managing directors: Camilla Deakin, Ruth Fielding
• *Little Wolf's Book of Badness (C4); Wilde Stories; Little Wolf's Adventure Academy; Mia, Cool Hunter*

M Power Media
0117 923 7333
enquiries@mpowermedia.uk.com
www.mpowermedia.uk.com
Managing director: Stef Brammar
• *Bristol City Council; Oxfam; Wells Cathedral School*

Macmillan Media
0870 350 2150
info@macmillanmedia.co.uk
www.macmillanmedia.co.uk
Managing director: Michael Macmillan
• *Corporate video*

Malachite
01790 763538
info@malachite.co.uk
www.malachite.co.uk
Managing director: Charles Mapleston
• *Fiore; Children of the Mafia; Organic Farm*

Maverick Television
0121 771 1812
mail@mavericktv.co.uk
www.mavericktv.co.uk
London office: 020 7631 1062
Chairman: Johnnie Turpie
• *Ten Years Younger; Celebrity Disfigurement*

Maya Vision International
020 7836 1113
info@mayavisionint.com
www.mayavisionint.com
Producer and director: Rebecca Dobbs
• *Great Mysteries (working title); Hitler's Search for the Holy Grail; Conquistadors; In Search of Shakespeare; Two Moons (feature)*

Mentorn
020 7258 6800
mentorn@mentorn.co.uk
www.mentorn.co.uk
Managing director: Charles Thompson
• *Robot Wars; Techno Games; Britain's Worst Driver*

Mint Productions
028 9024 0555
info@mint.ie
www.mint.ie
Belfast 028 9024 0555
Dublin 00 353 1 491 3333
Managing director: Steve Carson
• *Abu Hamza, Two Day Coup, De Lorean, Workers Strike, Crash, Emmet, All the Queen's Men, Who Kidnapped Shergar?*

Monkey
020 7749 3110
info@monkeykingdom.com
www.monkeykingdom.com
Managing director: Dom Loehnis
• *What Sadie Did Next; Swag; He's Starsky I'm Hutch*

Multi Media Arts
0161 374 5566
info@mmarts.com
www.mmarts.com
Managing director: Michael Spencer
• *Powerhouse; The Blizzard of Odd; Reality Bites*

Mute Marmalade
020 7449 2552
info@mutemarmalade.com
www.mutemarmalade.com
Managing director: Jonathan Bentata
• *Black Soles; The Runner; Making Mistakes*

Mykindofshow.com
020 7739 0234
mail@mykindofshow.com
www.mykindofshow.com
Managing director: Kirsten De Keyser
• *Follow That Tomato; Borscht, Blackbread and Champagne; Bin Sins; Six Degrees of Penetration; Tuscany To Go; Home Health Show*

Nexus Productions
020 7749 7500
info@nexusproductions.com
www.nexusproductions.com
Managing director: Chris O'Reilly
• *Catch Me if You Can; Goldfrapp; Erasure; Nike; T-Mobile; Aiwa; Monkey Dust*

October Films
020 7284 6868
info@octoberfilms.co.uk
www.octoberfilms.co.uk
Managing director: Tom Roberts
• *Suicide Bombers; Rugby World Cup – England's Story; Access to Evil*

Open Mind Productions
020 7437 0624
enquiries@openmind.co.uk
www.openmind.co.uk
Managing director: Roland Tongue
• *Paz; The Shiny Show; The Number Crew*

ORTV
020 8614 7200
info@ortv.co.uk
www.ortv.co.uk
Managing director: Nicholas Claxton
• *John McCarthy – Out of the Shadows; Heart of the Lioness; Saddam's Iraq*

Oxford Film And Television
020 7483 3637
email@oftv.co.uk
www.oftv.co.uk
Creative director:Nicholas Kent
• *Philip Larkin: Love and Death in Hull; Lionheart: the Crusade; Second Generation (all C4); Superfly, Terry Jones' Medieval Tales, National Trust (BBC)*

Paladin Invision
020 7371 2123
pitv@pitv.com
www.pitv.com
Managing directors: William Cran, Clive Syddall
• *Commanding Heights; Do You Speak American*

Pathe Pictures
020 7323 5151
orlaghcollins@pathe-uk.com
www.pathe.com
Managing director: Francois Ivernel
• *Natural History; Girl With a Pearl Earring; Millions*

Pepper's Ghost Productions
020 8546 4900
enquiries@peppersghost.com
www.peppersghost.com
Managing director: Paul Michael
• *Tiny Planets; Policecat Fuzz; Bus Stop; Kingfisher Tailor*

Pesky
020 7430 0200
hodgc@pesky.com
www.pesky.com
Directors: David Hodgson, Clare Underwood
• *Stress Maniacs (C4 pilot); Amazing Adrenalini Brothers; Thingamijig; I Could Murder A Curry*

Pilot Film and TV Productions
020 8960 2721
info@pilotguides.com
www.pilotguides.com
Director: John Pilot
• *Globe Trekker; Pilot Guides; Planet Food; Ian Wright Live*

Pioneer Productions
020 8748 0888
pioneer@pioneertv.com
www.pioneertv.com
Managing director: Stuart Carter
• *Naked Science; Danger Man; Tycoon Toys*

Planet 24 Productions
020 7612 0671
alice@planet24.co.uk
www.planet24.com
Managing director: Ed Forsdick
• *Mechanick; How to Pull…; Big Breakfast*

Planet Wild
0161 233 3090
office@planetwild.co.uk
www.planetwild.co.uk
Managing director: Paula Trafford
• *Cilla in Black and White; George Best's Story; Pushy Parents*

Presentable
029 2057 5729
all@presentable.co.uk
www.presentable.co.uk
Managing director: Megan Stewart
• *Celebrity Poker Club; Late Night Poker; Conversations with Ronan Williams*

The Press Association
020 7963 7474
broadcasting.info@pa.press.net
www.pabroadcasting.com
Managing director: Sean Curtis-Ward
• *A network of reporters, camera crews and editing facilities across the UK and Ireland*

Principal Films
020 7928 9287
films@principalmedia.com
www.principalmedia.com
Managing director: Richard Sattin
• *Concorde – A Love Story; Mountains and Man; Maidens of the Lost Ark*

Prism Entertainment
020 8969 1212
info@prism-e.com
www.prismentertainment.co.uk
Managing directors: Mike Crosby, Amelia Johnson
• *The Stables; FAQ series 3; Beat the Cyborgs*

Raw Charm
029 2064 1511
enquiries@rawcharm.tv
www.rawcharm.tv
Managing director: Pam Hunt
• *War Stories; Grave Detectives; Simon Weston's War Heroes*

Real Life Media Productions
0113 237 1005
info@reallife.co.uk
www.reallife.co.uk
Managing director: Ali Rashid
• *Mum, I'm a Muslim; Baby Baby; Britain's Most Dangerous Prisoner*

Red Fig
020 7944 0500
info@redfig.com
www.redfig.com
Marketing/PR: Heidi Scrimgeour
• *I'm A Celebrity… Get Me Out Of Here!; Popstars: The Rivals; Wild In Your Garden; The Big Conversation; Heaven and Earth; Asylum Day; Darkhouse; Justin Timberlake Karaoke Line*

Red Green and Blue Company
020 8746 0616
max@rgbco.com
www.rgbco.com
Production office:
1 Underwood Row
London N1 7LZ
020 7490 1788
Directors:Max Whitby, Cathy Collis
• *DNA Interactive*

Red Kite Animations
0131 554 0060
info@redkite-animation.com
www.redkite-animation.com
Managing director: Ken Anderson
• *The Secret World of Benjamin Bear; The Loch Ness Kelpie; Wilf the Witch's Dog*

Red Production Company
0161 827 2530
info@redlimited.co.uk
www.redproductioncompany.com
Managing director: Andrew Critchley
- *Blue Blood; Jane Hall Big Bad Bus Ride; Mine All Mine*

Reef Television
020 7836 8595
mail@reeftv.com
www.reef.tv
Managing director: Richard Farmbrough
- *Sun Sea & Bargain Spotting; Put Your Money Where Your House Is; Model Gardens*

Reel Life Television
020 7713 1585
enquiries@reel-life-tv.co.uk
www.reel-life-tv.co.uk
Managing directors: Chris Raine, Celine Smith
- *Songs of Praise; Moving On Up; Focus on Fear; Job Bank; Singled Out*

Renting eyeballs entertainment
020 7437 4417
malcolm.rasala@rentingeyeballs.com
www.rentingeyeballs.com
Managing director: Mark Maco
- *Commercials, promos, brand television, motion pictures*

Resource Base
023 8023 6806
post@resource-base.co.uk
www.resource-base.co.uk
Managing director: Karen Gilchrist, Hilary Durman
- *VEE-TV; Without You; World of Difference (C4); Lion Mountain; Who Cares? (BBC)*

Richmond Films and Television
020 8327 0430
PO Box 33154, London NW3 4AZ
mail@richmondfilms.com
Managing director: Sandra Hastie
- *In Two Minds; Privates; Wave Lengths*

Ricochet Films
020 7251 6966
mail@ricochet.co.uk
www.ricochet.co.uk
Managing director: Nick Powell
- *Who Rules the Roost; Fight Box; Living in the Sun*

Ronin Entertainment
020 7734 3884
mail@ronintv.com
www.ronintv.com
Managing directors: Richard Hearsey, Robin Greene
- *The Impressionable Jon Culshaw; Fort Boyard; It's a Knockout*

RS Productions
0191 224 4301
info@rsproductions.co.uk
www.rsproductions.co.uk
Managing director: Mark Lavender
- *Frozen; Elephants and Angels; Laughter When We're Dead; Thereby Hangs a Tale*

Sally Head Productions
020 8607 8730
admin@shpl.demon.co.uk
Managing director: Sally Head
- *Forefathers; Plastic Man; Tipping The Velvet; The Cry; Mayor of Casterbridge; The Return*

Samson Films
00 353 1 667 0533
info@samsonfilms.com
www.samsonfilms.com
Managing director: David Collins
- *Co-producer: Blind Flight; Honeymooners; Abduction Club; Most Fertile Man in Ireland. Feature development: Mir Friends; Immortal; Havoc*

Scream Films
020 8995 8255
info@screamfilms.com
www.screamfilms.com
Managing director: Susie Dark
- *Famous and Frightened; Dell Winton's Wedding; Terror Alert*

Screenhouse Productions
0113 266 8881
info@screenhouse.co.uk
www.screenhouse.co.uk
Chief executive: Barbara Govan
- *Star Date; Science Shack; Snapshot*

Seventh Art Productions
01273 777678
info@seventh-art.com
www.seventh-art.com
Managing director: Phil Grabsky
- *Tim Marlow on .... Edward Hopper; Easter in Art; Pelé – World Cup Hero; Great Artists II; The Boy Who Plays on the Buddhas of Bamiyan*

Shed Productions
020 8215 3387
shed@shedproductions.com
www.shedproductions.com
Managing director: Eileen Gallagher
- *Footballers Wives; Bad Girls*

Shine
020 7313 8000
info@shinelimited.com
www.shinelimited.com
Managing director: Elizabeth Murdoch
- *Dispatches; Fit to Eat; Take That*

SMG TV Productions
0141 300 3000
elizabeth.partyka@smg.plc.uk
www.smgtv.co.uk
Director: Surinder Gautama
- *Taggart; Club Reps: The Workers; Good Bye Mr Chips; Medics of the Glen; Squeak!; How 2*

Smith And Watson Productions
01803 863033
info@smithandwatson.com
www.smithandwatson.com
Managing director: Nick Smith
- *Building a Dream; Bill Wyman's Blues; A Story of Peter Rabbit and Beatrice Potter*

Smoking Dogs Films
020 7249 6644
info@smokingdogsfilms.com
www.smokingdogsfilms.com
Managing director: David Lawson
- *Urban Soul – Making of Modern R&B; The Wonderful World of Louis Armstrong; Goldie – When Satin Returns*

So Television
020 7960 2000
info@sotelevision.co.uk
www.sotelevision.co.uk
Director: Jon Magnusson
- *Comedy Lab; v Graham Norton (Channel 4)*

Specific Films
020 7580 7476
info@specificfilms.com
Managing director: Michael Hamlyn
- *Last Seduction II; Paws; Mr Reliable; Priscilla, Queen of the Desert*

Spire Films
01865 371979
mail@spirefilms.co.uk
Managing director: David Wilcox
- *Delia Smith; Romans*

Sunset + Vine
020 7478 7300
reception@sunsetvine.co.uk
www.sunsetvine.co.uk
Leeds 0113 284 2495
Managing director: John Leach
- *Cricket; Gillette World Sport; Gunball Rally*

Sunstone Films
020 7431 0535
sunstonefilms@aol.com
www.sunstonefilms.co.uk
- *Before Columbus; Lords of the Maya; Warhorse; Gladiators: The Brutal Truth*

Talent Television
020 7421 7800
entertainment@talenttv.com
www.talenttv.com
Creative director: John Kaye Cooper
- *Inside Clyde; Best of Friends; Casino, Casino*

Telemagination
020 7434 1551
mail@tmation.co.uk
www.telemagination.co.uk
Head of studio: Beth Parker
- *Pongwiffy; Little Ghosts; Something Else; Metalheads; Cramp Twins; Heidi (theatrical release)*

Television Junction
0121 248 4466
info@televisionjunction.co.uk
www.televisionjunction.co.uk
Managing directors: Paul Davies, Yvonne Davies
- *Double Act; Seeing Science; Think About It*

Tell-Tale Productions
020 8324 2308
info@tell-tale.co.uk
www.tell-tale.co.uk
Managing director: Karl Woolley
• *Tweenies; Boo*

Tern Television
0224 211123
www.terntv.com
73 Crown Street
Aberdeen AB11 6EX
0141243 5658
Managing directors: David Strachan, Gwyneth Hardy
• *Chancers; Fraserburgh; 2003 Reloaded; Mapman*

Tigress Productions
020 7434 4411
general@tigressproductions.co.uk or
general@tigressbristol.co.uk
www.tigressproductions.co.uk
2 St Paul's Road, Clifton
Bristol BS8 1LT
0117 933 5600
Managing director: Jeremy Bradshaw
• *Snakemaster; The Jeff Corwin Experience; Dolphin Murders; The Science of Combat*

Tinopolis
01554 880880
info@tinopolis.com
www.tinopolis.com
Managing director: Ron Jones
• *P'nawn Da; Wedi 7; Le Rygbi*

Torpedo
029 2076 6117
info@torpedoltd.co.uk
www.torpedoltd.co.uk
Chairman: Mark Jones
• *Fishlock's Sea Stories; Jigsaw; Horatio's Holiday*

Touch Productions
01747 828030
enquiries@touchproductions.co.uk
www.touchproductions.co.uk
Managing director: Malcolm Brinkworth
• *Feeding Martin (Meridian), Beasts of the Roman Games (C4); Life of a Ten Pound Note (BBC); The Missing Chink (C4); Party Maestro (BBC)*

TransAtlantic Films
020 8735 0505
mail@transatlanticfilms.com
www.transatlanticfilms.com
Cabalva, Whitney-On-Wye
Hereford HR3 6EX
01497 831800
Managing director: Corisande Albert
• *Amazing Animal Adaptors; Extreme Body Parts; Science of Love*

Turn On Television
0161 247 7700
mail@turnontv.co.uk
www.turnontv.co.uk
Managing director: Angela Smith
• *Viva La Diva; Bangkok Bound; Special Delivery*

TV6
020 7610 0266
mail@tv6.co.uk
www.tv6.co.uk
Managing director: Richard Reisz
• *Horizon: Percy Pilcher's Flying Machines (BBC); Horizon: King Solomon's Stone (BBC); Landscape Mysteries (BBC); Hidden Egypt (Nat Geo); Into the Great Pyramid (live, Fox Network)*

Unique Communications Group
020 7605 1200
ucg@uniquegroup.co.uk or
info@uniquecomms.com
www.uniquecomms.com
Managing director: Noel Edmonds
• *British Comedy Awards 2003 (ITV); Stars Behind Bars (Five); Harley Street (Living TV); I'm the Answer (ITV)*

Vera Productions
020 7436 6116
cree@vera.co.uk
Managing director: Elaine Morris
• *The Big Impression (BBC1), Between Iraq and A Hard Place (C4); Bremner Bird and Fortune (C4)*

Vivum Intelligent Media
020 7729 2749
nick@vivum.net
www.vivum.net
Managing director: Nick Rosen
• *2003 (BBC Radio 3,4 Channel 4) World Trade Centre series (PBS); documentary in Russia (BBC4); high-brow factual content*

Wag TV
020 7688 1711
post@wagtv.com
www.wagtv.com
Managing director: Martin Durkin
• *Inter Sex; Divine Designs; Dave Courtney's Underworld; The Great Scientist*

Wild Dream Films
01273 236168
mail@wild-dream.com
www.wild-dream.com
Managing director: Stuart Clarke
• *Map Makers; Ancient Discoveries series 1, 2*

Wild Rover Productions
028 9050 0980
enquiries@wild-rover.com
www.wild-rover.com
Managing director: Philip Morrow
• *Just For Laughs; A Day In The Westlife of Shane; Would You Pass the Eleven Plus?*

Wilton Films
020 7749 7282
info@wiltonfilms.com
cvs@wiltonfilms.com
www.wiltonfilms.com
Managing director: Paul Mitchell
• *Hotspots; Chechnya; The Alternative Rock 'n' Roll Years; Lords of the Spin*

Windfall Films
020 7251 7676
enquiries@windfallfilms.com
www.windfallfilms.com
Managing director: David Dugan
• *D-Day: The Ultimate Conflict; The Great Escape Revealed; Men of Iron*

World Of Wonder
020 7428 3444
wow@worldofwonder.co.uk
www.worldofwonder.net
Chief executive: Fenton Bailey
• *Matt's Old Masters; Housebusters; The Art Show – Spoils of War*

World Wide Pictures
020 7434 1121
info@worldwidegroup.ltd.uk
www.worldwidegroup.ltd.uk
Managing directors: Richard King, Ray Townsend, Chris Courtenay-Taylor
• *Bad Girls; videos for the Office of the Deputy Prime Minister*

World's End Productions
020 7751 9880
info@wordsendproductions.com
www.worldsendproductions.com
Managing directors: Jim Philips, Jerry Drew
• *Shoot Me; Going Down to South Park; Dead Casual; Live at Johnny's; Fighting Talk. Co-production with Celador: Johnny & Denise*

Zeal Television
020 8780 4600
www.zealtv.net
Chief executive: Peter Christiansen
Building the Dream; Come and Have a
• *Go if You Think You're Smart Enough; Resistance; Demolition; Super Human; Sushi TV*

Zeppotron
0870 333 1700
contact@zeppotron.com
www.zeppotron.com
Creative directors: Neil Webster, Ben Caudell, Charlie Brooker
• *People's Book of Records; Playing Tricks; The Cowboy Trap*

Zig Zag Productions
020 7353 7799
production@zigzag.uk.com
www.zigzagproductions.tv
Managing director: Danny Fenton
• *Fashion is Football Challenge; Inside the Mind of Frank Bruno; Three Lions; DIY Births; Celebrity Gladiators*

TV and film studios

3 Mills Studios
Three Mill Lane, London E3 3DU
020 7363 3336
info@3mills.com
www.3mills.com
Managing director: Daniel Dark

3 Sixty Media
Quay Street, Manchester M60 9EA
0161 827 2020
enquiry@3sixtymedia.com
www.3sixtymedia.com
Head of studios: Paul Bennett

Ardmore Studios
Herbert Road, Bray
Co Wicklow, Ireland
00 353 1 286 2971
film@ardmore.ie
www.ardmore.ie
Managing director: Kevin Moriarty

BBC Elstree Centre
Clarendon Road, Borehamwood
Herts WD6 1JF
020 8228 7102
www.bbc.co.uk
Senior facility manager: Sue Spree

BBC TV Centre Studios
BBC TV Centre
Wood Lane, Shepherds Bush
London W12 7RJ
020 8743 8000
bbcresources@bbc.co.uk
www.bbcresources.co.uk
Principal facilities manager: Gary Collins

Black Island Studios
9–11 Alliance Road, Acton
London W3 0RA
020 8956 5600
blackisland@compuserve.com
www.blackislandstudios.net
Managing director: Steve Guidici

Box Studios
15 Mandela Street
London NW1 0DU
020 7388 0020
mail@boxstudios.co.uk
www.boxstudios.co.uk
Directors: Philip Bier, Chris Gascoigne

Bray Studios
Down Place, Windsor Road
Water Oakley, Windsor
Berks SL4 5UG
01628 622111
B.earl@tiscali.co.uk
Studio manager: Beryl Earl

Broadley Studios
Broadley House, 48 Broadley Terrace
London NW1 6LG
020 7258 0324
markfrench@broadleystudios.com
www.broadleystudios.com
Managing director: Mark French

Canalot Production Studios
222 Kensal Road
London W10 6BN
020 8960 8580
andrea.kolokasi@workspacegroup.co.uk
www.workspacegroup.co.uk
Studio manager: Andrea Kolokasi

Capital Studios
13 Wandsworth Plain
London SW18 1ET
020 8877 1234
louise.prior@prospect-uk.com
www.capitalstudios.co.uk
Studio manager: Bobbi Johnstone

Central Studios
Location House, 5 Dove Lane
Bristol BS2 9HP
0117 955 4777
info@centralstudios.co.uk
www.centralstudios.co.uk
Studio manager: Dave Garbe

Corinthian Television Facilities
Chiswick Park, Building 12
566 Chiswick High Road
London W4 5AN
020 8100 1000
charlotte.alves@ctv.co.uk
www.ctv.co.uk/
Studio manager: Shelley Wallis

CTS and Lansdowne Recording Studios
Lansdowne House, Lansdowne Road
London W11 3LP
020 7727 0041
info@cts-lansdowne.co.uk
www.cts-lansdowne.co.uk
Studio manager: Chris Dibble

Depot Studios
29–31 Brewery Road
London N7 9QH
020 7609 1366
info@thedepotstudios.com
www.thedepotstudios.com
Studio manager: Helen Hilton

Desisti Lighting (UK)
15 Old Market Street
Thetford, Norfolk IP24 2EQ
01842 752909
docicti@globalnet.co.uk
www.desisti.co.uk
Director: John Reay-Young

Dukes Island Studios
2 Dukes Road, Acton
London W3 0SL
020 8956 5600
info@islandstudios.net
www.islandstudios.net/
Studio manager: Steve Guidici

Ealing Studios
Ealing Green, London W5 5EP
020 8567 6655
info@ealingstudios.com
www.ealingstudios.com
Studio manager: Jeremy Pelzer

East Side Studios
40A River Road, Barking
Essex IG11 0DW
020 8507 7572
info@eastsidestudios.com
www.eastsidestudios.com
Studio manager: Simon Price

Elstree Film and Television Studios
Shenley Road, Borehamwood
Herts WD6 1JG
020 8953 1600
info@elstreefilmtv.com
www.elstreefilmtv.com/
Directors: Julie Wicks, Neville Reid

Enfys
Unit 31 Portanmoor Road
East Moors, Cardiff
South Glamorgan, Wales CF2 5HB
029 2049 9988
mail@enfys.tv
www.enfys.tv
Studio manager: Sarah-Jane Salmon

Fountain TV Studios
128 Wembley Park Drive, Wembley
Middlesex HA9 8HQ
020 8900 5800
everyone@ftv.co.uk
www.ftv.co.uk
Studio manager: Tony Edwards

Greenford Studios
5–11 Taunton Road
Metropolitan Centre, Greenford
Middlesex UB6 8UQ
020 8575 7300
studios@panavision.co.uk
www.panavision.co.uk
Studio manager: Kate Tufano

Handstand studios
13 Hope Street, Liverpool L1 9BH
0151 708 7441
info@handstand-uk.com
www.handstand-uk.com
Studio manager: Han Duijvendak

Hillside
Merry Hill Road, Bushey
Herts WD23 1DR
020 8950 7919
mailbox@hillside-studios.co.uk
www.hillside-studios.co.uk
Operations manager: Peter Ball

Holborn Studios
49/50 Eagle Wharf Road
London N1 7ED
020 7490 4099
studiomanager@holborn-studios.co.uk
www.holborn-studios.co.uk
Studio manager: Marie McCartney

IAC
Moorside Road, Winchester
Hampshire S23 7US
01962 873000
info@iacl.co.uk
www.iacl.co.uk
Studio manager: Ian Rich

ICA Theatre
The Mall, London SW1 5AH
020 7930 0493
info@ica.org.uk
www.ica.org.uk
Technical manager: Lee Curran

Lichfield Studios
133 Oxford Gardens
London W10 6NE
020 8969 6161
kate@lichfieldstudios.co.uk
www.lichfieldstudios.com
Studio assistant: Kate Short

London Studios
London Television Centre
Upper Ground Floor
London SE1 9LT
020 7737 8888
sales@londonstudios.co.uk
www.londonstudios.co.uk/
Managing director: Debbie Hills

Metro Imaging
76 Clerkenwell Road
London EC1M 5TN
020 7865 0000
katarina@metroimaging.co.uk
www.metroimaging.co.uk
Studio manager: Steve Jackson

Millbank Studios
4 Millbank, London SW1P 3JA
020 7233 2020
facilities@millbank-studios.co.uk
www.millbank-studios.co.uk
Studio manager: Nicola Golding

Millennium Studios
5 Elstree Way, Borehamwood
Herts WD6 1SF
020 8236 1400
info@millenniumstudios.co.uk
www.millenniumstudios.co.uk
Managing director: Ronan Willson

Park Royal Studios
1 Barretts Green Road
London NW10 7AE
020 8965 9778
info@parkroyalstudios.com
www.parkroyalstudios.com
Studio manager: Francois van de Langkruis

Picture It Studios
50 Church Road
London NW10 9PY
020 8961 6644
chris@picit.net
www.picit.net
Studio manager: Chris Fellers

Pinewood Studios
Pinewood Road, Iver Heath
Bucks SL0 0NH
01753 651700
firstname.lastname@
pinewood-studios.co.uk
www.pinewoodshepperton.com
Studio manager: David Wight

Production House NI/Stage Services North
Unit 5, Prince Regent Retail Park
Prince Regent Road
Belfast BT5 6QP
028 9079 8999
info@productionhouse.net
Studio manager: Neil Lewis

Pylon Studios
Coal Hill Lane, Leeds LS13 1DJ
0113 204 7000
enquiries@pylonstudios.co.uk
www.pylonstudios.co.uk
Studio manager: Jo Scott

Q Broadcast
1487 Melton Road, Queniborough
Leicester LE7 3FP
0116 260 8813
paul@folosite.net
Studio manager: Martin Branson

RC Film & TV Set Construction
Unit C11 Dundonald Enterprise Park
Carrowreagh Road, Dundonald
Northern Ireland BT16 1QT
028 9055 7557
Managing director: Russell Fulton

Riverside Studios
Crisp Road, Hammersmith
London W6 9RL
020 8237 1000
online@riversidestudios.co.uk
www.riversidestudios.co.uk
Centre manager: Alex Cotterill

Sands Film Studios
Grices Wharf, 119 Rotherhithe Street
London SE16 4NF
020 7231 2209
OStockman@sandsfilms.co.uk
www.sandsfilms.co.uk
Managing director: Oliver Stockman

Savoy Hill Studios
Savoy Hill House, Savoy Hill
London WC2R 0BU
020 7497 0830
johnherbert@tabard.co.uk
Studio manager: John Herbert

Shepperton Studios
Studios Road, Shepperton
Middlesex TW17 0QD
01932 562611
firstname.lastname@
pinewood-studios.co.uk
www.pinewoodshepperton.com
Studio manager: David Godfrey

Space Studios
Boden House
114–120 Victoria Road
London NW10 6NY
020 8961 2412
dja@basegrp.com
Managing director: David Johnson

stu-dio
Cabul Road, London SW11 2PR
020 7228 5228
info@the-studio.co.uk
www.the-studio.co.uk
Studio manager: Gemma Masters

Teddington Studios
Broom Road, Teddington
Middlesex TW11 9NT
020 8977 3252
sales@teddington.tv
www.teddington.co.uk
Studio manager: Ray Gearing

The Worx
10 Heathmans Road, Fulham
London SW6 4TJ
020 7371 9777
enquiries@theworx.co.uk
www.the-worx.co.uk
Managing directors: Jackie Mallory, Jonathan Mallory

Twickenham Studios
The Barons, St Margarets
Twickenham, Middlesex TW1 2AW
020 8607 8888
caroline@twickenhamfilmstudios.com
www.twickenhamstudios.com/
Administrations manager: Caroline Tipple

VFX Company
Dukes Island Studios, Dukes Road
London W3 0SL
020 8956 5674
info@thevfxco.co.uk
www.thevfxco.co.uk
Operations manager: Digna Nigoumi

Waterfall Studios
2 Silver Road
Wood Lane, London W12 7SG
020 8746 2000
enquiries@waterfall-studios.com
www.waterfall-studios.com
Studio manager: Samantha Leese

Post-production

3sixty Media
Quay Street, Manchester M60 9EA
0161 839 0360
enquiry@3sixtymedia.com
www.3sixtymedia.com
Independent. Effects and virtual reality
Post-production manager: John Mariner
- *Island at War; Tonight with Trevor MacDonald; Blue Murder*

422 Manchester
4th Floor, South Central
11 Peter Street
Manchester M2 5QR
0161 839 6080
cooey@422.com
www.422manchester.com
Sister company 422 South. Animation, graphics, commercials, special effects and audio
Production director: Richard Wallwork
- *Chessington World of Adventures commercial; Most Haunted; Mastermind; A Question of Sport*

422 South
St John's Court, Whiteladies Road
Bristol BS8 2QY
0117 946 7222
debbiet@422.com
www.422south.com
Sister company 422 Manchester. Factual television and animation
Production director: Andy Davies-Coward
- *The Painter (Hewlett Packard); Extreme Machines; The Basil Brush Show*

Ascent Media Camden
13 Hawley Crescent
London NW1 8NP
020 7284 7900
www.ascent-media.co.uk
9 other sites. Film processing laboratory; video; tape; DVD
Managing director: Sam Webb
- *Poirot; Auf Weidersehen Pet; Hustle*

Anvil
Denham Media Park
North Orbital Road, Denham
Uxbridge, Middlesex UB9 5HL
01895 833522
firstname.secondname@thomson.net
www.anvil-post.com
Part of Technicolor (Thomson Group) Audio
Studio manager: Mike Anscombe
- *The Brief; Ultimate Force; Murder in Suburbia; Inspector Morse; Midsomer Murders; Waking the Dead; Poirot*

Arena Digital
74 Newman Street, London W1T 3EL
020 7436 4360
booking@arenadigital.co.uk
www.arenadigital.co.uk
Part of 2D video facilities. Effects; audio; documentaries; comedy
Managing directors: Terry Bettles, Dave Thompson
- *Bo' Selecta; Trouble at Top; Scambusters; Brassed off Britain*

Arion Communications
Global House, Denham Media Park
North Orbital Road, Denham
Uxbridge Middlesex UB9 5HL
01895 834484
sales@arion.co.uk
www.arion.co.uk
Independent. Telecine; DVD duplication; editing
Managing director: Neil Mockler
- *Hitchhiker's Guide to the Galaxy; Alien vs Predator; Tomb Raider; The Cradle of Life*

Barcud Derwen
Cibyn, Caernarfon
Gwynedd LL55 2BD
01286 684300
Cardiff 02920 611515
enq@barcud-derwen.co.uk
www.barcudderwen.com
Drama, graphics
Managing director: Tudor Roberts
- *Celebrity Poker; Tracy Beaker series; Mountains and Man*

Blue
58 Old Compton Street
London W1D 4UF
020 7437 2626
info@bluepp.co.uk
www.bluepp.co.uk
VTR plc Group. Special effects; graphics; commercial; audio
Managing director: David Cadel
- *BBC Imagine; Pompeii: The Last Day; Property People*

Capital FX
2nd Floor, 20 Dering Street
London W1S 1AJ
020 7493 9998
ian@capital-fx.co.uk
www.capital-fx.co.uk
Independent. Special effects; graphics; taped film transfer
Managing director: Ian Buckton
- *Harry Potter; Troy; Lord of the Rings*

Cine Wessex
Westway House
19 St Thomas Street
Winchester, Hampshire SO23 9HJ
01962 865454
info@cinewessex.co.uk
www.cinewessex.co.uk
Independent. Editing; camera kit and crew hire; 2D and 3D graphics; VHS, CD and DVD
Facilities director: Joe Conman
- *City Gardener; Mappin Murder; Room for Improvement*

Clear
Fenton House
55–57 Great Marlborough Street
London W1F 7JX
020 7734 5557
clear@clear.ltd.uk
www.clear.ltd.uk
Sister company Finally Cut. Visual effects, commercials and films
Senior producer/head of film: Steve Garrad
- *28 Days Later; BBC Talking Head preview; Millions*

Clear Cut Hirers
1 Springvale Terrace
London W14 0AE
020 7605 1700
fazal@clearcutpictures.com
www.clearcutpictures.com
Sister company Clear Cut Pictures. Dry hire post-production equipment
Managing director: Fazal Shah
- *Celeb Deck; Glastonbury Festival; Liquid News*

Clear Cut Pictures
1 Springvale Terrace
London W14 0AE
020 7605 1700
reception@clearcut pictures
www.clearcutpictures.com
Sister company Clear Cut Hirers. Graphics and digital rostrum; video and sound
Managing director: Jo Beighton
- *Crimewatch; Horizon; Money Programme*

Clickstream
37 Dean Street, London W1D 4PT
020 7437 0077
info@clickstream.co.uk
www.clickstream.co.uk
Part of VTR Group. Encoding; telestream; digital asset management
Managing director: Neil Lane
- *E-title project for European Union; Paramount; Movie Tone*

Code Design
Ingestre Court, Ingestre Place
London W1F 0JL
020 7343 6449
info@codedesign.co.uk
www.codedesign.co.uk
Part of M2 Group. Storyboarding; direction; studio shooting; graphics
Production manager: Bryony Evans
- *Troy; Q Channel Broadcasting; Waking the Dead*

Component
28 Newman Street
London W1T 1PR
020 7631 4477
mike@component.co.uk
www.component.co.uk
Independent. Pure graphics
Director: Mike Kenny
- *Hell's Kitchen; Destination D-Day; Without Prejudice; SAS Jungle; Clive Anderson Now*

Computamatch
117 Wardour Street
London W1F 0NU
020 7287 1316
edl@computamatch.co.uk
www.ascent-media.co.uk
Part of Ascent Group. Film negative cutting service
Managing director: Marilyn Sommer
• *5 Children and It; Guinness; Levi's*

Computer Film Services
66b Unit, York Road
Weybridge, Surrey KT13 9DY
01932 850034
enquiries@computerfilm.com
www.computerfilm.com
Independent. Digital disc recorders and post-production systems
Director: Peter Holland
• *Harry Potter; Lord of the Rings*

Crow TV
12 Wendell Road
London W12 9RT
020 8749 6071
info@crowtv.com
www.crowtv.com
Independent. Graphics; editing for television; pogle colour grade; online/offline editing; audio
Managing director: Paul Kingsley
• *Vincent, The Full Story; South Bank Show; The Challenge*

Cut and Run
Cinema House, 93 Wardour Street
London W1F 0UD
020 7432 9696
editors@cutandrun.co.uk
www.cutandrun.co.uk
Independent. Offline editing
Managing director: Steve Gandalphy
• *Commercials: Castrol; Rimmel; Diet Coke; UPS; Lynx*

DB Dubbing
4 St Pauls Road
Clifton, Bristol, Avon BS8 1LT
0117 904 8210
miles@dbdubbing.tv
Independent. Audio
Managing director: Miles Harris
• *Secret Nature; Built for the Kill; Eden Project*

De Lane Lea
75 Dean Street, London W1D 3PU
020 7432 3800
info@delanelea.com
www.delanelea.com
Part of Ascent group. Sound for post-production TV and film
Chief operating officer: Hugh Penalt-Jones
• *Cold Mountain; Harry Potter, the Prisoner of Azkaban; Two Brothers*

DGP
Portland House, 12–13 Greek Street
London W1D 4DL
020 7734 4501
info@dgpsoho.co.uk
www.dgpsoho.co.uk
Independent. Editing; graphics; DVD; authoring
Managing director: Julian Day
• *Murder City; Yahoo; Friends*

DVA Associates
7/8 Campbell Court, Bramley
Tadley, Hampshire RG26 5EG
01256 882032
info@dva.co.uk
www.dva.co.uk
Independent. Graphics; audio; DVD; commercials
Managing director: Barrie Gibson
• *SAS Survival Secrets; Life of David Kelly; Goalrush for Meridian*

Editworks
Austin House, 95–97 Ber Street
Norwich, Norfolk NR1 3EY
01603 624402
info@theeditworks.co.uk
Independent. Video
Managing director: Rob Manson
• *Commercials: Norwich Union; Virgin Money; Essex County Council for European Union*

Evolutions Television
5 Berners Street, London W1T 3LF
020 7580 3333
bookings@evolutionstelevision.com
www.evolutionstelevision.com
Independent. Graphics; documentaries; commercials; audio
Managing director: Simon Kanjee
• *Top of the Pops titles; Jump London; Other People's Houses*

The Farm
13 Soho Square
London W1D 3QF
020 7437 6677
info@farmgroup.tv
www.farmgroup.tv
Partner with Home and The Shed. Online/offline editing; audio dubbing; high definition edit and grading
Managing directors: Nicky Sargent, Vikki Dunn
• *Dunkirk; Friday night with Jonathan Ross; One Life*

Films at 59
59 Cotham Hill, Bristol
Avon BS6 6JR
0117 906 4300
info@filmsat59.com
www.filmsat59.com
Independent. Audio; high definition; equipment hire; online/offline dubbing
Managing director: Gina Lee Fucci
• *Teachers; Big Cat Diary; Building the Dream*

Finally Cut
1 Springvale Terrace
London W14 0AE
020 7556 6300
fclon@finalcut-edit.com
www.finalcut-edit.com
Sister company Clear. Offline editing
Producer: Zoe Henderson
• *Commercials: Sony PlayStation; Mountain; Mercedes "movement"*

Finishing Post
10, Gilt Way, Giltbrook
Nottingham, Notts NG16 2GN
0115 945 8800
info@finishing-post.co.uk
www.finishing-post.co.uk
Independent. Graphics; editing; DVD authoring
Managing director: Mark Harwood
• *Commercials: Jaguar; Peugeot; Heart of the Country*

Flare DVD
Ingestre Court, Ingestre Place
London W1F 0JL
020 7343 6565
sales@flare-DVD.com
www.flare-DVD.com
Part of M2 group. Short run duplication; DVD design; authoring; encoding facility
Managing director: Tom Jones
• *Kate Rusby; Hallmark; Fame Academy*

4x4
First Floor, 21 Ormeau Avenue
Belfast BT2 8HD
028 9027 1950
4@4x4post.com
www.4x4post.com
Independent. Effects; graphics; commercials; audio
Directors: Katy Jackson; Paula Campbell; Alan Perry; Jonathan Featherstone
• *Disability commercials; BTNI commercial; Just for a Laugh*

Framestore CFC
9 Noel Street, London W1F 8GH
020 7208 2600
info@framestore-cfc.com
www.framestore-cfc.com
Independent. Effects; computer generated commercials; films
Chief executive: William Sergeant
• *Thunderbirds; Walking with Sea Monsters*

Frontier Post
66–67 Wells Street
London W1T 3PY
020 7291 9191
info@frontierpost.co.uk
www.frontierpost.co.uk
Independent. Graphics; audio; online/offline grading
Managing director: Neil Hatton
• *Property Dreams; Howard Goodall's 20th Century Greats; Pagans of the Roman Empire*

Fusion Broadcast
56 Ballynahinch Road, Dromara
Dromore, County Down BT25 2AL
028 9753 1004
www.fusionbroadcast.co.uk
Independent. Crew supplying
Managing director: John Morriffey
• *BBC Northern Ireland; BBC Network*

Frontline Television
35 Bedfordbury, Covent Garden
London WC2 4DU
020 7836 0411
public@frontline-tv.co.uk
www.frontline-tv.co.uk
Independent. Editing; graphic design; audio; Avid online/offline; duplication
Managing director: Bill Cullen
• *Bum Fights; VTV programme for the Deaf; Curse of Reality TV*

Fusion Post Production
16 D'Arbly Street, London W1F 8EA
020 7758 0500
edit@fusionpost.co.uk
www.fusionpost.co.uk
Independent. Audio; online/offline grading; symphony online
Managing director: Adam de Wolff
• *BBC Holiday; How Clean is your House?; The Carrot or the Stick*

Future Post Production
25 Noel Street, London W1F 8GX
020 7434 6655
info@futurefilmgroup.com
www.futurefilmgroup.com
Part of Future Films Group. Sound; two dolby mix studios
Managing directors: Tim Levy, Stephen Margolis
• *King Arthur; Exorcist, The Beginning; Harry Potter 3*

Glassworks
33–34 Great Pulteney Street
London W1F 9NP
020 7434 1182
nina@glassworks.co.uk
www.glassworks.co.uk
Independent. Special effects; animation; all online
Managing director: Hector Macleod
• *Dream Keeper; Bjorkall is full of love; Sprite commercials*

Goldcrest Post-Production
1 Lexington Street
36–44 Brewer Street
London W1F 9LX
020 7437 7972
reception@goldcrest-post.co.uk
www.goldcrest-post.co.uk
Independent. Sound and telecine
Managing director: Peter Joly
• *Cold Mountain; Lord of Rings, Two Towers; Girl with a Pearl Earring*

Golden Square
11 Golden Square, London W1F 9JB
020 7300 3555
info@golden-square.co.uk
www.golden-square.co.uk
Independent. Commercials; special effects
Managing director: Phil Gillies
• *Campari; Tomb Raiders; Volkswagen*

Hackenbacker Audio Post Production
10 Bateman Street
London W1D 4AQ
020 7734 1324
reception@hackenbacker.com
www.hackenbacker.com
Independent. Audio; sound effects; films; trailers
Managing directors: Julian Slater, Nigel Heath
• *Shaun of the Dead; Girl with a Pearl Earring; Spooks*

The Hive
37 Dean Street, London W12 4PT
020 7565 1000
contact@hiveuk.com
www.hiveuk.com
Part of VTR Group. Telecine; online editing; special effects; 3 DVD and 2D graphics
Managing director: David Southwood
• *Direct Line sponsorship; BBC Bitesize; Hell's Kitchen promotion*

Home Post Productions
12–13 Richmond Buildings
Soho, London W1D 3HG
020 7292 0200
info@homepost.co.uk
www.farmgroup.tv
Independent. Graphics; audio; effects; commercials
Managing director: Janine Martin
• *Dunkirk; Friday night with Jonathan Ross; One Life*

Lip Sync Post
123 Wardour Street
London W1F 0UU
020 7534 9123
admin@lipsyncpost.co.uk
www.lipsync.co.uk
Independent. Sound; graphics; editing
Managing director: Norman Merry
• *Silent Witness; Touch the Void; Trolleywood*

Liquid TV
1–2 Portland Mews
London W1F 8JE
020 7437 2623
info@liquid.co.uk
www.liquid.co.uk
Independent. Title branding; special effects
Managing director: Asra Alikhan
• *Restoration; Film 2004; Horizon; Troy*

Lola
14–16 Great Portland Street
London W1W 8BL
020 7907 7878
info@lola-post.com
www.lola-post.com
Independent. Visualeffects; commercials; films and TV
Managing directors: Grahame Andrew, Rob Harvey
• *Troy; 5 children and It; Ancient Egyptians*

London Post
34–35 Dean Street
London W1D 4PR
020 7439 9080
dave@londonpost.co.uk
www.londonpost.co.uk
Part of Arena Digital. Audio; graphics; sound; editing; telecine
Managing director: Dave Thompson
• *Brassed off Britain; Blag; Celebrity Penthouse*

M2 Television
Ingestre Court, Ingestre Place
London W1F 0JL
020 7343 6543
Soho 020 73436543
Camden 020 73436789
info@m2tv.com
www.m2tv.com
Edit; visual; audio
Managing director: Tom Jones
• *Revenge; Human Mind; Bodysnatchers*

The Machine Room
54–58 Wardour Street
London W1D 4JQ
020 7734 3433
info@themachineroom.co.uk
www.themachineroom.co.uk
Part of VTR Group. Onlineediting; telecine suites; DVD; teramix machine; archive restoration department
Managing director: Danny Whybrow
• *Love Actually; Bad Girls; Footballers Wives*

Mediahouse
Hogarth Business Park
3 Burlington Lane, London W4 2TH
020 8233 5400
info@mediahouse.tv
www.mediahouse.tv/post_production/
IMG Mark McCormack Group. Video; graphics; DVD; transmission studio
Head of post-production: Karen Mullins
• *Bremner, Bird and Fortune; Planet's Funniest Animals*

Men-from-Mars
Unit 6, Walpole Court
Ealing Green, London W5 5ED
020 8280 9000
info@men-from-mars.com
www.men-from-mars.com
Part of Barcud Derwen. Visual effects for film and TV
Creative director: Philip Attfield; production director: Simon Frame
• *Gladiatress; Chasing Liberty; Jekyll and Hyde; Hamburg Cell; Sons of the Wind; De-Lovely; Trial and Retribution: Blue Eiderdown*

Metro Broadcast
5–7 Great Chapel Street
London W1F 8FF
020 7434 7700
Metro Suffolk Street 020 7202 2000
Metro Ecosse Edinburgh
0131 554 9421
Metro Ecosse Glasgow
0141 419 1660
info@metrobroadcast.com
www.metrobroadcast.com
Editing inc HD; crewing and equipment rental; audio and video restoration; DVD production; webcasting; duplications and standards conversion
Directors: Mark Cox, Paul Beale
- *EPKs for Mr Bean; Rugby World Cup promo; NHK various programmes, shot and edited in HD*

The Mill
40–41 Great Marlborough Street
London W1F 7JQ
020 7287 4041
info@mill.co.uk
www.mill.co.uk
Independent. Commercials; 3d animation; edition
Managing director: Pat Joseph
- *Commercials: Mercedes; Honda; O2*

MGB Facilities
Capital House, Sheepscar Court, Meanwood Road, Leeds
West Yorkshire LS7 2BB
0113 243 6868
contact@mgbtv.co.uk
www.mgbtv.co.uk
Independent. Graphics; commercials; DVD; animation
Managing director: Mike Gaunt
- *Hasbro commercial; Brazilian Football; DFS Furniture*

Molinare
34 Fouberts Place, London W1F 7PX
020 7478 7000
bookings@molinare.co.uk
www.molinare.co.uk
Independent. Graphics; DVD; audio
Managing director: Mark Foligno
- *Faking It; Make Me Honest; Poirot*

Moving Picture Company
127 Wardour Street
London W1F 0NL
020 7434 3100
mpc@moving-picture.com
www.moving-picture.com
Independent. Commercials; effects; animation; editing
Managing director: David Jeffers
- *Troy; Dunkirk; Guinness moth commercial*

Nats
10 Soho Square, London W1D 3NT
020 7287 9900
bookings@nats.ltb.uk
www.nats.ltd.uk
Independent. Editing; audio; telecine; effects; graphics
Managing director: Charlie Leonard
- *Seven Wonders of the Industrial World; Grand Design; The National Trust*

Oasis Television
6–7 Great Pulteney Street
London W1F 9NA
020 7434 4133
sales@oasistv.co.uk
www.oasistv.co.uk
Independent. Audio; editing; graphics; duplication
Managing director: Gareth Mullaney
- *State of Play; The Young Visitors; May 33rd*

One
71 Dean Street, London W1D 3SF
020 7439 2730
info@onepost.tv
www.onepost.tv
Part of Ascent Group. Commercials; telecine; animation
Managing director: Paul Jones
- *Jaguar; American Express; Aerosmith*

Optical Image
The Studio, Broome, Stourbridge
West Midlands DY9 0HA
01562 700404
info@optical-image.com
www.optical-image.com
Independent. Animation; DVD; duplication; effects; graphics
Managing director: David Clement
- *Sindy; Jellies; Butt Ugly Martians*

Outpost Facilities
Pinewood Studios, Pinewood Road
Iver, Buckinghamshire SL0 0NH
01753 630770
helen@outpostfacilities.co.uk
www.outpostfacilities.co.uk
Independent. Commercials; films; broadcast; TV
Managing director: Nigel Gourley
- *My Family; Everything I Know About Men; Teletubbies Everywhere*

P3 Post
40–42 Lexington Street
London W1F 0LN
020 7287 3006
reception@p3.tv
www.p3.tv
Independent. Effects; graphics; DVD; commercials
Managing director: Martin Price
- *Derren Brown; Celebs Exposed; Audi*

Pepper
3 Slingsby Place, London WC2E 9AB
020 7836 1188
mailuf@pepperpost.tv
www.pepperpost.tv
Independent. Effects; graphics; dramas
Managing director: Patrick Holzen
- *Dirty War; Midsomer Murders; White Noise*

Phaebus Communications Group
The Brewery Tower, The Deva centre
Trinity Way, Manchester M3 7BF
0161 605 9999
info@phaebus.co.uk
www.phaebus.co.uk
Two branches. DVD; authoring
Managing director: Steve Bettridge
- *BBC channel idents; Andy Pandy; Thomas Cook conference events*

Pink House
33 West Park Clifton
Bristol, Avon BS8 2LX
0117 923 7087
anita.nandwami@pinkhousepp.com
www.filmsat59.com
Part of Films at 59. Broadcast; audio; pictures; effects; commercials
Managing director: Anita Nandwami
- *Building the Dream; Big Cook Little Cook; Animal Camera*

Red Vision
Cambos House, 3 Canal Street
Manchester M1 3HE
0161 907 3764
London 020 7419 2010
Bristol 0117 946 6633
info@redvision.co.uk
www.redvision.co.uk
Computer graphics for film and TV
Managing director: David Mousley
- *Touching the Void; D-Day: Men and Machines*

Resolution
341 Old Street, London EC1V 9LL
020 7749 9300
London 020 7437 1336
info@resolution.tv
www.resolution.tv
Broadcast; commercials; offline/online; audio; graphics
Managing director: Mike Saunders
- *Big Brother; Top Gear; Fame Academy*

Rushes
66 Old Compton Street
London W1D 4UH
020 7437 8676
info@rushes.co.uk
www.rushes.co.uk
Part of Ascent media. Effects; telecine for commercial video
Managing director: Joce Capper
- *Commercials: Hewlett Packard; Offspring; Ford Mondeo (Tom and Jerry)*

Savalas
333 Woodlands Road
Glasgow G3 6NG
0141 339 0455
all@savalas.co.uk
www.savalas.co.uk
Independent. Music production; audio; sound design
Managing directors: Giles Lamb; Michael MacKinnon; Karl Henderson
- *Magdalene Sisters; Relocation, Relocation, Relocation; Sea of Souls*

2nd Sense Broadcast
Millennium Studios, Elstree Way
Borehamwood, Herts WD6 1SF
020 8236 1133
info@2ndsense.co.uk
www.2ndsense.co.uk
Independent. Audio
Managing director: Wendy Hewitt
- *Top of the Pops 2; Chuckle Vision; East Enders Revealed*

Skaramoosh
9–15 Neal Street
London WC2H 9PW
020 7379 9966
reception@skaramoosh.co.uk
www.skaramoosh.com
Independent. Effects; graphics; audio
Managing director: Daniel Slight
- *Strictly Come Dancing; Football Factory; Naked Science*

Soho Images
8–14 Meard Street
London W1F 0EQ
020 7437 0831
www.sohoimages.com
Part of Ascent Group. Commercials; telecine transfers; archive restoration; DVD
Managing director: Paul Collard
- *Murder in Mind; Bloody Sunday; Mrs Brown*

Sound Monsters
4 Grafton Mews, London W1T 5JE
020 7387 3230
info@soundmonsters.com
www.soundmonsters.com
Independent. Audio; sound; transfer; animation
Managing director: Cliff Jones
- *Death in Gaza; State of Texas; Real Great Escapes*

St Anne's Post
20 St Anne's Court
London W1F 0BH
020 7155 1500
info@saintannespost.co.uk
www.saintannespost.co.uk
Part of Ascent Group. Audio; editing; telecine
Managing director: Keith Williams
- *Brothers Grimm; Alfie; Night Detective*

Stream
61 Charlotte Street
London W1T 4PF
020 7208 1567
info@streamdm.co.uk
www.streamdm.co.uk
Part of Ascent Group. DVD; design compression; authoring facility
Managing director: Paul Kind
- *The Office; Where We're Calling From; My Big Fat Greek Wedding*

Suite
28 Newman Street
London W1T 1PR
020 7636 4488
shelley@suitetv.co.uk
www.suitetv.co.uk
Independent. Editing for TV
Managing director: Shelley Fox
- *The Office; Swiss Toni*

Sumners
Suite 401, Berkeley House
35 Whitworth Street West
Manchester M1 5NG
0161 228 0330
janet@sumners.co.uk
www.sumners.co.uk
Independent. Online/offline; graphics; very reality studio
Managing directors: Janet Sumner; Andrew Sumner
- *Best Sitcoms; Songs of Praise; Bank of Mum and Dad*

Television Set
22 Newman Street, London W1T 1PH
020 7637 3322
terry.bettles@tvsetgroup.co.uk
www.thetelevisionset.co.uk
2 branches. Restoration of old archives for reuse; audio; grading; telecine
Managing director: Terry Bettles
- *D-Day plus 60; Poirot remastering; Let it Be*

Television Services International
10 Grape Street, London WC2H 8TG
020 7379 3435
enquiries@tsi.co.uk
www.tsi.co.uk
Independent. Longform and shortform in light entertainment and documentaries
Managing director: Simon Peach
- *Ali G; My New Best Friend; Who Rules the Roost?*

3 Wise Men
Ingestre Court, Ingestre Place
London W1F 0JL
020 7343 6623
daz@3wisemen.tv
martin@3wisemen.tv
www.3wisemen.tv
Independent. Offline editing
Managing directors: Martin Sage, Darren Jonusas
- *Seven Industrial Wonders; Battlefield Britain; Horizon*

Todd-ao creative services
13 Hawley Crescent
London NW1 8NP
020 7284 7900
schedule@todd-ao.co.uk
www.todd-ao.co.uk
Part of Ascent Group. Telecine grading; negative film processing; video dailies; offline/online editing
Managing director: Samantha Webb
- *Monarch of the Glen; Canterbury Tales; Taggart*

Videosonics
13 Hawley Crescent
London NW1 8NP
020 7209 0209
info@videosonics.com
www.videosonics.com
Independent. Audio
Managing director: Denis Weinreich
- *Young Adam; Bright Young Things; Sexy Beast*

Vivid
68 Wells Street, London W1T 3QA
020 7290 0700
bookings@vividpost.com
www.vividpost.com
Independent. Documentaries; audio; picture
Managing director: Robin Bextor
- *Dinner Party Inspectors; Inside the Mind of a Suicide Bomber; Horizon Stronger*

VTR
64 Dean Street, London W1D 4QQ
020 7437 0026
reception@vtr.co.uk
www.vtr.co.uk
Independent. Effects; commercials; telecine. Managing director: Ant Frend
- *Christine Aguillera; McDonalds; Persil*

Wild Tracks Audio Studio
2nd Floor, 55 Greek Street
London W1D 3DT
020 7734 6331
bookings@wildtracks.co.uk
www.wildtracks.co.uk
Independent. Audio
Managing director: Graham Pickford
- *Canon; Bob the Builder; Pingu*

Yellow Moon
30 Shaw Road, Holywood
County Down BT18 9HX
028 9042 1826
general@yellowmoon.net
www.yellowmoon.net
Independent. Editing
Managing director: Greg Darby
- *Citizen Alec; Christine's Children; Sven-Goran Eriksson*

Film & music libraries

BBC Pebble Mill, Information & Archives
BBC Pebble Mill, Pebble Mill Road
Birmingham B5 7QQ
0121 432 8922
garry.campbell@bbc.co.uk
www.bbc.co.uk
Music, news requests, productions at Pebble Mill Studio

BFI National Film and TV Archives
Kingshill Way, Berkhamsted
Herts HP4 3TP
01442 876301
david.pierce@bfi.org.uk
www.bfi.org.uk
Large collection from 1895 to the present

East Anglian Film Archive
University of East Anglia
Norwich NR4 7TJ
01603 592 664
eafa@uea.ac.uk
www.uea.ac.uk/eafa
East Anglia

Film and Video Archive, Imperial War Museum
Department of Art, Lambeth Road
London SE1 6HZ
020 7416 5211
film@iwm.org.uk
www.iwm.org.uk/collections/film.htm
Large collection

Film Institute of Ireland/ Irish Film Archive
6 Eustace Street, Temple Bar
Dublin 2
00 353 1 679 5744
info@irishfilm.ie
www.irishfilm.ie
Films worldwide. Every Irish film ever made

GMTV Library Sales
London TV Centre, Upper Ground
London SE1 9TT
020 7827 7363 /6
librarysales@gmtv.co.uk
www.gmtv.co.uk

Huntley Film Archive
191 Wardour Street
London W1F 8ZE
020 7287 8000
films@huntleyarchives.com
www.huntleyarchives.com
Rare and vintage documentary film from 1895

Images Of War
31a Regents Park Road
London NW1 7TL
020 7267 9198
derek@dircon.co.uk
www.warfootage.com
Images of war archive. 1900 to first Gulf war

ITN Archive
200 Grays Inn Road
London WC1X 8XZ
020 7833 3000
sales@itnarchive.com
www.itnarchive.com
More than 500,000 hours of news and feature material

ITV Central
Gas Street, Birmingham B1 2JT
0121 643 9898
www.itv.com

JW Media Music
4 Whitfield Street, London W1T 2RD
020 7681 8900
info@jwmediamusic.com
www.jwmediamusic.com
Music

Media Archive for Central England
The Institute of Film Studies
University of Nottingham
University Park
Nottingham NG7 2RD
0115 846 6448
james.patterson@nottingham.ac.uk
www.nottingham.ac.uk/film/mace
East Midlands

National Screen and Sound Archive of Wales
Aberystwyth, Ceredigion SY23 3BU
01970 628 2828
agssc@llgc.org.uk
http://screenandsound.llgc.org.uk
Wales

North West Film Archive
Minshull House, 47–49 Chorlton Street
Manchester M1 3EU
0161 247 3097
n.w.filmarchive@mmu.ac.uk
www.nwfa.mmu.ac.uk
The North-west, 1897 to present day

Northern Region Film and Television Archive
University of Teesside, Borough Road
Middlesbrough TS1 3BA
01642 384022
leo@nrfta.org.uk
www.nrfta.org.uk
The North

Pathé Pictures
14–17 Market Place
London W1W 8AR
020 7323 5151
www.pathe.co.uk
Worldwide images

Royal Television Society, Library & Archive
Holborn Hall, 100 Grays Inn Road
London WC1X 8AL
020 7430 1000
info@rts.org.uk
www.rts.org.uk
Archive TV pictures, award ceremonies and monthly dinners

Scottish Screen Archive
1 Bowmont Gardens
Glasgow G12 9LR
0141 337 7400
archive@scottishscreen.com
www.scottishscreen.com/archivelive
Scotland since the 1890s

South East Film & Video Archive
University of Brighton
Grand Parade, Brighton BN2 0JY
01273 643 213
sefva@brighton.ac.uk
www.bton.ac.uk/sefva/sefilmarchivenews
The South-east: Kent, Surrey, East and West Sussex

South West Film and Television Archive
Melville Building, Royal William Yard
Stonehouse, Plymouth PL1 3RP
01752 202 650
info@tswfta.co.uk
www.tswfta.co.uk
Bristol to Dorset

Wessex Film and Sound Archive
Hampshire Record Office
Sussex Street, Winchester SO23 8TH
01962 847742
sadedm@hants.gov.uk
www.hants.gov.uk/record-office/film
Hants film and sound archive

Wiener Library
4 Devonshire Street
London W1W 5BH
020 7636 7247
info@wienerlibrary.co.uk
www.wienerlibrary.co.uk
Modern Jewish history

Yorkshire Film Archive
Yorkshire St John College
Mayors Walk, York YO31 7EX
01904 716 550
yfa@yorksj.ac.uk
Yorkshire only

TV associations

Association of Motion Picture Sound
28 Knox Street, London W1H 1FS
020 7723 6727
admin@amps.net
www.amps.net
Film and TV sound technicians

Bafta (British Academy of Film and Television Arts)
195 Piccadilly, London W1J 9LN
020 7734 0022
www.bafta.org
Awards, training and education

Barb (Broadcasters' Audience Research Board)
18 Dering Street, London W1S 1AQ
020 7529 5531
enquiries@barb.co.uk
www.barb.co.uk
Industry-owned audience data

Bectu (Broadcasting, Entertainment, Cinematograph and Theatre Union)
373–377 Clapham Road
London SW9 9BT
020 7346 0900
www.bectu.org.uk
Union for broadcasting, entertainment and theatre

British Film Council International
10 Little Portland Street
London W1W 7JG
020 7861 7860
info@ukfilmcouncil.org.uk
wwwukfilmcouncil.org.uk
Promotes UK as production centre

British Film Institute
21 Stephen Street, London W1T 1LN
020 7255 1444
publishing@bfi.org.uk
www.bfi.org.uk
Education, exhibitions and resources

British Universities Film and Video Council
77 Wells Street, London W1T 3QJ
020 7393 1500
ask@bufvc.ac.uk
www.bufvc.ac.uk/

Broadcasting Press Guild
Tiverton, The Ridge
Woking, Surrey GU22 7EQ
01483 764895
torin.douglas@bbc.co.uk

Cinema and Television Benevolent Fund
22 Golden Square, London W1F 9AD
020 7437 6567
charity@ctbf.co.uk
www.ctbf.co.uk
Trade charity

Drama Association of Wales
The Old Library Building
Singleton Road, Splott
Cardiff CF24 2ET
029 2045 2200
aled.daw@virgin.net

DigiTAG (Digital Terrestrial Television Action Group)
17a Ancienne Route
CH-1218 Grand Saconnex, Geneva
Switzerland
+41 22 717 2716
projectoffice@digitag.org
www.digitag.org
Not-for-profit international association

Digital Television Group
7 Old Lodge Place, St Margarets
Twickenham TW1 1RQ
020 8891 1830
office@dtg.org.uk
www.dtg.org.uk
Director general: Marcus Coleman
International industry-led consortium

Digital Video Broadcasting Project (DVB)
Project Office, 17a Ancienne Route
CH-1218 Grand Saconnex, Geneva
Switzerland
+41 22 717 2719
dvb@dvb.org
www.dvb.org
Not-for-profit international association

Directors' Guild of Great Britain
Acorn House
314–320 Gray's Inn Road
London WC1X 8DP
020 7278 4343
guild@dggb.org
www.dggb.org

Documentary Film-makers Group
225a Brecknock Road
London N19 5AA
020 7428 0882
info@dfglondon.com
www.dfglondon.com

Equity
Guild House, Upper St Martins Lane
London WC2H 9EG
020 7379 6000
info@equity.org.uk
www.equity.org.uk
Actors' union

Fact (Federation Against Copyright Theft)
Unit 7, Victory Business Centre
Worton Road, Isleworth
Middlesex TW7 6DB
020 8568 6646
contact@fact-uk.org.uk
www.fact-uk.org.uk
Industry-funded

Federation of Entertainment Unions
1 Highfield, Twyford, Nr Winchester
Hampshire SO21 1QR
01962 713134
harris@interalpha.co.uk

Film Archive Forum
c/o British Universities Film & Video Council
77 Wells Street, London W1T 3QJ
020 7393 1508
luke@bufvc.ac.uk
www.bufvc.ac.uk/faf

Film Council UK
10 Little Portland Street
London W1W 7JG
020 7861 7861
info@ukfilmcouncil.org.uk
www.ukfilmcouncil.org.uk
Promotes UK as a production centre

Film London
20 Euston Centre, Regents Place
London NW1 3JH
020 7387 8787
info@filmlondon.org.uk
www.filmlondon.org.uk
Strategic agency for film and media in London, to act as catalyst for film-making in London

FT2 – Film & TV Freelance Training
Fourth floor, Warwick House
9 Warwick Street, London W1R 5RA
020 7734 5141
info@ft2.org.uk
www.ft2.org.uk

Focal International
Pentax House, South Hill Avenue
South Harrow HA2 0DU
020 8423 5853
info@focalint.org
www.focalint.org
Trade association for libraries and researchers

Guild of British Camera Technicians
020 8813 1999
admin@gbct.org
www.gbct.org

Guild of Television Cameramen
01822 614405
administration@gtc.org.uk
www.gtc.org.uk

Guild of Vision Mixers
www.guildofvisionmixers.org.uk

Institute of Broadcast Sound
27 Old Gloucester Street
London WC1N 3XX
01483 575450
info@ibs.org.uk
www.ibs.org.uk

International Federation of Film Archives (FIAF)
1 Rue Defacqz
B-1000 Brussels, Belgium
00 322 538 3065
info@fiafnet.org
www.fiafnet.org

IVCA (International Visual Communication Association)
19 Pepper Street, Glengall Bridge
London E14 9RP
020 7512 0571
info@ivca.org
www.ivca.org
Promotes corporate visual communication

MCPS and PRS Alliance
29–33 Berners Street
London W1T 3AB
020 7580 5544
info@mcps-prs-alliance.co.uk
www.prs.co.uk
Collects and distributes music royalties

Musicians Union
60–62 Clapham Road
London SW9 0JJ
020 7582 5566
webmaster@musiciansunion.org.uk
www.musiciansunion.org.uk

Nasta (National Student Television Association)
c/o Glasgow University Student Television, John McIntyre Building
University Avenue
Glasgow G12 8QQ
0141 339 8541 x30
gust@frc.gla.ac.uk
www.nasta.org.uk
11 student-run TV stations

National Film Theatre
Belvedere Road, South Bank
Waterloo, London SE1 8XT
020 7928 3535
nft@bfi.org.uk
www.bfi.org.uk

New Producers Alliance (NPA)
9 Bourlet Close, London W1W 7BP
020 7580 2480
queries@npa.org.uk
www.npa.org.uk
Training and support for film-makers

Northern Ireland Film and Television Commission
Third Floor, Alfred House
21 Alfred Street, Belfast
Northern Ireland BT2 8ED
028 9023 2444
info@niftc.co.uk
www.niftc.co.uk
Commissions films for TV in Northern Ireland

Pact (Producers Alliance for Cinema and Television)
45 Mortimer Street
London W1W 8HJ
020 7331 6000
enquiries@pact.co.uk
www.pact.co.uk
Trade association for independent production companies

Picture Research Association
Head Office, 2 Culver Drive
Oxted, Surrey RH8 9HP
01883 730123
pra@lippmann.co.uk
www.picture-research.org.uk
Professional body for supply of visual material to media

Production Guild
N&P Complex, Pinewood Studios
Iver Heath
Buckinghamshire SL0 0NH
01753 651767
www.productionguild.com

Production Managers Association
Ealing Studios, Ealing Green
Ealing, London W5 5EP
020 8758 8699
pma@pma.org.uk
www.pma.org.uk

Professional Lighting and Sound Association – Plasa
38 St Leonards Road
Eastbourne BN21 3UT
01323 410335
www.plasa.org

Royal Television Society
Holborn Hall, 100 Gray's Inn Road
London WC1X 8AL
020 7430 1000
info@rts.org.uk
www.rts.org.uk
Membership and events organisation

Satellite and Cable Broadcasting Group
29 Harley Street, London W1G 9QR
020 7016 2608
chairman@scbg.org.uk
www.scbg.org.uk
The trade association for satellite and cable programme providers

Scottish Screen
Second Floor, 249 West George Street
Glasgow G2 4QE
0141 302 1700
info@scottishscreen.com
www.scottishscreen.com
Promotes film

Screenwriters' Workshop
Suffolk House, 1–8 Whitfield Place
London W1T 5JV
020 7387 5511
screenoffice@tiscali.co.uk
www.lsw.org.uk
Helps writers find work in film and television industries

Sgrin, Media Agency for Wales
The Bank, 10 Mount Stuart Square
Cardiff Bay, Cardiff CF10 5EE
029 2033 3300
sgrin@sgrin.co.uk
www.sgrin.co.uk
Film, TV and new media in Wales

Spoken Word Publishing Association (SWPA)
c/o Macmillan Audio
20 New Wharf Road
London N1 9RR
020 7014 6041
z.howes@macmillan.co.uk
www.swpa.co.uk
Spoken word audio

Voice of the Listener and Viewer (VLV)
101 Kings Drive, Gravesend
Kent DA12 5BQ
01474 352835
info@vlv.org.uk
www.vlv.org.uk
Represents citizens' and consumers' interests

Writernet
Cabin V, Clarendon Buildings
25 Horsell Road, Highbury
London N5 1XL
020 7609 7474
writernet@btinternet.com
www.writernet.org.uk

Trade press

Advance Production News
Crimson Communications
211a Station House
Greenwich Communication Centre
Greenwich High Road
London SE10 8JL
020 8305 6905
www.crimson.uk.com
Monthly. Listings for production companies. Editor: Alan Williams

BFI Film and Television Handbook
The British Film Institute
21 Stephen Street, London W1T 1LN
020 7255 1444
eddie.dyja@bfi.org.uk
www.bfi.org.uk/handbook
Annual. Editor: Eddie Dyja

Broadband TV News
3 Jansen Walk, Hope Street
London SW11 2AZ
020 7585 3849
office@broadbandtvnews.com
www.broadbandtvnews.com
Free weekly emails & subscription newsletters. Editor: Julian Clover

Broadcast
Emap Media
33–39 Bowling Green Lane
London EC1R 0DA
020 7505 8000
bcletters@emap.com
www.broadcastnow.co.uk
Weekly. Trade magazine for TV & radio. Editor: Conor Dignam

Broadcast Hardware International
Hardware Creations
48 The Broadway, Maidenhead
Berks SL6 1PW
01628 773935
cathy@hardwarecreations.tv
www.hardwarecreations.tv
10 pa. Editor: Dick Hobbs

Cable & Satellite Europe
Informa Media and Telecoms
Mortimer House
37–41 Mortimer Street
London W1T 3JH
020 7017 5533
media.enquiries@informa.com
www.informamedia.com
10 pa. Editor: Stuart Thomson

Cable & Satellite International
Perspective Publishing
402 The Fruit and Wool Exchange
Brushfield Street, London E1 6EP
020 7426 0101
justin@cable-satellite.com
www.cable-satellite.com
6pa. Editor: John Moulding

Channel 21 International magazine
C21 Medial, Top Floor, 25 Phipp Street
London EC2A 4NP
020 7729 7460
press@c21media.net
www.c21media.net
10pa. Editor: David Jenkins

Commonwealth Broadcaster
Commonwealth Broadcasting Association
17 Fleet Street, London EC4Y 1AA
020 7583 5550
cba@cba.org.uk
www.cba.org.uk
Quarterly. Editor: Elizabeth Smith

Contacts
The Spotlight, 7 Leicester Place
London WC2H 7RJ
020 7437 7631
info@spotlightcd.com
www.spotlightcd.com
Annual. Contacts for stage, film, TV and radio. Editor: Kate Poynton

Crewfinder
Adleader Publications
15 Chartwell Park, Belfast BT8 6NG
028 9079 7902
mail@adleader.co.uk
www.crewfinderwales.co.uk
Annual. Wales' film, TV and video directory. Proprietor: Stan Mairs

Digilook
7 Burgess Green, Deal
Kent CT14 0AU
07709 118854
andi@digilook.net
www.digilook.net
Web. Digital TV & radio
Editors: Andi Gasking, Alex Oughton

Digital Spy
6 Queen's Elm Square
London SW3 6ED
07814 776894
nwilkes@digitalspy.co.uk
www.digitalspy.co.uk
Web. Digital TV. Editor: Neil Wilkes

FilmBang
Marianne Mellin, 43 Hyndland Road
Glasgow G12 9UX
0141 334 2456
info@filmbang.com
www.filmbang.com
Annual. Scotland's film and video directory. Editor: Marianne Mellin

IBE
DMG Business Media
Queensway House, 2 Queens Way
Redhill, Surrey RH1 1QS
01737 855224
info@ibeweb.com
www.ibeweb.com
12pa. International broadcast engineering. Editor: Neil Nixon

Kemps Film, TV, Video Handbook (UK edition)
Reed Business Information
Windsor Court, East Grinstead House
East Grinstead
West Sussex RH19 1XA
01342 332073
kemps@reedinfo.co.uk
www.kftb.com
Annual. Guide to international production. Editor: Pat Huwson

The Knowledge
CMP Information
Riverbank House, Angel Lane
Tonbridge, Kent TN9 1SE
01732 377591
knowledge@cmpinformation.com
www.theknowledgeonline.com
Annual. Production directory

Line Up
Line Up Publications
The Hawthornes, 4 Conference Grove
Crowle WR7 4SF
01905 381725
editor@lineup.biz
www.ibs.org.uk
6pa. Journal of the Institute of Broadcast Sound. Editor: Hugh Robjohns

Multichannel News
Chilton Company, 37 The Towers
Lower Mortlake Road
Richmond TW9 2JR
020 8948 8561
chrisforrester@compuserve.com
www.multichannel.com
Weekly. Editor: Chris Forester

Pact directory of Independent producers
Producers Alliance for Cinema and Television (PACT)
45 Mortimer Street
London W1W 8HJ
020 7331 6000
enquiries@pact.co.uk
www.pact.co.uk
Annual. Directory of independent producers. Editor: Louise Bateman

Pro Sound News
CMP Information, Ludgate House
245 Blackfriars Road
London SE1 9UR
020 7921 8319
info@cmpinformation.com
www.cmpinformation.com
12pa. Audio industry
Editor: David Robinson

The Production Guide
Emap Information
33–39 Bowling Green Lane
London EC1R 0DA
020 7505 8000
theproductionguide@Emap.com
www.productionguideonline.com
Annual. Information on production
Editor: Mei Mei Rogers

Satellite Finance
Thompson Stanley Publishers
1–3 Leonard Street
London EC2A 4AQ
020 7251 2967
oliver.cann@satellitefinance.com
www.telecomfinance.com
11pa. Finance journal for executives
Editor: Oliver Cann

Screen Digest
Screen Digest, Lymehouse Studios
38 Georgiana Street
London NW1 0EB
020 7424 2820
editorial@screendigest.com
www.screendigest.com
Monthly. Editor: David Fisher

Screen International
Emap Media
33–39 Bowling Green Lane
London EC1R 0DA
020 7505 8080
screeninternational@hotmail.com
www.screendaily.com
Weekly. News service for global film industry. Editor: Colin Brown

Sports TV Yearbook
Perspective Media, PO Box 22499
London W6 9YS
020 7937 3636
pnicholson@sportsvisionnews.com
www.sportscentric.com
Annual. Editor: Jay Stuart

Stage Screen and Radio
Bectu, 373–377 Clapham Road
London SW9 9BT
020 7346 0900
janice@stagescreenandradio.org.uk
www.bectu.org.uk
10pa. Broadcasting union
Editor: Janice Turner

Televisual
Centaur Communications
50 Poland Street, London W1F 7AX
020 7970 4000
mundy.ellis@centaur.co.uk
www.mad.co.uk
Monthly. Trade magazine for TV
Editor: Mundy Ellis

TV International
Informa Media and Telecoms
Mortimer House
37–41 Mortimer Street
London W1T 3JH
020 7017 4269
toby.scott@informa.com
www.informamedia.com
Daily. International TV listings
Editor: Stewart Clarke

TBI (Television Business International)
Informa Media and Telecoms
Mortimer House
37–41 Mortimer Street
London W1T 3JH
020 7453 2300
kevin.scott@informa.com
www.informamedia.com
Annual. Directory to businesses
Editor: Kevin Scott

TV Technology and Production
IMAS Publishing UK
Atlantica House, 11 Station Road
St Ives, Cambs PE27 5BH
01480 461555
tvteurope@aol.com
www.imaspub.com
6pa. Broadcasting and production technology. Editor: Mark Hallinger

TVB Europe
CMP Information, Prospect House
1 Prospect Road, Dublin 9
00 353 1 882 4444
sgrice@cmpinformation.com
www.tvbeurope.com
Monthly. Broadcasting innovation and technology. Editor: Fergal Ringrose

VLV Bulletin
Voice of the Listener and Viewer
101 Kings Drive
Gravesend DA12 5BQ
01474 352835
vlv@btinternet.com
www.vlv.org.uk
Quarterly. Consumer campaigning body. Editor: Jocelyn Hay

Zerb
The Deeson Group
Ewell House, Gravney Road
Faversham, Kent ME13 8UP
01795 535468
alichap@mac.com
www.gtc.org.uk
2pa. For camera operators
Editor: Alison Chapman

Radio

These are exciting times to be in radio. The industry continues to grow quickly, thanks to the growth of digital radio and the advertising of yet more analogue licences. At the beginning of the 2004, there were more than 275 analogue and more than 300 digital stations. Britons devote around a third of their "media time" to radio – making it the second most popular medium behind TV, and the most popular until the early evening each day. But as digital radio becomes more popular, the BBC predicts that the amount of time we spend listening to the radio will increase by 10 per cent, or two hours a week, over the next five years.

Official radio listening figures are calculated by Rajar, an independent company owned by both the BBC and commercial radio. According to its latest figures, the BBC remains slightly bigger than the commercial sector: 32.4 million people listened to a BBC radio station for at least five minutes a week in the second quarter of 2004; 31.4 million listened to a commercial station in the same period. This statistic is known

National listening figures, second quarter 2004

Top 20 National stations	Reach (m)	Reach (%)	Share (%)
BBC Radio 2	13.4	27	16.2
BBC Radio 1	9.7	20	8.3
BBC Radio 4	9.5	19	1.1
Classic FM	6.5	13	4.5
BBC Radio Five Live	6.1	12	4.5
Heart*	3.3	7	2.3
Galaxy*	2.7	6	1.9
Magic*	2.7	5	1.8
Virgin*	2.6	5	1.6
Kiss*	2.5	5	1.3
TalkSport	2.2	4	1.8
BBC Radio 3	2.0	4	1.1
Capital Gold*	1.5	3	0.9
Jazz*	1.5	3	0.9
BBC World Service	1.4	3	0.6
Classic Gold*	0.9	2	0.8
The Hits	0.9	2	0.3
Smash Hits	0.7	1	0.2
Kerrang!	0.7	1	0.2
XFM*	0.7	1	0.4
All BBC national	**28.6**	**58**	**42.2**
All commercial national	**13.1**	**27**	**10.1**

*Total networks

Source: Rajar

Awards

Sony Radio Academy Awards, May 2004

- *Station of the year:* BBC Radio 4
- *Station of the year, audience over 1 million:* Heart 106.2
- *Station of the year, audience 300,000 to 1 million:* BBC Radio Suffolk
- *Station of the year, audience under 300,000:* BBC Radio Foyle
- *Station of the year, digital terrestrial:* PrimeTime Radio
- *Breakfast show of the year:* JK & Joel, Key 103
- *Entertainment award:* Jono and Harriet at Breakfast, Heart 106.2
- *DJ of the year:* Christian O'Connell, XFM
- *News programme of the year:* Crossing Continents – India (BBC Radio 4)
- *Speech broadcaster of the year:* Ian Robertson (BBC Radio Five Live)

Top 20 local/regional stations by reach

		Reach (m)	Reach (%)	Share (%)
95.8 Capital FM	London	2.11	20	6.6
Heart 106.2 FM	London	1.93	18	6.5
Kiss 100 FM	London	1.56	15	4.7
Magic 105.4	London	1.54	15	4.6
Galaxy 105	Leeds	1.01	24	8.5
100.7 Heart FM	Birmingham	0.94	27	11.0
BBC Radio Scotland		0.85	20	7.6
Capital Gold	London	0.78	7	2.5
105.4 Century FM	Manchester	0.75	15	6.4
Jazz FM	London	0.71	7	1.8
Real Radio	Scotland	0.69	26	15.1
Clyde 1 FM	Glasgow	0.68	37	17.6
Key 103	Manchester	0.64	24	9.2
LBC 97.3	London	0.60	6	3.0
XFM 104.9	London	0.58	6	1.7
96.4FM BRMB	Birmingham	0.57	28	9.3
BBC Radio Wales/Cymru		0.56	24	13.6
BBC Radio Ulster		0.55	41	26.9
BBC London 94.9		0.54	5	2.1
100–102 Century	North-east	0.53	25	11.7
All commercial local		**25.9**	**54**	**35.5**
All BBC local		**10.2**	**21**	**10.9**

Source, Rajar: second quarter 2004

as a station's "reach". BBC stations dominate in the national market, with a reach of 28.6 million to commercial's 13.1 million; but commercial stations dominate locally, with a reach of 25.9 million to the BBC's 10.2 million.

Not everyone, though, has faith in the official figures. In March 2004, Kelvin MacKenzie, chief executive of the Wireless Group – which owns the national station, TalkSport – sued Rajar for £66m, saying its pen-and-paper-based research undervalues his station and is fatally flawed. MacKenzie says electronically measured figures, such as those he has commissioned from the German researchers GfK, are more accurate. The difference is certainly big: according to Rajar, TalkSport had 1.8 million listeners in the first three months of 2004; but according to GfK it had 6.3 million. Virgin Radio, too, has said Rajar does not sample enough of its target 15- to 24-year-olds; GfK's figures put its reach at 3.3 million, 800,000 up on its Rajar figure. And most worryingly for Rajar, major media buyers Zenith Optimedia and PHD Group say that according to their tests, the GfK system is more accurate.

Rajar, for its part, is spending £500,000 on testing electronic measurement systems this summer, although it cannot award a new research contract until 2006. But it has said that MacKenzie's claims about its financial losses, outlined in a Wireless Group press release, are ludicrous. It appointed a new managing director, Sally De La Bedoyere, in January 2004.

BBC

BBC radio has five national analogue stations: Radio 1, for popular and chart music; Radio 2, for slightly older music listeners; Radio 3, for classical, world music and arts; Radio 4, the speech station with flagship news programmes such as Today; and Five Live, for rolling news and sport. The BBC also broadcasts the World Service, the international news station funded separately by the Foreign Office. On digital, it broadcasts all these stations plus five digital-only stations: 6Music, for modern music; 1xtra, for new street music; the Asian Network, for British Asians; BBC7, for comedy and drama; and Five Live Sports Extra.

The last few years have seen a marked change in the fortunes of Britain's two most popular stations, Radio 1 and Radio 2. In 1999, Radio 1 held the top spot: it reached 11.3 million listeners in the third quarter of that year, almost 2 million ahead of Radio 2. Now Radio 2 – home to Jonathan Ross, Mark Radcliffe and Terry Wogan – is the most popular: it recorded a reach of 13.4 million in the second quarter of 2004, compared to 9.7 million for Radio 1.

Wogan is still the most popular breakfast DJ, with 8 million listeners in the second quarter of 2004; but Radio 2 lost a successful leader in October 2003, when controller John Moir retired, to be replaced by Lesley Douglas. There are signs too that Radio 1's slide may be halting: buoyed by a TV campaign, Chris Moyles replaced Sara Cox as breakfast show host in January, and put on listeners to climb over 7 million. The BBC annual report said the station had been overhauled after projecting a "relentlessly single" outlook on life.

With some focus shifting away from international affairs, Radio 4 shed listeners. Its reach had gone over 10 million during the Iraq war in the first quarter of 2003, eclipsing Radio 1; but it was down 6.6 per cent to 9.37 million a year later. The Today programme, its flagship news and current affairs show – which broadcast the controversial report by Andrew Gilligan that led to the David Kelly affair and the Hutton report – lost 150,000 from its audience over the same period, down to 6.2 million.

Radio 5 also grew in popularity, with a reach of almost 6.1 million in the second quarter of 2004, up 300,000 year on year; this after reaching its second highest ever reach in January to March, some 6.5 million. Radio 3's reach remained steady at about 2 million.

There were criticisms for radio in the BBC annual report. Radio 1 had been overhauled after projecting a "relentlessly single" outlook on life even though half of 25- to 30-year-olds have children; and some Radio 3 listeners were "unhappy with the share of output given to non-classical music".

Finally, 2004 saw the sad death of broadcaster Alistair Cooke, who had presented Letter from America for 58 years.

Commercial radio

Radio advertising is back. According to the Advertising Association, ad spend on radio rose 6.8 per cent to £582m in 2003, despite the Iraq war in the first three months of the year; while in the first quarter of 2004, it grew 7 per cent year on year, in real terms, to £133m.

"The outlook for advertisers is a lot more chirpy and cheerful," said Kelvin Mackenzie, chairman and chief executive of the Wireless Group, which owns TalkSport and local stations; but what he meant was that he was feeling chirpy himself. His group made its first operating profit in 2003, some £2.3m; and ad sales increased by 19 per cent in the first three months of 2004. Similar rises were reported by other groups: GWR, owner of Classic FM, said its non-digital revenues were up 12 per cent year-on-year in the last three months of 2003; while Chrysalis, owner of the Galaxy network and Heart, said radio revenues rose 23 per cent year on year in the six months to the end of February, to £33.3m, with similar figures being sustained in the two months after that.

Life was not as rosy at SMG, owners of Virgin Radio: as the owner of two Scottish ITV1 franchises, it was perhaps left exposed by the ITV merger (see page 123). Its profits fell 25 per cent in 2003, and in March 2004 it was reported in MediaGuardian.co.uk to be sounding out buyers for Virgin.

From the listener's perspective, the top radio story in 2004 was the departure of Chris Tarrant from Capital Radio in London, after 17 years as host of the station's breakfast show. Tarrant finished his tenure on a high, as a total of 1.37 million people tuned in to his final three months, a rise of some 133,000 listeners. The performance helped Capital to the highest audience in London for the first quarter of 2004, at more than 2.3 million (7.9 per cent) – which meant it held on to the London top spot, after its rival Heart FM had briefly held it in October. In the same period, Heart's breakfast show had 833,000 listeners, down nearly 50,000; and its audience share was only 5.8 per cent. But in the second quarter of 2004, Tarrant's replacement, Johnny Vaughan, lost 180,000 listeners and Capital's breakfast lead over Heart was cut to 220,000. Overall, Capital led Heart by 2.1 million to 1.9 million. There was also speculation that Capital Radio Group might be in talks with GWR over a possible merger.

Johnny Vaughan: hosting his first Capital show

Jon Furniss

Elsewhere in the country, there was a boost for commercial radio as Ofcom announced that it was awarding at least 30 more FM radio stations in 2004 and 2005; Edinburgh, Manchester, Liverpool and Newcastle will be among the cities targeted. A fourth national commercial radio station may also be launched, some time in 2005.

Digital radio

Digital radio continued to expand in 2003 and 2004. Five years after the launch of the first digital radio service, there are more than 140 digital radio brands and more than 300 stations, according to the digital development bureau (DRDB), which markets the technology. Consumers can listen to the stations through a digital radio, through their televisions, and often through the internet, although not all stations are available via all media.

Digital radio sets have proved enormously popular. The number of sets sold, just 135,000 at the beginning of 2003, had reached 547,000 by June 2004; and the figure would rise to 1 million by the end of 2004, predicted the DRDB. At the beginning of 2004, digital radios accounted for more than two-thirds of the value of all "kitchen-style" radio sets sold.

Using a digital radio, listeners in most major towns can already receive between 30 and 50 radio stations, which in many cases is more than double what is available on analogue; this is because digital radio

National digital radio

On BBC network and Freeview	On Digital One and Freeview	On Freeview only
BBC Radio 1*	Oneword	The Hits
BBC Radio 2*		Heat
BBC Radio 3*	**On Digital One only**	Jazz FM*
BBC Radio 4*	Primetime Radio	Kerrang!
BBC Radio Five Live*	Talksport*	Kiss*
BBC Five Live Sports Extra	Virgin Radio*	Magic*
BBC 6Music	Core	Mojo
BBC World Service	Planet Rock	Q
BBC 1Xtra	Classic FM*	Smash Hits
BBC Asian Network	Life	

*also available on analogue

uses the radio spectrum more efficiently, so it is possible to broadcast more channels using the same frequency. The system works by dividing the spectrum into networks, or "multiplexes"; one of these is national and almost 50 are local. The BBC signal was expected to cover 85 per cent of the population by 2004, with commercial operators having already reached that target.

The number of people listening to the radio via their TV is growing faster: more than a quarter of adults said they listened to the radio in such a way in the first quarter of 2004, half as many again as in the same period the previous year. The rise is explained by the success of the Freeview digital terrestrial TV service: customers who bought a set-top box can access 20 national radio stations. Sky Digital subscribers also have access to more than 75 stations; and there are 81 stations included in BSkyB's free-to-air satellite service, announced in 2004.

At the beginning of 2004, meanwhile, some 15.5 per cent of adults said they listened to radio via the internet.

The BBC, under pressure for its £27m spend on digital radio with charter review approaching, was boosted by record audiences for three stations in the first three months of 2004. Five Live Sports Extra had a reasonable 369,000 listeners, up 112,000 from the end of 2003, as people tuned in for its Premiership football coverage; while BBC7, the speech and comedy station, had 398,000, up 131,000; and 6Music put on 32,000 to 187,000. 1Xtra seemed to follow the fortunes of its sister station, though; it had 248,000 listeners, down sharply on the 331,000 it had just six months before.

In commercial radio, a notable launch was Emap's Heat radio, a spin-off from the successful consumer magazine, which started transmission in February 2004.

Meanwhile, GWR chairman Ralph Bernard said in January that the government should announce a switch-off deadline for the radio analogue signal, as it has for TV. The move would be a boon for companies that have invested in digital terrestrial radio (such as GWR); but it would not go down well with the public, as it would leave millions of existing analogue radios defunct. The regulator, Ofcom, hinted that the switch could come soon after the TV switch-off in 2010, but BBC director of radio Jenny Abramsky was more cautious: "We have to do what is right for the listener, not for us," she said in July.

Community radio

The government is ready to extend its pilot of community radio stations – formerly known as access radio – nationwide. Since 2001, 16 non-profit community stations have been running across Britain (see page 202 for a full list and contact details); now the government wants to offer cash from a £500,000 fund to those who want to set up neighbourhood radio stations of their own. To protect the interests of local commercial radio, the bill includes restrictions: in an area where a community station broadcasts to 150,000 people or fewer and overlaps with another local commercial station, it will not be able to take advertising or sponsorship; while in other areas, advertising and sponsorship will be restricted to a maximum 50 per cent of funding.

Further reading

■ Press

MediaGuardian media.guardian.co.uk/radio

■ Books

Travels with My Radio FI GLOVER, EBURY PRESS 2002 Insightful radio travelogue

Local Radio Journalism PAUL CHANTLER AND SIM HARRIS, FOCAL PRESS 1997 Useful guide

On Air: A Career in TV & Radio CHRIS ALDEN, GUARDIAN BOOKS 2004 The essential careers guide to television and radio

■ Other resources

Digital Radio Development Bureau www.drdb.org

Radio Academy www.radioacademy.org

World Radio Network www.wrn.org

Digital multiplex licence-holders

Holder	Owners	Multiplexes Number	Location
NATIONAL			
BBC	Public	1	85% of country
Digital One		1	85% of country
Total national:		**2**	
LOCAL AND REGIONAL*			
BBC	Public	37	Throughout UK (local & regional)
Capital Radio Digital	Capital Radio	4	South of England; Cardiff & Newport
CE Digital	Capital Radio, Emap Radio	3	London, Birmingham, Manchester
Emap Digital Radio	Emap Performance	7	North of England
MXR	Chrysalis Radio Group, Capital Radio, Guardian Media Group, UBC Digital and Ford	5	The North, South Wales, West Midlands (all regional)
Now Digital	GWR Group	14	Throughout the South and the Midlands
Score Digital	Scottish Radio Holdings	6	Scotland, Northern Ireland
Switchdigital	The Wireless Group, Capital Radio, Clear Channel International and The Carphone Warehouse	3	London & Aberdeen (local), central Scotland (regional)
The Digital Radio Group	GWR Group, The Wireless Group, SMG, Carphone Warehouse, Emap	1	London
TWG/Emap Digital	The Wireless Group, Emap Performance	2	Swansea, Stoke-on-Trent
TWG Digital	The Wireless Group	1	Bradford/Huddersfield
Total local and regional:		**83**	
TOTAL:		**85**	

* Local licences unless stated

Sources: BBC, Digital Radio Development Bureau.

The seven-year switch **Jason Jenkins**

After years of nothing, the first signs have arrived that analogue radio may be killed off for good. A senior executive from the media regulator, Ofcom, has said that the plug could be pulled on the analogue radio signal shortly after the last analogue TV transmissions are broadcast some time in 2012 – and that Tessa Jowell, the current culture secretary, is listening favourably.

It's exactly the sort of statement that grabs headlines and makes radio executives excited – but when you start to look at the market, it seems rather premature to even be thinking about killing off FM.

Before switching off the analogue radio signal, a viable alternative needs to be in place so that people aren't left with silence. That alternative is digital radio, which, like digital TV, can offer better quality sound, a greater choice of programmes and extra services.

The idea is that, by switching off the analogue signal sooner rather than later and forcing everyone to use digital radio instead, Britain can cement itself as a radio pioneer, reaping economic benefits, and the government can raise cash by auctioning off the radio spectrum for next-generation wireless services.

No one doubts that the switch-off will come: the question is, when? The decision rests with the government, and it's a tricky one. Unlike analogue TVs, existing analogue radios can't be converted to digital – it's a question of buying an entirely new wireless to receive the digital signals.

If the analogue signal were switched off tomorrow, 100 million analogue radios would become useless overnight. Landfill sites everywhere would be full of the obsolete models, along with all the black and white tellies, Betamax video recorders and record players of yesteryear. And let's face it – no mainstream political party is ever going to go into an election with a promise to break granny's radio if they get in.

Realistically, most households will need to own at least one digital radio before any such drastic steps can be taken. Although the government has said that 95% of the population needs to be watching digital TV before the analogue TV signal is killed, no such target exists for radio.

Most industry sources reckon that one million digital radios will have been sold in the UK by the end of 2004 – an impressive achievement, considering that there were only about 35,000 units in the UK in 2002. Assuming that the government will apply similar criteria to digital radio as it will for TV, we're an unimaginably long way away from analogue switch-off.

Persuading more people to go digital will be helped partly by the fact that the hardware will continue to fall in price, but more by a series of technical innovations that will change the experience of listening to the wireless forever.

The most exciting of these is an electronic programme guide (EPG), which consumers will be able to start using early in 2005. This will be a digital version of a listing magazine, so you'll be able to see on your radio's display when the programme you want to listen to will be broadcast.

Digital radio pioneer Pure Digital plans to combine the EPG with the recording technology already available in its Bug radio, so not only will you be able to see when the next instalment of your favourite drama is playing, you'll be able to tell your radio to record it for you as well.

Coverage will improve, too, although it will be years before it is as good as FM in some areas. Currently, although household digital radios mostly work well, portable models suffer from the fact that the signal just isn't strong enough, and frequent cut-outs are common. Digital radios will become more common in cars, too – one area of the market that has remain largely immune from the digital revolution.

One question remains largely unanswered: what to do with the unused radio spectrum if and when the analogue signal is switched off. There aren't any concrete ideas at the moment, although the general consensus is that the spectrum won't be as valuable as the one freed up when analogue TV gets the heave-ho. Most people are assuming that the answer will emerge in the next 10-15 years as technology develops, and considering the tremendous advances that have been made in the last decade, this seems reasonable.

It may be too early to accurately predict the date analogue radio will be switched off – but with the news that, for the first time, more digital radios are being sold than analogue ones, it is a question that will come to occupy politicians' and regulators' time more and more.

Jason Jenkins is the deputy editor of gadget magazine T3

Radio Contacts

BBC radio

Broadcasting House
Portland Place
London W1A 1AA
020 7580 4468

Director of radio and music: Jenny Abramsky, 020 7765 4561
Head of radio news: Stephen Mitchell
Head of radio current affairs: Gwyneth Williams
Controller, radio production: Graham Ellis, 020 7765 4809
Controller, radio & music new media: Simon Nelson, 020 7765 2545
Publicity: Sue Lynas, 020 7765 4990
Digital radio publicist: Jamie Austin, 020 7765 0426

BBC Radio 1/1xtra
Yalding House
152–156 Great Portland Street
London W1N 6AJ
www.bbc.co.uk/radio1
www.bbc.co.uk/1xtra
Controller: Andy Parfitt; head of mainstream programmes: Ben Cooper, 020 7765 2236; head of specialist live music: Ian Parkinson, 020 7765 0365; breakfast show: Chris Moyles (Radio 1), Rampage (1xtra); press: Julian Payne, 020 7765 1030

BBC Radio 2
Western House
99 Great Portland Street
London W1A 1AA
www.bbc.co.uk/radio2
Controller: Lesley Douglas, 020 7765 3493; managing editor: Antony Bellekom, 020 7765 4612; editor, mainstream programmes: Phil Hughes, 020 7765 4159; editor, specialist programmes: Dave Barber, 0121 432 9854; breakfast show: Terry Wogan; press: Hester Nevill, 020 7765 5712

BBC Radio 3
Broadcasting House, Portland Place
London W1A 1AA
www.bbc.co.uk/radio3
Controller: Roger Wright, 020 7765 2523; head of speech programmes: Abigail Appleton, 020 7765 3277; head of music programming: John Evans, 020 7765 0481; controller, Proms, events & TV classical music: Nicholas Kenyon, 020 7765 4928; press: Sian Davis, 020 7765 5887

BBC Radio 4
Broadcasting House, Portland Place
London W1A 1AA
www.bbc.co.uk/radio4
Controller: Helen Boaden, 020 7765 3836; network manager: Denis Nowlan, 020 7765 4615; head of radio drama: Gordon House, 020 755 71006; editor, drama and entertainment: Caroline Raphael, 020 7765 1870; editor, radio light entertainment: John Pidgeon, 020 7765 4220; editors, general factual: Jane Ellison (features) 020 7765 0631, Prue Keely (strands) 020 7765 2585; editor, specialist factual: Andrew Caspari, 020 7765 2660; press: Marion Greenwood, 020 7765 2629

Today programmo
Room G630, Stage 6
Television Centre, Wood Lane
London W12 7RJ
www.bbc.co.uk/radio4/today
Editor: Kevin Marsh; presenters: John Humphrys, James Naughtie, Ed Stourton, Sarah Montague

BBC Radio Five Live & Five Live Sports Extra
Television Centre, Wood Lane
London W12 7RJ
www.bbc.co.uk/fivelive
Controller: Bob Shennan, 020 8624 8956; head of radio sport: Gordon Turnbull, 020 8225 6206; head of news, Radio Five Live: Ceri Thomas, 020 8624 8946; commissioning editor: Moz Dee, 020 8624 8948; press: Andy Bate, 020 8576 1694

BBC 6 Music
Western House
99 Great Portland Street
London W1A 1AA
www.bbc.co.uk/6music
Controller: Lesley Douglas, 020 7765 3493; head of programmes: Ric Blaxill; breakfast show: Phill Jupitus; see also Radio 2 contacts

BBC Asian Network
Epic House, Charles Street
Leicester LE1 3SH
0116 251 6688
www.bbc.co.uk/asiannetwork
Controller: Bijay Sharma; breakfast: Gagan Grewal; publicity: Dimple Poojara, 020 8225 6373

BBC 7
Broadcasting House, Portland Place
London W1A 1AA
www2.thny.bbc.co.uk/bbc7
Controller: Helen Boaden, 020 7765 3836; see also Radio 4 contacts

BBC World Service
Bush House, Strand
London WC2B 4PH
020 7557 2941
www.bbc.co.uk/worldservice
Director: Mark Byford

Nations & regions

BBC Radio Scotland
Queen Margaret Drive
Glasgow G12 8DG
0141 339 8844
scottishplanning@bbc.co.uk
www.bbc.co.uk/scotland
Controller: Ken MacQuarrie; news editor: Blair Jenkins
92–95 FM; 810 AM

BBC Radio Nan Gaidheal
52 Church Street, Stornoway
Isle of Lewis HS1 2LS
01851 705000
feedback@bbc.co.uk
www.bbc.co.uk/scotlandalba/radio
Editor: Marion MacKinnon; news editor: Norrie Maclennan
103–105 FM

BBC Radio Wales/Cymru
Broadcasting House
Llandaff, Cardiff CF5 2YQ
0870 010 0110
radiowales@bbc.co.uk
www.bbc.co.uk/radiowales
Managing editor: Julie Barton; head of news: Geoff Williams; breakfast show: Richard Ellis/Felicity Evans
93–104 FM

BBC Radio Ulster
Broadcasting House
Belfast BT2 8HQ
028 9033 8000
radioulster@bbc.co.uk
www.bbc.co.uk/radioulster
Head of radio: Ana Leddy; head of music: Declan McGovern; head of news: Andrew Colman
92–95.4 FM

BBC Radio Foyle
Northland Road, Derry
Londonderry BT48 7GD
028 7137 8600
radiofoyle@bbc.co.uk
www.bbc.co.uk/radiofoyle
Head of radio: Ana Leddy; head of news: Eimear O'Callaghan
792 AM; 93.1 FM

BBC local radio

BBC Radio Berkshire
PO Box 1044, Reading RG4 8FH
0118 946 4200
berkshireonline@bbc.co.uk
www.bbc.co.uk/berkshire
Editor: Marianne Bell; breakfast show: Jim Cathcart/Maggie Filburn. 104.1 FM; 95.4 FM; 104.4 FM; 94.6 FM

BBC Radio Bristol and Somerset Sound
PO Box 194, Bristol BS99 7QT
01179 741111
radio.bristol@bbc.co.uk
www.bbc.co.uk/radiobristol and www.bbc.co.uk/bristol
Managing editor, Bristol: Jenny Lacey; assistant editors: Dawn Trevett (Bristol), Simon Clifford (Somerset Sound); breakfast show: Nigel Dando/ Rachael Burden. 95.5, 94.9 FM; 1548, 1566 AM

BBC Radio Cambridgeshire
PO Box 96, 104 Hills Road
Cambridge CB2 1LD
01223 259696
cambs@bbc.co.uk
www.bbc.co.uk/cambridgeshire
News editor: Alison Daws; managing editor: David Martin; breakfast show: Trevor Dann & Emma McLean. 96 FM; 95.7 FM

BBC Radio Cleveland
PO Box 95FM, Newport Road
Middlesbrough TS1 5DG
01642 225211
bbcradiocleveland@bbc.co.uk
www.bbc.co.uk/tees
Managing editor: Andrew Glover; news editor: Peter Harris; breakfast show: Ken Snowdon. 95 FM

BBC Radio Cornwall
Phoenix Wharf
Truro, Cornwall TR1 1UA
01872 275421
radio.cornwall@bbc.co.uk
www.bbc.co.uk/cornwall
Managing editor: Pauline Causey; news editor: Ed Goodrich; breakfast show: Pam Spriggs & James Churchfield. 103.9 FM; 95.2 FM

BBC Radio Cumbria
Annetwell Street, Carlisle CA3 8BB
01228 592444
radio.cumbria@bbc.co.uk
www.bbc.co.uk/radiocumbria
Managing editor: Nigel Dyson; news editor: Tom Stight; breakfast show: Richard Corrie & Richard Nankivell. 95.6 FM; 96.1 FM; 104.1 FM

BBC Radio Derby
PO Box 104.5, Derby DE1 3HL
01332 361111
radio.derby@bbc.co.uk
www.bbc.co.uk/radioderby
Managing editor: Simon Cornes; news editor: John Atkin; breakfast show: Andy Whitaker. 1116 AM; 104.5 AM; 95.3 FM; 96FM

BBC Radio Devon
PO Box 1034, Plymouth PL3 5BD
01752 260323
radio.devon@bbc.co.uk
www.bbc.co.uk/devon
Managing editor: Sarah Softley; news editor: David Farwig; breakfast show: Monica Ellis. 103.4 FM

BBC Essex
198 New London Road
Chelmsford, Essex CM2 9XB
01245 616000
essex@bbc.co.uk
www.bbc.co.uk/essex
Managing editor: Margaret Hyde; news editor: Alison Hodgkins-Brown; breakfast show: Etholle George & John Hayes. 103.5 FM; 95.3 FM; 765 AM; 1530 AM; 729 AM

BBC Radio Gloucestershire
London Road, Gloucester GL1 1SW
01452 308585
radio.gloucestershire@bbc.co.uk
www.bbc.co.uk/gloucestershire
Managing editor: Mark Hurrell; news editor: Ivor Ward-Davis; breakfast show: Vernon Harwood. 104.7 FM; 1413 AM

BBC GMR
PO Box 951, Oxford Road
Manchester M60 1SD
0161 200 2000
gmr.newsdesk@bbc.co.uk
www.bbc.co.uk/england/gmr
Managing editor: Mike Briscoe; news editor: Matt Elliott; breakfast show: Heather Stott & Mark Edwardson. 95.1 FM; 104.6 FM

BBC Radio Guernsey
Bulwer Avenue, St Sampsons
Guernsey GY2 4LA
01481 200600
radio.guernsey@bbc.co.uk
www.bbc.co.uk/guernsey
Managing editor: Rod Holmes; news editors: Simon Alexander & Kay Longlay; breakfast show: Adrian Gidney. 93.2 FM; 1116 AM

BBC Hereford and Worcester
Hylton Road, Worcester WR2 5WW
01905 748485
bbchw@bbc.co.uk
www.bbc.co.uk/worcester
or /hereford
Managing editor: James Coghill; news editor: Jo Baldwin; breakfast show: Mike George. 104 FM; 104.6 FM; 94.7 FM

BBC Radio Humberside and BBCi Hull
Queens Court, Queens Gardens
Hull HU1 3RP
01482 323232
radio.humberside@bbc.co.uk
www.bbc.co.uk/humber
Managing editor: Simon Pattern; news editor: Mike Morris; breakfast show: Andy Comfort. 95.9 FM; 1485 AM

BBC Radio Jersey
18 Parade Road, St Helier
Jersey JE2 3PL
01534 870000
radio.jersey@bbc.co.uk
www.bbc.co.uk/jersey
Managing editor: Denzil Dudley; news editor: Sarah Scriven; breakfast show: Colin Bray. 88.8 FM

BBC Radio Kent
The Great Hall, Mount Pleasant Road
Tunbridge Wells, Kent TN1 1QQ
01892 670000
radio.kent@bbc.co.uk
www.bbc.co.uk/kent
Managing editor: Robert Wallace; news editors: Sally Dunk & Simon Longprice; breakfast show: Steve Ladner. 96.7 FM; 97.6 FM; 104.2 FM

BBC Radio Lancashire and BBC Open Centre
26 Darwen Street, Blackburn
Lancs BB2 2EA
01254 262411
radio.lancashire@bbc.co.uk
www.bbc.co.uk/lancashire
Managing editor: John Clayton; news editor: Chris Rider; breakfast show: Mike West. 95.5 FM

BBC Radio Leeds
Broadcasting Centre
2 St Peters Square, Leeds LS9 8AH
0113 244 2131
radio.leeds@bbc.co.uk
www.bbc.co.uk/leeds
Managing editor: John Ryan; news editor: Andy Evans; breakfast show: Andrew Edwards & Liz Rhodes. 92.4 FM

BBC Radio Leicester
Epic House, Charles Street
Leicester LE1 3SH
0116 251 6688
radio.leicester@bbc.co.uk
www.bbc.co.uk/leicester
Managing editor: Kate Squire; breakfast show: Ben Jackson. 104.9 FM

BBC Radio Lincolnshire
PO Box 219, Newport
Lincoln LN1 3XY
01522 511411
radio.lincolnshire@bbc.co.uk
www.bbc.co.uk/lincolnshire
Managing editor: Charlie Partridge; news editor: Andy Farrant; breakfast show: William Wright. 94.9 FM; 1368 FM; 104 FM

BBC London 94.9
35 Marylebone High Street
London W1U 4QA
020 7224 2424
yourlondon@bbc.co.uk
www.bbc.co.uk/london
Managing editor: David Robey; breakfast show: Danny Baker. 94.9 FM

BBC Radio Merseyside and BBC Open Centre
55 Paradise Street, Liverpool L1 3BP
0151 708 5500
radio.merseyside@bbc.co.uk
www.bbc.co.uk/liverpool
Managing editor: Mick Ord; news editor: Lee Bennion; breakfast show: Linda McDermot & Andy Ball. 95.8 FM

BBC Radio Newcastle
Broadcasting Centre, Barrack Road
Newcastle upon Tyne NE99 1RN
0191 232 4141
radio.newcastle@bbc.co.uk
www.bbc.co.uk/england/radionewcastle
Managing editor: Sarah Drummond; news editor: Doug Morris; breakfast show: Mike Parr. 95.4 FM

BBC Radio Norfolk
The Forum, Millennium Plain
Norwich NR2 1BH
01603 617411
radionorfolk@bbc.co.uk
www.bbc.co.uk/norfolk
Managing editor: David Clayton; news editor: Sarah Kings; breakfast show: Graham Barnard. 104.1 FM; 95.1 FM; 855 AM; 873 AM

BBC Radio Northampton
Broadcasting House, Abington Street
Northampton NN1 2BH
01604 239100
northampton@bbc.co.uk
www.bbc.co.uk/northamptonshire
Managing editor: Laura Moss; news editor: Mark Whall; breakfast show: Liz Caroll-Wheat. 104.2, 103.6 FM

BBC Radio Nottingham
London Road, Nottingham NG2 4UU
0115 955 0500
radio.nottingham@bbc.co.uk
www.bbc.co.uk/nottingham
Managing editor: Mike Bettison; news editor: Steve Beech; breakfast show: Karl Cooper. 103.8 FM

BBC Radio Oxford
PO Box 95.2, Oxford OX2 7YL
01865 311444
radio.oxford@bbc.co.uk
www.bbc.co.uk/radiooxford
Managing editor: Steve Taschini; news editor: Neil Bennett. 95.2 FM

BBC Radio Sheffield and BBC Open Centre
54 Shoreham Street
Sheffield S1 4RS
0114 273 1177
radio.sheffield@bbc.co.uk
www.bbc.co.uk/england/radiosheffield
Managing editor: Angus Moorat; news editor: Mike Woodcock; breakfast show: Everard Davy. 88.6 FM

BBC Radio Shropshire
2–4 Boscobel Drive
Shrewsbury SY1 3TT
01743 248484
radio.shropshire@bbc.co.uk
www.bbc.co.uk/shropshire
Managing editor: Tim Pemberton; news editor: John Shone; breakfast show: Eric Smith. 96 FM; 95.7 FM

BBC Radio Solent
Broadcasting House, Havelock Road
Southampton SO14 7PW
02380 631311
solent@bbc.co.uk
www.bbc.co.uk/radiosolent
Managing editor: Mia Costello; breakfast show: Julian Clegg. 96.1 FM

BBC Southern Counties Radio
Broadcasting Centre
Guildford GU2 7AP
01483 306306
southern.counties.radio@bbc.co.uk
www.bbc.co.uk/southerncounties
Managing editor: Mike Hapgood; news editor: Mark Carter; breakfast show: Sarah Gorrell, Ed Douglas, John Radford. 104–104.8 FM; 95–95.3 FM

BBC Radio Stoke and BBC Open Centre
Cheapside, Hanley
Stoke on Trent ST1 1JJ
01782 208080
radio.stoke@bbc.co.uk
www.bbc.co.uk/stoke
Managing editor: Sue Owen; news editor: Roy Hill; breakfast show: Kevin Fernihough, Janine Machin. 94.6 FM

BBC Radio Suffolk
Broadcasting House
St Matthew's Street, Ipswich
Suffolk IP1 3EP
01473 250000
radiosuffolk@bbc.co.uk
www.bbc.co.uk/suffolk
Managing editor: Gerald Main; news editor: Lis Henderson; breakfast show: Mark Murphy. 105.5 FM; 104.5 FM; 103 FM

BBC Radio Swindon
PO Box 1234, Swindon SN1 3RW
01793 513626
radio.swindon@bbc.co.uk
www.bbc.co.uk/wiltshire
Managing editor: Tony Worgan; news editor: Kirsty Ward; breakfast show: Peter Heaton-Jones. 103.6 FM

BBC Three Counties Radio
PO Box 3CR, Luton
Bedfordshire LU1 5XL
01582 637400
3cr@bbc.co.uk
www.bbc.co.uk/threecounties
Managing editor: Mark Norman; breakfast show: Roberto Perrone. 95.5 FM; 104.5 FM; 103 FM

BBC Radio Wiltshire
PO Box 1234
01793 513626
radio.wiltshire@bbc.co.uk
www.bbc.co.uk/wiltshire
Managing editor: Tony Worgan; news editor: Kirsty Ward; breakfast show: Sue Davies. 103.5 FM; 104.3 FM; 104.9 FM

BBC WM (Birmingham)
Pebble Mill Road
Birmingham B5 7QQ
0121 432 9000
radio.wm@bbc.co.uk
www.bbc.co.uk/birmingham
or www.bbc.co.uk/blackcountry
Managing editor: Keith Beech; breakfast show: Adrian Goldberg

BBC WM (Coventry)
1 Holt Court, Greyfriars Road
Coventry CV1 2WR
02476 860086
coventry.warwickshire@bbc.co.uk
www.bbc.co.uk/coventry
Managing editor: David Clargo; breakfast show: Ann Othen, Colin Hazelden, Sandie Dunleavy. 103.7 FM; 94.8 FM; 104 FM

BBC North Yorkshire – Radio York
20 Bootham Row, York YO30 7BR
01904 641351
northyorkshire.news@bbc.co.uk
www.bbc.co.uk/northyorkshire
Managing editor: Matt Youdale; news editor: Elly Fiorentini; breakfast show: Allan Watkiss, Anna Wallace 1260 AM; 666 AM; 104.3 FM; 103.7 FM; 95.5 FM

Resources

BBC Radio Resources
Brock House, 19 Langham Street
London W1A 1AA
020 7765 5394
radio.facilities@bbc.co.co.uk
www.bbcradioresources.com
Senior operations manager: Martin Hollister; head of research: Miles Hosking; marketing manager: Amanda Bates

Event Services
Brock House, 19 Langham Street
London W1A 1AA
020 7765 5100
rr-events-team@bbc.co.uk
Events manager: Mark Diamond; events assistant: Joanne Surtees

Outside Broadcasts
Brock House, 19 Langham Street
London W1A 1AA
020 7765 4889
duncan.smith@bbc.co.uk
Operations manager: Will Garrett; radio outside broadcasts manager: Duncan Smith

Studios

Birmingham Studios
Pebble Mill, Pebble Mill Road
Edgbaston, Birmingham
West Midlands B5 7QQ
0121 432 8888
bryn.george@bbc.co.uk
www.bbc.co.uk/birmingham
Operations co-ordinator: Liz Treacher; deputy controller: David Holdsworth

Bristol Broadcasting House
Whiteladies Road, Bristol BS8 2LR
0117 973 2211
www.bbc.co.uk/bristol
Operations co-ordinator: Maria Clutterbuck; open team leader: Iain Hunter

Broadcasting House Studios
Brock House, 19 Langham Street
London W1A 1AA
020 8743 8000
Communications and marketing manager: Amanda Bates; senior operations manager: Martin Hollister

Maida Vale Studios
1–129 Delaware Road
London W9 2LG
020 7765 2091
Facilities manager: John Hakrow

Manchester Studios
New Broadcasting House
PO Box 27, Oxford Road
Manchester M60 1SJ
0161 244 4607
Operations co-ordinator: Lilian O'Callaghan; operations manager: Richard Savage

Commercial radio

Commercial Radio Companies Association
77 Shaftesbury Avenue
London W1D 5DU
020 7306 2603
info@crca.co.uk
www.crca.co.uk
Chief executive: Paul Brown; research & commercial manager: Alison Winter

Main commercial radio groups

CN Group
Dalston Road, Carlisle
Cumbria CA2 5UA
01228 612600
news@cumbrian-newspapers.co.uk
www.cumbria-online.co.uk
Chief executive: Robin Burgess; director of technical services: Peter Simpson; general manager: Christopher Bisco

Capital Radio
30 Leicester Square
London WC2H 7LA
020 7766 6000
info@capitalradio.com
www.capitalradio.plc.uk
Chairman: Ian Irvins; chief executive: David Mansfield; operations director: Paul Davies; programme controller: Keith Pringle

Chrysalis Radio Group
The Chrysalis Building
13 Bramley Road, London W10 6SP
020 7221 2213
info@chrysalis.com
www.chrysalis.com
PLC chairman: Chris Wright; chief executives: Richard Huntingford (whole group), Phil Riley (radio); programming director: Jim Hicks; head of network news: Jonathan Richards; senior press officer: Huw Davies

Classic Gold Digital
Network Centre, Chiltern Road
Dunstable LU6 1HQ
01582 676200
www.classicgolddigital.com
Chairman: Tim Blackmore; managing director: John Baish; programme controller: Paul Baker

Emap Performance Network
Mappin House, 4 Winsley Street
London W1W 8HF
020 7436 1515
www.emap.com
Group managing director: Marcus Rich; advertising director: Dave King; programme director: Phil Roberts

GWR Group
Chiseldon House, Stonehill Green
Westlea, Swindon SN5 7HB
0118 928 4313
www.gwrgroup.musicradio.com
Executive chairman: Ralph Bernard; group operations director UK: Steve Orchard

Lincs FM
Witham Park, Waterside South
Lincoln LN5 7JN
01522 549900
enquiries@lincsfm.co.uk
www.lincsfm.co.uk
Chief executive: Michael Betton; director of programming: Jane Hill

SMG
200 Renfield Street
Glasgow G2 3PR
0141 300 3300
www.smg.plc.uk
Chief executive: Andrew Flanagan; chief executive, SMG Radio: John Pearson

Scottish Radio Holdings
Clydebank Business Park
Clydebank, Glasgow G81 2RX
0141 565 2200
www.srhplc.com
Chairman: Lord Gordon of Strathblane; chief executive: Richard Findlay; MD, radio: David Goode; MD, Score Digital: Grae Allan

The Wireless Group
18 Hatfields, London SE1 8DJ
020 7959 7800
www.talksport.net
Chairman and chief executive: Kelvin MacKenzie; MD, ILRS: Ashley MacKenzie; group programme director: Paul Chantler

Tindle Radio Holdings
Weaver's Yard, 6 West Street
Farnham, Surrey GU9 7DN
01252 735667
www.tindleradio.com
Chairman: Sir Ray Tindle; deputy chairman: Robert Stiby; directors: Colin Christmas, Kevin Stewart

UKRD Group
Cam Brea Studios, Wilson Way
Redruth, Cornwall TR15 3XX
01209 310435
enquiries@ukrd.co.uk
www.ukrd.com
Chairman: James St Aubyn; general managing director: William Rogers; commercial director: Rob van Pooss; programme director: Phil Angell; marketing director: Mark Beever

National commercial radio: AM, Digital One and Freeview

Digital One
7 Swallow Place, London W1B 2AG
020 7288 4600, press 07813 783181
info@digitalone.co.uk
www.ukdigitalradio.com
Chief executive: Quentin Howard
Joint venture backed by GWR and NTL

Freeview
Broadcast Centre, 201 Wood Lane
London W12 7TP
0870 880 9980
www.freeview.co.uk
General manager: Matthew Seaman

STATIONS

Capital Disney
30 Leicester Square
London WC2H 7LA
020 7766 6000
kevin.palmer@capitalradiogroup.com
www.capitaldisney.co.uk
Head of Communications Group Radio: Elly Smith; programme controller: Will Chambers
Digital One

Classic FM
7 Swallow Place, Oxford Circus
London W1B 2AG
020 7343 9000
www.classicfm.com
Editorial contact: Rob Weinberg; managing editor: Darren Henley
Digital One; 99.9–101.9 FM

Core
PO Box 2269, London W1A 5UQ
GWR Group
020 7911 7300
fresh@corefreshhits.com
www.corefreshhits.com
Digital content manager: Nick Piggott
Digital One, Sky, cable & internet

The Hits
Castle Quay, Castlefields
Manchester M15 4PR
0161 288 5000
studio@thehitsradio.com
www.thehitsradio.com
Station manager: Phil Mackenzie; programme controller: Anthony Gay
Freeview; DAB Digital Radio: Greater London

Jazz FM
26–27 Castlereagh Street
London W1H 5DL
020 7706 4100
jazzinfo@jazzfm.com
www.jazzfm.com
Managing director: Carter Tanner; programme director: Mark Walker
Freeview; DAB Digital Radio: central Scotland; Greater London; south Wales and Severn estuary; West Midlands; 102.2FM

Kerrang!
Kerrang House, 20 Lionel Street
Birmingham B3 1AQ
Emap Performance Network
0845 053 1052
brendan.moffett@emap.com
www.Emapdigitalradio.com
Programme controller: Andrew Jefferies; managing director: Lyn Wood
Freeview, satellite & Cable
Kerrang! Digital is broadcast from Mappin House, London. Tel: 020 7436 1515

Kiss
Mappin House, 4 Winsley Street
London W1W 8HF
Emap Performance Network
020 7975 8100
brendan.moffett@emap.com
www.kiss100.com
Managing director: Mark Story; programme director: Andy Roberts
100 FM; Greater London; Freeview, Sky, satellite, digital

Life
30 Leicester Square
London WC2H 7LA
020 7766 6000
studio@listentolife.com
Programme manager: Kevin Palmer
Digital One

Magic
900 Herries Road, Sheffield S6 1RH
0114 209 1034
natalie.johnson@emap.com
www.Emapdigitalradio.com
Managing director: Ian Clasper; programme director: Gary Stein
Freeview, Sky and cable

Oneword Radio
Landseer House
19 Charing Cross Road
London WC2H OES
020 7976 3030
info@oneword.co.uk
www.oneword.co.uk
Managing director: Simon Blackmore
Digital One, Freeview, Sky and internet

Planet Rock
PO Box 2269, London W1A 5UQ
GWR Group
020 7911 7300
joinus@planetrock.com
www.planetrock.com
Digital content manager: Nick Piggott
Digital One

Prime Time Radio
PO Box 5050, London SW1E 6ZR
0870 050 5050
david.atkey@primetimeradio.org
www.primetimeradio.org
Managing director: Ron Coles; operations director: David Atkey
Digital One, Sky, cable & internet

Q Radio
Mappin House, 4 Winsley Street
London W1W 8HF
Emap Performance Network
020 7436 1515
brendan.moffett@emap.com
www.q4music.com
Managing director: Mark Story; programme director: Simon Long
Freeview, Sky and cable

Smash! Hits
Mappin House, 4 Winsley Street
London W1W 8HF
Emap Performance Network
020 7436 1515
brendan.moffett@emap.com
www.Emapdigitalradio.com
Managing director: Ian Clasper; programme director: Andy Roberts
Freeview, Sky and cable

TalkSport
18 Hatfields, London SE1 8DJ
The Wireless Group
020 7959 7800
www.talksport.net
Managing director: Michael Franklyn; programme director: Mike Parry
Digital One; 1107 AM; 1053 AM; 1071 AM; 1089 AM

Virgin Radio
No 1 Golden Square
London W1F 9DJ
020 7434 1215
reception@virginradio.co.uk
www.virginradio.co.uk
Station manager: Steve Taylor; programme director: Paul Jackson
Digital One; 1197 AM; 1215 AM; 1233 AM; 1242 AM; 1260 AM, Sky

News services

ITN Radio
200 Grays Inn Road
London WC1X 8XZ
020 7430 4090
newsdesk: 020 7430 4814
radio@itn.co.uk
www.itn.co.uk
Provides news service for Independent Radio News (IRN), plus other feeds
Managing director: John Perkins; editor: Jon Godel

Independent Radio News (IRN)
6th Floor 200 Grays Inn Road
London WC1X 8XZ
020 7430 4090
newsdesk: 020 7430 4814
irn@itn.co.uk
news@irn.co.uk
www.irn.co.uk
Managing director: John Perkins; editor: Jon Godel

Commercial local radio: England

LONDON

107.3 Time FM
2–6 Basildon Road, Abbey Road
London SE2 OEW
020 8311 3112
www.timefm.com
South-east London. Station director: Neil Remain; head of news: Alex Hornall; breakfast show: Richard Price. 107.3 FM. Owner: London Media Group. All time favourites

95.8 Capital FM
30 Leicester Square
London WC2H 7LA
020 7766 6000
info@capitalradio.com
www.capitalfm.com
Greater London . Managing director: Keith Pringle; head of news: Justin Kings; breakfast show: Johnny Vaughan. 95.8 FM. Owner: Capital Radio. Pop

Capital Gold (1548)
30 Leicester Square
London WC2H 7LA
020 7766 6000
info@capitalradio.com
www.capitalgold.com
Greater London. Programme director: Andy Turner; head of news: Justin King; breakfast show: Mick Brown & Emma Hignett. 1548 AM. Owner: Capital Radio. Hits of the 60s, 70s and 80s

Choice 107.1 FM
291–299 Borough High Street
London SE1 1JG
020 7378 3969
info@choicefm.com
www.choicefm.com
North London. Programme controller: Ivor Etienne; news editor: Pam Joseph; breakfast show: Martin Jay & Asher. 107.1 FM. Owner: Capital Group. R&B

Club Asia
Asia House
227–247 Gascoigne Road
Barking, Essex IG11 7LN
020 8594 6662
info@clubasiaonline.com
www.clubasiaonline.com
Greater London. Managing director: Humerah Khan; creative director: Sumerah Ahmad; breakfast show: Missy D. 972 AM. Independent. London's young Asian hit music station

Easy Radio London
43–51 Wembley Hill Road
London HA9 8AU
020 8795 1035
info@easy1035.com
www.easy1035.com
Greater London. Programme controller & head of music: Natalie King; breakfast show: Chris Townsend. 1035 AM. Owner: Easy Radio Limited. Easy listening

Heart 106.2
The Chrysalis Building, Bramley Road
London W10 6SP
020 7468 1062
www.heart1062.co.uk
Greater London. MD: Steve Parkinson; programme director: Francis Currie; head of news: Jonathan Richards; breakfast show: Jono Coleman & Harriet Scott. 106.2 FM. Owner: Chrysalis Radio. Adult contemporary

Jazz FM 102.2
26–27 Castlereagh Street
London W1H 5DL
020 7706 4100
jazzinfo@jazzfm.com
www.jazzfm.com
Greater London. Managing director: Carter Tanner; programme director: Mark Walker; head of news: Nick Hatfield; breakfast show: Jon Scragg. 102.2FM. Owner: Guardian Media Group Radio. Smooth jazz & classic soul

Kiss 100
Mappin House, 4 Winsley Street
London W1W 8HF
020 7975 8100
firstname.lastname@kiss100.com
www.kiss100.com
Greater London. Managing director: Mark Story; programme director: Simon Long; breakfast show: Bam Bam 100 FM. Owner: Emap Performance Network. Garage, R&B

LBC 97.3 FM
The Chrysalis Building, Bramley Road
London W10 6SP
020 7314 7300
firstname.lastname@lbc.co.uk
www.lbc.co.uk
Greater London. Managing director: Mark Flanagan; programme director: Steve Kyte; head of news: Tom Bateman; breakfast show: Howard Hughes & Nick Ferrari. 97.3 FM. Owner: Chrysalis Group PLC. Talk radio

LBC News 1152 AM
The Chrysalis Building, Bramley Road
London W10 6SP
020 7314 7309
newsroom@lbc.co.uk
www.lbc.co.uk
Greater London. Head of network news: Jonathan Richards. 1152 AM. Owner: Chrysalis Group. News

London Greek Radio
437 High Road, London N12 OAP
0871 288 1000
sales@lgr.co.uk
www.lgr.co.uk
North London. Programme controller and head of news: G Gregoriou; breakfast show: Soula Viola Ri. 103.3 FM. Independent. Greek music

London Turkish Radio LTR
185B High Road, Wood Green
London N22 6BA
020 8881 0606
info@londontv.org
www.londonturkishradio.org
North London. Programme controller: Umit Dandul; head of news: Erkan Pastirmacioglu; breakfast show: Fatos Sarman. 1584 AM. Independent. Turkish & English music

Magic 105.4 FM
Mappin House, 4 Winsley Street
London W1W 8HF
020 7955 1054
firstname.lastname@emap.com
www.magic1054.co.uk
Greater London. Programming director: Trevor White; station director: Mark Storey; breakfast show: Graham Dean. 105.4 FM. Owner: Emap Performance Network. Adult contemporary

Premier Christian Radio
22 Chapter Street
London SW1P 4NP
020 7316 1300
premier@premier.org.uk
www.premier.org.uk
Greater London. Programme controller: Charmaine Noble-Mclean; head of news: Victoria Lawrence; breakfast show: John Pantry. 1413 AM; 1305 AM; 1413 AM; 1332 AM. Owner: Premier Media Group. Christian music

Spectrum Radio
4 Ingate Place, Battersea
London SW8 3NS
020 7627 4433
name@spectrumradio.net
www.spectrumradio.net
Greater London. General manager: Paul Hogan; sales: Millie Bentham. 558 AM. Independent. Multi-ethnic

Sunrise Radio
Sunrise House, Merrick Road
Southall, Middlesex UB2 4AU
020 8574 6666
Reception@sunriseradio.com
www.sunriseradio.com
Greater London. Chief executive: Tony Lit; MDs: Dr Avtar Lit (London), Andrew Housley (Midlands); head of news: David Landau; breakfast show: Tony Patti. 1458 AM. Independent. Asian music

Time FM
2–6 Basildon Road, Abbey Wood
London SE2 OEW
020 8311 3112
mark@time1068.com
www.1068.com
Thamesmead, Greater London. Station director: Mark Rasen; head of news: Alex Hornall; breakfast show: Gary Mulligan. 106.8 FM. Owner: London Media Group. Pop

Virgin 105.8
1 Golden Square
London W1F 9DJ
020 7434 1215
reception@virginradio.co.uk
www.virginradio.co.uk
Greater London. Programme director: Paul Jackson; head of news: Andrew Bailey; breakfast show: Pete & Geoff. 105.8 FM. Owner: SMG. Rock

Xfm
30 Leicester Square
London WC2H 7LA
020 7766 6600
info@xfm.co.uk
www.xfm.co.uk
Greater London. Managing director: Graham Bryce; programme controller: Andrew Phillips; head of news: Justin King. 104.9 FM. Owner: Capital Radio. Adult contemporary

SOUTH-EAST

103.2 Power FM
Radio House, Whittle Avenue, Segensworth
West Fareham PO15 5SH
01489 589911
info@powerfm.co.uk
www.powerfm.com
South Hampshire. Managing director: Peter Harris; programme controller: Craig Morris; head of news: Alison Law; breakfast show: Rick Jackson & Rachel Brooks. 103.2 FM. Owner: Capital Radio. 20 years to up-to-date pop

107.4 The Quay
Flagship Studios PO Box 1074
Portsmouth PO2 8YG
023 9236 4141
mail@quayradio.com
www.quayradio.com
Portsmouth. Programme controller: Paul Owen; head of news: Sam Mattersace; breakfast show: Simon Rose. 107.4 FM. Owner: Radio Investments. Pop

107.5 Sovereign Radio
14 St Mary's Walk, Hailsham
East Sussex BN27 1AF
01323 442700
info@1075sovereignradio.co.uk
www.1075sovereignradio.co.uk
Eastbourne. Brand manager: Nigel Ansell; commercial manager: Karen Dyball; breakfast show: Nigel Ansell. 107.5 FM. Owner: Radio Investments. Music

107.6 Kestrel FM
Paddington House, Festival Place
Basingstoke RG21 7LJ
01256 694000
studio@kestrelfm.com
www.kestrelfm.com
Basingstoke. Managing director: Paul Allen; programme manager: Andy Green; head of news: Mel Barham; breakfast show: Mandy O'Neil. 107.6 FM. Milestone Group. 70s, 80s, 90s and today

107.8 Arrow FM
Priory Meadow Centre, Hastings
East Sussex TN34 1PJ
01424 461177
info@arrowfm.co.uk
www.arrowfm.co.uk
Hastings. Managing director: Stuart Woodford; programme controller: Mike Buxton; head of news: Vicky Jones; breakfast show: Andy Knight 107.8 FM. Owner: Radio Investments. Adult contemporary

107.8 Radio Jackie
The Old Post Office 110–112, Tolworth Broadway
Surbiton, Surrey KT6 7JD
020 8288 1300
info@radiojackie.com
www.radiojackie.com
Kingston Upon Thames. Managing director: Peter Stremes; programme controller: Dave Owen; head of news: Rod Bradbury; breakfast show: Neil Long. 107.8 FM. Independent. Adult contemporary

107.8 SouthCity FM
City Studios, Marsh Lane
Southampton SO14 3ST
023 8022 0020
info@southcityfm.co.uk
www.southcityfm.co.uk
Southampton. Managing director: Gary Haberfield; programme director: Stuart McGinley; head of news: Stuart McGinley; breakfast show: Pat Sissons. 107.8 FM. Independent. Adult contemporary

2-Ten FM
PO Box 2020, Calcot, Reading
Berkshire RG31 7FG
0118 945 4400
tim.parker@creation.com
www.musicradio.com
Reading, Basingstoke, Newbury and Andover. Managing director: Jonathan Bradley; programme controller: Tim Parker; head of news: Susie Southgate; breakfast show: The Morning Crew. 103.4 FM; 97 FM; 102.9 FM. Owner: GWR Group. All types of music

96.4 The Eagle
Dolphin House, North Street
Guildford GU1 4AA
01483 300964
onair@964eagle.co.uk
www.964eagle.co.uk
Guildford. Managing director: Valeria Handley; programme director: Peter Gordon; head of news: Lucy Skitmore; breakfast show: Dave Johns. 96.4 FM. Owner: UKRD Group. Adult contemporary

Bright 106.4
The Market Place Shopping Centre, Burgess Hill
West Sussex RH15 9NP
01444 248127
reception@bright1064.com
www.bright1064.com
Burgess Hill and Haywards Heath. Managing director: Allan Moules; programme director: Mark Chapple; head of news: Alan Lewis; breakfast show: Mark Chappel. 106.4 FM. Independent. 70s, 80s, 90s & latest

Capital Gold (1170 and 1557)
30 Leicester Square
London WC2H 7LA
020 7766 6000
info@capitalgold.com
www.capitalgold.com
South Hampshire. Programme director: Andy Turner; head of news: Justin King; breakfast show: Kevin King. 1557 AM; 1170 AM. Owner: Capital Radio. Hits of the 60s, 70s and 80s

Capital Gold (1242 and 603)
30 Leicester Square
London WC2H 7LA
020 7766 6000
info@invictaradio.co.uk
www.capitalgold.com
Maidstone, Medway and East Kent. Programme director: Andy Turner; head of news: Justin King. 603 AM; 1242 AM. Owner: Capital Radio. Hits of the 60s, 70s and 80s

Capital Gold (1323 and 945)
30 Leicester Square
London WC2H 7LA
020 7766 6000
info@capitalgold.co.uk
www.capitalgold.com
Brighton, Eastbourne and Hastings. Programme director: Andy Turner; head of news: Justin King; breakfast show: Kevin King. 945 AM; 1323 AM. Owner: Capital Radio. Hits of the 60s, 70s and 80s

Classic Gold 1431/1485
The Chase, Calcot
Reading RG31 7RB
0118 945 4400
enquiries@classicgolddigital.com
www.classicgolddigital.com
Reading, Basingstoke and Andover. Managing director: Jonathan Bradley; programme controller: Don Douglas; head of news: Susie Southgate. 1431 AM; 1485 AM. Owner: Classic Gold Digital. 80s, 90s and modern

Classic Gold 1521
The Stanley Centre, Kelvin Way
Crawley, West Sussex RH10 2SE
01293 519161
studio@musicradio.com
www.musicradio.co.uk
Reigate and Crawley. Station manager: Amanda Masters; programme controller: Don Douglas; head of news: Gareth Davies; breakfast show: Dan Jennings & Emma Richards. 1521 AM. Owner: Classic Gold Digital. 60s & 70s

County Sound Radio 1566 AM
Dolphin House North Street
Guildford GU1 4AA
01483 300964
onair@countysound.co.uk
www.ukrd.com
Guildford. Managing director: Valerie Handley; programme director: Peter Gordon; head of news: Lucy Skitmore; breakfast show: Dave Johns. 1566 AM. Owner: UKRD Group. Adult contemporary

CTR 105.6 FM
6 Mill Street, Maidstone ME15 6XH
01622 662500
enq@ctrfm.com
www.ctrfm.com
Maidstone. Managing director: John Maxfield; head of news: Helen Fisher & Moira Mitchell; breakfast show: Mike Russell. 105.6 FM. Independent. Adult contemporary

Delta FM
65 Weyhill, Haslemere
Surrey GU27 1HN
01428 651971
studio@deltaradio.co.uk
www.deltaradio.co.uk
Alton, Hampshire. Managing director: David Way; sales manager: Andy Wise; head of news: Stuart Ireland; breakfast show: Bill Sheldrake. 101.6 FM; 102 FM; 97.1 FM; 101.6 FM Owner: UKRD Group and Tindell Newspapers. Yesterday and today

FM 103 Horizon
14 Vincent Avenue Crownhill
Milton Keynes MK8 OZP
01908 269111
reception@horizon.musicradio.com
www.musicradio.com
Milton Keynes. Station manager: Ian Stuart; programme controller: Trevor Marshall; breakfast show: Trevor Cueball & Roz. 103.3 FM. Owner: GWR Group. 80s, 90s and today

Invicta FM
Radio House
John Wilson Business Park
Whitstable, Kent CT5 3QX
01227 772004
info@invictaradio.co.uk
www.invictafm.com
Maidstone, Medway and East Kent. Sales director: Jake Worrall; programme controller: Rebecca Trbojevich; head of news: Clare Martin; breakfast show: The Morning Zoo. 95.9 FM; 102.8 FM; 96.1 FM; 97 FM; 103.1 FM. Owner: Capital Radio. Pop music

Isle of Wight Radio
Dodnor Park Newport
Isle of Wight PO30 5XE
01983 822557
admin@iwradio.co.uk
www.iwradio.co.uk
Isle of Wight. Programme controller: Tom Stroud; head of news: Andrew Carter; breakfast show: Andy Shier. 102 FM; 107 FM. Owner: Radio Investments. Adult contemporary & Pop

Juice 107.2
170 North Street, Brighton BN1 1EA
01273 386107
info@juicebrighton.com
www.juicebrighton.com
Brighton. Managing director: Stephen Stark; programme controller: Matt Bashford; head of news: Graham Levitt; breakfast show: Marc Brooks. 107.2 FM. Owner: Brighton & Hove Ltd. Commercial Dance

Kick FM
The Studios 42 Bone Lane, Newbury
Berkshire RG14 5SD
01635 841600
mail@kickfm.com
www.kickfm.com
Newbury. Managing director: Jeff Lee; head of news: John Statford; programme controller: Mark Watson; breakfast show: Mark Watson. 105.6 FM; 107.4 FM. Owner: Milestone Group. Adult contemporary

KMfm Canterbury
9 St George's Place, Canterbury
Kent CT1 1UU
01227 475950
reception@kmfm.co.uk
www.kentonline.co.uk/kmfm
Canterbury. Group programme controller: Mike Osborne; head of news: Julia Walsh; breakfast show: Chris Finn. 106 FM. Owner: KM Radio Adult Contemporary

KM-FM for Folkestone and Dover
93–95 Sandgate Road
Folkestone, Kent CT20 2BQ
01303 220303
Scork@kmfm.co.uk
www.kentonline/kmfm
Dover and Folkestone. Group programme controller: Mike Osborne; Head of Sales: Christine Saffrey; breakfast show: Johnny Lewis. 106.8 FM; 96.4 FM. Owner: KM Radio. 60s, 70s, 80s & 90s

Medway's KM-FM
Medway House, Ginsbury Close
Sir Thomas Longley Road
Stroud ME2 4DU
01634 227808
pcarter@kmfm.co.uk
www.kentonline.co.uk/kmfm
Medway Towns. Group programme controller: Mike Osborne; breakfast show: Russ Lowe. 100.4 FM; 107.9 FM. Owner: KM Radio. Adult contemporary

Mercury FM
The Stanley Centre, Kelvin Way
Crawley, West Sussex RH10 9SE
01293 519161
studio@musicradio.com
www.musicradio.com
Reigate and Crawley. Station manager: Amanda Masters; programme controller: Tim Parker; head of news: Gareth Davies; breakfast show: Dan Jennings & Emma Richards. 97.5 FM; 102.7 FM. Owner: GWR Group. 60s & 70s

Mix 96
Friars Square Studios
11 Bourbon Street
Aylesbury HP20 2PZ
01296 399396
info@mix96.co.uk
www.mix96.co.uk
Aylesbury. Managing director: Rachael Faulknet; programme controller: Nathan Cooper; head of news: Penny Harper; breakfast show: James O'Neil. 96.2 FM. Owner: Radio Investments. 70 to present day

Ocean FM
Radio House, Whittle Avenue, Segensworth
West Fareham PO15 5SH
01489 589911
info@oceanfm.co.uk
www.oceanfm.com
South Hampshire. Programme controller: Stuart Ellis; head of news: Alison Law; breakfast show: Pippa Head & David Perry. 96.7 FM; 97.5 FM. Owner: Capital Radio. 70s, 80s & 90s

Reading 107 FM
Radio House, Madejski Stadium,
Reading, Berkshire RG2 0FN
0118 986 2555
firstname@reading107fm.com
www.reading107fm.com
Reading. Managing director: Tony Grundy; programme controller: Tim Grundy; marketing director: Joannah Bishop; breakfast show: Tim Grundy. 107 FM. Independent. Beatles to Bangles

Soul City 107.5
Lambourne House, 7 Western Road
Romford, Essex RM1 3LD
0870 607 1075
info@soulcity1075.com
www.soulcity1075.com
Havering. Managing director: Chris Slack; sales director: Flip Pearce; programme director: Chris Slack; breakfast show: Tracy Young. 107.5 FM. Independent. Soul

Southern FM
Radio House, PO Box 2000
Brighton BN41 2SS
01273 430111
news@southernfm.co.uk
www.southernfm.com
Brighton/Eastbourne and Hastings. Sales director: Jack Manzoor; programme controller: Tony Aldridge; head of news: Lawrence King; breakfast show: Chris Baughen. 103.5 FM; 96.9 FM; 102.4 FM; 102 FM Owner: Capital Radio. Pop

Spirit FM
9–10 Dukes Court, Bognor Road
Chichester PO19 8FX
01243 773600
info@spiritfm.net
www.spiritfm.net
Chichester, Bognor Regis, Littlehampton. Managing director: Stephen Oates; programme controller: Duncan Barkes; head of news: Caroline Kingsmill. 102.3 FM; 96.6 FM. Independent. Easy listening

Splash FM
Guildbourne Centre, Worthing
West Sussex BN11 1LZ
01903 233005
mail@splashfm.com
www.splashfm.com
Worthing. Managing director: Roy Stannard; programme controller: Simon Osborne; news editor: Justin Stacey; breakfast show: Simon Osborne. 107.7 FM. Independent. 60s, 70s, 80s, 90s & today

Star 106.6
The Observatory Shopping Centre
Slough SL1 1LH
01753 551066
onair@star1066.co.uk
www.star1066.co.uk
Slough, Maidenhead, Windsor. Programme controller: Anthony Ballard; head of news: Rob Harris; breakfast show: Anthony Ballard. 106.6 FM. Owner: UKRD Group Adult contemporary

Swan FM
PO Box 1107, High Wycombe
Buckinghamshire HP13 6WQ
01494 446611
sales@swanfm.co.uk
www.swanfm.co.uk
High Wycombe. Commercial director: Rachael Faulkner; programme director and Head of News: Andy Muir; breakfast show: Andy Muir. 107.7 FM. Owner: Radio Investments Adult contemporary

Thanet's KM-FM
Imperial House, 2–14 High Street,
Margate, Kent CT9 1DH
01843 220222
initialsurname@kmgroup.co.uk
www.kentonline.co.uk/kmfm
Thanet. Group programme controller: Mike Osborne; head of news: Julia Walsh; breakfast show: Adam John. 107.2 FM. Owner: KM Radio. Classic hits from 70s and current

Wave 105 FM
5 Manor Court, Barnes Wallis Road,
Segensworth East
Fareham, Hampshire PO15 5TH
01489 481057
martin.ball@wave105.com
www.wave105.com
Solent. Managing director: Martin Ball; programme controller: John Dash; head of news: Jason Beck; breakfast show: Steve Power. 105.2 FM; 105.8 FM. Owner: ScottishRadio Holdings. 70s, 80s & 90s hits

West Kent's KM-FM
1 East Street, Tonbridge
Kent TN9 1AR
01732 369200
tunbridgestudio@kmfm.co.uk
www.kentonline.co.uk/radio
Tunbridge Wells and Sevenoaks. Group programme controller: Mike Osborne; head of news: Julia Walsh; breakfast show: Steve Watts. 96.2 FM; 101.6 FM. Owner: KM Radio. Adult contemporary

Win 107.2
PO Box 107
The Brooks Shopping Centre,
Winchester, Hants SO23 8FT
01962 841071
jo@winfm.co.uk
www.winfm.co.uk
Winchester. Station manager: Jo Talbot; head of news: Julie Massitter; breakfast show: David Adams. 107.2 FM. Owner: Radio Investments. Adult contemporary

SOUTH-WEST

104.7 Island FM
12 Westerbrook, St Sampsons
Guernsey GY2 4QQ
01481 242000
firstname@islandfm.guernsey.net
www.islandfm.guernsey.net
Guernsey. Managing director: Nick Cread; programme controller: Gary Burgess; head of news: Katie Collins; breakfast show: Gary Burgess. 104.7 FM; 93.7 FM. Owner: Tindle Radio. Chart music. Rock show in evenings

107.5 3TR FM
Riverside Studios, Boreham Mill,
Bishopstow, Warminster BA12 9HQ
01985 211111
admin@3trfm.com
www.3trfm.com
Warminster. Brand manager: Jonathan Fido; sales manager: Ann Holmes; head of news: Louisa Jackson; breakfast show: Kev Scott. 107.5 FM. Owner: Radio Investments. Classics

2CR FM
5–7 Southcote Road, Bournemouth
Dorset BH1 3LR
01202 259259
newsbournemouth@creation.com
www.musicradio.com
Bournemouth & Hampshire. Programme controller: Graham Mack; sales director: Jane Suttie; breakfast show: Graham Mack. 102.3 FM. Owner: GWR Group. 80 and 90s and chart music

97 FM Plymouth Sound
Earl's Acre, Plymouth PL3 4HX
01752 275600
mail@plymouthsound.musicradio.com
www.musicradio.com
Plymouth. Programme controller: Dave England; head of news: Lisa Hay; breakfast show: Leigh-Ann Venning & Martin Mills. 97 FM; 96.6 FM. Owner: GWR Group. 80s, 90s and today

97.4 Vale FM
Longmead Studios, Shaftesbury
Dorset SP7 8PL
01747 855711
studio@valefm.co.uk
www.valefm.co.uk
Shaftesbury. Programme controller: Stewart Smith; head of news: Kevin Gover; breakfast show: Karen Smith. 97.4 FM; 96.6 FM. Owner: Radio Investments. Adult contemporary

Bath FM
Station House, Ashley Avenue,
Lower Weston, Bath BA1 3DS
01225 471571
news@bath.fm
www.bath.fm
Bath. Managing director: Jo Woods; programme controller and head of news: Steve Collins. 107.9 FM. Independent. Adult contemporary

BCRfm
Royal Clarence House, York Buildings
High Street, Bridgwater TA6 3AT
01278 727701
studio@bcrfm.co.uk
www.bcrfm.co.uk
Bridgwater. Managing director: Mark Painter; programme controller: David Englefield; breakfast show: David Englefield. 107.4 FM. Independent. Music from last four decades

Channel 103 FM
6 Tunnell Street, St Helier
Jersey JE2 4LU
01534 888103
firstname@channel103.com
www.channel103.com
Jersey. Managing director: Linda Burnham; programme director: Matt Howells; head of news: Phil Bouchard; breakfast show: Peter Mac. 103.7 FM. Owner: Tindle Radio. Broad mix of pop and rock

Classic Gold 1152 AM
Earl's Acre, Plymouth PL3 4HX
01752 275600
Peter.Greig@musicradio.com
www.classicgolddigital.com
Plymouth. Programme controller: Don Douglas; head of news: Lisa Hay; breakfast show: Tony Blackburn. 1152 AM. Owner: GWR Group. 70s, 80s & 90s

Classic Gold 1260
One Passage Street
Bristol BS99 7SN
0117 984 3200
admin@classicgolddigital.com
www.classicgolddigital.com
Bristol and Bath. Managing director: Dirk Anthony; programme controller: Don Douglas; head of news: Vickie Brakewell; breakfast show: Tony Blackburn. 1260 AM. Owner: GWR Group. Chart music

Classic Gold 666/954
Hawthorn House
Exeter Business Park
Exeter EX1 3QS
01392 444444
colin.slade@musicradio.com
www.musicradio.com
Exeter/Torbay. Programme controller: Colin Slade; breakfast show: Tony Blackburn & Laura Pittson. 954 AM; 666 AM. Owner: GWR Group. Classic hits

Classic Gold 774
Bridge Studios, Eastgate Centre
Gloucester GL1 1SS
01452 313200
reception@musicradio.com
www.classicgolddigital.com
Gloucester/Cheltenham. Programme controller: Russel Wilcox; head of news: Mark Smith. 774 AM. Owner: Classic Gold Digital. Various sounds

Classic Gold 828
5 Southcote Road, Bournemouth
Dorset BH1 3LR
01202 259259
newsbournemouth@creation.com
www.classicgolddigital.co.uk
Bournemouth. Programme controller: Don Douglas; breakfast show: Tony Blackburn. 828 AM. Owner: Classic Gold Digital. Popular music

Classic Gold 936/1161 AM
Lime Kiln Studio, Lime Kiln
Wooton Bassett, Swindon SN4 7EX
01793 842600
reception@musicradio.com
www.musicradio.com
Swindon. Managing director: Dirk Anthony; programme controller: Sue Carter; breakfast show: Matt & H. 936 AM; 1161 AM. Owner: Classic Gold Digital. Popular music

Fire 107.6FM
Quadrant Studios
Old Christchurch Road
Bournemouth BH1 2AD
01202 318100
firstname@fire1076.com
www.fire1076.com
Bournemouth and Poole. Programme controller: Max Hailey; head of news: Justin Gladdis; breakfast show: Max & Northern. 107.6 FM. Owner: Radio Investments. Rhythmic & contemporary

FOX FM
Brush House, Pony Road
Oxford OX4 2XR
01865 871000
reception@foxfm.co.uk
www.foxfm.co.uk
Oxford and Banbury. Programme controller: Sam Walker; head of news: Hugh James; breakfast show: Carl & Jo. 102.6 FM; 97.4 FM. Owner: Capital Radio. Adult contemporary

Gemini FM
Hawthorn House
Exeter Business Park
Exeter EX1 3QS
01392 444444
gemini@geminifm.musicradio.com
www.musicradio.com
Exeter/Torbay. Programme controller: Gavin Marshall; head of news: Michelle Horsley; breakfast show: Ben Clarke & Rachael Hicks. 97 FM; 103 FM; 96.4 FM. Owner: GWR Group. Top 40

GWR FM and Classic Gold Digital
PO Box 2000
Woottonbassett SN4 7EX
01793 842600
reception@musicradio.com
www.musicradio.com
Swindon and West Wiltshire. Programme controller: Sue Carter; head of news: Deb Evans; breakfast show: Matt & H and Tony Blackburn. 102.2 FM; 96.5 FM; 97.2 FM. Owner: GWR Group. 70s, 80s & 90s & today

GWR FM (Bristol and Bath)
PO Box 2000, One Passage Street
Bristol BS99 7SN
0117 984 3200
reception@gwrfm.musicradio.com
www.musicradio.com
Bristol and Bath. Managing director: Dirk Anthony; programme controller: Paul Andrew; head of news: Vickie Brakewell; breakfast show: Tony & Michaela. 103 FM; 96.3 FM. Owner: GWR Group. Chart music

Ivel FM
The Studios, Middle Street
Yeovil, Somerset BA20 1DJ
01747 848488
all@ivelfm.co.uk
www.ivelfm.co.uk
Yeovil (Somerset). Programme controller: Steve Carpenter; head of news: Catherine DeCosta; breakfast show: Steve Carpenter. 105.6 FM. Owner: Radio Investments. 60s, 70s, 80s to present day

Lantern FM
2b Lauder Lane, Roundswell
Business Park
Barnstable EX31 3TA
01271 340340
jim.trevelyan@creation.com
www.musicradio.com
Barnstable. Sales director: Jim Trevelyan; programme controller: Paul Hopper; head of news: Dave Lewis; breakfast show: PJ and Spanky. 97.3 FM; 96.2 FM. Owner: GWR Group. Late 90s to present day

Orchard FM
Haygrove House, Taunton
Somerset TA3 7BT
01823 338448
orchardfm@musicradio.com
www.musicradio.com
Yeovil & Taunton. Programme controller: Steve Bulley; journalists: Nicola Maxey & Darren Bevan. 102.6 FM; 97.1 FM; 96.5 FM. Owner: GWR Group. Top 40

Passion 107.9
270 Woodstock Road
Oxford OX2 7NW
01235 547825
info@passion1079.com
www.passion1079.com
Oxford. Programme controller and station manager: Andy Green; breakfast show: Bodge at Breakfast. 107.9 FM. Owner: Milestone Group. Dance & pop

Pirate FM102
Carn Brea Studios, Wilson Way
Redruth, Cornwall TR15 3XX
01209 314400
enquiries@piratefm102.co.uk
www.piratefm102.co.uk
Cornwall & West Devon. Managing director: Beverley Warne; programme director: Bob McCreadie; head of news: Alistair Jell; breakfast show: Bob McCreadie. 102.2 FM; 102.8 FM. Owner: UKRD Group. Various pop

Quay West Radio
The Harbour Studios
The Esplanade, Watchet
Somerset TA23 0AJ
01984 634900
studio@quaywest.fm
www.quaywest.fm
West Somerset. Programme director: David Mortimer; head of news: Spencer Bishop; breakfast show: David Mortimer. 102.4 FM. Independent. Adult contemporary

Severn Sound
Bridge Studios, Eastgate Centre
Gloucester GL1 1SS
01452 313200
reception@musicradio.com
www.musicradio.com
Gloucester/Cheltenham. Programme controller: Russ Wilcox; sales manager: Mark Right; head of news: Mark Smith; breakfast show: Russ, Nicola & Darcy. 103 FM; 102.4 FM. Owner: GWR Group. Various sounds

South Hams Radio
Unit 1G, South Hams Business Park
Churchstow, Kingsbridge
Devon TQ7 3QH
01548 854595
southams@musicradio.com
South Hams. Station manager: David Fitzgerald; head of news: Stephanie Wright; breakfast show: Ian Calvert. 101.9 FM; 100.8 FM; 100.5 FM; 101.2 FM. Owner: GWR Group/ Independent. Adult contemporary

Spire FM
City Hall Studios, Malthouse Lane
Salisbury, Wiltshire SP2 7QQ
01722 416644
admin@spirefm.co.uk
www.spirefm.co.uk
Salisbury. Managing director: Ceri Hurford-Jones; programme controller: Roger Clark; breakfast show: Daren Cee. 102 FM. Owner: Radio Investments. Chart hits

Star 107
Unit 3 Brunel Mall, London Road
Stroud, Gloucester GL5 2BP
01453 767369
studio@star1079.co.uk
www.star1079.co.uk
Stroud. Head of sales: Rebecca Tansley; programme controller: Marie Greenwood; head of news: Alan Wood; breakfast show: Roger Noble. 107.2 FM; 107.9 FM. Owner: UKRD Group. 70s, 80s & 90s and greatest hits

Star 107.5
Cheltenham Film Studios, 1st Floor
West Suite Arle Court, Hatherley Lane
Cheltenham GL51 6PN
01242 699555
studio@star1075.co.uk
www.star1075.co.uk
Cheltenham
Managing director: Alan Knight; programme manager: Ian Timms; head of news: Dannielle Crawshaw. 107.5 FM. Owner: UKRD Group. 80s to today

Star 107.7 FM
11 Beaconsfield Road
Weston Super Mare BS23 1YE
01934 624455
name@star1077.co.uk
www.star1077.co.uk
Weston Super Mare. Programme controller: Scott Temple; head of news: Hayley Mellers; breakfast show: Derek Thompson. 107.7 FM; 107.1 FM; 106.5 FM. Owner: UKRD Group. 70s, 80s & 90s popular music

Vibe 101
26 Baldwin Street
Bristol BS1 1SE
0117 901 0101
info@vibe101.co.uk
www.vibe101.co.uk
South Wales & Severn Estuary. Managing director: Beverley Cleall-Harding; programme controller: Jason Staveley; head of news: Ben Moss; breakfast show: Ben & Alison. 97.2 FM; 101 FM. Scottish Radio Holdings. Dance and R&B

Wessex FM
Radio House, Trinity Street
Dorchester DT1 1DJ
01305 250333
admin@wessexfm.co.uk
www.wessexfm.com
Weymouth and Dorchester. Programme controller: Martin Lee; head of news: Kevin Gover; breakfast show: Phil Stocks. 97.2 FM; 96 FM. Owner: Radio Investments. Hits of 60s, 70s, 80s

102.7 Hereward FM
PO Box 225 Queensgate Centre
Peterborough PE1 1XJ
01733 460460
paul.green@musicradio.com
www.musicradio.com
Greater Peterborough. Programme controller: Paul Green; head of news: Sarah Spence; breakfast show: Matt & Sarah. 102.7 FM. Owner: GWR Group. Adult contemporary

103.4 The Beach
PO Box 103.4
Lowestoft, Suffolk NR32 2TL
0845 345 1035
sue.taylor@thebeach.co.uk
www.thebeach.co.uk
Great Yarmouth and Lowestoft. Managing director: David Blake; news editor: Kirsty Taylor; breakfast show: Tom Kay. 103.4 FM. Owner: Tindle Radio. Chart past and present

96.9 Chiltern FM
55 Goldington Road
Bedford, Beds MK40 3LT
01234 272400
simon.marshall@musicradio.com
www.musicradio.com
Bedford. Sales manager: Sharon Rush; programme controller: Stuart Davies; head of news: Mark Grinnell; breakfast show: Andy Gelder. 96.9 FM. Owner: GWR Group. 80s, 90s to today

97.6 Chiltern FM
Chiltern Road, Dunstable
Beds LU6 1HQ
01582 676200
stuart.davies@musicradio.co.uk
www.musicradio.com
Herts/Beds/Bucks. Programme controller: Stuart Davies; sales manager: Francis Flannigan; head of news: Mark Grinnell; breakfast show: Gareth Wesley & Karen Carpenter. 97.6 FM. Owner: GWR Group. Easy listening

Broadland 102
St George's Plain
47–49 Colgate, Norwich NR3 1DB
01603 630621
chris.marston@musicradio.com
www.musicradio.com
Norfolk and North Suffolk. Sales centre manager: Sophie Crocker; programme controller: Steve Martin; head of news: Harry Mitchell; breakfast show: Rob & Chrissy. 102.4 FM. Owner: GWR Group. 80s, 90s and today

Classic Gold 1332 AM
PO Box 225, Queensgate Centre
Peterborough PEI IXJ
01733 460460
don.douglas@classicgolddigital.com
www.classicgolddigital.com
Peterborough. Programme controller: Don Douglas; head of news: Sarah Spence; breakfast show: Tony Blackburn. 1332 AM. Owner: Opus Group. Classic Gold Digital. Classic hits

Classic Gold 792/828
Chiltern Road
Dunstable, Beds LU6 1HQ
01582 676200
john.baish@classicgolddigital.com
www.classicgolddigital.com
Luton/Bedford. Programme controller: John Baish; sales centre manager: Francis Flannighan; head of news: Mark Grinnell; breakfast show: Tony Blackburn & Laura Pitson. 792 AM; 828 AM. Owner: Opus Group. Classic Gold Digital. 60s to modern

Classic Gold Amber
St George's Plain
47–49 Colgate, Norwich NR3 1DB
01603 630621
paul.baker@classicgolddigital.com
www.classicgolddigital.com
Norwich. Programme controller: Paul Baker; sales centre manager: Sophie Crocker; breakfast show: Rob & Chrissy. 1152 AM. Owner: GWR Group. Classic Gold Digital. 80s, 90s and today

Classic Gold Amber
Alpha Business Park
6–12 White House Road
Ipswich IP1 5LT
01473 461000
paul.baker@classicgolddigital.com
www.classicgolddigital.com
Ipswich and Bury St Edmunds. Programme controller: Paul Baker; breakfast show: Tony Blackburn. 1251 AM; 1170 AM. Owner: Classic Gold Digital. 70s and 80s

Classic Gold Breeze
Radio House, Clifftown Road
Southend on Sea, Essex SS1 1SX
01702 333711
david.baker@classicgolddigital.com
www.classicgolddigital.com
Southend and Chelmsford. Programme controller: David Baker; head of news: Lee Murphy; breakfast show: David Baker. 1359 AM; 1431 AM. Owner: Opus Group. Classic Gold Digital. Classic 60s, 70s, 80s

Dream 100 FM
Northgate House, St Peter's Street
Colchester, Essex CO1 1HT
01206 764466
info@dream100.com
www.dream100.com
North Essex/South Suffolk. Managing director: Jamie Brodie; programme controller: Jonathan Hemmings; head of news: Andre Kimche; breakfast show: Chris Sturgess. 100.2 FM. Owner: Tindle Radio. 70s to today

Dream 107.7
Cater House, High Street
Chelmsford CM1 1AL
01245 259400
firstname.surname@dream107.com
www.dream107.com
Chelmsford. Managing director: Martyn Davies; programme controller and head of news: Nick Hull. 107.7 FM. Owner: Tindle Radio. Adult Contemporary

Essex FM
Radio House, Clifftown Road
Southend on Sea, Essex SS1 1SX
01702 333711
Lee.murphy@creation.com
www.musicradio.com
Southend and Chelmsford. Programme controller: Chris Cotton; head of news: Lee Murphy; breakfast show: David Baker. 102.6 FM; 96.3 FM; 97.5 FM. Owner: GWR Group. Classic 60s, 70s, 80s

Fen Radio 107.5 FM
5 Church Mews, Wisbech
Cambridgeshire PE13 1HL
01945 467107
studio@fenradio.co.uk
www.sound-wave.co.uk
Fenland. Station manager and programme director: Mark Pryke; programme manager: Richard Grant; sales director: Jason Smith; breakfast show: Richard Grant. 107.1 FM; 107.5 FM. Owner: UKRD Group. 70s to today

Hertbeat FM
The Pump House, Knebworth Park
Hertford, Hertfordshire SG3 6HQ
01438 810900
info@hertbeat.com
www.hertbeat.com
Hertfordshire. Station manager: Darrell Thomas; programme controller: Robert Owen; news editor: Rita Gibbon; breakfast show: Steve Folland. 106.9 FM; 106.7 FM. Independent. 80s/90s, specialist programmes weekend

KL.FM 96.7
18 Blackfriars Street
Kings Lynn, Norfolk PE30 1NN
01553 772777
admin@klfm967.co.uk
www.klfm967.co.uk
Kings Lynn and West Norfolk. Managing director: William Rogers; Station manager: Mark Pryke; programme controller: Steve Bradley; head of news: Euan Monahan; breakfast show: Steve Bradley. 96.7 FM. Owner: UKRD Group. Best of last 30 years

Lite FM
5 Church Street
Peterborough PE1 1XB
01733 898106
kev@lite1068.co.uk
www.lite1068.co.uk
Peterborough. Managing director: David Myatt; programme manager: Kevin Lawrence; head of news: Simon Potter; breakfast show: Kevin Lawrence. 106.8 FM. Owner: Forward Media Group. Adult contemporary

North Norfolk Radio
PO Box 962 The Studio, Breck Farm
Stody, Norfolk NR24 2ER
01263 860808
info@northnorfolkradio.com
www.northnorfolk.com
North Norfolk. Programme controller: Steve Wells; head of news: John Bultitude; breakfast show: Mike Ahern. 103.2 FM; 96.2 FM. Independent. Adult contemporary

Q103 FM
Enterprise House, The Vision Park
Chivers Way, Histon
Cambridgeshire CB4 9WW
01223 235255
firstname.surname@
q103.musicradio.com
www.musicradio.com
Cambridge and Newmarket. Area programme controller: Paul Green; sales director: Phil Caborn; head of news: Sarah Spence; breakfast show "Q103". 97.4 FM; 103 FM. Owner: GWR Group. Mix of today

SGR Colchester
Abbey Gate Two, 9 Whitewell Road
Colchester CO2 7DE
01206 575859
sgrcolchester@musicradio.com
www.musicradio.com
Colchester. Programme controller: Paul Morris; sales director: Brent Coulson; head of news: Peter Cook; senior Presenter: Paul Morris. 96.1 FM. Owner: GWR Group. 80s, 90s and today

SGR FM
Alpha Business Park
6–12 White House Road, Ipswich
Suffolk IP1 5LT
01473 461000
tracy.cooper@musicradio.com
www.musicradio.com
Suffolk. Programme controller: Tracy Cooper; head of news: Mike Jackson; breakfast show: Chris Skinner. 96.4 FM; 97.1 FM. Owner: GWR Group. 80s, 90s and current hits

Star 107.9
Radio House, Sturton Street
Cambridge CB1 2QF
01223 722300
admin@star107.co.uk
www.star1079.co.uk
Cambridge, Ely, New Market. Managing director: James Keen; programme controller: James Keen; head of news: Mathew Barratt; breakfast show: Andy Gall. 107.1 FM. Owner: UKRD Group. Mainstream adult contemporary

Ten 17
Latton Bush Centre, Southern Way
Harlow, Essex CM18 7BB
01279 431017
jill.adams@musicradio.com
www.musicradio.com
East Herts/west Essex. Programme director: Jeff O'Brien; news editor: Lee Murphy; breakfast show: Ian Burrage. 101.7 FM. Owner: GWR Group. Pop

Vibe FM
Reflection House
The Anderson Centre, Olding Road
Bury St Edmunds IP33 3TA
01284 715300
general@vibefm.co.uk
www.vibefm.co.uk
East of England. Managing director & programme controller: Gary Robinson; news editors: Dawn Ferguson & Neil Didsbury; breakfast show: Stuart Grant. 105–108 FM. Owner: ScottishRadio. Dance station

Watford's Mercury 96.6
Unit 5, The Metro Centre
Dwight Road, Watford WD18 9UP
01923 205470
firstname.surname@musicradio.com
www.musicradio.com
St Albans and Watford. Programme controller: Rebecca Dundon; head of news: Tricia Bullen; breakfast show: Danny Lacey. 96.6 FM. Owner: GWR Group. Popular music

EAST MIDLANDS

102.8 RAM FM
35–36 Irongate, Derby DE1 3GA
01332 205599
ramfm@musicradio.com
www.musicradiocom
Derby. Programme controller: James Daniels; Regional director: Chris Hughes; head of news: Lewis Scrimshaw; breakfast show: Rachael & Deano. 102.8 FM. Owner: GWR Group. All current pop music

107 Oak FM
7 Waldron Court
Prince William Road, Loughborough,
Leicestershire LE11 5GD
01509 211711
studio@oak107.co.uk
www.oak107.co.uk
Charnwood/NW Leicestershire. Managing director: Bill Johnston; programme manager: Mike Vitti; head of news: Yvonne Radley; breakfast show: Dave James. 107 FM. Owner: CN Group. 60s to today

96 Trent FM
29–31 Castle Gate
Nottingham NG1 7AP
0115 952 7000
dick.stone@musicradio.com
www.musicradio.com
Nottinghamshire. Area Regional director: Chris Hughes; programme controller: Dick Stone; head of news: Lewis Scrimshaw; breakfast show: Jo & Twiggy. 96.2 FM. Owner: GWR Group. All types of music

Centre FM
5-6 Aldergate
Tamworth, Staffordshire B79 7DJ
01827 318000
studio@centrefm.com
www.centre.fm
South-east Staffordshire. Managing director: Phil Richardson; programme manager: Mike Vitti; head of news: Chris Mills; breakfast show: Neil Jackson. 101.6 FM; 102.4 FM. Owner: CN Group. 80s, 90s and today

106 Century FM
City Link, Nottingham NG2 4NG
0115 910 6100
info106@centuryfm.co.uk
www.106centuryfm.com
East Midlands. Brand Managing director: Nick Davidson; Brand programme director: Giles Squire; breakfast show: Jim & Paula. 106 FM. Owner: Capital Radio. Contemporary 80s, 90s

Classic Gold 1557
Northamptonshire
19–21 St Edmunds Road
Northampton NN1 5DY
01604 795600
firstname.surname@
classicgolddigital.com
www.classicgolddigital.com
Northampton. Managing director: Colin Wilsher; programme controller: Don Douglas; head of news: Fiona Pryor; breakfast show: Lucinda Holman 1557 AM. Owner: Classic Gold Digital. Classic music

Classic Hits
PO Box 262, Worcester WR6 5ZE
01905 740600/ 01432 360246
info@classicgolddigital.fm
www.classichits.co.uk
Hereford and Worcester. Managing director: Chris Jefferies; programme controller: Tim Boswell; head of news: Andrew Currie; breakfast show: Tim Boswell. 954 AM; 1530 AM. Owner: Murfin Media International. Last four or five decades of hits

Classic Gold GEM
29–31 Castle Gate
Nottingham NG1 7AP
0115 952 7000
don.douglas@classicgolddigital.com
www.classicgolddigital.com
Nottingham/Derby. Managing director: John Daish; programme controller: Don Douglas; head of news: Lewis Scrimshaw; breakfast show: Tony Blackburn. 999 AM; 945 AM. Owner: Classic Gold Digital. Classic chart hits

Connect FM
Unit 1, Centre 2000
Kettering, Northants NN16 8PU
01536 412413
info@connectfm.com
www.connectfm.com
Kettering, Corby, Wellingborough. Group Managing director: David Myatt; Station manager: Martin Barr; programme manager: Danny Gibson, head of news: John Reading; breakfast show: Gregg Nunney. 107.4 FM; 97.2 FM. Owner: Forward Media Group. 70s, 80s & 90s and today

Dearne FM
PO Box 458, Barnsley S71 1YP
01226 321733
enquiries@dearnefm.co.uk
www.dearnefm.co.uk
Barnsley. Managing director: Keith Briggs; programme manager: Paul Bromley; head of news: Leanne Goacher; breakfast show: Kev Wilson. 97.1 FM; 102 FM. Owner: Lincs FM Group. 60s, 70s, 80s & 90s and current hits

Fosseway Radio
PO Box 107, Hinckley
Leicestershire LE10 1WR
01455 614151
enquiries@fossewayradio.co.uk
www.fossewayradio.co.uk
Hinckley/Nuneaton. Chief executive: Michael Betton; programme manager: Ian Ison; head of news: James Wall; breakfast show: Nick Guerney. 107.9 FM. Owner: Lincs FM. 70s, 80s & 90s and hits of today

Leicester Sound
6 Dominus Way
Meridian Business Park
Leicester LE19 1RP
0116 256 1300
reception@leicesterfm.musicradio.com
www.musicradio.com
Leicester. Programme controller: Craig Boddy; head of sales: Bina Chauhan; head of news: Liz Gameson; breakfast show: Rae & Kev. 105.4 FM. Owner: GWR Group. 90s and today

Lincs FM
Witham Park, Waterside South
Lincoln LN5 7JN
01522 549900
enquiries@lincsfm.co.uk
www.lincsfm.co.uk
Lincoln. Chief executive: Michael Betton; programme manager: John Marshall; news editor: Shaun Dunderdale; breakfast show: John Marshall. 102.2 FM; 97.6 FM; 96.7 FM. Owner: Lincs FM. Pop

Mansfield 103.2
The Media Suite,
Brunts Business Centre
Samuel Brunts Way, Mansfield
Notts NG18 2AH
01623 646666
info@mansfield103.co.uk
www.mansfield103.co.uk
Mansfield and District. Managing director: Tony Delahunty; programme controller & head of news: Katie Trinder; breakfast show: Katie Trinder. 103.2 FM. Independent. 70s, 80s & 90s and present day

Northants 96
19–21 St Edmunds Road
Northampton NN1 5DY
01604 795600
firstname.surname@musicradio.com
www.musicradio.com
Northampton. Managing director: Colin Wilsher; programme controller: Richard Neale; head of news: Fiona Pryor; breakfast show: Lucinda Holman. 96.6 FM. Owner: GWR Group. Pop

Peak 107 FM
Radio House, Foxwood Road
Chesterfield S41 9RF
01246 269107
info@peak107.com
www.peak107.com
Chesterfield/north Derbyshire/ south Sheffield/Peak District. Group programme controller: John Evington; head of news: Naz Premiji; breakfast show: Sean Goldsmith. 102 FM; 107.4 FM. Owner: TWG Wireless Group. 50/50 music mix

Rutland Radio
40 Melton Road
Oakham, Rutland LE15 6AY
01572 757868
enquiries@rutlandradio.co.uk
www.rutlandradio.co.uk
Rutland and Stamford. Station manager: Julie Baker; head of news: Richard Harding; breakfast show: Rob Persani. 97.4 FM; 107.2 FM. Owner: Lincs FM. Last 40 years' hits

Sabras Radio
Sabras Sound Ltd, Radio House
63 Melton Road, Leicester LE4 6PN
0116 261 0666
enq@sabrasradio.com
www.sabrasradio.com
Leicester. Managing director and programme controller: Don Kotak. 1260 AM. Independent. Asian music

Saga 106.6 FM
Saga Radio House, Alder Court
Riverside Business Park
Nottingham NG2 1RX
0115 986 1066
reception@saga1066fm.co.uk
www.saga1066fm.co.uk
East Midlands. Managing director: Phil Dixon; programme director: Paul Robey; head of news: Lisa Teanby; breakfast show: John Peters. 106.6 FM. Owner: Saga Group. Easy listening from past six decades

Signal 1
Stoke Road, Stoke on Trent ST4 2SR
01782 441300
info@signalradio.com
www.signal1.co.uk
Stoke on Trent. Group programme director: John Evington; managing director: Chris Hurst; head of news: Paul Sheldon; breakfast show: Andy Golding & Louise Stone. 96.4 FM; 102.6 FM; 96.9 FM. Owner: The Wireless Group. Pop music

Signal Two
Stoke Road, Stoke on Trent ST4 2SR
01782 441300
info@signalradio.com
www.signal1.co.uk
Stoke on Trent. ILR group programme director: Kevin Howard; managing director: Chris Hurst; head of news: Paul Sheldon; breakfast show: Johnny Owen. 1170 FM. Owner: The Wireless Group. Pop music

Trax FM
PO Box 444, Worksop
Notts S80 1HR
01909 500611
enquiries@traxfm.co.uk
www.traxfm.co.uk
Bassetlaw. Station manager: Paula Spence; programme controller: Rob Wagstaff; head of news: Tina Masters; breakfast show: Warren Miller. 107.9 FM. Owner: Lincs FM. Adult contemporary

WEST MIDLANDS

100.7 Heart FM
1 The Square, 111 Broad Street
Birmingham B15 1AS
0121 695 0000
news@heartfm.co.uk
www.heartfm.co.uk
West Midlands. Managing director: Paul Fairburn; programme director: Alan Carruthers; head of news: Chris Kowalik; breakfast show: Ed James. 100.7 FM. Owner: Chrysalis Radio. Easy listening

107.1 Rugby FM
Dunsmore Business Centre
Spring Street, Rugby CV21 3HH
01788 541100
mail@rugbyfm.co.uk
www.rugbyfm.co.uk
Rugby. Managing director & head of news: Martin Mumford. 107.1 FM. Owner: Milestone Radio Group. 60s, 70s, 80s & 90s and to date

107.4 Telford FM
PO Box 1074, Telford TF1 5HU
01952 280011
staff@telfordfm.co.uk
www.telfordfm.co.uk
Telford. Programme director: Pete Wagstaff; head of news: Ian Perry; breakfast show: Paul Shuttleworth 107.4 FM. Independent. Easy listening

107.7 The Wolf
10th Floor, Mander House
Wolverhampton WV1 3NB
01902 571070
firstname@thewolf.co.uk
www.thewolf.co.uk
Wolverhampton. Group programme director: John Evington; head of news: Julia Rae; breakfast show: Dickie Dodd. 107.7 FM. Owner: Wireless Group. 50/50 mix of yesterday and today

96.4 FM BRMB
Nine Brindleyplace, 4 Ozells Square
Birmingham B1 2DJ
0121 245 5000
info@brmb.co.uk
www.brmb.co.uk
Birmingham. Commercial controller: Jane Davis; programme controller: Adam Bridge; breakfast show: "The Big Brum Breakfast". 96.4 FM. Owner: Capital Radio. Chart music

Beacon FM
267 Tettenhall Road
Wolverhampton WV6 ODE
01902 461300
firstname.surname@creation.com
www.musicradio.com
Wolverhampton. Programme director: Chris Pegg; head of news: Adam Edward; breakfast show: Mark Jeeves & Jo Jesmond. 97.2 FM; 103.1 FM. Owner: GWR Group. Popular mix

Capital Gold (1152)
30 Leicester Square
London WC2H 7LA
020 7766 6000
info@capitalgold.co.uk
www.capitalgold.com
Birmingham. Programme director: Andy Turner; head of news: Justin King; breakfast show: Tom Ross. 1152 AM. Owner: Capital Radio. Hits of the 60s, 70s and 80s

Classic Gold 1359
Hertford Place, Coventry CV1 3TT
02476 868200
firstname.surname@classicgolddigital.com
www.classicgolddigital.com
Coventry. Programme controller: Luis Clark; breakfast show: Tony Blackburn. 1359 AM. Owner: Classic Gold Digital. 70s, 80s & 90s

Classic Gold WABC
267 Tettenhall Road
Wolverhampton WV6 ODE
01902 461300
firstname.surname@classicgolddigital.com
www.classicalgolddigital.com
Wolverhampton, Shrewsbury and Telford. Head of news: Adam Edward; breakfast show: Tony Blackburn. 990 AM; 1017 AM. Owner: Classic Gold Digital. Classic 80s, 90s onward

FM 102 – The Bear
The Guard House Studios
Banbury Road
Stratford Upon Avon CV37 7HX
01789 262636
info@thebear.co.uk
www.thebear.co.uk
Stratford Upon Avon. Station director: Chris Arnold; programme manager: Mike Vitti; head of news: Daniel Bruce; breakfast show: Howard Bentham. 102 FM. Owner: CN Group. Classic & current hits

Galaxy 102.2
1 The Square, 111 Broad Street
Birmingham B15 1AS
0121 695 0000
galaxy1022@galaxy1022.co.uk
www.galaxy1022.co.uk
Birmingham. Managing director: Paul Fairburn; programme director: Neil Greenslade; head of news: Chris Kowalik; breakfast show: Ed James. 102.2 FM. Owner: Chrysalis Radio. Easy listening

Kix 96
Watch Close Spon Street
Coventry CV1 3LN
024 7652 5656
firstname@kix.fm
www.kix.fm
Coventry. Sales director: Greg Parker; programme manager: Mike Vitti; head of news: Magdalene Kent; breakfast show: Stefan Latouche. 96.2 FM. Owner: CN Group. Pop and Dance

Mercia FM
Hertford Place, Coventry CV1 3TT
024 7686 8200
merciafm@musicradio.com
www.musicradio.com
Coventry. Programme controller: Luis Clark; head of news: Tony Attwater; breakfast show: Ru, Simon and James. 102.9 FM; 97 FM. Owner: GWR Group. 80s, 90s & modern

Radio XL 1296 AM
KMS House Bradford Street
Birmingham B12 OJD
0121 753 5353
arun@radioxl.net
www.radioxl.net
Birmingham. Managing director: Arun Bajaj; programme director: Sukjoinder Ghataore. 1296 AM. Independent. Indian and Asian mixes

Saga 105.7 FM
3rd Floor, Crown House
Beaufort Court, 123 Hagley Road
Edgbaston B16 8LD
0121 452 1057
onair@saga1057fm.co.uk
www.saga1057fm.co.uk
West Midlands. Managing director: Peter Tomlinson; programme director: Brian Savin; news editor: Colin Palmer; breakfast show: Les Ross. 105.7 FM. Owner: Saga Group. 40s upwards

Wyvern FM
5–6 Barbourne Terrace
Worcester WR1 3JZ
01905 612212
simon.monk@creation.com
www.musicradio.com
Hereford and Worcester. Programme controller: Simon Monk; head of news: Jonathan Dunbar; breakfast show: Lee Stone. 102.8 FM; 97.6 FM; 96.7 FM. Owner: GWR Group. Pop music

NORTH-EAST

Alpha 103.2
Radio House, 11 Woodland Road,
Darlington Co., Durham DL3 7BJ
01325 255552
sales@alpha1032.com
www.alpha1032.com
Darlington. Managing director: Angela Bridgen; programme manager: Ricky Durkin; head of news: Steve Mackay; breakfast show: Ricky Durkin. 103.2 FM. Owner: Radio Investments. Classic hits from last 30 years

Century FM
Church Street, Gateshead NE8 2YY
0191 477 6666
info@centuryfm.co.uk
www.100centuryfm.com
North-east England. Programme controller: Paul Drogan; head of news: Rick Martin; breakfast show: Liz and Gary. 96.2 FM; 96.4 FM; 100.7 FM; 101.8 FM. Owner: Capital Radio. 80s, 90s and today

Galaxy 105–106
Kingfisher Way
Silverlink Business Park
Tyne & Wear NE28 9NX
0191 206 8000
matt.mcclure@galaxy1056.co.uk
www.galaxy1056.co.uk
North-east England. Programme director: Matt McClure; Journalist: Mandy Simpson; breakfast show: Kate Fox. 105.3 FM; 105.6 FM; 105.8 FM; 106.4 FM. Owner: Chrysalis Radio. Dance and R&B

Magic 1152
Longrigg, Swalwell
Newcastle upon Tyne NE99 1BB
0191 420 0971
tony.mckenzie@metroandmagic.com
www.magic1152.co.uk
Tyne and Wear. Managing director: Sally Aitchaison; programme director: Tony McKenzie; breakfast show: Brian Moore. 1152 AM. Owner: Emap Performance Network. Classic 60s and 70s

Magic 1170
Radio House, Yales Crescent
Thornaby
Stockton-on-Tees TS17 6AA
01642 888222
colin.paterson@tfmradio.com
www.tfmradio.co.uk
Teesside. Managing director: Catherine Ellington; programme director: Colin Paterson; head of news: Myles Ashley; breakfast show: Peter Grant. 1170 AM. Owner: Emap Performance Network. Adult contemporary

Metro Radio
Longrigg, Swalwell
Newcastle upon Tyne NE99 1BB
0191 420 0971
tony.mckenzie@metroandmagic.com
www.magic1152.co.uk
Tyne and Wear. Managing director: Sally Aitchison; programme director: Tony McKenzie; breakfast show: Brian Moore. 97.1 FM; 102.6 FM; 103 FM; 103.2 FM. Owner: Emap Performance Network. Adult contemporary & chart

Sun FM
PO Box 1034, Sunderland SR5 2YL
0191 548 1034
progs@sun-fm.com
www.sun-fm.com
Sunderland. Brand controller: Simon Grundy; head of news: Mark Selling; breakfast show: Simon Grundy & Jill Hope. 103.4 FM. Owner: Radio Investments. Adult contemporary

TFM
Radio House, Yales Crescent
Thornaby
Stockton-on-Tees TS17 6AA
01642 888222
colin.paterson@tfmradio.com
www.tfmradio.co.uk
Teesside. Managing director: Catherine Ellington; programme director: Colin Paterson; head of news: Myles Ashley; breakfast show: Mojo & Cara. 96.6 FM. Owner: Emap Performance Network. Adult contemporary

YORKSHIRE AND HUMBERSIDE

96.3 Radio Aire
51 Burley Road, Leeds LS3 1LR
0113 283 5500
firstname.lastname@radioaire.com
www.radioaire.co.uk
Leeds. Managing director: Alexis Thompson; programme director: Stuart Baldwin; head of news: Richard Pervis; breakfast show: Cameron & Jamie. 96.3 FM. Owner: Emap Performance Network. Adult contemporary

96.9 Viking FM
The Boat House, Commercial Road
Hull HU1 2SG
01482 325141
reception@vikingfm.co.uk
www.vikingfm.co.uk
Hull. Programme director: Darrell Woodman; head of news: Kirsty Moore; breakfast show: Foxy & Tom. 97.2 FM. Owner: Radio Investments. Variety

97.2 Stray FM
The Hamlet, Hornbeam Park Avenue
Harrogate HG2 8RE
01423 522972
mail@972strayfm.co.uk
www.strayfm.com/
Harrogate. Managing director: Sarah Barry; programme director: Ray Stroud; head of news: Patrick Dunlop; breakfast show: Ed George. 97.2 FM. Owner: Radio Investments. 60s & 70s

Classic Gold 1278/1530 AM
Pennine House, Forster Square
Bradford, West Yorkshire BD1 5NE
01274 203040
general@pulse.co.uk
www.pulse.co.uk
Bradford, Halifax and Huddersfield. ILR group programme director: John Evington; managing director: Esther Morton; head of news: Richard Murie; breakfast show: Matt and Elisa. 1278 AM; 1530 AM. Owner: The Wireless Group. Oldies

Compass FM
26a Wellowgate
Grimsby DN32 0RA
01472 346666
enquiries@compassfm.co.uk
www.compassfm.co.uk
Grimsby. Programme director: Jane Hill; programme manager: Andy Marsh; head of news: Shaun Dunderdale; breakfast show: Richard Lyon. 96.4 FM. Owner: Lincs FM. Easy listening

Fresh Radio
Fresh Radio Ltd, Firth Mill, Firth Street
Skipton, North Yorkshire BD23 2PT
01756 799991
info@freshradio.co.uk
www.freshradio.co.uk
Yorkshire Dales with Skipton. Managing director: Dave Parker; head of news: James Wilson; breakfast show: Nick Bewes. 1431 AM; 1413 AM; 936 AM. Independent. Adult contemporary

Galaxy 105
Joseph's Well
Hannover Walk, off Park Lane
Leeds LS3 1AB
0113 213 0105
mail@galaxy105.co.uk
www.galaxy105.co.uk
Yorkshire. Managing director: David Lloyd; head of news & programme director: Mike Cass; breakfast show: Hirsty, Danny & JoJo. 105.8 FM; 105.6 FM; 105.1 FM; 105.6 FM; DAB; Sky; cable. Owner: Chrysalis Radio. Dance and R&B. Biggest station outside London

Hallam FM
Radio House 900 Herries Road
Sheffield S6 1RH
0114 209 1000
Programmes@hallamfm.co.uk
www.hallamfm.co.uk
South Yorkshire. Managing director: Iain Clasper; head of news & Programming: Chris Straw; breakfast show: Big John Breakfast Show. 102.9 FM; 103.4 FM; 97.4 FM. Owner: Emap Performance Network. All types of music

Home 107.9
The Old Stableblock, Lockwood Park
Huddersfield HD1 3UR
01484 321107
info@home1079.com
www.home1079.com
Huddersfield. Programme controller: Nick Hancock; sales director: Phil Chadderton; head of news: Steven Naylor; breakfast show: Nick Hancock. 107.9 FM. Owner: Radio Investments. Pop from last three decades

Magic 1161 AM
Commercial Road
Hull HU1 2SG
01482 325141
reception@magic1161.co.uk
www.magic1161.co.uk
Humberside (east Yorkshire and north Lincolnshire). Managing director: Mike Baldwin; programme director: Darrell Woodman; head of news: Kirsty Moore; breakfast show: Steve Jordan. 1161 AM. Owner: Emap Performance Network. 60s to present day

Magic 828
51 Burley Road
Leeds LS3 1LR
0113 283 5500
firstname.lastname@radioaire.com
www.radioaire.co.uk
Leeds. Managing director: Alexis Thompson; programme director: Stuart Baldwin; head of news: Richard Pervis; breakfast show: Paul Carrington. 828 AM. Owner: Emap Performance Network. Adult contemporary

Magic AM
Radio House, 900 Herries Road
Sheffield S6 1RH
0114 209 1000
Programmes@magicam.co.uk
www.magicam.co.uk
South Yorkshire. Managing director: Iain Clasper; head of news & Programming: Chris Straw; breakfast show: Howie & Emma at breakfast. 990 AM; 1.305 AM; 1545 AM. Owner: Emap Performance Network. Popular music

Minster FM
PO Box 123, Dunnington
York YO19 5ZX
01904 488888
general@minsterfm.com
www.minsterfm.com
York. Commercial station manager: Sarah Barry; programme controller: Ed Bretton; head of news: Tristan Hunkin; breakfast show: Ed Bretton. 104.7 FM; 102.3 FM. Owner: Radio Investments. Last few decades

Real Radio (Yorkshire)
Sterling Court, Capitol Park
Leeds WF3 1EL
0113 238 1114
info@realradiofm.com
www.realradiofm.com
South and West Yorkshire. Managing director: Mike Pennington; programme director: Terry Underhill; Head of News: James Rea; breakfast show: Terry Underhill. 107.6 FM; 106.2 FM; 107.7 FM. Owner: Guardian Media Group Radio. 90s and popular today

Ridings FM
PO Box 333, Wakefield WF2 7YQ
01924 367177
enquiries@ridingsfm.co.uk
www.ridingsfm.co.uk
Wakefield. Programme manager: Phil Butler; head of news: Andy Smith; breakfast show: Danny Lacey. 106.8 FM. Owner: Lincs FM. Popular music

Sunrise FM
Sunrise House, 30 Chapel Street
Little Germany, Bradford BD1 5DN
01274 735043
usha@sunriseradio.fm
www.sunriseradio.fm
Bradford. Managing director & programme controller: Usha Parmar; head of news: Gail Papworth. 103.2 FM. Independent. Asian music

The Pulse
Pennine House, Forster Square
Bradford, West Yorkshire BD1 5NE
01274 203040
general@pulse.co.uk
www.pulse.co.uk
Bradford, Huddersfield and Halifax. ILR group programme director: John Evington; managing director: Esther Morton; head of news: Richard Murie. 102.5 FM; 97.5 FM. Owner: The Wireless Group. Oldies

Trax FM
PO Box 44, Doncaster DN4 5GW
01302 341166
events@traxfm.co.uk
www.traxfm.co.uk
Doncaster. Programme controller: Rob Wagstaff; sales manager: Peggy Watson; head of news: Tine Master. 107.1 FM. Owner: Lincs FM. All sorts

Yorkshire Coast Radio
PO Box 962 Scarborough
North Yorkshire YO11 3ZP
01723 581700
studio@yorkshirecoastradio.com
www.yorkshirecoastradio.com
Bridlington, Scarborough, Whitby. Station manager & programme controller: Chris Sigsworth; head of news: Wesley Mallin; breakfast show: Chris Belly Bell. 96.2 FM; 103.1 FM. Owner: Radio Investments. Chart hits

Yorkshire Coast Radio
Bridlington's Best
PO Box 1024 Bridlington
East Yorkshire YO15 2YW
01262 404400
info@yorkshirecoastradio.com
www.yorkshirecoastradio.com
Bridlington. Programme controller: Chris Sigsworth; sales director: Gaynor Preston-Routledge; head of news: Wesley Mallin; breakfast show: Belly at Breakfast. 102.4 FM. Owner: Radio Investments. Adult Contemporary

NORTH-WEST

102.4 Wish FM
Orrell Lodge, Orrell Road
Orrell, Wigan WN5 8HJ
01942 761024
studio@wish_fm.com
Wigan. Programme director: John Evington; head of news: Alistair Clark; breakfast show: Danny & Jo. 102.4 FM. Owner: The Wireless Group. 80s, 90s, up to date

106.9 Silk FM
Radio House, Bridge Street
Macclesfield, Cheshire SK11 6DJ
01625 268000
mail@silkfm.com
www.silkfm.com
Macclesfield. Commercial manager: Rachael Barker; programme manager: Andy Bailey; head of news: Helen Croydon; breakfast show: Andy Clewes 106.9 FM. Owner: Radio Investments. Adult contemporary

107.2 Wire FM
Warrington Business Park, Long Lane
Warrington WA2 8TX
01925 445545
info@wirefm.com
www.wirefm.com
Warrington. ILR group programme director: John Evington; station director: Mathew Allitt; head of news: Mark Bell; breakfast show: Dominic Walker. 107.2 FM. Owner: The Wireless Group. Adult contemporary

2BR
Imex Lomeshaye Business Village
Nelson, Lancs BB9 7DR
01282 690000
info@2br.co.uk
www.2br.co.uk
Burnley. Managing director: Mark Matthews. 99.8 FM

96.2 The Revolution
PO Box 962, Oldham OL1 3JF
0161 621 6500
info@therevolution.uk.com
www.revolutiononline.co.uk
Oldham. Managing director: Dave Stankler; programme controller & head of news: Chris Gregg; breakfast show: Lee Clasby & Big Al. 96.2 FM. Owner UKRD & Hurst Kidd & Renny. Hits from yesteryear to current day

97.4 Rock FM
PO Box 974, Preston PR1 1YE
01772 477700
firstname.lastname@rockfm.co.uk
www.rockfm.co.uk
Preston and Blackpool. Programme director: Brian Paige; head of news: Clare Hannah; breakfast show: Dixie. 97.4 FM. Owner: Emap Performance Network. Adult contemporary

Asian Sound Radio
Globe House, Southall Street
Manchester M3 1LG
0161 288 1000
info@asiansoundradio.co.uk
www.asiansoundradio.com
East Lancashire. Managing director & programme director: Shujat Ali; head of news: Fiaz Mohammed; breakfast show: Sophie. 963 AM; 1377 AM. Independent. Asian hip-hop

The Bay
PO Box 969, St Georges Quay
Lancaster LA1 3LD
01524 848747
information@thebay.fm
www.thebay.fm
Morecambe Bay. 102.3 FM; 96.9 FM. Owner: CN Group

Century 105
Laser House, Waterfront Quay
Salford Quays
Manchester M5O 3XW
0161 400 0105
info1054@centuryfm.co.uk
www.1054centuryfm.com
North West England. Managing director: Nick Davidson; Brand programme director: Giles Squire; head of news: Matt Bowen; breakfast show: Tony Horne. 105.4 FM. Owner: Capital Radio. Pop

Classic Gold Marcher 1260 AM
The Studios, Mold Road
Wrexham LL11 4AF
01978 752202
firstname.surname@classicgolddigital.com
www.classicgolddigital.com
Wrexham and Chester. Programme controller: Don Douglas; head of news: Elina Cavanagh; breakfast show: Tony Blackburn. 1260 AM. Owner: Classic Gold Digital. Classical music

Dee 106.3
2 Chantry Court, Chester CH1 4QN
01244 391000
info@dee1063.com
www.dee1063.com
Chester. Sales director: Sarah Vel; Head of news: Lucy Liddard; breakfast show: Mike James. 106.3 FM. Independent. Adult contemporary

Dune FM
The Power Station, Victoria Way
Southport PR8 1RR
01704 502500
studio@dunefm.co.uk
www.dunefm.co.uk
Southport. Managing director: David Myatt; programme manager: Jonathan Dean; head of news: Charlotte Maher; breakfast show: Derek Marks. 107.9 FM. Media Forward Group. Adult contemporary

Galaxy 102
5th Floor, The Triangle, Hanging Ditch
Manchester M4 3TR
0161 279 0300
mail@galaxy102.co.uk
www.galaxy102.co.uk
Manchester. Managing director: David Lloyd; programme director: Vaughan Hobbs; Editorial: Lynsey Horn; breakfast show: Nicksy in the morning. 102 FM. Owner: Chrysalis Radio. Dance and R&B

Imagine FM
Regent House, Heaton Lane
Stockport SK4 1BX
0161 609 1400
info@imaginefm.com
www.imaginefm.co.uk
Stockport. ILR group programme director: John Evington; head of news & programme controller: Ashley Burne; breakfast show: Mathew Rudd. 104.9 FM. Owner: The Wireless Group. Hits 70s to 90s and today

Jazz FM 100.4
8 Exchange Quay
Manchester M5 3EJ
0161 877 1004
jazzinfo@jazzfm.com
www.jazzfm.com
North West England. Managing director: Roy Bennett; programming director: Steve Collins; programme controller: Derek Webster; breakfast show: Chris Best. 100.4 FM. Owner: Guardian Media Group Radio. Smooth and R&B

Juice 107.6
27 Fleet Street, Liverpool L1 4AR
0151 707 3107
mail@juiceliverpool.com
www.juice.fm
Liverpool. Managing director: Donna O'Driscoll; programme director: Grainne Landowski; head of news: Mike Baker; breakfast show: Paul Curran. 107.6 FM. Owner: Forever Broadcasting. R&B

KCR FM
The Studios, Cables Retail Park
Prescot, Knowsley L34 5NQ
0151 290 1501
kcrmusic@btconnect.com
www.kcr.fm
Knowsley. Managing director and programme controller: Ray Ferguson; head of news: John Donnelly; breakfast show: Dan & Jeff. 106.7 FM. Independent. 60s to modern

Key 103
Castle Quay, Castlefield
Manchester M15 4PR
0161 288 5000
first.name@key103.co.uk
www.key103.com
Manchester. Managing director: Gus McKenzie; programme director: Anthony Gay; head of news: John Pickford; breakfast show: "K". 103 FM. Owner: Emap Performance Network. Mainstream

Lakeland Radio
Lakeland Food Park, Plumgarths
Crook Road
Kendal, Cumbria LA8 8QJ
01539 737380
info@lakelandradio.co.uk
www.lakelandradio.co.uk
Kendal and Windermere. Station manager: Peter Fletcher; head of music: Colin Yare; breakfast show: Darren Milby. 100.8 FM; 100.1 FM. Independent. 60s to modern

Magic 1548
St Johns Beacon, 1 Houghton Street
Liverpool L1 1RL
0151 472 6800
firstname@magic1548.com
www.radiocity.co.uk
Liverpool. Managing director: Tom Hunter; programme director: Richard Maddock; head of news: Steve Hothersell; breakfast show: Phil Easton. 1548 AM. Owner: Emap Performance Network. Adult contemporary

Magic 999
St Pauls Square, Preston PR1 1YE
01772 477700
name.surname@magic999.co.uk
www.magic999.co.uk
Preston and Blackpool. Programme director: Brian Page; head of news: Clare Hannah; breakfast show: Dave Asher. 999 AM. Owner: Emap Performance Network. Adult contemporary

Manchester's Magic 1152
Castle Quay, Castlefield
Manchester M15 4PR
0161 288 5000
first.lastname@key103.co.uk
www.key103.co.uk
Manchester. Managing director: Gus McKenzie; programme director: Anthony Gay; head of news: John Pickford; breakfast show: Justin Moorhouse. 1152 AM. Owner: Emap Performance Network. 80s, 90s

MFM 103.4
The Studios, Mold Road, Gwersyllt
Nr Wrexham LL11 4AF
01978 752202
sarah.smithard@musicradio.com
www.mfmradio.co.uk
Wrexham and Chester. Area programme director: Graham Ledger; head of news: Elina Cavenagh; breakfast show: Dave & Beck. 103.4 FM. Owner: GWR Group. Pop music

Radio City 96.7
St Johns Beacon, 1 Houghton Street
Liverpool L1 1RL
0151 472 6800
firstname.surname@radiocity967.com
www.radiocity.co.uk
Liverpool. Managing director: Tom Hunter; programme director: Richard Maddock; head of news: Steve Hothersell; breakfast show: Kev Seed. 96.7 FM. Owner: Emap Performance Network. Pop

Tower FM
The Mill, Brownlow Way
Bolton BL1 2RA
01204 387000
info@towerfm.co.uk
www.towerfm.co.uk
Bolton and Bury. Sales director: Matt Ramsbottom; programme director: Gary Stein; head of news: Matt Hardman; breakfast show: Bix & Fairclough. 107.4 FM. Owner: Wire Group. Traditional music

Wave 96.5
965 Mowbray Drive, Blackpool
Lancashire FY3 7JR
01253 304965
wave@thewavefm.co.uk
www.wave965.com
Blackpool. Regional MD: Esther Morton; programme director: Helen Bowden; Station director: Mel Booth; breakfast show: Roy Lynch and Hayley Kay. 96.5 FM. Owner: The Wireless Group. Chart and retro

Wirral's Buzz 97.1
Media House, Claughton Road
Birkenhead CH41 6EY
0151 650 1700
sarah.smithard@musicradio.com
www.musicradio.com
Wirral. Managing director: Sarah Smithard; area programme controller: Graham Ledger; head of news: Alina Cavanagh; breakfast show: Loraine Gabriel & Jamie Scott. 97.1 FM. Owner: GWR Group. Chart 80s & 90s

Commercial local radio: Wales

106.3 Bridge FM
PO Box 1063, Bridgend CF31 1WF
01656 647777
firstname.surname@bridge.fm
www.bridge.fm
Bridgend. Managing director: Mark Franklyn; programme controller: Lee Thomas; head of news: Kayley Thomas; breakfast show: Mark Franklyn. 106.3 FM. Owner: Tindle Radio. Adult contemporary

96.4 FM The Wave
PO Box 1170, Swansea SA4 3AB
01792 511964
info@thewave.co.uk
www.thewave.co.uk
Swansea. ILR group programme director: John Evington; managing director: Esther Morton; head of news: Emma Thomas; breakfast show: Mark Powell. 96.4 FM. Owner: The Wireless Group. Chart hits

Capital Gold (1305 and 1359)
30 Leicester Square
London WC2H 7LA
020 7766 6000
first.surname@capitalgold.com
www.capitalgold.com
Cardiff and Newport. Programme director: Andy Turner; head of news: Justin King; breakfast show: Tony Wright. 1305 AM; 1359 AM. Owner: Capital Radio. 60s, 70s and 80s hits

Champion FM
Llys y Dderwen Parc Menai
Bangor LL57 4BN
01248 671888
sarah.smithard@musicradio.com
www.musicradio.com
Caenafon. Managing director: Sarah Smithard; Area programme controller: Graham Ledger; head of news: David Grundy; breakfast show: Kevin Williams. 103 FM. Owner: GWR Group. Modern music

Coast FM
PO Box 963, Bangor LL57 4ZR
01248 673272
sion.pritchard@musicradio.com
www.coastfm.co.uk
North Wales Coast. Managing director: Sarah Smithard; Area programme controller: Graham Ledger; head of news: David Grundy; breakfast show: Kevin Williams. 96.3 FM. Owner: GWR Group. Modern music

Radio Ceredigion
Yr Hen Ysgol Gymraeg Ffordd
Alexandra Aberystwyth
Ceredigion SY23 1LF
01970 627999
admin@ceredigionfmf9.co.uk
www.ceredigionradio.co.uk
Ceredigion. Programme controller: Mark Simon; head of news: Ceriel Davis; breakfast show: Thomo. 97.4 FM; 103.3 FM; 96.6 FM. Independent. Adult contemporary Welsh

Radio Maldwyn
The Studios, The Park, Newtown
Powys SY16 2NZ
01686 623555
radio.maldwyn@ukonline.co.uk
www.magic756.net
Montgomeryshire. Managing director & Operations director & programme controller: Austin Powell; head of news: Andrew Curry; breakfast show: Mark Edwards. 756 AM. Owner: Murfin Media International. Adult contemporary

Radio Pembrokeshire
Unit 14 The Old School Estate
Station Road, Narbarth
Pembrokeshire SA67 7DU
01834 869384
enquiries@radiopembrokeshire.com
www.radiopembrokeshire.com
Pembrokeshire/West Carmarthenshire. Managing director and programme controller: Keri Jones; head of news: Tim John; breakfast show: Keri Jones. 102.5 FM; 107.5 FM. Independent. Adult contemporary rock

Real Radio (South Wales)
PO Box 6105 Ty-Nant Court
Cardiff CF15 8YF
029 2031 5100
info@realradiofm.com
www.realradiofm.com
South Wales Regional. Programme director: Sarah Graham; head of news: Gareth Setter; breakfast show: Sam Graham & Steve Clark. 105.9 FM; 106 FM; 105.2 FM; 105.4 FM. Owner: Guardian Media Group Radio. 70s to modern

Red Dragon FM & Capital Gold
Atlantic Wharf
Cardiff Bay CF10 4DJ
029 2066 2066
mail@reddragonfm.co.uk
www.reddragonfm.co.uk
Cardiff and Newport. Programme controller: David Rees; head of news: Angharad Thomas; breakfast show: Jason Harrold & Zoe Hampson. 103.2 FM; 97.4 FM. Owner: Capital Radio. Chartmusic

Star 107.2
Bristol Evening Post Building
Temple Way, Bristol BS99 7HD
0117 910 6600
dev@star1072.co.uk
www.star1073.co.uk
Bristol. Station manager & Managing director: Dev Chakraborty; head of news: Stephanie Worman; breakfast director: Ian Downef. 107.2 FM. Owner: UKRD Group. Adult contemporary & soul

Sunshine 855
Unit 11, Burway Trading Estate,
Ludlow, Shropshire SY8 1EN
01584 873795
sunshine855@ukonline.co.uk
www.sunshine855.com
Ludlow. Managing director: Ginny Murfin; programme controller: Ginny Murfin; head of news: Andrew Currie; breakfast show: Nick Jones. 855 AM. Owner: Murfin Media International. Adult contemporary

Swansea Sound
PO Box 1170, Swansea SA4 3AB
01792 511170
info@swanseasound.co.uk
www.swanseasound.co.uk
Swansea. ILR group programme director: John Evington; managing director: Esther Morton; head of news: Emma Thomas; head of music: Andy Miles; breakfast show: Kevin Johns. 1170 AM. Owner: The Wireless Group. Chart hits

Valleys Radio
Festival Park Victoria
Ebbw Vale NP23 8XW
01495 301116
admin@valleysradio.co.uk
www.valleysradio.co.uk
Heads of South Wales valleys. ILR group programme director: John Evington; managing director: Chris Hurst; head of news: Emma Thomas; breakfast show: Tony Peters. 1116 AM; 999 AM. Owner: The Wireless Group. Adult contemporary

Commercial local radio: Scotland

96.3 QFM
65 Sussex Street
Glasgow G41 1DX
0141 429 9430
sales@q-fm.com
www.q96.net
Paisley. ILR group programme director: John Evington; managing director: Aaron Shields; head of news: Chris Martin; breakfast show: Derek McIntyre. 96.3 FM. Owner: The Wireless Group. All types

Argyll FM
27–29 Longrow, Campbeltown
Argyll PA28 6ER
01586 551800
argyllradio@hotmail.com
Kintyre, Islay and Jura. Managing director: Colin Middleton; programme controller: Kenny Johnson; head of news: Ian Henderson; breakfast show: Bill Young. 107.7 FM; 107.1 FM; 106.5 FM. Independent. Adult contemporary

Beat 106
Four Winds Pavilion, Pacific Quay
Glasgow G51 1EB
0141 566 6106
info@beat106.com
www.beat106.com
Central Scotland. Programme controller: Claire Pattenden; news editor: Vicky Lee; breakfast show: Paul Harper & Des Clarke. 106.1 FM; 105.7 FM. Owner: Capital Radio. Dance music

Central FM
201 High Street, Falkirk FK1 1DU
01324 611164
mail@centralfm.co.uk
www.centralfm.co.uk
Stirling and Falkirk. Programme controller: Tom Bell; head of news: Tadek Pszywa; breakfast show: Malky Brown. 103.1 FM. Owner: Radio Investments. Hits & memories

CFM (Carlisle)
PO Box 964, Carlisle CA1 3NG
01228 818964
reception@cfmradio.com
www.cfmradio.com
Carlisle. Managing director: Cathy Kirk; programme controller: David Bain; head of news: Bill McDonald; breakfast show: Robbie Dee. 96.4 FM; 102.5 FM. Owner: Scottish Radio Holdings. Best mix of music

CFM (West Cumbria)
PO Box 964
Carlisle CA1 3NG
01228 818964
reception@cfmradio.com
www.cfmradio.com
West Cumbria. Managing director: Cathy Kirk; programme controller: David Bain; head of news: Bill McDonald; breakfast show: Robbie Dee. 103.4 FM; 102.2 FM. Owner: Scottish Radio Holdings. Best mix of music

Clan FM
Radio House, Rowantree Avenue
Newhouse Ind. Estate, Newhouses
Lanarkshire ML1 5RX
01698 733107
reception@clanfm.com
www.clanfm.com
North Lanarkshire. Station manager: Janis Melville; programme controller: Darren Stenhouse; breakfast show: David Ross; Head of news: Andrew Thompson. 107.9 FM; 107.5 FM. Owner: Kingdom Group. Adult contemporary

Clyde 1 FM
Clydebank Business Park
Glasgow G81 2RX
0141 565 2200
info@clyde1.com
www.clyde1.com
Glasgow. Managing director: Paul Cooney; programme controller: Ross Macfadyen; head of news: Russell Walker; breakfast show: George Bowis. 97 FM; 103.3 FM; 102.5 FM. Owner: Scottish Radio Holdings. Pop

Clyde 2
Clydebank Business Park
Glasgow G81 2RX
0141 565 2200
info@clyde2.com
www.clyde2.com
Glasgow. Managing director: Paul Cooney; programme controller: Ross Macfadyen; head of news: Russell Walker; breakfast show: Mike Riddoch. 1152 AM. Owner: Scottish Radio Holdings. Hits from last few decades

Forth AM
Forth House, Forth Street
Edinburgh EH1 3LE
0131 556 9255
info@forth2.com
www.forth2.com
Edinburgh. Managing director: Sandy Wilkie; programme director: Nik Goodman; head of news: Paul Robertson; breakfast show: Darren Adam. 1548 AM. Owner: Scottish Radio Holdings. 60s, 70s, 80s, 90s & today

Forth FM
Forth House, Forth Street
Edinburgh EH1 3LE
0131 556 9255
info@forthone.com
www.forthone.com
Edinburgh. Managing director: Sandy Wilkie; programme director: Nik Goodman; head of news: Paul Robertson; breakfast show: Boogie & Vicky. 97.6 FM; 102.2 FM; 97.3 FM. Owner: Scottish Radio Holdings. Adult contemporary

Heartland FM
Atholl Curling Rink, Lower Oakfield
Pitlochry, Perthshire PH16 5HQ
01796 474040
mailbox@heartlandfm.co.uk
Pitlochry and Aberfeldy. Programme controller: Peter Ramsden; head of news: Margaret Stevenson; breakfast show: Bruce Patterson. 97.5 FM; 102.7 FM. Independent. Classic hits

Isles FM
PO Box 333
Stornoway, Isle of Lewis HS1 2PU
01851 703333
studio@isles.fm
www.isles.fm
Western Isles. Director of operations: David Morrison; head of news: Ian MacIver. 103 FM. Independent. Adult contemporary

Kingdom FM
Haig House, Haig Business Park
Markinch, Fife KY7 6AQ
01592 753753
info@kingdomfm.co.uk
www.kingdomfm.co.uk
Fife. Chief executive: Ian Sewell; programme director: Kevin Brady; head of news: Chris Hodge; breakfast show: Ian Gilmore. 95.2 FM; 105.4 FM; 96.6 FM; 106.3 FM; 96.1 FM. Independent. Across the board mix

Lochbroom FM
Radio House, Mill Street
Ullapool, Ross-shire IV26 2UN
01854 613131
radio@lochbroomfm.co.uk
www.lochbroomfm.co.uk
Ullapool. Chairman: Iain Boyd; head of music: Tiffany McCaulay. 96.8 FM; 102.2 FM. Independent. Adult contemporary

Moray Firth Radio (MFR)
Scorguie Place, Inverness IV3 8UJ
01463 224433
mfr@mfr.co.uk
www.mfr.co.uk
Inverness. Managing director: Danny Gallagher; senior presenter: Ray Atkins; breakfast show: Tich McCooey & Nicky Marr. 96.6 FM; 96.7 FM; 97.4 FM; 102.5 FM; 102.8 FM. Owner: Scottish Radio Holdings. Contemporary and chart

NECR
The Shed, School Road, Kintore
Aberdeenshire AB51 0UX
01467 632909
necrradio102.1fmsales@supanet.com
Inverurie. Managing director: Colin Strong; programme controller: John Dean; head of news: John Dean; breakfast show: John Dean. 102.1 FM; 102.6 FM; 97.1 FM; 103.2 FM; 101.9 FM; 106.4FM. Independent. Recent hits & classic gold. Specialist country, Irish and Scottish

Nevis Radio
Ben Nevis Estate, Claggan
Fort William PH33 6PR
01397 700007
studio@nevisradio.co.uk
www.nevisradio.co.uk
Fort William and parts of Lochaber. Head of News, Station manager and programme controller: Willie Cameron; breakfast show: Michael McCrae. 96.6 FM; 102.4 FM; 97 FM; 102.3 FM Independent. Daily chart music. Evening specialist

Northsound One
Abbotswell Road, West Tullos
Aberdeen AB12 3AJ
01224 337000
northsound@srh.co.uk
www.northsound1.co.uk
Aberdeen, north-east Scotland. Managing director: Adam Finlay; programme controller: Luke McCullough; head of news: Ross Govans; breakfast show: Andy James. 96.9 FM; 97.6 FM; 103 FM. Owner: Scottish Radio Holdings. Modern music

Northsound Two
Abbotswell Road, West Tullos
Aberdeen AB12 3AJ
01224 337000
northsound@srh.co.uk
www.northsound2.co.uk
Aberdeen, north-east Scotland. Managing director: Adam Finlay; programme controller: Luke McCullough; head of news: Ross Govans. 1035 AM. Owner: Scottish Radio Holdings. Modern music

Oban FM
132 George Street, Oban
Argyll PA34 5NT
01631 570057
obanfmradio@btconnect.com
www.obanfm.tk
Oban. Managing director: Neil Horne; programme director: Tina Tobertson; head of news: Coll McDougall. 103.3 FM. Independent. Gaelic to modern pop

Radio Borders
Tweedside Park, Galashiels TD1 3TD
01896 759444
programming@radioborders.com
www.radioborders.com
Borders. Programme controller: Stuart McCulloch; head of news: Denise Glass; breakfast show: Keith Clarkson. 96.8 FM; 103.1 FM; 103.4 FM; 97.5 FM Owner: Scottish Radio Holdings Hits & memories

Real Radio (Scotland)
PO Box 101, Parkway Court,
Glasgow Business Park
Glasgow G69 6GA
0141 781 1011
contact.name@realradiofm.com
www.realradiofm.com
Central Scotland. Managing director: Shaun Bowron; programme director: Jay Crawford; head of news: Heather Kane; breakfast show: Robin Galloway. 100.3 FM; 101.1 FM. Owner: Guardian Media Group Radio. Wide variety

River FM
Stadium House, Alderstone Road
Livingstone, West Lothian EH54 7DN
01506 420975
office@river-fm.com
www.river-fm.com
West Lothian. Programme controller: Donny Hughes; sales director: Susan Dignon; news editor: Campbell Hart; breakfast show: Mike Arthur. 107.7 FM; 103.4 FM. Kingdon Radio Group. Adult contemporary & charts

RNA FM
Radio North Angus Ltd
Abroath Infirmary, Rosemount Road
Abroath, Angus DD11 2AT
01241 879660
info@radionorthangus.co.uk
www.radionorthangus.co.uk
Arbroath/Carnoustie. Managing director and head of news: Malcolm Finlayson. 96.6 FM. Independent. Classic/Scottish and pop

SIBC
Market Street, Lerwick
Shetland ZE1 0JN
01595 695299
info@sibc.co.uk
www.sibc.co.uk
Shetland. Managing director & programme controller: Inga Walterson; head of news: Ian Anderson. 96.2 FM; 102.2 FM. Independent. Rock & pop

South West Sound
Unit 40, The Loreburne Centre
High Street, Dumfries DG1 2BD
01387 250999
info@westsound.co.uk
www.westsound.co.uk
Dumfries and Galloway. Managing director: Sheena Borthwick; programme director: Alan Toomey; head of news: Ian Wilson; breakfast show: Tommy Jargon. 96.5 FM; 97 FM; 103 FM. Owner: Scottish Radio Holdings. Chart music

Tay AM
6 North Isla Street
Dundee DD3 7JQ
01382 200800
tayam@radiotay.co.uk
www.radiotay.co.uk
Dundee/ Perth. Managing director & programme director: Arthur Ballingail; head of news: Amanda Mezullo; breakfast show: Grant Reed. 1584 AM; 1161 AM. Owner: Scottish Radio Holdings. Various music

Tay FM
6 North Isla Street
Dundee DD3 7JQ
01382 200800
tayam@radiotay.co.uk
www.radiotay.co.uk
Dundee/ Perth. Managing director & programme director: Arthur Ballingail; head of news: Amanda Mezullo; breakfast show: Graham Waggott. 102.8 FM; 96.4 FM. Owner: Scottish Radio Holdings. Various music

Two Lochs Radio
The Harbour Centre, Pier Road
Gairloch IV21 2BQ
01445 712712
info@2lr.co.uk
www.2lr.co.uk
Gairloch and Loch Ewe. Programme director: Colin Pickering; Chairman & Station manager: Alex Gray; breakfast show: Campbell Elder. 106.6 FM. Independent. Broad mix & Scottish Gaelic

Wave 102
8 South Tay Street
Dundee DD1 1PA
01382 901102
studio@wave102.co.uk
www.wave102.co.uk
Dundee. ILR group programme director: Peter Mas; managing director: Mike Robertson; head of news: Rebecca Wallis; breakfast show: Peter Mac. 102 FM. Owner: The Wireless Group. 70s to modern

Waves Radio Peterhead
7 Blackhouse Circle
Peterhead AB42 1BW
01779 491012
waves@radiophd.freeserve.co.uk
www.wavesfm.com
Peterhead. Managing director & programme controller: Norman Spence; head of news: Glenn Moir; breakfast show: Kenny King. 101.2 FM. Independent. Current & classic

West FM
Radio House, 54a Holmston Road
Ayr KA7 3BE
01292 283662
info@westfm.co.uk
www.westfmonline.com
Ayr. Managing director: Sheena Borthwick; programme director: Alan Toomey; head of news: Ian Wilson; breakfast show: Alan Toomey. 97.5FM; 96.7 FM. Owner: Scottish Radio Holdings. Wide variety including music

West Sound AM
Radio House 54a Holmston Road
Ayr KA7 3BE
01292 283662
info@westsound.co.uk
www.west-sound.co.uk
Ayr. Managing director: Sheena Borthwick; programme director: Alan Toomey; head of news: Ian Wilson; breakfast show: Alan Toomey. 1035 AM. Owner: Scottish Radio Holdings. Wide variety of music

Your Radio
Pioneer Park Studios, Unit 1–3
80 Castlegreen Street
Dumbarton G82 1JB
01389 734422
info@yourradio.com
www.yourradiocom
Dumbarton. Chairman: Jim Duncan; programme controller: Steven Scott; sales manager: Scott Gusfogg; breakfast show: Gary Pews. 103 FM; 106.9 FM. Independent. Popular music

Commercial local radio: Northern Ireland

City Beat 96.7
PO Box 967
Belfast BT9 5DF
028 9020 5967
misic@citybeat.co.uk
www.citybeat.co.uk
Belfast. Station director: Dorothy McDide; head of news: Mark Malett; breakfast show: Morris Jay. 96.7 FM. Owner: CN Group. Commercial chart

Cool FM
PO Box 974
Belfast BT1 1RT
028 9181 7181
music@coolfm.co.uk
www.coolfm.co.uk
Northern Ireland. Programme controller: David Sloan MBE; head of news: Harry Castles; breakfast show: Carl Kinsman. 97.4 FM. Owner: Scottish Radio Holdings. Pop

Downtown Radio
Newtownards, Co Down
Northern Ireland BT23 4ES
028 9181 5555
Programmes@downtown.co.uk
www.downtown.co.uk
Northern Ireland. Programme controller: David Sloan MBE; head of news: Harry Castles; breakfast show: Caroline & Roy. 97.1 FM; 103.1 FM; 103.4 FM; 102.4 FM; 1026 AM; 96.6 FM; 102.3 FM; 96.4 FM. Owner: Scottish Radio Holdings. Adult contemporary

Mid 106
2c Park Avenue, Burn Road
Cookstown BT80 8AH
028 8675 8696
firstnamelastname@midfm106fm.co.uk
www.mid106fm.co.uk
Mid-Ulster. Station director: Neil McLeod Berriskell; news manager: Donagh McKeown; senior Presenter: Francie Quinn; breakfast show: Francie Quinn. 106 FM. Owner: CN Group. 80s, 90s mix.

Q101.2 FM West
42A Market Street, Omagh
Co. Tyrone BT78 1EH
028 8224 5777
Manager@q101west.fm
www.q101west.fm
Omagh and Enniskillen. Programme controller: Frank McLaughlin; head of news: Sophie Wheeler; breakfast show: Stuart Gorclon. 101.2 FM. Owner: Q Radio Group. Chart & pop

Q102.9 FM
The Riverview Suite
87 Rossdowney Road, Waterside
Londonderry BT47 5SU
028 7134 4449
Manager@q102.fm
www.q102.fm
Londonderry. Managing director and programme controller: Frank McLaughlin; head of news: Roger Donnelly; breakfast show: Pete Wilson. 102.9 FM. Independent. 70s to today

Q97.2 Causeway Coast Radio
24 Cloyfin Road, Coleraine
Co Londonderry BT52 2NU
028 7035 9100
Manager@q972.fm
www.q972.fm
Coleraine. Programme controller: Frank McLaughlin; head of news: Bob Lee; breakfast show: Barrie Owler. 97.2 FM. Owner: Q Radio Group. Adult contemporary

Community radio

All FM
Manchester
0161 273 4072
info@allfm.org
www.allfm.org
Programme organiser: Dave Lenaghan 96.9 FM. Adult contemporary

Angel Community Radio
Havant
02392 481988
angelradio@37.com
www.cssd.com
Managing director: Tony Smith 101.1 FM

BCB 96.7 FM
Bradford
01274 771677
info@bcb.yorks.com
www.bcb.yorks.com/
Managing director: Mary Dowson; programme controller: Jonathan Pinfield 96.7 FM

Cross Rhythms City Radio
Stoke on Trent
0870 011 8008
admin@crossrhythms.co.uk
www.crossrhythms.co.uk
Chief executive officer: Chris Cole; programmes controller: Steve Perry 101.8 FM. Digital satellite channel 876

Desi Radio
Southall, London
020 8574 9591
info@desiradio.org.uk
www.desiradio.org.uk
Chair of the trustees: Amarjit Khera; programme controller: Ajit Singh 1602 AM. Panjabi, satellite,digital

Forest Of Dean Radio
Gloucester
01594 820722
contactus@fodradio.org
www.fodradio.org/
Programme manager: Roger Drury 1503 AM; 1521 AM. All ages

GTFM
Pontypridd
01443 406111
news@gtfm.fsnet.co.uk
www.gtfm.co.uk
Manager: Andrew Jones 106.9 FM. Adult contemporary

New Style Radio 98.7 FM
Birmingham
0121 456 3826
c_r_t@lineone.net
www.newstyleradio.co.uk
Manager: Barbara Richards; programme controller: Denis Edwards 98.7 FM. Reggae, all types music

Resonance 104.4 FM
London
020 7836 3664
info@resonance.com
www.resonancefm.com
Studio manager: Knut Aufermann; programmer: Ed Baxter 104.4 FM. Adult contemporary/pop

Sound Radio
Hackney, east London
020 8533 8899
info @soundradio.info
www.svt.org.uk/
Chief executive: Lol Gellor 1503 AM. Multilingual station

Takeover Radio
Leicester
0116 299 9600
office@takeoverradio.com
www.takeoverradio.com
Station manager: Graham Coley 103.2 FM. Children's

Wythenshawe FM
Manchester
0161 499 7982
info@wfmradio.org
www.wfmradio.org
Programme manager: Christine Brennan; programme organiser: Jason Kenyon 97.2 FM. Adult contemporary

Hospital, student and sporting event radio

1287 AM Insanity
01784 414268
studio@rhul.ac.uk
www.su.rhul.ac.uk
Station manager: Matt Jones
1287 AM. Student radio

1503 AM Radio Diamonds
01933 652000
mathew.rowe@airwair.co.uk
www.thediamonds.co.uk
General manager: Mathew Rowe
1503 AM. Matchday service for Rushden and Diamonds FC

Auckland Hospital radio
01388 455452
secretary@aucklandradio.com
www.aucklandradio.com
Station manager: Craig Robinson
1386 AM

Acorn FM
0781 640177
www.acornfm.co.uk
Programme controller: Niall Hayley
87.7 FM. North Devon College

Bailrigg FM
01524 593902
Manager@bailriggfm.co.uk
www.bailriggfm.co.uk
Station manager: Ali Cordrey
87.7 FM. Lancaster University

Basildon Hospital Radio
01268 282828
1287am@bhr.co.uk
www.bhr.org.uk
Chairman: Alan Newman
1287 AM

BFBS
01494 878703
bfbs@bfbs.com
www.bfbs.com
Station manager: Charles Foster
1287 AM. Forces radio

Blast 1386
0118 967 5068
blast1386@reading-college.ac.uk
www.blast1386.com
Station manager: Bob Goertz
1386 AM. Student radio

Bridge FM
01382 423000 x25151
studio@bridgefm.org.uk
www.bridgefm.org.uk
Chairman: Barry Hampton; programme controller: Bob McNally
87.7 FM. Hospital, Tayside

C4 Radio
01227 782424
c4radio@cant.ac.uk
www.c4radio.com
Station manager: Ian Eason
999 AM. Christchurch College radio

Canterbury Hospital Radio
01227 864161
www.chradio.org.uk
Studio manager: Martin Pauley
945 AM

Chichester Hospital Radio
01243 788122 x3000
studio@chr1431.org.uk
www.chr1431.org.uk
Presenter: Bill Barwell
1431 AM

City & Hemel Hospital Radio
01442 262222
general@hemelradio.com
www.hemelradio.com
Programme controller: Alan Etchells
1287 AM

Crush
01707 285005
uhsu.comms@herts.ac.uk
www.uhsu.herts.ac.uk
Programme controller: Ollie Cadman
1278 AM. College radio

CUR
committee@cur1350.co.uk
1350 AM

Dorton Radio Station
01732 592600
karen.campbell@risb.org.uk
www.rslb.org.uk
Station manager: Karen Campbell
1350 AM. Dorton College

Freak 1c
01772 894895
www.freak1c.co.uk
Station manager: Emily Bull
1350 AM
University of Central Lancashire

Frequency
01772 513200
surecreation@uclan.ac.uk
www.yourunion.co.uk
Station manager: Emily Bull
1350 AM. Student radio

Gara Sound
01623 464220
admin@garibaldi.org.uk
www.garibaldi.org.uk
Station manager: Dave Kenny
1386 AM. School radio

Garrison Radio
01748 830050
hq@garrisonradio.com
www.garrison.com
Station manager: Mark Page
1287 AM; 1350 AM. Army radio

GU2
01483 681350
studio@gu2.co.uk
www.gu2.co.uk
Station manager: Nathan Whittaker
1350 AM. Student

Hospital Radio Basingstoke
01256 313521
mail@hrbasingstoke.co.uk
www.hrbasingstoke.co.uk
Programme controller: Neil Ogden
945 AM

Hospital Radio Gwendolen
0116 256 1686
jsmethurst@ntlworld.com
www.beehive.thisisleicestershire.co.uk
Station manager: Dave Wilcocks
1287 AM

Hospital Radio Plymouth
01752 763441
www.plymouthhospitals.org.uk
Communications: Corinne Glen
87.7 FM

Hospital Radio Pulse
01527 512048
studio@hospitalradiopulse.com
www.hospitalradiopulse.com
Programme controller: Ian Barstow
1350 AM

Hospital Radio Reading
0118 950 7420
requests@hospitalradioreading.co.uk
www.hospitalradioreading.org.uk
Programme controller: Stephen Ham
945 AM

Hospital Radio Rossendale
01706 233334
945 AM

Hospital Radio Yare
01493 842613
www.radioyare.com
Chairman: Gerry Jarvis
1350 AM. James Paget, Northgate, Lowestoft Hospitals

IC Radio
020 7594 8100
info@icradio.com
www.icradio.com
Station manager: Mike Jones
999 AM
Imperial College halls of residence

Jam 1575
01482 466289
email@jam1575.com
www.jam1575.com
Station manager: Gareth Morris
1575 AM. Student radio

Kendal Radio
01539 795420
Info@kendalhospitalradio.com
www.kendalhospitalradio.org.uk
Studio manager: John Williamson
Hospital radio

Junction 11
0118 931 8698
www.1287am.com
Station manager: Joff Hopkins
1287 AM. Student radio

Kingstown Radio
01482 327711
onair@kingstownradio.com
www.kingstownradio.co.uk
Station manager: Nick Palmer
1350 AM. Hull hospital radio

Kool AM
020 8373 1072
pfmnews@email.com
www.koolam.co.uk
Programme controller: Joe Bone
1134 AM

Livewire
01603 592512
livewireradiouk@yahoo.co.uk
www.livewire1350.com
Station manager: Chris Davis
1350 AM. Union of UEA students

Loughborough Campus Radio
01509 635050
station@lcr1350.co.uk
www.lcr1350.co.uk
Head of media: Lucy Pritchard; station manager: Oliver Folkerd
1350 AM. Student radio

Manchester United Radio
0161 8721 413
Contact: Kenneth Ramsden
1413 AM
Manchester United matchday service

Mid-Downs Hospital Radio
01444 441350
studio@ndr.org.uk
Station manager: Alan French
1350 AM

Nevill Hall Sound
07771 722738
Station manager: Colin Palmer
1287 AM

Oakwell 1575 AM
01226 215753
enquiries@oakwell1575am.co.uk
www.oakwell1575am.co.uk
Station manager: Stuart Cocker
1575 AM. Matchday service for Barnsley FC

Palace Radio
020 8653 5799
info@palaceradio.net
www.palaceradio.net
Communications manager: Terry Byfield
1278 AM. Matchday service for Crystal Palace FC

Portsmouth Hospital Broadcasting
023 9228 6299
studio@phb945.co.uk
www.phb945.co.uk
Station manager: Barrie Swann
945 AM

Radio Airthrey
01786 467166
stationManager@airthrey.co.uk
www.airthrey.co.uk
Station manager: Matt Ludlow
1350 AM

Radio Branwen
01766 781911
radiobranwen@yahoo.co.uk
Station manager: Trevor Andrews
87.7 FM

Radio Brockley
020 8954 6591
studio@radiobrockley.org
www.radiobrockley.org
999 AM. The wards within Stanmore's Royal National Orthopaedic Hospital

Radio Brunel
01895 462238
studio@b1000.brunel.ac.uk
www.b1000.brunel.ac.uk
999 AM

Radio Cavell
0161 620 3033
info@radiocavell1350.org.uk
www.radiocavell.org.uk
Broadcasting manager: Phil Edmunds
1350 AM

Radio Donnington
01869 336200
enquiries@event-tech.biz
www.event-tech.biz
Liaison: Diane Smith
1602 AM. Motor racing

Radio Glangwili
01267 227504
87.7 FM

Radio Gosh
020 7405 9200 x5205
peter@radiogosh.co.uk
Chairman: Peter Losch
999 AM

Radio Heatherwood
01344 625818
www.radioheatherwood.org.uk
Station manager: Dave Smith
999 AM

Radio Hotspot
01473 326287
www.royalhospitalschool.org
Manager: Don Topley
1287 AM

Radio Knockhill
01383 723337
aardvark@pitlochry.org
Station manager: Garry Stagg
1602 AM. Motor racing

Radio Lonsdale
01229 877877
studio@radiolonsdale.co.uk
www.southlakes-uk.co.uk
Station manager: Julian Ackred
87.7 FM

Radio Nightingale
01709 304244
Admin@radionightingale.org.uk
www.radionightingale.org.uk
1350 AM

Radio North Angus
01382 424095
info@radionorthangus.co.uk
www.radionorthangus.co.uk
Secretary: Malcolm Finlayson
87.7 FM

Radio North Tees
01642 624337
info@radionorthtees.com
www.radionorthtees.com
Station manager: Elliot Kennedy
1575 AM

Radio Northwick Park
020 8869 3959
info@radionorthwickpark.org.uk
www.radionorthwickpark.org.uk
Programme controller: David Reece
945 AM

Radio Rainbow
01224 681818
radiorainbowinternational@hotmail.com
www.radio-rainbow.tnpod.com
945 AM

Radio Redhill
01737 768511
studio@radioredhill.co.uk
www.radioredhill.co.uk
Station manager: Nigel Gray
1287 AM

Radio Rockingham
01869 336200
enquiries@event-tech.biz
www.event-tech.biz
Liaison: Diane Smith
1602 AM. Rockingham speedway commentary

Radio Rovers
01254 261413
alan.yardley@creatv.co.uk
www.gjmedia.co.uk
Station manager: Alan Yardley
1404 AM. Blackburn Rovers matchday service

Radio Silverstone
01869 336200
enquiries@event-tech.biz
www.event-tech.biz
Liaison: Diane Smith
1602 AM. Motor racing

Radio Southlands
01273 446084
info@hospitalradiosouthlands.co.uk
www.hospitalradiosouthlands.co.uk
Programme controller: Adam James
846 AM

Radio Thruxton
01295 262000
enquiries@event-tech.biz
www.event-tech.biz
Liaison: Diane Smith
1602 AM. Motor racing

Radio Tyneside
0191 273 6970
info@radiotyneside.co.uk
www.radiotyneside.co.uk
1575 AM

Radio Warwick
024 7657 3077
studio@radiowarwick.ac.uk
www.radiowarwick.ac.uk
1251 AM

Radio West Suffolk
01284 713403
peteowen1350@hotmail.com
www.radiowestsuffolk.co.uk
Vice chairman: P Owen
1350 AM. West Suffolk Hospital

Radio Wexham
01753 570033
945 AM

Radio ysbty Glan Clwyd
01745 584229
Manager: Mrs M Jelly
1287 AM

Ram Air
01274 233267
studio@ramairfm.com
www.ramairfm.co.uk
Station manager: Mark Pickering
1350 AM

Range Radio
0161 861 9727
rap@whalleyrange.manchester.sch.uk
www.whalleyrange.manchester.sch.uk
Station manager: Roy Appleby
1350 AM

Red
01206 863211
red@essex.ac.uk
www.essexstudent.com
1404 AM

Rookwood Sound Hospital Radio
029 2031 3796
programming@rookwoodsound.co.uk
www.rookwoodsound.co.uk
Programme controller: Tim Evans
945 AM

Rugby Ref!Link
01225 835553
ppd@reflink.net
www.reflink.net
Managing director: Peter Downey
87.7 to 105 AM. Rugby referees

Solar AM
01744 733766
solar1287am@hotmail.com
Station manager: Terry Broughton
1287 AM

Sportslink UK
01225 835553
pd@officiallink.net
www.officiallink.net
Managing director: Peter Downey
87.7 to 105 AM. Tennis, dressage, racing

Stoke Mandeville Hospital Radio
01296 331575
info@smhr.co.uk
www.smhr.co.uk
1575 AM

Storm FM
01248 388000
admin@stormfm.com
www.stormfm.com
Manager: Alex Simpson
87.7 FM. University of Wales Bangor

Storm Radio
01206 500700
storm@colchsfc.ac.uk
Station manager: Neil Kelly
999AM

Subcity Radio
0141 341 6222
www.subcity.org.uk
Station manager: Rosie Scott
1350 AM

Surge 1287 AM
0870 357 2287
office@surgeradio.co.uk,
studio@surgeradio.co.uk
www.surgeradio.co.uk
Station manager: Matt Treacy; programme controller: Alex Duffy; head of music: Andrew Bailey
1287 AM. Student radio

Trust AM
01909 502909
studio@trustam.com
www.trustam.com
1278 AM
Bassetlaw district general hospital

Tunbridge Wells Hospital radio
01892 528528
info@hrtw.org.uk
www.hrtw.org.uk
Programme controller: Mark Burgess
1350 AM

UCA
01292 886433
ucaradio@paisley.ac.uk
www.ucaradiopaisley.ac.uk
Station manager: Marcus Bowinan
87.7 FM

UKC Radio
01227 824201
ukcr@kent.ac.uk
www.ukcr.net
Programme controller: Dan Thompson
1350 AM

Unity FM
01772 894876
info@unityfm.co.uk
Project manager: Paul Jenkins
107 FM. Culturally diverse music

University Radio Falmer
01273 678287
urf@sussex.ac.uk
Station manager: Fouad Sethra
999 AM

University Radio York
01904 433840
ury@york.ac.uk
www.ury.york.ac.uk
Programme controller: Adam Bell
1350 AM

URB
01225 386611
studio@bath.ac.uk
www.bath.ac.uk
Station manager: James Palmer
1449 AM

URF
01273 678999
Jonathan@urfonline.com
www.urfonline.com
Station manager: Jonathan Pascoe
1431 AM

URN
01273 678999
studio@urn1350.net
www.urn1350.net
Station manager: Phil Cotton
1350 AM

WCR AM
01902 317700
training@wcr1350.co.uk
www.wcr1350.co.uk
1350 AM

Whitechapel AM
020 7377 7000 x2928
info@whitechapelfm.org.uk
www.whitechapel.org.uk
999 AM

Withybush FM
01437 773562
studio@withybushfm.co.uk
www.withybushfm.co.uk
87.7FM

Xpression
01392 263568
stationManager@Xpressionfm.com
www.Xpressionfm.com
Station manager: Dan Fowler; programme controller: Ricky Bustin
87.7 FM

Xtreme
01792 295989
studio@xtremeradio.info
www.xtremeradio.info
1431 AM

Cable radio

Angel Radio
01983 242471
angelradio@37.com
www.angelfm.co.uk
Programme controller & Station manager: Martin Kirby
Nostalgia before 1960

BCB 96.7FM
01274 771677
info@bcb.yorks.com
www.bcb.yorks.com/
Station manager and programme controller: Jonathan Pinfield; project director: Mary Dowson
All types of music

Cablecom Investments
01638 532323
customer@cablecom.co.uk
www.cablecom.co.uk
Programme controller; Robert Barnes
News, pop music and documentary

Cable Radio
01273 418181
office@cableradio.co.uk
www.cableradio.co.uk
Station manager: R Mustapha
Adult contemporary

CRMK
01908 265266
Station manager: Mike Barry

Kerrang!
0114 209 1034
natalie.johnson@emap.com
www.Emapdigitalradio.com
Manager: Natalie Johnson

Kiss
0114 209 1034
natalie.johnson@emap.com
www.Emapdigitalradio.com
Manager: Natalie Johnson

Kool AM
020 8373 1075
pfmnews@email.com
www.koolam.co.uk
Programme controller: Joe Bone
1134 AM. Harlow

Radio Forth
0131 556 9255
marketing@radioforth.com
www.forthonline.com
Managing director: Sandy Wilkie; programme controller: Nik Goodman
548 AM; 97.3 FM. Adult contemporary

Radio Verulam
01442 398099
studio@radio-verulam.co.uk
www.radio-verulam.co.uk
Manager: Phil Richards

Smash! Hits
020 7436 1515
natalie.johnson@emap.com
www.Emapdigitalradio.com
Manager: Natalie Johnson

Satellite radio

Adventist World Radio
01344 401401
whitegates@AWR.org
www.awr.org
Programme controller: Bert Smit

All: Sports Live
0113 399 2043
cheryl.Westerman@teamtalk.com
Manager: Cheryl Westerman

Amrit Bani
020 8606 9292
info@amjritbani.com
www.amritbani.com
Operational director: Surjit Singh Dusanjh
Religious Asian broadcasting

Apna Radio
0121 555 8238
info@apnaradio.net
www.apnaradio.net
Director: Arfan Younis
Asian/English

The Arrow
0121 695 0000
paul.fairburn@chryslis.com
www.thearrow.co.uk
Managing director: Paul Fairburn

Asian Gold
020 8571 7200
info@asiangoldradio.com
www.asiangoldradio.com
Chief executive director: Zorawar Gakhal
Ethnic Asian

Assalam Radio
00 41 21 6476390
info@assalam.info
www.assalam.info
Manager: Mostepha Mohammed

Bloomberg Radio
020 7330 7575
digitalradio@bloomberg.net
www.bloomberg.co.uk
Radio Editor: Jack Reed

Calvary Chapel Radio
020 8466 5365/07779 507032
ccradio@btconnect.com
www.calvarychapelradio.co.uk
Managing director: Brian Brodersen; programme controller: Alison Johnstone-White; programmer: Mark Seddon
Christian radio

Capital Gold
020 7766 6006
www.capitalradio.co.uk
Manager: Gills Hind

Club Asia
020 8594 6662
info@clubasiaonline.com
www.clubasiaonline.com
Programme controller: Sumerad Ahmed
Young British Asians

Core
020 7911 7300
fresh@corefreshhits.com
www.corefreshhits.com
Digital content manager: Nick Piggott

Cross Rhythms
0870 011 8008
admin@crossrhythms.co.uk
www.crossrhythms.co.uk
Managing director: Chris Cole; Office manager: Jonathan Bellamy
Christian youth radio

Desi Radio – Southall
020 8574 9591
info@desiradio.org.uk
www.desiradio.org.uk
Chair of the trustees: Amarjit Khera; programme controller: Ajit Singh
Panjabi, satellite,digital

Easy Radio
020 8900 1035
info@easy1035.com
www.easy1035.com
Programme controller: Natalie King

ETBC London
020 8795 0045
atbcradio@yahoo.co.uk
www.atbclondon.com
Programme controller: Karjhi Gesu
Asian

EWTN
00 1 205 271 2900
www.ewtn.com
Global Catholic network

Family Radio
00 1 800 543 1495
www.familyradio.com
Christian gospel

FCUK FM
020 8749 7272
ian@deliciousdigital.com
www.fcuk.com
Managing director: O Raphael; director: Ian Taylor

Galaxy
0121 695 0000
www.galaxyfm.co.uk
Managing director: Paul Fair; programme controller: Neil Greenslade
Dance and R&B

Gaydar Radio
020 8893 9550
gary@qsoft.co.uk
Manager: Gary Frisch

Hallam FM
0114 209 1034
namesurname@hallamfm.co.uk
www.hallamfm.co.uk
Managing director: Ian Clasper; news editor: Katy Henderson

Heart 106.2
020 7465 6100
enquiries@heart1062.co.uk
www.heart1062.co.uk
Managing director: Steve Parkinson
106.2 FM. Greater London

Holiday FM
info@holidayfmradio.com
www.holidayfmradio.co.uk
Gran Canaria, Lanzarote, Tenerife, Fuerteventura, Katerini

Jazz FM
020 7298 7209
alistair@jazzfm.com
www.jazzfm.co.uk
Manager: Stuart Kilby

Laser Radio
01342 327842
laser@ukmail.com
www.laserradio.net
Managing director: Andrew Yeates
1557AM. Greater Amsterdam and Sky subscribers

LBC
020 7314 7300
newsroom@lbc.co.uk
www.lbc.co.uk
Managing director: Mark Flanagan; programme director: Steve Kyte

Magic
0114 209 1142
natalie.johnson@emap.com
www.emap.com
Station manager: Natalie Johnson

McColls FM
0113 399 2211
www.teamtalkbroadcast.com
Manager: Helen Jacklin

Mean Country
0870 150 0044
www.meanfiddler.com
Station manager: Dean James

The Mix
020 7911 7300
mail@themix.musicradio.com
www.musicradio.com
Station manager: Nick Piggott

Mojo
020 7436 1515
mojo@emap.com
www.mojo4music.com
Radio programme director: Scott Armstrong

Music Choice
020 7014 8700
contactus@musicchoice.co.uk
www.musicchoice.com
Station manager: Margo Daly; Head of News: Hannah Aiken

NPR Worldwide (National Public Radio)
00 1 202 513 2000
worldwide@npr.org
www.npr.org
Senior VP for programming: Jay Kernis; VP programming: Margaret Low Smith

On Air
020 7896 9000
voanews@voanews.com
www.voa.gov
Managing director: Tim Eris

Oneword
020 7976 3030
general@oneword.co.uk
www.oneword.co.uk
Managing director: Simon Blackmore

Panjab Radio
020 8848 8877
info@panjabradio.co.uk
www.panjabradio.co.uk
Station manager: Paramjit Kaur Nizzar
Panjab radio

Planet Rock
020 7911 7300
joinus@planetrock.com
www.planetrock.com
Digital content manager: Nick Piggott

Primetime Radio
0870 050 5050
david.atkey@primetimeradio.org
www.primetimeradio.org
Managing director Ron Coles; operations director: David Atkey

Premier Christian Radio
020 7316 1300
reception@premier.org.uk
www.premier.org.uk
Managing director: Peter Kerridge; programme controller: Charmain Noble-McLean
Christian & variety of styles

Q
0114 209 1142
natalie.johnson@emap.com
www.q4music.com
Managing director: Mark Story; programme director: Simon Long

Radio Al Mahabba
01274 721810
rthurgoo@hcjb.org.uk
www.hcjb.org
Managing director: RW Thurgood
Arabic music

Radio Caroline
020 8340 3831
caroline-pirate@btconnect.com
www.radiocaroline.co.uk
Programme controller & station manager: Peter Moore
Album rock music

Radio France Internationale (RFI)
00 33 1 5640 1212
www.rfi.fr

Radio London
01296 425644
sales@radiolondon.co.uk
www.radiolondon.co.uk
Station manager: Ray Anderson

Radio Telefis Eireann
info@rte.ie
www.rte.ie
Managing director of Radio: Adrian Moynes
Ireland's public service broadcaster

Real Radio
029 2031 5100
sarahgraham@realradio.com
www.realradiofm.com
Managing director: Andy Carter; programme director: Sarah Graham
60s to present day

SBN
020 7691 4777
info@campusmedia.co.uk
www.sbn.co.uk
Station manager: Marina Lois; assistant programmer: Deidre Melvin
Rock, hip-hop, Indian punk

Sky Radio 100.7 FM
00 31 35 699 1005
skyradio@skyradio.nl
www.skyradio.com

Smash Hits
020 7436 1515
info@emap.com
www.emap.com
Station manager: Andy Roberts

Spectrum Digital 1 and 2
020 7627 4433
enquiries@spectrumradio.net
www.spectrumradio.net
General manager: Paul Hogan

The Storm
020 7911 7300
reception@stormradio.co.uk
www.stormradio.co.uk
Station manager: Heidi Hanson
Adult contemporary

Sukh Sagar Radio
020 8571 7200
info@asiangoldradio.co.uk
www.asiangoldradio.co.uk
Chief executive: Zorawar Gakhal
Ethnic Asian

Sunrise Radio (UK and Europe)
020 8574 6666
reception@sunriseradio.com
www.sunriseradio.com
Managing director: Tony Lit; news editor: David Landau; programme controller: Tony Patti
Asian

talkGospel.com
020 7316 1300
enquiries@talkgospel.com
www.talkgospel.com
Chairman: Noble McLean

The Talking Bible
www.talkingbible.com

TBC Radio
07817 063682
info@tbcuk.com
www.tbcuk.com
Managing director: V. Ramarag
Asian music

TotalRock
020 7731 6696
bs@totalrock.com
www.totalrock.com
Station manager: Tony Wilson

Trans World Radio UK
01225 831390
web@twr.org.uk
www.twr.org.uk
Chief executive: Russell Farnworth; programme controller: Michael Pfundner
Christian music

Voice of America
020 7896 9000
voanews@voanews.com
www.voa.gov
Station manager: Tim Ayrisnger

WorldSpace UK
020 7494 8200
ukservice@worldspace.com
www.worldspace.com
Senior vice-president: Safia Safwat

XFM
020 7766 6606
firstname.lastname@xfm.co.uk
www.xfm.co.uk
Managing director: Garham Bryce; programme controller: Andy Ashton
Guitar-based

Radio associations

Assoc. for international Broadcasting
POBox 990, London SE3 9XL
020 8297 3993
info@aib.org.uk
www.aib.org.uk
Managing director: Simon Spandwick
Trade organisation for international broadcasters, manufacturers and consultants

Broadcasting Press Guild
Tiverton, The Ridge
Woking, Surrey GU22 7EQ
01483 764895
torin.douglas@bbc.co.uk
Managing director: Richard Last
Promotes professional interests of journalists who write or broadcast about the media

Commercial Radio Companies Association
The Radio Centre
77 Shaftesbury Avenue
London W1D 5DU
020 7306 2603
info@crca.co.uk
www.crca.co.uk
Trade body for commercial radio

Creators' Rights Alliance
British Music House
26 Berners Street
London W1T 3LR
020 7436 7296
info@creatorsrights.org
www.creatorsrights.org
Campaigns to protect creators' rights; operates in all media areas

Digital Radio Development Bureau (DRDB)
The Radiocentre
77 Shaftesbury Avenue
London W1D 5DU
020 7306 2630
info@drdb.org
www.drdb.org
Trade body; funded and supported by BBC and commercial radio multiplex operators

Musicians Union
60–62 Clapham Road
London SW9 0JJ
020 7582 5566
webmaster@musiciansunion.org.uk
www.musiciansunion.org.uk

Office of Communications (Ofcom)
Riverside House
2A Southwark Bridge Road
London SE1 9HA
020 7981 3000
mediaoffice@ofcom.org.uk
www.ofcom.gov.uk
New broadcasting super-regulator

Performing Right Society
29–33 Berners Street
London W1T 3AB
020 7580 5544
info@prs.co.uk
www.prs.co.uk
Collects and distributes royalties

Rad10
rad10@rad10.com
www.rad10.com
Free training resource for radio volunteers looking at going professional; offers advice for community radio groups

The Radio Academy
5 Market Place
London W1W 8AE
020 7255 2010
info@radioacademy.org
www.radioacademy.org
Professional body for radio; aims to encourage pursuit of excellence and a greater understanding of the medium

Radio Joint Audience Research (Rajar)
Gainsborough House
81 Oxford Street, London W1D 2EU
020 7903 5350
info@rajar.co.uk
www.rajar.co.uk

Voice of the Listener and Viewer (VLV)
101 Kings Drive
Gravesend, Kent DA12 5BQ
01474 352835
vlv@btinternet.com
www.vlv.org.uk
Independent, non-profit society working to ensure independence, quality and diversity in broadcasting

Women's Radio Group
27 Bath Road, London W4 1LJ
Fax: 020 8995 5442
wrg@zelo.demon.co.uk
www.womeninradio.org.uk
Training and networking charity

World Radio Network
PO Box 1212
London SW8 2ZF
020 7896 9000
email@wrn.org
www.wrn.org
Home to series of global radio networks; hosts transmission services for world's leading broadcasters

Radio trade press

Advance Production News
Crimson Communications
211a Station House, Greenwich Communication Centre
Greenwich High Road
London SE10 8JL
020 8305 6905
www.crimson.uk.com
Monthly. Listings for production companies. Editor: Alan Williams

Audio Media
IMAS Publishing UK
Atlantica House, 11 Station Road
St Ives, Cambs PE27 5BH
01480 461555
pr@audiomedia.com
www.audiomedia.com
Monthly. Professional audio. Editor: Paul Mac

Broadcast
Emap Media
33–39 Bowling Green Lane
London EC1R 0DA
020 7505 8000
bcletters@emap.com
www.broadcastnow.co.uk
Weekly. TV & radio industry. Editor: Conor Dignam

Broadcast Hardware International
Hardware Creations
48 The Broadway
Maidenhead, Berks SL6 1PW
01628 773935
cathy@hardwarecreations.tv
www.hardwarecreations.tv
10pa. Editor: Dick Hobbs

Commonwealth Broadcaster
Commonwealth Broadcasting Association, 17 Fleet Street
London EC4Y 1AA
020 7583 5550
cba@cba.org.uk
www.cba.org.uk
Quarterly. Editor: Elizabeth Smith

Contacts
The Spotlight, 7 Leicester Place
London WC2H 7RJ
020 7437 7631
info@spotlightcd.com
www.spotlightcd.com
Annual. Contacts for stage, film, TV and radio. Editor: Kate Poynton

Line Up
Line Up Publications
The Hawthornes
4 Conference Grove
Crowle WR7 4SF
01905 381725
editor@lineup.biz
www.ibs.org.uk
6pa. Journal of the Institute of Broadcast Sound. Editor: Hugh Robjohns

Pro Sound News
CMP Information, Ludgate House
245 Blackfriars Road
London SE1 9UR
020 7921 8319
info@cmpinformation.com
www.cmpinformation.com
12pa. Audio industry. Editor: David Robinson

QSheet
10 Northburgh Street
London EC1V 0AT
020 7253 8888
Monthly. Support material for presenters and producers. Contact: Nik Harta

Radcom
Radio Society of Great Britain
Lambda House
Cranbourne Road
Potters Bar EN6 3JE
01707 659015
radcom@rsgb.org.uk
www.rsgb.org
Monthly. Radio enthusiasts. Editor: Steve Telenius-Lowe

Radio Magazine
Radio Magazine
Crown House, 25 High Street
Rothwell, Northants NN14 6AD
01536 418558
info@theradiomagazine.co.uk
www.theradiomagazine.co.uk
Weekly. Radio news for industry. Editor: Paul Boon

Stage Screen and Radio
Bectu, 373–377 Clapham Road
London SW9 9BT
020 7346 0900
janice@stagescreenandradio.org.uk
www.bectu.org.uk
10pa. Broadcasting union. Editor: Janice Turner

VLV Bulletin
Voice of the Listener and Viewer
101 Kings Drive
Gravesend DA12 5BQ
01474 352835
vlv@btinternet.com
www.vlv.org.uk
Quarterly. Consumer campaigning body. Editor: Jocelyn Hay

New media

After the doom of the dotcom crash, 2005 brings renewed confidence in Britain's new media industry. Not only are more people accessing the internet, using broadband and shopping online more than ever before, but also some of the more exciting dreams of the dotcom boom – such as wireless networking and third-generation video phones – are starting to be fulfilled. The BBC, however, is under fire for its rapid expansion into the new media world; see the next page for more on that.

Year in technology

Internet access and broadband

It happened more slowly than the analysts predicted – but the internet has finally conquered the mass market. Ofcom announced in 2004 that, for the first time ever, the majority of British homes have **internet access**; the same research also showed that more than two-thirds of small businesses are now online. Europe-wide, according to a survey commissioned by the European Interactive Advertising Association, people now spend more time online than they do reading magazines. There is hope, too, of tackling Britain's digital divide: in 2004, the government pledged that every home in Britain would have "access to online services" within the next five years.

That is the good news. The bad news is that Britons are still, for now at least, accessing the internet in smaller numbers than other developed nations – particularly the US, Canada, Japan, Germany and South Korea. This could be because Britain has its significant minority of "never-users", but it could also be because of relatively slow access speeds: according to Ofcom, some 67 per cent of online British homes were using narrowband, dial-up connections, while 25 per cent, or 3.99 million, are connected to broadband.

There are three main ways to connect to broadband: cable, ADSL (the local exchange) or, most recently, through a wireless network. About 45 per cent of British homes have a **cable broadband** outside their house; they are represented by a total of 1.4 million customers, so most consumers possibly don't yet think it is worth the cash. The other main form of broadband is **ADSL** – bandwidth that "piggybacks" on the local telephone exchange, sold by former telecoms monopoly BT, either direct to the user or to a rival ISP. By 2005, almost all homes will be in areas where ADSL technology has been enabled, says BT – and not before time, say its rivals, who have waited for years to market the technology. In December 2003, meanwhile, Ofcom proposed to make the market more competitive, by forcing BT to offer its rivals a discount on the price it charges its wholesale customers; too little too

Broadband uptake, end of April 2004

Homes with internet access:	13 million
Total broadband connections	3.99m
DSL connections	2.45m
Cable modem connections	1.54m
Satellite	More than 6,000
Fixed wireless connections	More than 2,500

Source: Ofcom

late, said the ISPs, but expect to see a glut of adverts for ADSL broadband in 2004 and 2005.

Wireless internet

A note of optimism is the growth of wireless technologies. Just a few years ago, the only real form of wireless networking was basic Wap on a mobile phone; now there are several different ways of getting wireless broadband internet access.

Almost every new laptop now includes 802.11b, affectionately known as **Wi-fi**, which allows broadband access to users who are within a few hundred metres of the nearest "hotspot". Chip manufacturer Intel lists more than 5,000 hotspots in Britain, comparing favourably with 20,000 in the US and 1,000 in France. Access to such technologies can be expensive (BT Openzone, for example, costs about £85 a month), yet free access is offered not only by many public sector institutions, but also coffee shops and other public places. For some users, meanwhile, the sport of "warchalking" – gaining access to insecure wireless networks, either as hobbyist or malevolent hacker – has become too tempting to resist.

Mobile phone companies are also looking to cash in. In March Vodafone and T Mobile switched on their **3G** data networks, launching cards that give wireless internet access direct from a laptop – although at April 2004, coverage was limited to about 30 per cent of the country. Costs were about £400 a year to access 30 web pages a day. The cards should recoup some of the billions of pounds of investment made by mobile phone companies in 3G licences in 2001 – and represent a challenge to mobile phone network 3, owned by Hutchison Whampoa, which is focusing its resources entirely on 3G telephone handsets. 3 had 360,000 subsribers in January 2004, and at the beginning of the year launched an ad campaign starring the former Brookside actor Anna Friel. In a few years, the company hopes, the rise of video calling will make its investment worthwhile.

To complicate the situation further, some 12 per cent of people, mostly in urban areas, are also within range of a broadband wireless base station, under a little-known technology called Broadband Fixed Wireless Access (BFWA). One example is Liberty Broadband, which charges a monthly fee, aimed at the small businesses and home-office market. In December 2003, meanwhile, Ofcom announced the allocation of a further part of the radio spectrum to wireless, in an effort to deliver low-cost broadband outside towns and cities.

Voice calling

Meanwhile, the internet is beginning to encroach on the traditional territory of the telecoms company: the voice call. Voice-operated internet protocol, or VOIP, promises to make phone calls cheaper by routeing them across the internet instead of phone lines. There is already a British trade body, the Internet Telephony Service Providers Association; but the big telecoms companies are moving into the market to try and head the newcomers off.

The Graf report: BBC and new media

In July 2004, the BBC came under heavy criticism over its new media strategy. A government-commissioned report, by the former Trinity Mirror boss Philip Graf, said many of the corporation's 20,000 websites were too commercial, not justified by its public service remit, and should be closed. Sites covering areas such as fantasy football and local entertainment were not "sufficiently distinctive from commercial alternatives", said Graf; the corporation should prioritise coverage of news, current affairs and education. Part of the problem, he said, was that governors had not been experienced enough in new media.

In its 2003 annual report, the BBC had said it spent £72m on online services; Graf said the figure was nearer £90m including other costs.

BBC's commercial rivals, who had been lobbying the government on the issue, welcomed the report. Meanwhile, the corporation's new media chief, Ashley Highfield, announced next day that the BBC was shutting five of its sites – but these accounted for just 1-2 per cent of overall traffic. The corporation has four months to come up with its response.

Dotcom news

AP/Ben Margot

At the Googleplex: co-founders Sergey Brin (left) and Larry Page

The most significant dotcom mover of 2004 was the US company Google, the world's most popular search engine. After launching the news aggregator Google News and buying the blogging software company Pyra in 2003, Google began testing two more launches in March: Froogle, an e-commerce search engine, and Gmail, a free email service to rival Yahoo! and MSN Hotmail. The company, which is privately owned and has an office in Soho, was expected to float on the stock market in 2004; some estimates said it would float at £1.5bn, and on the Nasdaq technology market rather than the New York Stock Exchange. Google, just four years ago a plucky outsider in the search engine stakes, is now the second most popular web domain in Britain after MSN; the Gmail launch could take it to the top of the tree.

Meanwhile in March, Yahoo! acquired its own e-commerce search engine, spending £319m on the European online price comparison service Kelkoo. The revival in online advertising helped the portal post a £61m second-quarter profit in 2004; up from £27.6m in the same period of 2003; chief executive Terry Semel called it a "product renaissance".

As one big name rises, another falls. Freeserve, for years the UK's biggest internet provider, was rebranded in the summer to take the name of Wanadoo, its French parent company. Dixons, the store which once owned Freeserve and distributed its ubiquitous internet access CDs, had struck a deal with the rival internet service provider AOL.

The commercial sector was not alone in rebranding. In March the government unveiled its new portal, Directgov, to replace UK Online.

Top 10 web audiences

	Name	Unique audience (millions)	
		May 2004	May 2003
1	Microsoft	19.1	20.5*
2	Google	13.7	10.2
3	Yahoo!	12.0	9.2
4	BBC	8.8	8.1
5	eBay	8.7	7.4
6	Time Warner	8.1	7.2
7	Wanadoo	7.2	7.0
8	Ask Jeeves	6.8	**
9	British Telecom	5.7	6.3
10	Amazon	5.6	5.7

* Microsoft/MSN ** not in top 10 Source: Nielsen/NetRatings

E-envoy Andrew Pinder said of the move: "UK Online acted like a travel agent, and suggested a holiday to you. Directgov should take you to the destination."

Music downloads were another important sector in 2004; July saw Napster relaunch in its legal form; while OD2, the company behind several high-profile music download sites, was acquired by the US music technology company Loudeye.

Online advertising

Online advertising had a healthy 2003: advertisers spent more than £300m online, according to the Interactive Advertising Bureau, a market share of over 2 per cent.

But there were calls for more regulation of the sector. The much-hated "pop-up" advert was declared dead during the year, as more companies followed the example of the Google toolbar, which blocks pop-ups from users' screens; that said, major advertisers simply resorted to using Flash-based pop-overs (but not, thankfully, pop-unders) to get their messages across. Notably, one study – by a behavioural consultancy called Bunnyfoot Universality – said that nine out of 10 people who click on to some pop-up adverts are actually trying to close them down. It singled out an ad from Umbro during Euro 2004, which took users nearly a minute to close because they could not find the close button.

The Advertising Standards Authority, meanwhile, has ruled that search engines need to give due prominence to links that are paid-for adverts and those that are not. It singled out Freeserve (now Wanadoo) for the way it displayed ads.

One company that has done well out of the online advertising revival is Espotting, which was founded in 2001 – after the start of the dotcom crash. In the first quarter of 2004, the company announced its first profit.

Online ad spend

Year	Spend £m	Market share %
2003	376.0	2.2
2002	196.7	1.4
2001	165.7	1.2
2000	154.7	1.1
1999	51.0	0.4
1998	19.4	0.2

Source: Advertising Association

Online shopping

British spending on the internet almost doubled in 2003. According to figures from the transaction company Visa, online spending for the final quarter of the year – when most online purchases are made – grew 91 per cent to £1.8bn.

The big names also increased revenues and profits. Amazon posted profits of £62.6m in the first quarter of 2004, its third straight quarterly gain, and a huge improvement on a £5.6m loss a year before; significantly for Britain, its non-US sales accounted for more than half its revenue for the first time. The auction site eBay saw first-quarter earnings nearly double to £113m (from £61m), with more than 100 million people using the service.

Another old favourite, Lastminute.com, made £30.9m profits in the first quarter of 2004, up from £15m the year before.

Further reading

■ Press

MediaGuardian: New Media
media.guardian.co.uk/newmedia

Guardian Online
guardian.co.uk/online

New Media Age
www.nma.co.uk

■ Books

Weaving the Web TIM BERNERS LEE, TEXERE PUBLISHING 2000
History of the world wide web

Boo Hoo: A Dotcom story
ERNST MALMSTEN ET AL, RANDOM HOUSE 2002 Rise and fall of the dotcom dream

■ Web only

Online Journalism Review
www.ojr.org

The Register: irreverent tech news
www.theregister.co.uk

ZDNet: IT and tech news
www.zdnet.co.uk

■ Other resources

Association of Online Publishers
www.ukaop.org.uk

Google flak **Jane Perrone**

Googling, googlewhacking, google hacks, googlebombing, the Googleplex: no other dotcom brand has imprinted itself on the cultural landscape of the internet quite so successfully as Google.

The firm, founded in 1998 by Larry Page and Sergey Brin after they met while studying for a computer science PhD at Stanford, has gone from strength to strength. With its reputation spread largely through word of mouth, it built up a mammoth index of web pages currently numbering around 4.28 billion. It has become a near-ubiquitous online presence for just about anyone who has ever handled a mouse.

Google's rise harks back to the heady days of the late 1990s dotcom bubble, when every new start-up had a lava lamp-spotted headquarters staffed by the brightest young geeks. Many a starry-eyed hack has visited Google headquarters in Mountain View, California – the so-called Googleplex – to eat in the staff restaurant presided over by the former chef of the Grateful Dead. The subsequent enthusiastic media coverage has left Google with little need for aggressive PR.

The firm preaches an ethical approach to business: one of its stated central tenets is that "you can make money without being evil". But behind its slightly whimsical philosophy lies an extremely hard-headed approach that has enabled Google to stake a claim on some of the most highly competitive areas of the new media industry.

In fact, Google's growth reads like a potted history of some of the most crucial dotcom developments of the last few years. Its winning formula of an uncluttered search interface that gave users fast, accurate results, coupled with a targeted advertising programme that turned significant profits, helped Google to effectively wipe out search competitors such as AltaVista. The firm's purchase in February 2003 of Pyra Labs, the owners of free weblog-hosting service Blogger, represented a shrewd move into the burgeoning blogging craze; January 2004 saw the launch of its social networking site Orkut, again perfectly in tune with the net zeitgeist; in April 2004 Google raised the stakes in the free email market with the launch of its one-gigabyte service, Gmail. The company's announcement later that month [April 2004] of a $2.7bn (almost £1.5bn) initial public offering was the natural next step.

Not everything is rosy in Google's garden, however. Privacy campaigners say Google is collecting huge amounts of data about users of its search and email facilities without providing enough guarantees about how the information will be stored and used, or whether it would be shielded from exploitation by the US government – what campaign organisation Google Watch has called a "privacy time bomb". Other commentators argue that such privacy fears are based on the false assumption that unencrypted email is secure in the first place: in fact from the minute a message leaves your computer it is vulnerable to prying eyes, whichever email service you use.

Some internet seers predict that privacy will prove to be a red herring. The influential web designer Jason Kottke argues that while Google continues its skirmishes with Yahoo and Microsoft over the contested territories of search and free email, its ultimate goal could be to offer a viable cheap alternative to Microsoft Windows.

So could Google be planning to create an online computer operating system that would undercut Windows and revolutionise the computer business? Certainly it possesses legendary processing power: computer experts speak with hushed reverence about its cluster of up to 100,000 Linux-run servers. This giant computer could offer users the benefits of online back-up for their files and the flexibility of remote access to that data from any machine. It's an intriguing proposition, and one likely to send shivers down the spine of Microsoft executives.

They need not be too concerned – yet. Much hangs on whether, once Google has gone public and ceased to be accountable only to itself, it can shake off persistent privacy fears for good and maintain its cuddly public image as the internet user's friend.

Jane Perrone is assistant news editor at Guardian Unlimited [guardian.co.uk]

New media Contacts

Main search engines/portals

AltaVista/AlltheWeb
New London House
172 Drury Lane
London WC2B 5QR
Press: 020 7071 3510
angela.bloor@overture.com
www.altavista.co.uk,
www.alltheweb.com

Ask Jeeves
53 Parker Street
London WG2B 5PT
Switchboard: 020 7400 2222
info@askjeeves.co.uk
www.ask.co.uk

Excite UK
Viale G Baccelli, 70
00153 - Roma, Italy
Switchboard: +39 (06) 570231
Press: +39 (06) 57023208
bberger@staff.excite.it
www.excite.co.uk
emailed berger

Google UK
European Headquarters
Seagrave House
19/20 Earlsfort Terrace
Dublin 02, Ireland

Google UK
UK Sales Office
The Courtyard, 12 Sutton Row
London W1V 5FH
Switchboard: 020 7031 3000
Press: 020 7031 3130
UK@google.com
www.google.co.uk

Lycos UK
Lycos House, 3 Sutton Lane
Clerkenwell, London EC1M 5PU
Switchboard: 020 7250 7000
ukpressoffice@lycos-europe.com
www.lycos.co.uk

MSN
Microsoft House
10 Great Pulteney Street
London W1R 3DG
Press: 0870 2077 377
ukprteam@microsoft.com
www.msn.co.uk

Yahoo! UK
10 Ebury Bridge Road
London SW1W 8PZ
Switchboard: 020 7808 4200
Press: 020 7808 4590
agency@yahoo.co.uk
Press: jwayth@uk.yahoo-inc.com
www.yahoo.co.uk

Main software publishers

Activision UK
Parliament House, St Laurence Way
Slough, Berkshire SL1 2BW
Switchboard: 01753 756100
www.activision.com
Games

Adobe
3 Roundwood Avenue
Stockley Park, Uxbridge
Middlesex UB1 1AY
Switchboard: 020 8606 4000
www.adobe.co.uk
Design and publishing software

Apple Computer UK
2 Furzeground Way
Stockley Park East, Uxbridge
Middlesex UB11 1BB
020 8218 1000
millar.d@euro.apple.com
www.apple.com/uk
Operating systems for own computers

Atari UK
Landmark House
Hammersmith Bridge Road
London W6 9EJ
Switchboard: 020 8222 9700
www.uk.atari.com
Games

Codemasters
Stoneythorpe, Southam
Warwickshire CV47 2DL
Switchboard: 01926 814132
customerservice@codemasters.co.uk
www.codemasters.co.uk
Games

Eidos Interactive
Wimbledon Bridge House
1 Hartfield Road
Wimbledon SW19 3RU
Switchboard: 020 8636 3000
www.eidos.co.uk
Games

Electronic Arts
The Malt Building, Greenalls Avenue
Stockton Heath, Warrington
Cheshire WA4 6HL
01925 644000
http://uk.ea.com/
Independent developer and publisher of interactive entertainment software

Focus Multimedia
The Studios, Lea Hall Enterprise Park
Wheelhouse Road, Rugeley
Staffordshire WS15 1LH
01889 570156
info@focusmm.co.uk
www.focusmm.co.uk
Publisher of budget PC software

IBM Lotus
PO Box 41, North Harbour
Portsmouth, Hampshire PO6 3AU
Press: 020 7202 3129
www.lotus.com
Office software

Linux
59 East River St, #2
Ogdensburg, NY13669 USA
001 315 393 1202
pr@Linux.org
www.linux.org; www.linux.org.uk
Free operating system

MacAfee (Network Associates)
277 Bath Road
Slough, Berkshire SL1 5PP
Switchboard: 01753 217500
customerservice@nai.com
www.macafee.co.uk
Anti-virus

Macromedia Europe (UK)
Century Court, Millennium Way
Bracknell RG12 2XN
01344 458600
Press: smowatt@macromedia.com
www.macromedia.com/uk/
Web graphics and design

Microsoft UK
Microsoft Campus
Thames Valley Park
Reading, Berkshire RG6 1WG
Press: 0870 207 7377
ukprteam@microsoft.com
www.microsoft.com/uk
Operating systems, office software

Netscape
80 Hammersmith Road
London W14 8UD
020 7348 8000
UKMediaOffice@aol.com
Web browser

RealNetworks
2nd Floor, 32 Brook Street
London W1K 5DL
020 7290 1206
public_relations@real.com
www.real.co.uk
Audio and video

Symantec UK
Hines Meadow, St Cloud Way
Maidenhead, Berkshire SL6 8XD
01628 592365
Senior PR manager, Europe:
lmillington@symantec.com
www.symantec.com
Anti-virus

Main ISPs

AOL UK
80 Hammersmith Road
London W14 8UD
020 7348 8000
UKMediaOffice@aol.com
www.aol.co.uk

British Telecom
BT Centre, 81 Newgate Street
London EC1A 7AJ
020 7356 5000
www.bt.com

Claranet
Vinery Court, 50 Banner Street
London EC1Y 8TX
020 7903 3310
marketing@clara.net
www.clara.net

Demon
322 Regents Park Road
Finchley, London N3 2QQ
0845 270 0660
enquiries@demon.net
www.demon.net

Easynet
1 Brick Lane, London E1 6PU
Press: 020 7900 4444
www.easynet.net

Entanet
Stafford Park 6, Telford
Shropshire TF3 3AT
Press: 0870 770 4996
marketing@entagroup.com
www.enta.net

Nildram
1 Triangle Business Park
Stoke Mandeville
Buckinghamshire HP22 5BD
0800 197 1490
info@nildram.net
www.nildram.net

NTL UK
NTL House
Bartley Wood Business Park
Hook, Hampshire RG27 9UP
01256 752000
www.ntl.com

One.Tel
3rd Floor, Building 1
Chiswick Park High Road
London W4 5BY
020 7181 9991
marketing@onetel.co.uk
www.onetel.co.uk

Pipex
Pipex House, 4 Falcon Gate
Shire Park
Welwyn Garden City AL7 1TW
0845 077 2537
www.pipex.co.uk

PlusNet Technologies
Technology Building
Terry Street, Sheffield S9 2BU
0845 140 0200
www.Plus.net

Surfanytime
38 Queen Street
Glasgow G1 3DX
0870 141 7113
www.surfanytime.co.uk

Telewest
Unit 1, Genesis Business Park
Albert Way, Woking
Surrey GU21 3RW
Press: 020 7299 5888
www.telewest.co.uk

Tiscali UK
20 Broadwick Street
London W1F 8HT
Press: 020 7087 2115
www.tiscali.co.uk

Virgin.net
The Communications Building
48 Leicester Square
London WC2H 7LT
020 7664 6216
support@virgin.net
www.virgin.net

Vispa Internet
The Courtyard, 160a Moss Lane
Altrincham, Cheshire WA15 8AU
0870 1624 888
info@vispa.net
www.vispa.co.uk

Wanadoo
PO Box 73, Leeds LS10 1WZ
020 7553 7566
mediaqueries@freeserve.com
www.wanadoo.co.uk

Yahoo! UK
10 Ebury Bridge Road
London SW1W 8PZ
Press: 020 7808 4242
agency@uk.yahoo-inc.com
www.yahoo.co.uk

Main telecoms companies

British Telecom
BT Centre, 81 Newgate Street
PO Box 163, London EC1A 7AJ
Press: 020 7356 5000
www.bt.com

Cable and Wireless
124 Theobald's Road
Holborn, London WC1X 8RX
Press: 01908 845000
peter.eustace@cw.com
www.cableandwireless.co.uk

Colt
Beaufort House, 15 St Botolph Street
London EC3A 7QN
020 7863 5000
info@colt.net
www.colt.co.uk

Energis
Energis House, Forbury Road
Reading, Berkshire RG1 3JH
020 7206 5555
www.energis.co.uk

Hutchinson 3G UK
27b Floral Street, Covent Garden
London WC2E 9DP
020 7010 9312
www.three.co.uk

Kingston Communications
Carr Lane
Kingston upon Hull HU1 3RE
01482 602711
info.marketing@kcom.com
www.kcom.com

MCI WorldCom
Reading International Business Park
Basingstoke Road
Reading, Berkshire RG2 6DA
Press: 0118 905 5000
ukpressoffice@lists.mci.com
www1.worldcom.com/uk

mmO2
Wellington Street, Slough SL1 1YP
Press: 01753 628000
media@o2.co.uk
www.mmo2.co.uk

NTL UK
NTL House
Bartley Wood Business Park
Hook, Hampshire RG27 9UP
01256 752000
www.ntl.com

Orange
St James Court, Great Park Road
Almondsbury, Bristol BS32 4QJ
07973 100 150
www.orange.co.uk

Telewest
Unit 1, Genesis Business Park
Albert Way, Woking
Surrey GU21 3RW
Press: 020 7299 5888
www.telewest.co.uk

Thus
1/2 Berkley Square
99 Berkley Street, Glasgow G3 7HR
0141 567 1234
marketing@thus.net
www.thus.net

T-Mobile (UK)
Hatfield Business Park
Hatfield, Hertfordshire Al10 9BW
Press: 07017 150150
www.t-mobile.co.uk

Virgin Mobile
5th Floor, Communication Building
48 Leicester Square
London WC2H 7LT
Press: 0845 600 6272
www.virginmobile.com

Vodafone
Vodafone House
The Connection, Newbury
Berkshire RG14 2FN
0700 050 0100
www.vodafone.co.uk

UK news online

Ananova
Marshall Mill, Marshall Street
Leeds LS11 9YJ
0113 367 4600
www.ananova.com

bbc.co.uk
Bush House, The Strand
London WC2B 4PH
020 8743 8000
www.bbc.co.uk

Belfast Telegraph
Independent News and Media (Northern Ireland), Internet Department
124–144 Royal Avenue
Belfast BT1 1EB
028 9026 4000
www.belfasttelegraph.co.uk

FT
One Southwark Bridge
London SE1 9H2
020 7873 3000
joanna.manning-cooper@ft.com
www.ft.com

Guardian Unlimited
3–7 Ray Street, London EC1R 3DR
020 7278 2332
editor@guardianunlimited.co.uk
www.guardian.co.uk

The Independent
Independent House
191 Marsh Wall, London E14 9RS
020 7005 2000
www.independent.co.uk

ITN
200 Grays Inn Road
London WC1X 8X2
020 7430 4700
editor@itn.co.uk
www.itn.co.uk

Online Mirror
MGN, 1 Canada Square
Canary Wharf, London E14 5AP
020 7293 3000
www.mirror.co.uk

Reuters
85 Fleet Street, London EC4P 4AJ
020 7250 1122
simon.walker@reuters.com
www.reuters.co.uk

The Scotsman
Barclay House, 108 Holyrood Road
Edinburgh EH8 8AS
0131 620 8620
enquiries@scotsman.com
www.scotsman.com

The Sun Online
Level 6, 1 Virginia Street
London E98 1SN
020 7782 4000
corporate.info@the-sun.co.uk
www.thesun.co.uk

Telegraph
1 Canada Square
Canary Wharf, London E14 5DT
020 7538 5000
corporate.affairs@telegraph.co.uk
www.telegraph.co.uk

The Times
1 Pennington Street
Wapping, London E98 1TA
020 7782 5000
online.editor@thetimes.co.uk
www.timesonline.co.uk

High-profile online traders

Miscellaneous

Amazon UK
Patriot Court 1–9, The Grove
Slough, Berkshire SL1 1QP
Press: 020 8636 9280
www.amazon.co.uk
Books

eBay UK
pressenquiries@joepublicrelations.co.uk
www.ebay.co.uk
Auction

Friends Reunited
Press: 020 7734 1965
www.friendsreunited.co.uk

Groceries

Iceland
Second Avenue
Deeside Industrial Park, Deeside
Flintshire CH5 2NW
Press: 01244 842941
www.iceland.co.uk
Groceries frozen

Ocado
Titan Court, 3 Bishop Square
Hatfield Business Park
Hatfield AL10 9NE
01707 228000
news@ocado.com
www.ocado.com
http://corporate.ocado.com
Online supermarket service in partnership with Waitrose

J Sainsbury
33 Holborn, London EC1N 2HT
020 7695 7295
media.office@sainsburys.co.uk
www.j-sainsbury.co.uk

Tesco
New Tesco House, Delamare Road
Cheshunt, Hertford EN8 9SL
01992 644645
www.tesco.com

Travel

Ebookers
25 Farringdon Street
London EC4A 4AB
0870 010 7000
consumer & trade PR: 020 7958 3784
corporate & financial PR: 020 7489 2239
www.ebookers.com

Expedia UK
7 Soho Square, London W1D 3QB
Press: 020 7009 2806
expediapressoffice@expedia.co.uk
www.expedia.co.uk

Lastminute.com
4 Buckingham Gate
London SW1E 6JP
0871 222 3200
investor relations: 020 7802 4200
www.lastminute.com

Travelocity UK
0870 111 7080
UK PR: 020 7907 7130
travelocity@travelocity.com
UK PR: debbi@exposureltd.com
www.travelocity.co.uk

Banking

Egg
1 Waterhouse Square
138–142 Holborn
London EC1N 2NA
Press: 020 7526 2600
prteam@egg.com
www.egg.com

First Direct
40 Wakefield Road
Leeds LS98 1FD
020 7992 1571
www.firstdirect.com

Intelligent Finance
8 Lockside Ave, Edinburgh Park
South Gyle, Edinburgh EH12 9DJ
Press: 0131 658 2301
www.if.com

Smile
PO Box 600, Delf House
Skelmsdale, Lancashire
Press: 0161 8294252
www.smile.com

New media bodies

Association of Freelance Internet Designers
www.afid.net

Association of Online Publishers (AOP)
Queens House, 28 Kingsway
London WC2B 6JR
020 7400 7510
alex.white@ukaop.org.uk
www.ukaop.org.uk

British Interactive Media Association
Briarlea House, Southend Road
South Green, Billericay CM11 2PR
01277 658107
Press: 01932 706810
info@bima.co.uk
Press: katy.howell@immediatefuture.co.uk
www.bima.co.uk

British Internet Publishers Alliance (BIPA)
49 Park Town
Oxford OX2 6SL
01865 310732
www.bipa.co.uk

Entertainment and Leisure Software Publishers Association
167 Wardour Street
London W1F 8WL
020 7534 0580
www.elspa.com

HTML Writers Guild/ International Webmasters Association
119 E Union Street, Suite F
Pasadena, CA 91103 USA
+1 626 449 3709
membership-questions@hwg.org
www.hwg.org

Interactive Advertising Bureau
The Media Centre
131–151 Great Tichfield Street
London W1W 5BB
Press: 020 7886 8282
secretariat@iabuk.net
www.iabuk.net

Internet Corporation for Assigned Names and Numbers (ICANN)
www.icann.org

Internet Service Providers Association
23 Palace Street
London SW1E 5HW
020 7233 7234
admin@ispa.org.uk
www.ispa.org.uk

London Internet Exchange (Linx)
2nd Floor, Geneva House
3 Park Road, Peterborough PE1 2UX
Press: 01733 207700
www.linx.net

NetMedia
info@net-media.co.uk
www.net-media.co.uk

New media trade press

3G Mobile (informa UK)
Informa Telecoms Group
Mortimer House
37–41 Mortimer Street
London W1T 3JH
Press: 020 7017 5000
press@informa.com
www.telecoms.com
23pa

Computer Weekly
Quadrant House, The Quadrant
Sutton, Surrey SM2 5AS
020 8652 3500
editorial@computerweekly.com
www.computerweekly.co.uk
Weekly

Computing
VNU Business Publications
VNU House, 32–34 Broadwick Street
London W1A 2HG
Switchboard: 020 7316 9000
www.computing.co.uk
Weekly

Content Management Focus
Ark Publishing
86–88 Upper Richmond Road
Putney, London SW15 2UR
020 8785 2700
cmfocus@ark-group.com
www.cmfocus.com
10pa

IT Europa
656 The Crescent
Colchester Business Park
Colchester CO4 9YQ
01206 224400
contact@iteuropa.com
www.iteuropa.com
20pa

New Media Age
Centaur Communications
St Giles House, 50 Poland Street
London W1F 7AX
020 7970 4000
michael.nutley@centaur.co.uk
www.newmediazero.com
Weekly

The Online Reporter
Information Express
PO Box 2077, Verney Park
Buckingham MK18 1WQ
01280 820560
simon@g2news.com
www.g2news.com
Weekly

The Register
www.theregister.co.uk
Website

Revolution
Haymarket Business Publications
174 Hammersmith Road
London W6 7JP
020 8267 4947
donlawrencejones@haynet.com
www.revolutionmagazine.com
Monthly

VNUnet.com
VDU House, 32–34 Broadwick Street
London W1A 2HG
020 7316 9725
www.vnunet.com
Website

World Telemedia
Network for Online Commerce Services
Tulip House
70 Borough High Street
London SE1 1XF
0870 7327327
info@noconline.org
www.noconline.org
Quarterly

ZDNet UK and Silicon.com
International House
1 St Katherines Way
London E1W 1UN
020 7903 6800
silicon.marketing@silicon.com
www.silicon.com
www.zdnet.co.uk
Website

Books

There is encouraging growth in the publishing industry. According to the Books and Consumer survey for 2003, book sales are up on the previous year — and they are worth more too. True, 2003 was a Potter year – Harry Potter and the Order of the Phoenix dominated bestseller charts throughout the second half of the period, selling a staggering 1.7 million copies in its first day alone – but the total number of books sold grew from 273 million to 286 million, and would have grown even if Potter was taken out of the figures. Even more encouraging is the value of those books: £2.17bn in 2003, up 8 per cent on the previous year – or a 5 per cent growth if, again, you discount Potter.

But ah, that word. "Discount" is exactly what booksellers have been doing, and even Potter is not immune. The Books and Consumer figures show that, over the past four years, some 45 per cent of books have been sold at a discount against the recommended retail price; the statistic will surprise no one who has walked into a bookshop and been tempted by a three-for-two offer. Harry Potter and the Order of the Phoenix, for example, was reported to be on sale at discounts of 30 per cent in its first two weeks; this led the editor of the Bookseller, Nicholas Clee, to remark in the Guardian that had they all been sold at full price, they would have made publisher Bloomsbury some £20m more. The practice remains as controversial as ever: it helps larger booksellers to dominate the market, selling more books at a lower average price; and it squeezes the royalties of authors who have discount clauses in their contracts – so attracting criticism from top agents such as Jonny Geller.

Pottermania: staff guard boxes of books in 2003

The controversy does not end there. Partly thanks to the proliferation in discounting, some booksellers now say that recommended prices should no longer be printed on books at all. The move would be popular with buyers of Christmas presents, of course, and catastrophic for sales of permanent marker pens – but in other ways the advantages are mixed. It would not benefit the heaviest discounters, because they use the recommended prices to plug their own price cuts. And authors don't like it much either: apart from their discount clauses, they try to tie their royalties as far as possible to the higher, recommended price. Writing in the Guardian in March 2004, the author Philip Pullman said that such a move would be disastrous. "The book trade needs to nurture those who produce the books," he wrote, "because without us, the whole edifice would collapse."

As far as publishers are concerned, meanwhile, the rise in book sales has been accompanied by a consolidation of purchasing power into ever bigger firms. The big four of Random House, Penguin, HarperCollins and Hodder Headline have carved larger than ever market shares, according to Nielsen BookScan, with Bloomsbury just behind them, buoyed by the success of two of the industry's most recent publishing phenomena, Schott's Original Miscellany and Harry Potter. Even among these publishers, there has been consolidation: in January 2004 HarperCollins closed its literary imprint Flamingo, merging it with Fourth Estate. Among the upmarket bookselling chains, meanwhile, Ottakar's bought out medium-sized rival Hammick's.

In January 2004, it appeared that the good news on book sales might soon get even better: the number of books sold in that month were 66 per cent up on 2003, according to the CBI.

Bestsellers

So what were the success stories of the year? Harry Potter and the Order of the Phoenix was a predictable front-runner, but after that, the big winners were harder to pick. Eats, Shoots and Leaves, a paean to correct punctuation by the journalist Lynne Truss, published by Canongate, struck a nerve among pedantic booklovers everywhere, to become the "Schott's" of 2003. The autobiography of England's football captain David Beckham – who received a £2m advance from HarperCollins – did well at the beginning of the 2003–04 football season; but it faded sharply as Rugby World Cup fever took hold, making Martin Johnson's own volume the stocking-filler of choice for sport-loving dads. Novelist

Guardian Fastsellers 2003

	Title	Genre	Author	Imprint	RRP	Total	Gross
1	Dr Atkins' New Diet Revolution	Diet (B)	Robert Atkins	Vermilion	£7.99	1,145,713	£9.2m
2	The Summons	Thriller (A)	John Grisham	Arrow	£6.99	1,102,278	£7.7m
3	Quentins	Novel (A)	Maeve Binchy	Orion	£6.99	909,413	£6.4m
4	The Lovely Bones	Novel (A+B)	Alice Sebold	Picador	£7.99	797,536	£6.4m
5	Life of Pi	Novel (B)	Yann Martel	Canongate	£7.99	775,499	£6.2m
6	Angels	Chick lit (B)	Marian Keyes	Penguin	£6.99	626,511	£4.4m
7	Can You Keep a Secret	Chick lit (B)	Sophie Kinsella	Black Swan	£6.99	563,642	£3.9m
8	Man and Wife	Novel (B)	Tony Parsons	HCF	£6.99	550,155	£3.8m
9	I Don't Know How She Does It	Novel (B)	Allison Pearson	Vintage	£6.99	513,200	£3.6m
10	No.1 Ladies' Detective Agency	Novel (B)	Alexander McCall Smith	Abacus	£6.99	507,355	£3.5m

For current bestsellers list, see guardian.co.uk/books

Mark Haddon, for his part, had spectacular success with his Whitbread prizewinning book, The Curious Incident of the Dog in the Night-time, published by Cape.

Book events

2003, of course, was the year of the Big Read. The BBC's much-hyped attempt to get the population reading, while increasing its own Saturday-night ratings in the process, was a success. Twenty-one books competed in a phone-in vote to decide Britain's Best-Loved Book (winner: The Lord of the Rings). The event led to increased sales for the books, each of which received a half-hour plug from celebrities as diverse as Meera Syal and William Hague; and also led to an increase in the number of book groups around the country.

Other prominent events did their bit: World Book Day books went straight to the top of the bestseller charts in March; Lit Idol, won by Canadian writer Paul Cavanagh, dominated headlines from the London Book Fair; while a new literary prize was announced, the £10,000 Orange Award for New Writers, which will be awarded for the first time in 2005. Better send off that manuscript now.

The Big Read: final table	
1	The Lord of the Rings, JRR Tolkien
2	Pride and Prejudice, Jane Austen
3	His Dark Materials, Philip Pullman
4	The Hitchhiker's Guide to the Galaxy, Douglas Adams
5	Harry Potter and the Goblet of Fire, JK Rowling
6	To Kill a Mockingbird, Harper Lee
7	Winnie the Pooh, AA Milne
8	Nineteen Eighty-Four, George Orwell
9	The Lion, the Witch and the Wardrobe, CS Lewis
10	Jane Eyre, Charlotte Brontë
11	Catch-22, Joseph Heller
12	Wuthering Heights, Emily Brontë
13	Birdsong, Sebastian Faulks
14	Rebecca, Daphne du Maurier
15	The Catcher in the Rye, JD Salinger
16	The Wind in the Willows, Kenneth Grahame
17	Great Expectations, Charles Dickens
18	Little Women, Louisa May Alcott
19	Captain Corelli's Mandolin, Louis de Bernieres
20	War and Peace, Leo Tolstoy
21	Gone with the Wind, Margaret Mitchell

www.bbc.co.uk/arts/bigread

"The book trade needs to nurture those who produce the books, because without us, the whole edifice would collapse"

Philip Pullman

Major rights deals, 2003–04				
July 03	Vikram Seth	Two Lives, literary memoir	Little, Brown	£1.4m
July 03	Paul Burrell	A Royal Duty	Penguin	£1.3m
August 03	David Beckham	My Side	HarperCollins	£2m
October 03	Ricky Tomlinson	autobiography	Little, Brown	£850,000
December 03	Philip Kerr	The Children of the Lamp	DreamWorks	seven figures
January 04	Louise Rennison	Two-book deal	HarperCollins	"substantial six-figure sum"
February 04	Peter Robinson	Four-book deal	Hodder & Stoughton	£1.4m
March 04	Zadie Smith	Two-book deal	Hamish Hamilton	unknown

Awards

British book awards 2004
www.britishbookawards.com
- *Imprint of the year:* Abacus
- *Small publisher of the year:* Profile
- *Bookseller of the year:* Ottakar's

Orange prize 2004
www.orangeindex.co.uk/2004prize/
- Small Island, by Andrea Levy (Review)

Lit Idol 2004
- Paul Cavanagh

Man Booker prize 2003
www.bookerprize.co.uk
- Vernon God Little, by DBC Pierre (Faber & Faber)

Guardian first book award 2003
http://books.guardian.co.uk/firstbook2003
- Mountains of the Mind, by Robert Macfarlane (Granta)

Guardian children's fiction prize 2003
http://books.guardian.co.uk/guardianchildrensprize2003
- The Curious Incident of the Dog in the Night-time, by Mark Haddon (David Fickling)

Whitbread awards 2003
www.whitbread-bookawards.co.uk
- *Book of the year:* The Curious Incident of the Dog in the Night-time, by Mark Haddon (David Fickling)
- *First novel:* Vernon God Little, by DBC Pierre (Faber & Faber)
- *Biography:* Orwell, The Life by DJ Taylor (Chatto Windus) Children's: The Fire-Eaters by David Almond (Hodder Children's)
- *Poetry:* Landing Light by Don Paterson (Faber and Faber)

Out from the crowd **Toby Mundy**

In an effort to dismiss the idea that publishing is a profession, the critic and editor Raymond Mortimer once described it as "at once an art, a craft and a business". His depiction seems as true today as it did when he said it nearly 50 years ago. But what is it that publishers actually do? What does it mean "to publish" a book?

The word to publish, of course, has its origin in the Latin *publicare*, to make public. But in 2005 it also describes the method by which a new book is differentiated from the other 119,000-odd titles that will be published this year. To publish a book effectively is to find a way to distinguish it from the avalanche of competition – and so attract the attention and money of booksellers and consumers.

But how does a publisher make a book stand out? When the book buyer is faced with such superabundance, when more and more handsomely produced books are published than ever before, how does a publisher, acting on behalf on the author, ensure that the author's book is the one that is noticed?

The task becomes slightly less daunting when one realises that the book trade and the media – and the support of both is usually crucial to the success of a book – respond best to books that fall into one of two categories: the Original and the Proven.

Originality comes in many forms: it could describe something about the book's subject matter, or the way that subject matter is addressed. It could describe the author's relationship to her themes, or something about the author herself. Wherever these points of originality are, the publisher's job is to work with the author to find them and then to communicate them effectively to the three groups that hold the destiny of a book in their hands: the bookseller, the media and, through the media, the public.

There is also the Proven. Authors can be proven (think John Grisham, but also David Beckham), as can plots (hapless 20something woman searches the city for love) and genre (science fiction, for example). Because the media is so hungry for novelty, it is harder to persuade it to get excited about proven plots and genre. But the print media loves proven authors, who adorn the interviews and features pages like movie stars. Publishers, meanwhile, work to try and find the tipping point for a book, the moment when its sales surge upwards driven by word-of-mouth recommendation. At this point, literary alchemy takes place that transforms an original author into a proven seller. Such a writer then becomes, as they say in Hollywood, bankable.

The publisher's job is to construct a narrative about the book that foregrounds the degree to which it is either original or proven. But that narrative is not simply what we say about a work. It also describes its look and feel: is the book published in an appealing shape, with an arresting jacket, at a surprisingly attractive price? Does the blurb sing? These are all publishing decisions – that is, decisions made in order to make the book more prominent, which in turn one hopes will maximise its sales.

All publishers are optimists, and most believe that good writing, if genuinely original, can find its way to the surface of public consciousness. But it is also true that bad publishing – poor decisions about price, format and jacket design, allied to false or hyperbolic declarations about the book's strengths – can hobble a writer's chances. At which point, the publisher has failed.

Toby Mundy is the managing director and publisher of Atlantic Books

Books Contacts

A&C Black (Publishers)
(see Bloomsbury Publishing)

AA Publishing
The Automobile Association
14th Floor, Fanum House
Basingstoke, Hampshire RG21 4EA
01256 491519
ian.harvey@theaa.com
www.theaa.co.uk
Maps, atlases and guidebooks

Abacus
(see Time Warner Books)

ABC-Clio
26 Beaumont Street
Oxford OX1 2NP
01865 517222
salesuk@abc-clio.com
www.abc-clio.com
Academic and general reference

Absolute Press
Scarborough House
29 James Street West
Bath BA1 2BT
01225 316013
info@absolutepress.co.uk
www.absolutepress.co.uk
Non-fiction

Abson Books London
5 Sidney Square
London E1 2EY
020 7790 4737
absonbooks@aol.com
Language glossaries

Acair
7 James Street, Stornoway
Isle of Lewis HS1 2QN
01851 703020
enquiries@acairbooks.com
www.acairbooks.com
Scottish history and culture, Gaelic

Acumen Publishing
15A Lewins Yard, East Street
Chesham
Buckinghamshire HP5 1HQ
01494 794398
steven.gerrard@
acumenpublishing.co.uk
www.acumenpublishing.co.uk
Philosophy, history and politics

Addison-Wesley
(see Pearson Education)

African Books Collective
The Jam Factory
27 Park End Street
Oxford OX1 1HU
01865 726686
abc@africanbookscollective.com
www.africanbookscollective.com

Age Concern England
1268 London Road
London SW16 4ER
020 8765 7200
media@ace.org.uk
www.ageconcern.org.uk

Aidan Ellis Publishing
Whinfield, Herbert Road
Salcombe, South Devon TQ8 8HN
01548 842755
mail@aidanellispublishing.co.uk
www.aepub.demon.co.uk
General publishing and non-fiction

Albatross Publishing
The Coach House, Grange Court
Grange Road, Tongham
Surrey GU10 1DW
01252 781994
sbutler@z-guides.com
www.z-guides.com
Reference and non-fiction

Allen & Unwin
(see Orion Publishing Group)

Allen Lane
(see Penguin Books)

Allison & Busby
Suite 111, Bon Marche Centre
241 Ferndale Road
London SW9 8BJ
020 7738 7888
all@alisonandbusby.com
www.alisonandbusby.com
Crime; literary fiction and non-fiction

Allyn & Bacon
(see Pearson Education)

Amber Lane Press
Cheorl House, Church Street
Charlbury, Oxfordshire OX7 3PR
01608 810024
jamberlane@aol.com
www.amberlanepress.co.uk
Plays and theatre

Andersen Press
20 Vauxhall Bridge Road
London SW1V 2SA
020 7840 8701
andersenpress@randomhouse.co.uk
www.andersenpress.co.uk
Children's books and fiction

Anness Publishing
Hermes House
88–89 Blackfriars Road
London SE1 8HA
020 7401 2077
sbaldwin@anness.com
General non-fiction

Anthem Press
(see Wimbledon Publishing Press)

Antique Collectors' Club
Sandy Lane, Old Martlesham
Woodbridge, Suffolk IP12 4SD
01394 389950
sales@antique-acc.com
www.antique-acc.com

Anvil Press Poetry
Neptune House
70 Royal Hill, London SE10 8RF
020 8469 3033
anvil@anvilpresspoetry.com
www.anvilpresspoetry.com

APA Publications
58 Borough High Street
London SE1 1XF
020 7403 0284
berlitz@apaguide.co.uk
www.berlitzpublishing.co.uk
Owned by Langenscheidt Publishing Group. Travel and languages. Imprint: Berlitz Publishing

Appletree Press
The Old Potato Station
14 Howard Street South
Belfast BT7 1AP
028 9024 3074
reception@appletree.ie
www.appletree.ie
Cookery and Celtic interest

Arc Publications
Nanholme Mill, Shaw Wood Road
Todmorden
Lancashire OL14 6DA
01706 812338
info@arcpublications.co.uk
www.arcpublications.co.uk
Contemporary poetry

Arcadia Books
15–16 Nassau Street
London W1W 7AB
020 7436 9898
arc.publications@btconnect.com
www.arcadiabooks.co.uk
Literary fiction, biography, gender studies and travel

Architectural Association Publications
36 Bedford Square
London WC1B 3ES
020 7887 4000
publications@aaschool.ac.uk
www.aaschool.info/publications/
Publishing arm of Architectural Association School of Architecture

Arcturus Publishing
26/27 Bickels Yard
151–153 Bermondsey Street
London SE1 3HA
020 7407 9400
info@arcturuspublishing.com
www.arcturuspublishing.com
Non-fiction

Arrow
(see Random House Group)

Ashgate Publishing
Gower House, Croft Road
Aldershot, Hampshire GU11 3HR
01252 331551
info@ashgatepublishing.com
www.ashgate.com
Social sciences, humanities, art & professional

Ashgrove Publishing
55 Richmond Avenue
London N1 0LX
020 7831 5013
gmo73@dial.pipex.com
www.ashgrovepublishing.com
Owned by Hollydata Publishers
Mind, body & spirit

Ashley Drake Publishing
PO Box 733, Cardiff CF14 2YX
029 2069 1282
post@ashleydrake.com
www.ashleydrake.com
Imprints: Welsh Academic Press (academic titles in English); St David's Press (general trade); Y Ddraig Fach (children's books in Welsh); Gwasg Addysgol Cymru (educational in Welsh)

Ashmolean Museum Publications
(see Oxford University)

Atlantic Books
Ormond House
26–27 Boswell Street
London WC1N 3JZ
020 7269 1610
enquiries@groveatlantic.co.uk
www.groveatlantic.co.uk
Literary fiction, non-fiction and reference. Imprints: Guardian Books, Observer Books

Atom
(see Time Warner Books)

Aurum Press
25 Bedford Avenue
London WC1B 3AT
020 7637 3225
editorial@aurumpress.co.uk
www.aurumpress.co.uk
Non-fiction

Australian Consolidated Press UK
Moulton Park Business Centre
Red House Road, Moulton Park
Northampton NN3 6AQ
01604 497531
acpukltd@aol.com
Home interest

Authentic Media
9 Holdom Avenue, Bletchley
Milton Keynes MK1 1QR
01908 364200
info@authenticmedia.co.uk
www.authenticmedia.co.uk
Imprints: Authentic (Christian life); Paternoster (academic and theological titles and theses)

Autumn Publishing
Appledram Barns
Birdham Road, Near Chichester
West Sussex PO20 7EQ
01243 531660
autumn@autumnpublishing.co.uk
www.autumnpublishing.co.uk
Early learning. Imprint: Byeway Books

Award Publications
1st Floor, 27 Longford Street
London NW1 3DZ
020 7388 7800
info@awardpublications.co.uk
Children's fiction and reference. Imprint: Horus Editions

Axis Publishing
8C Accommodation Road
London NW11 8ED
020 8731 8080
wallace@axispublishing.co.uk
www.axispublishing.co.uk
Health and sport

Bantam/Bantam Press
(see Random House Group)

Barefoot Books
124 Walcot Street
Bath BA1 5BG
01225 322400
info@barefootbooks.co.uk
www.barefootbooks.com
Children's picture books

Barny Books
The Cottage, Hough on the Hill
Near Grantham
Lincolnshire NG32 2BB
01400 250246/ 01522 790009
Children's books, adult fiction and non-fiction

Barrington Stoke
Sandeman House, Trunks Close
55 High Street
Edinburgh EH1 1SR
0131 557 2020
info@barringtonstoke.co.uk
www.barringtonstoke.co.uk
Remedial children's reading

Batsford
(see Chrysalis Books)

BBC Bookshop
PO Box 308, Sittingbourne
Kent ME9 8LW
0870 241 5490
bbcshop@bbc.co.uk
www.bbcshop.com

Beaumont Publishing (London)
Grosvenor House, 1 High Street
Edgware, Middlesex HA8 7TA
020 8951 1700
info@beaumont-publishing.com
www.beaumont-publishing.co.uk
Educational materials

Benjamin Cummings
(see Pearson Education)

Bentwyck Henry Publishers
36 Hart Street
Henley-On-Thames
Oxfordshire RG9 2AU
01491 413100
bentwyckhenrybks@aol.com
www.bentwyckhenry.co.uk
General non-fiction and fiction

Berg Publishers
1st Floor Angel Court
81 St Clements Street
Oxford OX4 1AW
01865 245104
enquiry@bergpublishers.com
www.bergpublishers.com
Various academic. Imprint: Oswald Wolff Books

Berghahn Books
3 Newtec Place, Magdalen Road
Oxford OX4 1RE
01865 250011
editorialuk@berghahnbooks.com
www.berghahnbooks.com
Academic books and journals

BFI Publishing
British Film Institute
21 Stephen Street
London W1T 1LN
020 7255 1444
publishing@bfi.org.uk
www.bfi.org.uk/books
Part of the British Film Institute

BFP Books
Focus House, 497 Green Lanes
London N13 4BP
020 8882 3315
info@thebfp.com
www.thebfp.com/home.html
Publishing arm of the Bureau of Freelance Photographers

BIOS Scientific Publishers
(see T&F Informa)

Birlinn
West Newington House
10 Newington Road
Edinburgh EH9 1QS
0131 668 4371
info@birlinn.co.uk
www.birlinn.co.uk
History and folklore

Black & White Publishing
99 Giles Street, Edinburgh EH6 6BZ
0131 625 4500
mail@blackandwhitepublishing.com
www.blackandwhitepublishing.com
General fiction and non-fiction

Black Spring Press
Burbage House, 83–85 Curtain Road
London EC2A 3BS
020 7613 3066
general@blackspringpress.co.uk
Fiction and non-fiction

Black Swan
(see Random House Group)

Blackie & Co Publishers
107–111 Fleet Street
London EC4A 2AB
020 7936 9021
editors@blackiepublishers.com
www.blackiepublishers.com
Fiction and non-fiction

Blackstaff Press
4c Heron Wharf
Sydenham Business Park
Belfast BT3 9LE
028 9045 5006
marketing@blackstaffpress.com
www.blackstaffpress.com
Fiction, non-fiction and poetry

Blackwell Publishing
108 Cowley Road
Oxford OX4 1JF
01865 791100
www.blackwellpublishing.com
Journals and textbooks

Bloodaxe Books
Highgreen, Tarset
Northumberland NE48 1RP
01434 240500
bloodaxepublicity@yahoo.co.uk
www.bloodaxebooks.com
Poetry

Bloomsbury Publishing
38 Soho Square
London W1D 3HB
020 7494 2111
www.bloomsbury.com
Adult and children's fiction and non-fiction (including Harry Potter)

A&C Black (Publishers)
Alderman House, 37 Soho Square
London W1D 3QZ
020 7758 0200
enquiries@acblack.com
www.acblack.com
Reference and non-fiction; Writers' and Artists' Yearbook

BMJ Books
BMA House, Tavistock Square
London WC1H 9JR
020 7383 6245
orders@bmjbooks.com
www.bmjbooks.com
Part of the British Medical Journal Publishing Group. Clinical medicine

The Bodley Head
(see Random House Group)

Book Guild
Temple House, 25 High Street
Lewes, East Sussex BN7 2LU
01273 472534
info@bookguild.co.uk
www.bookguild.co.uk
Fiction and non-fiction

Boulevard Books & The Babel Guides
71 Lytton Road, Oxford OX4 3NY
01865 712931
raybabel@dircon.co.uk
www.babelguides.com
Contemporary world fiction and guides

Bowker
Farringdon House, Wood Street
East Grinstead
West Sussex RH19 1UZ
01342 310450
worldcustserv@bowker.com
www.bowker.co.uk
Part of the Cambridge Information Group (CIG). Reference and biography

Boydell & Brewer
PO Box 9, Woodbridge
Suffolk IP12 3DF
01394 610600
boydell@boydell.co.uk
www.boydell.co.uk
Non-fiction, principally medieval studies

Boxtree
(see Macmillan Publishers)

Bradt Travel Guides
19 High Street, Chalfont St Peter
Buckinghamshire SL9 9QE
01753 893444
info@bradt-travelguides.com
www.bradtguides.com
Travel guides

Brasseys
(see Chrysalis Books)

Breedon Books Publishing Co
Breedon House, 3 Parker Centre
Mansfield Road, Derby DE21 4SZ
01332 384235
sales@breedonpublishing.co.uk
www.breedonbooks.co.uk
Local history and heritage, sport

Breese Books
10 Hanover Crescent, Brighton
East Sussex BN2 9SB
01273 687555
mbreese999@aol.com
www.sherlockholmes.net,
www.abracadabra.co.uk,
www.martinbreese.com
Conjuring books and Sherlock Holmes pastiches

British Academy
10 Carlton House Terrace
London SW1Y 5AH
020 7969 5200
secretary@britac.ac.uk
www.britac.ac.uk

British Library
96 Euston Road
London NW1 2DB
020 7412 7469
blpublications@bl.uk
www.bl.uk

British Museum Press
46 Bloomsbury Street
London WC1B 3QQ
020 7323 1234
customerservices@britishmuseum.co.uk
www.britishmuseum.co.uk

Brooklands Books
PO Box 146, Cobham
Surrey KT11 1LG
01932 865051
sales@brooklands-books.com
www.brooklands-books.com
Motoring titles and technical catalogues

Brown Watson
The Old Mill, 76 Fleckney Road
Kibworth Beauchamp
Leicestershire LE8 0HG
0116 279 6333
books@brownwatson.co.uk
www.brownwatson.co.uk
General children's interest

Brown, Son & Ferguson
4–10 Darnley Street
Glasgow G41 2SD
0141 429 1234
info@skipper.co.uk
www.skipper.co.uk
Nautical textbooks and Scottish plays

Browntrout Publishers
Redland Office Centre
157 Redland Road
Redland, Bristol BS6 6YE
0117 973 9191
sales@browntroutuk.com
www.browntrout.com
Fine art and photography products

Brunner-Routledge
(see T&F Informa)

Bryntirion Press
Bryntirion, Bridgend
Mid-Glamorgan CF31 4DX
01656 655886
office@emw.org.uk
www.emw.org.uk
Owned by the Evangelical Movement of Wales. Christian books in English and Welsh

Business Education Publishers
The Teleport, Doxford International
Sunderland, Tyne & Wear SR3 3XD
0191 525 2410
info@bepl.com
www.bepl.com

Butterworth
(see Reed Elsevier)

C Hurst & Co (Publishers)
Africa Centre, 38 King Street
Covent Garden, London WC2E 8JZ
020 7240 2666
hurst@atlas.co.uk
www.hurstpub.co.uk
Contemporary history

Cadogan Guides
Highlands House
165 The Broadway, Wimbledon
London SW19 1NE
020 8544 8053
info@cadoganguides.co.uk
www.cadoganguides.com
Owned by US firm, Morris Publications. Travel guides

Calder Publications
51 The Cut, London SE1 8LF
020 7633 0599
info@calderpublications.com
www.calderpublications.com
Formerly John Calder (Publishers)
Biography, drama, music, poetry and translations

Cambridge University Press
The Edinburgh Building
Shaftesbury Road
Cambridge CB2 2RU
01223 312393
information@cambridge.org
www.cambridge.org

Camden Press
43 Camden Passage
London N1 8EA
020 7226 4673
Social issues. Imprint: Mindfield

Campbell Books
(see Macmillan Publishers)

Canongate Books
14 High Street
Edinburgh EH1 1TE
0131 557 5111
info@canongate.co.uk
www.canongate.net
Literary fiction and non-fiction, music

Capall Bann Publishing
Auton Farm, Milverton
Somerset TA4 1NE
01823 401528
enquiries@capallbann.co.uk
www.capallbann.co.uk
British traditional works and folklore

Capstone Publishing
(see John Wiley & Sons)

Carcanet Press
4th Floor, Alliance House
30 Cross Street
Manchester M2 7AQ
0161 834 8730
pnr@carcanet.u-net.com
www.carcanet.co.uk
Poetry, academic works, literary biography, fiction in translation

Cardiff Academic Press
St Fagans Road, Fairwater
Cardiff CF5 3AE
029 2056 0333
cap@drakeed.com
www.drakeed.com/cap

Carfax
(see T&F Informa)

Carlton Publishing Group
20 Mortimer Street
London W1T 3JW
020 7612 0400
enquiries@carltonbooks.co.uk
www.carlton.com
Owned by Carlton Communications
Illustrated entertainment and leisure titles. Imprints: Carlton Books, Granada Media, Manchester United Books

Carroll & Brown Publishers
20 Lonsdale Road
London NW6 6RD
020 7372 0900
mail@carrollandbrown.co.uk
Lifestyle

Cassell Reference/Cassell Military
(see Orion Publishing Group)

Catholic Truth Society (CTS)
40–46 Harleyford Road
London SE11 5AY
020 7640 0042
editorial@cts-online.org.uk
www.cts-online.org.uk
Roman Catholic books, including Vatican documents

Causeway Press
PO Box 13, 129 New Court Way
Ormskirk, Lancashire L39 5HP
01695 576048
causeway.press@btinternet.com
Educational textbooks

Cavendish Publishing
The Glass House, Wharton Street
London WC1X 9PX
020 7278 8000
info@cavendishpublishing.com
www.cavendishpublishing.com
Academic and practitioner law books

CBA (Publishing Department)
Bowes Morrell House
111 Walmgate, York YO1 9WA
01904 671417
info@britarch.ac.uk
www.britarch.ac.uk
Publishing arm of the Council for British Archaeology. Archaeology, practical handbooks

CBD Research
Chancery House, 15 Wickham Road
Beckenham, Kent BR3 5JS
020 8650 7745
cbd@cbdresearch.com
www.cbdresearch.com
Directories

Century
(see Random House Group)

Chambers Harrap Publishers
7 Hopetoun Crescent
Edinburgh EH7 4AY
0131 556 5929
admin@chambersharrap.com
www.chambersharrap.com
Dictionaries and reference

Channel 4 Books
(see Random House Group)

Chapman Publishing
4 Broughton Place
Edinburgh EH1 3RX
0131 557 2207
chapman-pub@blueyonder.co.uk
www.chapman-pub.co.uk
Scottish writers including poetry, drama, short stories

Chartered Institute of Personnel and Development
CIPD House, Camp Road
London SW19 4UX
020 8263 3387
publish@cipd.co.uk (books) and editorial@peoplemanagement.co.uk (magazine)
www.cipd.co.uk
Part of CIPD Enterprises

Chatto & Windus
(see Random House Group)

Chicken House Publishing
2 Palmer Street, Frome
Somerset BA11 1DS
01373 454 488
chickenhouse@doublecluck.com
www.doublecluck.com
Children's fiction

Child's Play (International)
Ashworth Road, Bridgemead
Swindon, Wiltshire SN5 7YD
01793 616286
allday@childs-play.com
www.childs-play.com

Chris Andrews Publications
15 Curtis Yard, North Hinksey Lane
Oxford OX2 0LX
01865 723404
chris.andrews1@btclick.com
www.cap-ox.co.uk
Owns the Oxford Picture Library
Coffee table books, calendars and diaries

Christian Focus Publications
Geanies House, Fearn
Tain, Ross-shire IV20 1TW
01862 871011
info@christianfocus.com
www.christianfocus.com
Christian books for adults and children

Chrysalis Books
The Chrysalis Building, Bramley Road
London W10 6SP
020 7314 1400
www.chrysalisbooks.co.uk

Batsford
Specialist and technical illustrated non-fiction: embroidery, lace, chess, bridge, practical art, film and furniture

Brasseys
Military

Children's Books

Collins & Brown
Illustrated non-fiction: photography, crafts and practical arts; national magazine branded books; health, mind, body & spirit (formerly Vega)

Conway Maritime
Maritime history, ship modelling and naval

Paper Tiger
Non-fiction, illustrated: science fiction and fantasy art

Pavilion
High-end coffee table books: celebrity, lifestyle, interiors, cookery, garden, art and photography

Putnams
Aeronautical

Robson Books
Sports, humour and biography, esp. celebrity; small amount of fiction

Church Warden Publications
PO Box 420, Warminster
Wiltshire BA12 9XB
01985 840189
churchwardens@btinternet.com
Churches and heritage

Cicerone Press
2 Police Square, Milnthorpe
Cumbria LA7 7PY
01539 562069
info@cicerone.co.uk
www.cicerone.co.uk
Guidebooks for outdoor enthusiasts

Cico Books
1st Floor, 32 Great Sutton Street
London EC1V 0NB
020 7253 7960
mail@cicobooks.co.uk
Lifestyle and interiors

Cisco Press
(see Pearson Education)

Co & Bear Productions (UK)
565 Fulham Road
London SW6 1ES
020 7385 0888
bvincenzini@cobear.co.uk
www.scriptumeditions.co.uk
High quality illustrated books. Imprint: Scriptum Editions

Colin Smythe
PO Box 6, Gerrards Cross
Buckinghamshire SL9 8XA
01753 886000
sales@colinsmythe.co.uk
www.colinsmythe.co.uk
Anglo-Irish literature and criticism

Collins
(see HarperCollins Publishers)

Collins & Brown
(see Chrysalis Books)

Colourpoint Books
Colourpoint House
Jubilee Business Park
21 Jubilee Road, Newtownards
Co. Down BT23 4YH
028 9182 0505
info@colourpoint.co.uk
www.colourpoint.co.uk
School textbooks, transport, Irish interest

Compass Maps
The Coach House, Beech Court
Winford BS40 8DW
01225 445555
info@popoutmaps.com
www.mapgroup.net
Pocket-size maps and guides

Compendium Publishing
1st Floor, 43 Frith Street
London W1D 4SA
020 7287 4570
compendiumpub@aol.com
historical

Constable & Robinson
3, The Lanchesters
162 Fulham Palace Road
London W6 9ER
020 8741 3663
enquiries@constablerobinson.com
www.constablerobinson.com
Fiction and non-fiction: lifestyle, reference, children's, current affairs and politics

Continuum International Publishing Group
Tower Building, 11 York Road
London SE1 7NX
020 7922 0880
info@continuumbooks.com
www.continuumbooks.com
Academic and religious. Imprints: Athlone, Pinter, Sheffield Academic Press, Geoffrey Chapman, Mowbray, TandT Clark, Burns and Oates, Morehouse, Claridge Press

Conway Maritime
(see Chrysalis Books)

Corgi
(see Random House Group)

Countryside Books
2 Highfield Avenue
Newbury, Berkshire RG14 5DS
01635 43816
info@countrysidebooks.co.uk
www.countrysidebooks.co.uk
Local interest, walking

CRC
(see T&F Informa)

Crecy Publishing
Unit 1a, Ringway Trading Estate
Shadowmoss Road
Manchester M22 5LH
0161 499 0024
enquiries@crecy.co.uk
www.crecy.co.uk
Aviation and naval military history

Cressrelles Publishing Co
10 Station Road Industrial Estate
Colwall, Malvern
Worcestershire WR13 6RN
01684 540154
simonsmith@cressrelles4drama.fsbusiness.co.uk
Plays and theatre texts. Imprints: Actinic Press

Crowood Press
The Stable Block, Crowood Lane
Ramsbury, Marlborough
Wiltshire SN8 2HR
01672 520320
enquiries@crowood.com
www.crowood.com
Aviation, military history, country, sports, hobby and leisure pursuits

Curzon Press
(see T&F Informa)

CW Daniel Company
1 Church Path, Saffron Walden
Essex CB10 1JP
01799 521909
cwdaniel@ukonline.co.uk
www.cwdaniel.com
New Age

Dalesman Publishing Co
Stable Courtyard, Broughton Hall
Skipton, North Yorkshire BD23 3AZ
01756 701381
editorial@dalesman.co.uk
www.dalesman.co.uk
Magazines and regional books (Yorkshire, Lake District and Peak District)

Darton, Longman & Todd
1 Spencer Court
140–142 Wandsworth High Street
London SW18 4JJ
020 8875 0155
mail@darton-longman-todd.co.uk
www.darton-longman-todd.co.uk
Spirituality, theology and the Christian church

David & Charles Publishers
Brunel House, Forde Close
Newton Abbot, Devon TQ12 4PU
01626 323200
mail@davidandcharles.co.uk
www.davidandcharles.co.uk
A subsidiary of F&W (A US company) Illustrated non-fiction

David Fickling Books
(see Random House Group)

David Fulton (Publishers)
(see Granada Learning)

Debrett's
Brunel House
55–57 North Wharf Road
London W2 1LA
020 7915 9633
people@debretts.co.uk
www.debretts.co.uk
Specialist reference works

Dedalus
Langford Lodge, St Judith's Lane
Sawtry, Cambridgeshire PE28 5XE
01487 832382
info@dedalusbooks.com
www.dedalusbooks.com
English contemporary fiction and European fiction in translation, alternative lifestyle

Dewi Lewis Publishing
8 Broomfield Road, Heaton Moor
Stockport SK4 4ND
0161 442 9450
mail@dewilewispublishing.com
www.dewilewispublishing.com
Fiction, photography and visual arts

Diva Books
Unit M, Spectrum House
32/34 Gordon House Road
London NW5 1LP
020 7424 7400
www.millivres.co.uk
Part of the Millivres Prowler Group Literary lesbian fiction. Imprint: Red Hot Diva (lesbian erotic fiction)

Donhead Publishing
Lower Coombe, Donhead St Mary
Shaftesbury, Dorset SP7 9LY
01747 828422
jillpearce@donhead.com
www.donhead.com
Building, architecture and heritage

Dorling Kindersley
(see Penguin Books)

Doubleday/Doubleday Picture Books
(see Random House Group)

Drake Educational Associates
St Fagans Road, Fairwater
Cardiff CF5 3AE
029 2056 0333
info@drakeav.com
www.drakeav.com
Audio-visual, educational

Dref Wen
28 Church Road, Whitchurch
Cardiff CF14 2EA
029 2061 7860
sales@drefwen.com
Welsh language

Duncan Baird Publishers
Castle House, 75–76 Wells Street
London W1T 3QH
020 7323 2229
enquiries@dbairdpub.co.uk
General non-fiction

Duncan Petersen Publishing
31 Ceylon Road
London W14 0PY
020 7371 2356
dp@macunltd.net
www.charmingsmallhotels.co.uk
Non-fiction

Eagle Publishing
6 Kestrel House, Mill Street
Trowbridge, Wiltshire BA14 8BE
01225 781111
eaglepublishing1@aol.com
Christian books and music

Ebury Press
(see Random House Group)

Eden
(see Random House Group)

Edinburgh University Press
22 George Square
Edinburgh EH8 9LF
0131 650 4218
Timothy.Wright@eup.ed.ac.uk
www.eup.ed.ac.uk

Edward Elgar Publishing
Glensanda House, Montpellier Parade
Cheltenham
Gloucestershire GL50 1UA
01242 226934
info@e-elgar.co.uk
www.e-elgar.com
Economics, business and environment

Egmont Books
239 Kensington High Street
London W8 6SA
020 7761 3500
egmont@egmont.com
www.egmont.com
Children's entertainment. Imprints: Heinemann Young Books, Methuen Children's Books, Hamlyn Children's Books, Mammoth, Dean

Eland Publishing
Third Floor, 61 Exmouth Market
Clerkenwell, London EC1R 4QL
020 7833 0762
info@travelbooks.co.uk
www.travelbooks.co.uk
Travel, poetry, literature and history of the Islamic world

Elliot Right Way Books
Kingswood Buildings
Lower Kingswood
Tadworth, Surrey KT20 6TD
01737 832202
info@right-way.co.uk
www.right-way.co.uk
Practical non-fiction paperbacks

Elliott & Thompson
27 John Street
London WC1N 2BX
020 7831 5013
gmo73@dial.pipex.com
www.elliottthompson.com
History, biography, literary and fiction

Elm Consulting
Seaton House, Kings Ripton
Huntingdon
Cambridgeshire PE28 2NJ
01487 773254
sritchie@elm-training.co.uk
www.elm-training.co.uk
Educational aids

Elsevier
(see Reed Elsevier)

Emissary Publishing
PO Box 33, Bicester
Oxfordshire OX26 4ZZ
01869 323447
Humorous paperbacks

Emma Treehouse
2nd Floor, The Old Brewhouse
Lower Charlton Trading Estate,
Shepton Mallet, Somerset BA4 5QE
01749 330529
treehouse-books@btconnect.com
www.emmatreehouse.com
Children's pre-school

Encyclopaedia Britannica (UK)
2nd Floor, Unity Wharf
Mill Street, London SE1 2BH
020 7500 7800
enquiries@britannica.co.uk
www.britannica.co.uk

English Heritage (Publishing)
Kemble Drive, Swindon SN2 2GZ
01793 414619
customers@english-heritage.org.uk
www.english-heritage.org.uk
General and specialist history

Enitharmon Press
26B Caversham Road
London NW5 2DU
020 7482 5967
books@enitharmon.co.uk
www.enitharmon.co.uk
Poetry, literary criticism, fiction, art and photography, memoirs and translations

Euromonitor
60–61 Britton Street
London EC1M 5UX
020 7251 8024
info@euromonitor.com
www.euromonitor.com
Business reference, market analysis and information directories

Europa Publications
(see T&F Informa)

Evans Publishing Group
(see Thomson Learning)

Everyman
(see Orion Publishing Group)

Everyman's Library
Northburgh House
10 Northburgh Street
London EC1V 0AT
020 7566 6350
books@everyman.uk.com
An Imprint of Alfred A. Knopf (a subsidiary of Random House US) Literature, poetry, children's and travel

Exley Publications
16 Chalk Hill, Watford
Hertfordshire WD19 4BG
01923 248328
editorial@exleypublications.co.uk
www.helenexleygiftbooks.com
Giftbooks, quotation anthologies and humour

Expert Books
(see Random House Group)

FA Thorpe (Publishing)
(see Ulverscroft Group)

Faber & Faber
3 Queen Square, London WC1N 3AU
020 7465 0045
info@faber.co.uk
www.faber.co.uk
Fiction, non-fiction and poetry

Facet Publishing
7 Ridgmount Street
London WC1E 7AE
020 7255 0590/ 0505 (text phone)
info@facetpublishing.co.uk
www.facetpublishing.co.uk
Publishing arm of CILIP (Chartered Institute of Library and Information Professionals). Library and information science

Fernhurst Books
Duke's Path, High Street
Arundel, West Sussex BN18 9AJ
01903 882277
sales@fernhurstbooks.co.uk
www.fernhurstbooks.co.uk
Sailing and watersports

Findhorn Press
305a The Park, Findhorn, Forres
Morayshire IV36 3TE
01309 690582
books@findhorn.org
www.findhornpress.com
New Age, personal development

First & Best in Education
Unit K, Earlstrees Court
Earlstrees Road, Corby
Northamptonshire NN17 4HH
01536 399004
info@firstandbest.co.uk
www.firstandbest.co.uk
Educational books for schools. Imprints: School Improvement Reports

Fitzwarren Publishing
2 Orchard Drive
Aston Clinton, Aylesbury
Buckinghamshire HP22 5HR
01296 632627
pen2paper@btopenworld.com
Legal handbooks for the layman

Flicks Books
29 Bradford Road, Trowbridge
Wiltshire BA14 9AN
01225 767728
flicks.books@dial.pipex.com
Cinema and related media

Floris Books
15 Harrison Gardens
Edinburgh EH11 1SH
0131 337 2372
floris@florisbooks.co.uk
www.florisbooks.co.uk
Scientific, religion, holistic health and children's

Fodor's
(see Random House Group)

Folens Publishers
Unit 20, Apex Business Centre,
Boscombe Road, Dunstable
Bedfordshire LU5 4RL
0870 609 1237
folens@folens.com
www.folens.com
Educational books. Imprint: Belair

Footprint Handbooks
6 Riverside Court
Lower Bristol Road, Bath BA2 3DZ
01225 469141
pressoffice@footprintbooks.com
www.footprintbooks.com
Travel. Activity guides to hundreds of cities and countries, inc the South American Handbook, longest-running guidebook in English

For Dummies
(see John Wiley & Sons)

Fountain Press
Newpro UK , Old Sawmills Road
Faringdon, Oxfordshire SN7 7DS
01367 242411
sales@newprouk.co.uk
Photography and natural history

Fourth Estate
(see HarperCollins Publishers)

Frances Lincoln Publishers
4 Torriano Mews, Torriano Avenue
London NW5 2RZ
020 7284 4009
reception@frances-lincoln.com
www.franceslincoln.com
Highly illustrated non-fiction

Frank Cass
(see T&F Informa)

Free Association Books
57 Warren Street
London W1T 5NR
020 7388 3182
info@fabooks.com
www.fabooks.com
Psychoanalysis and psychotherapy, social science, psychology

Frommer's
(see John Wiley & Sons)

FT Prentice Hall
(see Pearson Education)

Gaia Books
66 Charlotte Street
London W1T 4QE
020 7323 4010
info@gaiabooks.com
www.gaiabooks.co.uk
Illustrated natural health, mind body spirit, natural living and environmental issues

Gairm Publications
29 Waterloo Street
Glasgow G2 6BZ
0141 221 1971
Gaelic

Garland Science
(see T&F Informa)

Garnet Publishing
8 Southern Court, South Street
Reading, Berkshire RG1 4QS
0118 959 7847
enquiries@garnet-ithaca.demon.co.uk
www.garnet-ithaca.co.uk
Imprints: Garnet (Middle East); Ithaca Press (business books)

Geddes & Grosset
David Dale House
New Lanark ML11 9DJ
01555 665000
caroline@geddesandgrosset.co.uk
www.geddesandgrosset.co.uk
Children's and reference books. Imprint: Beanobooks (children's)

Geological Society Publishing House
Unit 7, Brassmill Enterprise Centre
Brassmill Lane, Bath BA1 3JN
01225 445046
sales@geolsoc.org.uk
www.bookshop.geolsoc.org.uk
Publishing arm of the Geological Society. Undergraduate and postgraduate texts in the earth sciences

George Mann Books
PO Box 22, Maidstone
Kent ME14 1AH
01622 759591
Original non-fiction and selected reprints

Gibson Square Books
15 Gibson Square
London N1 0RD
020 7689 4790
publicity@gibsonsquare.com
www.gibsonsquare.com/
Biography and personal experience. Imprints: Gibson Square; New Editions

Giles de la Mare Publishers
PO Box 25351, London NW5 1ZT
020 7485 2533
gilesdelamare@dial.pipex.com
www.gilesdelamare.co.uk
Art and architecture, biography, history, music

Gollancz
(see Orion Publishing Group)

GMP (Gay Men's Press)
Unit M, Spectrum House
32/34 Gordon House Road
London NW5 1LP
020 7424 7400
www.millivres.co.uk
Part of the Millivres Prowler Group Literary gay fiction. Imprint: Zipper Books (gay male erotic fiction)

Gomer Press
Llandysul, Ceredigion SA44 4QL
01559 362371
gwasg@gomer.co.uk
www.gomer.co.uk
Adult fiction and non-fiction. Imprint: Pont Books

Good Web Guide
65 Bromfelde Road
London SW4 6PP
020 7720 8919
marketing@thegoodwebguide.co.uk
www.thegoodwebguide.co.uk

Granada Learning Group
Television Centre, Quay Street
Manchester M60 9EA
0161 827 2927
info@granada-learning.co.uk
www.granada-learning.co.uk

David Fulton Publishers
The Chiswick Centre
414 Chiswick High Road
London W4 5TF
020 8996 3610
mail@fultonpublishers.co.uk
www.fultonpublishers.co.uk
Books for Initial Teacher Training courses, continuing professional development and for special educational needs teachers

Leckie and Leckie
8 Whitehill Terrace, St Andrews
Fife KY16 8RN
01334 475656
enquiries@leckieandleckie.co.uk
www.leckieandleckie.co.uk
Study guides for students preparing for the Scottish Standard Grade and Higher exams

Letts Educational
The Chiswick Centre
0845 602 1937
mail@lettsed.co.uk
www.lettsed.co.uk
Examination study and revision guides

nferNelson
The Chiswick Centre
020 8996 8444
information@nfernelson.co.uk
www.nfer-nelson.co.uk
Tests, assessments and assessment services

SEMERC
Television Centre
0161 827 2927
www.semerc.com
ICT special needs

Granta Books
2–3 Hanover Yard, Noel Road
London N1 8BE
020 7704 9776
lcampbell@granta.com>
www.granta.com
Literary fiction and general non-fiction

Green Books
Foxhole, Dartington, Totnes
Devon TQ9 6EB
01803 863260
edit@greenbooks.co.uk
www.greenbooks.co.uk
Green issues

Greenhill Books/ Lionel Leventhal
Park House, 1 Russell Gardens
London NW11 9NN
020 8458 6314
lionelleventhal@greenhillbooks.com
www.greenhillbooks.com
Aviation, military, Napoleonic. Imprint: Chatham Publishing (naval)

Gresham Books
46 Victoria Road, Summertown
Oxford OX2 7QD
01865 513582
info@gresham-books.co.uk
www.gresham-books.co.uk
Hymn and service books

Griffith Institute
(see Oxford University)

Grub Street
4 Rainham Close
London SW11 6SS
020 7924 3966/ 7738 1008
post@grubstreet.co.uk
www.grubstreet.co.uk
Lifestyle and military

Guild of Master Craftsman Publications
166 High Street, Lewes
East Sussex BN7 1XU
01273 477374
pubs@thegmcgroup.com
www.gmcbooks.com
Craft and woodworking

Guinness World Records
338 Euston Road
London NW1 3BD
020 7891 4567
press@guinnessworldrecords.com
www.guinnessworldrecords.com

Gullane
(see Pinwheel)

Gwasg Carreg Gwalch
12 Iard yr Orsaf, Llanrwst
Conwy LL26 0EH
01492 642031
books@carreg-gwalch.co.uk
www.carreg-gwalch.co.uk
Welsh fiction and non-fiction; books on Wales

Halsgrove
Halsgrove House, Lower Moor Way
Tiverton Business Park, Tiverton
Devon EX16 6SS
01884 243242
sales@halsgrove.com
www.halsgrove.com
South-west regional books, cookery, biography and art

Hambledon and London
102 Gloucester Avenue
London NW1 8HX
020 7586 0817
office@hambledon.co.uk
www.hambledon.co.uk
History and biography

Hamish Hamilton
(see Penguin Books)

Harcourt Education
(see Reed Elsevier)

Harlequin Mills & Boon
Eton House, 18–24 Paradise Road
Richmond, Surrey TW9 1SR
020 8288 2800
www.millsandboon.co.uk
Subsidiary of Canadian company, Harlequin. Popular fiction

Harley Books
Martins, Great Horkesley
Colchester, Essex CO6 4AH
01206 271216
harley@keme.co.uk
www.harleybooks.com
Natural history

HarperCollins Publishers
77–85 Fulham Palace Road
London W6 8JB
020 8741 7070
webcontact@harpercollins.co.uk
www.harpercollins.co.uk

Collins
Reference books, cartography, education, dictionaries
www.collins.co.uk

General Books

- HarperCollins Childrens Books
  Picture books, fiction and properties (Dr Seuss, Paddington Bear, Noddy etc.)
  www.harpercollinschildrensbooks.co.uk
- HarperEntertainment
  Imprints: Entertainment (media-related); Collins Willow (sports); Tolkien and Estates (works by JRR Tolkien, Agatha Christie, CS Lewis); HarperCollins Audio
  www.tolkien.co.uk
- HarperFiction
  Imprints: HarperCollins Fiction (crime and popular fiction); Voyager (sci-fi and fantasy)
  www.voyager-books.co.uk
  www.collins-crime.co.uk
  www.readinggroups.co.uk
- HarperPress
  Imprints: HarperCollins Non-Fiction (history, current affairs, travel and biography); Fourth Estate (innovative fiction and non fiction); HarperPerennial (literary paperbacks)
- Thorsons
  Health, mind, body & spirit, and personal development books. Imprint: Thorsons and Element (colour illustrated) www.thorsons.co.uk

Harvard University Press/ MIT Press
Fitzroy House, 11 Chenies Street
London WC1E 7EY
020 7306 0603
info@HUP-MITpress.co.uk
http://mitpress.mit.edu
European office of US company

Harvill Secker
(see Random House Group)

Haynes Publishing
Sparkford, Near Yeovil
Somerset BA22 7JJ
01963 440635
sales@haynes.co.uk
www.haynes.co.uk
Owns Sutton Publishing. Car and motorcycle service and repair manuals

Hazleton Publishing
5th Floor, Mermaid House
2 Puddledock, London EC4V 3DS
020 7332 2000
info@hazletonpublishing.com
www.hazletonpublishing.com
Motorsport annuals

Heinemann
(see Reed Elsevier)

Helicon Publishing
RM , New Mill House
183 Milton Park, Abingdon
Oxfordshire OX14 4SE
0870 920 0200
helicon@rm.com
www.helicon.co.uk
CD-ROMs and online reference and cartography

Helm Information
The Banks, Mountfield
Nr Robertsbridge
East Sussex TN32 5JY
01580 880561
amandahelm@helm-information.co.uk
www.helm-information.co.uk
Academic

Helter Skelter Publishing
South Bank House
Black Prince Road
London SE1 7SJ
020 7463 2204
info@helterskelterpublishing.com
www.helterskelterpublishing.com
Obscure music. Co-imprint with SAF Publishing: Firefly Publishing (mainstream rock and pop)

Hesperus Press
4 Rickett Street, London SW6 1RU
020 7610 3331
agallenzi@hesperuspress.com
www.hesperuspress.com
Classic fiction in paperback

Highbury Leisure Publications
Berwick House, 8/10 Knoll Rise
Orpington, Kent BR6 0PS
01689 899200
www.splpublishing.co.uk
Formerly Highbury Nexus. Leisure and hobbies

Hobsons Publishing
Challenger House, 42 Adler Street
London E1 1EE
020 7958 5000
info@hobsons.co.uk
www.hobsons.com/uk
Part of the Daily Mail & General Trust Course and career guides

Hodder Headline Group
338 Euston Road
London NW1 3BH
020 7873 6000
www.hodderheadline.co.uk and
www.madaboutbooks.com
Owned by WHSmith

Hodder Headline Ireland
8 Castlecourt Centre
Castleknock, Dublin 15
+353 1 824 6288
Adult fiction and non-fiction. Imprint: HHI Lir (fiction)

Hodder Headline Scotland
2A Christie Street
Paisley PA1 1NB
0141 848 1609
bob.mcdevitt@hodder.co.uk

General
- Hodder & Stoughton *Imprints: Sceptre (literary); NEL (crime); Coronet (commercial fiction); Mobius (mind, body & spirit); Flame (fiction)*
- Headline *Imprints: Review (literary); Headline (commercial fiction and non-fiction)*
- John Murray *Fiction, history, travel, literature and memoir*

Education
- Hodder Arnold *Imprints: teach yourself (home reference); Hodder + Stoughton (reference including FA Guides and Michelle Thomas)*
- Hodder Murray *Curriculum materials*
- Hodder Gibson *Textbooks and revision support for the Scottish market 0141 848 1609 hoddergibson@hodder.co.uk*

Religious
- Hodder Religious *Imprints: Hodder & Stoughton (gift and inspirational); HY [help yourself] (home reference); HCB (Hodder Christian Books); NIV [New International Version] (bible translation)*

Children's
- Hodder Children's Books *Fiction for children and young adults*
- Hodder Wayland *Non-fiction educational books www.hodderwayland.co.uk*

Honeyglen Publishing
56 Durrels House, Warwick Gardens
London W14 8QB
020 7602 2876
History and fiction

Honno Welsh Women's Press
c/o Canolfan Merched Y Wawr
Vulcan Street, Aberystwyth
Ceredigion SY23 1JH
01970 623150
post@honno.co.uk
www.honno.co.uk
Reprints of classics, children's, fiction, poetry and short stories

House of Lochar
Isle of Colonsay, Argyll PA61 7YR
01951 200232
lochar@colonsay.org.uk
www.houseoflochar.com
Mostly Scottish titles. Imprint: Colonsay Books

House of Stratus
Thirsk Industrial Park
Thirsk, North Yorkshire YO7 3BX
01845 527700
sales@houseofstratus.com
www.houseofstratus.com
Quality literary fiction and non-fiction

How To Books
3 Newtec Place, Magdalen Road
Oxford OX4 1RE
01865 793806
info@howtobooks.co.uk
www.howtobooks.co.uk
Reference and self-help books

Hutchinson
(see Random House Group)

Ian Allan Publishing
Riverdene Business Park
Molesey Road, Hersham
Surrey KT12 4RG
01932 266600
info@ianallanpub.co.uk
www.ianallan.com
Maritime, road, rail, aviation, militaria and military history. Imprints: Midland Publishing, OPC Railway, Classic Publications, Lewis Masonic

Ian Henry Publications
20 Park Drive, Romford
Essex RM1 4LH
01708 749119
iwilkes@ianhenry.fsnet.co.uk
History and Sherlock Holmes

IB Tauris
(see Thomson Learning)

Icon Books
The Old Dairy, Brook Road
Thriplow, Royston SG8 7RG
01763 208008
info@iconbooks.co.uk
www.iconbooks.co.uk
History, children's fiction and non-fiction, adult non-fiction

IMP Fiction
PO Box 14691, London SE1 2ZA
01440 788 561
info@impbooks.com
www.impbooks.com
Original fiction

Independent Music Press
PO Box 14691, London SE1 2ZA
01440 788 561
info@impbooks.com
www.impbooks.com
Music biography and youth culture

Interpet
Interpet House, Vincent Lane
Dorking, Surrey RH4 3YX
01306 873840
kevin@interpet.co.uk
Pet, aquatic and water gardening books

Inter-Varsity Press
38 De Montfort Street
Leicester LE1 7GP
0116 255 1754
ivp@uccf.org.uk
www.ivpbooks.com
Christian belief and lifestyle. Imprints: IVP, Apollos, Crossway

Isis Publishing
(see Ulverscroft Group)

Ithaca Press
(see Garnet Publishing)

James Clarke & Co Lutterworth Press
PO Box 60, Cambridge CB1 2NT
01223 350865
publishing@jamesclarke.co.uk
www.jamesclarke.co.uk
Parent company of The Lutterworth Press. Theological, directory and reference

James Currey Publishers
73 Botley Road, Oxford OX2 0BS
01865 244111
editorial@jamescurrey.co.uk
www.jamescurrey.co.uk
Academic books on Africa, the Caribbean and third world

Jane's Information Group
163 Brighton Road, Coulsdon
Surrey CR5 2YH
020 8700 3700
info.uk@janes.com
www.janes.com
Defence, aerospace and transport

Janus Publishing Company
105–107 Gloucester Place
London W1U 6BY
020 7580 7664
publisher@januspublishing.co.uk
www.januspublishing.co.uk
Fiction and non-fiction. Imprint: Empiricus Books

Jarrold Publishing
Whitefriars, Norwich
Norfolk NR3 1JR
01603 763300
publishing@jarrold.com
www.jarrold-publishing.co.uk
Heritage and leisure, walking guides. Imprints: Pitkin, Unichrome

Jessica Kingsley Publishers
116 Pentonville Road
London N1 9JB
020 7833 2307
post@jkp.com
www.jkp.com
Social and behavioural sciences

John Blake Publishing
3 Bramber Court, 2 Bramber Road
London W14 9PB
020 7381 0666
words@blake.co.uk
www.blake.co.uk
General non-fiction, esp. true crime, popular culture, general biography. Includes Richard Cohen, Smith Gryphon and Blake Publishing. Imprints: Metro Books (health, fitness, cookery and lifestyle)

John Hunt Publishing
46a West Street, New Alresford
Hampshire SO24 9AU
01962 736880
maria@johnhunt-publishing.com
www.johnhunt-publishing.com, www.o-books.net
Children's and world religions. Imprint: O Books (mind, body and spirit)

John Murray
(see Hodder Headline Group)

John Wiley & Sons
The Atrium, Southern Gate
Chichester PO19 8SQ
01243 779777
cs-books@wiley.co.uk
www.wileyeurope.com
Scientific, technical and medical; professional and trade; textbooks and educational materials

Capstone Publishing
Business and personal development
www.capstoneideas.com

For Dummies
Reference series

Frommer's
Travel guides

Jossey-Bass
Management, education and religion

The Unofficial Guide
Travel, computing

Visual/Redhat Press/ Wrox
Computing

Wiley
Scientific, technical and medical; professional and trade; textbooks and educational materials

Wiley Interscience
Scientific, technical and medical; print and online reference materials

Wiley-Academy
Architecture

Wiley-Liss
Life and medical

Wiley-VCH
Scientific, technical and medical

Jonathan Cape
(see Random House Group)

Kahn & Averill
9 Harrington Road
London SW7 3ES
020 8743 3278
kahn@averill23.freeserve.co.uk
Books on music

Kenilworth Press
Addington, Buckingham
Buckinghamshire MK18 2JR
01296 715101
editorial@kenilworthpress.co.uk
www.kenilworthpress.co.uk
Equestrian

Kenneth Mason Publications
The Book Barn, Westbourne
Emsworth, Hampshire PO10 8RS
01243 377977
info@researchdisclosure.com
www.researchdisclosure.com
Lifestyle, nutrition and nautical. Imprint: Research Disclosure

Kevin Mayhew Publishers
Buxhall, Stowmarket
Suffolk IP14 3BW
01449 737978
info@kevinmayhewltd.com
www.kevinmayhewltd.com
Religious titles

Kingfisher Publications
New Penderel House
283–288 High Holborn
London WC1V 7HZ
020 7903 9999
sales@kingfisherpub.com
www.kingfisherpub.com
Children's fiction and non-fiction

Kluwer Academic/ Plenum Publishers
100 Borough High Street
London SE1 1LB
020 7863 3000
mail@plenum.co.uk
www.wkap.nl
Owned by Candover & Cinven Scientific, technical and medical textbooks. Imprints: Consultants Bureau, Plenum Press, Human Science Press

Kluwer Law International
145 London Road
Kingston-on-Thames
Surrey KT2 6SR
020 8247 1694
sales@kluwerlaw.com
www.kluwerlaw.com
Part of Aspen Publishers, a Wolters Kluwer company. International law. Imprints: Graham and Trotman, Kluwer Law and Taxation, Martinus Nyhoff

Kogan Page
120 Pentonville Road
London N1 9JN
020 7278 0433
kpinfo@kogan-page.co.uk
www.kogan-page.co.uk
Business and management

Kyle Cathie
122 Arlington Road
London NW1 7HP
020 7692 7215
general.enquiries@kyle-cathie.com
www.KyleCathie.com
Lifestyle

Ladybird
(see Penguin Books)

Landmark Publishing
Ashbourne Hall, Cokayne Avenue
Ashbourne, Derbyshire DE6 1EJ
01335 347349
landmark@clara.net
www.landmarkpublishing.co.uk
Travel guides, and industrial and local history

Laurence King Publishing
71 Great Russell Street
London WC1B 3BP
020 7430 8850
enquiries@laurenceking.co.uk
www.laurenceking.co.uk
Illustrated arts

Lawrence & Wishart
99A Wallis Road
London E9 5LN
020 8533 2506
lw@lwbooks.co.uk
www.lwbooks.co.uk
Current and world affairs

Leckie and Leckie
(see Granada Learning)

Lennard Associates
Windmill Cottage, Mackerye End
Harpenden, Hertfordshire AL5 5DR
01582 715866
stephenson@lennardqap.co.uk
Sporting yearbooks. Imprints and divisions include: Lennard Publishing, Queen Anne Press

Letts Educational
(see Granada Learning)

LexisNexis
(see Reed Elsevier)

Lion Hudson
Mayfield House, 256 Banbury Road
Oxford OX2 7DH
01865 302750
enquiries@lionhudson.com
www.lionhudson.com
Formed through merger of Lion Publishing and Angus Hudson Christian books. Imprints: Lion, Lion Children's, Candle, Monarch

Little, Brown
(see Time Warner Books)

Little Tiger Press
Magi Publications, 1 The Coda Centre
189 Munster Road
London SW6 6AW
020 7385 6333
info@littletiger.co.uk
www.littletigerpress.com
Children's picture and novelty books. Imprints: Little Tiger, Caterpillar Books

Liverpool University Press
4 Cambridge Street
Liverpool L69 7ZU
0151 794 2233
sbell@liv.ac.uk
www.liverpool-unipress.co.uk

Lonely Planet Publications
72-82 Rosebery Avenue
Clerkenwell, London EC1R 4RW
020 7841 9000
go@lonelyplanet.co.uk
www.lonelyplanet.com
Travel guides

Longman
(see Pearson Education)

Lutterworth Press
(see James Clarke & Co Lutterworth Press)

Macmillan Publishers
4 Crinan Street
London N1 9XW
020 7843 3600
www.macmillan.com

Nature Publishing Group
4 Crinan Street
020 7843 4000
www.nature.com
Scientific journals and reference publishing

Macmillan Education
Macmillan Oxford
4 Between Towns Road
Oxford OX4 3PP
01865 405700
www.macmillaneducation.com
ELT learning materials for international markets

Palgrave Macmillan
Brunel Road, Houndmills
Basingstoke, Hampshire RG21 6XS
01256 329242
www.palgravo.com
Academic, scholarly and reference publishing in the social sciences and humanities

Pan Macmillan
20 New Wharf Road
London N1 9RR
020 7014 6000
www.panmacmillan.com
Fiction and non-fiction for adults and children

- Imprints: *Macmillan, Pan, Picador, Young Picador, Boxtree, Sidgwick and Jackson, Papermac, Macmillan Children's Books, Campbell Books, Priddy Books*
- US imprints: *Picador USA; St Martin's Press; Farrar, Straus and Giroux Inc.; Henry Holt; Tor*
- Australian imprints: *Pan Macmillan Australia, Pancake*
- South African imprints: *Pan Macmillan South Africa, Picador Africa*
- Irish imprints: *Gill and Macmillan*

Magna Large Print Books
(see Ulverscroft Group)

Mainstream Publishing Co (Edinburgh)
7 Albany Street, Edinburgh EH1 3UG
0131 557 2959
editorial@mainstreampublishing.com
www.mainstreampublishing.com
General non-fiction and popular paperbacks

Management Books 2000
Forge House, Limes Road
Kemble, Cirencester
Gloucestershire GL7 6AD
01285 771441
mb.2000@virgin.net
www.mb2000.com
Working books for working managers

Manchester University Press
Oxford Road, Manchester M13 9NR
0161 275 2310
mup@man.ac.uk
www.manchesteruniversitypress.co.uk

Manson Publishing
73 Corringham Road
London NW11 7DL
020 8905 5150
www.mansonpublishing.com
Scientific, technical, medical and veterinary

Marion Boyars Publishers
24 Lacy Road, London SW15 1NL
020 8788 9522
catheryn@marionboyars.com
www.marionboyars.co.uk
Formerly Calder and Boyars. Literary fiction, fiction in translation, social affairs, film, music, drama

Marshall Cavendish
119 Wardour Street
London W1F 0UW
020 7565 6000
www.marshallcavendish.co.uk
Adults and children's and educational

Marston House
Marston House, Marston Magna
Yeovil, Somerset BA22 8DH
01935 851331
alphaimage@marstonhouse.ndo.co.uk
Fine art, architecture, ceramics and horticulture

Martin Dunitz
(see T&F Informa)

McGraw-Hill Education
Shoppenhangers Road
Maidenhead, Berkshire SL6 2QL
01628 502500
www.mcgraw-hill.co.uk
Business, economics, computing and engineering

Professional
Professional, business & general reference books covering computing, science, technical and medical, languages, architecture, careers, politics, management, finance, parenting, health, sports & fitness. Imprints: McGraw-Hill Professional, McGraw-Hill Trade, McGraw-Hill Osborne, McGraw-Hill Medical Publishing, McGraw-Hill Contemporary, Harvard Business School Press, AMACOM, Berrett-Koehler, CMP

Higher Education
University textbooks on business, economics, accounting, finance, marketing, computing science, decision sciences. Imprints: McGraw-Hill Education, McGraw-Hill Irwin

- Open University Press: *Higher education, education, health & social welfare, cultural and media studies, psychology, criminology, sociology, counselling, study guides*

Schools
Early childhood, primary and secondary school books. Imprints: Kingscourt, Glencoe and SRA, Macmillan, The Learning Group

Mercat Press
10 Coates Crescent
Edinburgh EH3 7AL
0131 225 5324
enquiries@mercatpress.com
www.mercatpress.com
Fiction and non-fiction of Scottish interest

Merlin Press
PO Box 30705, London WC2E 8QD
020 7836 3020
local rate: 0845 4581579
info@merlinpress.co.uk
www.merlinpress.co.uk
Economics, history, leftwing politics. Imprints: Green Print, Merlin Press

Merrell Publishers
42 Southwark Street
London SE1 1UN
020 7403 2047
mail@merrellpublishers.com
www.merrellpublishers.com
Art, architecture, design and photography

Methodist Publishing House
4 John Wesley Road
Werrington, Peterborough
Cambridgeshire PE4 6ZP
01733 325002
sales@mph.org.uk
www.mph.org.uk
Owned by the Methodist Church Christian books. Imprint: Epworth Press

Methuen Publishing
215 Vauxhall Bridge Road
London SW1V 1EJ
020 7798 1600
sales@methuen.co.uk
www.methuen.co.uk
Drama and general fiction and non-fiction. Imprint: Politicos (politics)

Michael Joseph
(see Penguin Books)

Michael O'Mara Books
9 Lion Yard, Tremadoc Road
London SW4 7NQ
020 7720 8643
enquiries@michaelomarabooks.com
www.michaelomarabooks.com
Biography, popular history, humour, children's and pre-school

Michelin Travel Publications
Hannay House, 39 Clarendon Road
Watford, Hertfordshire WD17 1JA
01923 205240
www.viamichelin.com
Travel books and maps

Microsoft Press
Thames Valley Park, Reading
Berkshire RG6 1WG
0870 601 0100
mspinfo@microsoft.com
www.microsoft.com/mspress/uk
Computing manuals to accompany Microsoft products; also system administration, business solutions and security

Miles Kelly Publishing
Unit 17 & 18, Bardfield Centre
Great Bardfield, Essex CM7 4SL
01371 811309
rob@mileskelly.net
www.mileskelly.net
Children's titles

Milet Publishing
6 North End Parade, London W14 0SJ
020 7603 5477
info@milet.com
www.milet.com
Children's books

Mills & Boon
(see Harlequin Mills & Boon)

MIT Press
(see Harvard University Press/ MIT Press)

Motor Racing Publications
PO Box 1318, Croydon
Surrey CR9 5YP
020 8654 2711
mrp.books@virgin.net
www.mrpbooks.co.uk
Motor racing, road cars, performance and classic cars

MQ Publications
12 The Ivories, 6–8 Northampton St
London N1 2HY
020 7359 2244
kim@mqpublications.com
www.mqpublications.com
Illustrated cookbooks

Multi-Sensory Learning
Highgate House, Groom's Lane
Creaton, Northampton NN6 8NN
01604 505000
info@msl-online.net
www.msl-online.net
Resources on learning difficulties esp. dyslexia

Murdoch Books UK
Erico House, 6th Floor
93–99 Upper Richmond Road
Putney, London SW15 2TG
020 8785 5995
aelliott@murdochbooks.co.uk
Recipe, craft, gardening

National Trust Publications
36 Queen Anne's Gate
London SW1H 9AS
020 7222 9251
enquiries@thenationaltrust.org.uk
www.nationaltrust.org.uk/bookshop
Publishing arm of The National Trust

Nautical Data
The Book Barn, Westbourne
Emsworth, Hampshire PO10 8RS
01243 389352
info@nauticaldata.com
www.nauticaldata.com

NCVO Publications
Regent's Wharf, 8 All Saints Street
London N1 9RL
020 7713 6161
ncvo@ncvo-vol.org.uk
www.ncvo-vol.org.uk
Publishing imprint of the National Council for Voluntary Organisations Directories, public policy and governance; trusteeship and HR in the voluntary sector

Neil Wilson Publishing
Suite 303, The Pentagon Centre
36 Washington Street
Glasgow G3 8AZ
0141 221 1117
info@nwp.co.uk
www.nwp.co.uk
www.11-9.co.uk
www.vitalspark.co.uk
www.angelshare.co.uk
www.theinpinn.co.uk
Scottish and Irish interest: food and drink, outdoor pursuits, history, humour and biography

Nelson Thornes
Delta Place, 27 Bath Road
Cheltenham
Gloucestershire GL53 7TH
01242 267100
info@nelsonthornes.com
www.nelsonthornes.com
Part of the Wolters Kluwer Group Educational

New Beacon Books
76 Stroud Green Road
London N4 3EN
020 7272 4889
newbeaconbooks@lineone.net
Black-oriented fiction, history, politics, poetry and language

New Holland Publishers (UK)
Garfield House, 86–88 Edgware Road
London W2 2EA
020 7724 7773
postmaster@nhpub.co.uk
www.newhollandpublishers.com
Non-fiction, lifestyle and self-improvement

New Riders
(see Pearson Education)

nferNelson
(see Granada Learning)

Nicholas Brealey Publishing
3–5 Spafield Street
London EC1R 4QB
020 7239 0360
rights@nbrealey-books.com
www.nbrealey-books.com
Includes Intercultural Press. Cultural business, self-help and travel. US imprint: Intercultural Press

Nick Hern Books
The Glasshouse, 49a Goldhawk Road
London W12 8QP
020 8749 4953
info@nickhernbooks.demon.co.uk
www.nickhernbooks.co.uk
Theatre and film

Nielsen BookData
3rd Floor, Midas House
62 Goldsworth Road, Woking
Surrey GU21 6LQ
0870 7778710
info@bookdata.co.uk
www.nielsenbookdata.com
"The Red Book" directory of publishers

NMS Enterprises... Publishing
National Museums of Scotland
Chambers Street
Edinburgh EH1 1JF
0131 247 4026
publishing@nms.ac.uk
www.nms.ac.uk
History, art, archaeology, natural history, popular Scottish history, culture, biography and geology

Nottingham University Press
Manor Farm, Church Lane
Thrumpton, Nottingham NG11 0AX
0115 983 1011
editor@nup.com
www.nup.com
Scientific textbooks

Oberon Books
521 Caledonian Road
London N7 9RH
020 7607 3637
oberon.books@btinternet.com
www.oberonbooks.com
Play texts. Imprint: Absolute Classics (translations of classical plays)

Octagon Press
PO Box 227, London N6 4EW
020 8348 9392
octagon@octagonpress.com
www.octagonpress.com
Philosophy, psychology, travel and Eastern religion

Octopus Publishing Group
2–4 Heron Quays, London E14 4JP
020 7531 8400
info@octopus-publishing.co.uk
www.octopus-publishing.co.uk
and www.conran-octopus.co.uk
and www.hamlyn.co.uk
and www.mitchell-beazley.co.uk
and www.philips-maps.co.uk
Owned by Hachette. Illustrated adult reference books

Oldcastle Books
PO Box 394, Harpenden
Hertfordshire AL5 1XJ
01582 761264
info@noexit.co.uk
info@pocketessentials.com
www.noexit.co.uk
www.pocketessentials.com
www.gamblingbooks.co.uk
Imprints: No Exit Press and Crime Time (crime/noir fiction); Pocketessentials (compact reference books on film, tv, literature, ideas and history); High Stakes (gambling)

Omnibus Press
Music Sales, 8–9 Frith Street
London W1D 3JB
020 7434 0066
music@musicsales.co.uk
www.omnibuspress.com
Imprints: Omnibus Press (music-related biography); Vision On (upmarket music-related photo books). US imprint: Schirmer Books (self-help books, music industry)

Oneworld
(see Thomson Learning)

Onlywomen Press
40 St Lawrence Terrace
London W10 5ST
020 8354 0796
onlywomenpress@aol.com
www.onlywomenpress.com
Lesbian and feminist fiction, non-fiction theory and poetry

Open University Press
(see McGraw-Hill Education)

Orbit Press
(see Time Warner Books)

Orion Publishing Group
Orion House
5 Upper Saint Martin's Lane
London WC2H 9EA
020 7240 3444
info@orionbooks.co.uk
www.orionbooks.co.uk
- Gollancz: *Sci-fi and fantasy*
- Orion Children's Books

Weidenfeld & Nicolson
History, reference, non-fiction, illustrated and literary fiction, military
- Cassell Military: *Illustrated and paperback*
- Cassell Reference
- Everyman: *Classics in paperback*
- Phoenix: *Contemporary fiction*

Peter Halban
22 Golden Square
London W1F 9JW
020 7437 9300
books@halbanpublishers.com
www.halbanpublishers.com
Fiction, memoirs, history, biography and books of Jewish interest

Allen & Unwin (Australian imprint)
www.allen-unwin.com.au

Osprey Publishing
Elms Court, Chapel Way
Botley, Oxford OX2 9LP
01865 727022
info@ospreypublishing.com
www.ospreypublishing.com
Military history, aviation

Oxford University

Ashmolean Museum Publications
Ashmolean Museum
Beaumont Street, Oxford OX1 2PH
01865 278010
publications@ashmus.ox.ac.uk
www.ashmol.ox.ac.uk
Art and archaeology

Griffith Institute
Sackler Library, 1 St John's Street
Oxford OX1 2LG
01865 278099
griffox@herald.ox.ac.uk
www.ashmol.ox.ac.uk/Griffith.html
Egyptology

Oxford University Press
Great Clarendon Street
Oxford OX2 6DP
01865 556767
enquiry@oup.com
www.oup.com
A department of Oxford University Academic. Imprint: Oxford Children's Books

Palgrave Macmillan
(see Macmillan Publishers)

Pan/Pan Macmillan
(see Macmillan Publishers)

Papermac
(see Macmillan Publishers)

Paper Tiger
(see Chrysalis Books)

Pavilion
(see Chrysalis Books)

Peachpit Press
(see Pearson Education)

Pearson Education
Edinburgh Gate, Harlow
Essex CM20 2JE
01279 623623
HEEnquiriesUK@pearsoned-ema.com
www.pearsoned.co.uk

Allyn & Bacon
Education, humanities and social sciences

Addison-Wesley
Computer programming

Benjamin Cummings
Science

Cisco Press
Cisco systems materials

FT Prentice Hall
Global business

Longman
Educational materials for schools, English language teaching (ELT) materials, higher education textbooks (law, humanities, social sciences)

New Riders
Graphics and design

Peachpit Press
Web development

Penguin Books
(see separate entry under Penguin Books)

Penguin Longman
ELT books
- *Penguin English (for teachers) www.penguinenglish.com*
- *Penguin Readers (for students) www.penguinreaders.com*

Prentice Hall
Academic and reference textbooks: business, computer science, engineering and IT

Prentice Hall Business
Practical and personal development

QUE Publishing
Computing

SAMS Publishing
Reference books for programmers and developers, web developers, designers, networking and system administrators

York Notes
Literature guides for students

Pegasus Elliot & Mackenzie Publishers
Sheraton House, Castle Park
Cambridge CB3 0AX
01223 370012
editors@pegasuspublishers.com
www.pegasuspublishers.com
Fiction and non-fiction, crime and erotica. Imprints: Vanguard Press, Nightingale Books, Chimera

Pen & Sword Books
47 Church Street, Barnsley
South Yorkshire S70 2AS
01226 734222
enquiries@pen-and-sword.co.uk
www.pen-and-sword.co.uk
Military, naval and aviation history. Imprints: Leo Cooper, Wharncliffe Publishing

Penguin Books
80 Strand, London WC2R 0RL
020 7010 3000
penguin@penguin.co.uk
www.penguin.co.uk
Owned by Pearson

Dorling Kindersley
Information books and resources for children and adults

ePenguin
ebooks

Penguin Audiobooks
- Penguin General Books: *Imprints: Penguin Paperbacks; Hamish Hamilton; Michael Joseph; Viking)*

Penguin Ireland
25 St Stephen's Green, Dublin 2
00 353 1 661 7695
info@penguin.ie
www.penguin.ie

Penguin Press
Imprints: Allen Lane (reference inc. Roget's Thesaurus and Pears Cyclopaedia); Penguin Classics; Penguin Modern Classics)

Puffin
Children's
Rough Guides
Travel guides, phrase books, music guides and reference
roughguide@penguin.co.uk
Warne
Children's, inc. Beatrix Potter, Spot, Ladybird

Persephone Books
59 Lamb's Conduit Street
London WC1N 3NB
020 7242 9292
info@persephonebooks.co.uk
www.persephonebooks.co.uk
Reprint fiction and non-fiction, focus on women

Perseus Books Group
PO Box 317, Oxford OX2 9RU
01865 865466
info@perseusbooks.com
www.perseusbooksgroup.com
UK office of US Perseus Books Group Non-fiction. Imprints: PublicAffairs (current affairs), Da Capo Press (music, history, film and biography), Basic Books (current affairs, history, popular science), Counterpoint (literature and fiction), Basic Civitas Books (African American studies), Westview Press (social sciences, humanities, science)

Peter Haddock Publishing
Pinfold Lane, Bridlington
East Yorkshire YO16 6BT
01262 678121
sales@phpublishing.co.uk
www.phpublishing.co.uk
Children's books

Peter Halban Publishers
(see Orion Publishing Group)

Peter Owen Publishers
73 Kenway Road, London SW5 0RE
020 7373 5628
admin@peterowen.com
www.peterowen.com
Biography, non-fiction, literary fiction, literary criticism, history and the arts

Phaidon Press
Regent's Wharf, All Saints Street
London N1 9PA
020 7843 1000
enquiries@phaidon.com
www.phaidon.com
Arts

Pharmaceutical Press
1 Lambeth High Street
London SE1 7JN
020 7735 9141
pharmpress@rpsgb.org.uk
www.pharmpress.com
The publications division of the Royal Pharmaceutical Society of Great Britain. Medicine

Philip Berrill International
60 Leyland Road, Southport
Merseyside PR9 9JA
01704 534725
philipberrill@hotmail.com
Art and mind, body & spirit guides

Philip Wilson Publishers
109 The Timber Yard
7–27 Drysdale Street
London N1 6ND
020 7033 9900
pwilson@philip-wilson.co.uk
www.philip-wilson.co.uk
Art, museums and exhibition materials

Phillimore & Co
Shopwyke Manor Barn, Chichester
West Sussex PO20 2BG
01243 787636
bookshop@phillimore.co.uk
www.phillimore.co.uk
Local and family history

Phoenix
(see Orion Publishing Group)

Piatkus Books
5 Windmill Street, London W1T 2JA
020 7631 0710
info@piatkus.co.uk
www.piatkus.co.uk
Fiction, biography, history, health and business

Picador
(see Macmillan Publishers)

Piccadilly Press
5 Castle Road, London NW1 8PR
020 7267 4492
books@piccadillypress.co.uk
www.piccadillypress.co.uk
Children's, teenage and parental books

Pimlico
(see Random House Group)

Pinwheel
Winchester House
259–269 Old Marylebone Road
London NW1 5XJ
020 7616 7200
www.pinwheel.co.uk
Imprints: Gullane (children's picture); Pinwheel (novelty); Andromeda (education)

Pluto Press
(see Thomson Learning)

Pocket Books
(see Simon & Schuster UK)

The Policy Press
University of Bristol, Fourth Floor
Beacon House, Queen's Road
Bristol BS8 1QU
0117 331 4054
tpp-info@bristol.ac.uk
www.policypress.org.uk
Social sciences

Politico's Publishing
(see Methuen Publishing)

Polity Press
65 Bridge Street
Cambridge CB2 1UR
01223 324315
info@polity.co.uk
www.polity.co.uk
General academic

Portland Press
59 Portland Place
London W1B 1QW
020 7637 5873
editorial@portlandpress.com
www.portlandpress.com
Biochemistry and medicine

Prentice Hall/ Prentice Hall Business
(see Pearson Education)

Prestel Publishing
4 Bloomsbury Place
London WC1A 2QA
020 7323 5004
sales@prestel-uk.co.uk
www.prestel.com
Art, architecture, photography and design

Priddy Books
(see Macmillan Publishers)

Profile Books
58a Hatton Garden
London EC1N 8LX
020 7404 3001
info@profilebooks.co.uk
www.profilebooks.co.uk
Non-fiction. Imprint: Economist Books

Proquest Information and Learning
The Quorum, Barnwell Road
Cambridge CB5 8SW
01223 215512
marketing@proquest.co.uk
www.proquest.co.uk
Educational

Psychology Press
(see T&F Informa)

Publishing House
Trinity Place, Barnstaple
Devon EX32 9HJ
01271 328892
publishinghouse@vernoncoleman.com
www.vernoncoleman.com
Fiction, health, humour, animals and politics

Puffin
(see Penguin Books)

Pushkin Press
12 Chester Terrace
London NW1 4ND
020 7266 9136
sasha@pushkinpress.com
www.pushkinpress.com
Translated classic and contemporary European literature

Putnams
(see Chrysalis Books)

Quadrille Publishing
Alhambra House
27–31 Charing Cross Road
London WC2H 0LS
020 7839 7117
enquiries@quadrille.co.uk
www.quadrille.co.uk
Lifestyle

Quartet Books
27 Goodge Street, London W1T 2LD
020 7636 3992
quartetbooks@easynet.co.uk
Part of the Namara Group
Contemporary literary fiction

Quarto Publishing
The Fitzpatrick Building
188–194 York Way
London N7 9QP
020 77006700
info@quarto.com
www.quarto.com
Highly illustrated non-fiction

QUE Publishing
(see Pearson Education)

Radcliffe Medical Press
18 Marcham Road, Abingdon
Oxfordshire OX14 1AA
01235 528820
contact.us@radcliffemed.com
www.radcliffe-oxford.com

Random House Group
Random House
20 Vauxhall Bridge Road
London SW1V 2SA
020 7840 8400
enquiries@randomhouse.co.uk
www.randomhouse.co.uk

Random House Division
- Arrow: *Mass-market paperback fiction and non-fiction*
- Century: *General fiction and non-fiction including commercial fiction, autobiography, biography, history and self-help*
- Chatto & Windus: *Memoirs, current affairs, essays, literary fiction, history, poetry, politics, philosophy and translations*
- Harvill Secker: *Literary fiction, literature in translation, English literature, quality thrillers, some non-fiction*
- Hutchinson: *General fiction and non-fiction including belles-lettres, current affairs, politics, travel and history*
- Jonathan Cape: *Biography and memoirs, current affairs, fiction, history, photography, poetry, politics and travel*
- Pimlico: *Quality non-fiction paperbacks specialising in history, biography, popular culture and the arts*
- Random House Business Books
- Vintage: *Quality paperback fiction and non-fiction*
- William Heinemann: *General fiction and non-fiction especially history, literary fiction, crime, science, thrillers and women's fiction*
- Yellow Jersey Press: *Narrative sports books*

Ebury Press Division
- Ebury Press: *Autobiography, biography, popular history, cookery, popular science, humour, diet and health*
- Fodor's: *Travel guides*
- Rider: *Mind, body & spirit*
- Vermilion: *Popular reference, lifestyle, crafts, interior design*

Random House Children's Books
Transworld Publishers
61–63 Uxbridge Road
London W5 5SA
020 8231 6800
- *Imprints: Hutchinson, Jonathan Cape, The Bodley Head, Doubleday Picture Books, David Fickling Books, Corgi, Red Fox*

Transworld Publishers
61–63 Uxbridge Road
London W5 5SA
020 8579 2652
info@transworld-publishers.co.uk
www.booksattransworld.co.uk
- *Imprints: Bantam, Bantam Press, Corgi & Black Swan, Doubleday, Eden, Expert Books, Channel 4 Books*

Ransom Publishing
Rose Cottage, Howe Hill
Watlington, Oxfordshire OX49 5HB
01491 613711
jenny@ransom.co.uk
www.ransom.co.uk
Education

Reader's Digest Association
11 Westferry Circus, Canary Wharf
London E14 4HE
020 7715 8000
gbeditorial@readersdigest.co.uk
www.readersdigest.co.uk
Cookery, history, reference, gardening and DIY

Reaktion Books
79 Farringdon Road
London EC1M 3JU
020 7404 9930
info@reaktionbooks.co.uk
www.reaktionbooks.co.uk
Architecture, Asian and cultural studies, film and travel

Reardon Publishing
56 Upper Norwood Street
Leckhampton, Cheltenham
Gloucestershire GL53 0DU
01242 231800
reardon@bigfoot.com
www.reardon.co.uk
Member of the Outdoor Writers Guild
Cotswold area local interest

Red Bird Publishing
Kiln Farm, East End Green
Brightlingsea, Colchester
Essex CO7 0SX
01206 303525
info@red-bird.co.uk
www.red-bird.co.uk
Special-effects books for children

Red Fox
(see Random House Group)

Redhat Press
(see John Wiley & Sons)

Reed Elsevier
1–3 Strand, London WC2N 5JR
020 7930 7077
Press: 020 7166 5657/5670
www.reedelsevier.com

Science and Medical Division
32 Jamestown Road
Camden Town, London NW1 7BY
020 7424 4200
eurobkinfo@elsevier.com
Press: PressOffice@elsevier.com
www.elsevier-international.com
- Elsevier Science and Technology
  Imprints: Academic Press (physical, applied and life sciences); Morgan Kaufmann (databases, computer networking, human computer interaction, computer graphics, multimedia information and systems, artificial intelligence, and software engineering); Syngress Media (computing reference works for IT professionals)
- Elsevier Health Sciences
  Imprints: Saunders (medical), Mosby (medicine, nursing, allied health and veterinary medicine), Churchill Livingstone (medical), Butterworth-Heinemann (technology, medicine and management), Hanley & Belfus (medical); Bailliere Tindall (nursing and midwifery); BC Decker (medicine, health sciences, and dentistry); GW Medical Publishing (abuse, maltreatment, sexually transmitted diseases, and domestic violence)

Education Division
- *Harcourt Education*
  Halley Court, Jordan Hill
  Oxford OX2 8EJ
  01865 311366
  uk.schools@harcourteducation.co.uk
  www.harcourteducation.co.uk
  Textbooks and educational resources. Imprints: Ginn, Heinemann (Primary, Secondary, FE & Vocational), Rigby UK

Business Division
- *Reed Business Information*
  Quadrant House, The Quadrant,
  Sutton, Surrey SM2 5AS
  020 8652 3500
  Press: 020 8652 3296
  www.reedbusiness.co.uk
  Business directories, magazines, e-newsletters, websites and cd-roms

Legal Division
- *LexisNexis Butterworths Tolley*
  Halsbury House, 35 Chancery Lane
  London WC2A 1EL
  020 7400 2500
  Press: 020 7400 2753
  competitive.intelligence@lexis-nexis.com
  www.lexisnexis.co.uk
  Legal and business materials in print and online, including The Advertiser Red Books. Butterworths Services provide access to a library of UK law

Regency House Publishing
Nial House, 24–26 Boulton Road
Stevenage, Hertfordshire SG1 4QX
01438 314488
regency-house@btconnect.com
Art and transport

Richmond House Publishing Company
70–76 Bell Street, Marylebone
London NW1 6SP
020 7224 9666
sales@rhpco.co.uk
www.rhpco.co.uk
Theatre and entertainment directories

Rider
(see Random House Group)

Robert Hale
Clerkenwell House
45–47 Clerkenwell Green
London EC1R 0HT
020 7251 2661
enquire@halebooks.com
www.halebooks.com

Robson Books
(see Chrysalis Books)

Rodale Books
7–10 Chandos Street
London W1G 9AD
020 7291 6000
www.rodale.co.uk
Lifestyle

Roget's Thesaurus
(see Penguin Books)

RotoVision
Sheridan House
112/116A Western Road, Hove
East Sussex BN3 1DD
01273 727268
sales@rotovision.com
www.rotovision.com
Graphic arts and design

Rough Guides
(see Penguin Books)

Roundhouse Publishing
Millstone, Limers Lane
Northam, North Devon EX39 2RG
01237 474474
roundhouse.group@ukgateway.net
www.roundhouse.net
Cinema and media

Routledge
(see T&F Informa)

Ryland, Peters & Small
Kirkman House
12–14 Whitfield Street
London W1T 2RP
020 7436 9090
info@rps.co.uk
www.rylandpeters.com
Illustrated lifestyle

SAF Publishing
149 Wakeman Road
London NW10 5BH
020 8969 6099
info@safpublishing.com
www.safpublishing.com
Experimental rock and jazz music. Co-imprint with Helter Skelter Publishing: Firefly Publishing (mainstream rock and pop)

Sage Publications
1 Olivers Yard, 55 City Road
London EC1Y 1SP
020 7374 0645
market@sagepub.co.uk
www.sagepub.co.uk
Social sciences and humanities. Imprint: Paul Chapman (education and training)

Saint Andrew Press
Church of Scotland
121 George Street
Edinburgh EH2 4YN
0131 225 5722
standrewpress@cofscotland.org.uk
www.standrewpress.com
Owned by the Church of Scotland Christian, moral and ethical

Samuel French
52 Fitzroy Street, London W1T 5JR
020 7387 9373
theatre@samuelfrench-london.co.uk
www.samuelfrench-london.co.uk
Plays

SAMS Publishing
(see Pearson Education)

Sangam Books
57 London Fruit Exchange
Brushfield Street, London E1 6EP
020 7377 6399
sangambks@aol.com
Educational textbooks

Saqi Books
26 Westbourne Grove
London W2 5RH
020 7221 9347
editorial@saqibooks.com
www.saqibooks.com
Academic and illustrated; books on Balkans, Middle East and Arab world; Asia and European fiction

SB Publications
19 Grove Road
Seaford, East Sussex BN25 1TP
01323 893498
sbpublications@tiscali.co.uk
www.sbpublications.co.uk
Local history, travel, guides

Scholastic
Villiers House, Clarendon Avenue
Leamington Spa
Warwickshire CV32 5PR
01926 887799
enquiries@scholastic.co.uk
www.scholastic.co.uk
Education

Scholastic Children's Books
Commonwealth House
1–19 New Oxford Street
London WC1A 1NU
020 7421 9000
scbenquiries@scholastic.co.uk
www.scholastic.co.uk
Fiction. Imprints: Hippo, Point

Scitech Educational
Kent Innovation Centre
Millennium Way
Thanet Reach Business Park,
Broadstairs, Kent CT10 2QQ
01843 609300
maria.thompson@scitech-ed.com
www.scitech-ed.com
Learning resources and e-learning programs

SCM Canterbury Press
9–17 St Albans Place
London N1 0NX
020 7359 8033
admin@scm-canterburypress.co.uk
www.scm-canterburypress.co.uk
Theology and hymn books

Scala Publishers
Northburgh House
10 Northburgh Street
London EC1V 0AT
020 7490 9900
info@scalapublishers.com
Art

Scottish Cultural Press/ Scottish Children's Press
Unit 6
Newbattle Abbey Business Park
Newbattle Road, Dalkeith EH22 3LJ
Cultural: 0131 660 6366
Children's: 0131 660 4757
info@scottishbooks.com
www.scottishbooks.com
Cultural: Scottish interest books for adult, tourist and academic readers

Search Press
Wellwood, North Farm Road
Tunbridge Wells, Kent TN2 3DR
01892 510850
searchpress@searchpress.com
www.searchpress.com
Art and crafts

SEMERC
(see Granada Learning)

Seren
First Floor, 38–40 Nolton Street
Bridgend CF31 3BN
01656 663018
general@seren-books.com
www.seren-books.com
Wales. Imprint: Border Lines Biographies

Serpent's Tail
4 Blackstock Mews
London N4 2BT
020 7354 1949
info@serpentstail.com
www.serpentstail.com
Contemporary and gay fiction and non-fiction

Severn House Publishers
9–15 High Street, Sutton
Surrey SM1 1DF
020 8770 3930
info@severnhouse.com
www.severnhouse.com
Hardback fiction for the library market: romance, science fiction, horror, fantasy and crime

Shepheard-Walwyn (Publishers)
Suite 604, The Chandlery
50 Westminster Bridge Road
London SE1 7QY
020 7721 7666
books@shepheard-walwyn.co.uk
www.shepheard-walwyn.co.uk
Ethical economics, perennial philosophy, biography, gift books, books of Scottish interest

Shetland Times
Gremsta, Lerwick
Shetland ZE1 0PX
01595 693622
publishing@shetland-times.co.uk
www.shetlandtoday.co.uk
Shetland interest

Shire Publications
Cromwell House, Church Street
Princes Risborough
Buckinghamshire HP27 9AA
01844 344301
shire@shirebooks.co.uk
www.shirebooks.co.uk
Original non-fiction paperbacks

Short Books
15 Highbury Terrace
London N5 1UP
020 7226 1607
rebecca@shortbooks.biz
www.shortbooks.co.uk
Non-fiction for adults and children

Sidgwick and Jackson
(see Macmillan Publishers)

Sigma Press
5 Alton Road, Wilmslow
Cheshire SK9 5DY
01625 531035
info@sigmapress.co.uk
www.sigmapress.co.uk
Outdoor, heritage, myth, biography

Simon & Schuster UK
Africa House, 64–78 Kingsway
London WC2B 6AH
020 7316 1900
enquiries@simonandschuster.co.uk
web: www.simonsays.co.uk
General fiction and non-fiction. Imprint: Earthlight (science fiction), Scribner (trade paperback), Pocket Books (mass-market fiction and children's), Simon & Schuster Children, Free Press (literary fiction)

Skoob Russell Square
10 Brunswick Centre
off Bernard Street
London WC1N 1AE
020 7278 8760
books@skoob.com
www.skoob.com
Literary guides, cultural studies, esoterica, poetry, new writing from Orient

Soundings
(see Ulverscroft Group)

Souvenir Press
43 Great Russell Street
London WC1B 3PD
020 7580 9307
souvenirpress@ukonline.co.uk
Academic. Imprints include: Condor, Human Horizons, Independent Voices, Pictorial Presentations, Pop Universal, The Story-Tellers

Spellmount
The Village Centre, High Street
Staplehurst, Kent TN12 0BJ
01580 893730
enquiries@spellmount.com
www.spellmount.com
History and military history

Spon Press
(see T&F Informa)

Springer-Verlag London
Ashbourne House, The Guildway
Old Portsmouth Road, Guildford
Surrey GU3 1LR
01483 418800
postmaster@svl.co.uk
www.springeronline.com
Computer science, medical, engineering, astronomy, maths

Stainer & Bell
PO Box 110, 23 Gruneisen Road
London N3 1DZ
020 8343 3303
post@stainer.co.uk
www.stainer.co.uk
Music and hymns

Stanley Gibbons Publications
7 Parkside, Christchurch Road
Ringwood, Hampshire BH24 3SH
01425 472363
rpurkis@stanleygibbons.co.uk
www.stanleygibbons.co.uk
Philatelic reference catalogues and handbooks

TSO (The Stationery Office)
St Crispins, Duke Street
Norwich, Norfolk NR3 1PD
01603 622211
customer.services@tso.co.uk
www.thestationeryoffice.com

Summersdale Publishers
46 West Street, Chichester
West Sussex PO19 1RP
01243 771107
enquiries@summersdale.com
www.summersdale.com
Travel, martial arts, self-help, cookery, humour and gift books

Summertown Publishing
29 Grove Street, Summertown
Oxford OX2 7JT
01865 454130
chris@summertown.co.uk
www.summertown.co.uk
English-language teaching

Sutton Publishing
Phoenix Mill, Thrupp, Stroud
Gloucestershire GL5 2BU
01453 731114
sales@sutton-publishing.co.uk
www.suttonpublishing.co.uk
Owned by Haynes Publishing
Biography, countryside, history, transport, military and aviation

Sweet & Maxwell Group
100 Avenue Road
London NW3 3PF
020 7393 7000
marketinginformation@sweetandmaxwell.co.uk
www.sweetandmaxwell.co.uk
Part of the Thomson Corporation
Legal and professional. Imprints: W Green (Scotland), Round Hall

T&F Informa
Haines House, 21 John Street
London WC1N 2BP
www.tfinforma.com
- BIOS Scientific Publishers: *Biology and medicine*
- Brunner-Routledge psychology and counselling
- Carfax: *Social science and humanities*
- CRC: *Science and medical*
- Curzon Press: *Asian and Middle Eastern studies*
- Europa Publications: *International affairs, politics and economics*
- Frank Cass: *Military and strategic studies. Also Jewish interest imprints: Vallentine Mitchell, Jewish Chronicle Publications*
- Garland Science: *Biology*
- Martin Dunitz: *Medical*
- Psychology Press: *Psychology*
- Routledge: *Humanities & social sciences textbooks/general non-fiction*
- Routledge Curzon: *Politics and Middle Eastern studies*
- Routledge Falmer: *Education*
- Spon Press: *Architecture and planning*
- Taylor & Francis: *Science and reference esp. ergonomics, geographical information systems, biotechnology and engineering*

Taschen UK
13 Old Burlington Street
London W1S 3AJ
020 7437 4350
contact@taschen.com
www.taschen.com
Art and pop culture

Taylor & Francis
(see T&F Informa)

Templar Publishing
Pippbrook Mill, London Road
Dorking, Surrey RH4 1JE
01306 876361
info@templarco.co.uk
www.templarco.co.uk
Illustrated and novelty books for children

Terence Dalton
Water Street, Lavenham
Sudbury, Suffolk CO10 9RN
01787 249291
terence@lavenhamgroup.co.uk
www.terencedalton.com
Part of the Lavenham Group. Non-fiction: aeronautical, aviation, maritime and local interest

Thalamus Publishing
4 Attorney's Walk, Bull Ring
Ludlow, Shropshire SY8 1AA
01584 874977
roger@thalamus-books.com
Family reference

Thames & Hudson
181A High Holborn
London WC1V 7QX
020 7845 5000
mail@thameshudson.co.uk
www.thamesandhudson.com
Cultural non-fiction

Thomas Cook Publishing
PO Box 227
Unit 15/16 Coningsby Road
Peterborough PE3 8SB
01733 416477
publishing-sales@thomascook.com
www.thomascookpublishing.com
Guide books and timetables

Thomson Learning
50–51 Bedford Row
London WC1R 4LR
020 7067 2500
communications@thomsonlearning.com
www.thomsonlearning.co.uk
Part of the Thomson Corporation Educational. Imprints: Scientific Press, Cherry Tree Books (children's), Business Press, Arden Shakespeare, Computer Press, Course Technology, Premier Press, Texere, Wadsworth

Continuum International Publishing Group
Tower Building, 11 York Road
London SE1 7NX
020 7922 0880
info@continuumbooks.com
www.continuumbooks.com
Academic and religious. Imprints: Athlone, Pinter, Sheffield Academic Press, Geoffrey Chapman, Mowbray, TandT Clark, Burns and Oates, Morehouse, Claridge Press

Evans Publishing Group
2A Portman Mansions
Chiltern Street, London W1U 6NR
020 7487 0920
sales@evansbrothers.co.uk
www.evansbooks.co.uk
Children's and educational. Imprints: Cherrytree Books, Evans Brothers, Zero to Ten

IB Tauris
6 Salem Road, London W2 4BU
020 7243 1225
enquiries@ibtauris.com
www.ibtauris.com
Culture, history and politics. Imprint: New Press

Oneworld
185 Banbury Road
Oxford OX2 7AR
01865 310597
info@oneworld-publications.com
www.oneworld-publications.com
Religion, history and philosophy

Pluto Press
345 Archway Road, Highgate
London N6 5AA
020 8348 2724
pluto@plutobooks.com
www.plutobooks.com
Academic and political non-fiction

Thorsons
(see HarperCollins Publishers)

Time Out Group
c/o L Aldrich Publishing Consultancy
The Studio, 14 Priory Avenue
London W4 1TX
020 7813 3000
www.timeout.com
Guide and travel books

Time Warner Books (UK)
Brettenham House, Lancaster Place
London WC2E 7EN
020 7911 8000
email.uk@twbg.co.uk
www.timewarnerbooks.co.uk
Imprints: Little, Brown (non-fiction); Abacus (fiction, travel); Time Warner (paperback fiction); Virago Press (women authors only: fiction, non-fiction and poetry); Atom (teen sci-fi); Orbit Press (sci-fi and fantasy)

Titan Publishing
144 Southwark Street
London SE1 0UP
020 7620 0200
editorial@titanmail.com
www.forbiddenplanet.com
Comic books, graphic novels, spin-offs

Tolkien
(see HarperCollins Publishers)

Top That Publishing
Marine House, Tide Mill Way
Woodbridge, Suffolk IP12 1AP
01394 386651
www.topthatpublishing.com
Children. Imprint: Kudos (adult range)

Transworld Publishers
(see Random House Group)

Travel Publishing
7A Apollo House, Calleva Park
Aldermaston, Berkshire RG7 8TN
0118 981 7777
info@travelpublishing.co.uk
www.travelpublishing.co.uk
Imprints: Hidden Places, Hidden Inns, Golfers Guides, Country Living Rural Guides, Off the Motorway

Trentham Books
Westview House, 734 London Road
Stoke-on-Trent
Staffordshire ST4 5NP
01782 745567
tb@trentham-books.co.uk
www.trentham-books.co.uk
Education, culture and law for professional readers

Trident Press
Empire House, 175 Piccadilly
London W1J 9TB
020 7491 8770
admin@tridentpress.com
www.tridentpress.com
TV tie-ins, history, travel, geography, culture

Trotman & Co
2 The Green, Richmond
Surrey TW9 1PL
020 8486 1150
mail@trotman.co.uk
www.careers-portal.co.uk
Careers and education

Ulverscroft Group
The Green, Bradgate Road
Anstey, Leicester LE7 7FU
0116 236 4325
sales@ulverscroft.co.uk
www.ulverscroft.com

FA Thorpe Publishing
Fiction and non-fiction large print books. Imprints and divisions include: Linford Romance, Linford Mystery, Linford Western, Charnwood (HB) and Ulverscroft (HB)

Isis Publishing
7 Centremead, Osney Mead
Oxford OX2 0ES
01865 250333
sales@isis-publishing.co.uk
www.isis-publishing.co.uk
Large-print books

Magna Large Print Books
Magna House, Long Preston
Nr. Skipton, North Yorkshire
BD23 4ND
01729 840225
Large-print books; audio fiction and non-fiction

Soundings
Isis House, Kings Drive
Whitley Bay, Tyne & Wear NE26 2JT
0191 253 4155
gillian@soundingsne.fsbusiness.co.uk
Audio books

Ulverscroft Large Print Books
University of Exeter Press
Reed Hall, Streatham Drive
Exeter, Devon EX4 4QR
01392 263066
uep@exeter.ac.uk
www.ex.ac.uk/uep/

University of Hertfordshire Press
Learning and Information Services, Hatfield Campus Learning Resources Centre
College Lane, Hatfield
Hertfordshire AL10 9AB
01707 284681
uhpress@herts.ac.uk
www.herts.ac.uk/UHPress/
Literary criticism and theatre studies, Romani studies, regional and local history, parapsychology. Imprints: Interface Collection, Hertfordshire Publications

University of Wales Press
10 Columbus Walk, Brigantine Place
Cardiff CF10 4UP
029 2049 6899
press@press.wales.ac.uk
www.wales.ac.uk/press
Imprints: GPC Books, Gwasg Prifysgol Cymru

University Presses of California, Columbia & Princeton
1 Oldlands Way, Bognor Regis
West Sussex PO22 9SA
01243 842165
lois@upccp.demon.co.uk
www.ucpress.edu
www.columbia.edu/cu/cup
www.pup.princeton.edu

Unofficial Guides
(see John Wiley & Sons)

Usborne Publishing
83–85 Saffron Hill
London EC1N 8RT
020 7430 2800
mail@usborne.co.uk
www.usborne.com
Non-fiction books for children, including computer guides, puzzle-books, pre-school and books on music

Vallentine Mitchell/ Jewish Chronicle Publications
(see Frank Cass, T&F Informa)

Vermilion
(see Random House Group)

Viking
(see Penguin Books)

Vintage
(see Random House Group)

Virago Press
(see Time Warner Books)

Virgin Books
Units 5 & 6, Thames Wharf Studios
Rainville Road, London W6 9HA
020 7386 3300
info@virgin-books.co.uk
www.virginbooks.com
TV, film, music, sport and pop culture. Imprints: Black Lace and Nexus (erotic fiction)

Vista House
27 Greenhead Road, Huddersfield
West Yorks HD1 4EN
01484 427200
editorialinfo@vistahouse.co.uk
www.vistahouse.co.uk
Fiction and non-fiction. Imprint: First Authors

Visual
(see John Wiley & Sons)

Voyager
(see HarperCollins Publishers)

W Foulsham & Co
The Publishing House
Bennetts Close, Slough
Berkshire SL1 5AP
01753 526769
info@foulsham.com
Lifestyle

Walker Books
87 Vauxhall Walk, London SE11 5HJ
020 7793 0909
enquiry@walker.co.uk
www.walkerbooks.co.uk
Children's big books, book charts, game books. Series: Giggle Club

Wallflower Press
4th Floor, 26 Shacklewell Lane
London E8 2EZ
020 7690 0115
info@wallflowerpress.co.uk
www.wallflowerpress.co.uk
Film, media and cultural studies

Warne
(see Penguin Books)

Watts Publishing Group
96 Leonard Street
London EC2A 4XD
020 7739 2929
gm@wattspub.co.uk
www.wattspublishing.co.uk
Part of Groupe Lagardere. Children's non-fiction, reference, fiction, picture and novelty. Imprints: Franklin Watts, Orchard Books, Cats Whiskers, Aladdin/Watts

Weidenfeld & Nicolson
(see Orion Publishing Group)

Wimbledon Publishing Press
75–76 Blackfriars Road
London SE1 8HA
020 7401 4200
enquiries@wpcpress.com
www.wpcpress.com
Textbooks for languages, maths, biology and accountancy. Imprint: Anthem Press

Wharncliffe Publishing
(see Pen & Sword Books)

Which?
2 Marylebone Road
London NW1 4DF
020 7770 7000
editor@which.net
www.which.net
Publishing arm of the Consumers' Association

Whittet Books
Hill Farm, Stonham Road, Cotton
Stowmarket, Suffolk IP14 4RQ
01449 781877
annabel@whittet.dircon.co.uk
www.whittetbooks.com
Natural history, pets and rural interest, livestock and horticulture

Whurr Publishers
19B Compton Terrace
London N1 2UN
020 7359 5979
info@whurr.co.uk
www.whurr.co.uk
Occupational therapy, nursing, special education, psychology, audiology and communication disorders

Wild Goose Publications
Iona Community, 4th Floor
The Savoy House
140 Sauchiehall Street
Glasgow G2 3DH
0141 332 6292
admin@ionabooks.com
www.iona.books.com
Publishing house of the Iona Community. Religion, spiritualism and human rights

Wiley
(see John Wiley & Sons)

William Heinemann
(see Random House Group)

Windhorse Publications
11 Park Road, Moseley
Birmingham B13 8AB
0121 449 9191
info@windhorsepublications.com
www.windhorsepublications.com
Meditation and Buddhism

WIT Press
Ashurst Lodge, Ashurst
Southampton
Hampshire SO40 7AA
023 8029 3223
marketing@witpress.com
www.witpress.com
Scientific and technical

Women's Press
27 Goodge Street
London W1T 2LD
020 7636 3992
sales@the-womens-press.com
www.the-womens-press.com
Part of the Namara Group

Woodhead Publishing
Abington Hall, Abington
Cambridge CB1 6AH
01223 891358
wp@woodhead-publishing.com
www.woodhead-publishing.com
Formerly Abington Publishing Engineering, textiles, finance and investment, food technology and environmental science

Wordsworth Editions
8b East Street, Ware
Hertfordshire SG12 9HJ
01920 465167
enquiries@wordsworth-editions.com
www.wordsworth-editions.com
Literary classics, reference, poetry, children's classics, military history and folklore

Working White
Chancery Court, Lincolns Inn
Lincoln Road
High Wycombe HP12 3RE
01494 429318
info@workingwhite.co.uk
www.workingwhite.co.uk
Children's big books, book charts, game books. Series: Giggle Club

Wrox
(see John Wiley & Sons)

WW Norton & Company
Castle House, 75–76 Wells Street
London W1T 3QT
020 7323 1579
office@wwnorton.co.uk
Academic and professional non-fiction

X Press
PO Box 25694, London N17 6FP
020 8801 2100
vibes@xpress.co.uk
www.xpress.co.uk
Black interest. Imprints: Nia, 20/20

Y Lolfa Cyf
Talybont, Ceredigion SY24 5AP
01970 832304
ylolfa@ylolfa.com
www.ylolfa.com
Welsh and Celtic interest. Imprints and divisions include: Dinas

Yale University Press (London)
47 Bedford Square
London WC1B 3DP
020 7079 4900
sales@yaleup.co.uk
www.yalebooks.co.uk

Yellow Jersey Press
(see Random House Group)

York Notes
(see Pearson Education)

Young Picador
(see Macmillan Publishers)

Zambezi Publishing
PO Box 221
Plymouth, Devon PL2 2YJ
01752 367300
info@zampub.com
www.zampub.com
New-Age and self-help

Zed Books
7 Cynthia Street
London N1 9JF
020 7837 4014
www.zedbooks.co.uk
International and third-world affairs and development studies

Literary agents

AM Heath & Co*
79 St Martin's Lane
London WC2N 4RE
020 7836 4271
www.amheath.com
Fiction, general non-fiction and children's

AP Watt*
20 John Street
London WC1N 2DR
020 7405 6774
apw@apwatt.co.uk
www.apwatt.co.uk
Full-length typescripts, including children's books, screenplays for film and TV

Abner Stein*
10 Roland Gardens
London SW7 3PH
020 7373 0456
abner@abnerstein.co.uk
US agents and authors, some full-length fiction and general non-fiction

Alan Brodie Representation
211 Piccadilly
London W1J 9HF
020 7917 2871
info@alanbrodie.com
www.alanbrodie.com
Theatre, film and TV scripts

Alexandra Nye
Craigower', 6 Kinnoull Avenue
Dunblane, Perthshire FK15 9JG
01786 825114
Fiction and topical non-fiction, esp. literary fiction and history

Andrew Mann*
1 Old Compton Street
London W1D 5JA
020 7734 4751
manscript@onetel.net.uk
Fiction; general non-fiction; film, TV, theatre and radio scripts

Andrew Nurnberg Associates*
Clerkenwell House
45–47 Clerkenwell Green
London EC1R 0HT
020 7417 8800
all@nurnberg.co.uk
Foreign rights

Annette Green Authors' Agency*
1 East Cliff Road
Tunbridge Wells, Kent TN4 9AD
01892 514275
annettekgreen@aol.com
Literary and general fiction; non-fiction; fiction for teenagers; upmarket popular culture

Artellus
30 Dorset House, Gloucester Place
London NW1 5AD
020 7935 6972
artellus@artellusltd.co.uk
General fiction and non-fiction

The Agency (London)*
24 Pottery Lane, Holland Park
London W11 4LZ
020 7727 1346
info@theagency.co.uk
www.theagency.co.uk
Theatre, film, TV, radio and children's writers and illustrators; also film and TV rights in novels and non-fiction

Andrew Lownie Literary Agency*
17 Sutherland Street
London SW1V 4JU
020 7828 1274
lownie@globalnet.co.uk
www.andrewlownie.co.uk
Non-fiction

Barbara Levy Literary Agency*
64 Greenhill, Hampstead High Street
London NW3 5TZ
020 7435 9046
General fiction, non-fiction, TV presenters, film and TV rights

Bill McLean Personal Management
23B Deodar Road
London SW15 2NP
020 8789 8191
Scripts for all media

Blake Friedmann*
122 Arlington Road
London NW1 7HP
020 7284 0408
carole@blakefriedmann.co.uk (books)
isobel@blakefriedmann.co.uk (books)
julian@blakefriedmann.co.uk (Film and TV)
conrad@blakefriedmann.co.uk (Film and TV)
www.blakefriedmann.co.uk
Literary, TV & films

BookBlast
PO Box 20184
London W10 5AU
020 8968 3089
info@bookblast.com
www.bookblast.com
Horror, crime, science fiction, fantasy, poetry, short stories, academic, children's books and lifestyle

Brie Burkeman*
14 Neville Court, Abbey Road
London NW8 9DD
0709 223 9113
brie.burkeman@mail.com
Commercial and literary fiction and non-fiction, scripts, poetry, short stories. Independent film and television consultant to literary agents

Bell Lomax Agency
James House, 1 Babmaes Street
London SW1Y 6HF
020 7930 4447
agency@bell-lomax.co.uk
Fiction and non-fiction, biography, children's, business and sport

Campbell Thomson & McLaughlin*
1 King's Mews, London WC1N 2JA
020 7242 0958
Fiction and general non-fiction

* *member of the Association of Authors' Agents*

Capel & Land*
29 Wardour Street, London W1D 6PS
020 7734 2414
robert@capelland.co.uk
Fiction and non-fiction; film, TV, theatre and radio scripts and children's books

Caroline Davidson Literary Agency
5 Queen Anne's Gardens
London W4 1TU
020 8995 5768
High quality fiction of originality and non-fiction

Caroline Sheldon Literary Agency*
Thorley Manor Farm, Thorley
Yarmouth PO41 0SJ
01983 760205
Fiction, commercial and literary novels, especially women's and children's fiction

Casarotto Ramsay and Associates
National House
60–66 Wardour Street
London W1V 4ND
020 7287 4450
agents@casarotto.uk.com
www.casarotto.uk.com
Scripts for TV, theatre, film and radio

Cat Ledger Literary Agency*
20–21 Newman Street
London W1T 1PG
020 7861 8226
cat.ledger@virgin.net
Non-fiction: popular culture, biography, politics, investigative journalism and fiction (non-genre)

Cecily Ware Literary Agents
19C John Spencer Square
London N1 2LZ
020 7359 3787
info@cecilyware.com
Scripts for TV and film in all areas

Chapman & Vincent*
The Mount, Sun Hill, Royston
Herts SG8 9AT
01763 245005
info@chapmanvincent.co.uk
Non-fiction

Christine Green Authors' Agent*
6 Whitehorse Mews
Westminster Bridge Road
London SE1 7QD
020 7401 8844
info@christinegreen.co.uk
www.christinegreen.co.uk
Literary and general fiction and non-fiction

Conville & Walsh*
2 Ganton Street, Soho
London W1F 7QL
020 7287 3030
sara@convilleandwalsh.com
Literary and commercial fiction; serious and narrative non-fiction

Curtis Brown Group*
Haymarket House, 28/29 Haymarket
London SW1Y 4SP
020 7396 6600
cb@curtisbrown.co.uk
www.curtisbrown.co.uk
Writers, directors, designers and presenters

The Christopher Little Literary Agency*
10 Eel Brook Studios
125 Moore Park Road
London SW6 4PS
020 7736 4455
christopher@christopherlittle.net
www.christopherlittle.net
Commercial and literary full-length fiction and non-fiction; film scripts for established clients

Darley Anderson Literary, TV & Film Agency*
Estelle House, 11 Eustace Road
London SW6 1JB
020 7385 6652
enquiries@darleyanderson.com
Fiction: young male, American, Irish, women's, crime/mystery and humour; non-fiction; children's fiction; selected scripts for film and TV

David Godwin Associates
55 Monmouth Street
London WC2H 9DG
020 7240 9992
assistant@
davidgodwinassociates.co.uk
Literary and general fiction, non-fiction, biography

David Grossman Literary Agency
118b Holland Park Avenue
London W11 4UA
020 7221 2770
dgal@aol.com
Full-length fiction and general non-fiction especially controversial

David Higham Associates*
5–8 Lower John Street
Golden Square, London W1F 9HA
020 7434 5900
dha@davidhigham.co.uk
www.davidhigham.co.uk
Fiction; general non-fiction: biography, history, current affairs; children's; scripts

David O'Leary Literary Agents
10 Lansdowne Court
Lansdowne Rise, London W11 2NR
020 7229 1623
d.oleary@virgin.net
Fiction (popular and literary) and non-fiction, esp. thrillers, history, popular science, Russia and Ireland (history and fiction)

Deborah Owen*
78 Narrow Street, Limehouse
London E14 8BP
020 7987 51191
do@deborahowen.co.uk
International fiction and non-fiction

Dench Arnold Agency
10 Newburgh Street
London W1F 7RN
020 7437 4551
www.dencharnold.com
Scripts for TV and film

Dinah Wiener*
12 Cornwall Grove, Chiswick
London W4 2LB
020 8994 6011
dinahweiner@enterprise.net
Fiction and general non-fiction: popular science, cookery

Dorian Literary Agency*
Upper Thornehill, 27 Church Road
St Marychurch, Torquay
Devon TQ1 4QY
01803 312095
General fiction especially popular; children's (over 10 yrs)

Dorie Simmonds Agency*
67 Upper Berkeley Street
London W1H 7QX
020 7486 9228
dhsimmonds@aol.com
General fiction and commercial non-fiction, children's books and associated rights

Duncan McAra
28 Beresford Gardens
Edinburgh EH5 3ES
0131 552 1558
duncanmcara@hotmail.com
Literary fiction and non-fiction

Ed Victor*
6 Bayley Street, Bedford Square
London WC1B 3HE
020 7304 4100
Mostly commercial fiction and non-fiction; children's

Edwards Fuglewicz*
49 Great Ormond Street
London WC1N 3HZ
020 7405 6725
efla@ftech.co.uk
Fiction: literary, some commercial; non-fiction: biography, history, popular culture

Elaine Steel
110 Gloucester Avenue
London NW1 8HX
020 8348 0918
ecmsteel@aol.com
Writers and directors in film, television and publishing

Elizabeth Puttick Literary Agency*
46 Brookfield Mansions
Highgate West Hill, London N6 6AT
020 8340 6383
agency@puttick.com
www.puttick.com
General non-fiction, esp. self-help, mind, body & spirit, health and fitness, lifestyle and business

Elspeth Cochrane Personal Management
14/2 Second Floor
South Bank Commercial Centre
140 Battersea Park Road
London SW11 4NB
020 7622 0314
ecochrane@pji.uk.com
Fiction, non-fiction, biographies, screenplays, scripts for all media

Eric Glass
25 Ladbroke Crescent
London W11 1PS
020 7229 9500
eglassltd@aol.com
Fiction, non-fiction and scripts

Eunice McMullen Children's Literary Agent
Low Ibbotsholme Cottage
Off Bridge Lane, Troutbeck Bridge
Windermere, Cumbria LA23 1HU
01539 448551
eunicemcmullen@totalise.co.uk
Children's material

Faith Evans Associates*
27 Park Avenue North
London N8 7RU
020 8340 9920
Fiction and non-fiction

Felicity Bryan*
2A North Parade, Banbury Road
Oxford OX2 6LX
01865 513816
agency@felicitybryan.com
Fiction and non-fiction

Felix de Wolfe
Garden Offices, 51 Maida Vale
London W9 1SD
020 7289 5770
info@felixdewolfe.com
Theatrical agency

Fox & Howard Literary Agency
4 Bramerton Street
London SW3 5JX
020 7352 8691
Non-fiction: biography, history and popular culture, reference, business and lifestyle

Frances Kelly Agency*
111 Clifton Road
Kingston Upon Thames
Surrey KT2 6PL
020 8549 7830
Illustrated and academic non-fiction

Futerman, Rose & Associates*
Heston Court Business Park
19 Camp Road, Wimbledon
London SW19 4UW
020 8947 0188
guy@futermanrose.co.uk
www.futermanrose.co.uk
Commercial and literary fiction, non-fiction, biography, film and television scripts specialising in book-to-film projects

Gillon Aitken Associates*
18–21 Cavaye Place
London SW10 9PT
020 7373 8672
reception@Gillonaitken.co.uk
Fiction and non-fiction

Greene & Heaton*
37 Goldhawk Road
London W12 8QQ
020 8749 0315
info@greeneheaton.co.uk
www.greeneheaton.co.uk
Wide range of fiction and general non-fiction; clients include Bill Bryson, Hugh Fearnley-Whittingstall, Michael Frayn, PD James and Sarah Waters

Gregory & Co*
3 Barb Mews, London W6 7PA
020 7610 4676
info@gregoryandcompany.co.uk
www.gregoryandcompany.co.uk
Fiction: literary, commercial, crime, suspense and thrillers; general non-fiction

ICM
Oxford House, 76 Oxford Street
London W1D 1BS
020 7636 6565
duncanheath@icmlondon.co.uk
Film, TV and theatre scripts

IMG Literary UK
McCormick House, 3 Burlington Lane
Chiswick, London W4 2TH
020 8233 5000
www.imgworld.com
Celebrity books, commercial fiction, non-fiction, sports-related and how-to business books

Intercontinental Literary Agency*
33 Bedford Street
London WC2E 9ED
020 7379 6611
ila@ila-agency.co.uk
Translation rights only

Jane Conway-Gordon*
1 Old Compton Street
London W1D 5JA
020 7494 0148
Fiction and general non-fiction

Jane Judd Literary Agency*
18 Belitha Villas, London N1 1PD
020 7607 0273
General fiction and non-fiction: biography, investigative journalism, health, women's interests and travel

Janklow & Nesbit (UK)
29 Adam & Eve Mews
London W8 6UG
020 7376 2733
queries@janklow.co.uk
Fiction and non-fiction, commercial and literary; US and translation rights handled by Janklow and Nesbit Associates in New York

Jeffrey Simmons
15 Penn House, Mallory Street
London NW8 8SX
020 7224 8917
jas@london-inc.com
www.jeffreysimmons.com
Biography, cinema and theatre, quality and commercial fiction, history, law and crime, politics and world affairs, parapsychology and sport

Jill Foster
9 Barb Mews, Brook Green
London W6 7PA
020 7602 1263
Scripts for TV, film and radio

JM Thurley Management
Archery House, 33 Archery Square
Walmer, Deal CT14 7JA
01304 371721
jmthurley@aol.com
Full-length fiction, non-fiction, TV and films

John Johnson*
Clerkenwell House
45/47 Clerkenwell Green
London EC1R 0HT
020 7251 0125
johnjohnson@btinternet.com
A division of Johnson & Alcock
General fiction and non-fiction

John Welch, Literary Consultant & Agent
Mill Cottage, Calf Lane
Chipping Camden
Gloucestershire GL55 6JQ
01386 840237
johnwelch@waitrose.com
Military, naval and aviation history, general history, and a little biography

Jonathan Clowes*
10 Iron Bridge House
Bridge Approach, London NW1 8BD
020 7722 7674
jonathanclowes@aol.com
Fiction and non-fiction; scripts, especially situation comedy, film and television rights; clients include Doris Lessing, David Nobbs, Len Deighton

Josef Weinberger Plays
12–14 Mortimer Street
London W1T 3JJ
020 7580 2827
general.info@jwmail.co.uk
www.josef-weinberger.com
Scripts for the theatre; play publisher and licensor of stage rights; publishes plays and acts as UK agent for US agents including the Dramatists Play Service

Judith Chilcote Agency*
8 Wentworth Mansions
Keats Grove, London NW3 2RL
020 7794 3717
judybks@aol.com
Commercial fiction, TV tie-ins, biography and lifestyle

* *member of the Association of Authors' Agents*

Judith Murdoch Literary Agency*
19 Chalcot Square
London NW1 8YA
020 7722 4197
Full-length fiction only

Judy Daish Associates
2 St Charles Place
London W10 6EG
020 8964 8811
judy@judydaish.demon.co.uk
Scripts for TV, theatre, film and radio

Juri Gabriel
35 Camberwell Grove
London SE5 8JA
020 7703 6186
Quality fiction and non-fiction

Juvenilia
Avington, near Winchester
Hampshire SO21 1DB
01962 779656
juvenilia@clara.co.uk
Baby to teen fiction and picture books; non-fiction and scripts for TV and radio

Knight Features
20 Crescent Grove
London SW4 7AH
020 7622 1467
peter@knightfeatures.co.uk
Motorsports, cartoon books, puzzles, business, history, factual and biographical material

Laurence Fitch
Mezzanine, Quadrant House
80–82 Regent street
London W1B 5AU
020 7734 9911
information@laurencefitch.com
www.laurencefitch.com
Children's and horror books, scripts for theatre, film, TV and radio

Lavinia Trevor Agency*
The Glasshouse
49A Goldhawk Road
London W12 8QP
020 8749 8481
General literary and commercial fiction; non-fiction including popular science

LAW (Lucas Alexander Whitley)*
14 Vernon Street, London W14 0RJ
020 7471 7900
Commercial and literary fiction, non-fiction and children's books; film and TV scripts for established clients

Limelight Management*
33 Newman Street
London W1T 1PY
020 7637 2529
limelight.management@virgin.net
www.limelightmanagement.com
General non-fiction

Lisa Eveleigh Literary Agency*
3rd Floor, 11/12 Dover Street
London W1S 4LJ
020 7399 2803
eveleigh@dial.pipex.com
Literary and commercial fiction and non-fiction

Louise Greenberg Books*
The End House, Church Crescent
London N3 1BG
020 8349 1179
louisegreenberg@msn.com
Literary fiction and non-fiction

Lutyens and Rubinstein*
231 Westbourne Park Road
London W11 1EB
020 7792 4855
susannah@lutyensrubinstein.co.uk
Adult fiction and non-fiction

Maggie Pearlstine Associates*
31 Ashley Gardens
Ambrosden Avenue
London SW1P 1QE
020 7828 4212
post@pearlstine.co.uk
General non-fiction and fiction, history, current affairs, biography, health and politics

Manuscript ReSearch
PO Box 33, Bicester
Oxfordshire OX26 4ZZ
01869 323447
Scripts for film and TV

Margaret Hanbury Literary Agency*
27 Walcot Square
London SE11 4UB
020 7735 7680
maggie@mhanbury.demon.co.uk
Quality fiction and non-fiction; clients include JG Ballard, Simon Callow, George Alagiah, Judith Lennox, children's books, plays/scripts and poetry

Marjacq Scripts
34 Devonshire Place
London W1G 6JW
020 7935 9499
philip@marjacq.com
and luke@marjacq.com
www.marjacq.com
All fiction and non-fiction, screenplays, radio plays and film and tv rights

Martinez Literary Agency
60 Oakwood Avenue, Southgate
London N14 6QL
020 8886 5829
High quality fiction, children's books, lifestyle, autobiography, biography, popular music, sport and memorabilia books

Mary Clemmey Literary Agency*
6 Dunollie Road, London NW5 2XP
020 7267 1290
Fiction and non-fiction, high quality for an international market.

MBA Literary Agents*
62 Grafton Way, London W1T 5DW
020 7387 2076
agent@mbalit.co.uk
Fiction and non-fiction books, TV, film, theatre and radio scripts

Merric Davidson Literary Agency
12 Priors Heath, Goudhurst
Cranbrook, Kent TN17 2RE
01580 212041
authors@mdla.co.uk
www.mdla.co.uk
Fiction especially contemporary; authors include Francesca Clementis, Alison Habens, Simon Scarrow

Mic Cheetham Literary Agency
11–12 Dover Street
London W1S 4LJ
020 7495 2002
info@miccheetham.com
www.miccheetham.com
General and literary fiction, fantasy and science fiction, crime and some specific non-fiction

Michael Alcock Management (division of Johnson & Alcock)*
45/47 Clerkenwell Green
London EC1R 0HT
020 7837 8137
alcockmgt@aol.com
General non-fiction, literary and commercial mainstream fiction

Micheline Steinberg Associates
Fourth Floor
104 Great Portland Street
London W1W 6PE
020 7631 1310
info@steinplays.com
Plays for stage, TV, radio and film

Michelle Kass Associates*
36–38 Glasshouse Street
London W1B 5DL
020 7439 1624
Literary fiction and film

Maggie Noach Literary Agency*
22 Dorville Crescent
London W6 0HJ
020 8748 2926
m-noach@dircon.co.uk
Fiction and general non-fiction

Marsh Agency
11/12 Dover Street
London W1S 4LJ
020 7399 2800
enquiries@marsh-agency.co.uk
www.marsh-agency.co.uk
International rights specialists selling English and foreign-language writing

Narrow Road Company
182 Brighton Road
Coulsdon, Surrey CR5 2NF
020 8763 9895
narrowroad@freeuk.com
Scripts for TV, theatre, film and radio

Owen Robinson Literary Agents
20 Tolbury Mill, Bruton
Somerset BA10 0DY
01749 812836
jpr@owenrobinson.netlineuk.net
Fiction and non-fiction

Paterson Marsh*
11/12 Dover Street
London W1S 4LJ
020 7399 2800
steph@patersonmarsh.co.uk
www.patersonmarsh.co.uk
World rights, especially psychoanalysis and psychotherapy

Paul Kiernan
PO Box 120, London SW3 4LU
Fiction, non-fiction: biography, lifestyle; scripts for TV, film, theatre and radio

Peake Associates*
14 Grafton Crescent
London NW1 8SL
020 7267 8033
peakeassoc@aol.com
www.tonypeake.com
Fiction and non-fiction

Peters Fraser & Dunlop Group (PFD)*
Drury House, 34–43 Russell Street
London WC2B 5HA
020 7344 1000
postmaster@pfd.co.uk
www.pfd.co.uk
Fiction and children's, plus scripts for film, theatre, radio and TV

Pollinger*
9 Staple Inn, Holborn
London WC1V 7QH
020 7404 0342
info@pollingerltd.com
www.pollingerltd.com
Formerly Laurence Pollinger and Pearn, Pollinger & Higham. General trade, non-fiction, children's fiction and non-fiction

PVA Management
Hallow Park, Worcester WR2 6PG
01905 640663
books@pva.co.uk
Non-fiction only

Real Creatives Worldwide
14 Dean Street, London W1D 3RS
020 7437 4188
boiltheocean@rentingeyeballs.com
www.realcreatives.com
Represents writers and creative media professionals

Robert Smith Literary Agency*
12 Bridge Wharf
156 Caledonian Road
London N1 9UU
020 7278 2444
robertsmith.literaryagency@virgin.net
Non-fiction; biography, health and nutrition, cookery, lifestyle, showbusiness and true crime

Robin Wade Literary Agency
1 Cormorant Lodge
Thomas More Street
London E1W 1AU
020 7488 4171
rw@rwla.com
www.rwla.com
General fiction and non-fiction

Roger Hancock
4 Water Lane, London NW1 8NZ
020 7267 4418
info@rogerhancock.com
Scripts for comedy, drama and light entertainment

Rogers, Coleridge & White*
20 Powis Mews, London W11 1JN
020 7221 3717
Fiction, non-fiction and children's books

Rosemary Bromley Literary Agency
Avington, Near Winchester
Hampshire SO21 1DB
01962 779656
juvenilia@clara.co.uk
Non-fiction and scripts for TV and radio

Rosemary Sandberg
6 Bayley Street, London WC1B 3HB
020 7304 4110
rosemary@sandberg.demon.co.uk
Children's picture books and novels, adult non-fiction

Rosica Colin
1 Clareville Grove Mews
London SW7 5AH
020 7370 1080
Full-length manuscripts plus theatre, film, television and sound broadcasting

Rupert Crew*
1A King's Mews, London WC1N 2JA
020 7242 8586
rupertcrew@compuserve.com
Volume and subsidiary rights in fiction and non-fiction properties

Rupert Heath Literary Agency
The Beeches, Furzedown Lane
Amport, Hampshire SP11 8BW
01264 771899
enquiries@rupertheath.com
www.rupertheath.com
Fiction, history, biography, science, the arts and popular culture

Rod Hall Agency
3 Charlotte Mews, London W1T 4DZ
020 7637 0706
office@rodhallagency.com
www.rodhallagency.com
Drama for film, TV and theatre

Sayle Screen
11 Jubilee Place, London SW3 3TD
020 7823 3883
info@saylescreen.com
www.saylescreen.com
Writers and directors for film, TV, theatre and radio

Sheil Land Associates*
43 Doughty Street
London WC1N 2LH
020 7405 9351
info@sheilland.co.uk
Full-length general, commercial and literary fiction and non-fiction, including theatre, film, radio and TV scripts

Sheila Ableman Literary Agency
122 Arlington Road
London NW1 7HP
020 7485 3409
sheila@ableman.freeserve.co.uk
Non-fiction including history, science and biography

Shelley Power Literary Agency*
13 rue du Pre Saint Gervais
75019 Paris, France
00 33 1 42 383649
shelley.power@wanadoo.fr
Fiction, business, true crime, film and entertainment

Shirley Stewart Literary Agency
3rd Floor, 21 Denmark Street
London WC2H 8NA
020 7836 4440
Literary fiction and non-fiction

Sinclair-Stevenson
3 South Terrace, London SW7 2TB
020 7581 2550
Biography, current affairs, travel, history, fiction, the arts

Sayle Literary Agency*
Bickerton House
25–27 Bickerton Road
London N19 5JT
020 7263 8681
Fiction, crime and general; general non-fiction

Sharland Organisation
The Manor House, Manor Street
Raunds
Northamptonshire NN9 6JW
01933 626600
tsoshar@aol.com
Scripts for film, TV, theatre and radio; non-fiction; specialises in national and international film, television and theatre negotiations

Susijn Agency
3rd Floor, 64 Great Titchfield Street
London W1W 7QH
020 7580 6341
info@thesusijnagency.com
www.thesusijnagency.com
Sells rights worldwide in English and non-English language literature: literary fiction and non fiction

Tamar Karet Literary Agency
56 Priory Road, Crouch End
London N8 7EX
020 8340 6460
tamar@btinternet.com
Fiction, leisure, biography, history, social affairs and politics

Tanja Howarth Literary Agency*
19 New Row, London WC2N 4LA
020 7240 5553
tanja.howarth@virgin.net
Fiction and non-fiction from British writers; represents German authors in Britain on behalf of German publishers

* *member of the Association of Authors' Agents*

Teresa Chris Literary Agency
43 Musard Road, London W6 8NR
020 7386 0633
TeresaChris@litagency.freeserve.co.uk
Fiction: crime, general, women's, commercial and literary and non-fiction

The Tennyson Agency
10 Cleveland Avenue
Wimbledon Chase
London SW20 9EW
020 8543 5939
agency@tenagy.co.uk
www.tenagy.co.uk
Theatre, film, radio and TV scripts

Toby Eady Associates
3rd Floor, 9 Orme Court
London W2 4RL
020 7792 0092
jessica@tobyeady.demon.co.uk
www.tobyeadyassociates.co.uk
Fiction, non-fiction, especially China, Middle East and Africa

Valerie Hoskins Associates
20 Charlotte Street
London W1T 2NA
020 7637 4490
vha@vhassociates.co.uk
Scripts for film, TV and radio, especially feature films, animation and TV

Vanessa Holt*
59 Crescent Road, Leigh-on-Sea
Essex SS9 2PF
01702 473787
vanessa@holtlimited.freeserve.co.uk
General fiction especially crime, commercial and literary; non-fiction; non-illustrated children's

The Wylie Agency (UK)
17 Bedford Square
London WC1B 3JA
020 7908 5900
mail@wylieagency.co.uk
Fiction and non-fiction

Watson, Little*
Capo Di Monte, Windmill Hill
London NW3 6RJ
020 7431 0770
sz@watsonlittle.com
www.watsonlittle.com
Commercial and literary fiction and non-fiction for adults and children

William Morris Agency (UK)*
52/53 Poland Street
London W1F 7LX
020 7534 6800
ldnmailroom@wma.com
www.wma.com
Fiction; general non-fiction; TV and film scripts

* *member of the Association of Authors' Agents*

William Neill-Hall
Old Oak Cottage, Ropewalk
Mount Hawke, Truro
Cornwall TR4 8DW
01209 891427
wneill-hall@msn.com
General non-fiction; clients include George Carey, Philip Yancey and Eugene Peterson

Zebra Agency
Broadland House, 1 Broadland
Shevington, Lancashire WN6 8DH
077193 75575
admin@zebraagency.co.uk
www.zebraagency.co.uk
Non-fiction and general fiction; scripts for TV, radio, film and theatre

Useful contacts

Academi (Yr Academi Gymreig)
Mount Stuart House
Mount Stuart Square
Cardiff CF10 5FQ
029 2047 2266
post@academi.org
www.academi.org
Welsh national literature promotion agency

Alliance of Literary Societies
22 Belmont Grove, Havant
Hampshire PO9 3PU
023 9247 5855
rosemary@sndc.demon.co.uk
www.sndc.demon.co.uk

Association for Scottish Literary Studies
c/o Department of Scottish History
9 University Gardens
University of Glasgow
Glasgow G12 8QH
0141 330 5309
office@asls.org.uk
www.asls.org.uk
Charity promoting language and literature of Scotland

Association of Christian Writers
All Saints Vicarage
43 All Saints Close, Edmonton
London N9 9AT
020 8884 4348
admin@christianwriters.org.uk
www.christianwriters.org.uk
Support, training and encouragement

Association of Freelance Writers
The Writers Bureau, Sevendale House
7 Dale Street
Manchester M1 1JB
0161 228 2362
www.writersbureau.com

Association of Illustrators
81 Leonard Street
London EC2A 4QS
020 7613 4328
info@a-o-theaoi.com
www.theaoi.com
Trade association

Association of Learned and Professional Society Publishers
South House, The Street, Clapham
Worthing, West Sussex BN13 3UU
01903 871686
marketing@alpsp.org
www.alpsp.org
For not-for-profit academic and professional publishers

AuthorsOnline
40 Castle Street, Hertford
Hertfordshire SG14 1HR
0870 7500544
theeditor@authorsonline.co.uk
www.authorsonline.co.uk
Self publishing and authors' services

Authors' Club
40 Dover Street, London W1S 4NP
020 7499 8581
mem@authorsclub.co.uk
www.authorsclub.co.uk
Anyone involved with written word; administers Best First Novel award and Sir Banister Fletcher award

Authors' Licensing & Collecting Society (ALCS)
Marlborough Court, 14–18 Holborn
London EC1N 2LE
020 7395 0600
alcs@alcs.co.uk
www.alcs.co.uk
UK collecting society for writers and successors

Bibliographical Society
c/o The Institute of English Studies, University of London
Room 304, Senate House
Mallet Street, London WC1E 7HU
020 7862 8679
admin@bibsoc.org.uk
www.bibsoc.org.uk
Aims to encourage study of bibliography and history of publishing

Books 4 Publishing
Lasyard House, Underhill Street
Bridgnorth, Shropshire WV16 4BB
0870 777 3339
editor@books4publishing.com
www.books4publishing.com
Online showcase for unpublished writers

Booksellers Association of the UK & Ireland
Minster House
272 Vauxhall Bridge Road
London SW1V 1BA
020 7834 5477
mail@booksellers.org.uk
www.booksellers.org.uk
Trade association. Coordinates World Book Day with Publishers Association; administers Whitbread Book Awards

Booktrust
Book House, 45 East Hill
London SW18 2QZ
020 8516 2977
info@booktrust.org.uk
www.booktrust.org.uk and
www.booktrusted.com
Educational charity

British Centre for Literary Translation
University of East Anglia, Norwich
Norfolk NR4 7TJ
01603 592134/592785
bclt@uea.ac.uk
www.literarytranslation.com

British Copyright Council
Copyright House
29–33 Berners Street
London W1T 3AB
01986 788122
copyright@bcc2.demon.co.uk
www.britishcopyright.org.uk
Creators' watchdog

British Science Fiction Association
1 Long Row Close, Everdon
Daventry, Northants NN11 3BE
01327 361661
bsfa@enterprise.net
www.bsfa.co.uk
Also publishes Matrix, Vector & Focus magazines

British Society of Comedy Writers
61 Parry Road, Ashmore Park
Wolverhampton
West Midlands WW11 2PS
01902 722729
info@bscw.co.uk
www.bscw.co.uk

Children's Books Ireland
17 Lower Camden Street
Dublin 2, Ireland
00 353 1872 5854
info@childrensbooksireland.com
www.childrensbooksireland.com
Promotes children's literature

Cle, The Irish Book Publishers' Association
43/44 Temple Bar
Dublin 2, Republic of Ireland
00 353 1 670 7393
info@publishingireland.com
www.publishingireland.com
Provides expertise and resources; access to directory of Irish Association of Freelance Editors, Proofreaders and Indexers

Combrogos
10 Heol Don, Whitchurch
Cardiff CF14 2AU
029 2062 3359
Arts and media research and editorial services; books about Wales or by Welsh authors; contact Dr Meic Stephens

Comedy Writers' Association UK
Wisteria Cottage, Coombe Meadow
Bovey Tracey, Newton Abbot
Devon TQ13 9EZ
info@cwauk.co.uk
www.cwauk.co.uk

Crime Writers' Association (CWA)
media.enquiries@thecwa.co.uk;
info@thecwa.co.uk
www.thecwa.co.uk

Critics' Circle
c/o Catherine Cooper
69 Marylebone Lane
London W1U 2PH
020 7224 1410
www.criticscircle.org.uk
Critics of drama, music, cinema & dance

Directory & Database Publishers Association
PO Box 23034, London W6 0RJ
020 8846 9707
rosemarypettit@onetel.net.uk
www.directory-publisher.co.uk
Trade association

Drama Association of Wales
The Old Library Building
Singleton Road, Splott
Cardiff CF24 2ET
029 2045 2200
aled.daw@virgin.net
www.amdram.co.uk

English Association
University of Leicester
University Road, Leicester LE1 7RH
0116 252 3982
engassoc@le.ac.uk
www.le.ac.uk/engassoc
Promotes knowledge, understanding and enjoyment of English language and literature

English PEN
Lancaster House
33 Islington High Street
London N1 9LH
020 7713 0023
enquiries@englishpen.org
www.englishpen.org
Association of writers and literary professionals. Fights for right to freedom of expression

Federation of Worker Writers and Community Publishers (FWWCP)
Burslem School of Art, Queen Street
Stoke on Trent ST6 3EJ
01782 822327
thefwwcp@tiscali.co.uk
www.thefwwcp.org uk
For independent writing workshops and community publishers

Fellowship of Authors and Artists
PO Box 158, Hertford SG13 8FA
0870 747 2514
fellowship@compassion-in-business.co.uk
www.author-fellowship.co.uk
Promotes writing and art as therapy and self-healing

Garden Writers' Guild
c/o Institute of Horticulture
14/15 Belgrave Square
London SW1X 8PS
020 7245 6943
gwg@horticulture.org.uk
www.gardenwriters.co.uk
Promotes high quality garden writing, photography & broadcasting

Gaelic Books Council (Comhairle nan Leabhraichean)
22 Mansfield Street
Glasgow G11 5QP
0141 337 6211
brath@gaelicbooks.net
www.gaelicbooks.net

Horror Writers Association
PO Box 50577, Palo Alto
CA 94303 USA
hwa@edclayton.com
www.horror.org/UK/

Independent Publishers Guild
P O Box 93, Royston
Hertfordshire SG8 5GH
01763 247014
info@ipg.uk.com
www.ipg.uk.com

Independent Theatre Council
12 The Leathermarket
Weston Street, London SE1 3ER
020 7403 1727
c.jones@itc-arts.org
www.itc-arts.org
Offers legal advice and training opportunities

Institute of Linguists
Saxon House, 48 Southwark Street
London SE1 1UN
020 7940 3100
info@iol.org.uk
www.iol.org.uk
Professional association; accredited exam board; commercial contracts for government

Institute of Translation and Interpreting (ITI)
Fortuna House, South Fifth Street
Milton Keynes
Buckinghamshire MK9 2EU
01908 325250
info@iti.org.uk
www.iti.org.uk

International Booksearch Service
8 Old James Street
London SE15 3TS
020 7639 8900
sarah.fordham@btinternet.com
www.scfordham.com
Finds out-of-print books

Irish Writers Centre
19 Parnell Square, Dublin 1
Republic of Ireland
00 353 1 872 1302
info@writerscentre.ie
www.writerscentre.ie
Promotes Irish writers, living in Ireland, organises readings and workshops
Also houses:

Irish Playwrights and Screenwriters Guild:
moffats@indigo.ie
www.writerscentre.ie/IPSG.html

Irish Translators' and Interpreters' Association
translation@eircom.net
or secretary-itia@ntlworld.ie
www.translatorsassociation.ie

Irish Writers' Union
words@neteireann.com
www.ireland-writers.com

ISBN Agency
Woolmead House, Bear Lane
Farnham, Surrey GU9 7LG
0870 7778712
isbn@nielsenbookdata.co.uk
www.whitaker.co.uk/isbn
Book numbering agency

Manuscript ReSearch
selfpublish@
manuscriptresearch.co.uk
www.manuscriptresearch.co.uk
Services for self-publishing authors

Medical Writers' Group
The Society of Authors
84 Drayton Gardens
London SW10 9SB
020 7373 6642
info@societyofauthors.org
www.societyofauthors.org
Specialist group within Society of Authors

National Archives
Kew, Richmond, Surrey TW9 4DU
020 8876 3444
enquiry@nationalarchives.gov.uk
www.nationalarchives.gov.uk
National resource for documents relating to British history; brings together the Public Record Office and the Historical Manuscripts Commission

National Association for Literature Development
PO Box 140, Ilkley
West Yorkshire LS29 7WP
01943 862107
steve@nald.org
www.nald.org

National Association of Writers Groups
The Arts Centre, Biddick Lane
Washington
Tyne & Wear NE38 2AB
01262 609228
nawg@tesco.net
www.nawg.co.uk
Connecting writers' groups around the country; yearly festivals and competitions

National Association of Writers in Education
PO Box 1, Sheriff Hutton
York YO60 7YU
01653 618429
paul@nawe.co.uk
www.nawe.co.uk

New Writing North
7/8 Trinity Chare, Quayside
Newcastle Upon Tyne NE1 3DF
0191 488 8580
mail@newwritingnorth.com
www.newwritingnorth.com
Literature development agency for northern arts region

Nielsen BookData
3rd Floor, Midas House
62 Goldsworth Road, Woking
Surrey GU21 6LQ
0870 7778710
info@bookdata.co.uk
www.nielsenbookdata.com
Bibliographic data

Nielsen BookScan
3rd Floor, Midas House
62 Goldsworth Road, Woking
Surrey GU21 6LQ
0870 7778710
info@nielsenbookscan.co.uk
www.nielsenbookscan.co.uk
International sales data monitoring

Player-Playwrights
9 Hillfield Park, London N10 3QT
020 8883 0371
p-p@dial.pipex.com
www.playerplaywrights.co.uk
Gives opportunities to writers new to stage, radio and TV

Public Lending Right
Richard House, Sorbonne Close
Stockton-on-Tees TS17 6DA
01642 604699
registrar@plr.uk.com
www.plr.uk.com

Publishers Association
29B Montague Street
London WC1B 5BH
020 7691 9191
mail@publishers.org.uk
www.publishers.org.uk
Trade association

Publishers Licensing Society
37–41 Gower Street
London WC1E 6HH
020 7299 7730
pls@pls.org.uk
www.pls.org.uk
Licensing of photocopying materials in schools and universities

Publishers Publicity Circle
65 Airedale Avenue
London W4 2NN
020 8994 1881
ppc-@lineone.net
www.publisherspublicitycircle.co.uk
Forum for book publicists and freelance PRs

Romantic Novelists' Association
38 Stanhope Road, Reading
Berks RG2 7HN
trisha_ashley@hotmail.com
www.rna-uk.org

Royal Society of Literature
Somerset House, Strand
London WC2R 1LA
020 7845 4676
info@rslit.org
www.rslit.org
Holds monthly lectures promoting literature

Science Fiction Foundation
37 Coventry Road, Ilford IG1 4QR
sff@sjbradshaw.cix.co.uk
www.sf-foundation.org
Writers, academics and critics with an active interest in science fiction

Scottish Book Trust
Sandeman House, Trunk's Close
55 High Street, Edinburgh EH1 1SR
0131 524 0160
info@scottishbooktrust.com
www.scottishbooktrust.com
Arts organiser, promotes reading and writing in Scotland; holds a resource library

Scottish Print Employers Federation
48 Palmerston Place
Edinburgh EH12 5DE
0131 220 4353
info@spef.org.uk
www.spef.org.uk
Advice, expertise, education and training

Scottish Publishers Association
Scottish Book Centre
137 Dundee Street
Edinburgh EH11 1BG
0131 228 6866
info@scottishbooks.org
www.scottishbooks.org
Training and marketing

Scottish Youth Theatre
3rd Floor Forsythe House
111 Union Street, Glasgow G1 3TA
0141 221 5127
info@scottishyouththeatre.org
www.scottishyouththeatre.org

Society for Children's Book Writers & Illustrators
8271 Beverley Boulevard
Los Angeles, CA 90048, USA
001 323 7821010
scbwi@scbwi.org
www.scbwi.org

Society for Editors and Proofreaders (SfEP)
Riverbank House
1 Putney Bridge Approach
London SW6 3JD
020 7736 3278
admin@sfep.org.uk
www.sfep.org.uk
Courses and support system

Society of Authors
84 Drayton Gardens
London SW10 9SB
020 7373 6642
info@societyofauthors.org
www.societyofauthors.org
Trade union for professional authors

Society of Civil and Public Service Writers
Adrian Danson, Editor
38 Cumberland Road
Bromley BR2 8PQ
editor@scpsw.co.uk
www.scpsw.co.uk

Society of Indexers
Blades Enterprise Centre
John Street, Sheffield S2 4SU
0114 292 2350
admin@indexers.org.uk
www.indexers.org.uk

Society of Women Writers & Journalists
Calvers Farm, Thelveton, Diss
Norfolk IP21 4NG
01379 740550
zoe@zoeking.com
www.swwj.com

Society of Young Publishers
Endeavour House
189 Shaftesbury Avenue
London WC2H 8TJ
info@thesyp.org.uk
www.thesyp.org.uk
Provides a forum, organises readings and meetings

South and Mid-Wales Association of Writers (SAMWAW)
c/o IMC Consulting Group
Denham House, Lambourne Crescent
Cardiff CF14 5ZW
029 2076 1170
info@imcconsultinggroup.co.uk
www.samwaw.org.uk
Open to all writers

Spoken Word Publishing Association (SWPA)
c/o Macmillan Audio
20 New Wharf Road
London N1 9RR
020 7014 6041
z.howes@macmillan.co.uk
www.swpa.co.uk

Sports Writers' Association of Great Britain
c/o Sport England External Affairs
16 Upper Woburn Place
London WC1H 0QP
020 7273 1500
petta.naylor@sportengland.org
www.sportswriters.org.uk

Translators Association
84 Drayton Gardens
London SW10 9SB
020 7373 6642
info@societyofauthors.org
www.societyofauthors.org

Welsh Books Council (Cyngor Llyfrau Cymru)
Castell Brychan, Aberystwyth
Ceredigion SY23 2JB
01970 624151
castellbrychan@cllc.org.uk
www.cllc.org.uk and
www.gwales.com
For Welsh writers

West Country Writers' Association
High Wootton, Wootton Lane
Limpstone, Exmouth
Devon EX8 5AY
01395 222749
judy@josser.freeserve.co.uk
www.westcountrywriters.co.uk
Annual congress in May

Women in Publishing
info@wipub.org.uk
www.wipub.org.uk

Writernet
Cabin V, Clarendon Buildings
25 Horsell Road, Highbury
London N5 1XL
020 7609 7474
info@writernet.org.uk
www.writernet.org.uk
Information and guidance for playwrights and performance writers

Writers, Artists and their Copyright Holders (Watch)
The Harry Ransom Humanities Research Center
21st and Guadalupe, PO Box 7219
Austin, Texas 78713-7219, USA
+1 512 471 8944
hrcweb@hrc.utexas.edu
www.watch-file.com

Writers' Guild of Great Britain
15 Britannia Street
London WC1X 9JN
020 7833 0777
admin@writersguild.org.uk
www.writersguild.org.uk
Trade union for professional writers

Books trade press

Annual Bibliography of English Language and Literature
Modern Humanities Research Association
c/o Cambridge University Library
West Road, Cambridge CB3 9DR
01223 333058
abell@bibl.org
www.mhra.org.uk/Publication/Journals/abell.html
Annual

Books
Publishing News, 7 John Street
London WC1N 2ES
0870 870 2345
info@publishingnews.co.uk
www.publishingnews.co.uk
Weekly

Books in the Media
VNU Entertainment Media
Fifth Floor, Endeavour House
189 Shaftesbury Avenue
London WC2H 8TJ
020 7420 6006
webeditor@bookseller.co.uk
www.thebookseller.com
Weekly

The Bookseller
VNU Entertainment Media
5th Floor Endeavour House
189 Shaftesbury Avenue
London WC2H 8TJ
020 7420 6006
joel.rickett@bookseller.co.uk
www.thebookseller.com
Weekly

Booksellers Association Directory of Members
The Booksellers Association of the UK and Ireland
272 Vauxhall Bridge Road
London SW1V 1BA
020 7802 0802
mail@booksellers.org.uk
www.booksellers.org.uk
Annual

BookWorld Magazine
Christchurch Publishers
2 Caversham Street
London SW3 4AH
020 7351 4995
leonard.holdsworth@btopenworld.com
Monthly

Digital Demand – The Journal of Printing and Publishing Technology
PIRA International, Randalls Road
Leatherhead KT22 7RU
01372 802080
publications@pira.co.uk
www.piranet.com
6pa

London Review of Books
Nicholas Spice, 28 Little Russell Street
London WC1A 2HN
020 7209 1141
edit@lrb.co.uk
www.lrb.co.uk
Fortnightly

Publishing News
Publishing News, 39 Store Street
London WC1E 7DS
0870 870 2345
mailbox@publishingnews.co.uk
www.publishingnews.co.uk
Weekly

Writers Forum
Writers International, PO Box 3229
Bournemouth BH1 1ZS
01202 589828
editorial@writers-forum.com
www.writers-forum.com
12pa

Writers News/ Writing Magazine
Warner Group Publications
1st Floor, Victoria House
143–145 The Headrow
Leeds LS1 5RL
0113 200 2929
derek.hudson@writersnews.co.uk
www.writersnews.co.uk
Monthly

Global media

Mousing boom: Disney fought off hostile bid

The world's media are dominated by a few mostly US-based giants, plus around 40 very large European and American firms. Between them, the top 10 (see table below) own most of the famous names in press, publishing and broadcasting, among them CNN, Time, CBS, Fox, Sky and Random House - and control about three-quarters of global advertising spend. In 2003 all of these made more money, or lost less, than in 2002, as the global media industry climbed out of a two-year recession.

The upturn came just in time for Walt Disney, which in February rejected a £26bn hostile bid from a rival cable company, Comcast. The company posted £306m profits for the second half of 2003, up 71 per cent on the year before. The figures were a fillip for its beleaguered chief executive, Michael Eisner, who was stripped of the chairmanship of the company at an annual meeting in March.

Vivendi, the French company which in 2002 suffered the biggest loss in its country's history, also saw improved fortunes. In October the company agreed to sell its Universal entertainments arm to General Electric, a deal which in 2004 created the merged entertainment giant NBC Universal; a GE subsidiary which, if separately listed, would make the media top 10 in its own right. Vivendi went on to report its first quarterly profit in two years in December 2003 — £91.5m - but dipped back to a £4m loss in the following quarter. Meanwhile in June, the former Vivendi chairman Jean-Marie Messier was placed under formal investigation - one step short of being charged - for his role in alleged share dealing.

In October 2003, Time Warner tried to forget the circumstances of its past few years of losses, by dropping the word "AOL" from its corporate brand. Following its merger with the internet provider, Time Warner had made the biggest loss in US history in 2002, some £60bn; the failure was a spectacular example of the misplaced optimism of dotcom era. But the firm bounced back by making a profit of more than £1.4bn in 2003.

Gannett, regional publisher and owner of Britain's Newsquest, made a slightly smaller profit of $1.2bn in 2003, 4 per cent up on 2002. Rupert Murdoch's News Corporation was similarly successful, after its acquisition of US cable company DirecTV: its $760m profits in the second quarter of 2003-04 were its eighth consecutive quarter of year-on-year growth. Clear Channel, for its part, made $187m in 2002.

Viacom's year was less successful. After reporting the lowest top-10 loss in 2002, it posted the highest in 2003 — £206m, thanks to its writedown of the struggling video rental chain Blockbuster. Its subsidiary, MTV, then suffered adverse publicity in 2004, when the singer Janet Jackson exposed a star-spangled breast during an entertainment break in American football's Superbowl. Nipplegate was a welcome boon for regional newspaper columnists and talkshow hosts nationwide, and was repeated ad infinitum on the world wide web. The company then had a brief but destructive spat with US cable distributor Echostar, which led to its channels — including CBS and MTV — disappearing from the "Dish" network; in the aftermath of the row, Viacom hinted that it might vertically integrate by buying a distributor for itself. Mel Karmazin, the company's president, quit in June 2004.

Rupert Murdoch's News Corporation posted a 69 per cent increase in profits in January to March 2004, some £258m.

Global journalism

In October 2003, Reporters Sans Frontières published its second annual index of world press freedom, based on a survey of journalists (see table). The table reminded the world that whereas in some countries, freedom to speak and publish is an alienable human right, in other countries it barely exists. As in the previous year, Finland, Iceland, the Netherlands and Norway took joint first place; North Korea was again last, with Cuba a close challenger. Britain fell six places in the table to 27th, even though its absolute standard improved; for its part, the US slipped 14 places. The index also saw an improvement in press freedom in Iraq since the US-led invasion of the country; but the US was also criticised over the deaths of journalists during the Iraq war, so its score there was one of the lowest. Press freedom in Israel and the occupied territories, meanwhile, was measured separately for the first time; the survey found a predictable difference between the two. Judged geographically, there was also a decline in press freedom in other Middle East countries as a result of the Iraq war.

The Zimbabwe Daily News, a newspaper that has been something of a cause célèbre for international press freedom, fought a losing battle to stay alive in the face of the most intense intimidation from the government of Robert Mugabe. The newspaper was ordered to close in September 2003, when the government's "Media and Information Commission" refused it a licence; it printed one edition in October 2003, and was closed again with the arrest of 18 journalists; and although it resumed operations in January 2004 when a Harare judge ruled that the commission's credentials were invalid, it was finally forced to stop publishing in February when the supreme court ruled that it was a criminal offence to publish any newspaper, or even be a journalist, without a government licence.

In June, a BBC cameraman, Simon Cumbers, was killed and a security

Top 10 global media companies

		market cap	*(last year)*	
1	General Electric	£182.6bn	*(1 – £175.5bn)*	Owns NBC Universal; several US regional channels; significant non-media interests
2	Time Warner	£40.4bn	*(3 – £42.7bn)*	Owns HBO, CNN, Time, Warner Books, AOL
3	Viacom	£30.2bn	*(2 – £49.0bn)*	Owns CBS, MTV, Nickelodeon, Simon & Schuster, outdoor advertising
4	News Corporation	£28.2bn	*(6 – £25.5bn)*	Owns BSkyB, News International, HarperCollins, DirecTV (US), Star TV (Asia)
5	Walt Disney	£26.7bn	*(5 – £26.9bn)*	Owns ABC, several US papers, Disney channels, Miramax, theme parks
6	Comcast	£20.6bn	*(4 – £42.3bn)*	Owns E! entertainment, Golf Channel
7	Vivendi	£15.1bn	*(10 – £12.2bn)*	Owns Canal Plus
8	Bertelsmann	£13.4bn*	*(8 – £14.8m*)*	Owns Random House, Five, Ballantine, BMG
9	Gannett	£12.0bn	*(9 – £12.8bn)*	Owns Newsquest, US Today
10	Clear Channel	£11.7bn	*(7 – £15.3bn)*	Owns hundreds of US regional radio stations, outdoor advertising

*Bertelsmann is privately owned; figure refers to total assets declared by the company NB Sony excluded from list, as media interests are mostly music

correspondent, Frank Gardner, seriously injured in a gun attack in Saudi Arabia, renewing fears about the safety of journalists globally. "The attack on them marks the moment at which journalists ceased to be regarded as onlookers and became, against their wishes and instincts, combatants instead," wrote the BBC's world affairs editor in the Sunday Telegraph.

Meanwhile in the US, the fallout from the New York Times plagiarism scandal continued. The reporter Jayson Blair had been plagiarising and fabricating articles for the newspaper for two years, a revelation that led to the resignations of two executives and a Pulitzer-winning writer; so in 2004 he published a book of his experiences, half *apologia*, half *mea culpa*, for which he received a reported advance of about half a million dollars. The book described how New York Times reporters would often

World Press Freedom Index 2003 – Reporters Sans Frontières

Rank	Country	Index	2002 rank and index
Top of the table			
1=	Finland	0.5	(1st=, 0.5)
	Iceland	0.5	(1st=, 0.5)
	Netherlands	0.5	(1st=, 0.5)
	Norway	0.5	(1st=, 0.5)
5=	Denmark	1.0	(10th, 3.0)
	Trinidad and Tobago	1.0	not measured in 2002
7	Belgium	1.17	(12th, 3.5)
8	Germany	1.33	(7th=, 1.5)
9	Sweden	1.50	(7th=, 1.5)
10	Canada	1.83	(5th, 0.75)
...			
27	UK	4.25	(21st, 6.0)
...			
31=	US (own territory)	6.0	(17th, 4.75)
...			
44	Israel (own territory)	8.0	measured separately for first time
Bottom of the table			
130	Palestinian Authority	39.25	(82nd, 27.0)
...			
135	US (in Iraq)	41.0	(130th, 79.0)
...			
141	Zimbabwe	41.5	(122nd, 48.25)
...			
146	Israel (occupied territories)	49.0	measured separately for first time
...			
148	Russia	49.5	(121st, 48.0)
...			
158	Turkmenistan	82.8	(136th, 91.5)
159	Vietnam	89.17	(131st, 81.25)
160	Iran	89.33	(122nd, 48.25)
161	China	91.25	(138th, 97.0)
162	Eritrea	91.50	(132nd, 83.67)
163	Laos	94.83	(133rd, 89.0)
164	Burma	95.50	(137th, 96.83)
165	Cuba	97.83	(134th, 97.0)
166	North Korea	99.50	(139th and last, 97.5)

Source: Reporters Sans Frontières. Index drawn up by asking journalists, researchers and legal experts to answer 50 questions about press freedom, covering issues such as murders or arrests of journalists, censorship, pressure, state monopolies in various fields, punishment of press law offences, and regulation

fly to cities across America after writing a story, for the sole purpose of adding a date and location stamp – an absurd practice known as a "toe-touch". In March, the deposed editor Howard Raines wrote a tirade in Atlantic Monthly, in which, among other criticisms, he said the paper needed reform to get off "its glide path toward irrelevance".

History then repeated itself at USA Today, where it was reported that the Pultizer-winning journalist Jack Kelley – a much bigger fish than Jayson Blair – had been faking major foreign news stories for several years. A team of five reporters and an editor had been appointed to go through more than 700 stories the reporter had written in the course of the previous decade.

America's media empire **Chris Alden**

On the face of it, it was just a financial decision. Rupert Murdoch's News Corporation – owner of DirecTV, Sky, Fox and more than 175 newspapers worldwide – announced in April that it was abandoning the Australian stock market, to set up home in New York instead.

To the NewsCorp bean counters, the move was logical. NewsCorp – the world's fastest growing media company, commercially aggressive and an advocate of global deregulation – is a perfect fit for US investors. Only last year it bought DirecTV, America's biggest cable TV platform; while Fox, its biggest brand, has long been the voice of the American right.

From a global perspective, it was more controversial. The Australian market, in particular, stands to lose its biggest company almost overnight, leading to inevitable instability in the short term.

In the long term, the effects may not only be seen down under. NewsCorp has interests in more than 60 countries worldwide, not least the UK. When the move goes ahead, it will mean that for the first time, more than a third of the British national newspaper market – the Sun, the News of the World, the Times and the Sunday Times, not to mention the biggest commercial broadcaster, BSkyB – are part of an American company.

In itself, that is no bad thing. But NewsCorp is just the latest in a series of US companies to have controlling interests in UK media.

In local papers, Newsquest – owned by US giant Gannett since 1999 – is our second largest publisher, controlling one-sixth of the market.

Three of our biggest magazine publishers – IPC Media, Condé Nast & The National Magazine Company – are US-controlled; and so are two of our biggest books publishers, HarperCollins (another NewsCorp company) and Time Warner.

In advertising, the three biggest players are the US supergroups: WPP, Omnicom and Interpublic. Two of the main companies in the outdoor advertising market, Clear Channel and Viacom Outdoor, are again US-owned.

The Communications Act 2003 also allows companies such as NewsCorp and Clear Channel to buy into the British terrestrial broadcasting market – as long as they can comply with a "public interest test". The test, introduced after lobbying from Labour peer Lord Puttnam, was designed to protect the plurality and diversity of Britain's media market.

But with the advent of new technology, so the pressure to deregulate grows.

Take the internet. Britain's three biggest search engines, Microsoft, Google and Yahoo!, are already US-owned; our two biggest online retailers, Amazon and eBay, are US companies; while our second biggest internet provider is – you guessed it – America Online.

With the exception of the BBC and Guardian Unlimited and companies such as LastMinute.com, much of Britain's new media business is just a localised offshoot of California.

There can be a profound imbalance, of course, when companies in one country gain too much control over the media in another. And as Greeks in an American empire, as Macmillan had it, it is Britain's responsibility to remain independent of dominant global interests. Nowhere is that so crucial than in our media.

Seen in that light, it was right and proper that our public service broadcaster, the BBC, should seek to assert its independence from government in its coverage of a US-led war – even though that coverage culminated in the tragic death of David Kelly, and the Hutton report.

And that is also why, during charter renewal, the focus should be on maintaining the BBC's reputation as an independent player on the global stage – which means protecting its system of funding.

If that were overlooked, investors in the News Corporation – if not one of the other seven US giants in the world's top 10 media companies – would be the ones to gain.

Global media Contacts

Global media groups

Bertelsmann
Carl-Bertelsmann-Strasse 270
33311 Gütersloh, Germany
00 49 5241 800
media services: 020 7840 8400
info@bertelsmann.com
www.bertelsmann.com

Clear Channel
200 East Basse Road, San Antonio
TX 78209, USA
00 1 210 822 2828
lisacdollinger@clearchannel.com
www.clearchannel.com

ComCast
1500 Market Street, Philadelphia
PA 19102, USA
00 1 215 763 6600
www.comcast.com

Gannett
7950 Jones Branch Drive
McLean VA 22107, USA
00 1 703 854 6000
www.gannett.com
NewsQuest Media Group
58 Church Street, Weybridge
Surrey KT13 8DP
01932 821212
www.newsquest.co.uk

General Electric/NBC
USA
00 1 203 373 2039
www.ge.com/en

NewsCorp
1211 Avenue of Americas
8th Floor, New York, NY 10036, USA
00 1 212 852-7017
investor@newscorp.com
press: abutcher@newscorp.com
www.newscorp.com

Sony
550 Madison Avenue, New York
NY 10022, USA
00 1 212 833 8000
www.sony.com; www.sony.co.uk

Time Warner
1 Time Warner Centre
58th and 8th Avenue, New York
NY 10019, USA
00 1 212 484 8600
www.timewarner.com

Viacom
1515 Broadway, New York
NY 10036, USA
00 1 212 258 6000
www.viacom.com

Vivendi Universal
42 avenue de Friedland
75380 Paris Cedex 08, France
00 33 1 7171 1000
www.vivendiuniversal.com
New York office
800 Third Avenue, New York
NY 10022, USA
00 1 212 572 7000

Walt Disney Company
500 South Buena Vista Street
Burbank, CA 91521, USA
00 1 818 560 1000
http://disney.go.com

Global news outlets

Europe

Corriere della Sera
via Solferino, 28, Milano, Italy
00 39 026 339
www.corriere.it
Italian daily

Cyprus Mail
24 Vassiliou Voulgaroctonou Street
PO Box 21144, 1502 Nicosia, Cyprus
00 357 22 818 585
editor@cyprus-mail.com
www.cyprus-mail.com
English-language daily

Deutsche Welle
Public Broadcasting Service
Kurt-Schumacher-Str. 3
53113 Bonn, Germany
00 49 228 429 0
www.dw-world.de
German broadcaster. European focus

Diario de Noticias
Av. da Liberdade, 266
1250-149 Lisboa, Portugal
dnot@dn.pt
www.dt.pt
Portuguese daily

EuroNews
BP 161, 60 Chemin de Mouilles
69131 Lyon Ecully, France
00 33 4 7218 8000
info@euronews.net
www.euronews.net
Pan-European TV news

le Figaro
37 rue du Louvre
75002 Paris, France
00 33 1 5865 0101
www.lefigaro.fr
Rightwing quality daily

Frankfurter Allgemeine
Hellerhofstraße 2
60327 Frankfurt am Main, Germany
00 49 69 75910
reduktion@faz.de
www.faz.de
Right-leaning daily

Gazeta Wyborcza
8/10 Czerska Street
Warsaw, Poland
00 48 22 555 4001
postmaster@gazeta.pl
www.gazeta.pl
Poland's most popular daily

International Herald Tribune
6 bis, rue des Graviers
92521 Neuilly Cedex, France
00 33 1 4143 9322
iht@iht.com
www.iht.com/info/contact.html

Kathimerini
D Falireos & E Makariou St 2
185-47 N Faliron, Piraeus, Greece
00 30 210 480 8000
editor@ekathimerini.com
www.ekathimerini.com
English-language daily

Libération
11, rue Béranger
75154 Paris Cedex 03, France
00 33 01 42 76 17 89
www.libe.com
Left-leaning quality daily

le Monde
21 bis, rue Claude-Bernard
75242 Paris Cedex 05, France
00 33 1 4217 2000
mail@mondepub.fr
www.lemonde.fr
France's bestselling quality daily

Moscow Times
Building 4, Ulitsa Vyborgskaya 16
125212 Moscow, Russia
00 7 095 232 3200
moscowtimes@imedia.ru
www.moscowtimes.ru
Respected English-language daily

el Mundo
Calle Pradillo, 42, 28002 Madrid
Spain
00 34 91 586 48 00
cartas.director@elmundo.es
www.elmundo.es
Progressive Spanish daily

el País
Miguel Yuste 40, Madrid 28037
Spain
00 34 91 337 8200
redaccion@prisacom.com
www.elpais.es
Spain's biggest daily paper

Prague Post
Stepanska 20, Prague 1
110 00, Czech Republic
00 420 02 9633 4400
info@praguepost.com
www.praguepost.com
The Czech Republic's best English-language daily

Radio France Internationale
116, avenue du President Kennedy
Paris 75016, France
00 33 1 5640 1212
www.rfi.fr
A French "world service"

Radio Netherlands
Box 222, 1200 JG Hilversum
The Netherlands
00 31 35 672 4211
www.rnw.nl
Holland's best English-language news service

la Repubblica
Piazza Indipendenza, 11/b
Roma 00185, Italy
00 39 6 49821
larepubblica@repubblica.it
www.repubblica.it
(In Italian.) Liberal Rome-based daily

der Standard
Schenkenstrasse 4/6
A-1010 Wien, Austria
00 43 1 53 1700
chefredaktion@derStandard.at
www.derstandard.at
(In German.) Liberal daily

Süddeutsche Zeitung
Sendlinger Strasse 8
80331 Munchen, Germany
00 49 89 21830
www.sueddeutsche.de
(In German.) Major Munich-based paper. Broadly liberal

De Telegraaf
Alle rechten voorbehouden
Amsterdam, The Netherlands
00 31 20 585 9111
business@telegraaf.nl
www.telegraaf.nl
Holland's largest national daily. In Dutch

▶▶ **IRISH OUTLETS: page 72**

Middle East

Al Ahram
Galaa St., Cairo, Egypt
00 20 2578 6441
weeklyeditor@ahram.org.eg
http://weekly.ahram.org.eg

Al-Jazeera
PO Box 22300, Doha, Qatar
00 974 438 2777
info@aljazeera.net.qa
http://english.aljazeera.net
www.aljazeera.com
Arabic-language satellite channel, based in Qatar

Aljazeera Publishing
London, UK
0870 432 0671

Daily Star
Marine Tower 6th floor
Rue de La Ste Famille, Gemaizeh
Achrafieh, Beirut, Lebanon
00 961 1 587277
letters@dailystar.com.lb
www.dailystar.com.lb
Lebanese daily

Ha'aretz
21 Schocken St, PO Box 233
Tel Aviv 61001, Israel
00 972 3 512 1212
secretary@haaretz.co.il
www.haaretzdaily.com/
English edition of Israel's moderate national daily, published in Tel Aviv

Jerusalem Post
Jerusalem Post Building
PO Box 81, Jerusalem 91000, Israel
00 972 2 531 5666
eedition@jpostmail.com
www.jpost.com
Conservative English-language daily

Jordan Times
Jordan Press Foundation
PO Box 6710
Queen Rania Al Abdullah Street
Amman, Jordan
00 962 6 560 0800 x392
jotimes@jpf.com.jo
www.jordantimes.com
Jordan's only English-language daily

Middle East Times
12, rue Mohamed Bayoumi
Ard El Golf, Heliopolis, Cairo, Egypt
00 202 291 3752/3583/3174
00 202 414 7081
editor@middleastimes.net,
egyptnews@metimes.com
www.metimes.com
Quality English-language weekly, based in Egypt

US and Canada

CBS Broadcasting Inc
524 West 57th Street, New York
NY 10019, USA
00 1 212 975 4321
www.cbs.com
News network

CNN
One CNN Center, Atlanta
GA 30348, USA
00 1 404 827 1995
cnn@cnn.com
www.cnn.com
News network

International Herald Tribune
6 bis, rue des Graviers
92521 Neuilly Cedex, France
00 33 1 4143 9322
iht@iht.com
www.iht.com
International daily, owned by the New York Times

LA Times
202 W 1st St, Los Angeles
CA 90012, USA
00 1 213 237 5000
www.latimes.com
Biggest west-coast daily

NBC
30 Rockefeller Plaza, New York
NY 10112, USA
00 1 212 664 4444
press@nbcmv.com
www.nbc.com/
News network

New York Times
229 West 43rd Street, New York
New York 10036, USA
00 1 212 556 1234
editorial@nytimes.com
www.nytimes.com
National paper of record, rocked this year by plagiarism scandal that cost two senior resignations

Wall St Journal
200 Liberty Street, New York
NY 10281, USA
00 1 800 568 7625
wsj.ltrs@wsj.com.
www.wsj.com
Conservative financial daily

Wall St Journal Europe
Boulevard Brand Whitlock, No. 87
1200 Brussels, Belgium
00 32 2 741 1211
europesupport@wsj.com
www.europesubs.wsj.com/
Global Business News for Europe

Washington Post
1150 15th Street NW, Washington
DC 20071, USA
00 1 202 334 6000
www.washingtonpost.com
The New York Times' main rival

Canada

Toronto Globe and Mail
444 Front Street West, Toronto
Ontario M5V 2S9, Canada
00 1 416 585 5000
newsroom@GlobeAndMail.ca
www.theglobeandmail.com
Quality daily, Canada

Africa

Daily Mail and Guardian
PO Box 91667, Auckland Park
Johannesburg 2006, South Africa
00 27 11 727 7000
newsdesk@mg.co.za
www.mg.co.za
South African daily

Daily Nation, Kenya
Nation Centre, Kimathi Street
Nairobi, Kenya
www.nationmedia.com
Kenya's biggest daily paper

Daily News, Zimbabwe
00 27 31 308 2107
pather@nn.independent.co.za
www.dailynews.co.za
Daily independent paper

The East African
Kenya
comments@nationaudio.com
www.nationaudio.com/News/EastAfrican/current

East African Standard
Likoni Road, PO Box 30080
Nairobi, Kenya
00 254 20 552510/6
editorial@eastandard.net
www.eastandard.net

Le Matin, Algeria
Algeria
www.lematin-dz.net
(In French.) Moderate, secular paper

Monitor, Uganda
PO Box 12141, Plot 29-35, 8th Street
Industrial Area, Kampala, Uganda
00 256 041 232367
info@monitor.co.ug
www.monitor.co.ug
Major independent daily

SABC
Private Bag X1, Auckland Park
2006, South Africa
00 27 11 714 5150
feedback@sabcnews.com
www.sabcnews.com
South African broadcaster

Sunday Times (South Africa)
PO Box 1742, Saxonwold 2132
South Africa
00 27 11 280 3000
suntimes@sundaytimes.co.za
www.suntimes.co.za

Asia

Asahi Shimbun
Tokyo, Japan
00 81 3354 50131
www.asahi.com
Japanese daily

Dawn – Pakistan
Haroon House
Dr Ziauddin Ahmed Road
Karachi 74200, Pakistan
00 92 21 111 444 777
webmaster@dawn.com
www.dawn.com
English-language daily

Hindustan Times
Hindustan Times House
18-20, K.G. Marg, New Delhi 1, India
00 91 11 2336 1234
feedback@hindustantimes.com
www.hindustantimes.com

Jakarta Post – Indonesia
Jl. Palmerah Selatan 15
Jakarta 10270, Indonesia
00 62 21 5300476
editorial@thejakartapost.com
www.thejakartapost.com

JoongAng Ilbo
7, Sunhwa-dong, Jung-gu
Seoul 100-759, Korea
00 82 2 751 9215
iht@joongang.co.kr
http://joongangdaily.joins.com
Korean daily

South China Morning Post – Hong Kong
16F Somerset House, Taikoo Place
979 King's Road, Quarry Bay
Hong Kong
00 852 2565 2222
www.scmp.com
English-language daily

Star News Asia
8th Floor, One Harbourfront,
18 Tak Fung Street, Hunghom
Kowloon, Hong Kong
00 852 2621 8888
http://focusasia.startv.com/starnewsasia.cfm
Broadcaster

Straits Times
Singapore
00 65 6319 5397
STI@sph.com.sg
http://straitstimes.asia1.com.sg
Singapore's most widely circulated English-language paper: close ties to the government

Taipei Times (Taiwan)
Nanking East Rd, Sec 2, #137, 5Fl
Taipei, ROC - 104, Taiwan
00 886 2 2518 2728
inquiries@taipeitimes.com
www.taipeitimes.com

Latin America and Caribbean

o Estado de Sao Paulo
Sao Paulo, Brazil
00 55 11 3856 2122
www.estado.estadao.com.br

el Mercurio
Santiago, Chile
00 56 2330 1111
mcampos@mercurio.cl
www.elmercurio.cl
Daily

la Nacion
Buenos Aires, Argentina
00 54 11 4309 7200
consultas@lanacion.com.ar
www.lanacion.com.ar

el Tiempo
Eldorado Avenue, Bogotá, Colombia
comercial@eltiempo.com.co
http://eltiempo.terra.com.co

el Universal
Mexico City, Mexico
00 52 55 5709 1313/6917
paul64@eluniversal.com.mx
www.el-universal.com.mx

Caribbean

Jamaica Gleaner
7 North Street, PO Box 40
Kingston, Jamaica
00 1 876 922 3400
feedback@jamaica-gleaner.com
www.jamaica-gleaner.com

Pacific

ABS-CBN (Philippines)
9/F ELJ Communications Centre
Eugenio Lopez Jr Street
Quezon City, Philippines
00 63 2 924 4101
feedback@abs-cbn.com
www.abs-cbnnews.com/
News network

New Zealand Herald
PO Box 32, Auckland, New Zealand
00 64 9 379 5050
www.nzherald.co.nz

The Age, Melbourne
250 Spencer Street
Melbourne 3000, Australia
00 61 3 9600 4211
www.theage.com.au

Sydney Morning Herald
201 Sussex St, GPO Box 506
Sydney NSW 2000, Australia
00 61 2 9282 1569
readerlink@smh.com.au
www.smh.com.au
Quality daily

Global journalism bodies

AMARC (World Association of Community Broadcasters)
705 Bourget Street, Suite 100
Montreal, Quebec, H4C 2M6
Canada
00 1 514 982 0351
amarc@amarc.org
www.amarc.org

Article XIX
Lancaster House
33 Islington High Street
London N1 9LH
020 7278 9292
info@article19.org
www.article19.org
Combats censorship

Committee to Protect Journalists
330 7th Avenue 12th Floor
New York NY 10001, USA
00 1 212 465 1004
info@cpj.org
www.cpj.org
Independent, non-profit body defending right of journalists to report without fear of reprisal

Foreign Press Association in London
11 Carlton House Terrace
London SW1Y 5AJ
020 7930 0445
secretariat@foreign-press.org.uk
www.foreign-press.org.uk

Institute for War and Peace Reporting
Lancaster House
33 Islington High Street
London N1 9LH
020 7713 7130
alan@iwpr.net
www.iwpr.net
Training in conflict areas

International Centre for Journalists
1616 H Street NW, Third Floor
Washington DC 20006, USA
00 1 202 737 3700
www.icfj.org

International Consortium of Investigative Journalists
910 17th Street, NW, 7th Floor
Washington, DC 20006, USA
00 1 202 466 1300
www.icij.org

International Federation of Journalists
IPC-Residence Palace, Bloc C
Rue de la Loi 155, B-1040 Brussels
Belgium
00 32 2 235 2200
ifj@ifj.org
www.ifj.org

International Federation of the Periodical Press
Queens House
55–56 Lincoln's Inn Fields
London WC2A 3LJ
020 7404 4169
info@fipp.com
www.fipp.com
Works for benefit of magazine publishers worldwide

International Freedom of Expression
489 College Street, Suite 403
Toronto, Ontario, M6G 1A5
Canada
00 1 416 515 9622
ifex@ifex.org
www.ifex.org

International News Safety Institute
Residence Palace, Block C
International Press Centre
155 Rue de la Loi
1040 Brussels, Belgium
00 32 2 235 2201
rodney.pinder@newssafety.com
www.newssafety.com
Safety network for journalists in conflict zones

International Press Institute
Spiegelgasse 2, A-1010 Vienna
Austria
00 43 1 512 90 11
ipi@freemedia.at
www.freemedia.at
Network of editors, executives and senior journalists

International Women's Media Foundation
1625 K Street NW, Suite 1275
Washington, DC 20006, USA
00 1 202 496 1992
info@iwmf.org
www.iwmf.org

InterNews
1640 Rhode Island Avenue NW
7th Floor, Washington, USA
00 1 202 833 5740
www.internews.org

InterWorld Radio
Panos Institute, 9 White Lion Street
London N1 9PD
020 7239 7630/1/2/3
editor@interworldradio.org
www.interworldradio.org

Overseas Press and Media Association
OPMA Secretariat
15 Magrath Avenue
Cambridge CB4 3AH
01223 512631
membership@opma.co.uk
www.opma.co.uk

Panos London
9 White Lion Street
London N1 9PD
020 7278 1111
info@panoslondon.org.uk
www.panos.org.uk
Journalism in developing countries

Reporters Sans Frontieres
5 Rue Geoffroy-Marie
75009 Paris, France
00 33 1 4483 8484
rsf@rsf.org
www.rsf.org

World Association of Newspapers
7 Rue Geoffroy St. Hilaire
75005 Paris, France
00 33 1 4742 8500
contact_us@wan.asso.fr
http://www.wan-press.org/

World Press Freedom Committee
11690-C Sunrise Valley Drive
Reston, VA 20191, USA
00 1 703 715 9811
freepress@wpfc.org
www.wpfc.org

World Press Photo
Jacob Obrechtstraat 26
1071 KM Amsterdam
The Netherlands
00 31 20 676 6096
office@worldpressphoto.nl
www.worldpressphoto.nl

Global media bodies

Association for International Broadcasting
PO Box 990, London SE3 9XL
020 8297 3993
info@aib.org.uk
www.aib.org.uk
Trade association

Association for Progressive Communications
PO Box 29755, Melville 2109
South Africa
00 27 11 726 1692
webeditor@apc.org
www.apc.org
Internet and ICTs for social justice and development
APC secretariat
Presidio Building 1012
Torney Avenue, PO Box 29904
San Francisco, CA 94129, USA

European Audio-Visual Observatory
76, allee de la Robertsau
67000 Strasbourg, France
00 33 388 144400
obs@obs.coe.int
www.obs.coe.int
European media observatory. Operates within framework of Council of Europe

European Broadcasting Union
17A, Ancienne Route
CH-1218 Grand-Saconnex
Switzerland
00 41 22 717 2111
ebu@ebu.ch
www.ebu.ch/en/index.php

GSM Association
6–8 Old Bond Street
London W1S 4PH
020 7518 0530
info@gsmworld.com
www.gsmworld.com

International Advertising Association
521 Fifth Avenue, Suite 1807
New York, NY 10175, USA
00 1 212 557 1133
iaa@iaaglobal.org
www.iaaglobal.org

International Classified Media Association (ICMA)
ICMA Head Office, Rokin 36-II
1012 KT Amsterdam
The Netherlands
00 31 20 638 2336
info@icmaonline.org
www.icmaonline.org

International Communications Forum
icforum@yahoo.co.uk
www.icforum.org

International Institute of Communications
Regent House, 24–25 Nutford Place
London W1H 5YN
020 7323 9622
enquiries@iicom.org
www.iicom.org

International Newspaper Marketing Association
10300 North Central Expressway
Suite 467, Texas 75231, USA
00 1 214 373 9111
inma@inma.org
www.inma.org

International Public Relations Association
Cheltonian House, Portsmouth Road
Esher, Surrey KT10 9AA
01372 461 188
secretariat@ipra.org
www.ipra.org

International Publishers Association
Av. de Miremont 3
1206 Geneva, Switzerland
00 41 22 346 3018
secretariat@ipa-uie.org
www.ipa-uie.org

International Telecommunication Union
Place des Nations
CH-1211 Geneva 20, Switzerland
00 41 22 730 51 11
itumail@itu.int
www.itu.int

International Webcasting Association
4206 F Technology Court
Chantilly, VA 20151, USA
00 1 301 650 2467
info@webcasters.org
www.webcasters.org

World Federation of Advertisers
120, Avenue Louise
1050 Brussels, Belgium
00 32 2 502 57 40
www.wfanet.org

World Radio Network
PO Box 1212, London SW8 2ZF
020 7896 9000
email@wrn.org
www.wrn.org

World Summit on the Information Society
Executive Secretariat
Place des Nations
1211 Geneva 20, Switzerland
00 41 22 730 60 48
wsismedia@itu.int
www.itu.int/wsis

Global media trade press

Advertising Age Global
711 Third Ave, New York
NY 10017-4036, USA
00 1 212 210 0100
editor@adage.com
www.adageglobal.com
Website

The Fourth Estate
Suite 3, 79 Roscoe Street
Bondi Beach, Sydney NSW 2026
Australia
00 61 416 178 908
michael@walsh.net
www.fourth-estate.com
Website & newsletter. Editor: Mike Walsh. Digital techology & media

MediaChannel
575 8th Avenue, #2200
New York, NY 10018, USA
00 1 212 246 0202
editor@mediachannel.org
www.mediachannel.org
Website. Executive director: Timothy Karr; executive editor: Danny Schechter

Middle East Media Guide
PO Box 74375
Dubai, UAE
00 971 50 553 0209
editor@middleeastmediaguide.com
www.middleeastmediaguide.com
Annual. Editor: Ben Smalley

Online Journalism Review
3502 Watt Way, Los Angeles
CA 90089-0281, USA
00 1 213 821 1285
editor@ojr.org
www.ojr.org
Website. Editor: Larry Pryor

PR Week
Haymarket Professional Publications
174 Hammersmith Road
London W6 7JP
020 8267 4429
prweek@haynet.com
www.prweek.com
Weekly. Editor-in-chief: Kate Nicholas; news editor: Ravi Chandiramani

World Press Freedom Review
IPI Headquarters, Spiegelgasse 2
A-1010 Vienna, Austria
00 43 1 512 90 11
ipi@freemedia.at
www.freemedia.at/wpfr/world.html
Website. Director: Johann P Fritz

Advertising

Award winners

Cannes International Advertising Festival, Grand Prix awards

- *Press:* Cops, DDB London, UK (VW Polo)
- *Television:* Force is with Cristal Beer, OMD, Chile (Cristal Beer)
- *Outdoor:* Missile Car, J Walter Thompson, Malaysia (CH-9 Media)
- *Film:* Mountain, TBWA\London, UK (Sony Computer Entertainment)

British Television Advertising Awards

- *Advertising agency of the year:* Clemmow Hornby Inge
- *Commerical of the year:* Cog, Wieden & Kennedy (Honda Accord)
- *Production company of the year:* Partizan

Shout it from the rooftops: Britain's advertising recession is over. As the advertisement company WPP put it when it reported increasing revenues in June, the industry is emerging "from an economic period that none of us hopes to revisit". Ad spend in Britain was worth more than £3.6bn in the first quarter of 2004, according to the Advertising Association, up 3.5 per cent in real terms on the year before. In 2003, total spend was just over £17.2bn; although this was a slight fall in real terms on 2002, there was a strong recovery in the second half of the year. Even more promising was the spend expected in 2004, featuring both Euro 2004 and the Olympics: the media buyer, Zenith Optimedia, expected growth in ad spending to be 3.5 per cent in real terms over the course of the year, and 3.1 per cent in 2005. Outdoor advertising, radio and the internet were expected to perform best of all, it said.

About the industry

In theory, advertising is split into two main areas: ad agencies, which handle industry accounts and come up with creative ideas; and media agencies, which control the purchase of ad space. There are about 1,600 ad agencies in Britain and more than 300 media agencies. In practice though, many big firms are owned by one of the major, mostly US-based, advertising "supergroups", who control not only the main ad and media agencies, but many of the PR and direct marketing agencies as well.

All advertising expenditure, by medium

	2003 £m	2002 £m	2001 £m	2000 £m	1999 £m	1998 £m
National newspapers	1,902	1,933	2,062	2,252	1,991	1,824
Regional newspapers	2,986	2,894	2,834	2,762	2,483	2,389
Consumer magazines	784	785	779	750	727	709
Business & professional magazines	1,048	1,088	1,202	1,270	1,195	1,209
Directories	1,040	990	959	868	831	780
Press production costs	634	643	669	702	650	620
Total press	**8,394**	**8,333**	**8,514**	**8,604**	**7,877**	**7,531**
Television	4,374	4,332	4,147	4,646	4,320	4,029
Direct mail	2,431	2,378	2,228	2,049	1,876	1,666
Outdoor & transport	901	816	788	810	649	613
Radio	582	545	541	595	516	460
Internet	376	233	166	155	51	19
Cinema	173	180	164	128	123	97
Total all media	**17,231**	**16,817**	**16,548**	**16,988**	**15,412**	**14,415**

Source: Advertising Association

Many ad agencies also offer below-the-line marketing services. These services include market research, sales promotion and direct marketing – direct mail expenditure alone reached £1.4bn in 2002, with the average British household receiving 13 advertisements in the mail a month. Figures show that such services performed strongly even during the advertising recession. Public relations is also traditionally considered a below-the-line service; but the industry now has such a high profile that it is worth considering it as a separate chapter (see page 281).

Financial performance

In accordance with the improved outlook, these giants began to fare better in 2003. At the huge **WPP**, which owns the ad agencies Young & Rubicam, J Walter Thompson and Ogilvy & Mather, media buyers MindShare and Mediaedge:cia, and PR firms Hill & Knowlton and Burson-Marsteller – plus a stake in the leading media buyer Carat – profits rose 18 per cent to £473.4m in 2003, and 2004 promised to be even better. The group also won the £340m account of HSBC bank. Meanwhile **Omnicom**, which owns the TBWA and Abbott Mead Vickers BBDO agencies, said profits rose by 7 per cent in the third quarter of 2003 to £80m; while **Publicis**, the French group that owns Saatchi & Saatchi and Zenith Optimedia, made £100m in 2003.

But in the first quarter of 2004, losses nearly doubled year-on-year at **Interpublic**, which owns ad agencies McCann-Erickson and Lowe, reaching £9m; and **Havas**, the French advertising giant, lost £119m in 2003, having announced in September that it was cutting 1,600 jobs.

2003 was a good year for independent agencies. Miles Calcraft Briginshaw Duffy, Clemmow Hornby Inge and Mother all performed well in Campaign magazine's list of the top agencies by billings (see box).

Ratecards

£10,000 might buy you:

- Twenty 10-second spots in the ITV Anglia region (7 peak-time, 13 off-peak); includes production
- A full-page colour ad in the Guardian's G2 section
- The outside back cover of a classic car magazine
- 230,000 page impressions on a "skyscraper" ad on Guardian Unlimited
- A 30-second targeted slot on 207 cinema screens in north-east England (cost per week)
- Three 30-second breakfast slots each weekday on a London radio station

(Based on industry rate cards available in 2004: Granada, the Guardian and Guardian Unlimited, Emap, Pearl & Dean and Virgin Radio)

Campaign magazine's top 20 UK agencies 2003

1	Abbott Mead Vickers BBDO	£350m
2	McCann–Erickson	£303m
3	J Walter Thompson	£286m
4	Publicis	£280m
5	Ogilvy & Mather	£253m
6	Euro RSCG London	£238m
7	TBWA\London	£237m
8	M&C Saatchi	£233m
9	Lowe	£219m
10	Saatchi & Saatchi	£213m
11	Leo Burnett	£208m
12	Rainey Kelly Campbell Roalfe/Y&R	£187m
13	Grey Worldwide London	£177m
14	DDB London	£176m
15	Bartle Bogle Hegarty	£142m
16	WCRS	£139m
17	Mother	£99m
18	Bates UK*	£95m
19	DLKW & Partners	£89m
20	Banks Hoggins O'Shea/FCB	£83m

* became part of J Walter Thompson in 2003
Source: Campaign Report – The Top 300 Agencies, February 2004
(Data supplied by Nielsen Media Research)

Cog: Honda ad won British TV award

Creative performance

Among the most effective campaigns of 2004 were the "118 118" runner ads by the agency, WCRS. But they were also controversial: the ads were dropped in March 2004 when the 70s athlete, David Bedford, complained that the runners were based on his image, and threatened to sue. Ofcom, then the broadcast advertising regulator, had upheld Bedford's complaint, ruling that the ads were a "comically exaggerated representation" of him. WCRS, meanwhile, was bought by its management from Havas in a £20m deal.

Meanwhile "Cog", the acclaimed Wieden & Kennedy ad for Honda that mysteriously failed to win the Grand Prix at Cannes in 2003, made up for that by taking top prize at the British Television Advertising Awards.

Regulation

The British advertising industry was further deregulated in 2004. Historically, the industry had been monitored in two ways: TV & radio advertising had been controlled by broadcast regulators, while non-broadcast advertising was handled by the Advertising Standards Authority (ASA), a self-regulatory body. That changed in December 2003, when Ofcom, the new "light-touch" regulator across the broadcast industry, inherited its powers; and in May, it surprised no one by announcing it would pass control of TV advertising to the ASA. Under its plan – improved in the Lords in July – the Advertising Standards Authority (Broadcast) would handle public complaints about TV adverts; while another new body, the Broadcast Committee of Advertising Practice, would set, monitor and review overall standards.

Ofcom's plans did, however, come at an awkward time for the industry. Also in May, the Commons health select committee published a report

Top 20 media brands 2003
(Agencies ranked by Nielsen media research billings)

1	MediaCom	£611m
2	Zenith Optimedia	£606m
3	MindShare	£557m
4	Carat	£519m
5	OMD UK	£427m
6	Initiative London	£415m
7	Starcom Motive	£389m
8	Universal McCann London	£325m
9	PHD	£263m
10	Starcom MediaVest	£260m
11	Manning Gottlieb OMD	£255m
12	Vizeum UK	£206m
13	Mediaedge:cia	£199m
14	Walker Media	£173m
15	Media Planning Group	£137m
16	MediaVest (Manchester)	£105m
17	BrandConnection	£90m
18	The Allmond Partnership	£77m
19	Feather Brooksbank	£62m
20	Universal McCann Manchester	£62m

Source: Campaign Report – The Top 300 Agencies, February 2004 (Data supplied by Nielsen Media Research)

attacking the ability of the industry to regulate itself effectively, as it announced that the nation's "obesity crisis" could cost £7.4bn a year. The report said it was "disturbed at the ineffectiveness" of self-regulation, with particular regard to an ad for Wotsits in which, it said, Abbott Mead Vickers BBDO was briefed to get children to pester their parents to buy the crisps; the ASA, for its part, pointed out that is the Broadcasting Advertising Clearance Centre that pre-clears scripts, and that body does not see ad agency briefs. But the report led to the speculation that the government might ban junk food manufacturers from advertising during children's TV programmes: Labour MP Debra Shipley put forward a private member's bill proposing just such a move in May; but the plan is opposed by cabinet ministers.

A leaked awards entry by Abbott Mead Vickers BBDO, meanwhile, highlighted the importance of celebrity endorsements to the sale of junk food: the agency said that campaigns involving Gary Lineker, the former England footballer, had led to 1.4 billion extra bags of Walkers crisps being sold in seven years.

Meanwhile in north London, a local council has come up with a novel method of stopping illegal outdoor advertising, or flyposting; by taking individual marketing executives to court under antisocial behaviour legislation. Two executives who worked at Sony, Catherine Davies and Jo Headland, faced the prospect of up to five years in jail for defacing local amenities, after Camden council took the action; faced with a PR disaster, Sony agreed it would no longer use flyposters to advertise artists.

Further reading

■ Press

MediaGuardian
media.guardian.co.uk/advertising

Campaign
www.campaignlive.com

Marketing
www.marketing.haynet.com

Marketing Week
www.mad.co.uk/mw

Media Week
www.mediaweek.co.uk

Promotions & Incentives
www.pandionline.com

Adbusters magazine
www.adbusters.org

■ Books

How to Get into Advertising
ANDREA NEIDLE, CONTINUUM 2002

Ogilvy on Advertising
DAVID OGILVY, PRION 1995

Shared Beliefs, Institute of Practitioners in Advertising 2001

■ Film

How to Get Ahead in Advertising, 2001 Richard E Grant in post-Withnail black comedy

■ Other resources

Advertising Association
www.adassoc.org.uk

Institute of Practitioners in Advertising
www.ipa.co.uk

Mother love **Will Orr and Ed Collin**

The signs are that the worst of advertising's longest recession may be over. In July 2004, according to the World Advertising Research Centre, UK TV ad spend is reported to be up 4.8%. It's been a painful time for many – but it's also demonstrated how competitive advertising can be.

Advertising is a cut-throat business, but it's always one with opportunities for talented people to do things better. Conflict laws prevent complete consolidation, and ensure there is always business to pitch for. As a result, the market is over-supplied and clients have real choice.

The recession has forced clients to look very carefully at the value their agencies are providing and to take advantage of the choices on offer. The result has been a flourishing independent sector, with agencies like Mother and Clemmow Hornby Inge growing rapidly through the recession. The idea that blue-chip clients are the preserve of large, network-owned agencies has been shattered, with the likes of British Gas, Coca Cola and Orange looking to smaller agencies.

At the heart of this trend is a truism that agencies are nothing more than the people who work for them. Clients want direct access to talented, experienced individuals, which is something the smaller independent agencies credibly offer. In addition they can provide a fundamental benefit of independence: personal motivation. The opportunity for fame and fortune afforded by starting an agency means the partners are likely to be at the top of their game. There's an obvious shared agenda between client and agency: make our brand famous and your agency will become famous too.

It would be wrong to write off the network-owned agencies and the "super-groups" who own them. At a global level the market has consolidated rapidly in the last few years, and a few big players dominate. What is certain, however, is that the independents are forcing the likes of WPP to think carefully about their strategies.

One strategy has been to acquire companies across the spectrum of communication disciplines and assemble an integrated offering for clients. As clients seek greater integration across a wider mix of channels, the logic was that the groups would be best-placed to capitalise. Boots' appointment of a Mother-led consortium to its £90m integrated account was, as a result, one of the most talked-about pitches of the last year.

If that's the case domestically, the challenge for independent agencies is to develop an international offering. Bartle Bogle Hegarty, still 51% privately owned, has shown what can be done, but the groups can still point to global clients who favour the benefits of scale. HSBC, for example, recently appointed WPP to its £350m marketing services account. The fact that the client asked the holding companies rather than individual agencies to pitch is something we expect to see more of in the coming year.

Looking ahead, it's an exciting time to be in advertising. The recession has demonstrated that our industry rewards talent and entrepreneurial spirit. As Campaign magazine put it in summarising the last year, "the best are winning and, in an industry that depends on the potency of its ideas for its very existence, that has to be a good thing".

Will Orr and Ed Collin are strategists at Mother

Advertising Contacts

Advertising agencies

1576 Advertising
0131 473 1576
www.1576.co.uk

Abbott Mead Vickers BBDO
020 7616 3500
www.amvbbdo.com

AGA Group
020 7330 8888
www.aga.co.uk

AMD Girardot
020 7349 6376
www.amdgirardot.com

Arc Integrated Marketing
020 7751 1662
Barnsley 01285 740707
Edinburgh 0131 556 0115
www.arcconnect.co.uk

Archibald Ingall Stretton
020 7467 6100
www.archibaldingallstretton.com

ARM Direct
020 7224 3040
www.arm-direct.co.uk

Attinger Jack
01225 758222
www.aja.co.uk

Awa-Map
0161 907 3000
www.map-plc.co.uk

Banc
020 7437 5552
Leeds 0113 234 2022
www.banc.co.uk

Banks Hoggins O'Shea FCB
020 7947 8000
www.london.fcb.com

Barkers Scotland
0141 248 5030
Edinburgh 0131 229 7493
www.barkersscotland.co.uk

Barrett Cernis
020 7663 3575
www.barrett.cernis.co.uk

Barrington Johnson Lorains & Partners
0161 831 7141
www.bjl.co.uk

Bartle Bogle Hegarty
020 7734 1677
www.bartleboglehegarty.com

Bates UK
020 7262 5077
www.batesuk.com

BDH\TBWA
0161 908 8600
www.bdhtbwa.co.uk

BDS Beechwood
020 7439 4142
www.bds-beechwood.com

Bespoke Communications
020 7436 0266
www.bespokecommunications.com

Big Communications
0116 299 1144
www.bigcommunications.co.uk

Black & White Advertising
0191 493 2493

Blair Fowles
01202 558111
www.blairfowles.co.uk

Bray Leino
01598 760700
www.brayleino.co.uk

The Bridge
0141 552 8384
www.thebridgeuk.com

Burkitt DDB
020 7320 9300
www.burkittddb.com

Camp Chipperfield Hill Murray
020 7881 3200
www.cchm.co.uk

Campbell Doyle Dye
020 7483 9805
www.cddlondon.com

Carney Richardson
01491 834981

Carter Gosling
01225 465415

cdp-travissully
020 7437 4224
www.cdp-travissully.com

Charterhouse Advertising & Marketing
0161 848 9050
www.charterhouse-advertising.co.uk

Cheetham Bell JWT
0161 832 8884
www.cheethambelljwt.com

Chemistry Communications Group
020 7736 5355
www.chemistrygroup.co.uk

Citigate Albert Frank
020 7282 8000
Edinburgh 0131 555 0425
www.citigateaf.com

Citigate Smarts
0141 222 2040
Edinburgh 0131 555 0425
Manchester 0161 829 0740
www.citigatesmarts.co.uk

Clark McKay & Walpole
020 7487 9750
www.cmw-uk.com

Claydon Heely Jones Mason
020 7924 3000
www.claydonheeley.com

Clayton Graham Advertising
0141 353 3012
www.claytongraham.co.uk

Clear Marketing Communications
0161 448 8008

Clemmow Hornby Inge
020 7462 8500
www.chiadvertising.com

Coltas
0141 204 5665
www.coltas.com

Connectpoint Advertising
0161 817 4200
www.connectpoint.co.uk

Conzept
020 7633 0008

Craik Jones Watson Mitchell Voelkel
020 7734 1650
www.craikjones.co.uk

Crammond Dickens Lerner
020 7240 8100
www.cdl-uk.com

Cravens Advertising
0191 232 6683
Leeds 0113 2753399
www.cravens.co.uk

CWA Creative
0116 232 7400
www.cwa.co.uk

Da Costa & Co
020 7916 3791

David Gent Creative
01706 220388
www.davidgent.com

DDB London
020 7262 7755
www.ddblondon.com

Delaney Lund Knox Warren & Partners
020 7836 3474
www.dlkw.co.uk

Dewynters
020 7321 0488
www.dewynters.com

DFGW
020 7292 7213
www.dfgw.com

Dig For Fire
0114 281 1200

DKA
020 7636 6992

Doner Cardwell Hawkins
020 7734 0511
www.donercardwellhawkins.co.uk

Draft Worldwide
0131 466 6300
London 020 7323 4586
020 7589 0800, 020 7863 9773
Edinburgh 0131 662 0600
01865 884444
www.draftworldwide.com

Eardrum
020 7287 2211
www.eardrum.co.uk

Edge Ideas
020 7379 7799

EHS Brann
020 7017 1000
Cirencester 01285 644744
Leeds 0113 207 0400
www.ehs.co.uk

Elliott Borra Perlmutter
020 7836 7722
www.ebpcreative.com

Euro RSCG
020 7379 3991
www.eurorscg.co.uk
Euro RSCG Wnek Gosper
020 7240 4111
www.eurorscg.co.uk
Factor 3
01242 254242
Fallon
020 7494 9120
www.fallon.com
Farm Communications
020 7428 1300
www.creativebrief.com
Faulds
020 7908 7510
Edinburgh 0131 557 6003
www.faulds.co.uk
FEREF
020 7580 6546
www.feref.co.uk
Fox Kalomaski
020 7691 8090
www.foxkalomaski.co.uk
Frog Communications
020 8969 0999
GCAS
028 9032 3418
www.gcasgroup.com
Genesis Advertising
028 9031 3344
www.genesis-advertising.co.uk
Gillett & Bevan
0161 228 0023
www.gillett-bevan.com
Golley Slater & Partners
020 7379 8886
Bristol 0117 921 1131
Cardiff 029 2038 8621
www.golleyslater.com
Goode International
01491 873323
www.goode.co.uk
Gould & Portmans
020 7831 3121
www.g-p.co.uk
Grey London
020 7636 3399
www.grey.co.uk
Harrison Troughton Wunderman
020 7611 6333
www.htw.wunderman.com
HDM Agency
020 7321 2227
www.hdmagency.co.uk
Heresy
020 7349 6800
www.heresynetwork.com
HHCL/Red Cell
020 7436 3333
www.hhclredcell.com
Hooper Galton
020 7494 6300
www.hoopergalton.co.uk
Huet & Co
0161 835 3100
www.huet.co.uk
IC Group
01772 679383
www.icgonline.co.uk
Inferno
020 7292 7070
www.inferno-group.com
Interfocus Network
020 7376 9000
www.interfocus.co.uk
J Walter Thompson
020 7656 7000
www.jwt.com
JDA Group
0113 290 4290
www.jda.co.uk
Joshua Agency
020 7453 7900
www.joshua-agency.co.uk
Kaleidoscope Advertising Design & Marketing
0151 707 2220
www.kadm.co.uk
Karmarama
020 7612 1777
Kastner & Partners
020 7689 6989
Lavery Rowe
020 7378 1780
Birmingham 0121 212 2230
www.laveryrowe.com
Lawton Communications Group
023 8082 8500
www.lawton.co.uk
Leagas Delaney
020 7758 1758
www.leagasdelaney.com
Leith Advertising Agency
020 7758 1400
Edinburgh 0131 561 8600
www.leith.co.uk
Leo Burnett
020 7591 9111
www.leoburnett.com
Levy McCallum
028 9031 9220
www.levymccallum.co.uk
Link ICA
01622 767700
www.linkica.co.uk
Lowe & Partners
020 7584 5033
www.loweworldwide.com
Lowe Broadway
020 7344 8888
www.lowebroadway.com
M&C Saatchi
020 7543 4500
www.mcsaatchi.com
Maher Bird Associates
020 7287 1718
www.mba.co.uk
Marr Associates
01828 632800
www.marr.co.uk
Martin Tait Redheads
0191 232 1926
www.mtra.co.uk
Masius
020 7751 1664
www.masius.com
Matters Media
020 7224 6030
McCann-Erickson Advertising UK
020 7837 3737
www.mccann.co.uk
Mercier Gray
020 7420 7900
www.merciergray.com
Merle
0141 242 1800
www.merleagency.com
Miles Calcraft Briginshaw Duffy
01344 458600
www.mcbd.co.uk
Minerva
020 7631 6900
www.amvadvance.com
Mitchell Patterson Grime Mitchell
020 7734 8087
www.mpgm.co.uk
Mortimer Whittaker O'Sullivan
020 7379 8844
www.mwo.co.uk
Mostly Media
01935 478238
www.mostlymedia.co.uk
Mother
020 7012 1999
www.motherlondon.com
Mustoe Merriman Levy
020 7379 9999
www.mmhl.co.uk
Nexus/H UK
01892 517777
www.nexus-h.co.uk
Oakbase
01244 391391
www.oakbase.co.uk
Odiorne Wilde Narraway
020 7930 0432
Ogilvy & Mather
020 7345 3000
www.ogilvy.com
Ogilvy Primary Contact
020 7468 6900
www.primary.co.uk
Palmer Hargreaves Wallis Tomlinson
01926 452525
Birmingham 0121 233 9494
www.thisiswt.co.uk
Peacock Marketing & Design
020 7580 8868
www.peacockdesign.com
Ping Communications
01422 241237
Poulter
0113 285 6500
www.poulterpartners.com
Proximity Media
020 7298 1000
www.proximitylondon.com
Publicis
020 7935 4426
www.publicis.co.uk
Publicity Bureau
01302 730303
www.tp-bureau.co.uk
PWLC
0113 398 0120
www.pwlc.uk.com
Quiet Storm
020 7907 1140
www.quietstormltd.com
Radford Advertising & Marketing
0161 832 8807

Radioville
020 7534 5999
www.radioville.co.uk
Rainey Kelly Campbell Roalfe/Y&R
020 7611 6568/9
www.rkcryr.com
Rapier
020 7369 8000
www.rapieruk.com
Raw Media
01305 259444
www.rawmedia.co.uk
Redman Jones & Partners
0161 828 2600
www.redmanjones.co.uk
Rhythmm
0117 942 9786
www.rhythmm.co.uk
Robson Brown
0191 232 2443
Manchester 0161 877 2004
www.robson-brown.co.uk
RPM3
020 7434 4343
www.rpm3.co.uk
Saatchi & Saatchi
020 7636 5060
www.saatchi-saatchi.com
Scholz & Friends London
020 7961 4000
www.s-f.com
Senior King Communications Group
020 7734 5855
www.seniorkinggroup.co.uk
Sheppard Day Associates
020 7821 2222
www.sheppard-day.com
Sold Out Advertising
020 7704 0409
www.soldout.co.uk
Soul
020 7292 5999
www.souladvertising.com
Space City Productions
020 7371 4000
www.spacecity.co.uk
Springer & Jacoby UK
020 7012 6000
www.sjsimplicity.co.uk
SPS Advertising
01392 464545
St Luke's Communications
020 7380 8888
www.stlukes.co.uk
SWK Communications
020 7637 6800
Target NMI
020 7436 5000
www.targetnmi.com
TBA
020 7380 0953
www.tbaplc.co.uk
TBWA\GGT and TBWA\London
020 7573 6666
www.tbwa.co.uk
Team Saatchi
020 7436 6636
www.saatchi.com
Tequila
020 7557 6100
www.tequila-uk.com
TEQUILA\ Manchester
0161 908 8100
www.tequilamanchester.com
Tugboat Agency
020 7436 4433
Typestyle Advertising
01625 536144
www.typestyle.co.uk
UK Advertising & Marketing Services
01322 228899
www.ukams.co.uk
Union Advertising Agency
0113 226 6050
Edinburgh 0131 625 6000
www.union.co.uk
Vallance Carruthers Coleman Priest
020 7802 5803
www.vccp.com
WAA
0121 321 1411
www.waa.co.uk
Walker Agency
01202 414200
www.thewalkeragency.co.uk
Walsh Trott Chick Smith
020 7907 1200
www.wtcs.co.uk
Ware Anthony Rust
01223 566212
www.war.uk.com
WARL Change Behaviour
020 7400 0900
www.warl.com
WCRS
020 7806 5099
www.wcrs.com
WFCA Integrated
01892 511085
www.wfca.co.uk
Wieden & Kennedy
020 7299 7500
www.wklondon.com
Windmill Partnership
020 7371 2868
www.windmillpartnership.com
Worth Communications
020 8439 8200
www.worthcommunications.com
WWAV Rapp Collins
020 8735 8000
www.wwavrc.co.uk
Wyatt International
0121 454 8181
www.wyattinternational.com
Young & Rubicam EMEA
020 7387 9366
www.yandr.com
Young Phillips
01202 298969

Media consultancies

All Response Media
020 7017 1450
www.allresponsemedia.com
Allmond Partnership
020 7766 5600
www.theallmondpartnership.com
AMS Media Group
020 7843 6900
www.amsgroup.co.uk
Attinger Jack
01225 758222
www.aja.co.uk
BJK & E Media
020 7379 8080
www.bjke.co.uk
BLM Media
020 7437 1317
www.blm-group.com
BrandConnection
020 7676 2850
www.brandconnection.com
Bray Leino
01598 760700
www.brayleino.co.uk
Brilliant Independent Media Specialists
0113 394 0000
www.brilliantmedia.co.uk
Bygraves Bushell Valladares & Sheldon
020 7734 4445
www.bbvs.co.uk
Carat
020 7430 6000
www.carat.co.uk
Feather Brooksbank
0131 555 2554
Manchester 0161 834 9793
Glasgow 0141 332 3382
www.featherbrooksbank.co.uk
Initiative Media London
020 7663 7000
www.initiativemedia.com
John Ayling & Associates
020 7439 6070
Manning Gottlieb OMD
020 7470 5300
www.omd.com
Matters Media
020 7224 6030
Leeds 0113 209 4495
www.mattersmedia.com
Media Campaign Services
020 7389 0800
www.mediacampaign.co.uk
Media Insight
020 7969 4141
www.mediainsight.com
Media Planning Group
020 7393 2546
www.mpg.com
Mediability
01625 441911
www.mediability.co.uk
MediaCom
020 7874 5500
Edinburgh 0131 555 1500
Manchester 0161 839 6600
www.mediacomuk.com

Mediaedge:cia
www.mediaedgecia.com
MediaVest
020 7190 8000
Manchester 0161 211 8032
www.mediavest.co.uk
MediaVision
0161 838 4444
Edinburgh 0131 554 0033
www.media-vision.co.uk
MindShare
020 7969 4227
www.mindshareworld.com
OMD
020 7893 4893
www.omdmedia.com
PHD Compass
020 7446 0555
www.phd.co.uk
Starcom MediaVest
020 7453 4444
www.starcommedia.com
Total Media
020 7937 3793
www.totalmedia.co.uk
Total Media North
0121 523 1144
www.totalmedia.co.uk
Universal McCann Birmingham
0121 713 3500
www.mccann.co.uk
Universal McCann EMEA
020 7833 5858
www.universalmccann.com
Universal McCann Manchester
01625 822300
www.mccannmcr.com
Universal McCann UK
020 7833 5858
www.mccann.co.uk
Vizeum UK
020 7395 0882
www.vizeum.co.uk
Walker Media
020 7447 7500
www.walkermedia.com
WWAV Rapp Collins Media
020 8735 8000
www.wwavrc.co.uk
Zed Media
020 7224 8500
www.zedmedia.co.uk
ZenithOptimedia UK
020 7224 8500
www.zenithoptimedia.com
Zentropy Partners
020 7554 0500
www.zentropypartners.co.uk

Outdoor media

Clear Channel UK
020 7478 2200
www.clearchannel.co.uk
JC Decaux
020 7298 8000
www.jcdecaux.co.uk
Maiden
020 7838 4000
www.maiden.co.uk
Primesight
020 7882 1200
www.primesight.co.uk
Viacom Outdoor
020 7482 3000
www.viacom-outdoor.co.uk

New media agencies

Agency.com
020 7964 8500
www.i-traffic.com
AKQA
020 7494 9200
www.akqa.com
CCG.XM
020 7724 7228
www.ccgxm.com
Citigate Online – London
020 7535 9803
www.citigatemc.com
Dare Digital
020 7612 3600
www.daredigital.com
Digit
020 7684 6769
www.digitlondon.com
Digital Marketing Direct – London
020 7282 2800
www.incepta.co.uk
Digitas Europe
020 7494 6700
www.digitas.com
EURO RSCG Circle
020 7240 4111
www.eurorscginteraction.co.uk
Global Beach
020 7384 1188
www.globalboach.com
Glue London
020 7739 2345
www.gluelondon.com
Grey Interactive UK
020 7453 8320
www.greyinteractive.co.uk
i-level
020 7340 2700
www.i-level.com
Incepta Online
020 7282 2800
www.inceptaonline.com
itraffic
020 7964 8500
www.itraffic.com
Lateral
020 7613 4449
www.lateral.net
MediaVest IP
020 7751 1661
www.mediavest.co.uk
Modem Media
020 7874 9400
www.modemmedia.com
Outrider
0161 930 9000
London 020 7803 2390
www.outrider.com
Oyster Partners
020 7446 7500
www.oyster.co.uk
Profero
020 7387 2000
www.profero.co.uk
Rufus Leonard
020 7404 4490
www.rufusleonard.com
Syzygy
020 7460 4080
www.syzygy.net
Tangozebra
020 7535 9850
www.tangozebra.com
Wheel
020 7348 1000
Glasgow 0141 225 6560
www.wheel.co.uk
Zentropy
020 7554 0500
www.zentropypartners.co.uk

Direct marketing & sales promotion

Arc Integrated Marketing
020 7751 1662
www.arcmarketing.co.uk
Black Cat
020 7656 7310
www.black-cat.co.uk
Brann
0113 207 0400
www.ehsbrannleeds.com
Carlson Marketing Group
020 8875 0875
www.carlson-europe.com
Clark McKay & Walpole
020 7487 9750
www.clarkmckayandwalpole.com
Claydon Heeley Jones Mason
020 7924 3000
www.chjm.com
Craik Jones Watson Mitchell Voelkel
020 7734 1650
www.craikjones.co.uk
Dialogue Marketing Partnership
020 8783 3100
www.dialmkg.com
Draft Worldwide
020 7589 0800
www.draftworldwide.com
dunnhumby
020 8832 9222
www.dunnhumby.com
Dynamo Marketing
020 7386 0699
www.dynamo.net.uk

EHS Brann
01285 644744
London 020 7017 1000
Leeds 0113 207 0400
www.ehsbrann.com
www.ehsbrannleeds.com

Finex Communications
020 7361 7777
www.finexgroup.com

GHA Holdings
01903 885672
www.g-h-a.co.uk

Harrison Troughton Wunderman
020 7611 6333
www.wunderman.com

Haygarth
020 8971 3300
www.haygarth.co.uk

Joshua Agency
020 7453 7900
www.joshua-agency.co.uk

KLP Euro RSCG
020 7478 3478
www.klpeurorscg.co.uk

Marketing Store Worldwide
020 7745 2100
Birmingham 01675 467404
Leeds 0113 246 8266
www.themarketingstore.com

McCann-Erickson Relationship Marketing
020 7153 8075
www.mrmworldwide.com

OgilvyOne
020 7566 7000
www.ogilvy.com

Perspectives Red Cell
020 8568 4422
www.perspectivesredcell.com

Proximity London
020 7298 1000
www.proximitylondon.com

Rapier
020 7369 8000
www.rapier.ltd.uk

TBWA\GGT
020 7439 4282
www.tbwa-ggt.com

TDA
01242 633 111
www.tdaltd.com

Tequila
020 7557 6100
www.tequila-uk.com

Triangle Communications
020 7637 0322
www.trianglecommunications.co.uk

Tullo Marshall Warren
020 7349 4000
www.tmw.co.uk

WWAV Rapp Collins
020 8735 8000
www.wwavrc.co.uk

Useful associations – advertising

Advertising Association
020 7828 2771
www.adassoc.org.uk

Advertising Standards Authority
020 7580 5555
www.asa.org.uk

Chartered Institute of Marketing
01628 427500
www.cim.co.uk

Committee of Advertising Practice
020 7828 4224
www.cap.org.uk

Direct Marketing Association
020 7291 3300
www.dma.org.uk

Incorporated Society of British Advertisers
020 7291 9020
www.isba.org.uk

International Advertising Association
00 1 212 557 1133
www.iaaglobal.org

Institute of Practitioners in Advertising
020 7235 7020
www.ipa.co.uk

Market Research Society
020 7490 4911
www.marketresearch.org.uk

Nielsen/NetRatings
01865 384067
www.nielsen-netratings.com

Outdoor Advertising Association of Great Britain
020 7973 0315
www.oaa.org.uk

World Federation of Advertisers
00 32 2 502 5740
www.wfanet.org

Trade press

Advertising Age Global
711 Third Ave, New York
NY 10017-4036, USA
00 1 212 210 0414
editor@adage.com
www.adageglobal.com
Website. Editor: Hoag Levins

Brand Strategy
Centaur Communications
St Giles House, 50 Poland Street
London W1F 7AX
020 7943 8160
elen.lewis@centaur.co.uk
www.mad.co.uk/bs
Monthly. Editor: Elen Lewis

Campaign
Haymarket Business Publications
174 Hammersmith Road
London W6 7JP
020 8267 4683
campaign@haynet.com
www.brandrepublic.com
Weekly. Editor: Caroline Marshall

Creative Review
Centaur Communications
St Giles House, 50 Poland Street
London W1F 7AX
020 7970 4000
patrick.burgoyne@centaur.co.uk
www.creativereview.co.uk
Monthly. Editor: Patrick Burgoyne

Design Week
Centaur Communications
St Giles House, 50 Poland Street
London W1F 7AX
020 7970 4000
lyndark@centaur.co.uk
www.designweek.co.uk
Weekly. Editor: Lynda Relph-Knight

Marketing
Haymarket Business Publications
174 Hammersmith Road
London W6 7JP
020 8267 5000
marketing@haynet.com
www.marketingmagazine.co.uk
Weekly. Editor: Craig Smith

Marketing Direct
Haymarket Business Publications
174 Hammersmith Road
London W6 7JP
020 8267 5000
bill.britt@haynet.com
www.mxdirect.co.uk
Monthly. Editor: Bill Britt

Marketing Week
Centaur Communications
St Giles House, 50 Poland Street
London W1F 7AX
020 7970 4000
mw.editorial@centaur.co.uk
www.marketing-week.co.uk
Weekly. Editor: Stuart Smith

Media Week
Quantum Business Media
Quantum House, 19 Scarbrook Road
Croydon CR9 1LX
020 8565 4326
editorial@mediaweek.co.uk
www.mediaweek.co.uk
Weekly. Editor: Tim Burrowes. Covers media agencies, media sales and marketers

Shots
Emap Information
33–39 Bowling Green Lane
London EC1R 0DA
020 7505 8000
lyndy.stout@shots.net
www.shots.net
International advertising, 6pa. Editor: Lyndy Stout

PR

The PR industry is rebuilding confidence after a dismal few years. Since 1997 the industry has seen its reputation fall to a new low as its work – particularly the political kind – began to be known as "spin doctoring" even by the general public; while the advertising recession, for its part, hit the sector hard. From 2001 to 2003, more than half of Britain's "most admired" companies did not increase PR spending, according to a report by the Institute of Public Relations (IPR); while in 2003, some 12 of PR Week's top-twenty firms made less money than they did even in 2002. That had its effect on the bottom lines of PR and marketing groups: Chime Communications, which owns Bell Pottinger, saw profits fall 35 per cent in the first half of 2003; while Incepta, which owns Citigate Dewe Rogerson, lost £1.5m before tax in the year to February 2004 – a period in which it cut 150 jobs.

That said, 2004 has seen renewed optimism among PR consultants. According to the Communications Agency Federation's barometer report for the first quarter of 2004, some 84 per cent of firms say the market for new business is "busy" or "buoyant"; and more than 60 per cent say they are optimistic about the future.

The new mood is exemplified by the appointment of Anne Gregory, a former BBC reporter and professor of public relations at Leeds Metropolitan University, as the president of the IPR, in July 2003. She earned election by promising to rid the industry of its "spin doctor" tag; she has also called for a new code of practice to good PR, perhaps controlled by a self-regulatory body similar to the Press Complaints Commission for journalists. Over at the Public Relations Consultants Association, there was also a change at the top: its new chairman, Crispin Manners, started out in May 2004.

2004 saw a joint report into the industry by the IPR and the Department of Trade and Industry. The report identified some 120 elements of good practice in PR, for consultants to pore over at their leisure; it also noted how good PR is increasingly at the heart of strategic management; two of the biggest PR disasters of 2004, the Dasani launch and the Shell oil reserve scandal (see "disasters and coups", below), would appear to support this view. It also noted that PR needed to improve its audience research, and to improve how the performances of PR firms can be fairly compared; and it called for progress in improving training of PR professionals. In that respect, an interesting statistic was a survey by Benchmark Research, reported in the Financial Times in May 2004, saying the PR industry wastes £592m a year on poorly targeted press releases. If that figure could be reduced, PR would doubtless start to get a better press of its own.

Government & politics

Perhaps the most controversial aspect of PR is its role in public life. How far should a PR man – and Alastair Campbell, the former head of communications at Downing Street, will, of course, immediately spring to mind – be involved in the strategic thinking of an elected government? This was one of the questions addressed by the Hutton inquiry, after the BBC journalist Andrew Gilligan quoted the Iraq weapons expert, Dr David Kelly, as accusing Downing Street of knowingly "sexing up" a dossier into Iraqi weapons capabilities. Lord Hutton cleared Campbell of all blame on that score (see page 116), but Campbell had resigned in any case in September 2003. Then in January 2004, an inquiry into government communications, led by the Guardian Media Group chief executive Bob Phillis, recommended a new civil service post of "permanent secretary, government communications"; the post was filled by Howell James, a close friend of Peter Mandelson and the former press secretary to John Major, an appointment which the Guardian said had "a faint whiff of cronyism". The report also notably criticised the government for not grasping "the potential of modern communications as a service provided for citizens".

In March 2004, official figures showed that Downing Street press office costs had increased to almost £1.4m, from about £600,000 in 1997.

There was also a change for the Tories, as Guy Black, the former president of the Press Complaints Commission, became director of communications for the Conservative party.

2004 also saw the increasing use of private PR firms by the public sector. In January, it was revealed that the financial PR firm, Finsbury, had won a contract from university vice-chancellors to sell the prime minister's plans on top-up fees; in October 2003, the Environment Agency appointed Burson-Marsteller – which also represents oil, GM, tobacco and chemical industries – to act for the government's pollution watchdog, a move that environmentalist groups called "barmy"; and in March, Bell Pottinger was appointed to promote democracy in Iraq, a contract it won from the US government.

Meanwhile in April, James Herbert, the former head of global media relations at Shell, began to handle PR for the NHS's £6bn national programme for IT.

PR disasters

- **March 2004:** It emerges that Dasani, a bottled water marketed by Coca Cola, is tap water from Sidcup – reminding consumers of Del Boy's "Peckham spring", and crippling a £7m launch. PR man Mark Borkowski writes in the Guardian that the launch could have been saved by focusing on bottled water as a convenience product.
- **April 2004:** The world's largest oil company, Shell, deliberately misled investors about its financial health by overstating oil and gas reserves, an internal inquiry concludes.
- **April 2004:** The Financial Services Authority finds Peter Bracken, the former head of communications at recruitment consultant Whitehead Mann, guilty of insider dealing.

Moving into PR

2004 also saw another senior journalist leave the newspaper world to join the PR industry. David Yelland, the Sun editor who had been shunted upstairs at NewsCorp with the arrival of Rebekah Wade, joined Britain's biggest agency, Weber Shandwick, in June. He follows Roland Rudd, the former FT journalist who set up Finsbury PR, and Rory Godson, former Sunday Times business editor, who last year joined Goldman Sachs as a PR adviser, and this year announced he was setting up his own consultancy. Earlier, in November 2003, Mike Granatt, the director general of the now defunct Government Information and Communications Service, had become a partner in PR firm Luther Pendragon.

Celebrity PR

The name of Max Clifford remains synonymous with a certain kind of PR. The publicist's client list last year included Kerry McFadden, winner of I'm A Celebrity ... Get me Out of Here!; a 17-year-old girl at the heart of rape allegations involving eight Premiership footballers; and the UK Independence Party. Although he consistently denied it, it was also reported in MediaGuardian.co.uk that Clifford brokered a deal between Rebecca Loos, the woman who claimed to have had an affair with David Beckham, and the News of the World.

Football and PR are never very far apart, it seems: Beckham himself appointed a new PR manager in June 2004, in the form of Simon Oliveira; Karen Parlour, ex-wife of Arsenal footballer Ray Parlour, appointed Mark Borkowski in May as she fought to win half of the player's earnings; while in September 2003, the partner of Sven Goran Eriksson, Nancy Dell'Olio, hired the former FA head of communications, Paul Newman.

Further reading

■ Press

MediaGuardian
media.guardian.co.uk/marketingandpr

PR Week
www.prweek.com

■ Books

Public Relations Handbook
ALISON THEAKER 2001

■ Films

The Sweet Smell of Success, 1957
Tony Curtis as a slimy press agent: unmissable

■ Other resources

Institute of Public Relations
www.ipr.org.uk

Public Relations Consultants Association
www.prca.org.uk

Good publicity **Julia Hobsbawm**

The relationship between PR and journalism has always been fraught. No journalist worth their salt would admit to liking, let alone relying on, PR; an attitude that has prevailed for over 100 years, but which now needs to change – for the sake of public good, and for the sake of all our publics.

PR's origins were the same late 19-century ones as those of journalism. Both came out of an information age heralded by the rise of mass newspapers, followed rapidly by cinema, radio, and, half-way into the 20th century, television. Then, public relations was inspired by journalism, and it still is: the most highly prized recruits in any PR firm are still those who know the news machine at first hand.

The first objective of PR is not objectivity; it is bias. But it is, according to the code of conduct laid down by the Institute of Public Relations, one which must have integrity. Telling the truth runs through good public relations – contrary to the myths of spin, which are exaggerated in most sections of the business. And it's a good thing that PR is there to tell the truth, because today's pressurised young journalists rely on our profession more than their forebears ever did.

The always-on world of media means most journalists need to report a story in a fraction of the time they used to, getting briefed on topics they may know next to nothing about at short notice, and gaining access to spokespeople sooner rather than later. This is where PR comes into its own. According to its official global definition, public relations is "the planned and sustained effort to establish and maintain mutual understanding and goodwill between an organisation and its publics". The media is one such public, and a conduit to many others.

What I would call "proper PR" has at its heart the desire and ability to make journalism's life easier. Not, as some critics would suggest, by using media dependence to manipulate facts that hacks no longer have the time to check – or not in Britain, anyway, as they tend to much more in the US – but by being a necessary informer, guide, matchmaker between their client and the media wishing to report them.

While journalism reserves the right to its opinion, one which we hope is expressed fairly, PR aims to put its clients across to people in a favourable light, often via journalism, while not dissembling.

But in many quarters, journalism still believes it has the right to be critical by virtue of its so-called independence – and it believes public relations disowns such a right, because it puts the vested interest of clients first. So there is a perceived natural communications order, a kind of moral food chain which journalism sits atop, while PR languishes down below.

I think tomorrow's PR people need to challenge these preconceptions, and to do so today; not least because to claim real independence, in a media dominated by its proprietors and by advertising, is pushing the definition to its limits.

But I admit it: there is such a thing as poor PR. By this I mean PR which is either badly done – for which I include the sins of shoddy targeting, phoning journalists on deadline, or otherwise distracting them with trivia – or PR done for the wrong reasons.

I disagree with the "taxi rank" principle which suggests everyone is entitled to PR representation and just needs to flag down help when they need it. I think that the tools of PR – variously deployed by despots and democrats alike – are too powerful to be made universally available or to be applied just because they can be.

If PR fails from time to time, so does journalism. But these are still two professions to be proud of belonging to, both with equally high aspirations – to tell the truth, and to do so persuasively.

I think that not only is proper PR vital for the lifeblood of today's rapid-turnaround culture of journalism, but it feeds a healthy global information machine. Properly self-regulated PR, like properly self-regulated journalism, is surely the engine of any democracy.

So tomorrow's PRs are every bit the legitimate friend, and not foe, of journalists. And you can quote me on that.

Julia Hobsbawm is professor of public relations at the London School of Communication, and runs the PR consultancy HMC – Hobsbawm Media + Marketing Communications. Her book on truth and integrity in PR and journalism will be published by Atlantic Books in September 2005.

PR Contacts

PR agencies

3 x 1
Glasgow
0141 353 5131
info@3x1.com
www.3x1.com

AD Communications
Esher, Surrey
01372 464470
richard@adcommunications.co.uk
www.adcommunications.co.uk

AS Biss & Co
London
020 7340 6200
tellmemore@asbiss.com
www.asbiss.com

Ashley Communications
Northwood, Middlesex
01923 826150
info@ashleycomms.com

Atlas Media Group
Leeds
0113 306 0000
London 020 7323 7170
info@atlasmediagroup.co.uk
www.atlasmediagroup.co.uk

Attenborough Associates
London
020 7734 4455
info@attenborough.net
www.attenborough.net

August One
London
020 8434 5555
info.uk@augustone.com
www.augustone.com

Aurelia Public Relations
London
020 7351 2227
info@aurelia-london.co.uk
www.aurelia-london.com

Automotive PR
London
020 7494 8050
info@automotivepr.com
www.automotivepr.com

AxiCom
London
020 8392 4050
lyle.closs@axicom.com
www.axicom.com

B2B Communications
Chessington, Surrey
020 8974 2404
enquiries@b2bcommunications.co.uk
www.b2bcommunications.co.uk

Band & Brown Communications
London
020 7419 7000
nick.band@bbpr.com
www.bbpr.com

Barclay Stratton
London
020 8877 8600
James.Laird@barclaystratton.co.uk
www.barclaystratton.com

Barkers Scotland
Glasgow
0141 248 5030
pr@barkers-scot.com
www.barkersscotland.co.uk

Barrett Dixon Bell
Altrincham, Cheshire
0161 925 4700
info@bdb.co.uk
www.bdb.co.uk

BCLO PR
Bristol
0117 973 1173
info@bclo.co.uk
www.bclo.com

Beattie Communications Group/ Beattie Media
London
020 7398 3300
Dundee 01382 562883
Edinburgh 0131 220 8269:
Falkirk 01324 602550
Glasgow 01698 787878
Leeds 0113 213 0300
London West 020 7930 0453
www.beattiemedia.co.uk

Bell Pottinger
London
020 7861 2400
pbingle@bell-pottinger.co.uk
www.bppa.co.uk

Berkeley PR International
Reading
0118 988 2992
Derbyshire 01629 826942
Bristol 0117 925 7489
enquiries@berkeleypr.co.uk
www.berkeleypr.co.uk

BGB & Associates
London
020 7233 2300
pr@bgb.co.uk
www.bgb.co.uk

The BIG Partnership
Glasgow
0141 333 9585
info@bigpartnership.co.uk
www.bigpartnership.co.uk

Binns & Co Public Relations
London
020 7786 9600
Bristol 0117 317 9477
Edinburgh 0131 226 8009
York 01347 844 844
www.binnspr.co.uk

Biosector 2
London
020 7016 3300
www.biosector2.com

Bite Communications
London
020 8741 1123
moreuk@bitepr.com
www.bitepr.com

Biss Lancaster Euro RSCG
London
020 7022 4000
bisslancaster@bisslancaster.com
www.bisslancaster.com

BMB Reputation Managers
Luton
01582 725454
sussana.orchard@bmb.uk.com
www.bmb.uk.com

Brahm PR
Leeds
0113 230 4000
www.brahm.com

Brands2Life
London
020 7386 6200
info@brands2life.com
www.brands2life.com

Brave PR
London
020 7802 8111
charlotte.a@bravepr.com
www.bravepr.com

Brazen
Manchester
0161 923 4994
nina@brazenpr.com
www.brazenpr.com

The Bright Consultancy
Henley-in-Arden, West Midlands
01564 795535
ian@bright-consultancy.co.uk
www.bright-consultancy.co.uk

Broadgate
London
020 7726 6111
contact@bgate.co.uk
www.bgate.co.uk

Brodeur Worldwide
London
020 7298 7070
www.brodeuruk.com

Brower Lewis Pelham PR
London
020 7935 2735
www.blppr.com

Brunswick
London
020 7404 5959
www.brunswickgroup.com

Buchanan Communications
London
020 7466 5000
Leeds 01943 883990
mirandar@buchanan.uk.com
www.buchanan.uk.com

Buffalo Communications
London
020 7292 8680
info@buffalo.co.uk
www.buffalo.co.uk

Burson-Marsteller
London
020 7831 6262
www.bm.com

Cairns & Associates
London
020 7235 7773
inforequest@cairnsassociates.co.uk

Camargue
London
020 7636 7366
Cheltenham 01242 577277
www.camarguepr.com

Camron PR
London
020 7420 1700
genevieve@camron.co.uk
www.camron.co.uk

Capital MS&L
London
020 7878 3181
steffan.williams@capitalmsl.com
www.capitalmsl.co.uk

Capitalize
London
020 7940 1700
info@capitalize.co.uk
www.capitalize.co.uk

Carat
London
020 7430 6000
joe_rudkin@carat.co.uk
www.carat.co.uk

Carrot Communications
London
020 7953 4010
richard.houghton@carrotcomms.co.uk
www.carrotcomms.co.uk

Chambers Cox PR
London
020 7592 3100
info@ccpr.co.uk
www.ccpr.co.uk

Chameleon PR
London
020 7721 7875
www.chameleonmkg.com

Cherton Enterprise
Belfast
028 9065 4007
staff@cherton.co.uk
www.cherton.co.uk

CIB Communications
Leatherhead, Surrey
01372 371800
gavint@cibcommunications.co.uk
www.cibcommunications.co.uk

Citigate Communications
London
020 7282 2880
Birmingham 0121 456 3199
info@citigatec.co.uk
www.citigatecommunications.co.uk

Citigate Dewe Rogerson
London
020 7638 9571
www.citigatedr.co.uk

Citigate Northern Ireland
Holywood
028 9039 5500
www.citigateni.co.uk

Citigate Public Affairs
London
020 7838 4800
Edinburgh 0131 200 6040
Cardiff 029 2078 6434
warwick.smith@citigatepa.co.uk
www.citigatepa.com

Citigate Smarts
Edinburgh
0131 555 0425
Glasgow 0141 222 2040
Manchester 0161 829 0740
Leeds 0113 297 9899
www.smarts.co.uk

Citypress PR
Manchester
0161 606 0260
mail@citypress.co.uk
www.citypress.co.uk

Clareville Communications
London
020 7736 4022
mail@clareville.co.uk
www.clareville.co.uk

CLEAR Communication Consultancy & Training
London
020 7432 2500
clear@clearco.co.uk
www.clearco.co.uk

Cohesive Communications
London
020 7470 8777
Chepstow 01291 626200
info@cohesive.uk.com
www.cohesive.uk.com

Cohn & Wolfe
London
020 7331 5300
jonathan_shore@cohnwolfe.com
www.cohnwolfe.com

Colette Hill Associates
London
020 7622 8252
cha@chapr.co.uk
www.chapr.co.uk

College Hill
London
020 7457 2020
pr@collegehill.com
www.collegehill.com
Financial PR

Colman Getty PR
London
020 7631 2666
Edinburgh 0131 477 7950
pr@colmangettypr.co.uk
www.colmangettypr.co.uk

The Communication Group
London
020 7630 1411
enquiries@thecommunicationgroup.co.uk
www.thecommunicationgroup.co.uk

Communique PR
Manchester
0161 228 6677
London 020 7300 6300
www.communiquepr.co.uk

Companycare Communications
Reading
0118 939 5900
info@companycare.com
www.companycare.com

Consolidated Communications
London
020 7287 2087
sarahr@consol.co.uk
www.consol.co.uk

Corixa Communications
Bristol
0117 949 3394
info@corixa.co.uk
www.corixa.co.uk

Counsel Public Relations
London
020 7402 2272
nigel.dickie@counsel-huntsworth.com
www.counsel-huntsworth.com

Countrywide Porter Novelli
London
020 7853 2222
Edinburgh 0131 470 3400
Leeds 0113 381 5100
Banbury 01295 224400
www.cpn.co.uk

Cow Communications
London
020 7684 6969
dirk.singer@cowpr.com
www.cowpr.com

Cubitt Consulting
London
020 7367 5100
simon.brocklebank-fowler@cubitt.com
www.cubitt.com

Darwall Smith Associates
London
020 7553 3700
gill@dsapr.co.uk
www.dsapr.co.uk

Dialogue Agency
Twickenham
020 8607 0340
enquiry@dialogueagency.com
www.dialogueagency.com

DTW
Guisborough, Cleveland
01287 610404
Canterbury 01227 454023
office@dtw.co.uk
www.dtw.co.uk

Edelman
London
020 7344 1200
london@edelman.com
www.edelman.co.uk

Edson Evers
Stafford
01785 255146
info@edsonevers.com

EHPR (Elizabeth Hindmarch Public Relations)
Windsor, Berkshire
01753 842017
London 020 7031 0380
info@ehpr.co.uk
www.ehpr.co.uk

EML
Kingston-upon-Thames, Surrey
020 8408 8000
eml@eml.com
www.eml.com

Eulogy!
London
020 7927 9999
pr@eulogy.co.uk
www.eulogy.co.uk

EuroPR Group
London
020 8879 3033
info@europrgroup.com
www.europrgroup.com

Financial Dynamics
London
020 7831 3113
www.fd.com

Finsbury PR
London
020 7251 3801
info@finsbury.com
www.finsbury.com

Firefly Communications
London
020 7386 1400
claire.walker@fireflycomms.com
www.fireflycomms.com

Fishburn Hedges
London
020 7839 4321
sarah.croom-johnson@fishburn-hedges.co.uk
www.fishburn-hedges.co.uk

Flagship Group
London
020 7886 8440
www.flagshipgroup.co.uk

Fleishman-Hillard (UK)
London
020 7306 9000
Edinburgh 0131 226 2162
Dublin 00 353 1 618 8444
www.fleishman.com

Focus PR
London
020 7432 9432
vision@focuspr.co.uk
www.focuspr.co.uk

Four Communications
London
0870 420 3212
info@fourplc.com
www.fourplc.com

Fox Parrack Hirsch
London
020 7436 4336
tparrack@fphcom.com
www.fphcom.com

Freud Communications
London
020 7580 2626
jackie@freudcommunications.com
www.freudcommunications.com

Galliard Healthcare Communications
London
020 7663 2250
www.galliardhealth.com

Garnett Keeler Public Relations
Surbiton, Surrey
020 8399 1184
pr@garnett-keeler.com
www.garnett-keeler.com

GCI/APCO
London
020 7072 4000
awheeler@gciuk.com
www.gciuk.com

Geronimo PR
London
020 8238 8550
karen.harris@geronimopr.com
www.geronimopr.co.uk

GMX Communications
London
020 7808 7976
Southampton 023 8071 3000
Manchester 0161 234 0040
info@gmxpa.com
www.gmxcommunications.com

Golin/Harris Weber
London
020 7067 0600
www.golinharris.com

Golley Slater PR
London
020 7379 8886
Cardiff 029 2038 8621
Birmingham 0121 4542323
Bristol 0117 921 1131
Cirencester 01285 741111
Leeds 0113 297 9737
Manchester 0161 237 3495
Newcastle 0191 245 9020
Twickenham 020 8744 2630
tgilbert-harris@golleyslater.co.uk
www.golleyslater.com

Good Relations
London
020 7861 3030
afossey@goodrelations.co.uk
www.goodrelations.co.uk

Gough Allen Stanley
Bromsgrove, Worcs
01527 579902
info@gough.co.uk
www.gough.co.uk

Grandfield
London
020 7417 4170
enquiries@grandfield.com
www.grandfield.com

Grant Butler Coomber
London
020 8322 1922
carob@gbc.co.uk
www.gbc.co.uk

Grayling
London
020 7255 1100
info@uk.grayling.com
www.grayling.com

Great Circle Communications
Edinburgh
0131 225 4646
frontdesk@greatcircle.co.uk
www.greatcircle.co.uk

Green Issues Communications
London
020 7321 3767
Reading 0118 959 1211
Manchester 0161 209 3850
Cardiff 01446 772223
post@greenissues.com
www.greenissues.com

Hallmark Public Relations
Winchester
01962 892900
inspired@hallmarkpr.com
www.hallmarkpr.com

Halogen PR
London
020 7487 9191
Cheltenham 01242 227499
gerwyn@halogenuk.com
www.halogenuk.com

Harrison Cowley
London
020 7404 6777
Birmingham 0121 236 7532
Bristol 0117 929 2311
Cardiff 029 2034 4717
Edinburgh 0131 556 6600
Leeds 0113 244 2424
Manchester 0161 839 5666
Southampton 023 8033 7237
info@harrisoncowley.com
www.harrisoncowley.com

Haslimann Taylor
Birmingham
0121 355 3446
patzih@haslimanntaylor.com
www.haslimanntaylor.com

Haygarth
London
020 8971 3300
stephen.m@haygarth.co.uk
www.haygarth.co.uk

Henry's House
London
020 7291 3000
www.henryshouse.com

Herald Communications
London
020 7340 6300
info@heraldcommunications.com
www.heraldcommunications.com

Hill & Knowlton
London
020 7413 3000
info@hillandknowlton.co.uk
www.hillandknowlton.co.uk

Hills Balfour
London
020 7922 1100
info@hillsbalfour.com
www.hillsbalfour.com

HMC – Hobsbawm Media + Marketing Communications
020 7430 9444
www.hmclondon.co.uk

The Hoffman Agency
Egham, Surrey
01784 487 920
lhoffman@hoffman.com
www.hoffman.com

Hotwire PR
London
020 7608 2500
alexia.sciplino@hotwirepr.com
www.hotwirepr.com

Houston Associates
London
020 8778 1900
info@houston-associates.com
www.houston-associates.com

Howell Petersen
Newport
01633 255015
Cardiff 029 2072 9400
London 020 7290 2627
info@howellpetersen.com
www.howellpetersen.com

ICAS PR
Hemel Hempstead
01442 261199
London 020 7632 2400
pr@icas.co.uk
www.icas.co.uk

The Ideas Network
London
020 7351 4719
victoria@ideasnetwork.co.uk
www.ideasnetwork.co.uk

The Impact Agency
London
020 7580 1770
linda@impactagency.co.uk
www.theimpactagency.com

Insight Marketing & Communications
London
020 7861 3999
Heathrow 020 8564 6397
Manchester 01625 500800
info@insightmkt.com
www.insightmkt.com

The ITPR Group
Chertsey, Surrey
01932 578800
ashleyc@itpr.co.uk
www.itpr.co.uk

Jackie Cooper PR
London
020 7208 7208
Info@jcpr.com
www.jcpr.com

JBP Public Relations
0117 907 3400
www.jbp.co.uk

Johnson King
London
020 7357 7799
info@johnsonking.co.uk
www.johnsonking.co.uk

Kaizo
London
020 7580 8852
crispin.manners@kaizo.net
www.kaizo.net

Kavanagh Communications
Cobham, Surrey
01932 866010
anne@kavanaghcommunications.com
www.kavanaghcommunications.com

Keene Public Affairs Consultants
London
020 7287 0652
kpac@keenepa.co.uk
www.keenepa.co.uk

Kelso Consulting
London
020 7072 2310
info@kelsopr.com
www.kelsopr.com

Kenyon Fraser
Liverpool
0151 706 9966
pr@kenyons.co.uk
www.kenyons.co.uk

Kestrel WorldCom
London
020 8543 2299
kestrel@kestrelcomms.co.uk
www.kestrelworldcom.com

Ketchum
London
020 7611 3500
greatwork@ketchum.com
www.ketchum.com

Kinross & Render
London
020 7592 3100
info@kinrossrender.com
www.kinrossrender.com

Kysen PR
London
020 7323 3230
contactus@kysenpr.co.uk
www.kysenpr.co.uk

Lansons Communications
London
020 7490 8828
pr@lansons.com
www.lansons.com

Lawson Dodd
London
020 7535 1355
iam@lawsondodd.co.uk
www.lawsondodd.co.uk

Leader Communications
Warwickshire
01564 796200
www.leader.co.uk

Leedex Euro RSCG
London
020 7497 0110
Manchester 0161 236 2277
Edinburgh 0131 524 1500
Leeds 0113 242 4999
www.leedex.com

Lexis Public Relations
London
020 7908 6488
intray@lexispr.co.uk
www.lexispr.com

Lighthouse PR
London
020 7968 4949
mail@lighthousepr.com
www.lighthousepr.com

London Communications Agency
London
020 7479 2830
lca@londoncommunications.co.uk
www.londoncommunications.co.uk

M: Communications
London
020 7153 1530
info@mcomgroup.com
www.mcomgroup.com

MacLaurin (now part of Trimedia UK)
London
020 7371 3333
www.trimediauk.com

Manning Selvage & Lee
London
020 7878 3000
nicholas.walters@mslpr.co.uk
www.mslpr.co.uk

Mantra Public Relations
London
020 7907 7800
info@mantra-pr.com
www.mantra-pr.com

Market Engineering
Banbury, Oxon
01295 277050
richard.gotch@m-eng.com
www.marketengineering.co.uk

Mary Rahman PR
London
020 7749 1136
07958 399740
www.mr-pr.com

Mason Williams
London
020 7534 6080
Manchester 0161 273 5923
info@mason-williams.com
www.mason-williams.co.uk

McCann-Erickson Public Relations
Solihull
0121 713 3500
Contact@mccann.com
www.mccann.com

McCluskey International
London
020 8237 7979
info@mccluskey.co.uk
www.mccluskeyinternational.co.uk

Media Strategy
London
020 7400 4480
enquiries@mediastrategy.co.uk
www.mediastrategy.co.uk

Medicom Group
Hampton Court, Surrey
020 8481 8100
mellis@medicomgroup.com
www.medicomgroup.com

MediTech Media
London
020 7398 0500
Manchester 0161 236 2367
info@meditech.co.uk
www.meditech-media.com

Midas PR
London
020 7584 7474
info@midaspr.co.uk
www.midaspr.co.uk

Midnight Communications
Brighton
0870 458 4182
enquiries@midnight.co.uk
www.midnight.co.uk

Mulberry Marketing Communications
London
020 7928 7676
info@mulberrymc.com
www.mulberrymc.com

Munro & Forster Communications
London
020 7815 3900
contact@munroforster.com
www.munroforster.com

Neesham PR
Berkhamsted
01442 879222
admin@neesham.co.uk
www.neesham.co.uk

Nelson Bostock Communications
London
020 7229 4400
info@nelsonbostock.com
www.nelsonbostock.com

Nexus Communications Group
London
020 7373 4537
www.nexuspr.com

NorthBank Communications
Congleton
01260 296500
London 020 7886 8150
info@northbankcommunications.com
www.northbankcommunications.com

Ogilvy
London
020 7309 1000
www.ogilvypr.com

Pagoda PR
Edinburgh
0131 447 8999
Belfast 028 9092 3468
info@pagodapr.com
www.pagodapr.co.uk

Partners Group
York
01904 610077
postbox@partners-group.co.uk
www.partners-group.co.uk

Pegasus PR
Worthing, West Sussex
01903 821550
info@pegasuspr.co.uk
www.pegasuspr.co.uk

Penrose Financial
London
020 7786 4888
gillianm@penrose.co.uk
www.penrose.co.uk

PFPR Communications
Maidstone
01622 691361
info@pfpr.com
www.pfpr.com

Phipps Public Relations
London
020 7759 7400
info@phippspr.co.uk
www.phippspr.com

Pinnacle Marketing Communications
Pinner, Middlesex
020 8869 9339
simon@pinnacle-marketing.com
www.pinnacle-marketing.com

Piranhakid
London
020 7413 3198
jason.gallucci@piranhakid.com
www.piranhakid.com

Portfolio Communications
London
020 7240 6959
mark.westaby@portmet.co.uk
www.portfoliocomms.com

Positive Profile
London
020 7489 2028
henryg@positiveprofile.com
www.positiveprofile.com

PPS Group
London
020 7629 7377
Almondsbury 01454 275 630
Birmingham 0121 7671863
Manchester 0161 8322139
Edinburgh 0131 2261951
Cardiff 029 2066 0194
info@ppsgroup.co.uk
www.ppsgroup.co.uk

Prowse & Co
Leatherhead, Surrey
01372 363386
reception@prowse.co.uk
www.prowse.co.uk

Ptarmigan Consultants
Leeds
0113 242 1155
www.ptarmiganpr.co.uk

Public Relations Consultants Association
London
020 7233 6026
pressoffice@prca.org.uk
www.prca.org.uk

Purple PR
London
020 7439 9888
enquiries@purplepr.com
www.purplepr.com

QBO Bell Pottinger
London
020 7861 2424
dwilson@qbo-bellpottinger.co.uk
www.qbo-bellpottinger.co.uk

QuayWest Communications
Coggeshall, Essex
01376 563156
s.morrison@quay-west.co.uk
www.quay-west.co.uk

Radiator PR
London
020 7404 8264
www.radiatorpr.com

Rainier PR
London
020 7494 6570
Cambridge 01223 421010
rainier@rainierpr.co.uk
www.rainierpr.co.uk

The Red Consultancy
London
020 7465 7700
red@redconsultancy.com
www.redconsultancy.com

Red Door Communications
London
020 8392 8040
www.rdcomms.com

Regester Larkin
London
020 7831 3839
enquiries@regesterlarkin.com
www.regesterlarkin.com

Republic
London
020 7379 5000
www.republicpr.com

Resolute Communications
London
020 7357 8187
info@resolutecommunications.com
www.resolutecommunications.com

Revolver Communications
London
020 7251 5599
enquiries@revolvercomms.com
www.revolvercomms.com

Richard Lewis Communications
Southampton
01962 771111
info@crossculture.com
www.crossculture.com

Six Degrees (formerly Roger Staton Associates and Marbles)
Marlow, Buckinghamshire
01628 480280
mail@sixdegreespr.com
www.rsagroup.com

Ruder Finn UK
London
020 7462 8900
mailbox@ruderfinn.co.uk
www.ruderfinn.com

salt
London
020 8870 6777
sophie@saltlondon.com
www.saltlondon.com

Seal Communications
Birmingham
0121 455 7788
London 020 7935 0726
stevedann@sealgroup.co.uk
www.sealgroup.co.uk

Shine Communications
London
020 7553 3333
brilliance@shinecom.com
www.shineon-line.com

Shire Health Group
London
020 7313 6300
matt.degruchy@shirehealthlondon.com
www.shirehealthlondon.com

Sinclair Mason
Leeds
0870 60 60 960
sallyh@sinclairmason.com
www.sinclairmason.co.uk

Spark Marketing Communications
London
020 7357 8612
info@sparkcomms.co.uk
www.sparkcomms.co.uk

Spin Media
Manchester
0161 236 9909
enquiries@spinmedia.co.uk
www.spinmedia.co.uk

Spreckley Partners
London
020 7388 9988
info@spreckley.co.uk
www.spreckley.co.uk

Staniforth
London
020 7940 7999
Manchester 0161 274 0100
urgent@staniforth.co.uk
www.staniforth.co.uk

Starfish Communications
London
020 7323 2121
fearfield@star-fish.net
www.star-fish.net

Storm Communications
London
020 7240 2444
Bucks 01494 670444
info@stormcom.co.uk
www.stormcom.co.uk

StrategicAlliance International
Old Amersham, Bucks
01494 434434
nicholasf@strategicpr.net
www.strategicpr.net

Strategy Communications
Bristol
0117 983 6400
London 020 7849 6663
enquiries@strategycomms.co.uk
www.strategycomms.co.uk

Target Public Relations
Cheltenham
01242 633100
www.targetgroup.co.uk

Taylor Alden
London
020 8543 3866
Newbury, Berkshire 01635 521103
pr@tayloralden.co.uk
www.tayloralden.com

Taylor Herring
London
020 8206 5151
james@taylorherring.com
www.taylorherring.com/

TBWA UK Group
London
020 7573 6666
Edinburgh 0131 225 3952
www.tbwa.com

Text 100
London
020 8996 4100
michelled@text100.co.uk
www.text100.com

Trimedia Communications
London
020 7371 3333, 020 7898 9036
Glasgow 0141 333 6440
www.trimediauk.com

Twelve Consultancy
London
020 7631 0737
mail@twelvepr.co.uk
www.twelvepr.co.uk

Warman Group
Birmingham
0121 605 1111
bob@warmangroup.com
www.warmangroup.com

Weber Shandwick
London
020 7067 0000
Aberdeen 01224 806600
Belfast 028 9076 1007
Edinburgh & Glasgow 0131 556 6649
Manchester 0161 238 9400
Cardiff 029 2022 3928
Liverpool 0151 236 5050
Dublin 00 353 1 676 0168
www.webershandwick.co.uk

Westbury Communications
London
020 7751 9170

What Matters
St Albans, Hertfordshire
01582 793994
www.whatmatters.co.uk

Whiteoaks Consultancy
Farnham, Surrey
01252 727313
London 020 7751 2480
comms@whiteoaks.co.uk
www.whiteoaks.co.uk

Wild Card PR
London
020 7307 9670
deck@wildcardpr.co.uk
www.wildcardpr.co.uk

William Murray PR
London
020 8256 1360
www.williammurraypr.co.uk

Willoughby PR
Birmingham
0121 456 3004
joannes@willoughby-pr.co.uk
www.willoughby-pr.co.uk

Write Image
London
020 7959 5400
info@write-image.co.uk
www.write-image.com

Wyatt International
Birmingham
0121 454 8181
info@wyatt-inter.co.uk
www.wyattinternational.com

Yellow Door Creative Marketing
London
020 7580 0707
www.yellow-door.co.uk

Associations

Association of Public Relations Consultants
020 7233 6026
www.prca.org.uk

Institute of Public Relations
020 7253 5151
Press: 020 7553 3772
www.ipr.org.uk

PRJobSeek.com
020 8894 5739
www.prjobseek.com

PR trade press

Hollis UK PR Annual
Hollis Publishing, Harlequin House
7 High Street
Teddington TW11 8EL
020 8977 7711
prannual@hollis-pr.co.uk
www.hollis-pr.com
Press and PR contacts. Annual. Editor: Sarah Hughes

PR Week
Haymarket Business Publications
174 Hammersmith Road
London W6 7JP
020 8267 4429
prweek@haynet.com
www.prweek.com
Weekly. Editor-in-Chief: Kate Nicholas

Contact (PRWeek Black Book)
Haymarket Business Publications
174 Hammersmith Road
London W6 7JP
020 8267 4496
sales@haynet.com
www.prweek.co.uk
Press and PR contacts. Annual

Agents

The more creative your role in the media, the greater the chance that there is an agent to represent you. The best authors, script-writers, actors, directors and presenters will always be in demand, but the number of wannabes far exceeds the number of talents. So the agent's role is to be the middle man: to find the talent, sell it, and make themselves a profit into the bargain.

There are more than 200 literary agents in Britain, of whom about 75 are members of the association of authors' agents; while the Agents' Association has more than 400 entertainment agencies among its members. Agencies can range from large multinational organisations such as PFD or ICM, the world-leading talent agency which this year opened a literary agency in London, to tiny operations managed by just one overworked soul. The best agents will have an eye for talent, a wide range of industry contacts, and above all a hard head for a business deal.

Literary agents

It is increasingly difficult to acquire the services of a good literary agent; but then, it is harder still to sell a novel or a script without one. A good agent will not only advise an author in an editorial capacity, at least to make a script more saleable; they will also be able to sell writing for much more than writers could on their own. In particular, agents aim to separate rights for different media (such as paperback, film, television, multimedia and novelisation in the case of a script), for different markets (such as potentially lucrative US rights) and even, in this post-Potter world, for merchandising. Thus they hope to earn more for the writer than if all the rights were sold at once. In return, they charge a commission which normally ranges from 10 per cent to 15 per cent.

Agents complain that they are so busy trying to sell their existing authors that they have little time to find new talent. The result is that many agents, at one point or another, are either not accepting new writers or only accepting writers recommended to them by people they know and trust. Those that do receive unsolicited manuscripts are deluged: some agents receive up to 50 a day, which will usually mean the agent is looking for a reason to reject them.

The advice to an author seeking any agent, then, is to make life as easy as possible for them. Don't send work to an agent who doesn't accept unsolicited manuscripts, or who doesn't handle the genre you write in; you'll only be wasting your time and theirs. Check the agent's website to find the authors they already handle: this will help you target the agents who you know will like the kind of work you write. Spend a few moments finding out how the agent prefers to see a manuscript – complete, or in the form of a few chapters plus synopsis – and how they like the type to be set (normally use a simple font such as Times New Roman, on decent-quality white paper, double-spaced to allow room for notes; don't forget to enclose a stamped addressed envelope). Asked when they like to see a manuscript, many agents will helpfully reply that the best time is when you've improved it as best you can: make of that what you will. Finally, if an agent offers to represent you, trust your instinct: an agent who likes you and your writing will be your best advocate. To put it another way, the better your relationship with your agent, the more likely you are to sell your work.

Finally, don't lose hope: one day it could be your script that is being sold by a top agent like Jonny Geller for a seven-figure sum at the Frankfurt Book Fair. It won't be, but it could.

Talent agents

Talent agencies have a reputation – cemented in films such as Little Voice and Some Like It Hot – as a hard-headed, wheeling-and-dealing bunch. In the real world they come in a vast variety of forms: specialisms include television presenters, voice-overs for radio ads, directors of short films, actors, singers, make-up artists, cruise ship entertainers, lookalikes and of course models; many agencies will handle some but not all of these, even though they work under the broad umbrella of "entertainment". Agents employed by artists charge about 15 per cent commission, rising to 20 per cent for musicians and models in particular; or they may act as talent-brokers, earning their commission as a mark-up charged to the event hirer. There are few hard and fast rules – but the agents' association does have a code of conduct; artists should never, for example, pay a fee to join an agency's books. Other bodies include the personal managers' association, which represents actors' agents; and the association of voice-over agents.

So you wanna be a star? **Lisa O'Carroll**

Media agents are not powerful and they are the first to admit it. They don't make TV programmes, publish books, or guarantee polished performances on Newsnight or Radio 4. And they certainly don't pay well. But if you are talented and you need to stand out from the crowd, engaging an agent can be one way of grabbing the attention of that producer, editor, or researcher, who could make you a modest living or even a million.

For those starting out in their careers, hiring an agent is an expensive route to fame and fortune – typically they take a 12.5% to 15% cut of your salary or fee. Unscrupulous ones will even try and take a slice of your current earnings, something that you should absolutely refuse. Trying to persuade an agent to take you on board can also be difficult, particularly if you are untried or untested. Even those with years of experience may not fit the bill – too old, too ugly, or just too high maintenance – and can be callously cast aside because they aren't worth the agent's time.

Anyone who has touted a TV or book script around literary agents will know what a soul-destroying experience it is to get yet one Dear John letter after another. That said, media agents are a must for those with experience or expertise. Only the most successful in their trade can afford private salary and shares negotiations with the top boss; the likes of Sir Trevor McDonald or John Humphrys, for example.

But even those in the upper reaches of their careers have a use for agents – Jeremy Paxman has one, as do Desmond Lynam, Cilla Black and John Motson. At this level an agent's services are likely to be all-encompassing: everything from after-dinner bookings, handling the press (a full-time job in a crisis) to pay negotiations and the delicate subject of advice on hair, make-up and wardrobe.

But while an agent can make most of their money from the fees of their better-earning clients, they will typically have dozens of presenters on their books and should be just as keen to give a leg-up to those on the lower rungs of the ladder.

Good agents will know all the top executives in TV, radio and newspapers and will work day and night to push their clients. They will know, before the presenter, which programmes are being planned and what the controller of any channel or producer of any programme is looking for. Most will also have a good relationship with newspapers, which is valuable for PR and gaining and maintaining a high profile, thereby maximising your market window.

With the explosion of TV stations, there is also a growing demand for pundits and a parallel blossoming in the number of agents willing to deal with experts in their field, who have no media experience. Household names such as Sir Roy Strong, Robert Winston, Simon Schama and Dr David Starkey all have agents. But there is also a plethora of lesser known archaeologists, architects, gardeners and designers, who have found agents indispensable, particularly at the start of their career.

For those who suddenly find themselves thrust into the spotlight, reality TV stars are a warning not to take the first agent you find. Ask for advice from producers, directors and all those who have more experience. Listen to what the public relations people say and, although it may not seem like a good idea at the time, journalists will also have valuable observations on individuals.

There are thousands of agents operating in London – picking the right one could paralyse or kick-start your career.

Lisa O'Carroll edits MediaGuardian.co.uk

Agents Contacts

Associations

Agents Association
54 Keyes House, Dolphin Square
London SW1V 3NA
020 7834 0515
association@agents-uk.com
www.agents-uk.com

Association of Authors' Agents
A P Watt, 20 John Street
London WC1N 2DR
020 7405 6774
aaa@apwatt.co.uk
www.agentsassoc.co.uk

Personal Managers' Association
1 Summer Road, East Molesey
Surrey KT8 9LX
020 8398 9796
info@thepma.com

Agents

Alexander Personal Management
PO Box 834, Hemel Hempstead
Hertfordshire HP3 9ZP
01442 252907
apm@apmassociates.net
www.apmassociates.net
Actors, voiceovers

Amanda Howard Associates
21 Berwick Street
London W1F 0PZ
020 7287 9277
mail@amandahowardassociates.co.uk
www.amandahowardassociates.co.uk
Actors, directors, composers, voiceovers, writers

Andrew Manson
288 Munster Road
London SW6 6BQ
020 7386 9158
post@andrewmanson.com
www.talentroom.com
Actors, voiceovers (for US)

Another Tongue Voices
10–11 D'arblay Street
London W1F 8DS
020 7494 0300
info@anothertongue.com
www.anothertongue.com
Voiceovers

Arlington Enterprises
1–3 Charlotte Street
London, W1T 1RD
020 7580 0702
info@arlington-enterprises.co.uk
www.arlingtonenterprises.co.uk
TV presenters

Billy Marsh Associates
76A Grove End Road
St John's Wood
London NW8 9ND
020 7449 6930
talent@billymarsh.co.uk
TV presenters and personalities

Bryan Drew
Mezzanine, Quadrant House
80–82 Regent Street
London W1B 5AU
020 7437 2293
bryan@bryandrewltd.com
www.bryandrewltd.com
Actors, writers, voiceovers

Calypso Voices
25–26 Poland Street
London W1F 8QN
020 7734 6415
calypso@calypsovoices.com
www.calypsovoices.com
Actors for voiceover work

Take Three Management
110 Gloucester Avenue
Primrose Hill, London NW1 8HX
020 7209 3777
info@take3management.com
www.take3management.co.uk
TV presenters, after dinner speakers

Castaway
7 Garrick Street
London WC2E 9AR
020 7240 2345
sheila@castaway.org.uk
www.castaway.org.uk
Voiceovers

Celebrity Management
12 Nottingham Place
London W1U 5NE
020 7224 5050
info@celebrity.co.uk
www.celebrity.co.uk
Celebrity booking

Chase Personal Management
Model Plan 4th Floor
4 Golden Square
London W1F 9HT
020 7287 8444
sue@sammon.fsnet.co.uk
www.modelplan.co.uk
Presenters and celebrities

Complete Talent Agency
200 London Road, Hadleigh
Benfleet, Essex SS7 2PD
01702 427100
info@entertainers.co.uk
www.entertainers.co.uk
Celebrity guests, speakers and comedians
Also at:
The Old Forge, Kingfield Road
Woking, Surrey GU22 9EG

Conway Van Gelder
3rd Floor, 18–21 Jermyn Street
London SW1Y 6HP
020 7287 1070
kate@conwayvg.co.uk
www.conwayvangelder.com
Actors, commercials, voiceovers, directors

Crawfords
PO Box 44394, London SW20 0YP
020 8947 9999
cr@wfords.com
www.crawfords.tv
Actors and models for TV commercials

Curtis Brown Group
Haymarket House, 28–29 Haymarket
London SW1Y 4SP
020 7396 6600
cb@curtisbrown.co.uk
www.curtisbrown.co.uk
Writers, directors, actors, playwrights and celebrities

David Anthony Promotions
PO Box 286, Warrington
Cheshire WA2 8GA
01925 632496
dave@davewarwick.co.uk
www.davewarwick.co.uk
TV presenters

Downes Presenters Agency
96 Broadway, Bexleyheath
Kent DA6 7DE
020 8304 0541
downes@presentersagency.com
www.presentersagency.com
TV presenters

Dynamic FX
Regent House, 291 Kirkdale
London SE26 4QD
020 8659 8130
mail@dynamicfx.co.uk
www.dynamicfx.co.uk
Magical entertainment

Eric Glass
25 Ladbroke Crescent, Notting Hill
London W11 1PS
020 7229 9500
eglassltd@aol.com
Actors, writers

Evans O'Brien
115 Humber Road
London SE3 7LW
020 8293 7077
info@evansobrien.co.uk
www.evansobrien.co.uk
Voiceovers

Excellent Talent Company
53 Goodge Street, London W1T 1TG
020 7636 1636
ruth@excellentvoice.co.uk
www.excellentvoice.co.uk
Voiceovers and TV presenters

Extras Unlimited
9 Hansard Mews, London W14 8BJ
020 7603 9995
www.extrasunlimited.com
Extras

FBI Agency
PO Box 250, Leeds LS1 2AZ
07050 222747
casting@fbi agency.ltd.uk
www.fbi-agency.uk
Models, dancers, walk-ons, presenters, actors, stand-ins

Foreign Versions
60 Blandford Street
London W1U 7JD
020 7935 0993
info@foreignversions.co.uk
www.foreignversions.com
Translators and voiceovers in foreign languages

Fox Artist Management
Concorde House
101 Shepherds Bush Road
London W6 7LP
020 7602 8822
fox.artist@btinternet.com
www.foxartistmanagement.tv
TV presenters

Gordon & French
12–13 Poland Street
London W1F 8QB
020 7734 4818
mail@gordonandfrench.net
Actors and voiceovers

Hobson's Voices
62 Chiswick High Road
London W4 1SY
020 8995 3628
voices@hobson-international.com
www.hobsons-international.com
Actors, voiceovers, kids, singers

ICM Artists (London)
4–6 Soho Square
London W1D 3PZ
020 7432 0800
infoUK@icmtalent.com
www.icmtalent.com
Conductors and musicians

Icon Actors Management
Tanzaro House, Ardwick Green North
Manchester M12 6FZ
0161 273 3344
info@iconactors.net
www.iconactors.net
Actors

International Artists
4th Floor, Holborn Hall
193–197 High Holborn
London WC1V 7BD
020 7025 0600
reception@intart.co.uk
www.intart.co.uk
Presenters, actors and comedians

J Gurnett Personal Management
2 New Kings Road
London SW6 4SA
020 7736 7828
mail@jgpm.co.uk
www.jgpm.co.uk
TV and radio presenters

Jacque Evans Management
Suite 1, 14 Holmesley Road
London SE23 1PJ
020 8699 1202
jacque@jacqueevans.com
www.jacqueevans.com
Presenters, journalists, broadcasters and experts

James Grant Management
Syon Lodge, 201 London Road
Isleworth, Middlesex TW7 5BH
020 8232 4100
enquiries@jamesgrant.co.uk
www.jamesgrant.co.uk
TV presenters

Jane Morgan Management
Thames Wharf Studios
Rainville Road
London W6 9WA
020 7386 5345
enquiries@janemorganmgt.com
www.janemorganmgt.com

Jeremy Hicks Associates
11–12 Tottenham Mews
London W1T 4AG
020 7636 8008
info@jeremyhicks.com
www.jeremyhicks.com
Presenters, writers, comedians and chefs

JLA (Jeremy Lee Associates)
4 Stratford Place, London W1C 1AT
020 7907 2800
talk@jla.co.uk
www.jla.co.uk
Presenters, speakers, entertainers

John Miles Organisation
Cadbury Camp Lane
Clapton-in-Gordano
Bristol BS20 7SB
01275 854675
john@johnmiles.org.uk
www.johnmiles.org.uk
Presenters

John Noel Management
2nd Floor, 10A Belmont Street
London NW1 8HH
020 7428 8400
john@johnnoel.com
www.johnnoel.com
TV presenters and radio djs

Julie Ivelaw-Chapman
The Chase, Chaseside Close
Cheddington, Beds LU7 0SA
01296 662441
jic@collectorsworldwide.co.uk
Broadcasters

KBJ Management
7 Soho Street, London W1D 3DQ
020 7434 6767
candida@kbjmgt.co.uk
www.kbjmgt.co.uk
Presenters and comics

Knight Ayton Management
114 St Martin's Lane
London WC2N 4BE
020 7836 5333
info@knightayton.co.uk
www.knightayton.co.uk
TV presenters and news people

Lip Service
60–66 Wardour Street
London W1F 0TA
020 7734 3393
bookings@lipservice.co.uk
www.lipservice.co.uk
Voiceovers

Liz Hobbs Group
1st Floor, 65 London Road
Newark, Notts NG24 1RZ
0870 070 2702
info@lizhobbsgroup.com
www.lizhobbsgroup.com
Musical theatre, actors and presenters

Mark Summer Management & Agency
9 Hansard Mews, London W14 8BJ
0870 443 5621
info@marksummers.com
www.marksummers.com
Choreographers and actors, adults and children

Markham & Froggatt Personal Management
4 Windmill Street, London W1T 2HZ
020 7636 4412
reception@markhamfroggatt.co.uk
http://markhamfroggatt.com
Actors, voiceovers and radio

McLean-Williams Management
212 Piccadilly, London W1J 9HG
020 7917 2806
alex@mclean-williams.com
Actors

MPC Entertainment
MPC House, 15–16 Maple Mews
London NW6 5UZ
020 7624 1184
mpc@mpce.com
www.mpce.com
Radio, TV and sports personalities

NCI Management
51 Queen Anne Street
London W1G 9HS
020 7224 3960
nicola@nci-management.com
www.nci-management.com
TV presenters

Noel Gay Artists
19 Denmark Street
London WC2H 8NA
020 7836 3941
mail@noelgay.com
www.noelgay.com
TV presenters, voiceovers, writers, directors

Off The Kerb Productions
3rd Floor, Hammer House
113–117 Wardour Street
London W1F 0UN
020 7437 0607
offthekerb@aol.com
www.offthekerb.co.uk
Comedians
Also at
22 Thornhill Crescent
London N1 1BJ
020 7700 4477
info@offthekerb.co.uk

PFD
Drury House, 34–43 Russell Street
London WC2B 5HA
020 7344 1000
postmaster@pfd.co.uk
www.pfd.co.uk
Writers, directors, producers, actors, technicians, composers, sportsmen and women, public speakers and illustrators

PHA Casting
Tanzaro House, Ardwick Green North
Manchester M12 6FZ
0161 273 4444
info@pha-agency.co.uk
www.pha-agency.co.uk
Models, extras, actors

Princess Talent Management
Princess Studios, Whiteleys Centre
151 Queensway, London W2 4SB
020 7985 1985
talent@princesstv.com
www.princesstv.com
TV and radio presenters

PVA Management
Hallow Park, Hallow
Worcester WR2 6PG
01905 640663
clients@pva.co.uk
TV and radio presenters and classical musicians

Qvoice
4th Floor, Holborn Hall
193–197 High Holborn
London WC1V 7BD
020 7025 0660
info@qvoice.co.uk
www.qvoice.co.uk
Voiceovers

Rabbit Vocal Management
2nd Floor, 18 Broadwick Street
London W1F 8HS
020 7287 6466
info@rabbit.uk.net
www.rabbit.uk.net
Voiceovers

Rhubarb
Bakerloo Chambers
304 Edgware Road
London W2 1DY
020 7724 1300
enquiries@rhubarb.co.uk
www.rhubarb.co.uk
Voiceovers

Richard Stone Partnership
2 Henrietta Street
London WC2E 8PS
020 7497 0849
all@richstonepart.co.uk
Actors, presenters, voiceovers, comedians

RK Commercials
205 Chudleigh Road
London SE4 1EG
020 8690 6542
enquiries@rkcommercials.com
www.rkcommercials.com
Actors for commercials and presenting work

Roseman Organisation
51 Queen Anne Street
London W1G 9HS
020 7486 4500
info@theroseman organisation.co.uk
www.therosemanorganisation.co.uk
News and TV presenters

Roxane Vacca Management
73 Beak Street, London W1F 9SR
020 7734 8085
mail@roxanevaccavoices.com
www.roxanevaccavoices.com
Actors and voiceovers

Sally Hope Associates
108 Leonard Street
London EC2A 4XS
020 7613 5353
casting@sallyhope.biz
www.sallyhope.biz
Actors, voiceovers, directors, designers, lighting, hair and make up etc

Shining Management
82C Shirland Road
London W9 2EQ
020 7286 6092
info@shiningvoices.com
www.shiningvoices.com
Voiceovers

Sicron Entertainment
19 Cromwell Road
Colchester, Essez CO2 7EN
01206 525423
simon@sicron.co.uk
www.sicron.co.uk

Speak
59 Lionel Road North, Brentford
Middlesex TW8 9QZ
020 8758 0666
info@speak.ltd.uk
www.speak.ltd.uk
Voiceovers

Speak-Easy
1 Dairy Yard, High Street
Market Harborough, Leics LE16 7NL
0870 013 5126
enquiries@speak-easy.co.uk
www.speak-easy.co.uk
TV presenters and voiceovers

Storm Artists Management
1st Floor, 5 Jubilee Place
London SW3 3TD
020 7437 4313
info@stormartists.co.uk
www.stormmodels.com
Actors, composers and voiceover

Susi Earnshaw Management
5 Brook Place, Barnet
Herts EN5 2DL
020 8441 5010
casting@susiearnshaw.co.uk
www.susiearnshaw.co.uk
Actors and musical theatre performers

Susy Wootton Voices
75 Shelley Street, Kingsley
Northampton NN2 7HZ
0870 765 9660
suzy@suzywoottonvoices.com
www.suzywoottonvoices.com
Voiceovers

Talking Heads
2/4 Noel Street, London W1F 8GB
020 7292 7575
voices@talkingheadsvoices.co.uk
www.talkingheadsvoices.co.uk
Voiceovers

Tongue & Groove
3 Stevenson Square
Manchester M1 1DN
0161 228 2469
info@tongueandgroove.co.uk
www.tongueandgroove.co.uk
Voiceovers

Unique Management Group
Beaumont House
Kensington Village, Avonmore Road
London W14 8TS
020 7605 1100
celebrities@uniquegroup.co.uk
www.unique-management.co.uk
TV presenters, radio hosts

Venture Artistes
91 Walton Street, Oxford OX2 6EB
07000 402001
venture-artistes@msn.com
TV and radio presenters

Vincent Shaw Associates
51 Byron Road, London E17 4SN
020 8509 2211
info@vincentshaw.com
www.vincentshaw.com
Actors

Vocal Point
25 Denmark Street
London WC2H 8NJ
020 7419 0700
enquiries@vocalpoint.net
www.vocalpoint.net
Voiceovers

Voice & Script International
Aradco House, 132 Cleveland St
London W1T 6AB
020 7692 7700
info@vsi.tv
www.vsi.tv
Translators and voiceovers in foreign languages

Voice Shop
Bakerloo Chambers
304 Edgware Road
London W2 1DY
020 7402 3966
info@voice-shop.co.uk
www.voice-shop.co.uk
Voiceovers

Voice Squad
62 Blenheim Gardens
London NW2 4NT
020 8450 4451
bookem@voicesquad.com
www.voicesquad.com
English- and foreign-language voiceovers and translations

Voicebank, The Irish Voice Over Agency
The Barracks, 76 Irishtown Road
Dublin 4
00 353 1 6687234
voicebank@voicebank.ie
www.voicebank.ie
Voiceovers

Voicecall
67A Gondar Gardens, Fortune Green
London NW6 1EP
020 7209 1064
voicecall@blueyonder.co.uk
www.voicecall-online.co.uk
Voiceovers

Whatever Artists Management
1 York Street, London W1U 6PA
020 7487 3111
wam@agents-uk.com
www.wamshow.biz
Artists in light entertainment

Yakety Yak
8 Bloomsbury Square
London WC1A 2NE
020 7430 2600
info@yaketyyak.co.uk
www.yaketyyak.co.uk
Voiceovers

Media law

Legally, it has been a tough year for the media – and not just because of the Hutton inquiry (see page 116 for more on that). 2004 also saw a crucial defeat for the Daily Mirror at the House of Lords on privacy; and in July, the Financial Times found itself facing possibly the biggest ever libel claim at an English court.

Privacy

Perhaps the most confusing area of law is that of privacy. The question of how far an individual's right to privacy outweighs the right to freedom of expression – both enshrined in the European convention of human rights – is a vexed one that is testing the courts. In June 2003, the media select committee of MPs, led by Gerald Kaufman, called for government to "clarify the protection that individuals can expect from unwarranted intrusion by anyone ... into their private lives" – in other words, to draft a privacy law.

The government's answer, which came in October 2003, was no. It said a privacy law was "unnecessary and undesirable", saying "existing legislation is capable of dealing adequately with questions of privacy".

In May 2004, we saw that existing legislation in action, when the model **Naomi Campbell** won a privacy case against the Daily Mirror at the House of Lords. Judges ruled, on a 3-2 split verdict, that Campbell should receive damages for "breach of privacy" after the newspaper published a photograph of her attending a Narcotics Anonymous clinic.

The verdict did not mean, however, that a de facto privacy law had been established. The judges agreed only that it was in the public interest for the paper to say Campbell was an addict and receiving treatment, because since she had denied taking drugs in the past it was legitimate to set the record straight. But they added that it was not legitimate to publish details of her treatment; nor the photograph, which was taken covertly using a long lens.

Perhaps more worrying for sections of the tabloid press was a verdict won by **Princess Caroline of Monaco** in the European court of human rights, which ruled in June that the German press had violated her right to privacy by publishing photographs of her and her children in a public place.

Two **royal stories** dominated the legal agenda in England in November. First the Guardian won the right to identify Michael Fawcett, one of Prince Charles's former aides, as the man who obtained a libel injunction banning publication in a Sunday paper of allegations about him (which, incidentally, the Guardian chose not to publish). Second, the Daily Mirror settled a legal row with the Queen after it exposed palace security by getting a reporter to work under cover as a royal footman; the newspaper kept the profits from its scoop, but agreed not to publish further revelations if the palace dropped its breach of privacy claim.

In the big story of 2003, **Hello!** was faced with a bill of £3.5m in costs and damages after it published pictures, taken surreptitiously, of Catherine Zeta Jones's wedding reception after she had signed an official deal with its rival, OK! magazine. It had to pay three-quarters of Zeta Jones's costs of £2m, £1m damages to OK!, and its own £1m costs; it will have been glad, though, that Zeta Jones's damages came to less than £15,000.

Freedom of the press

In April 2004, a criminal case against News of the World journalist **David McGee** was thrown out of court. The journalist had got a job at Woodhill prison, where Soham murderer Ian Huntley was awaiting trial, despite providing a bogus address, false references and giving his job as journalist. When he took photographs of Huntley with a concealed camera, he was charged with the offence of smuggling a camera into a prison – but the case was thrown out on public interest grounds.

In March, meanwhile, the government admitted it was wrong to prevent the parliamentary ombudsman disclosing information on ministers' conflicts of interest – after a legal challenge from the Guardian.

Libel

In July, the government agreed to review the use of no-win, no-fee agreements in libel cases – after a high court judge said the system "is bound to have a chilling effect on a newspaper exercising its right to freedom of expression". Lord Justice Brooke's remarks were aimed at the firm of solicitors, Carter-Ruck, whose client Musa King is suing the Sunday Telegraph for libel. The court heard that if King won, Carter-Ruck would earn double the fee from the client, costs which the newspaper might have to pay; but if he lost, the newspaper would not get its costs back because he had no funds. If he won, the court said, King would be unlikely to get more than £150,000 in damages; but legal costs would exceed £1m; the court said there was a gulf between what the client and his lawyers stood to gain and what the Sunday Telegraph stood to lose whichever way the case went.

Law and the media, 2003–04

- **July 2003, privacy:** Actress Jennifer Aniston wins £40,000 damages from the Daily Sport, after it published photographs of her topless, taken with a telephoto lens.
- **October 2003, libel:** The Sun apologises to Nicole Kidman and agrees to pay libel damages and costs over false allegations that she had an affair with actor Jude Law.
- **October 2003, libel:** Actress Diana Rigg wins £30,000 in libel damages from the Daily Mail and the London Evening Standard, over reports that wrongly portrayed her as an embittered woman who held British men in low regard.
- **December 2003, privacy:** Policeman Brian Paddick wins "substantial damages" and an apology from the Mail on Sunday, after it published private and confidential information provided by his former lover and ex-fiancée and falsely claimed he took drugs.
- **February 2004, libel:** Harrods loses a high court libel action against the Wall Street Journal, over an article which it said equated it with the disgraced company Enron.
- **May 2004, privacy:** Model Naomi Campbell wins landmark privacy case against Daily Mirror in the House of Lords (see text).
- **May 2004, privacy:** Lord Coe, chairman of London's Olympic bid, fails to win an injunction halting publication of an interview with his former lover Vanessa Lander.
- **June 2004, privacy:** European court of human rights says German press have violated Princess Caroline of Monaco's right to privacy, by publishing photographs of her and her children in a public place.
- **July 2004, privacy:** Actor Ewan McGregor wins a settlement from several newspapers, including the Sun and the Daily Record, over pictures of him and his family on holiday.

December 2003, meanwhile, saw the death at 89 of **Peter Carter-Ruck**, head of the firm involved with the Sunday Telegraph, and the one-time "king of libel" who was the scourge of Fleet Street and, of course, the satirical magazine Private Eye. According to a former colleague, David Hooper, Carter-Ruck "did for freedom of speech what the Boston Strangler did for door-to-door salesmen".

Unlike the Sunday Telegraph case, no-win, no-fee is hardly an issue in the case of **Collins Stewart Tullett**, an investment bank which, in March, sued the Financial Times for libel. The bank said millions of pounds were wiped off its share price as a result of coverage of an unfair dismissal suit brought by an ex-employee of the company – and sought some £240m from the newspaper, believed to be the highest ever in English law.

Internet law

In June 2003, a second libel action was brought in a country outside that in which a newspaper is primarily published – thanks to the internet. Cheickh Bangoura, who lives in Canada, sued the Washington Post over an article it published in 1997, which at the time was only available in Ontario over the internet and to seven paying subscribers. The court agreed that it could hear the case.

The case follows that of a Melbourne mining boss, who in December 2002 was allowed to sue Dow Jones in Australia over an online version of an article published in the US.

Contempt and court reporting

In the light of press coverage of the Soham murders, the attorney general, Lord Goldsmith, spent much of 2003 worrying about contempt of court. In November, he described some pre-trial press reports of Ian Huntley and Maxine Carr as unacceptable – and promised to introduce tougher guidelines on the reporting of criminal trials.

Lord Goldsmith was not helped by the actions of two Shropshire radio presenters Mark Peters and Lisa Freame, from **Beacon FM** – who, during the trial, went so far as to host a phone-in asking whether Huntley's defence was believable. The broadcast, on November 26, appeared to breach existing rules prohibiting comment on the guilt or innocence of a person on trial. Nor was he helped by the home secretary, David Blunkett, who in the same month appeared to make prejudicial remarks following the arrest of an alleged al-Qaida terrorist in Gloucester.

Also in November, the outgoing director of public prosecutions, Sir David Calvert-Smith, said the publicity surrounding cases involving high-profile individuals was getting out of hand. "I think there is a huge problem. As a prosecutor, I would be very happy to see the media exercise greater restraint ... Even if they are not technically breaking the law, they are either making it more difficult, or actually impossible, to bring offenders to justice."

In March 2004, the Daily Star heard it was to face contempt proceedings for revealing the identities of two footballers arrested after a teenager alleged she was raped at the Grosvenor House hotel, London.

Meanwhile in July, the government launched a pilot study into the use of cameras in courtrooms. It is making dummy programmes of civil court cases, in an effort to assess whether trials should be televised.

Media law Contacts

Media law firms

A&L Goodbody
International Financial Services Centre
North Wall Quay, Dublin 1
00 353 1 649 2000
London: 020 7382 0800
law@algoodbody.ie
www.algoodbody.ie
Specialist media & entertainment law group, Ireland. IP & e-commerce; film financing; production law; contracts, defamation

Adlex Solicitors
76A Belsize Lane
London NW3 5BJ
020 7317 8404
adamt@adlexsolicitors.co.uk
www.adlexsolicitors.co.uk
Internet law; co-branding; software licensing; IT; IP; trademark registration

Akin Gump Strauss Hauer & Feld
Citypoint, Level 32
One Ropemaker Street
London EC2Y 9AW
020 7012 9600
londoninfo@akingump.com
www.akingump.com
IP; licensing; finance; media infringement (esp digital music online); defamation; employment inc 'credit' disputes, contracts, confirmation of minors' contracts

Allen & Overy
One New Change
London EC4M 9QQ
020 7330 3000
claire@meeghan@allenovery.com
www.allenovery.com
IP, finance, regulatory, antitrust issues; for IT, publishing, film, video, radio & TV, programming, live performance, music, sports, ads & PR

Arnold & Porter (UK)
Tower 42, 25 Old Broad Street
London EC2N 1HQ
020 7786 6100
www.arnoldporter.com
Patents, trademarks, copyright & trade secrets

Ashurst
Broadwalk House, 5 Appold Street
London EC2A 2HA
020 7638 1111
enquiries@ashursts.com
www.ashursts.com
Commercial agreements, satellite, transactions & litigation; acquisitions, disposals, mergers; advice on European & UK law, licensing, regulation esp. pan-European broadcasting; regulators, govts, broadcasters, producers, telecoms, multiplex & satellite operators; specialist film practice

Astburys
210 High Street, Lewes
East Sussex BN7 2NH
01273 403935
jastbury@astburys-law.co.uk
www.astburys-law.co.uk
Services for broadcasting, publishing & advertising

BM Nyman & Co
181 Creighton Avenue
London N2 9BN
020 8365 3060
bernie.nyman@iname.com
Publishing law

Baily Gibson
30 High Street, High Wycombe
Buckinghamshire HP11 2AG
01494 442661
Beaconsfield: 01494 672661
wycombe@bailygibson.co.uk
www.bailygibson.co.uk
e-commerce, IP

Baker & Mckenzie
100 New Bridge Street
London EC4V 6JA
020 7919 1000
info@bakernet.com
www.bakerinfo.com
e-commerce, IT licensing; broadcast, media regulation inc pay-per-view contracts, digital copyright, convergence of media & network technologies

Beachcroft Wansbroughs
100 Fetter Lane, London EC4A 1BN
020 7242 1011
London Eastcheap: 020 7208 6800
Birmingham: 0121 698 5200
Bristol: 0117 918 2000
Manchester: 0161 934 3000
Leeds: 0113 251 4700
Winchester: 01962 705500
info@bwlaw.co.uk
www.bwlaw.co.uk
interactive commerce & new media inc branding, data protection & privacy, franchising, IP, IT

Beale & Company
Garrick House, 27–32 King Street
Covent Garden, London WC2E 8JB
020 7240 3474
Dublin: 00 353 1 799 6213
reception@beale-law.com
www.beale-law.com
IT inc software, hardware supply & retail, e-commerce, internet, web design, database licensing

Berwin Leighton Paisner
Adelaide House, London Bridge
London EC4R 9HA
020 7760 1000
media@blplaw.com
www.blplaw.com
IP; e-business & IT; data protection; finance; film & TV production; cable & network operator agreements; transponder leasing, broadcast & telecoms regulation; publishing & multimedia inc video games; software, sport, performing arts; marketing law & sponsorship

Bevan Ashford
Head Office, 35 Colston Avenue
Bristol, Avon BS1 4TT
0117 923 0111
Birmingham: 0121 634 5000
London: 020 7822 7822
info@bevanashford.co.uk
www.bevanashford.co.uk
IP & IT law

Bird & Bird
90 Fetter Lane, London EC4A 1JP
020 7415 6000
london@twobirds.com
www.twobirds.com
IP; IT; broadcasting; film finance; advertising; sponsorship; film production; music; publishing

Blake Lapthorn Linnell
Holbrook House
14 Great Queen Street
London WC2B 5DG
020 7430 1709
Oxford: 01865 248607
Southampton: 023 8063 1823
Fareham: 01489 579990
Portsmouth: 023 9222 1122
info@bllaw.co.uk
www.bllaw.co.uk
IP; IT

Bournemouth Media School
Talbot Campus, Fern Barrow
Poole, Dorset BH12 5BB
01202 595191
eforbes@bournemouth.ac.uk
http://media.bournemouth.ac.uk
Media law consultancy to press, broadcast, film and creative industries. *See also careers & training*

Briffa
Business Design Centre
Upper Street, Islington
London N1 0QH
020 7288 6003
info@briffa.com
www.briffa.com
IP inc brand protection; personality rights in sport; rights for ad industry & designers

Brightley Commercial
Lower Landrine, Mitchell
Newquay, Cornwall TR8 5BB
01872 519087
robert@brightley.com
www.brightley.com
IP; contracts

Bristows
3 Lincoln's Inn Fields
London WC2A 3AA
020 7400 8000
info@bristows.com
www.bristows.com
IP & media law, inc publishing, ads & marketing, defamation, sponsorship & merchandising, TV distribution, privacy & competition law

Campbell Hooper
35 Old Queen Street
London SW1H 9JD
020 7222 9070
ch@campbellhooper.com
www.campbellhooper.com
IP; commercial & media dispute resolutions; defamation & media management; theatre; merchandising & sponsorship; advertising & marketing law; brand & domain name management; ICT; e-commerce; software licensing; data protection; licensing agreements

CapitalLaw
Discovery House
Scott Harbour, Cardiff
South Glamorgan CF10 4HA
029 2045 2770
law@capitallaw.co.uk
www.capitallaw.co.uk
Formerly Palser Grossman. IP claims, litigation & dispute resolution

Carter-Ruck
London International Press Centre
76 Shoe Lane, London EC4A 3JB
020 7353 5005
lawyers@carter-ruck.com
www.carter-ruck.com
Defamation, media, human rights, IP & employment law

Charles Lucas & Marshall
1 Wood Street, Swindon SN1 4AN
01793 511055
Newbury: 01635 521212
Wantage: 01235 771234
Hungerford: 01488 682506
ask@clmsolicitors.co.uk
www.clmsolicitors.co.uk
IT contracts & agreements

Charles Russell
8–10 New Fetter Lane
London EC4A 1RS
020 7203 5000
Guildford: 01483 252525
Cheltenham: 01242 221122
enquiry@cr-law.co.uk
www.charlesrussell.co.uk
Telecoms, IT, e-commerce, competition & regulatory law specialists; data protection team; internet law; media & entertainment work for Film, TV, Literary & music sectors inc reputation management and IP

Clarke Willmott
Equity Court
73–75 Millbrook Road East
Southampton, Hampshire SO15 1RJ
023 80483200
Bristol: 0117 9416600
Taunton: 01823 442266
info@clarkewillmott.com
www.clarkewillmott.com
Sports & media law – contact Linda Gregory on 023 8048 3232, email lgregory@clarkewillmott.com

Class Law
1 Great Cumberland Place
London W1H 8DQ
020 7724 2526
mail@classlaw.co.uk
www.classlaw.co.uk
Finance, employment contracts, IT

Clifford Chance Limited Liability
10 Upper Bank Street, Canary Wharf
London E14 5JJ
020 7006 1000
info@cliffordchance.com
www.cliffordchance.com
Full IP service: patents, trademarks, copyright, design, trade secrets & unfair competition

Clifford Miller
Burnhill Business Centre
50 Burnhill Road, Beckenham
Kent BR3 3LA
020 8663 0044
mail@millercompany.demon.co.uk
www.cliffordmiller.com
IP; competition (anti-trust); IT Law

Clintons
55 Drury Lane, Covent Garden
London WC2B 5RZ
020 7379 6080
info@clintons.co.uk
www.clintons.co.uk
Film & TV: finance, development, IP, production, catalogue acquisition & disposal, distribution & exploitation, rights clearance; radio: contracts, digital exploitation, IP, licence agreements, licence applications, regulation. Talent agencies: contracts & indiv freelance broadcast & bi-media service agreements. Publishing: contracts, libel, disputes, rights exploitation

Cobbetts Lee Crowder
Ship Canal House, King Street
Manchester M2 4WB
0845 404 2404
Birmingham: 0121 236 4477
Leeds: 0845 404 2404
info@cobbetts.co.uk
www.cobbetts.co.uk
IP; ICT; media law: software development, outsourcing, data protection, distance selling & ad regulations; defamation; experience in gaming, music publishing & events, interactive TV, new media, film & TV

Collins Long
24 Pepper Street, London SE1 0EB
020 7401 9800
jamescollins@collinslong.com
www.collinslong.com
Media & entertainment law: contracts, litigation, development, production, financing, distribution

Collyer-Bristow
4 Bedford Row, London WC1R 4DF
020 7242 7363
cblaw@collyerbristow.com
www.collyerbristow.com
IP; IT & e-commerce; artists & managers, composers & publishers, record producers & distributors, scriptwriters, indies, film producers, actors & performers

Constant & Constant
Sea Containers House
20 Upper Ground, London SE1 9QT
020 7261 0006
twoconstants@constantlaw.com
www.constantlaw.com
Media & e-commerce: development, production & financing; distribution & sales; broadcasting & publishing; advertising; IP

Couchman Harrington Associates
8 Bloomsbury Square
London WC1A 2LQ
020 7611 9660
enquiries@chass.co.uk
www.chass.co.uk
Sports law, IP & broadcasting

Coudert Brothers
60 Cannon Street
London EC4N 6JP
020 7248 3000
london@coudert.com
www.coudert.com
IP; international & domestic film financing & tax planning; international licensing; telecoms

Courts & Co
15 Wimpole Street, London W1G 9SY
020 7637 1651
law@courtsandco.com
www.courtsandco.com
IP inc electronic delivery of AV material; Community trademarks in EU & Madrid Protocol; members of International Trademark Association

■ *IP = Intellectual property*

Covington & Burling – Registered Foreign Lawyers & Solicitors – London
265 Strand, London WC2R 1BH
020 7067 2000
jrupp@cov.com
www.cov.com
IP & data protection; broadcasting, mass media, telecoms, multichannel video distribution, satellite, PCS/cellular

Cripps Harries Hall
Wallside House
12 Mount Ephraim Road
Tunbridge Wells, Kent TN1 1EG
01892 515121
reception@crippslaw.com
www.e-cripps.co.uk
IP; tech; copyright & other media rights; defamation, libel & slander; sport

Cuff Roberts
100 Old Hall Street, Liverpool
Merseyside L3 9TD
0151 237 7777
email@cuffroberts.co.uk
www.cuffroberts.co.uk
Services to music & sports industries

Cumberland Ellis Peirs (incorporating Barth & Partners)
Columbia House, 69 Aldwych
London WC2B 4RW
020 7242 0422
suzanneeva@cep-law.co.uk
www.cep-law.co.uk
Services for governing bodies of sport; event organisers; participants; advertisers, sponsors & broadcasters

Davenport Lyons
1 Old Burlington Street
London W1S 3NL
020 7468 2600
dl@davenportlyons.com
www.davenportlyons.com
Specialist areas: defamation; film & TV; music; IP; publishing; ads; IT, e-commerce, interactive & new media; sport

David Price Solicitors and Advocates
21 Fleet Street, London EC4Y 1AA
020 7353 9999
enquiries@lawyers-media.com
www.lawyers-media.com
Defamation (libel & slander), breach of confidence & privacy, contempt & copyright, pre-publication advice, internet defamation

Dawsons
2 New Square, Lincoln's Inn
London WC2A 3RZ
020 7421 4800
info@dawsons-legal.com
www.dawsons-legal.com
IT, e-commerce & internet; IP; defamation, breach of confidence; music publishing, group management & artists' recording agreements; finance & production, distribution & exploitation for film & TV; rights clearance; sponsorship, broadcast, ambush marketing, merchandising, endorsements for sports

Dean Marsh & Co
20 Bowling Green Lane
London EC1R 0BD
020 7553 4400
info@deanmarsh.com
www.deanmarsh.com
Music & entertainment

Denton Wilde Sapte
Five Chancery Lane, Clifford's Inn
London EC4A 1BU
020 7242 1212
info@dentonwildesapte.com
www.dentonwildesapte.com
IP; services for ads & marketing, broadcasting, IT, live performance, music, publishing, sponsorship, sport & telecoms; film & TV production, film financing

Dickinson Dees
St Ann's Wharf, 112 Quayside
Newcastle Upon Tyne
Tyne And Wear NE99 1SB
0191 279 9000
marketing@dickinson-dees.com
www.dickinson-dees.com

DLA
3 Noble Street, London EC2V 7EE
0870 011 1111
www.dla.com
Defamation, confidentiality & privacy, digital media, data protection and freedom of information, publishing, gaming, contractual, IT. Clients include Time Warner Book Group, ITV plc, Thomson, IPC

DMA Legal
14 Coach & Horses Yard
Savile Row, London W1S 2EJ
020 7534 5850
info@dmalegal.com
www.dmalegal.com
IP, defamation, contracts, licensing, distribution, multi media agreements, royalty arrangements

DMH Solicitors
100 Queens Road, Brighton
East Sussex BN1 3YB
01273 329833
james.quarmby@dmh.co.uk
www.dmh.co.uk
All areas

Dorsey & Whitney
21 Wilson Street
London EC2M 2TD
020 7588 0800
Cambridge: 01223 451036
london@dorsey.com
www.dorseylaw.com
IP litigation

DWF
5 Castle Street, Liverpool
Merseyside L2 4XE
0151 907 3000
Manchester: 0161 603 5000
enquiries@dwf.co.uk
www.dwf.co.uk
IP; contracts

Dyer Burdett & Co
64 West Street, Havant
Hampshire PO9 1PA
023 9249 2472
mail@dyerburdett.com
www.dyerburdett.com
IP; TV, radio, film, & theatre production & licensing, sport

Edwin Coe
2 Stone Buildings
London WC2A 3TH
020 7691 4000
mail@edwincoe.com
www.edwincoe.com
IP

Eversheds
Senator House, 85 Queen Victoria St
London EC4V 4JL
020 7919 4500
Birmingham: 0121 232 1000
Cambridge: 01223 443666
Ipswich: 01473 284428
Leeds: 0113 243 0391
Manchester: 0161 831 8000
Cardiff: 029 2047 1147
Newcastle: 0191 241 6000
Norwich: 01603 272727
Nottingham: 0115 950 7000
www.eversheds.com
E-commerce, IT; music, TV & related areas; IP

Farrer & Co
66 Lincoln's Inn Fields
London WC2A 3LH
020 7242 2022
enquiries@farrer.co.uk
www.farrer.co.uk
IP & media law

Fennemores
200 Silbury Boulevard
Central Milton Keynes
Buckinghamshire MK9 1LL
01908 678241
info@fennemores.co.uk
www.fennemores.co.uk
Data protection & contracts in e-business & tech

Ferdinand Kelly
21 Bennetts Hill, Birmingham
West Midlands B2 5QP
0121 643 5228
ferdinand-kelly@dial.pipex.com
www.ferdinandkelly.co.uk
E-commerce, franchising, IT, IP

Field Fisher Waterhouse
35 Vine Street, London EC3N 2AA
020 7861 4000
info@ffwlaw.com
www.ffwlaw.com
Services to broadcasters & publishers esp licensing book & magazine publishing rights in TV programmes; IP

Fieldings Porter
Silverwell House, 32 Silverwell Street
Bolton, Lancashire BL1 1PT
01204 387742
info@fpsols.co.uk
www.fieldingsporter.co.uk
IP disputes

Finers Stephens Innocent
179 Great Portland Street
London W1W 5LS
020 7323 4000
mstephens@fsilaw.co.uk
www.fsilaw.com
Specialist areas: ads & sales promotion; anti-counterfeiting; copyright; cultural property; defamation; design rights; IT & e-commerce; obscenity; publishing; sports law; trademark & brand management; visual arts; photo agencies & libraries; TV & film

Fladgate Fielder
25 North Row, London W1K 6DJ
020 7323 4747
fladgate@fladgate.com
www.fladgate.com
IP, IT & sports law

Foot Anstey Sargent
21 Derrys Cross, Plymouth
Devon PL1 2SW
01752 675000
Exeter: 01392 685351
tony.jaffa@foot-ansteys.co.uk
www.foot-ansteys.co.uk/businessadvice/media
Specialist media, commercial, & employment advice to newspapers, publishers & ISPs

Freshfields Bruckhaus Deringer
65 Fleet Street, London EC4Y 1HS
020 7936 4000
www.freshfields.com
IP/IT; specialist telecoms, media & tech (TMT) group

Gamlins
31–37 Russell Road, Rhyl
Denbighshire LL18 3DB
01745 343500
www.gamlins.co.uk
IP; largest law firm in north Wales

Gateley Wareing
14 Regent Street, Nottingham
Nottinghamshire NG1 5BQ
0115 983 8200
Birmingham: 0121 234 0000
Leicester: 0116 285 9000
gw@gateleywareing.com
www.gateleywareing.co.uk
IP, esp in computers & software; tech sector: trademarks, patents, e-commerce, databases & rights

George Davies
Fountain Court, 68 Fountain Street
Manchester, Lancashire M2 2FB
0161 236 8992
mail@georgedavies.co.uk
www.georgedavies.co.uk
IP, contracts & franchising; also sports personalities & major sporting bodies

Gersten & Nixon
National House, 60–66 Wardour Street
London W1F 0TA
020 7439 3961
law@gernix.co.uk
www.gernix.co.uk
All aspects of media & entertainment law

Goodman Derrick
90 Fetter Lane, London EC4A 1PT
020 7404 0606
pherbert@gdlaw.co.uk
www.gdlaw.co.uk
Media law: disputes & litigation; contracts & documentation; programme clearance; regulatory advice. Film: banking, securitisation; distribution, writer & talent contracts; mergers & acquisitions; sponsorship & merchandising agreements; script clearance

Gray & Co
Habib House, 9 Stevenson Square,
3rd Floor, Piccadilly
Manchester, Lancashire M1 1DB
0161 237 3360
grayco@grayand.co.uk
www.grayand.co.uk
Entertainment industry in Manchester & north-west; esp. music & record companies; film & TV contracts & finance

Greenwoods
Monkstone House
City Road, Peterborough
Cambridgeshire PE1 1JE
01733 887700
sblackwell@greenwoods.co.uk
www.greenwoods.co.uk
IP; e-commerce; IT

Grundberg Mocatta Rakison
4th Floor Imperial House
15–19 Kingsway
London WC2B 6UN
020 7632 1600
post@gmrlaw.com
www.gmrlaw.com
IP

H2O
The Media Centre
3–8 Carburton Street
London W1W 5AJ
020 7886 0740
enquiries@h2o-law.com
www.h2o-law.com
Art & photography: advise artists & photographers on IP, contracts & licensing; Publishing: manages authors rights, advises on contract & dispute issues, IP & libel vetting

Hale And Dorr
Alder Castle House, 10 Noble Street
London EC2V 7QJ
020 7645 2400
webmaster@haledorr.com
www.haledorr.com
IP; services for telecoms, internet, e-commerce & software industries

Halliwell Landau
St James Court, Brown Street
Manchester M2 2JF
020 7929 1900
London: 020 7929 1900
info@halliwells.co.uk
www.halliwells.co.uk
IP, commercial & tech law; IT & e-commerce sectors

Hamlins
Roxburghe House
273–287 Regent Street
London W1B 2AD
020 7355 6000
admin@hamlins.co.uk
www.hamlins.co.uk
IP & copyright

Hammonds
7 Devonshire Square, Cutlers Gardens
London EC2M 4YH
0870 839 0000
enquiries@ hammonds.com
www.hammonds.com
ICT, e-commerce, data protection, media, sport & entertainment team

Harbottle & Lewis
Hanover House, 14 Hanover Square
London W1S 1HP
020 7667 5000
robert.porter@harbottle.com
www.harbottle.com
All areas inc film, TV, broadcasting, sport, music, publishing, advertising & theatre; IP; defamation

Harrison Curtis
8 Jockey's Fields, London WC1R 4BF
020 7611 1720
mail@harrisoncurtis.co.uk
www.harrisoncurtis.co.uk
Principal areas: music, film & TV, e-commerce, theatre, ads & marketing, sport

Haynes Phillips
73 Farringdon Road
London EC1M 3JQ
020 7242 2213
hello@haynesphillips.com
www.haynesphillips.com
IP; music: contracts, rights, licensing, management, merchandising, music publishing, videos

Herbert Smith
Exchange House, Primrose Street
London EC2A 2HS
020 7374 8000
contact@herbertsmith.com
www.herbertsmith.com
Litigation, competition, corporate & IT/IP, piracy, copyright & defamation; TV & radio, books & publishing, media, music, ads & marketing

Hewitsons
Shakespeare House
42 Newmarket Road, Cambridge
Cambridgeshire CB5 8EP
01223 461155
Northampton: 01604 233233
mail@hewitsons.com
www.hewitsons.com
IP; IT inc internet, e-commerce, ICT

Hextalls
28 Leman Street, London E1 8ER
020 7488 1424
info@hextalls.com
www.hextalls.com
Telecoms, media & tech dept serving music, entertainment, publishing & telecoms sector

■ *IP = Intellectual property*

Hill Dickinson
Sun Court, 66–67 Cornhill
London EC3V 3RN
020 7695 1000
Liverpool: 0151 236 5400
Manchester: 0161 817 7200
Chester: 01244 896600
law@hilldicks.com
www.hilldickinson.com
Agency; broadcasting, theatre & film; e-commerce; endorsement, merchandising & sponsorship; IT; libel & slander; publishing; sports law

HLW
Princess House, 122 Queen Street
Sheffield, South Yorkshire S1 2DW
0114 276 5555
info@hlwlaw.co.uk
www.hlw-solicitors.co.uk
IP

Holme Roberts & Owen
Heathcoat House, 20 Savile Row
London W1S 3PR
020 7320 6464
information@hro.com
www.hro.com
IP; film, telecoms, sport & entertainment

Howard Kennedy
Harcourt House
19 Cavendish Square
London W1A 2AW
020 7636 1616
Info@howardkennedy.com
www.howardkennedy.com
IP; film, TV, music, theatre, sports

Howell-Jones Partnership
75 Surbiton Road
Kingston upon Thames
Surrey KT1 2AF
020 8549 5186
kingston@hjplaw.co.uk
www.hjplaw.co.uk
IP

Humphreys & Co
14 King Street, Bristol
Avon BS1 4EF
0117 929 2662
lawyers@humphreys.co.uk
www.humphreys.co.uk
IP; sports contracts; IT; also advises artists, publishers, writers, managers & record companies in music & entertainment industries

Ingram Winter Green
Bedford House, 21A John Street
London WC1N 2BL
020 7845 7400
backchat@iwg.co.uk
www.iwg.co.uk
E-business & IT; clients in TV, print media, film, radio, music, printing & ad industries; film finance, syndication, distribution, regulation & broadcasting complaints

James Chapman & Co
76 King Street, Manchester
Lancashire M2 4NH
0161 828 8000
mike.blood@james-chapman.co.uk
www.james-chapman.co.uk
Sports law

Kemp Little LLP
Saddlers House, Gutter Lane
London EC2V 6BR
020 7710 1610
amanda.millar@kemplittle.com
www.kemplittle.com
IP; IT & telecoms regulation

Kendall Freeman
43 Fetter Lane, London EC4A 1JU
020 7583 4055
info@kendallfreeman.com
www.kendallfreeman.com
Formerly DJ Freeman. Dispute resolution & arbitration

Kent Jones and Done
Churchill House, Regent Road
Stoke-On-Trent
Staffordshire ST1 3RQ
01782 202020
mail@kjd.co.uk
www.kjd.co.uk
IT, e-commerce, tech licensing, trademarks & copyright, entertainment

Kidd Rapinet
14 & 15 Craven Street
London WC2N 5AD
020 7925 0303
Slough: 01753 532541
info@krlondon.co.uk
www.kiddrapinet.co.uk
IP inc copyright protection & licensing

Kimbells LLP
Power House, Davy Avenue
Knowlhill, Milton Keynes
Buckinghamshire MK5 8RR
01908 668555
alison.foxton@kimbells.com
www.kimbells.com
IT & IP

Kirkland & Ellis International
Tower 42, 25 Old Broad Street
London EC2N 1HQ
020 7816 8700
info@kirkland.com
www.kirkland.com
IP inc transactions & litigation relating to internet & e-commerce

McGrigors, London
1–2 Dorset Rise, London EC4Y 8EN
020 7694 2500
www.mcgrigors.com
IP

Kuit Steinart Levy
3 St. Marys Parsonage, Manchester
Lancashire M3 2RD
0161 832 3434
ksllaw@kuits.com
www.kuits.com
Licensing & brand acquisitions; sports merchandising; e-commerce

Latham & Watkins
99 Bishopsgate, Eleventh Floor
London EC2M 3XF
020 7710 1000
joe.blum@lw.com
www.lw.com
IP & tech; acquisition, financing, sale, licensing & dispute resolution

Lawdit Solicitors
Station House, 17 Saxon Road
Southampton, Hampshire SO15 1JJ
023 8023 5979
info@lawdit.co.uk
www.lawdit.co.uk
IP inc domain names, data protection, e-commerce, IT contracts, media law, trademarks & websites

Lawrence Graham
190 Strand, London WC2R 1JN
020 7379 0000
jonathan.riley@lawgram.com
www.lawgram.com
IP; dispute resolution; telecoms

Lawrence Jones
Sea Containers House,
20 Upper Ground, Blackfriars Bridge
London SE1 9LH
020 7620 1311
contact@lawrencejones.co.uk
www.lawrencejones.co.uk
IT inc internet & e-commerce; sports law

Laytons
Carmelite, 50 Victoria Embankment
Blackfriars, London EC4Y 0LS
020 7842 8000
Bristol: 0117 930 9500
Guildford: 01483 407000
Manchester: 0161 834 2100
london@laytons.com
www.laytons.com
IP, IT & related UK & EU competition law

Leathes Prior
74 The Close, Norwich
Norfolk NR1 4DR
01603 610911
info@leathesprior.co.uk
www.leathesprior.co.uk
IP inc counterfeiting, domain names, passing-off & trade libel; e-commerce & IT

Lee & Thompson
Greengarden House
15–22 St. Christophers Place
London W1U 1NL
020 7935 4665
mail@leeandthompson.com
www.leeandthompson.com
Film/TV inc financing; music industry agreements & copyright law

Lennox Bywater
9 Limes Avenue, London NW7 3NY
020 8906 1206
lennox.bywater@virgin.net
www.lennoxbywater.com
Sports law

Leonard Lowy & Co
500 Chiswick High Road
London W4 5RG
020 8956 2785
lowy@leonardlowy.co.uk
www.leonardlowy.co.uk
Music industry

Lester Aldridge
Russell House, Oxford Road
Bournemouth, Dorset BH8 8EX
01202 786161
info@LA-law.com
www.lesteraldridge.com
IP

Lewis Silkin
12 Gough Square
London EC4A 3DW
020 7074 8000
mark.king@lewissilkin.com
www.lewissilkin.com
Media brands & tech department

Linklaters
One Silk Street, London EC2Y 8HQ
020 7456 2000
enquiries@linklaters.com
www.linklaters.com
IP; IT & comms law – inc telecoms & satellites; broadcasting; IT; e-commerce & internet; outsourcing; data protection

Lovells
Atlantic House, Holborn Viaduct
London EC1A 2FG
020 7296 2000
information@lovells.com
www.lovells.com
IP; tech, media & telecoms

Macfarlanes
10 Norwich Street
London EC4A 1BD
020 7831 9222
iain.mackie@macfarlanes.com
www.macfarlanes.com
IP: IT; e-commerce; advertising & marketing

Maclay Murray & Spens London
151 St Vincent Street
Glasgow G2 5NJ
0141 248 5011
London: 020 7606 6130
Edinburgh: 0131 226 5196
Aberdeen: 01224 356130
magnus.swanson@mms.co.uk
www.mms.co.uk
IP & tech in sectors of software, electronics & engineering, film & media, internet & e-commerce

Magrath & Co
52–54 Maddox Street
London W1S 1PA
020 7495 3003
admin@magrath.co.uk
www.magrath.co.uk
Law inc IP & agreements, for recording artists & recording companies, actors, sports people, TV & filmmakers

Manches
Aldwych House, 81 Aldwych
London WC2B 4RP
020 7404 4433
manches@manches.com
www.manches.com
IT, IP, internet, publishing & media inc sponsorship, merchandising, financing, litigation, defamation, data protection, ad & sales promotion laws

Mann & Partners
New Court Chambers
23–25 Bucks Road, Douglas
Isle Of Man IM99 2EN
01624 695800
law@mannandpartners.com
www.mannandpartners.com
IP

Marcus J O' Leary
Anvil Court, Denmark Street
Wokingham, Berkshire RG40 2BB
0118 989 7110
moleary@mjol.co.uk
www.mjol.co.uk
National IT IP firm. Clients include Microsoft & Dell

Marks & Clerk solicitors
Queens House
55–56 Lincoln's Inn Fields
London WC2A 3LJ
020 7400 3002
solicitors@marks-clerk.com
www.marks-clerk.com
IP; IT; Publishing

Patent and trademark attorneys
57–60 Lincoln's Inn Fields
London WC2A 3LS
020 7400 3000
Birmingham: 0121 643 5881
Cambridge: 01223 345520
Cheltenham: 01242 524520
Coventry: 024 7622 2756/ 7145
Edinburgh: 0131 225 4500
Glasgow: 0141 221 5769
Leeds: 0113 389 5600
Leicester: 0116 233 8181
Liverpool: 0151 236 5147
Manchester: 0161 233 5800
Oxford: 01865 397900
St. Albans: 01727 854215
london@marks-clerk.com
www.marks-clerk.com
Patents; trademarks; copyright; domain names; licensing

Marriott Harrison
12 Great James Street
London WC1N 3DR
020 7209 2000
astacha@marriottharrison.co.uk
www.marriottharrison.com
Film & entertainment law

Marshall Ross & Prevezer
4 Frederick's Place
London EC2R 8AB
020 7367 9000
mail@mrp-law.co.uk
www.mrp-law.co.uk
IP disputes

Martineau Johnson
Phillips House, St Phillips Place
Birmingham B3 2PP
0121 200 3300
lawyers@martjohn.com
www.martineau-johnson.co.uk
IP; IT inc hardware acquisition, software licensing, internet & e-commerce

Masons
30 Aylesbury Street
London EC1R 0ER
020 7490 4000
info@masons.com
www.masons.com
IP; IT inc resolution of IT & telecoms disputes

Massers
15 Victoria Street, Nottingham
Nottinghamshire NG1 2JZ
0115 8511666
www.masser.co.uk
IP & copyright disputes

McClure Naismith
Pountney Hill House
6 Laurence Pountney Hill
London EC4R 0BL
020 7623 9155
Glasgow: 0141 204 2700
Edinburgh: 0131 220 1002
london@mcclurenaismith.com
www.mcclurenaismith.com
IP/IT; dispute resolution & litigation

McCormicks
Britannia Chambers, 4 Oxford Place
Leeds, West Yorkshire LS1 3AX
0113 246 0622
Harrogate: 01423 530630
p.mccormick@mccormicks-solicitors.com
www.mccormicks-solicitors.com
IP; defamation; sponsorship

Media Legal Services
The Burrows, Poundfield Lane
Cookham SL6 9RY
07976 869954
jane_isaacs@hotmail.com
Advice to TV industry

Memery Crystal
44 Southampton Buildings
London WC2A 1AP
020 7242 5905
info@memerycrystal.com
www.memerycrystal.com
Digital tech inc software development, licensing agreements; IP

Merricks
207–208 Moulsham Street
Chelmsford CM2 0LG
01245 491414
London: 020 7959 0202
Info@MerricksLLP.com
www.merricksllp.com
All aspects

MLM
Pendragon House, Fitzalan Court
Newport Road, Cardiff
South Glamorgan CF24 0BA
029 2046 2562
enquiries@mlmsolicitors.com
www.mlmsolicitors.com
IP; IT; tech companies, TV companies & broadcasters

■ *IP = Intellectual property*

Moorcrofts
Mere House, Mere Park
Dedmere Road
Marlow, Buckinghamshire SL7 1PB
01628 470000
info@moorcrofts.com
www.moorcrofts.com
Corporate, IP & regulation. Clients include RDF, Video Arts & Shop on Box

Morgan Cole
Buxton Court, 3 West Way
Oxford, Oxfordshire OX2 0SZ
01865 262600
Cardiff: 029 2038 5385
Reading: 0118 955 3000
London: 020 7822 8000
info@morgan-cole.com
www.morgan-cole.com
IP

Morrison & Foerster MNP
21 Garlick Hill, London EC4V 2AU
020 7815 1150
london@mofo.com
www.mofo.com
IP, new media & tech, telecoms & other regulation, & all aspects of project & corporate finance

Myers Fletcher & Gordon
15 Cambridge Court
210 Shepherds Bush Road,
Hammersmith, London W6 7NJ
020 7610 4433
mfg@mfglon.co.uk
www.mfg-law.com
Copyright, entertainment law, internet & appropriation of personality, IP dispute litigation

Nabarro Nathanson
Lacon House, Theobalds Road
London WC1X 8RW
020 7524 6000
www.nabarro.com
E-commerce, telecoms, IT

Neil McQueen Duncan & Egner
Floor E, Milburn House, Dean Street
Newcastle Upon Tyne
Tyne And Wear NE1 1LF
0191 232 7469
info@solicitorsupontyne.co.uk
www.solicitorsupontyne.co.uk
Copyright & patent law

New Media Law LLP
102 Dean Street, London W1D 3TQ
020 7734 9777
ian.penman@newmedialaw.biz
www.newmedialaw.biz
Copyright & contract law for music, TV & film

Nexus Solicitors
Carlton House, 16–18 Albert Square
Manchester, Lancashire M2 5PE
0161 819 4900
help@nexussolicitors.co.uk
www.nexussolicitors.co.uk
Sports & media inc sponsorship, endorsement agreements, merchandising & licensing, football transfers, event regulation, publishing etc

Nicholson Graham & Jones
110 Cannon Street
London EC4N 6AR
020 7648 9000
marketing@ngj.co.uk
www.ngj.co.uk
IP & technologies

Norton Rose
Kempson House
35–37 Camomile Street
London EC3A 7AN
020 7283 6000
marketing@nortonrose.com
www.nortonrose.com
Advice on rights management, marketing law & dispute resolution

Olswang
90 High Holborn, London WC1V 6XX
020 7067 3000
john.enser@olswang.com
www.olswang.com
Media & comms

Orchard
6 Snow Hill, London EC1A 2AY
020 7246 6100
info@orchardlaw.com
www.orchardlaw.com
Film, marketing, music, publishing, TV & radio; IT; internet

Osborne Clarke
26 Old Bailey, London EC4M 7HW
020 7809 1000
info@osborne-clarke.co.uk
www.osborneclarke.com
IP; IT & telecoms; advertising & marketing

Peachey & Co
95 Aldwych, London WC2B 4JF
020 7316 5200
oml@peachey.co.uk
www.PEACHEY.co.uk
Broadcasting; creative media (ads & marketing); new media; software & IT services; sport; telecoms

Penningtons
Bucklersbury House
83 Cannon Street
London EC4N 8PE
020 7457 3000
information@penningtons.co.uk
www.penningtons.co.uk
E-business & IP

Pictons
Keystone Building, 60 London Road
St. Albans, Hertfordshire AL1 1NG
01727 798000
marketing@pictons.co.uk
www.pictons.co.uk
Tech IP

Pinsents
Dashwood House
69 Old Broad Street
London EC2M 1NR
020 7418 7000
Leeds: 0113 244 5000
Birmingham: 0121 200 1050
Manchester: 0161 250 0100
susan.biddle@pinsents.com
www.pinsents.com
IP

Putsman.Wlc.
Britannia House
50 Great Charles Street, Birmingham
West Midlands B3 2LT
0121 237 3000
info@pwlc.co.uk
www.pwlc.co.uk
IP etc for TV production; band & media managers; celeb agents; publishers; media personalities; signed bands & artists; casting agents; venues

RT Coopers
Office 5, Telfords Yard,
6/8 The Highway
London E1W 2BS
020 7488 2985
enquiries@rtcoopers.com
www.rtcoopers.com
Film, TV, music, IP, copyright, branding, licensing, publishing etc

Rawlison Butler
Griffin House, 135 High Street
Crawley, West Sussex RH10 1DQ
01293 527744
info@rawlisonbutler.com
www.rawlisonbutler.com
IP & brand protection; IT & e-commerce; data protection; EU & UK competition law; contracts

Reed Smith
Minerva House, 5 Montague Close
London SE1 9BB
020 7403 2900
tfoster@reedsmith.com
www.reedsmith.co.uk
Pre-publication & pre-broadcast inc libel, invasion of privacy etc; non-litigation such as protecting IP, general corporate, negotiation of industry-related agreements, labour & employment, comms regulatory, & ad branding

Reid Minty
14 Grosvenor Street, Mayfair
London W1K 4PS
020 7318 4444
lawyers@reidminty.co.uk
www.reidminty.co.uk
Defamation: libel, slander & malicious falsehood

Reynolds Porter Chamberlain
Chichester House
278–282 High Holborn
London WC1V 7HA
020 7242 2877
enquiries@rpc.co.uk
www.rpc.co.uk
Content-related issues for press, publishers, TV

Richard Howard & Co
45–51 Whitfield Street
London W1T 4HB
020 7831 4511
richard.howard@richardhoward.co.uk
www.richardhoward.tv
TV, paper & electronic publishing, multimedia & telecoms; IP

Richards Butler International
Beaufort House, 15 St. Botolph Street
London EC3A 7EE
020 7247 6555
pma@richardsbutler.com
www.richardsbutler.com
IP; telecoms; IT, data protection & e-business

Ricksons
6 Winckley Square, Preston
Lancashire PR1 3JJ
01772 556677
james.cowell@ricksons.co.uk
www.ricksons.co.uk
E-commerce & computer contracts; IP; confidentiality agreements & data protection

Robert Muckle
Norham House
New Bridge Street West
Newcastle Upon Tyne
Tyne And Wear NE1 8AS
0191 232 4402
enquiries@robertmuckle.co.uk
www.robertmuckle.co.uk
IP; IT; dispute resolution

Roiter Zucker
Regent House
5–7 Broadhurst Gardens
Swiss Cottage, London NW6 3RZ
020 7328 9111
mail@roiterzucker.co.uk
www.roiterzucker.co.uk
IP & disputes

Rollits
Wilberforce Court, High Street
Hull, North Humberside HU1 1YJ
01482 323239
info@rollits.com
www.rollits.com
IP & telecoms

Rooks Rider
Challoner House
19 Clerkenwell Close
London EC1R 0RR
020 7689 7000
lawyers@rooksrider.co.uk
www.rooksrider.co.uk
IP

Rosenblatt
9–13 St. Andrew Street
London EC4A 3AF
020 7955 0880
info@rosenblatt-law.co.uk
www.rosenblatt-law.co.uk
Defamation & IP

Ross & Craig
12a Upper Berkeley Street
London W1H 7QE
020 7262 3077
reception@rosscraig.com
www.rosscraig.com
Co-production arrangements; IP & copyright; film & TV funding; rights acquisition; production & artistes' contracts; defamation

Rowberry Morris
17 Castle Street, Reading
Berkshire RG1 7SB
0118 958 5611
admin@rowberrymorris.co.uk
www.rowberrymorris.co.uk
All aspects of media law. Specialist unit advises new bands & writers

SJ Berwin
222 Gray's Inn Road
London WC1X 8XF
020 7533 2222
info@sjberwin.com
www.sjberwin.com
IP; film, TV & radio work (content & carriage), music, telecoms, sport, animation, digital media, e-commerce & online

Salans
Clements House
14–18 Gresham Street
London EC2V 7NN
020 7509 6000
rabrahams@salans.com
www.salans.com
IP; IT & comms law

Schillings
Royalty House, 72–74 Dean Street
London W1D 3TL
020 7453 2500
legal@schillings.co.uk
www.schillings.co.uk
IP & media management

Seddons
5 Portman Square
London W1H 6NT
020 7725 8000
postmaster@seddons.co.uk
www.seddons.co.uk
Entertainment & music industry

Shepherd And Wedderburn
Bucklersbury House
83 Cannon Street
London EC4N 8SW
020 7763 3200
london@shepwedd.co.uk
www.shepwedd.co.uk
IP & trademark litigation, copyright, sport law

Sheridans
14 Red Lion Square
London WC1R 4QL
020 7775 9469
staylor@sheridans.co.uk
www.sheridans.co.uk
Agreements; music, book & magazine publishing; distribution; licensing; merchandising; sponsorship; trademarks & domain names

Simkins Partnership
45–51 Whitfield Street
London W1T 4HB
020 7907 3000
antony.gostyn@simkins.com
www.simkins.com
Film & TV; music; theatre; ads; sport; publishing; photography; e-commerce

Simmons & Simmons
Citypoint, 1 Ropemaker Street
London EC2Y 9SS
020 7628 2020
enquiries@simmons-simmons.com
www.simmons-simmons.com
IP litigation

Simons Muirhead & Burton
50 Broadwick Street, Soho
London W1F 7AG
020 7734 4499
info@smab.co.uk
www.smab.co.uk
Film & TV regulatory & production law; dispute resolution, copyright & libel advice

Slaughter & May
One Bunhill Row, London EC1Y 8YY
020 7600 1200
www.slaughterandmay.com
IP; IT; tech, media & telecoms

Spearing Waite
41 Friar Lane, Leicester
Leicestershire LE1 5RB
0116 262 4225
info@spearingwaite.co.uk
www.spearingwaite.co.uk
Franchising, agency & licensing; IP

Spring Law
40 Craven Street
London WC2N 5NG
020 7930 4158
tim.perry@springlaw.co.uk
www.Springlaw.co.uk
IP, franchise arrangements, sponsorship, rights exploitation, distribution, merchandising, licensing, marketing, ads & promotions

Squire Sanders & Dempsey
Royex House, 5 Aldermanbury Square
London EC2V 7HR
020 7776 5200
ssdinfo@ssd.com
www.ssd.com
Comms law inc IP, internet, licensing, regulatory restructuring, satellite comms, broadcasting & cable

Steele & Co
11 Guilford Street
London WC1N 1DH
020 7421 1720
finplan@steele.co.uk
www.steele.co.uk
For record labels, agents, managers, event organisers, artists, publishers, writers, broadcasters, unions & professional bodies

Stringer Saul
17 Hanover Square
London W1S 1HU
020 7917 8500
info@stringersaul.co.uk
www.stringersaul.co.uk
IP; IT & internet; publishing

■ *IP = Intellectual property*

Tarlo Lyons
Watchmaker Court, 33 St John's Lane
London EC1M 4DB
020 7405 2000
www.tarlo-lyons.com
IP; digital media; IT; data protection; ads; website development & e-commerce; information security & fraud; telecoms

Taylor Wessing
Carmelite, 50 Victoria Embankment
London EC4Y 0DX
020 7300 7000
www.talyorwessing.com
Patents, copyright & other IP

Teacher Stern Selby
37–41 Bedford Row
London WC1R 4JH
020 7242 3191
g.shear@tsslaw.com
www.tsslaw.com
IT; IP; internet & e-commerce; data protection; telecoms & risk management

Thompsons
Congress House
23–28 Great Russell Street
London WC1B 3LW
020 7290 0000
info@thompsons.law.co.uk
www.thompsons.law.co.uk
Represents several media unions

Thomson Snell & Passmore
3 Lonsdale Gardens
Tunbridge Wells, Kent TN1 1NX
01892 510000
mcarter-jones@ts-p.co.uk
www.ts-p.co.uk
E-commerce & IP law

Travers Smith Braithwaite
10 Snow Hill, London EC1A 2AL
020 7295 3000
travers.smith@traverssmith.com
www.TraversSmith.com
IT & e-commerce; media & IP; contracts

Martin Truman & Co Solicitors
76 Fore Street, Topsham
Exeter, Devon EX3 0HQ
01392 879414
info@truelegal.co.uk
www.truelegal.co.uk
Internet, web & e-law

Turner Parkinson
Hollins Chambers, 64a Bridge Street
Manchester, Lancashire M3 3BA
0161 833 1212
tp@tp.co.uk
www.tp.co.uk
IP; computer contracts & e-commerce

Tweedie & Prideaux
5 Lincoln's Inn Fields
London WC2A 3BT
020 7405 1234
enquiry@tweedieandprideaux.co.uk
www.tweedieandprideaux.co.uk
Media & IT law

Veale Wasbrough
Orchard Court, Orchard Lane
Bristol
South Gloucestershire BS1 5WS
0117 925 2020
www.vwl.co.uk
IP esp tech, computer systems & e-commerce

Wake Smith
68 Clarkehouse Road, Sheffield
South Yorkshire S10 2LJ
0114 266 6660
legal@wake-smith.com
www.wake-smith.co.uk
Media & entertainment law; global tech licensing contracts; agency, distribution & marketing agreements

Watson Farley & Williams
15 Appold Street, London EC2A 2HB
020 7814 8000
lchappell@wfw.com
www.wfw.com
Telecoms, media & tech: for operators, regulators, equipment & maintenance providers, internet services, content providers, e-commerce users & developers

Weightman Vizards
High Holborn House
52–54 High Holborn
London WC1V 6RL
020 7067 4506
www.weightmanvizards.com
IP & commercial contracts

Wiggin & Co
95 Promenade, Cheltenham
Gloucestershire GL50 1WG
01242 224114
law@wiggin.co.uk
www.wiggin.co.uk
Broadcast media, telecoms, e-commerce, advertising, publishing, gaming, music, IP, content & regulation

Willoughby & Partners
The Isis Building, Thames Quay
193 Marsh Wall, London E14 9SG
020 7345 8888
Oxford: 01865 791990
rouse@iprights.com
www.iprights.com
IP services worldwide in TV, film, entertainment & publishing sectors inc agreements, rights, licensing & defence of infringement

Wilmer Cutler & Pickering
4 Carlton Gardens
London SW1Y 5AA
020 7872 1000
www.wilmer.com
For broadcasters, publishers, cable programmers, ISPs, journalists, personalities & others

Wollastons
Brierly Place, New London Road
Chelmsford, Esssex CM2 0AP
01245 211211
enquiries@wollastons.co.uk
www.wollastons.co.uk
IP inc agreements, licensing, trademark registration, infringement of copyright, passing off, breach of confidence, warranties & liability, internet trade & portal development

Wragge & Co
3 Waterhouse Square
142 Holborn, London EC1N 2SW
0870 903 1000
mail@wragge.com
www.wragge.com
Media business services from content creation & exploitation to financing & corporate development

Wright Hassall
9 Clarendon Place, Leamington Spa
Warwickshire CV32 5QP
01926 886688
email@wrighthassall.co.uk
www.wrighthassall.co.uk
IP; broadcasting rights, contracts & TV channel building; sponsorship; publishing inc copy review & clearance; advertising; data protection; e-commerce; sports finance & business; dispute resolution & avoidance; music agreements & contracts

Wright Johnston & Mackenzie
302 St Vincent Street
Glasgow G2 5RZ
0141 248 3434
enquiries@wjm.co.uk
www.wjm.co.uk
IP & dispute resolution

■ *IP = Intellectual property*

Copyright associations

Authors' Licensing & Collecting Society (ALCS)
Marlborough Court, 14–18 Holborn
London EC1N 2LE
020 7395 0600
alcs@alcs.co.uk
www.alcs.co.uk
UK collecting society for writers & their successors

British Copyright Council
Copyright House
29–33 Berners Street
London W1T 3AB
01986 788122
copyright@bcc2.demon.co.uk
Copyright watchdog

Copyright Licensing Agency
90 Tottenham Court Road
London W1T 4LP
020 7631 5555
cla@cla.co.uk
www.cla.co.uk
Administers copying rights

Design and Artists Copyright Society (DACS)
Parchment House
13 Northburgh Street
London EC1V 0JP
020 7336 8811
info@dacs.org.uk
www.dacs.org.uk
Copyright & collecting society for visual artists

Federation Against Copyright Theft (Fact)
Unit 7, Victory Business Centre
Worton Road, Isleworth
Middlesex TW7 6DB
020 8568 6646
contact@fact-uk.org.uk
www.fact-uk.org.uk
Anti-piracy

Irish Copyright Licensing Agency
Irish Writers' Centre
19 Parnell Square, Dublin 1
Republic of Ireland
00 353 1 872 9202
icla@esatlink.com
Operates scheme for providing & requesting copyright

Patent Office
Concept House, Cardiff Road
Newport NP10 8QQ
0845 950 0505
enquiries@patent.gov.uk
www.patent.gov.uk
Patents, trademarks, design & copyright

Performing Right Society
29–33 Berners Street
London W1T 3AB
020 7580 5544
see website
www.prs.co.uk
Collects & distributes music royalties

Public Lending Right
Richard House, Sorbonne Close
Stockton-on-Tees TS17 6DA
01642 604699
registrar@plr.uk.com
www.plr.uk.com
Library payment scheme for authors

Publishers Licensing Society
37–41 Gower Street
London WC1E 6HH
020 7299 7730
pls@pls.org.uk
www.pls.org.uk
Supports Copyright Licensing Agency

UK Copyright Bureau
110 Trafalgar Road, Portslade
East Sussex BN41 1GS
info@copyrightbureau.co.uk
www.copyrightbureau.co.uk
Copyright service for creators

Writers, Artists and their Copyright Holders (Watch)
David Sutton
Director of Research Projects
University of Reading Library
PO Box 223, Whiteknights
Reading RG6 6AE
0118 931 8783
UK: d.c.sutton@reading.ac.uk
US: hrcweb@hrc.utexas.edu
www.watch-file.com
Database containing primarily names & addresses of copyright holders & contacts for authors & artists whose archives are housed in libraries in North America & UK

Media law journals

Entertainment and Media Law Reports
Sweet and Maxwell
100 Avenue Road, London NW3 3PF
020 7393 7000
marketinginformation@sweetandmaxwell.co.uk
www.sweetandmaxwell.co.uk
6pa

Entertainment Law Review
Sweet and Maxwell
100 Avenue Road, London NW3 3PF
020 7393 7000
marketinginformation@sweetandmaxwell.co.uk
www.sweetandmaxwell.co.uk
8pa

International Journal of Communications Law and Policy
Offentlich-rechtliche Abteilung
Universitatsstrasse 14–15
48143 Munster, Germany
00 49 251 832 8411
www.digital-law.net/IJCLP
2pa, Jan & July

IP Law and Business
International Publications
020 7936 9401
rmenzies@amlaw-international.com
www.ipww.com
12pa & annual digest issue

Media Law and Policy
New York Law School
57 Worth Street, New York
NY 10013-2960, USA
001 212 431 2899 x4305
aabrigo@nyls.edu
www.nyls.edu/pages/1572.asp

Media Lawyer
01229 716622
Media_lawyer@pa.press.net
www.medialawyer.press.net
Bi-monthly

Diversity

It was Greg Dyke's last stand. Just 48 hours before the Hutton verdict ended his tenure as director general, the BBC's boss was in bullish mood: his controversial quotas for the recruitment of ethnic minority staff – set in 2000, when he called the organisation "hideously white" – had been narrowly met. For the first time at the BBC, at the end of 2003, more than 10 per cent of staff, and more than 4 per cent of senior BBC managers, were from ethnic minorities. Cultural diversity, went the message, was not an issue that the corporation would no longer ignore.

Some criticisms remain. More than one-third of people in London are from ethnic minorities – and as that is where the corporation does much of its recruiting, the 10 per cent figure still seems low. Comedian Lenny Henry wrote in November 2003 that more black and Asian people still needed to be involved in the decision-making in TV: "It has changed significantly in the last 10 years," he told a discussion on the Guardian Unlimited website, "but I think our problem is we are impatient for change." Nonetheless, on the same day as it announced its 2003 figures, the BBC announced further targets for the end of 2007, of 12.5 per cent of staff and 7 per cent of senior managers. Change is slow, but it is happening.

Statistics show that the BBC is ahead of the game. In broadcasting, the sector skills council (Skillset) reported in 2004 that just 7.4 per cent of people from ethnic minorities work in film and TV. In advertising, the Institute of Practitioners in Advertising reported in 2003 that only 4 per cent of agencies' employees are from ethnic minorities; in creative jobs, the record was even worse. (The number of campaigns featuring black and Asian people did, however, rise to about 7 per cent in 2004.) In publishing, Bookseller magazine ran an informal survey of cultural diversity in its industry: it found that 14 per cent of the staff sample was of black or Asian ethnic origin. The top jobs, it said, were dominated by white, middle-class men. No comprehensive study of ethnic minority representation yet covers newspapers and magazines.

Getting the staff in is one thing: persuading people from ethnic minorities to join the audience is another. There is "little evidence so far that the BBC is attracting more people from ethnic minorities to its output", the BBC's governors wrote in the 2003 annual report. So in May 2004, the corporation launched its "Asian Archers", Silver Street, a soap on its digital Asian Network. Producers hoped the programme would fare better than The Crouches, BBC1's first all-black sitcom, which received a pasting from the critics: Michael Eboda, editor of community newspaper New Nation, called that programme "about as funny as being carjacked". Behind his criticism was an impression that the characters were no more than "working-class white people of a different hue"; the writer, he noted, was white. "We have our own culture,"

"We are impatient for change"

Lenny Henry

he wrote, "be it African or Caribbean or even black British. But this is not evident in The Crouches."

In October, meanwhile, a BBC undercover investigation exposed a police recruit who wore a clan-style hood at a training centre as he simulated the beating of an Asian colleague. The report was widely heralded as an important piece of investigative public service journalism about race.

The past year has seen a number of high-profile media figures also hauled over the coals over race-related remarks. In August 2003, broadcasting regulators upheld a complaint against the provocative LBC DJ Nick Ferrari, for encouraging listeners to make racist comments. The following January, the chat show Kilroy was taken off air after its presenter, Robert Kilroy-Silk, made anti-Arab remarks in the Sunday Express; the replacement programme, Now You're Talking, continued to be made by Mr Kilroy-Silk's production company until mid-June. In April, Ron Atkinson resigned from his roles as football pundit at both ITV and the Guardian after making racist remarks about the Chelsea defender Marcel Desailly. Finally, and most bizarrely, the Express owner Richard Desmond shocked Telegraph executives by goose-stepping around a meeting with them in April, suggesting that all Germans were Nazis. There is clearly still a long way to go.

The minority press

Quite apart from the ethnic minority journalists in "mainstream" media, there is a thriving ethnic minority press. The contacts section of this book lists magazines and newspapers serving a rich diversity of minority communities – see page 325.

The top story in the sector was the sale of the Voice, Britain's best-known black publication. The newspaper was the brainchild of Val McCalla, who launched the newspaper from an east London council flat in 1982. Following his death in August 2002, his estate faced the decision as to how to sell the title. After prolonged interest from the Ethnic Media Group – which owns the newspaper's main rival, New Nation – it was finally bought in June 2004 by the Jamaica Gleaner, a highly regarded Caribbean newspaper, for an undisclosed sum.

In 2003, minority magazine publishers also joined forces to try to persuade advertisers of the importance of the "black pound". The ethnic minority market is worth up to £32bn, according to the Institute of Practitioners in Advertising, yet there is a dearth of advertising in black community newspapers – so the Black Independent Publishers Association was set up to try to combat the problem. Meanwhile, the IPA also reported that advertisers rarely try to target ethnic minority people unless there is a specific "ethnic brief".

One issue that continues to exercise ethnic minority journalists is the "multiculturalism" debate – or rather, how far multiculturalism should be sacrificed for the sake of inclusivity. The answer, it seems, is not much. After the head of the Commission for Racial Equality, Trevor Phillips, said minorities should strive to behave like white Britons, the online magazine Asians in Media conducted a survey of more than 200 minority journalists – of whom 57 per cent thought Mr Phillips should stand down. More than 70 per cent said his comments were not justified, although more than 90 per cent did believe in greater integration along with the retention of non-British cultures.

Women

The widespread sexism of the media industry of the 1970s is now largely a thing of the past, but there remain problems. In particular, women find it difficult to break into the higher echelons of management: just 13 of the 2004 MediaGuardian 100 were women, although they included the culture and media secretary, the chief executive at Trinity Mirror, the director of television at the BBC, and the editor of the Sun.

In broadcasting, the Skillset 2003 survey showed that women make up just 38 per cent of the workforce: they were only a significant majority in certain roles, such as make-up and hairdressing (94 per cent), wardrobe (80 per cent) and cinema cleaners (71 per cent). But the survey did show that women are beginning to break into technical roles such as camera operating, traditionally the domain of men: 18 per cent this year, well up on 10 per cent the year before.

Age

Ageism remains the media's dirty little secret. Many media companies – in common with the rest of industry – still recruit younger, relatively inexperienced (and cheaper) staff in preference to someone over 40. Nevertheless, it was good to see Michael Parkinson, 69 years young, signing a contract rumoured to be worth £1.5m as he was poached by ITV; while Bruce Forsyth, 76, returned to BBC1's Saturday primetime with Strictly Come Dancing, his career relaunched by a spectacular performance as presenter of Have I Got News For You.

Disability

Disability is another area where the media could do better. Just 1.1 per cent of people employed in broadcasting are disabled; but after media secretary Tessa Jowell last year called on broadcasters to recruit a representative number, the BBC responded by launching "disabled quotas". The corporation says it wants at least one disabled character in each high-profile BBC1 series; one disabled contestant in 50 on high-profile quiz shows; and one disabled person in high-profile factual and leisure shows such as Changing Rooms and Bargain Hunt. It also pledged to boost the numbers of disabled people on its other main channels.

My generation **Sunny Hundal**

It was the chairman of the Commission for Racial Equality, Trevor Phillips, who this year reignited the multiculturalism debate among ethnic minority journalists in Britain. In a series of public remarks including an interview to the Times, he discouraged non-white Britons from emphasising their "foreignness", saying they should "retain a core of Britishness" instead.

"When we stress our foreignness instead of claiming our right to be British," he said, "we surrender our place in society. We all know how patronised we feel when people talk to us as though we are foreigners, even though their intent is to make us feel at home. The fact is that we are at home already."

For those remarks, ethnic minority journalists took against him. In a poll of nearly 200 media professionals by Asians in Media magazine, more than 70% disagreed with him – and 57% said he should resign.

Nevertheless, during the summer, I noticed a huge proportion of young British Asians expressing their Britishness – by supporting England in Euro 2004, and flying the St George flag with pride.

Why the seeming disparity between the two points of view?

Like most of my friends and peers, I am a British citizen. I love London and feel a part of this city and this country. I take part in the media and the political process. I go to the pub, listen to Jazz FM and I fanatically followed Spitting Image. At the same time I eat Indian food, frequently speak in Panjabi, watch Bollywood movies, listen to Indian music and attend Asian events.

In the context of this hybrid culture, most approaches to multiculturalism are fraught with danger, because they don't take into account the wide range of opinions on how we ethnic minorities see ourselves and fit into the UK. There are the liberals, conservatives, traditionalists, progressives, the highly religious and secular Asians too, same as any.

Take media as an example. From an Asian media rooted in foreign languages, the industry is increasingly aiming for a growing second- to third-generation demographic where English is the primary language of communication. Magazines, radio stations and websites catering for the young affluent generation are booming.

The paradox is that while we are increasingly soaked in British culture, we want to retain the right to pick and choose between British and Asian culture. The Asian media becomes part of this equation. Supporting England and feeling British does not have to mean playing down, or not taking pride in, Asian heritage and roots.

The middle ground between them, of course, should be explored in the media – but the media has become part of the problem. People like Phillips stress cultural homogeneity partly because they want to neutralise a sensationalist rightwing press, bent on whipping up hysteria against immigrants. But can you really appease a monster?

There is only one way out of this: if you can't beat them, join them. Whether to ensure better representation on TV, counteract press hysteria, or just to promote a wider range of news stories from minority communities, we need to get more people from ethnic minorities into the media.

From the media's point of view, it not only makes commercial sense to reach out to new markets – but because it helps add perspective to often one-sided news.

But with the lack of diversity in the media workforce, perpetuated by the current paranoid climate, minorities are distrustful of our industry.

Before anyone asks Asians to be more "British", it might help to examine how the media can be complicit in pushing them the other way.

Sunny Hundal is founder and editor of Asians in Media [www.asiansinmedia.org], an online magazine reporting on the media

Diversity Contacts

Media diversity associations

Age Concern
Astral House, 1268 London Road
London SW16 4ER
020 8765 7200
www.ageconcern.co.uk

Age Positive
Department for Work and Pensions
Room W8d, Moorfoot
Sheffield S1 4PQ
agepositive@dwp.gsi.gov.uk
www.agepositive.gov.uk/
Age diversity in employment

Broadcaster and Creative Industries Disability Network
Employers' Forum on Disability
Nutmeg House, 60 Gainsford Street
London SE1 2NY
020 7403 3020
jenny.stevens@employers-forum.co.uk
www.employers-forum.co.uk
Employers organisation

Commission for Racial Equality (CRE)
St Dunstan's House
201–211 Borough High Street
London SE1 1GZ
020 7939 0000
info@cre.gov.uk
www.cre.gov.uk

Creative Collective
239a Uxbridge Road
Shepherds Bush, London W12 9DL
020 8576 6300
info@thecreativecollective.com
www.thecreativecollective.com
Aims to develop social policy on diversity and to empower community groups to harness media

Cultural Diversity Network (CDN)
c/o Channel 4, 124 Horseferry Road
London SW1P 2TX
diversitydatabase@channel4.co.uk
www.cdndiversitydatabase.tv
Database for ethnic minorities in broadcasting

Digital Media Access Group
Applied Computing
University of Dundee
Dundee DD1 4HN
01382 345050
info@dmag.org.uk
www.dmag.org.uk/aboutus/default.asp
Promotes new media accessibility

Disability Rights Commission
Freepost MID02164
Stratford upon Avon CV37 9BR
0845 762 2633
enquiry@drc-gb.org
www.drc-gb.org

Diversity Database
BBC Television Centre
London W12 7RJ
020 8743 8000
diversity.database@bbc.co.uk
www.bbc.co.uk/info/policies/diversity.shtml

Emma Awards
67–69 Whitfield Street
London W1T 4HF
020 7636 1233
mail@emma.tv
www.emma.tv
Multicultural media awards

Equal Opportunities Commission
Arndale House, Arndale Centre
Manchester M4 3EQ
0845 601 5901
info@eoc.org.uk
www.eoc.org.uk

International Association of Women in Radio and Television
Radio Norway International, Norwegian Broadcasting NRK
0340, Oslo, Norway
00 47 230 48441
nik@netactive.co.za
www.iawrt.org

International Women's Media Foundation
1625K Street NW, Suite 1275
Washington, DC 20006, USA
00 1 202 496 1992
info@iwmf.org
www.iwmf.org

PressWise Trust
38 Easton Business Centre
Felix Road, Bristol BS5 0HE
0117 941 5889
pw@presswise.org.uk
www.presswise.org.uk
Independent media ethics charity

Society of Women Writers & Journalists
Calvers Farm, Thelveton
Diss IP21 4NG
01379 740 550
zoe@zoeking.com
www.swwt.co.uk

Spoken Word Publishing Association (SWPA)
c/o Macmillan Audio
20 New Wharf Road
London N1 9RR
020 7014 6041
audio@penguin.co.uk
www.swpa.co.uk

Women and Equality Unit
35 Great Smith Street
London SW1P 3BQ
0845 001 0029
info-womenandequalityunit@dti.gsi.gov.uk
www.womenandequalityunit.gov.uk

Women in Film and Television
6 Langley Street
London WC2H 9JA
020 7240 4875
emily@wftv.org.uk
www.wftv.org.uk

Women in Journalism
wijUK@aol.com
www.womeninjournalism.co.uk

Women in Publishing
info@wipub.org.uk
www.wipub.org.uk

Women's Radio Group
27 Bath Road, London W4 1LJ
020 8995 5442
wrg@zelo.demon.co.uk
www.womeninradio.org.uk
Training, info and production facilities

Minority press

Disability

Big Print
Big Print, 2 Palmyra Square North
Warrington WA1 1JQ
01925 242222
sales@big-print.co.uk
www.big-print.co.uk
Weekly. Large print news. Editor: Trevor Buckley

Break Times
Winged Fellowship Trust
20–32 Pentonville Road
London N1 9XD
020 7833 2594
admin@wft.org.uk
www.wft.org.uk
2pa. Physical disabilities and carers. Editor: James Hale

Breathe Easy
The British Lung Foundation
73–75 Goswell Road
London EC1V 7ER
020 7688 5555
info@britishlungfoundation.com
www.lunguk.org/
Quarterly, Lung disease. Editor: Humphrey Cochrane

Communication
The National Autistic Society
393 City Road, London EC1V 1NG
020 7833 2299
publications@nas.org.uk
www.nas.org.uk
3pa. Autism. Editor: Anne Cooper

Devon Link
Devon County Council and
Torbay Council
Room A123
Social Services Directorate
County Hall, Topsham Road
Exeter EX2 4QR
01392 382332
joanne.white@devon.gov.uk
Quarterly. People with physical & sensory disabilities, & carers. Editor: Joanne White

Disability Now
Scope, 6 Market Road
London N7 9PW
020 7619 7323
editor@disabilitynow.org.uk
www.disabilitynow.org.uk
Monthly. Editor: Mary Wilkinson

Disability Times
112 Craven Road
London W5 2TL
020 8566 1202
dtnews@btclick.com
www.disabilitytimes.co.uk
9pa. Editor: Teresa Moore

Disabled and Supportive Carer
Euromedia Associates
Unit 8, Chorley West Business Park
Ackhurst Road, Chorley PR7 1NL
0870 444 8955
editorial@euromedia-al.com
6pa. Editor: Richard Cheeseborough

Disabled Motorist
Cottingham Way
Thrapston NN14 4PL
01832 734724
LesleyEBrowne@aol.com
www.ddmc@ukonline.co.uk
Monthly. Editor: Lesley Browne

DISH Update
DISH, 45 Grosvenor Road
St Albans AL1 3AW
01727 813815
info@dish4info.co.uk
www.dish4info.co.uk
Quarterly. Hertfordshire. Editor: Jane Fookes

Epilepsy Today
Epilepsy Action, New Anstey House
Gate Way Drive, Yeadon
Leeds LS19 7XY
0113 2108800
smitchell@epilepsy.org.uk
www.epilepsy.org.uk
Quarterly. Editor: Sue Mitchell

FreeHand
Abucon, 13 Vincent Square
London SW1P 2LX
020 7834 1066
info@abucon.co.uk
www.abucon.co.uk
6pa. Elderly disabled in their own homes. Editor: Liza Jones

Jigsaw
DISH, 45 Grosvenor Road
St Albans AL1 3AW
01727 813815
info@dish4info.co.uk
www.dish4info.co.uk
Quarterly. Young people. Editor: Jane Fookes

London Disability News
Greater London Action on Disability
336 Brixton Road, London SW9 7AA
020 7346 5800
b.humphreys@glad.org.uk
www.glad.org.uk
10pa. Editor: Michael Turner

Motability Lifestyle
CBC Media, Unit 4–5 Greenwich Quay
Clarence Road, London SE8 3EY
020 8469 9700
mike.trounce@cbcmedia.co.uk
www.cbcmedia.co.uk
Quarterly. Motability vehicles. Editor: Mike Trounce

MS Matters
MS Society, 372 Edgware Road
London NW2 6ND
020 8438 0700
info@mssociety.org.uk
www.mssociety.org.uk
6pa. Editor: Debbie Reeves

New Beacon
Royal National Institute of the Blind
Falcon Park, Neasden Lane
London NW10 1RN
020 7878 2307
beacon@rnib.org.uk
www.rnib.org.uk
11pa. For those with sight problems. Editor: Ann Lee

New Pathways
The MS Resource Centre
Unit 7, Peartree Business Centre
Peartree Road, Stanway
Colchester CO3 0JN
01206 505444
info@msrc.co.uk
www.msrc.co.uk
6pa. MS issues. Editor: Judy Graham

Ouch!
Room 2507, BBC White City
201 Wood Lane
London W12 7TS
020 8450 1018
ouch@bbc.co.uk
www.bbc.co.uk/ouch
Website. Producer: Damon Rose

One in Seven Magazine
The Royal National Institute for
Deaf People
19–23 Featherstone Street
London EC1Y 8SL
020 7296 8000
oneinseven@rnid.org.uk
www.rnid.org.uk
6pa. For the deaf. Editor: Dawn Egan

The Parkinson Magazine
Parkinson's Disease Society of the UK
215 Vauxhall Bridge Road
London SW1V 1EJ
020 7931 8080
bcormie@parkinsons.org.uk
www.parkinsons.org.uk
Quarterly. Editor: Barbara Cormie

Pinpoint
Disability West Midlands
Prospect Hall, College Walk
Selly Oak, Birmingham B29 6LE
0121 414 1616
pinpoint@dwm.org.uk
www.dwm.org.uk
6pa. Editor: Pete Millington

Positive Nation
The UK Coalition of People Living
with HIV and Aids (UKC)
250 Kennington Lane
London SE11 5RD
020 7564 2121
editor@positivenation.co.uk
www.positivenation.co.uk
10pa. Issues for people with HIV/AIDS. Editor: Amanda Elliott

Pure
The National Kidney Research Fund
Kings Chambers, Priestgate
Peterborough PE1 1FG
01733 704650
louisecox@nkrf.org.uk
www.nkrf.org.uk
Quarterly. Editor: Louise Cox

RADAR Bulletin
Royal Association for Disability
and Rehabilitation
12 City Forum, 250 City Road
London EC1V 8AF
020 7250 3222
radar@radar.org.uk
www.radar.org.uk
11pa. Civil rights issues for the disabled. Editor: John Stanford

Soundaround
Soundaround Associations
74 Glentham Road, Barnes
London SW13 9JJ
020 8741 3332
freephone for advice: 0800 917 6008
nigel@soundaround.org
www.soundaround.org
Monthly. Visually impaired, worldwide. Editor: Nigel Vee

Stroke News
The Stroke Association
Stroke House, 240 City Road
London EC1V 2PR
020 7566 0300
www.stroke.org.uk
Quarterly

Talk
The National Deaf Children's Society
15 Dufferin Street, London EC1Y 8UR
020 7490 8656
ndcs@ndcs.org.uk
www.ndcs.org.uk
6pa. For deaf children. Editor: Jo Kelly

Talking Sense
Sense, National Deafblind and
Rubella Association
11–13 Clifton Terrace, Finsbury Park
London N4 3SR
020 7272 7774
enquiries@sense.org.uk
www.sense.org.uk
3pa. Deafblind. Editor: Colin Anderson

Typetalk Update
Paver Downes Associates
2 Queens Square, Liverpool L1 1RH
0151 293 0505
hogan@paverdownes.co.uk
www.typetalk.org
6pa. Down's syndrome. Editor: Rachel Brough

Viewpoint
Mencap, 123 Golden Lane
London EC1Y 0RT
020 7696 5599
viewpoint@mencap.org.uk
www.mencap.org.uk/viewpoint
6pa. Learning disabilities. Editor: Faiza Fareed

Yes!
Yes! Promotions, 36–38 Avenue Road
Hartlepool TS24 8AT
01429 282009
enquiries@yesmagazine.org.uk
www.yesmagazine.org.uk
6pa. Disability positive thinking. Editor: Stephen Wharton

Gay and lesbian

3sixty
Newsquest (Sussex), Argus House
Crowhurst Road, Hollingbury
Brighton BN1 8AR
01273 561618
info@3sixtymag.co.uk
www.3sixtymag.co.uk
Monthly. Editor: Geoff Tourle

Attitude
Northern and Shell
Northern and Shell Tower
4 Selsdon Way, London E14 9GL
020 7308 5090
attitude@nasnet.co.uk
Monthly. Editor: Adam Mattera

AXM
Blue Maverick Media
2 Charlotte Road, London EC2A 3DH
020 7749 1970
mike@axm-mag.com
www.axm-mag.com
Monthly. Editor: Mike Dent

Dent
All Points North Publications
Walk 34, Middleton Road
Leeds LS27 8BB
0870 125 5555
editor@bent.com
www.bent.com
11–12pa. Editor: Christopher Amos

Boyz
PP and B, 63–69 New Oxford Street
London WC1A 1DG
020 7845 4300
hudson@boyz.co.uk
www.boyz.co.uk
Weekly. Editor: David Hudson

Diva
Millivres-Prowler
Unit M, Spectrum House
32–34 Gordon House Road
London NW5 1LP
020 7424 7400
edit@divamag.co.uk
www.divamag.co.uk
Monthly. Editor: Jane Czyzselska

G3
G3 Magazine, Oxford House
49a Oxford Road, London N4 3EY
020 7272 0093
info@g3magazine.co.uk
www.g3magazine.co.uk
Monthly. Editor: Sarah Garrett

Gay Times
Millivres-Prowler
Unit M, Spectrum House
32–34 Gordon House Road
London NW5 1LP
020 7424 7400
edit@gaytimes.co.uk
www.gaytimes.co.uk
Monthly. Editor: Vicky Powell

Gay.com UK
22–23 Carnaby Street
London W1F 7DB
020 7734 3700
info@uk.gay.com
www.uk.gay.com
Editor: Christine Townsend

Midlands Zone
What's On Magazine Group
5–6 Shoplatch
Shrewsbury SY1 1HF
01743 281777
info@zonemag.com
Monthly. Editor: Martin Monahan

Outnorthwest
Unity House
15 Pritchard Street (off Charles Street)
Manchester M1 7DA
0161 235 8035
editor@outnorthwest.com
www.outhnorthwest.com
Monthly free, published by the Lesbian and Gay Foundation. Editor: Grahame Robertson

Pink Paper
PP and B, 63–69 New Oxford Street
London WC1A 1DG
020 7845 4300
editorial@pinkpaper.co.uk
www.pinkpaper.com
Weekly. Editor: Tris Reid-Smith

Refresh
CBC Media, Unit 4–5 Greenwich Quay
Clarence Road, London SE8 3EY
020 8469 9700
refresh@cbcmedia.co.uk
www.refreshmag.co.uk
Monthly. Editor: David Tickner

ScotsGay
Pageprint, PO Box 666
Edinburgh EH7 5YW
0131 539 0666
editorial@scotsgay.co.uk
www.scotsgay.co.uk
Monthly. Editor: John Hein

Stonewall Newsletter
Stonewall, 46 Grosvenor Gardens
London SW1W OEB
020 7881 9440
info@stonewall.org.uk
www.stonewall.org.uk
Quarterly. Editor: Jodie West

UKBlackOut.com
0870 204 8071
www.ukblackout.com
Website. For black lesbians and gays

Cultural and ethnic minorities

Ad-Diplomasi News Report
PO Box 138, Chelsea
London SW3 6BH
020 7286 1372
www.ad-diplomasi.com
Monthly. Arabic. Editor: Raymond Atallah

African Times
Ethnic Media Group
Unit 2 Whitechapel Technology Centre
65 Whitechapel Road
London E1 1DU
020 7650 2000
africantimes@ethnicmedia.co.uk
www.ethnicmedia.co.uk
Weekly. Editor: Eminike Pio

Al Arab
Al Arab Publishing House
159 Acre Lane, London SW2 5UA
020 7274 9381
editor@alarab.co.uk
www.alarab.co.uk
Daily. Editor: As Elhouni

Al-Jamila
Saudi Research and Marketing UK
Arab Press House, 184 High Holborn
London WC1V 7AP
020 7831 8181
aljamila@hhsaudi.com
www.arab.net
Monthly. Upper and middle-income Arab women. Editor: Sanaa Al-Hadethee

Al-Majalla
Saudi Research and Marketing UK
Arab Press House, 184 High Holborn
London WC1V 7AP
020 7831 8181
al-majalla@hhsaudi.com
www.al-majalla.com
Weekly. Arab matters. Editor: Fahed Al-Tayash

Anglo-Hellenic Review
Anglo-Hellenic League
23 Jeffreys Street, London NW1 9PS
020 7267 3877
paul.watkins@virgin.net
www.hellenicbookservice.com/ahr.htm
2pa. Cultural affairs covering Greece and Britain. Editor: Paul Watkins

Asharq Al-Awsat
Saudi Research and Marketing UK
Arab Press House, 184 High Holborn
London WC1V 7AP
020 7831 8181
editorial@asharqalawsat.com
www.aawsat.com
Daily. Saudi Arabia. Editor: Mohammed Alutam

Asian Express
Smart Asian Media, 211 Picadilly
London W1J 9HF
020 7917 2744
info@asianxpress.newspapers.com
www.asianxpressnewspaper.com
Weekly. Editor: Vallabh Kaviraj

Asian News
01706 898933
www.theasiannews.co.uk
Website. Editor: Steve Hammond

Asian Times
Ethnic Media Group
Unit 2 Whitechapel Technology Centre
65 Whitechapel Road
London E1 1DU
020 7650 2000
asiantimes@ethnicmedia.co.uk
www.ethnicmedia.co.uk
Weekly. Editor: Isaac Hamza

Asians in Media
243 North Hyde Lane
Southall, Middlesex UB2 5TE
020 7737 0749
sunny.hundal@asiansinmedia.org
www.asiansinmedia.org
Weekly. Guide to the British Asian media industry. Editor: Sunny Hundal

barfiCulture
www.barficulture.com
Website. British Asians. Editor: Sunny Hundal

Blacknet
46 Deptford Broadway
London SE8 4PH
0870 746 5000
information@blacknet.co.uk
www.blacknet.co.uk
Community website for black people in Britain. Editor: Junior Wilson

Black Information Link
Suite 12, 9 Cranmer Road
London SW9 6EJ
020 7582 1990
blink1990@blink.org.uk
www.blink.org.uk
Website

Canada Post
RoseMaple Media, PO Box No 2
No. 4 Circular Road
London W5 2QA
020 7840 9765
info@canadapost.co.uk
www.canadapost.co.uk
Monthly. Editor: Paula Adamick

Caribbean Times
Ethnic Media Group
Unit 2 Whitechapel Technology Centre
65 Whitechapel Road
London E1 1DU
020 7650 2000
caribbeantimes@ethnicmedia.co.uk
www.ethnicmedia.co.uk
Weekly. Editor: Ron Shillingford

Chinatown
CTM Publishing, Enterprise Centre
14a Rochdale Road
Manchester M4 4JR
0161 839 5400
enquiries@chinatownthemagazine.com
www.chinatownthemagazine.com/
Bi-monthly. English-language for Chinese

Clickwalla.com
MeMedia, Clerkenwell House
67 Clerkenwell Road
London EC1R 5BL
020 7693 8400
info@memediagroup.com
www.clickwalla.com
Website

Daily Jang London
Jang Publications, 1 Sanctuary Street
London SE1 1ED
020 7403 5833
editor@jang.globalnet.co.uk
www.jang.com.pk
Daily. Asian. Editor: Zahoor Niazi

Des Pardes
8 The Crescent, Southall UB1 1BE
020 8571 1127
despadesuk@btconnect.com
Weekly. Indian expatriates. Editor: GS Virk

Dziennik Polski
The Polish Daily (Publishers)
63 Jeddo Road, London W12 9ED
020 8740 1991
editor@dziennikpolski.co.uk
www.polishdailynews.com
Daily. Polish community in UK. Editor: Jaroslaw Kovninski

Eastern Eye
65 Whitechapel Road
London E1 1DU
020 7650 2000
aeditor@easterneyeuk.co.uk
www.ethnicmedia.co.uk
Weekly. Second- and third-generation UK Asians. Editor: Aram Singh

Eikoku News Digest
News Digest International
8–10 Long Street, London E2 8HQ
020 7749 8000
info@newsdigest.co.uk
www.newsdigest.co.uk
Weekly. Japanese. Editor: Mikiko Toshima

Filipino Observer
PO Box 20376, London NW11 8FE
020 8731 7195
editor@filipino.co.uk
Monthly. Editor: Bong Forrouzan

Garavi Gujarat
1 Silex Street, London SE1 ODW
020 7928 1234
garav@gujarat.co.uk
www.gg2.net
Weekly. Editor: Ramniknal Solanki

Gujarat Samachar
Asian Business Publications
8–12 Hoxton Market, off Coronet Street
London N1 6HG
020 7749 4080
support@abplgroup.com
www.gujarat-samachar.com/
Weekly. Editor: C Patel

Hia
Saudi Research and Marketing UK
Arab Press House, 184 High Holborn
London WC1V 7AP
020 7831 8181
hia@hhsaudi.com
Monthly. Arab women. Editor: Mai Badr

India weekly
Ethnic Media Group
White Chapel Technology Centre
65 Whitechapel Road
London E1 1DU
020 7650 2000
newsdesk@indiaweekly.co.uk
www.indiaweekly.co.uk
Weekly. Editor: Dr Premenaddy

Irish Post
Cambridge House, Cambridge Grove
Hammersmith, London W6 OLE
020 8741 0649
irishpost@lrishpost.co.uk
www.irishpost.co.uk
Weekly. Editor: Frank Murphy

Irish World
934 North Circular Road
London NW2 7JR
020 8453 7800
sales@theirishworld.com
www.theirishworld.com
Weekly. Editor: Donal Mooney

Janomot Bengali Newsweekly
Creative Media Publications
Unit 2, 20B Spelman Street
London E1 5LQ
020 7377 6032
janomot@easynet.co.uk
Weekly. Older Bangladeshi immigrants. Editor: Nabob Udden

Jewish Chronicle
25 Furnival Street, London EC4A 1JT
020 7415 1500
webmaster@thejc.com
www.jchron.co.uk
Weekly and website

Jewish Telegraph
Maccabi Complex, May Terrace
Glasgow G46 6LD
0141 621 4422
mail@jewishtelegraph.com
www.jewishtelegraph.com
Weekly. Editor: Paul Harris

La Voce degli Italiani
Scalabrine Fathers, 20 Brixton Road
London SW9 6BU
020 7735 5164
redaction@lavoce.com
www.lavoce.com
55pa. Italians in Europe. Editor: Cari Lettori

London Turkish Gazette
177 Green Lanes, Palmers Green
London N13 4UR
020 8889 5025
news@londragazete.com
www.londragazete.com
Weekly. Editor: Artun Goksan

London Welsh Magazine
London Welsh Association
157–163 Gray's Inn Road
London WC1X 8UE
020 7837 3722
gethinest@aol.com
Quarterly. Editor: Gethin Williams

Maghreb Review
45 Burton Street, London WC1H 9AL
020 7388 1840
maghrab@maghrabreview.com
www.maghrabreview.com
Quarterly. North Africa, Sub Sahara Africa, Middle East & Islam. Editor: Mohammed Ban-madani

MIL Matchmaker Magazine
Matchmaker International
PO Box 430, Pinner HA5 2TW
020 8868 1879
info@perfect-partner.com
www.perfect-partner.com
Quarterly. Asians seeking partners. Editor: Mr Bharat Raipthatha

Mauritian Abroad
Sankris Publishing, 32 Ethelbert Road
Faversham ME13 8SQ
01795 539499
eveer77807@aol.com
Quarterly. Editor: Krish Veeramah

Mauritius News
583 Wandsworth Road
London SW8 3JD
020 7498 3066
editor@mauritiusnews.co.uk
www.mauritiusnews.co.uk
Monthly. Editor: Mr Chellen

Milap Weekly
Masbro Centre, 87 Masbro Road
London W14 0LR
020 7385 8966
Weekly. Urdu-speaking community. Editor: Ramesh Soni

Muslim News
Visitcrest, PO Box 380
Harrow HA2 6LL
020 8863 8586
editor@muslimnews.co.uk
www.muslimnews.co.uk
Monthly. Editor: A. Versi

Navin Weekly
Masbro Centre, 87 Masbro Road
London W14 0LR
020 7385 8966
Weekly. South Asian community. Editor: Ramesh Soni

NetAsia.co.uk
www.netasia.co.uk
Website

New Nation
Ethnic Media Group
Unit 2 Whitechapel Technology Centre
65 Whitechapel Road
London E1 1DU
020 7650 2000
newsdesk@newnation.co.uk
www.ethnicmedia.co.uk
Weekly. Black news. Editor: Michael Eboda

New Zealand News UK
Southern Link Media, 2nd Floor
Quadrant House, 250 Kennington Lane
London SE11 5RD
020 7820 0885
editor@southernlink.co.uk
www.nznewsuk.co.uk
Weekly. Editor: Rachael Walsh

Noticias Latin America
PO Box 34783, London N7 7WD
020 7686 1633
informacion@noticias.co.uk
www.noticias.co.uk
Monthly. Editor: Albrairto Rojas

Notiun Din Bengali Newsweekly
Din Publishers, 46g Greatorex Street
London E1 5NP
020 7247 6280
news@notiundin.dlus.com
Weekly. Editor: Mohib Choudhury

Occasions Magazine
Ethnic Media Group
Unit 2, 65 White Chapel Road
Edgware, London E1 1DU
020 7650 2000
reva@dircon.co.uk
www.occasions.co.uk
Quarterly. Asians worldwide. Editor: Terry Tan

Parikiaki
534a Holloway Road
London N7 6JP
020 7272 6777
parikiakinews@yahoo.co.uk
Weekly. Cypriots in UK. Editor: Bambos Charalambous

Perdesan Monthly
PTI Media, 24 Cotton Brook Road
Sir Francis Ley Industrial Estate
Derby DE23 8YJ
01332 372851
punjabtimes@aol.com
Monthly. Asian community. Editor: Mr Purewal

Punjab Times International
PTI Derby Media
24 Cotton Brook Road
Sir Francis Ley Industrial Estate
Derby DE23 8YJ
01332 372851
punjabtimes@aol.com
Weekly. Punjabi community in UK. Editor: A Purewal

Red Hot Curry
Unit 9, Fulton Close, Argyle Way
Stevenage, Herts SG1 2AF
01438 365582
www.redhotcurry.com
Website. Asian community website. Editor: Mrs Lopa Patel

Sayidaty
Saudi Research and Marketing UK
Arab Press House, 184 High Holborn
London WC1V 7AP
020 7831 8181
sayidaty@hhsaudi.com
www.sayidaty.net
Weekly. Arab issues. Editor: Hani Nakshbandi

Sikh Courier International
The World Sikh Foundation
88 Mollison Way, Edgware
Middlesex HA8 5QW
020 8864 9228
thesikhcourier@aol.com
www.sikhfoundation.org
2pa. Sikhs. Editor: Sukhbir Singh

Snoop
Britasian Media, 5a High Street
Southall UB1 3HA
020 8571 7700
raj@snooplife.co.uk
www.snooplife.com
Monthly. Second- and third-generation UK Asians. Editor: Raj Kaushal

SomethingJewish.co.uk
PO Box 1554, Hanwell
London W7 1ZF
07976 220273
editor@somethingjewish.co.uk
www.somethingjewish.co.uk
Web. UK Jewish website. Editor: Leslie Bunder

TNT Magazine
Trader Media Group
14–15 Child's Place
Earls Court, London SW5 9RX
020 7373 3377
ian.wakeling@tntmag.co.uk
www.tntmagazine.com
Weekly. International travellers. Editor: Lyn Eyb

Ukrainian Thought
Association of Ukrainians in GB
49 Linden Gardens
London W2 4HG
020 7229 8392
Weekly. Ukrainian. Editor: Dr Swiatomyr Forstun

Ultra Journey
Japan Journals, 93 Newman Street
London W1T 3EZ
020 7255 3838
info@japanjournals.com
www.japanjournals.com
Monthly. Japanese. Editor: Ko Tejima

Weekly Gleaner
Unit 220–223, Elephant and Castle Shopping Centre
London SE1 6TE
020 7277 1714
editorial@gleaner1.demon.co.uk
http://jamaica-gleaner.com
Weekly. Caribbean and Jamaican. Editor: Michael Oban

Weekly Journey
Japan Journals, 93 Newman Street
London W1T 3EZ
020 7255 3838
lina@japanjournals.com
www.japanjournals.com
Weekly. Japanese in Britain. Editor: K Tejima

Zoneast
Elm Media Communications
4th Floor, 44 Gerrard Street
London W1D 5QG
020 7439 2288
zoneast@hotmail.com
Monthly. Chinese in Europe. Editor: Mrs Lei Wang

Religion

All The World
The Salvation Army
101 Queen Victoria Street
London EC4P 4EP
020 7332 0101
kevin-sims@salvationarmy.org
www.salvationarmy.org
Quarterly. Editor: Kevin Sims

Amar Deep Hindi Weekly
2 Chepstow Road
London W7 2BG
020 8840 3534
alphabet@globalnet.co.uk
Weekly. India and diaspora. Editor: M Kaushal

Baptist Times
Baptist Times, PO Box 54
129 Broadway, Didcot OX11 8XB
01235 517670
btadmin@bluecom.net
Weekly. Church leaders. Editor: Hazel Southam

Catholic Herald
Herald House, Lambs Passage
London EC1Y 8TQ
020 7588 3101
editorial@catholicherald.co.uk
www.catholicherald.co.uk
Weekly. Acting Editor: Luke Coppen

Catholic Times
Gabriel Communications, 1st Floor
St James' Buildings, Oxford Street
Manchester M1 6FP
0161 236 8856
kevin.flaherty@the-universe.net
www.ctonline.org
Weekly. Editor: Mark Moretti

Challenge
Authentic Media, PO Box 300
Carlisle CA3 0QS
01228 554320
steven.bunn@whsmithnet.co.uk
www.paternoster-publishing.com
Monthly. Christian. Editor: Debbie Bunn

Christian Aid News
Christian Aid, PO Box 100
London SE1 7RT
020 7620 4444
press@christian-aid.org
www.christian-aid.org.uk
Quarterly. Editor: Susan Roberts

Christian Herald
Christian Media Centre
Garcia Estate, Canterbury Road
Worthing, West Sussex BN13 1EH
01903 821082
editor@christianherald.org.uk
www.christianmedia.org.uk
Weekly. Evangelical Christian community. Editor: Russ Bravo

Christianity and Renewal
Premier Media Group (PMG)
PO Box 17911, London SW1P 4YX
020 7316 1450
john.buckeridge@premier.org.uk
www.christianityandrenewal.com
Monthly. Editor: John Buckeridge

Daily Bread
Scripture Union Publishing
207–209 Queensway, Bletchley
Milton Keynes MK2 2EB
01908 856000
laurels@scriptureunion.org.uk
www.dailybread.org.uk
Quarterly. Adult Bible readers. Editor: James Davies

Home and Family
The Mothers' Union
Mary Sumner House, 24 Tufton Street
London SW1P 3RB
020 7222 5533
homeandfamily@themothersunion.org
www.themothersunion.org
Quarterly. Editor: Jill Worth

Jewish Chronicle
25 Furnival Street
London EC4A 1JT
020 7415 1500
webmaster@thejc.com
www.jchron.co.uk
Weekly and website

Jewish Telegraph
Maccabi Complex, May Terrace
Glasgow G46 6LD
0141 621 4422
mail@jewishtelegraph.com
www.jewishtelegraph.com
Weekly. Editor: Paul Harris

Jewish.net
07976 220273
admin@jewishnet.net
www.jewishnet.net
Website. Director: Don Winer

The Life
Scripture Union Publishing
207–209 Queensway, Bletchley
Milton Keynes MK2 2EB
01908 856000
media@scriptureunion.org.uk
www.scriptureunion.org.uk/thelife
Quarterly. Editor: Adam Pettrie

Life and Work
Board of Communications
121 George Street
Edinburgh EH2 4YN
0131 225 5722
magazine@lifeandwork.org
www.lifeandwork.org
Monthly. Church of Scotland. Editor: Lynne Robertson

The Muslim News
Visitcrest, PO Box 380
Harrow HA2 6LL
020 8863 8586
editor@muslimnews.co.uk
www.muslimnews.co.uk
Monthly. Editor: A Versi

New Day
The Leprosy Mission, Goldhay Way
Orton, Goldhay
Peterborough PE2 5GZ
01733 370505
post@tlmew.org.uk
www.leprosymission.org
2pa. Editor: Mr Simon Watkinson

Presbyterian Herald
Church House, Fisherwick Place
Belfast BT1 6DW
028 9032 2284
herald@presbyterianireland.org
www.presbyterianrianireland.org
Monthly. Presbyterian. Editor: Rev Arthur Clarke

Scottish Catholic Observer
19 Waterloo Street, Glasgow G2 6BT
0141 221 4956
editorial@scottishcatholicobserver.com
www.scottishcatholicobserver.com
Weekly. Editor: Harry Conroy

Sikh Courier International
World Sikh Foundation
33 Wargrave Road, Harrow HA2 8LL
020 8864 9228
thesikhcourier@aol.com
www.sikhfoundation.org
2pa. Editor: Sukhbir Singh

SomethingJewish.co.uk
PO Box 1554, Hanwell
London W7 1ZF
07976 220273
editor@somethingjewish.co.uk
www.somethingjewish.co.uk
Web. UK Jewish website. Editor: Leslie Bunder

Ummah.com
info@ummah.com
www.ummah.org.uk
Website. Muslim/Islam

The Universe
Gabriel Communications
1st Floor, St James' Building
Oxford Street, Manchester M1 6FP
0161 236 8856
newsdesk@the-universe.net
www.totalcatholic.com
Weekly. Roman Catholics and Ireland. Editor: Joe Kelly

War Cry
101 Newington Causeway
Elephant and Castle
London SE1 6BN
020 7367 4900
warcry@salvationarmy.org.uk
www.salvationarmy.org.uk/warcry
Monthly. Christian current affairs. Editor: Major Nigel Bovey

Careers & training

University of Lincoln

Lincoln School of Journalism

BA (Hons) Journalism

Degree courses in Journalism at Lincoln's new School of Journalism aim to provide students with the key editorial skills of research, newsgathering, news evaluation and journalistic writing plus a thorough knowledge of law and public affairs in the context of intensive journalism practice. After a comprehensive grounding in essential skills, single honours students can specialise in television, radio, print or on-line media.

Students undertaking a joint honours programme can combine their journalism with one of the following: Advertising; Criminology; English; History; International Relations; Media Communications; Politics; Public Relations.

Postgraduate opportunities

The School will launch a new MA in Journalism in September 2005. This programme will cater both for graduates who wish to prepare themselves for a career in journalism and working journalists and other professionals who wish to develop research interests. The School's research interests include: journalism and literature; press and broadcasting history; the role of the popular press; press conduct and regulation and the political impact of the media.

The School is based in the UK's newest campus in the heart of the historic and beautiful city of Lincoln. Facilities include: industry-standard newsrooms, radio and television studios and editing facilities.

For further details about the undergraduate programme, please contact the Enquiry Centre, University of Lincoln, Brayford Pool, Lincoln LN6 7TS
Telephone: 01522 886644 or Email: enquiries@lincoln.ac.uk

For further information about postgraduate opportunities, please contact the Head of School, Professor John Tulloch
Telephone: 01522 886898 or Email: jtulloch@lincoln.ac.uk

UNIVERSITY OF
LINCOLN

Ask any student if they would like a career in the media, and they would probably say yes. Ask anyone in the media industry if they would rather still be a student, and they would most likely give the same answer. While a "creative" career might sound glamorous, everyone else thinks so too; and many employers, recognising this, get away with paying low or mediocre salaries for long hours, and even then offer little formal training to help employees develop. To get a foot in the door, most people will probably at some stage have to work for free; to develop professionally, many end up having to train at their own expense. Some give it up and go off to become accountants instead.

That said, if accountancy is not for you, there are many different kinds of media roles to choose from. In press and publishing you could be a news reporter, a writer of features or specialist articles, a subeditor, a production editor, a commissioning editor, or a writer for the web; in broadcasting, you could be a journalist, a presenter, a researcher, a camera operator, a director or producer. You could be a creative director in advertising, a PR agent, or a media buyer whose job it is to know the industry inside out (tip: read this book). And most, if not all these areas, need their designers, graphic artists, production gurus, marketers, sales managers, distributors and managers who – in theory at least – make the whole enterprise tick. Which is better than spending all day sitting in front of a spreadsheet.

Entry-level: courses and work experience

There are two ways of getting into any media career: first, go off and train yourself to do the job; second, do the job. You don't always have to do the first. You always have to do the second.

More and more entrants into the media are well qualified, with good degrees in media studies or other subjects; but having such a degree will not necessarily make you stand out from the crowd. Indeed, rightly or wrongly – and partly as a result of articles written by hacks who worked their way up through the regional press – "media studies" still has a poor reputation among employers as a soft option. What can make the difference is a practical qualification which suggests you have the commitment and ability to do the job.

Many parts of the media have accrediting bodies for postgraduate and training courses. In journalism, this is the National Council for the Training of Journalists (NCTJ); the courses it accredits are run either through a training contract at a regional or a local paper – the traditional route, with much to recommend it – or, popularly but competitively, at a university. Courses try to be as practical as possible: those in newspaper journalism, for example, will include all the knowledge you need plus 100wpm of shorthand; while journalism students at Preston are issued with a stylebook as if working in a newsroom. Courses will also include work experience, although students usually need work experience to get on the course in the first place.

In broadcasting, journalism courses are accredited by the Broadcast Journalism Training Council (BJTC). There are also a few highly competitive broadcast training schemes, often funded by Skillset – the skills council for the broadcast industry in general. In most parts of TV and radio, many people start as a "runner" or in a similar junior training position and gain experience and qualifications as they progress, often from BBC Training.

In PR, the Institute of Public Relations approves training courses. Many successful journalism schools now also run PR courses alongside their journalism courses, a trend that started in the US, and which has split opinion in the Observer's media pages. Patrick Weever, editor of anti-spin.com, wondered if it was possible for "the same person to teach spin and unspin"; while Chris Rushton, head of journalism and PR at Sunderland University, wrote that "to exclude knowledge of each other's professional, ethical and commercial imperatives is to blinker horizons and limit debate".

The real key to getting any job in the media, though, is work experience. The best way to get work experience is to target an individual in the organisation closest to where you want to work; send them your CV and follow it up a day or two later with a phone call. Be persistent but polite; if they are busy (and they will always say they are), ask when would be the best time to call, or – as a last resort – if there is someone else they think might be able to help you. When doing work experience, dress fairly smartly, put on your most plausible manner, and try to be as helpful as you can. If in doubt, make tea.

The job market

Jobs in the media are advertised in the Guardian on a Monday, on Guardian Unlimited Jobs (jobs.guardian.co.uk) and in other newspapers and the trade press. Most jobs that are advertised nationally attract large numbers of applications; so spend time targeting your CV and covering letter, by thinking hard about how your skills and experience best relate to the job description. Keep the CV down to one page (two at most); use a simple font such as Times New Roman (Arial if you love sans serif); and get someone who knows how to spell to read it through (not just Bill Gates).

Remember, most jobs aren't advertised: with the happy exception of the inclusive BBC, many media organisations simply recruit internally or give a job to a freelance who's been around a while. So if you're looking for a job, the best place to be is working: carry on working for free, or if you are experienced enough, charge freelance rates. So don't apply for jobs simply because they're advertised in the Guardian; better to target the right job for you, or you'll end up back where you started in a few months.

One other problem to bear in mind when looking for a job: the vast majority of media jobs – perhaps up to 80 per cent — are based in London and the south-east. National newspapers, TV production and advertising are based almost exclusively in London; most magazines are in London, with small concentrations elsewhere; while only radio, some TV, and (of course) the regional press are truly nationwide.

Freelancing

Many people who work in the media are freelances; that is, they are self-employed workers who are paid by the day or by the job. Many experienced journalists and producers become freelances out of choice, for the relative freedom it offers; there are others who are freelance by necessity because they are looking for a job. In broadcasting, according to the Skillset survey 2003, a quarter of the workforce was freelance; though this under-represented the actual freelance population, as many will not have been working on the day of the survey. Many newspaper and magazine journalists also work on a freelance basis, either writing from home or coming into the office to do reporting or subediting shifts.

There are a few major advantages to freelancing: you get to be your own boss, no one tells you what time you have to get up in the morning, and above all you have the freedom to move your career in whatever direction you choose. That's about the size of it. On the other hand, there are many major disadvantages: you never know where the next pay cheque is coming from; you have little power against companies who pay too little, too late, or attempt to appropriate the rights for your work; and you have to fill in a tax return. Remember, you should be entitled to statutory holiday pay in addition to the pay you receive, but many companies will not pay up unless you ask for it.

In broadcasting, you will work a lot of short-term contracts; so ask to see a contract up front, check their rates of pay with the broadcasters' union Bectu, and watch out for terms covering intellectual copyright and statutory holiday pay (companies often try to include holiday pay in the headline figure). In journalism, the biggest issue is rates of pay: publishers are paying reporters and subeditors less and less in real terms each year for a shift, usually by setting arbitrarily low "ceilings" for a day rate. It is up to freelances and the NUJ to work together to get the pay they deserve.

From top to bottom

Advertising

- Sir Martin Sorrell, chief executive of WPP: almost £2.5m in 2003, including pension and bonuses
- Trainee account executive: typically £18,000

Newspapers

- Paul Dacre, editor-in-chief of the Daily Mail: £899,000 in 2003
- Qualified senior journalists at the Blackpool Evening Gazette: £16,000 (source: NUJ)

Broadcasting

- Greg Dyke, former director general of the BBC: £321,000 in 2003–04, plus a £488,000 pay-off
- Minimum salary, BBC Resources, 2003–04: £11,834 (source: Bectu)

Magazines

- Tom Moloney, chief executive, Emap: £702,000 salary and bonuses in 2003
- Minimum salary, Emap Healthcare: £21,000

Further training

Training and professional development, or the lack of it, is a serious problem for the media. A survey for Media Week magazine in 2003 showed that four out of 10 employees wanted to quit their jobs; nearly 60 per cent felt that it was a lack of training that had affected their ability to make progress in their careers.

In the broadcast industry, Skillset subsidises 60 per cent of the cost of a range of short courses for freelances; but freelances will often have to pay the rest themselves. The BBC also subsidises training, and the industry body Pact can organise training for its members; but regular freelances will often have less formal training than if they worked for a big in-house team such as the BBC.

Further reading

■ Press

Guardian Unlimited Jobs
jobs.guardian.co.uk/media

■ Books

McNae's Essential Law for Journalists
LCJ MCNAE, BUTTERWORTHS 2001

Broadcast Journalism ANDREW BOYD, FOCAL PRESS 2000

Writing Feature Articles BRENDAN HENNESSY, FOCAL PRESS 1996

How to Get into Advertising ANDREA NEIDLE, CONTINUUM 2002

In Print: A Career in Journalism CHRIS ALDEN, GUARDIAN BOOKS 2004
The essential careers guide to newspapers and magazines

On Air: A Career in TV & Radio CHRIS ALDEN, GUARDIAN BOOKS 2004
The essential careers guide to television and radio

■ Other resources

Skillset
www.skillset.org

Skillsformedia
www.skillsformedia.com

NCTJ
www.nctj.com

Broadcast Journalism Training Council
www.bjtc.org.uk

Pact
www.pact.co.uk

A Mickey Mouse degree? **Steven Barnett**

I still remember my grandfather's reaction when I told him what I was going to study at university back in 1971. "Classics? What's the point of that? Who on earth's going to offer you a job after three years learning Latin and Greek? Go and do something useful." Like media studies, perhaps, which in the early 70s was about to be inaugurated as a degree course at Regent Street Poly – the first of its kind in the country.

That poly is now the University of Westminster, and media studies courses have proliferated at about the rate that classics is being abandoned. Some media studies courses are better than others – although they are traditionally lumped together by smug, ill-informed politicians trying to make a cheap point about the state of higher education. At some point, this bigotry usually extends to jibes about Mickey Mouse degrees, and ends with a weary lament about the decline of "proper" university subjects – like classics.

Any aspiring, or even existing, media studies undergraduate should have their defences prepared for the inevitable sneer – which follows a long and honourable tradition from the dismissal of English literature at the turn of the century to contempt for sociology in the 1960s. So here are three arguments to help you turn the tables on your accusers.

First, good media studies courses do not consist of sitting around watching EastEnders. In most cases, you can expect to learn about and understand the basics of a number of intellectual disciplines – including economics, philosophy, sociology, history and literature.

Debates about the nature and role of the press complaints commission, for example, can be placed in the wider context of the right to free expression, going back to Aristotle and Milton. The Human Rights Act is based on a philosophical contradiction which policymakers are still trying to unravel: free speech versus the right to privacy. Most debate about the new Communications Act presupposes an understanding of the economics of the media – conspicuously lacking in many commentators. And that's before we get into the theory and practice of journalism.

This leads to the second point, which is that no media studies degree is a passport to a job in journalism or anywhere else. Most national newspaper editors – tabloid and broadsheet – still fall into the sneer category, preferring ability and experience on the Skegness Sentinel to any kind of media degree. Don't walk into an editor's office waving your hard-earned upper second in media studies and expect to impress.

But it won't do any harm either. In areas like broadcasting, web design, PR or advertising, having some kind of specialist or technical knowledge on which to build can give you an edge over non-specialist graduates – as long as it's combined with all the other individual qualities of flair, drive, common sense and intelligence that good employers look for. Michael Jackson did not become chief executive of Channel 4 because he started with a media studies degree from Westminster, but it was a start.

Finally, all good university courses serve the same purpose, almost regardless of content: to produce self-motivated, critical, thinking adults for whom the ability to pursue independent inquiry is more important than the acquisition of knowledge for its own sake. Once you have the tools for self-improvement, you can teach yourself history, Serbo-Croat, advanced needlework or even classics. When someone asks what's the point of doing media studies, the answer is simple: what's the point of doing English, history or classics?

It will still be a while before the sneerers stop looking down their noses, but I'm hoping that one day we may see their final humiliation: when the first media studies graduate is appointed a professor of classics. My grandfather would have approved.

Steven Barnett (classics at Pembroke College, Cambridge, 1971–74) is professor of communications at the University of Westminster.

Careers & training Contacts

Media training bodies

BKSTS – The Moving Image Society
Pinewood Studios, Iver Heath
Bucks SL0 0NH
01753 656656
training@bksts.com
www.bksts.com
Film foundation, TV and digital tech, foundation sound for film and video, broadcasting engineering

Broadcast Journalism Training Council
The Secretary, 18 Miller's Close
Rippingale, Lincolnshire PE10 0TH
01778 440025
Sec@bjtc.org.uk
www.bjtc.org.uk
Accredits courses

City & Guilds
1 Giltspur Street
London EC1A 9DD
020 7294 2800
enquiry@city-and-guilds.co.uk
www.city-and-guilds.co.uk
Vocational qualifications

FT2 – Film and Television Freelance Training
Fouth Floor, Warwick House
9 Warwick Street
London W1B 5LY
020 7734 5141
info@ft2.org.uk
www.ft2.org.uk
Training for new broadcast freelancers

Film Education
21–22 Poland Street
London W1F 8QQ
020 7851 9450
postbox@filmeducation.org
www.filmeducation.org

Film First Foundation
9 Bourlet Close, London W1W 7BP
020 7580 2111
info@firstfilm.co.uk
www.firstfilm.co.uk
Training for new film writers, producers and directors

British Universities Film & Video Council
77 Wells Street, London W1T 3QJ
020 7393 1500
ask@bufvc.ac.uk
www.busvc.ac.uk
To promote the use of media within higher education

National Council for the Training of Journalists
Latton Bush Centre
Southern Way, Harlow
Essex CM18 7BL
01279 430009
info@NCTJ.com
www.nctj.com
Runs schemes for print journalists. Accredits courses

Periodicals Training Council
Queens House, 28 Kingsway
London WC2B 6JR
020 7404 4166
info1@ppa.co.uk
www.ppa.co.uk/ptc
Training arm of PPA

PMA Training
PMA House, Free Church Passage
St Ives, Cambridgeshire PE27 5AY
020 7490 7280
admin@pma-group.com
www.pma-group.com
Runs workshops and postgrad training

Skillset
Skillset: The Sector Skills Council for the Audio Visual Industries
Prospect House
80–110 New Oxford Street
London WC1A 1HB
020 7520 5757
info@skillset.org
www.skillset.org
Owned by broadcast industry; accredits courses, publishes handbooks and runs Skillsformedia service (www.skillsformedia.com)

BBC Training and development: Broadcast Training
BBC Training & Development
35 Marylebone High Street
London W1U 4PX
0870 122 0216
training@bbc.co.uk
www.bbctraining.com
All strands of broadcast training

yourcreativefuture.org
education@designcouncil.org.uk
www.yourcreativefuture.org
Guide to a creative career; sponsored by government, Design Council and Arts Council

Universities and training providers

Aberdeen, University of
King's College, Aberdeen AB24 3FX
01224 272000
www.abdn.ac.uk
▪ *MLitt visual culture.* ▪ *BA film studies with various other options; Mlitt/ MPhil/PhD film and visual studies (by research).*

Abertay, Dundee, University of
40 Bell Street, Dundee DD1 1HG
01382 308000
enquiries@abertay.ac.uk
www.abertay.ac.uk
▪ *BA (Hons) media, culture and society.*

Anglia Polytechnic University
East Road, Cambridge CB1 1PT
or Bishop Hall Lane, Chelmsford, Essex CM1 1SQ
01223 363271
answers@apu.ac.uk
www.apu.ac.uk
▪ *BA (Hons) writing (combined award); BA (Hons) communication studies.*

Barnsley College
PO Box 266, Church Street, Barnsley S70 2YW
01226 216569/216287
programme.enquiries@barnsley.ac.uk
www.barnsley.ac.uk
▪ *Fdg journalism & media production (with University of Huddersfield).*

Universities and training providers

General media: see public relations (communications).
Press/journalism & writing: also see publishing, general media (English) and broadcasting (broadcast journalism, screenwriting etc).
Broadcasting & film: also see press (writing) and multimedia (animation and digital).
Public relations & communications: excl. single advertising and marketing qualifications.
Publishing industry: also see press (writing) and new media (online and web publishing).
Multimedia, digital & new media: includes animation and special effects; also see broadcasting (television)

	general media	press/journalism & writing	broadcasting & film	public relations & communications	publishing industry	multimedia, digital & new media
Aberdeen, University of	●		●			
Abertay, Dundee, University of	●					
Anglia Polytechnic University		●				
Barnsley College		●	●			
Basingstoke College of Technology	●					●
Bath, University of			●			●
Bath Spa University College	●		●	●		●
Bell College		●	●			
Birkbeck, University of London	●		●			●
Birmingham University	●					
Blackburn College	●		●			●
Bolton Institute of Higher Education	●	●	●	●		●
Arts Institute at Bournemouth			●			●
Bournemouth University		●	●	●		●
Bradford College			●	●		●
Bradford, University of	●		●			●
Brighton, University of		●		●		
Bristol, University of			●			
Brunel University			●	●		●
Buckingham University				●		●
Bucks Chilterns University College		●	●			●
Canterbury Christ Church University College	●	●	●			●
Cardiff University		●	●	●		
Cardonald College		●	●	●		
Carmarthenshire College (Coleg Sir Gar)			●			
Central England in Birmingham, University of		●	●	●		●
Central Lancashire, University of		●	●	●		●
University College Chester	●	●	●		●	●
Chichester College	●		●			
University College Chichester	●		●			
City Literary Institute		●				
City Of Wolverhampton College		●	●			
City University, London		●	●		●	
Cleveland College of Art & Design			●			
Coleg Menai	●					●
Cornwall College		●		●		●
Coventry University	●	●	●	●		●
Crawley College		●				
Cumbria Institute of the Arts		●				
Darlington College Of Technology	●	●	●			●
De Montfort University	●		●	●		●
Derby, University of	●		●			
Doncaster College						●
Dublin Institute of Technology	●	●		●		●

	general media	press/journalism & writing	broadcasting & film	public relations & communications	publishing industry	multimedia, digital & new media
Dundee, University of						●
Ealing, Hammersmith and West London College	●					●
East Anglia, University of			●			
University of East London	●	●	●	●		●
East Surrey College		●	●			
Edge Hill College of Higher Education		●	●	●		
Falmouth College of Arts		●	●			
Fife College of Further Education		●		●		●
Glasgow Caledonian University		●		●		●
Glasgow College of Building and Printing		●	●		●	●
Glasgow School of Art						●
Glasgow, University of		●				
Gloucestershire University		●	●	●		●
Goldsmiths College	●	●	●	●		●
Greenwich University	●	●	●	●		●
Grimsby College		●	●			●
Guildford College of Further and Higher Education			●			
Harlow College		●				
Harrow College		●	●			
Henley College Coventry	●		●			●
Hertfordshire, University of	●	●	●	●		●
Highbury College, Portsmouth		●	●			
Hopwood Hall College			●			●
University of Huddersfield		●	●	●		
Hull College	●		●			
Journalism Training Centre		●				
Kensington and Chelsea College		●	●			●
Kent Institute of Art and Design			●	●		●
Kent, University of			●	●		●
King's College London	●		●			
Kingston University	●	●	●			●
Lambeth College	●	●	●			●
Lancaster University	●		●	●		●
Leeds College of Art and Design				●		●
Leeds Metropolitan University	●		●	●		●
Leeds Trinity & All Saints University College	●	●	●			
Leeds, University of			●			
Leicester, University of				●		
Lincoln, University of	●	●	●	●		●
Liverpool Community College		●	●			
Liverpool John Moores University	●	●	●			
Liverpool, University of			●	●		●
London College of Communication, School of Media		●	●			
London College of Fashion		●	●	●		
London College of Music & Media			●	●		●
London Film School			●			
London Metropolitan University	●	●	●	●		●
London School of Economics and Political Science				●		●
London South Bank University	●	●	●			●
Luton, University of	●	●	●	●		●

	general media	press/journalism & writing	broadcasting & film	public relations & communications	publishing industry	multimedia, digital & new media
Manchester Metropolitan University	●		●			●
Mid-Cheshire College			●			●
Middlesex University	●	●	●	●	●	●
Napier University		●	●		●	●
National Broadcasting School			●			
National Film and Television School			●			
NE Wales Institute of Higher Education	●		●			●
Neath Port Talbot College			●			●
New College Nottingham	●		●			●
Newcastle College			●			●
Newcastle Upon Tyne University			●			
North East Surrey College of Technology – Nescot			●			●
North East Worcestershire College			●			
North Tyneside College			●			
North West Kent College		●	●			●
Northbrook College Sussex	●	●	●	●		
Northumbria University	●	●	●	●		●
Norwich School of Art and Design		●			●	●
noSweat Journalism Training		●				
Nottingham Trent University	●	●	●			●
Nottingham, University of			●			
Open University	●					
Oxford Brookes University				●	●	●
Paisley University	●		●	●		●
Peterborough Regional College	●	●	●			
Plymouth College of Art and Design			●	●		●
Plymouth, University of			●			●
Portsmouth, University of	●	●	●			
The Press Association/Editorial Centre		●				
Queen Margaret University College, Edinburgh	●		●	●		
Queen Mary, University of London			●			●
Queen's University of Belfast			●			●
The Radio and TV School			●			
Ravensbourne College of Design and Communication			●			●
Robert Gordon University				●	●	●
Roehampton University of Surrey		●	●			
Royal Holloway, University of London	●	●	●			
Salford, University of		●	●			●
Salisbury College			●			●
Sandwell College			●			●
School of Oriental and African Studies, University of London	●			●		
Sheffield College		●	●			
Sheffield Hallam University	●	●	●	●		●
Sheffield University		●	●	●		●
Solihull College	●					●
South Birmingham College			●	●		●
South Devon College	●		●			
South East Essex College	●	●	●		●	●
South Nottingham College			●			●

	general media	press/journalism & writing	broadcasting & film	public relations & communications	publishing industry	multimedia, digital & new media
South Thames College	●	●	●			●
Southampton Institute	●	●	●	●		●
Southport College						●
St Helen's College		●	●	●		●
College of St Mark and St John	●			●		
St Mary's College		●				
Staffordshire University, Faculty of Arts, Media and Design	●	●	●			●
Stevenson College Edinburgh			●	●	●	
Stirling, University of	●	●	●	●	●	
Stockport College of Further and Higher Education	●		●			
Stratford Upon Avon College	●		●			
Strathclyde, University of		●				
Sunderland, University of		●	●	●		●
Surrey Institute of Art and Design		●	●			●
Surrey, University of				●		●
Sussex, University of	●		●			●
Sutton Coldfield College	●	●				
Tameside College						●
Teesside, University of	●		●	●		
Thames Valley University			●	●		●
Trinity College		●	●			
UHI Millennium Institute	●		●	●		
Ulster, Univcrsity of	●	●	●		●	
University College London			●			
University College Northampton	●	●	●	●		
University College Winchester (formerly King Alfred's College)	●	●	●			
University College Worcester	●		●	●		●
University of Wales Institute, Cardiff			●	●		●
University of Wales, Aberystwyth			●	●		
University of Wales, Bangor	●	●	●	●		
University of Wales, Lampeter	●		●			
University of Wales, Newport			●		●	●
University of Wales, Swansea	●	●	●			
Wakefield College	●					●
Warwick, University of	●	●				
Warwickshire College	●	●		●		●
West Herts College	●		●	●		●
West Kent College		●	●	●		
West of England, University of the	●		●			●
Westminster, University of	●	●	●	●		●
Wirral Metropolitan College	●		●			
Wolverhampton, University of	●	●	●	●		●
York St John College	●		●			
Yorkshire Coast College of Further Education						●

Basingstoke College of Technology
Worting Road, Basingstoke RG21 8TN
01256 354141
info@bcot.ac.uk
www.bcot.ac.uk
- *BTEC FirstDip/NatCert/NatDip media.*
- *BTEC NatCert/NatDip/HND multimedia.*

Bath, University of
Claverton Down, Bath BA2 7AY
01225 383019
admissions@bath.ac.uk
www.bath.ac.uk
- *HND audio and visual tech (at Salisbury College); HND media production (at Wiltshire College, Chippenham).* - *HND multimedia and design (at Wiltshire College, Chippenham).*

Bath Spa University College
Newton Park, Newton Street Low, Bath BA2 9BN
01225 875875
enquiries@bathspa.ac.uk
www.bathspa.ac.uk
- *BA (Hons) creative studies in English.* - *Fdg/BA (Hons) commercial music; BA (Hons) creative music tech.* - *BA/BSc media communication (combined award).* - *Fdg design for digital technologies.*

Bell College
Almada Street, Hamilton, Lanarkshire ML3 0JB
01698 283100
enquiries@bell.ac.uk or r.bergman@bell.ac.uk
www.bell.ac.uk
- *HND/BA journalism.* - *PGDip in broadcast journalism (BJTC).*

Birkbeck, University of London
Malet Street, Bloomsbury, London WC1E 7HX
0845 601 0174
info@bbk.ac.uk
www.bbk.ac.uk
- *CertDip media practice, Fdg media & business applications, BA humanities and media studies, MA cultural & critical studies.*
- *CertDip film and media studies; BA film and media; MA/MA(Res) history of film and visual media; MPhil/PhD film/TV/media studies.*
- *Dip new media management, Dip web design and development.*

Birmingham University
Edgbaston, Birmingham B15 2TT
0121 414 3344
postmaster@bham.ac.uk
www.bham.ac.uk
- *BA media, culture and society (single and joint).*

Blackburn College
Feilden Street, Blackburn BB2 1LH
01254 55144
studentservices@blackburn.ac.uk
www.blackburn.ac.uk
- *NatDip media.* - *Pre-entry media production.* - *Fdg multimedia (with Lancaster University).*

Bolton Institute of Higher Education
Deane Road, Bolton BL3 5AB
01204 900600
enquiries@bolton.ac.uk
www.bolton.ac.uk
- *BA (Hons) fashion design and media.* - *BA (Hons) creative writing.*
- *BA (Hons) photography and video/ media, writing and production/ writing for stage, screen and radio.* - *BA (Hons) creative advertising and new media.* - *BA (Hons) animation and illustration; HND/BSc (Hons) multimedia and website development.*

Arts Institute at Bournemouth
Wallisdown, Poole, Dorset BH12 5HH
01202 533011
general@aib.ac.uk
www.aib.ac.uk
- *BA (Hons) film and animation production.* - *Fdg interactive media.*

Bournemouth University
Bournemouth Media School, Weymouth House
Fern Barrow, Poole, Dorset BH12 5BB
01202 524111
bms@bournemouth.ac.uk
www.bournemouth.ac.uk
- *BA multimedia journalism (NCTJ, BJTC, PTC); MA/PGDip multimedia journalism (BJTC).* - *BA/MA TV production; MA radio production/ broadcast and film management.* - *BA PR (IPR)/ advertising and marketing comms (CIM)/ comms and media; PGDip/MA PR practice/ corporate communication.* - *BA multimedia journalism (NCTJ, BJTC, PTC)/ interactive media production; PGDip/ MA multimedia journalism (BJTC); MA interactive media.*

Bradford College
Great Horton Road, Bradford BD7 1AY
01274 433004
admissions@bilk.ac.uk
www.bradfordcollege.ac.uk
- *PGDip/MA politics of visual representation/ representation in film.*
- *BA (Hons) graphic media communication.* - *BTEC NatDip multimedia design.*

Bradford, University of
Richmond Road, Bradford BD7 1DP
01274 232323; media: 01274 233084
eimcugadmissions@bradford.ac.uk
www.eimc.brad.ac.uk
- *EuroMA media, communication and cultural studies.* - *BSc media tech and production.* - *BSc computer animation and special effects/ electronic imaging and media comms (with pre-entry year)/ multimedia computing/ creative media and technologies; BA digital media; MSc creative media and technologies with computer animation and special effects/ creative media and technologies with multimedia systems.*

Brighton, University of
Mithras House, Lewes Road, Brighton BN2 4AT
01273 600900
admissions@brighton.ac.uk
www.brighton.ac.uk
- *BA (Hons) sports journalism (NCTJ).* - *BA (Hons) communication and media studies.*

Bristol, University of
Senate House, Tyndall Avenue, Bristol BS8 1TH
0117 928 9000
admissions@bristol.ac.uk
www.bristol.ac.uk
- *MA film and TV production; MA TV studies.*

Brunel University
Uxbridge, Middlesex UB8 3PH
01895 274000
admissions@brunel.ac.uk
www.brunel.ac.uk
- *BA creative music tech/ film and TV studies (also with American studies/ drama/English/history/music); MA documentary practice.*
- *BSc communication and media studies; MA media, communication and tech.* - *BSc multimedia tech and design; MSc digital broadcast systems/ multimedia computing for e-commerce/ multimedia information systems.*

Buckingham University
Hunter Street, Buckingham MK18 1EG
01280 814080
admissions@buckingham.ac.uk
www.buckingham.ac.uk
- *BA (Hons) English studies/psychology with media comms; BA (Hons) communication (EFL) and media studies; BSc (Hons) marketing with media comms.* - *BA (Hons) English literature/ English studies with multimedia journalism.*

Bucks Chilterns University College
Queen Alexander Road, High Wycombe, Bucks HP11 2JZ
01494 522141
marketing@bcuc.ac.uk
www.bcuc.ac.uk
- *BA (Hons) media studies (with creative writing/English studies).*
- *BA (Hons) media studies (with drama production/ video production/ film studies).* ▪ *Fdg/BSc (Hons) internet and multimedia computing; BSc (Hons) multimedia product design.*

Canterbury Christ Church University College
Department of Media, North Holmes Road, Canterbury
Kent CT1 1QU
01227 767700
admissions@cant.ac.uk
www.cant.ac.uk
- *BA (Hons) media and cultural studies (single, joint and combined); MA pop culture and the media.* ▪ *MA journalism.* ▪ *BA (Hons) film, radio and TV studies (single, joint and combined); MA media production.*
- *HND multimedia computing; BA (Hons) digital culture, arts and media (joint and combined)/ digital media.*

Cardiff University
Dept of Journalism and Media Studies, PO Box 927
King Edward VII Avenue, Cardiff CF10 3NB
029 2087 4000
jomec@cardiff.ac.uk
www.cardiff.ac.uk/jomec
- *PGDip magazine/newspaper journalism; MA journalism studies, European journalism, international journalism.* ▪ *BA (Hons) journalism, film and media (single and joint); PGDip broadcast journalism.* ▪ *PGDip public and media relations (IPR); MA international PR.*

Cardonald College
690 Moss Park Drive, Glasgow G52 3AY
0141 272 3333
enquiries@cardonald.ac.uk
www.cardonald.ac.uk
- *HND practical journalism (NCTJ).* ▪ *HNC/HND TV operations and production.* ▪ *HNC/HND comms and media.*

Carmarthenshire College (Coleg Sir Gar)
Pibwrlwyd Campus, Carmarthen SA31 2NH
01554 748000
admissions@colegsirgar.ac.uk
www.colegsirgar.ac.uk
- *Short course in DJ tech; NatDip media production/ music tech; BA (Hons) media production.*

Central England in Birmingham, University of
Corporation Street, Birmingham B4 7DX
0121 331 5000
media@uce.ac.uk
www.uce.ac.uk
- *BA (Hons) media and communication (culture and society/ journalism/ media photography); MA international press journalism.* ▪ *BA (Hons) media and communication (culture and society/ radio and TV and video); PGDip broadcast journalism (BJTC); MA international broadcast journalism; MA media production.* ▪ *BA (Hons) media and communication (PR); MA media and communication.* ▪ *BA (Hons) media and communication (multimedia).*

Central Lancashire, University of
Department of Journalism, Preston, Lancashire PR1 2HE
01772 894730
meward@uclan.ac.uk
www.ukjournalism.org
- *BA (Hons) journalism (NCTJ, BJTC) (single and combined)/ journalism and English/ international journalism/ sports journalism (seeking NCTJ); PGDip newspaper journalism (NCTJ); MA newspaper journalism (NCTJ)/ international journalism/ magazine journalism (seeking NCTJ).* ▪ *PGDip/ MA broadcast journalism (BJTC).* ▪ *BA (Hons) PR (combined, joint and with sandwich) (IPR)/ media comms/ PR and marketing/ marketing and PR/ PR and management; MA strategic communication (IPR); MSc international applied communication.* ▪ *MA online journalism (BJTC).*

University College Chester
Parkgate Road, Chester CH1 4BJ
01244 375444
enquiries@chester.ac.uk
www.chester.ac.uk
- *BA media studies (combined); MA media and cultural studies.*
- *BA journalism (NCTJ) (single and combined); BA media (multimedia journalism) (single and combined).* ▪ *BA media (commercial music production/ multimedia journalism/ radio production/ TV production (Granada Media & Education Partnership Scheme)) (single and combined); MA radio production/ screen studies/ TV production.*
- *BA publishing (single and combined)* ▪ *BA media (multimedia journalism/ web production) (single and combined).*

Chichester College
Westgate Fields, Chichester, West Sussex PO19 1SB
01243 536196
www.chichester.ac.uk
- *BTEC firstDip/ NatDip media.* ▪ *BTEC HND media (radio production).*

University College Chichester
Bishop Otter Campus, College Lane, Chichester
West Sussex PO19 6PE
01243 816002
admissions@ucc.ac.uk
www.ucc.ac.uk
- *BA (Hons) media studies.* ▪ *Fdg/BA (Hons) media production.*

City Literary Institute
Stukeley Street, London WC2B 5LJ
020 7430 0542
www.citylit.ac.uk
- *Short courses: introduction to freelance journalism, freelance journalism stage 2, travel journalism, freelance writing for newspapers and magazines.*

City Of Wolverhampton College
Wulfrun Campus, Paget Road, Wolverhampton WV6 0DU
01902 836000
mail@wolverhamptoncollege.ac.uk
www.wolverhamptoncollege.ac.uk; www.mediacove.com
- *Pre-entry journalism (NCTJ); BA (Hons) journalism and editorial design (W'ton Uni).* ▪ *HND media design (video) (W'ton Uni); Fdg broadcast journalism (W'ton Uni).*

City University, London
Department of Journalism, Northampton Square
London EC1V 0HB
020 7040 5060
journalism dept: 020 7040 8221
ugadmissions@city.ac.uk
www.city.ac.uk
- *BA journalism with social science/ contemporary history; PGDip newspaper journalism/ magazine journalism (PTC); PGDip/MA international journalism; MA creative writing; doctorate journalism.*
- *PGDip broadcast journalism (BJTC)/ TV current affairs journalism (BJTC).* ▪ *MA publishing studies; MA/MSc electronic publishing.*

Cleveland College of Art & Design
Green Lane, Linthorpe, Middlesbrough TS5 7RJ
01642 288888
admissions@ccad.ac.uk
www.ccad.ac.uk
- *Fdg TV and film production.*

Coleg Menai
Ffriddoedd Road, Bangor, Gwynedd, North Wales LL57 2TP
01248 370125
student.services@menai.ac.uk
www.menai.ac.uk
- *NatDip media.* ▪ *NatDip e-media.*

Cornwall College
Trevenson Campus, Pool, Redruth, Cornwall TR15 3RD
01209 611611
enquiries@cornwall.ac.uk
www.cornwall.ac.uk
- *Fdg newspaper and magazine journalism; PGDip journalism (NCTJ).*
- *Fdg graphic and communication design.* ▪ *Fdg multimedia design.*

Coventry University
Priory Street, Coventry CV1 5FB
024 7688 7050
rao.cor@coventry.ac.uk
www.coventry.ac.uk
▪ *PGCert/PGDip/MA media arts.* ▪ *PGCert/PGDip/MA automotive journalism/ international media journalism.* ▪ *BA media production/ media studies and music or theatre.* ▪ *BA multimedia & communication design/ communication design/ applied communication; BA/PGCert/ PGDip/ MA communication, media and culture.* ▪ *BA multimedia & communication design; PGCert/PGDip/MA design and digital media.*

Crawley College
College Road, Crawley, West Sussex RH10 1NR
01293 442200
information@crawley-college.ac.uk
www.crawley-college.ac.uk
▪ *Pre-entry newspaper journalism (NCTJ).*

Cumbria Institute of the Arts
Brampton Road, Carlisle, Cumbria CA3 9AY
01228 400300
info@cumbria.ac.uk
www.cumbria.ac.uk
▪ *BA (Hons) journalism (NCTJ).*

Darlington College Of Technology
Cleveland Avenue, Darlington, County Durham DL3 7BB
01325 503127
enquire@darlington.ac.uk
www.darlington.ac.uk
▪ *BTEC FirstDip media.* ▪ *Pre-entry and PG journalism (NCTJ); Fdg journalism (University of Teesside).* ▪ *BTEC NatCert media (audio production); BTEC NatDip media (moving image).* ▪ *Pre-entry and PG digital photo-journalism (NCTJ); BTEC NatDip multimedia; Fdg digital media (University of Teesside).*

De Montfort University
The Gateway, Leicester LE1 9BH
0116 255 1551
enquiry@dmu.ac.uk
www.dmu.ac.uk
▪ *BA (Hons) media studies.* ▪ *HND music tech; BA (Hons) (single and joint)/BSc (Hons) music, tech and innovation; BSc (Hons) audio and recording tech/ broadcast tech/ media production; BA (Hons) film studies/ photography and video.* ▪ *BA/BA (Hons) advertising and marketing comms.* ▪ *BA (Hons) multimedia design (single and joint); BSc media tech/ multimedia computing.*

Derby, University of
School of Arts, Design & Technology, Kedleston Road
Derby DE22 1GB
01332 590500
admissions@derby.ac.uk
www.derby.ac.uk
▪ *BA (Hons) media studies.* ▪ *Fdg commercial video and photography/ video production; BA (Hons) film and TV studies/ film and video.*

Doncaster College
Waterdale, Doncaster DN1 3EX
01302 553553
infocentre@don.ac.uk
www.don.ac.uk
▪ *NatDip multimedia/ new media; HNC/HND multimedia.*

Dublin Institute of Technology
Fitzwilliam House, 30 Upper Pembroke Street, Dublin 2
00 353 1 402 3000; school of media: 00 353 1 402 3098
www.dit.ie
▪ *BA media arts; MA media studies.* ▪ *BA/MA journalism.* ▪ *MA PR.* ▪ *MA digital media technologies.*

Dundee, University of
Nethergate, Dundee DD1 4HN
01382 344000
srs@dundee.ac.uk
www.dundee.ac.uk
▪ *BA time-based art/ animation and electronic media; BSc interactive media design; PGDip/MSc electronic imaging; MSc animation and visualisation.*

Ealing, Hammersmith and West London College
Gliddon Road, Barons Court, London W14 9BL
0800 980 2175
Marketing@wlc.ac.uk
www.wlc.ac.uk
▪ *BTEC FirstDip/ NatDip media.* ▪ *Fdg digital animation; NatDip/HND multimedia.*

East Anglia, University of
Norwich, Norfolk NR4 7TJ
01603 456161
admissions@uea.ac.uk
www.uea.ac.uk
▪ *BA film and TV studies/ film and English or American studies; MA film studies/ film studies with archiving.*

University of East London
Docklands Campus, Longbridge Road, Dagenham E16 2RD
020 8223 3000
admiss@uel.ac.uk
www.uel.ac.uk
▪ *Pre-entry year media; BA (Hons) media studies/ media and creative industries; MA media studies/ global media.* ▪ *BA (Hons) journalism.* ▪ *MA independent film, video and new screen media/ film, TV and history/ sonic culture: sound, arts and media in the digital age.* ▪ *BA (Hons) media and advertising/ comms studies.* ▪ *BA (Hons) interactive media; BSc (Hons) media and comms technologies/ multimedia studies/ e-learning and multimedia; MA cybernetic culture: media, digital arts and the body machine/ multimedia production: cultures and theories/ sonic culture: sound, arts and media in the digital age.*

East Surrey College
Reigate School of Art Design and Media
Gatton Point, Claremont Road, Redhill, Surrey RH1 2JX
01737 772611
studentservices@esc.ac.uk
www.esc.ac.uk
▪ *C&G Dip media techniques – journalism; PGDip journalism (NCTJ).* ▪ *C&G Dip media techniques – TV and video; HND moving image (documentary and drama production).*

Edge Hill College of Higher Education
St Helen's Road, Ormskirk, Lancashire L39 4QP
01695 584274
enquiries@edgehill.ac.uk
www.edgehill.ac.uk
▪ *BA (Hons) journalism (NCTJ).* ▪ *BA (Hons) film studies/ with film and TV production/ media (film and TV).* ▪ *BA (Hons) PR (subject to IPR approval).*

Falmouth College of Arts
Woodlane Campus, Falmouth, Cornwall TR11 4RH
01326 370400
admissions@falmouth.ac.uk
www.falmouth.ac.uk
▪ *BA (Hons) journalism/ English with media studies; PgDip/MA professional writing.* ▪ *BA (Hons) broadcasting/ film studies; PgDip/MA broadcast journalism (BJTC)/ TV production.*

Fife College of Further Education
St Brycedale Avenue, Kirkcaldy, Fife, Scotland KY1 1EX
01592 268591
enquiries@fife.ac.uk
www.fife.ac.uk
▪ *HNC/HND practical journalism.* ▪ *HNC/HND communication with media; HNC/HND events management.* ▪ *AdvDip interactive graphic design.*

Glasgow Caledonian University
70 Cowcaddens Road, Glasgow G4 0BA
0141 331 3000
enquiries@gcal.ac.uk
www.gcal.ac.uk
▪ BA/BA (Hons) journalism (seeking NCTJ); PGDip journalism studies (NCTJ). ▪ BA/BA(Hons) marketing (with specialist route in media)/ communication and mass media. ▪ BA/BA (Hons) applied graphics tech with multimedia; BSc/BSc (Hons) mutlimedia tech; MA digital media design.

Glasgow College of Building and Printing
60 North Hanover Street, Glasgow G1 2BP
0141 332 9969
enquiries@gcbp.ac.uk
www.gcbp.ac.uk
▪ HNC/HND journalism: broadcast and print. ▪ HNC/HND journalism: broadcast and print. ▪ HNC/HND publishing studies. ▪ HNC/HND digital media for publishing and print/ multimedia design and production.

Glasgow School of Art
167 Renfrew Street, Glasgow G3 6RQ
0141 353 4500
i.johnston@gsa.ac.uk
www.gsa.ac.uk
▪ MPhil 2D/3D motion graphics.

Glasgow, University of
Glasgow G12 8QQ
0141 330 2000
admissions@gla.ac.uk
www.gla.ac.uk
▪ MPhil creative writing.

Gloucestershire University
The Park, Cheltenham GL50 2QF
01242 532700
gthatcher@glos.ac.uk
www.glos.ac.uk
▪ BA/BSc (Hons) creative writing; BA (Hons) journalism and professional writing. ▪ BA (Hons) broadcast journalism/ video; BA/BSc (Hons) film studies; PGCert/PGDip/MA film and media. ▪ BA/BSc (Hons) media comms. ▪ BA design for interactive media; BA/BSc multimedia.

Goldsmiths College
Dept. of Media and Communications
University of London, New Cross, London SE14 6NW
020 7919 7171
media-comms@gold.ac.uk
www.goldsmiths.ac.uk
▪ BA (Hons) media with modern literature/anthropology/ sociology; BA (Hons) international media. ▪ MA journalism (PTC)/ comparative international journalism/ script writing. ▪ Short courses: introduction to video/ to TV studio/ to single-camera production and video editing/ surrealism in the cinema; MA feature film/ radio (BJTC, NUJ)/ screen doc/ screen drama direction/ TV journalism (BJTC). ▪ FCert/BA (Hons)/ MA/ MRes/ MPhil/ PhD media and comms; MA political comms/ trans-national comms and global media. ▪ MA digital media: tech and cultural form/ image and communication (photography or electronic graphics).

Greenwich University
Old Royal Naval College, Park Row, Greenwich
London SE10 9LS
020 8331 8000
courseinfo@greenwich.ac.uk
www.gre.ac.uk
▪ BA creative industries. ▪ HND professional writing; BA creative writing (with options)/ media writing (with options). ▪ HND lens-based media/ TV production tech; Fdg creative industry (music tech); BA film studies (with options). ▪ BA media and communication/ media culture and comms. ▪ Fdg creative industry (multimedia); HND multimedia; HND/BA graphic and digital design; BA design tech/ 3D digital design; BSc multimedia tech; BSc/PGDip/MSc multimedia and internet tech; PGCert/PGDip/MA/PhD critical studies, new media and practising arts.

Grimsby College
Nuns Corner, Grimsby DN34 5BQ
01472 311222
infocent@grimsby.ac.uk
www.grimsby.ac.uk
▪ BA (Hons) digital media production (journalism/ photography) (with Lancaster University). ▪ HNC/HND media production/ music production; HND moving image; BA (Hons) digital media production (TV, film and video) (with Lancaster University). ▪ BA (Hons) digital media production (multimedia) (with Lancaster University).

Guildford College of Further and Higher Education
Stoke Park, Guildford, Surrey GU1 1EZ
01483 448500
info@guildford.ac.uk
www.guildford.ac.uk
▪ NatDip/HND/BA (Hons) media production.

Harlow College
Velizy Avenue, Town Centre, Harlow, Essex CM20 3LH
01279 868000
full-time@harlow-college.ac.uk
www.harlow-college.ac.uk
▪ Pre-entry newspaper journalism (NCTJ); BA (Hons) journalism (PTC and Middlesex University); PG pre-entry newspaper journalism (NCTJ)/ magazine journalism (NCTJ, PTC).

Harrow College
Brookshill, Harrow Weald, Middlesex HA3 6RR
020 8909 6000
www.harrow.ac.uk
▪ NCTJ journalism. ▪ Short courses: film studies/introduction to video production and editing.

Henley College Coventry
Henley Road, Bell Green, Coventry CV2 1ED
024 7662 6300
info@henley-cov.ac.uk
www.henley-cov.ac.uk
▪ BTEC media; HND media. ▪ BTEC media (moving image). ▪ BTEC media (e-media production)/ art, design and media; HND multimedia.

Hertfordshire, University of
College Lane, Hatfield AL10 9AB
01707 284000
admissions@herts.ac.uk
www.herts.ac.uk
▪ BA (Hons) media cultures (combined). ▪ BA (Hons) journalism (combined). ▪ BA (Hons) film (combined)/ digital and lens media; BSc (Hons) music: commercial composition and tech/ music tech/ sound design tech; MA interactive broadcast media. ▪ BA (Hons) English language and communication (single and joint); MA graphic communication. ▪ BA (Hons) digital publishing (combined)/ digital animation/ digital modelling/ digital and lens media/ model design and special effects; BA/BSc (Hons) software systems for the arts and media; MA 3D digital animation/ 3D modelling and special effects/ hyperfictions.

Highbury College, Portsmouth
Dept. of Media and Journalism, Dovercourt Road
Portsmouth, Hampshire PO6 2SA
023 9238 3131
info@highbury.ac.uk
www.highbury.ac.uk
▪ Pre-entry newspaper journalism (NCTJ)/ magazine journalism (PTC); HND media (journalism). ▪ PGDip in broadcast journalism (BJTC).

Hopwood Hall College
St Mary's Gate, Rochdale OL12 6RY
01706 345346
enquiries@hopwood.ac.uk
www.hopwood.ac.uk
▪ BTEC FirstDip/NatDip media (moving image). ▪ Fdg new media design (Manchester Metropolitan University).

University of Huddersfield
Queensgate, Huddersfield HD1 3DH
01484 422288
admissions@hud.ac.uk
www.hud.ac.uk
▪ *BA(Hons) media and print journalism.* ▪ *BA(Hons) media and TV production/ media and radio journalism.* ▪ *BA(Hons) PR with media and design management (IPR).*

Hull College
Queens Gardens, Hull HU1 3DG
01482 329943
info@hull-college.ac.uk
www.hull-college.ac.uk
▪ *BTEC FirstDip media.* ▪ *BTEC NatAward/NatDip media (moving image/audio).*

Journalism Training Centre
Unit G, Mill Green Business Park, Mill Green Road
Mitcham, Surrey CR4 4HT
020 8640 3696
info@jtctraining.com
www.jtctraining.ac.uk
▪ *Short courses: sports writing, sub-editing, feature writing; PGDip journalism (acc. PTC, approved by NUJ).*

Kensington and Chelsea College
Hortensia Road, London SW10 0QS
020 7573 3600
l.gibbons@kcc.ac.uk
www.kcc.ac.uk
▪ *Cert/Dip media studies – introduction to journalism/screenwriting (with Birkbeck, University of London).* ▪ *LOCN music tech/ video production.* ▪ *LOCN sound design for multimedia; BTEC NatCert/ HNC multimedia.*

Kent Institute of Art and Design
Oakwood Park, Maidstone, Kent ME16 8AG
01622 620000
info@kiad.ac.uk
www.kiad.ac.uk
▪ *BA (Hons) video media arts; MA artists' film, video and photography.* ▪ *BA (Hons) fashion promotion.* ▪ *BTEC NatDip multimedia; Fdg graphic design and interactive media; BA (Hons) animation; BSc (Hons) multimedia tech and design.*

Kent, University of
The Registry, Canterbury, Kent CT2 7NZ
01227 764000
recruitment@kent.ac.uk
www.kent.ac.uk
▪ *BA (Hons) film and contemporary arts; BSc (Hons) music tech; MA/MPhil/PhD film studies.* ▪ *BEng (Hons) internet and multimedia comms.* ▪ *Fdg computing and multimedia; BSc (Hons) multimedia tech and design; BEng (Hons) internet and multimedia comms; PGDip/MSc broadband and mobile communication networks; MSc information and communication technologies.*

King's College London
School of Humanities, Strand, London WC2R 2LS
020 7836 5454
ceu@kcl.ac.uk
www.kcl.ac.uk
▪ *MA cultural and creative industries.* ▪ *BA film studies with various options; MA visual and performing arts – National Film Theatre/ contemporary cinema cultures.*

Kingston University
River House, 53–57 High Street, Kingston-upon-Thames
Surrey KT1 1LQ
020 8547 2000
admissions-info@kingston.ac.uk
www.kingston.ac.uk
▪ *BA(Hons) media and cultural studies (combined).* ▪ *BA(Hons) journalism (combined); MA writing for the contemporary media.* ▪ *BA(Hons) film studies (combined)/ TV studies (combined); BA (Hons)/ DipHE/CertHE audio tech and music industry studies; MA production design for film and TV/ screen design for film and TV (motion graphics)/ film studies/ composing for film and TV; MA/DPhil media, film and drama (by research).* ▪ *Fdg/MA graphic comms; BSc(Hons) computer information systems-multimedia information systems/ media tech (combination); MA illustration and animation/ composing for new media.*

Lambeth College
Belmore Street, Wandsworth Road, London SW8 2JY
020 7501 5010
courses@lambethcollege.ac.uk
www.lambethcollege.ac.uk
▪ *BTEC FirstDip media.* ▪ *Fdg journalism (London Metropolitan University); pre-entry newspaper journalism (NCTJ).* ▪ *BTEC NatDip media (moving image); C&G Cert video production techniques; BTEC NatAward radio; BTEC NatCert music tech and audio electronics; NCFE Cert music tech.* ▪ *BTEC FirstDip multimedia and photography; BTEC NatDip multimedia.*

Lancaster University
Bailrigg, Lancaster LA1 4YW
01524 65201
ugadmissions@lancaster.ac.uk
www.lancs.ac.uk
▪ *BA (Hons) English language and the media.* ▪ *BA (Hons) film and cultural studies/ film with sociology or philosophy; PGDip/MSc media production and distribution.* ▪ *BSc comms and computer systems/ information tech and media comms.* ▪ *BSc comms and computer systems/ information tech and media comms.*

Leeds College of Art and Design
Blenheim Walk, Leeds, West Yorkshire LS2 9AQ
0113 202 8000
info@leeds-art.ac.uk
www.leeds-art.ac.uk
▪ *BA (Hons) visual comms.* ▪ *BTEC HND multimedia.*

Leeds Metropolitan University
Civic Quarter, Leeds LS1 3HE
0113 283 2600
course-enquiries@lmu.ac.uk
www.lmu.ac.uk
▪ *Fdg/MSc creative tech; BA (Hons) media and popular culture.* ▪ *CertHE/ Fdg film and TV production; HNC/HND moving image production; BA (Hons)/ MA film and moving image production; BSc (Hons) creative music and sound tech/ music tech; PGDip/MA screenwriting (fiction).* ▪ *IPR AdvCert/Dip (apply direct to IPR: 020 7253 5151); HND business and PR; BSc (Hons) marketing media and systems; BA (Hons) PR/ PR with a European language; MA PR/ PR management.* ▪ *HNC/HND/ BSc (Hons) multimedia tech; BA (Hons) web media management.*

Leeds Trinity & All Saints University College
School of Media, Brownberrie Lane, Horsforth
Leeds LS18 5HD
0113 283 7100
enquiries@tasc.ac.uk
www.tasc.ac.uk
▪ *BA media (single, joint and combined).* ▪ *BA business journalism/ lifestyle journalism; BSc psychology with journalism; MA/PgDip print journalism (NCTJ).* ▪ *MA/PgDip in bimedia journalism (BJTC)/ radio journalism (BJTC).*

Leeds, University of
Institute of Communications Studies, Leeds LS2 9JT
0113 243 1751
admissions@leeds.ac.uk
www.leeds.ac.uk
▪ *BA broadcasting.*

Leicester, University of
University Road, Leicester LE1 7RH
0116 252 2522
admissions@le.ac.uk
www.le.ac.uk
▪ *BSc comms and society; MA mass comms (inc distance learning option)/ globalisation and comms; MSc media and communication research; PhD/MPhil mass comms.*

Lincoln, University of
Brayford Pool, Lincoln LN6 7TS
01522 882000
enquiries@lincoln.ac.uk
www.lincoln.ac.uk
▪ *MPhil media studies; MA/MRes media and cultural studies.* ▪ *BA (Hons) journalism – print, internet, radio and TV; MA journalism (from Sep 2005).* ▪ *BA (Hons) media production/ TV and film design/ digital and interactive TV; MA documentary and factual programme production; MPhil/PhD film studies/ media production.* ▪ *BA (Hons) PR (IPR)/ media comms.* ▪ *BA (Hons) animation/ interactive multimedia/ interactive and screen-based graphics; BSc (Hons) multimedia tech/ media tech.*

Liverpool Community College
Journalism School, The Arts Centre, 9 Myrtle Street
Liverpool L7 7JA
0151 252 1515
www.liv-coll.ac.uk
▪ *NCTJ prelimCert print journalism/ fast track/ periodical journalism/ day release.* ▪ *FCert broadcast journalism (BJTC provisional).*

Liverpool John Moores University
JMU Tower, 24 Norton Street, Liverpool L3 8PY
0151 231 5090
recruitment@livjm.ac.uk
www.livjm.ac.uk
▪ *BA/BA(Hons) media & cultural studies.* ▪ *BA/BA (Hons)/MA journalism/ international journalism.* ▪ *BA/BA(Hons) media professional studies with TV/ media professional studies with radio (subject to validation)/ screen studies/ popular music studies; MA screenwriting.*

Liverpool, University of
Liverpool L69 3BX
0151 794 2000
uksro@liv.ac.uk
www.liv.ac.uk
▪ *BA (Hons) European film studies and modern languages (joint).* ▪ *BA (Hons) communication, media and popular music (joint).* ▪ *BSc (Hons) computer and multimedia systems/ design and tech with multimedia; BEng (Hons)/ MEng (Hons) electronic and multimedia systems.*

London College of Communication, School of Media
Elephant & Castle, London SE1 6SB
020 7514 6569
info@lcc.arts.ac.uk
www.lcc.arts.ac.uk
▪ *Fdg/BA (Hons)/MA journalism; PGCert periodical journalism.* ▪ *PGDip broadcast journalism; MA documentary research.*

London College of Fashion
20 John Prince's Street, London W1G 0BJ
020 7514 7344
enquiries@fashion.arts.ac.uk
www.fashion.arts.ac.uk
▪ *BA (Hons) fashion promotion – pathways in journalism; PGCert fashion: fashion and lifestyle journalism; MA fashion journalism.* ▪ *BA (Hons) fashion promotion – pathways in broadcast; MA fashion media.* ▪ *BA (Hons) fashion promotion – pathways in PR.*

London College of Music & Media
▶▶ see **Thames Valley University**

London Film School
24 Shelton Street, London WC2H 9UB
020 7836 9642
info@lfs.org.uk
www.lfs.org.uk
▪ *MA filmmaking.*

London Metropolitan University
31 Jewry Street, London EC3N 2EY
020 7320 1616
enquiries.city@londonmet.ac.uk
www.londonmet.ac.uk
▪ *BA (Hons) media studies (single and joint); MA media and cultural industries.* ▪ *Fdg journalism; BA (Hons) journalism studies.* ▪ *Fdg audio production for broadcast media; BA (Hons) film and broadcast production/ film studies (single and joint)/ sound and media; MA filmmaking.* ▪ *Dip PR (IPR); BA (Hons) advertising and marketing communication (links with CIM, IDM and IPR subject to accreditation) (single and joint)/ comms (joint)/ comms and visual culture (single and joint)/ mass comms (joint)/ professional comms/ PR (single and joint) (IPR subject to accreditation); MA mass comms/ comms management.* ▪ *Fdg multimedia BA (Hons) digital media (single and joint); BSc (Hons) multimedia (single and joint); MA digital media.*

London School of Economics and Political Science
Houghton Street, London WC2A 2AE
020 7405 7686
pressoffice@lse.ac.uk
www.lse.ac.uk
▪ *MSc media and comms/ media and comms regulation and policy.* ▪ *MSc new media, information and society.*

London South Bank University
103 Borough Road, London SE1 0AA
020 7928 8989
enquiries@lsbu.ac.uk
www.lsbu.ac.uk
▪ *BSc (Hons) media and society; MA culture and media.* ▪ *BA (Hons) writing for media arts; MA media writing.* ▪ *BA (Hons) digital video production/ sonic media/ film studies (combined).* ▪ *Fdg/BSc multimedia computing; BA (Hons) digital media arts; BSc (Hons) special effects; MA new media.*

Luton, University of
Park Square, Luton, Beds LU1 3JU
01582 734111
enquiries@luton.ac.uk
www.luton.ac.uk
▪ *PGCert/PGDip/MA media, culture and tech.* ▪ *BA (Hons) journalism/ journalism studies and PR.* ▪ *Fdg media, art and design (also at Dunstable College)/ media production (at Barnfield College, Milton Keynes College and Bedford College)/ music tech (at Dunstable College); BA (Hons) media performance/ media production/ music tech/ TV production; PGCert/ PGDip/MA media production (doc).* ▪ *BA (Hons) PR/ journalism studies and PR/ media practices (mass comms)/ media practices and marketing; PGCert/PGDip/MA media arts (mass comms).* ▪ *Fdg digital imaging and design for media (at Milton Keynes College); MA new media and internet technologies.*

Manchester Metropolitan University
Faculty of Art & Design, Ormond Building
Lower Ormond Street, Manchester M15 6BX
0161 247 1701
www.mmu.ac.uk
▪ *MA media arts/ visual culture.* ▪ *BA (Hons) contemporary film and video.* ▪ *BA (Hons) illustration with animation.*

Mid-Cheshire College
Hartford Campus, Chester Road, Northwich
Cheshire CW8 1LJ
01606 744444
info@midchesh.ac.uk
www.midchesh.ac.uk
▪ *Short course: sound recording studio techniques; NatDip media (moving image)/ music tech.* ▪ *NCFE multimedia design; NatDip/HNC/ Fdg multimedia.*

Middlesex University
White Hart Lane, London N17 8HR
020 8411 5000
admissions@mdx.ac.uk
www.mdx.ac.uk
▪ *BA (Hons) media and cultural studies (single and joint).* ▪ *BA (Hons) journalism/ journalism and communication studies (single and joint)/ creative and media writing (single and joint); MA writing.* ▪ *BA (Hons) recording arts and BA digital film arts/ film making (apply directly to SAE Institute 020 7609 2653); BA TV production; BA (Hons) film studies (single and joint); BA/BSc (Hons) sonic arts.* ▪ *BA (Hons) journalism and communication studies (single and joint); MA media and communications management.* ▪ *BA (Hons) publishing and media (single and joint).* ▪ *BA (Hons) multimedia arts and BA digital film arts (apply directly to SAE Institute 020 7609 2653); HNC/HND multimedia; BSc (Hons) information tech (with multimedia pathway); MSc multimedia application development.*

Napier University
School of Communication Arts, Craighouse Campus
Craighouse Road, Edinburgh EH10 5LG
0131 455 6150
www.napier.ac.uk
▪ *Short courses: design for print/ intro to journalism/ intro to print process/ journalism and media/ writing for specialists/ writing for press and broadcast media/ intermediate sub-editing/ refresher for journalists/ sub-editing for beginners; BA/BA (Hons)/ PGDip/MSc journalism; PGDip/MSc international English language journalism.* ▪ *Short courses: intro to screenwriting/ project management for film production/ science fiction and comic culture/ working in TV and film art departments/ handling the media – TV/ writing for the press and broadcast media; BA/BA (Hons) photography, film and imaging; MA screen project development.* ▪ *Short courses: basic and specialist copy-editing, proofreading, e-Publishing, introduction to book commissioning/ introduction to book marketing/issues with electronic or digital publishing/ book arts/ design for print/ introduction to the print process/ writing for specialists; BA/BA (Hons) publishing media; PGDip/MSc publishing.* ▪ *short course: new media writing; BEng/BEng (Hons) multimedia systems; BSc/BSc (Hons) multimedia tech.*

National Broadcasting School
The Innovation Centre, University of Sussex
Brighton BN1 9SB
01273 704510
www.nationalbroadcastingschool.com
▪ *Cert radio presentation and programming (CRCA)/ radio journalism and news presentation (CRCA/NCTJ).*

National Film and Television School
Beaconsfield Studios, Station Road, Beaconsfield
Bucks HP9 1LG
01494 671234
admin@nftsfilm-tv.ac.uk
www.nftsfilm-tv.ac.uk
▪ *ExecDip script development; Dip digital post-production/ sound recording for film and TV/ TV production: factual entertainment/ special effects; MA animation direction/ cinematography/ composing for film and TV/ documentary direction/ editing/ fiction direction/ sound post-production/ producing/ production design/ screenwriting/ TV production: factual entertainment (subject to validation).*

NE Wales Institute of Higher Education
Plas Coch, Mold Road, Wrexham LL11 2AW
01978 290666
enquiries@newi.ac.uk
www.newi.ac.uk
▪ *BA (Hons) media studies (single and with options).* ▪ *HND film and TV design; BA (Hons) film studies (with options)/ design: moving image; HND/Fdg/BEng (Hons)/BSc (Hons) sound broadcast and production.* ▪ *Fdg digital media; HNC/HND/BSc (Hons) multimedia computing; Fdg/BEng (Hons) digital technologies; BA (Hons) design: multimedia design; MA animation.*

Neath Port Talbot College
Dwr-y-Felin Road, Neath SA10 7RF
01639 648000
enquiries@nptc.ac.uk
www.nptc.ac.uk
▪ *HNC/HND broadcast media; BA(Hons) music performance and production (popular music).* ▪ *HNC/ HND computing (multimedia).*

New College Nottingham
City Campus, Adams Building, Stoney Street, Lace Market
Nottingham NG1 1NG
0115 910 0100
enquiries@ncn.ac.uk
www.ncn.ac.uk
▪ *BTEC FirstDip/HND media.* ▪ *C&G TV and video production.*
▪ *BTEC NatDip media (e-media); HND multimedia.*

Newcastle College
Rye Hill Campus, Scotswood Road
Newcastle Upon Tyne NE4 5BR
0191 200 4000
enquiries@ncl-coll.ac.uk
www.ncl-coll.ac.uk
▪ *BTEC HND music production; Fdg stage management and technical production/ TV and media practice.* ▪ *Fdg illustration and animation/ multimedia design.*

Newcastle Upon Tyne University
Newcastle Upon Tyne NE1 7RU
0191 222 6000
admissions-enquiries@ncl.ac.uk
www.ncl.ac.uk
▪ *MA/PGDip film studies.*

North East Surrey College of Technology – Nescot
Reigate Road, Ewell, Epsom, Surrey KT17 3DS
020 8394 3038
info@nescot.ac.uk
www.nescot.ac.uk
▪ *NatDip media production/ music tech.* ▪ *NatDip multimedia; Fdg media and multimedia (OUVS).*

North East Worcestershire College
Peakman Street, Redditch, Worcestershire B98 8DW
01527 570020
info@ne-worcs.ac.uk
www.ne-worcs.ac.uk
▪ *HNC/HND media (moving image); NatDip music tech.*

North Tyneside College
Embleton Avenue, Wallsend, Tyne and Wear NE28 9NJ
0191 229 5000
infocent@ntyneside.ac.uk
www.northtyneside.ac.uk
▪ *HNC/HND TV and video production; BTEC NatDip media production (moving image).*

North West Kent College
Oakfield Lane, Dartford, Kent DA1 2JT
0800 074 1447
course.enquiries@nwkcollege.ac.uk
www.nwkcollege.ac.uk
▪ *NatDip media studies; Dip advanced music tech (joint).*
▪ *NatDip multimedia.* ▪ *Higher NatDip professional writing.*

Northbrook College Sussex
Little Hampton Road, Worthing, West Sussex BN12 6NU
01903 606060
admissions@nbcol.ac.uk
www.nbcol.ac.uk
▪ *BA (Hons) media arts.* ▪ *BA (Hons) digital journalism (subject to validation).* ▪ *HND media – the moving image.* ▪ *BA (Hons) communication design.*

Northumbria University
Ellison Place, Newcastle Upon Tyne NE1 8ST
0191 232 6002
ca.marketing@northumbria.ac.uk
www.northumbria.ac.uk
▪ *BA (Hons) visual culture; MA art practices (media).* ▪ *MA creative writing.* ▪ *BA (Hons) media production/ English and film studies.* ▪ *BSc (Hons) communication.* ▪ *BA (Hons) multimedia design.*

Norwich School of Art and Design
St George Street, Norwich, Norfolk NR3 1BB
01603 610561
info@nsad.ac.uk
www.nsad.ac.uk
▪ *MA writing the visual.* ▪ *BA (Hons) publishing.* ▪ *BA (Hons) animation; MA animation and sound design/ digital practices.*

noSweat Journalism Training
25b Lloyd Baker Street, London WC1X 9AT
020 7713 1000
info@nosweatjt.co.uk
www.nosweatjt.co.uk
▪ *NCTJ PrelimCert (reporters) p/t, f/t, intakes Sep & Mar; magazine journalism (working towards acc. PTC), p/t, f/t, intakes Feb, Jun & Oct; short courses: feature writing, Quark subbing, travel writing, sports reporting etc. Course director: Stephen Ward – steve@nosweatjt.co.uk*

Nottingham Trent University
Burton Street, Nottingham NG1 4BU
0115 941 8418
cbj@ntu.ac.uk
www.ntu.ac.uk
▪ *BA (Hons) media and cultural studies (single and joint).* ▪ *PGDip/MA newspaper journalism/ newspaper journalism (international).* ▪ *BA (Hons) design for TV; BSc (Hons) audio-visual tech/ audio visual production; PGDip/ MA TV journalism/ TV journalism (international)/ radio journalism/ radio journalism (international).* ▪ *BSc (Hons) multimedia tech/ multimedia production; PGDip/MA online journalism/ online journalism (international); PGDip/MSc applied multimedia.*

Nottingham, University of
University Park, Nottingham NG7 2RD
0115 951 5151
undergraduate-enquiries@
nottingham.ac.uk
www.nott.ac.uk
▪ *BA (Hons) music with film studies/ film studies with options; MA film studies.*

Open University
Walton Hall, Milton Keynes MK7 6AA
01908 274066
general-enquiries@open.ac.uk
www.open.ac.uk
▪ *MA cultural and media studies.*

Oxford Brookes University
Gypsy Lane Campus, Headington, Oxford OX3 0BP
01865 484848
admissions@brookes.ac.uk
www.brookes.ac.uk
▪ *BA (Hons)/BSc (Hons) communication, media and culture (single and combined).* ▪ *BA (Hons)/BSc (Hons) publishing (single or combined); MA publishing/ international publishing/ publishing and language; MBA with specialism in publishing (AMBA).* ▪ *BSc (Hons) multimedia production; MSc e-commerce computing; MA interactive media publishing.*

Paisley University
Paisley, Scotland PA1 2BE
0800 027 1000
uni-direct@paisley.ac.uk
www.paisley.ac.uk
▪ *BA (Hons) media/ creative practice.* ▪ *BA (Hons) cinema/ commercial music.* ▪ *BA (Hons) events management; MSc multimedia comms.* ▪ *BSc (Hons) media tech/ multimedia systems/ business information tech and multimedia/ computer animation and multimedia; BA (Hons) digital art/ computer animation and digital art.*

Peterborough Regional College
Park Crescent, Peterborough PE1 4DZ
01733 767366
info@peterborough.ac.uk
www.peterborough.ac.uk
▪ *BTEC NatDip media (publishing/journalism); HNC/HND media.* ▪ *C&G 7790 journalism (media techniques); HNC/HND journalism; Fdg print journalism.* ▪ *NCFE studio recording and music tech; BTEC NatDip media (audio/radio)/ media (moving image/video).*

Plymouth College of Art and Design
Tavistock Place, Plymouth PL4 8AT
01752 203434
enquiries@pcad.ac.uk
www.pcad.ac.uk
▪ *Fdg moving image.* ▪ *BA (Hons) environmental visual comms/ photomedia and design communication.* ▪ *Fdg animation and creative media/ photography and electronic imaging/ multimedia design; BA (Hons) photomedia and design communication.*

Plymouth, University of
Drake Circus, Plymouth, Devon PL4 8AA
01752 600600
prospectus@plymouth.ac.uk
www.plymouth.ac.uk
▪ *HND sound engineering and multimedia integration; HND media moving image (taught at Truro College); HND media production (taught at South Devon).* ▪ *HND sound engineering and multimedia integration; BSc (Hons) medialab arts/ multimedia production and tech.*

Portsmouth, University of
University House, Winston Churchill Avenue, Portsmouth
Hampshire PO1 2UP
023 9284 8484
info.centre@port.ac.uk
www.port.ac.uk
▪ *BA (Hons) media studies.* ▪ *BA (Hons) media studies with creative writing.* ▪ *BA (Hons) media studies with drama/ entertainment tech.*

The Press Association / Editorial Centre
Hanover House, Marine Court, St Leonards-on-Sea
Hastings, East Sussex TN38 0DX
01424 435991
editorial-centre@mistral.co.uk
www.editorial-centre.co.uk
▪ *Combined Dip journalism and NVQ Level 4 journalism; PADip sub-editing.*

Queen Margaret University College, Edinburgh
Corstophine Campus, Clerwood Terrace
Edinburgh EH12 8TS
0131 317 3000
marketing@qmuc.ac.uk
www.qmuc.ac.uk
▪ *BA (Hon) media (also with culture/ management/psychology).* ▪ *BA (Hons) film and media.* ▪ *BA (Hons) PR and media/ marketing/ psychology (all IPR pending)/ media and marketing.*

Queen Mary, University of London
Mile End Road, London E1 4NS
020 7882 5555
external-relations@qmw.ac.uk
www.qmw.ac.uk
▪ *BA film studies and drama.* ▪ *MSc multimedia systems tech/ digital music processing.*

Queen's University of Belfast
University Road, Belfast BT7 1NN
028 9024 5133
www.qub.ac.uk
▪ *BA (Hons) film studies; BSc (Hons) music tech; MA film studies.* ▪ *Fdg creative multimedia (offered at North Down Institute of Further and Higher Education) leading to BSc (Hons) creative multimedia.*

The Radio and TV School
High Street, Staplehurst, Kent TN12 0AX
01580 895256
mail@radioandtvschool.com
www.radioandtvschool.com
▪ *Broadcast certificates of achievement – one-to-one courses in radio presentation and production techniques; also courses in TV and voice-over.*

Ravensbourne College of Design and Communication
Walden Road, Chislehurst, Kent BR7 5SN
020 8289 4900
info@rave.ac.uk
www.ravensbourne.ac.uk
▪ *Fdg/BA broadcasting courses.* ▪ *BA interaction and moving image design; PG digital, new media and online journalism.*

Robert Gordon University
School Hill, Aberdeen AB10 1FR
01224 262000
admissions@rgu.ac.uk
www.rgu.ac.uk
▪ *BA/BA (Hons) corporate communication; GCert/PGDip/MSc corporate communication and public affairs.* ▪ *BA/BA (Hons) publishing/ publishing with journalism; PGCert/PGDip/MSc publishing studies.* ▪ *BSc (Hons) computing for internet and multimedia (British Computer Society)/ computing for graphics and animation (BCS).*

Roehampton University of Surrey
Erasmus House, Roehampton Lane, London SW15 5PU
020 8392 3000
enquiries@roehampton.ac.uk
www.roehampton.ac.uk
▪ *BA journalism and news media/ creative writing; MA creative writing and professional writing.* ▪ *BA TV studies/ film studies/ film studies and screen practice/ journalism and news media.*

Royal Holloway, University of London
Egham, Surrey TW20 0EX
01784 434455
undergrad-office@rhul.ac.uk
www.rhul.ac.uk
▪ *BA media arts; BSc science and the media.* ▪ *MA creative writing.*
▪ *BA German/French/Italian with film studies; MA TV production/ feature film screenwriting/ screen studies/ documentary by practice.*

Salford, University of
Salford, Greater Manchester M5 4WT
0161 295 5000
ugadmissions-exrel@salford.ac.uk
www.salford.ac.uk
▪ *BA (Hons) journalism and design studies/English/languages/ politics/ sociology (NCTJ); BSc (Hons) journalism and broadcasting (NCTJ).*
▪ *HND audio and video systems/ professional sound and video tech/ media production; BSc (Hons) acoustics/ audio tech/ audio, video and broadcast tech/ journalism and broadcasting (NCTJ); BA (Hons) media and performance/ TV and radio/ popular music and recording; PGDip/MA TV documentary production/ TV and radio scriptwriting.*
▪ *BSc (Hons) media tech.*

Salisbury College
Southampton Road, Salisbury, Wiltshire SP1 2LW
01722 344344
enquiries@salisbury.ac.uk
www.salisbury.ac.uk
▪ *C&G 1820 (parts 1 & 2) sound engineering; BTEC NatDip music tech; HND TV and film; BA (Hons) photomedia (film and TV).* ▪ *Fdg computer aided design (3D modelling and animation)/ multimedia; BA (Hons) photomedia (multimedia).*

Sandwell College
Oldbury Business Centre, Pound Road, Oldbury
West Midlands B68 8NA
0800 622006
enquiries@sandwell.ac.uk
www.sandwell.ac.uk
▪ *NatDip music tech; HNC professional sound and video; HNC/HND media production (moving image)/ music production; HND professional sound engineering; BSc (Hons) TV tech and production (with University of Central England, Birmingham).* ▪ *BTEC NatDip multimedia.*

School of Oriental and African Studies, University of London
Thornaugh Street, Russell Square, London WC1H 0XG
020 7637 2388
study@soas.ac.uk
www.soas.ac.uk
▪ *MA critical Media and cultural studies/ anthropology of media.*
▪ *MA global media and postnational communication.*

Sheffield College
The Norton Centre, Dyche Lane, Sheffield S8 8BR
0114 260 3603
mail@sheffcol.ac.uk
www.sheffcol.ac.uk
▪ *NCTJ journalism/ reporter; NCTJ journalism/ photography; NCTJ pre-entry journalism/ photography.* ▪ *BTEC HND media production.*

Sheffield Hallam University
Psalter Lane Campus, Sheffield S11 8UZ
0114 225 5555
admissions@shu.ac.uk
www.shu.ac.uk
▪ *BA (Hons) visual culture and its management; BA (Hons)/PGCert/ PGDip/MA media studies.* ▪ *PGCert/ PGDip/MA writing.* ▪ *BA (Hons) film and literature/ film and media production; BA (Hons)/PGCert/PGDip/ MA film studies; PGCert/PGDip/MA broadcast journalism/ film and digital production.* ▪ *BA (Hons) communication studies.* ▪ *BA (Hons) multimedia and communication design/ information design and multimedia; PGCert/PGDip/MSc e-learning, multimedia and consultancy.*

Sheffield University
Department of Journalism Studies, 18–22 Regent Street
Sheffield S1 3NJ
0114 222 2500
journalism@sheffield.ac.uk
www.sheffield.ac.uk/journalism
▪ *BA (Hons) journalism studies (NCTJ, BJTC)/ journalism and French/ Germanic studies/ Hispanic studies/ Russian; PGDip/MA print journalism (NCTJ).* ▪ *PGDip/MA broadcast journalism (BJTC).* ▪ *MA political communication.* ▪ *MA web journalism.*

Solihull College
Blossomfield Road, Solihull B91 1SB
0121 678 7001
enquiries@solihull.ac.uk
www.solihull.ac.uk
▪ *BTEC FirstDip/NatDip/HND media. HNC/HND multimedia; HNC/HND photography and digital imaging.*

South Birmingham College
Cole Bank Road, Birmingham B28 8ES
0121 694 5000
info@sbc.ac.uk
www.sbirmc.ac.uk
▪ *Short course: introduction to digital video editing; NOCN sound engineering; NCFE/OCN/BTEC NatCert/NatDip music tech; OCN/BTEC NatCert/NatDip media production; CollegeCert scriptwriting for film and TV (fiction).* ▪ *HND media and communication.* ▪ *BTEC NatCert/NatDip/ HND multimedia.*

South Devon College
Newton Road, Torquay, Devon TQ2 5BY
01803 400700
www.southdevon.ac.uk
▪ *FirstDip media studies.* ▪ *NatDip media moving image; HND media production.*

South East Essex College
Carnarvon Road, Southend-on-Sea, Essex SS2 6LS
01702 220400
marketing@southend.ac.uk
www.southend.ac.uk
▪ *BTEC FirstDip media.* ▪ *BA (Hons) journalism.* ▪ *Short courses: TV presenting skills/ radio broadcasting skills/ sound engineering (stage 1 and 2)/ video production and editing; NCFE intermediate music tech; BTEC NatDip moving image; HNC/HND performing arts (music production); BA (Hons) TV production and screen media/ music production.* ▪ *BTEC NatDip publishing.* ▪ *Short course in basic 3D animation; BSc (Hons) e-media/ digital animation.* ▪ *Centre of Vocational Excellence for media technology*

South Nottingham College
Greythorn Drive, West Bridgford, Nottingham NG2 7GA
0115 914 6464
enquiries@south-nottingham.ac.uk
www.south-nottingham.ac.uk
▪ *HNC/HND media production.* ▪ *HNC/HND multimedia/ photography and digital imaging/ print, media and digital design.*

South Thames College
Wandsworth High Street, London SW18 2PP
020 8918 7777
studentservices@south-thames.ac.uk
www.south-thames.ac.uk
▪ *BTEC FirstDip/NatAward media; HNC media (inc 16mm film making).*
▪ *Short course: intro to journalism.* ▪ *Short courses: introduction to low-budget film production/ scriptwriting/ final cut – desktop video/ 16mm film production; HNC media (inc 16mm film making)/ media production; NCFE/ NatCert/HNC/NatDip music tech; NatAward music for media.* ▪ *NatCert multimedia; BTEC introDip media and multimedia.* ▪ *Centre of Vocational Excellence for Music Business, Design and Production*

Southampton Institute
East Park Terrace, Southampton, Hampshire SO14 0RB
023 8031 9000
fmas@solent.ac.uk
www.solent.ac.uk
▪ *Fdg/BA (Hons) creative industries; BA (Hons) media with cultural studies; MA media.* ▪ *BA (Hons) journalism (NCTJ, PTC, BJTC)/ media writing/ writing fashion and culture.* ▪ *BSc (Hons) audio tech (BKSTS)/ film and video tech (BKSTS)/ media tech/ music studio tech (BKSTS); BA (Hons) film and TV studies/ film studies; PGDip/MA film.* ▪ *HND advertising and media comms; BA (Hons) marketing with media and design/ PR and communication.* ▪ *BA (Hons) animation/ digital media/ multimedia design; MA interactive production.*

Southport College
Mornington Road, Southport PR9 0TT
01704 500606
www.southport.mernet.ac.uk
▪ *BTEC NatDip multimedia.*

St Helen's College
St Helens, Merseyside WA10 1PZ
01744 623580
enquire@sthelens.ac.uk
www.sthelens.ac.uk
▪ *BTEC HND media (writing); Fdg vocational writing (subject to validation).* ▪ *Fdg factual TV and video production; BA (Hons) TV and video production (both through Liverpool John Moores University).*
▪ *BA (Hons) digital graphic communication (subject to validation).*
▪ *Fdg interactive multimedia arts and animation (Liverpool John Moores University); BA (Hons) digital graphic communication (subject to validation); BA (Hons) digital arts (LJM Uni).*

College of St Mark and St John
Derriford Road, Plymouth PL6 8BH
01752 777188
promotion@marjon.ac.uk
www.marjon.ac.uk
▪ *BA (Hons) media (with University of Exeter).* ▪ *BA (Hons) PR (with University of Exeter).*

St Mary's College
Waldegrave Road, Twickenham TW1 4SX
020 8240 4000
recruit@smuc.ac.uk
www.smuc.ac.uk
▪ *BA (Hons) professional and creative writing.*

Staffordshire University
Faculty of Arts, Media and Design, College Road
Stoke-on-Trent, Staffordshire ST4 2XW
01782 294869
amdadmissions@staffs.ac.uk
www.staffs.ac.uk
▪ *BA (Hons) media studies (joint award).* ▪ *BA (Hons) journalism/ sports journalism (NCTJ).* ▪ *BA (Hons) broadcast journalism (NCTJ)/ broadcasting factual/ broadcasting music/ film, TV and radio studies/ film studies/ design: media production; MA broadcast journalism (NCTJ).* ▪ *BA (Hons) interactive multimedia.*

Stevenson College Edinburgh
Bankhead Avenue, Edinburgh EH11 4DE
0131 535 4700
info@stevenson.ac.uk
www.stevenson.ac.uk
▪ *HNC/HND TV operations/ audio-visual tech; Fdg film and TV.*
▪ *HNC advertising and PR.* ▪ *Fdg publishing.*

Stirling, University of
Stirling FK9 4LA
01786 467046
recruitment@stir.ac.uk
www.stir.ac.uk
▪ *MSc/PGDip media management (available online learning); Mres/ PGDip media research.* ▪ *BA (Hons) journalism studies (single and combined).* ▪ *BA (Hons) film and media studies (single and combined)/ European film and media/ journalism studies (single and combined).*
▪ *MSc PR; MSc/PGCert/PGDip PR (online learning).* ▪ *MLitt publishing studies.*

Stockport College of Further and Higher Education
Wellington Road South, Stockport, Cheshire SK1 3UQ
0845 230 3106
admissions@stockport.ac.uk
www.stockport.ac.uk
▪ *BTEC FirstDip media.* ▪ *BTEC NatDip media broadcasting; HND media: broadcasting/media broadcasting (moving image).*

Stratford Upon Avon College
The Willows North, Alcester Road, Stratford-upon-Avon
Warwickshire CV37 9QR
01789 266245
college@stratford.ac.uk
www.stratford.ac.uk
▪ *BTEC firstDip media; HND media.* ▪ *BTEC NatDip media (moving image).*

Strathclyde, University of
16 Richmond Street, Glasgow G1 1XQ;
0141 552 4400
Scottish Centre for Journalism Studies
Crawfurd Building, Jordanhill Campus
76 Southbrae Drive, Glasgow G13 1PP
0141 950 3281
www.strath.ac.uk
▪ *BA in journalism and creative writing; PgDip/MLitt in Journalism Studies (NCTJ).*

Sunderland, University of
Langham Tower, Ryhope Road, Sunderland SR2 7EE
0191 515 2000
media dept: 0191 515 2112
student-helpline@sunderland.ac.uk
www.sunderland.ac.uk
▪ *BA (Hons) journalism (routes inc newspaper and magazine) (NCTJ); PGDip/ MA journalism (NCTJ).* ▪ *BA (Hons) media production (TV and radio or video and new media); MA media production (TV and video); MA radio (production and management).* ▪ *BA (Hons) PR (IPR).*
▪ *BA (Hons) media production (video and new media).*

Surrey Institute of Art and Design
Falkner Road, Farnham, Surrey GU9 7DS
01252 722441
registry@surrart.ac.uk
www.surrart.ac.uk
▪ *BA (Hons) journalism (PTC, BJTC, recognised by NCTJ)/ fashion journalism.* ▪ *BA (Hons) film and video (BKSTS).* ▪ *BA (Hons) digital screen arts.*

Surrey, University of
Guildford, Surrey GU2 7XH
01483 300800
information@surrey.ac.uk
www.surrey.ac.uk
▪ *BA culture, media and communication.* ▪ *BSc (Hons) sociology, culture and new media.*

Sussex, University of
Falmer, Brighton BN1 9RH
01273 606755
information@sussex.ac.uk
www.sussex.ac.uk
▪ *BA English and media studies/ media practice and theory/ media studies and anthropology/ media studies and European languages/ media and cultural studies; PGDip media and cultural studies; MA gender and media.* ▪ *Film studies cert (centre for continuing education); BA film studies (with options)/ music and media studies; MA/MPhil film studies.* ▪ *MA digital media.*

Sutton Coldfield College
34 Lichfield Road, Sutton Coldfield
West Midlands B74 2NW
0121 355 5671
infoc@sutcol.ac.uk
www.sutcol.ac.uk
▪ *Cert media techniques.* ▪ *Cert newspaper journalism (NCTJ).*

Tameside College
Beaufort Road, Ashton-under-Lyne
Greater Manchester OL6 6NX
0161 908 6600
www.tameside.ac.uk
▪ *Fdg new media design (with Manchester Metropolitan University).*

Teesside, University of
Middlesbrough, Tees Valley TS1 3BA
01642 342015
hotline@tees.ac.uk
www.tees.ac.uk
▪ *BA (Hons) media studies.* ▪ *Fdg TV and Film Production; BA (Hons) TV production professional practice/ media production professional practice/ media and music tech.* ▪ *BA (Hons) PR (IPR).*

Thames Valley University
London College of Music & Media, St Mary's Road
Ealing, London W5 5RF
0800 036 8888
www.tvu.ac.uk
▪ *BA (Hons) film: video production with film studies; MA film and the moving image/ video: feature film production/ video production with film studies.* ▪ *BA (Hons) PR.* ▪ *BA (Hons) digital broadcast media/ new media journalism.*

Trinity College
Carmarthen, Wales SA31 3EP
01267 676767
registry@trinity-cm.ac.uk
www.trinity-cm.ac.uk
▪ *BA/MA creative writing.* ▪ *BA media studies/ film studies/ theatr, cerdd a'r cyfryngau (theatre, music and media); MA cyfryngau (media).*

UHI Millennium Institute
Caledonia House, 63 Academy Street, Inverness IV1 1LU
01463 279000
eo@uhi.ac.uk
www.uhi.ac.uk
▪ *BA creative media (subject to OUVS) – offered at Perth College UHI; BA Gaelic and media studies (gàidhlig agus na meadhanan) (OUVS) – fluency in Gaelic required, offered at Sabhal Mòr Ostaig UHI and Lews Castle College UHI.* ▪ *HNC media production – offered at Inverness College UHI; HND TV and multimedia – fluency in Gaelic required, offered at Sabhal Mòr Ostaig UHI; HND video production – offered at Perth College UHI.* ▪ *HNC/HND communication with media – offered at Moray College UHI.*

Ulster, University of
Cromore Road, Co Londonderry, Northern Ireland BT52 1SA
0870 040 0700
online@ulster.ac.uk
www.ulster.ac.uk
▪ *BA (Hons) combinations with media, English, European studies, languages, history and geography; PGDip/MA media studies.* ▪ *BA (Hons) combinations with media, journalism & publishing, English, languages; PGDip/MA newspaper journalism.* ▪ *BA (Hons) film studies (single and combined)/ media (single and combined); MA film and TV management (proposed).* ▪ *BA (Hons) combinations with media, journalism & publishing, English, French, German, Irish, Spanish.*

University College London
Gower Street, London WC1E 6BT
020 7679 2000
www.ucl.ac.uk
▪ *MA film studies.*

University College Northampton
Boughton Green Road, Northampton NN2 7AL
01604 735500
study@northampton.ac.uk
www.northampton.ac.uk
▪ *BA (Hons) media and cultural studies/ media studies.* ▪ *BA (Hons) journalism.* ▪ *BA (Hons) film and TV studies.* ▪ *BA (Hons) advertising with PR.*

University College Winchester (formerly King Alfred's College)
Hampshire SO22 4NR
01962 841515
admissions@winchester.ac.uk
www.winchester.ac.uk
▪ *Fdg creative industries; BA media studies.* ▪ *MA contemporary popular knowledges/ creative and critical writing/ writing for children.* ▪ *BA drama, community theatre and media/ film and American studies/ film studies/ screen production.*

University College, Worcester
Henwick Grove, Worcester WR2 6AJ
01905 855000
admissions@worc.ac.uk
www.worc.ac.uk
▪ *HND media; BA (Hons) media and cultural studies.* ▪ *HND film making/ music for the moving image.* ▪ *BA (Hons) communication design.* ▪ *BA (Hons) creative digital media/ interactive digital media/ time-based digital media.*

University of Wales Institute, Cardiff
PO Box 377, Western Avenue, Cardiff CF5 2YB
029 2041 6070
uwicinfo@uwic.ac.uk
www.uwic.ac.uk
▪ *BA (Hons) broadcast media and popular culture.* ▪ *BA (Hons) graphic communication.* ▪ *BA (Hons)/BA/BSc (Hons) design for interactive media.*

University of Wales, Aberystwyth
Old College, King Street, Aberystwyth, Ceredigion SY23 2AX
01970 623111
www.aber.ac.uk
▪ *BA/MA/PhD theatre, film and TV studies (with Welsh, French, Spanish, German, English, IT, international politics or politics).* ▪ *BA/MA/PhD media and communication studies.*

University of Wales, Bangor
Gwynedd LL57 2DG
01248 351151
admissions@bangor.ac.uk
www.bangor.ac.uk
▪ *BA (Hons) creative studies.* ▪ *BA (Hons) cyfathrebu a newyddiaduraeth (communication & journalism); journalism with history/English/Welsh (anrhydedd cymraeg gyda newyddiaduraeth)/ PGDip newyddiaduraeth ymarferol (practical journalism); MPhil/PhD creative & critical writing.*
▪ *BA (Hons) astudiaethau ffilm a'r cyfryngau (film & the media)/ astudiaethau theatr a'r cyfryngau (theatre and media studies (also with Welsh))/ English with film studies or theatre studies; BA (Hons) English language/French/German with film studies; PGDip/MA cynhyrchu cyfryngol (media production).* ▪ *BA (Hons) cyfathrebu a newyddiaduraeth (communication & journalism); cyfathrebu a'r cyfryngau (communication and the media).*

University of Wales, Lampeter
Ceredigion SA48 7ED
01570 422351; dept of film and media: 01570 424790
admissions@lamp.ac.uk
www.lamp.ac.uk
▪ *PGDip/MA Welsh media.* ▪ *BA/PGDip/MA media production.*

University of Wales, Newport
Caerleon Campus, PO Box 179, Newport
South Wales NP18 3YG
01633 430088
uic@newport.ac.uk
www.newport.ac.uk
▪ *BA (Hons) cinema studies and scriptwriting/ creative sound and music (both subject to validation); BA (Hons) film and video/ documentary film and TV; MA documentary photography/ film; MA/MSc sports media (subject to validation).* ▪ *BA (Hons) new media publishing (subject to validation).* ▪ *BA (Hons) animation/multimedia; BA (Hons) new media publishing (subject to validation); MA animation/ design (new media and tech).*

University of Wales, Swansea
Singleton Park, Swansea SA2 8PP
01792 205678
admissions@swansea.ac.uk
www.swansea.ac.uk
▪ *BA (Hons) media studies; MA media talk.* ▪ *MA comparative journalism/ creative and media writing.* ▪ *BA (Hons) screen studies.*

Wakefield College
Margaret Street, Wakefield, West Yorks WF1 2DH
01924 789789
info@wakcoll.ac.uk
www.wakcoll.ac.uk
▪ *FirstDip media.* ▪ *NatDip e-media; Fdg multimedia and web design.*

Warwick, University of
Coventry CV4 7AL
024 7652 3523
www.warwick.ac.uk
▪ *MA creative and media enterprises.* ▪ *BA English and creative writing.*

Warwickshire College
Leamington Centre, Warwick New Road, Leamington Spa
Warwickshire CV32 5JE
0800 783 6767
www.warkscol.ac.uk
▪ *HND media.* ▪ *PG journalism (NCTJ).* ▪ *HND visual communication.*
▪ *HNC/HND multimedia.*

West Herts College
Hampstead Road, Watford WD17 3EZ
01923 812000
admissions@westherts.ac.uk
www.westherts.ac.uk
▪ *BTEC NatDip media.* ▪ *NatDip media (moving image); Fdg media, design and production – media production.* ▪ *PGDip PR (sponsored by PRCA and approved by IPR).* ▪ *Short course: 3D computer animation; BTEC NatDip multimedia; Fdg media, design and production – graphics and new media design.*

West Kent College
Brook Street, Tonbridge, Kent TW9 2PW
01732 358101
marketing@wkc.ac.uk
www.wkc.ac.uk
▪ *Pre-entry newspaper journalism (NCTJ).* ▪ *HNC/HND TV production tech; BA (Hons) broadcast journalism.* ▪ *BA (Hons) media and communication.*

West of England, University of the
Frenchay Campus, Coldharbour Lane, Bristol BS16 1QY
0117 965 6261
enquiries@uwe.ac.uk
www.uwe.ac.uk
▪ *pre-entry media; BA (Hons)/MA cultural and media studies.*
▪ *BA (Hons) time-based media; BSc (Hons) music systems engineering/ music systems with mathematics; PGDip/MA communication media (screenwriting); MA film and video.* ▪ *BSc (Hons) multimedia computing/ digital comms with mathematics; PGDip/MA communication media (animation/ interactive media).*

Westminster, University of
309 Regent Street, London W1B 2UW
020 7911 5000
www.wmin.ac.uk
▪ *BA contemporary media practice; MA media management.* ▪ *BA media studies with pathway in journalism/ medical journalism; PGDip periodical journalism; MA journalism (for international students)/ journalism studies.* ▪ *BA media studies with pathways in TV production or radio production/ film and TV production/ commercial music; PGDip broadcast journalism (BJTC); MA film: culture and industry/ screenwriting and producing/ audio production/ music business management.* ▪ *Cert/Dip media and communication studies; BA media studies with pathway in PR; MA comms/ communication policy/ public communication and PR.* ▪ *BA animation; BSc digital and photographic imaging/ multimedia computing; MSc digital and photographic imaging/ interactive multimedia/ computer animation; MA hypermedia studies/ design for interaction.*

Wirral Metropolitan College
Conway Park Campus, Europa Boulevard, Conway Park
Birkenhead, Wirral CH41 4NT
0151 551 7777
enquiries@wmc.ac.uk
www.wmc.ac.uk
▪ *BA media studies.* ▪ *MOCN radio and sound production.*

Wolverhampton, University of
Wulfruna Street, Wolverhampton WV1 1SB
01902 321000
enquiries@wlv.ac.uk
www.wlv.ac.uk
▪ *BA (Hons) media and cultural studies.* ▪ *BA (Hons) journalism and editorial design (NCTJ)/ creative and professional writing.* ▪ *HND digital media (design for screen)/ digital media – video production; Fdg broadcast journalism; BA (Hons) film studies/ literary, film and theatre studies/ TV graphics/ video; MA art and design network – video.*
▪ *BA (Hons) media and communication studies/ PR.* ▪ *BA (Hons)/MA animation/ design for multimedia/ digital media/ graphic communication/ multimedia communication; BSc (Hons) computing (multimedia)/ virtual reality design; MSc computer science (multimedia tech).*

York St John College
Lord Mayor's Walk, York YO31 7EX
01904 624624
admissions@yorksj.ac.uk
www.yorksj.ac.uk
▪ *Fdg creative industries and technologies; BA (Hons) comparative media.* ▪ *BA (Hons) film and TV production.*

Yorkshire Coast College of Further Education
Lady Edith's Drive, Scarborough, North Yorks YO12 5RN
01723 372105
admissions@ycoastco.ac.uk
www.yorkshirecoastcollege.ac.uk
▪ *Fdg applied digital media (design) (University of Hull/NTI); HND graphic and multimedia design.*

In-house newspaper training courses

Archant
Prospect House, Rouen Road
Norwich, Norfolk NR1 1RE
01603 772803/628311
david.allison@archant.co.uk
www.archant.co.uk

Bristol United Press
Bristol United Press
Temple Way, Bristol BS99 7HD
0117 934 3000
a.ocallaghan@bepp.co.uk
www.thisisbristol.com
Owned by Northcliffe since 2000

Johnston Training Centre
Upper Mounts
Northampton NN1 3HR
01604 467755
ilvi.smith@northantsnews.co.uk
www.johnstonpress.co.uk

Midland News Association
MNA Training Centre
Rock House, Old Hill, Tettenhall
Wolverhampton WV6 8QB
01902 742126
c.clark@expressandstar.co.uk
www.expressandstar.com
Mostly in-house but takes a few non-company trainees

Newsquest Media Group
58 Church Street
Weybridge KT13 8DP
01932 821212
ebudiar@newsquest.co.uk
www.newsquest.co.uk

Press Association
The Press Association
292 Vauxhall Bridge Road
London SW1V 1AE
020 7963 7000
information@pa.press.net
www.pa.press.net/

Trinity Mirror Training Centre
Trinity Mirror Editorial Training
Thomson House, Groat Market
Newcastle-upon-Tyne NE1 1ED
0191 201 6043
tony.johnston@ncj.media.co.uk

Glossary

Press

ABC: The Audit Bureau of Circulation, the company that monitors and verifies magazines and newspaper sales. "ABCs" is the popular term for the circulation figures it publishes: see explainer.

average issue readership: The number of people who, when surveyed, say they have read a newspaper or magazine within the lifespan of the issue. Also known as AIR.

Brad: British Rate and Data, a company that records every periodical that carries advertising in Britain

broadsheet: Larger size of paper, used by the news sections of most quality UK papers; usually 580mm × 380mm.

bulks: Copies of newspapers distributed free to targeted places such as hotels and airlines. See explainer on ***ABCs.***

byline: A journalist's name next to an article. Reporters live for bylines like salesmen live for bonuses.

circulation: The number of copies a newspaper or magazine sells or distributes in a defined period (usually a month). Not the same as average issue readership.

copy: Words for publication.

DPS: Double-page spread.

freesheet: A newspaper or magazine distributed free of charge, and usually paid for by advertising.

journalist: Someone who works on the editorial side of a newspaper or magazine.

leader: Editorial opinion column expressing the views of the newspaper (or its owner).

masthead: The bit with the title of the newspaper or magazine at the top of the front page.

news agency: Company that sells news stories to a newspaper or magazine, usually delivered electronically to each journalist's desktop over the ***wires***. The biggest are Reuters, the UK-based Press Assocation (PA) and the US-based Associated Press (AP).

Newspaper Society: Body representing the regional press.

PPA: The Periodical Publishers Association. Represents magazine publishers in Britain.

reporter: Someone who writes news stories. Just one of many kinds of journalist.

scoop: The act of printing a news story (or, these days, a celebrity interview) before a rival. The "scoop culture" has been criticised for getting in the way of balanced news reporting.

standfirst: The short paragraph at the top of a feature article, below the headline, that summarises it for the reader. Usually written by a subeditor.

subeditor: Someone who lays out and edits the copy in a newspaper or magazine. Will also write the headline, standfirst and other page furniture such as picture captions.

tabloid: Smaller size of paper, used by more downmarket titles and (recently) the features sections of some quality papers; usually half the size of broadsheet.

wires: Electronic delivery of news and pictures, sent by agencies to a journalist's desktop.

TV

analogue television: Television transmitted in "radio waves"; in other words, not digitally. Most terrestrial TV in Britain is still transmitted in analogue.

Barb: The Broadcasters Audience Research Board, which measures television audiences.

BBC: The British Broadcasting Corporation. Britain's public service broadcaster.

best boy: In broadcasting, the second-in-command of a lighting team.

BSkyB: Britain's only satellite broadcaster, owned by Rupert Murdoch's News Corporation.

cable television: Television delivered through a cable under the ground into the home. Largely concentrated in urban areas. Can be digital or analogue.

digital television: Television transmitted in binary format; can be delivered by cable, by satellite or terrestrially. Allows greater choice of channels, better quality and interactive services.

encryption: The encoding of television signals for security purposes, usually so they can only be watched by paying subscribers.

free-to-air: A television service that can be received without decoding or paying a fee.

Freeview: A commercial free-to-air digital terrestrial service; a partnership between BBC, BSkyB and the transmission firm Crown Castle.

grip: Someone who handles the equipment that enables a camera to move.

ITV network: The 15 regional franchises that together make up the ITV1 channel.

ITV plc: Company, formed from the merger of Carlton and Granada, that controls 11 of the 15 ***ITV network*** franchises, including all those in England and Wales.

licence fee: How the BBC generates most of its revenue. A colour licence cost £121 in 2004.

multichannel television: TV that includes more than just the five analogue terrestrial channels. If you receive cable, satellite or digital terrestrial, you are defined as being in a "multichannel home".

multiplex: A single digital terrestrial transmission comprising several channels. There are six television multiplexes in all.

Ofcom: Broadcasting super-regulator.

Pact: Producers' alliance for cinema and television. Represents independent television production companies.

pay-per-view: An individual programme which the viewer has to pay to see.

pay-TV: A general term for subscription services that the viewer has to pay to see.

radio spectrum: The total capacity of radio frequencies that can be received. A small part of the electromagnetic spectrum, which is made up of a range of phenomena including gamma rays, X-rays, ultraviolet radiation and visible light.

satellite television: Television received through a satellite dish, controlled in Britain by BSkyB. BSkyB has switched all its television services to digital.

terrestrial television: Television beamed from a ground transmitter directly to the home; can be analogue or digital.

watershed: Before 9pm, nothing may shown on television that is considered unsuitable for children; after 9pm, nothing may shown that is considered unsuitable for adults. 9pm is therefore the "watershed".

Radio

access radio: The old name for ***community radio***.

analogue radio: Radio transmitted in waves; in other words, not digitally. Most terrestrial radio in Britain is still transmitted in analogue.

audience share: In Rajar figures, the percentage of all radio listening hours that a station accounts for within its transmission area.

BBC: The British Broadcasting Corporation. Britain's public service broadcaster.

community radio: Not-for-profit, community-based radio. Formerly ***access radio***.

DAB digital radio: Digital terrestrial radio.

digital radio: Shorthand for digital terrestrial radio. More accurately, refers to any radio transmitted in binary format – either through ***DAB digital radio***, or via a television or the internet.

multiplex: A single digital terrestrial transmission, comprising several channels. There are two national and almost 50 local multiplexes.

Ofcom: Broadcasting super-regulator.

Rajar: Radio Joint Audience Research, the company that calculates radio audience figures.

radio spectrum: The total capacity of radio signals that can be received

reach: In Rajar figures, the number of people aged 15 or over who tune to a radio station within at least a quarter-hour period over the course of a week, and have listened to the station for at least five minutes within that quarter-hour.

Books

A-format, B-format: The two main "sizes" in which paperbacks are published. A-format are smaller (110mm x 178mm) and usually more downmarket; B-format are larger (130mm x 198mm) and usually further upmarket.

acquisition editor: Someone in a publishing house who identifies and negotiates to acquire new titles for publication.

advance: Initial payment to authors against which any royalties are offset.

commissioning editor: Someone in a publishing house who looks for authors to write particular books for publication; sometimes also an acquiring editor.

imprint: The name of the publisher; usually a brand operating under the auspices of a large publishing house.

literary agent: Person who finds marketable authors and tries to sell rights in their work to publishers, taking a commission in the process.

Nielsen Bookscan: Company that produces bestseller lists and other analysis of the British book industry.

royalties: Payment received by the author as a percentage of sales. Usually set off against the advance.

rights: The main commodity in the books business. Rights can be separated out to include film, television, multimedia, merchandising and rights to publish abroad.

New media

3G: Third-generation mobile phones, capable of video messaging, location mapping and other technical wizardries.

ADSL: Broadband over a BT phone line (but not necessarily bought from BT).

blog: Diary-style web page in which new entries are added at the top and old ones drift to the bottom; popular among those who want a web page but don't necessarily know much about the internet. Short for "weblog".

broadband: High-speed internet access, usually 512kbps (kilobytes per second) as opposed to the 52kbps of a standard modem.

browser: Software usually used to surf, or "browse", the internet. Internet Explorer and Netscape Communicator are the most popular.

coverage: The percentage of the country or the population that can be reached by a mobile phone network.

search engine: Service allowing you to find a word, image anywhere on the world wide web. Google is the best.

short message service (SMS): Text messaging.

Wi-fi: Wireless internet access.

Media law

Communications Act 2003: Legislation under which Ofcom became the super-regulator for the broadcasting industry.

contempt of court: A crime which carries imprisonment or a fine. Journalists could be in contempt of a court by, among other things, publishing information about a defendant or other person granted privacy under a court order or injunction; or by speculating about the guilt or innocence of a defendant; or by publishing a photograph of a defendant when identity is an issue.

culture select committee: Influential cross-party parliamentary committee that examines issues in culture, media and sport.

DCMS: Government's department of culture, media and sport. Headed by culture secretary Tessa Jowell.

European convention on human rights: European Union legislation, incorporated in British law through the Human Rights Act 1998. Includes articles protecting right to freedom of expression, but also the right to privacy.

European court of human rights: Highest European court dealing with human rights law.

law commission: Senior lawyers who meet to recommend changes in the law.

libel: A civil "tort", for which a complainant may sue for damages. Generally speaking, a journalist commits libel by publishing or broadcasting something that is defamatory, even by implication, of a person or a small enough group of people; *unless* the journalist can prove that what they wrote or published was true, or it was fair comment based firmly in fact, or it was an accurate, contemporaneous report of something said in parliament or court. But that isn't the half of it: see the latest edition of *McNae's Essential Law for Journalists*.

Advertising & PR

Advertising Association: Body representing the advertising and promotional marketing industries.

Advertising Standards Authority: Regulator for advertising.

below the line: Marketing services such as PR, direct marketing, market research and sales promotion are said to be "below the line"; advertising directly in media is "above the line".

creatives: In advertising, art directors and copywriters, who often work in pairs on an ad.

display: Advertising in the main body of a publication (as opposed to classified).

demographic data: Information defining a population according to factors such as age, sex and income; used to target an ad or marketing campaign.

Institute of Public Relations: PR professional organisation.

media agency: Agency that controls the purchase of advertising space.

pitch: The lifeblood of the advertising industry is the pitch for an account.

press release: Information sent by PR agencies and other publicists to journalists.

Public Relations Consultants Association: PR trade body.

solus: In publishing, the only advert on a page.

Careers & training

Bectu: Broadcasting, entertainment, cinematograph and theatre union. Represents workers in broadcasting, film, theatre, entertainment, leisure and interactive media.

BJTC: Broadcast journalism training council. Accredits broadcast journalism courses.

FT2: Freelance Training for Film and Television, a respected training body.

NCTJ: National council for the training of journalists. Accredits newspaper and magazine journalism courses.

NUJ: National union of journalists. Represents journalists.

Pact: Producers' alliance for cinema and television. Represents independent television production companies.

Skillset: National training organisation for broadcast, film, video and interactive media.

Libraries & research

Specialist libraries and archives

Bank of England Information Centre
Threadneedle Street
London EC2R 8AH
020 7601 4715
informationcentre@bankofengland.co.uk
www.bankofengland.co.uk
Central banking and finance

Barbican Library
Barbican Centre, Silk Street
London EC2Y 8DS
020 7638 0569
barbicanlib@corpoflondon.gov.uk
www.cityoflondon.gov.uk
Arts lending library

BBC Written Archives Centre
Peppard Road, Caversham Park
Reading, Berkshire RG4 8TZ
0118 948 6281
wac.enquiries@bbc.co.uk
www.bbc.co.uk/heritage

bfi National Library, British Film Institute
21 Stephen Street, London W1P 1LN
020 7255 1444
library@bfi.org.uk
www.bfi.org.uk/nationallibrary/index.html
World's largest collection of documentation on film and television

British Architectural Library
Royal Institute of British Architects
66 Portland Place, London W1B 1AD
020 7580 5533
bal@inst.riba.org
www.architecture.com

British Library
Reader Admissions Office
St Pancras, 96 Euston Road
London NW1 2DB
0870 4441500
reader-admissions@bl.uk
www.bl.uk

British Newspaper Library
Colindale Avenue, London NW9 5HE
020 7412 7332
newspaper@bl.uk
www.bl.uk/catalogues/newspapers.html

CAA Library and Information Centre
Aviation House, Gatwick Airport
West Sussex RH6 0YR
01293 573725
infoservices@caa.co.uk
www.caa.co.uk

Catholic Central Library
Lancing Street, London NW1 1ND
020 7383 4333
librarian@catholic-library.org.uk
www.catholic-library.org.uk

City Business Library
1 Brewers' Hall Garden
London EC2V 5BX
020 7332 1812
cbl@corpoflondon.gov.uk
www.cityoflondon.gov.uk/citybusinesslibrary

City of Westminster Archives Centre
10 St Ann's Street
London SW1P 2DE
020 7641 5180
archives@westminster.gov.uk
www.westminster.gov.uk/archives

DigiReels Media Monitoring
Paramount House
162–170 Wardour Street
London W1F 8ZX
020 7437 7743
peter.godden@digireels.co.uk
www.digireels.co.uk
Online ad database

Foreign and Commonwealth Office, Library and information services E213
King Charles Street
London SW1A 2AH
020 7270 3925
library.enquiries@fco.gov.uk
www.fco.gov.uk

Forestry Commission Library
Forest Research Station
Alice Holt Lodge, Wrecclesham
Farnham, Surrey GU10 4LH
01420 222555
library@forestry.gsi.gov.uk
www.forestry.gov.uk/forest_research

French Institute Library
Institut francais, 17 Queensberry Place
London SW7 2DT
020 7073 1350
library@ambafrance.org.uk
www.institut.ambafrance.org.uk

Goethe-Institut Library
50 Princes Gate, Exhibition Road
London SW7 2PH
020 7596 4000
mail@london.goethe.org
www.goethe.de/london
German literature & reference

Harry Price Library of Magical Literature
University of London Library
Senate House, Malet Street
London WC1E 7HU
020 7862 8470
historic@ull.ac.uk
www.ull.ac.uk/historic/collections.shtml
Magic

Institute of Education Library (London)
20 Bedford Way, London WC1H 0AL
020 7612 6080
lib.enquiries@ioe.ac.uk
www.ioe.ac.uk
Over 300,000 volumes including special sections on educational studies. 2,000 periodicals

Instituto Cervantes
102 Eaton Square
London SW1W 9AN
020 7201 0757
biblon@cervantes.es
www.cervantes.es
Spain

International Booksearch Service
020 7639 8900
sarah.fordham@btinternet.com
www.scfordham.com
Finds out-of-print books

Italian Cultural Institute
39 Belgrave Square
London SW1X 8NX
020 7396 4425
library@italcultur.org.uk
www.italcultur.org.uk

Linen Hall Library
17 Donegall Square North
Belfast BT1 5GB
028 9032 1707
info@linenhall.com
www.linenhall.com
Ireland and politics

Llyfrgell Genedlaethol Cymru/ National Library of Wales
Aberystwyth, Ceredigion SY23 3BU
01970 632800
holi@llgc.org.uk
www.llgc.org.uk

London Metropolitan Archives (LMA)
40 Northampton Road, Clerkenwell
London EC1R 0HB
020 7332 3820
ask.lma@corpoflondon.gov.uk
www.cityoflondon.gov.uk/lma
Largest local authority archive in the UK

Murder Files
Dommett Hill Farm, Hare Lane
Buckland St Mary
Somerset TA20 3JS
01460 234065
enquiry@murderfiles.com
www.murderfiles.com
UK murders since 1400

National Archives
Kew, Richmond, Surrey TW9 4DU
020 8392 3444
enquiry@nationalarchives.gov.uk
www.nationalarchives.gov.uk
11th-20th century national records

National Film and TV Archive
Kingshill Way, Berkhamsted
Herts HP4 3TP
01442 876301
david.pierce@bfi.org.uk
www.bfi.org.uk
Contains more than 275,000 films and 200,000 TV programmes, dating from 1895 to the present

National Library of Scotland
George IV Bridge
Edinburgh EH1 1EW
0131 226 4531
enquiries@nls.uk
www.nls.uk

National Meteorological Archive
The Scott Building, Sterling Centre
Eastern Road, Bracknell
Berkshire RG12 2PW
01344 861629
metarc@metoffice.com
www.metoffice.com

National Museum of Scotland
NMS Enterprises, Chambers Street
Edinburgh EH1 1JF
0131 247 4026
nmsphoto@nms.ac.uk
www.nms.ac.uk

Natural History Museum Library
Cromwell Road, London SW7 5BD
020 7942 5460
library@nhm.ac.uk
www.nhm.ac.uk/library/index.html

Office for National Statistics
1 Drummond Gate
London SW1V 2QQ
0845 601 3034
info@statistics.gov.uk
www.statistics.gov.uk

Polish Library
238–246 King Street
London W6 0RF
020 8741 0474
bibliotekapolska@posk.library.fsnet.co.uk

Royal Geographical Society Library (with the Institute of British Geographers)
1 Kensington Gore
London SW7 2AR
020 7591 3000
press@rgs.org
www.rgs.org

Royal Society Library
6 Carlton House Terrace
London SW1Y 5AG
020 7451 2606
library@royalsoc.ac.uk
www.royalsoc.ac.uk
Science

Royal Society of Medicine Library
1 Wimpole Street, London W1G 0AE
020 7290 2940
library@rsm.ac.uk
www.rsm.ac.uk

Science Fiction Foundation Research Library
Liverpool University Library
PO Box 123, Liverpool L69 3DA
0151 794 3142
asawyer@liverpool.ac.uk
www.liv.ac.uk/~asawyer/sffchome.html

Science Museum Library
Imperial College Road
London SW7 5NH
020 7942 4242
smlinfo@nmsi.ac.uk
www.sciencemuseum.org.uk

Theatre Museum Library & Archive
1e Tavistock Street
London WC2E 7PR
020 7943 4700
tmenquiries@vam.ac.uk
www.theatremuseum.org

United Nations Information Centre
Millbank Tower (21st Floor)
21–24 Millbank, London SW1P 4QH
020 7630 1981
info@uniclondon.org
www.unitednations.org.uk

Westminster Music Library
Victoria Library
160 Buckingham Palace Road
London SW1W 9UD
020 7641 4292
musiclibrary@westminster.gov.uk
www.westminster.gov.uk/libraries/special/music

Wiener Library
4 Devonshire Street
London W1W 5BH
020 7636 7247
info@wienerlibrary.co.uk
www.wienerlibrary.co.uk
Modern Jewish history

Women's Library
25 Old Castle Street
London E1 7NT
020 7320 2222
moreinfo@thewomenslibrary.ac.uk
www.thewomenslibrary.ac.uk

Zoological Society Library
Regent's Park, London NW1 4RY
020 7449 6293
library@zsl.org
www.zsl.org

Research data

Audit Bureau of Circulations (ABC)
Saxon House, 211 High Street
Berkhamsted, Hertfordshire HP4 1AD
01442 870800
marketing@abc.org.uk
www.abc.org.uk
Circulation figures for newspapers and magazines

Broadcasters' Audience Research Board (Barb)
18 Dering Street, London W1S 1AQ
020 7529 5531
enquiries@barb.co.uk
www.barb.co.uk
TV audience data

Communications Research Group
Anvic House, 84 Vyse Street
Jewellery Quarter
Birmingham B18 6HA
0121 523 9595
research@crghq.com
www.crghq.com
Market and audience research

LemonAd United Kingdom
Nielsen/NetRatings UK, 2nd Floor
4 Elder Street, London E1 6BT
020 7420 9268
barney@netcrawling.com
www.lomonad.com
Advertising monitoring in Europe

National Readership Survey (NRS)
40 Parker Street, London WC2B 5PQ
020 7242 8111
stevemillington@nrs.co.uk
www.nrs.co.uk
Newspaper and magazine readership estimates

Nielsen BookScan
3rd Floor Midas House
62 Goldsworth Road
Woking, Surrey GU21 6LQ
01483 712222
info@nielsenbookscan.co.uk
www.nielsenbookscan.co.uk
International sales data monitoring and analysis service for the English-language book industry worldwide

Nielsen/NetRatings
ACNielsen House, London Road
Headington, Oxford OX3 9RX
01865 742742
www.acneilson.com
Marketing research worldwide

Rajar
Gainsborough House
81 Oxford Street, London W1D 2EU
020 7903 5350
info@rajar.co.uk
www.rajar.co.uk
Measures and profiles the audiences of UK radio stations

Library associations

Association of Independent Libraries
Leeds Library, 18 Commercial Street
Leeds, West Yorkshire LS1 6AL
0113 245 3071
admin@hlsi.demon.co.uk
www.independentlibraries.co.uk/

Association of UK Media Libraries
Editorial Information Services, Financial Times
One Southwark Bridge
London SE1 9HL
020 7873 3920
Margaret.Katny@bbc.co.uk
www.aukml.org.uk

Chartered Institute of Library and Information Professionals
7 Ridgmount Street
London WC1E 7AE
020 7255 0500
info@cilip.org.uk
www.cilip.org.uk

Chartered Institute of Library and Information Professionals in Scotland
1st Floor, Building C, Brandon Gate
Leechlee Road, Hamilton ML3 6AU
01698 458888
cilips@slainte.org.uk
www.slainte.org.uk

Focal International
Pentax House, South Hill Avenue
South Harrow HA2 0DU
020 8423 5853
info@focalint.org
www.focalint.org
Trade association of commercial film/audiovisual libraries & film professionals

Museum Libraries & Archives Council
16 Queen Anne's Gate
London SW1H 9AA
020 7273 1444
info@mla.gov.uk
www.mla.gov.uk
Council for museums, archives and libraries

Media awards

Press

Amnesty International Media Awards
020 7814 6278
www.amnesty.org.uk/mediaawards
Human rights journalism

British Garden Writers Guild
020 7245 6943
www.gardenwriters.co.uk/awards

British Press Awards
020 8565 4392
www.britishpressawards.com
Organised by Press Gazette

British Society of Magazine Editors
020 8906 4664
www.bsme.com

Emmas (Ethnic Multicultural Media Academy awards)
020 7636 1233
www.emma.tv
Multicultural media

Foreign Press Association Annual Media Awards
020 7930 0445
www.foreign-press.org.uk
International journalism by British media

Glenfiddich Food & Drink awards
020 8334 1235
www.glenfiddich.com/foodanddrink

Guardian Student Media Awards
020 7278 2332
www.media.guardian.co.uk/studentmediaawards
Student journalists, designers and photographers

The Herald Scottish Student Press Awards 2003
0141 302 7000
www.theherald.co.uk
Open to full-time students in Scotland

ICIJ Award for Outstanding International Investigative Reporting
00 1 202 481 1234
www.icij.org

Local Reporting Awards
020 7636 7014
www.newspapersoc.org.uk
Under-30s

Medical Journalism Awards
023 8035 4728
www.norwichunion.co.uk/medical_journalism_awards

NetMedia European Online Journalism Awards
020 7637 7097
www.net-media.co.uk

Newspaper Awards
01869 340788
www.newspaperawards.newstech.co.uk
Technical innovation in newspaper and new media production

Observer Hodge Award
01727 799987
www.observer.co.uk/hodgeaward
Young photographers

Picture Editors' Awards
administrator@pictureawards.net
www.pictureawards.net
Photographic journalism

Plain English Media Awards
01663 744409
www.plainenglish.co.uk/mediaawards
Campaign against gobbledygook

PPA Awards
020 7404 4166
www.ppa.co.uk
Magazines

PPAi interactive Awards
020 7400 7532
www.ppai.co.uk
Online publishing

Press Gazette Student Journalism Awards
020 8565 3056
www.pressgazette.co.uk
Open to students enrolled on a journalism course

Race in the Media Awards
020 7939 0000
www.cre.gov.uk
Organised by Commission for Racial Equality

Regional Press Awards
020 8565 3056
www.regionalpressawards.co.uk
Organised by Press Gazette

What the Papers Say Awards
Fax: 0870 7058562
www.whatthepaperssay.co.uk
National newspaper journalists

TV and radio

Bafta Awards
020 7734 0022
www.bafta.com
Film, TV and interactive industries

British Comedy Awards
020 7605 1200
www.britishcomedyawards.co.uk

Broadcast Awards
020 7505 8452
www.broadcastnow.co.uk
Programme ideas and execution

Indie Awards (Pact)
020 7331 6000
www.pact.co.uk

National TV Awards
020 7241 8000
Winners picked by viewers

NTL Commercial Radio Awards
020 7306 2603
www.crca.co.uk

Royal Television Society Awards
020 7691 2470
www.rts.org.uk

Sony Radio Academy Awards
020 7255 2010
www.radioacademy.org/awards

Student Radio Awards
www.studentradio.org.uk

Books

British Book Design and Production Awards
01865 484453
www.publishers.org.uk

Guardian First Book Award
020 7278 2332
www.guardian.co.uk/firstbook
First-time writers of fiction, poetry, biography, memoirs, history, politics, science and current affairs

Orange Prize for Fiction
020 7471 6848
www.orangeprize.co.uk
Women's fiction

The Man Booker Prize
020 7631 2666
www.themanbookerprize.com
Best novel in English by citizen of Commonwealth, Ireland, Pakistan or South Africa

Whitbread
020 7202 2822
www.whitbread-bookawards.co.uk
Contemporary British writing

Advertising & PR

Advertising, Marketing & Digital Media Awards
020 7693 0428
www.newspapersoc.org.uk

British Television Advertising Awards
020 7734 6962
www.btaa.co.uk

Campaign Direct Awards
020 8267 4090
www.brandrepublic.com/magazines/campaign

Campaign Media Awards
020 8267 4090
www.brandrepublic.com/magazines/campaign

Campaign Poster Advertising Awards
020 8267 4090
www.brandrepublic.com/magazines/campaign

Cannes Lions International Advertising Festival Awards
020 7291 8444
www.canneslions.com

Creative Juice Awards
020 7636 7014
www.newspapersoc.org.uk
Young creative teams with maximum of three years' experience

Institute of Public Relations Excellence Awards
020 7253 5151
www.ipr.org.uk

London International Advertising Awards
020 8426 1670
www.liaawards.com

Marketing Week Effectiveness Awards
020 7970 4772
www.marketingweek.co.uk

Media Week Awards
020 8565 3056
www.mediaweekawards.co.uk

PR Week Awards
020 8267 4017
www.prweek.com

The Pride Awards
01158 419699
www.ipr.org.uk/prideawards/

TUC/Bank of Scotland Press and PR Awards
020 7467 1242
www.tuc.org.uk
Journalism about Scottish issues and on Scottish publications

Contacts book

Government: **UK government**

Downing Street

Prime Minister's Office
10 Downing Street
London SW1A 2AA
020 7270 3000
Press: 020 7930 4433
www.no-10.gov.uk
*Prime minister: Tony Blair**

Cabinet Office
70 Whitehall, London SW1A 2AS
020 7276 3000
Press: 020 7276 1191
www.cabinet-office.gov.uk
Cabinet Office minister: Douglas Alexander
Leader of the Lords: Baroness Amos; leader of the Commons and Privy Seal: Peter Hain*; deputy leader: Phil Woolas; party chairman: Ian McCartney**

Government departments

Treasury
1 Horse Guards Road
London SW1A 2HQ
020 7270 5000
Press: 020 7270 5238
www.hm-treasury.gov.uk
*Chancellor of the Exchequer: Gordon Brown**
Chief secretary: Paul Boateng; paymaster general: Dawn Primarolo; financial secretary: Ruth Kelly; economic secretary: John Healey*

Deputy Prime Minister
26 Whitehall, London SW1A 2WH
020 7944 4400
Press: 020 7944 4651
www.odpm.gov.uk
*Deputy prime minister: John Prescott**
Local government minister: Nick Raynsford; regeneration minister: Lord Rooker; housing/planning minister: Keith Hill; parliamentary secretaries: Yvette Cooper, Phil Hope

Constitutional Affairs
54 Victoria Street
London SW1E 6QW
020 7210 8500
Press: 020 7210 8512
www.lcd.gov.uk
*Constitutional affairs secretary: Lord Falconer**

Culture, Media and Sport
2–4 Cockspur Street
London SW1Y 5DH
020 7211 6000
Press: 020 7211 6215
www.culture.gov.uk
*Culture secretary: Tessa Jowell**
Arts minister: Estelle Morris; sports minister: Richard Caborn; minister for media: Lord McIntosh

Defence
Horseguards Avenue
London SW1A 2HB
020 7218 9000
Press: 020 7218 3256
www.mod.uk
*Defence secretary: Geoff Hoon**
Minister: Adam Ingram; parliamentary secretaries: Lord Bach, Ivor Caplin

Education and Skills
Great Smith Street
London SW1P 3BT
020 7925 5000
Press: 020 7925 6789
www.dfes.gov.uk
*Education secretary: Charles Clarke**
Schools standards minister: David Miliband; universities minister: Alan Johnson; minister for children: Margaret Hodge; parliamentary secretaries: Baroness Ashton, Ivan Lewis, Stephen Twigg

Environment, Food and Rural Affairs
17 Smith Square, London SW1P 3JR
020 7238 3000
Press: 020 7238 6600
www.defra.gov.uk
*Environment secretary: Margaret Beckett**
Rural affairs minister: Alun Michael; environment minister: Elliot Morley; parliamentary secretaries: Ben Bradshaw, Lord Whitty

Foreign Office
Whitehall, London SW1A 2AH
020 7270 1500
Press: 020 7008 3100
www.fco.gov.uk
*Foreign secretary: Jack Straw**
Europe minister: Denis MacShane; minister for trade: Mike O'Brien; Middle East minister: Baroness Symons; parliamentary secretaries: Michael Jay, Bill Rammell, Chris Mullin

Health
79 Whitehall, London SW1A 2NS
020 7210 4850
Press: 020 7210 5231
www.doh.gov.uk
*Health secretary: John Reid**
Ministers: John Hutton, Rosie Winterton; parliamentary secretaries: Lord Warner, Melanie Johnson, Stephen Ladyman

Home Office
Queen Anne's Gate
London SW1H 9AT
0870 000 1585
Press: 020 7273 4545
www.homeoffice.gov.uk
*Home secretary: David Blunkett**
Ministers: Hazel Blears, Des Browne, Baroness Scotland, Beverley Hughes; parliamentary secretaries: Michael Wills, Paul Goggins, Fiona Mactaggart, Caroline Flint

** cabinet minister*

International Development
1 Palace Street
London SW1E 5HE
020 7023 0000
Press: 020 7023 0600
www.dfid.gov.uk
*International development secretary: Hilary Benn**
Parliamentary secretary: Gareth Thomas

Trade and Industry
1 Victoria Street
London SW1H 0ET
020 7215 5000
Press: 020 7215 5954
www.dti.gov.uk
*Trade and industry secretary: Patricia Hewitt**
Energy, e-commerce and postal services minister: Stephen Timms; industry and regions minister: Jacqui Smith; minister for trade: Mike O'Brien; parliamentary secretaries: Nigel Griffiths, Lord Sainsbury, Gerry Sutcliffe

Transport
76 Marsham Street
London SW1P 4DR
020 7944 8300
Press: 020 7944 3066 (roads)
020 7944 3108 (marine, aviation, railways)
www.dft.gov.uk
*Transport secretary: Alistair Darling**
Minister: Kim Howells; parliamentary secretaries: David Jamieson, Tony McNulty

Work and Pensions
79 Whitehall, London SW1A 2NS
020 7238 0800
Press: 020 7238 0866
www.dwp.gov.uk
*Pensions secretary: Andrew Smith**
Minister: Jane Kennedy (work), Malcolm Wicks (pensions); parliamentary secretaries: Baroness Hollis, Chris Pond, Maria Eagle, Baroness Ashton

Law Officers' Department
9 Buckingham Gate
London SW1E 6JP
020 7271 2422
Press: 020 7271 2440
www.lslo.gov.uk
Attorney general: Lord Goldsmith
Solicitor general: Harriet Harman

Privy Council
2 Carlton Gardens
London SW1Y 5AA
020 7210 3000
Press: 020 7210 1092
www.privy-council.org.uk
President: Baroness Amos (also leader of the Lords)*

** cabinet minister*

Wales

Wales Office
Whitehall, London SW1A 2ER
020 7270 0549
Press: 020 7270 0565;
029 2089 8267
www.walesoffice.gov.uk
*Wales secretary: Peter Hain**
parliamentary secretary: Don Touhig

National Assembly for Wales
Cardiff Bay, Cardiff CF99 1NA
029 2082 5111
Press: 029 2089 8931;
029 2089 8763 (first minister)
www.wales.gov.uk
First minister: Rhodri Morgan; education and lifelong learning: Jane Davidson; economic development and transport: Andrew Davies; environment, planning and countryside: Carwyn Jones; finance, local government and public services: Sue Essex; health and social services: Jane Hutt; culture, sport and the welsh language: Alun Pugh; business Karen Sinclair; social justice and regeneration: Edwina Hart

Scotland

Scotland Office
Whitehall, London SW1A 2AU
020 7270 6828
Press: 0131 244 9053
www.scottishsecretary.gov.uk
*Scottish secretary: Alistair Darling**
parliamentary secretary: Anne Mcguire

Scottish Executive
St Andrews House
Edinburgh EH1 3DG
0131 556 8400
Press: 0131 244 1111
www.scotland.gov.uk
First minister: Jack Mcconnell; deputy first minister, and enterprise & lifelong learning: Jim Wallace (E&LL deputy: Lewis Macdonald); education and young people: Peter Peacock (deputy: Evan Robson); transport: Nicol Stephen; environment and rural development: Allan Wilson; tourism, culture and sport: Frank McAveety; justice: Cathy Jamieson (deputy: Hugh Henry); finance and public services: Andy Kerr (deputy: Tavish Scott); health and community care: Malcolm Chisholm (deputy: Tom McCabe); communities: Margaret Curran (deputy: Mary Mulligan); parliamentary business: Tavish Scott; Lord advocat: Colin Boyd; solicitor general: Elish Angiolini

Northern Ireland

Northern Ireland Office
11 Millbank
London
SW1P 4PN
020 7210 3000, 028 9052 0700
Press: 020 7210 6518 / 028 9052 8220
www.nio.gov.uk

Northern Ireland Assembly
(suspended October 2002)
www.ni-assembly.gov.uk

Northern Ireland Executive
(suspended October 2002)
www.northernireland.gov.uk

Local and regional government

Local Government Association
020 7664 3131
www.lga.gov.uk
County Councils Network
020 7664 3011
www.lga.gov.uk/ccn/
Audit Commission for Local Authorities
020 7828 1212
www.audit-commission.gov.uk
Convention of Scottish Local Authorities
0131 474 9200
www.cosla.gov.uk
Improvement and Development Agency
020 7296 6600
www.idea.gov.uk
Local government ombudsman
0845 602 1983
www.lgo.org.uk
Scotland
0870 011 5378
www.scottishombudsman.org.uk
Wales
01656 661325
www.ombudsman-wales.org

Professional bodies

Association of Council Secretaries and Soliticors
01772 40404
www.acses.org.uk
Association of Electoral Administrators
0151 281 8246
www.aea-elections.co.uk
Association of Local Authority Chief Executives
01923 727282
www.alace.org.uk

England

London

Greater London Authority
020 7983 4000
www.london.gov.uk
Association of London Government
020 7934 9999
www.alg.gov.uk
Corporation of London
020 7606 3030
www.corpoflondon.gov.uk

LONDON BOROUGHS

Barking and Dagenham
020 8592 4500
Barnet
020 8359 2000
Bexley
020 8303 7777
Brent
020 8937 1234
Bromley
020 8464 3333
Camden
020 7278 4444
Croydon
020 8686 4433
Ealing
020 8825 5866
Enfield
020 8379 1000
Greenwich
020 8854 8888
Hackney
020 8356 5000
Hammersmith and Fulham
020 8748 3020
Haringey
020 8489 0000
Harrow
020 8863 5611
Havering
01708 434343
Hillingdon
01895 250111
Hounslow
020 8583 2000
Islington
020 7527 2000
Kensington and Chelsea
020 7937 5464
Kingston upon Thames
020 8546 2121
Lambeth
020 7926 1000
Lewisham
020 8314 6000
Merton
020 8274 4901
Newham
020 8430 2000
Redbridge
020 8554 5000
Richmond upon Thames
020 8891 1411
Southwark
020 7525 5000
Sutton
020 8770 5000
Tower Hamlets
020 7364 5000
Waltham Forest
020 8496 3000
Wandsworth
020 8871 6000
Westminster
020 7641 6000

County councils

Bedfordshire
01234 363222
Buckinghamshire
01296 395000
Cambridgeshire
01223 717111
Cheshire
01244 602424
Cornwall
01872 322000
Cumbria
01228 606060
Derbyshire
01629 580000
Devon
01392 382000
Dorset
01305 251000
Durham
0191 383 3000
East Sussex
01273 481000
Essex
01245 492211
Gloucestershire
01452 425000
Hampshire
01962 841841
Hertfordshire
01992 555555
Kent
01622 671411
Lancashire
01772 254868
Leicestershire
0116 232 3232
Lincolnshire
01522 552222
Norfolk
01603 222222
North Yorkshire
01609 780780
Northamptonshire
01604 236236
Northumberland
01670 533000
Nottinghamshire
0115 982 3823
Oxfordshire
01865 792422
Shropshire
01743 251000
Somerset
01823 355455
Staffordshire
01785 223121
Suffolk
01473 583000
Surrey
020 8541 8800
Warwickshire
01926 410410
West Sussex
01243 777100
Wiltshire
01225 713000
Worcestershire
01905 763763
Isle of Wight
01983 821000
Rutland
01572 722577

City and district councils

AVON

see Somerset & Avon

BEDFORDSHIRE

Bedford
01234 267422
Luton
01582 546000
Mid Bedfordshire
01525 402051
South Bedfordshire
01582 472222

BERKSHIRE

Bracknell Forest
01344 424642
Reading
01189 390900
Slough
01753 552288
West Berkshire
01635 424000
Windsor and Maidenhead
01628 798888
Wokingham
01189 746000

BUCKINGHAMSHIRE

Aylesbury Vale
01296 585858
Chiltern
01494 729000
Milton Keynes
01908 691691
South Bucks
01753 533333
Wycombe
01494 461000

CAMBRIDGESHIRE

Cambridge
01223 457000
Peterborough
01733 563141
East Cambridgeshire
01353 665555

Fenland
01354 654321
Huntingdonshire
01480 388388
South Cambridgeshire
01223 443000

CHANNEL ISLANDS

Isles of Scilly
01720 422537
States of Jersey
01534 603000
www.gov.je
States of Guernsey
01481 717000
www.gov.gg

CHESHIRE

Chester
01244 324324
Congleton
01270 763231
Crewe and Nantwich
01270 537777
Ellesmere Port and Neston
0151 356 6789
Halton
0151 424 2061
Macclesfield
01625 500500
Vale Royal
01606 862862
Warrington
01925 444400

CLEVELAND

Hartlepool
01429 266522
Middlesbrough
01642 245432
Redcar and Cleveland
01642 444000

CORNWALL

Caradon
01579 341000
Carrick
01872 224400
Kerrier
01209 614000
North Cornwall
01208 893333
Penwith
01736 362341
Restormel
01726 223300

COUNTY DURHAM

Durham
0191 386 6111
Chester-le-Street
0191 387 1919
Derwentside
01207 218000
Easington
0191 527 0501
Sedgefield
01388 816166
Teesdale
01833 690000
Wear Valley
01388 765555

CUMBRIA

Carlisle
01228 817000
Allerdale
01900 326333
Barrow-in-Furness
01229 894900
Copeland
01946 852585
South Lakeland
01539 733333

DERBYSHIRE

Derby
01332 293111
Amber Valley
01773 570222
Bolsover
01246 240000
Chesterfield
01246 345345
Derbyshire Dales
01629 761100
Erewash
0115 907 2244
High Peak
0845 129 7777
North East Derbyshire
01246 231111
South Derbyshire
01283 221000

DEVON

Exeter
01392 277888
Plymouth
01752 668000
East Devon
01395 516551
Mid Devon
01884 255255
North Devon
01271 327711
South Hams
01803 861234
Teignbridge
01626 361101
Torbay
01803 201201
Torridge
01237 428700
West Devon
01822 813600

DORSET

Bournemouth
01202 451451
Christchurch
01202 495000
East Dorset
01202 886201
North Dorset
01258 454111
Poole
01202 633633
Purbeck
01929 556561
West Dorset
01305 251010
Weymouth and Portland
01305 838000

EAST SUSSEX

Brighton and Hove
01273 290000
Eastbourne
01323 410000
Hastings
01424 781066
Lewes
01273 471600
Rother
01424 787878
Wealden
01892 653311

ESSEX

Basildon
01268 533333
Braintree
01376 552525
Brentwood
01277 261111
Castle Point
01268 882200
Chelmsford
01245 606606
Colchester
01206 282222
Dagenham
01325 380651
Epping Forest
01992 564000
Harlow
01279 446611
Maldon
01621 854477
Rochford
01702 546366
Southend-on-Sea
01702 215000
Tendring
01255 425501
Thurrock
01375 652652
Uttlesford
01799 510510

GLOUCESTERSHIRE

Gloucester
01452 522232
Cheltenham
01242 262626
Cotswold
01285 623000
Forest of Dean
01594 810000
South Gloucestershire
01454 868686
Stroud
01453 766321
Tewkesbury
01684 295010

GREATER MANCHESTER

Manchester
0161 234 5000
Bolton
01204 333333
Bury
0161 253 5000
Oldham
0161 911 3000
Rochdale
01706 647474
Salford
0161 794 4711
Stockport
0161 480 4949
Tameside
0161 342 8355
Trafford
0161 912 2000
Wigan
01942 244991

HAMPSHIRE

Portsmouth
023 9282 2251
Southampton
023 8022 3855
Basingstoke and Deane
01256 844844
East Hampshire
01730 266551
Eastleigh
02380 688000
Fareham
01329 236100
Gosport
023 9258 4242
Hart
01252 622122
Havant
023 9247 4174
New Forest
023 8028 5000
Rushmoor
01252 398398
Test Valley
01264 368000
Winchester
01962 840222

HEREFORDSHIRE

Hereford
01432 260000

HERTFORDSHIRE

St Albans
01727 866100
Broxbourne
01992 785555
Dacorum
01442 228000
East Hertfordshire
01279 655261
Hertsmere
020 8207 2277
North Hertfordshire
01462 474000
Stevenage
01438 242242
Watford
01923 226400
Welwyn Hatfield
01707 357000

KENT

Canterbury
01227 862000
Ashford
01233 637311

Dartford
01322 343434
Dover
01304 821199
Gravesham
01474 564422
Maidstone
01622 602000
Medway
01634 306000
Sevenoaks
01732 227000
Shepway
01303 850388
Swale
01795 424341
Thanet
01843 577000
Tonbridge and Malling
01732 844522
Tunbridge Wells
01892 526121

LANCASHIRE

Lancaster
01524 582000
Preston
01772 906000
Blackburn with Darwen
01254 585585
Blackpool
01253 477477
Burnley
01282 425011
Chorley
01257 515151
Fylde
01253 658658
Hyndburn
01254 388111
Pendle
01282 661661
Ribble Valley
01200 425111
Rossendale
01706 217777
South Ribble
01772 421491
West Lancashire
01695 577177
Wyre
01253 891000

LEICESTERSHIRE

Leicester
0116 254 9922
Blaby
0116 275 0555
Charnwood
01509 263151
Harborough
01858 821100
Hinckley and Bosworth
01455 238141
Melton
01664 502502
North West Leicestershire
01530 454545
Oadby and Wigston
0116 288 8961

LINCOLNSHIRE

Lincoln
01522 881188
Boston
01205 314200
East Lindsey
01507 601111
North East Lincolnshire
01472 313131
North Kesteven
01529 414155
North Lincolnshire
01724 296296
South Holland
01775 761161
South Kesteven
01476 406080
West Lindsey
01427 676676

MERSEYSIDE

Liverpool
0151 233 3000
Knowsley
0151 489 6000
Sefton
01704 533133
St Helens
01744 456000
Wirral
0151 638 7070

NORFOLK

Norwich
01603 622233
Breckland
01362 695333
Broadland
01603 431133
Great Yarmouth
01493 856100
Kings Lynn and West Norfolk
01553 616200
North Norfolk
01263 513811
South Norfolk
01508 533633

NORTH AND EAST YORKSHIRE

York
01904 613161
Craven
01756 700600
East Riding of Yorkshire
01482 887700
Hambleton
01609 779977
Harrogate
01423 500600
Kingston upon Hull
01482 609100
Richmondshire
01748 829100
Ryedale
01653 600666
Scarborough
01723 232323
Selby
01757 705101

Stockton-on-Tees
01642 393939

NORTHAMPTONSHIRE

Corby
01536 402551
Daventry
01327 871100
East Northamptonshire
01832 742000
Kettering
01536 410333
Northampton
01604 233500
South Northamptonshire
01327 322322
Wellingborough
01933 229777

NORTHUMBERLAND

Alnwick
01665 510505
Berwick-upon-Tweed
01289 330044
Blyth Valley
01670 542000
Castle Morpeth
01670 535000
Tynedale
01434 652200
Wansbeck
01670 532200

NOTTINGHAMSHIRE

Nottingham
0115 915 5555
Ashfield
01623 450000
Bassetlaw
01909 533533
Broxtowe
0115 917 7777
Gedling
0115 901 3901
Mansfield
01623 463463
Newark and Sherwood
01636 650000
Rushcliffe
0115 981 9911

OXFORDSHIRE

Oxford
01865 249811
Cherwell
01295 252535
South Oxfordshire
01491 823000
Vale of White Horse
01235 520202
West Oxfordshire
01993 702941

SHROPSHIRE

Bridgnorth
01746 713100
North Shropshire
01939 232771
Oswestry
01691 671111
Shrewsbury and Atcham
01743 281000

South Shropshire
01584 813000
Telford & Wrekin
01952 202100

SOMERSET AND AVON

Bath and North East Somerset
01225 477000
Bristol
0117 922 2000
Mendip
01749 343399
North Somerset
01934 888888
Sedgemoor
01278 435435
South Somerset
01935 462462
Taunton Deane
01823 356356
West Somerset
01984 632291

SOUTH YORKSHIRE

Doncaster
01302 734444
Rotherham
01709 382121
Sheffield
0114 272 6444

STAFFORDSHIRE

Stoke-on-Trent
01782 234567
Cannock Chase
01543 462621
East Staffordshire
01283 508000
Lichfield
01543 308000
Newcastle-under-Lyme
01782 717717
South Staffordshire
01902 696000
Stafford
01785 619000
Staffordshire Moorlands
01538 483483
Tamworth
01827 709709

SUFFOLK

Babergh
01473 822801
Forest Heath
01638 719000
Ipswich
01473 432000
Mid Suffolk
01449 720711
St Edmundsbury
01284 763233
Suffolk Coastal
01394 383789
Waveney
01502 562111

SURREY

Elmbridge
01372 474474

Epsom and Ewell
01372 732000
Guildford
01483 505050
Mole Valley
01306 885001
Reigate and Banstead
01737 276000
Runnymede
01932 838383
Surrey Heath
01276 707100
Tandridge
01883 722000
Waverley
01483 523333
Woking
01483 755855

TYNE AND WEAR

Gateshead
0191 433 3000
Newcastle upon Tyne
0191 232 8520
North Tyneside
0191 200 6565
South Tyneside
0191 427 1717
Sunderland
0191 553 1000

WARWICKSHIRE

North Warwickshire
01827 715341
Nuneaton and Bedworth
024 7637 6376
Rugby
01788 533533
Stratford-on-Avon
01789 267575
Warwick
01926 450000

WEST MIDLANDS

Birmingham
0121 303 9944
Coventry
024 7683 3333
Dudley
01384 818181
Sandwell
0121 569 2200
Solihull
0121 704 6000
Walsall
01922 650000
Wolverhampton
01902 556556

WEST SUSSEX

Adur
01273 263000
Arun
01903 737500
Mid Sussex
01444 458166
Chichester
01243 785 166
Crawley
01293 438000
Horsham
01403 215100
Worthing
01903 239999

WEST YORKSHIRE

Bradford
01274 752111
Calderdale
01422 357257
Kirklees
01484 221000
Leeds
0113 234 8080
Wakefield
01924 306090

WILTSHIRE

Kennet
01380 724911
North Wiltshire
01249 706111
Salisbury
01722 336272
Swindon
01793 463000
West Wiltshire
01225 776655

WORCESTERSHIRE

Worcester
01905 723471
Bromsgrove
01527 873232
Malvern Hills
01684 892700
Redditch
01527 64252
Wychavon
01386 565000
Wyre Forest
01562 820505

Government offices for the regions

East of England
01223 372500
www.go-east.gov.uk
East Midlands
0115 971 9971
www.go-em.gov.uk
London
020 7217 3328
www.go-london.gov.uk
North-east
0191 201 3300
www.go-ne.gov.uk
North-west
0161 952 4000
www.go-nw.gov.uk
South-east
01483 882255
www.go-se.gov.uk
South-west
0117 900 1700
www.gosw.gov.uk
West Midlands
0121 212 5050
www.go-wm.gov.uk
Yorkshire and the Humber
0113 280 0600
www.goyh.gov.uk

Regional development agencies

West Midlands
0121 380 3500
www.advantagewm.co.uk
East Midlands
0115 988 8300
www.emda.org.uk
East of England
01223 713900
www.eeda.org.uk
London
020 7680 2000
www.lda.gov.uk
North-west
01925 400100
www.nwda.co.uk
North-east
0191 229 6200
www.onenortheast.co.uk
South-east
01483 484220
www.seeda.co.uk
South-west
01392 214747
www.southwestrda.org.uk
Yorkshire
0113 394 9600
www.yorkshire-forward.com

Wales

National Assembly for Wales
029 2082 5111
Press: 029 2089 8931
See above for ministers etc
Cardiff
029 2087 2087
Swansea
01792 636000
Carmarthenshire
01267 234567
Ceredigion
01545 570881
Denbighshire
01824 706000
Flintshire
01352 752121
Gwynedd
01286 672255
Isle of Anglesey
01248 750057
Monmouthshire
01633 644644
Newport
01633 656656
Pembrokeshire
01437 764551
Powys
01597 826000

COUNTY BOROUGH COUNCILS

Blaenau Gwent
01495 350555
Bridgend
01656 643643
Caerphilly
01443 815588
Conwy
01492 574000
Merthyr Tydfil
01685 725000
Neath Port Talbot
01639 763333
Rhondda Cynon Taff
01443 424000
Torfaen
01495 762200
Vale of Glamorgan
01446 700111
Wrexham
01978 292000

Scotland

Scottish Executive
0131 556 8400
www.scotland.gov.uk
See above for ministers etc

Aberdeen
01224 522000
Dundee
01382 434000
Edinburgh
0131 200 2000
Glasgow
0141 287 2000

Aberdeenshire
01467 620981
Angus
01307 461460
Argyll and Bute
01546 602127
Clackmannanshire
01259 450000
Dumfries and Galloway
01387 260000
East Ayrshire
01563 576000
East Dunbartonshire
0141 578 8000
East Lothian
01620 827827
East Renfrewshire
0141 577 3000
Falkirk
01324 506070
Fife
01592 414141
Highland
01463 702000
Inverclyde
01475 717171
Midlothian
0131 270 7500
Moray
01343 543451
North Ayrshire
01294 324100
North Lanarkshire
01698 302222
Orkney Islands
01856 873535
Perth and Kinross
01738 475000
Renfrewshire
0141 842 5000
Scottish Borders
01835 824000
Shetland Islands
01595 693535
South Ayrshire
01292 612000
South Lanarkshire
01698 454444
Stirling
0845 277 7000
West Dunbartonshire
01389 737000
West Lothian
01506 777000
Western Isles
01851 703773

Northern Ireland

Belfast
028 9032 0202
Lisburn
028 9250 9250

ANTRIM

Antrim
028 9446 3113
Ballymena
028 2566 0300
Ballymoney
028 2766 0200
Carrickfergus
028 9335 1604
Larne
028 282 72313
Moyle
028 207 62225
Newtownabbey
028 9034 0000

ARMAGH

Armagh
028 37 529600
Craigavon
028 38 312400

CO. DERRY

Coleraine
028 7034 7034
Derry
028 7136 5151
Limavady
028 7772 2226
Magherafelt
028 7939 7979

DOWN

Ards
028 9182 4000
Banbridge
028 4066 0600
Castlereagh
028 9049 4500
Down
028 4461 0800
Newry and Mourne
028 3031 3031
North Down
028 9127 0371

FERMANAGH

Fermanagh
028 6632 5050

TYRONE

Cookstown
028 8676 2205
Dungannon and South Tyrone
028 8772 0300
Omagh
028 8224 5321
Strabane
028 7138 2204

Government: **Parliament & politics**

Parliaments and assemblies

Parliament
020 7219 3000
www.parliament.uk
Commons information office
020 7219 4272
Lords information office
020 7219 3107
National Assembly for Wales
029 2082 5111
Press: 029 2089 8099
www.wales.gov.uk
Scottish Parliament
0131 348 5000
Press: 0131 348 5605
www.scottish.parliament.uk

Main political parties

Labour party
0870 590 0200
www.labour.org.uk
Conservative party
020 7222 9000
www.conservatives.com
Liberal Democrat party
020 7222 7999
www.libdems.org.uk

Regional parties

WALES

Plaid Cymru
029 2064 6000
www.plaidcymru.org
Welsh Labour party
029 2087 7700
www.welshlabour.org.uk
Welsh Conservative party
029 2061 6031
www.welshconservatives.com
Welsh Liberal Democrats
029 2031 3400
www.demrhydcymru.org.uk

SCOTLAND

Scottish Conservative party
0131 247 6890
www.scottishtories.org.uk
Scottish Labour party
0141 572 6900
www.scottishlabour.org.uk
Scottish Liberal Democrats
0131 337 2314
www.scotlibdems.org.uk
Scottish National party
0131 525 8900
www.snp.org.uk
Scottish Socialist party
0870 752 2504
www.scottishsocialistparty.org.uk

NORTHERN IRELAND

Alliance party
028 9032 4274
www.allianceparty.org
Progressive Unionist party
028 9032 6233
www.pup-ni.org.uk
Sinn Fein
00 353 1 872 6100
www.sinnfein.ie
Social Democratic and Labour party
028 9024 7700
www.sdlp.ie
UK Unionist party
028 9052 1482
www.ukup.org
Democratic Unionist party
www.dup.org.uk
The Ulster Unionist party
028 9076 5500
www.uup.org

Minor parties

British National party
0870 757 6267
www.bnp.org.uk
Communist League party
mail@communistleague.org.uk
www.communistleague.org.uk
Communist party of Britain
office@communist-party.org.uk
www.communist-party.org.uk
Co-operative party
020 7367 4158
www.co-op-party.org.uk
English Independence party
020 7278 5221
www.englishindependenceparty.com
Green party
020 7272 4474
www.greenparty.org.uk
Liberal party
01562 68361
www.libparty.demon.co.uk
Separate from the Liberal Democrats
National Front
0121 246 6838
www.natfront.com
Natural Law party
01622 815380
www.natural-law-party.org.uk
Official Monster Raving Loonies
01252 878382
www.omrlp.com
Scottish Green party
0131 661 8543
www.scottishgreens.org.uk
Socialist Alliance
020 7609 2999
www.socialistalliance.net
Socialist party
020 8988 8777
www.socialistparty.org.uk
Socialist Party of Great Britain
www.worldsocialism.org
UK Independence party
0121 333 7737
www.independence.org.uk
Workers Revolutionary party
020 7232 1101
www.wrp.org.uk

Parliamentary and electoral bodies

Electoral Commission
020 7271 0500
www.electoralcommission.gov.uk
Electoral Reform Society
020 7928 1622
www.electoral-reform.org.uk
Hansard Society
020 7395 4000
www.hansardsociety.org.uk
Parliamentary Counsel
020 7210 6644
www.parliamentary-counsel.gov.uk

Thinktanks

Adam Smith Institute
020 7222 4995
www.adamsmith.org
Free market economics
Bow Group
020 7431 6400
www.bowgroup.org
Centre-right
Centre for Economic Policy Research
020 7878 2900
www.cepr.org
European network of research fellows
Centre for Global Energy Studies
020 7235 4334
www.cges.co.uk
Centre for Policy Studies
020 7222 4488
www.cps.org.uk
Established 1974 by Margaret Thatcher and Keith Joseph
Centre for Reform
020 7631 3566
www.cfr.org.uk
Centre for the Study of Financial Innovation
020 7493 0173
www.csfi.org.uk
Chatham House
020 7957 5700
www.riia.org
Royal Institute for International Affairs
Civitas
020 7799 6677
www.civitas.org.uk

Demos
0845 458 5949
www.demos.co.uk
Fabian Society
020 7227 4900
www.fabian-society.org.uk
Centre-left
Federal Trust
020 7735 4000
www.fedtrust.co.uk
Foreign Policy Centre
20 7401 5350
www.fpc.org.uk
Established 1998 by Labour government
Institute for African Alternatives
020 7482 4660
www.ifaanet.org
International Institute for Environment and Development
020 7388 2117
www.iied.org
Institute for European Environmental Policy
020 7799 2244
www.ieep.org.uk
Institute for Global Ethics
020 7486 1954
www.globalethics.org/uk
Institute for Health Sector Development
020 7253 2222
www.ihsd.org
Institute for Jewish Policy Research
020 7935 8266
www.jpr.org.uk
Institute for Public Policy Research
020 7470 6100
www.ippr.org.uk
Centre-left
International Institute for Strategic Studies
020 7379 7676
www.iiss.org
Institute of Economic Affairs
020 7799 8900
www.iea.org.uk
UK's original free market thinktank
Institute of Fiscal Studies
020 7291 4800
www.ifs.org.uk
Institute of Ideas
020 7269 9220
www.instituteofideas.com
New Economics Foundation
020 7820 6300
www.neweconomics.org
New Policy Institute
020 7721 8421
www.npi.org.uk
New Politics Network
020 7278 4443
www.new-politics.net
Overseas Development Institute
020 7922 0300
www.odi.org.uk
Policy Studies Institute
020 7468 0468
www.psi.org.uk
Politeia
020 7240 5070
www.politeia.co.uk
Scottish Council Foundation
0131 225 4709
www.scottishcouncilfoundation.org
Smith Institute
020 7823 4240
www.smith-institute.org.uk
Social Affairs Unit
020 7637 4356
www.socialaffairsunit.org.uk
Social Market Foundation
020 7222 7060
www.smf.co.uk

Alternative and protest

Anarchist Federation
info@afed.org.uk
www.afed.org.uk
Anti-Nazi League
020 7924 0333
www.anl.org.uk
Big Green Gathering
01458 834629
www.big-green-gathering.com
British Democracy Campaign
www.britishdemocracycampaign.com
Campaign Against Racism and Facism (CARF)
020 7837 1450
www.carf.demon.co.uk
Charter 88
0845 450 7210
www.charter88.org.uk
Creative Exchange
020 8432 0550
www.creativexchange.org
Democracy Movement
0870 511 0440
www.democracymovement.org.uk
Freedom Association
01746 861267
www.tfa.net
Globalise Resistance
020 7053 2071
www.resist.org.uk
Green Events
020 7424 9100
www.greenevents.fsnet.co.uk
GreenNet
020 7713 1941
www.gn.apc.org
Indymedia
www.indymedia.org.uk
Network of independent media activists
Love Music Hate Racism
020 7924 0333
www.lmhr.org.uk
OneWorld
020 7239 1400
www.oneworld.net
Anti-globalisation
Peoples' Global Action
www.agp.org
Protest Net
rabble-rouser@protest.net
www.protest.net
Reclaim the Streets
rts@gn.apc.org
www.reclaimthestreets.net
Red Star Research
07960 865601
www.red-star-research.org.uk
Revolutionary Communist Group
020 7837 1688
www.revolutionarycommunist.com
Rising Tide
01865 241097
www.risingtide.org.uk
Squall
squall@squall.co.uk
www.squall.co.uk
Subvertise
webmaster@subvertise.org
www.subvertise.org
Radical advertising
The Land is Ours
07961 460171
www.tlio.org.uk
Undercurrents News Network (UNN)
01792 455900
www.undercurrents.org
Alternative news videos
Unite Against Fascism
unite@natfhe.org.uk
www.uaf.org.uk
Urban 75
07961 430719
www.urban75.com
Wombles
wombles@hushmail.com
www.wombles.org.uk
Anarchist and libertarian

Freemasons

Freemasons
020 7831 9811
www.grandlodge.org.uk

Government: **Global politics**

Government departments

Foreign Office
020 7270 1500
Press: 020 7008 3100
www.fco.gov.uk

International Development
020 7023 0000
Press: 020 7023 0600
www.dfid.gov.uk

International

United Nations
00 1 212 963 4475
Press fax: 00 1 212 963 7055
www.un.org

UN Commission on International Trade Law (UNCITRAL)
00 43 1 26060 4061
www.uncitral.org

UN Conference on Trade & Development (UNCTAD)
00 41 22 917 5809
www.unctad.org

UN Educational, Scientific & Cultural Organisation (Unesco)
00 33 1 4568 1000
www.unesco.org

UN High Commissioner for Human Rights (UNHCHR)
00 41 22 917 9011
www.unhchr.ch

UN High Commissioner for Refugees (UNHCR)
00 41 22 739 8111
www.unhcr.ch

UN Relief & Works Agency for Palestinian Refugees (UNRWA)
00 972 8 677 7333
www.un.org/unrwa

UN World Food Programme
020 7592 9292
www.wfp.org

Unicef
020 7405 5592
Press: 020 7430 0162
www.unicef.org.uk

International Labour Organisation (ILO)
00 41 22 799 6111
www.ilo.org

International Maritime Organisation (IMO)
020 7735 7611
www.imo.org

International Monetary Fund (IMF)
00 1 202 623 7000
www.imf.org

International Whaling Commission
01223 233971
www.iwcoffice.org

Nato
Press: 00 32 2 707 5041
www.nato.int

OneWorld
020 7239 1400
www.oneworld.net/uk

World Bank
UK Press: 020 7930 8511
HQ Washington 00 1 202 473 1000
www.worldbank.org

World Health Organisation (WHO)
00 41 22 791 2111
www.who.int

World Trade Organisation (WTO)
00 41 22 739 5111
www.wto.org

EU Institutions

European Parliament
London 020 7227 4300
Edinburgh 0131 557 7866
Press: 00 32 2 284 2929
www.europarl.eu.int

European Commission
00 800 6789 1011
Press: 00 32 2 295 0086
www.europa.eu.int/comm/

Committee of the Regions of the European Union
00 32 2 282 2211
Press: 00 32 2 282 2155
www.cor.eu.int

Council of the European Union
00 32 2 285 6111
Press: 00 32 2 285 6550
www.ue.eu.int

Court of Justice of the European Communities
00 352 43031
Press: 00 352 4303 3668/3382
www.curia.eu.int

European Central Bank
00 49 69 13440
www.ecb.int

European Convention
00 32 2 285 5071/2
http://european-convention.eu.int/

European Court of Auditors
00 352 4398 45410
www.eca.eu.int

European Economic and Social Committee
00 32 2 546 9011
Press: 00 32 2 546 9396
www.esc.eu.int

European Environment Agency
00 45 33 367100
http://org.eea.eu.int

European Investment Bank
00 352 4379 3122
www.eib.org

The European Ombudsman
00 33 3 8817 2313
www.euro-ombudsman.eu.int

European Police Office
00 31 70 302 5000
www.europol.eu.int

Office for Official Publications of the European Communities
00 352 29291
www.publications.eu.int

Translation Centre for the Bodies of the European Union
00 352 42 17111
www.cdt.eu.int

Western European Union
00 32 2 500 4412
www.weu.int

Other European contacts

Congress of Local and Regional Authorities of Europe
00 33 3 8841 3194
www.coe.int/t/e/clrae/

Council of Europe
00 33 3 8841 2033
www.coe.int

Council of European Municipalities and Regions
00 32 2 511 7477
00 33 1 4450 5959
Press: 00 32 2 500 0534
www.ccre.org

European Court of Human Rights
00 33 3 8841 2018
www.echr.coe.int

European Space Agency
00 33 1 5369 7654
Press: 00 33 1 5369 7155
www.esa.int

European University Institute, Florence
00 39 055 46851
www.iue.it

European Youth Parliament
01993 709940
National contact for UK:
01458 832144
www.eyp.org; www.eypuk.com/

Organisation for Economic Cooperation and Development
00 33 1 4524 8200
Press: 00 33 1 4524 9700
www.oecd.org

Organisation for Security and Cooperation in Europe
00 43 1 514360
Press: 00 43 1 5143 6180
www.osce.org

Eurocorps
Press: 00 33 388 433061
www.eurocorps.org

Political parties

Confederal Group of the European United Left / Nordic Green Left
00 32 2 284 2683/2686;
Press: 00 32 475 646628
www.europarl.eu.int/gue/

European Liberal Democrats
00 32 2 284 3169
www.eldr.org

Greens-European Free Alliance
00 32 2 284 3044/2117
00 33 3 8817 4042/5879
Press: 00 32 2 284 4683
00 33 3 8817 4760
www.greens-efa.org

Group for a Europe of Democracies and Diversities
fax: 00 32 2 284 9144
www.europarl.eu.int/edd/

Group of European People's Party (Christian Democrats) and European Democrats
00 32 2 284 2234
Press: 00 32 2284 2228
00 33 3 8817 4144
www.epp-ed.org

Parliamentary Group of the Party of European Socialists
Press: 00 32 2 28 43099
00 33 3 88 1 74873
www.socialistgroup.org

Union for Europe of the Nations Group
00 32 2 284 2971
www.europarl.eu.int/uen/

Pro-Europe and anti-Europe lobbies

Britain in Europe
020 7725 4200
www.britainineurope.org.uk
Pro-Britain in Europe

European Movement
020 7725 4300
www.euromove.org.uk
Pro-European

The No Campaign
info@no-euro.com
www.no-euro.com
Pro-Europe, anti-euro

Federation of Small Businesses
01253 336000
www.fsb.org.uk
Powerful anti-euro lobby

Bruges Group
020 7287 4414
www.brugesgroup.com
Eurosceptic thinktank

Commonwealth and British international

British Executive Service Overseas
020 7630 0644
www.beso.org

British Council
0161 957 7755
Press: 020 7389 4268
www.britcoun.org

Commonwealth Institute
020 7603 4535
www.commonwealth.org.uk

Commonwealth Secretariat
020 7747 6500
www.thecommonwealth.org

British overseas territories

Anguilla
Small east Caribbean island. 35 sq miles, 13,000 approx. pop
Governor, Anguilla:
00 1 264 497 2621

Bermuda
100 small islands, 20 inhabited, 600 miles off North Carolina, USA. 58 sq miles. 64,900 approx. pop
Governor, Hamilton:
001 441 292 3600

British Antarctic Territory
Uninhabited part of Antarctica, including South Orkney and South Shetland islands. 660,000 sq miles
Commissioner, London:
020 7270 2742

British Indian Ocean Territory
Group of Chagos Archipelago islands in central Indian Ocean, south of India. 23 sq miles of land, 21,000 sq miles sea. Uninhabited, except for UK-US base at Diego Garcia
Commissioner, London:
020 7008 2890

British Virgin Islands
Eastern Caribbean group of 46 islands, 11 inhabited, near Anguilla. 58 sq miles. 20,250 pop
Governor, Tortola:
00 1 284 494 2345

Cayman Islands
Three tax-free, wealthy islands south of Cuba. 102 sq miles. 43,100 approx. pop.
Governor, Georgetown:
00 1 345 949 7900

Falkland Islands
Largest islands in the south Atlantic. 4,700 sq miles. 2,900 approx. pop, plus military
Governor, Stanley: 00 500 27433

Gibraltar
2.3 sq mile promontory of southern-most Spain. 27,800 approx. pop.
Governor: 00 350 45440

Montserrat
East Caribbean volcanic island, 39 sq miles. 9,200 approx. pop
Governor, Olveston:
001 664 491 2688

Pitcairn Islands
Eastern group in Pacific, between north New Zealand and Peru. 47 sq miles (across all 4 islands), 46 approx. pop, all Seventh Day Adventists. Home of mutineers from HMS Bounty, 1790
Governor, Auckland:
00 64 09 366 0186

St Helena
Island in south Atlantic, 1,100 miles off Angola. 47 sq miles. 6,000 pop, with two dependencies
Governor, Jamestown: 00 290 2555

Ascension Island
700 miles north-west of St Helena. 34 sq miles, 980 pop
Administrator: 00 247 6311

Tristan da Cunha
Island group 1,850 miles west of Cape Town. 285 pop. 38 sq miles
Administrator: 00 870 682 087155

South Georgia & Sandwich Islands
Scattered islands east and south-east of Cape Horn. 1,507 sq miles. South Georgia is military, South Sandwich unhinhabited and volcanic
Commissioner, Stanley:
00 500 27433

Turks & Caicos Islands
30 Caribbean islands, north of Haiti. 166 sq miles. 20,000 approx. pop
Governor, Grand Turk:
00 1 649 946 2309

International aid

ActionAid
020 7561 7561
www.actionaid.org.uk

Baby Milk Action
01223 464420
www.babymilkaction.org

Book Aid International
020 7733 3577
www.bookaid.org

British Leprosy Relief Association
01206 562286
www.lepra.org.uk

British Overseas NGOs for Development (Bond)
020 7837 8344
www.bond.org.uk

British Red Cross
020 7235 5454
www.redcross.org.uk

Care International
020 7934 9334
www.careinternational.org.uk

Casa Alianza
info@casa-alianza.org
www.casa-alianza.org

Catholic Agency for Overseas Development
020 7733 7900
www.cafod.org.uk

Christian Aid
020 7620 4444
www.christian-aid.org.uk

Christian Vision
0121 522 6087
www.christianvision.com

Church Mission Society
020 7928 8681
www.cms-uk.org
Disasters Emergency Committee
020 7387 0200
www.dec.org.uk
International Care and Relief
01892 519 619
www.icrcharity.com
International Committee of Red Cross
HQ Geneva 00 41 22 734 6001
Press: 00 41 22 730 2282
www.icrc.org
International HIV/AIDS Alliance
01273 718 900
www.aidsalliance.org
International Rescue Committee
001 212 551 3000
www.theirc.org
Islamic Relief
0121 605 5555
www.islamic-relief.org.uk
Médecins sans Frontières (UK)
020 7404 6600
www.uk.msf.org
Methodist Relief and Development Fund
020 7467 5132
www.mrdf.org.uk
Muslim Aid
020 7609 4425
www.muslimaid.org.uk
Oxfam
0870 333 2700; 01865 311311
www.oxfam.org.uk
Plan UK
020 7482 9777
www.plan-uk.org
Sightsavers
01444 446600
www.sightsavers.org.uk
Tear Fund
0845 355 8355; 020 8977 9144
www.tearfund.org
Voluntary Services Overseas
020 8780 7200
www.vso.org.uk
WaterAid
020 7793 4500
www.wateraid.org.uk
World Emergency Relief
0870 429 2129
www.wer-uk.org
World Vision UK
Print press: 01908 841020
Broadcast press: 01908 841020
www.worldvision.org.uk

Human rights

ActionAid
020 7561 7561
www.actionaid.org.uk
Amnesty International
020 7814 6200/6274
www.amnesty.org.uk
Anti-Slavery
020 7501 8920
www.antislavery.org
Asian Human Rights Commission
00 852 2698 6339
www.ahrchk.net
Association for Civil Rights in Israel
00 9722 652 1218
www.acri.org.il
British Institute of Human Rights
020 7848 1818
www.bihr.org
British Refugee Council
020 7820 3000
www.refugeecouncil.org.uk
Burma Campaign
020 7324 4710
www.burmacampaign.org.uk
Campaign Against Criminalising Communities
020 7586 5892
www.cacc.org.uk
Campaign Against Sanctions on Iraq
info@casi.org.uk
www.casi.org.uk
Campaign Against the Arms Trade
020 7281 0297
www.caat.org.uk
Campaign to End Genocide
00 1 202 546 3950
www.endgenocide.org
Centre for Research on Globalisation
00 1 705 720 6500
http://globalresearch.ca
Coalition against Slavery in Mauritania and Sudan
00 1 212 774 4287
http://members.aol.com/casmasalc
Coalition for the International Criminal Court
00 1 212 687 2176; 00 31 70 363 4484
www.iccnow.org
Concern Worldwide
020 7738 1033
www.concern.net
Derechos Human Rights
hr@derechos.org
www.derechos.org
Eliminate Child Labour in Tobacco
00 41 22 306 1444
www.eclt.org
European Roma Rights Centre
00 36 1 4132200
http://errc.org
Free Tibet Campaign
020 7324 4605
www.freetibet.org
Gendercide Watch
gendercide_watch@hotmail.com
www.gendercide.org
Global Action to Prevent War
info@globalactionpw.org
www.globalactionpw.org
Global Fund for Women
00 1 415 202 7640
www.globalfundforwomen.org
Human Rights Watch
020 7713 1995
www.hrw.org
International Fellowship of Reconciliation
00 31 72 512 3014
www.ifor.org
International Physicians for the Prevention of Nuclear War
00 1 617 868 5050
www.ippnw.org
Kurdish Human Rights Project
020 7287 2772
www.khrp.org
Labour Behind the Label
01603 610993
www.labourbehindthelabel.org
One World Action
020 7833 4075
www.oneworldaction.org
Safer World
020 7324 4646
www.saferworld.co.uk
Stop the War Coalition
020 7053 2153/4/5/6
www.stopwar.org.uk
Transcend
00 1 914 773 3440
www.transcend.org
Unrepresented Nations and Peoples Organisation
00 31 70 364 6504
www.unpo.org
War Resistors International
info@wri-irg.org
www.wri-irg.org
Womankind Worldwide
020 7549 5700
www.womankind.org.uk
World Commission for Peace and Human Rights Council
00 92 51 411704
www.worphco.cjb.net
World Organization For Human Rights USA
00 1 202 296 5702
www.woatusa.org

Government: **Overseas embassies in UK**

Afghanistan
020 7589 8891
www.afghanembassy.co.uk
Albania
020 7828 8897
Algeria
020 7221 7800
www.consalglond.u-net.com/
Andorra
020 8874 4806
Angola
020 7299 9850
www.angola.org.uk
Antigua and Barbuda
020 7486 7073
www.antigua-barbuda.com
Argentina
020 7318 1300
www.argentine-embassy-uk.org
Armenia
020 7938 5435
Australia
020 7379 4334
www.australia.org.uk
Austria
020 7235 3731
www.austria.org.uk
Azerbaijan
020 7938 5482
Bahamas
020 7408 4488
Bahrain
020 7201 9170
Bangladesh
020 7584 0081
www.bangladeshhighcommission.co.uk
Barbados
020 7631 4975
Belarus
020 7937 3288
http://belembassy.org/uk
Belgium
020 7470 3700
www.diplobel.org/uk
Belize
020 7723 3603
www.bzhc-lon.co.uk
Bolivia
020 7235 4248
www.embassyofbolivia.co.uk
Bosnia and Herzegovina
020 7373 0867
Botswana
020 7499 0031
Brazil
020 7499 0877
www.brazil.org.uk
Brunei
020 7581 0521
Bulgaria
020 7584 9400
www.bulgarianembassy.org.uk
Burma
020 7499 8841
www.myanmar.com
Burundi
00 32 2 230 45 35
nearest embassy is in Belgium
Cameroon
020 7727 0771
Canada
020 7258 6600
www.canada.org.uk
Chile
020 7580 6392
www.echileuk.demon.co.uk
China
020 7299 4049
www.chinese-embassy.org.uk
Colombia
020 7589 9177
www.colombianembassy.co.uk
Congo
020 7622 0419
Congo (Democratic Republic)
020 7278 9825
Costa Rica
020 7706 8844
Croatia
020 7387 2022
Cuba
020 7240 2488
Cyprus
020 7499 8272
Czech Republic
020 7243 1115
www.czech.org.uk
Denmark
020 7333 0200
www.denmark.org.uk
Dominica, Commonwealth of
020 7370 5194
www.dominica.co.uk
Dominican Republic
020 7727 6285
www.serex.gov.do
Ecuador
020 7584 2648
Egypt
020 7499 3304
El Salvador
020 7436 8282
Eritrea
020 7713 0096
Estonia
020 7589 7690
www.estonia.gov.uk
Ethiopia
020 7589 7212
www.ethioembassy.org.uk
Fiji
020 7584 3661
Finland
020 7838 6200
www.finemb.org.uk
France
020 7073 1000
www.ambafrance-uk.org
Gabon
020 7823 9986
Gambia, The Republic of
020 7937 6316
Georgia
020 7603 7799
Germany
020 7824 1300
www.german-embassy.org.uk
Ghana
020 7235 4142
www.ghana-com.co.uk
Greece
020 7229 3850
www.greekembassy.org.uk
Grenada
020 7631 4277
Guatemala
020 7351 3042
Guinea
020 7839 2625
Guyana
020 7229 7684
Holy See
020 8946 1410
Honduras
020 7486 4880
Hungary
020 7235 5218
www.huemblon.org.uk
Iceland
020 7259 3999
www.iceland.org.uk
India
020 7836 8484
www.hcilondon.org
Indonesia
020 7499 7661
www.indonesianembassy.org.uk
Iran
020 7225 3000
www.iran-embassy.org.uk
Ireland
020 7235 2171
Israel
020 7957 9500
http://london.mfa.gov.il/
Italy
020 7312 2200
www.embitaly.org.uk
Ivory Coast
020 7235 6991
Jamaica
020 7823 9911
www.jhcuk.com
Japan
020 7465 6500
www.uk.emb-japan.go.jp
Jordan
020 7937 3685
www.jordanembassyuk.org
Kazakhstan
020 7581 4646
www.kazakhstanembassy.org.uk
Kenya
020 7636 2371
Korea, DPR (North Korea)
020 8992 4965
Korea, Republic of (South Korea)
020 7227 5500

Kuwait
020 7590 3400
www.kuwaitculturaluk.com
Kyrgyz Republic
020 7935 1462
www.kyrgyz-embassy.org.uk
Latvia
020 7312 0040
www.london.am.gov.lv/en
Lebanon
020 7229 7265
Lesotho
020 7235 5686
www.lesotholondon.org.uk
Liberia
020 7221 1036
Libya
020 7589 6120
Lithuania
020 7486 6401
http://amb.urm.lt
Luxembourg
020 7235 6961
Macedonia
020 7935 2823
www.macedonianembassy.org.uk
Madagascar
020 8746 0133
Malawi
020 7491 4172
Malaysia
020 7235 8033
Maldives
020 7224 2135
Malta
020 7292 4800
Mauritania
020 7478 9323
Mauritius
020 7225 3331
Mexico
020 7499 8586
www.embamex.co.uk
Moldova
00 32 2 732 9300
nearest embassy is in Belgium
Monaco
020 7225 2679
Mongolia
020 7937 0150
www.embassyofmongolia.co.uk
Morocco
020 7581 5001
Mozambique
020 7383 3800
Namibia
020 7636 6244
Nepal
020 7229 1594
www.nepembassy.org.uk
Netherlands
020 7590 3200
www.netherlands-embassy.org.uk
New Zealand
020 7930 8422
www.nzembassy.com
Nicaragua
020 7938 2373
http://freespace.virgin.net
/emb.ofnicaragua/
Nigeria
020 7839 1244
www.nigeriahighcommissionuk.com
Norway
020 7591 5500
www.norway.org.uk
Oman
020 7225 0001
Pakistan
020 7664 9200
www.pakmission-uk.gov.pk
Panama
020 7493 4646
Papua New Guinea
020 7930 0922
Paraguay
020 7937 1253
www.paraguayembassy.co.uk
Peru
020 7838 9223
www.peruembassy-uk.com
Philippines
020 7937 1600
www.philemb.co.uk
Poland
0870 774 2700
www.polishembassy.org.uk
Portugal
020 7235 5331
www.portembassy.gla.ac.uk
Qatar
020 7493 2200
Romania
020 7937 9666
www.roemb.co.uk
Russia
020 7229 2666
Rwanda
020 7930 2570
www.ambarwanda.org.uk
Saint Christopher and Nevis (St Kitts and Nevis)
020 7460 6500
St Lucia
020 7370 7123
St Vincent and the Grenadines
020 7565 2874
Samoa
00 02 6608454
San Marino
020 7299 9850
Saudi Arabia
020 7917 3000
www.saudiembassy.org.uk
Senegal
020 7937 7237
www.senegalembassy.co.uk
Serbia and Montenegro
020 7370 6105
www.yugoslavembassy.org.uk
Seychelles
020 7224 1660
Sierra Leone
020 7287 9884
www.slhc-uk.org.uk
Singapore
020 7235 8315
www.mfa.gov.sg/london/
Slovakia
020 7243 0803
www.slovakembassy.co.uk
Slovenia
020 7222 5400
www.gov.si/mzz/dkp/vlo/eng
Solomon Islands
00 32 2 732 7085
Somalia
no embassy
South Africa
020 7451 7299
www.southafricahouse.com
Spain
020 7235 5555
Sri Lanka
020 7262 1841
www.slhclondon.org
Sudan
020 7839 8080
www.sudan-embassy.co.uk
Surinam
00 31 070361 7445
Swaziland
020 7630 6611
Sweden
020 7917 6400
www.swedish-embassy.org.uk
Switzerland
020 7616 6000
www.swissembassy.org.uk
Syria
020 7245 9012
www.syrianembassy.co.uk
Tanzania
020 7499 8951
www.tanzania-online.gov.uk
Thailand
020 7589 2944
Togo
00 33 1 4380 1213
Tonga
020 7724 5828
Trinidad and Tobago
020 7245 9351
Tunisia
020 7584 8117
Turkey
020 7393 0202
www.turkconsulate-london.com
Turkmenistan
020 7255 1071
Uganda
020 7839 5783
Ukraine
020 7727 6312
www.ukremb.org.uk
United Arab Emirates
020 7581 1281
United States
020 7499 9000
www.usembassy.org.uk
Uruguay
020 7589 8835
Uzbekistan
020 7229 7679
www.uzbekembassy.org
Venezuela
020 7584 4206
www.venezlon.demon.co.uk
Vietnam
020 7937 1912
www.vietnamembassy.org.uk
Yemen
020 7584 6607
www.yemenembassy.org.uk
Zambia
020 7589 6655
Zimbabwe
020 7836 7755
www.zimbabwelink.com

Government: **Overseas diplomatic contacts**

Key: E Embassy HC High Commission CG Consulate-General C Consulate *Source: Foreign Office*

Albania
E: Tirana *00 355 42 34973/4/5*
Algeria
E: Algiers *00 213 21 23 00 68*
Andorra
E: *00 376 839 840*
Angola
E: Luanda *00 244 2 334582/3, 392991, 387681*
Antigua and Barbuda
HC: St John's *00 1 268 462 0008/9, 463 0010*
Argentina
E: Buenos Aires *00 54 11 4808 2200*
Armenia
E: Yerevan *00 3741 264301*
Australia
HC: Canberra *00 61 2 6270 6666*
CG: Brisbane *00 61 7 3223 3200*
CG: Melbourne *00 61 3 9652 1600*
CG: Perth *00 61 8 9224 4700*
CG: Sydney *00 61 2 9247 7521*
C: Adelaide *00 61 8 8212 7280*
Austria
E: Vienna *00 43 1 716 130 www.britishembassy.at*
C: Bregenz *00 43 5574 78586*
C: Graz *00 43 316 8216 1621*
C: Innsbruck *00 43 512 588320*
C: Salzburg *00 43 662 848133*
Azerbaijan
E: Baku *00 99 412 975188/89/90*
Bahamas
HC: Nassau *00 1 242 325 7471*
Bahrain
E: *00 973 574100 www.ukembassy.gov.bh*
Bangladesh
HC: Dhaka *00 880 2 8822705 www.ukinbangladesh.org*
Barbados
HC: Bridgetown *00 1 246 430 7800*
Belarus
E: Minsk *00 375 172 105920*
Belgium
E: Brussels *00 32 2 287 6211*
Belize
HC: Belmopan *00 501 822 2146 www.britishhighbze.com*
Bolivia
E: La Paz *00 591 2 2433424*
Bosnia and Herzegovina
E: Sarajevo *00 387 33 28 2200 www.britishembassy.ba*
Botswana
HC: Gaborone *00 267 395 2841*
Brazil
E: Brasilia *00 55 61 329 2300 www.reinounido.org.br*
CG: Rio de Janeiro *00 55 21 2555 9600*
CG: São Paulo *00 55 11 3094 2700*
www.gra-bretanha.org.br
C: Belém *00 55 91 222 5074/223 0990*
C: Belo Horizonte *00 31 3261 2072*
C: Curitiba *00 55 41 322 1202*
C: Fortaleza *00 55 85 466 8580/8582*
C: Manáus *00 55 92 613 1819*
C: Porto Alegre *00 55 51 341 0720*
C: Rio Grande *00 55 53 233 7700*
C: Salvador *00 55 71 243 7399*
C: Santos *00 55 13 3211 2300*

Brunei
HC: Bandar Seri Begawan *00 673 2 222231/223121*
www.britishhighcommission.gov.uk/brunei
Bulgaria
E: Sofia *00 359 2 933 9222 www.british-embassy.bg*
C: Varna *00 359 52 6655 555*
Burma
E: Rangoon *00 95 1 256918, 380322, 370863/5*
Burundi
E-LIAISON: Bujumbura *00 257 827 602*
Cambodia
E: Phnom Penh *00 855 23 427124, 428295*
Cameroon
HC: Yaoundé *00 237 2220545/2220796*
C: Douala *00 237 3422177/3428145*
Canada
HC: Ottawa *00 1 613 237 1530 www.britain-in-canada.org*
CG: Montreal *00 1 514 866 5863*
CG: Toronto *00 1 416 593 1290*
CG: Vancouver *00 1 604 683 4421*
C: Halifax/Dartmouth *00 1 902 461 1381*
C: St John's *00 1 709 579 2002*
C: Winnipeg *00 1 204 896 1380*
C: Quebec City *00 1 418 521 3000*
Chad
E: Ndjamena *00 235 523970*
Chile
E: Santiago *00 56 2 370 4100 www.britemb.cl*
C: Valparaíso *00 56 32 213063*
C: Punta Arenas *00 56 61 211535*
China
E: Beijing *00 86 10 5192 4000*
CG: Shanghai *00 86 21 6279 7650*
CG: Guangzhou *00 86 20 8335 1354*
CG: Chongqing *00 86 23 6381 0321*
CG: Hong Kong Special Administrative Region
00 852 2901 3000 www.britishconsulate.org.hk
CG: Macao *00 853 6850886*
Colombia
E: Bogotá *00 57 1 317 6690, 6310, 6321*
C: Cali *00 57 2 896 1235*
C: Medellin *00 57 4 377 9966*
Congo (Democratic Republic)
E: Kinshasa *00 243 98169100/111/200*
Costa Rica
E: San José *00 506 258 2025 www.britishembassycr.com*
Croatia
E: Zagreb *00 385 1 600 9100*
C: Split *00 385 21 341 464*
C: Dubrovnik *00 385 20 324 597*
Cuba
E: Havana *00 53 7 204 1771*
Cyprus
HC: Nicosia *00 357 22 861100*
Czech Republic
E: Prague *00 420 2 5740 2111*
Denmark
E: Copenhagen *00 45 35 44 5200*
C: Aabenraa *00 45 7462 3500*
C: Aalborg *00 45 9811 3499*
C: Aarhus *00 45 8730 7777*
C: Esbjerg *00 45 7911 1900*
C: Fredericia *00 45 7592 2000*

C: Herning *00 45 9627 7300*
C: Odense *00 45 6614 4714*
C: Torshavn, Faroe Islands *00 45 29835 9977*

Djibouti
C: *00 253 25 0917*

Dominica, Commonwealth of
HC: Roseau *00 1 246 430 7800*

Dominican Republic
E: Santo Domingo *00 1 809 472 7111*
C: Puerto Plata *00 1 809 586 4244/8464*

East Timor
E: Dili *00 670 332 2838*

Ecuador
E: Quito *00 593 2 2970 800/801*
C: Guayaquil *00 593 4 2560400 x 318*
C: Galápagos *00 593 5 526157/9*

Egypt
E: Cairo *00 20 2 794 0850/2/8 www.britishembassy.org.eg*
CG: Alexandria *00 20 3 5467001, 5467002, 5223717, 5220507*
C: Suez *00 20 62 334102*

El Salvador
E: Guatemala City *00 502 367 5425*
HC: San Salvador *00 503 281 5555*

Eritrea
E: Asmara *00 291 1 120145*

Estonia
E: Tallinn *00 372 667 4700 www.britishembassy.ee*

Ethiopia
E: Addis Ababa *00 251 1 612354*

Fiji
HC: Suva *00 679 3229100*
www.britishhighcommission.gov.uk/fiji

Finland
E: Helsinki *00 358 9 2286 5100 www.britishembassy.fi*
C: Jyväskylä *00 358 14 446 9211*
C: Kotka *00 358 5 2344281*
C: Kuopio *00 358 17 265 7777*
C: Åland Islands *00 358 18 13591, 47720*
C: Oulu *00 358 83 310 7117*
C: Rovaniemi *00 358 16 317831*
C: Tampere *00 358 3 256 5701*
C: Turku *00 358 2 274 3410*
C: Vaasa *00 358 6 2822000*

France
E: Paris *00 33 1 4451 3100 www.amb-grandebretagne.fr*
CG: Bordeaux *00 33 5 5722 2110*
CG: Lille *00 33 3 2012 8272*
CG: Lyon *00 33 4 7277 8170*
CG: Marseille *00 33 4 9115 7210*
C: Amiens *00 33 3 2272 0848*
C: Boulogne-sur-Mer *00 33 3 2187 1680*
C: Calais *00 33 3 2196 3376*
C: Cherbourg *00 33 2 3388 6560*
C: Dunkirk *00 33 3 2866 1198*
C: Fort de France, Martinique *00 596 618892*
C: French Guiana (Cayenne) *00 594 311034*
C: French Polynesia (Papeete) *00 689 706382*
C: Guadeloupe *00 590 825757*
C: La Réunion *00 33 2 6234 7576*
C: Le Havre *00 33 2 3519 7888*
C: Lorient *00 33 2 9787 3620*
C: Montpellier *00 33 4 6715 5207*
C: Nantes *00 33 2 5172 7260*
C: New Caledonia *00 687 273627/282153*
C: St Malo-Dinard *00 33 2 2318 3030*
C: Saumur *00 33 2 4152 9054*
C: Toulouse *00 33 5 6115 0202*
C: Tours *00 33 2 4743 5058*

Gabon
C: Libreville *00 241 762200/742041*

Gambia, The Republic of
HC: Banjul *00 220 4495133/4*

Georgia
E: Tbilisi *00 995 32 955497/998447/988796*

Germany
E: Berlin *00 49 30 204570 www.britischebotschaft.de*
CG: Düsseldorf *00 49 211 94480*
www.british-consulate-general.de
CG: Frankfurt *00 49 69 1700020*
CG: Hamburg *00 49 40 448 0320*
CG: Munich *00 49 89 211090*
CG: Stuttgart *00 49 711 162690*
C: Bremen *00 49 421 590708*
C: Hanover *00 511 3883808*
C: Kiel *00 49 431 331971*
C: Nuremburg *00 49 911 2404 303*

Ghana
HC: Accra *00 233 21 7010650, 221665*
www.britishhighcommission.gov.uk/ghana

Greece
E: Athens *00 30 210 727 2600 www.british-embassy.gr*
ViceC: Corfu *00 30 26610 30055*
ViceC: Kos *00 30 22420 21549*
ViceC: Patras *00 30 2610 277329*
ViceC: Syros *00 30 22810 82232/88922*
ViceC: Zakynthos *00 30 26950 22906/48030*
C: Heraklion (Crete) *00 30 2810 224012*
C: Rhodes *00 30 22410 27247/22005*
C: Thessaloniki *00 30 2310 278006*

Grenada
HC: St George's *001 473 440 3536/3222*

Guatemala
E: Guatemala City *00 502 367 5425*

Guinea
CG: Conakry *00 224 455807/456020*

Guyana
HC: Georgetown *00 592 22 65881/2/3/4*

Haiti
C: Port-au-Prince *00 509 257 3969*

Holy See
E: Rome *00 39 06 699 23561*

Honduras
C: San Pedro Sula *00 504 550 2337*

Hungary
E: Budapest *00 36 1 266 2888 www.britishembassy.hu*

Iceland
E: Reykjavik *00 354 550 5100*
ViceC: Akureyri *00 354 463 0102*

India
HC: New Delhi *00 91 11 2687 2161*
DepHC: Chennai *00 91 44 5219 2151*
DepHC: Kolkata *00 91 33 2288 5172/3/4/5/6*
DepHC: Mumbai *00 91 22 2283 0517/2330/3602*

Indonesia
E: Jakarta *00 62 21 315 6264*
C: Medan *00 62 61 821 0559*

Iran
E: Tehran *00 98 21 6705011-19*

Ireland
E: Dublin *00 353 1 205 3700 www.britishembassy.ie*

Israel
E: Tel Aviv *00 972 3 725 1222 www.britemb.org.il*
CG: Jerusalem *00 972 2 541 4100 www.britishconsulate.org*
CG: West Jerusalem *00 972 2 671 7724*

Italy
E: Rome *00 39 06 4220 0001 www.britain.it*
CG: Milan *00 39 02 723001*
C: Bari *00 39 080 554 3668*
C: Cagliari *00 39 070 828628*
C: Catania *00 39 095 715 1864*
C: Florence *00 39 055 284133*
C: Genoa *00 39 010 416828*
C: Naples *00 39 081 423 8911*
C: Palermo *00 39 091 326412*

C: Trieste *00 39 040 3478303*
C: Turin *00 39 011 6509202*
C: Venice *00 39 041 5055990*
Ivory Coast
E: Abidjan *00 225 20300800 www.britaincdi.com*
Jamaica
HC: Kingston *00 1 876 510 0700*
Japan
E: Tokyo *00 81 3 5211 1100 www.uknow.or.jp*
C: Sapporo *00 81 11 613 1123*
CG: Osaka *00 81 6 6120 5600*
C: Nagoya *00 81 52 223 5031*
Jordan
E: Amman *00 962 6 5923100 www.britain.org.jo*
Kazakhstan
E: Almaty *00 73272 506191/2*
Kenya
HC: Nairobi *00 254 20 2844000*
Kiribati
HC: Tarawa *00 686 22501*
Korea, DPR (North)
E: Pyongyang *00 850 2 381 7980-3*
Korea (South)
E: Seoul *00 82 2 3210 5500 www.uk.or.kr*
Kuwait
E: *00 965 240 3334/5/6*
Kyrgystan
HC: Bishkek *00 996 312 680185*
Laos
E: Vientiane *00 856 21 413606*
Latvia
E: Riga *00 371 777 4700 www.britain.lv*
Lebanon
E: Beirut *00 961 1 990400*
Lesotho
HC: Maseru *00 266 223 13961 www.bhc.org.ls*
Liberia
00 231 226056
Libya
E: Tripoli *00 218 21 335 1084*
Lithuania
E: Vilnius *00 370 5 246 2900 www.britain.lt*
Luxembourg
E: *00 352 22 98 64/65/66*
Macedonia
E: Skopje *00 389 2 3299 299 www.britishembassy.org.mk*
Madagascar
E: Antananarivo *00 261 20 22 49378/79/80*
C: Toamasina *00 261 20 533 25 48/69*
Malawi
HC: Lilongwe *00 265 1 772 400*
Malaysia
HC: Kuala Lumpur *00 60 3 2170 2200 www.britain.org.my*
Malta
HC: Valletta *00 356 2323 0000*
Mauritania
HC: Nouakchott *00 222 525 8331*
Mauritius
HC: Port Louis *00 230 202 9400*
Mexico
E: Mexico City *00 52 55 5 242 8500*
C: Monterrey *00 52 818 356 5359*
Moldova
E: Chisinau *00 3732 238991*
Monaco
C: *00 377 9350 9954*
Mongolia
E: Ulaanbaatar *00 976 11 458133*
Morocco
E: Rabat *00 212 37 729696 www.britain.org.ma*
CG: Casablanca *00 212 2243 7700*
C: Agadir *00 212 48 823401/2*
C: Marrakech *00 212 44 435095*
C: Tangier *00 212 39 941557*
Mozambique
HC: Maputo *00 258 1 320 111*
Namibia
HC: Windhoek *00 264 61 274800*
Nepal
E: Kathmandu *00 977 1 4410583/4411281/4414588/4411590*
Netherlands
E: The Hague *00 31 70 427 0427 www.britain.nl*
CG: Amsterdam *00 31 20 676 4343*
C: Willemstad (Curacao) *00 599 9 747 3322*
New Zealand
HC: Wellington *00 64 4 924 2888 www.britain.org.nz*
CG: Auckland *00 64 9 303 2973*
C: Christchurch *00 64 3 337 9933*
Nicaragua
E: San Jose *00 506 258 2025*
Nigeria
HC: Abuja *00 234 9 413 2010/2011/2796/2880*
DepHC: Lagos *00 234 1 261 9531/9537/9541/9543*
Norway
E: Oslo *00 47 2313 2700 www.britain.no*
C: Alesund *00 47 7012 4460*
C: Bergen *00 47 5594 4705*
C: Bodo *00 47 7556 5800*
C: Kristiansand *00 47 3812 2070*
C: Stavanger *00 47 5152 9713*
C: Tromso *00 47 7762 4500*
C: Trondheim *00 47 7360 0200*
Oman
E: Muscat *00 968 609000*
www.britishembassy.gov.uk/oman
Pakistan
HC: Islamabad *00 92 51 2822131/5*
DepHC: Karachi *00 92 21 5872431-6*
Palestine National Authority
CG: Jerusalem *00 972 2 541 4100*
CG: West Jerusalem *00 972 2 671 7724*
Panama
E: Panama City *00 507 269 0866*
Papua New Guinea
HC: Port Moresby *00 675 325 1643/1645/1659/1677*
Paraguay
E: Asunción *00 595 21 612611*
Peru
E: Lima *00 51 1 617 3000*
C: Arequipa *00 51 54 241 340*
C: Cusco *00 51 84 226671/239974*
C: Iquitos *00 51 94 22 2732*
C: Piura *00 51 74 333300/326233*
C: Trujillo *00 51 44 235548*
Philippines
E: Manila *00 63 2 816 7116*
C: Angeles City *00 63 45 323 4187*
C: Cebu *00 63 32 346 0525*
C: Olongapo *00 63 47 2522222*
Poland
E: Warsaw *00 48 22 3110000 www.britishembassy.pl*
C: Gdansk *00 48 58 3414365, 3461558*
C: Katowice *00 48 32 206 9801*
C: Kraków *00 48 12 421 7030*
C: Lublin *00 48 81 742 0101*
C: Pozna *00 48 61 851 7290*
C: Szczecin *00 48 91 487 0302*
C: Wroclaw *00 48 71 344 8961*
Portugal
E: Lisbon *00 351 21 392 4000 www.uk-embassy.pt*
C: Oporto *00 351 22 618 4789*
C: Portimão *00 351 282 490 750*

Qatar
E: Doha *00 974 4421991*
Romania
E: Bucharest *00 40 21 201 7200*
Russia
E: Moscow *00 7 095 956 7200*
CG: St Petersburg *00 7 812 320 3200*
CG: Yekaterinburg *00 7 3432 564931 www.britain.sky.ru*
C: Novorossiysk *00 7 8617 618100*
C: Vladivostok *00 7 4232 411312*
Rwanda
E: Kigali *00 250 85771 / 85773 / 84098 / 86072 www.britishembassykigali.org.rw*
St Kitts and Nevis
HC: Basseterre *001 268 462 0008/9*
St Lucia
HC: Castries *001 758 45 22484/5*
St Vincent
HC: Kingstown *001 784 457 1701*
Samoa
HC: Apia *00 64 4 924 2888*
San Marino
E: *00 39 055 284133*
São Tomé and Principe
C: São Tomé *00 239 12 21026/7*
Saudi Arabia
E: Riyadh *00 966 1 488 0077*
CG: Jeddah *00 966 2 622 5550/7/8*
Senegal
E: Dakar *00 221 823 7392 / 9971*
Serbia and Montenegro
E: Belgrade *00 381 11 2645055 / 3060900 / 3615660 http://britemb.org.yu*
Seychelles
HC: Victoria *00 248 283666*
Sierra Leone
HC: Freetown *00 232 22 232 961 / 362 / 563*
Singapore
HC: *00 65 6424 4200 www.britain.org.sg*
Slovakia
E: Bratislava *00 421 2 5998 2000 www.britemb.sk*
Slovenia
E: Ljubljana *00 386 1 200 3910 www.british-embassy.si*
Solomon Islands
HC: Honiara *00 677 21705/6*
Somalia
E: Mogadishu *00 252 1 20288/9*
South Africa
HC: Pretoria *00 27 12 421 7500 www.britain.org.za*
CG: Cape Town *00 27 21 405 2400*
C: Durban *00 27 31 305 3041*
C: East London *00 27 43 726 9380*
C: Port Elizabeth *00 27 41 363 8841*
Spain
E: Madrid *00 34 91 700 82 00*
CG: Barcelona *00 34 93 366 6200 www.ukinspain.com*
CG: Bilbao *00 34 94 415 7600 / 7711 / 7722*
C: Alicante *00 34 96 521 6022*
C: Las Palmas, Canary Islands *00 34 928 262 508*
C: Málaga *00 34 95 235 2300*
C: Palma *00 34 971 712445 / 712085 / 716048 / 718501 / 712696*
C: Santa Cruz de Tenerife (Canary Islands) *00 34 922 28 6863 / 6653*
C: Santander *00 34 942 220000*
C: Vigo *00 34 986 437133*
ViceC: Ibiza *00 34 971 301818 / 303816 / 301058*
ViceC: Menorca *00 34 971 363373*
Sri Lanka
HC: Colombo *00 94 11 2 437336/43*
Sudan
E: Khartoum *00 249 11 777105*
Surinam
C: Paramaribo *00 597 402 558 / 870*
Swaziland
HC: Mbabane *00 268 404 2581/2/3/4*
Sweden
E: Stockholm *00 46 8 671 3000 www.britishembassy.com*
CG: Gothenburg *00 46 31 339 3300*
C: Sundsvall *00 46 60 164000*
Switzerland
E: Berne *00 41 31 359 7700 www.britain-in-switzerland.ch*
CG: Geneva *00 41 22 918 2400*
ViceC: Basel *00 41 61 483 0977*
ViceC: Lugano *00 41 91 950 0606*
ViceC: Montreux / Vevey *00 41 21 943 3263*
ViceC: Valais *00 41 27 480 3210*
ViceC: Zurich *00 41 1 383 6560*
Syria
E: Damascus *00 963 11 373 9241 / 2 / 3 / 7*
C: Aleppo *00 963 21 2672200 / 2661206*
C: Lattakia *00 963 41 461615*
Tajikistan
E: Dushanbe *00 992 91 901 5079*
Tanzania
HC: Dar es Salaam *00 255 22 211 0101*
Thailand
E: Bangkok *00 66 2 305 8333 www.britishemb.or.th*
C: Chiang Mai *00 66 53 263015*
Togo
C: Lomé *00 228 2264606*
Tonga
HC: Nuku'alofa *00 676 24285 / 24395*
Trinidad and Tobago
HC: Port of Spain *001 868 6222748 / 6281234 / 6281068 www.britain-in-trinidad.org*
Tunisia
E: Tunis *00 216 71 341 444*
Turkey
E: Ankara *00 90 312 455 3344 www.britishembassy.org.tr*
ViceC: Antalya *00 90 242 244 5313*
CG: Istanbul *00 90 212 334 6400*
C: Bodrum *00 90 252 319 0093/4*
C: Izmir *00 90 232 463 5151*
C: Marmaris *00 90 252 412 6486*
Turkmenistan
E: Ashgabat *00 993 12 363462/3/4 www.britishembassy.gov.uk/turkmenistan*
Uganda
HC: Kampala *00 256 31 312000*
Ukraine
E: Kiev *00 380 44 490 3660*
United Arab Emirates
E: Abu Dhabi *00 971 2 6101100 www.britain-uae.org*
E: Dubai *00 971 4 309 4444*
United States
E: Washington *00 1 202 588 6500 www.britainusa.com*
CG: Atlanta *00 1 404 954 7700*
CG: Boston *00 1 617 245 4500*
CG: Chicago *00 1 312 970 3800*
CG: Houston *00 1 713 659 6270*
CG: Los Angeles *00 1 310 481 0031*
CG: New York *00 1 212 745 0200*
CG: San Francisco *00 1 415 617 1300*
C: Anchorage *00 1 907 786 4848*
C: Charlotte *00 1 704 383 4359*
C: Dallas *00 1 214 521 4090*
C: Denver *00 1 303 592 5200*
C: Kansas City *00 1 913 469 9786*
C: Miami *00 1 305 374 1522*
C: Minneapolis *00 1 612 338 2525*
C: Nashville *00 1 615 743 3061*
C: New Orleans *00 1 504 524 4180*
C: Philadelphia *00 1 215 557 7665*

C: Phoenix *00 1 602 978 7200*
C: Pittsburgh *00 1 412 562 8872*
C: Portland *00 1 503 227 5669*
C: Puerto Rico *00 1 787 758 9828*
C: St Louis *00 1 636 227 1334*
C: Salt Lake City *00 1 801 297 6922*
C: San Diego *00 1 619 459 8231*
C: San Jose *00 1 408 747 7140 x1200 or x1400*
C: Seattle *00 1 206 622 9255*
ViceC: Orlando *00 1 407 426 7855*

Uruguay
E: Montevideo *00 598 2 622 3630/50*

Uzbekistan
E: Tashkent *00 99871 120 6451/6288/7852/7853/7854 www.britishembassy.gov .uk/uzbekistan*

Vanuatu
HC: Port-Vila *00 678 23100 www.britishhighcommission.gov.uk/vanuatu*

Venezuela
E: Caracas *00 58 212 263 8411 www.britain.org.ve*
C: Maracaibo *00 58 2 61 797 7003*
C: Margarita *00 58 2 95 264 6993*
C: Mérida *00 58 2 74 266 4665*
C: San Cristobal *00 58 2 3460434/3471872*

Vietnam
E: Hanoi *00 84 4 936 0500 www.uk-vietnam.org*
CG: Ho Chi Minh City *00 84 8 8298433*

Yemen
E: Sana'a *00 967 1 264081/82/83/84*
CG: Aden *00 967 2 232712/3/4*
C: Hodeidah *00 967 3 238130/1*

Zambia
HC: Lusaka *00 260 1 251133*

Zimbabwe
E: Harare *00 263 4 77 2990/4700 www.britainzw.org*

Websites

The Foreign Office is in the process of building new websites for Britain's embassies abroad. Where a website is not listed, visit **www.britishembassy.gov.uk** for a country list

Arts

Government departments

Culture, Media and Sport
020 7211 6000
Press: 020 7211 6200
www.culture.gov.uk

Education and Skills
020 7925 5000
Press: 020 7925 6789
www.dfes.gov.uk

Arts councils

Arts Council England
020 7973 6517; 0845 300 6200
www.artscouncil.org.uk

Arts Council for Northern Ireland
028 9038 5200
www.artscouncil-ni.org

Design Council
020 7420 5200
www.design-council.org.uk

Film Council
020 7861 7861
www.filmcouncil.org.uk

Scottish Arts Council
0131 226 6051
www.scottisharts.org.uk

Galleries and museums

Association of Independent Museums
samm@ltm.co.uk
www.museums.org.uk/aim

British Library
020 7412 7000
www.bl.uk

British Museum
020 7323 8000 (switchboard)
020 7323 8299 (information desk)
www.thebritishmuseum.ac.uk

Geffrye Museum
020 7739 9893
www.geffrye-museum.org.uk

Imperial War Museum
020 7416 5320
www.iwm.org.uk

Institute of Contemporary Arts
020 7930 3647
www.ica.org.uk

Museum of London
020 7600 3699
0870 444 3852 (local rate)
0870 444 3851 (automated information line)
www.museum-london.org.uk

Museums Association
020 7426 6970
www.museumsassociation.org

National Art Collections Fund
020 7225 4800
www.artfund.org

National Galleries of Scotland
0131 624 6200
www.nationalgalleries.org
www.natgalscot.ac.uk

National Gallery
020 7839 3321; 020 7747 2885
www.nationalgallery.org.uk

National Maritime Museum
020 8858 4422 (admin)
020 8312 6565 (recorded information line)
www.nmm.ac.uk

National Museum of Science and Industry
0870 870 4868
www.nmsi.ac.uk

National Museums Liverpool
0151 207 0001
www.liverpoolmuseums.org.uk

National Portrait Gallery
020 7306 0055;
Press: 020 7312 2452
www.npg.org.uk

Natural History Museum
020 7942 5000
020 7942 5011 (information)
www.nhm.ac.uk

Royal Academy of Arts
020 7300 8000; 020 7439 7438
www.royalacademy.org.uk

Royal College of Art
020 7590 4444
www.rca.ac.uk

Royal Marines Museum
023 9281 9385
www.royalmarinesmuseum.co.uk

Tate
020 7887 8000
www.tate.org.uk

Victoria and Albert Museum
020 7942 2000
www.vam.ac.uk

24 Hour Museum
01273 820044
www.24hourmuseum.org.uk

Performing arts

Almeida Theatre Company
020 7226 7432
www.alemida.co.uk
British Film Institute
020 7255 1444
www.bfi.org.uk
Edinburgh Festival Fringe
0131 226 0026
Press: 0131 226 0024
www.edfringe.com
English National Ballet
020 7581 1245
www.ballet.org.uk
English National Opera
020 7836 0111
Press: 020 7845 9378
www.eno.org
National Theatre
020 7452 3333
Information: 020 7452 3400
www.nt-online.org
Musicians Benevolent Fund
020 7636 4481
www.mbf.org.uk
Royal Academy of Dance
020 7326 8000
www.rad.org.uk
Royal Ballet School
020 8748 6334
www.royal-ballet-school.org.uk
Royal College of Music
020 7589 3643
www.rcm.ac.uk
Royal Opera House, Covent Garden
020 7240 1200
www.royalopera.org
Royal Shakespeare Company
01789 403404
www.rsc.org.uk
South Bank Centre
020 7921 0600
www.sbc.org.uk
Theatres Trust
020 7836 8591
www.theatrestrust.org.uk

History and heritage

Alexandra Palace and Park
020 8365 2121
www.alexandrapalace.com
Ancient Monuments Society
office@ancientmonumentssociety.org.uk
www.ancientmonumentssociety.org.uk
Architectural Heritage Fund
020 7925 0199
www.ahfund.org.uk
British Archaeological Association
www.britarch.ac.uk/baa
Civic Trust
020 7170 4299
www.civictrust.org.uk
Council for British Archaeology
01904 671 417
www.britarch.ac.uk
Cultural Heritage search engine
www.culturalheritage.net
English Heritage
0870 333 1181
Press: 020 7973 3250
www.english-heritage.org.uk
Garden History Society
020 7608 2409
www.gardenhistorysociety.org
Historic Royal Palaces
020 8781 9750
Press: 020 7488 5662/3
www.hrp.org.uk
Banqueting House
0870 751 5178
Hampton Court Palace
0870 752 7777
Kensington Palace State Apartments
0870 751 5170
Kew Palace and Queen Charlotte's Cottage
0870 751 5179
Tower of London
0870 756 6060
Historical Diving Society
enquiries@thehds.com
www.thehds.com
Historical Manuscripts Commission
020 8876 3444
www.hmc.gov.uk
Historical Metallurgy Society
01792 233223
http://hist-met.org
Institute of Historic Building Conservation
01747 873133
www.ihbc.org.uk
International Council on Monuments & Sites in UK
020 7566 0031
www.icomos.org/uk
Jewish Historical Society of Britain
020 7723 5852
www.users.dircon.co.uk/~jhse
Keltek Trust
bells@keltek.org
www.keltek.org
Church bell preservation society
Landmark Trust
01628 825920
www.landmarktrust.org.uk
National Association of Decorative & Fine Arts Associations
020 7430 0730
www.nadfas.org.uk
National Trust
0870 609 5380
www.nationaltrust.org.uk
National Trust for Scotland
0131 243 9300
www.nts.org.uk
Royal Commisssion on the Ancient & Historic Monuments of Wales
01970 621200
www.rcahmw.org.uk
Save Britain's Heritage
020 7253 3500
www.savebritainsheritage.org
Scottish Railway Preservation Society
01506 825855
www.srps.org.uk
Society for the Protection of Ancient Buildings
020 7377 1644
www.spab.org.uk
Ulster Architectural Heritage Society
028 9055 0213
www.uahs.co.uk
United Kingdom Institute for Conservation of Historic & Artistic Works
020 7721 8721
www.ukic.org.uk
Vivat Trust
0845 090 0194
www.vivat.org.uk

Business

Government departments

Treasury
020 7270 5000, press 020 7270 5238
www.hm-treasury.gov.uk
Trade and Industry
020 7215 5000, press 020 7215 5954
www.dti.gov.uk
Work and Pensions
020 7238 0800, press 020 7238 0866
www.dwp.gov.uk

Central banks

Bank of England
020 7601 4444
www.bankofengland.co.uk
European Central Bank
00 49 69 13440
www.ecb.int

FTSE-100 companies

3i Group
020 7928 3131
www.3i.com
Abbey National
0870 607 6000; press: 020 7756 5952
www.abbeynational.com
Alliance & Leicester
0116 201 1000; press: 0116 200 3355
www.alliance-leicester-group.co.uk;
www.newscast.co.uk
Alliance Unichem
01932 870550
www.alliance-unichem.com
Allied Domecq
0117 978 5000
www.allieddomecqplc.com
Amvescap
020 7638 0731
Press: 001 404 479 2886
www.amvescap.com
Anglo American
020 7698 8500; press: 020 7698 8555
www.angloamerican.co.uk
Antofagasta
020 7808 0988
www.antofagasta.co.uk
Associated British Foods
020 7282 1076
www.abf.co.uk
AstraZeneca
01582 836000
www.astrazeneca.co.uk;
www.astrazenecapressoffice.com
Aviva
020 7283 2000; press: 020 7662 8221
www.aviva.com
BAA
020 7834 9449; press: 020 7932 6654
www.baa.co.uk
BAE Systems
01252 373232
www.baesystems.com
Barclays
0845 7555555
www.barclays.co.uk
BG Group
0118 935 3222; press: 0118 929 3717
www.bg-group.com
BHP Billiton
020 7802 4000; press: 020 7802 4177
www.bhpbilliton.com
BOC Group
01276 477222; press: 01276 807594
www.boc.com
Boots Group
0115 9506111; press: 020 7608 1000
www.boots-plc.com;
www.newscast.co.uk
BP
020 7496 4000; press: 020 7496 4076
www.bp.com
Bradford & Bingley
01274 555555
B&B Corporate press: 020 7067 5627
MarketPlace and B&B Savings press: 020 7067 5632
Property Services and B&B Lending press: 020 7067 5631
www.bbg.co.uk
British Airways
0870 850 9850; press: 020 8738 5100
www.britishairways.com
British American Tobacco
0870 850 9850; press: 020 8738 5100
www.bat.com
British Land
020 7486 4466; press: 020 7251 3801
www.britishland.com
BSkyB
0870 240 3000
www.sky.com
BT Group
020 7356 5000
National journalists: 020 7356 5369
Regional journalists: 0845 726 2624
www.btplc.com
Bunzl
020 7495 4950
www.bunzl.com
Cable & Wireless
01908 845 000; press: 020 7315 4495
www.cw.com
Cadbury Schweppes
020 7409 1313; press: 020 7409 1313
Cadbury Schweppes European Beverages press: 01923 250 999
Cadbury World press: 0121 451 4180
Cadbury Trebor Bassett press: 01923 483483
Cadbury International press: 0121 458 2000
www.cadburyschweppes.com
Capita Group
020 7799 1525
www.capita.co.uk
Carnival
00 1 305 599 2600; 023 8052 5231
www.poprincesscruises.com
Centrica
01753 494000; press: 01753 494085
www.centrica.co.uk
Compass Group
01932 573000
www.compass-group.com
Daily Mail & General Trust
020 7291 3870; press: 020 7938 6000
www.dmgt.co.uk
Diageo
020 7927 5200
www.diageo.com
Dixons Group
0870 850 3333; press: 0845 609 0805
www.dixons-group-plc.co.uk
Emap
020 7278 1452
Emap plc and Emap Communications press: 020 7278 1452
Emap Consumer Media press: 020 7859 8411
Emap Performance press: 020 7436 1515
www.emap.com
Enterprise Inns
0121 733 7700
www.enterpriseinns.com
Exel Group
01344 302000; press: 01908 244306
www.exel.com
Friends Provident
0870 6071352
City and corporate press enquiries: 020 7760 3133
Product, services and product performance press enquiries: 01722 311 447
www.friendsprovident.co.uk
Gallaher Group
01932 859777
www.gallaher-group.com
Glaxo SmithKline
020 8047 5000; press: 020 8047 5502
www.gsk.com
Gus
020 7495 0070; press: 020 7251 3801
Experian International: 0115 941 0888
Argos: 01908 690333
Homebase: 020 8784 7200
www.gus.co.uk
Hanson
020 7245 1245; press: 01454 316 000
www.hansonplc.com
Hays
0191 566 1900
www.hays-travel.co.uk

HBOS
0870 600 5000
HBOS press:
pressoffice@HBOSplc.com
Halifax retail banking press:
01422 333253
Bank of Scotland retail banking
Press: 0131 243 7195
or 0845 606 6696
Bank of Scotland corporate banking:
0845 606 6696
www.hbosplc.com

Hilton Group
020 7856 8000
Hilton Group plc and Hilton International press: 020 7856 8293
Ladbrokes Worldwide press:
020 8515 5651
Livingwell press: 01908 308856
www.hiltongroup.com

HSBC
020 7991 8888; press: 020 7992 1573
www.hsbc.com

ICI
020 7009 5000
www.ici.com

Imperial Tobacco
0117 963 6636; press: 0117 933 7241
www.imperial-tobacco.com

Intercontinental Hotel Group
01753 410100
www.intercontinental.com

ITV
020 7843 8000
Press: 020 7843 8218/8219
www.itv.com

J Sainsbury
020 7695 6000; press: 020 7695 7295
www.j-sainsbury.co.uk

Johnson Matthey
020 7269 8400
www.matthey.com

Kingfisher
020 7372 8008
www.kingfisher.co.uk

Land Securities Group
020 7413 9000
Land Securities Trillium:
020 7796 5500
Press: melissa.winsor@landsecurities.com
www.landsecurities.co.uk

Legal & General Group
020 7528 6200
Press: 01737 375353/375351
www.legalandgeneral.com

Liberty International
020 7960 1200
www.liberty-international.co.uk

Lloyds TSB
Press: 020 7356 2493
www.mediacentre.lloydstsb.com

Man Group
020 7144 1000; press: 020 7653 6620
www.mangroupplc.com

Marks & Spencer
020 7935 4422; press: 020 7268 1919
www.marksandspencer.com

MMO2
0113 272 2000; press: 01753 628402
www.mmo2.com

Wm Morrison Supermarkets
01274 494166
www.morereasons.co.uk

National Grid Transco
01926 653000; NETA: 0800 777770
www.nationalgrid.com/uk

Next
0845 600 7333; press: 0116 284 2503
http://order.next.co.uk/aboutnext/

Northern Rock
0191 285 7191
www.northernrock.co.uk

Old Mutual
020 7002 7000; press: 020 7002 7133
www.oldmutual.com

Pearson
020 7010 2000; press: 020 7825 8076
plc press: 020 7010 2314/2307
Pearson Education press:
001 212 782 3482
Penguin UK press: 020 7010 3000
FT Group press: 020 7873 4447
www.pearson.com

Prudential
020 7220 7588
Group press office: 020 7548 3719
UK Insurance operations press:
020 7150 2203
M&G press: 020 7548 3222
EGG plc press: 020 7526 2600
www.prudential.co.uk

Reckitt Benckiser
01753 217800
www.reckitt.com

Reed Elsevier
Press corporate:
020 7166 5657/5670
Science and medical press:
00 31 20 485 2994
Legal press: 001 937 865 8838
Education press: 001 407 345 3987
Business press: 020 8652 3296
www.r-e.com

Rentokil Initial
01342 833022; press: 01342 830255
www.rentokil-initial.co.uk

Reuters Group
020 7250 1122; press: 020 7542 8404
www.reuters.com

Rexam
020 7227 4100
www.rexam.com

Rio Tinto
020 7930 2399; press: 020 7753 2305
www.riotinto.com

Rolls Royce
020 7222 9020
www.rolls-royce.com

Royal & Sun Alliance
01403 232323
UK press: 020 7337 5146
Worldwide press enquiries:
020 7569 6023
www.royalsunalliance.com

Royal Bank of Scotland
020 7250 1122
Group press: 0131 523 4414
Corporate Banking and Financial Markets press: 0131 523 4414
Royal Bank press: 020 7672 1928
NatWest press:
020 7672 1932/1931/1927
Coutts press: 020 7957 2427
RBS Insurance press: 0845 878 2367
Direct Line Financial Services press:
0141 308 4100
Lombard press: 020 7672 1921
RBS Cards press: 020 7672 5086
Ulster Bank press: 00 353 1 608 4573
The One Account press:
01603 707154
www.rbs.co.uk

SABMiller
020 7659 0100; press: 020 7659 0120
www.sab.co.za

Sage Group
0191 294 3000;
www.sage.co.uk

Schroders
020 7658 6000
www.schroders.com

Scottish & Newcastle
0131 528 2000; press: 0131 528 2131
www.scottish-newcastle.com

Scottish & Southern Energy
0870 702 0125
www.scottish-southern.co.uk

Scottish Power
0845 2727111; press: 0141 636 4515
www.scottishpower.plc.uk

Severn Trent Water
0121 722 4000
Severn Trent plc press:
0121 722 4273
Water press: 0121 722 4121
Biffa press: 01494 521 221
www.stwater.co.uk

Shell Transport & Trading Company
020 7934 1234
Chemicals: 01244 685000
Global Solutions: 0151 373 5000
Bitumen: 01932 568211
Marine Personnel (IOM):
01624 821500
Oils (Lubricants Centre):
0151 357 1161
Oils: 0161 499 4000
Ship Management: 01624 824344
Aircraft: 020 8730 5200
Gas Direct: 020 7257 0100
Shell Gas (LPG): 0870 830 1100
Northern Ireland: 01232 553800
Exploration and Production:
01224 882000 (Aberdeen)
01263 720661 (Norwich)
01307 462225 (Angus)
01595 4888 (Isle of Shetland)
01502 522000 (Suffolk)
01383 892001 (Fife)
www.shell.com

Shire Pharmaceuticals
01256 894 000; press: 01256 894280
www.shiregroup.com

Smith & Nephew
020 7401 7646
R&D: 01904 824000
Orthopaedics: 01223 568100
Endoscopy: 01480 423200
Wound management: 01482 222200
Extruded films: 01430 440757
Press photos: www.newscast.co.uk
020 7608 1000
www.smith-nephew.com

Smiths Group
020 8458 3232; press: 020 8457 8306
www.smiths-group.com
Standard Chartered
020 7280 7500; press: 020 7280 7163
www.standardchartered.com
Tesco
01992 632222
www.tesco.com
Tomkins
020 8871 4544
www.tomkins.co.uk
Unilever
01932 263000
www.unilever.co.uk
United Utilities
0800 1954141
www.unitedutilities.com
Vodafone
01635 33251
Group press enquiries: 01635 674268
UK press: 07000 500100
www.vodafone.co.uk
Whitbread
020 7606 4455
Group plc press: 020 7806 5442
Restaurant brands: 01582 424200
Restaurants press: 01582 844486
Marriott and Travel Inn:
01582 422022
Hotels press: 01582 499105
David Lloyd Leisure: 01582 844899
Sports press: 01582 844257
Whitbread Leisure Vouchers:
01582 396666
www.whitbread.co.uk
Wolseley
0118 929 8700
www.wolseley.com
WPP Group
020 7408 2204; press: 020 7408 2204
www.wpp.com
Xstrata
020 7968 2800; press: 020 7968 2812
www.xstrata.com
Yell Group
0121 455 0000; press: 0118 950 6999
www.yellgroup.com

Regulators and government agencies

Advertising Standards Authority
020 7580 5555
www.asa.org.uk
British and Irish Ombudsman Association
020 8467 7455
www.bioa.org.uk
British Board of Film Classification
020 7440 1570
www.bbfc.co.uk
British Standards Institution
020 8996 9000
www.bsi-global.com
Competition Commission
020 7271 0100; press: 020 7271 0242
www.competition-commission.org.uk
Council of Mortgage Lenders
020 7437 0075
www.cml.org.uk
Financial Ombudsman Service
020 7964 1000
www.financial-ombudsman.org.uk
Financial Services Authority
020 7066 1000
www.fsa.gov.uk
Food Standards Agency
020 7276 8000
www.foodstandards.gov.uk
Health and Safety Executive
08701 545500
www.hse.gov.uk
Health and Safety Executive for Northern Ireland
0800 0320 121; 028 9024 3249
www.hseni.gov.uk
Independent Committee for the Supervision of Telephone Information Services
020 7940 7474; press: 020 7940 7408
www.icstis.org.uk
Information Commissioner
01625 545700; press: 020 7282 2960
www.dataprotection.gov.uk
National Lottery Commission
020 7016 3400; press: 020 7016 3430
Camelot: 0845 910 0000
Lottery funding: 0845 275 0000
www.natlotcomm.gov.uk
Ofcom
020 7981 3000; press: 020 7981 3033
www.ofcom.gov.uk
Office of Fair Trading
020 7211 8000; 08457 224499
Government liaison unit:
020 7211 8178
Press: 020 7211 8900
www.oft.gov.uk
Office of the Rail Regulator
020 7282 2000
Press: 020 7282 2002/2007
www.rail-reg.gov.uk
Ofgem
020 7901 7000; press: 020 7901 7006
www.ofgas.gov.uk/ofgem
Ofwat
0121 625 1300; press: 0121 625 1450
www.ofwat.gov.uk
Ombudsman for Estate Agents
01722 333306
www.oea.co.uk
Pensions Ombudsman
020 7834 9144
www.pensions-ombudsman.org.uk
Serious Fraud Office
020 7239 7272
www.sfo.gov.uk
Small Business Service
0845 001 0031
www.sbs.gov.uk
Trading Standards Institute
0870 872 9000; press: 0870 872 9030
www.tsi.org.uk

Industry bodies

Trade Association Forum
020 7395 8283
www.taforum.org
Confederation of British Industry
press: 020 7395 8239
www.cbi.org.uk
Ethnic Minority Business Forum
embf@sbs.gsi.gov.uk
www.ethnicbusiness.org
Federation of Small Businesses
01253 336000
www.fsb.org.uk

Consumer bodies

Consumer Support Networks
020 7840 7223
www.csnconnect.org.uk
Consumers' Association
020 7770 7000; 0845 307 4000
Press: 020 7770 7062/7373
www.which.net/corporate
General Consumer Council for Northern Ireland
028 9067 2488
www.gccni.org.uk
Internet Watch Foundation UK
01223 237700
To submit a report: 0845 600 8844
Press: 01223 237 700
www.iwf.org.uk
National Association of Citizens Advice Bureaux
www.adviceguide.org.uk
National Consumer Council
020 7730 3469
www.ncc.org.uk
Scottish Consumer Council
0141 226 5261
www.scotconsumer.org.uk
Welsh Consumer Council
029 2025 5454
www.wales-consumer.org.uk

Unions

TUC
Trades Union Congress
020 7636 4030
www.tuc.org.uk

ANGU
Abbey National Group Union
01442 891122
www.angu.org.uk

Accord
0118 934 1808
www.accord-myunion.org

ALGUS
Alliance and Leicester Group Union of Staff
0116 285 6585
www.algus.org.uk

Amicus
020 7505 3000
www.aeeu.org.uk
manufacturing, technical & skilled persons
www.msf.org.uk
engineering and electrical

Aslef
Associated Society of Locomotive Engineers and Firemen
020 7317 8600
www.aslef.org.uk

ACM
Association for College Management
0116 275 5076
www.acm.uk.com

AEP
Association of Educational Psychologists
0191 384 9512
www.aep.org.uk

AFA
Association of Flight Attendants
001 202 712 9799
www.afanet.org

AMO
Association of Magisterial Officers
020 7403 2244
www.amo-online.org.uk

ATL
Association of Teachers and Lecturers
020 7930 6441
Press: 020 7782 1509
www.askatl.org.uk

AUT
Association of University Teachers
020 7670 9700
www.aut.org.uk

BFAWU
Bakers, Food and Allied Workers Union
01707 260150
www.bfawu.org

BSU
Britannia Staff Union
01538 399627
www.britanniasu.org.uk

BALPA
British Air Line Pilots Association
020 8476 4000
Press: 020 7924 7555
www.balpa.org.uk

BACM-TEAM
British Association of Colliery Management – Technical, Energy and Administrative Management
01302 815551
www.bacmteam.org.uk

BDA
British Dietetic Association
0121 200 8080
www.bda.uk.com

BOS
British and Irish Orthoptic Society
020 7387 7992
www.orthoptics.org.uk

Bectu
Broadcasting, Entertainment, Cinematograph and Theatre Union
020 7346 0900
www.bectu.org.uk

CSMTS
Card Setting Machine Tenters Society
01924 400206

CATU
Ceramic and Allied Trades Union
01782 272755
www.catu.org.uk

CSP
Chartered Society of Physiotherapy
020 7306 6666
www.csp.org.uk

CWU
Communication Workers Union
020 8971 7200
www.cwu.org

CDNA
Community and District Nursing Association
020 8231 0180
www.cdna.tvu.ac.uk

CYWU
Community and Youth Workers' Union
0121 244 3344
www.cywu.org.uk

Connect
020 8971 6000
www.connectuk.org
professionals in communications

Diageo Staff Association
020 8963 5249
staff grades at Diageo, including Guinness, in the UK

EIS
Educational Institute of Scotland
0131 225 6244
www.eis.org.uk

EFTU
Engineering and Fastener Trade Union
0121 420 2204

Equity
020 7379 6000
Press: 020 7670 0259
www.equity.org.uk
performers and artists

FDA
020 7343 1111
Press: 020 7343 1121
www.fda.org.uk
senior managers and professionals in public service

FBU
Fire Brigades Union
020 8541 1765
www.fbu.org.uk

GULO
General Union of Loom Overlookers
01254 51760

GMB
020 8947 3131
Press: 020 8971 4202
www.gmb.org.uk
general union

GPMU
Graphical, Paper and Media Union
England: 01234 351521
Ireland: 00 353 1 663 2048
www.gpmu.org.uk

HCSA
Hospital Consultants and Specialists Association
01256 771777
www.hcsa.com

ISTC
020 7239 1200
Press: 020 7239 1243
www.istc-tu.org
steel and metal industry and communities

MU
Musicians' Union
020 7582 5566
www.musiciansunion.org.uk

NAPO
The Trade Union and Professional Association for Family Court and Probation Staff
020 7223 4887
www.napo.org.uk

NATFHE
020 7837 3636
Press: 020 7520 3207/1032
www.natfhe.org.uk
university and college lecturers

NACODS
National Association of Colliery Overmen, Deputies and Shotfirers
01226 203743

NACO
National Association of Co-operative Officials
0161 351 7900

NAEIAC
National Association of Educational Inspectors, Advisers and Consultants
01226 383420
www.naeiac.org

NASUWT
National Association of Schoolmasters Union of Women Teachers
0121 453 6150
www.teachersunion.org.uk

NUDAGO
National Union of Domestic Appliances and General Operatives
020 7387 2578
www.gftu.org.uk

NUJ
National Union of Journalists
020 7278 7916
www.nuj.org.uk

KFAT
National Union of Knitwear, Footwear and Apparel Trades
0116 255 6703
www.kfat.org.uk
manufacturing, retail and logistics

NULMW
National Union of Lock and Metal Workers
01902 366651

NUMAST
National Union of Marine, Aviation and Shipping Transport Officers
020 8989 6677
www.numast.org

NUM
National Union of Mineworkers
01226 215555

RMT
National Union of Rail, Maritime and Transport Workers
020 7387 4771
www.rmt.org.uk

NUT
National Union of Teachers
020 7388 6191
www.teachers.org.uk

NGSU
Nationwide Group Staff Union
01295 710767
www.ngsu.org.uk

POA
Prison Officers Association
020 8803 0255
www.poauk.org.uk

PFA
Professional Footballers' Association
0161 236 0575
www.givemefootball.com

Prospect
020 7902 6600
www.prospect.org.uk
engineers, scientists, managers and specialists

PCS
Public and Commercial Services Union
020 7924 2727
Press: 020 7801 2820
www.pcs.org.uk

SWSWU
Sheffield Wool Shear Workers Union
17 Galsworthy Road
Sheffield S5 8QX

SCP
Society of Chiropodists and Podiatrists
0845 450 3720
www.scpod.org

SoR
Society of Radiographers
020 7740 7200
www.sor.org

T&G
Transport and General Workers' Union
020 7611 2500
www.tgwu.org.uk

TSSA
Transport Salaried Staffs' Association
020 7387 2101
www.tssa.org.uk

UBAC
01653 697634
staff in the Bradford and Bingley Group and Alltel Mortgage Solutions

UCAC
Undeb Cenedlaethol Athrawon Cymru
01970 615 577

UNIFI
020 8946 9151
www.unifi.org.uk
finance sector

UCATT
Union of Construction, Allied Trades and Technicians
020 7622 2442
www.ucatt.org.uk

USDAW
Union of Shop, Distributive and Allied Workers
0161 224 2804/249 2400
www.usdaw.org.uk

Unison
0845 355 0845
www.unison.org.uk
public service union

WGGB
Writers' Guild of Great Britain
020 7833 0777
www.writersguild.org.uk

YISA
Yorkshire Independent Staff Association
01482 862058

Employment bodies

Pay & Employment Rights Service
01924 439587
www.pers.org.uk

Employment Tribunals
020 7273 8603; enquiry line: 0845 795 9775
www.employmenttribunals.gov.uk

Equal Opportunities Commission (EOC)
0845 601 5901
www.eoc.org.uk

Equality Commission for Northern Ireland
028 9050 0600
www.equalityni.org

Investors in People UK
020 7467 1900
www.iipuk.co.uk

Labour Relations Agency
028 9032 1442
www.lra.org.uk

Low Pay Commission
020 7215 5773
Press:: 020 7215 6052
www.lowpay.gov.uk

Education

Government department

Education and Skills
020 7925 5000
Press: 020 7925 6789
www.dfes.gov.uk

Government agencies

Adult Learning Inspectorate
0870 240 7744
www.ali.gov.uk
Arts and Humanities Research Board
0117 987 6500
www.ahrb.ac.uk
Council for Science and Technology
020 7215 6518
www.cst.gov.uk
Education and Learning Wales
08456 088 066
www.elwa.ac.uk
Higher Education Funding Council for England (HEFCE)
0117 931 7317
www.hefce.ac.uk
Learning and Skills Council
0870 900 6800
www.lsc.gov.uk
Learning and Skills Development Agency
020 7297 9000
www.lsda.org.uk
Learning and Teaching Scotland
0141 337 5000
www.ltscotland.com
National Grid for Learning
www.ngfl.gov.uk
Ofsted
020 7421 6800
www.ofsted.gov.uk
Qualifications and Curriculum Authority
020 7509 5555
www.qca.org.uk
Scottish Qualifications Authority
0845 279 1000
www.sqa.org.uk
Sector Skills Development Agency
01709 765444
www.ssda.org.uk
Student Loans Company
0800 40 50 10
www.slc.co.uk
Teacher Training Agency (TTA)
0845 600 0991
www.canteach.gov.uk
Ucas
01242 222444
www.ucas.com

Professional bodies

Association of Teachers and Lecturers
020 7930 6441
www.askatl.org.uk
Association of University Administrators
0161 275 2063
www.aua.ac.uk
Association of University Teachers
020 7670 9700
www.aut.org.uk
British Educational Research Association
01636 819090
www.bera.ac.uk
National Association of School-masters Union of Women Teachers
0121 453 6150
www.teachersunion.org.uk
National Union of Students
020 7272 8900 (England)
0131 556 6598 (Scotland)
028 9024 4641 (Ireland)
029 2037 5980 (Wales)
www.nus.org.uk
National Union of Teachers
020 7388 6191
www.teachers.org.uk

Voluntary bodies

Afasic
020 7490 9410
www.afasic.org.uk
Speech, language & communication charity
Campaign for Learning
020 7930 1111
www.campaign-for-learning.org.uk
CEDC
024 7658 8440
www.cedc.org.uk
Education Extra
020 8709 9900
www.educationextra.org.uk
Out-of-hours learning
Learning Through Action
0870 770 7985
www.learning-through-action.org.uk
Life Education Centres
suecullen@lifeeducation.org.uk
www.lifeeducation.org.uk
National Literacy Trust
020 7828 2435
www.literacytrust.org.uk
UFI/ Learn Direct
020 7681 6523
www.ufi.com

Universities

Aberdeen, University of
01224 272090/1
www.abdn.ac.uk
Abertay Dundee, University of
01382 308080
www.abertay.ac.uk
Aberystwyth – University of Wales
01970 622021
www.aber.ac.uk
Anglia Polytechnic University
0845 271 3333
www.apu.ac.uk
Aston University, Birmingham
0121 359 3611
www.aston.ac.uk
Bangor – University of Wales
01248 382016
www.bangor.ac.uk
Bath Spa University College
01225 875875
www.bathspa.ac.uk
Bath, University of
01225 323019
www.bath.ac.uk
Bell College
01698 283100
www.bell.ac.uk
Birmingham, University of
0121 414 3344
www.bham.ac.uk
Bishop Grosseste College
01522 527347
www.bgc.ac.uk
Bolton Institute of Higher Education
01204 900600
www.bolton.ac.uk
Bournemouth University
01202 524111
www.bournemouth.ac.uk
Bournemouth, Arts Institute at
01202 533011
www.aib.ac.uk
Bradford, University of
01274 233081
www.bradford.ac.uk
Brighton, University of
01273 600900
www.brighton.ac.uk
Bristol, University of
0117 928 9000
www.bris.ac.uk
Brunel University
01895 274000
www.brunel.ac.uk
Buckingham Chilterns University College
01494 603015
www.bcuc.ac.uk
Buckingham, University of
01280 814080
www.buckingham.ac.uk

Cambridge, University of
01223 332200
www.cam.ac.uk
Christ's College: 01223 334900
www.christs.cam.ac.uk
Churchill College: 01223 336000
www.chu.cam.ac.uk
Clare College: 01223 333246
www.clare.cam.ac.uk
Corpus Christi College: 01223 338057
www.corpus.cam.ac.uk
Downing College: 01223 334800
www.downing.cam.ac.uk
Emmanuel College: 01223 334290
www.emma.cam.ac.uk
Fitzwilliam College: 01223 332000
www.fitz.cam.ac.uk
Girton College: 01223 338999
www.girton.cam.ac.uk
Gonville & Caius College:
01223 332447
www.caius.cam.ac.uk
Homerton College: 01223 411141
www.homerton.cam.ac.uk
Hughes Hall: 01233 334893
www.hughes.cam.ac.uk
Jesus College: 01223 339495
www.jesus.cam.ac.uk
Kings College: 01223 339313
www.kings.cam.ac.uk
Lucy Cavendish College
01223 332190
www.lucy-cav.cam.ac.uk
Magdalene College: 01223 332100
www.magd.cam.ac.uk
New Hall: 01223 762100
www.newhall.cam.ac.uk
Newnham College: 01223 334700
www.newn.cam.ac.uk
Pembroke College: 01223 338100
www.pem.cam.ac.uk
Peterhouse College: 01223 338200
www.pet.cam.ac.uk
Queen's College: 01223 335540
www.quns.cam.ac.uk
Robinson College: 01223 339100
www.rob.cam.ac.uk
Selwyn College: 01223 335846
www.sel.cam.ac.uk
Sidney Sussex College: 01223 338800
www.sid.cam.ac.uk
St Catharine's College: 01223 338300
www.caths.cam.ac.uk
St Edmund's College: 01223 336250
www.stedmunds.cam.ac.uk
St John's College: 01223 338703
www.joh.cam.ac.uk
Canterbury Christ Church University College
01227 767700
www.cant.ac.uk
Cardiff – University of Wales Institute
029 2041 6070
www.uwic.ac.uk
Cardiff University
029 2087 4404/4839
www.cardiff.ac.uk
Central England in Birmingham, University of
0121 331 5595
www.uce.ac.uk

Central Lancashire, University of
01772 892400
www.uclan.ac.uk
Central School of Speech and Drama
020 7722 8183
www.cssd.ac.uk
City University
020 7040 5060
www.city.ac.uk
Conservatoire for Dance & Drama
London Contemporary Dance School
020 7387 0161
www.theplace.org.uk
Royal Academy of Dramatic Art (Rada)
020 7636 7076
www.rada.org.uk
Coventry University
024 7688 7688
www.coventry.ac.uk
Cumbria Institute of the Arts
01228 400300
www.cumbria.ac.uk
Dartington College of Arts
01803 862224
www.dartington.ac.uk
De Montfort University
0116 255 1551
www.dmu.ac.uk
Derby, University of
08701 202330
www.derby.ac.uk
Dundee, University of
01382 344160
www.dundee.ac.uk
Durham, University of
0191 374 2000
www.dur.ac.uk
East Anglia, University of
01603 456161
www.uea.ac.uk
East London, University of
020 8223 3000
www.uel.ac.uk
Edge Hill College
01695 575171
www.edgehill.ac.uk
Edinburgh College of Art
0131 221 6000
www.eca.ac.uk
Edinburgh, University of
0131 650 4360
www.ed.ac.uk
Essex, University of
01206 873666
www.essex.ac.uk
Exeter, University of
01392 263035
www.ex.ac.uk
Falmouth College of Arts
01326 211077
www.falmouth.ac.uk
Glamorgan, University of
01443 483348
www.glam.ac.uk
Glasgow Caledonian
0141 331 3000
www.caledonian.ac.uk
Glasgow School of Art
0141 353 4500
www.gas.ac.uk
Glasgow, University of
0141 330 3219
www.gla.ac.uk

Gloucestershire, University of
01242 532825
www.chelt.ac.uk, www.glos.ac.uk
Goldsmiths College, University of London
020 7919 7171
www.goldsmiths.ac.uk
Greenwich, University of
020 8331 8000
www.gre.ac.uk
Harper Adams University College
01952 820820
www.harper-adams.ac.uk
Heriot-Watt University
0131 449 5111
www.hw.ac.uk
Hertfordshire, University of
01707 284800
www.herts.ac.uk
Huddersfield, University of
01484 422288
www.hud.ac.uk
Hull, University of
01482 346311
www.hull.ac.uk
Imperial College, London
020 7589 5111
www.ic.ac.uk
Keele University
01782 584005
www.keele.ac.uk
Kent, University of
01227 827272
www.ukc.ac.uk
Kent Institute of Art & Design
01622 757286
www.kiad.ac.uk
King's College London
020 7836 5454
www.kcl.ac.uk
Kingston University
020 8457 2000
www.kingston.ac.uk
Lampeter – University of Wales
01570 422351
www.lamp.ac.uk
Lancaster University
01524 65201
www.lancs.ac.uk
Leeds Metropolitan University
0113 283 3113
www.lmu.ac.uk
Leeds, University of
0113 233 2332
www.leeds.ac.uk
Leicester, University of
0116 252 5281
www.le.ac.uk
Lincoln, University of
01522 882000
www.lincoln.ac.uk
Liverpool Hope University College
0151 291 3000
www.hope.ac.uk
Liverpool John Moores University
0151 231 5090
www.livjm.ac.uk
Liverpool, University of
0151 794 5928
www.liv.ac.uk
London Metropolitan University
020 7423 0000
www.londonmet.ac.uk

London School of Economics and Political Science (LSE)
020 7955 7124
www.lse.ac.uk
London – University of the Arts
Camberwell College of Arts
020 7514 6302
www.camberwell.arts.ac.uk
Central St Martin's College of Art & Design
020 7514 7000
www.csm.arts.ac.uk
Chelsea College of Art & Design
020 7514 7777
www.chelsea.arts.ac.uk
London College of Communication
020 7514 6569
www.lcc.arts.ac.uk
London College of Fashion
020 7514 7407
www.fashion.arts.ac.uk
Loughborough University
01509 263171
www.lboro.ac.uk
Luton, University of
01582 489286
www.luton.ac.uk
Manchester Metropolitan University
0161 247 2000
www.mmu.ac.uk
Manchester, University of
0161 275 2077
www.man.ac.uk
Middlesex University
020 8411 5898
www.mdx.ac.uk
Napier University
0500 353570
www.napier.ac.uk
Newcastle upon Tyne, University of
0191 222 6000
www.ncl.ac.uk
Newman College
0121 476 1181
www.newman.ac.uk
Newport – University of Wales
01633 432432
www.newport.ac.uk
North East Wales Institute of Higher Education
01978 290666
www.newi.ac.uk
Northern School of Contemporary Dance
0113 219 3000
www.nscd.ac.uk
Northumbria, University of
0191 227 4777
www.unn.ac.uk
Norwich School of Art & Design
01603 610561
www.nsad.ac.uk
Nottingham Trent University
0115 941 8418
www.ntu.ac.uk
Nottingham, University of
0115 951 5151
www.nottingham.ac.uk
Oxford Brookes University
01865 484040
www.brookes.ac.uk

Oxford, University of
01865 288000
www.ox.ac.uk
Admissions: 01865 270000
www.admissions.ox.ac.uk
Balliol College: 01865 277777
www.balliol.ox.ac.uk
Brasenose College: 01865 277510
www.bnc.ox.ac.uk
Christ Church: 01865 276151
www.chch.ox.ac.uk
Corpus Christi College: 01865 276693
www.ccc.ox.ac.uk
Exeter College: 01865 279660
www.exeter.ox.ac.uk
Harris Manchester College: 01865 271009
www.hmc.ox.ac.uk
Hertford College: 01865 279400
www.hertford.ox.ac.uk
Jesus College: 01865 279720
www.jesus.ox.ac.uk
Keble College: 01865 272711
www.keble.ox.ac.uk
Lady Margaret Hall: 01865 274300
www.lmh.ox.ac.uk
Lincoln College: 01865 279800
www.lincoln.ox.ac.uk
Magdalen College: 01865 276063
www.magd.ox.ac.u
Mansfield College: 01865 270970
www.mansfield.ox.ac.uk
Merton College: 01865 276310
www.merton.ox.ac.uk
New College: 01865 279590
www.new.oc.ac.uk
Oriel College: 01865 276555
www.oriel.ox.ac.uk
Pembroke College: 01865 276412
www.pmb.ox.ac.uk
The Queen's College: 01865 279120
www.queens.ox.ac.uk
Regent's Park College: 01865 288120
www.rpc.ox.ac.uk
Somerville College: 01865 270600
www.some.ox.ac.uk
St Anne's College: 01865 274825
www.stannes.ox.ac.uk
St Catherine's College: 01865 275800
www.stcatz.ox.ac.uk
St Edmund Hall: 01865 279008
www.she.ox.ac.uk
St Hilda's College: 01865 276884
www.sthildas.ox.ac.uk
St Hugh's College: 01865 274910
www.st-hughs.ox.ac.uk
St John's College: 01865 277317
www.sjc.ox.ac.uk
St Peter's College: 01865 278892
www.spc.ox.ac.uk
Trinity College: 01865 279910
www.trinity.ox.ac.uk
University College: 01865 276602
www.univ.ox.ac.uk
Wadham College: 01865 277946
www.wadham.ox.ac.uk
Worcester College: 01865 278391
www.worcester.ox.ac.uk
Paisley, University of
0141 848 3727
www.paisley.ac.uk

Plymouth, University of
01752 232137
www.plymouth.ac.uk
Portsmouth, University of
023 9284 8484
www.port.ac.uk
Queen Margaret University College
0131 317 3000
www.qmuc.ac.uk
Queen Mary, University of London
020 7882 5555
www.qmul.ac.uk
Queen's University Belfast
028 9033 5081
www.qub.ac.uk
Ravensbourne College of Design & Communication
020 8325 8320
www.rave.ac.uk
Reading, University of
0118 987 5123
www.reading.ac.uk
Robert Gordon University, Aberdeen
01224 262000
www.rgu.ac.uk
Roehampton – University of Surrey
020 8392 3232
www.roehampton.ac.uk
Rose Bruford College
020 8300 3024
www.bruford.ac.uk
Royal Academy of Music
020 7873 7374
www.ram.ac.uk
Royal Agricultural College
01285 652531
www.royagcol.ac.uk
Royal College of Music
020 7589 3640
www.rcm.ac.uk
Royal Holloway, University of London
01784 434455
www.rhul.ac.uk
Royal Northern College of Music
0161 907 5210
www.rncm.ac.uk
Royal Scottish Academy of Music & Drama
0141 332 4101
www.rsamd.ac.uk
Royal Veterinary College
020 7468 5148
www.rvc.ac.uk
Royal Welsh College of Music & Drama
029 2034 2854
www.rwcmd.ac.uk
St Andrews, University of
01334 462150
www.st-andrews.ac.uk
St George's Hospital Medical School
020 8725 5992
www.sghms.ac.uk
St Mark & St John College
01752 636890
www.marjon.ac.uk
St Martin's College
01524 384384
www.ucsm.ac.uk

St Mary's College
020 8240 4000
www.smuc.ac.uk
Salford, University of
0161 295 4545
www.salford.ac.uk
School of Oriental and African Studies (SOAS)
020 7637 2388
www.soas.ac.uk
School of Pharmacy, University of London
020 7753 5831
www.ulsop.ac.uk
Scottish Agricultural College
0800 269453
www.sac.ac.uk/education
Sheffield Hallam University
0114 225 5555
www.shu.ac.uk
Sheffield, University of
0114 222 2000
www.sheffield.ac.uk
South Bank University
020 7815 7815
www.sbu.ac.uk
Southampton Institute
023 8031 9039
www.solent.ac.uk
Southampton, University of
023 8059 5000
www.soton.ac.uk
Staffordshire University
01782 294000
www.staffs.ac.uk
Stirling, University of
01786 467044
www.stir.ac.uk
Stranmillis University College
028 9038 1271
www.stran-ni.ac.uk
Strathclyde, University of
0141 552 4400
www.strath.ac.uk
Sunderland, University of
0191 515 3000
www.sunderland.ac.uk
Surrey Institute of Art & Design, University College
01252 722441
www.surrart.ac.uk
Surrey, University of
01483 879305
www.surrey.ac.uk
Sussex, University of
01273 606755
www.sussex.ac.uk
Swansea – University of Wales
01792 205678
www.swan.ac.uk
Swansea Institute of Higher Education
01792 481000
www.sihe.ac.uk
Teesside, University of
01642 218121
www.tees.ac.uk
Thames Valley University
020 8579 5000
www.tvu.ac.uk
Trinity & All Saints College
0113 283 7123
www.tasc.ac.uk
Trinity College, Carmarthen
01267 676767
www.trinity-cm.ac.uk
Trinity College of Music
020 8305 3888
www.tcm.ac.uk
UHI Millennium Institute
01643 27900
www.uhi.ac.uk
Ulster, University of
08700400 700
www.ulster.ac.uk
University College Chester
01244 375444
www.chester.ac.uk
University College Chichester
01243 816000
www.ucc.ac.uk
University College London
020 7679 2000
www.ucl.ac.uk
University College Northampton
01604 735500
www.northampton.ac.uk
University College Winchester
01962 841515
www.winchester.ac.uk
University College Worcester
01905 740800
www.worc.ac.uk
Warwick, University of
024 7652 3523
www.warwick.ac.uk
West of England, University of the
0117 344 3333
www.uwe.ac.uk
Westminster, University of
020 7911 5000
www.westminster.ac.uk
Wimbledon School of Art
020 8408 5000
www.wimbledon.ac.uk
Wolverhampton, University of
01902 322222
www.wlv.ac.uk
Writtle College
01245 424200
www.writtle.ac.uk
York St John College
01904 624624
www.yorksj.ac.uk
York, University of
01904 430000
www.york.ac.uk

Environment

Government and agencies

Department for the Environment, Food and Rural Affairs
020 7238 3000
Press: 020 7238 6600
www.defra.gov.uk

British Waterways Board
01923 226422
www.britishwaterways.co.uk

Countryside Agency
01242 521381
www.countryside.gov.uk

Environment Agency
0845 933 3111
www.environment-agency.gov.uk

Food Standards Agency
020 7276 8000
www.foodstandards.gov.uk

Forestry Commission
0845 367 3787
Press: 0131 314 6249
www.forestry.gov.uk

Meat and Livestock Commission
01908 677577
Press:: 01908 844160
www.mlc.org.uk

The Pesticides Safety Directorate
01904 640500
www.pesticides.gov.uk

United Kingdom Atomic Energy Authority
01235 820220
www.ukaea.org.uk

Rural and environmental bodies

Country Landowners Society
020 7235 0511
www.cla.org.uk

English Heritage
0870 333 1181
www.english-heritage.org.uk

English Nature
01733 455000
Press: 01733 455040
www.english-nature.org.uk

Friends of the Earth
0808 800 1111; 020 7490 1555
www.foe.co.uk

Game Conservancy Trust
01425 652381
www.gct.org.uk

Greenpeace
020 7865 8100
Press: 020 7865 8255
www.greenpeace.org.uk

National Farmers Union
020 7331 7200
www.nfu.org.uk

National Trust
0870 609 5380; 020 7222 9251
www.nationaltrust.org.uk

National Trust for Scotland
0131 243 9300
www.nts.org.uk

Ramblers Association
020 7339 8500
Press: 020 7339 8531/8532
www.ramblers.org.uk

Worldwide Fund for Nature UK
01483 426444
www.wwf-uk.org

National parks

Brecon
01874 624437
www.breconbeacons.org

Dartmoor
01626 832093
www.dartmoor-npa.gov.uk

Exmoor
01398 323665
www.exmoor-nationalpark.gov.uk

Lake District
01539 724555
www.lake-district.gov.uk

Norfolk & Suffolk Broads
01603 610734
www.broads-authority.gov.uk

Northumberland
01434 605555
www.northumberland-national-park.org.uk

North Yorkshire Moors
01439 770657
www.moors.uk.net

Peak District
01629 816200
www.peakdistrict.org

Pembrokeshire Coast
0845 345 7275
www.pembrokeshirecoast.org.uk

Snowdonia
0845 130 6229
www.ccw.gov.uk

Yorkshire Dales
01969 650456 or 01756 752748
www.yorkshiredales.org.uk

Voluntary sector

Animal welfare

Animal Aid
01732 364546
www.animalaid.org.uk

Animal Defenders
020 8846 9777
www.animaldefenders.org.uk

Animal Health Trust
0870 050 2424
www.aht.org.uk

Bat Conservation Trust
020 7627 2629
www.bats.org.uk

Battersea Dogs Home
020 7622 3626
www.dogshome.org

Blue Cross
Press: 020 7932 4060
www.bluecross.org.uk
Pet welfare charity

British Deer Society
01425 655434
www.bds.org.uk

British Hedgehog Protection Trust
01584 890801
www.software-technics.com/bhps

British Union for Abolition of Vivisection
0207 700 4888
www.buav.org

Brooke Hospital for Animals
020 7930 0210
www.brooke-hospital.org.uk
Working animals in developing world

Butterfly Conservation Trust
0870 774 4309
www.butterfly-conservation.org

Canine Lifeline UK
0870 758 1401
www.caninelifeline.fsnet.co.uk

Cat Action Trust
01555 660784
www.catactiontrust.co.uk

Cats Protection
0870 209 9099
www.cats.org.uk

Celia Hammond Animal Trust
01892 783820
www.celiahammond.org

Dog Trust
020 7837 0006
www.dogstrust.org.uk

Donkey Sanctuary
01395 578222
www.thedonkeysanctuary.org.uk

Exotic Animal Welfare Trust (Formerly The Reptile Trust)
01388 730500
www.eawt.co.uk

Farm Animal Welfare Council
020 7904 6721
www.fawc.org.uk

Fauna & Flora International
01223 571000
www.fauna-flora.org

Federation of Zoos
www.zoofederation.org.uk

Feline Advisory Board
0870 742 2278
www.fabcats.org

Humane Slaughter Society
01582 831919
www.hsa.org.uk

Hunt Saboteurs Organisation
0845 450 0727
www.huntsabs.org.uk

International Dolphin Watch
01482 632650
www.idw.org

International Fund for Animal Welfare
020 7587 6700
www.ifaw.org

International League for the Protection of Horses
0870 870 1927
www.ilph.org

League Against Cruel Sports
0845 330 8486
www.league.uk.com

London Wildlife Trust
020 7261 0447
www.wildlondon.org.uk

Mammal Society
020 7350 2200
www.abdn.ac.uk/mammal

Mare & Foal Sanctuary
01626 853085
www.mareandfoal.org.uk

Marine Conservation Society
01989 566017
www.mcsuk.mcmail.com

National Federation of Badger Groups
020 7228 6444
www.nfbg.org.uk

Otter Trust
01986 893470
www.ottertrust.org.uk

People and Dogs Society
01924 897732
www.padsonline.org

People for the Ethical treatment of Animals (PETA)
020 7357 9229
www.peta.org

PDSA (People's Dispensary for Sick Animals)
01952 290999
www.pdsa.org.uk

Rare Breeds Survival Trust
024 7669 6551
www.rare-breeds.com

Redwings Horse Sanctuary
01603 737432
www.redwings.co.uk

Royal Society for the Prevention of Cruelty to Animals
0870 555 5999; 0870 010 1181
www.rspca.org.uk

Royal Society for the Protection of Birds
01767 680551
www.rspb.org.uk

Save the Rhino
020 7357 7474
www.savetherhino.org

Scottish Society for the Prevention of Cruelty to Animals
0131 339 0222
www.scottishspca.org

Scottish Wildlife Trust
0131 312 7765
www.swt.org.uk

Society for the Protection of Animals Abroad
020 7831 3999
www.spana.org
environment

TRAFFIC
01223 277427
www.traffic.org
Combats damaging trade in plants & animals

Ulster Wildlife Trust
028 4483 0282
www.ulsterwildlifetrust.org

Uncaged
0114 272 2220
www.uncaged.co.uk
Anti-vivisection campaigner

Veteran Horse Society
01239 881300
www.veteran-horse-society.co.uk

Whale & Dolphin Conservation Society
0870 870 0027
www.wdcs.org.uk

Wildfowl & Wetlands Trust
01453 890333; 01453 891900
www.wwt.org.uk

The Wildlife Trusts
0870 036 7711
www.wildlifetrusts.org

Wood Green Animal Shelters
08701 904090
www.woodgreen.org.uk

World Society for the Protection of Animals
020 7587 5000
www.wspa-international.org;
www.wspa.org.uk

WWF UK
01483 426444
www.wwf.org.uk

Conservation

Black Environment Network
01286 870715
www.ben-network.co.uk

British Association for Shooting and Conservation
01244 573030
www.basc.org.uk

British Trust for Conservation Volunteers
01302 572 244
www.btcv.org

Campaign for Real Events
andi@c-realevents.demon.co.uk
www.c-realevents.demon.co.uk
Provides renewable energy & 'alt tech' support for events

Campaign to Protect Rural England
020 7981 2800
www.cpre.org.uk

Centre for Alternative Technology
01654 705950
www.cat.org.uk

Community Composting Network
0114 258 0483
www.communitycompost.org

Community Service Volunteers – Environment
0121 322 2008
www.csvenvironment.org.uk

Conservation Foundation
020 7591 3111
www.conservationfoundation.co.uk

Council for Environmental Education
0118 950 2550
www.cee.org.uk

Council for National Parks
020 7924 4077
www.cnp.org.uk

Earth First! In Britain
www.earthfirst.org.uk

Earth Rights
01279 870391
www.earthrights.org.uk
Environmental public interest law firm

Earthwatch Institute
01865 318838
www.uk.earthwatch.org
Conservation of natural environments & cultural heritage

Eco-Village Network
0117 373 0346
www.eco village.org

Energywatch
0845 906 0708
www.energywatch.org.uk

Environmental Campaigns
01942 612639
www.encams.org

European Rivers Network
00 33 47 102 0814
www.rivernet.org
Based in Southern France

Forest Action Network
001 250 799 5800
www.fanweb.org

Forum for the Future
01242 265715
www.forumforthefuture.org.uk

Future Forests
0870 199 9988
www.futureforests.com

Gaia Energy Centre
01840 213321
www.gaiaenergy.co.uk
Promotes renewable energy

Game Conservancy Trust
01425 652381
www.gct.org.uk

People and Planet
01865 245678
www.peopleandplanet.org
UK student action on human rights, poverty & the environment

Rising Tide
0161 226 6814
www.risingtide.org.uk
Action against climate change

Royal Society for Nature Conservation
0870 036 1000
www.rsnc.org

Solar Energy Society
01865 484 367
www.thesolarline.com

Surfers Against Sewage
0845 458 3001
www.sas.org.uk

UNEP World Conservation Monitoring Centre
01223 277314
www.unep-wcmc.org

Woodland Trust
01476 581111; 01476 581135
www.woodland-trust.org.uk

Farming and food

Farm
020 7352 7928
www.farm.org.uk
Campaigners for the future of independent & family farms

Farm Animal Welfare Council
020 7904 6721
www.fawc.org.uk

Farming & Wildlife Advisory Group
02476 696699
www.fwag.org.uk

Biodynamic Agricultural Association
01453 759501
www.anth.org.uk/biodynamic

Campaign for Real Ale
01727 867201
www.camra.org.uk

Compassion in World Farming
01730 264208
www.ciwf.org.uk

Dig it up!
dig-it-up@envoy.dircon.co.uk
www.dig-it-up.uk.net
Action against planting of GM rape crops

Eat the View
01242 533222
www.eat-the-view.org.uk

Food from Britain
020 7233 5111
www.foodfrombritain.com
Promoting sustainable local products

Five Year Freeze Campaign
020 7837 0642
www.fiveyearfreeze.org
Anti-GM activists group

Food & Drink Federation
020 7836 2460
www.fdf.org.uk

Food Dudes
01248 38 3973
www.fooddudes.co.uk
Teaching children about healthy eating

Foundation for Local Food Initiatives
0845 458 9525
www.localfood.org.uk

Free Range Activism Website
fraw@gn.apc.org
www.fraw.org.uk

Future Harvest
info@futureharvest.org
www.futureharvest.org
Promoting environmentally sound agricultural methods

Henry Doubleday Research Society
024 7630 3517
www.hdra.org.uk
Researches & promotes organic methods & produce

Herb Society
01295 768899
www.herbsociety.co.uk
Herbs for health

National Association of Farmers Markets
0845 230 2150
www.farmersmarkets.net

National Federation of City Farms
0117 923 1800

Permaculture Society
0845 458 1805
www.permaculture.org.uk

Pesticide Action Network
020 7274 8895
www.pan-uk.org

Soil Association
0117 314 5000
www.soilassociation.org

Sustain
020 7837 1228
www.sustainweb.org
Alliance for better food & farming

UK Food Group
020 7523 2369
www.ukfg.org.uk
Network for NGOs working on global food & agriculture issues

Veggies Catering Campaign
0845 458 9595
www.veggies.org.uk

Willing Workers on Organic Farms
01273 476286
www.wwoof.org/wwoof_uk

Gardening

Royal Horticultural Society
020 7821 3039
www.rhs.org.uk

Health

Department of Health
020 7210 4850; press 020 7210 5221
www.doh.gov.uk
NHS Executive
0113 254 5000
www.doh.gov.uk/nhs.htm
Scottish Executive DoH
0131 556 8400; press 0131 244 2797
www.scotland.gov.uk
Northern Ireland DoH
028 9052 0500; press 028 9052 0636
www.dhsspsni.gov.uk

Government agencies

Commission for Health Improvement
020 7448 9200
www.chi.nhs.uk
Health and Safety Executive
0870 1545 500
www.hse.gov.uk
Health Protection Agency
020 7339 1300
www.hpa.org.uk
Health Service Ombudsman
0845 015 4033
www.ombudsman.org.uk/hse
Human Fertilisation and Embryology Authority
020 7291 8200
www.hfea.gov.uk
Human Genetics Commission
020 7972 1518
www.hgc.gov.uk
Medical Research Council
020 7636 5422
www.mrc.ac.uk
Medicines Commission
020 7084 2652
www.mhra.gov.uk
Medicines Regulatory Agency
020 7284 2000
www.mca.gov.uk
Mental Health Task Force
0845 4647
www.doh.gov.uk/mentalhealthtaskforce
Microbiological Research Authority
01980 612100
www.camr.org.uk
National Blood Authority
0113 214 8606
www.blood.co.uk
National Institute for Clinical Excellence (NICE)
020 7067 5800
www.nice.org.uk
National Patient Safety Agency
020 7927 9500
www.npsa.nhs.uk

Strategic health authorities, England

Avon, Gloucestershire and Wiltshire
01249 858500
www.agwsha.nhs.uk
Bedfordshire and Hertfordshire
01727 812929
www.bhha.nhs.uk
Birmingham and the Black Country
0121 695 2222
www.bbcha.nhs.uk
Cheshire and Merseyside
01925 406000
www.cmha.ngs.uk
County Durham and Tees Valley
01642 666700
www.countydurhamteesvalley.nhs.uk
Cumbria and Lancashire
01772 647000
www.clha.nhs.uk
Dorset and Somerset
01935 384000
www.dorsetsomerset.nhs.uk
Essex
01376 302100
www.essex.nhs.uk
Greater Manchester
0161 2372011
www.gmsha.nhs.uk
Hampshire and Isle of Wight
023 8072 5400
www.hiow.nhs.uk
Kent and Medway
01622 713107
www.kentandmedway.nhs.uk
Leicestershire, Northamptonshire and Rutland
0116 295 7500
www.inrsha.nhs.uk
Norfolk, Suffolk and Cambridgeshire
01223 597500
www.nscstha.nhs.uk
North-East Yorkshire and Northern Lincolnshire
01904 724500
www.neynlha.nhs.uk
North Central London
020 7756 2500
www.northcentral.nhs.uk
North-East London
020 7655 6600
www.nelondon.nhs.uk
North-West London
020 7756 2500
www.nwlha.nhs.uk
Northumberland, Tyne and Wear
0191 210 6400
www.ntwha.nhs.uk
Shropshire and Staffordshire
01785 252233
www.sasha.nhs.uk
South-East London
020 7716 7000
www.selondon.nhs.uk
South-West London
020 8545 6000
www.swlondon.nhs.uk
South-West Peninsula
01752 315001
www.swpsha.nhs.uk
South Yorkshire
0114 263 0300
www.southyorkshire.nhs.uk
Surrey and Sussex
01293 778899
www.surreysussex.nhs.uk
Thames Valley
01865 337000
www.tvha.nhs.uk
Trent
0115 968 4444
www.tsha.nhs.uk
West Midlands South
01527 587500
www.wmssha.nhs.uk
West Yorkshire
0113 295 2000
www.wysha.nhs.uk

Local health boards, Wales

Anglesey
01248 751229
www.angleseylhb.wales.nhs.uk
Blaenau Gwent
01495 325400
www.blaenaugwentlhb.wales.nhs.uk
Bridgend
01656 754498
www.bridgendlhb.wales.nhs.uk
Caerphilly
01443 862056
www.caerphilly.lhb.wales.nhs.uk
Cardiff
029 2055 2212
www.cardifflhb.wales.nhs.uk
Ceredigion
01570 424100
www.ceredigionlhb.wales.nhs.uk
Conwy
01492 536586
www.conwylhb.wales.nhs.uk
Denbighshire
01745 589601
www.denbighshirelhb.wales.nhs.uk
Flintshire
01352 744103
www.flintshirelhb.wales.nhs.uk
Gwynedd
01286 672451
www.gwyneddlhb.wales.nhs.uk
Merthyr Tydfil
01685 358508
www.merthyrtydfillhb.wales.nhs.uk

Monmouthshire
01291 636400
www.monmouthshirelhb.wales.nhs.uk

Neath/Port Talbot
01639 890916
www.neathporttalbotlhb.wales.nhs.uk

Newport
01633 436200
www.newportlhb.wales.nhs.uk

Pembrokeshire
01437 771220
www.pembrokeshirelhb.wales.nhs.uk

Powys
01874 711661
www.powys-lhb.wales.nhs.uk

Rhondda Cynon Taff
01443 824400
www.rhonddacynontafflhb.wales.nhs.uk

Swansea
01792 784800
www.swansealhb.wales.nhs.uk

Torfaen
01495 745868
www.torfaenlhb.wales.nhs.uk

Vale of Glamorgan
029 2035 0600
www.valeofglamorganlhb.wales.nhs.uk

Wrexham
01978 346500
www.wrexhamlhb.wales.nhs.uk

NHS boards, Scotland

Argyll and Clyde
0141 842 7200
www.show.scot.nhs.uk/achb

Ayrshire and Arran
01292 611040
www.show.scot.nhs.uk/aahb

Borders
01896 825500
www.nhsborders.org.uk

Dumfries and Galloway
01387 272700
www.show.scot.nhs.uk/dghb

Fife
01334 656200
www.show.scot.nhs.uk/fhb

Forth Valley
01786 463031
www.show.scot.nhs.uk/nhsfv

Grampian
01224 663456
www.nhsgrampian.org

Greater Glasgow
0141 201 4444
www.nhsgg.org.uk

Highland
01463 717123
www.show.scot.nhs.uk/hhb

Lanarkshire
01698 281313
www.show.scot.nhs.uk/lhb

Lothian
0131 536 9000
www.nhslothian.nhs.uk

Orkney
01856 885400
www.show.scot.nhs.uk/ohb

Tayside
01382 818479
www.show.scot.nhs.uk

Western Isles
01851 702997
www.show.scot.nhs.uk.wihb

Scottish Ambulance Service
0131 446 7000
www.scottishambulance.com

NHS Health Scotland
0131 536 5500
www.healthscotland.com

NHS Quality Improvement, Scotland
0131 623 4300
www.show.scot.nhs.uk

NHS State Hospitals Board for Scotland
01555 840293
www.show.scot.nhs.uk

Health & social services boards, Northern Ireland

Eastern
028 9032 1313
www.ehssb-n-l-nhs.uk

Northern
028 2565 3333
www.nhssb.n.l.nhs.uk

Southern
028 3741 0041
www.shssb.org.uk

Western
028 7186 0086
www.whssb.org.uk

Professional bodies

British Medical Association
020 7387 4499
www.bma.org.uk

General Medical Council
020 7915 3720
www.gmc-uk.org

Royal College of Nursing
020 7409 3333
www.rcn.org.uk

Academy of Medical Royal Colleges
020 7408 2244
www.aomrc.org.uk

Royal College of Anaesthetists
020 7813 1900
www.rcoa.ac.uk

Royal College of General Practitioners
020 7581 3232
www.rcgp.org.uk

Royal College of Obstetricians & Gynaecologists
020 7772 6200
www.rcog.org.uk

Royal College of Ophthalmologists
020 7935 0702
www.rcophth.ac.uk

Royal College of Paediatrics and Child Health
020 7307 5600
www.rcpch.ac.uk

Royal College of Pathologists
020 7451 6700
www.rcpath.org

Royal College of Physicians of Edinburgh
0131 225 7324
www.rcpe.ac.uk

Royal College of Physicians of Ireland
00 353 1 661 6677
www.rcpi.ie

Royal College of Physicians of London
020 7935 1174
www.rcplondon.ac.uk

Faculty of Public Health Medicine
020 7935 0243
www.fphm.org.uk

Royal College of Physicians & Surgeons of Glasgow
0141 221 6072
www.rcpsglasg.ac.uk

Royal College of Psychiatrists
020 7235 2351
www.rcpsych.ac.uk

Royal College of Radiologists
020 7636 4432
www.rcr.ac.uk

Royal College of Surgeons of Edinburgh
0131 527 1600
www.rcsed.ac.uk

Royal College of Surgeons of England
020 7405 3474
www.rcseng.ac.uk

Royal College of Surgeons in Ireland
00 353 1 402 2100
www.rcsi.ie

British Dental Association
020 7935 0875
www.bda-dentistry.org.uk

Patients Association
020 8423 9111
www.patients-association.com

Voluntary sector

General health

Action Medical Research
01403 210406
www.action.org.uk

Alzheimer's Society
020 7306 0606
www.alzheimers.org.uk

Arthritis Care
020 7380 6500
www.arthritiscare.org.uk

Arthritis Research Campaign
01246 558 033
www.arc.org.uk

Association for International Cancer Research
01334 477910
www.aicr.org.uk

Bliss
0500 618140
www.bliss.org.uk
National charity for premature or sick babies

Breakthrough Breast Cancer
020 7405 5111
www.breakthrough.org.uk

Breast Cancer Campaign
020 7749 3700
www.bcc-uk.org
Breast Cancer Care
020 7384 2984
www.breastcancercare.org.uk
British Dietetic Association
0121 200 8080
www.bda.uk.com
British Heart Foundation
020 7935 0185
www.bhf.org.uk
British Pregnancy Advisory Service
08457 304030
www.bpas.org
Cancer and Leukaemia in Childhood – CLIC
0117 311 2600
www.clic.uk.com
Cancer Research UK
020 7242 0200
www.cancerresearchuk.org
Consensus Action on Salt and Health
020 8725 2409
www.actionsalt.org.uk
Cystic Fibrosis Trust
020 8464 7211
www.cftrust.org.uk
Diabetes UK
020 7424 1000
www.diabetes.org.uk
Great Ormond St Children's Charity
020 7916 5678
www.gosh.org
Guy's & St Thomas' Charitable Foundation
020 7955 4996
www.charitablefoundation.org.uk
Healthwise
0151 649 3400
www.healthwise.org.uk
Campaigning and providing helplines
Healthy Living Scotland
0845 278 8878
www.healthyliving.gov.uk
Institute of Cancer Research
020 7352 8133
www.icr.ac.uk
International HIV/AIDS Alliance
01273 718 900
www.aidsalliance.org
International Obesity Taskforce
020 7691 1900
www.iotf.org
Leeds Teaching Hospitals Charitable Foundation
0113 392 3640
www.leedsth.nhs.uk
Leukaemia Research Fund
020 7405 0101
www.lrf.org.uk
www.leukaemia-research.org.uk
Macmillan Cancer Relief
020 7840 7821
www.macmillan.org.uk
Marie Curie Cancer Care
020 7599 7700
www.mariecurie.org.uk
Marie Stopes International
020 7574 7400
www.mariestopes.org.uk
Reproductive healthcare worldwide
Meningitis Trust
01453 768000
www.meningitis-trust.org
Mind (National Association for Mental Health)
020 8519 2122
www.mind.org.uk
Motor Neurone Disease Association
01604 250505
www.mndassociation.org
Multiple Sclerosis Society
020 8438 0700
www.mssociety.org.uk
Muscular Dystrophy Campaign
020 7720 8055
www.muscular-dystrophy.org
National Asthma Campaign
020 7226 2260
www.asthma.org.uk
National Heart Forum
020 7383 7638
www.heartforum.org.uk
National Kidney Research Fund
01733 704 650
www.nkrf.org.uk
Parkinson's Disease Society of the UK
020 7931 8080
www.parkinsons.org.uk
St John Ambulance
020 7324 4210
www.sja.org.uk
Stroke Association
020 7566 0300
www.stroke.org.uk
Terrence Higgins Trust
020 7831 0330
www.tht.org.uk
HIV/Aids
The Wellcome Trust
020 7611 8888
www.wellcome.ac.uk
World Cancer Research Fund UK
020 7343 4200
www.wcrf-uk.org
Yorkshire Cancer Research
01423 501269
www.ycr.org.uk

Drugs, alcohol and addiction

Addaction
020 7251 5860
www.addaction.org.uk
Adfam
020 7928 8898
www.adfam.org.uk
Families, drugs and alcohol
Alchemy Project
0845 165 1197
www.alchemyproject.co.uk
Alcohol Concern
020 7928 7377
www.alcoholconcern.org.uk
Alcohol Focus Scotland
0141 572 6700
www.alcohol-focus.scotland.org.uk
Alcoholics Anonymous
01904 644 026
www.alcoholics-anonymous.org.uk
Arrest Referral Forum
07739 983058
www.drugreferral.org
Support for workers on drugs referral projects
ASH: Action on Smoking and Health
01484 517065
www.ash.org.uk
Association of Nurses in Substance Abuse
0870 2413503
www.ansa.uk.net
Clouds
01747 830733
www.clouds.org.uk
Treatment for addiction
Crew 2000
0131 220 3404
www.crew2000.co.uk
Drugscope
020 7928 1211
www.drugscope.org.uk
Information resource
European Association for the Treatment of Addiction
020 7922 8753
www.eata.org.uk
Legalise Cannabis Alliance
07984 255015
www.lca-uk.org
Life or Meth
www.lifeormeth.com
Methamphetamine awareness campaign
Narcotics Anonymous
020 7251 4007
www.ukna.org
National Treatment Agency
020 7972 2274
www.nta.nhs.uk
No Smoking Day – March 9
0870 770 7909
www.nosmokingday.org.uk
Parents Against Drug Abuse
0845 702 3867
www.btinternet.com/~padahelp
Promis Recovery Centre
01304 841700
www.promis.co.uk
Multi-addiction awareness and treatment

Release
020 7729 9904
www.release.org.uk
Provides for health, welfare and legal needs of drug users

Re-Solve
01785 817885
helpline: 0808 800 2345
www.re-solv.org
The society for the prevention of solvent abuse

Ride Foundation
01372 467708
www.ridefoundation.org.uk
Drug awareness programmes for schools

Sargent Cancer Care for Children
020 8752 2800
www.sargent.org

Scottish Drugs Forum
0141 221 1175
www.sdf.org.uk

Stroke Association
020 7566 0300
www.stroke.org.uk

Substance Misuse Management in General Practice
0161 905 8581
www.smmgp.demon.co.uk

Transform
0117 941 5810
www.tdpf.org.uk
Anti-prohibition campaign

UK harm reduction alliance
www.ukhra.org
Campaigning for health and ethical treatment of drug users

First wave of foundation hospitals: England

Basildon Hospital
01268 533911

Bassetlaw District General Hospital, Worksop
01909 500990

Bradford Royal Infirmary, Bradford
01274 542200

Cherry Tree Hospital, Stockport
0161 483 1010

Countess of Chester Hospital, Chester
01244 365 000

Doncaster Royal Infirmary & Montagu Hospital, Doncaster
01302 366666

Edith Cavell Hospital, Peterborough
01733 874000

Homerton University Hospital, London
020 8510 5555

Moorfields Eye Hospital, London
020 7253 3411

Orsett Hospital, Grays
01268 533911

Peterborough District Hospital, Peterborough
01733 874000

Retford Hospital, Retford
01777 705261

Royal Devon & Exeter Hospital, Exeter
01392 411611

Royal Marsden Hospital, London
020 7352 8171

St Luke's Hospital, Bradford
01274 734744

Stamford & Rutland Hospital, Stamford
01780 764151

Stepping Hill Hospital, Stockport
0161 483 1010

Tickhill Road Hospital, Doncaster
01302 796000

Health helplines

NHS Direct
0845 4647

Alcoholics Anonymous
08457 697555

Alzheimers Helpline
08453 000336

Arthritic Care Helpline
0800 289170

Asthma Helpline
08457 010203

British Allergy Foundation Helpline
01322 619864

Cancerlink
0800 132095

Carers Line
0808 808 7777

Contraceptive Education Service
08453 101334

Diabetes UK Careline
020 7424 1030

Doctors' Supportline
08707 650001

Drinkline
0800 917 8282

Drugscope
0800 776600

Healthwise
0151 649 3400

Help with Health Costs Advice Line
0800 917 7711

Menopause and HRT Helpline
01293 413000

Miscarriage Association Helpline
01924 200799

National Aids Helpline
0800 567123

National Asthma Helpline
08457 010203

National Drugs Helpline
0800 776600

NHS Asian Tobacco Helpline
0800 169 0881 (Urdu)
0800 169 0882 (Punjabi)
0800 169 0883 (Hindi)
0800 169 0884 (Gujerati)
0800 169 0885 (Bengali)

NHS Careers Helpline
0845 606 0655

NHS Pregnancy Smoking Helpline
0800 169 9169

NHS Smoking Helpline
0800 169 0169

Organ Donor Line
0845 606 0400

Parents Against Drug Abuse
0845 702 3867

Re-Solve
0808 800 2345

RNID Tinnitus Helpline
0808 808 6666

Smokers Quitline
0800 002200

Still Births and Neonatal Deaths Helpline
020 7436 5881

Talk to Frank
0800 776600

Women's Health Concern Helpline
01628 483612

Women's Health Enquiry Line
020 7251 6580

NHS hospitals: England

Abberton Day Hospital, Colchester
01206 228704
Abingdon Community Hospital, Abingdon
01235 522717
Accrington Victoria Community Hospital, Accrington
01254 263555
Acre Day Hospital, Worthing
01903 216807
Acton Hospital, London
020 8383 1133
Acute Mental Health Services, Shaftesbury
01747 824949
Addenbrooke's Hospital, Cambridge
01223 245151
Adult Psychiatry Day Hospital, Manchester
0161 447 4367
Airedale General Hospital, Keighley
01535 652511
Alcester Hospital, Alcester
01789 762470
Aldeburgh & District Community Hospital, Aldeburgh
01728 452778
Alder Hey Children's Hospital, Liverpool
0151 228 4811
Alderney Hospital, Poole
01202 735537
Alexander Day Hospital, Manchester
0161 748 4022 ext 2766
Alexandra Hospital, Redditch
01527 503030
Alfred Bean Hospital, Driffield
01377 241124
All Saints Hospital, Birmingham
0121 623 5500
All Saints Hospital, Eastbourne
01323 417400
Allenby Ward, Louth County Hospital, Louth
01507 600100
Alnwick Infirmary
01665 626700
Alton Community Hospital, Alton
01420 82811
Altrincham General Hospital, Altrincham
0161 928 6111
Amberstone Hospital, Hailsham
01323 440022
Amersham Hospital, Amersham
01494 434411
Ancoats Hospital, Manchester
0161 795 4567
Andover War Memorial Community Hospital, Andover
01264 358811
Arundel & District Hospital
01903 882543
Ashburton & Buckfastleigh Hospital
01364 652203
Ashby & District Hospital, Ashby de la Zouch
01530 414222
Ashby Rehabilitation Centre, Lincoln
01522 577055
Ashfield Community Hospital, Kirkby in Ashfield
01623 785050
Ashford Hospital
01932 872000
Ashington Hospital
01670 521212
Ashley House, Grantham
01476 573985
Ashmore House, Poole
01202 660846
Ashurst Child And Family Health Centre, Southampton
023 8074 3000
Aston Hall Hospital (Learning Disabilities), Aston on Trent
01332 792412
Atkinson Morley's Hospital & Wolfson Neurorehabilitation Centre, Wimbledon
020 8946 7711
Atu Day Hospital, Manchester
0161 447 4312
Avondale Unit (Adult Acute Psychiatry), Preston
01772 710651
Axminster Hospital, Axminster
01297 32071

B

Babington Hospital, Belper
01773 824171
Barking Hospital, London
020 8983 8000
Barnes Hospital, Cheadle
0161 491 2300
Barnes Hospital, London
020 8878 4981
Barnet Community Healthcare NHS Trust
020 8370 6520
Barnet Hospital, London
020 8216 4000
Barnet Psychiatric Unit
020 8216 4400
Barnsley District General Hospital
01226 730000
Barrow Hospital, Bristol
01275 392811
Bartlet Hospital, Felixstowe
01394 284292
Barton Under Needwood Cottage Hospital, Barton Under Needwood
01283 712323
Basingstoke BSU, Basingstoke
01256 473202
Battle Hospital, Reading
0118 958 3666
Beccles & District War Memorial Hospital, Beccles
01502 712164
Beckenham Hospital, Beckenham
020 8289 6600
Becontree Day Hospital, Dagenham
020 8984 1234
Bedford Hospital, Bedford
01234 355122
Beech House Mental Health Day Hospital, Camberley
01276 670911
Beech House, Boston
01205 354988
Beighton Community Hospital, Sheffield
0114 271 6572
Bensham Hospital, Gateshead
0191 482 0000
Berkeley Hospital, Berkley
01453 562000
Berwick Infirmary, Berwick on Tweed
01289 307484
Bethlem Royal Hospital, Manchester
020 8777 6611
Bexhill Hospital, Bexhill on Sea
01424 730077
Bexley Hospital, Bexley
01322 625754
Bicester Community Hospital, Bicester
01869 876500
Bideford Hospital, Bideford
01237 420200
Biggleswade Hospital, Biggleswade
01767 224906
Billinge Hospital, Wigan
01942 244000
Bingley Hospital, Bingley
01274 563438
Birch Hill Hospital, Rochdale
01706 377777
Birchfield, Shoreham by Sea
01273 455622
Birmingham and Midland Eye Centre, Birmingham
0121 554 3801
Birmingham Heartlands Hospital
0121 424 1263
Birmingham Skin Centre, Birmingham
0121 554 3801
Birmingham Women's Hospital
0121 472 1377
Bishop Auckland General Hospital
01388 455000
Bishops Castle Community Hospital, Bishops Castle
01588 638220
Blackberry Hill Hospital, Bristol
0117 965 6061
Blackburn Royal Infirmary, Blackburn
01254 263555
Blackpool Victoria Hospital
01253 300000
Blandford Community Hospital, Blandford
01258 456541
Bletchley Community Hospital, Milton Keynes
01908 376415
Bloxwich Hospital, Walsall
01922 858600
Blyth Community Hospital, Blyth
01670 396400
Bognor Regis War Memorial Hospital, Bognor Regis
01243 865418
Bolingbroke Hospital, Wandsworth Common
020 7223 7411
Bolsover Local Hospital
01246 827901
Booth Hall Children's Hospital, Manchester
0161 795 7000
Bootham Park Hospital, York
01904 610777
Bovey Tracey Hospital, Bovey Tracey
01626 832279
Bradford on Avon Community Hospital, Bradford-on-Avon
01225 862975
Bradwell Hospital, Newcastle
01782 425400
Bramcote Hospital, Nuneaton
024 7638 8200

Brampton War Memorial Community Hospital, Brampton
01697 72534
Brentry Hospital, Bristol
0117 908 5000
Brentwood Community Hospital
01277 212244
Bridgnorth Hospital, Bridgnorth
01746 762641
Bridgwater Community Hospital
01278 451501
Bridlington & District Hospital
01262 606666
Bridport Community Hospital
01308 422345
Brighton General Hospital
01273 696955
Bristol Eye Hospital
0117 923 0000
Bristol General Hospital
0117 923 0000
Bristol Homoeopathic Hospital
0117 973 1231
Bristol Royal Hospital for Children
0117 927 6998
Bristol Royal Infirmary
0117 923 0000
Brixham Hospital
01803 882153
Broadgreen Hospital, Liverpool
0151 706 2000
Bromley Hospital
020 8289 7000
Bromyard Community Hospital, Bromyard
01885 488080
Brookfields Hospital, Cambridge
01223 723001
Brooklands, Birmingham
0121 779 6981
Broomfield Hospital, Chelmsford
01245 440761
Brumby Hospital, Scunthorpe
01724 290402
Buckingham Hospital, Buckingham
01280 813243
Buckland Hospital, Dover
01304 200 0624
Bucknall Hospital, Stoke-on-Trent
01782 273510
Budleigh Salterton Hospital, Budleigh Salterton
01395 442020
Burden Neurological Hospital, Bristol
0117 956 7444
Burnley General Hospital
01282 425071
Burton House Day Hospital, Manchester
0161 447 4509
Bushey Fields Hospital, Dudley
01384 457373
Butleigh Hospital, Glastonbury
01458 850237
Buxton Hospital
01298 214000

C

Calderdale Royal Hospital, Halifax
01422 357171
Calderstones Hospital, Clitheroe
01254 822121
Cambourne/Redruth Community Hospital, Redruth
01209 881688
Cannock Chase Hospital, Cannock
01543 572757
Cardiothoracic Centre Liverpool, Liverpool
0151 228 1616
Carlton Court, Lowestoft
01582 538008
Carter Bequest Hospital, Middlesbrough
01642 850911
Cassel Hospital, Richmond
020 8237 2922
Castle Hill Hospital, Cottingham
01482 875875
Castle Hill House, Poole
01202 747416
Castle Hospital, Okehampton
01837 52411
Castleberg Hospital, Settle
01729 823515
Castleford Normanton & District Hospital, Castleford
01977 605500
Caterham Dene Hospital, Caterham
01883 837500
Cathedral View Day Hospital, Gloucester
01452 307814
Cavendish Hospital, Buxton
01298 79236
Central Middlesex Hospital, London
020 8965 5733
Chadwell Heath Hospital, Romford
020 8983 8000
Chalfonts & Gerrards Cross Hospital, Chalfont St Peter
01753 883821
Chapel Allerton Hospital, Leeds
0113 392 4595
Chard & District Hospital, Chard
01460 63175
Charing Cross Hospital, London
020 8846 1234
Charles Clifford Dental Hospital, Sheffield
0114 271 7800
Chase Farm Hospital, Enfield
020 8366 6600
Chase Hospital, Whitehall
01420 488801
Cheadle Hospital, Stoke-on-Trent
01538 487500
Chelsea and Westminster Hospital, London
020 8746 8000
Cheltenham General Hospital, Cheltenham
01242 222222
Cherry Knowle Hospital, Sunderland
0191 565 6256
Chesham Hospital
01494 783961
Cheshunt Community Hospital, Cheshunt
01992 622157
Chester le Street Hospital
0191 333 6262
Chesterfield & North Derbyshire Royal Hospital, Chesterfield
01246 277271
Chesterton Hospital, Cambridge
01223 363415
Chippenham Community Hospital, Chippenham
01249 447100
Chipping Norton Community Hospital, Chipping Norton
01608 628000
Chorley & South Ribble District General Hospital, Chorley
01257 261222
Christchurch Hospital, Christchurch
01202 486361
Christie Hospital, Manchester
0161 446 3000
Churchill Hospital, Headington
01865 741841
Cirencester Hospital, Cirencester
01285 884632
City General Hospital, Stoke-on-Trent
01782 715444
City Hospital, Birmingham
0121 554 3801
Clacton & District Hospital, Clacton on Sea
01255 253520
Clacton Hospital, Clacton
01255 201 717
Clatterbridge Hospital, Wirral
0151 334 4000
Clay Cross Community Hospital
01246 863031
Clayponds Hospital, London
020 8560 4011
Clayton Hospital, Wakefield
01924 201688
Clevedon Hospital, Clevedon
01275 341473
Clifton Hospital, Lytham St Annes
01253 306204
Clitheroe Hospital
01772 782216
Coalville Community Hospital, Coalville
01530 510510
Cobham Cottage Hospital, Cobham
01932 584200
Cockermouth Cottage Hospital, Cockermouth
01900 822226
Colchester General Hospital, Colchester
01206 747474
Colindale Hospital, London
020 8200 1555
Coltman Street Day Hospital, Hull
01482 328807
Colwood Hospital, Haywards Heath
01444 441881
Community Day Hospital, Runcorn
01928 753047
Congleton & District War Memorial Hospital, Congleton
01260 272227
Conquest Hospital, St Leonards on Sea
01424 755255
Cookridge Hospital, Leeds
0113 392 4253
Coppetts Wood Hospital, London
020 7794 0500
Coquetdale Cottage Hospital, Morpeth
01669 620555
Corbett House, Stourbridge
01384 456111
Corby Community Hospital, Corby
01536 400070
Coronation Hospital, Ilkley
01943 609666
Cossham Hospital, Bristol
0117 9671661
Cottage Day Hospital, Oldham
0161 627 8068
County Hospital, Durham
0191 333 6262

County Hospital, Hereford
01432 355 444
Coventry and Warwickshire Hospital, Coventry
024 7622 4055
Cranleigh Village Hospital, Cranleigh
01483 782400
Crawley Hospital, Crawley
01293 600300
Crediton Hospital, Crediton
01363 775588
Crewkerne Hospital, Crewkerne
01460 72491
Cromer Hospital, Cromer
01263 513571
Crowborough War Memorial Hospital, Crowborough
01892 652284
Cumberland Infirmary, Carlisle
01228 523444

D

Dane Garth, Mental Health Unit, Barrow in Furness
01229 870870
Darent Valley Hospital, Dartford
01322 428100
Darlington Memorial Hospital
01325 380100
Dartmouth & Kingswear Hospital, Dartmouth
01803 832255
Dawlish Hospital, Dawlish
01626 863219
Day Hospital for the Elderly, Grimsby
01472 874111
Defoe Day Hospital, Colchester
01206 228928
Delancey Assessment & Rehabilitation Hospital, Cheltenham
01242 222222
Dellwood Hospital, Reading
0118 958 9195
Dental Hospital, Bristol
0117 923 0000
Derby City General Hospital
01332 340131
Derby Royal Infirmary
01332 347141
Derbyshire Children's Hospital, Derby
01332 340131
Dereham Hospital
01362 692391
Derriford Hospital, Plymouth
01752 777111
Devizes Community Hospital
01380 723511
Devonshire Road Hospital, Blackpool
01253 303364
Devonshire Royal Hospital, Buxton
01298 72222
Dewsbury and District Hospital, Dewsbury
01924 512000
Diana, Princess of Wales Children's Hospital, Birmingham
0121 333 9999
Diana, Princess of Wales Hospital, Grimsby
01472 874 111
Didcot Community Hospital
01235 517900
Dilke Memorial Hospital, Gloucester
01594 598100
Doddington Hospital, March
01354 644299
Doncaster Gate Hospital, Rotherham
01709 304802
Dorking Hospital
01737 768511
Dorothy Pattison Hospital, Walsall
01922 858000
Dorset County Hospital, Dorchester
01305 251150
Dryden Road Day Hospital, Gateshead
0191 402 6600
Dunston Hill Hospital, Gateshead
0191 482 0000

E

Ealing Hospital, Southall
020 8967 5000
Earls House Hospital, Durham
0191 333 6262
East Cleveland Hospital, Saltburn by Sea
01287 676205
East Cornwall Hospital, Bodmin
01208 251560
East Ham Memorial Hospital, London
020 8586 5000
East Surrey and Crawley Hospitals, Redhill
01737 768511
Eastbourne District General Hospital, Eastbourne
01323 417400
Eastman Dental Hospital, London
020 7915 1000
Edenbridge & District War Memorial Hospital, Edenbridge
01732 862137
Edgware Community Hospital
020 8952 2381
Edward Bolitho House NHS Nursing Home, Penzance
01736 575555
Edward Hain Hospital, St Ives
01736 576100
Edward Street Hospital, West Bromwich
0121 553 7676
Elizabeth Garrett Anderson Hospital, London
020 7387 9300
Ellen Badger Hospital, Shipston-on-Tour
01608 661410
Ellesmere Port Hospital
01244 365000
EMI Unit (Hillview) Day Hospital, Blackburn
01254 293365
Enfield Community Care Centre, Enfield
020 8366 6600
Epsom General Hospital, Epsom
01372 735735
Erith & District Hospital, Erith
020 8302 2678
Essex County Hospital, Colchester
01206 747474
Evesham Community Hospital, Evesham
01386 502538
Exmouth Hospital, Exmouth
01395 226005

F

Fair Mile Hospital, Wallingford
020 8366 9174/9193
Fairfield General Hospital, Bury
0161 764 6081
Fairford Hospital, Fairford
01285 712212
Fairmile Hospital, Wallingford
01491 651281
Fall Birch Hospital, Bolton
01204 695 5714
Falmouth Hospital
01326 434700
Farnham Community Hospital, Farnham
01483 782000
Farnham Road Mental Health & Community Hospital Health Services, Guildford
01483 443535
Faversham Cottage Hospital, Faversham
01795 562066
Feilding Palmer Hospital, Lutterworth
01455 552150
Felixstowe General Hospital, Felixstowe
01394 282214
Fenwick Hospital, Lyndhurst
023 8028 2782
Fieldhead Hospital, Wakefield
01924 327000
Finchley Memorial Hospital, London
020 8349 3121
Fleet Community Hospital, Fleet
01483 782700
Fleetwood Hospital
01253 303364
Florence Desmond Day Hospital, Guildford
01483 571122
Fordingbridge Hospital, Fordingbridge
01425 652255
Fowey Hospital
01726 832241
Franklyn Hospital, Exeter
01392 208400
Freeland Court Day Hospital, Clacton on Sea
01255 253602
Freeman Hospital, Newcastle General Hospital, Royal Victoria Infirmary, Newcastle Upon Tyne
0191 284 3111
Frenchay Hospital, Bristol
0117 970 1070
Friarage Hospital, Northallerton
01609 779911
Frimley Park Hospital, Frimley
01276 604604
Fulbourn Hospital, Cambridge
01223 243961
Furness General Hospital, Barrow-in-Furness
01229 870870

G

Gables Day Hospital, Braintree
01376 555700
General Hospital, Hereford
01432 355444
George Eliot Hospital, Nuneaton
024 7635 1351
Glenfield Hospital, Leicester
0116 287 1471
Gloucestershire Royal Hospital, Gloucester
01452 528555
Goldie Leigh Hospital, London
020 8311 5128

Good Hope District General Hospital, Sutton Coldfield
0121 378 2211
Goodmayes Hospital, Ilford
020 8983 8000
Goole & District Hospital, Goole
01405 720720
Gordon Hospital, London
020 8746 5505
Gorse Hill Hospital, Leicester
0116 225 5200
Goscote Hospital, Walsall
01922 710710
Gosport War Memorial Hospital, Gosport
023 9252 4611
Grantham & District Hospital, Grantham
01476 565232
Gravesend & North Kent Hospital, Gravesend
01474 564333
Graylingwell Hospital, Chichester
01243 787970
Great Ormond Street Hospital for Children, London
020 7405 9200
Great Western Hospital, Swindon
01793 604020
Green Lane Hospital, Devizes
01380 731200
Grimsby Maternity Hospital, Grimsby
01472 874111
Grove Hospital, Derby
01332 792210
Guild Park, Preston
01772 865531
Guisborough General Hospital, Guisborough
01287 284000
Gulson Hospital
024 7655 3344
Guy's Hospital, London
020 7955 5000

H

Hallam Day Hospital, West Bromwich
0121 553 1831
Hallam Street Hospital, West Bromwich
0121 607 3900
Halstead Hospital, Halstead
01787 291010
Haltwhistle War Memorial Hospital, Northumberland
01434 320225
Ham Green Hospital, Bristol
01275 812661
Hammersmith Hospital, London
020 8383 4692
Hammerwich Hospital, Burntwood
01543 686224
Hanham Hall Hospital, Bristol
0117 908 5000
Harefield Hospital, Harefield
01895 823737
Harold Wood Hospital, Romford
01708 345533
Harpenden Memorial Hospital, Harpenden
01582 460429
Harrogate District Hospital, Harrogate
01423 885959
Harry Watton House, Birmingham
0121 623 5500
Hartismere Hospital, Eye
01379 870543
Harwich & District Hospital, Harwich
01255 201200
Harwich Day Hospital, Harwich
01255 207400
Haslemere Community Hospital, Haslemere
01483 782300
Havant War Memorial Hospital, Havant
023 9248 4256
Hawkhurst Cottage Hospital, Hawkhurst
01580 753345
Head and Neck Centre, Shrewsbury
01743 261000
Heanor Memorial Hospital
01773 710711
Heart Hospital, London
020 7573 8888
Heath Lane Hospital, West Bromwich
0121 553 7676
Heathorwood Hospital, Ascot
01753 633000
Hellesdon Hospital & Wensum Meadows, Norwich
01603 421421
Helston Community Hospital
01326 435800
Hemel Hempstead General Hospital, Hemel Hempstead
01442 213141
Herbert Hospital, Bournemouth
01020 765323
Hertford County Hospital, Hertford
01707 328111
Herts & Essex General Hospital, Bishop's Stortford
01279 444455
Herts & Essex Hospital, Bishop's Stortford
01279 655191
Hexham General Hospital, Hexham
01434 655655
High Royds Hospital, Leeds
01943 876151
High Wood Hospital, Brentwood
01708 465000
Highbury Hospital, Nottingham
0115 977 0000
Highcroft Hospital, Birmingham
0121 623 5500
Highfield Day Hospital, Chester le Street
0191 333 6262
Hill Crest Mental Health Unit, Redditch
01527 500575
Hillingdon Hospital, Uxbridge
01895 238282
Hinchingbrooke Hospital, Huntingdon
01480 416416
Hinckley & District Hospital, Hinckley
01455 441800
Hinckley Sunnyside Hospital, Hinckley
01455 251188
Hitchin Hospital, Hitchin
01438 314333
Holme Valley Memorial Hospital, Holmfirth
01484 681711
Holsworthy Hospital, Holsworthy
01409 253424
Holywell Rehabiltation Unit, St Albans
01727 897411
Homeopathic Hospital, Tunbridge Wells
01892 542977
Honiton Hospital, Honiton
01404 540540
Hope Hospital, Salford
0161 789 7373
Horn Hall Hospital, Stanhope
01388 528233
Horncastle War Memorial Hospital, Horncastle
01507 522349
Hornsea Cottage Hospital, Hornsea
01964 533146
Hornsey Central Hospital, London
020 8219 1700
Horsham Hospital (Community and Mental Health), Horsham
01403 227000
Horsham Hospital, Horsham
01403 227000
Horton Hospital, Banbury
01295 275500
Hospital for Tropical Diseases, London
020 7387 9300 or 020 7387 4411
Hospital of St Cross, Rugby
01788 572831
Hospital of St John and St Elizabeth, London
020 7806 4000
Huddersfield Royal Infirmary
01484 342000
Hull Royal Infirmary, Hull
01482 328541
Hulton Hospital, Bolton
01204 390390
Hyde Hospital, Cheshire
0161 366 8833
Hythe Hospital, Southampton
023 8084 6046

I

Ilfracombe Hospital, Ilfracombe
01271 863448
Ilkeston Community Hospital
0115 930 5522
Ipswich Hospital, Ipswich
01473 712233
Isebrook Hospital, Wellingborough
01933 440099

J

James Cook University Hospital, Middlesbrough
01642 850850
James Paget Hospital, Great Yarmouth
01493 452452
John Coupland Hospital, Gainsborough
01427 816500
John Radcliffe Hospital, Oxford
01865 741166
John Taylor Hospice, Birmingham
0121 255 2400
Johnson Hospital, Spalding
01775 722386
Julian Hospital, Norwich
01603 421421

K

Kelling Hospital, Holt
01263 713333
Kendray Hospital, Barnsley
01226 777811
Kent & Canterbury Hospital, Canterbury
01227 766877
Kent and Sussex Hospital, Tunbridge Wells
01892 526111
Kent County Ophthalmic & Aural Hospital, Maidstone
01622 673444
Kettering General Hospital, Kettering
01536 492000
Keycol Hospital, Sittingbourne
01634 810900
Keynsham Hospital, Bristol
0117 986 2356
Kidderminster Hospital, Kidderminster
01562 823424
King Edward VII Hospital, Windsor
01753 860441
King George Hospital, Ilford
020 8983 8000
King's College Hospital, London
020 7737 4000
King's Mill Hospital, Sutton in Ashfield
01623 622515
Kings Park Hospital, Bournemouth
01202 303757
Kingsbury Community Hospital, London
020 8903 1323
Kingston General Hospital, Hull
01482 328631
Kingston Hospital, Kingston upon Thames
020 8546 7711
Kingsway Hospital, Derby
01332 362221
Kington Cottage Hospital, Kington
01544 230317
Knutsford and District Community Hospital, Knutsford
01565 632112

L

Lambert Memorial Hospital, Thirsk
01845 522292
Lamellion Hospital, Liskeard
01579 335300
Langdon Hospital, Dawlish
01626 888372
Lanthorne Hospital, Leytonstone
020 8539 5511
Larchwood Hospital, Haywards Heath
01444 252248
Launceston General Hospital
01566 765650
Lea Castle Hospital, Kidderminster
01562 850461
Leatherhead Hospital, Leatherhead
01372 384384
Ledbury Cottage Hospital, Ledbury
01531 632488
Leeds General Infirmary
0113 243 2799
Leeds Road Hospital, Bradford
01274 494194
Leeds/Wakefield BSU, Leeds
0113 264 8164
Leek Moorlands Hospital, Leek
01538 487100
Leicester Frith Hospital, Leicester
0116 225 5200
Leicester General Hospital, Leicester
0116 249 0490
Leicester Royal Infirmary, Leicester
0116 254 1414
Leigh House Hospital, Winchester
01962 825800
Leigh Infirmary, Leigh
01942 672333
Leighton Hospital, Crewe
01270 255141
Leominster Community Hospital, Leominster
01568 614211
Lichfield Victoria Hospital, Lichfield
01543 442000
Lincoln County Hospital, Lincoln
01522 512512
Lings Bar Hospital, Nottingham
0115 945 5577
Lister Hospital, Stevenage
01438 314333
Little Bromwich Centre for Elderly Mental Health, Birmingham
0121 623 5500
Little Plumstead Hospital, Norwich
01603 711227
Littlehampton Hospital, Littlehampton
01903 717101
Littlemore Mental Health Centre, Oxford
01865 778911
Liverpool Women's Hospital, Liverpool
0151 708 9988
Livingstone Hospital, Dartford
01322 622222
London Chest Hospital
020 7377 7000
Longton Cottage Hospital, Stoke-on-Trent
01782 425600
Lord Mayor Treloar Hospital, Alton
01420 82811
Lothingland Community Unit, Lowestoft
01502 560111
Loughborough General Hospital, Loughborough
01509 611600
Loughborough Hospital, Loughborough
01509 611600
Louth County Hospital, Louth
01507 600100
Loversall Hospital, Doncaster
01302 796000
Lowestoft Hospital, Lowestoft
01502 587311
Lucy Baldwyn Hospital, Stourport-on-Severn
01299 827327
Ludlow Hospital, Ludlow
01584 872201
Luton & Dunstable Hospital, Luton
01582 491122
Lymington Hospital, Lymington
01590 677011
Lymington Infirmary, Lymington
01590 676081
Lynfield Mount Hospital, Bradford
01274 494194
Lytham Hospital, Lytham St Annes
01253 303980

M

Macclesfield District General Hospital, Macclesfield
01625 421000
Maidstone Hospital, Maidstone
01622 729000
Malmesbury Community Hospital, Malmesbury
01666 823358
Malton Norton & District Hospital, Malton
01653 693041
Malvern Community Hospital, Malvern
01684 612600
Manchester Royal Eye Hospital, Manchester
0161 276 1234
Manchester Royal Infirmary, Manchester
0161 276 1234
Manor Hospital (Walsall), Walsall
01922 721172
Mansfield Community Hospital, Mansfield
01623 785050
Mapleton Day Hospital (Elderly Services), Derby
01332 340131
Market Harborough & District Hospital, Market Harborough
01858 410500
Marlow Community Hospital
01628 482292
Martello Court Day Hospital, Clacton on Sea
01255 253540
Mary Hewetson Community Hospital, Keswick
01768 772012
Maternity Hospital, Hull
01482 376215
Maudsley Hospital, London
020 7703 6333
Mayday University Hospital, Croydon
020 8401 3000
Meadowbrook Hospital, Manchester
0161 772 3700
Medway Maritime Hospital, Gillingham
01634 830000
Melksham Community Hospital, Melksham
01225 703088
Melton Mowbray & District War Memorial Hospital, Melton Mowbray
01664 854901
Memorial Hospital, London
020 8856 5511
Memorial Hospital, Woolwich
020 8836 6000
Middlesbrough General Hospital, Middlesbrough
01642 850850
Midhurst Eastbourne & District Cottage Hospital, Midhurst
01730 813105
Mile End Hospital, London
020 7377 7000
Milford Rehabilitation Hospital, Godalming
01483 782000
Milford-on-sea Hospital, Milford-on-sea
01590 648100
Mill View hospital, Hove
01273 696011

Millbrook Macclesfield District General Hospital, Macclesfield
01625 663306

Millom Cottage Hospital, Millom
01229 772631

Milton Keynes General NHS Hospital, Milton Keynes
01908 660033

Minehead & West Somerset Hospital, Minehead
01643 707251

Molesey Hospital, West Molesey
020 8941 4481

Monkwearmouth Hospital, Sunderland
0191 565 6256

Montfield Hospital, Lerwick
01595 743000

Moore Cottage Hospital, Cheltenham
01451 820228

Moorgreen Hospital, Southampton
023 8047 2258

Moreton District Hospital, Moreton in Marsh
01608 650456

Moretonhampstead Hospital, Newton Abbot
01647 440217

Morpeth Cottage Hospital, Morpeth
01670 395600

Morton Ward, John Coupland Hospital, Gainsborough
01427 614751

Moseley Hall Hospital, Birmingham
0121 4424321

Mossley Hill Hospital, Liverpool
0151 250 3000

Mount Gould Hospital, Plymouth
01752 268011

Mount Hospital, Eastleigh
01703 612335

Mount Vernon Hospital, Barnsley
01226 777835

Mount Vernon Hospital, Northwood
01923 826111

N

National Hospital for Neurology & Neurosurgery, London
020 7837 3611

Nelson Hospital, Merton
020 8296 2000

New Cross Hospital, Wolverhampton
01902 307999

Newark Hospital
01636 681681

Newbury Community Hospital, Newbury
01635 32500

Newcastle Dental Hospital, Newcastle upon Tyne
0191 232 5131

Newcastle General Hospital, Newcastle Upon Tyne
0191 273 8811

Newham General Hospital, London
020 7476 4000

Newhaven Downs House, Newhaven
01273 513441

Newholme Hospital, Bakewell
01629 812525

Newmarket Hospital, Newmarket
01638 564000

Newquay and District Hospital
01637 893600

Newton Abbot Hospital, Newton Abbot
01626 354321

Newton Community Hospital, Newton-le-Willows
01925 222731

Newtown Hospital, Worcester
01905 763333

Norfolk & Norwich University Hospital, Norwich
01603 286286

North Cambridgeshire Hospital, Wisbech
01945 585781

North Devon District Hospital, Barnstaple
01271 322577

North Hampshire Hospital, Basingstoke
01256 473202

North Manchester General Hospital Day Surgery Unit, Manchester
0161 795 4567

North Manchester General Hospital, Manchester
0161 795 4567

North Middlesex University Hospital, London
020 8887 2000

North Riding Infirmary, Middlesbrough
01642 850850

North Staffordshire Royal Infirmary, Stoke-on-Trent
01782 715444

North Tyneside General Hospital, North Shields
0191 259 6660

North Walsham Cottage Hospital, North Walsham
01692 500560

Northampton General Hospital, Northampton
01604 634700

Northern Centre for Cancer Treatment, Newcastle Upon Tyne
0191 273 8811

Northern General Hospital, Sheffield
0114 243 4343

Northgate Hospital, Great Yarmouth
01493 452452

Northgate Hospital, Morpeth
01670 394000

Northowram Hospital, Halifax
01422 201101

Northwick Park Hospital, Harrow
020 8864 3232

Northwood & Pinner Community Hospital, Northwood
01923 824182/3/4

Nottingham City Hospital, Nottingham
0115 969 1169

Nunnery Fields Hospital, Canterbury
01227 766877

O

Okehampton & District Hospital, Okehampton
01837 52188

Old Manor Hospital, Salisbury
01722 336262

Oldchurch Hospital, Romford
01708 345533

Ongar War Memorial Hospital, Ongar
01277 362629

Ormskirk and District General Hospital, Ormskirk
01695 577111

Orpington Hospital
01689 815000

Ottery St Mary Hospital, Ottery St Mary
01404 816000

Oxford Community Hospital, Oxford
01865 225501

Oxted and Limpsfield Hospital, Oxted
01883 714334

P

Paignton Hospital, Paignton
01803 557425

Palmer Community Hospital, Jarrow
0191 451 6000

Papworth Hospital, Cambridge
01480 830541

Park Hospital for Children, Headington
01865 226213

Park View Resource Centre, King's Lynn
01553 613613/ext.5502

Parklands Hospital, Basingstoke
01256 817718

Patrick House, Sutton Coldfield
0121 685 6685

Patrick Stead Hospital, Halesworth
01986 872124

Paulton Memorial Hospital, Bristol
01761 412315

Pembury Hospital, Pembury
01892 823535

Pendle Community Hospital, Nelson
01282 474900

Penn Hospital, Wolverhampton
01902 444141

Penrith Hospital, Penrith
01768 245300

Pershore Cottage Hospital, Pershore
01386 502070

Peterlee Community Hospital, Peterlee
01642 617617

Petersfield Hospital, Petersfield
01730 263221

Pilgrim Hospital, Boston
01205 364801

Pinderfields General Hospital, Wakefield
01924 201688

Plaistow Hospital, London
020 8586 6200

Plympton Hospital, Plymouth
01752 338484

Poltair Hospital, Penzance
01736 575578

Pontefract General Infirmary, Pontefract
01977 600600

Poole Hospital, Poole
01202 665511

Portland Hospital for Women and Children, London
020 7580 4400

Portland Hospital, Portland
01305 820341

Preston Hall Hospital, Aylesford
01622 710161

Prestwich Hospital, Manchester
0161 772 9121

Primrose Hill Hospital, Jarrow
0191 451 6375

Princess Alexandra Hospital, Harlow
01279 444455

Princess Anne Hospital, Southampton
023 8077 7222
Princess Louise Hospital, London
020 8969 2488
Princess Margaret Hospital, Swindon
01793 604020
Princess Marina Hospital, Northampton
01604 752323
Princess of Wales Community Hospital, Bromsgrove
01527 488000
Princess of Wales Hospital and Oliver Zangwill Centre For Neuropsychologica, Ely
01353 652000
Princess Royal Hospital, Haywards Heath
01444 441881
Princess Royal Hospital, Hull
01482 701151
Princess Royal Hospital, Telford
01952 641222
Princess Royal University Hospital, Orpington
01689 814000
Prudhoe Hospital, Prudhoe
01670 394000
Purley War Memorial Hospital, Purley
020 8401 3000
Putney Hospital, London
020 8789 6611

Q

Queen Alexandra Hospital, Cosham
023 9228 6941
Queen Alexandra Hospital, Portsmouth
023 9228 6000
Queen Elizabeth Hospital, Gateshead
0191 482 0000
Queen Elizabeth Hospital, King's Lynn
01553 613613
Queen Elizabeth Hospital, London
020 8836 6000
Queen Elizabeth II Hospital, Welwyn Garden City
01707 328111
Queen Elizabeth Medical Centre, Birmingham
0121 4721311
Queen Elizabeth Psychiatric Hospital, Birmingham
0121 627 2999
Queen Elizabeth The Queen Mother Hospital, Margate
01843 225544
Queen Mary's Hospital for Children, Carshalton
020 8296 2000
Queen Mary's Hospital, London
020 7794 0500
Queen Mary's Hospital, Sidcup
020 8302 2678
Queen Victoria Hospital (Morecambe), Morecambe
01524 411661
Queen Victoria Hospital, East Grinstead
01342 410210
Queen Victoria Memorial Hospital, Herne Bay
01227 594700
Queen Victoria Memorial Hospital, Welwyn
01707 365291
Queen's Hospital, Burton-on-Trent
01283 566333
Queen's Medical Centre, Nottingham
0115 924 9924
Queens Park Hospital, Blackburn
01254 263555
Queen's Park Psychiatric Day Hospital, Blackburn
01254 293427

R

Radcliffe Infirmary, Oxford
01865 311188
Rainbow Cottage, Bournemouth
01202 534692
Ramsbottom Cottage Hospital, Bury
01706 823123
Rathbone Hospital, Liverpool
0151 250 3000
Ribchester Hospital, Preston
01772 782216
Richardson Hospital, Barnard Castle
01833 637436
Richmond Healthcare Hamlet, Richmond
020 8940 3331
Richmond Royal, Richmond
020 8940 3331
Richmond Victoria Hospital, Richmond
01748 822109
Ridge Lea Hospital, Lancaster
01524 586200
Ridings, Shoreham by Sea
01273 455622
Ripley Hospital
01773 743456
Ripon Community Hospital, Ripon
01765 602546
Rochdale Infirmary, Rochdale
01706 377777
Rochford Hospital, Wickford
01702 578000
Romsey Hospital, Romsey
01794 512343
Rosie Hospital, Cambridge
01223 245151
Ross Community Hospital, Ross-on-Wye
01989 562100
Rossall Hospital, Fleetwood
01253 303800
Rotherham District General Hospital, Rotherham
01709 820000
Roundwell Place Day Centre, Stoke-on-Trent
01782 425740
Rowley Regis Hospital
0121 607 3465
Royal Albert Edward Infirmary, Wigan
01942 244000
Royal Alexandra Hospital for Sick Children, Brighton
01273 328145
Royal Berkshire & Battle Hospitals, Reading
0118 987 5111
Royal Bolton Hospital
01204 390390
Royal Bournemouth Hospital, Bournemouth
01202 303626
Royal Brompton Hospital, London
020 7352 8121
Royal Cornwall Hospital, Truro
01872 250000
Royal Eye Infirmary, Plymouth
01752 662078
Royal Free Hospital, London
020 7794 0500
Royal Halifax Infirmary
01422 357222
Royal Hallamshire Hospital, Sheffield
0114 271 1900
Royal Hampshire County Hospital, Winchester
01962 863535
Royal Lancaster Infirmary, Lancaster
01524 65944
Royal Leamington Spa Rehabilitation Hospital, Warwick
01926 317700
Royal Liverpool University Hospital, Liverpool
0151 706 2000
Royal London Homeopathic Hospital, London
020 7837 8833
Royal London Hospital
020 7377 7000
Royal Manchester Children's Hospital, Manchester
0161 794 4696
Royal National Hospital for Rheumatic Diseases, Bath
01225 465941
Royal National Orthopaedic Hospital, Stanmore
020 8954 2300
Royal National Throat, Nose and Ear Hospital, London
020 7837 8855
Royal Oldham Hospital
0161 624 0420
Royal Orthopaedic Hospital, Birmingham
0121 685 4000
Royal Preston Hospital
01772 716 565
Royal Shrewsbury Hospital, Shrewsbury
01743 261 000
Royal South Hants Hospital, Southampton
023 8063 4288
Royal Surrey County Hospital, Guildford
01483 571122
Royal Sussex County Hospital, Brighton
01273 696955
Royal United Hospital, Bath
01225 428331
Royal Victoria Hospital, Folkestone
01303 850202
Royal Victoria Infirmary, Newcastle Upon Tyne
0191 232 5131
Royston Hospital, Royston
01763 242134
Runwell Hospital, Wickford
01268 366000
Rushden Hospital, Rushden
01933 440666
Russells Hall, Wordsley, Corbett & Guest Hospitals, Stourbridge
01384 456111
Ruth Lancaster James Cottage Hospital, Alston
01434 381218
Rutland Memorial Hospital, Rutland
01572 722552
Rutson Hospital, Northallerton
01609 779911
Ryhope Hospital, Sunderland
0191 565 6256

Saffron Walden Community Hospital, Saffron Walden
01799 562900
St Albans City Hospital, St Albans
01727 866122
St Andrew's Hospital, Bow
020 7476 4000
St Anne's Hospital, Altrincham
0161 928 5851
St Anns Hospital, London
020 8442 6000
St Ann's Hospital, Poole
01202 708881
St Austell Community Hospital
01726 291100
St Barnabas Hospital, Saltash
01752 843101
St Bartholomew's Day Hospital, Liverpool
0151 489 6241
St Bartholomew's Hospital, London
020 7377 7000
St Bernards Hospital, Southall
020 8354 8027
St Catherines Hospital, Birkenhead
0151 678 7272
St Catherines Hospital, Bradford
01274 227599
St Catherine's Hospital, Doncaster
01302 796000
St Charles Hospital, London
020 8969 2488
St Christophers Hospital, Fareham
01329 286321
St Clements Hospital, Ipswich
01473 715111
St Clements Hospital, London
020 7377 7000
St Edmunds Hospital, Northampton
01604 637221
St Edwards Hospital, Leek
01538 360421
St Francis Unit, City Hospital, Nottingham
0115 969 1169
St Georges Hospital, Hornchurch
01708 465000
St George's Hospital, Lincoln
01522 512512
St George's Hospital, London
020 8672 1255
St George's Hospital, Morpeth
01670 512121
St Georges Hospital, Stafford
01785 257888
St Helens Hospital
0151 426 1600
St Helier Hospital, Carshalton
020 8296 2000
St James Hospital, Portsmouth
023 9282 2444
St James's University Hospital, Leeds
0113 243 3144
St Johns & Amyand House, Twickenham
020 8744 9943
St Johns Health Centre, Twickenham
020 8891 3101
St John's Hospital, Chelmsford
01245 491149
St Lawrences Hospital, Bodmin
01208 251300
St Leonard's Hospital, Ringwood
01202 871165
St Leonards Hospital, Sudbury
01787 371341
St Leonard's, London
020 7301 3000
St Luke's Hospital, Huddersfield
01484 343000
St Lukes Hospital, London
020 8219 1800
St Luke's Hospital, Market Harborough
01858 410300
St Luke's Hospital, Middlesbrough
01642 850850
St Margaret's Hospital, Epping
01279 444455
St Mark's Hospital, Maidenhead
01628 632012
St Mark's, Harrow
020 8235 4000
St Martins Hospital, Bath
01225 832383
St Martin's Hospital, Canterbury
01227 459371
St Mary's Hospital for Women and Children (Manchester), Manchester
0161 276 1234
St Mary's Hospital, Isles of Scilly
01720 422392
St Marys Hospital, Kettering
01536 410141
St Mary's Hospital, Leeds
0113 279 0121
St Mary's Hospital, London
020 7886 6666
St Mary's Hospital, Melton Mowbray
01664 854800
St Mary's Hospital, Newport
01983 524081
St Marys Hospital, Portsmouth
023 9228 6892
St Michael's Hospital, Aylsham
01263 732341
St Michael's Hospital, Braintree
01376 551221
St Michael's Hospital, Bristol
0117 921 5411
St Michael's Hospital, Hayle
01736 753234
St Michael's Hospital, Lichfield
01543 414555
St Michael's Hospital, Warwick
01926 496241
St Monica's Hospital, York
01347 821214
St Nicholas Hospital, Gosforth
0191 273 6666
St Nicholas Hospital, Newcastle upon Tyne
0191 273 6666
St Oswalds Hospital, Ashbourne
01335 342121
St Pancras Hospital, London
020 7530 3500
St Peter's Hospital, Chertsey
01932 872000
St Peter's Hospital, Maldon
01621 854344
St Richard's Hospital, Chichester
01243 788122
St Thomas' Hospital, London
020 7928 9292
Salisbury District Hospital, Salisbury
01722 336262
Sanderson Hospital, Gosforth
0191 285 0171
Sanderson Hospital, Newcastle upon Tyne
0191 285 0171
Sandwell General Hospital, West Bromwich
0121 553 1831
Savernake Hospital, Marlborough
01672 514571
Scarborough General Hospital, Scarborough
01723 368111
Scott Clinic, St Helens
0151 430 6300
Scott Hospital, Plymouth
01752 284370
Scunthorpe General Hospital, Scunthorpe
01724 282282
Seacroft Hospital, Leeds
0113 264 8164
Seaton & District Community Hospital, Seaton
01297 23901
Sedgefield Community Hospital, Stockton-on-Tees
01740 626600
Selby War Memorial Hospital, Selby
01757 702664
Selly Oak Hospital, Birmingham
0121 627 1627
Sevenoaks Hospital, Sevenoaks
01732 455155
Sharoe Green Hospital, Preston
01772 716565
Sheffield Children's Hospital, Sheffield
0114 271 7000
Sheldon Nursing Home, Birmingham
0121 4756100
Shelton Hospital, Shrewsbury
01743 261000
Shepherd House, Worthing
01903 843390
Sheppey Community Hospital, Isle of Sheppey
01795 879100
Shepton Mallet Community Hospital
01749 342931
Shipley Hospital
01274 773390
Shire Hill Hospital, Glossop
01457 866021
Shotley Bridge Day Hospital for the Elderly, Consett
01207 583583
Shotley Bridge General Hospital, Consett
01207 214444
Sidmouth Hospital, Sidmouth
01395 512842
Sir Alfred Jones Memorial Hospital, Liverpool
0151 250 3000
Sir GB Hunter Memorial Hospital, Tyne & Wear
0191 220 5953
Sir Robert Peel Hospital, Tamworth
01827 263800
Sittingbourne Memorial Hospital, Sittingbourne
01795 418300
Skegness & District Hospital, Skegness
01754 762401

Skipton General Hospital
01756 792 233
Small Heath Health Centre, Birmingham
0121 685 7204
Smallwood Health Centre, Redditch
01527 60121
Smallwood House, Redditch
01527 488600
Snowdon House, Southampton
023 8029 3636
Solihull Hospital
0121 424 2000
South Hams Hospital, Kingsbridge
01548 852349
South Molton Hospital, South Molton
01769 572164
South Moor Hospital, Stanley
0191 333 6262
South Petherton Hospital, South Petherton
01460 241106
South Shore Hospital, Blackpool
01253 306106
South Tyneside District Hospital, South Shields
0191 454 8888
Southampton General Hospital, Southampton
023 8077 7222
Southend Hospital, Westcliff-on-Sea
01702 435555
Southlands Hospital, Shoreham by Sea
01273 455622
Southmead Hospital, Bristol
0117 950 5050
Southmoor Hospital, Pontefract
01977 465 630
Southport & Formby District General Hospital, Southport
01704 547471
Southport & Ormskirk District General Hospital, Southport
01704 547471
Southport General Infirmary, Southport
01704 547471
Southwold & District Hospital, Southwold
01502 723333
Southwood Hospital, London
020 8340 8778
Southwood House, Bridgwater
01278 456561
Springbourne House, Bournemouth
01202 300024
Springfield University Hospital, London
020 8672 9911
Staffordshire General Hospital, Stafford
01785 257731
Standish Hospital, Stonehouse
01453 822481
Stanfield Hospital, Stoke-on-Trent
01782 835721
Stead Memorial Hospital, Redcar
01642 282282
Steppingley Hospital, Steppingley
01525 716601
Stewart Day Hospital, St Helens
01744 458380
Stoke Mandeville Hospital, Aylesbury
01296 315000
Stonebury Day Hospital, Lydney
01594 598260
Stoney Ridge Hospital, Bingley
01274 495737
Stow Lodge Centre, Stowmarket
01449 614024
Stratfield House, Wellington
01823 661663
Stratford upon Avon Hospital, Stratford-upon-Avon
01926 495321
Stratton Hospital, Bude
01288 352161
Stretford Memorial Hospital, Manchester
0161 881 5353
Stroud General Hospital, Stroud
01453 562200
Stroud Maternity Hospital, Stroud
01453 562140
Stroud Road Mental Health Centre, Gloucester
01452 891200
Sunderland Eye Infirmary, Sunderland
0191 5283616
Sunderland Royal Hospital, Sunderland
0191 565 6256
Surbiton Hospital, Surbiton
020 8399 7111
Surrey BSU, Farnham
01483 782000
Sussex Eye Hospital, Brighton
01273 606126
Sutherland Centre, Stoke-on-Trent
01782 425560
Sutton Coldfield Cottage Hospital
0121 255 4000
Swaffham Community Hospital, Swaffham
01760 721363
Swanage Hospital, Swanage
01929 422282
Sycamores Day Hospital, Oldham
0161 627 8101

T

Tameside General Hospital, Ashton-Under-Lyne
0161 331 6000
Tatchbury Mount, Southampton
023 8087 4000
Taunton & Somerset Hospital, Taunton
01823 333444
Tavistock General Hospital, Tavistock
01822 612233
Teddington Memorial Hospital, Teddington
020 8408 8210
Teignmouth Hospital, Teignmouth
01626 772161
Tenbury District Hospital, Tenbury Wells
01584 810643
Tewkesbury Hospital, Tewkesbury
01684 293303
Thame Community Hospital, Thame
01844 212727
Thanet Mental Health Unit, Margate
01843 225544
Thetford Cottage Hospital
01842 752490
Thornbury Hospital, Bristol
01454 412636
Thorpe Coombe Hospital, Walthamstow
020 8520 8971
Thurrock Community Hospital, Grays
01375 390044
Tiddington Fields, Stratford-upon-Avon
01789 414923
Tiverton & District Hospital, Tiverton
01884 253251
Tolworth Hospital, Tolworth
020 8390 0101
Tonbridge Cottage Hospital, Tonbridge
01732 353653
Torbay District General Hospital, Torquay
01803 614567
Torrington Hospital, Torrington
01805 622208
Totnes Community Hospital, Totnes
01803 862622
Towers Hospital, Leicester
0116 225 6000
Townlands Hospital, Henley-on-Thames
01491 572544
Trafford General Hospital, Manchester
0161 748 4022
Trengweath Hospital, Redruth
01209 881900
Trowbridge Community Hospital, Trowbridge
01225 752558

U

Uckfield Community Hospital, Uckfield
01825 769999
Ulverston Hospital, Ulverston
01229 583635
University College London Hospital
020 7636 8333
University Hospital Aintree, Liverpool
0151 525 5980
University Hospital Lewisham, London
020 8333 3000
University Hospital of Hartlepool, Hartlepool
01429 266654
University Hospital of North Durham, Dryburn
0191 333 2333
University Hospital of North Tees, Stockton-on-Tees
01429 266654
Upton Hospital, Slough
01753 821441
Upton Road Day Hospital, Bexleyheath
020 8303 3577

V

Verrington Hospital, Wincanton
01963 32006
Victoria Central Hospital, Wirral
0151 678 7272
Victoria Cottage Hospital, Emsworth
01243 376041
Victoria Cottage Hospital, Maryport
01900 812634
Victoria Eye Hospital (Hereford), Hereford
01432 355444
Victoria Hospital, Deal
01304 865400
Victoria Hospital, Frome
01373 463591
Victoria Hospital, Lewes
01273 474153
Victoria Hospital, Swindon
01793 481182

Victoria House, Margate
01843 224541
Victoria Infirmary, Northwich
01606 74331
Violet Hill Day Hospital, Stowmarket
01449 673872

W

Walkergate Hospital, Newcastle Upon Tyne
0191 219 4300
Wallingford Community Hospital, Wallingford
01491 208500
Walnuttree Hospital, Sudbury
01787 371404
Walsgrave Hospital, Coventry
024 7660 2020
Walton Centre for Neurology and Neurosurgery, Liverpool
0151 525 3611
Walton Community Hospital
01932 220060
Walton Hospital, Chesterfield
01246 277271
Wanford House Hospital, Exeter
01392 403433
Wansbeck General Hospital, Ashington
01670 521212
Wantage Community Hospital, Wantage
01235 205801
Wareham Health Centre, Wareham
01929 556422
Wareham Hospital, Wareham
01929 552433
Warley Hospital, Brentwood
01708 465000
Warminster Community Hospital, Warminster
01985 212076
Warrington Hospital, Warrington
01925 635911
Warrington, Halton, St Helens & Knowsley BSU, Warrington
01925 635911
Warwick Hospital, Warwick
01926 495321
Warwickshire, Solihull & Coventry BSU, Coventry
024 7622 4055
Waterloo Day Hospital, Liverpool
0151 928 7243
Waterside Hospital, Londonderry
01504 860007
Watford General Hospital, Watford
01923 244366
Wathwood Hospital, Rotherham
01709 873106
Wayland Hospital, Attleborough
01953 452181
Welland Hospital, Spalding
01775 766800
Wellington & District Cottage Hospital, Wellington
01823 662663
Wells & District Hospital
01749 673154
Wells Cottage Hospital, Wells next the Sea
01328 710218
Wembley Community Hospital, Wembley
020 8903 1323
Wesham Park Hospital, Preston
01253 303280
West Bank Hospital, Telford
01952 243482
West Cheshire Hospital, Chester
01244 365000
West Cornwall Hospital, Penzance
01736 874000
West Cumberland Hospital, Whitehaven
01946 693181
West Haven Hospital, Weymouth
01305 786116
West Heath Hospital, Birmingham
0121 627 1627
West Howe Clinic, Bournemouth
01202 572501
West Lane Hospital, Middlesbrough
01642 850619
West Middlesex University Hospital, Isleworth
020 8560 2121
West Norwich Hospital, Norwich
01603 286286
West Park Hospital, Wolverhampton
01902 444000
West Suffolk Hospital, Bury St Edmunds
01284 713000
West View Hospital, Tenterden
01580 763677
Westbourne, Plymouth
01752 550741
Westbury Community Hospital, Westbury
01373 823616
Westcliffe Hospital, Stoke-on-Trent
01782 425860
Western Community Hospital, Southampton
023 8047 5401
Western Eye Hospital, London
020 7886 3231
Western House Hospital, Ware
01920 468954
Westminster Memorial Hospital, Shaftesbury
01747 851535
Westmorland General Hospital, Kendal
01539 732288
Weston General Hospital, Weston-super-Mare
01934 636363
Weston Park Hospital, Sheffield
0114 226 5000
Westwood Hospital, Beverley
01482 886600
Westwood Hospital, Beverley
01482 875875
Wexham Park Hospital, Slough
01753 633000
Weybridge Hospital
01932 852931
Weymouth Community Hospital, Weymouth
01305 760022
Wharfdale General Hospital, Leeds
0113 392 2000
Whelley Hospital, Wigan
01942 244000
Whipps Cross University Hospital, London
020 8539 5522
Whipton Hospital, Exeter
01392 208333
Whiston Hospital, Prescot
0151 426 1600
Whitby Hospital, Whitby
01947 604851
Whiteabbey Hospital, Newtownabbey
028 9086 5181
Whitstable & Tankerton Hospital, Tankerton
01227 594400
Whittington Hospital, London
020 7272 3070
Whitton Clinic, Whitton
020 8894 0306/4293
Whitworth Hospital, Matlock
01629 580211
Wigton Community Hospital, Wigton
016973 66600
Willesden Community Hospital, London
020 8459 1292
William Harvey Hospital, Ashford
01233 633331
William Julien Courtauld Hospital, Braintree
01376 551221
Williton & District Hospital, Williton
01984 632422
Wimborne Hospital, Wimborne
01202 841101
Winchcombe & District Hospital, Winchcombe
01242 602341
Windsor Day Hospital, Shepton Mallet
01749 343911
Wirral Hospital (Arrowe Park & Clatterbridge), Wirral
0151 678 5111
Withernsea Hospital, Withernsea
01964 614666
Withington Hospital, Manchester
0161 445 8111
Witney Community Hospital, Witney
01993 602900
Woking Community Hospital
01483 715911
Wokingham Hospital
0118 949 5000
Wolverhampton Eye Infirmary, Wolverhampton
01902 307999
Women's Hospital, Doncaster Royal Infirmary
01302 366666
Wonford House Hospital, Exeter
01392 403475
Woodlands Hospital, Manchester
0161 790 4222
Woodlands Hospital, St Leonards on Sea
01424 755255
Woods Hospital, Glossop
01457 860783
Woodside Health Centre, London
020 8656 0213
Worcester Royal Infirmary (Newtown Branch)
01905 763333
Worcestershire Royal Hospital, Worcester
01905 763333
Wordsley Hospital, Stourbridge
01384 456111
Wordsworth House Child Development Centre, Southampton
023 8079 6657
Workington Infirmary, Workington
01900 602244

Worthing Hospital, Worthing
01903 205111
Wotton Lawn Acute Hospital, Gloucester
01452 891500
Wrightington Hospital, Wigan
01257 252211
Wycombe Hospital, High Wycombe
01494 526161
Wythenshawe Hospital, Manchester
0161 998 7070
Yeatman Hospital, Sherborne
01935 813991
Yeovil District Hospital, Yeovil
01935 475122
York District Hospital, York
01904 631313
Zachary Merton Community Hospital, Rustington
01903 784155

NHS hospitals: Wales

Aberaeron Cottage Hospital
01545 570225
Aberdare General Hospital, Aberdare
01685 872411
Abergele Hospital
01745 832295
Abergoed Hospital, Abergoed
01443 821821
Abertillery & District Hospital, Abertillery
01496 214123
Amman Valley Hospital, Ammanford
01269 822226
Barry Hospital
01446 704000
Blaina & District Hospital, Nantyglo
01495 290230
Brecon War Memorial Hospital, Brecon
01874 622443
Bro Cerwyn Psychiatric Day Hospital, Haverfordwest
01437 773157
Bro Ddyfi Community Hospital, Powys
01654 702266/7
Bro Morgannwg NHS Trust, Bridgend
01656 752752
Bronglais General Hospital, Aberystwyth
01970 623131
Bronllys Hospital, Brecon
01874 711255
Bryn Beryl Hospital, Pwllheli
01758 701122
Brynhaul Day Hospital, Llanelli
01554 756567
Brynmair Day Hospital, Llanelli
01554 772768
Bryntirion Hospital, Llanelli
01554 756567
Builth Cottage Hospital, Builth Wells
01982 552221
Caerphilly District Miners' Hospital, Caerphilly
029 2085 1811
Cardigan and District Memorial Hospital
01239 612214
Chepstow Community Hospital, Chepstow
01291 636636
Chirk Community Hospital, Chirk
01691 772430
Colwyn Bay Community Hospital
01492 515218
Conwy Hospital
01492 592333
County Hospital, Torfeen
01495 768768
Cymla Hospital
01639 641161
Deeside Community Hospital, Deeside
01244 830461
Denbigh Community Hospital
01745 812624
Dolgellau & Barmouth Hospital, Dolgellau
01341 422479
Ebbw Vale Hospital, Ebbw Vale
01495 302483
Fairwood Hospital, Swansea
01792 203192
Glan Clwyd District General Hospital, Rhyl
01745 583910
Glanrhyd Hospital, Bridgend
01656 752752
Groeswen Hospital, Port Talbot
01639 641161
Hensol Hospital, Pontyclun
01656 752752
Hill House Hospital, Swansea
01792 203551
HM Stanley Hospital, St Asaph
01745 583275
Knighton Hospital, Knighton
01547 528633
Llandough Hospital, Penarth
029 2071 1711
Llandrindod Wells Hospital, Llandrindod Wells
01597 822951
Llandudno General Hospital, Llandudno
01492 860066
Llanfrechfa Grange Hospital, Cwmbran
01633 623623
Llangollen Community Hospital
01978 860226
Llanidloes War Memorial Hospital, Llanidloes
01686 412121
Lluesty Hospital, Holywell
01352 710581
Llwynypia Hospital, Rhondda
01443 440440
Maesgwyn Hospital, Bryncethin
01656 720371
Maesteg Hospital, Maesteg
01654 732732
Maindiff Court Hospital, Abergavenny
01873 735500
Mid-Wales Hospital, Brecon
01874 711661
Monmouth Hospital, Monmouth
01600 713522
Montgomery County Infirmary, Newtown
01686 627722
Morriston Hospital, Swansea
01792 702222
Mountain Ash General, Mountain Ash
01685 872411
Neath General Hospital, Neath
01639 862000
Neath Port Talbot Hospital, Port Talbot
01639 862000
Nevill Hall Hospital, Abergavenny
01873 732732
Oakdale Hospital, Blackwood
01495 225207
Port Talbot Hospital
01639 641161
Porth Hospital, Porth
01443 440440
Prestatyn Community Hospital
01745 853487
Prince Charles Hospital, Merthyr Tydfil
01685 721721
Prince Philip Hospital, Llanelli
01554 756567
Princess of Wales Hospital, Bridgend
01656 752752
Redwood Memorial Hospital, Rhymney
01685 840314
Robert Jones & Agnes Hunt Orthopaedic and District Hospital, Oswestry
01691 404000
Royal Alexandra Hospital, Rhyl
01745 343188
Royal Glamorgan Hospital, Llantrisant
01443 443443
Royal Gwent Hospital, Newport
01633 234234
Ruthin Hospital
01824 702692
St Brynach's Day Hospital, Haverfordwest
01437 764545

St Cadoc's Hospital, Newport
01633 436700
St David's Hospital (Carmarthen), Carmarthen
01267 237481
St Tydfil's Hospital, Merthyr Tydfil
01685 723244
St Woolos Hospital, Newport
01633 234234
Singleton Hospital, Swansea
01792 205666
South Pembrokeshire Hospital, Pembroke Dock
01646 682114
Swn-Y-Gwynt Day Hospital, Ammanford
01269 595473
Tenby Cottage Hospital, Tenby
01834 842040
Tonna Hospital, Neath
01639 641161
Tredegar General Hospital
01495 722271
Tregaron Hospital
01974 298203
Ty Sirhowy Health Centre, Blackwood
01495 229010
Tywyn & District War Memorial Hospital, Tywyn
01654 710411
University Hospital of Wales, Cardiff
029 2074 7747
Velindre Hospital, Cardiff
029 2061 5888
Victoria Memorial Hospital, Welshpool
01938 553133
West Wales General Hospital, Carmarthen
01267 235151
Whitchurch Hospital, Cardiff
029 2069 3191
Whitechurch Hospital, Whitechurch
01948 666292
Withybush General Hospital, Haverfordwest
01437 764545
Wrexham Maelor Hospital, Wrexham
01978 291100
Ystrad Mynach Hospital, Hangoed
01443 812201
Ystradgynlais Community Hospital, Swansea
01639 844777

NHS hospitals: Scotland

Aberdeen Maternity Hospital, Aberdeen
01224 840606
Aberdeen Royal Infirmary, Aberdeen
01224 681818
Aberfeldy Cottage Hospital, Aberfeldy
01887 820314
Aboyne Hospital, Aboyne
01339 886433
Acorn Street Day Hospital, Glasgow
0141 556 4789
Adamson Hospital, Fife
01334 652901
Ailsa Hospital, Ayr
01292 610556
Alexander Hospital, Coatbridge
01236 422661
Annan Hospital, Annan
01461 203425
Arbroath Infirmary, Arbroath
01241 872584
Argyll & Bute Hospital, Argyll
01546 602323
Arran War Memorial Hospital, Lamlash
01770 600777
Ashludie Day Hospital, Dundee
01382 527830
Astley Ainslie Hospital, Edinburgh
0131 537 9000
Ayr Hospital, Ayr
01292 614500
Ayrshire Central Hospital
01294 274191
Balfour Hospital, Kirkwall
01856 885400
Bangour Village Hospital, Broxburn
01506 419666
Bannockburn Hospital, Bannockburn
01786 813016
Belford Hospital, Fort William
01397 702481
Belhaven Hospital, Dunbar
01368 862246
Bellsdyke Hospital, Larbert
01324 570700
Benbecula Hospital, Benbecula
01870 603603
Birch Avenue Day Hospital, Perth
01738 553920/553500
Birkwood Hospital, Lesmahagow
01555 892382
Blairgowrie Cottage Hospital, Blairgowrie
01250 874466
Blawathill Hospital, Glagow
0141 954 9000
Bo'ness Hospital, Bo'ness
01506 823032
Bonnybridge Hospital
01324 814685
Borders General Hospital, Melrose
01896 826000
Brechin Infirmary, Brechin
01356 622291
Brooksby House Hospital, Largs
01475 672285
Caithness General Hospital, Wick
01955 605050
Cameron Hospital, Fife
01592 712472
Campbell Hospital, Banff
01261 842202
Campbeltown Hospital, Argyll
01586 552224
Canniesburn Hospital, Glasgow
0141 2115845
Castle Douglas Hospital, Castle Douglas
01556 502333
Chalmers Hospital, Banff
01261 812567
Chalmers Hospital, Edinburgh
0131 536 1000
City Hospital, Aberdeen
01224 663131
City Hospital, Edinburgh
0131 536 1000
Clackmannan County Day Hospital, Alloa
01259 723840
Clackmannan County Hospital, Alloa
01259 723840
Cleland Hospital, Motherwell
01698 860293
Coathill Hospital, Coatbridge
01698 245000
Coldstream Cottage Hospital, Coldstream
01890 882417
Corstorphine Hospital, Edinburgh
0131 537 6250
Cottage Day Hospital, Dumbarton
01389 763151
County Hospital, Invergordon
01349 852496
Cresswell Maternity Hospital, Dumfries
01387 246246
Crieff Hospital, Crieff
01764 653173
Crosshouse Hospital, Kilmarnock
01563 521133
Dalrymple Hospital, Dumfries
01776 706900
Davidson Cottage Hospital, Girvan
01465 712571
Dingleton Hospital, Melrose
01896 822727
Dr Gray's Hospital, Elgin
01343 543131
Dr MacKinnon Memorial Hospital, Isle of Skye
01471 822137
Drumchapel Hospital, Glasgow
0141 211 6000
Dumbarton Joint Hospital, Dumbarton
01389 762317
Dumfries and Galloway Royal Infirmary, Dumfries
01387 246246
Dunaros Hospital/Salen Sick Bay Hospital, & Eventide Home, Isle of Mull
01680 300392
Dunbar Hospital, Caithness
01847 893263
Dunoon & District General Hospital, Dunoon
01369 704341
Dunrowan Day Hospital, Falkirk
01324 639009
Dykebar Hospital, Paisley
0141 884 5122
Eastern General Hospital, Edinburgh
0131 536 7000
Edenhall Hospital, Musselburgh
0131 536 8000
Edinburgh Dental Institute, Edinburgh
0131 536 4900
Edington Cottage Hospital, North Berwick
01620 897040
Falkirk & District Royal Infirmary, Falkirk
01324 624000
Fernbank Street Day Hospital, Glasgow
0131 537 6246
Fleming Hospital, Aberlour
01340 871464
Florence Street Day Hospital, Glasgow
0141 429 2878
Forfar Infirmary, Angus
01307 464551
Forth Park Hospital, Kirkcaldy
01592 643355

Fraserburgh Hospital, Fraserburgh
01346 513151
Garrick Hospital, Stranraer
01776 702323
Gartnavel General Hospital, Glasgow
0141 211 3000
Gartnavel Royal Hospital, Glasgow
0141 211 3600
Gesto Hospital, Edinbane
01470 582262
Gilbert Bain Hospital, Lerwick
01595 743000
Glasgow Homoeopathic Hospital, Glasgow
0141 211 3000
Glasgow Royal Infirmary
0141 211 4000
Glaxo Day Hospital, Dundee
01382 532101 ex 170
Glen O'Dee Hospital, Banchory
01330 822233
Glencoe Hospital, Glencoe
01855 811254
Glenrothes Hospital, Glenrothes
01592 743505
Hairmyres Hospital, Glasgow
01355 585000
Hartwoodhill Hospital, Shotts
01698 245000
Hawick Cottage Hospital
01450 372162
Hawkhead Hospital, Paisley
0141 889 8151
Hawkhill Day Hospital, Dundee
01382 668300
Haylodge Hospital, Peebles
01721 722080
Herdmanflat Hospital, Haddington
0131 536 8300
Holmhead Hospital, Cumnock
01290 422220
Ian Charles Hospital, Grantown-on-Spey
01479 872528
Insch & District War Memorial Hospital, Insch
01464 820213
Inverclyde Royal Hospital, Greenock
01475 633777
Inverurie Hospital, Inverurie
01467 620454
Irvine Memorial Hospital, Pitlochry
01796 472050
Islay Hospital, Isle of Islay
01496 810219
Johnstone Hospital, Johnstone
01505 331471
Jubilee Hospital, Huntly
01466 792116
Kello Hospital, Biggar
01899 220077
Kelso Hospital
01573 223441
Kildean Hospital, Stirling
01786 458600
Kilsyth Victoria Memorial Hospital, Kilsyth
01236 822172
Kincardine Community Hospital, Stonehaven
01569 762022
Kincardine O'Neill War Memorial Hospital, Torphins
01339 882302
King's Cross Hospital, Dundee
01382 660111
Kirkcudbright Hospital, Kirkcudbright
01557 330549
Kirklands Hospital, Bothwell
01698 245000
Kirklandside Hospital, Kilmarnock
01563 524355
Knightswood Hospital, Glasgow
0141 211 6900
Knoll Hospital, Duns
01361 883373
Lady Home Hospital, Lanark
01555 851210
Lady Margaret Hospital, Isle of Cumbrae
01475 530307
Ladysbridge Hospital, Banff
01261 861361
Law Hospital, Carluke
01698 361100
Lawson Memorial Hospital & Cambusavie Unit, Sutherland
01408 633157
Lawson Memorial Hospital, Sutherland
01408 633157
Leanchoil Hospital, Forres
01309 672284
Leverndale Hospital, Glasgow
0141 211 6400
Liberton Hospital, Edinburgh
0131 536 7800
Lightburn Hospital, Glasgow
0141 211 1500
Little Cairnie Hospital, Arbroath
01241 872584
Loanhead Hospital, Loanhead
0131 440 0174
Lochmaben Hospital, Lochmaben
01387 810255
Lockhart Hospital, Lanark
01555 662496
Lorn and Islands District General Hospital, Oban
01631 567500
Lynebank Hospital, Fife
01383 623623
MacKinnon House, Glasgow
0141 531 3100
Macmillan House, Perth
01738 639303
Maud Hospital, Maud
01771 613236
Meigle Community Day Hospital, Meigle
01828 640211
Merchiston Hospital, Johnstone
01505 328261
Mid Argyll Hospital, Argyll
01546 602952
Migdale Hospital, Sutherland
01863 766211
Moffat Hospital, Moffat
01683 220031
Monklands Hospital, Airdrie
01236 748748
Montrose Royal Infirmary, Montrose
01674 830361
Murray Royal Hospital, Perth
01738 621151/8
Netherlea Hospital, Newport-on-Tay
01382 543223
Newton Stewart Hospital, Newton Stewart
01671 402015
Ninewells Hospital, Dundee
01382 660111
Nithbank Hospital, Dumfries
01387 241950
Orleans Day Hospital, Dundee
01382 667322
Parkhead Hospital, Glasgow
0141 211 8300
Perth Royal Infirmary, Perth
01738 623311
Peterhead Hospital, Peterhead
01779 478234
Portree Hospital, Portree
01478 613200
Princes Street Day Hospital, Stirling
01786 474230
Princess Alexandra Eye Pavilion, Edinburgh
0131 536 3899
Princess Margaret Rose Orthopaedic Hospital, Edinburgh
0131 536 4600
Princess Royal Maternity Hospital, Glasgow
0141 211 5400
Queen Margaret Hospital, Dunfermline
01383 623623
Queen Mother's Hospital, Glasgow
0141 201 0550
Raigmore Hospital, Inverness
01463 704000
Randolph Wemyss Memorial Hospital, Buckhaven
01592 712427
Ravenscraig Hospital, Greenock
01475 633777
Red Deer Day Hospital, Glasgow
01355 244254
Roadmeetings Hospital, Carluke
01555 772271
Roodlands Hospital, Haddington
0131 536 8300
Roseangle Day Hospital, Dundee
01382 24073
Rosemount Day Hospital, Arbroath
01241 872584
Ross Memorial Hospital, Dingwall
01349 663313
Rosslynlee Hospital, Midlothian
0131 536 7608
Roxburghe House, Aberdeen
01224 681818
Royal Aberdeen Children's Hospital, Aberdeen
01224 681818
Royal Alexandra Hospital, Paisley
0141 887 9111
Royal Cornhill Hospital, Aberdeen
01224 663131
Royal Dundee Liff Hospital, Dundee
01382 423038
Royal Edinburgh Hospital
0131 537 6000
Royal Hospital for Sick Children, Edinburgh
0131 536 0000
Royal Hospital for Sick Children, Glasgow
0141 2010000
Royal Infirmary of Edinburgh, Edinburgh
0131 5361000
Royal Northern Infirmary, Inverness
01463 242860
Royal Scottish National Hospital, Larbert
01324 570700

Royal Victoria Hospital, Dundee
01382 423123
Royal Victoria Hospital, Edinburgh
0131 5375000
St Andrews Memorial Hospital, Fife
01334 472327
St John's Hospital at Howden, Livingston
01506 419666
St Margaret's Hospital, Auchterarder
01764 662246
St Michael's Hospital, Linlithgow
01506 842053
St Vincent's Hospital, Kingussie
01540 661219
Sauchie Hospital, Alloa
01259 722060
Seafield Hospital, Buckie
01542 832081
Shettleston Day Hospital, Glasgow
0141 778 8381
Sister Margaret Hospital, Jedburgh
01835 863212
Southern General Hospital, Glasgow
0141 201 1100
Southfield Hospital, Edinburgh
0131 664 1788
Spynie Hospital, Moray
01343 543131
Stephen Hospital, Dufftown
01340 820215
Stirling Royal Infirmary, Stirling
01786 434000
Stobhill Hospital, Glasgow
0141 201 3000
Stonehouse Hospital, Larkhall
01698 793521
Stracathro Hospital, Brechin
01356 647291
Strathclyde Hospital, Motherwell
01698 245000
Stratheden Hospital, Fife
01334 652611
Strathmartine Hospital, Dundee
01382 423000
Sunnyside Royal Hospital, Montrose
01674 830361
Thomas Hope Hospital, Langholm
01387 380417
Thornhill Hospital, Thornhill
01848 330205
Threshold Day Hospital, Dundee
01382 322026
Tippethill House, Bathgate
01501 740342
Tor-Na-Dee Hospital, Aberdeen
01224 681818
Town & Country Hospital, Caithness
01955 604025
Town & Country Hospital, Nairn
01667 452101
Turner Memorial Hospital, Keith
01542 882526
Turriff Cottage Hospital, Turriff
01888 563293
Udston Hospital, Hamilton
01698 823255
Ugie Hospital, Peterhead
01779 472011
Vale of Leven District General Hospital, Alexandria
01389 754121
Victoria Annex Hospital, Isle of Bute
01700 502943
Victoria Hospital, Isle of Bute
01700 503938
Victoria Hospital, Kirkcaldy
01592 643355
Victoria Infirmary, Glasgow
0141 201 6000
Victoria Infirmary, Helensburgh
01436 672158
Weddenburn House Day Hospital, Dundee
01382 346000
Westbank Day Hospital, Falkirk
01324 624111
Wester Moffat Hospital, Airdrie
01236 763377
Western General Hospital, Edinburgh
0131 537 1000
Western Infirmary, Glasgow
0141 211 2000
Western Isles Hospital, Stornoway
01851 704704
Weston Day Hospital, Fife
01334 652163
Whitehills Hospital, Angus
01307 464551
Whittingham Gardens Day Hospital, Glasgow
0141 211 3616
Whytemans Brae Day Hospital, Fife
01592 643355
Whytemans Brae Hospital, Fife
01592 643355
Wishaw General Hospital, Wishaw
01698 361100
Woodend Hospital, Aberdeen
01224 663131
Woodlands Hospital, Aberdeen
01224 663131.

NHS hospitals: Northern Ireland

Albert Bridge Road Day Hospital, Belfast
01232 456007
Alexandra Gardens Day Hospital, Belfast
01232 773311
Altnagelvin Area Hospital, Londonderry
028 7134 5171
Antrim Hospital, Antrim
028 9442 4000
Ards Hospital, Newtownards
01247 812661
Armagh Community Hospital, Armagh
01861 522381
Bangor Hospital, Bangor
01247 454184
Beaver Park Hospital, Belfast
028 9069 9069
Belfast City Hospital
028 9032 9241
Braid Valley Hospital, Ballymena
01266 655200
Causeway Hospital, Coleraine
028 7032 7032
Coleraine Hospital
028 904 4177
Craigavon Area Hospital
028 3833 4444
Daisy Hill Hospital, Newry
02830 835000
Dalriada Hospital, Ballycastle
028 2070 2066
Downe Hospital, Downpatrick
028 4461 3311
Erne Hospital, Enniskillen
028 6632 4711
Forster Green Hospital, Belfast
028 9079 3681
Gransha Hospital, Londonderry
01504 860261
Holywell Hospital, Antrim
028 9446 5211
Lagan Valley Hospital, Lisburn
028 9266 5141
Longstone Hospital, Armagh
01861 522381
Lurgan Hospital (Day Hospital)
01762 323262
Mater Hospital, Belfast
028 9074 1211
Mid-Ulster Hospital, Magherafelt
028 7963 1031
Mourne Hospital, Newry
016937 62235
Moyle Hospital, Larne
01574 275431
Muckamore Abbey Hospital, Muckamore
028 9446 3333
Mullinure Hospital, Armagh
01861 522381
Musgrave Park Hospital, Belfast
028 9066 9501
Robinson Memorial Hospital, Ballymoney
028 2766 0332
Route Hospital, Ballymoney
028 27666600
Royal Belfast Hospital for Sick Children, Belfast
028 9024 0503
Royal Maternity Hospital, Belfast
01232 894656
Royal Victoria Hospital, Belfast
028 9026 3000
St Luke's Hospital (Armagh), Armagh
01861 522381
Shaftsbury Square Hospital, Belfast
01232 329808
South Tyrone Hospital, Dungannon
01868 722381
Stradreagh Hospital, Londonderry
01504 860261
Royal Hospitals, Belfast
028 9024 0503
Thompson House Hospital, Lisburn
01846 665646
Tyrone and Fermanagh Hospital, Omagh
028 8224 5211
Tyrone County Hospital, Omagh
028 8224 5211
Ulster Hospital, Dundonald
028 9048 4511

Hospitals: Ireland

Abbeyleix District Hospital, Laois
00 353 502 31204
Adelaide and Meath Hospital (Tallaght Hospital), Dublin
00 353 1 414 2000
Bantry General Hospital, Bantry
00 353 27 50133
Beaumont Hospital, Dublin
00 353 1 837 7755
Birr District Hospital, Offaly
00 353 509 20819
Carlow District Hospital, Carlow
00 353 59 91 36400
Castlecomer District Hospital, Castlecomer
00 353 56 44 412 46
Cavan General Hospital, Lisdarn
00 353 49 436 1399
Cherry Orchard Hospital, Dublin
00 353 1 626 4702
Cork University Hospital, Cork
00 353 21 45 46400
Ennis General Hospital, Ennis
00 353 65 682 4464
Erinville Hospital
00 353 21 4275211
Gorey District Hospital, Gorey
00 353 55 211 02
James Connolly Memorial Hospital, Dublin
00 353 1 821 3844
Letterkenny General Hospital, Letterkenny
00 353 74 91 258 88
Limerick Regional Hospital, Limerick
00 353 61 301111
Longford/Westmeath General Hospital, Westmeath
00 353 44 40 221
Lourdes Regional Orthopaedic Hospital, Kilkenny
00 353 56 77 52465
Louth County Hospital, Dundalk
00 353 42 933 4701
Mallow General Hospital, Mallow
00 353 22 212 51
Mater Misericordiae Hospital, Dublin
00 353 1 803 2000
Mayo General Hospital, Castlebar
00 353 94 90 21733
Mercy Hospital, Cork
00 353 21 4271971
Merlin Park Regional Hospital, Galway
00 353 91 757631
Monaghan General Hospital, Monaghan
00 353 47 81811
Naas General Hospital, Kildare
00 353 45 897 221
Nenagh General Hospital, Nenagh
00 353 67 31 491
Our Lady of Lourdes, Drogheda
00 353 41 983 7601
Our Lady's County and Surgical Hospital, Cashel
00 353 62 61022
Our Lady's Hospital, Navan
00 353 46 90 21210
Portiuncula Hospital, Galway
00 353 90 96 42140
Portlaoise Regional Hospital, Portlaoise
00 353 502 21364
Roscommon General Hospital, Roscommon
00 353 90 66 26200
St Brigid's District Hospital, Carrick on Suir
00 353 51 640 025
St Columcille's Hospital, Dublin
00 353 1 282 5800
St Finbarr's Hospital, Cork
00 353 21 4966555
St James's Hospital, Dublin
00 353 1 453 7941
St John's Hospital, Limerick
00 353 61 415 822
St Joseph's Hospital, Clonmel
00 353 52 77000
St Luke's General Hospital, Kilkenny
00 353 56 77 85 000
St Mary's Hospital, Dublin
00 353 1 677 8132
St Mary's Orthopaedic Hospital, Cork
00 353 21 4303264
St Michael's Hospital, Dublin
00 353 1 280 6901
St Nessan's Orthopaedic Hospital, Croom
00 353 61 397276
St Teresa's District Hospital, Clogheen
00 353 52 652 05
St Vincent University Hospital, Dublin
00 353 1 269 4533
St Vincent's District Hospital, Dungarvan
00 353 58 411 25
Sligo General Hospital, Sligo Town
00 353 7191 71111
South Infirmary / Victoria Hospital, Cork
00 353 21 451 7700
Temple Street – The Children's Hospital, Dublin
00 353 1 87 84200
Tralee General Hospital, Tralee
00 353 66 718 4000
Tullamore Regional Hospital, Tullamore
00 353 506 21501
University College Hospital, Galway
00 353 91 544 544
Waterford Regional Hospital, Waterford
00 353 51 848000
Wexford General Hospital, Wexford Town
00 353 53 42233

Private hospitals

Abbey Caldew Hospital
01228 531713
Abbey Carrick Glen Hospital
01292 288882
Abbey Gisburne Park
01200 445693
Abbey Kings Park Hospital
01786 451669
Abbey Park Hospital
01229 813388
Abbey Sefton Hospital
0151 257 6700
Alexandra Hospital, Cheadle
0161 428 3656
Ashtead Hospital
01372 221400
Beaumont Hospital
01204 404404
Benenden Hospital
01580 240333
Berkshire Independent Hospital
0118 902 8000
Birkdale Clinic
01709 828928
Birth Centre
020 8767 8294
BMI Albyn Hospital
01224 595993
BMI Bath Clinic
01225 835555
BMI Bishops Wood Hospital
01923 835814
BMI Chatsworth Suite
01246 544400
BMI Chelsfield Park Hospital
01689 877855
BMI Esperance Hospital
01323 411188
BMI Fernbrae Hospital
01382 667203
BMI Meriden Wing
01203 602772
BMI Park Hospital
0115 967 0670
BMI Ross Hall Hospital
0141 810 3151
BMI Shirley Oaks Hospital
020 8655 5500
BMI The Alexandra Hospital Victoria Park
0161 257 2233
BMI The Beardwood Hospital
01254 507607
BMI The Beaumont Hospital
01204 404499
BMI The Blackheath Hospital
020 8318 7722
BMI The Chaucer Hospital
01227 825100
BMI The Chiltern Hospital
01494 890890
BMI The Clementine Churchill Hospital
020 8872 3872
BMI The Droitwich Spa Hospital
01905 793333
BMI The Fawkham Manor Hospital
01474 879900
BMI The Foscote Hospital
01295 252281
BMI The Garden Hospital
020 8457 4500
BMI The Goring Hall Hospital
01903 506699
BMI The Hampshire Clinic
01256 357111
BMI The Harbour Hospital
01202 244200
BMI The Highfield Hospital
01706 655121

BMI The Kings Oak Hospital
020 8370 9500
BMI The London Independent Hospital
020 7780 2400
BMI The Manor Hospital
01234 364252
BMI The Nuneaton Hospital
024 7635 7500
BMI The Paddocks Hospital
01844 276000
BMI The Princess Margaret Hospital
01753 743434
BMI The Priory Hospital
0121 440 2323
BMI The Ridgeway Hospital
01793 814848
BMI The Runnymede Hospital
01932 877800
BMI The Sandringham Hospital
01553 769770
BMI The Sarum Road Hospital
01962 844555
BMI The Saxon Clinic
01908 665533
BMI The Shelborne Hospital
01494 888700
BMI The Sloane Hospital
020 8466 6911
BMI The Somerfield Hospital
01622 208000
BMI The South Cheshire Hospital
01270 500411
BMI Three Shires Hospital
01604 620311
BMI Winterbourne Hospital
01305 263252
Bridge Centre, The
020 7403 3363
British Pregnancy Advisory Sevice
0845 730 4030
Bupa Alexandra Hospital
01634 687166
Bupa Belvedere Hospital
01723 365363
Bupa Cambridge Lea Hospital
01223 266900
Bupa Dunedin Hospital
0118 958 7676
Bupa Fylde Coast Hospital
01253 394188
Bupa Gatwick Park Hospital
01293 785511
Bupa Hartswood Hospital
01277 232525
Bupa Hospital Bristol
0117 973 2562
Bupa Hospital Bushey
020 8950 9090
Bupa Hospital Cardiff
029 2073 5515
Bupa Hospital Clare Park
01252 850216
Bupa Hospital Elland
01422 324000
Bupa Hospital Harpenden
01582 763191
Bupa Hospital Hastings
01424 757400
Bupa Hospital Leeds
0113 269 3939
Bupa Hospital Leicester
0116 272 0888
Bupa Hospital Little Aston
0121 353 2444
Bupa Hospital Manchester
0161 226 0112
Bupa Hospital Norwich
01603 456181
Bupa Hospital Portsmouth
023 9245 6000
Bupa Hospital Southampton
023 8077 5544
Bupa Hospital Tunbridge Wells
01892 740047
Bupa Hospital Washington
0191 415 1272
Bupa Hull And East Riding Hospital
01482 659471
Bupa Methley Park Hospital
01977 518518
Bupa Murrayfield Hospital Edinburgh
0131 334 0363
Bupa Murrayfield Hospital Wirral
0151 648 7000
Bupa North Cheshire Hospital
01925 265000
Bupa Parkway Hospital
0121 704 1451
Bupa Redwood Hospital
01737 277277
Bupa Regency Hospital
01625 501150
Bupa Roding Hospital
020 8551 1100
Bupa South Bank Hospital
01905 350003
Bupa St Saviour's Hospital
01303 265581
Bupa Wellesley Hospital
01702 462944
Bupa Yale Hospital
01978 291306
Chalfont Centre for Epilepsy
01494 874646
Cheadle Royal
0161 428 9511
Churchill Private Clinic
020 7928 5633
Claremont Hospital
0114 263 0330
Cromwell Hospital
020 7460 2000
Devonshire Hospital
020 7486 7131
Duchy Hospital
01872 226100
Euxton Hall Hospital
01257 276261
Fairfield Independent Hospital
01744 739311
Farm Place
01306 627742
Fawkham Manor Hospital
01474 879900
Fitzwilliam Hospital
01733 261717
Florence Nightingale Clinic Chelsea
0800 783 0594
Florence Nightingale Hospital Liverpool
0151 928 8351
Florence Nightingale, The
020 7258 3828
Foscote Private Hospital
01295 252281
Fulwood Hall Hospital
01772 704111
Gainsborough Clinic, The
020 7928 5633
Goring Hall Hospital
01903 506699
Grovelands Priory Hospital
020 8882 8191
Guthrie Clinic, The
020 7346 3192/3
Hampshire Clinic
01256 357111
Harbour Hospital
01202 244200
Harley Street Clinic
020 7935 7700
Hayes Grove Priory Hospital
020 8462 7722
HCI International Medical Centre
0141 951 5000
Heart Hospital, The
020 7573 8888
Heath House Priory Hospital
0117 952 5255
Highbank Rehabilitation Centre
01706 829540
Highgate Private Hospital
020 8341 4182
Holly House Hospital
020 8505 3311
Holy Cross Hospital
01428 643311
Horder Centre for Arthritis, The
01892 665577
Hospital of St John and St Elizabeth
020 7806 4000
Hull IVF Unit
01482 676541
Huntercombe Manor Hospital
01628 667881
International Centre for Excellence in Dentistry
020 7905 1234
King Edward VII Hospital
01730 812341
King Edward VII's Hospital Sister Agnes
020 7486 4411
King's Oak Hospital
020 8370 9500
Lister Hospital, The
020 7730 3417
London Bridge Hospital
020 7407 3100
London Clinic, The
020 7935 4444
London Independent Hospital
020 7780 2400
London IRYO Centre
020 8202 7272
Lourdes Hospital
0151 733 7123
Manchester Fertility Services
0161 862 9567
Mcindoe Surgical Centre
01342 330300
Mount Alvernia Hospital
01483 570122
Mount Stuart Hospital
01803 313881
New Hall Hospital
01722 422333
New Victoria Hospital
020 8949 9000
North Downs Hospital
01883 348981
Nuffield Hospital Acland
01865 404142
Nuffield Hospital Birmingham
0121 456 2000
Nuffield Hospital Bournemouth
01202 291866
Nuffield Hospital Brentwood
01277 695695
Nuffield Hospital Brighton
01273 624488
Nuffield Hospital Bristol
0117 973 0391
Nuffield Hospital Bury St Edmunds
01284 701371
Nuffield Hospital Cambridge
01223 303336
Nuffield Hospital Cheltenham
01242 246500
Nuffield Hospital Grosvenor Chester
01244 680444
Nuffield Hospital Chesterfield
0117 987 2727
Nuffield Hospital Chichester
01243 530600
Nuffield Hospital Derby
01332 517891

Nuffield Hospital Enfield
020 8366 2122
Nuffield Hospital Exeter
01392 276591
Nuffield Hospital Glasgow
0141 334 9441
Nuffield Hospital Guildford
01483 555800
Nuffield Hospital Harrogate
01423 567136
Nuffield Hospital Haywards Heath
01444 456999
Nuffield Hospital Hereford
01432 355131
Nuffield Hospital Hove
01273 779471
Nuffield Hospital Huddersfield
01484 533131
Nuffield Hospital Hull
01482 623500
Nuffield Hospital Ipswich
01473 279100
Nuffield Hospital Lancaster
01524 62345
Nuffield Hospital Leamington Spa
01926 427971
Nuffield Hospital Leeds
0113 388 2000
Nuffield Hospital Leicester
0116 276 9401
Nuffield Hospital Lincoln
01522 578000
Nuffield Hospital Mid Yorkshire
0113 258 8756
Nuffield Hospital Newcastle-under-Lyme
01782 625431
Nuffield Hospital Newcastle
0191 281 6131
Nuffield Hospital Christchurch Park Suffolk
01473 256071
Nuffield Hospital Nottingham
0115 920 9209
Nuffield Hospital Plymouth
01752 775861
Nuffield Hospital Purey Cust York
01904 641571
Nuffield Hospital Shrewsbury
01743 282500
Nuffield Hospital Taunton
01823 286991
Nuffield Hospital Teesside
01642 360100
Nuffield Hospital Thames Valley Slough
01753 662241
Nuffield Hospital Tunbridge Wells
01892 531111
Nuffield Hospital Wessex Eastfield
023 8026 6377
Nuffield Hospital Woking
01483 227800
Nuffield Hospital Wolverhampton
01902 754177
Nuffield Hospital HRH Princess Christians Windsor
01753 853121
Nuneaton Private Hospital
024 7635 7500
Oaklands Hospital
0161 787 7700
Oaks Hospital, The
01206 752121
Orchard Hospital, The
01983 520022
Paddocks Hospital
01844 346951
Park Hill Hospital
01302 730300
Parkside Hospital
020 8971 8000
Pinehill Hospital
01462 422822
Portland Hospital for Women and Children, The
020 7580 4400
Princess Grace Hospital, The
020 7486 1234
Priory Clinic Nottingham, The
0115 969 3388
Priory Hospital Chelmsford, The
01245 345345
Priory Hospital Glasgow, The
0141 636 6116
Priory Hospital Marchwood, The
023 8084 0044
Priory Hospital North London, The
020 8882 8191
Priory Hospital Roehampton, The
020 8876 8261
Priory Hospital Sturt, The
01737 814488
Priory Hospital Woking, The
01483 489211
Priory Hospital, The
0161 904 0050
Priory Ticehurst House, The
01580 200391
Renacres Hall Hospital
01704 841133
Rivers Hospital, The
01279 600282
Rowley Hall Hospital
01785 223203
Royal Hospital for Neuro-disability
020 8780 4500
St Anthony's Hospital
020 8337 6691
St Hugh's Hospital
01472 251100
St John of God Hospital
01748 811535
St Joseph's Hospital
01633 820300
St Luke's Hospital for the Clergy
020 7388 4954
Sancta Maria Hospital
01792 479040
Sarum Road Hospital
01962 841555
Saxon Clinic
01908 665533
Shelburne
01494 888700
Sketchley Hall
01455 890023
South Cheshire Private Hospital
01270 500411
Springfield Hospital
01245 234000
Stamford Hospital, The
020 8636 9000
Stockton Hall Hospital
01904 400500
Surgicare Birmingham
01827 263831
Surgicare Manchester
0161 945 8688
Thornbury Hospital
0114 266 1133
Ulster Independent Clinic
028 9066 1212
Unsted Park Hospital
01483 892061
Waterside Suite
01934 647000
Wellington Hospital, The
020 7586 5959
Werndale Hospital
01267 211500
Wessex Maternity Centre
023 8046 4721
West Midlands Hospital
01384 560123
Winfield Hospital
01452 331111
Woodbourne Priory Hospital
0121 434 4343
Woodland Hospital
01536 414515
Woodlands Hospital
01325 341700
Yorkshire Clinic
01274 560311
Yorkshire Laser Centre
01724 290456

Law

Home Office
0870 000 1585
Press: 020 7273 4545
www.homeoffice.gov.uk

Attorney General's Office
020 7271 2400
Press: 020 7271 2440

Department for Constitutional Affairs
020 7210 8614
Press: 020 7210 8512
www.dca.gsi.gov.uk

Crown Office and Procurator Fiscal Service, Scotland
0131 226 2626
www.crownoffice.gov.uk

Scottish Executive
0131 556 8400; press office, justice desk: 0131 244 2718
www.scotland.gov.uk

Court, legal and prison services

Appeals Service
020 7712 2600
www.appeals-service.gov.uk

Court Service
020 7189 2000
Press: 020 7210 8510
www.courtservice.gov.uk

Court Service, Northern Ireland
028 9032 8594
Press: 028 9041 2345
www.courtsni.gov.uk

Crown Prosecution Service
020 7796 8000
Publicity office: 020 7796 8442
www.cps.gov.uk

Scottish Courts Administration
0131 229 9200
www.scotcourts.gov.uk

Magistrates Court Service Inspectorate
020 7217 4344
www.mcsi.gov.uk

Prison Service
020 7217 6000
Press: 020 7273 4545
Victim helpline: 0845 758 5112
www.hmprisonservice.gov.uk

Scottish Prison Service
0131 244 8745
www.sps.gov.uk

N Ireland Prison Service
028 9052 5065
www.niprisonservice.gov.uk

Appeal courts

Court of Appeal
Civil: 020 7947 6533
Criminal: 020 7947 7388
Press: 020 7210 8512
www.courtservice.gov.uk

High Court
020 7947 6000
Press: 020 7210 8512
www.courtservice.gov.uk

Supreme Courts, Scotland – High Court (criminal); Court of Session (civil)
0131 225 2595

High Court of Justiciary, Scotland
0131 240 6906
Press: 0131 244 2939

Supreme Court of Northern Ireland
028 9072 4661
Press: 028 9041 2385

Judicial Committee of the Privy Council
020 7276 0483 / 0485 / 0487

Other agencies

Civil Justice Council
020 7947 6670
www.civiljusticecouncil.gov.uk

Criminal Cases Review Commission
0121 633 1800
www.ccrc.gov.uk

Criminal Records Bureau
0870 909 0811
www.crb.gov.uk

Customs and Excise
0845 010 9000
Press: 020 7865 5471 / 020 7865 5095 / 020 8929 4637
www.hmce.gov.uk

Law Commission
020 7453 1220
www.lawcom.gov.uk

Legal Services Commission
020 7759 0000
www.legalservices.gov.uk

Legal Services Ombudsman
0845 601 0794
www.olso.org

Scottish Legal Services Ombudsman
0131 556 9123
www.slso.org.uk

Youth Justice Boards for England and Wales
020 7271 3033
Press: 020 7271 3014 / 2988
www.youth-justice-board.gov.uk

Professional bodies

Administrative Law Bar Association
020 7353 1633
www.adminlaw.org.uk

Association of Personal Injury Lawyers
0115 958 0585
www.apil.com

Association of Women Barristers
020 7842 7070
www.womenbarristers.co.uk

Bar Council
020 7242 0082
Press: 020 7222 2525
www.barcouncil.org.uk

Chancery Bar Association
020 8883 1700
www.chba.org.uk

Commercial Bar Association
020 7404 2022
www.combar.com

Family Law Bar Association
020 7242 1289
www.flba.co.uk

Institute of Barristers' Clerks
020 7831 7144
www.barristersclerks.com

Institute of Legal Executives
01234 841000
Press: 01234 845715
www.ilex.org.uk

Justices' Clerks' Society
0151 255 0790
www.jc-society.co.uk

Law Society
020 7242 1222
Press: 020 7320 5811
www.lawsoc.org.uk

Legal Aid Practitioners' Group
020 7336 8565
www.lapg.co.uk

Magistrates' Association
020 7387 2353
www.magistrates-association.org.uk

Solicitors' Criminal Law Association
01273 676725
www.clsa.co.uk

Solicitors' Family Law Association
01689 850227
Press: 020 7923 2922
www.sfla.org.uk

Crown courts

Central Criminal Court – Old Bailey
020 7248 3277
Aylesbury Crown Court
01296 434401
Basildon Combined Court
01268 458000
Birmingham Crown Court
0121 681 3300
Blackfriars Crown Court
020 7922 5800
Bolton Combined Court Centre
01204 392881
Bournemouth Crown Court
01202 502800
Bradford Combined Court Centre
01274 840274
Bristol Crown Court
0117 976 3030
Burnley Combined Court Centre
01282 416899
Cambridge Crown Court
01223 224666
Canterbury Combined Court Centre
01227 819200
Cardiff Crown Court
029 2041 4400
Carlisle Combined Court Centre
01228 520619
Central Criminal Court
020 7248 3277
Chelmsford Crown Court
01245 603000
Chester Crown Court
01244 317606
Chichester Combined Court Centre
01243 520742
Court of Appeal (Criminal Division)
020 7947 6011
Coventry Combined Court Centre
024 7653 6166
Croydon Combined Court Centre
020 8410 4700
Derby Combined Court Centre
01332 622600
Doncaster Crown Court
01302 322211
Durham Crown Court
0191 386 6714
Exeter Combined Court Centre
01392 210655
Gloucester Crown Court
01452 529351
Great Grimsby Combined Court Centre
01472 311811
Guildford Crown Court
01483 468500
Harrow Crown Court
020 8424 2294
Hereford Crown Court
01432 276118
Hove Trial Centre
01273 229200
Inner London Crown Court
020 7234 3100
Ipswich Crown Court
01473 228 585
Isleworth Crown Court
020 8380 4500
Kingston-upon-Hull Combined Court Centre
01482 586161
Kingston-upon-Thames Crown Court
020 8240 2500
Lancaster Crown Court
01772 832300
Leeds Combined Court Centre
0113 2830040
Leicester Crown Court
0116 222 5800
Lewes Combined Court Centre
01273 480400
Lincoln Crown Court
01522 525222
Liverpool Combined Court Centre
0151 473 7373
Luton Crown Court
01582 522000
Maidstone Combined Court Centre
01622 202000
Manchester Crown Court (Crown Square)
0161 954 1702
Manchester Crown Court at Minshull St
0161 954 7500
Merthyr Tydfil Combined Court Centre
01685 358222
Middlesex Guildhall Crown Court
020 72020370
Mold Crown Court
01244 356709
Newcastle-upon-Tyne Combined Court Centre
0191 201 2000
Newport (South Wales) Crown Court
01633 266211
Newport, I.O.W. Crown Court
01983 821569
Northampton Combined Court
01604 470400
Norwich Combined Court Centre
01603 728200
Nottingham Crown Court
0115 910 3551
Oxford Combined Court Centre
01865 264200
Peterborough Combined Court Centre
01733 349161
Plymouth Combined Court
01752 677400
Portsmouth Combined Court Centre
023 9289 3000
Preston Combined Court Centre
01772 844759
Reading Crown Court
0118 967 4400
Salisbury Combined Court Centre
01722 325444
Sheffield Combined Court Centre
0114 281 2400
Shrewsbury Crown Court
01743 355775
Snaresbrook Crown Court
020 8530 0000
Southampton Combined Court Centre
023 8021 3200
Southwark Crown Court
020 7522 7200
St. Albans Crown Court
01727 753220
Stafford Combined Court Centre
01785 610730
Stoke-on-Trent Combined Court
01782 854000
Swansea Crown Court
01792 484700
Swindon Combined Court
01793 690514
Taunton Crown Court
01823 326685
Teesside Combined Court Centre
01642 340000
Truro Combined Court Centre
01872 222340
Warrington Combined Court Centre
01925 256700
Warwick Combined Court Centre
01926 492276
Weymouth and Dorchester Combined Court Centre
01305 752510
Winchester Combined Court Centre
01962 841212
Wolverhampton Combined Court Centre
01902 481000
Wood Green Crown Court
020 8881 1400
Woolwich Crown Court
020 8312 7000
Worcester Combined Court
01905 730807
York Crown Court
01904 645121

Northern Ireland courts

Court Service, Northern Ireland
028 9032 8594
Press: 028 9041 2345
www.courtsni.gov.uk
Antrim
028 9446 2661
Armagh
028 3752 2816
Ballymena
028 2564 9416
Belfast
028 9023 5111
Craigavon
028 3834 1324
Downpatrick
028 4461 4621
Enniskillen
028 6632 2356
Londonderry
028 7136 3448
Newry
028 3025 2040
Omagh
028 8224 2056

Sheriff courts, Scotland

Scottish Courts Administration
0131 229 9200
www.scotcourts.gov.uk
Aberdeen
01224 657200
Airdrie
01236 751121
Alloa
01259 722734
Arbroath
01241 876600
Ayr
01292 268474
Banff
01261 812140
Campbeltown
01586 552503
Cupar
01334 652121
Dingwall
01349 863153
Dornoch
01862 810224
Dumbarton
01389 763266
Dumfries
01387 262334
Dundee
01382 229961
Dunfermline
01383 724666
Dunoon
01369 704166
Duns
01361 883719
Edinburgh
0131 225 2525

Elgin
01343 542505
Falkirk
01324 620822
Forfar
01307 462186
Fort William
01397 702087
Glasgow
0141 429 8888
Greenock
01475 787073
Haddington
0162082 2936
Hamilton
01698 282957
Inverness
01463 230782
Jedburgh
01835 863231
Kilmarnock
01563 520211
Kirkcaldy
01592 260171
Kirkcudbright
01557 330574
Kirkwall
01856 872110
Lanark
01555 661531
Lerwick
01595 693914
Linlithgow
01506 842922
Lochmaddy
01876 500340
Oban
01631 562414
Paisley
0141 887 5291
Peebles
01721 720204
Perth
01738 620546
Peterhead
01779 476676
Portree
01478 612191
Rothesay
01700 502982
Selkirk
01750 21260
Stirling
01786 462191
Stonehaven
01569 762758
Stornoway
01851 702231
Stranraer
01776 702138
Tain
01862 892518
Wick
01955 602846

County courts

Aberdare
01685 888575
Aberystwyth
01970 636370
Accrington
01254 237490
Aldershot & Farnham
01252 796800
Altrincham
0161 975 4760
Ashford
01233 632464
Aylesbury
01296 393498
Banbury
01295 265799
Barnet
020 8343 4272
Barnsley
01226 203471
Barnstaple
01271 372252
Barrow-In-Furness
01229 820046
Basildon Combined Court
01268 458000
Basingstoke
01256 318200
Bath
01225 310282
Bedford
01234 760400
Birkenhead
0151 666 5800
Birmingham Civil Justice Centre
0121 681 4441
Bishop Auckland
01388 602423
Blackburn
01254 680640
Blackpool
01253 754020
Blackwood
01495 223197
Bodmin
01208 74224/ 73735
Bolton Combined Court Centre
01204 392881
Boston
01205 366080
Bournemouth
01202 502800
Bow
020 8536 5200
Bradford Combined Court Centre
01274 840274
Brentford
020 8231 8940
Bridgend
01656 768881
Brighton
01273 674421
Bristol
0117 929 4414
Bromley
020 8290 9620

Burnley Combined Court Centre
01282 416899
Burton Upon Trent
01283 568241
Bury
0161 764 1344
Bury St Edmunds
01284 753254
Buxton
01298 23734
Caernarfon
01286 684600
Cambridge
01223 224500
Canterbury Combined Court Centre
01227 819200
Cardiff Civil Justice Centre
029 2037 6400
Carlisle Combined Court Centre
01228 520619
Carmarthen
01267 228010
Central London
020 7917 5000
Chelmsford
01245 264670
Cheltenham
01242 519983
Chester Civil Justice Centre
01244 404200
Chesterfield
01246 501200
Chichester
01243 520700
Chorley
01257 262778
Clerkenwell
020 7359 7347
Colchester
01206 572743
Consett
01207 502854
Conwy & Colwyn
01492 530807
Coventry Combined Court Centre
024 7653 6166
Crewe
01270 212255
Croydon Combined Court Centre
020 8410 4700
Darlington
01325 463224
Dartford
01322 629820
Derby Combined Court Centre
01332 622600
Dewsbury
01924 466135
Doncaster
01302 381730
Dudley
01384 480799
Durham
0191 386 5941
Eastbourne
01323 735195

Edmonton
020 8807 1666
Epsom
01372 721801
Evesham
01386 442287
Exeter Combined Court Centre
01392 210655
Gateshead
0191 477 2445
Gloucester Crown &
01452 834900
Grantham
01476 563638
Gravesend
01474 321771
Great Grimsby Combined Court Centre
01472 311811
Guildford
01483 595200
Halifax
01422 344700
Harlow
01279 443291
Harrogate
01423 503921
Hartlepool
01429 268198
Hastings
01424 435128
Haverfordwest
01437 772060
Haywards Heath
01444 456326
Hereford
01432 357233
Hertford
01992 503954
High Wycombe
01494 436374
Hitchin
01462 443750
Horsham
01403 252474
Huddersfield
01484 421043
Huntingdon
01480 450932
Ilford
020 8478 1132
Ipswich
01473 214256
Keighley
01535 602803
Kendal
01539 721218
Kettering
01536 512471
Kidderminster
01562 822480
King's Lynn
01553 772067
Kingston-upon-Hull Combined Court Centre
01482 586161
Kingston-Upon-Thames
020 8546 8843
Lambeth
020 7091 4410/4420
Lancaster
01524 68112

Leeds Combined Court Centre
0113 283 0040
Leicester
0116 222 5700
Leigh
01942 673639
Lewes Combined Court Centre
01273 480400
Lincoln
01522 883000
Liverpool Combined Court Centre
0151 473 7373
Llanelli
01554 757171
Llangefni
01248 750225
Lowestoft
01502 586047
Ludlow
01584 872091
Luton
01582 506700
Macclesfield
01625 412800
Maidstone Combined Court Centre
01622 202000
Manchester
0161 954 1800
Mansfield
01623 656406
Mayor's & City of London Court
020 7796 5400
Medway
01634 810720
Melton Mowbray
01664 485100
Merthyr Tydfil Combined Court Centre
01685 358222
Middlesborough at Teesside Combined Court
01642 340000
Milton Keynes
01908 302800
Mold
01352 707330
Morpeth & Berwick
01670 512221
Neath and Port Talbot
01639 642267/8
Nelson
01282 601177
Newark
01636 703607
Newbury
01635 40928
Newcastle-upon-Tyne Combined Court Centre
0191 201 2000
Newport (Gwent)
01633 227150
Newport (Isle Of Wight)
01983 526821
North Shields
0191 257 5866
Northampton Combined Court
01604 470400
Northwich
01606 42554
Norwich Combined Court Centre
01603 728200
Nottingham
0115 910 3500
Nuneaton
024 7638 6134
Oldham
01612 904200
Oswestry
01691 652127
Oxford Combined Court Centre
01865 264200
Penrith
01768 862535
Penzance
01736 362987
Peterborough Combined Court Centre
01733 349161
Plymouth Combined Court
01752 677400
Pontefract
01977 702357
Pontypool
01495 762248
Pontypridd
01443 490800
Poole
01202 741150
Portsmouth Combined Court Centre
023 9289 3000
Preston Combined Court Centre
01772 844700
Rawtenstall
01706 214614
Reading
0118 987 0500
Redditch
01527 67822
Reigate
01737 763637
Rhyl
01745 330216
Romford
01708 775353
Rotherham
01709 364786
Rugby
01788 542543
Runcorn
01925 256700
Salford
0161 745 7511
Salisbury Combined Court Centre
01722 325444
Scarborough
01723 366361
Scunthorpe
01724 289111
Sheffield Combined Court Centre
0114 281 2400
Shoreditch
020 7253 0956
Shrewsbury
01743 289069
Skegness
01754 762429
Skipton
01756 793315
Slough
01753 690300
South Shields
0191 456 3343
Southampton Combined Court Centre
023 8021 3200
Southend
01702 601991
Southport
01704 531541
St Albans
01727 856925
St Helens
01744 27544
Stafford Combined Court Centre
01785 610730
Staines
01784 459175
Stockport
01614 747707
Stoke-on-Trent Combined Court
01782 854000
Stourbridge
01384 394232
Stratford Upon Avon
01789 293056
Sunderland
0191 568 0750
Swansea Civil Justice Centre
01792 510350
Swindon Combined Court
01793 690514
Tameside
0161 331 5614
Tamworth
01827 62664
Taunton
01823 335972
Teesside Combined Court Centre
01642 340000
Telford
01952 291045
Thanet
01843 221722
Torquay & Newton Abbot
01803 616791
Trowbridge
01225 752101
Truro Combined Court Centre
01872 222340
Tunbridge Wells
01892 515515
Uxbridge
020 8561 8562
Wakefield
01924 370268
Walsall Hearing Centre
01922 728855
Wandsworth
020 8333 4351
Warrington Combined Court Centre
01925 256700
Warwick Combined Court Centre
01926 492276
Watford
01923 699400/401
Wellingborough
01933 226168 / 222393
Welshpool and Newtown
01938 552004
West London
020 7602 8444
Weston Super Mare
01934 626967
Weymouth and Dorchester Combined Court Centre
01305 752510
Whitehaven
01946 67788
Wigan
01942 246481
Willesden
020 8963 8200
Winchester Combined Court Centre
01962 841212
Wolverhampton Combined Court Centre
01902 481000
Woolwich
020 8854 2127
Worcester Combined Court
01905 730807
Worksop
01909 472358
Worthing
01903 221920
Wrexham
01978 351738
Yeovil
01935 474133
York
01904 629935

Law centres

Law Centres Federation
020 7387 8570
www.lawcentres.org.uk
Barnet Law Centre
020 8203 4141
Battersea Law Centre
020 7585 0716
Bradford Law Centre
01274 306 617
Brent Community Law Centre
020 8451 1122
Bury Law Centre
0161 272 0666
Cambridge House Law Centre
020 7703 3051
Camden Community Law Centre
020 7284 6510
Cardiff Law Centre
029 2049 8117
Carlisle Law Centre
01228 515 129
Central London Law Centre
020 7839 2998
Chesterfield Law Centre
01246 550 674
Coventry Law Centre
024 7622 3053
Derby Law Centre
01332 344 557
Devon Law Centre
01752 519 794
Enfield Law Centre
020 8807 8888
Gateshead Law Centre
0191 478 2847
Gloucester Law Centre
01452 423492
Greenwich Community Law Centre
020 8305 3350
Hackney Community Law Centre
020 8985 8364
Hammersmith & Fulham Law Centre
020 8741 4021
Harehills & Chapeltown Law Centre
0113 249 1100
Hillingdon Law Centre
020 8561 9400
Hounslow Law Centre
020 8570 9505
Humberside Law Centre
01482 211 180
Isle of Wight Law Centre
01983 524715
Islington Law Centre
020 7607 2461
Lambeth Law Centre
020 7737 9780
Leicester Law Centre
0116 255 3781
Lewisham Law Centre
020 8692 5355
Liverpool 8 Law Centre
0151 709 7222
Luton Law Centre
01582 481 000
North Manchester Law Centre
0161 205 9031
South Manchester Law Centre
0161 225 5111
Newcastle Law Centre
0191 230 4777
North Kensington Law Centre
020 8969 7473
Nottingham Law Centre
0115 978 7813
Oldham Law Centre
0161 627 0925
Paddington Law Centre
020 8960 3155
Plumstead Community Law Centre
020 8855 9817
Rochdale Law Centre
01706 657766
Saltley & Nechells Law Centre
0121 328 2307
Sheffield Law Centre
0114 273 1888
South Manchester Law Centre
0161 225 5111
Southwark Law Centre
020 7732 2008
Springfield Law Centre
020 8767 6884
Stockport Law Centre
0161 476 6336
Thamesmead Law Centre
020 8311 0555
Tottenham Law Centre
020 8808 5354
Tower Hamlets Law Centre
020 7247 8998
Trafford Law Centre
0161 872 3669
Vauxhall Law and Information Centre
0151 330 0239
Wandsworth & Merton Law Centre
020 8767 2777
Warrington Community Law Centre
01925 651 104
Wiltshire Law Centre
01793 486926
Wythenshawe Law Centre
0161 498 0905/6
Law Centre (NI) – (Belfast office)
028 9024 4401
Law Centre (NI) – (Western Area office)
028 7126 2433

Legal advice

Activists Legal Project
01865 243772
www.activistslegalproject.org.uk
Legal information for activists
Asylum Aid
020 7377 5123
Advice line: 020 7247 8741
www.asylumaid.org.uk
CHAS Central London
020 7723 5928
www.chascl.org.uk
Children's Legal Centre
Admin: 01206 872466
Advice line: 01206 873820
www.childrenslegalcentre.com
Community Legal Service
020 7759 1020
www.justask.org.uk
Counsel & Care
Admin: 020 7241 8555
Advice line: 0845 300 7585
www.counselandcare.org.uk
Detainee Support & Help Unit
020 7703 5435
www.dshu.org.uk
Disability Law Service
020 7791 9800
Environmental Law Foundation
020 7404 1030
www.elflaw.org
Housing Justice
020 7723 5928
www.housingjustice.org.uk
Joint Council for the Welfare of Immigrants
020 7251 8708
www.jcwi.org.uk
Legal Action Group
020 7833 2931
www.lag.org.uk
Legal Services Research Centre
020 7759 2349
www.lsrc.org.uk
Liberty (the National Council for Civil Liberties)
Advice line: 0845 123 2307
www.yourrights.org.uk
Maternity Alliance
020 7490 7639
Information line: 020 7490 7638
www.maternityalliance.org.uk
National Youth Advocacy Service
0151 649 8700
Young people helpline: 0800 616101
www.nyas.net
Prisoners' Families Helpline
0808 808 2003
www.prisonersfamilieshelpline.org.uk
Public Law Project
020 7697 2190
www.publiclawproject.org.uk
Refugee Legal Centre
020 7780 3200
Advice line: 020 7780 3220
www.refugee-legal-centre.org.uk
Scottish Human Rights Centre
0141 332 5960
www.scottishhumanrightscentre.org.uk
UK Legal
0845 2801976
www.uklegal.com

Prisons

Prison Service
020 7217 6000
www.hmprisonservice.gov.uk
Press: 020 7273 4545
Victim helpline: 0845 758 5112
Scottish Prison Service
0131 244 8745
www.sps.gov.uk
N Ireland Prison Service
028 9052 5065
www.niprisonservice.gov.uk

Agencies

Parole Board for England and Wales
020 7217 5314
Press: 020 7217 5266
www.paroleboard.gov.uk
Prisons and Probation Ombudsman for England and Wales
020 7035 2876, 0845 010 7938
www.ppo.gov.uk
Scottish Parole Board
0131 244 8755
www.scottishparoleboard.gov.uk
Scottish Prisons Inspectorate
0131 244 8481
Chief Inspector of Prisons
0870 267 4298
www.homeoffice.gov.uk

Professional bodies

Prison Governors Association
020 7217 8591
www.prisongovernors.org.uk
Prison Officers Association
020 8803 0255
www.poauk.org.uk
National Association of Prison Visitors
01234 359763
NAPO
020 7223 4887
www.napo.org.uk
(the trade union and professional association for family court and probation staff)

Campaign groups

Action for Prisoners' Families
020 7384 1987
www.prisonersfamilies.org.uk
Apex Trust
020 7638 5931
www.apextrust.com
Campaign for Freedom of Information
020 7831 7477
www.cfoi.org.uk
Campaign for the Accountability of American Bases
01943 466405
www.caab.org.uk
Committee on the Administration of Justice (Northern Ireland)
028 90961122
www.caj.org.uk
Crimestoppers
020 8254 3200
Freephone: 0800 555 111
www.crimestoppers-uk.org
Howard League for Prison Reform
020 7249 7373
www.howardleague.org
Inquest
020 7263 1111
www.inquest.org.uk
Justice
020 7329 5100
www.justice.org.uk
Liberty
020 7403 3888
www.liberty-human-rights.org.uk
Minority Rights Group
020 7422 4200
www.minorityrights.org
National Association for the Care & Resettlement of Offenders
020 7582 6500
www.nacro.org.uk
Prison Reform Trust
020 7251 5070
www.prisonreformtrust.org.uk
Prisoners Family and Friends
020 7403 4091
www.prisonersfamiliesandfriends.org.uk
Unit for the Arts & Offenders
01227 470 629
www.a4offenders.org.uk
Unlock (National Association of Ex-Offenders)
01634 247350
www.unlockprison.org.uk
Women in Prison
020 7226 5879
www.womeninprison.org.uk

Prisons for men

Acklington
01670 762300
Albany
01983 556300
Altcourse*
0151 522 2000
Ashfield*
0117 303 8000
Juvenile, under 18
Ashwell
01572 774100
Aylesbury
01296 444000
Young offenders, closed
Bedford
01234 373000
Belmarsh
020 8331 4400
High security
Birmingham
0121 345 2500
Blakenhurst
01527 400500
Blantyre House
01580 213200
Blundeston
01502 734500
Brinsford
01902 532450
Young offenders, closed
Bristol
0117 372 3100
Brixton
020 8588 6000
Brockhill
01527 552650
Buckley Hall
01706 514300
Bullingdon
01869 353100
Camp Hill
01983 554600
Canterbury
01227 862800
Cardiff
029 2043 3100
Castington
01670 382100
Young offenders, closed
Channings Wood
01803 814600
Chelmsford
01245 272000
Coldingley
01483 804300
Dartmoor
01822 892000
Deerbolt
01833 633200
Young offenders, closed
Doncaster*
01302 760870
Dorchester
01305 214500
Dovegate*
01283 829400
Downview
020 8929 3300
Durham
0191 332 3400
High security
Elmley
01795 882000
Erlestoke
01380 814400
Everthorpe
01430 426500
Featherstone
01902 703000
Feltham
020 8844 5000
Young offenders, closed
Ford
01903 663000
Forest Bank*
0161 925 7000
Foston Hall
01283 584300
Frankland
0191 332 3000
High security
Full Sutton
01759 375100
High security
Garth
01772 443300
Gartree
01858 436600
Glen Parva
0116 264 3100
Young offenders, closed
Gloucester
01452 453000
Grendon
01296 443000
Guys Marsh
01747 856400
Young offenders, closed
Haverigg
01229 713000
Hewell Grange
01527 552000
High Down
020 8722 6300
Highpoint
01440 823100
Hindley
01942 855000
Prisoners serving under two years
Hollesley Bay
01394 412400
Young offenders, closed
Holme House
01642 744000
Hull
01482 282200
Huntercombe
01491 643100
Young offenders, closed
Kingston
023 9289 1100
Kirkham
01772 675400

** Private prisons*

Kirklevington Grange
01642 792600
A resettlement prison
Lancaster Farms
01524 563450
Latchmere House
020 8588 6650
Leeds
0113 203 2600
Leicester
0116 228 3000
Lewes
01273 405100
Leyhill
01454 264000
Lincoln
01522 663000
Lindholme
01302 848800
Littlehey
01480 333000
Liverpool
0151 530 4000
Long Lartin
01386 835100
High security
Lowdham Grange*
0115 966 9200
Maidstone
01622 775300
Manchester
0161 817 5600
High security
Moorland
01302 523000
Morton Hall
01522 866700
The Mount
01442 836300
Northallerton
01609 785100
Prisoners serving under two years
North Sea Camp
01205 769300
Norwich
01603 708600
Young offenders, closed
Nottingham
0115 872 3000
Onley
01788 523400
Young offenders, closed
Parc*
01656 300200
Parkhurst
01983 554000
Pentonville
020 7023 7000
Portland
01305 825600
Prescoed
01291 675000
Preston
01772 444550
Ranby
01777 862000
Reading
0118 908 5000
Rochester
01634 838100

Rye Hill*
01788 523300
Young offenders, closed
Shepton Mallett
01749 823300
Shrewsbury
01743 273000
Send
01483 471000
Stafford
01785 254421
Standford Hill
01795 884500
Stocken
01780 485100
Stoke Heath
01630 636000
Sudbury
01283 584000
Swaleside
01795 884100
Swansea
01792 485300
Swinfen Hall
01543 484000
Young offenders, open
Thorn Cross
01925 605100
Young offenders, closed
Usk
01291 671600
The Verne
01305 825000
Wakefield
01924 246000
High security
Wandsworth
020 8588 4000
Warren Hill
01394 412400
Wayland
01953 858100
Wealstun
01937 848500
The Weare
01305 825400
Wellingborough
01933 232700
Werrington
01782 463300
Juvenile, under 18
Wetherby
01937 544200
Young offenders, closed
Whatton
01949 859200
Whitemoor
01354 602350
High security
Winchester
01962 723000
Wolds*
01430 421588
Woodhill
01908 722000
High security
Wormwood Scrubs
020 8588 3200
Wymott
01772 444000

Prisons for women

Askham Grange
01904 772000
Bronzefield*
enquiries@ukds.co.uk
Bullwood Hall
01702 562800
Cookham Wood
01634 202500
Drake Hall
01785 858100
Young offenders, open
East Sutton Park
01622 845000
Eastwood Park
01454 382100
Edmunds Hill
01440 823100
Exeter
01392 415800
Holloway
020 7979 4400
Low Newton
0191 376 4000
New Hall
01924 844200
Young offenders, closed
Risley
01925 733000
Styal
01625 553000

Prisons in Scotland

Aberdeen
01224 238300
Men and women
Barlinnie
0141 7702000
Castle Huntly
01382 319333
Men, employment training and transitional/through-care
Cornton Vale
01786 832591
Women and young offenders
Dumfries
01387 261218
Men and women
Edinburgh
0131 444 3000
Glenochil
01259 760471
Greenock
01475 787801
Inverness
01463 229000
Men and women
Kilmarnock*
01563 548800
Low Moss
0141 7624848
Noranside
01382 319333
Men, employment training and transitional/through-care

Perth
01738 622293
Peterhead
01779 479101
A dedicated facility for the location and treatment of men convicted of sexual offences who are sentenced to 4 years or more
Polmont
01324 711558
Young offenders
Shotts
01501 824000
High security

Prisons in Northern Ireland

Hydebank Wood
028 9025 3666
Young offenders, men and women
Maghaberry
028 9261 1888
High security and immigration detainees
Magilligan
028 7776 3311
Medium security

Immigration removal centres

Dover
01304 246400
Haslar
023 9260 4000

* *Private prisons*

Religion

Inter Faith Network for the UK
020 7931 7766
www.interfaith.co.uk

Anglicanism

Anglican Communion
020 7313 3900
www.anglicancommunion.org
Archbishop of Canterbury
020 7898 1200
www.archbishopofcanterbury.org
Archbishop of York
01904 707021
www.bishopthorpepalace.co.uk/archbishop
Church in Wales
029 2034 8200
www.churchinwales.org.uk
Church of England
020 7898 1000
www.cofe.anglican.org
Church of Ireland
00 353 1 497 8422
www.ireland.anglican.org
Record Centre
020 7898 1400
www.lambethpalacelibrary.org
Scottish Episcopal Church
0131 225 6357
www.scotland.anglican.org

Catholicism

Catholic Church
020 7233 8196
www.catholic-ew.org.uk
Media Office: 020 7901 4800
Provinces/ Archbishops
Armagh 028 3752 2045
Birmingham 0121 236 5535
Edinburgh 0131 452 8244
Glasgow 0141 226 5898
Cardiff 029 2022 0411
Liverpool 0151 522 1000
Southwark 020 7928 5592
Westminster 020 7798 9055
Catholic Enquiry Office
020 8458 3316
www.life4seekers.co.uk
Information about Catholic life and beliefs

Other Christian

Baptist Union
01235 517700
www.baptist.org.uk
Church of Christ, Scientist
020 7371 0600
www.themotherchurch.org
Church of Jesus Christ of Latter Day Saints (Mormons)
0121 712 1200
www.lds.org
Church of Scotland
0131 657 2000
www.churchofscotland.org.uk
Churches Together in Britain & Ireland
020 7654 7254
www.ctbi.org.uk
Congressional Federation
0115 911 1460
www.congregational.org.uk
Council of Churches for Britain
020 7654 7254
www.interchurchfamilies.org
Eastern Orthodox Churches
Greek: 020 7723 4787
Russian: 020 7584 0096
www.eastern-christian-churches.net
Free Church Federal Council
020 7387 8413
www.churches-together.org.uk
Free Church of England
020 7387 2564
www.fcofe.freeserve.co.uk
Free Presbyterian Church of Scotland
0131 229 0649
www.fpchurch.org.uk
Independent Methodist Churches
01942 223526
www.fimc.org.uk
International Churches of Christ
020 7247 6480
www.icoc.org.uk
Jehovah's Witnesses
020 8906 2211
www.watchtower.org
Jesus Army
0845 123 5550
www.jesusarmy.org.uk
Lutheran Council of GB
020 7554 2900
www.lutheran.org.uk
Methodist Church
020 7486 5502
www.methodist.org.uk
Moravian Church
020 8883 3409
www.moravian.org.uk
New Testament Church of God
01604 643311
www.ntcg.org.uk
Pentecostal Assemblies of God
0115 921 7272
www.aog.org.uk
Presbyterian Church in Ireland
028 9032 2284
www.presbyterianireland.org
Presbyterian Church of Wales
029 2062 7465
www.ebcpcw.org.uk
Quakers
020 7663 1000
www.quaker.org.uk
Salvation Army
020 7332 0101
www.salvationarmy.org
Seventh Day Adventist Church
01923 672251
www.adventist.org
Unification Church
020 7223 0721
www.unification.org
Unitarian Churches
020 7240 2384
www.unitarian.org.uk
United Free Church of Scotland
0141 332 3435
www.ufcos.org.uk
United Reform Church
020 7916 2020
www.urc.org.uk
World Council of Churches
00 41 22 791 6111
www.wcc-coe.org

Buddhism

BuddhaNet
support@buddhanet.net
www.buddhanet.net
Buddhist Centre London
020 7916 2282
www.buddhismlondon.demon.co.uk
The Buddha Vihara
020 8470 1879
www.buddha-vihara.org.uk
The Buddhist Society
020 7834 5858
www.thebuddhistsociety.org.uk
Cardiff Buddhist Centre
029 2046 2492
www.cardiffbuddhistcentre.com
Edinburgh Buddhist Centre
0131 228 3333
www.edinburghbuddhistcentre.org.uk
Friends of the Western Buddhist Order
020 8981 1225
www.fwbo.org
Network of Buddhist Organisations
0845 345 8978
www.nbo.org.uk
Potala Buddhist Centre, Belfast
028 9023 8090
www.potalacentre.org.uk
Society Krishna Consciousness
01923 857244
www.iskcon.org.uk

Islam

Islamic Centre of England
020-7604 5500
www.ic-el.org

Islamic Cultural Centre
020 7724 3363
www.islamicculturalcentre.co.uk

Islamic Digest
id5@islamicdigest.net
www.islamicdigest.org

Muslim Council of Britain
020 8432 0585
www.mcb.org.uk

Muslim Directory
020 8799 4455
www.muslimdirectory.co.uk

Hinduism

Hindu Centre, London
020 7485 8200

Hindunet
hsc@hindunet.org
www.hindunet.org

Hindu Links
www.hindulinks.org

Judaism

Board of Deputies of British Jews
020 7543 5400
www.bod.org.uk

Jewish Network
07974 439668
www.jewish.co.uk

Reform Synagogue
020 8349 4731
www.refsyn.org.uk

United Synagogue
020 8343 8989
www.unitedsynagogue.org.uk

Sikhism

Sikh Missionary Society
020 8574 1902
www.sikhs.org

Sikhnet
mail@khalsa.com
www.sikhnet.com

Sikh Women's Network
www.Sikhwomen.com

Spiritualism and paganism

Aetherius Society
020 7736 4187
www.aetherius.org

British Druid Order
sparrowhawk@britishdruidorder.co.uk
www.druidorder.demon.co.uk

Order of Bards, Ovates & Druids
01273 470 888
www.druidry.org

Pagan Federation
01295 277244
www.paganfed.org

PaganLink
www.paganlink.org

Satanism
HPNadramia@churchofsatan.com
www.churchofsatan.com

Spiritualist Association of Great Britain
020 7235 3351
www.spiritualuk.com

Spiritualists' National Union
01279 816 363
www.snu.org.uk

Theosophical Society
020 7935 9261
www.thesociety.org

Transcendental Meditation
0870 514 3733
www.transcendental-meditation.org.uk.

Other religions

Church of Scientology
01342 318229
www.scientology.org

Baha'i Community of UK
020 7584 2566
www.bahai.org.uk

Jainism
vinod@jainworld.com
www.jainworld.com

World Zoroastrian Organisation
President@w-z-o.org
www.w-z-o.org

Humanism and atheism

Association of Irish Humanists
00 353 12869870
www.irish-humanists.org

British Humanist Assoc
020 7079 3580
www.humanism.org.uk

Gay and Lesbian Humanist Association
019268 58450
www.galha.freeserve.co.uk/galha.htm

International Humanist and Ethical Union
020 7831 4816
www.iheu.org

National Secular Society
020 7404 3126
www.secularism.org.uk

Rationalist Press Association
020 7436 1151
www.rationalist.org.uk

South Place Ethical Society
020 7242 8037
www.ethicalsoc.org.uk

Society

Key contact

Institute of Fundraising
020 7627 3436
www.institute-of-fundraising.org.uk

Government departments

Deputy Prime Minister
020 7944 4400
Press: 020 7944 4651
www.odpm.gov.uk
Health
020 7210 4850
Press: 020 7210 5231
www.doh.gov.uk
Home Office
0870 0001585
Press: 020 7273 4545
www.homeoffice.gov.uk
Work and Pensions
020 7238 0800
Press: 020 7238 0866
www.dwp.gov.uk

Government agencies

British Council
Info: 0161 957 7755
Switchboard: 020 7930 8466
www.britcoun.org
Charity Commission
0870 333 0123
Press: 020 7674 2322
www.charity-commission.gov.uk
Children and Family Court Advisory Service
020 7510 8776 (after September 28 2004)
www.cafcass.gov.uk
Child Support Agency
Helpline: 08457 133133
Press: 020 7238 0866
www.csa.gov.uk
Commission for Racial Equality (CRE)
020 7939 0000
www.cre.gov.uk
Connexions
0808 001 3219
www.connexions.gov.uk
Advice and support for 13–19 year olds
Housing Corporation
020 7393 2000
www.housingcorp.gov.uk
Funding and regulation of housing associations
Immigration and Nationality Directorate
0870 606 7766
www.ind.homeoffice.gov.uk
Office of the Immigration Services Commissioner
020 7211 1500
www.oisc.gov.uk

Major charities

Action for Blind People
020 7635 4800
www.afbp.org
ActionAid
020 7561 7561
www.actionaid.org
Age Concern England
020 8765 7200
www.ageconcern.org.uk
www.ace.org.uk/
Alzheimer's Society
020 7306 0606
www.alzheimers.org.uk
Arthritis Research Campaign
01246 558033
www.arc.org.uk
Association for International Cancer Research
01334 477910
www.aicr.org.uk
Barnardo's
020 8550 8822
www.barnardos.org.uk
Battersea Dogs' & Cats' Home
020 7622 3626
www.dogshome.org
BBC Children in Need Appeal
020 8576 7788
www.bbc.co.uk/pudsey
www.firstpages.com/CIN/WR
Benenden Hospital Trust
01580 240333
Birmingham Diocesan Trust
0121 236 5535
Blue Cross (Incorporating Our Dumb Friends' League)
020 7932 2370
www.bluecross.org.uk
British and Foreign Bible Society
01793 418100
www.biblesociety.org.uk
British Heart Foundation
020 7935 0185
www.bhf.org.uk
British Red Cross Society
020 7235 5454
www.redcross.org.uk
British Tennis Foundation
020 7381 7140
www.lta.org.uk
Cambridge Foundation
01223 332288
www.cam.ac.uk
Cancer Research UK
020 7242 0200
www.cancerresearchuk.org
Catholic Agency for Overseas Development
020 7733 7900
www.cafod.org.uk
Cats Protection
0870 209 9099
www.cats.org.uk
ChildLine
020 7650 3200
www.childline.org.uk
Children with Leukaemia Foundation
020 7404 0808
www.leukaemia.org
Children's Society
020 7841 4400
www.childrenssociety.org.uk
Choice Support
020 8693 6088
www.choicesupport.co.uk
Christian Aid
020 7620 4444
www.christianaid.org.uk
Christian Vision
0121 522 6087
www.christianvision.com
Christie Hospital Charitable Fund
0161 446 3000
Church of Jesus Christ of Latter Day Saints Great Britain
0121 712 1248
Church of Scotland Unincorporated Boards and Committees
0131 225 5722
Comic Relief
020 7820 5555
www.comicrelief.com
Community Integrated Care
0151 420 3637
www.c-i-c.co.uk
Concern Worldwide
00 353 1475 4162
www.concern.net
Diabetes UK
020 7424 1000
www.diabetes.org.uk
Disasters Emergency Committee
020 7387 0200
www.dec.org.uk
Dogs Trust
020 7837 0006
www.dogstrust.org.uk
Donkey Sanctuary
01395 578222
www.thedonkeysanctuary.org.uk
Fremantle Trust
01296 393055
www.fremantletrust.org
Great Ormond Street Hospital Children's Charity
020 7916 5678
www.gosh.org
Guide Dogs for the Blind Association
0118 983 5555
www.gdba.org.uk;
www.guidedogs.org.uk
Help the Aged
020 7278 1114
www.helptheaged.org.uk
International Planned Parenthood Federation
020 7487 7900
www.ippf.org

Islamic Relief
0121 605 5555
www.islamic-relief.org.uk
Jewish Care
020 8922 2000
www.jewishcare.org
Leonard Cheshire
020 7802 8200
www.leonard-cheshire.org
Leukaemia Research Fund
020 7405 0101
www.lrf.org.uk
www.leukaemia-research.org.uk
Liverpool Roman Catholic Archdiocesan Trust
0151 522 1020
Macmillan Cancer Relief
020 7840 7840
www.macmillan.org.uk
Marie Curie Cancer Care
020 7599 7729
www.mariecurie.org.uk
Mencap
020 7454 0454
www.mencap.org.uk
MIND (The National Association for Mental Health)
020 8519 2122
www.mind.org.uk
Motability
01279 635999
www.motability.co.uk
Multiple Sclerosis Society
020 8438 0700
www.mssociety.org.uk
National Asthma Campaign
020 7226 2260
www.asthma.org.uk
National Council of YMCAs
020 8520 5599
www.ymca.org.uk
National Galleries of Scotland
0131 624 6200
www.nationalgalleries.org;
www.natgalscot.ac.uk
National Missing Persons Helpline
Press: 020 8392 4510
www.missingpersons.org
National Museum of Science and Industry
0870 870 4868
www.nmsi.ac.uk
National Society for the Prevention of Cruelty to Children NSPCC
020 7825 2500
www.nspcc.org.uk
National Trust
020 7222 9251
www.nationaltrust.org.uk
National Trust for Scotland
0131 243 9300
www.nts.org.uk
NCH
020 7704 7000
www.nch.org.uk
Oxfam
01865 311311
www.oxfam.org.uk
Parkinson's Disease Society of the United Kingdom
020 7931 8080
www.parkinsons.org.uk
PDSA
01952 290999
www.pdsa.org.uk
Plan International (UK)
020 7482 9777
www.plan-uk.org
Portsmouth Roman Catholic Diocesan Trustees Registered
023 9282 5430
Prince's Trust
020 7543 1234
www.princes-trust.org.uk
Rank [Arthur] Centre Addington Fund
024 7685 8207
RNIB – Royal National Institute of the Blind
020 7388 1266
www.rnib.org.uk
RNID
020 7296 8000
www.rnid.org.uk
Roman Catholic Diocese of Hexham & Newcastle
0191 243 3300
www.st-vincents.com
Roman Catholic Diocese of Southwark
020 7928 5767
Royal British Legion
020 7973 7200
www.britishlegion.org.uk
www.poppy.org.uk
Royal Horticultural Society
020 7821 3039
www.rhs.org.uk
Royal Marsden Hospital Charity
020 7352 8171
www.royalmarsden.org
Royal National Lifeboat Institution RNLI
01202 663000
www.lifeboats.org.uk;
www.rnli.org.uk
Royal Society for the Prevention of Cruelty to Animals RSPCA
0870 010 1181
www.rspca.org.uk
Royal Society for the Protection of Birds RSPB
01767 680551
www.rspb.org.uk
Salford Diocesan Trust
0161 736 1421
Salvation Army Trust
020 7367 4783
www.salvationarmy.org.uk
Samaritan's Purse International
020 8559 2044
www.samaritanspurse.org.uk
Save the Children (UK)
020 7703 5400
www.savethechildren.org.uk
Scope
020 7619 7100
www.scope.org.uk
Sense – National Deafblind and Rubella Association
020 7272 7774
www.sense.org.uk
Sheffield City Trust
0114 276 7777
Shelter
020 7505 2000
www.shelter.org.uk
Sight Savers International
01444 446600
www.sightsavers.org
St John Ambulance
020 7324 4000
www.sja.org.uk
Stroke Association
020 7566 0300
www.stroke.org.uk
Tate
020 7887 8000
www.tate.org.uk
Tearfund
020 8977 9144
www.tearfund.org
Unicef
020 7405 5592
www.unicef.org.uk
United Jewish Israel Appeal
020 8369 5000
www.ujia.org
United Kingdom Evangelization Trust
020 8502 5600
www.stewardshipservices.org
Victoria and Albert Museum
020 7942 2000
www.vam.ac.uk
Watch Tower Bible and Tract Society of Britain
020 8906 2211
WaterAid
020 7793 4500
www.wateraid.org
Westminster Roman Catholic Diocesan Trust
020 7798 9036
World Emergency Relief
0870 429 2129
www.wer-uk.org
World Vision UK
01908 841000
www.worldvision.org.uk
WWF UK
01483 426444
www.wwf.org.uk

Other charities and campaign groups

Children

Acorns Children's Hospice Trust
0121 248 4815
www.acorns.org.uk
Adoption and Fostering Information Line
www.adoption.org.uk
Anna Freud Centre
020 7794 2313
www.annafreudcentre.org
Psychoanalysis for children
Barnardo's
020 8550 8822
www.barnardos.org.uk
BBC Children in Need
020 8576 7788
www.bbc.co.uk/cin

Bliss
0870 770 0337
www.bliss.org.uk
National charity for premature or sick babies

Care and Relief For The Young
01489 788300
www.cry.org.uk

Child Concern
0161 832 8113
www.childconcern.org.uk

ChildHope
020 7833 0868
www.childhopeuk.org
Defending street children worldwide

ChildLine
020 7650 3240
www.childline.org.uk

Children and Armed Conflict Unit
01206 873483
www.essex.ac.uk/armedcon

Children with Leukaemia Foundation
020 7404 0808
www.leukaemia.org
top 100

Children's Society
0845 300 1128
www.childrenssociety.org.uk

Coram Family
020 7520 0300
www.coram.org.uk
Working with vulnerable children

End Child Poverty
020 7843 1913
www.ecpc.org.uk

EveryChild
020 7729 8191
www.everychild.org.uk

Foyle Foundation
020 7430 9119
www.foylefoundation.org.uk

Girlguiding UK
020 7834 6242
www.girlguiding.org.uk

Great Ormond Street Hospital Children's Charity
020 7916 5678
www.gosh.org

Hope
01442 234561
www.hope-for-children.org
International charity for handicapped, orphaned, poor and exploited children

Hope and Homes for Children
01722 790111
www.hopeandhomes.org

Hyperactive Children's Support Group
01243 551313
www.hacsg.org.uk

International Planned Parenthood Federation
020 7487 7900
www.ippf.org

Kids Clubs Network
0870 770 2498
www.4children.org.uk

National Children's Bureau
020 7843 6000
www.ncb.org.uk

National Youth Agency
0116 285 3700
www.nya.org.uk

NCH
020 7704 7000
www.nch.org.uk

NSPCC
020 7825 2500
www.nspcc.org.uk

Plan International (UK)
020 7482 9777
www.plan-uk.org
top 100

Prince's Trust
020 7543 1234
www.princes-trust.org.uk

Relate
press: 0845 456 1210
www.relate.org.uk
Relationship Guidance

Ride Foundation
01372 467708
www.ridefoundation.org.uk
Drug awareness, life skills and citizenship programmes for schools

Sargent Cancer Care for Children
020 8752 2800
www.sargent.org

Save the Children
020 7703 5400
www.savethechildren.org.uk

Second Chance
023 9287 2790
www.second-chance.org.uk
Camping and fishing for disavantaged children

Task Brazil
020 7394 1177
www.taskbrasil.org.uk
UK charity for street children in Brazil

The Site
020 7226 8008
Press:: 020 7288 7309
www.thesite.org.uk
Advice and help for young people

Trident Trust
020 7014 1400
www.thetridenttrust.org.uk

Unicef
020 7405 5592
www.unicef.org.uk

United Kingdom Missing Children
www.missingkids.co.uk

Variety Club Children's Charity
020 7428 8100
www.varietyclub.org.uk

War Child UK
020 7916 9276
www.warchild.org.uk

Whizz Kidz
020 7233 6600
www.whizz-kidz.org.uk

World Villages for Children
020 7629 3050
www.worldvillages.org

Young Enterprise
01865 776845
www.young-enterprise.org.uk

Women

The 300 Group
01403 733797
www.300group.org.uk

Abortion Rights
020 7278 5539
www.abortionrights.org.uk

Breast Cancer Campaign
020 7749 3700
www.bcc-uk.org

Breast Cancer Care
020 7384 2984
www.breastcancercare.org.uk

British Association of Women Entrepreneurs
020 7935 0085
www.bawe-uk.org

Campaign Against Domestic Violence
020 8520 5881
www.cadv.org.uk

Child and Woman Abuse Studies Unit
020 7133 5014
www.cwasu.org

Emily's List
contact@emilyslist.org.uk
www.emilyslist.org.uk
Campaign for Labour women MPs

European Women's Lobby
00 32 2 217 9020
www.womenlobby.org

Everywoman
0870 746 1800
www.everywoman.co.uk

FEM Vision
0118 973 2291
www.femvision.org

The Fawcett Society
020 7253 2598
www.fawcettsociety.org.uk

Feminist Library
020 7928 7789

Justice for Women
0113 262 0293
www.jfw.org.uk

League of Jewish Women
020 7242 8300
www.leagueofjewishwomen.org.uk

Marie Stopes International
020 7574 7400
www.mariestopes.org.uk

Meet A Mum Association
01525 217064
www.mama.org.uk

National Association for Premenstrual Syndrome
0870 777 2178
www.pms.org.uk

National Council of Women
020 7354 2395
www.ncwgb.org

National Federation of Women's Institutes
020 7371 9300
www.womens-institute.co.uk

Older Feminist Network
020 8346 1900
www.ofn.org.uk

Rights of Women
020 7251 6575
www.row.org.uk
Scottish Women's Aid
0131 475 2372
www.scottishwomensaid.co.uk
Single Parent Action Network
0117 951 4231
www.spanuk.org.uk
Suzy Lamplugh Trust
020 8876 0305
www.suzylamplugh.org
Womankind Worldwide
020 7549 5700
www.womankind.org.uk
Women and Manual Trades
020 7251 9192
www.wamt.org
Women Connect
020 7226 5375
www.womenconnect.org.uk
Women's Aid
0800 800034
www.womensaid.org.uk
Women's Aid, Ireland
028 2563 9301
www.womens-aid.org.uk
The Women's Library
020 7320 2222
www.thewomenslibrary.ac.uk
Women's Link
020 7248 1200
www.womenslink.org.uk
Women's National Commission
020 7276 2555
www.thewnc.org.uk
YWCA (London)
01865 304200
www.ywca-gb.org.uk

Citizenship

Association for Citizenship Teaching
020 7367 0510
www.teachingcitizenship.org.uk
Information and direct action across a number of areas
Citizenship Foundation
020 7367 0518
www.citizenshipfoundation.org.uk
Time for Citizenship
www.timeforcitizenship.com

Community

Anchor Trust
020 7759 9100
Press:: 020 7759 9104
www.anchor.org.uk
Army Benevolent Fund
020 7591 2000
www.armybenfund.org
Business in the Community
0870 600 2482
www.bitc.org.uk
Changemakers
01458 834767
www.changemakers.org.uk
Citizens Advice Bureaux
020 7833 2181
www.nacab.org.uk
Civil Service Benevolent Fund
020 8240 2400
www.csbf.org.uk
Coalfields Regeneration Trust
01709 760272
www.coalfields-regen.org.uk
Commonwealth Ex-Services League
020 7973 7200
Communities that Care
020 7619 0123
www.communitiesthatcare.org.uk
Community Development Foundation
020 7226 5375
www.cdf.org.uk
Community Foundation
0191 222 0945
www.communityfoundation.org.uk
Serving Tyne & Wear and Northumberland
Community Integrated Care
0151 420 3637
www.c-i-c.co.uk
Community Service Volunteers
020 7278 6601
www.csv.org.uk
Directory of Social Change
020 7391 4800
www.dsc.org.uk
Duke of Edinburgh's Award
01753 727400
www.theaward.org
Erskine Hospital
0141 812 1100
www.erskine.org.uk
For ex-servicemen
Groundwork
0121 236 8565
www.groundwork.org.uk
Community improvement schemes in rundown areas
Gurkha Welfare Trust
020 7251 5234
www.gwt.org.uk
JustdoSomething
020 7608 8123
www.justdosomething.net
Nacro
020 7582 6500
www.nacro.org.uk
Crime reduction charity
National Federation of Community Organisations
020 7837 7887
www.communitymatters.org.uk
Neighbourhood Renewal Unit
neighbourhoodrenewal@odpm.gsi.gov.uk
www.neighbourhood.gov.uk
Norwood Ravenswood Foundation
020 8420 6831
www.nwrw.org
Outward Bound Trust
020 7928 1991
www.outwardbound-uk.org
Police Rehabilitation Centre
01491 874499
www.flinthouse.co.uk
Prince's Trust
020 7543 1234
www.princes-trust.org.uk
Princess Royal Trust for Carers
0141 221 5066
www.carers.org
Quest Trust
01225 466307
www.quest-net.org
Raleigh International Trust
020 7371 8585
www.raleighinternational.org
Rathbone Community Industry
08707 461045
www.rathbonetraining.co.uk
Learning and training support for the disadvantaged
Royal Air Force Benevolent Fund
020 7580 8343
www.rafbf.org.uk
Royal Air Forces Association
0116 268 8770
www.rafa.org.uk
Royal British Legion
020 7973 7200
www.britishlegion.org.uk;
www.poppy.org.uk
Samaritans
020 8394 8300
www.samaritans.org
Scottish Community Foundation
0131 524 0300
www.scottishcommunityfoundation.com
Soldiers, Sailors, Airmen and Families Association – Forces Help
020 7403 8783
www.ssafa.org.uk
Sue Ryder Care
020 7400 0440
www.suerydercare.org
National volunteering campaign for community welfare
Time Bank
020 7401 5420
www.timebank.org.uk
Victim Support
020 7735 9166
www.victimsupport.org
Voluntary Service Overseas
020 8780 7200
www.vso.org.uk

Disability

Disability Rights Commission
0845 762 2633
www.drc-gb.org
Independent body established by statute
Action for Blind People
020 7635 4800
www.afbp.org
Afasic
020 7490 9410
www.afasic.org.uk
For children and young adults with communication impairments
British Wheelchair Sports Foundation
01296 395995
www.britishwheelchairsports.org

Christian Blind Mission
01223 426161
www.cbmuk.org.uk
Council for Disabled Children
020 7843 6000
www.ncb.org.uk
Dogs For the Disabled
01295 252600
www.dogsforthedisabled.org
Elizabeth Foundation for Pre-School Deaf Children
023 9237 2735
www.elizabeth-foundation.org
Employment Opportunities for People with Disabilities
020 7448 5420
www.opportunities.org.uk
emPower
020 8788 1777
www.empowernet.org/empower
Aiming to influence policy on disability equipment services
First Asian Support Trust
0161 740 3399
www.fast-uk.org
Support for Asians with disabilities
Guide Dogs for the Blind
0870 600 2323
www.gdba.org.uk
Leonard Cheshire
020 7802 8200
www.leonard-cheshire.org
Creating opportunities with disabled people
Mencap
020 7454 0454
www.mencap.org.uk
Motability
01279 635999
www.motability.co.uk
top 100
National Autistic Society
020 7833 2299
www.nas.org.uk
National Deaf Children's Society
020 7490 8656
www.ndcs.org.uk
Northern Counties School for the Deaf
0191 281 5821
www.northern-counties-school.co.uk
Physically Handicapped and Able Bodied Children
020 8667 9443
www.phabengland.org.uk
Riding for the Disabled
0845 658 1082
www.riding-for-disabled.org.uk
RNIB – Royal National Institute of the Blind
020 7388 1266
www.rnib.org.uk
top 100
RNID
020 7296 8000
www.rnid.org.uk
Institute for the deaf
Royal Hospital for Neuro-disability
020 8780 4500
www.rhn.org.uk
Royal London Society for the Blind
01732 592500
www.rlsb.org.uk
Royal Star and Garter Home
020 8940 3314
www.starandgarter.org
Scope
020 7619 7100
www.scope.org.uk
top 100
Sense – National Deafblind and Rubella Association
020 7272 7774
www.sense.org.uk
top 100
Sight Savers International
01444 446600
www.sightsavers.org
top 100
St Dunstan's
020 7723 5021
www.st-dunstans.org.uk
The Shaw Trust
01225 716350
www.shaw-trust.org.uk
Provides training and work opportunities
United Response
020 8246 5200
www.united-response.co.uk
Support for those with learning difficulties and mental health problems
West Midlands Special Needs Transport
0121 333 3107
www.ringandride.org.uk
Westminster Society for Mentally Handicapped Children and Adults
020 8968 7376
www.wspld.org.uk
World Vision UK
01908 841000
www.worldvision.org.uk
top 100

Asylum and refugees

Asylum Aid
020 7377 5123
www.asylumaid.org.uk
Immigration Advisory Service
020 7967 1200
www.iasuk.org
Immigration Law Practitioners' Association
020 7251 8383
www.ilpa.org.uk
Joint Council for the Welfare of Immigrants
020 7251 8708
www.jcwi.org.uk
Human rights for immigrants & asylum seekers in UK
Migration Research Unit
020 7679 7569
www.geog.ucl.ac.uk/mru
Refugee Action
020 7654 7700
www.refugee-action.org.uk
Refugee Council
020 7346 6700
www.refugeecouncil.org.uk
Scottish Asylum Seekers Consortium
0141 248 2396
www.asylumscotland.org.uk
Scottish Refugee Council
0141 248 9799
www.scottishrefugeecouncil.org.uk

Diversity

Equal Opportunities Commission
0845 601 5901
www.eoc.org.uk

RACE

1990 Trust
020 7582 1990
www.blink.org.uk
Black community organisation
Black Enterprise
020 7498 5656
www.blackenterprise.co.uk
Ethnic Minority Foundation
020 8432 0307
www.emf-cemvo.co.uk

AGE

Age Concern England
020 8765 7200
www.ageconcern.org.uk
Help the Aged
020 7278 1114
www.helptheaged.org.uk
Age Positive
www.agepositive.gov.uk/
Age diversity in employment

SEXUALITY

Armed Forces Lesbian and Gay Association
0870 740 7755
www.aflaga.org.uk
Beyond Barriers
0141 574 0242
www.beyondbarriers.org.uk
Gay and Lesbian Association of Doctors and Dentists
0870 765 5606
www.gladd.org.uk
Lesbian and Gay Christian Movement
020 7739 1249
www.lgcm.org.uk
Lesbian and Gay Employment Rights
gay: 020 7704 6066
lesbian: 020 7704 8066
www.lager.dircon.co.uk
Lesbian and Gay Foundation
0161 235 8035
www.lgf.org.uk

Metro Centre
020 8265 3311
www.themetro.dircon.co.uk
Services for people questioning their sexuality

Outrage
020 8240 0222
http://outrage.nabumedia.com
Direct action for gay rights

Out-Side-In
osiuk@hotmail.com
www.users.globalnet.co.uk/~quequeg/osi.html
Support for gay prisoners

Queerspace
info@queerspace.org.uk
www.queerspace.org.uk
Northern Ireland

Stonewall
020 7881 9440
www.stonewall.org.uk

The Gay Vote
www.thegayvote.co.uk

UK Lesbian and Gay Immigration Group
0870 606 7766
www.uklgig.org.uk

▸▸ DIVERSITY IN THE MEDIA, page xx

Housing

Broadway
020 7089 9500
www.broadwaylondon.org
Working to house the homeless

Centrepoint
020 7426 5300
www.centrepoint.org.uk
Agency for young homeless

Chartered Institute of Housing
020 7837 4280
www.cih.org
Promoting high standards in housing provision

Connection at St Martin's
020 7766 5555
www.connection-at-stmartins.org.uk
Facilities for London's homeless

Crash
020 8742 0717
www.crash.org.uk
Construction and property industry homeless charity

Crisis
0870 011 3335
www.crisis.org.uk
Homeless charity

Defend Council Housing
020 7987 9989
www.defendcouncilhousing.org.uk

Empty Homes Agency
020 7828 6288
www.emptyhomes.com

FEANTSA
office@feantsa.org
www.feantsa.org
European federation of homeless organisations

Foyer Federation
020 7430 2212
www.foyer.net
Accommodation and opportunities for the young

Groundswell
020 7737 5500
www.groundswell.org.uk
Support projects for the homeless

Homeless Link
020 7960 3010
www.homeless.org.uk
UK membership network for homeless agencies

Homes for Homeless People
01582 481426
www.homeline.dircon.co.uk

Housing Quality Network
01723 350099
www.hqnetwork.org.uk
Aims to improve quality of housing services

Joseph Rowntree Foundation
01904 629241
www.jrf.org.uk
Policy research and action on housing and social care

National Housing Federation
020 7067 1010
www.housing.org.uk
Representing the independent social housing sector

Paddington Churches Housing Association
020 8537 4141
www.pcha.org.uk
London housing association founded 1965

Peabody Trust
020 7021 4000
www.peabody.org.uk
London housing association

Room
020 7929 9494
www.room.org.uk
Forum for debate on housing and regeneration issues

Rural Housing Trust
020 7793 8114
www.ruralhousing.org.uk
Affordable housing in English villages

Shelter
020 7505 2000
www.shelter.org.uk

Thamesreach
020 7702 4260
Press:: 020 7702 5646
www.thamesreach.org.uk
London homeless charity

UK Co-Housing Network
coordinator@cohousing.co.uk
www.cohousing.co.uk
Network of resident-developed neighbourhoods

Society helplines

Afasic
0845 355 5577

Benefit Enquiry Line
0800 882200

Childline
0800 1111

Churches Child Protection Advisory Service
0845 120 4551

Deafblind UK
0800 132 320

Disability Alliance – Rights Advice Line
020 7247 8763

Disability Living Allowance
0845 712 3456

Elder Abuse Response line
0808 808 8141

Gamblers Anonymous
0870 050 8880

Gay Men's Employment Rights
020 7704 6066

Gingerbread Advice Line
0800 018 4318

Kidscape
0845 120 5204

Learning Disability Helpline
0808 808 1111

Lesbian Employment Rights
020 7704 8066

National Missing Persons Helpline
0500 700700

NSPCC National Child Protection Helpline
0808 800 5000

Parent Line
0808 800 2222

Refugee Helpline
0800 413 848

Relate
0845 130 4010

Runaway Helpline
0808 800 7070

Samaritans
08457 90 90 90

Saneline
0845 767 8000

Shelter London Line
0800 800444

Supportline for Survivors of Professional Abuse
0845 4 500 300

Victim Supportline
0845 303 0900

Welfare Foods Helpline
0800 056 2665

Winter Warmth Advice Line
0800 085 7000

Women's Aid National Domestic Violence Helpline
0845 702 3468

Sport

Government department

Department for Culture, Media and Sport
020 7211 6000
Press: 020 7211 6215
www.culture.gov.uk

Official bodies

UK Sport
020 7211 5100
Press: 020 7211 5106
www.uksport.gov.uk

Sport England
020 7273 1500; press 0870 5210 255
www.sportengland.org
Regional offices:
East 01234 345222
East Midlands 0115 982 1887
London 020 8778 8600
North 0191 384 9595
North-west 0161 834 0338
South-east 0118 948 3311
South-west 01460 73491
West Midlands 0121 456 3444
Yorkshire 0113 243 6443

Sport Scotland
0131 317 7200
www.sportscotland.org.uk
Glenmore lodge 01479 861256
Cumbrae 01475 530757
Inverclyde 01475 674 666

Sports Council for N Ireland
028 9038 1222
www.sportni.net

Sports Council for Wales
029 2030 0500
www.sports-council-wales.co.uk

Football

Governing bodies

FA
020 7745 4545
www.the-fa.org

FA Premier League
020 7298 1690
www.premierleague.com

Football League
0870 4420 1888
www.football-league.co.uk

Nationwide Conference
01322 411021
www.football.nationwide.co.uk

Irish Football Association
028 9066 9458
www.irishfa.com

Scottish Football Association
0141 616 6000
www.scottishfa.co.uk

Football Association of Wales
029 2037 2325
www.faw.org.uk

Women's Football Association
01707 651840
www.thefa.com/womensl

Scottish Women's Football Association
0141 353 1162
www.scottishfa.co.uk/affiliates

Uefa
00 4122 994 4444
www.uefa.com

Fifa
00 41222 7777
www.fifa.com

World Cup: Germany 2006
www.fifaworldcup.com
Deutsche Fussball-Bund (German FA)
00 49 69 67880
www.dfb.de

National stadiums

Millennium Stadium, Cardiff
0870 013 8600
www.millenniumstadium.com

Wembley Stadium
020 8795 9000
www.wembleystadium.com

Premiership 2004–05

Arsenal FC
020 7704 4000
www.arsenal.com

Aston Villa FC
0121 327 2299
www.avfc.co.uk

Birmingham FC
0121 772 0101
www.blues.premiumtv.co.uk

Blackburn Rovers FC
01254 691919
www.rovers.co.uk

Bolton Wanderers FC
01204 673673
www.bwfc.co.uk

Charlton AFC
020 8333 4000
www.cafc.co.uk

Chelsea FC
020 7385 5545
www.chelseafc.co.uk

Crystal Palace FC
020 8768 6000
www.cpfc.co.uk

Everton FC
0151 330 2307
www.evertonfc.com

Fulham FC
020 7893 8383
www.fulham-fc.co.uk

Liverpool FC
0151 330 2200
www.liverpoolfc.net

Manchester City FC
0161 224 5000
www.mcfc.co.uk

Manchester United FC
0161 868 8000
www.manutd.com

Middlesbrough FC
01642 877700
www.mfc.co.uk

Newcastle United FC
0191 201 8400
www.nufc.co.uk

Norwich City FC
01603 760 760
www.canaries.co.uk

Portsmouth FC
023 9261 8777
www.pompeyfc.co.uk

Southampton FC
0870 220 0000
www.saintsfc.co.uk

Tottenham Hotspur FC
020 8365 5000
www.spurs.co.uk

West Bromwich Albion FC
0121 525 4714
www.wba.co.uk

Coca-Cola Football League Championship

Brighton and Hove Albion FC
01273 695 400
www.seagulls.co.uk

Burnley FC
0870 443 1882
www.burnleyfootballclub.com

Cardiff City FC
029 20 221001
www.cardifffc.co.uk

Coventry City FC
024 762 34000
www.ccfc.co.uk

Crewe Alexandra FC
01270 213 014
www.crewealex.net

Derby County FC
01332 667 503
www.dcfc.co.uk

Gillingham FC
01634 851 854
www.gillinghamfootballclub.com

Ipswich Town FC
01473 400500
www.itfc.co.uk

Leeds United FC
0113 367 3000
www.lufc.co.uk

Leicester City FC
0116 291 5279
www.lcfc.co.uk

Millwall FC
020 723 21222
www.millwallfc.co.uk

Nottingham Forest FC
0115 982 4444
www.nottinghamforest.co.uk

Plymouth Argyle FC
01752 562561
www.pafc.co.uk

Preston North End FC
0870 442 1964
www.pnefc.net

Queens Park Rangers FC
020 8743 0262
www.qpr.co.uk

Reading FC
0118 968 1100
www.readingfc.co.uk

Rotherham FC
01709 512 434
www.themillers.co.uk

Sheffield United FC
0114 221 5757
www.sufc.co.uk

Stoke City FC
01782 592 222
www.stokecityfc.com

Sunderland FC
0191 551 5000
www.safc.com

Watford FC
01923 496000
www.watfordfc.com

West Ham United FC
020 8548 2748
www.whufc.co.uk

Wigan Athletic FC
01942 774000
www.wiganathletic.tv

Wolverhampton Wanderers FC
01902 655000
www.wolves.co.uk

Coca-Cola League One

AFC Bournemouth
01202 726300
www.afcb.co.uk

Barnsley FC
01226 211211
www.barnsleyfc.co.uk

Blackpool FC
0870 443 1953
www.blackpoolfc.co.uk

Bradford City FC
01274 773355
www.bradfordcityfc.co.uk

Brentford FC
0870 900 9229
www.brentfordfc.co.uk

Bristol City FC
0117 963 0630
www.bcfc.co.uk

Chesterfield FC
01246 209765
www.chesterfield-fc.co.uk

Colchester United FC
01206 508800
www.cu-fc.co.uk

Doncaster Rovers FC
01302 539441
www.doncasterroversfc.co.uk

Hartlepool United FC
01429 272584
www.hartlepoolunited.co.uk

Huddersfield Town FC
01484 484100
www.htafc.com

Hull City FC
0870 837 0003
www.hullcityafc.net

Luton Town FC
01582 411622
www.lutontown.co.uk

Milton Keynes Dons FC
01908 607090
www.mkdons.com

Oldham Athletic FC
0870 753 2000
www.oldhamathletic.co.uk

Peterborough United FC
01733 563947
www.theposh.com

Port Vale FC
01782 655800
www.port-vale.co.uk

Sheffield Wednesday FC
0114 221 2121
www.swfc.co.uk

Stockport County FC
0161 286 8888
www.stockportcounty.com

Swindon Town FC
01793 333700
www.swindontownfc.co.uk

Torquay United FC
01803 328666
www.torquayunited.com

Tranmere Rovers FC
0151 609 3333
www.tranmererovers.co.uk

Walsall FC
01922 622791
www.saddlers.co.uk

Wrexham AFC
01978 262129
www.wrexhamafc.co.uk

Coca-Cola League Two

Boston United FC
01205 364406
www.bostonunited.co.uk

Bristol Rovers FC
0117 909 6648
www.bristolrovers.co.uk

Bury FC
0161 764 4881
www.buryfc.co.uk

Cambridge United FC
01223 566500
www.cambridge-united.co.uk

Cheltenham Town FC
01242 573558
www.ctfc.com

Chester City FC
01244 371376
www.chestercityfc.net

Darlington FC
01325 387000
www.darlington-fc.net

Grimsby Town FC
01472 605050
www.gtfc.co.uk

Kidderminster Harriers FC
01562 823931
www.harriers.co.uk

Leyton Orient FC
020 8926 1111
www.leytonorient.net

Lincoln City FC
01522 880011
www.redimps.com

Macclesfield Town FC
01625 264686
www.mtfc.co.uk

Mansfield Town FC
0870 756 3160
www.mansfieldtown.net

Northampton Town FC
01604 757773
www.ntfc.co.uk

Notts County FC
0115 952 9000
www.nottscountyfc.co.uk

Oxford United FC
01865 537500
www.oufc.co.uk

Rochdale FC
01706 644648
www.rochdaleafc.co.uk

Rushden & Diamonds FC
01933 652000
www.thediamondsfc.com

Scunthorpe United FC
01724 747670
www.scunthorpe-united.co.uk

Shrewsbury Town FC
01743 360111
www.shrewsburytown.co.uk

Southend United FC
01702 304050
www.southendunited.co.uk

Swansea City FC
01792 633400
www.swanseacity.net
Wycombe Wanderers FC
01494 472100
www.wycombewanderers.co.uk
Yeovil Town FC
01935 423662
www.ytfc.net

Football: other bodies

Professional Footballers' Association
0161 236 0575
www.thepfa.co.uk
Referees Association
024 7660 1701
www.footballreferee.org
Football Supporters' Federation
01634 319461
www.fsf.org.uk
Let's Kick Racism Out of Football
020 7684 4884
racism hotline 0800 169 9414
www.kickitout.org
Show Racism the Red Card
0191 291 0160
www.srtrc.org

Olympics

International Olympic Committee
00 4121 621 6111
www.olympic.org
International Paralympic Committee
00 49 228 209 7200
www.paralympic.org
British Olympic Association
020 8871 2677
www.olympics.org.uk
British Paralympic Association
020 7662 8882
www.paralympics.org.uk

Other sports

AMERICAN FOOTBALL

British American Football Association
01661 843179
www.bafa.org

ANGLING

National Federation of Anglers
01283 734835
www.the-nfa.org.uk
National Federation of Sea Anglers
01364 644643
www.nfsa.org.uk
Salmon and Trout Association
020 7283 5838
www.salmon-trout.org.uk

ARCHERY

The Grand National Archery Society
01952 677888
www.gnas.org

ATHLETICS

International Association of Athletics Federations
00 377 9310 8888
www.iaaf.org
UK Athletics
0870 9986 800
www.ukathletics.org

BADMINTON

Badminton Association of England
01908 268400
www.baofe.co.uk
Welsh Badminton Union
029 2022 2082
www.welshbadminton.force9.co.uk
Scottish Badminton Union
0141 445 1218
www.scotbadminton.demon.co.uk
Ulster Branch Badminton Union of Ireland
028 9038 3810
www.badmintonireland.com

BALLOONING

British Balloon & Airship Club
0117 9531231
www.bbac.org

BASEBALL

British Baseball Federation
020 7453 7055
www.baseballsoftballuk.com

BASKETBALL

English Basketball Association
0870 7744225
www.basketballengland.org.uk
Basketball Association of Wales
029 2049 6696
www.hoopscymru.net
Basketball Scotland
0131 317 7260
www.basketball-scotland.com
Ulster Basketball Association
028 9064 8000
www.ulsterbasketball.com

BIATHLON

British Biathlon Union
01874 730562
www.britishbiathlon.com

BOBSLEIGH

British Bobsleigh Association
01225 826802
www.british-bobsleigh.com

BOWLING

English Bowling Association
01903 820222
www.bowlsengland.com
Welsh Bowling Association
01446 733745
www.welsh-bowling-association.org.uk
Scottish Bowling Association
0141 221 8999
www.scottish-bowling.co.uk
Irish Bowling Association
028 9044 8348

BOXING

Amateur Boxing Association of England
020 8778 0251
www.abae.org.uk
Amateur Boxing Scotland
07900 003206
www.garnockboxing.com
British Boxing Board of Control
029 2036 7000
www.bbbofc.com
International Boxing Federation
00 1 973 414 0300
www.ibf-usba-boxing.com
Irish Amateur Boxing Association
00 353 1 453 3371
www.iaba.ie
World Boxing Association (Venezuela)
00 58 414 343 6499
www.wbaonline.com
World Boxing Organisation
00 1 787 765 4444
www.wbo-int.com

CANOEING

British Canoe Union
0115 982 1100
www.bcu.org.uk

CAVING

National Caving Association
020 8422 9668
www.nca.org

CRICKET

England and Wales Cricket Board
020 7432 1200
www.ecb.co.uk
Scottish Cricket Union
0131 313 7420
www.cricketeurope.org/scotland
Marylebone Cricket Club
020 7616 8500
www.lords.org.uk

CROQUET

Croquet Association
01242 242318
www.croquet.org.uk

CURLING

British Curling Association
01506 670138
www.britishcurlingassociation.org.uk
Royal Caledonian Curling Club
0131 333 3003
www.royalcaledoniancurlingclub.org

CYCLING

British Cycling Federation
0870 871200
www.bcf.uk.com

EQUESTRIANISM

British Equestrian Federation
024 7669 8871
www.bef.co.uk
British Show Jumping Association
024 7669 8800
www.bsja.co.uk

FENCING

British Fencing Association
020 8742 3032
www.britishfencing.com

GOLF

English Golf Union
01526 354500
www.englishgolfunion.org
Welsh Golfing Union
01633 430830
www.welshgolf.org
Scottish Golf Union
01382 549500
www.scottishgolfunion.org
Golfing Union of Ireland (Ulster Branch)
028 9042 3708
www.gui.ie
Ladies Golf Union
01334 475811
www.lgu.org
R&A, St Andrews
01334 460000
www.randa.org
Open Championship
www.opengolf.com
St Andrews Links
01334 466666
www.standrews.org.uk

GYMNASTICS

British Gymnastics
01952 820330
www.baga.co.uk

HANDBALL

British Handball Association
01706 229354
www.britsport.com/handball

HOCKEY

Great Britain Olympic Hockey Board
01628 470630
www.hockeyonline.co.uk
English Hockey Association
01908 544644
www.englandhockey.co.uk
Welsh Hockey Union
029 2057 3940
www.welsh-hockey.co.uk
Scottish Hockey Union
0131 453 9070
www.scottish-hockey.org.uk
Irish Hockey Assoc (Ulster Branch)
028 9038 3819
www.hockey.ie

HORSE RACING

The Jockey Club
01638 664151
www.thejockeyclub.co.uk
The Tote
020 8874 6411
www.tote.co.uk
Ascot
01344 622211
www.ascot.co.uk
Aintree (Grand National)
0151 523 2600
www.aintree.co.uk
Epsom (Derby)
01372 726311
www.epsomderby.co.uk

ICE HOCKEY

Ice Hockey UK
0115 924 1441
www.icehockeyuk.co.uk

ICE SKATING

National Ice Skating Association of UK
0115 853 3100
www.iceskating.org.uk

MARTIAL ARTS

British Aikido Board
020 8304 8430
www.aikido-baa.org.uk
British Ju-Jitsu Association
0870 774 1122
www.bjjagb.com
British Judo Association
01509 631670
www.britishjudo.org.uk
British Kendo Association
john.howell@kendo.org.uk
www.kendo.org.uk
English Karate Governing Body
01302 337645
www.ekgb.org.uk
Tae Kwon-Do Association of Great Britain
0800 052 5960
www.tagb.biz

KORFBALL

British Korfball Association
020 8395 2306
www.korfball.co.uk

LACROSSE

English Lacrosse Association
07976 258191; press 07931 376811
www.englishlacrosse.co.uk

LUGE

Great Britain Luge Association
01684 576604
www.gbla.org.uk

MODERN PENTATHLON

Modern Pentathlon Association of Great Britain
01225 386 808
www.mpagb.org.uk

MOTOR SPORTS

Auto-Cycle Union
01788 566400
www.acu.org.uk
motorcycling
Federation Internationale de L'Automobile (FIA)
00 33143 124455
www.fia.com
motor sports
Royal Automobile Club Motor Sports Association
01753 681736
www.msauk.org
motor sports

MOUNTAINEERING

British Mountaineering Council
0870 010 4078
www.thebmc.co.uk

NETBALL

All England Netball Association Ltd
01462 442344
www.england-netball.co.uk
Welsh Netball Association
029 2023 7048
www.welshnetball.co.uk
Netball Scotland
0141 572 0114
www.netballscotland.com

ORIENTEERING

British Orienteering Federation
01629 734042
www.britishorienteering.org.uk

PARACHUTING

British Parachute Association
0116 278 5271
www.bpa.org.uk

PETANQUE

British Petanque Association
024 7645 7815
www.britishpetanque.org.uk

POLO

Hurlingham Polo Association
01367 242828
www.hpa-polo.co.uk

POOL

English Pool Association
01706 642770
www.epa.org.uk

ROUNDERS

National Rounders Association
0114 248 0357
www.nra-rounders.co.uk

ROWING

Amateur Rowing Association
020 8748 3632
www.ara-rowing.org

RUGBY

The Rugby Football League
0113 232 9111
www.rugby-league.org
British Amateur Rugby League Association
01484 544131
www.barla.org.uk
Rugby Football Union
020 8892 2000
www.rfu.com
Welsh Rugby Union
www.wru.co.uk
Scottish Rugby Union
0131 346 5000
www.sru.org.uk
Irish Rugby Union
00 353 1 647 3800
www.irishrugby.ie
Rugby Football Union for Women
020 8831 7996
www.rfu-women.co.uk

SAILING

Royal Yachting Association
08453 450400
www.rya.org.uk

SCUBA DIVING

British Sub-Aqua Club
0151 350 6200
www.bsac.com

SHOOTING

Great Britain Target Shooting Federation
01702 219395
www.gbtsf-worldclass.co.uk

SKIING AND SNOWBOARDING

British Ski & Snowboard Federation
0131 445 7676
www.snowsportgb.com
Snowsport Scotland
0131 445 4151
www.snowsportscotland.org

SOFTBALL

British Softball Federation
020 7453 7055
www.baseballsoftballuk.com

SQUASH

England Squash
0161 231 4499
www.englandsquash.com
Scottish Squash
0131 317 7343
www.scottishsquash.org
Squash Wales
01633 682108
www.squashwales.co.uk
Ulster Squash
028 9038 1222
www.ulstersquash.com

SURFING

British Surfing Association
01673 876 474
www.britsurf.co.uk

SWIMMING

Amateur Swimming Federation of Great Britain
01509 618700
www.britishswimming.org

TABLE TENNIS

English Table Tennis Association
01424 722525
www.englishtabletennis.org.uk

TENNIS

Lawn Tennis Association
020 7381 7000
www.lta.org.uk
Tennis and Rackets Association
020 7386 3448
www.irtpa.com

TENPIN BOWLING

British Tenpin Bowling Association
020 8478 1745
www.btba.org.uk

TRIATHLON

British Triathlon Association
01702 391230
www.britishtriathlon.co.uk

VOLLEYBALL

English Volleyball Association
01509 631699
www.volleyballengland.org

WATER SKIING

British Water Ski Federation
01932 575 364
www.britishwaterski.co.uk

WEIGHTLIFTING

British Weight Lifting Association
01952 604201
www.bawla.com

WRESTLING

British Amateur Wrestling Association
01246 236443
www.britishwrestling.org

YOGA

British Wheel of Yoga
01529 306851
www.bwy.org.uk

Institutes of sport

English Institute of Sport
0870 759 0400
www.eis2win.co.uk
Scottish Institute of Sport
01786 460100
www.sisport.com

National sports centres

Bisham Abbey, Bucks
01628 476911
wwwbishamabbey.lc.thehealthhub .co.uk
Crystal Palace, south London
020 8778 9876
www.crystalpalacensc.co.uk
Cumbrae, Ayrshire
01475 530757
www.nationalcentrecumbrae.org.uk
Glenmore Lodge, Aviemore
01479 861256
www.glenmorelodge.org.uk
Inverclyde, Largs
01475 674666
www.nationalsportscentreinverclyde .org.uk
Lilleshall, Shropshire
01952 603003
www.lilleshallnsc.co.uk
National Water Sports Centre – Holme Pierrepont, Nottinghamshire
01159 821212
www.nationalsportscentres.co.uk
Plas Menai, Gwynedd
01248 670964
www.plasmenai.co.uk
Plas y Brenin, Conwy
01690 720214
www.pyb.co.uk
Tollymore, County Down
028 4372 2158
www.tollymoremc.com
Welsh Institute, Cardiff
029 2030 0500
www.welsh-institute-sport.co.uk

Sport and education

British Universities Sports Association
020 7357 8555
www.busa.org.uk
Central Council of Physical Recreation
020 7854 8500
www.ccpr.org.uk
National Council for School Sport
0115 923 1229
www.ncss.org.uk
Physical Education Association of UK
0118 931 6240
www.pea.uk.com
Youth Sport Trust
01509 226600
www.youthsporttrust.org

Sport and disability

British Amputee and Les Autres Sports Association
0120 449 4308
www.patient.co.uk
British Blind Sport
08700 789000
www.britishblindsport.org.uk
British Deaf Sports Council
fax 01268 510621
www.britishdeafsportscouncil.org.uk
British Wheelchair Sports Foundation
01296 395995
www.britishwheelchairsports.org
United Kingdom Sports Association for People with Learning Disability
020 7354 1030
www.uksports association.org
Wheelchair Sports Foundation
01296 395995
www.britishwheelchairsports.org

Other bodies

National Lottery Charities Board
0845 791 C3589191
wwwc-f.org.uk
Sports Aid Foundation
020 7273 1975
www.sportsaid.org.uk
Sports Coach UK
0113 274 4802
www.sportscoachuk.org
Women's Sports Foundation
020 7273 1740
www.wsf.org.uk

Travel

Government agencies

Department for Transport
020 7944 8300
Press: 020 7944 3066 (roads)
020 7944 3108 (marine, aviation, railways)
www.dft.gov.uk

Commission for Integrated Transport
cfit@dft.gsi.gov.uk
www.cfit.gov.uk

Transport 2000
01628 524900
www.transport2000.org.uk
National independent transport advisory body

Transport in London

Transport for London
020 7941 4500
Press: 020 7941 4434
www.tfl.gov.uk/tfl

London Underground
020 7222 5600
www.tube.tfl.gov.uk

London Transport Users Committee
020 7505 9000

London River Services
020 7941 2400
www.tfl.gov.uk/river

London Buses
0845 300 7000
www.tfl.gov.uk/buses

Congestion charge
enquiries@cclondon.com
www.cclondon.com

Passenger transport executives

www.pteg.net

Centro (West Midlands)
0121 214 7001
www.centro.org.uk

GMPTE (Greater Manchester)
0161 242 6000
www.gmpte.gov.uk

Merseytravel
0151 227 5181
www.merseytravel.gov.uk

Nexus (Tyne and Wear)
0191 203 3333
www.nexus.org.uk

South Yorkshire
0114 221 1279
www.sypte.co.uk

Strathclyde
0141 332 6811
www.spt.co.uk

Metro (West Yorkshire)
0113 251 7272
www.wymetro.com

Rail

Rail: official bodies

Network Rail
Headquarters: 020 7557 8000
Helpline: 08457 114141
National press: 020 7557 8292
Scotland 0141 555 4109
North West 0161 228 8582
North East 01904 522825
East Anglia 020 7557 8107
Midlands 0121 345 3100
West Country and Wales 01793 515267
South & South East 020 7922 4747
www.networkrail.co.uk

Strategic Rail Authority
020 7654 6000
www.sra.gov.uk

Office of the Rail Regulator
Library: 020 7282 2001
Press: 020 7282 2002 / 2007
www.rail-reg.gov.uk

Rail Safety & Standards Board
020 7904 7777
www.railwaysafety.org.uk

Health and Safety Executive: railways
0870 154 5500
www.hse.gov.uk/railways
Continental route planning & ticket sales

National Rail Enquiries
08457 484950
www.nationalrail.co.uk

Rail: passenger councils

London Transport Users Committee (LTUC)
020 7505 9000
www.ltuc.org.uk

Wales
029 2022 7247
www.railpassengers.org.uk

Midlands
0121 212 2133
www.railpassengers.org.uk

Southern England
020 7240 5308
www.railpassengers.org.uk

North-west England
0161 244 5982
www.railpassengers.org.uk

Western England
0117 926 5703
www.railpassengers.org.uk

Eastern England
01733 312188
www.railpassengers.org.uk

North-eastern England
01904 787711
www.railpassengers.org.uk

Scotland
0141 221 7760
www.railpassengers.org.uk

General Consumer Council Northern Ireland
028 9067 2488
www.gccni.org.uk

Rail: train operating companies

Association of Train Operating Companies
020 7841 8000
www.atoc.org

Anglia Railways Train Services
01473 693929
www.angliarailways.co.uk

Arriva Trains Northern
0870 602 3322
www.arrivatrainsnorthern.co.uk

C2C
0845 601 4873
www.c2c-online.co.uk

Central Trains
0121 654 2040
www.centraltrains.co.uk

Chiltern Railways
0845 600 5165
www.chilternrailways.co.uk

Docklands Light Rail
020 7363 9700
www.tfl.gov.uk/dlr

English Welsh & Scottish Railways
020 7713 2486
www.ews-railway.co.uk

Eurostar
0870 518 6186
www.eurostar.com

First Great Eastern
0845 950 5000
www.ger.co.uk

First Great Western
0845 600 5604
www.firstgreatwestern.co.uk

First North Western
0845 600 1159
www.firstnorthwestern.co.uk

Freightliner
020 7200 3902
www.freightliner.co.uk

Gatwick Express
020 8750 6622
www.gatwickexpress.co.uk

GNER
0845 722 5333
www.gner.co.uk

Heathrow Express
0845 600 1515
www.heathrowexpress.co.uk

Hull Trains
01482 606388
www.hulltrains.co.uk

Island Line
01983 812591
www.island-line.co.uk

Midland Mainline
0845 722 1125
www.midlandmainline.com
NI Railways
028 9089 9455
www.nirailways.co.uk
Scotrail
0845 601 5929
www.scotrail.co.uk
Silverlink
County: 0845 601 4868
Metro: 0845 601 4867
www.silverlink-trains.com
Southern
0870 830 6000
www.southcentraltrains.co.uk
South West Trains
0845 600 0650
www.swtrains.co.uk
Think Thameslink
0845 330 6333
www.thameslink.co.uk
Thames Trains
0845 330 7182
www.thamestrains.co.uk
Valley Lines
029 2044 9944
www.valleylines.co.uk
Virgin Trains
0870 789 1234
www.virgintrains.co.uk
Wales & Borders Trains
0191 387 1387
www.walesandborders.co.uk
West Anglia Great Northern Railway (WAGN)
0845 781 8919
www.wagn.co.uk
Wessex Trains
0845 600 0880
www.wessextrains.co.uk

Air travel

Air: official bodies

Airport Operators Authority
020 7222 2249
www.aoa.org.uk
Air Transport Users Council
020 7240 0061
www.auc.org.uk
British Airline Pilots Association
020 8476 4000
www.balpa.org
British Airports Authority
020 7834 9449
www.baa.co.uk
Civil Aviation Authority
020 7379 7311
www.caa.co.uk
International Air Transport Association
020 8607 6200
www.iata.org
National Air Traffic Services
020 7309 8666
www.nats.co.uk

Airports

London Heliport (Battersea)
020 7228 0181
www.weston-aviation.com
London City
020 7646 0000
www.londoncityairport.com
London Gatwick
0870 000 2468; press: 01293 505000
www.baa.co.uk/main/airports/gatwick
London Heathrow
0870 000 0123
Press: 020 8745 7224
Heathrow Express press: 020 7313 0308
www.baa.com/main/airports/heathrow
London Stansted
0870 000 0303
Press: 01279 680534
www.baa.com/main/airports/stansted
London Luton
01582 405100
www.london-luton.co.uk
Aberdeen
0870 040 0006
Press: 0131 272 2111
www.baa.co.uk/main/airports/aberdeen
Barra
01871 890212
www.hial.co.uk/barra-airport.html
Belfast (City)
028 9045 7745
www.belfastcityairport.com
Belfast International Airport (Aldergrove)
028 9448 4848
www.belfastairport.com
Benbecula
01870 602051
www.hial.co.uk/benbecula-airport.html
Biggin Hill
01959 578500
www.bigginhillairport.com
Birmingham
0121 767 5511
www.bhx.co.uk
Blackpool
01253 343434
www.blackpoolairport.com
Bournemouth
01202 364000
www.flybournemouth.com
Bristol
0870 1212747
www.bristolairport.co.uk
RAF Brize Norton
01993 842551
www.raf.mod.uk/rafbrizenorton
Cambridge City Airport
01223 373765
www.cambridgecityairport.com
Campbeltown
01586 553797
www.hial.co.uk/campbeltown-airport.html
Cardiff International Airport
01446 711111
www.cial.co.uk
Carlisle
01228 573641
www.carlisleairport.co.uk
Channel Islands:
Alderney
01481 822551
www.alderney.gov.gg/index.php/pid/40
Guernsey
01481 237766
www.guernsey-airport.gov.gg
Jersey
01534 492000
www.jersey-airport.com
Coventry
024 7676 2220
www.coventryairport.co.uk
RNAS Culdrose
01326 574121
www.royal-navy.mod.uk
Dundee
01382 643242
www.dundeecity.gov.uk/airport
East Midlands
01331 852852
www.eastmidlandsairport.com
Edinburgh
0870 040 0007
Press: 0131 272 2111
www.baa.co.uk/main/airports/edinburgh
Exeter
01392 367433
www.exeter-airport.co.uk
Glasgow
0870 040 0008
Press: 0131 272 2111
www.baa.co.uk/main/airports/glasgow
Gloucester
01452 857700
www.gloucestershireairport.co.uk
Inverness
01667 464000
www.hial.co.uk/inverness-airport.html
Ipswich
01473 720111
Islay
01496 302361
www.hial.co.uk/islay-airport.html
Isle of Man (Ronaldsway)
01624 821600
www.iom-airport.com
Kent International, Manston
01843 825063
www.kia-m.com
Lands End
01736 788771
Leeds Bradford International Airport
0113 250 9696
www.lbia.co.uk
Liverpool (Speke)
0151 288 4000
Liverpool John Lennon Airport
0870 750 8484
www.liverpooljohnlennonairport.com
Lydd
01797 322400
www.lydd-airport.co.uk
Manchester
0161 489 3000
Press: 0161 489 2700
www.manairport.co.uk

Newcastle
0870 122 1488
www.newcastleairport.com
Newquay Cornwall Airport
01637 860551
Norwich
01603 411923
www.norwichairport.co.uk
Orkney (Kirkwall)
01856 872421
www.hial.co.uk/kirkwall-airport.html
Penzance Heliport
01736 351200
www.islesofscillyhelicopter.com
Plymouth City Airport
01752 204090
www.plymouthcity.co.uk/airport.html
Prestwick
01292 511115
www.gpia.co.uk
St Mary's, Isles of Scilly
01720 422677
Sheffield City Airport
0114 201 1998
www.sheffieldcityairport.com
Shetland
01950 460654
Shoreham (Brighton City)
01273 296900
www.shorehamairport.co.uk
Southampton
0870 040 0009
Press: 023 8062 7141
www.baa.co.uk/main/airports/southampton
Southend
01702 608100
www.southendairport.net
Stornoway
01851 707400
www.hial.co.uk/stornoway-airport.html
Sumburgh
01950 461000
www.hial.co.uk/sumburgh-airport.html
Teesside
01325 332811
www.teessideairport.com
Tiree
01879 220456
www.hial.co.uk/tiree-airport.html
Tresco Heliport
01720 422970
www.tresco.co.uk
Wick
01955 602215
www.hial.co.uk/wick-airport.html

Airlines

Aer Lingus
00 353 1 886 8844
www.aerlingus.ie
Aeroflot
00 1 212 944 2300
www.aeroflot.com
Air Berlin
0870 738 8880
www.airberlin.com
Air Canada
0871 220 1111
www.aircanada.ca
Air France
0845 084 5010
www.airfrance.com
Air India
020 7495 7950
www.airindia.com
Air Malta
00 356 2169 0890
www.airmalta.com
Air New Zealand
020 8600 7600
www.airnewzealand.com
Air Polonia
00 48 22 575000
www.airpolonia.com
Air Scotland
0141 222 2363
www.air-scotland.com
Air Seychelles
01293 596 656
www.airseychelles.net
Air Wales
0870 777 3131
www.airwales.com
Alitalia
020 8745 8297/8
www.alitalia.com
Alaska Airlines
01992 441517
www.alaskaair.com
America West Airlines
00 1 480 693 0800
www.americawest.com
American Airlines
00 1 817 967 2000
www.aa.com
ANA Europe
0870 837 8866
www.anaskyweb.com
ATA
00 1 800 225 2995
www.ata.com
Austrian Airlines
020 7766 0300
www.aua.com
Avianca (Columbia)
0870 5767747
www.avianca.com
Basiq Air
020 7365 4997
www.basiqair.com
British Airways
0870 850 9850
www.british-airways.com
BMI (British Midland)
01332 854000
www.britishmidland.com
Cathay Pacific
00 852 2747 5563
www.cathaypacific.com
China Airlines
020 7436 9001
www.china-airlines.com
Continental Airlines
01293 776464
www.continental.com
Cyprus Airways
020 8897 2190
www.cyprusair.com
Delta Express
0800 414767
www.delta.com
EasyJet
0871 750 0100
www.easyjet.com
El Al Israel Airlines
020 7957 4250
www.elal.com
Emirates
0870 243 2222
www.emirates.com
EUJet
0870 414 1414
www.eujet.com
Finnair
0870 241 4411
www.finnair.com
Flybe
01392 366669
www.flybe.com
Flyglobespan
0870 556 1522
www.flyglobespan.com
Germanwings
020 8321 7255
www.germanwings.com
Gulf Air
0870 777 1700
www.gulfairco.com
Hellas Jet
0870 751 7222
www.hellas-jet.com
HLX (Hapag-Lloyd Express)
0870 606 0 519
www.hlx.com
Iberia
0845 601 2854
www.iberia.com
Icelandair
00 354 50 50 100
www.icelandair.net
Japan Airlines
0845 774 7700
www.jal.com
JAT – Yugoslav Airlines
020 7629 2007
www.jat.com
Jet 2
0871 226 1737
www.jet2.com
Kenya Airways
01784 888222
www.kenya-airways.com
KLM Royal Dutch
0870 243 0541
www.klm.com
Kuwait Airways
020 7412 0006/10
www.kuwait-airways.com
LanChile
0800 917 0572
www.lanchile.com
LOT – Polish Airlines
0870 414 0088
www.lot.com
Lufthansa
020 8750 3500
www.lufthansa.com
Malaysia Airlines
020 7341 2000
www.malaysia-airlines.com
Monarch
01582 400000
www.monarch-airlines.com

Olympic Airways
0870 606 0460
www.olympic-airways.gr
Portugalia Airlines
0161 489 5039
www.pga.pt
Qantas Airways
0845 774 7767
www.qantas.com
Royal Air Maroc
00 212 2248 9731
www.royalairmaroc.com
Royal Jordanian Airlines
020 7878 6300
www.rja.com.jo
RyanAir
0871 246 0000
www.ryanair.co.uk
SAS Scandinavian Airlines
020 8990 7059
www.scandinavian.net
Saudi Arabian Airlines
020 7798 9898
www.saudiairlines.com
Singapore Airlines
0121 233 2066
www.singaporeair.com
Sky Europe
020 7365 0365
www.skyeurope.com
South African Airways
020 8897 3645
www.flysaa.com
Spanair
00 97 174 5020
www.spanair.com
Sri Lankan Airlines
020 8538 2001
www.airlanka.com
Swiss
00 41 61 582 0000
www.swiss.com
Thai Airways
0870 606 0911
www.thaiairways.com
United Airlines
0845 844 4777
www.ual.com
V Bird
090 1488 1488
www.v-bird.com
Varig – Brazilian Airlines
020 8321 7170
www.varig.co.uk
Virgin Atlantic
01293 562345
www.virgin-atlantic.com
Virgin Express
0870 730 1134
www.virgin-express.com
Volare
00 380 44 452 1115
www.volare.kiev.ua
Wizz Air
info@wizzair.com
www.wizzair.com
Yemen Airways
020 8759 0385
www.yemenairways.co.uk

Water travel

Boats and shipping: authorities

Associated British Ports
020 7430 1177
www.abports.co.uk
Association of Inland Navigation Authorities
01642 590257
www.aina.org.uk
British Marine Industries Federation
01784 473377
www.bmif.co.uk
British Ports Association
020 7242 1200
www.britishports.org.uk
British Waterways Board
01923 201120
www.british-waterways.org
Hydrographic Office
01823 723366
www.hydro.gov.uk
Inland Waterways Association
01923 711114
www.waterways.org.uk
International Maritime Organisation
020 7735 7611
www.imo.org
Lloyd's Register – Fairplay
01737 379000
www.fairplay.co.uk
Lloyd's Register
020 7423 2040
www.lr.org
London River Services
020 7941 4500
www.tfl.gov.uk/river
Lloyd's List
020 7553 1374
www.lloydslist.com
Maritime & Coastguard Agency
023 8032 9100
www.mcagency.org.uk
Register of Shipping & Seamen
029 2074 7333
Marine information services
Royal Institute of Navigation
020 7591 3130
www.rin.org.uk
Royal Yachting Association
0845 345 0400
www.rya.org.uk
UK Harbours Directory
www.harbours.co.uk

Ports

Aberdeen
01224 597000
www.aberdeen-harbour.co.uk
Ardrossan
01294 463972
Ayr
01292 281687
www.abports.co.uk
Barrow
01229 822911
www.abports.co.uk
Barry
0870 609 6699
www.abports.co.uk
Belfast
028 9055 4422
www.belfast-harbour.co.uk
Boston
01205 365571
www.portofboston.co.uk
Brightlingsea
01206 302370
Bristol
0117 982 0000
www.bristolport.co.uk
Brixham
01803 853321
Cardiff
0870 609 6699
www.abports.co.uk
Cowes
01983 293952
www.cowes.co.uk
Dartmouth
01803 832337
www.dartharbour.org.uk
Dover
01304 240400
www.doverport.co.uk
Dundee
01382 224121
www.forthports.co.uk
Ellesmore Port (Manchester Ship Canal)
01928 567465
www.shipcanal.co.uk
Eyemouth
01890 750223
Falmouth
01326 312285
www.falmouthport.co.uk
Felixstowe
01394 604500
www.portoffelixstowe.co.uk
Fife
01383 413366
www.forthports.co.uk
Fleetwood
01253 872323
www.abports.co.uk
Garston
0151 427 5971
www.abports.co.uk
Goole
01405 762691
www.abports.co.uk
Grangemouth
01324 482591
www.forthports.co.uk
Great Yarmouth
01493 335500
www.gypa.co.uk
Grimsby
01472 359181
www.abports.co.uk
Harwich
01255 243030
www.hha.co.uk
Heysham
01524 852373
Hull
01482 327171
www.abports.co.uk

Immingham
01472 359181
www.abports.co.uk
Inverness Harbour Trust
01463 715715
www.invernessharbour.co.uk
Ipswich
01473 231010
www.abports.co.uk
Isle of Man
01624 686628
King's Lynn
01553 691555
www.abports.co.uk
Larne
028 2887 2100
www.portoflarne.co.uk
Leith
0131 555 8750
www.forthports.co.uk
Lerwick
01595 692991
www.lerwick-harbour.co.uk
Liverpool
0151 949 6000
www.merseydocks.co.uk
Port of London
020 7743 7900
www.portoflondon.co.uk
Londonderry
028 7186 0555
www.londonderryport.com
Lowestoft
01553 691555
www.abports.co.uk
Medway Ports
01795 596596
www.medwayports.com
Milford Haven
01646 696100
www.mhpa.co.uk
Montrose Port Authority
01674 672302
www.montroseport.co.uk
Mostyn Docks, Holywell
01745 560335
Newport
0870 609 6699
www.abports.co.uk
Peterhead
01779 474020
www.peterhead-bay.co.uk
Plymouth
01752 662191
www.abports.co.uk
Poole
01202 440200
www.phc.co.uk
Portsmouth
023 9229 7395
www.portsmouthand.co.uk
Port Talbot
0870 609 6699
www.abports.co.uk
Ramsgate
01843 587661
www.ramsgatenewport.co.uk
Rosyth
01383 413366
www.forthports.co.uk
Saundersfoot
01834 812094
Scarborough
01947 602354
Seaham
0191 516 1700
www.seaham.com/business/port
Shoreham
01273 598100
www.portshoreham.co.uk
Silloth
016973 31358
www.abports.co.uk
Southampton
023 8048 8800
www.abports.co.uk
Stonehaven
01569 762 741
Stornoway
01851 702688
www.stornoway-portauthority.com
Sunderland
0191 553 2100
www.portofsunderland.org.uk
Swansea
0870 609 6699
www.abports.co.uk
Tees & Hartlepool
01642 877000
www.thpal.co.uk
Teignmouth
01626 774044
www.abports.co.uk
Tilbury
01375 852200
www.forthports.co.uk
Troon
01292 281687
www.abports.co.uk
Tyne, Port of
0191 455 2671
www.portoftyne.com
Weymouth
01305 838000
www.weymouth.gov.uk
Whitby, Port of
01947 602354
www.portofwhitby.co.uk

Ferries

Brittany Ferries
08703 665 333
www.brittany-ferries.com
Caledonian MacBrayne
01475 650 100
www.calmac.co.uk
Condor Ferries Limited
01202 207207
www.condorferries.co.uk
DFDS Seaways Limited
01255 240240
www.dfdsseaways.co.uk
Fjord Line
0191 296 1313
www.fjordline.com
Hoverspeed Limited
0800 1211 1211
www.hoverspeed.com
Hovertravel
01983 811000
www.hovertravel.co.uk
Irish Ferries Limited
08705 171717
www.irishferries.com
Isle of Man Steam Packet Company
08705 523 523
www.steam-packet.com
Norfolk Line
00 31 7035 27400
www.norfolkline.com
Orkney Ferries
01856 872044
www.orkneyferries.co.uk
P&O Ferries
020 7930 4343
www.poferries.com
Red Funnel Ferries
020 7436 2449
www.ferryinformationservice.co.uk
Sea Containers Irish Sea Operations
020 7805 5000
www.seacontainers.com
SeaFrance Limited
01304 828300
www.seafrance.com
Stena Line
00 46 3185 8000
www.stenaline.com
Superfast Ferries Scotland
0870 234 0870
www.superfast.com
Swansea Cork Ferries
01792 456116
www.swansea-cork.ie
Wightlink Limited
0870 582 7744
www.wightlink.co.uk
Woolwich Ferry
020 8921 5967
www.yellins.co.uk/woolwichferry

Road travel

Motoring bodies

AA
0870 600 0371; HQ: 0870 544 8866; press: 01256 492927
www.theaa.co.uk
British Motorcyclists Federation
0116 284 5380
www.bmf.co.uk
British Parking Association
01444 447 300
www.britishparking.co.uk
Coach Operators Federation
somerbus@tinyworld.co.uk
http://users.tinyworld.co.uk/somerbus/COFmembers.html
Confederation of Passenger Transport
020 7240 3131
www.carlton-group.co.uk/passtransport.html
DVLA (Drivers & Vehicles Licensing Authority)
Licence: 0870 240 0009
Vehicle: 0870 240 0010
Press: 01792 782318
www.dvla.gov.uk

Greenflag
0845 246 1557; press: 0113 399 1427
www.greenflag.com
Institute of Logistics & Transport
01536 740100
www.iolt.org.uk
Institute of the Motor Industry
01992 511 521
www.motor.org.uk
International Road Transport Union
www.iru.org
Licensed Taxi Drivers Association
020 7286 1046
www.ltda.co.uk
Motor Industry Research Association
01268 290100
www.mira.co.uk
National Federation of Bus Users
023 9281 4493
www.nfbu.org
RAC
01628 843888; press: 020 8917 2742
www.rac.co.uk
Road Haulage Association
01932 841515
www.rha.net
Road Operators Safety Council
01865 775552
www.rosco.org.uk
Society of Motor Manufacturers
020 7235 7000
www.smmt.co.uk
Transport & General Workers Union
020 7611 2500
www.tgwu.org.uk
World Road Association (PIARC)
00 33 1 47 96 8121
www.piarc.org

Pedestrians, cyclists and campaign groups

Brake
01484 559909
www.brake.org.uk
Road Safety charity
British Cycling Federation
0870 871 2000
www.bcf.uk.com
Campaign Against Drinking & Driving
01275 892225
www.cadd.org.uk
Cycle Campaign Network
ccn@cyclenetwork.org.uk
www.cyclenetwork.org.uk
Cyclists Touring Club
0870 873 0060
Press: 0870 873 0063
www.ctc.org.uk
Environmental Transport Association
0800 212810
www.eta.co.uk
Environmental campaigner & provider of roadside recovery service
European Federation of Road Victims
fevr@worldcom.ch
www.fevr.org
Lift Share
08700 780225
www.liftshare.com
Online car-sharing scheme
Living Streets
020 7820 1010
www.livingstreets.org.uk
Fighting for cleaner, safer streets
London Cycling Campaign
020 7928 7220
www.lcc.org.uk
Motorcycle Action Group
0870 444 8448
www.mag-uk.org
National Cycle Network
0845 113 0065
Press: 0117 927 7555
www.sustrans.org.uk
Nationwide Cycle Registration
0117 964 2187
www.cycleregistration.com
Ramblers Association
020 7339 8500
Press: 020 7339 8531/8532
www.ramblers.org.uk
Reclaim the Streets
rts@gn.apc.org
http://rts.gn.apc.org/
RoadPeace
020 8838 5102
www.roadpeace.org
Slower Speeds Initiative
info@slower-speeds.org.uk
www.slower-speeds.org.uk
Smart Moves
01484 483061
www.smartmoves.co.uk
Sustrans
0845 113 0065
Press: 0117 927 7555
www.sustrans.org.uk
Sustainable transport charity

Buses

Arriva
Press: 0191 520 4000
www.arriva.co.uk
Firstgroup
020 7291 0505
Press: 0101 627 7218
www.firstgroup.com
The Go-ahead Group
0191 232 3123
www.go-ahead.com
London United Busways
020 8400 6665
www.lonutd.co.uk
Lothian Buses Plc
0131 554 4494
www.lothianbuses.co.uk
Metroline
020 8218 8888
www.metroline.co.uk
National Express
08705 808080
www.nationalexpress.com
Scottish Citylink
0141 332 9644
www.citylink.co.uk
Stagecoach
Press: 01738 442111
www.stagecoachplc.com
Ulsterbus
028 9066 6630
www.ulsterbus.co.uk

Tourism

Air Travel Organisers' Licensing (ATOL)
020 7453 6424
www.caa.co.uk/cpg/atol
Association of British Travel Agents
020 7637 2444
Press:: 020 7307 1900
www.abtanet.com
British Tourist Authority
020 8846 9000
www.britishtouristauthority.org
Tourism Concern
020 7133 3330
www.tourismconcern.org.uk
Youth Hostels Association
01629 592600
www.yha.org.uk

Utilities

Gas and electricity

Ofgem – regulator
020 7901 7003
Press: 020 7901 7006
www.ofgem.gov.uk

Energywatch
0845 906 0708
www.energywatch.org.uk

National Grid Transco
0800 777770; 01926 653000
www.nationalgrid.com/uk
www.transco.uk.com

British Gas
0845 600 5001
www.gas.co.uk

EDF Energy
020 7242 9050
www.edfenergy.com

npower
0845 070 9494
Press: 0845 070 2807
www.npower.co.uk

Powergen
024 7642 4000
www.powergen.co.uk

Scottish and Southern
01738 456000
Press: 0870 900 0410
www.scottish-southern.co.uk

Scottish Power
0141 248 8200
www.scottishpower.com

Water

Ofwat – regulator
0121 625 1300
Press: 0121 625 1416 / 1496 / 1442
www.ofwat.gov.uk

Anglian
01480 323900
Press: 0870 600 5600
www.anglianwater.co.uk

Welsh
01443 452300
Press: 029 2055 6140
www.dwrcymru.co.uk

Northumbrian
0870 608 4820
www.nwl.co.uk

Severn Trent
0121 722 4000
Press: 0121 722 4380
www.stwater.co.uk

South West
01392 446688
Press: 01392 443021
www.southwestwater.co.uk

Southern
01903 264444
www.southernwater.co.uk

Thames
0118 373 8000
www.thames-water.com

United Utilities
01925 234000
www.unitedutilities.com

Wessex
01225 526000
Press: 01225 526323 / 526329
www.wessexwater.co.uk

Yorkshire
01274 691111
www.yorkshirewater.com

Post

Postal Services Commission – regulator
020 7593 2100
www.postcomm.gov.uk

Royal Mail
press.office@royalmail.com
www.royalmail.com

Telecoms

Ofcom – regulator
020 7981 3040
Press: 020 7981 3033
www.ofcom.gov.uk

British Telecom
020 7356 5000
Press: 020 7356 5369
www.bt.com

Cable and Wireless
020 7315 4000
Press: 020 7315 4495
www.cableandwireless.co.uk

Colt
020 7863 5000
www.colt.co.uk

Energis
020 7206 5555
Press: 0118 919 3499
www.energis.co.uk

Hutchinson 3G
01628 765000; press: 020 7010 9312
www.three.co.uk

Kingston Communications
01482 602100
www.kcltd.co.uk

MCI WorldCom
0118 905 5000
www1.worldcom.com/uk

mmO2
0113 272 2000
www.mmo2.com

NTL
01256 752000
www.ntl.com

Orange
01454 624600; press: 020 7984 2001
www.orange.co.uk

Telewest
01483 750 900
www.telewest.co.uk

Thus
0800 027 58487
www.thus.co.uk

T-Mobile
0800 956 5001
Press: 07017 150 150
www.t-mobile.co.uk

Virgin Mobile
01225 895555; press: 020 7484 4300
www.virginmobile.com

Vodafone
01635 33251; press: 07000 500100
www.vodafone.co.uk

Emergency & services

see separate panel on page 457 for police, fire, ambulance

Police

Home Office
0870 000 1585; press: 020 7273 4545
www.homeoffice.gov.uk

Police Service
(see panel for regional contacts)
www.police.uk

British Transport Police
0800 405040
Communications centres:
0141 335 3198 (Scotland)
0113 247 9517 (North Eastern)
0161 228 5685 (North Western)
0121 654 2244 (Western)
www.btp.police.uk

Centrex (national police training)
01256 602100; press: 01256 602725
www.centrex.police.uk

Forensic Science Service
www.forensic.gov.uk

HM Inspectors of Constabulary
01527 882000
www.homeoffice.gov.uk/hmic/hmic.htm

Independent Police Complaints Commission (IPCC)
0845 300 2002
Press: 020 7166 3214
www.ipcc.gov.uk/

Interpol
fax: 00 33 4 7244 7163
www.interpol.int

Metropolitan Police, London
020 7230 1212; press: 020 7230 2171
www.met.police.uk

Ministry of Defence Police
0870 607 4455; press: 0870 607 4455
www.mod.uk/mdp/

Missing Persons Helpline
0500 700700; press: 020 8392 4510
www.missingpersons.org

National Crime Squad
Press: 020 7238 2500
www.nationalcrimesquad.police.uk

National Criminal Intelligence Service
020 7238 8000
Press: 020 7238 8431
www.ncis.gov.uk

Northern Ireland Police Service
028 9065 0222
www.psni.police.uk

Northern Ireland Policing Board
028 9040 8500
Press: 028 9040 8539 / 8623
www.nipolicingboard.org.uk

Police Forces in Scotland
www.scottish.police.uk

Police IT Organisation (national computer)
020 8358 5555
www.pito.org.uk

Port of Dover Police
01304 240400
www.doverport.co.uk/portofdover/portoperations/port_of_dover_police/index.htm

Scottish Drug Enforcement Agency
enquiries@sdea.pnn.police.uk
www.sdea.police.uk

Scottish Police Information Strategy
0141 582 1000
www.spis.police.uk

UK Atomic Energy Constabulary
www.ukaea.org.uk/ukaeac/index

Professional bodies

Police Federation
020 8335 1000
www.polfed.org

Police Federation for Northern Ireland
028 9076 4200
www.policefed-ni.org.uk

Police Superintendents' Association
0118 984 4005
www.policesupers.com

Association of Chief Police Officers
020 7227 3434
www.acpo.police.uk

Association of Chief Police Officers in Scotland
www.scottish.police.uk

Association of Police Authorities
020 7664 3185
www.apa.police.uk

Institute of Traffic Accident Investigators
01332 292447
www.itai.org

British Association for Women in Policing
01706 216331
www.bawp.org

Fire

Office of the Deputy Prime Minister
020 7944 4400
Press: 020 7944 4651
www.odpm.gov.uk

Fire Policy Division
020 7944 6923

HM Fire Service Inspectorate
020 7944 5569

Northern Ireland Fire Brigade
028 9266 4221
www.nifb.org.uk

Fire Kills campaign
www.firekills.gov.uk

Professional bodies

Fire Brigades Union
020 8541 1765
www.fbu.org.uk

Chief and Assistant Chief Fire Officers' Association (CACFOA)
01827 302300
www.fire-uk.org

Fire Protection Association
020 7902 5300
www.thefpa.co.uk

Ambulance

Department of Health
020 7210 4850
Press: 020 7210 5231
www.doh.gov.uk

Ambulance Service Association
020 7928 9620
www.the-asa.org

Association of Professional Ambulance Personnel
0870 167 0999
www.apap.org.uk

Search and rescue

Mountain Rescue Council of England and Wales
secretary@mountain.rescue.org.uk
www.mountain.rescue.org.uk
Links to all mountain rescue bodies in the UK

RAF Mountain Rescue Association
www.rafmra.org.uk

Search and Rescue Dog Association
chairman@nsarda.org.uk
www.nsarda.org.uk

Maritime and Coastguard Agency
0870 600 6505
www.mcga.gov.uk

Military

Ministry of Defence
0870 607 4455
www.mod.uk

British Army
www.army.mod.uk

Royal Air Force
www.raf.mod.uk

Royal Navy
www.royal-navy.mod.uk

MI5
Press: 020 7273 4545 (Home Office)
www.mi5.gov.uk
UK's defensive security intelligence agency

MI6
Press: 020 7008 3100 (Foreign Office)
www.fco.gov.uk
Secret intelligence service

GCHQ (Government Communications Headquarters)
Press: 01242 221491 ext 33847
www.gchq.gov.uk

Territorial Army
0845 603 8000
www.ta.mod.uk
Reserve force

Ministry of Defence Police
0870 607 4455
Press: 0870 607 4455
www.mod.uk/mdp/

Military associations

Army Base Repair Organisation
01264 383295
www.abrodev.co.uk

Army Training and Recruitment Agency
01980 615041
www.atra.mod.uk

Central Data Management Authority
01793 555391
www.cdma.mod.uk
Tri-service organisation helping enable IS interoperability.

Commonwealth War Graves Commission
01628 634221; press: 01628 507163
www.cwgc.org

Computer Emergency Response Team
020 7218 8715
www.mod.uk/cert

Defence Analytical Services Agency
020 7807 8792
www.dasa.mod.uk
UK defence statistics

Defence Procurement Agency
0117 913 0000
www.mod.uk/dpa

Defence Scientific Advisory Council
020 7218 0333
www.mod.uk/dsac
Provides independent advice to the defence secretary

Hydrographic Office
01823 337900
Helpdesk: 01823 723366
www.hydro.gov.uk
Responsible for surveying the seas around the UK

International Visits Control Office
0870 607 4455 (MoD)
www.mod.uk/ivco
Provides security clearance and advice for visitors to and from the UK defence industry

Military Heraldry Society
01952 408830 / 270221

Military Historical Society
020 7730 0717

Orders and Medals Research Society
020 8680 2701
www.omrs.org.uk

Reserve Forces' and Cadets' Associations in Scotland
Lowland: 0141 945 4951
Highland: 01382 668283
www.rfca.org.uk

Royal British Legion
08457 725 725
Press: 020 7973 7296
www.britishlegion.org.uk

Sabre
0800 389 5459
www.sabre.mod.uk
Supporting Britain's reservists and employers

SSAFA Forces Help
020 7403 8783
www.ssafa.org.uk
National charity helping serving and ex-service men, women and their families

Veterans Agency
0800 169 2277 / 01253 866043
www.veteransagency.mod.uk
MoD contact for veterans and dependants

Emergency planning

Government

Air Accidents Investigation Branch
01252 510300
24-hour Accident Reporting line: 01252 512299
www.aaib.dft.gov.uk

Civil Contingencies Secretariat
020 7276 3000
www.ukresilience.info
Formerly the Emergency Planning Division

Emergency Planning College, Easingwold
01347 822877
Press: 01347 821 406
www.ukresilience.info/college
Government training college

Emergency Services Action Team
020 7210 4850
www.doh.gov.uk/esat.htm

London Fire and Emergency Planning Authority
020 7587 2000
www.london-fire.gov.uk

London Prepared
020 7276 3000
www.londonprepared.gov.uk

National Infrastructure Security Co-ordination Centre (NISCC)
020 7821 1330
www.niscc.gov.uk

National Radiological Protection Board
01235 831600
www.nrpb.org

Scottish Executive Justice Department
0131 556 8400
www.scotland.gov.uk

Anti-Terrorist Hotline
0800 789321

Professional body

Emergency Planning Society
0845 600 9587
www.emergplansoc.org.uk

Voluntary services

Basics
0870 165 4999
www.basics.org.uk
Medical help at disasters

British Red Cross
020 7235 5454
www.redcross.org.uk

Casualties Union
08700 780590
www.casualtiesunion.org.uk
Simulated injuries for emergency exercises

Royal Life Saving Society
01789 773 994
www.lifesavers.org.uk

Royal National Lifeboat Institution
0800 543210
www.rnli.org.uk

St Andrews Ambulance Association
Aberdeen 01224 877271
Fife 01592 631758
Glasgow 0141 332 4031
Edinburgh 0131 229 5419
Dundee 01382 322389
www.firstaid.org.uk

St John Ambulance
08700 104950
www.sja.org.uk

Victim Support
020 7735 9166
Press: 020 7896 3809
www.victimsupport.com
Supports fire and crime victims

■ Fire, police and ambulance

Avon
FIRE 0117 926 2061
PRESS x216
POLICE 01275 818181
PRESS 01275 816350
AMBULANCE 0117 927 7046
PRESS 0117 928 0265/ 0870 241 0857

Bedfordshire
FIRE 01234 351081
PRESS 01234 326198
POLICE 01234 841212
PRESS 01234 842390
AMBULANCE 01234 408999
PRESS 01234 408999

Berkshire
FIRE 0118 945 2888
PRESS 0118 932 2214/ 2283
POLICE 01865 846000
PRESS 01865 846699
AMBULANCE 0118 936 5500
PRESS 0118 936 5500

Buckinghamshire
FIRE 01296 424666
PRESS 0797 1216014
POLICE 01865 846000
PRESS 01865 846699
AMBULANCE 01908 262422
PRESS 01908 262422

Cambridgeshire
FIRE 01480 444500
PRESS 01480 444558
POLICE 01480 422630
PRESS 01480 422393
AMBULANCE 01603 424255
PRESS 01603 422729

Cheshire
FIRE 01606 868700
PRESS 01606 868657/ 868422/ 868786
POLICE 01244 350000
PRESS 01244 612030
AMBULANCE 0151 260 5220
PRESS 0151 261 2585

Cleveland
FIRE 01429 872311
PRESS x4160 / x4151
POLICE 01642 326326
PRESS 01642 301245/ 54
AMBULANCE 01904 666000
PRESS 01904 666041

Cornwall
FIRE 01872 273117
PRESS 01872 322785
POLICE 0870 577 7444
PRESS 01392 452151/200
AMBULANCE 01392 261500
PRESS 01392 261506

Cumbria
FIRE 01900 822503
PRESS 01900 822503
POLICE 01768 891999
PRESS 01768 217009
AMBULANCE 01228 596909
PRESS 01228 596909

Derbyshire
FIRE 01332 771221
PRESS 01332 771221
POLICE 0845 123 3333
PRESS 01773 572033/ 572034/ 572979
AMBULANCE 0115 929 6151
PRESS 0115 929 6151

Devon
FIRE 01392 872200
PRESS 01392 872318
POLICE 0870 577 7444
PRESS 01392 452151/ 452200
AMBULANCE 01392 261500
PRESS 01392 261506

Dorset
FIRE 01305 251133
PRESS 01305 252040
POLICE 01929 462727
PRESS 01202 223893/ 07626 932345 *(VB)*
AMBULANCE 01202 438970
PRESS 07970 157025

Durham
FIRE 0191 384 3381
PRESS 0191 384 3381
POLICE 0191 386 4929
PRESS 0191 375 2157
AMBULANCE 0191 273 1212
PRESS 0191 273 1212

East Sussex
FIRE 0845 130 8855
PRESS 01323 462388
POLICE 0845 607 0999
PRESS 01273 404173
AMBULANCE 01273 489444
PRESS 01273 897859

Essex
FIRE 01277 222531
PRESS 01277 222531
POLICE 01245 491491
PRESS 01245 452450
AMBULANCE 01245 443344
PRESS 01245 444444

Gloucestershire
FIRE 01452 753333
PRESS 07626 067134
POLICE 0845 090 1234
PRESS 01242 276070
AMBULANCE 01452 753030
PRESS 01452 753030

Greater Manchester
FIRE 0161 736 5866
PRESS 0161 608 4090
POLICE 0161 872 5050
PRESS 0161 856 2220
AMBULANCE 0161 796 7222
PRESS 0161 834 9836

Hampshire
FIRE 023 8064 4000
PRESS 023 8062 6812
POLICE 0845 045 4545
PRESS 01962 871619
AMBULANCE 01962 863511
PRESS 01962 843165

Hereford
FIRE 01905 24454
PRESS 01905 725060
POLICE 0845 744 4888
PRESS 01432 347340
AMBULANCE 01886 834200
PRESS 01886 834200

Hertfordshire
FIRE 01992 507507
PRESS 01992 507546
POLICE 01707 354000
PRESS 01707 354588
AMBULANCE 01234 408999
PRESS 01234 408999

Humberside
FIRE 01482 565333
PRESS 01482 567466
POLICE 01482 326111
PRESS 01482 578372
AMBULANCE see Lincolnshire (south of Humber) or North Yorkshire (north)

Isle of Wight
FIRE 01983 823194
PRESS 01983 823107
POLICE 0845 045 4545
PRESS 01962 871619
AMBULANCE 01983 534111
PRESS 01983 534184

Kent
FIRE 01622 692121
PRESS 01622 692121
POLICE 01622 690690
PRESS 01622 652231/2/3
AMBULANCE 01622 747010
PRESS 01622 740331

Lancashire
FIRE 01772 862545
PRESS 01772 866939 / 07769 907887 *(VB)*
POLICE 01772 614444
PRESS 01772 412658/ 412444
AMBULANCE 01772 862666
PRESS 01772 773005

Leicestershire
FIRE 0116 287 2241
PRESS 0116 229 2194
POLICE 0116 222 2222
PRESS x2798
AMBULANCE 0115 929 6151
PRESS 0115 929 6151

Lincolnshire
FIRE 01522 582222
PRESS 01522 552302
POLICE 01522 532222
PRESS 01522 558026
AMBULANCE 01522 545171
PRESS 01522 832638

London
FIRE 020 7587 2000
PRESS 020 7587 6100
METROPOLITAN POLICE 020 7230 1212
PRESS 020 7230 2171
CITY OF LONDON POLICE 020 7601 2222
AMBULANCE 020 7921 5100
PRESS 020 7921 5113

Merseyside
FIRE 0151 296 4000
PRESS 0151 296 4419
POLICE 0151 709 6010
PRESS 0151 777 8566
AMBULANCE 0151 260 5220
PRESS 0151 261 2585

Norfolk
FIRE 01603 810351
PRESS 01603 819759
POLICE 01953 424242
PRESS 01953 423666/ 07626 952342 *(VB)*
AMBULANCE 01603 424255
PRESS 01603 422729

North Yorkshire
FIRE 01609 780150
PRESS 01609 788595
POLICE 01609 783131
PRESS 01609 789959
AMBULANCE 01904 666000
PRESS 01904 666041

Northamptonshire
FIRE 01604 797000
PRESS 01536 516400
POLICE 01604 700700
PRESS 01604 703197
AMBULANCE 01908 262422
PRESS 01908 262422

Northumberland
FIRE 01670 534701
PRESS 01670 533208
POLICE 01661 872555
PRESS 01661 868888
AMBULANCE 0191 273 1212
PRESS 0191 273 1212

Nottinghamshire
FIRE 0115 967 0880
PRESS 0115 977 4918
POLICE 0115 967 0999
PRESS 0115 967 2080
AMBULANCE 0115 929 6151
PRESS 0115 929 6151

Oxfordshire
FIRE 01865 842999
PRESS 01865 842999
POLICE 01865 846000
PRESS 01865 846699
AMBULANCE 01865 740100
PRESS 01865 740117

Rutland
FIRE 0116 287 2241
PRESS 0116 229 2194
POLICE 0116 222 2222
PRESS x2798
AMBULANCE 0115 929 6151
PRESS 0115 929 6151

Shropshire
FIRE 01743 260200
PRESS 01743 260286
POLICE 0845 744 4888
PRESS 01743 237491
AMBULANCE 01384 215555
PRESS 01384 246395

VB = VOICE BANK

Somerset
FIRE 01823 364500
PRESS 01823 364582
POLICE 01275 818181
PRESS 01275 816350
AMBULANCE 01392 261500
PRESS 01392 261506

South Yorkshire
FIRE 0114 272 7202
PRESS 0114 253 2353
POLICE 0114 220 2020
PRESS 0114 252 3848
AMBULANCE 01709 820520
PRESS 01709 302026

Staffordshire
FIRE 01785 813234
PRESS 01785 285000
POLICE 01785 257717
PRESS 01785 234864
AMBULANCE 01785 253521
PRESS 01785 273309

Suffolk
FIRE 01473 588888
PRESS 01473 264392
POLICE 01473 613500
PRESS 01473 613996/7
AMBULANCE 01603 424255
PRESS 01603 422729

Surrey
FIRE 01737 242444
PRESS 01737 224027
POLICE 01483 571212
PRESS 01483 482322
AMBULANCE 01737 353333
PRESS 01737 363815

Tyne and Wear
FIRE 0191 232 1224
PRESS 0191 235 9470
POLICE 01661 872555
PRESS 01661 868888
AMBULANCE 0191 273 1212
PRESS 0191 273 1212

Warwickshire
FIRE 01926 423231
PRESS 01926 423231
POLICE 01926 415000
PRESS North: x3366, 07626 952404 *(VB)*; South: x4266, 07626 955647 *(VB)*
AMBULANCE 01926 881331
PRESS 01926 881331

West Midlands
FIRE 0121 380 6906
PRESS 0121 380 6101
POLICE 0845 113 5000
PRESS 0121 626 5858
AMBULANCE 01384 215555
PRESS 01384 246395

West Sussex
FIRE 01243 786211
PRESS 01243 752448
POLICE 0845 607 0999
PRESS 01273 404173
AMBULANCE 01273 489444
PRESS 01273 897859

West Yorkshire
FIRE 01274 682311
PRESS 01274 655717
POLICE 01924 375222
PRESS 01924 292045
AMBULANCE 01924 582000
PRESS 01924 582204

Wiltshire
FIRE 01380 723601
PRESS 01380 723601
POLICE 01380 722341/ 735735
PRESS 01380 734126
AMBULANCE 01249 443939
PRESS 01249 443939

Worcestershire
FIRE 01905 24454
PRESS 01905 725060
POLICE 0845 744 4888
PRESS 01905 331871
AMBULANCE 01886 834200
PRESS 01886 834200

Wales

Mid Wales
FIRE 01267 221444
PRESS 01267 221444
POLICE 01267 222020
PRESS 01267 222274
AMBULANCE 01745 532900
PRESS 01745 532925

West Wales
FIRE 01267 221444
PRESS 01267 221444
POLICE 01267 222020
PRESS 01267 222274
AMBULANCE 01745 532900
PRESS 01745 532925

North Wales
FIRE 01745 343431
PRESS 01745 343431
POLICE FORCES (ENG.) 0845 607 1002
POLICE FORCES (WELSH) 0845 607 1001
PRESS 01492 511157/8/9
AMBULANCE 01745 532900
PRESS 01745 532925

South Wales
FIRE 01443 232000
PRESS 01443 232164
POLICE 01656 655555
PRESS 01656 869291
AMBULANCE 01745 532900
PRESS 01495 765466 / 01745 532925

Scotland

Central Scotland
FIRE 01324 716996
PRESS 01324 716996
POLICE 01786 456000
PRESS 01786 456370
AMBULANCE 0131 446 7000
PRESS 07974 017937

Dumfries and Galloway
FIRE 01387 252222
PRESS 01387 252222
POLICE 01387 252112
PRESS 01387 260576
AMBULANCE 0131 446 7000
PRESS 07974 017937

Fife
FIRE 01592 774451
PRESS x2082 *(VB)*/ x2069
POLICE 01592 418500
PRESS 01592 418813
AMBULANCE 0131 446 7000
PRESS 07974 017937

Grampian
FIRE 01224 696666
PRESS 01224 696666
POLICE 0845 600 5700
PRESS 01224 386431
AMBULANCE 0131 446 7000
PRESS 07974 017937

Highland and Islands
FIRE 01463 227000
PRESS 01463 227009
POLICE 01463 715555
PRESS 01463 720396
AMBULANCE 0131 446 7000
PRESS 07974 017937

Lothian and Borders
FIRE 0131 228 2401
PRESS 0131 228 2401
POLICE 0131 311 3131
PRESS 0131 311 3423
AMBULANCE 0131 446 7000
PRESS 07974 017937

Strathclyde
FIRE 01698 300999
PRESS 01698 338207
POLICE 0141 532 2000
PRESS 0141 532 2658
AMBULANCE 0131 446 7000
PRESS 07974 017937

Tayside
FIRE 01382 322222
PRESS 01382 322222
POLICE 01382 322222
PRESS 01382 322222
AMBULANCE 0131 446 7000
PRESS 07974 017937

Northern Ireland

HQ, Lisburn
FIRE 028 9266 4221
PRESS 028 9266 4221
POLICE 028 9065 0222
PRESS 028 9070 0084
AMBULANCE 028 9040 0999
PRESS 028 9040 0999

VB = VOICE BANK

Index

Contacts index

A

B

C

D

E

F

G

H

J

K

L

M

N

O

P

S

T

U

V

W

Subject index